READING OF THE EMANCIPATION PROCLAMATION

NEW YORK,
JOHNSON, FRY & COMPANY,
27 BEEKMAN STREET

NATIONAL HISTORY

OF THE

WAR FOR THE UNION,

Civil, Military and Naval.

FOUNDED ON

OFFICIAL AND OTHER AUTHENTIC DOCUMENTS.

BY

EVERT A. DUYCKINCK,

Author of "National Portrait Gallery of Eminent Americans," "Cyclopedia of American Literature," Etc.

Illustrated with Highly-Finished Steel Engravings.

INCLUDING

BATTLE SCENES BY SEA AND LAND, AND FULL-LENGTH PORTRAITS OF NAVAL AND MILITARY HEROES, FROM ORIGINAL PAINTINGS,

BY ALONZO CHAPPEL AND THOMAS NAST.

IN THREE VOLUMES.—VOLUME III.

NEW YORK:

JOHNSON, FRY AND COMPANY,

27 BEEKMAN STREET.

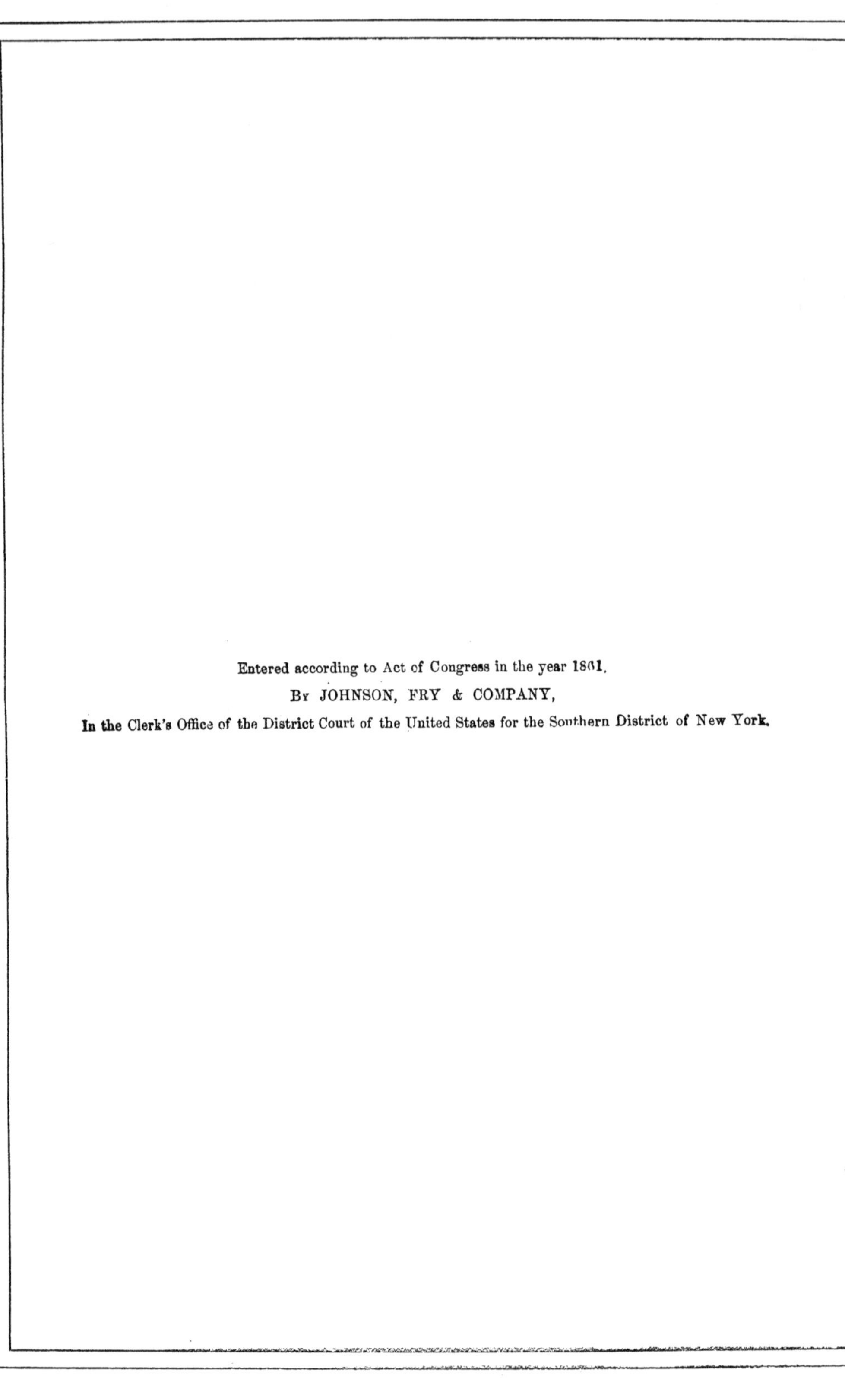

CONTENTS OF VOLUME III.

CONTENTS.

CHAPTER LXXX.

GENERAL BURNSIDE'S CAMPAIGN IN VIRGINIA, AND BATTLE OF FREDERICKSBURG—DECEMBER, 1862.

On entering upon his new command, as the successor of General McClellan, General Burnside, on the 10th November, issued the following address to his soldiers:—"In accordance with General Order No. 182, issued by the President of the United States, I hereby assume command of the Army of the Potomac. Patriotism and the exercise of my every energy in the direction of the army, and by the full and hearty coöperation of its officers and men, will, I hope, under the blessing of God, insure its success. Having been a sharer of the privations and a witness of the bravery of the old Army of the Potomac in the Maryland campaign, and fully identified with them in their feeling of respect and esteem for General McClellan, entertained through a long and most friendly association with him, I feel that it is not as a stranger I assume command. To the Ninth Army Corps, so long and intimately associated with me, I need say nothing. Our histories are identical. With diffidence for myself, but with a proud confidence in the unswerving loyalty and determination of the gallant army now intrusted to my care, I accept its control with the steadfast assurance that the just cause must prevail."

As intimated in this address, it was with reluctance that General Burnside accepted a command which had been offered to him twice before and refused. Entertaining the most friendly feelings towards General McClellan, he held the opinion that that officer "could command the Army of the Potomac better than any other general in it."* Yielding to a sense of duty, however, he obeyed the orders of the Government, and immediately prepared to enter upon a new and decided course. Having previously urged upon General McClellan the advantages of taking the army to Richmond by the way of Fredericksburg, on the Rappahannock, instead of following up the enemy on the recent line of operations to Gordonsville, he was confirmed in this plan by an interview with General Halleck, who visited the camp immediately after he had taken command. Accordingly, having at his headquarters, at Warrenton, organized the army in three grand divisions—the right composed of the 2d and 9th corps, to be commanded by Major-General Sumner; the left, the 1st and 6th corps, assigned to Major-General Franklin; the centre, the 3d and 5th corps, to Major-General Hooker, while the 11th corps, under Major-General Sigel, constituted the reserve—he prepared to carry the new movement into effect. His immediate design was to employ the attention of the enemy in front of Warrenton, and make a rapid movement of the army to Fredericksburg. To cross the river at the latter place, he called at an early moment, after taking command of the army, for a sufficient pontoon train to be forwarded from Washington, and meet his advance on the Rappahannock. A depot of supplies he requested should be established at Acquia Creek, and other pro-

* Testimony before the War Committee, Washington, December 19, 1862.

visions sent overland towards Fredericksburg.

A summons from the War Department, meanwhile, recalled all absent officers to the Army of the Potomac, while to give tone and character to the army in its movement, by impressing it with a sense of religious duty, and reminding it of the loftiest obligations of patriotism, President Lincoln, on the 16th of November, issued the following order :—"The President, Commander-in-Chief of the Army and Navy, desires and enjoins the orderly observance of the Sabbath by the officers and men in the military and naval service. The importance for man and beast of the prescribed weekly rest, the sacred rights of Christian soldiers and sailors, a becoming deference to the best sentiments of a Christian people, and a due regard for the Divine Will, demand that Sunday labor in the army and navy be reduced to the measure of strict necessity. The discipline and character of the national forces should not suffer, nor the cause they defend be imperiled, by the profanation of the day or name of the Most High. At this time of public distress, adopting the words of Washington in 1776, 'Men may find enough to do in the service of God and their country, without abandoning themselves to vice and immorality.' The first general order issued by the Father of his Country, after the Declaration of Independence, indicates the spirit in which our institutions were founded, and should ever be defended : 'The General hopes and trusts that every officer and man will endeavor to live and act as becomes a Christian soldier, defending the dearest rights and privileges of his country.'"

The new movement was commenced on the 15th, by the right army division of General Sumner, the advance of which reached Falmouth, opposite Fredericksburg, on the 18th, when, if the pontoon trains ordered had been on hand, the passage of the river might have been securely effected, the communications kept open, and an important advantage gained for the campaign, as there were few of the enemy at that time at Fredericksburg. General Sumner, knowing the military importance of the heights in the rear of the town, and anxious to occupy them, would have crossed at once by a ford ; but as there was a prospect of a rise in the river, and the division might be cut off from supplies and from the rest of the army, their movement was forbidden by General Burnside. Thus early was the new march to Richmond arrested. Delay had occurred at Washington, and the non-arrival of the pontoons compelled the army, as it came up, to rest on the left bank of the river, while the enemy, by a parallel movement on the opposite side, moved in force to the rear of Fredericksburg, and occupying a range of hills—a most defensible position—confronted the Union army at that place. General Burnside, disappointed in his projected rapid movement towards the Confederate capital, and prospect of meeting the enemy before General Jackson, who, it was understood, had lingered in the valley of the Shenandoah, could come up with his command, was compelled for a time to watch the enemy on the opposite bank, while he laid new plans to bring the army of General Lee under inevitably disadvantageous circumstances for himself to an engagement. Both armies were now in easy communication with their respective bases: the Confederates by direct railway line with Richmond, sixty-five miles distant, and the intermediate depots ; while the Union army, after a brief period of busy preparation, received its supplies from Washington by water to the storehouses at Acquia Creek, and thence over a railway of fourteen miles to the camp at Falmouth. The high grounds on either side of the river gave to each army an excellent defensive position.

On his first arrival in the vicinity of Falmouth, on the 17th of November, General Sumner had exchanged a few shots with a battery across the river, which he had silenced. A few days after, on the 21st, we find him in correspondence with the civil authorities of Fredericksburg, complaining of shots fired under cover of the houses of the city upon his troops, of the employment of the mills and railroads of the place in clothing and forwarding armed bodies in rebellion against the United States; "a condition of things" which, he said, "must terminate." He accordingly, by direction of General Burnside, demanded the surrender of the city at or before five o'clock in the afternoon. Failing an affirmative reply, sixteen hours were to be allowed for the removal of women and children, at the expiration of which time he stated that he should proceed to shell the town. Mayor Slaughter, having secured the concurrence of the military authorities, replied that the acts complained of should cease, and the threatened bombardment was for the time abandoned. The city, however, was not surrendered, it being understood that neither army should occupy it for the present.

The question was, now, in what way should the attack upon General Lee's army be made—for an early demonstration of some kind was not to be long delayed, the removal of General McClellan absolutely requiring a show at least of prompt and vigorous action on the part of his successor. As General Sumner afterwards said of the military counsels of this period, in the Army of the Potomac, he was in favor of crossing the Rappahannock, "because I knew that neither our Government nor our people would be satisfied to have our army retire from their position, or go into winter quarters, until we knew the force which was on the other side of the river; and the only way in which we could learn that was by going over there and feeling of them." The bridges over the creeks, on the Acquia Railroad, having been rebuilt, and cars and engines brought down the Potomac, the line was in operation, and the army well supplied with provisions, by the end of November. The anxiously expected pontoons, moreover, had at length arrived. Professor Low was also announced, "with an entirely new set of balloon apparatus." The presence of President Lincoln one day in camp, followed by a hasty visit of General Burnside to Washington on the 29th, looked to immediate action. The result of the General's interview with the War Department was said to be entirely satisfactory. He would now "be let alone—allowed to follow out his own plans, in his own time and way, free from bureaucratic dictation at Washington, and confident that he will have from the Government all the assistance he asks for."* The beginning of December saw the Union camps in active preparation for a movement upon the enemy, not without embarrassment from the inclemency of the weather — winter setting in with severity. The enemy, meanwhile, were growing more formidable in their intrenchments—General Jackson, it was understood, having now joined the army of Lee. On the 2d, a picket of Pennsylvania cavalry, stationed down the river at King George Court-House, was surprised by a party of the enemy, who crossed the river in small boats, capturing Captain Johnson and a number of his officers and men. For his negligence in this affair, the Union officer was promptly dismissed the service by General Burnside. It was in the vicinity of this misadventure, at Skinker's Neck, some twelve miles below Falmouth, that it was first intended to cross the Rappahannock, and attack the enemy on their flank, and a movement for this purpose was commenced; but the intention was abandoned when it was found that the foe had concentrated troops on the opposite shore. General Burnside, however, kept up a demonstration in that quarter to draw off as many troops of the enemy as possible,

* Army Correspondence, *New York Times*, December 5, 1862.

while he projected a main attack upon their centre at Fredericksburg. "I felt satisfied," says he, "that they did not expect us to cross here, but down below; and that this was the place to fight the most decisive battle, because, if we could divide their forces by piercing their lines at one or two points, separating their left from their right, then a vigorous attack with the whole army would succeed in breaking their army in pieces." In these movements, General Burnside had his eye upon a road which the enemy had constructed in the rear of the line of heights on which they were so advantageously posted behind Fredericksburg. To penetrate to and occupy that road would sever the rebel army, when, with this movement on their flank and rear, a direct attack might be made on their front, the enemy be taken at a disadvantage, and their main works, it was expected, be carried by storm. Such was the general plan of the coming engagement, proposed by General Burnside, and agreed upon by a council of officers on the 10th of December. Preparations were accordingly made that night for the passage of the river at and in the immediate vicinity of Fredericksburg. The pontoons were brought down to the water side, and a series of batteries, numbering about a hundred and fifty pieces, were placed in position on the surrounding hills commanding the opposite sides of the river, to protect the construction of the bridges, and cover the crossing of troops. There were six pontoon bridges to be thrown across the stream, which was about three hundred yards wide; four immediately in front of Fredericksburg, within a short distance of each other, and the other two about a mile and a half below. In the passage of the river, the left division of General Franklin was to use the latter, while the right and centre of Sumner and Hooker were to cross at the town. The work was well advanced during the darkness of the night, and was partially concealed by the morning's fog. The bridges below the city, in consequence of the batteries commanding the opposite plain, were constructed with slight resistance; not so, however, those above, where the shelter of the buildings in the town gave the best opportunity of annoyance by the enemy's sharp-shooters. The work on the upper bridges commenced about four o'clock. The pontoons were pushed out over the ice, which had been formed along the banks, and a number of them launched into the stream, were arranged in order by the engineers, when the process was interrupted by a severe musketry fire from the opposite shores. The firing of two signal-guns from the rebel batteries at this time, at five o'clock, announced the discovery of the meditated attack. The attempt to cross the river had failed to be a surprise, and could now be accomplished only in face of the most serious opposition. To protect the bridge-builders, who were suffering severely, several of the batteries, posted about a mile from the river, opened their fire. "The effect," says a correspondent in an eloquent account of the movements of the day, "was singular enough, and it was difficult to believe that the whole affair was not a phantasmagoria. It was still quite dark, the horizon around being lit up only by the flash of projectiles, which reappeared in explosive flame on the other side of the river. Daylight came, but with it came not clearness of vision for on-lookers. The mist and smoke not only did not lighten, but grew more opaque and heavy, hugging the ground closely. Our gunners, however, still continued to launch their missiles at a venture. The rebel batteries hardly returned our fire, and this chariness of their ammunition they preserved all day —not a dozen rounds being fired during the whole forenoon. Towards eight o'clock a large party of general officers, among them General Burnside, the corps commanders, and many others of high rank, had congregated in front of and on the balcony of General Sumner's head-quarters, Phillips' House, situated about a mile directly back of the Lacy House. The performance could be heard, but not seen—the stage was obstinately hidden from view, and all were impatient that the curtain should rise. Aids and couriers came and went with messages to and from the batteries and bridges. At half-past nine o'clock official notification was received that the two bridges on the extreme left were completed, and General Franklin sent to General Burnside to know if he should cross his force at once. The reply was that he should wait until the upper bridges also were completed.

"Meantime, with the latter but little progress was made. During the next couple of hours half a dozen attempts were made to complete the bridges, but each time the party was repulsed with severe loss. On the occasion of one essay, Captain Brainerd, of the 50th New York Volunteer Engineers, went out on the bridge with eleven men. Five immediately fell by the balls of the rebel sharp-shooters. Captain Perkins led another party, and was shot through the neck, and the 66th and 57th New York Regiments, which were supporting the 50th and 15th New York Volunteer Engineers—General Woodbury's brigade—suffered severely. It was a hopeless task, and we made little or no progress. The rebel sharp-shooters, posted in the cellars of the houses of the front street, not fifty yards from the river, behind stone walls and in rifle-pits, were able to pick off with damnable accuracy any party of engineers venturing on the half-completed bridges. The case was perfectly clear. Nothing can be done till they are dislodged from their lurking-places. There is but one way of doing this effectually—shell the town. At ten o'clock General Burnside gives the order, 'Concentrate the fire of all your guns on the city, and batter it down!' You may believe they were not loth to obey. The artillery of the right—eight batteries—was commanded by Colonel Hays; Colonel Tompkins, right centre—eleven batteries; Colonel Tyler, left centre—seven batteries; Captain De Russy, left—nine batteries. In a few moments these thirty-five batteries, forming a total of one hundred and seventy-nine guns, ranging from 10-pounder Parrotts to 4½-inch siege guns, posted along the convex side of the arc of a circle, formed by the bend of the river and land opposite Fredericksburg, opened on the doomed city. The effect was, of course, terrific, and, regarded merely as a phenomenon, was among the most awfully grand conceivable. Perhaps what will give you the liveliest idea of its effect is a succession, absolutely without intermission, of the very loudest thunder peals. It lasted thus for upward of an hour, fifty rounds being fired from each gun, and I know not how many hundred tuns of iron were thrown into the town. The congregated generals were transfixed. Mingled satisfaction and awe was upon every face. But what was tantalizing was, that though a great deal could be heard, nothing could be seen, the city being still enveloped in fog and mist. Only a denser pillar of smoke, defining itself on the back-ground of the fog, indicated where the town had been fired by our shells. Another and another column showed itself, and we presently saw that at least a dozen houses must be on fire. Towards noon the curtain rolled up, and we saw that it was indeed so. Fredericksburg was in conflagration. Tremendous though this firing had been, and terrific though its effect obviously was on the town, it had not accomplished the object intended. It was found by our gunners almost impossible to obtain a sufficient depression of their pieces to shell the front part of the city, and the rebel sharp-shooters were still comparatively safe behind the thick stone walls of the houses.

"During the thick of the bombardment a fresh attempt had been made to complete the bridge. It failed, and evidently nothing could be done till a party could be thrown over to clean out the rebels and cover the bridge-head. For this mission General Burnside called for volunteers, and Colonel Hall, of Fort Sumter fame, immediately responded that he had a brigade that would do the business. Accordingly, the 7th Michigan and 19th Massachusetts, two small regiments, numbering in all about four hundred men, were selected for the purpose. The plan was that they should take the pontoon boats of the first bridge, of which there were ten lying on the bank of the river, waiting to be added to the half-finished bridge, cross over in them, and landing, drive out the rebels. Nothing could be more admirable or more gallant than the execution of this daring feat. Rushing down the steep banks of the river, the party found temporary shelter behind the pontoon boats lying scattered on the bank, and behind the piles of planking destined for the covering of the bridge, behind rocks, etc. In this situation they acted some fifteen or twenty minutes as sharp-shooters, they and the rebels observing each other. In the mean time new and vigorous artillery firing was commenced on our part, and just as soon as this was fairly developed, the 7th Michigan rose from their crouching-places, rushed for the pontoon boats, and pushing them into the water, rapidly filled them with twenty-five or thirty each. The first boat pushes off. Now, if ever, is the rebels' opportunity. Crack! Crack! Crack! from fifty lurking-places go rebel rifles at the gallant fellows, who, stooping low in the boat, seek to avoid the fire. The murderous work was well done. Lustily, however, pull the oarsmen, and presently, having passed the middle of the stream, the boat and its gallant freight come under cover of the opposite bluffs. Another and another boat follows. Now is their opportunity. Nothing could be more amusing, in its way, than the result. Instantly they see a new turn of affairs. The rebels pop up by the hundred, like so many rats, from every cellar, rifle-pit and stone wall, and scamper off up the streets of the town. With all their fleetness, however, many of them were much too slow. With incredible rapidity the Michigan and Massachusetts boys sweep up the hill, making a rush for the lurking-places occupied by the rebels, and gaining them, each man capturing his two or three prisoners. The pontoon boats on their return trip took over more than a hundred of these fellows. You can imagine with what intense interest the crossing of the first boat-load of our men was watched by the numerous spectators on the shore, and with what enthusiastic shouts their landing on the opposite side was greeted. It was an authentic piece of human heroism, which moves men as nothing else can. The problem was solved. This flash of bravery had done what scores of batteries and tuns of metal had failed to accomplish. The country will not forget that little band. The party once across, and the rebels cleaned out, it took the engineers but a brief period to complete the bridge. They laid hold with a will, plunging waist-deep into the water, and working as men work who are under inspiration. In less than half an hour the bridge was completed, and the head of the column of the right grand division, consisting of General Howard's command, was moving upon it over the Rappahannock. A feeble attempt from the rebel batteries was made to shell the troops in crossing, but it failed completely."*

At the second bridge the New York Volunteer Engineers pursued their task with like gallantry, a detachment of Colonel Fairchild's 89th New York Regiment coming to their aid, crossing the river in boats, and rivaling the Michigan and

* W. Swinton, Correspondence *New York Times*. Fredericksburg, Va., December 11, 1862.

Massachussetts men in the capture of a number of the Mississippi and Alabama sharp-shooters stationed in the town. The New York Volunteer Engineers at the third bridge, protected by the fire of the batteries, accomplished their task with little loss, while the fourth was constructed by the engineer corps of Sappers and Miners—the enemy offering no resistance.* Such was the gallant work of the army in providing the means of passing the river in face of the enemy. The evening of the 11th saw Fredericksburg, that portion of the city, at least, fronting the river, in possession of an advance-guard of Sumner's right division, while a brigade of New England troops, of Franklin's division, were also encamped on the opposite shore at the lower crossing. A hundred men, it was reported, were killed and wounded while driving the enemy out of Fredericksburg. The town had suffered less from the heavy bombardment than might have been expected. A number of the houses had been riddled, and some twenty burnt; the churches had been more or less damaged by the missiles—the total injury being estimated by an intelligent observer at not exceeding two hundred thousand dollars. To this was to be added the loss from pillage, which the establishment of guards and other efforts did not altogether prevent. The inhabitants had generally left the city, though a number remained, who took refuge from the bombardment in the cellars.

On early morning and forenoon of the next day, Friday, the 12th, under cover of a dense fog, the remainder of General Sumner's division crossed the river and occupied the town, being protected from the enemy's batteries in the rear by the shelter of the houses in the streets running parallel with the rebel works. The upper portion of the town was occupied by the skirmishers, while the pickets of both armies faced one another at the outskirts. Both corps of General Franklin's division, General Reynolds' and General Smith's, crossed below, and were in position by one o'clock in the afternoon; the former extending from the river towards the hills, the latter nearly parallel to the old Richmond road, with its right across Deep Run. General Hooker's division remained on the left bank of the river, held in readiness, if the movement succeeded, "to spring upon the enemy in their retreat." The crossing of the troops was made with comparatively little annoyance from the enemy's batteries, which, as the opinion was afterwards expressed by General Franklin, had the enemy so willed, might have defeated the movement. The main part of the force being now over the river, and under the enemy's fire, the attack could not be long delayed. Early the next morning, accordingly, orders were given by General Burnside for the advance upon the rebel position. General Franklin, on the left, was instructed to hold his command in readiness for a rapid movement down the old Richmond road, while he sent out a division, well supported, with the line of retreat open, to seize a position on the heights, which, with a similar movement by a column from General Sumner's command, farther to the westward, would, it was expected, compel the enemy to evacuate the ridge. The movement upon the heights in General Franklin's division was assigned to General Reynolds, and under him was carried out by General Meade. General Gibbon was to support it on the right, and General Doubleday was held in reserve. "As soon as General Meade," we quote the narrative of the operations of the day by General Franklin, "was in motion, a large force of the enemy was turned on our extreme left, and General Reynolds stopped Meade and sent Doubleday's division to drive them off. They were in such position that they could fire into

* Special army correspondence New York *Times*, Fredericksburg, December 12, 1862.

Meade's rear as he advanced, so that it was absolutely necessary that he should be stopped until the enemy could be driven off. While he was stopped and Doubleday was advancing, I sent for one of General Stoneman's divisions, which was on the other side of the river at the bridges. This division—General Birney's division—I directed to be crossed, and before it reached the field I sent an aid-de-camp to direct General Birney to report to General Reynolds. General Birney did so report, but before he got up General Meade had advanced into the woods; had a severe fight with the enemy; had driven them, so he reported to me, so that his men were on the crown of the hill, when they were fallen upon by an immensely superior force of the enemy, and driven back. By this time two regiments of Birney's division had arrived on the field, and General Reynolds immediately put them in; but they were also driven back, and it was not until the main body of Birney's division came up that they were able to retrieve themselves at all so as to hold any part of the woods. While this was going on, General Gibbon had also advanced on Meade's right, as a support. He had become engaged with the enemy, was wounded about half-past two, and had to leave the field, and shortly afterwards his division retired. By this time the second division of General Stoneman, which I had also ordered up, came up and took the place of Gibbon's division, and those two divisions—Birney's and Sickles'—together held the line for the remainder of the day, it being now about three o'clock."* This closed the serious fighting on the left. There was skirmishing and cannonading on Sunday, the troops holding their position that and the following day, when the army was withdrawn across the river.

The assault on the right in the rear of the town by General Sumner's division, made with great heroism, utterly failed. "I selected for the attack," says that officer, "the corps of General French and General Hancock, two of the most gallant officers in our army, and two corps that had neither of them ever turned their backs to the enemy. They made repeated assaults, but were driven back in spite of all the efforts that could be made by their officers. The principal obstacle that they found was a long stone wall, which was the outwork of the enemy. That wall was some four hundred or five hundred yards in length, as represented to me, and had been raised and strengthened. The enemy had artillery that enfiladed that wall on both sides; they held their fire until our troops arrived at a certain point, when they rose up and poured a perfect volley over this wall, their artillery enfilading our column at the same time. No troops could stand such a fire as that. I do not think it a reproach to those two divisions that they did not carry that position; they did all that men could do. I had General Howard's division in readiness to support those two, and one strong division of Wilcox's corps—the 9th corps, General Burnside's old corps—detached to keep open communication with General Franklin's right. That division was not under fire during the day. Some of the other divisions of the 9th corps were more or less engaged. General Hooker had a part of his grand division in the town, and one of his corps under General Humphries was engaged. They made a gallant attack, but were driven back."

A passage from General Hooker's testimony, describing this last attack, will sufficiently exhibit the desperate character of this conflict. "I brought up," said he, "every available battery in the city, with a view to break away the enemy's barriers by the use of artillery. I proceeded against the barriers as I would against a fortification, and endeavored to breach a hole sufficiently large for a 'forlorn hope' to enter. I had

* General Franklin's testimony before the War Committee, Washington, March 28, 1863.

two batteries posted on the left of the road, within four hundred yards of the position upon which the attack was to be made, and I had other parts of batteries posted on the right of the road at the distance of five or six hundred yards. I had all these batteries playing with great vigor until sunset upon that point, but with no apparent effect upon the rebels or upon their works. During the last part of the cannonading I had given directions to General Humphrey's division to form, under the shelter which a small hill afforded, in column for assault. When the fire of the artillery ceased I gave directions for the enemy's works to be assaulted. General Humphrey's men took off their knapsacks, overcoats and haversacks. They were directed to make the assault with empty muskets, for there was no time there to load and fire. When the word was given the men moved forward with great impetuosity. They ran and hurrahed, and I was encouraged by the great good feeling that pervaded them. The head of General Humphrey's column advanced to within, perhaps, fifteen or twenty yards of the stone wall, which was the advanced position which the rebels held, and then they were thrown back as quickly as they had advanced. Probably the whole of the advance and the retiring did not occupy fifteen minutes. They left behind, as it was reported to me, 1,760 of their number, out of about 4,000."*

The grand movement of the day—for the contest was continued till night—had failed. The forces of Jackson, who held the Confederate right, had repulsed the insufficient force with which Meade had advanced to the attack, and Longstreet, on the enemy's left, with the aid of his batteries and defences, held his formidable line untouched. "The repulse," as General Sumner said, "was what frequently happens in campaigns — the works were stronger than we believed them to be. They were tier upon tier for two or three tiers. If we had carried the first tier, we could not have held it, because their next tier was a much more formidable row of fortifications, only a mile distant and on a higher position still; and no doubt large masses of infantry were between the two crests: and having got on the top of one crest, we would have been compelled to contend with large masses of fresh troops, over whom their own batteries could fire."*

Disheartening as was the situation at the close of the day, General Burnside did not despair of yet retrieving the fortunes of battle by one gigantic effort. After passing the night with the officers and men on the field on the right, he returned to his headquarters across the river, and directed General Sumner to order the 9th army corps, which he had originally commanded, and which now consisted of eighteen old regiments and some new ones, to make a direct attack upon the enemy's works. "I thought," says General Burnside, "that these regiments, by coming quickly up after each other, would be able to carry the stone wall and the batteries in front, forcing the enemy into their next line, and by going in with them they would not be able to fire upon us to any great extent." The column of attack was actually formed, when, just before the time appointed for its starting, General Sumner interposed and recommended that this new assault be abandoned. A council of the division and corps commanders was called, when they were found unanimously of the same opinion. The attack was therefore relinquished. On the afternoon of the same day General Burnside ordered the return across the river of all the forces except enough to hold the town and the bridge-heads, intending to retain the bridges for recrossing should it be

* Testimony before the War Committee, December 20, 1862.

* Testimony of General Sumner before the War Committee, Washington, December 19, 1862.

thought advisable. That night, supported by the advice of General Hooker, who thought the town untenable, Genhral Burnside resolved to withdraw the whole command, which he justly considered "a perilous operation." The order was sent over after midnight, when it had commenced raining, which, "to some extent," says General Burnside, "was an assistance to us, but a very bad thing in the moving of troops." The difficult undertaking—a proof of the excellent discipline of the army—was successfully accomplished. "I consider the crossing of the river, under the circumstances," said General Sumner, "a very creditable thing; and I also consider the retreat, under the circumstances, as very creditable. There was not a gun or anything else lost. The entire army returned without an accident." The movement was assisted by the wind blowing from the enemy's lines, and by the darkness of the night. The sound of the moving artillery was deadened on the bridges by a covering of earth. In a brief dispatch to General Halleck, General Burnside announced the termination of the movement from which so much had been expected. "The Army of the Potomac was withdrawn to this side of the Rappahannock River, because I felt fully convinced that the position in front could not be carried, and it was a military necessity either to attack the enemy or retire. A repulse would have been disastrous to us under existing circumstances."

On the day previous to the withdrawal of the troops, a report was made by General Lee to the Secretary of War at Richmond, in which in few words and an utter absence of pretence he narrated, as follows, the stirring incidents of the late engagement: "On the night of the 10th instant the enemy commenced to throw three bridges over the Rappahannock—two at Fredericksburg, and the third about a mile and a quarter below, near the mouth of the Deep Run. The plain on which Fredericksburg stands is so completely commanded by the hills of Stafford, in possession of the enemy, that no effectual opposition could be offered to the construction of the bridges on the passage of the river without exposing our troops to the destructive fire of his numerous batteries. Positions were therefore selected to oppose his advance after crossing. The narrowness of the Rappahannock, its winding course and deep bed, afforded opportunity for the construction of bridges at points beyond the reach of our artillery, and the banks had to be watched by skirmishers. The latter, sheltering themselves behind the houses, drove back the working parties of the enemy at the bridges opposite the city; but at the lowest point of crossing, where no shelter could be had, our sharp-shooters were themselves driven off, and the completion of the bridge was effected about noon on the 11th. In the afternoon of that day the enemy's batteries opened upon the city, and by dark had so demolished the houses on the river bank as to deprive our skirmishers of shelter, and, under cover of his guns, he effected a lodgment in the town. The troops which had so gallantly held their position in the city under the severe cannonade during the day, resisting the advance of the enemy at every step, were withdrawn during the night, as were also those who, with equal tenacity, had maintained their post at the lowest bridge. Under cover of darkness and a dense fog, on the 12th, a large force passed the river, and took position on the right bank, protected by their heavy guns on the left. On the morning of the 13th, his arrangements for attack being completed about nine o'clock, the movement veiled by a fog, he advanced boldly in large force against our right wing. General Jackson's corps occupied the right of our line, which rested on the railroad; General Longstreet's the left, extending along the heights to the Rappahannock, above Fredericksburg; General Stuart, with two brigades of cavalry, was posted in the extensive plain on our extreme right. As soon as the advance of the enemy was discovered through the fog, General Stuart, with his accustomed promptness, moved up a section of his horse artillery, which opened with effect upon his flank, and drew upon the gallant Pelham a heavy fire, which he sustained unflinchingly for about two hours.

"In the mean time the enemy was fiercely encountered by General A. P. Hill's division, forming General Jackson's right, and after an obstinate combat repulsed. During this attack, which was protracted and hotly contested, two of General Hill's brigades were driven back upon our second line. General Early, with part of his division, being ordered to his support, drove the enemy back from the point of woods he had seized and pursued him into the plain until arrested by his artillery. The right of the enemy's column, extending beyond Hill's front, encountered the right of General Hood, of Longstreet's corps. The enemy took possession of a small copse in front of Hood, but were quickly dispossessed and repulsed with loss. During the attack on our right the enemy was crossing troops over his bridges at Fredericksburg, and massing them in front of Longstreet's line. Soon after his repulse on our right he commenced a series of attacks on our left, with a view of obtaining possession of the heights immediately overlooking the town. These repeated attacks were repulsed in gallant style by the Washington Artillery, under Colonel Walton, and a portion of McLaw's division, which occupied these heights. The last assault was made after dark, when Colonel Alexander's battalion had relieved the Washington Artillery, whose ammunition had been exhausted, and ended the contest for the day. The enemy was supported in his attacks by the fire of strong batteries of artillery on the right bank of the river, as well as by the numerous heavy batteries on the Stafford Heights. Our loss during the operations, since the movements of the enemy began, amounts to about eighteen hundred killed and wounded. Among the former, I regret to report the death of the patriotic soldier and statesman, Brigadier-General Thomas R. R. Cobb, who fell upon our left; and among the latter, that brave soldier and accomplished gentleman, Brigadier-General M. Gregg, who was very seriously, and, it is feared, mortally wounded, during the attack on our right. The enemy to-day has been apparently burying his dead. His troops are visible in their first position in line of battle, but with the exception of some desultory cannonading and firing between skirmishers, he has not attempted to renew the attack. About five hundred and fifty prisoners were taken during the engagement, but the full extent of his loss is unknown."

General Maxcy Gregg, alluded to in this dispatch, presently died of his wound in the battle. He was a prominent politician in South Carolina, his native State, and had long advocated the principles leading to the rebellion, having, as a young man, taken an active part in the disunion measures of 1832. Leaving his profession of the law, at the outbreak of the war, he participated in the attack on Sumter, and afterwards carried his regiment — the first from South Carolina—into Virginia, and from that time to the present had been conspicuous in the field. He had a high reputation for bravery and self-possession in battle.

The peculiar circumstances under which General Burnside had reluctantly accepted the command, with the expectation necessarily excited in the public mind by the course which he had chosen, acting upon his sensitive character, induced him to address a letter to General Halleck, in which, after candidly reviewing the campaign so unhappily interrupted by the passage of the river, he candidly assumed the whole burden of the affair. "But for the fog and the unexpected and unavoidable delay in building the bridges, which gave the enemy twenty-four hours to concentrate his forces in his strong position, we would," he said, "almost certainly have succeeded, in which case the battle would have been, in my opinion, far more decisive than if we had crossed at the places first selected. As it was, we came very near success. Failing in accomplishing the main object, we remained in order of battle two days—long enough to decide that the enemy would not come out of his strongholds to fight us with his infantry—after which we recrossed to this side of the river unmolested without the loss of men or property. As the day broke our long lines of troops were seen marching to their different positions as if going on parade—not the least demoralization or disorganization existed. To the brave officers and soldiers who accomplished the feat of thus recrossing the river in the face of the enemy I owe everything. For the failure in the attack I am responsible, as the extreme gallantry, courage and endurance shown by the brave officers and soldiers was never exceeded, and would have carried the points had it been possible. To the families and friends of the dead I can only offer my heartfelt sympathies, and for the wounded I can only offer my earnest prayers for their comfortable and final recovery. The fact that I decided to move from Warrenton to this line rather against the opinion of the President, Secretary of War and yourself, and that you left the whole movement in my hands, without giving me orders, makes me responsible."*

In response to this letter from General Burnside, President Lincoln issued, on the 22d of December, the following address to the Army of the Potomac:—

"I have just read your Commanding General's preliminary report of the battle of Fredericksburg. Although you were not successful, the attempt was not an error, nor the failure other than an accident. The courage with which you, in an open field, maintained the contest against an intrenched foe, and the consummate skill and success with which you crossed and recrossed the river in the face of the enemy, show that you possess all the qualities of a great army which will yet give victory to the cause of the country and of popular government. Condoling with the mourners for the dead and sympathizing with the severely wounded, I congratulate you that the number of both is comparatively so small. I tender to you, officers and soldiers, the thanks of the nation." Simultaneously with the publication of this letter, it was announced that the President had declined to accept the resignation of General Burnside, which he had tendered.

The entire Union loss in this battle of Fredericksburg was reported at 1,128 killed; 9,105 wounded, and 2,078 missing. The corps of General Couch, in Sumner's division, and that of General Reynolds, in Franklin's division, suffered most heavily; the former losing 377 killed, and 3,068 wounded; the latter, 279 killed, and 2,217 wounded. The entire loss of Sumner's division was 5,311; that of General Hooker 3,548; that of General Franklin 3,452. Hancock's division lost 1,870; Meade's 1,624. As, according to the estimate of General Sumner, there were hardly 50,000 of the Union army under fire, excluding, of course, the troops held in reserve, it would appear that the casualties amounted to nearly one-fourth of the entire number in action. General Burnside estimated the number of the rebel army at less than 100,000. General Sumner thought that the forces on both sides were about equal. The Confederate loss, though heavy, was doubtless much less, the enemy being greatly protected by their works.

* General Burnside to General Halleck, Falmouth, December 19, 1862.

A sad record of mortality this, summing up the result of another great indecisive battle of the war. Posterity, reading the fearful story of the rebellion, and contemplating its train of calamity, will yet shudder at the record of the fruitless slaughter, when many of its horrible details—for all will never be written—shall be fully brought to light. In this chronicle, hurrying from one battle-ground to another, we can pause only over a few of the fallen brave, whose rank in the field, or previous history, demands particular notice. The Union army lost in the battle of Fredericksburg several distinguished officers. The eminent cavalry officer, Brigadier-General George D. Bayard, who had been actively employed in the recent campaigns in Virginia, fell at a critical moment of the engagement on the left. He had just reached General Franklin's headquarters, when, as he was sitting under a tree, he was struck by a ball on the thigh. Learning that the wound was mortal, he calmly resigned himself to his fate. "He was perfectly sensible," says a correspondent on the field, "and never once lost that self-possession which has always characterized him on the field of battle." General Bayard was a native of New York, a graduate of West Point, of 1856, when he commenced his military career as 2d Lieutenant of the 4th Cavalry. In 1861 he was promoted to a Captaincy, and about the same time was placed in command of the 1st Pennsylvania Volunteer Cavalry, attached to General McCall's reserve corps. In June, 1862, he was appointed a Brigadier-General of volunteers commanding cavalry.

Brigadier-General Conrad F. Jackson, who fell in the same action, a citizen of Pennsylvania, and civilian before the war, also entered upon the war the colonel of a regiment in McCall's reserve corps. He was attached to General Ord's brigade, before Washington, and took part in the battle at Dranesville, in December, 1861. He was in the peninsula before Richmond, in General McClellan's campaign, and subsequently promoted to the command of Ord's brigade, on the departure of that officer for the West, was actively engaged with the Army of the Potomac in the recent battles in Maryland. He died a soldier's death on the battle-field, pierced in the head by a rifle-ball, while leading his troops in a charge.

The Rev. Arthur Buckminster Fuller, of Massachusetts, a Unitarian clergyman of distinction, brother of the eminent authoress, Margaret Fuller, was with the army as chaplain. With earnest enthusiasm he offered his services, in a military capacity, at the first crossing of the river in the occupation of Fredericksburg. Accompanying the 19th Massachusetts Regiment, he had taken a musket, and was employed as a skirmisher in the principal street, when he was struck by a rebel ball, and survived but a few moments. He died at the age of forty. Educated in his youth by his distinguished sister, he had graduated at Harvard, and commenced his public career as the principal of an academy in Illinois. Becoming a Unitarian minister, he had charge at different times of several churches in Massachusetts, resigning a pastoral charge to enter the army out of a pure spirit of devotion to his country. He is said to have been "one of the most genial of men," his humanitarian services on the battle field being equally rendered to friend and foe.

Lieutenant-Colonel Joseph Bridgman Curtis, a young officer of promise, fell at the age of twenty-six in this battle—another offering to the patriotic cause: of an honored family in New York, he left the desirable position of engineer of the Central Park, of that city, to engage in the war with a volunteer regiment. He was subsequently with the North Carolina expedition, and distinguishing himself at Roanoke Island, was promoted, at General Burnside's request, to the Lieutenant-Colonelcy of the 4th Rhode Island.

The regiment was with the Army of the Potomac on the peninsula, and afterwards in Maryland. "At the battle of Antietam it was in front of the battle on the left, and was so terribly cut up that it had to be withdrawn from the field. But young Curtis did not go with it. Unwilling to be an inactive spectator, and filled with the excitement of battle, he seized the musket and cartridge-box of a dead soldier, fell into the ranks of a Pennsylvania regiment, hurrying to the front, and did duty as a private to the end of the fight. At Fredericksburg the command of the regiment devolved on him, the colonel being disabled by a wound, and he fell at the head of his men while leading them on with the fearlessness that always marked his courage in the field."*

After this disastrous battle of Fredericksburg, the usual enforced repose, which follows in the repair of losses, the care of the wounded and the burial of the dead, succeeded on the Rappahannock. With the exception of an occasional skirmish, for the following month all was again reported quiet in the Army of the Potomac. Both parties, however, were preparing to renew the "never-ending, still beginning" contest on the old still unsated Virginia battle-ground. On the last day of the year General Lee took occasion to animate the courage of his troops in the following congratulatory order, referring to their recent victory: —"The General commanding takes this occasion to express to the officers and soldiers of the army his high appreciation of the fortitude, valor, and devotion displayed by them, which, under the blessing of Almighty God, have added the victory of Fredericksburg to the long list of their triumphs. An arduous march, performed with celerity under many disadvantages, exhibited the discipline and spirit of the troops and their eagerness to confront the foe. The immense army of the enemy completed its preparations for attack without interruption, and gave battle in its own time and on ground of its own selection. It was encountered by less than 20,000 of this brave army, and its columns, crushed and broken, hurled back at every point with such fearful slaughter that escape from entire destruction became the boast of those who had advanced with the full confidence of victory. That this great result was achieved with a loss small in point of numbers, only augments the admiration with which the Commanding General regards the prowess of the troops, and increases his gratitude to Him who hath given us the victory. The war is not yet ended. The enemy is still numerous and strong, and the country demands of the army a renewal of the heroic efforts in her behalf. Nobly has it responded to her call in the past, and she will never appeal in vain to its courage and patriotism. The signal manifestations of Divine mercy that have distinguished the eventful and glorious campaign of the year just closing, give assurance of hope that under the guidance of the same Almighty hand the coming year will be no less fruitful of events that will insure the safety, peace and happiness of our beloved country, and add new lustre to the already imperishable name of the Army of Northern Virginia."

* Obituary, *New York Tribune*, December 17, 1862.

CHAPTER LXXXI.

GENERAL FOSTER'S OPERATIONS IN NORTH CAROLINA, TO DECEMBER, 1862.

WHEN General Burnside, in the previous summer, left North Carolina with a large portion of his army to reinforce General McClellan before Richmond, the charge of the department was placed in the hands of his former division commander, General Foster, who was about the same time promoted to the rank of Major-General of volunteers. There was little of special interest, beyond an occasional reconnoissance into the interior, for some time occurring in the region, the efforts of both parties being concentrated on the grand movements in Virginia. Additional troops were from time to time sent from the new levies in New England and incorporated with the force at Newbern. It was always an efficient command, and, in the hands of General Foster, was not likely to lose its former prestige. The necessity of a proper support of the department was shown in a rebel attack of cavalry and infantry upon the small Union force holding the town of Washington on the Pamlico River. The assault was made on the 6th of September, at early dawn of a foggy morning, when a party of Union troops had just left the place in another direction. The town, taken by surprise, was swept by the rebels before its defenders were fairly aroused. Vigorous resistance was then made by the garrison and the returning troops of the expedition, and opportune aid was rendered by Captain Renshaw, in command of the gunboat Louisiana in the river, who shelled their position. A second gunboat, the Picket, was accidentally exploded in the action. Notwithstanding they were thus harassed, the enemy succeeded in making good their retreat, carrying with them four pieces of artillery, which they had found inadequately protected.* The Union loss in this affair was eight killed and thirty-six wounded, and that of the enemy thirty-three killed and about one hundred wounded.† It was in consequence of threatened depredations of this nature that General Foster, at the beginning of November, led an expedition through the eastern counties of the State, the details of which are related in his report to General Halleck of November 12th. "The 1st brigade, under command of Colonel T. J. C. Amory, together with the artillery, cavalry and wagon train, were marched from Newbern across the country to Washington; the balance of my forces, including the 2d brigade, Colonel Stevenson, and the 3d brigade, Colonel Lee, were embarked on transports, and landed at Washington, where they were joined by Colonel Amory's command on Saturday evening, the 2d inst. On Sunday, the 3d, all the forces, including artillery, left Washington, under my command, for Williamson. On the evening of the same day we encountered the enemy, posted in a strong position at a small creek, called Little Creek. I immediately ordered Colonel Stevenson commanding the 2d brigade, who was then in the advance, to make all haste in driving them from the opposite side of the creek, and push on at once. The engagement lasted one hour, when the enemy being driven from their rifle-pits by the effective fire of Belger's Rhode Island battery, retired to Rawle's Mills,

* Correspondence of the *Boston Traveller*, Newbern, N. C., September 7, 1862. *Rebellion Record*, v. 609.

† Report of General Halleck, November 25, 1862.

one mile further on, where they made another stand in a recently constructed field-work. Belger's Battery and two batteries of the 3d New York Artillery were immediately ordered into position, and after a spirited engagement of half an hour succeeded in driving the enemy from their works, and across a bridge, which they burned. That night, while the pioneers built the burnt bridge, the forces bivouacked on the field and proceeded the next morning to Williamson, where we arrived about noon. We started from there, after a short rest, in pursuit of the enemy, bivouacking about five miles from that place. On the following day we reached and occupied the fortifications at Rainbow Banks, three miles below Hamilton, and then pushed on to Hamilton. There we expected to find some iron-clad boats, said to be in the process of construction at Hamilton, but discovered nothing of the kind. On the 6th we left Hamilton, in pursuit of the enemy towards Tarboro', and encamped on the same night within ten miles of that place. It was my intention to pursue the enemy towards Tarboro', but the exhausted condition of my men, most of whom had been sick during the last two months and had not yet recovered their strength, and the provisions being entirely exhausted, so that I had to subsist the command by foraging, as well as the fact that the enemy were being largely reinforced by rail, changed my plans, and on the following morning, the 7th inst., I countermarched the column, making Hamilton the same night, where we remained till the next morning, when we marched for Williamson in the midst of a severe snow-storm. At Williamson we remained a day, in order to give the men an opportunity to rest. At daylight the next day, the 10th inst., we started for Plymouth, where we arrived that night. The following day the troops were all reëmbarked for Newbern. During the engagement at Rawle's Mills and at Hamilton we captured five prisoners, who were paroled at Williamson. The loss on our side consisted in six killed and eight wounded. The expedition was instrumental in saving the town and forces at Plymouth from destruction and capture, as I found upon my arrival at the place that the enemy's forces, while lying in the vicinity, besides being engaged in foraging, had reconstructed a bridge over the creek, three miles outside the town, for the transportation of their artillery to the opposite bank. I also learned, from information gathered on the spot, that an immediate attack was to have been made on the place; but upon hearing of my advance from Washington, and seeing the danger of their capture, they beat a precipitate and hasty retreat."

The next military movement of importance in the department was set on foot simultaneously with the attack described in the last chapter, by General Burnside upon the enemy at Fredericksburg. This was an attempt to break the line of the important coast railway passing from Richmond to Wilmington and thence to Charleston and the other chief cities of the Southwest. Goldsborough, one of its chief stations lying about fifty miles to the northwest of Newbern, which contained the head-quarters of the Union army, was the point aimed at. General Foster having welded his mixed levies into efficient fighting brigades, set out on the morning of the 11th of December, a cool and clear winter day, from Newbern with a force embracing General Wessells's brigade of General Peck's division, the brigades of Colonels Amory, Stevenson and Lee, the 3d New York and 1st Rhode Island batteries, with sections of the 23d and 24th New York Independent batteries, and the 3d New York cavalry. Fourteen miles were made the first day on the main road by Kinston, when further progress was found to be obstructed by felled trees for half a mile and more. This compelled a halt, the army bivouacking for the night on a plantation which had hiiherto escaped the devastation of war, while the pioneers cleared the road. Pushing on at daylight, the cavalry advance, about four miles beyond, near Trenton, met a body of rebel cavalry and infantry, which, "after a sharp but brief skirmish," was routed with severe loss. "On arriving," continues General Foster in his report, "at the Vine Swamp road, I ordered Captain Hall, with three companies of cavalry, to push on up the main Kinston road as a demonstration, while the main column proceeded by the Vine Swamp road to the left, thereby avoiding the obstructions and the enemy on the main road. Captain Hall encountered the enemy in some force; but, after a severe fight, whipped them, taking eighteen prisoners, and killing a number. The march of the main column was somewhat delayed by the bridge over Beaver Creek being destroyed. This was rebuilt, and I pushed on, leaving a regiment (51st Massachusetts) and a section of artillery (23d New York) at the bridge to hold it, and to protect the intersection of the main road and the road I was on, to support Captain Hall, and to prevent any force driving him back and occupying the cross-roads in our rear. The main column pushed on about four miles, and bivouacked for the night. There was some cavalry skirmishing during the day.

"On Saturday, the 13th, we again started, leaving the second main road (the one I was on) to the right, and leaving at this intersection the 46th Massachusetts and one section of artillery (the 24th New York) to hold the position and feint on the second main road. We reached Southwest Creek, the bridge over which was destroyed, and the enemy posted on the opposite bank, some four hundred strong, with three pieces of artillery. The creek was not fordable, and ran at the foot of a deep ravine, making a very bad position for us. I ordered a battery in as good a position as could be obtained, and under their fire the 9th New Jersey, which had the advance, pushed gallantly across the creek—by swimming, by fragments of the bridge and by a mill-dam—and formed on the opposite bank; at the same time the 85th Pennsylvania, of General Wessells's brigade, forced a passage, by the felling of trees and fording, about half a mile below the bridge, and engaged the enemy's left, who thereupon retired and deserted his breastworks. I had ordered the 23d Massachusetts, of Colonel Amory's brigade, to cross at the mill to support the 9th New Jersey, and also crossed the remainder of General Wessells's brigade. Colonel Heckman, with the 9th New Jersey, advanced, and was fired upon when about one mile from the creek with canister and musketry. The regiment charged at double-quick, drove the enemy, took some prisoners, and captured a 6-pounder gun, caisson, etc., complete. General Wessells bivouacked on the further side of the creek, with the 9th New Jersey in advance. The balance of the command, with the artillery, remained on this side of the creek. The 9th New Jersey; Company K, 3d New York cavalry, and Morrison's battery, 3d New York artillery, had quite a skirmish with the enemy, but drove him, and camped for the night. From the south side of the creek I sent a company of cavalry to strike, and proceed up the Kinston road No. 2. I was on No. 3. The company proceeded up the road towards Kinston, and found the enemy posted by a bridge, which was prepared to be destroyed. The company charged them, and they retired with some loss, destroying the bridge. The enemy's force at this place was estimated at one regiment and four pieces of artillery. Major Garrard, with three companies of cavalry and one section of artillery, proceeded on a reconnoissance on a road leading to Whitehall. After following this road ten miles, and meeting no opposition, they rejoined the main column.

"Sunday, the 14th inst., I advanced the column, and when about one mile from Kinston encountered the enemy in strong force. They were posted in strong position in the woods, taking advantage of the ground, which formed a natural breastwork; their position was secured on their right by a deep swamp, and their left was partially protected by the river. The 9th New Jersey were deployed as skirmishers, and General Wessells's brigade, with Morrison's battery, 3d New York artillery, were ordered to advance to the right and left of the road, the battery being sent to our extreme right, supported by one of General Wessells's regiments. Colonel Amory's brigade was then advanced, the 17th Massachusetts being sent to support Colonel Heckman on the right, and two regiments (23d and 45th Massachusetts) advanced up the road. My artillery (three batteries) I posted in a large field on the right of the road, and about three-fourths of a mile in rear of line of attack, (the only position they could be placed in.) I then ordered Colonel Stevenson's brigade, with Belger's Rhode Island battery, forward. The 24th Massachusetts supported this battery, and the 5th Rhode Island, 10th Connecticut, and 44th Massachusetts were ordered forward, the two former on the left of the road and the latter on the right, to support the regiments there in pushing the enemy and turning that flank. The 10th Connecticut advanced steadily to the extreme front, relieving two of Wessells's brigade who were short of ammunition, and, after receiving a horrible fire for some twenty minutes, made a most gallant charge, in conjunction with the 96th New York volunteers, of General Wessells's brigade, which, with the advance already made (slowly but surely) of the whole line, forced the enemy to retreat precipitately for the bridge over the Neuse, which they crossed, firing the bridge, which had been prepared for that purpose. Several regiments were so close, however, that about four hundred prisoners were taken from the enemy. A line was formed to the river, and the fire extinguished before great damage was done. The 9th New Jersey, 17th Massachusetts, and General Wessells's brigade were at once crossed, pushed into the town and halted. I ordered the bridge to be at once repaired for the crossing of cavalry and artillery. General Evans retired about two miles from town with his command and formed line of battle. I sent a flag of truce to inquire whether he proposed to surrender. He declined. I immediately prepared to attack him, but, knowing he had three light batteries and one section to start with, was unwilling to sacrifice my men, and waited for my artillery to cross. I ordered batteries E and I, 3d New York artillery, to shell the enemy with their 20-pounder Parrotts (— in number) from the opposite bank, and crossed Colonel Amory's brigade with all dispatch; but before I could attack, the enemy had retired, and, it being by this time night, I was unable to pursue, and, moreover, my object was accomplished. The troops bivouacked in the fields beyond the town that night, a provost-guard was established for the protection of the town, and all necessary precautions were taken. I sent Company K, 3d New York cavalry, down the Neuse, to a work commanding the river. They reported it deserted, with six guns in position, and the work to be of great strength. I sent the company back with teams to bring up the guns and blow up the magazine—the two heavy guns, one 8-inch columbiad and one 32-pounder, which the men were unable to remove. Captain Cole destroyed the magazine and brought off four field-pieces complete. Besides these we had two others, deserted by the enemy, and the one taken by the 9th New Jersey. I left a strong guard in the town, under Major Fitzsimmons, to make a demonstration on the Goldsboro' road on that side of the river. Colonel Ledlie, 3d New York artillery, remained to destroy commissary and quartermaster's stores and to burn the bridge. Major Fitzsimmons advanced some nine miles in the direction of Goldsboro', when, hearing the whistle of a locomotive, he fired three shots in the direction of the sound, upon which the train immediately returned in the direction of Goldsboro'. Colonel Ledlie, before leaving Kinston, destroyed a locomotive, a railroad monitor, etc. I advanced, without opposition, to within three and a half miles of Whitehall, when I halted for the night. I sent Major Garrard, with three companies of cavalry, to make a reconnoissance to Whitehall. He found one regiment and four guns on our side of the bridge over the Neuse; but they quickly retreated as he approached, firing the bridge effectually.

"The next morning, (16th,) I ordered Major Garrard, with five companies, 3d New York cavalry, and one section of artillery, (23d New York,) to proceed to Mount Olive, a station on the Wilmington and Weldon Railroad, fourteen miles below Goldsboro'. In passing Whitehall, *en route* for Mount Olive, his command was fired upon from the opposite side of the river. He placed his guns in position, and returned the fire till the main column arrived, when he limbered up, and proceeded towards Mount Olive, which point he reached without opposition. Here he destroyed the railroad track for about a mile. He then proceeded along the line of the railroad for four miles, and destroyed the bridge over Goshen Swamp. The track between Mount Olive and the Goshen Swamp bridge was torn up and burned in five places. The column having arrived at Whitehall, and finding the bridge burned, and the enemy in some force, with infantry and artillery on the other side, and this being the direct road to Goldsboro', I determined to make a strong feint, as if to rebuild and cross. The 9th New Jersey and Colonel Amory's brigade were sent forward and posted on the bank of the river to engage the enemy. I then ordered up several batteries and posted them on a hill, overlooking the enemy's intrenchments. They opened, and silenced, after an hour's firing, the enemy's guns. The enemy still maintained their admirable position with sharp-shooters; but, deeming my object accomplished, I moved the command forward towards Goldsboro', having sharpshooters in rear to continue the fight. We bivouacked that night eight miles from Goldsboro', encountering no further opposition.

"On the morning of the 17th I advanced on Goldsboro'. I ordered Major Fitzsimmons, with two companies of cavalry, to make a feint in the direction of Dudley's Station and Everettsville. They scattered a small force of the enemy there in every direction, burned two trestlework culverts, destroyed a train of four railroad cars, water-station, depot etc., as well as some small arms, which they were not able to carry off, and captured a flag of the enemy. They then returned by a short cut to the main column. I also ordered Major Garrard, with four companies of cavalry and one section of artillery, to make a feint in the direction of a bridge over the Neuse on our right, called Thompson's bridge. He found the enemy in force, supposed to be one regiment of infantry and four pieces of artillery, and the bridge already burned. I then directed, in order to make the feint more complete, and to further distract the enemy, one regiment, (43d Massachusetts,) and Angel's battery, (3d New York artillery,) to the support of the cavalry and to engage the enemy, which they did, silencing, after an hour's brisk engagement, the enemy's fire. Colonel Lee's brigade was in advance of the main column, and came upon the enemy in small force on the edge of the woods lining the railroad track. Riggs's battery (3d New York artillery) was placed in position, and opened upon them, when the enemy retired. The 9th New Jersey were ordered to strike the railroad track and follow it up direct to the bridge, which they were to burn. Three regiments of Colonel Lee's brigade were ordered to their support, (the 25th, 27th, and 3d Massachusetts.) The remaining regiment was thrown on the left to protect our flank in that quarter. General Wessells's brigade was advanced and formed on the hill overlooking the track, etc. Three regiments were thrown to the left, and the remaining regiments in line, to be available at any point. My artillery was brought forward and placed in position, firing to the front and left, principally at the bridge. The enemy replied with artillery from the other side of the river. Colonel Heckman advanced steadily up the track, fighting the enemy's infantry posted at the bridge, and receiving a fire from the artillery in a monitor car, on the track of the bridge. After two hours he reached the bridge, and under a heavy fire, Lieutenant Graham, 23d New York battery, acting as aid-de-camp to Colonel Heckman, fired the bridge. All who had attempted it were picked off, as was wounded Lieutenant B. N. Mann, 17th Massachusetts, who accompanied him. I brought all my artillery to bear to prevent any effort to save the bridge, and when the fire was doing its work, ordered a countermarch for Newbern, leaving Colonel Lee to form the rear-guard. Colonel Lee was forming his brigade to leave the field, deeming the fight over, when three regimental colors were seen across the railroad track, the men protected by the embankment on which the track was laid. Colonel Lee placed Morrison's battery in position, and recalled his regiment in line. The enemy advanced with cheers across the railroad steadily in line upon Colonel Lee's brigade. Morrison's battery opened on the advancing line with spherical case, which did good effect; but they advanced steadily until within three hundred yards of the battery, where, unable to stand the fearful loss they were sustaining from the battery, they broke and retreated. Their retreat was unexpectedly covered by a masked battery, in the woods, on our left. Belger's Rhode Island battery, which had been brought back, opened in reply to the battery, and on two regiments which came in view supporting their guns. Riggs's battery, 3d New York artillery, was placed on an eminence on our left, and in line with the enemy; then, bringing a cross-fire to bear, they were thereby forced to return, as also a regiment in the woods on our right. Colonel Lee, having orders not to attempt any further move, again formed his brigade and batteries, and proceeded to join the column, which I had halted on hearing the firing from Colonel Lee. This was a bold attempt of the enemy to entrap and secure Colonel Lee's brigade and Morrison's battery. Owing to the efficiency of Colonel Lee and Morrison's battery, it was a disastrous failure. With a strong cavalry rear-guard, I then started on my return by the direct road, took and transported my sick and wounded men from Whitehall and Kinston, bringing them all safely to Newbern. On the 13th, a fleet of small boats left Newbern, under Commander Murray, United States Navy, to attack the works on the river at Kinston; but, owing to the lowness of the water in the river, only one small boat—the Allison, under Colonel Manchester, marine artillery—was brought into action. The works being too strong, she, after a gallant resistance, was obliged to retire."

In this expedition the military qualities of the new army in North Carolina were fully tested, and the conduct of officers and men was pronounced by the commander "most excellent." He particularly mentions Lieutenant-Colonel Leggett's 11th Regiment of Connecticut volunteers, as "behaving in the most gallant and dashing manner, making a charge under a fire which in twenty minutes killed and wounded 90 men out of 340." He also records "the conduct of Lieutenant George W. Graham, 23d New York battery, acting as aid to Colonel Heckman. Throughout the entire march he was conspicuous for his venturesome courage, and at Goldsboro', in company with Lieutenant B. N. Mann, 17th Massachusetts volunteers, advanced and fired the bridge, under the fire of the enemy's infantry and artillery. He only escaped capture by jumping from the bridge down the bank. Lieutenant Mann was wounded." 496 prisoners taken during the expedition were paroled. The Union loss showed an aggregate of 90 killed, 478 wounded, and 9 missing. Colonel Gray, of the 96th New York Regiment, an officer who, "though but a few days in the department, had already won the esteem of all," was among the killed.

From the report of the Confederate Major-General G. W. Smith, dated Goldsboro', December 29th, we learn some interesting particulars of the resistance offered to General Foster's expedition. Mention, it will be seen, is made of "the daring incendiary," Lieutenant Graham, who succeeded in burning the bridge. "Brigadier-General Evans," says he, "with 2,000 men held the enemy in check at Southwest Creek, beyond Kinston, on the 13th, and on the 14th, delayed their advance for some time, and succeeded in withdrawing his force, with small loss, to the left bank of the Neuse River, at Kinston. He held them at bay until the 16th, when they advanced on the opposite side of the river, and made an attack at Whitehall bridge, about eighteen miles below Goldsboro', in which they were driven back by General Robertson with severe loss. Small reinforcements arrived from Petersburg and Wilmington on the 15th, one regiment of which was placed in position to cover the railroad bridge over the Neuse, near this place. A battalion of artillery, which had made a successful retreat from the works of the obstructions below Kinston, after the enemy occupied the latter point in force, was stationed on this side of the river, at the railroad bridge, and about half a mile above, at the county bridge. On the 16th a regiment arrived from Wilmington, and one from Petersburg, both of which were sent to the river, and under General Clingman's command, to protect the two bridges. On the morning of the 17th, having no cavalry, and being unable to obtain information by other means, I directed Lieutenant-Colonel Stevens, of the engineers, with two brigades and five pieces of artillery, to make a reconnoissance, for the purpose of ascertaining the position and numbers of the enemy. General Evans' brigade had then reached Goldsboro' by rail, and remaining on board, only awaiting the clearing of the track and watering of the engines, to move by rail to the position already occupied by General Clingman with his three regiments. about one mile and a half beyond the railroad bridge. The capacity of the water-tanks being inadequate for the amount of transportation accumulated here at that time, the cars were delayed until after twelve o'clock, for want of water; pending which, the enemy appeared in force before General Clingman's three regiments, and he withdrew across the county bridge to this side of the river. The artillery of the enemy was playing upon the railroad bridge, and Evans's brigade had at last to move forward by the county road, and cross, if at all, the bridge a half mile above the railroad. About three o'clock in the afternoon, one bold and daring incendiary succeeded in reaching the bridge, and, covered by the wing wall of the abutment, lighted a flame, which soon destroyed the superstructure, leaving the masonry abutments and pier intact. At that time reinforcements which I had ordered from Richmond were hourly expected. It was very important for us now to save the county bridge, the only means remaining of crossing the river in this vicinity. Evans's and Clingman's brigades were ordered to cross, supported by Pettigrew's brigade, and the Mississippi brigade just coming in was ordered to move forward at once. The enemy were driven back from their position on the line of the railroad ; but on account of the lateness of the hour, the nature of the ground, and the fact that our artillery, cavalry, and a large portion of the reinforcements had not yet arrived, it was not advisable to attack their strong second position that evening. During the night the enemy made a hurried retreat to their fortifications and gunboats, moving with such celerity that it was useless to attempt pursuit with any other arm than cavalry, of which at that time, unfortunately, we had none." General Smith reported his loss at 71 killed, 268 wounded, and about 400 missing.

CHAPTER LXXXII.

THE ARMY OF THE CUMBERLAND—BATTLE OF MURFREESBORO', DECEMBER 31, 1862—JANUARY 3, 1863.

IMMEDIATELY after the second battle of Corinth, General Rosecrans was called from the Army of the Mississippi to the command of the newly created 14th Army Corps, known from the department to which it was assigned as the Army of the Cumberland. The corps was composed of the late Army of the Ohio, recently commanded by General Buell—a force which had been developed and gathered in Kentucky by successive accretions, and hardened in various conflicts, from the time when, early in the war, the defence of the State was first undertaken by its gallant supporter, General Rousseau, in the formation of a camp near Louisville. It was in the direct succession of the army organized and commanded by Generals Anderson, Sherman, and Buell, which had repeatedly defended the State against invasion, and had carried its victorious banners through Tennessee to the heart of the enemy's country.* The new Department of the Cumberland, in which the corps was now to be employed, comprised all of the State of Tennessee lying east of the Tennessee River, and such portions of Northern Alabama and Georgia as should be occupied by the United States forces. General Rosecrans arrived at Louisville on the 27th of October and assumed command of the army, which, with the exception of the troops at Nashville, was then concentrated at Bowling Green and Glasgow. There was much to be done in organizing and equipping the force shattered in the recent arduous campaign, and, what was of the first importance, the broken line of communication with Nashville had to be restored and supplies collected preparatory to future military movements. As Louisville was the real base of operations, distant one hundred and eighty-three miles from Nashville, it was necessary, particularly in the present low state of the Cumberland River, to reopen the railroad between the two places. This was accomplished as far as Mitchelville, on the State line, in Tennessee, thirty-five miles north of Nash-

* An interesting account of the Kentucky forces will be found in the comprehensive volume entitled "Annals of the Army of the Cumberland, by an Officer." Philadelphia, 1863.

ville, by the 6th of November, when the advance corps of General McCook passed by this route to the latter city.

Nashville was thus relieved from the presence of the enemy who were threatening the position, though General Negley, in command there, had just defeated a formidable incursion of Forrest's and Morgan's rebel cavalry. A joint attack was made on November 5th, before dawn, on both the north and south sides of the river, above and below the city. In the former, Morgan was gallantly repulsed by the Illinois troops; while Forrest's command, drawn within range of the guns of Fort Negley, were driven back, when General Negley went out to meet them. "Finding the enemy on the south," says he in his report, "taking a position beyond our picket-lines, Colonel Roberts, with two regiments of infantry and one section of artillery, was ordered to advance on the Murfreesboro' road, while I took the 69th Ohio infantry, with parts of the 78th Pennsylvania, 14th Michigan, Colonel Stokes's and Wynkoop's cavalry, and two sections of artillery, numbering in all about one thousand four hundred, and pursued that portion of the enemy on the Franklin pike. They were speedily driven from every position by our artillery, until we reached a distance of seven miles from the city. Colonel Stokes's cavalry was here ordered to charge upon the enemy's rear, and then retreat with the view of bringing him to a stand. But the main body of the enemy, with their artillery, had suddenly turned into a lane to the left; while our cavalry, in the excitement of the chase, pursued a small portion of the enemy within five miles of Franklin, capturing some prisoners, killing several, and taking a drove of cattle. Previous to the return of Stokes's cavalry the enemy appeared in considerable force upon our left, in front and rear, with the evident intention of cutting off the cavalry and our retreat. The infantry and artillery were immediately moved forward a mile to the support of our cavalry, which was ordered to rejoin the column immediately. Upon receiving intelligence from my videttes that the enemy were in force a mile to our rear, masking a battery close to the road, the head of our column was immediately faced to the rear and hastened forward to the position occupied by the enemy, fortunately getting our artillery into position and action, forcing the enemy to retire, which he did in great confusion and with considerable loss; after which he succeeded in getting his artillery into position, and a brisk firing ensued for about half an hour, during which time our forces had to be frequently shifted to avoid their range. Ascertaining that the enemy greatly outnumbered our forces, and were aiming to make a charge on both our flanks, the troops were slowly retired upon favorable grounds towards the city; at the same time the cavalry were so disposed as to divert the coming charge of the enemy on our rear, and lead them upon the 14th Michigan infantry. The object succeeded admirably, an entire regiment of cavalry making the charge, receiving a fire so destructive as to drive them back in great disorder. The enemy then planted several guns on the turnpike, which were driven off before they could load their pieces. Our forces were retired in good order towards the city, the enemy making one more attempt to get in our rear nearer the city, but were immediately driven off by a regiment of infantry and a section of artillery which had been ordered forward as a reserve. The concerted plans of the enemy, who had Hanson's brigade of four Kentucky regiments and two Tennessee regiments of infantry and five batteries of artillery, were defeated, and our troops enabled to give additional proof of their efficiency and valor."

General Rosecrans immediately followed the advance of McCook with the remainder of the army taking up a position in front of Nashville. On the 26th, the railway communication from Louisville to the city was completed, relieving the army of the tedious wagon transportation from Mitchelville. A month was now spent in bringing up the large supplies which the exhausted stores of the garrison and the risk of further interference with the railroad by the enemy rendered necessary. To guard the road, a considerable force of General Thomas's corps was stationed at Gallatin. An outpost of this command, a brigade of about two thousand raw Ohio, Illinois, and Indiana troops, commanded by Colonel A. B. Moore, which had been thrown forward to Hartsville, was, on Sunday the 7th of December, attacked by a rebel force under General Morgan. The enemy, numbering two regiments of Kentucky infantry, several regiments of cavalry, and a Kentucky battery, came up at sunrise, and after an engagement of an hour and a half, unequally sustained by the national troops, compelled the latter to surrender. The Union loss was about fifty killed and twice as many wounded. Morgan then retreated, carrying off his prisoners in the direction of Murfreesboro'. The affair, which was severely commented on in the Union journals, was made the subject of a special order by the Confederate commander-in-chief, General Bragg. "This brilliant exploit," said he, "was achieved by a portion of Morgan's cavalry brigade, together with detachments from the 2d and 9th Kentucky regiments of infantry, under Colonel Hunt—the whole under Brigadier-General Morgan. After a remarkable march of more than forty miles through snow and ice, they forded the Cumberland under cover of darkness, and at daylight precipitated themselves upon the enemy. Our success was complete. With a force of not more than one thousand two hundred men in action, we inflicted a loss upon the enemy of five hundred killed and wounded, and captured eighteen hundred prisoners, with all their arms, munitions, and other stores. Our own loss was small, compared with the result—not exceeding one hundred and twenty-five in killed and wounded. The memory of the gallant men who fell to rise no more, will be revered by their comrades and forever honored by their country." In a previous report of the same engagement, General Bragg stated the Union killed and wounded at two hundred.* The number of prisoners taken is stated in the national accounts at about thirteen hundred. Two days after, this event was somewhat redeemed by a spirited encounter between Colonel Stanley Matthews, in command of a well-supported foraging train sent out from the camp at Nashville, and the rebel General Wheeler. The latter attacked the train in force, and were gallantly repulsed.

Having secured his supplies at Nashville, General Rosecrans was in a measure indifferent to the efforts of the enemy to cut off his communications. He took advantage, indeed, of the absence of a part of their force on these excursions, to advance upon their main army "The enemy," says he, in his official report of the protracted engagement which ensued, "expecting us to go into winter quarters at Nashville, had prepared his own winter quarters at Murfreesboro', with the hope of possibly making them at Nashville; and had sent a large cavalry force into West Tennessee to annoy Grant; and another large force into Kentucky to break up the railroad. In the absence of these forces, and with adequate supplies in Nashville, the moment was judged opportune for an advance on the rebels. Polk's and Kirby Smith's forces were at Murfreesboro', and Hardee's corps on the Shelbyville and Nolinsville pike, between Triune and Eaglesville, with an advance-guard at Nolinsville, while no troops lay in front at Nashville, on the Franklin, Nolinsville and Murfreesboro' Turnpike. The

* *Rebellion Record*, v. 244.

plan of the movements was as follows: McCook, with three divisions, to advance by Nolinsville pike to Triune. Thomas, with two divisions (Negley's and Rousseau's), to advance on his right by the Franklin and Wilson pikes, threatening Hardee's right, and then to fall in by the cross-roads to Nolinsville. Crittenden, with Wood's, Palmer's and Van Cleve's divisions, to advance by the Murfreesboro' pike to Lavergne. With Thomas's two divisions at Nolinsville, McCook was to attack Hardee at Triune, and if the enemy reinforced Hardee, Thomas was to support McCook. If McCook beat Hardee, or Hardee retreated, and the enemy met us at Stewart's Creek, five miles south of Lavergne, Crittenden was to attack him. Thomas was to come in on his left flank, and McCook, after detaching a division to pursue or observe Hardee, if retreating south, was to move with the remainder of his force on their rear.

"The movement began on the morning of December 26th. McCook advanced on Nolinsville pike, skirmishing his way all day, meeting with stiff resistance from cavalry and artillery, and closing the day by a brisk fight, which gave him possession of Nolinsville and the hills one and a half miles in front, capturing one gun by the 101st Ohio and 15th Wisconsin Regiments, his loss this day being about seventy-five killed and wounded. Thomas followed on the right, and closed Negley's division on Nolinsville, leaving the other (Rousseau's) division on the right flank. Crittenden advanced to Lavergne, skirmishing heavily on his front over a rough country, intersected by forests and cedar brakes, with but slight loss. On the 26th, General McCook advanced on Triune, but his movement was retarded by a dense fog. Crittenden had orders to delay his movement until McCook had reached Triune and developed the intentions of the enemy at that point, so that it could be determined which Thomas was to support. McCook arrived at Triune, and reported that Hardee had retreated, and that he had sent a division in pursuit. Crittenden began his advance about eleven o'clock, A. M., driving before him a brigade of cavalry, supported by Maury's brigade of rebel infantry, and reached Stewart's Creek, the 3d Kentucky gallantly charging the rear-guard of the enemy and saving the bridge, on which had been placed a pile of rails that had been set on fire. This was Saturday night. McCook having settled the fact of Hardee's retreat, Thomas moved Negley's division on to join Crittenden at Stewart's Creek, and moved Rousseau's to Nolinsville. On Sunday the troops rested, except Rousseau's division, which was ordered to move on to Stewardston, and Willich's Brigade, which had pursued Hardee as far as Riggs's Cross-roads, and had determined the fact that Hardee had gone to Murfreesboro', when they returned to Triune. On Monday morning McCook was ordered to move from Triune to Wilkinson's Cross-roads, six miles from Murfreesboro', leaving a brigade at Triune. Crittenden crossed Stewart's Creek by the Smyrna bridge, on the main Murfreesboro' pike, and Negley by the ford two miles above, their whole force to advance on Murfreesboro', distant about eleven miles. Rousseau was to remain at Stewart's Creek until his train came up, and prepare himself to follow. McCook reached Wilkinson's Cross-roads by evening, with an advance brigade at Overall's Creek, saving and holding the bridge, meeting with but little resistance. Crittenden's corps advanced, Palmer leading, on the Murfreesboro' pike, followed by Negley, of Thomas's corps, to within three miles of Murfreesboro', having had several brisk skirmishes, driving the enemy rapidly, saving two bridges on the route, and forcing the enemy back to his intrenchments.

"About three P. M., a signal message coming from the front, from General

Palmer, that he was in sight of Murfreesboro', and the enemy were running, an order was sent to General Crittenden to send a division to occupy Murfreesboro'. This led General Crittenden, on reaching the enemy's front, to order Harker's Brigade to cross the river at a ford on his left, where he surprised a regiment of Breckinridge's division, and drove it back on its main lines, not more than five hundred yards distant, in considerable confusion; and he held this position until General Crittenden was advised, by prisoners captured by Harker's brigade, that Breckinridge was in force on his front, when, it being dark, he ordered the brigade back across the river, and reported the circumstances to the Commanding General on his arrival, to whom he apologized for not having carried out the order to occupy Murfreesboro'. The General approved of his action, of course, the order to occupy Murfreesboro' having been based on the information received from General Crittenden's advance division, that the enemy were retreating from Murfreesboro'. Crittenden's corps, with Negley's division, bivouacked in order of battle, distant seven hundred yards from the enemy's intrenchments, our left extending down the river some five hundred yards. The Pioneer brigade bivouacking still lower down, prepared three forts, and covered one of them, while Wood's division covered the other two, Van Cleve's division being in reserve. On the morning of the 30th, Rousseau, with two brigades, was ordered down early from Stewart's Creek, leaving one brigade there, and sending another to Smyrna to cover our left and rear, and took his place in reserve, in rear of Palmer's right, while General Negley moved on through the cedar brakes, until his right rested on the Wilkinson pike. The Pioneer corps cut roads through the cedars for his ambulances and ammunition wagons. The Commanding General remained with the left and centre, examining the ground, while General McCook moved forward from Wilkinson's Cross-roads, slowly and steadily, meeting with heavy resistance, fighting his way from Overall's Creek until he got into position, with a loss of some one hundred and thirty-five killed and wounded. Our small division of cavalry, say 3,000 men, had been divided into three parts, of which General Stanley took two, and accompanied General McCook, fighting his way across from the Wilkinson to the Franklin pike and below it, Colonel Zahn's brigade leading gallantly, and meeting with such heavy resistance that McCook sent two brigades from Johnson's division which succeeded in fighting their way into position, while the 3d brigade which had been left at Triune, moved forward from that place, and arrived at nightfall near General McCook's head-quarters. At four o'clock in the afternoon, General McCook had reported his arrival on the Wilkinson pike, joining Thomas; the result of the combat in the afternoon near Greison's home, and the fact that Sheridan was in position there, that his right was advancing to support the cavalry; also that Hardee's corps, with two divisions of Polk's, was on his front, extending down towards the Salem pike. Without any map of the ground, which was to us *terra incognita*, when General McCook informed the General commanding that his corps was facing strongly towards the east, the General commanding told him that such a direction to his line did not appear to him a proper one, but that it ought, with the exception of his left, to face much more nearly south, with Johnson's division in reserve; but that this matter must be confided to him, who knew the ground over which he had fought.

"At nine P. M. the corps commanders met at the head-quarters of the General commanding, who explained to them the following plan of the battle: McCook was to occupy the most advantageous position, refusing his right as much as practicable and necessary to secure it, to receive the attack of the enemy ; or, if that did not come, to attack himself sufficient to hold all the force on his front. Thomas and Palmer to open with skirmishing, and gain the enemy's centre and left, as far as the river. Crittenden to cross Van Cleve's division at the lower ford, covered and supported by the Sappers and Miners, and to advance on Breckinridge. Wood's division to follow by brigades, crossing at the upper ford and moving on Van Cleve's right, to carry everything before them into Murfreesboro'. This would have given us two divisions against one ; and as soon as Breckinridge had been dislodged from his position, the batteries of Wood's division, taking position on the heights east of Stone River, in advance, would see the enemy's work in reverse, would dislodge them and enable Palmer's division to press them back and drive them westward across the river or through the woods ; while Thomas, sustaining the movement on the centre, would advance on the right of Palmer, crushing their right ; and Crittenden's corps advancing, would take Murfreesboro' ; and then moving westward on the Franklin road, get in their flank and rear, and drive them into the country towards Salem, with the prospect of cutting off their retreat, and probably destroying their army. It was explained to them that this combination, insuring us a vast superiority on our left, required for its success that General McCook should be able to hold his position for three hours ; that if necessary to recede at all, he should recede as he had advanced on the preceding day, slowly and steadily, refusing his right, thereby rendering our success certain. Having thus explained the plan, the General commanding addressed General McCook as follows : 'You know the ground ; you have fought over its difficulties. Can you hold your present position for three hours?' To which General McCook replied, 'Yes, I think I can.' The General commanding then said : 'I don't like the facing so much to the east, but must confide that to you, who know the ground. If you don't think your present the best position, change it ;' and the officers then retired to their commands.

"At daylight on the morning of the 31st, the troops breakfasted and stood to their arms, and by seven o'clock were preparing for the battle. The movement began on the left by General Van Cleve, who crossed at the lower fords ; Wood prepared to sustain and follow him. The enemy meanwhile had prepared to attack General McCook, and by half-past six o'clock advanced in heavy columns—regimental front—his left attacking Willich's and Kirk's brigades of Johnson's division, which, being disposed without support, were, after a sharp but fruitless contest, crumbled to pieces and driven back, leaving Edgarton's and part of Goodspeed's battery in the hands of the enemy. The enemy following up, attacked Davis's division, and speedily dislodged Post's brigade ; Carlin's brigade was compelled to follow, as Woodruff's brigade, from the weight of testimony, had previously left its position on his left. Johnson's brigade, on retiring, inclined too far to the west, and were too much scattered to make a combined resistance, though they fought bravely at one or two points before reaching Wilkinson's pike. The reserve brigade of Johnson's division, advancing from its bivouac near Wilkinson's pike, towards the right, took a good position, and made a gallant but ineffectual stand, as the whole rebel left was moving up on the ground abandoned by our troops. Within an hour from the time of the opening of the battle, a staff-officer from General McCook arrived, announcing to me that the right wing was heavily pressed, and needed assistance ; but I was not advised of the rout of Willich's and Kirby's brigades, nor of the rapid withdrawal of Davis's division, necessitated thereby—moreover, having supposed his wing posted more compactly and his right more refused than it really was, the direction of the noise of battle did not indicate to me the true state of affairs. I consequently directed him to return, and direct General McCook to dispose his troops to the best advantage, and to hold his ground obstinately. Soon after a second officer from General McCook arrived, and stated that the right wing was being driven—a fact that was but too manifest, by the rapid movement of the noise of battle towards the north. General Thomas was immediately dispatched to order Rousseau—there in reserve—into the cedar brakes to the right and rear of Sheridan. General Crittenden was ordered to suspend Van Cleve's movement across the river, on the left, and to cover the crossing with one brigade, and move the other two brigades westward across the fields towards the railroad, for a reserve. Wood was also directed to suspend his preparations for crossing, and to hold Hascall in reserve.

"At this moment fugitives and stragglers from McCook's corps began to make their appearance through the cedar brakes, in such numbers that I became satisfied that McCook's corps was routed. I therefore directed General Crittenden to send Van Cleve in to the right of Rousseau, Wood to send Colonel Harker's brigade further down the Murfreesboro' pike, to go in and attack the enemy on the right of Van Cleve, the Pioneer brigade meanwhile occupying the knoll of ground west of Murfreesboro' pike, and about four hundred or five hundred yards in rear of Palmer's centre, supporting Stokes's battery. Sheridan, after sustaining four successive attacks, gradually swung his right from a south-easterly to north-westerly direction, repulsing the enemy four times, losing the gallant General Sill, of his right and Colonel Roberts of his left brigades, when having exhausted his ammunition—Negley's division being in the same predicament, and very heavily pressed—after desperate fighting, they fell back from the position held at the commencement, through the cedar woods, in which Rousseau's division, with a portion of Negley's and Sheridan's met the advancing enemy and checked his movements. The ammunition train of the right wing, endangered by its sudden discomfiture, was taken charge of by Captain Thruston, of the 1st Ohio, regular ordnance officer, who by his energy and gallantry, aided by a charge of cavalry and such troops as he could pick up, carried it through the woods to the Murfreesboro' pike, around to the rear of the left wing, thus enabling the troops of Sheridan's division to replenish their empty cartridge-boxes. During all this time Palmer's front had likewise been in action, the enemy having made several attempts to advance upon it. At this stage it became necessary to readjust the line of battle to the new state of affairs. Rousseau and Van Cleve's advance having relieved Sheridan's division from the pressure, Negley's division and Cruft's brigade, from Palmer's division, withdrew from their original position in front of the cedars, and crossed the open field to the east of the Murfreesboro' pike, about four hundred yards in rear of our front line, where Negley was ordered to replenish his ammunition, and form in close column in reserve. The right and centre of our line now extended from Hazen to the Murfreesboro' pike in a north-westerly direction. Hascall supporting Hazen, Rousseau filling the interval to the Pioneer brigade. Negley in reserve, Van Cleve west of the Pioneer brigade, McCook's corps refused on his right and slightly to the rear on the Murfreesboro' pike, the cavalry being still further to the rear on the Murfreesboro' pike and beyond Overall's Creek. The enemy's infantry and cavalry attack on our extreme right was repulsed by

Van Cleve's division, with Harker's brigade and the cavalry. After several attempts of the enemy to advance on this new line, which were thoroughly repulsed, as also their attempts on the left, the day closed, leaving us masters of the original ground on our left, and our new line advantageously posted, with open ground in front swept at all points by our artillery.

"We had lost heavily in killed and wounded, and a considerable number in stragglers and prisoners; also twenty-eight pieces of artillery, the horses having been slain, and our troops being unable to withdraw them by hand over the rough ground, but the enemy had been thoroughly handled, and badly damaged at all points, having had no success where we had open ground and our troops were properly posted; none, which did not depend on the original crushing of our right, and the superior masses which were, in consequence, brought to bear upon the narrow front of Sheridan's and Negley's divisions, and a part of Palmer's, coupled with the scarcity of ammunition, caused by the circuitous road which the train had taken, and the inconvenience of getting it from a remote distance through the cedars. Orders were given for the issue of all the spare ammunition, and we found that we had enough for another battle, the only question being where that battle was to be fought. It was decided, in order to complete our present lines, that the left should be retired some two hundred and fifty yards to a more advantageous ground, the extreme left resting on Stone River above the lower ford and extending to Stokes's battery. Starkweather's and Walker's brigades arriving near the close of the evening, the former bivouacked in close column in reserve in rear of McCook's left, and the latter was posted on the left of Sherman near the Murfreesboro' pike, and next morning relieved Van Cleve, who returned to his position in the left wing. After careful examination, and free consultation with corps commanders, followed by a personal examination of the ground in rear as far as Overall's Creek, it was determined to await the enemy's attack in that position, to send for the provision train, and order up fresh supplies of ammunition, on the arrival of which, should the enemy not attack, offensive operations should be resumed.

"No demonstration on the morning of the 1st of January. Crittenden was ordered to occupy the points opposite the ford on his left with a brigade. About two o'clock in the afternoon the enemy, who had shown signs of movement and massing on our right, appeared at the extremity of a field a mile and a half from the Murfreesboro' pike, but the presence of Gibson's brigade with a battery occupying the woods near Overall's Creek, and Negley's division and a portion of Rousseau's on the Murfreesboro' pike opposite the field, put an end to this demonstration, and the day closed with another demonstration by the enemy on Walker's brigade, which ended in the same manner. On Friday morning the enemy opened four heavy batteries on our centre, and a strong demonstration of attack a little further to the right, but a well-directed fire of artillery soon silenced his batteries, while the guns of Walker and Sheridan put an end to his effort there. About three o'clock P. M., while the Commanding General was examining the position of Crittenden's left across the river, which was now held by Van Cleve's division, supported by a brigade from Palmer's, a double line of skirmishers was seen to emerge from the woods in a south-easterly direction, advancing across the fields, and they were soon followed by heavy columns of infantry—battalion front, with three batteries of artillery. Our only battery on that side of the river had been withdrawn from an eligible point; but the most available spot was pointed out, and it soon opened fire upon the enemy.

The line, however, advanced steadily to within one hundred yards of the front of Van Cleve's division, when a short and fierce contest ensued. Van Cleve's division, giving way, retired in considerable confusion across the river, followed closely by the enemy. General Crittenden immediately directed his chief of artillery to dispose the batteries on the hill on the west side of the river, so as to open on them, while two brigades of Negley's division, from the reserve, and the Pioneer brigade, were ordered up to meet the onset. The firing was terrific, and the havoc terrible. The enemy retreated more rapidly than they had advanced. In forty minutes they lost two thousand men. General Davis, seeing some stragglers from Van Cleve's division, took one of his brigades and crossed at a ford below, to attack the enemy on his left flank, and by General McCook's order the rest of his division was permitted to follow; but when he arrived, two brigades of Negley's division and Hazen's brigade of Palmer's division had pursued the flying enemy well across the field, capturing four pieces of artillery and a stand of colors. It was now after dark, and raining, or we should have pursued the enemy into Murfreesboro'. As it was, Crittenden's corps passed over, and, with Davis, occupied the crests, which were intrenched in a few hours. Deeming it possible that the enemy might again attack our right and centre thus weakened, I thought it advisable to make a demonstration on our right, by a heavy division of camp fires, and by laying out a line of battle with torches, which answered the purpose.

"On Saturday, January 3d, it rained heavily from three o'clock in the morning; the plowed ground over which our left would be obliged to advance was impassable for artillery; the ammunition train did not arrive until ten o'clock, it was therefore deemed unadvisable to advance, but batteries were put in position on the left by which the ground could be swept, and even Murfreesboro' reached by the Parrott guns. A heavy and constant picket firing had been kept up on our right and centre, and extending to our left, which at last became so annoying, that in the afternoon I directed the corps commanders to clear their fronts. Occupying the woods to the left of Murfreesboro' pike with sharpshooters, the enemy had annoyed Rousseau all day, and General Thomas and himself requested permission to dislodge them and their supports which covered a ford. This was granted, and a sharp fire from four batteries was opened for ten or fifteen minutes, when Rousseau sent two of his regiments, which, with Speer's Tennesseeans and the 85th Illinois Volunteers, that had come out with the wagon-train, charged upon the enemy, and after a sharp contest, cleared the woods and drove the enemy from his trenches, capturing from seventy to eighty prisoners. Sunday morning, the 4th of January, it was not deemed advisable to commence offensive movements, and news soon reached us that the enemy had fled from Murfreesboro'. Burial parties were sent out to bury the dead, and the cavalry was sent to reconnoitre. Early on Monday morning General Thomas advanced, driving the rear guard of rebel cavalry before him six or seven miles towards Manchester. McCook and Crittenden's corps following took position in front of the town, occupying Murfreesboro'. We learned that the enemy's infantry had reached Shelbyville by twelve o'clock M. on Sunday, but owing to the impracticability of bringing up supplies and the loss of five hundred and fifty-seven artillery horses, further pursuit was deemed unadvisable.

"It may be of use," adds General Rosecrans, "to give the following general summary of the operations and results of the series of skirmishes, closing with the battle of Stone River and occupation of Murfreesboro'. We moved on the enemy with the following forces:

Infantry	41,421
Artillery	2,223
Cavalry	3,296
Total	46,940

We fought the battle with the following forces:

Infantry	37,977
Artillery	2,223
Cavalry	3,200
Total	43,400

We lost in killed:

Officers	92
Enlisted men	1,441
Total	1,533

We lost in wounded:

Officers	384
Enlisted men	6,861
Total	7,245
Total killed and wounded,	8,778

Being 20.03 per cent of the entire force in action. Our loss in prisoners is not fully made out, but the Provost Marshal General says, from present information, they will fall short of 2,800. If there are many more bloody battles on record, considering the newness and inexperiences of the troops, both officers and men, or if there has been more true fighting qualities displayed by any people, I should be pleased to know it.

"As to the condition of the fight we may say, that we operated over an unknown country against a position which was 15 per cent better than our own, every foot of ground and approaches being well known to the enemy, and that these disadvantages were fatally exhumed by the faulty position of our right wing. The force we fought is estimated as follows. We have prisoners from 132 regiments of infantry (consolidations counted as one), averaging from those in General Bushrod Johnson's division, 411 each, say, for certain 350 men each, will give—

132 Regiments Infantry, say 350 men each	46,000
12 Battalions Sharpshooters, say 100 men each	1,200
23 Batteries of Artillery, say 80 men each	1,840
29 Regiments of Cavalry, and } 400 24 Organizations of Cavalry, } 70	13,250
220	62,490

Their average loss, taken from the statistics of Clayburn, Breckinridge, and Withers's divisions, was about 2,080 each; this, for six divisions of infantry, and one of cavalry, will amount to 14,560 men, or to ours nearly as 165 to 100. Of 14,560 rebels struck by our missiles, it is estimated that 20,000 rounds of artillery hit 728 men; 2,000,000 rounds of musketry hit 13,832 men. Averaging 27 cannon shots to hit one man, 145 musket shot to hit one man. Our relative loss was as follows:

	Per Cent.
Right wing, 15,983, musketry and artillery, loss	20.72
Centre, 10,866, musketry and artillery, loss	18.4
Left wing, 13,288, musketry and artillery, loss	24.6

On the whole, it is evident that we fought superior numbers on unknown ground, inflicting much more injury than we suffered, were always superior on equal ground with equal numbers, and failed of a most crushing victory on Wednesday by the extension and direction of our right wing."

Turning to the official report of General Bragg of these seven days' engagements, we are informed that on the Union advance from Nashville, the divisions of his army were stationed, Polk's corps and three brigades of Breckinridge's division of Hardee's corps, at Murfreesboro', the balance of Hardee's corps at Eagleville, about twenty miles west, and McCown's division twelve miles east of Murfreesboro'; the three cavalry brigades of Wheeler, Wharton and Pegram occupying the entire front and covering all approaches within ten miles of Nashville. "On Sunday, the 26th, his main force of infantry and artillery was concentrated in front of Murfreesboro', whilst the cavalry, supported by three brigades of infantry and three batteries of artillery, impeded the advance of the enemy by constant skirmishing and sudden unexpected attacks." We have seen how this resistance was met and how the Union army succeeded in securing its line of battle resting on Stone River. In anticipation of the conflict, General Bragg arranged his forces, Polk's corps forming the left wing in front of the river, Hardee's corps constituting the right wing in its rear: Withers's division to form the first line on Polk's corps; Cheatham's, the second: Breckinridge's division the first line in Hardee's corps, Cleburn's the second: McCown's division to form reserve opposite centre on high ground, Jackson's brigade in reserve to the right flank. "Late on Monday, the 29th, it became apparent," says General Bragg, "the enemy was extending to the right, to flank us on the left. McCown's division in reserve was promptly thrown to that flank, and added to the command of Lieutenant-General Polk. The enemy not meeting our expectations of making an attack on Tuesday, which was consumed in artillery firing and heavy skirmishing, with the exception of a dash late in the evening on the left of Withers's division, which was repulsed and severely punished, it was determined to assail him on Wednesday morning, the 31st. For this purpose, Cleburn's division, Hardee's corps, was moved from the second line on the right to the corresponding position on the left, and Lieutenant-General Hardee was ordered to that point and assigned to the command of that and McCown's division. This disposition—the result of necessity—left me no reserve; but Breckinridge's command on the right, not now threatened, was regarded as a source of supply for any reinforcements absolutely necessary to other parts of the field. Stone River at its low stage was fordable at almost every point for infantry, and at short intervals perfectly practicable for artillery. This disposition completed, Lieutenant-General Hardee was ordered to assail the enemy at daylight on Wednesday, the 31st, the attack to be taken up by General Polk's command in succession to the right flank, the move to be made by a constant wheel to the right on Polk's right flank as a pivot; the object being to force the enemy back on Stone River, and, if practicable, by the aid of cavalry cut him off from his base of operations and supplies by the Nashville pike. The lines were now bivouacked at a distance in places of not more than five hundred yards, the camp-fires of the two being within distinct view. Wharton's cavalry brigade had been held on our left to watch and check the movements of the enemy in that direction, and to prevent his cavalry from gaining the railroad in our rear, the preservation of which was of vital importance. In this he was aided by Brigadier-General A. Buford, who had a small command of six hundred new cavalry. The duty was most ably, gallantly, and successfully performed. On Monday night, Brigadier-General Wheeler proceeded with his cavalry brigade and one regiment from Pegram's, as ordered, to gain the enemy's rear. By Tuesday morning, moving on the Jefferson pike around the enemy's left flank, he had gained the rear of the whole army, and soon attacked the trains, their guards, and the numerous stragglers. He succeeded in capturing several hundreds of wagons loaded with supplies and baggage. After clearing the road, he made his way entirely around and joined the cavalry on our left.

"The failure of General McCown to execute, during the night, an order for a slight change in the line of his division, and which had to be done the next morning, caused some delay in the general and vigorous assault by Lieutenant-General Hardee. But about seven o'clock, the rattle of musketry and the roar of artillery announced the beginning of the conflict. The enemy was taken completely by surprise; general and staff-officers were not mounted; artillery horses not hitched and infantry not formed; a hot and inviting breakfast of coffee and other luxuries, to which our gallant and hardy men had long been strangers, was found upon the fire unserved, and was left whilst we pushed on to the enjoyment of a more inviting feast, that of captured artillery, flying battalions, and hosts of craven prisoners begging for the lives they had forfeited by their acts of brutality and atrocity. Whilst thus routing and pushing the enemy on his front, Lieutenant-General Hardee announced to me by a messenger that the movement was not being as promptly executed by Major-General Cheatham's command on his right, the left of General Polk's corps, as he expected, and that his line was completely exposed to an enfilade fire from the enemy's artillery in that point. The necessary instructions for prompt movement at that point were immediately dispatched, and in a short time our whole line, except Breckinridge's command, was warmly engaged. From this time we continued to drive the enemy more or less rapidly until his line was thrown entirely back at right ranges to his first position, and occupied the cut of the railroad along which he had massed his reserves and posted very strong batteries. The enemy's loss was very heavy in killed and wounded, far exceeding our own, as appeared from a critical examination of the field, now almost entirely in our possession. Of artillery alone we had secured more than twenty-five pieces. Whilst the infantry and artillery were yet engaged in this successful work, Brigadier-General Wharton with his cavalry command was most actively and gallantly engaged on the enemy's right and rear, where he inflicted a heavy loss in killed and wounded, captured a full battery of artillery endeavoring to escape, and secured and sent in near two thousand prisoners. These important successes and results had not been achieved without heavy sacrifices on our part, as the resistance of the enemy, after the first surprise, was most gallant and obstinate. Finding Lieutenant-General Hardee so formidably opposed by the movements of the enemy to his front, reinforcements for him were ordered from Major-General Breckinridge, but the orders were countermanded, as will hereafter appear, and Polk's corps pressed forward with vigor, hoping to draw the enemy back or route him on the right, as he had already been on the left. We succeeded in driving from every position except the strong one held by his extreme left flank, resting on Stone River, and carried by a concentration of artillery of superior range and calibre, which seemed to bid us defiance. The difficulty of our general advance had been greatly enhanced by the topography of the country. All parts of our line had to pass in their progress over grounds of the roughest character, covered with huge stones and studded with the densest growth of cedar, the branches reaching the ground and forming an almost impassable 'brake.' Our artillery could rarely be used, while the enemy, holding defensive lines, had selected formidable positions for his batteries, and the dense cover for his infantry, from both of which he had to be dislodged by our infantry alone.

"The determined and unwavering gallantry of our troops, and the uninterrupted success which attend their repeated charges against their stronghold, defended by double their numbers, fully justified the unbounded confidence I have ever reposed in them and had so often expressed. To meet our successful advance and retrieve his losses in the front of his left, the enemy early transferred a portion of his reserve from his left to that flank, and by two o'clock had succeeded in concentrating such a force on Lieutenant-General Hardee's front as to check his further progress. Our two lines had by this time become almost blended, so weakened were they by losses, exhaustion, and extension to cover the enemy's whole front. As early as ten o'clock A. M. Major-General Breckinridge was called on for one brigade, and soon after a second, to reinforce or act as a reserve to Lieutenant-General Hardee. His reply to the first call represented the enemy crossing Stone River in heavy force in his immediate front, and on receiving the second order, he informed me that they had already crossed in heavy force, and were advancing to attack his lines. He was immediately ordered not to await attack, but to advance and meet them. About this same time a report reached me that a heavy force of the enemy's infantry was advancing on the Lebanon road, about five miles on Breckinridge's front. Brigadier-General Pegram, who had been sent to that road to cover the flank of the infantry with his cavalry brigade, two regiments detached with Wheeler and Wharton was ordered forward immediately to develope any such movement. The orders from the two brigades of Breckinridge were countermanded, whilst dispositions were made at his request to reinforce him. Before this could be carried out, the move ordered disclosed the fact that no force had crossed Stone River; that the only enemy in our immediate front then was a small body of sharpshooters, and that there was no advance on the Lebanon road. These unfortunate misrepresentations on that part of the field which, with proper caution, could not have existed, withheld from active operations three fine brigades until the enemy had succeeded in checking our progress, had reestablished his lines, and had collected many of his broken battalions. Having now settled the question that no movement was being made against our right, and none to be apprehended, Breckinridge was ordered to leave two brigades to support the battery at 'A,' on his side of Stone River—and with the balance of the force to cross to the left and report to Lieutenant-General Polk. By the time this could be accomplished it was too late to send this force to Lieutenant-General Hardee's support, who was unable to make further progress, and he was directed to maintain his position. Lieutenant-General Polk was directed with these reinforcements to throw all the force he could collect upon the enemy's extreme left, and thereby either carry that strong point which had so far resisted us so successfully—or, failing in that, at least to draw off from Hardee's front the formidable opposition there concentrated. The three brigades of Jackson, Preston, and Adams were successively reported for their work.

"How gallantly they moved to their task, and how much they suffered in the determined effort to accomplish it, will better appear from reports of subordinate commanders, and the statement of the losses therewith. Upon this flank, their strongest defensive position resting on the river-bank, the enemy had concentrated not less than twenty pieces of artillery, masked almost from view, but covering an open space in front of several hundred yards, supported right and left and rear by heavy masses of infantry. This position proved impracticable, and after two unsuccessful efforts, the attempt to carry it by infantry was abandoned. Our heaviest batteries of artillery and rifled guns of long range were now concentrated in front, and their fires opened upon this position. After a cannonade of some time, the enemy's fire slackened, and finally ceased near nightfall. Lieutenant-General Hardee had slightly retired his line from the farthest point he had attained, for better position and cover, without molestation from the enemy. Lieutenant-General Polk's infantry, including the three reinforcing brigades, uniting their front with Hardee's right, and extending to our extreme right flank, formed a continuous line, very nearly perpendicular to the original line of both—then leaving nearly the whole field with all its trophies, the enemy's dead and many of his wounded, his hospitals and stores in our full possession. The body of Brigadier-General Sill, one of their division commanders, was found where he had fallen, and was sent to town and decently interred, though he had forfeited all claim to such consideration by the acts of cruelty, barbarity and atrocity, but a few days before committed under his authority on the women and children and old men living near the road on which he had made a reconnoissance. During the afternoon, Brigadier-General Pegram, discovering a hospital and large numbers of stragglers in the rear of the enemy's lines and across Stone River, charged them with his cavalry and captured about one hundred and seventy prisoners. Both armies, exhausted by a conflict of full ten hours' duration, rarely surpassed for its continued intensity and heavy losses sustained, sunk to rest with the sun, and perfect quiet prevailed for the night.

"At dawn on Thursday morning, the 1st of January, orders were sent to the several commanders to press forward their skirmishers, feel the enemy, and report any change in his position. Major-General Breckinridge had been transferred to the right of Stone River to resume the command of that position, now held by two of his brigades. It was soon reported that no change had occurred, except the withdrawal of the enemy from the advanced position occupied by his left flank. Finding, upon further examination, that this was the case, the right flank of Lieutenant-General Polk's corps was thrown forward to occupy the ground for which we had so obstinately contended the evening before. This shortened our lines considerably, and gave us possession of the centre battlefield, from which we gleaned the spoils and trophies throughout the day, and transferred them rapidly to the rear. A careful reconnoissance of the enemy's position was ordered, and the most of the cavalry was put in motion for the roads in his rear, to cut off his trains and develope any movement. It was soon ascertained that he was still in very heavy force all along our front, occupying a position strong by nature, and improved by such work as could be done at night by his reserves. In a short time reports from the cavalry informed me that heavy trains were moving towards Nashville, some of the wagons loaded, and all the ambulances filled with wounded. These were attacked at different places; many wagons were destroyed, and hundreds of prisoners paroled. No doubt this induced the enemy to send large escorts of cavalry, artillery, and infantry with later trains, and then the impression was made on our ablest commanders that a retrograde movement was going on. Our forces, greatly wearied and much reduced by heavy losses, were held ready to avail themselves of any change in the enemy's position; but it was deemed unadvisable to assail him as there established. The whole day after these dispositions was passed without an important movement on either side, and was consumed by us in gleaning the battlefield, burying the dead and replenishing ammunition.

"At daylight on Friday, the 2d, orders to feel the enemy and ascertain his position were repeated, with the same result. The cavalry brigades of Wheeler and Wharton had returned during the night, greatly exhausted from long continued service, with but little rest or food to either man or horse. Both commanders reported the indications, from the enemy's movements, the same. Allowing them only a few hours to feed and rest, and sending the two detached regiments back to Pegram's brigade, Wharton was ordered to the right flank, across Stone River, to assume command in that quarter, and keep me advised of any change. Wheeler, with his brigade, was ordered to gain the enemy's rear again, and remain until he could definitely report whether any retrograde movement was being made. Before Wharton had taken his position, observation excited my suspicions in regard to a movement having been made by the enemy across Stone River, immediately in Breckinridge's front. Reconnoissance by several staff-officers soon developed the fact that a division had quietly crossed, unopposed, and established themselves on and under cover of an eminence, from which Lieutenant-General Polk's line was commanded and enfiladed. The dislodgment of this force or the withdrawal of Polk's line was an evident necessity. The latter involved consequences not to be entertained. Orders were accordingly given for the concentration of the whole of Major-General Breckinridge's division in front of the position to be taken. The addition to his command of the ten Napoleon guns (12-pounders) under Captain F. H. Robertson, an able and accomplished artillery officer, and for the cavalry forces of Wharton and Pegram, about two thousand men, to join in the attack on his right. Major-General Breckinridge was sent for, and advised of the movement and its objects, the securing and holding the position which protected Polk's flank, and gave us command of the enemy's by which to enfilade him. He was informed of the forces placed at his disposal, and instructed, with them, to drive the enemy back, crown the hill, intrench his artillery, and hold the position.

"To distract their attention from our real object, a heavy artillery-fire was ordered to be opened from Polk's front, at the exact hour at which the movement was to begin; at other points throughout both lines, all was quiet. General Breckinridge, at half-past three P. M., reported he would advance at four. Polk's batteries promptly opened fire, and were soon answered by the enemy. A heavy cannonade of some fifteen minutes was succeeded by the musketry, which soon became general. The contest was short and severe; the enemy was driven back and the eminence gained; but the movement as a whole was a failure, and the position was again yielded. Our forces were moved, unfortunately, so far to the left as to throw a portion of them into and over Stone River, where they encountered heavy masses of the enemy, whilst those against whom they were intended to operate on our side of the river, had a destructive enfilade on our whole line. Our second line was so close to the first as to receive the enemy's fire, and returning it took their friends in the rear. The cavalry force was left entirely out of the action. Learning from my own staff-officers, sent to the scene, of the disorderly retreat being made by General Breckinridge's division, Brigadier-General Patton Anderson's fine brigade of Mississippians, the nearest body of troops, was promptly ordered to his relief. On reaching the field and moving forward, Anderson found himself in front of Breckinridge's infantry, and soon encountered the enemy's light troops, close upon our artillery, which had been left without support. This noble brigade, under its cool and gallant chief, drove the enemy back and saved all the guns not captured before its arrival. Captain F. H. Robertson, after the disabling wound received by Major Graves, chief of artillery, took the entire charge of the artillery of the division, in addition to his own. To his gallantry, energy, and fearlessness, is due the smallness of our loss sustained before the arrival of support, only three guns. Before the end of the whole movement it was quite dark. Anderson's command held a position next the enemy, corresponding nearly with our original line, whilst Breckinridge's brigade commanders collected their scattered men as far as practicable in the darkness, and took irregular positions on

Anderson's left and rear. At daylight in the morning, they were moved forward to the front, and the whole line was established without opposition. During the night General Cleburn's division was retransferred to its original position on the right, and Lieutenant-General Hardee directed to resume command there and restore our line.

"On Saturday morning, the 3d, our forces had been in line of battle five days and nights, with but little rest, having o reserves; their baggage and tents had been loaded and the wagons were four miles off; their provisions, if cooked at all, were most imperfectly prepared with scanty means; the weather had been severe from cold and almost constant rain, and we had no change of clothing, and in many places could not have fire. The necessary consequence was the great exhaustion of both officers and men, many having to be sent to the hospitals in the rear, and more still were beginning to straggle from their commands, an evil from which we had so far suffered but little. During the whole of the day the rain continued to fall with little intermission, and the rapid rise in Stone River indicated that it would soon be unfordable. Late on Friday night I had received the captured papers of Major-General McCook, commanding one *corps d'armée* of the enemy, showing their effective strength to have been very nearly, if not quite, seventy thousand men. Before noon reports from Brigadier-General Wheeler satisfied me that the enemy, instead of retiring, was receiving reinforcements. Common prudence and the safety of my army, upon which even the safety of our cause depended, left no doubt in my mind as to the necessity for my withdrawal from so unequal a contest. My orders were accordingly given about noon for the movement of the train and for the necessary preparations of troops. Under the efficient management of the different staff departments every thing had been secured and transferred to the rear, including prisoners captured, artillery and small arms, subsistence, means of transportation, and nearly all of our wounded able to bear moving. No movement of any kind was made by the troops on either side during this most inclement day, until just at night, when a sharp skirmish occurred between Polk's right and the enemy's left flank, resulting in nothing decisive. The only question with me was, whether the movements should be made at once or delayed twenty-four hours to save a few of our wounded. As it was possible that we should lose by exhaustion as many as we should remove of the wounded, my inclination to remain was yielded. The whole force, except the cavalry, was put in motion at eleven o'clock P. M., and the army returned in perfect order to its present position beyond Duck River, without receiving a single shot. Our cavalry held the position before Murfreesboro' until Monday morning, the 5th, when it quietly retired, as ordered, to cover our front.

"We had left one thousand two hundred badly wounded, one half of whom we have since heard have died from the severity of their wounds; about three hundred sick, too feeble to bear transportation, and a number of well men and officers as medical attendants. In addition to this, the enemy had captured about eight hundred prisoners from us. As the one thousand two hundred wounded are counted once under that head among our losses, they should be expunged from the general total. As our offset to this loss, we had received considerably over six thousand prisoners, had captured over thirty pieces of cannon, six thousand stand of small arms, ambulances, mules and horses, with a large amount of other valuable property, all of which was secured and appropriated to proper uses. Besides all this secured, we destroyed not less than eight hundred wagons, mostly laden with various articles, such as arms, ammunition, provisions, baggage, clothing, medicine, and hospital stores. We had lost only three pieces of artillery, all in Breckinridge's repulse. A number of stands of colors, nine of which are forwarded with this report, were also captured on the field. Others known to have been taken have not been sent in. A tabular statement of our forces, showing the number of fighting men we had in the field on the morning of the 31st of December, to have been less than thirty-five thousand, of which thirty thousand were infantry and artillery. Our losses, it will be seen, exceeded ten thousand, nine thousand of whom were killed or wounded. Among the gallant dead the nation is called to mourn, none could have fallen more honored or regarded than Brigadier-Generals James E. Rains and R. M. Hanson. They yielded their lives in the heroic discharge of their duties, and leave their honored names as a legacy to their descendants. Brigadier-Generals J. R. Chalmers and D. W. Adams received disabling wounds on Monday, I am happy to say not serious, but which deprived us of their valuable services. Having been under my immediate command since the beginning of the war, I can bear evidence to their devotion and to the conspicuous gallantry which has marked their services on every field."

Such, in the words of the rival commanders, is the military narrative of the battle of Murfreesboro'—one of the most determined and equally sustained conflicts of the war. It will be forever memorable among the great conflicts of the struggle for the Union in the West. A volume would not exhaust its incidents or relate the story in detail of the bravery displayed on the field. The official reports on one side, as published by the National Congress, occupy an octavo of nearly six hundred pages. In these actions, particularly of the Western troops, there is a rare individuality, every officer feeling the responsibility of his command, and the soldiers fully aware of the honor of their State or district at stake. In ordinary armies all separate interests of this kind are merged in an indiscriminate mass; but a volunteer force bears its local banner into the field and must account at home for its preservation. Space would fail us to recount the celebrities of the Army of the Cumberland. General Rosecrans in his report of Murfreesboro' liberally sets forth their merits. Of the leading Generals in the grand division of the right, the centre, and the left, McCook, Thomas, and Crittenden, we need not here speak, the previous record of the war bearing ample testimony to their merits in the field. The same may be said of Brigadier-General David S. Stanley. "Already," says General Rosecrans, "distinguished for four successive battles, Island No. 10, May 27th before Corinth, Iuka, and the battle of Corinth, at this time in command of our ten regiments of cavalry, he fought the enemy's forty regiments of cavalry, and held them at bay and beat them wherever he could meet them. He ought to be made a Major-General for his services and also for the good of the service." A recommendation which was extended by General Rosecrans to include "such brigadiers as Negley, Jefferson C. Davis, Johnson, Palmer, Hascall, Van Cleve, Wood, Mitchell, Cruft, and Sheridan." General Stanley, a native of Ohio, and graduate of West Point, having served with distinction on the Western frontier, and at the outbreak of the rebellion held the rank of Captain of the 4th Regular cavalry. He was then in command in Arkansas, and was thus brought into relation with the early military movements of General Lyon in Missouri. After the battle of Wilson's Creek he was appointed Brigadier-General of Volunteers, and subsequently was engaged in the battles enumerated by General Rosecrans. He was now in his thirty-fifth year. He was presently, according to the suggestion made, created Major-General of Volunteers.

General James S. Negley, who was also raised to this rank, was a native of Pennsylvania. Born in 1826 of an influential family he was early attracted to a military life, leaving college, before he was of age, to enlist as a private in an infantry company raised for the Mexican war. Various legal and other obstacles were placed in his way by his friends, but he broke through them all, took his place in the army, and surviving a serious illness, was with the column of General Scott to the close of the war. Returning to Pennsylvania, he was engaged in rural pursuits, always giving attention to military affairs, when he was summoned at the beginning of the war by Governor Curtin to organize the volunteers in Western Pennsylvania. He subsequently raised a brigade, with which he was ordered to Kentucky, and when Tennessee was open to occupation by the Union troops was stationed in an important command, with his headquarters in that state at Columbia. When the army was withdrawn from the Southern frontier he returned to Nashville, which he fortified with great skill and as we have seen, held in defiance of the enemy till the arrival of the main army under General Rosecrans. Much depended upon his efforts during this period, and to the admiration of the country, he gallantly maintained his trust.

Brigadier-General Richard W. Johnson, a native of Kentucky, was a graduate of West Point, 1849. After several years' service in the infantry, he was transferred to the cavalry, Colonel A. S. Johnston's regiment, and was with that officer in Texas, remaining in the state till the defection of General Twiggs, when he made his way with a portion of his command to the North. On the organization of the new armies, he was first Lieutenant-Colonel of a regiment of Kentucky cavalry, and then a Brigadier-General of volunteers in General Buell's department. He was engaged at Corinth, and, subsequently, as we have narrated, in an encounter at Gallatin with the rebel Morgan, in which his command was overpowered, and he was compelled to surrender. He was paroled, and afterwards exchanged, and had recently been appointed to his command in the army of the Cumberland.

Brigadier-General John McAuley Palmer, since promoted to a Major-Generalship, born in Kentucky, in 1817, removed with his parents to Illinois in his boyhood. Early embued with a love of knowledge and desire for intellectual advancement, he had worked his way from a youth of poverty to eminence in the legal profession and many positions of political importance in the State. An influential member of the Republican party, he had been one of the electors at large in Illinois, voting for President Lincoln, and had been sent as a delegate to the Peace Congress at Washington. He entered the military service early in the war as Colonel of an Illinois regiment, was with Fremont in Missouri, and subsequently with General Pope at New Madrid, accompanying the latter officer to Mississippi. He was in the action at Farmington before Corinth, was afterwards attached to Buell's army and shared with General Negley the recent protection of Nashville.

General Hascall, a native of New York, was a graduate of West Point of 1852, and after a brief service in the artillery, resigned and settled in Indiana. He reëntered the service at the beginning of the war as Colonel of a regiment from that State, and had since been engaged in the West.

General Van Cleve, born in New Jersey, also a graduate of West Point, of the class of 1831, had, likewise, after several years' service in the infantry, resigned his commission and taken up his residence in the West. The war found him in Minnesota, where he entered the field in command of an infantry regiment from that State, fought at Mill Spring, was promoted to a Brigadier-

Generalship for his gallantry, and was with General Buell in his campaigns in Tennessee and Kentucky. In the action at Murfreesboro' a wound received on the 31st of December compelled him to retire from the field the next day.

General Thomas Jefferson Wood, also a graduate of West Point, of the year 1845, had served with General Taylor in the Mexican war in the dragoons, was subsequently much employed as a cavalry officer in the West, visited Europe on a leave of absence, returning in time to participate in the organization of the new army in 1861. He was at Pittsburgh Landing and subsequently with the army of General Buell. He held the rank in the regular service of Colonel of the 2d Cavalry. General Mitchell, a native of Ohio,entered the volunteer service in the war with Mexico, from civil life, resuming his profession of a lawyer at the end of the contest. He removed to Kansas, and at the outbreak of the present war entered the service at the head of a regiment from that State. General Cruft entered the service at the beginning of the war as a Colonel of an Indiana regiment of volunteers. General Sheridan, since promoted to a Major-Generalship of volunteers, was a native of Ohio and graduate of West Point of 1853. He was actively employed on the Pacific coast, rising, to a Captaincy in the 13th regular Infantry. From the beginning of the present war he had been employed in the West in General Halleck's department, in which he had greatly distinguished himself. His services at Chaplin Hills or Perryville, in the previous October, will be remembered by the reader. No one fought more gallantly in the present action at Murfreesboro'.

To these notices of the living which exhibit the ranks of life from which the officers of the Western armies were drawn, we have to add the usual accompaniment to the narratives of all great battles, some memorial of the dead. In relation to the numbers engaged and the severity of the conflict, the loss of higher officers was comparatively light. "Words of my own," says General Rosecrans, "cannot add to the renown of our brave and patriotic officers and soldiers who fell on the field of honor, nor increase respect for their memory in the hearts of our countrymen. The names of such men as Lieutenant-Colonel J. P. Garesché, the pure and noble Christian gentleman and chivalric officer, who gave his life an early offering on the altar of his country's freedom; the gentle, true, and accomplished General Sill; the heroic, ingenious, and able Colonels Roberts, Millikin, Shaffer, McKee, Reed, Foreman, Fred. Jones, Hawkins, Knell, and the gallant and faithful Major Carpenter of the 19th Regulars, and many other field-officers, will live in our country's history, as will those of many others of inferior rank, whose soldierly deeds on this memorable battlefield won for them the admiration of their companions, and will dwell in our memories in long future years after God, in his mercy, shall have given us peace and restored us to the bosom of our homes and families." Brigadier-General Joshua W. Sill, the only general officer killed in the engagement, born in Ohio, entered West Point in 1849, graduated and was appointed to the ordnance department, and after several years' service, chiefly on the Pacific, resigned his commission in 1860. Accepting a professorship of mathematics and civil engineering in the Brooklyn Collegiate and Polytechnic Institute, he had not long discharged his duties when the outbreak of the rebellion again summoned him to arms. He was at once employed in Ohio in the organization of the new forces, took the field at the head of an Ohio regiment with General Nelson in Kentucky, was with General Mitchell in Tennessee, and in the summer of 1862 was promoted to a Brigadiership. In the subsequent movements of the army in Tennessee, he was highly distinguished as an efficient leader. The epithets of General Rosecrans just cited, characterize him as combining the highest qualities of the soldier and the gentleman. They are confirmed by the eulogy of his biographer: "Gifted with more than ordinary abilities, he had by unwearied and successful culture trained them to a high degree of perfection. The unsullied purity of his life was rare and admirable. He was gentle and sensitive to excess: yet in unswerving integrity, cool, practical sagacity, chivalrous courage and unyielding resolution, he verified his title to the noblest attributes of manhood."*

Colonel Julius P. Garesché, who has also received the distinguished eulogy of General Rosecrans, was chief of his staff. Born in the island of Cuba of American parentage, he graduated at West Point in 1841, with an appointment in the artillery. He was in service in Mexico, and had of late been employed at the national capital as Assistant Adjutant-General, with the rank of major. His first active service in the field during the war was in the staff of General Rosecrans. A zealous member of the Roman Catholic church, he carried to the army a rare reputation for Christian beneficence and charity.

These eulogies might readily be extended and will one day from the lips of survivors be duly gathered and recorded. Many others, also, must pass away from all memory in this world. Touching this class there is a feeling tribute, worthy a better cause, in the conclusion of the rebel General Bragg's report of this battle. "To the private soldier," says he, "a fair word of praise is due, and though it is so seldom given, and so rarely expected, that it may be considered out of place, I cannot, in justice to myself, withhold the opinion ever entertained, and so often expressed during our struggle for independence. In the absence of instructions and discipline of our armies, and of the confidence which long associations produce between veterans, we have in a great measure to trust to the individuality and self-reliance of the private soldiers, without the incentive or the motive which controls the officer who hopes to live in history. Without the hope of reward, actuated by a sense of duty and patriotism, he has in this great contest justly judged that the cause was his own, and gone into it with a determination to conquer or die, to be free or not to be at all; no encomium is too high, no honor too great, for such a soldier. However much of credit and glory may be given, and probably justly given, to the leaders in the struggle, history will yet award the main honor, when it is due to the private soldier, who, without hope or reward, and with no other incentive than a conscientiousness of rectitude has encountered all the hardships, and has suffered all the privations. Well has it been said: The first monument our confederacy raises, when our independence shall have been won, should be a lofty shaft, pure and spotless, bearing this inscription: 'To the unknown and unrecorded dead.'"

The battle of Murfreesboro', though it fell short of a decisive victory, was a serious blow to the enemy and was justly hailed as a triumph to the North—securing as it did possession of a vast and important frontier, menaced by the foe. On receipt of the intelligence at Washington, President Lincoln expressed the sentiment of the loyal states in this telegraphic response to General Rosecarns. "God bless you and all with you. Please tender to all, and accept for yourself the nation's gratitude for your and their skill, endurance and dauntless courage." The Secretary of War, General Halleck, also, a few days after, tendered his congratulations: "General rebel telegrams fully confirm your telegrams from the battlefield. The victory was well earned and one of the most brilliant of the war.

* Obituary in "Army of the Cumberland," by a lady contributor, Canandaigua, N. Y.

You and your brave army have won the gratitude of your country and the admiration of the world. The field of Murfreesboro' is made historical, and future generations will point out the place where so many heroes fell gloriously in defence of the Constitution and the Union. All honor to the army of the Cumberland. Thanks to the living and tears for the lamented dead."

During the movement upon Murfreesboro' an expedition was sent by order of Major-General Wright from his department in Kentucky to cut off the communications of the enemy by the destruction of the East Tennessee railroad. It was fitted out under the supervision of Major-General Granger, and placed under the immediate command of Brigadier-General Carter of the 2d Tennessee regiment. A force of about a thousand men, all told, composed of battalions of Ohio, Pennsylvania and Michigan cavalry, were collected at the end of December in the south-eastern corner of Kentucky. On the 28th, they crossed the Cumberland mountain into Virginia, and thence across Powell's mountain into Tennessee. Continuing their route over Clinch mountain, they entered Blountsville on the 30th, and proceeded to the Union station on the Virginia and East Tennessee railroad, where they took by surprise and captured one hundred and fifty of a North Carolina regiment, with Major McDowell in command, destroyed the railroad bridge over the Holston river, and a large quantity of stores and arms. A portion of the force then advanced to Carter's station, ten miles distant, where they destroyed the bridge across the Watauga river and other railroad property. Having thus effectually severed this main military line of the enemy, General Carter, with the loss of but ten men in several encounters, made good his retreat across the mountains into Kentucky. His congratulatory order, dated Richmond, Ky., January 9, 1863, celebrates this gallant exploit which General Halleck pronounced for daring and brilliant achievement without a parallel in the history of the war. "In taking leave," said General Carter, "of the officers and soldiers comprising the expeditionary force in East Tennessee, the General Commanding desires to thank you in his own name and that of our common country, for the faithful manner in which you performed the difficult duties assigned you. In twenty days you marched four hundred and seventy miles, one hundred and seventy of which was in the enemy's country without tents, and with only such rations as you could carry in your haversacks, in every instance. When you met the rebels you captured, destroyed, or put them to flight. You burned two most important railroad bridges at a time when it was taxed to its utmost capacity, took some four hundred prisoners, killed a number, destroyed six to seven hundred stand of arms, a locomotive, tender and cars, besides a considerable amount of valuable stores. You moved day and night, exposed to rain, snow, and bitter cold, and much of the time with only such scanty rations as you could procure in your rapid march. You bore such hardships and privations as few of our soldiers have been called upon to encounter, without a murmur or a single word of complaint. You have acquitted yourselves like worthy soldiers of the Republic. 'Through the Lord you have done valorously.' Your country is proud of your achievements. To your valor and endurance are due the success of our undertaking. With such men few things are impossible. We drop a tear to the memory of our brave comrades who sleep in the valley of East Tennessee, and tender to their surviving friends our heartfelt sympathies. Let it be our pride to emulate their heroism and devotion to our most glorious and holy cause."

CHAPTER LXXXIII.

AFFAIRS IN ARKANSAS AND MISSISSIPPI—GENERAL SHERMAN'S EXPEDITION TO VICKSBURG—DECEMBER, 1862.

When General Halleck, in April, 1862, then in command of the Department of Missouri, left his headquarters at St. Louis to take command of the army before Corinth, he committed the military charge of the State to General John M. Schofield, with the parting injunction to "take care of Missouri." The officer to whom this important duty was thus entrusted was a native of New York, who had removed at an early age to Illinois, been appointed a cadet from that State, and graduated at West Point in 1853, receiving the rank of 2d Lieutenant in the 2d Artillery. After two years of service in South Carolina and Florida, he was appointed instructor in natural philosophy at West Point, discharged this duty for five years, when he obtained a leave of absence to occupy a similar professorship in Washington University at St. Louis. There he was found at the outbreak of the rebellion, when he was recalled to active service in the organization of the new levies in Missouri. He was with General Lyon as his chief-of-staff in the last campaign of that gallant officer, and in the following November was commissioned Brigadier-General of Volunteers and assigned to the command of all the militia of the State. This new force was raised and equipped under various difficulties, and in April, 1862, numbered nearly 14,000 men, mostly cavalry, in the field. A still larger volunteer force similarly composed was also attached to General Schofield's command, which at this period embraced about three-fourths of the State, comprising the northern, central, and eastern portions. Missouri was then comparatively quiet after the Union victory at Pea Ridge, large numbers of its citizens who had joined the rebel army were suffered to return to their homes on taking the oath of allegiance, and the guerrilla bands were for the time broken up. General Curtis was operating in Arkansas, threatening its capital, Little Rock. At his request, in June, Missouri was erected into a separate military district and placed in command of General Schofield. He had an effective force of about 17,000 men, volunteer and militia, who were distributed through the State in six divisions. Of these, Colonel John McNeil, of the Missouri State militia, commanded the north-eastern; Brigadier-General Ben Loan, the north-western; Brigadier-General James Totten, the central; Brigadier-General F. B. Brown, the south-western; Colonel J. M. Glover, 3d Missouri cavalry, at Rolla, and Colonel Lewis Merrill, United States Volunteer cavalry, at St. Louis. The movement about this time of General Curtis to Helena, left the southern frontier of Missouri again exposed, and a new and insidious attempt was made by the enemy to push their fortunes in the State. Rebel Missourians in large numbers were sent home from the Confederate army to obtain recruits and stir up revolt. "Many of these," says General Schofield, "succeeded in secretly passing our lines and eluding arrest, some were arrested and others voluntarily surrendered themselves, professing their desire to return to their allegiance and were permitted to take the oath of allegiance and return to their homes as loyal citizens. These emissaries spread themselves over the State, and while maintaining outwardly the character of loyal citizens, or evading our troops, secretly enrolled, organized and officered a very large number of men, estimated by their friends at from thirty to fifty thousand. Places of rendezvous were designated where all were to assemble at an appointed signal, and by a sudden *coup-de-main*, seize the important points in the State, surprise and capture our small detachments guarding railroads, etc., thus securing arms and ammunition, and coöperate with an invading army from Arkansas." This system of attack and pillage was so industriously carried out that the Union forces, though making every resistance, proved unequal to the protection of the State. As no reinforcements in sufficient numbers could be obtained from abroad, General Schofield called upon the Governor for authority to organize all the militia of the State and call into the field such a force as the situation might demand. The Governor consented, and the measure was carried into effect. As a consequence of the enrollment, the more desperate of the rebels joined the guerrilla bands, others hid themselves, while loyal citizens, especially in those districts which had been harassed by their foes, eagerly obeyed the call. The whole State was agitated with the question of military service. It was a problem what to do with the disaffected in St. Louis. It would not do to place arms in their hands; it seemed unfair to the others to excuse them from military duty, thus setting a premium on disloyalty. The question was settled by admitting only those of approved loyalty to bear arms, while, as there were many men of wealth among "the friends of the South," it was resolved that the latter should be made to contribute handsomely from their means. A tax of five hundred thousand dollars was assessed upon the rebels of St. Louis county, "to be used in arming, clothing and subsisting the enrolled militia when in active service, and in providing for those families of militia men and volunteers which might be left destitute. Those living in the country were taxed in furnishing subsistence to the troops in pursuit of the enemy." In one week after the issuing the order of enrollment, at the end of July, about 20,000 men had been organized, armed, and called into active service.

Two months of "desperate and sanguinary guerrilla war" now ensued, the principal theatre of operations being Colonel McNeil's north-eastern division above the Missouri and bordering on the Mississippi. The rebel bands in this region under Porter, Poindexter, Cobb, and others of less note, amounted to more than 5,000 men in parties varying in numbers according to their success. By carefully guarding the Missouri river the communication of these marauders with the South was effectually cut off. "Porter's band," says General Schofield in his narrative of the events of the year already cited, "was immediately pursued by the Union cavalry, almost without intermission, for twelve days, during which time he was driven over a distance of nearly five hundred miles and forced to fight our troops nine sharp engagements. His force increased during the first few days, from two to three hundred to three thousand, which it reached on the 6th of August at Kirksville, where he was attacked by Colonel McNeil, with about one thousand cavalry and six pieces of artillery. The engagement was very desperate, and lasted about four hours. It resulted in a total defeat of the rebels. Their loss was one hundred and eighty killed, about five hundred wounded, and a large number taken prisoners or scattered. Several wagon-loads of arms fell into our hands. In this single engagement Porter's force was reduced from three thousand to about eight hundred, and his power and influence entirely broken. Our loss at Kirksville was twenty-eight killed and about sixty wounded. Our troops behaved with great gallantry, and were handled with consumate skill by their commander, Colonel McNeil. Poindexter's gang had increased to about twelve hundred men before a sufficient force could be collected to break him up. About the 8th of August, Colonel Guitar, 9th cavalry, Missouri State Militia, with about six hundred men and two pieces of artillery, started in pursuit of Poindexter, overtaking and attacking him while crossing the Chartain River, on the night of the 10th. A very large number of the enemy were killed, wounded, and drowned. Many horses and arms, and all their spare ammunition and other supplies, were captured. Poindexter moved rapidly northward to effect a junction with Porter, but was intercepted and driven back by the troops of the north-western division, under General Loan, which force at the same time drove Porter back upon McNeil, and compelled him to disperse his band to save it from destruction. Poindexter being forced back by Loan, was again struck by Guitar, and, after a running fight of nearly forty-eight hours, his entire force was killed, captured, or dispersed. The bandit leader himself, after wandering alone through the woods for several days, fell into the hands of the militia. Colonel Guitar and his troops deserve great credit for their gallantry and untiring energy. To the promptness and energy of General Loan and his command, in throwing themselves between Porter and Poindexter, was due in a great degree the speedy destruction of the latter. The rebel forces under Porter and Poindexter having been broken up, the band of robbers under Cobb soon dispersed or broke up into small parties, the more securely to continue their systematical plunder and murder of loyal men. To dispose of these fragments of the recently formidable bands of guerrillas, then scattered over the entire State, was necessarily a work of time. Many of them still held together with great tenacity in small bands, and endeavored to continue the system of petty war which had been going on for some time previous to the general insurrection. But through the activity of our troops, and the important aid of our militia, now organized in large numbers, and thoroughly acquainted with the country and people, the outlaws were soon hunted down, and either killed, captured, or driven out of the State. It would be impossible to give a detailed report of all the minor affairs in which our troops were engaged during this period, or to do justice to the many gallant officers and men who were distinguished in this arduous and most unpleasant service. From the 1st of April to the 20th of September our troops met the enemy in more than one hundred engagements, great and small, in which our numbers varied from forty or fifty to ten or twelve hundred, and those of the enemy from a few men to four or five thousand. In not more than ten of these were our troops defeated. Our entire loss, so far as reported, was seventy-seven killed, one hundred and fifty-six wounded, and three hundred and forty-seven prisoners—most of the latter taken in the capture of Independence and Newark. That of the enemy was five hundred and six killed, about eighteen hundred wounded, and five hundred and sixty prisoners taken in battle, beside the large number who have recently surrendered or fled from the State. The whole number killed, wounded, captured, and driven away cannot fall short of ten thousand."

While these operations were going on north of the Missouri river, an ineffectual attempt to relieve their friends in that quarter was made by the rebels of the South. On the 11th of August the garrison at Independence was compelled to surrender to a body of the enemy, and immediately after the central and south-western divisions of Generals Totten and Brown were aroused to meet the rebel

General Coffy, who was pushing north with about 1,500 cavalry. Major Foster of the 7th Militia, sent out from Lexington with about 800 men and two pieces of artillery to effect a junction with Colonel Warren, in command of 1,500 men from Clinton, and attack the force under Hughes and Quantrel; disappointed in making the combination singly, met the combined forces of Coffy and Hughes at Lone Jack. A severe conflict ensued, Major Foster was very severely wounded, his two pieces of artillery captured and his command forced to fall back to Lexington. The engagement, however, saved the latter town from a serious meditated attack of the enemy. A strong force under General Blunt, then commanding the department of Kansas, energetically coöperating with Generals Totten and Loan, the further movements of the rebels in this quarter were promptly arrested and Coffy was pursued to the Arkansas line. The central division was now placed under the administration of General Loan, and order in that region was gradually restored. The enemy meanwhile were gathering strength in Arkansas. They had been largely recruited from Southern Missouri by home conscription, and by the addition of a considerable body of troops from Texas. General Schofield estimates their entire force in the middle of September at about fifty thousand. General Hindman was chief in command at that time. There were various demonstrations on the border of portions of this army by the rebel officers Cooper, Rains, McBride and Parsons, which led General Schofield to take the field in person and concentrate a large force at Springfield, while he called on General Steel, at Helena, to coöperate in a movement against the enemy. At the close of the month Major-General Curtis took command of the Department of the Missouri, General Schofield retaining command of the troops in the field in the South-west. The latter had at this time an effective force at and near Springfield of 4,800 infantry, 5,600 cavalry and 16 pieces of artillery, a total of 10,800 men, of whom, after providing for keeping open the line of communication, over 8,000 were available for active operations. General Blunt, in command at Kansas, was also now placed under General Schofield's orders, and summoned all the troops he could muster, to join with a considerable force sent out from Springfield to Sarcoxie to watch the enemy. There was an engagement at Newtonia in this quarter, on the 30th, between about 4,500, under the Union General Salomon, and a superior force of the enemy, which resulted in the retreat of the former without serious loss. To repair this disaster, General Schofield hurried to Sarcoxie, where he was joined on the 3d of October by General Blunt, when, with their joint forces, about 10,000 in all, they advanced upon the enemy at Newtonia. The latter failing to receive expected support from General Rains at once began to retreat, and were pursued for thirty miles into the border of Arkansas. General Schofield presently advanced to the old battleground at Pea Ridge, and learning that the enemy had divided his force sent General Blunt in pursuit of the rebel General Cooper in the direction of Maysville, while he himself marched with Totten's and Herron's divisions after Rains in the direction of Huntsville. General Blunt, after a hard night's march, attacked Cooper in his camp at old Fort Wayne, near Maysville, and after a short but sharp engagement on the 22d of October, captured all his artillery, four pieces, and completely routed him, the enemy flying in great disorder across the river to Fort Gibson. His loss in this affair was very small, that of the enemy considerable. On arriving at Maysville, after an arduous forced march over the White River mountains, General Schofield found the enemy in that quarter in full retreat across the mountains. They were shortly after pursued by General Herron's command and driven from a position in the neighborhood of Fayetteville. Other movements followed, leading to no decided engagement. At the end of November, General Schofield in consequence of illness relinquished his command of the army of the frontier.*

In the course of the measures taken in Northern Missouri for the suppression of the guerrilla warfare, an event occurred which became the subject of much comment both at home and abroad. It was thus related in the *Palmyra Courier*, the paper of the town where the affair took place. "When the rebels entered Palmyra, an old resident of the place, Andrew Allsman by name, mysteriously disappeared, and it was supposed he was murdered. When General McNeil returned to Palmyra after that event, and ascertained the circumstances under which Allsman had been abducted, he caused to be issued a notice that if the missing man was not returned within ten days he would retaliate upon the rebel prisoners in his hands. The ten days elapsed and no tidings came of the man. On the eleventh day, ten rebel prisoners, already in custody, were selected to pay with their lives the penalty demanded. Their names were Willis Baker, Thomas Humston, Morgan Bixler and John Y. McPheeters, Lewis county; Herbert Hutson, John M. Wade, Marion Lair, Ralls county; Captain Thomas A. Sidner, Monroe county; Eleazer Lake, Scotland county; Hiram Smith, Knox county. These parties were informed on Friday evening (17th October) that unless Mr. Allsman was returned to his family by one o'clock on the following day they would all be shot at that hour." A little after noon accordingly, the next day, the missing man not having made his appearance, the ten men were taken to the Fair Grounds outside the town for execution, which, after a prayer with the prisoners by the Rev. R. Rhodes, was carried out, the condemned sitting each at the foot of his coffin and receiving the fire of a detachment of thirty soldiers of the 2d Missouri State Militia. Thus narrated, this execution certainly required explanation. It was readily taken advantage of by the Confederate President Davis, who, as we shall see, held it up to public execration, with the execution of Mumford at New Orleans by General Butler, already narrated, while the friends of the South everywhere took up the cry of "cold-blooded, monstrous cruelty," and other approbious epithets.

Without entering upon the particular merits of this case, or undertaking to defend the course pursued, it may be sufficient generally to remark that it grew out of, and was justified to many by the anomalous system of guerrilla warfare, in numerous instances, instigated and pursued by the rebels. It was the punishment meted out as a stern lesson to a class who had carried on to the fearful injury of an unoffending loyal people, a remorseless system of robbery and murder. "Such wretches as Quantrell, compared with whom Dick Turpin and Jack Sheppard were humane gentlemen," wrote a journalist of the day, "have done nothing except steal horses, kill cattle, burn houses, and shoot, not only unarmed men, but women and children as well. We know of one neighborhood in southern Missouri where every loyal family—to the number of over a dozen—has been killed off; where one poor fellow saw his two sons, his wife and two small children, successively shot by assassins who lurked in the woods near his house, while he only escaped by concealing himself in a swamp till he was nearly starved to death. Nor does this case stand alone. All over Missouri, last year, loyal farmers ploughed their fields and tended their crops with guns at their sides, and, too often, after every precaution, they were shot down in their fields, or found their cattle,

* Report of General Schofield of operations in Missouri and Arkansas, for the year ending November 30, 1862.

their chief dependence, driven off or cruelly killed and left on the ground. Many months of such barbarities exasperated the peaceful people ; not only the loyal men, but very many of the secessionists, united to put a stop to them ; but in vain. Encouraged by Jefferson Davis, Quantrell and his fellow ruffians went on. At last, General McNeil, an officer, as it happens, in the State and not in the United States service, made an example of ten of these assassins."*

After the retirement of General Schofield the army was reörganized in three divisions, the first being commanded by General Blunt, the second by General Herron, the third having been assigned to General Totten, who about this time being called to St. Louis, quitted the field. A reserve force of militia was commanded by General Brown. General Blunt, who was described at this time by a correspondent as "a bold, dashing soldier, rough in his exterior, unpretending in his manners, but full of courage and fire," was a native of Maine, who had passed hi s early years as a sailor ; removing from the seaboard to Ohio, he had graduated as a physician at a medical college in that State, practiced the profession there for a number of years and then emigrated to Kansas, where he became a prominent leader of the Free-Soil party. He entered the military service at the outbreak of the rebellion as Lieutenant-Colonel of the 3d Kansas volunteers, subsequently commanded the cavalry of General Lane's brigade, and in April, 1862, was appointed Brigadier-General of volunteers, and assigned to the command of the department. He was now in his thirty-sixth year. General Herron, a native of Pennsylvania, one of the youngest officers in the service, and previous to the war a banker in Dubuque, entered the army as Lieutenant-Colonel of an Iowa regiment of volunteers, fought in the battle of Pea Ridge, where he was wounded, taken prisoner, and being exchanged, received his appointment of Brigadier-General of volunteers in July. The rebel General Hindman, to whom these officers were now opposed, was a native of Tennessee, who had served in the Mexican war as 2d Lieutenant of a Mississippi regiment of volunteers, and had in the administration of President Buchanan represented Arkansas in Congress. He had early in the war entered the Confederate army, and had seen various service in Kentucky, at Memphis, and in the battle of Shiloh, where he was injured by the fall of his horse which was shot under him in the action.

A month after the enemy were driven from their camps by General Schofield's command, the contest was resumed in north-western Arkansas. On the 26th of November, General Blunt while encamped with his division of the army of the frontier at Lindsay's Prairie, fifteen miles south of Maysville, received information that the rebel General Marmaduke was at Cane Hill, approaching his position with an estimated force of eight thousand men, the advance of the army of Hindman who was hastening with additional troops to the place. Determining to anticipate this combination, General Blunt, on the morning of the 27th, with about five thousand men and thirty pieces of artillery set out to attack the enemy. All the transportation and commissary trains were left in charge of a guard, the men taking with them four days' rations of hard bread and salt. The distance to be travelled to reach the enemy was thirty-five miles, twenty-five of which were made by seven o'clock on the evening of the first day. Avoiding the easily defensible main road on which the enemy's pickets were posted, General Blunt resumed his march at five the next morning, taking an obscure and unfrequented road which brought his advance upon the foe in the vicinity of their camp at Cave Hill. His main column havingbeen detained in the ascent of a moun-

* *New York Evening Post*, December 6, 1862.

tain seven miles in the rear, he made the best disposition of the small body of cavalry with the battery and two mountain howitzers he had with him, opening the contest with an "artillery duel." The enemy retreating to their reserve, the battery was again brought to bear upon them from a better position, when they withdrew to the town. Here General Blunt brought up his forces for a decisive struggle, when the enemy further retreated, to the Boston Mountains, taking up an advantageous position on one of the heights. From this they were dislodged by a determined charge of the 2d Kansas cavalry, dismounted, the 3d Indian Cherokee regiment, and the 11th Kansas infantry. The pursuit was now continued with sharp skirmishing till dark, Marmaduke making good his retreat in the direction of Van Buren, General Blunt returning with his command to Cane Hill. The Union casualties in this series of engagements were four killed and thirty-six wounded, four of them mortally, among the latter was Lieutenant-Colonel Jewett of the 6th Kansas, "a brave and gallant officer," says General Blunt in his report, "whose noble example is worthy of emulation." The enemy's loss in killed was estimated at seventy-five, including several officers, the wounded not known, as they were carried from the field. The notorious Quantrel and his band were engaged in the fight with Colonel Shelby and Emmett McDowell, commanding the rear guard in the retreat across the Boston Mountains.*

Following this retreat of the enemy came another engagement between the united divisions of Generals Blunt and Herron and the rebel army led by General Hindman. General Blunt since the late action had, though threatened by the enemy, maintained his position in their late quarters at Cane Hill, while General Herron was hastening by forced marches from Missouri to join him, bringing with him a force of between six and seven thousand men,—Illinois, Iowa and Wisconsin regiments,—and twenty-four pieces of artillery. To prevent this junction, General Hindman, on the morning of Sunday the 7th of December, turning General Blunt's position at Cane Hill, came upon and attacked General Herron's force on Crawford's Prairie, ten miles south of Fayetteville. The action was thus reported the following day from the battlefield in a dispatch by General Blunt to General Curtis: "This place on yesterday was the scene of a hard-fought and bloody field, resulting in a complete victory of the Army of the Frontier. The rebel forces, under Generals Hindman, Marmaduke, Parsons, and Frost, numbered twenty-four thousand. I had been holding the enemy on the Boston Mountains for two days, skirmishing with their advance, holding them in check until General Herron could come up with reinforcements. On the 7th they drove in my outposts, and got possession of a road by which they commenced a flank movement on my left during the night, while they made a heavy feint in front. Their object was to cut off communication between myself and General Herron, who was to be at Fayetteville at daylight. They attacked General Herron at about ten o'clock A. M., who, by gallant and desperate fighting, held them in check for three hours, until I came and attacked them in the rear. The fighting was desperate on both sides, and continued until it was terminated by the darkness of the night. My command bivouacked on their arms, ready to renew the conflict at daylight in the morning. But the enemy had availed themselves of the night to retreat across the Boston Mountains. The loss on both sides has been heavy. My loss in killed is small in proportion to the number of wounded. The enemy's loss, compared with ours, was at least four to one. My artillery

* Dispatches of Brigadier-General Blunt, Cane Hill, Arkansas, November 30, December 3, 1862.

made terrible destruction in their ranks. They had greatly the advantage in numbers and position. Yet Generals Hindman and Marmaduke acknowledged to me in an interview under a flag of truce, that they had been well whipped. Among the enemy's killed, is Colonel Stein, formerly Brigadier-General of the Missouri State Guard. The 19th and 20th Iowa, 37th Illinois, and 26th Indiana regiments, of General Herron's division, suffered severely. General Herron deserves great credit for the promptness with which he reinforced me, by forced marches from near Springfield, and also for his gallantry upon the field."

In a subsequent dispatch to General Halleck by General Curtis, dated St. Louis, December 11th, we have some additional particulars of this important engagement:—"Further details are received from Generals Blunt and Herron from the battleground, Prairie Grove, near Fayetteville, Arkansas. Our loss in killed and wounded is now estimated at one thousand, and that of the enemy at over two thousand. The rebels left many of their dead and most of their wounded for us to care for. Extensive hospitals will be improvised in Fayetteville. Persons returned from the battlefield represent that the enemy are twenty-eight thousand strong. Their artillery was much crippled. We took four caissons filled with ammunition, and a large number of small arms. General Blunt moves forward to-day on Cane Hill. General Herron remains at Prairie Grove burying the dead and wounded. The enemy muffled their wheels and moved off in the night, continuing their retreat to Van Buren, and probably crossing the Arkansas River. Colonel McFarland, of the 19th Iowa regiment, is killed. Colonel Black, of the 37th Illinois, and Major Thomas, of the 20th Iowa regiment, and a large number of subaltern officers, are wounded. It was a hard fought battle, and a complete victory."

The year closed with another expedition of General Blunt, and defeat of the enemy, at Van Buren, on the Arkansas River. It is thus narrated in his dispatch to General Curtis, on the 28th of December, from the scene of the engagement:—"The Stars and Stripes now wave in triumph over Van Buren. On learning that Hindman had been reinforced, and contemplated making another attempt to force his way to Missouri, I determined to attack him. Leaving my transportation north of the mountains, I marched from Prairie Grove at eight o'clock yesterday morning, upon this place, a distance of fifty miles. At ten o'clock this morning, my advance came upon two regiments of rebel cavalry at Dripping Springs, eight miles north of the river. Dashing upon them with three thousand cavalry and four mountain howitzers, a brisk running fight took place, which was kept up into the town, resulting in the capture of all their transportation, forty wagons, with six mule-teams, camp and garrison equipage, one hundred prisoners, a large amount of ammunition, four steamboats and a ferry-boat. The latter was taken in attempting to cross the river with rebel troops, and was shelled from the howitzer. When in the middle of the stream the boat was disabled and a number of men killed. The remainder jumped overboard and swam to the shore. Three large steamers, heavily laden with supplies, had got up steam and attempted to escape down the river, but were pursued by cavalry five miles and brought to by the fire of their carbines, and returned back to the levee. The enemy then brought their artillery to the opposite bank of the river and commenced shelling the town, for the purpose of driving out my cavalry, but resulting in no other damage than the destruction of some buildings. My artillery coming up, soon silenced their batteries. Quite a number of the enemy have been killed. During the day's operations the only casualties on our side are five or six men slightly wounded."

To the cares of the government in the West, in addition to the control of "border ruffianism" and insurrection in Missouri and Arkansas, a serious revolt of the Indian tribes on the remote frontier was to be met by a military force. There had been growing symptoms of disaffection since the beginning of the war, excited, it is said, by rebel emissaries, and doubtless to a considerable extent by difficulties which had arisen in regard to the payment of annuities under former treaty stipulations. But in whatever way the cause was to be accounted for, a deep feeling of hostility existed in the northwestern tribes, particularly with those in the reservations in Minnesota, which broke out in the latter State in August, in one of the most barbarous massacres ever inflicted on the white population of the country in Indian warfare. The Sioux, under their chief, Little Crow, set on foot and perpetrated an indiscriminate assault, devastating the border settlements and murdering the inhabitants with the most atrocious outrages and cruelties, sparing neither age nor sex; more than two hundred of the settlers at the agencies and along the frontier, it is calculated, were killed in these attacks, and by some the number was made very much larger—while thousands, abandoning their homes and property, escaped in cruel flight. The military power in the State was invoked for vengeance. Governor Ramsay called for mounted volunteers in addition to the troops at his disposal, and Colonel Sibley, at the head of the force, set out to punish the insurgents. He relieved the town of New Ulm, a German settlement which had been resolutely defended by its citizens led by Judge Flandrau, and drove the savage foe from the vicinity of Fort Ridgely, where the garrison had been several times assailed. As the enemy fled they continued their work of massacre, appearing in parties in different portions of the State. Though suffering in various conflicts where they came in contact with the United States forces, as at Fort Ridgely and Abercrombie, it was more than a month from the first outbreak before the main band was effectually met and defeated by Colonel Sibley, on the 23d of September, in an engagement in the vicinity of Yellow Medicine River. Several hundred prisoners were now taken, and were with difficulty preserved from the fury of the inhabitants, who were excited to vengeance by the gross barbarities and violence which had been inflicted by the Sioux. About five hundred were tried by court-martial and three hundred of them sentenced to be executed. Their case was then brought before President Lincoln. On receiving a dispatch, in November, from General Pope, who was in command in the department, he ordered transcripts of the records of the trial to be forwarded to him, of which, December 11th, he caused a careful examination to be made. "First," said he, in a message to Congress, in reply to a resolution calling for information on the subject, "anxious," in his own words, "to not act with so much clemency as to encourage another outbreak on the one hand, nor with so much severity as to be real cruelty on the other, I ordered the execution of such as had been proved guilty of violating females; contrary to my expectations, only two of this class were found. I then directed a further examination and classification of all who were proven to have participated in massacres as distinguished from participation in battles. This class numbered forty, and included two convicted of female violation. One of the number is strongly recommended by the commission which tried him, for commutation to ten years' imprisonment. I have ordered the other thirty-nine to be executed on Friday, the 19th inst." In this decision, which he arrived at and maintained in the face of a loud popular outcry for vengeance, the President was actuated by the customary moderation and equity of his character. Thirty-eight of the Indians thus marked out were executed by hanging on a single scaffold at Mankato, Minnesota, on the 26th day of December.

At the end of December, active operations were resumed against Vicksburg. While General Grant with his army remained in Northern Mississippi with his headquarters at Holly Springs, General W. T. Sherman, in command of the army corps on the Mississippi, having collected a fleet of transports at Memphis, there and at Helena, embarked his forces, numbering, it is said, about forty thousand men, with whom on the 26th he entered the Yazoo. A landing was effected a few miles above the mouth on the left bank, at a point in a direct line distant from Vicksburg about six miles. Across the country, above and below the city, from Haine's Bluff on the Yazoo to Warrenton on the Mississippi extended a line of hills, which with the swamps and lagoons in front afforded an excellent means of defence. On sending out his reconnoitering parties, it was soon ascertained by General Sherman that, what with the natural advantages of the situation and the improvement of it by the enemy, the attempt to take Vicksburg from this direction was one of no ordinary difficulty. At the very outset the fleet was checked in its endeavors to ascend the Yazoo by a formidable battery at Haine's Bluff, which it was an object to silence by a flank attack from the river preparatory to an advance of the army in front. The gunboat Benton was severely injured in a bombardment of this work, and her gallant commander, Captain Gwin, mortally wounded. This occurred on the morning of the 27th. "The whole army,"—in the absence of official reports we follow the narrative of a correspondent—"was drawn up in line of battle and prepared to make assaults on the enemy's works at several different points. General Steele's division was on the left; General A. J. Smith's on the right; General G. W. Morgan's on the left centre, and General M. L. Smith's on the right centre. After the line of battle was formed, General Morgan L. Smith's division took the advance, and moved rapidly on the enemy, encountering them about three-quarters of a mile from Chickasaw Bayou. Skirmishing immediately began, and was kept up throughout the day, the enemy contesting every inch of the road, but being gradually pushed back toward the bayou. The evening before, a portion of General Steele's division had been reëmbarked on the transports, and landed above Chickasaw Bayou, for the purpose of attempting to take a battery in the rear, which commanded the only point where a crossing could be made on the extreme right. This was at a place known as Mrs. Lake's plantation, and the rebels had a force there in possession of field and house. Owing to the mud and other difficulties, the landing of this portion of General Steele's division occupied the whole of the day of the 26th, and it did not reach the scene of operations until the morning of the 27th. While General M. L. Smith's division was skirmishing with the enemy on the right centre, General Blair's brigade and General Morgan's division had advanced on the left by different routes, and came into position nearly side by side, close by Mrs. Lake's plantation. Skirmishing took place with the enemy's infantry, and at the same time a masked battery opened on General Blair's brigade. He ordered Hoffman's battery to return the fire with shell, and in a few minutes the rebel battery was silenced, and their infantry retreated from the plantation to the cover of a thicket not far off. By nightfall the enemy had been driven a quarter of a mile from where they were first encountered, and the contest then ceased, both forces resting on their arms, ready to renew the conflict in the morning.

During the night silence and darkness prevailed in both camps. Not a fire was lighted, or a sound made, by which either would betray its position to the other. In the night a light wind sprung up, blowing toward the river from the enemy's position, and the night became clear and frosty. Amid the prevailing silence, and aided by the wind, the sound of cars constantly running could be heard on the Jackson and Vicksburg Railroad, no doubt bearing reinforcements to the enemy. During the night, the enemy was no doubt busily engaged in erecting rifle-pits and breastworks, as, on the following morning, long lines of them could be seen where none were visible the night before. Several new batteries were also seen on the heights beyond.

"At daylight on Sunday morning, the 28th, the enemy commenced the battle by a heavy cannonade on General Blair's brigade and General Morgan's division from the battery across the bayou, which the detachment from General Steele's division had been sent out to flank, and at the same time the conflict was renewed by General M. L. Smith's division, and the enemy in his front, General Smith leading in person. After an hour's hard fighting, he drove the enemy from their position, and seeing that he could drive them across the bayou, started out to the front with his Chief of Staff, Charles McDonald, Acting Adjutant-General, and two orderlies, to look for a place where he could cross his army in the pursuit, designing to keep the enemy between him and their batteries until he was ready to make a charge on the latter. He discovered a point where a sandbar had formed in the bayou, and which could be passed without difficulty, and as he was in the act of turning his horse to return to his command, a volley was fired at him from a force concealed in an adjacent canebrake. One of the shots took effect in his hip, the ball passing in an oblique direction, and lodging in his spine, where it was wedged so tightly that the surgeons could not remove it. The wound is not supposed to be mortal, but it disables him from further service at present. He evinced great coolness on the occasion, merely turning to his Chief of Staff, and remarking: 'Charley, I've got one of them.' He then rode on for half a mile as if nothing had happened, hoping to get to the rear without his men knowing that he was wounded, fearing its demoralizing effect on them. He was unable to proceed further, as he rapidly became faint from loss of blood, and had to be taken in an ambulance to his headquarters on one of the transports. The ball has since been extracted, while he was under the influence of chloroform, and his prospect of recovery is now good. He was wounded at a very inopportune moment, and the result was the loss of the advantage he had gained over the enemy, who now retreated successfully across the bayou and took refuge behind their intrenchments. The command then devolved temporarily upon General Stuart, who kept up during the day a constant skirmishing with his forces, but without accomplishing anything of importance. The opportunity of successfully storming the enemy's batteries in that position was lost by the delay necessarily occasioned by the change of commanders, and it could not be regained. In the mean time General Blair's brigade was busily engaged in building a bridge across the bayou by Mrs. Lake's house, which it succeeded in doing under a very heavy fire, and the brigade passed over in safety, with the loss of but few men. Among these was Colonel John B. Wyman, 13th Illinois infantry, who was killed by a ball passing through his right breast, and emerging below the right shoulder-blade. He was an efficient officer and accomplished gentleman, and greatly beloved by all who knew him. . . The day passed without any considerable results. The rattling of musketry and booming of cannon had been incessant throughout the day, but when evening came all the firing ceased, except an occasional gun fired at night by our batteries, and which met with no response. It afterward appeared that the enemy spent the night in constructing a second line of rifle-pits, about two hundred yards in rear of the first. No accurate estimate could be made of our loss during the day, but from the best accounts attainable it appeared to be small, not exceeding fifty killed and two hundred wounded. The army was still bivouacking, but tents were sent out for the wounded, into which they were conveyed, and received all the attention possible. At sundown, when the firing ceased, General Blair's brigade returned from across the bayou and took a position on General Morgan's right, and to the left of General M. L. Smith's division. At the extreme right was General A. J. Smith's division, where it had remained all day; and General Steele was in the rear on the left, as a reserve.

"On Monday morning the enemy still remained intrenched in force on the opposite bank of the bayou, and their line of defences could be seen extending for at least two miles up the bluffs. Batteries were seen planted at every assailable point, and it was evident that the rebels had exerted a most commendable industry during the night and had prepared to make the most determined resistance to our anticipated assault. The position was naturally strong, and all the appliances of military art and skill had been brought into requisition to make it a second Gibraltar. Far back on the highest peak of the hill they had erected a signal station, overlooking all the battleground, and far removed from the reach of shot or shell. By the aid of a glass the persons in charge of the station could be easily seen; and, during the entire day, every movement of our troops was signaled to the commanding general. Many spectators were also posted there with glasses, among whom were a number of women.

"It had been arranged that at an early hour on Monday morning a concerted attack should be made on the enemy's works, at four different points, and to do this it was found necessary to construct three bridges across the bayou so that artillery could be taken over. Accordingly, by daylight, parties were sent out to undertake this dangerous enterprise. Wherever men appeared with this view, the enemy immediately commenced a heavy cannonade upon them, and their batteries appeared to have been so skillfully placed as to command every point where a bridge was possible. General A. J. Smith, at the extreme right, put a bridge across within two miles of Vicksburg, but it was not brought into requisition. General Blair had already got a bridge across at Mrs. Lake's house, and General Stuart, commanding General Morgan L. Smith's division, decided to attempt the crossing at the sandbar, where General Smith had intended to cross when he was wounded. The bank of the bayou, opposite this bar, was about fifteen feet high, and it was further increased by an embankment or levee of three feet in height. This bank was very steep, and the land being sandy, the sides had caved in, so that the brow overhung about a foot and a half. To ascend it was utterly impossible without digging a road, and this would have to be done under a deadly fire from the enemy. The road across the sandbar was about two hundred yards in length, exposed to a double cross-fire, and the only approach to it was over a flat bottom, covered with fallen trees. After consultation with Colonel Giles Smith, brother of General M. L. Smith, who had now been assigned the command of the division, General Stuart resolved to attempt the enterprise. The 6th Missouri regiment, under command of Lieutenant-Colonel Blood, was detailed to lead the van. It was necessary first to send two companies over to dig away the bank, so that when the brigade came over it could rush up and storm the works. The duty was so perilous that Colonel Blood was unwilling to detail any companies, and called for volunteers—one company to take picks and spades, and the other muskets. Company F, Captain Bouton, and Company K, Captain Buck, volunteered for the duty. The plan was to make an excavation under the bank, without breaking the surface through, but so that it could be caved in at any moment. Amid the plaudits of their comrades, the two brave companies started on their perilous march. A perfect storm of bullets met them on the way, and with the loss of more than a tenth of their number, they effected the crossing. No more desperate enterprise was ever undertaken, and none more successfully achieved. Once under the protection of the bank, they commenced plying pick and spade in a manner indicating their appreciation of the fact that they had no time to spare.

"In the mean time, to keep down the enemy's sharpshooters, who were endeavoring to reach over and fire at them down the bank, the 13th regulars were posted on the right, and the batteries from General Steele's and General Morgan's divisions on the left. These kept up a continual fire until the work was completed. Meanwhile, General Morgan prepared to assault the hill from the south side of the bayou, supported by Generals Blair and Thayer, but General Blair having already crossed the bayou, led the assault himself. The signal for General Stuart's brigade to attempt the crossing at the sandbar was to be heavy firing from General Morgan's division, the assault then to be made in concert. General Blair, being in the advance, led his brigade upon the first line of rifle-pits, and after a hard but brief struggle drove the enemy to their second line. Between the two lay a sort of ditch or small slough, with mud and quicksand in the bottom. As General Blair advanced, his horse got inextricably mired, and the General coolly slid down his head, and led his brigade the remainder of the way on foot. The other mounted officers, seeing the difficulty, abandoned their horses also. On arriving at the second line of rifle-pits another charge was made, supported by Hoffman's battery, and the enemy was again routed and driven into a thicket, or willow grove. The 13th Ohio then came up, and in a hand-to-hand conflict drove them from the thicket and took possession of it, but were in turn driven out by a heavy cannonade from the enemy's batteries on the hill. The enemy then commenced retreating up the hill, General Blair's brigade pursuing them, when all of a sudden, the enemy, from a masked battery, opened a most deadly and destructive fire upon them, with grape and canister. In a few minutes, the ground was covered with the dead and dying. The brigade went into the action with less than one thousand nine hundred men, and of this number six hundred and forty-five were lost in killed, wounded and taken prisoners. Colonel Thomas C. Fletcher, 31st Missouri infantry, was wounded and taken prisoner, and Lieutenant-Colonel Dister was killed. The 31st Missouri lost sixteen officers in killed and wounded, and the 29th Missouri, nine. Of the 58th Ohio, only one hundred and seventy-five men were left. This ended the assault on the hill at this point, and General Blair, with the remainder of his brigade, fell back to his position on the right of General Morgan. The heavy firing from General Morgan's division, which was to have been the signal, not being heard, and the excavation under the bank being completed, the men sheltered themselves under it the best they could and waited as patiently as the circumstances would permit for the next move. Our sharpshooters of the 13th regulars still kept up a fire to prevent firing from the bank, and in some instances their aim was too low, and the consequence was that they shot dead two of our own men. The men sent up a shout, 'Fire higher,' and the rebels on the banks attempted to drown their voices by superior numbers shouting: 'Fire lower.' The parties were so close together that when the rebels reached their guns over the bank and depressed them, those below could easily have crossed bayonets with them. Conversation could be easily carried on, and one rebel cried out: 'What regiment is below?' On being answered that it was the '6th Missouri,' he replied: 'It is too brave a regiment to be on the wrong side.'

"It was now nearly evening, and the men had tasted no food since before day, and one of them called out: 'Have you got anything to eat up there, I'm hungry?' Immediately a large loaf of corn-bread was thrown on the bank to them, and was welcomed heartily. The signal for the assault still being unheard, and a heavy rain coming up, it was deemed advisable by Captain Bouton to send back a messenger for further orders, and private Mallsby volunteered to undertake the dangerous exploit. He crossed in safety, and in a few minutes the remainder of the gallant 6th, led by Lieutenant-Colonel Blood, started over to their assistance, amid a renewed shower of bullets, and made the passage with the loss of one-sixth their number. Colonel Blood was wounded in the left shoulder by a ball, which, striking against a memorandum, glanced, or it would have passed through his body. His wound is not dangerous. Lieutenant Vance was the only officer killed. By the time Lieutenant-Colonel Blood got his regiment across, the day was hopelessly lost by the repulse of the army at other points, and about dark he received orders to retire at discretion. Under cover of the rain and darkness he brought his regiment back, a company at a time, until all were over, without the loss of a man, and only two wounded slightly. Not until the night was pitchy dark did the firing all cease, and floods of rain were now descending as if we were to have a second edition of Noah. The ground where the fighting was done was all low and marshy, and soon the water and mud were several inches deep. No preparations whatever had been made for the wounded, all the accommodations having been exhausted on the wounded of the day before, and all that pitiless night and all the next day, the wounded lay in their agony on that oozy bed, under a soaking rain, uncared for, and many who had fallen on their faces and were unable to turn themselves, smothered in the mud, and many more died from the exposure. It was horrible to think of. The only means I had of arriving at any idea of our loss is by common rumor, which places it at about two thousand in killed, wounded and captured. That is the estimate, made in the rough, by the Commanding General, according to common report.* The heaviest loss was in General Blair's brigade, consisting of the 13th Illinois infantry, 29th, 30th and 31st Missouri infantry, and Hoffman's Ohio battery. This brigade acted most heroically, and General Blair showed himself an able and brave commander."

"The heavy rains of the night and the consequent condition of the low, swampy ground, prevented the possibility of any military operations the next day, by land. General Sherman sent out parties with flags of truce, to bury the dead and bring away the wounded, and the whole day was consumed in the discharge of this melancholy duty. It was discovered that the enemy had carried off all the slightly wounded as prisoners of war, leaving only those who were unable to walk. All the dead had been robbed of their haversacks, and many of the bodies stripped of their outer clothing. During the day, many rebel soldiers came down to the flags of

* It was stated 600 killed, 1,400 wounded, and 400 prisoners.

truce and manifested a disposition to be quite friendly, and in some instances assisting in burying the dead. They also brought a few Vicksburg papers of that morning, containing a glowing account of the battle, and jubilating over the repulse of the Yankees. They estimated the numbers engaged in the battle, at three thousand on the part of the rebels, and fifteen thousand on the part of the Federals. The weather had cleared off as suddenly in the morning as the rain had come up on the evening before, and the beauty of the day, with its soft and languid air, illy harmonized with the mournful work in which our army was engaged. By night, the last sad office of burying the dead was completed, and the wounded were borne from the field to the hospital-boats. The condition of the ground was still such as to prevent any operations on the Yazoo swamps, and General Steele proposed to General Sherman that a division be sent up the Yazoo on the transports, as near to Haines's Bluff as they could get without coming within range of the guns from the battery, and that the troops then land and assault the works in the rear while the gunboats engaged the batteries in front. After consultation with the other division commanders, General Sherman approved the plan, and detailed General Steele's division to carry it into execution. At an early hour in the afternoon, the troops designated were embarked on the transports, reinforced by the 6th and 8th Missouri regiments from General Morgan L. Smith's division. The expedition was ordered to sail at daylight on the following morning, but when daylight came it was accompanied by a dense fog which did not clear away until nearly noon. The expedition was then abandoned. After the fog cleared away, the troops were again landed, and during the remainder of the day remained idly and listlessly in camp, in momentary expectation of receiving an order for a movement of some kind. Toward evening a horseman was seen riding along the shore distributing orders to the various boats, and soon the roll of the drums along the lines indicated the reading of an order. Groups of anxious listeners gathered around each regimental commander as he read the order, which proved to be an order for every regiment to embark on its original transport, and be ready to move by daylight in the morning. . . . By three o'clock the following afternoon the last boat passed out at the mouth of the Yazoo, where just one week before it had sailed in so triumphantly. The expedition which was to have taken Vicksburg so easily, ingloriously and ignominiously fled, leaving the exulting foe in undisputed possession of the battleground."

At the mouth of the Yazoo the fleet was met by the steamer Tigress, having on board General McClernand. General Sherman reported to him, and issued the following order :—"Headquarters Right Wing Army of the Tennessee, Steamer Forest Queen, Milliken's Bend, January 4, 1863. Pursuant to the terms of General Order No. 1, made this day by General McClernand, the title of our army ceases to exist, and constitutes in the future the Army of the Mississippi, composed of two 'army corps,' one to be commanded by General G. W. Morgan, and the other by myself. In relinquishing the command of the Army of the Tennessee, and restricting my authority to my own 'corps,' I desire to express to all commanders, to the soldiers and officers recently operating before Vicksburg, my hearty thanks for the zeal, alacrity, and courage, manifested by them on all occasions. We failed in accomplishing one great purpose of our movement, the capturing of Vicksburg, but we were part of a whole. Ours was but part of a combined movement, in which others were to assist. We were on time. Unforeseen contingencies must have delayed the others. We have destroyed the Shreveport road, we have attacked the defences of Vicksburg, and pushed the attack as far as prudence would justify, and having found it too strong for our single column, we have drawn off in good order and good spirits, ready for any new move. A new commander is now here to lead you. He is chosen by the President of the United States, who is charged by the Constitution to maintain and defend it, and he has the undoubted right to select his own agents. I know that all good officers and soldiers will give him the same hearty support and cheerful obedience they have hitherto given me. There are honors enough in reserve for all, and work enough, too. Let each do his appropriate part, and our nation must in the end emerge from this dire conflict, purified and ennobled by the fires which now test its strength and purity. All officers of the general staff not attached to my person will hereafter report in person and by letter to Major-General McClernand, commanding the Army of the Mississippi, on board the steamer Tigress, at our rendezvous at Gaines's Landing, and at Montgomery Point."*

* Correspondence of the *Missouri Democrat*, Milliken's Bend, La., Jan. 3, 1863. Moore's *Rebellion Record*, vi. p. 310.

CHAPTER LXXXIV.

NATIONAL AFFAIRS AT HOME AND ABROAD TO THE CLOSE OF 1862.

The adjournment of Congress in July was an important point in the history of the national affairs. It was the moment of a new and extraordinary effort to meet the growing requirements of the war. The year had opened with the battle of Mill Springs in Kentucky, followed by the victories at Forts Henry and Donelson, and the capture of Nashvill. A great rebel army had been successfully met in the contest at Pea Ridge in March, and in the same month the victory at Newbern had followed upon the brilliant affair at Roanoke Island. April had seen the Union armies victorious on the Mississippi at Island No. 10, while the greatest achievement of the war had been accomplished in the brilliant conquest of New Orleans and its powerful river defences. Forts Macon and Pulaski, the same month, had yielded to the perseverance and consummate science of the land and naval forces. The men of the West had fully measured their strength with the best troops of the enemy at Pittsburg Landing and maintained their ground in the arduous struggle. Norfolk had been surrendered and Yorktown fallen in May, preparatory to the advance to the close proximity of Richmond by the Army of the Potomac. June witnessed the disastrous conflicts in which this splendid force was wasted on the banks of the Chickahominy; disappointing the hopes of the nation, which looked to the early capture of the rebel capital as a certain means of the speedy suppression of the rebellion. Failure in this quarter neutralized the brilliant victories of the Southwest and of the Atlantic coast. It was evident that new and larger armies must be called into the field to meet the necessities of the war. Congress saw this, and, as we have seen, made ample provision for a gigantic contest in the future. It remained for the executive and the departments to use the power which had been given them. The foremost need was the supply of men. The six hundred thousand and more reported by the Secretary of War in the previous December, great as the number then appeared, wasted by the vicissitudes of war and scattered over an immense territory, scantily supplied the vast area. It now appeared necessary to double this mighty force. Two calls of 300,000 each in addition to temporary services of large bodies of militia summoned for special emergencies to the Potomac and the Ohio before the close of the year, raised the number of men enlisted for service to more than a million. We have already recorded the call of the President, by concert with the Governors of the loyal States, on the first of July, for 300,000 volunteers for the war. It was generally received with favor, and the most strenuous efforts were made by popular harangues, the raising of bounties and other measures, to carry it into effect. A second great meeting was held in the city of New York in Union Square, with the intention of reviving the influence of that held on the same spot at the beginning of the war; but though it was successful in devising means for carrying on the struggle, it fell short of its predecessor in numbers and enthusiasm, which indeed could hardly be expected to be repeated. The war once accepted was now to be maintained by ordinary means. One thing was forcibly inculcated by the speakers, that the contest should henceforth be waged with greater vigor. "We have dealt too mildly," said President Charles King, of Columbia College, "with those whom but a little while ago we regarded as our friends. They are no longer friends but deadly enemies. They make war in earnest. They omit no means of strengthening their hands and weakening ours. They fight us like incarnate fiends; let us at least meet them like our deadliest foes. I only speak common sense when I say that war is a fierce game; that they only prevail who wage it in earnest."* It was felt by all that the contest was one in which there could be no retreat. The life of the nation was involved in the struggle, and the only policy to be pursued was that for the effectual suppression of the rebellion. The sentiment was everywhere expressed by the loyal leaders of the North. Liberty, the people were reminded, was a precious possession, and, like all things valuable, a proportionate price must be paid for its acquisition. Our ancestors had purchased it dearly in the war of the Revolution; if the present generation would retain it, they must not grudge at least a portion of their fathers' efforts.

A foremost step in the progress of the war was indicated in the executive order which was issued by direction of the President from the War Department on the 22d of July, within a week of the adjournment of Congress. By this it was ordered, "first, that military commanders within the States of Virginia, North Carolina, Georgia, Florida, Alabama, Mississippi, Louisiana, Texas and Arkansas, in an orderly manner seize and use any property, real or personal, which may be necessary or convenient for their several commands, for supplies, or for other military purposes; and that while property may be destroyed for proper military objects, none shall be destroyed in wantonness or malice; second, that military and naval commanders shall employ as laborers, within and from said States, so many persons of African descent as can be advantageously used for military or naval purposes, giving them reasonable wages for their labor; third, that as to both property, and persons of African descent, accounts shall be kept sufficiently accurate and in detail to show quantities and amounts, and from whom both property and such persons shall have come, as a basis upon which compensation can be made in proper cases."

On the 4th of August an additional requisition was made. It was ordered that a draft of 300,000 militia be im-

* Proceedings at the Mass Meeting at Union Square, New York, July 15th, 1862.

mediately called into the service of the United States to serve for nine months, unless sooner discharged, and in case any State should on the 15th of August not have furnished its quota of the previous call, the deficiency was also to be made up by a special draft from the militia. This new edict set in motion through the loyal States the novel machinery of a thorough military enrollment, with the momentous contingency hanging over the population of enforced service in the field. It of course stimulated the payment of bounties to avoid, if possible, the unpalatable draft; for though the fairest and most certain means of meeting the demands of the State in a time of war, this is the most inconvenient and obnoxious to the people who are more accessible to the motives of interest or other appeals to voluntary action than to the simple claim of duty demanded by the State. The draft, in fact, was so unpopular that it was generally avoided. In some States, as Pennsylvania, Connecticut, Massachusetts, Wisconsin it was practically carried out; but what with the necessary delay for enrollments and the activity shown in securing voluntary enlistments making up the numbers required, it was in most cases postponed and again postponed till at the close of the year it was finally lost sight of. The short term of service under the recent militia act, with the liberal bounties offered, favored the supply of men, so that at the meeting of Congress the Secretary of War was enabled to report under the calls of July and August, 420,000 new troops in the field, of whom 320,000 were volunteers for three years or during the war. Before reaching this satisfactory result, the Secretary had passed through an embarrassing and perplexing series of measures, which called down upon him no little unfriendly animadversion. A few days after the publication of the order for the draft, he had on the 8th of August issued another "to prevent the evasion of military duty and for the suppression of disloyal practices." Under this no citizen liable to be drafted into the militia was allowed to go to a foreign country, and any person liable to draft who absented himself from his country or State before such draft was made, it was ordered, should "be arrested by any Provost Marshal or other United States or State officer wherever he may be found within the jurisdiction of the United States, and conveyed to the nearest military post or depot, and placed on military duty for the term of the draft." The expenses of such arrest and conveyance with the sum of five dollars as a reward to the officer making the arrest, were to be deducted from the refugee's pay, and the writ of *habeas corpus* was moreover ordered to be suspended in respect to all persons so arrested and detained for disloyal practices. By another order of the Secretary of the same date, "all United States Marshals and Superintendents or Chiefs of Police of any town, city or district were authorized and directed to arrest and imprison any person or persons who may be engaged, by act, speech or writing, in discouraging volunteer enlistments, or in any way giving aid and comfort to the enemy, or in any other disloyal practice against the United States." Such arrest was to be immediately reported to Major Turner, Judge Advocate, at Washington, "that such person may be tried before a military commission." By an order of the 27th of August, Secretary Stanton declared that all attempts to procure substitutes in anticipation of the draft were to be regarded as discouraging enlistments and subjecting persons engaged in such attempts to arrest under the previous order. Under these orders, strictly interpreted by subordinates, various arrests were made and the course of ordinary trial interrupted. A passport system was introduced for foreign travellers. These novel regulations were attended with many vexations and much complaint on the score of oppressiveness and illegality. The general reading of this order was modified by a "circular" from the War office of the 11th August, stating that it was not the intention to interfere with the transit from State to State of any persons but those who design to evade military duty," while "any person detained may be released on giving bonds to the United States in the sum of $1,000 conditional for the performance of military duty if he should be drafted, or the providing of a proper substitute." They were borne with for a month, when the obnoxious restrictions on travel were entirely removed and any arrests under the orders, it was directed, were to be made only upon the express warrant of the Judge Advocate of the War Department, or by the Military Commander or Governor of the particular State.

The reinforcement of the army was the first and most pressing duty of the President, but his course with reference to the confiscation act and the treatment of the slaves of rebels was regarded by the public with hardly less interest. By the terms of the confiscation act, as we have seen, while the seizure of the property of certain officers of the so-called Confederate States was absolutely ordered, an opportunity was offered to other persons in the rebel states to protect their effects by renouncing the rebellion and returning to their allegiance to the United States. If after public warning or proclamation by the President they did not within sixty days avail themselves of this privilege, their property was to be subject to the penalties of the act. This notice was given by the President in a simple, official proclamation on the 25th of July. Whilst the Confederate government was maintained with its relentless vigor, there was of course little opportunity, had the people desired it, to embrace this offer of security. It was, whether from choice or necessity, neglected, and consequently at the close of the following September a vast proportion of the entire wealth of the South became — where there was means of enforcing the decree—subject to confiscation.

The policy to be pursued with reference to the slaves, was evidently a matter of great anxiety to the President. He saw and felt the evil that slavery had brought upon the country; he deplored it as a man and lamented it as a citizen; he knew the strength this system of undisturbed labor gave to the rebellion and yet was reluctant, out of regard to the sentiment of the border States and a disclination hastily to disturb the settled order of society in a vast portion of the country, to strike the blow which might prove fatal to the institution. He felt the full burden of his responsibility on this subject, and brought to his decision the considerations of conscience and religion no less than of patriotism. To a Committee of the Synod of the Reformed Presbyterian Church which waited upon him in July, to impress their anti-slavery views, be replied:—

"Had slavery no existence among us, and were the question asked, Shall we adopt such an institution? we should agree as to the reply which should be made. If there be any diversity in our views it is not as to whether we should receive slavery when free from it, but as to how we may get rid of it already among us. Were an individual asked whether he would wish to have a wen on his neck, he could not hesitate as to the reply; but were it asked whether a man who has such a wen should at once be relieved of it by the application of the surgeon's knife, there might be diversity of opinion, perhaps the man might bleed to death, as the result of such an operation. Feeling deeply my responsibility to my country and to that God to whom we all owe allegiance, I assure you I will try to do my best, and so may God help me."

To give unity and force to the recruiting operations under the recent call for troops, the President, on the 24th of September, issued the following proclamation, in which the suspension of the *habeas corpus* act was distinctly announced: "Whereas, it has become necessary to call into service, not only volunteers, but also portions of the militia of the States, by draft, in order to suppress the insurrection existing in the United States; and disloyal persons are not adequately restrained by the ordinary processes of the law from hindering this measure and from giving aid and comfort in various ways to the insurrection; Now, therefore, be it ordered: First—That during the existing insurrection, and as a necessary measure for suppressing the same, all rebels and insurgents, their aiders and abettors, within the United States, and all persons discouraging volunteer enlistments, resisting militia drafts, or guilty of any disloyal practice, affording aid and comfort to the rebels against the authority of the United States, shall be subject to martial law, and liable to trial and punishment by courts-martial or military commissions. Second—That the writ of *habeas corpus* is suspended in respect to all persons arrested, or who are now or hereafter during the rebellion shall be imprisoned in any fort, camp, arsenal, military prison or other place of confinement, by any military authority, or by the sentence of any court-martial or military commission."

On the 14th of August, President Lincoln made a fresh appeal in behalf of the policy of colonization which he had advocated before the Border State members at the recent session of Congress. This time he addressed the negroes themselves through a deputation of free colored men in Washington, who came to him by invitation. His remarks, as reported, present a striking proof of his solicitude, mingled with fears for the welfare of the race. Having all been seated, he informed them that a sum of money had been appropriated by Congress and placed at his disposition, for the purpose of aiding the colonization, in some country, of the people, or a portion of them, of African descent, thereby making it his duty, as it had long been his inclination, to favor that cause. He spoke of the grounds which made this separation desirable. "You and we," said he, "are different races. We have between us a broader difference than exists between almost any other two races. Whether it is right or wrong I need not discuss; but this physical difference is a great disadvantage to us both, as I think. Your race suffer very greatly, many of them, by living among us, while ours suffer from your presence. In a word, we suffer on each side. If this is admitted, it affords a reason, at least, why we should be separated. You, here, are freemen, I suppose. Perhaps you have long been free, or all your lives. Your race are suffering, in my judgment, the greatest wrong inflicted on any people. But even when you cease to be slaves you are yet far removed from being placed on an equality with the white race. You are cut off from many of the advantages which the other race enjoys. The aspiration of men is to enjoy equality with the best when free, but on this broad continent not a single man of your race is made the equal of a single man of ours. Go where you are treated the best, and the ban is still upon you. I do not propose to discuss this, but to present it as a fact with which we have to deal. I cannot alter it if I would. It is a fact about which we all think and feel alike, I and you. We look to our condition. Owing to the existence of the two races on this continent, I need not recount to you the effects upon white men growing out of the institution of slavery. I believe in its general evil effects on the white race. See our present condition—the country engaged in war! our white men cutting one anothers' throats—none knowing how far it will extend—and then consider what we know to be the truth. But for your race among us there could not be war, although many men engaged on either side do not care for you one way or the other. Nevertheless, I repeat, without the institution of slavery, and the colored race as a basis, the war could not have an existence. It is better for us both, therefore, to be separated." The President then admitting that emigration might in certain instances be attended with loss of comforts enjoyed by some in the United States, reminded those before him of the spirit of self-sacrifice by which they might lead the way to the prosperity of their less fortunate brethren. "It is a cheering thought throughout life," said he, "that something can be done to ameliorate the condition of those who have been subject to the hard usages of the world. It is difficult to make a man miserable while he feels he is worthy of himself and claims kindred to the great God who made him. In the American Revolutionary war sacrifices were made by men engaged in it, but they were cheered by the future. General Washington himself endured greater physical hardships than if he had remained a British subject, yet he was a happy man, because he was engaged in benefiting his race; something for the children of his neighbors, having none of his own." He then spoke of the claims of Liberia, and in reference to its distance from the country of their nativity, remarked: "I do not know how much attachment you may have toward our race. It does not strike me that you have the greatest reason to love them." This led to the suggestion of planting a colony in Central America—a scheme which was then plausibly advocated, but which was subsequently ascertained to be without any adequate inducements in the unsettled political condition and other unfavorable circumstances of that country. When months had passed and the subject been tested in various ways, the President in his December Message to Congress was compelled to admit that the Spanish-American republics were not favorable to the measure, while "the free persons of African descent," for whose benefit it was intended, were generally indisposed to avail themselves of the invitation to Liberia and Hayti which was extended to them.

The arguments of the President were good and conveyed to his audience with tact and feeling, but the "napkin was too narrow" to bind up the wounds of the country. Colonization, at the best, like ordinary emigration, could offer a refuge only to the few. The great question of emancipation, in connection with the war, could not wait this slow inadequate solution. The President was meanwhile pressed, by his Republican supporters, whose influence at the present crisis it seemed necessary to look to for the proper maintenance of the war, for some larger declaration of his policy on the vexed question of slavery. It was not his habit to practice any unnecessary reserve on this or other matters. Accordingly, when the voice of the public appeared to him sufficiently authoritative, he gave in the following letter to the editor of the *New York Tribune*, in which journal the appeal had been urgently pressed, a statement of his position: "Executive Mansion, Washington, August 22, 1862. Hon. Horace Greeley—Dear Sir: I have just received yours of the 19th instant, addressed to myself through the *New York Tribune*. If there be in it any statements or assumptions of facts which I may know to be erroneous, I do not now and here controvert them. If there be any inferences which I may believe to be falsely drawn, I do not now and here argue against them. If there be perceptible in it an impatient and dictatorial tone, I waive it in deference to an old friend whose heart I have always supposed to be right. As to the policy I 'seem to be pursuing,' as you say, I have not meant to leave any one in doubt. I would save the Union. I would save it the shortest way under the Constitution. The sooner the national authority can be restored the nearer the Union will be—the Union as it was. If there be those who would not save the Union unless they could at the same time save slavery, I do not agree with them. If there be those who would not save the Union unless they could at the same time destroy slavery, I do not agree with them. My paramount object is to save the Union, and not either to save or destroy slavery. If I could save the Union without freeing any slave I would do it, and if I could save it by freeing all the slaves I would do it, and if I could save it by freeing some and leaving others alone I would also do that. What I do about slavery and the colored race I do because I believe it helps to save this Union, and what I forbear I forbear because I do not believe it would help to save the Union. I shall do less whenever I shall believe what I am doing hurts the cause, and I shall do more whenever I believe doing more will help the cause. I shall try to correct errors, when shown to be errors, and I shall adopt new views so fast as they shall appear to be true views. I have here stated my purpose according to my view of official duty, and I intend no modification of my oft-expressed personal wish that all men everywhere could be free. Yours, A. LINCOLN."

The President thus placed slavery in subordination to the Union. The preservation of the State he felt to be his first duty to which all others were incidental. The letter was another note of warning to the Southern States preparatory to the final overture. This came exactly one month after in the memorable Emancipation Proclamation. As an evidence of the continued anxiety in the mean time regarding the measure on the President's mind, we have the narrative of another notable interview at the White House with a delegation from Chicago, on the 13th of September. In answer to the memorial which was read, urging emancipation on religious grounds, the President replied: "The subject presented is one upon which I have thought much for weeks past, and I may even say for months. I am approached with the most opposite opinions and advice, and that by religious men, who are equally certain that they represent the Divine will. I am sure that either the one or the other class is mistaken in that belief, and that perhaps, in some respects, both. I hope it will not be irreverent for me to say, that if it is probable that God would reveal his will to others on a point so connected with my duty, it might be supposed he would reveal it directly to me. For, unless I am more deceived in myself than I often am, it is my earnest desire to know the will of Providence in this matter. And if I can learn what it is I will do it! These are not, however, the days of miracles, and I suppose it will be granted that I am not to expect a direct revelation. I must study the plain, physical facts of the case, ascertain what is possible, and learn what appears to be wise and right."

It is a habit of the President in these interviews candidly to present the various embarrassments of a question, from a habit of fairness, so that they may be answered, arguing the case, as it were, aloud, before himself, and reserving his judicial decision on a review of the whole. He thus went on illustrating the subject by various anecdote, and in the course of his remarks made use of an expression which presently passed into the currency of a proverb. "What good," said he, "would a proclamation of emancipation from me do; especially as we are now situated? I do not want to issue a document that the whole world will see must necessarily be inoperative, *like the Pope's bull against the comet.* Would my word free the slaves, when I cannot even enforce the Constitution in the rebel States?" To this and other like suggestions the delegation replied, that though different opinions might be argued, the truth was somewhere, and if religiously sought would be found, that emancipation would appeal to a new class at the South, give a glorious principle to the war, and secure the sympathy of Europe against intervention. The President to these various arguments rejoined: "I admit that slavery is the root of the rebellion, or, at least, its *sine qua non*. The ambition of politicians may have instigated them to act, but they would have been impotent without slavery as their instrument. I will also concede that emancipation would help us in Europe, and convince them that we are incited by something more than ambition. I grant further, that it would help somewhat at the North, though not so much, I fear, as you and those you represent imagine. Still, some additional strength would be added in that way to the war. And then unquestionably it would weaken the rebels by drawing off their laborers, which is of great importance; but I am not so sure we could do much with the blacks. If we were to arm them, I fear that in a few weeks the arms would be in the hands of the rebels; and indeed thus far we have not had arms enough to equip our white troops. I will mention another thing, though it meet only your scorn and contempt. There are 50,000 bayonets in the Union army from the border slave States. It would be a serious matter if, in consequence of a proclamation such as you desire, they should go over to the rebels. I do not think they all would—no so many indeed as a year ago, or as six months ago—not so many to-day as yesterday. Every day increases their Union feeling. They are also getting their pride enlisted, and want to beat the rebels. Let me say one thing more: I think you should admit that we already have an important principle to rally and unite the people in the fact that constitutional government is at stake. This is a fundamental idea, going down about as deep as anything." In conclusion, he said: "Do not misunderstand me, because I have mentioned these objections. They indicate the difficulties that have thus far prevented my action in some such way as you desire. I have not decided against a proclamation of liberty to the slaves, but hold the matter under advisement. And I can assure you, that the subject is on my mind, by day and night, more than any other. Whatever shall appear to be God's will, I will do."*

Having thus exhausted ratiocination on the subject, the President was prepared to come to a conclusion. That judgment was deliberately pronounced in his Proclamation of September 22d, at conclusion of the sixty days of warning under the Confiscation Act, and following close after a season of military disasters upon the brilliant victory at Antietam. It thus read: "I, Abraham Lincoln, President of the United States of America, and Commander-in-Chief of the Army and Navy thereof, do hereby proclaim and declare that hereafter as heretofore the war will be prosecuted for the object of practically restoring the constitutional relation between the United States and the people thereof in those states in which that relation is, or may be, suspended or disturbed; that it is my purpose upon the next meeting of Congress to again recommend the adoption of a practical measure tendering pecuniary aid to the free acceptance or rejection of all the slave states, so called, the people whereof may not then be in rebellion against the United States, and which states may then have voluntarily adopted, or thereafter may voluntarily adopt, the immediate or gradual abolishment of slavery within their respective limits, and that the effort to colonize persons of African descent, with their consent, upon the continent or elsewhere, with

* Report of the delegation by W. W. Patton and John Dempster. Chicago, Ill., September 21, 1862.

the previously obtained consent of the government existing there, will be continued; that on the first day of January, in the year of our Lord one thousand eight hundred and sixty-three, all persons held as slaves within any state, or any designated part of a state, the people whereof shall then be in rebellion against the United States shall be then, thenceforward and forever, free, and the executive government of the United States, including the military and naval authority thereof, will recognize and maintain the freedom of such persons, and will do no act or acts to repress such persons, or any of them, in any efforts they may make for their actual freedom; that the Executive will, on the first day of January aforesaid, by proclamation, designate the states and parts of states, if any, in which the people thereof respectively shall then be in rebellion against the United States; and the fact that any state, or the people thereof, shall on that day be in good faith represented in the Congress of the United States by members chosen thereto, at elections wherein a majority of the qualified voters of such state shall have participated, shall, in the absence of strong countervailing testimony, be deemed conclusive evidence that such state and the people thereof have not been in rebellion against the United States."

In the same document the President also called attention to an additional article of war enacted by the recent Congress, "prohibiting all officers or persons in the military or naval service of the United States from employing any of the forces under their respective commands for the purpose of returning fugitives from service or labor who may have escaped from any persons to whom such service or labor is claimed to be due, and any officer who shall be found guilty by a court-martial of violating this article, shall be dismissed from the service." He also further enjoined upon the military and naval service obedience and enforcement of the provisions attached to the Confiscation Act emancipating the refugee or captured slaves of rebels; requiring proof of the loyalty of the claimants of fugitive slaves in any of the States, and forbidding any military or naval officer deciding on the validity of such claim or surrendering such fugitive. In a final clause it was added, "the Executive will in due time recommend that all citizens of the United States who shall have remained loyal thereto throughout the rebellion shall (upon the restoration of the constitutional relation between the United States and their respective states and people if the relation shall have been suspended or disturbed) be compensated for all losses by acts of the United States, including the loss of slaves." Such was the Emancipation Proclamation of President Lincoln given at length to the world,—a military act justified by a military necessity. It was everywhere hailed by friends and feared and denounced by opponents, while they affected to treat it with contempt, borrowing an instrument of assault from its author, as "the Pope's bull against the comet." The emancipating legislation of Congress now had its full sanction, and from this time as the Union armies were advanced the slave of the rebel owner walked a free man within the lines.

When the national Congress again met, on the 1st of December, President Lincoln, mindful of the purpose which he had expressed in his Proclamation, again called attention to what he termed compensated emancipation. The larger part of his message was in fact devoted to the subject. Repeating the language of his inaugural address on the inadequacy of disunion as a remedy for the differences between the people of the two sections, he sagaciously pointed out the physical and geographical laws which rendered union a matter of political necessity. "A nation," said he, "may be said to consist of its territory, its people and its laws. The territory is the only part which is of certain durability. 'One generation passeth away and another generation cometh, but the earth abideth forever.' It is of the first importance to duly consider and estimate this ever-enduring part. That portion of the earth's surface which is owned and inhabited by the people of the United States is well adapted to be the home of one national family, and it is not well adapted for two or more. Its vast extent and its variety of climate and production are of advantage in this age for one people, whatever they might have been in former ages. Steam and telegraphs, in intelligence, have brought these to be an advantageous combination for one united people. There is no line, straight or crooked, suitable for a national boundary upon which to divide. Trace through from east to west, upon the line between the free and slave country, and we shall find a little more than one-third of its length are rivers easy to be crossed and populated, or soon to be populated thickly upon both sides, while nearly all its remaining length are merely surveyor's lines, over which people may walk back and forth without any consciousness of their presence. No part of this line can be made any more difficult to pass by writing it down on paper or parchment as a national boundary. The fact of separation, if it comes, gives up on the part of the sectional obligations upon the seceding section the Fugitive Slave clause, along with all other constitutional obligations upon the section seceded from, while I should expect no treaty stipulation would ever be made to take its place.

"But there is another difficulty. The great interior region bounded east by the Alleghanies, north by the British dominions, west by the Rocky Mountains, and south by the line along which the culture of corn and cotton meets, and which includes part of Virginia, part of Tennessee, all of Kentucky, Ohio, Indiana, Michigan, Wisconsin, Illinois, Missouri, Kansas, Iowa, Minnesota, and the Territories of Dakotah, Nebraska, and part of Colorado, has about ten millions of people, and will have fifty millions within fifty years, if not prevented by any political folly or mistake. It contains more than one-third of the country owned by the United States, certainly more than one million of square miles. If half as populous as Massachusetts already is, it would have more than seventy-five millions of people. A glance at the map shows that, territorially speaking, it is the great body of the Republic. The other parts are but marginal borders to it, the magnificent region sloping west from the Rocky Mountains to the Pacific being the deepest and also the richest in undeveloped resources. In the production of provisions, grains, grasses, and all which proceed from them, this great interior region, is naturally one of the most important in the world. Ascertain from the statistics the small proportion of the region which has as yet been brought into cultivation, and also the large and rapidly increasing amount of its products, and we shall be overwhelmed with the magnitude of the prospect presented; and yet this region has no sea-coast, touches no ocean anywhere. As part of one nation, its people now find, and may forever find, their way to Europe by New York, to South America and Africa by New Orleans, and to Asia by San Francisco. But separate our common country into two nations, as designed by the present rebellion, and every man of this great interior region is thereby cut off from some one or more of these outlets, not, perhaps, by a physical barrier, but by embarrassing and onerous trade regulations. And this is true wherever the dividing or boundary line may be fixed. Place it now between the now free and slave country, or place it south of Kentucky, or north of Ohio, and still the truth remains that none south of it can trade to any place north of it, and none north of it can trade to any port or place south of it, except upon terms dictated by a government, foreign to them. These outlets, east, west, and south, are indispensable to the well-being of the people inhabiting and to inhabit this vast interior region. Which of the three may be the best, is no proper question. All are better than either, and all of right belong to that people and to their successors forever. True to themselves, they will not ask where a line of separation shall be, but will vow rather that there shall be no such line. Nor are the marginal regions less interested in these communications to and through them to the great outside world. They, too, and each of them, must have access to this Egypt of the West, without paying toll at the crossing of any national boundary. Our national strife springs not from our permanent part, not from the land we inhabit, not from our national homestead. There is no possible severing of this, but would multiply, and not mitigate, evils among us. In all its adaptations and aptitudes, it demands union, and abhors separation. In fact, it would ere long force reunion, however much of blood and treasure the separation might have cost."

From this view of the geographical necessities of the situation the President, inferring the present struggle to be but temporary, proceeded with great earnestness to the presentation of a scheme of peaceful emancipation. "Our strife," said he, "pertains to ourselves, to the passing generations of men, and it can, without convulsion, be hushed forever with the passing of one generation. In this view, I recommend the adoption of the following resolution and articles amendatory of the Constitution of the United States: *Resolved*, By the Senate and House of Representatives of the United States of America, In Congress assembled, two-thirds of both Houses concurring, that the following Articles be proposed to the Legislatures or Conventions of the several States, as Amendments to the Constitution of the United States, all or any of which Articles, when ratified by three-fourths of the said Legislatures or Conventions, to be valid as a part or parts of the said Constitution, viz.: ARTICLE — Every State wherein Slavery now exists which shall abolish the same therein at any time or times before the first day of January, in the year of our Lord one thousand nine hundred, shall receive compensation from the United States, as follows, to wit: The President of the United States shall deliver to every such State bonds of the United States, bearing interest at the rate of —— for each slave shown to have been therein by the Eighth Census of the United States, said bonds to be delivered to such State by installments, or in one parcel, at the completion of the abolishment, accordingly as the same shall have been gradual or at one time within such State; and interest shall begin to run upon any such bond only from the proper time of its delivery as aforesaid. Any State having received bonds as aforesaid, and afterwards reintroducing or tolerating slavery therein, shall refund to the United States the bonds so received or the value thereof and all interest paid thereon. ARTICLE — All slaves who shall have enjoyed actual freedom, by the chances of the war, at any time before the end of the Rebellion, shall be forever free; but all owners of such, who shall not have been disloyal, shall be compensated for them at the same rates as is provided for States adopting abolishment of slavery, but in such a way that no slave shall be twice accounted for. ARTICLE—Congress may appropriate money and otherwise provide for colonizing free colored persons, with their own consent, at any place or places without the United States.

"I beg indulgence to discuss these proposed articles at some length. Without slavery, the rebellion could never have existed; without slavery, it could not continue. Among the friends of the Union there is great diversity of sentiment and of policy in regard to slavery and the African race among us. Some would perpetuate slavery, some would abolish it suddenly, and without compensation; some would abolish it gradually, and with compensation; some would remove the freed people from us, and some would retain them with us; and there are yet other minor diversities. Because of these diversities, we waste much strength in struggles among ourselves; by mutual concession, we should harmonize and act together. This would be compromise; but it would be compromise among the friends and not the enemies of the Union. These articles are intended to embody a plan of such mutual concessions. If the plan shall be adopted, it is assumed that emancipation will follow, at least in several of the States.

"As to the first article, the main points are: first, The emancipation; secondly, The length of time for consummating it—thirty-seven years; and, thirdly, The compensation. The emancipation will be unsatisfactory to the advocates of perpetual slavery; but the length of time should greatly mitigate their dissatisfaction. The time spares both races from the evils of sudden derangement; in fact, from the necessity of any derangement, while most of those whose habitual course of thought will be disturbed by the measure will have passed away before its consummation. They will never see it. Another class will hail the prospect of emancipation, but will deprecate the length of time. They will feel that it gives too little to the now living slaves. But it really gives them much. It saves them from the vagrant destitution which must largely attend immediate emancipation in localities where their numbers are very great, and it gives the inspiriting assurance that their posterity shall be free forever. The plan leaves to each State choosing to act under it to abolish slavery now or at the end of the century, or at any intermediate time, or by degrees extending over the whole or any part of the period; and it obliges no two States to proceed alike. It also provides for compensation, and generally the mode of making it. This, it would seem, must further mitigate the dissatisfaction of those who favor perpetual slavery and especially those who are to receive the compensation. Doubtless, some of those who are to pay and not to receive, will object. Yet the measure is both just and economical. In a certain sense liberation of the slaves is the destruction of property; property acquired by descent or by purchase, the same as any other property. It is no less true for having been often said that the people of the South are no more responsible for the original introduction of this property than are the people of the North; and when it is remembered how unhesitatingly we all use cotton and sugar, and share the profits of dealing in them, it may not be quite safe to say that the South has been more responsible than the North for its continuance. If, then, for a common object, this property is to be sacrificed, is it not just that it be done at a common charge? And if with less money, or money more easily paid, we can preserve the benefits of the Union by this means than we can by the war alone, is it not also economical to do it?

"Let us consider it then. Let us ascertain the sum we have expended in the war since compensated emancipation was proposed last March, and consider, whether, if that measure had been promptly accepted by even some of the slave States, the same sum would not have done more to close the war than has been otherwise done. If so, the measure would save money, and in that view, would be a prudent and economical measure. Certainly, it is not so easy to pay something as it is to pay nothing.

But it is easier to pay a large sum than it is to pay a larger one, and it is easier to pay any sum, when we are able, than it is to pay it before we are able. The war requires large sums and requires them at once. The aggregate sum necessary for compensated emancipation, of course, would be large; but it would require no ready cash, nor the bonds even, any faster than the emancipation progresses. This might not, and probably would not, close before the end of the thirty-seven years. At that time, we shall probably have 100,000,000 of people to share the burden, instead of 31,000,000, as now; and, not only so, but the increase of our population may be expected to continue for a long time after the period as rapidly as before, because our territory will not have become full. I do not state this inconsiderately. At the same ratio of increase which we have maintained on an average from our first National Census in 1790, until that of 1860, we should, in 1900, have a population of 103,208,415. And why may we not continue that ratio far beyond that period? Our abundant room, our broad national homestead is our ample resources. Were our territory as limited as are the British Isles, very certainly our population could not expand as stated. Instead of receiving the foreign-born, as now, we should be compelled to send part of the native-born away; but such is not our condition. We have 2,963,000 square miles. Europe has 3,800,000, with a population averaging seventy-three and one-third persons to the square mile. Why may not our country at some time average as many? Is it less fertile? Has it more waste surface by mountains, rivers, lakes, deserts, or other causes? Is it inferior to Europe in any natural advantage? If, then, we are at some time to be as populous as Europe, how soon? As to when this may be, we can judge by the past and the present. As to when it will, if ever, depends much on whether we maintain the Union. Several of our States are already above the average European population of seventy-three and one-third to the square mile. Massachusetts has one hundred and fifty-seven, Rhode Island one hundred and thirty-three, Connecticut, ninety-nine, New York and New Jersey each eighty; and two other great States, Pennsylvania and Ohio, are not far below, the former having sixty-three, and the latter fifty-nine. The States, already above the European average, except New York, have increased in as rapid ratio since passing that point as ever before, while no one of them is equal to some other parts of our country in natural capacity for sustaining a dense population. Taking the nation in the aggregate, and we find its population and ratio of increase for the several decennial periods to be as follows:

1720—3,929,827
1800—5,305,937—35.02 per cent ratio of increase.
1810—7,239,814—36.45 per cent ratio of increase.
1820—9,638,131—33.12 per cent ratio of increase.
1830–12,866,020—33.49 per cent ratio of increase.
1840–17,069,453—32.67 per cent ratio of increase.
1850–23,191,876—35.87 per cent ratio of increase.
1860–31,443,790—35.58 per cent ratio of increase.

This shows an average decennial increase of 34.60 per cent. in population through the seventy years from our first to our last census taken. It is seen that the ratio of increase at no one of these seven periods is either two per cent. below or two per cent. above the average; thus showing how inflexible, and consequently how reliable, the law of increase in our case is. Assuming that it will continue, it gives the following results: 1870, 42,323,341; 1880, 56,967,216; 1890, 76,677,872; 1900, 103,208,415; 1910, 138,918,526; 1920, 186,984,335; 1930, 251,680,914. These figures show that our country may be as populous as Europe now is, at some point between 1920 and 1930, say about 1925—our territory at seventy-three and one-third persons to the square mile, being of a capacity to contain 247,186,000. And we will reach this, too, if we do not ourselves relinquish the chances by the folly and evils of disunion, or by long and exhausting war, springing from the only great element of national discord among us. While it cannot be foreseen exactly how much one huge example of secession breeding lesser ones indefinitely would retard the population, civilization, and prosperity, no one can doubt that the extent of it would be very great and injurious. The proposed emancipation would shorten the war, perpetuate peace, insure this increase of the population and proportionately of the wealth of the country. With these we should pay all the emancipation would cost, together with our other debt, easier than we should pay our other debt without it. If we had allowed our old national debt to run at six per cent per annum, simple interest, from the end of our Revolutionary struggle till to-day without paying anything on either principal or interest, each man of us would owe less upon that debt now than each man owed upon it then; and this because our increase of men through the whole period has been greater than six per cent.; has run faster than the interest upon the debt. Thus time alone relieves a debtor nation, so long as its population increases faster than unpaid interest accumulates on its debt. This fact would be no excuse for delaying the payment of what is justly due; but it shows the great importance of time in this connection, the great advantage of a policy by which we shall not have to pay until we number a hundred millions, what by a different policy we should have to pay now, when we number but 31,000,000. In a word, it shows that a dollar will be much harder to pay for the war than will be a dollar for emancipation on the proposed plan—and then the latter will cost no blood; no precious life. It will be a saving of both.

"As to the second article, I think it would be impracticable to return to bondage the class of persons therein contemplated. Some of them doubtless, in the property sense, belong to loyal owners, and hence provision is made in this article for compensating such. The third article relates to the future of the freed people. It does not oblige, but merely authorizes, Congress to aid in colonizing such as may consent. This ought not to be regarded as objectionable on the one hand or on the other, inasmuch as it comes to nothing unless by mutual consent of the people to be deported and the American voters, through their representatives in Congress. I cannot make it better known than it already is that I strongly favor colonization, and yet I wish to say there is an objection urged against the colored persons remaining in the country which is largely imaginary, if not sometimes malicious. It is insisted that their presence would injure and displace white labor and white laborers. If there ever could be a proper time for mere arguments, that time surely is not now. In times like the present, men should utter nothing for which they would not willingly be responsible through time and in eternity. Is it true, then, that colored people can displace any more white labor by being free than by remaining slaves? If they stay in their old places, they jostle no white laborers. If they leave their old places, they leave them open to white laborers. Logically, there is neither more nor less of it. Emancipation, even, without deportation, would probably enhance the wages of white labor, and very surely would not reduce them. Thus the customary amount of labor would still have to be performed. The freed people would surely not do more than their old proportion of it, and very probably for a time would do less, leaving an increased part to white laborers, bringing their labor into greater demand, and consequently enhancing the wages of it. With deportation, even to a limited extent, enhancing wages to white labor is mathematically certain. Labor is like any other commodity in the market; increase the demand for it, and you increase the price of it. Reduce the supply of black labor by colonizing the black laborers out of the country, and by precisely so much you increase the demand for and wages of white labor. But it is dreaded that the freed people will swarm forth and cover the whole land. Are they not already in the land? Will liberation make them any more numerous? Equally distributed among the whites of the whole country, there would be but one colored to seven whites. Could the one in any way greatly disturb the seven? There are many communities now having more than one free colored person to seven whites, and this without any apparent consciousness of evil from it. The District of Columbia, and the States of Maryland and Delaware are all in this condition. The District has more than one free colored person to six whites; and yet in its frequent petitions to Congress, I believe it has never presented the presence of free colored persons as one of its grievances. But why should emancipation south send the freed people north? People of any color seldom run unless there be something to run from. Heretofore, colored people to some extent have fled north from bondage; and now perhaps from both bondage and destitution; but if gradual emancipation and deportation be adopted, they will have neither to flee from. Their old masters will give them wages, at least until new laborers can be procured; and the freed men in turn will gladly give their labor for the wages till new homes can be found for them in congenial climes and with people of their own blood and race. This proposition can be trusted on the mutual interests involved. And, in any event, cannot the North decide for itself whether to receive them? Again, as practice proves more than theory in any case, has there been any irruption of colored people northward because of the abolishment of slavery in this District last Spring? What I have said of the proportion of free colored persons to the whites in the District is from the census of 1860, having no reference to persons called contrabands, nor to those made free by the act of Congress abolishing slavery here. The plan consisting of these articles is recommended, not but that a restoration of the national authority would be accepted without its adoption. Nor will the war, nor proceedings under the Proclamation of September 22, 1862, be stayed because of the recommendation of this plan. Its timely adoption, I doubt not, would bring restoration, and thereby stay both. And notwithstanding this plan the recommendation that Congress provide by law for compensating any State which may adopt emancipation before this plan shall have been acted upon is hereby earnestly renewed. Such would only be an advance part of the plan, and the same arguments apply to both.

"This plan is recommended as a means, not in exclusion of, but additional to, all others for restoring and preserving the national authority throughout the Union. The subject is presented exclusively in its economical aspect. The plan would, I am confident, secure peace more speedily than can be done by force alone, while it would cost less, considering amounts and manner of payment, and times of payment, and the amounts would be easier paid than will be the additional cost of the war, if we rely solely upon force. It is much—very much—that it would cost no blood at all. The plan is proposed as permanent constitutional law. It cannot become such without the concurrence of, first, two-thirds of Congress, and afterward three-fourths of the States. The requisite three-fourths of the States will necessarily include seven of the slave States. Their concurrence, if obtained, will give assurance of their severally adopting emancipation at no distant day upon the new constitutional terms. This assurance would end the struggle now and save the Union forever. I do not forget the gravity which should characterize a paper addressed to the Congress of the nation by the Chief Magistrate of the nation; nor do I forget that some of you are my seniors, nor that many of you have more experience than I in the conduct of public affairs; yet I trust that, in view of the great responsibility resting upon me, you will perceive no want of respect to yourselves in any undue earnestness I may seem to display. Is it doubted, then, that the plan I propose, if adopted, would shorten the war, and thus lessen its expenditure of money and of blood? Is it doubted that it would restore the national authority and national prosperity, and perpetuate both indefinitely? Is it doubted that we here, Congress and Executive, can secure its adoption? Will not the good people respond to a united and earnest appeal from us? Can we, can they, by any other means, so certainly or so speedily assure these vital objects? We can succeed only by concert. It is not 'Can any of us imagine better,' but 'Can we all do better?' Object wheresoever is possible, still the question recurs, 'Can we do better?' The dogmas of the quiet past are inadequate to the stormy present. The occasion is piled high with difficulties, and we must rise with the occasion. As our case is new, so we must think anew, and act anew. We must disenthrall ourselves, and then we shall save our country. Fellow citizens, we cannot escape history. We of this Congress and this administration will be remembered in spite of ourselves. No personal significance or insignificance can spare one or another of us. The fiery trial through which we pass will light us down in honor or dishonor to the latest generation. We say we are for the Union. The world will not forget that we say this. We know how to save the Union. The world knows we do know how to save it. We, even we here, hold the power, and bear the responsibility. In giving freedom to the slave, we assure freedom to the free, honorable alike in what we give and what we preserve. We shall nobly save or meanly lose the last, best hope of earth. Other means may succeed; this could not fail. The way is plain—peaceful—generous—just—a way which, if followed, the world will forever applaud, and God must forever bless." Thus earnestly the President sought—while recognizing slavery as the essential element at work in the rebellion, and adhering to the military policy which his Proclamation had sanctioned—to ward off from the loyal slaveholder the evils of a violent abolition of the injurious institution.

Accompanying the President's message was a second huge volume of papers relating to foreign affairs, affording ample evidence of the difficulties with which the government was beset in its maritime and other international relations, and of the zeal and ability displayed by the Secretary of State in asserting the rights and protecting the welfare of the country, of the general situation abroad, the President summing up the results of the year's voluminous diplomacy without prejudice, remarked with mingled hesitation and confidence: "If the condition of our relations with other nations is less gratifying than it has usually been at former periods, it is certainly more satisfactory than a nation so unhappily distressed as we are might reasonably have apprehended. In the month of June last, there were some grounds to expect that the maritime powers, which, at the beginning of our domestic difficulties, so unanimously and unnecessarily, as we think, recognized the insurgents as a belligerent, would soon recede from that position, which has proved only less injurious to themselves than to our own country, but the temporary reverses which afterward befell the national arms, and which were exaggerated by our own disloyal citizens abroad, have hitherto delayed that act of simple justice. The civil war which has so radically changed for the moment the occupations and habits of the American people, has necessarily disturbed the social conditions and affected very deeply the prosperity of the nations with which we have carried on a commerce, that has been steadily increasing throughout a period of half a century. It has at the same time excited political ambitions and apprehensions, which have produced a profound agitation throughout the civilized world. In this unusual agitation, we have forborne from taking part in any controversy between foreign states and between parties or factions in such states. We have attempted no propagandism and acknowledged no revolution. But we have left to every nation the exclusive conduct and management of its own affairs. Our struggle has been, of course, contemplated by foreign nations with reference less to its own merits than to its supposed and often exaggerated effects, and the consequences resulting to those nations themselves. Nevertheless, complaint on the part of this Government, even if it were just, would certainly be unwise."

The correspondence of Secretary Seward through Mr. Adams with the British Government covers not only the purely foreign relations of the country, but supplies an instructive commentary on the progress of affairs at home. A running criticism on the war, in fact, appeared necessary to meet the interpretations or prejudices of a court which professed to be guided in its policy by the course of events. To ward off recognition of the Confederacy with its possible sequel intervention, it was requisite that the power and motives of the North in the struggle for national existence should be fully displayed; accordingly the utmost vigilance was maintained by the Secretary of State and the United States Minister at London in meeting every adverse exhibition of opinion on the war. They had not only to repel injury from abroad, but to vindicate as in the explanations regarding the blockade, the obstruction of the harbor of Charleston, and even such acts as the order of General Butler concerning the women in New Orleans, the domestic policy of the country against meddlesome interference. Of more serious importance were the continued remonstrances against the fitting out of vessels intended for the Confederate service, in the British ports. Two cases of this kind became particularly prominent by the subsequent injuries inflicted by these rebel steamers on American commerce.

The first of these was the Oreto, afterwards named the Florida. She was fitted out at Liverpool early in the year, when her destination for the rebel service was detected by the American Consul and brought to the notice of the British Government, which instituted an examination of her cargo. Her clearance being adroitly made out for the island of Sicily, she was permitted to leave the harbor without interruption at the end of March. On her appearance at Nassau another ineffectual attempt was made to detain her. Subsequently, in September, she boldly, in the guise of a British man-of-war, ran by the blockading vessels into Mobile — a performance which called forth from the Secretary of the Navy the instant dismissal from the service of Commander Preble of the United Sates steam sloop Oneida at this station. From Mobile, at the end of December, the Florida made her way out in safety as a Confederate war vessel, under the command of Captain John Newland Maffit, formerly of the United States navy, to enter upon a series of depredations upon Northern commerce.

A second war steamer of larger dimensions, fitted out this season in England for the Confederates, the "290," subsequently known as the "Alabama," became the subject of further correspondence between Mr. Adams and Earl

Russell. The complaint was referred in June to the Lords Commissioners of the Treasury, who reported, that while it was apparent that the vessel was intended for a ship of war there was not sufficient evidence of her destination to warrant detention. The case becoming stronger a second appeal, backed by the advice of Mr. Collier, Queen's Counsel, was made to arrest her, but pending this application, while an order for her detention was on its way to Liverpool, the vessel on the 29th of July, suddenly left the port of Liverpool without register or clearance. She took her departure with a party of ladies and gentlemen ostensibly on a trial trip; dismissing her visitors on getting out of the Mersey. It had been popularly reported — a rather transparent jest — that she was being built for the Emperor of China. Mr. Adams telegraphed to Captain Craven, in command of the United States steamer Tuscarora, at Southampton, to intercept her at sea, a risk of capture which the rebel vessel avoided by taking the channel to the north of Ireland, while her pursuer lay in wait in St. George's channel. She then proceeded, undisturbed, to one of the Azores, where, according to a previous arrangement, she awaited the arrival of a bark from the Thames laden with her stores and armament. Her appearance meanwhile at the island was excused to the Portuguese authorities on the plea of making repairs to her engines. The bark presently came and claimed the hospitality of the harbor, pretending to have sprung aleak, when she was placed in quarantine. Under pretence of preventing her sinking, Captain Bullock, of the "290," brought his vessel alongside and relieved her of her heavy cargo; the Portuguese protesting at the violation of quarantine, and the Captain blustering, feigning a passion and declaring "that he was doing no more for the bark than any Englishman would do for another in distress." When this business was completed, the British screw steamer Bahama made her appearance, bringing the notorious Captain Semmes and the late officers of the Sumter and an additional crew and armament. Being thus equipped, Captain Semmes mustered the crew on deck and read his commission in the Confederate navy and the order of Jefferson Davis to take command of the Confederate sloop of war now named the Alabama. In this way, as the story was told to the delight of the English public—a leading British journal pronouncing it "fairly to be compared, both for interest and drollery, with any scene either of Cooper or any other naval novelist"—the Alabama was fairly launched on her career of piratical adventure. Space would fail us to repeat the story of her depredations which repeated in various forms the evil exploits of her famous commander in the Sumter. Before the close of the year twenty-eight vessels, mostly owned at New York and the Eastward, the greater part of which were burnt, had become her prey. The Confederate flag, unrecognized by any foreign nation and having no port into which to carry and adjudicate her prizes, she was compelled to take the pirate's method of plundering, and burning. Occasionally a vessel, as the California steamship Ariel, which she arrested on the 7th of December, on the eastern point of Cuba, was released on giving bonds for the ship and cargo in a heavy sum, charitably allowed to be paid on the establishment of the independence of the Confederate States, but generally the practice was robbery and destruction.

This course of proceeding naturally excited the vehement indignation of the merchant sufferers in New York and elsewhere, who were loud in their remonstrances at the neglect or indifference of the British Government in permitting the fitting out of such an enemy to civilization; the home government sent one vessel of war after another in fruitless search of the adroitly managed cruiser, while her successive depredations and the advantages which she received as a recognized "belligerent" were promptly brought before the British Cabinet with the hope at least of arresting similar injuries in the future. The intention of the British Government was doubtless to maintain a neutral course between the contending parties; the difficulties which arose in its way grew out of the nature of this undertaking, which, from the start, gave undue credit to the rebellion, and from the obstacles interposed by ship-builders and others in concealing or covering up their illegal aid which they rendered to the Confederates. It was not to be wondered at that mercantile cupidity should favor the Southern cause when it was almost universally recognized as an axiom with the British public that the separation of the two portions of the United States was complete and irrevocable. In a previous chapter* we have recorded the sentiments of eminent Englishmen uttered during the first year of the struggle to this effect,—convictions which were not likely to be diminished by the continuance of the war. Parliament, when the question of recognition was brought up by such unfriendly agitators as Mr. Lindsay, at the suggestion of the ministry, postponed any action on the subject; but the idea was not so much rejected as held in reserve to wait the opportunities of the future. Out of parliament, a prominent cabinet minister, Mr. Gladstone, the Chancellor of the Exchequer, in a speech at a banquet at Newcastle, on the 7th of October, did not hesitate to assert in the most decided manner, while expressing his concern for the welfare of the North, his belief of the final dissolution of the Union. "We may," said he, "have our own opinions about slavery—we may be for the South or against the South, but there is no doubt, I think, about this, Jefferson Davis and the other leaders of the South have made an army—they are making, it appears, a navy—and they have made what is more than either, they have made a nation. I cannot say that I, for one, have viewed with any regret their failure to establish themselves in Maryland. It appears to be too probable that, if they had been able to establish themselves in Maryland, the consequences of their military success in any aggressive movement would have been that a political party favorable to them would have been formed in that State—that they would have contracted actual or virtual engagements with that political party, and that the existence of these engagements, hampering them in their negotiations with the Northern States, might have formed a new obstacle to peace. Gentlemen, from the bottom of our hearts we should desire that no new obstacle to peace may be formed. We may anticipate with certainty the success of the Southern States, so far as regards effecting their separation from the North. I, for my own part, cannot but believe that that event is as certain as any event yet future and contingent can be. But it is from feeling that that great event is likely to arise, and that the North will have to suffer that mortification, that I earnestly hope that England will do nothing to inflict additional shame, sorrow, or pain upon those who have already suffered much, and will probably have to suffer more. It may be that a time might arrive when it would be the duty of Europe to offer a word of expostulation, or of friendly aid toward composing the quarrel. If it be even possible that such a time as that may arrive, how important it is that when that word comes, it should address itself to minds which are not embittered by the recollection that unkind things have been said and done toward them in Europe, and above all, in England, the country, which, however they may find fault with it from time to time, we know holds the highest place in their admiration and respect." If such was

* Ch. 47, ante p. 152 and sequel.

the language of a friendly statesman, what could be expected from those whose prejudices or interests were committed to advocacy of the Southern cause. The avowal of Mr. Gladstone that the Confederates were a nation and would remain so, was echoed by the London *Times*, the representative of the average British opinions. "By this time," was its language, "this is probably the expectation of ninety-nine Englishmen out of a hundred. Many have their own opinions as to the origin of this war, the results to ourselves and other points; yet agree in the utter impossibility of the old Union being ever restored, or any union effected, unless, possibly, under a military empire." Mr. Gladstone, in his speech just mentioned, was thought to favor the idea of a recognition of the Confederacy by the Government of which he was a member; but if his remarks sanctioned this interpretation, they were neutralized by the opposite expression of opinion of another officer of the Cabinet, Sir George Cornewall Lewis, the Secretary of War, who took occasion, publicly, to oppose the assertion that the South had yet established itself as a nation. As it was upon the power of the South to maintain itself that recognition depended the Government, whatever the expectations of ruling statesmen might be, could wait a little longer for the fact.

On this subject of British opinion the minister, Mr. Adams, felt compelled to write to his government at Washington, in September: "The breaking out of the insurrection has brought to light the existence of national feelings in England towards the United States, the strength of which had scarcely been suspected in America. As the struggle has gone on, the nature and extent of them has become so clear and unmistakable as to defy all disavowal. Having their root in the same apprehensions of the force of a foreign State which exists in the case of France, they take the same direction towards efforts to curtail, if not to neutralize, its energies. The popular sentiment of Great Britain, as now developed, should be a warning to the statesmen of America by which to regulate their action, at least for two generations. It dictates the necessity of union at home far more imperatively even than the wretchedness which now fills the country with grief from end to end."*

Friendly voices, however, were not wanting in England, raised in appeal or warning against interference with the efforts of the government at Washington. "It would be idle," said the eminent member of Parliament, economist and friend of liberal institutions, Mr. Cobden, to his constituents at Rochdale, on the 29th of October, "for England or France, or both together to talk of intervention. The idea of employing force must be abandoned. The cause is utterly unmanageable by force; but if by interference we could get cotton, what price would we pay for it? It would be cheaper to keep the whole population of the cotton district, aye, even on turtle, champagne, and venison, than to send to America to obtain cotton by force of arms. Six months of war would cost more than would maintain the entire people of these districts ten years."

The sturdy champion of popular rights, Mr. Bright, was also again heard in an eloquent address, in December, to the operatives of Lancashire. Alluding to the gratuitous prophecy of disunion by Mr. Gladstone, he remarked that he was "happy to say that, although the chancellors of the exchequer can often decide to a penny what shall be the rate of taxation in England, they cannot determine what is to be the fate of a whole continent." For himself he looked to a higher authority. "I believe," said he, "the question is not in the hands of Lord Palmerston, nor President Lincoln, but in the hands of that Supreme Ruler who is

* Mr. Adams to Mr. Seward. London, September 12, 1862.

bringing about one of those great events in history which men will not often regard when passing before them, but which they look on with astonishment after they have taken place." Picturing the cause of the South, desirous "to secure that a handful of white men shall lord it over millions of men made black by the very Hand that made us white, to retain the power to breed negroes, to lash negroes, to chain them, to buy and sell negroes, to deny them the enjoyment of the commonest family ties, to break their hearts by rending them at their pleasure, to close their mental eyes against a glimpse of that knowledge which separates us from the brute creation," he asked, indignantly, "who are they who speak in favor of England becoming so eagerly the ally of this great conspiracy against human nature." Turning from his own land, "how is it," he asked, "that on the continent of Europe there is not a liberal newspaper nor a liberal politician that durst say, or even thought of saying, one word in favor of that portentous and momentous shape which now asks to be received into the family of nations? The late Count Cavour had no difficulty in deciding on this point. Ask Garibaldi — ask Kossuth whether slavery has nothing to do with this strife. Ask Victor Hugo, the poet of freedom and exponent of the yearnings of all mankind for the better time— ask any man in Europe who opens his lips or indites a sentence for freedom, on which side your sympathies should lie." The different expressions of opinion in England he attributed to the control of the London Press by the aristocratic classes. One of the most eminent statesmen in the country, he said, had remarked to him: "I had not an idea how much influence the example of the Republic was having upon opinion here until I discovered the universal congratulations on the prospect of that Republic breaking up." The people, however, he remarked, do not err. "Free States are the home of the workingman. In fifteen years 2,500,000 of our countrymen and countrywomen have left us for the United States, every one of whom, speaking generally, is in a much better position in point of comfort than if they had remained here; as if, as one of America's own poets had said:

> 'For her free latch-string never was drawn in
> Against the poorest child of Adam's kin.'

In America there are no six millions of grown men excluded by the Constitution from political rights; there is a free church, a free school, a free hand, a free vote, a free career for the child of the humblest. No! countrymen who work for your living, remember that there will be one wild shriek of freedom to startle all mankind if that republic is overthrown. Slavery has been the huge blot upon its fame; it is a hideous outrage against human right and divine law; the pride and passion of men will not permit its peaceable extinction; the slave owners of our colonies, if they had been strong enough, would have revolted too. I believe there was no mode short of a miracle more stupendous than any recorded in Holy Writ which would in our time, or in a century, have brought the abolition of slavery in America but the suicide the South has committed and the war they are now waging." He did not, he reiterated in conclusion, hold to the opinion of those who thought the struggle hopeless for the North. "I cannot believe that civilization in its journey with the sun will sink into endless night to gratify the ambition of the leaders in this revolt, who seek 'to wade through slaughter to a throne and shut the gates of mercy on mankind.' I have another and far brighter vision before my gaze. It may be but a vision, but I will still cherish it. I see one vast confederation stretching from the frozen North, in one unbroken line, to the glowing South, and from the wide billows of the Atlantic to the calmer waters of the Pacific main, and I see one people and one law and one language and one faith, and over all that wide continent the home of freedom and a refuge for the oppressed of every race."

The spirit of this eloquent oration was echoed in a contemporary address by the workingmen of Manchester to President Lincoln, especially called forth by the Proclamation of Emancipation. "We honor," said they, "your free States as a singularly happy abode for the working millions, where industry is honored. . . . Our interests are identified with yours. We are truly one people, though locally separated. And if you have any ill-wishers here, be assured they are chiefly those who oppose liberty at home, and that they will be powerless to stir up quarrels between us from the very day in which your country becomes, undeniably and without exception, the home of the free."

Meanwhile the war bore heavily upon the industrial interests of England and France, the looms of Lyons and the cotton spinning of Manchester. Large demands were made upon British charity, not unaided by liberal contributions from the Northern States of America, to relieve the distress of the English operatives thrown out of employ. But trade in other quarters was active, the stock of manufactured goods on hand rose greatly in value, and breadstuffs from America were cheaply and abundantly furnished. The nation, confident of a revolt in the dismemberment of the Union, which was looked upon as favorable to its interests, was content to bear with present evils while its leaders were not inclined to provoke unnecessary hostility on the part of the United States, by such further act of interference as the recognition of the Southern Confederacy, or even any direct offer of mediation. The Emperor of the French, however, foreseeing, from his insight into the military elements of the war, the probable long continuance of the struggle, and frankly admitting that at the outset in granting belligerent rights to the South, "It was with the general belief of statesmen in Europe that the two sections would never come together again,"*—seemed less inclined to be patient. The American Minister at Paris, Mr. Dayton, was from time to time reminded of the commercial wants of France, and anxiously interrogated as to the prospects of the war. This uneasiness was more formally expressed in a diplomatic dispatch of M. Drouyn De L'Huys, the French Minister of Foreign Affairs, who had succeeded to M. Thouvenel, addressed on the 30th October, to Lord Russell and Prince Gortchakoff, the Ministers of State of England and Russia. In this the concurrence of those nations was solicited in an offer of mediation by the three powers, in which it was proposed that they should "exert their influence at Washington as well as with the Confederates, to obtain an armistice for six months, during which every act of war, direct or indirect, should provisionally cease on sea as well as on land, and it might be, if necessary, ulteriorly prolonged." The design of this overture was represented as of a purely friendly character; while the calamities of the civil war suffered in America, the apprehension of servile war, "which would be the culminating point of so many irreparable disasters," and the sufferings of Europe were given as motives for the proceeding. It was represented that there had been established from the very beginning of the war an equilibrium of forces between the belligerents, which had been since almost constantly maintained, and after the spilling of so much blood, they are, to-day, in this respect, in a situation, which has not sensibly changed," and that the two armies were in fact "in a condition that would not allow either party to hope, within a brief delay, for any decided advantage to turn the balance and accelerate the conclusion of a peace." There was also an

* Mr. Dayton to Mr. Seward, Paris, March 25, 1862.

allusion to certain "favorable dispositions towards peace, which were beginning to manifest themselves in the North as well as in the South." The Russian minister was the first to reply to this proposition. On the 8th of November he expressed his opinion through the legation at Paris, that, "what ought especially to be avoided, was the appearance of any pressure whatever, of a nature to wound public opinion in the United States, and to excite susceptibilities very easily aroused at the bare idea of foreign intervention," adding, that from the information which had been received, he was "inclined to believe that a combined step between France, England and Russia, no matter how conciliatory and how cautiously made, if it were taken with an official and collective character, would run the risk of causing precisely the very opposite of the object of pacification, which is the aim of the wishes of the three courts." The proposal was therefore declined. The English minister, a few days after, informed the French Government that the overture was at least premature, thus expressing the grounds of refusal: "Is the end proposed attainable at the present moment? Such is the question anxiously and carefully examined by Her Majesty's Government. After weighing all the information which has been received from America, Her Majesty's Government are led to the conclusion that there is no ground at the present moment to hope that the Federal Government would accept the proposal suggested, and a refusal from Washington at the present time would prevent any speedy renewal of the offer. Her Majesty's Government think, therefore, that it would be better to watch carefully the progress of opinion in America, and if, as there appears reason to hope, it may be found to have undergone, or may undergo hereafter, any change, the three courts might then avail themselves of such change to offer their friendly counsel, with a greater prospect than now exists, of its being accepted by the two contending parties." The conference proving thus inconclusive, no further action was taken by France. The vigilance of the American Secretary of State had anticipated any semblance of interference in his circular of the 18th of August, to the representatives abroad, in which he ably stated the position of the European powers towards the United States, and forcibly repelled all ideas of appeal, mediation and intervention. "Europeans," said he, "tell us that the task of subduing the insurrection is too great, that the conclusion is already foregone, and the Union must be lost. They fail, however, to satisfy us of either their right or their ability to advise upon it, while they no longer affect to conceal the prejudices or the interests which disqualify them for any judgment in the case."

An intercepted letter from the Confederate commissioner, Rost, who had been sent out to Spain, written in March of this year, 1862, to Hunter, the rebel Secretary of State, disclosed the disheartening Southern prospects at that time in Europe. He was able to make no impression upon the Spanish Foreign Secretary, Collantes, whose mind he found preoccupied with the Northern arguments of Mr. Seward, who was not likely at the moment to favor the cause which had just received so severe a blow at Mill Spring, Fort Henry and Donelson. To meet this unhappy piece of intelligence the rebel ambassador unfolded a map of the United States, and pointed out the distances from those points to New Orleans and Texas along the line of the Mississippi river, which he said the invading army intended to follow. "I stated," says he, "that throughout this distance there were no roads upon which the transport of the *material* of an army would be effected, while we had nearly three thousand leagues of railway which could be used for purposes of defence and destroyed as the enemy advanced, and that, besides, the Northern troops could stand neither the heat of our summer nor the maladies incident to the climate." The estimate of these difficulties is worth noting as a measure of the work to be accomplished, and which was accomplished by the army of the Union the following year. If the Spaniard was slow in perceiving the advantages of an alliance with the Confederacy, England and France were represented in this letter as equally insensible. The Emperor Napoleon, Messrs. Mason and Slidell had been informed, considered the disruption of the Union and of its rising navy as a great misfortune to France, and was, of late, inclined to hope that it might be reconstructed; and further, that he would, under no circumstances, incur the enmity of the North by taking the lead in recognizing us; while the present administration in England was to a great extent composed of abolitionists and wanted the support of the abolition faction for the maintenance in power, deluding itself at the same time with the vain hope that if the civil war was protracted and the culture of cotton ceased, in whole or in part, the monopoly of that staple would pass from the Confederate States to India, as a compensation for the present sufferings of the British manufacturing population." In conclusion of the whole matter, Mr. Rost expressed this discouraging opinion:—"Owing to the enormous preparations made by the North to subjugate us, I believe that nothing is now to be expected from any of them until the Northern government is ready to treat with us as an independent Power. If it be so, and the war is to last many years, as the President intimates in his inaugural, it will be for him to determine whether it is consistent with our dignity to keep longer abroad commissioners, who, he knows, are under no circumstances to be received or listened to." But, however, gratifying it might be to Northern readers to peruse this candid revelation in their journals, the efforts of the intriguing Southern representatives abroad were by no means abandoned, and the topics of foreign intervention continued to be agitated with more or less anxiety to the North with the varying fortunes of the war.

In noting the influences brought to bear upon foreign opinion we should not forget the extra ambassadorial service this year of three persons of distinction, the Catholic Archbishop Hughes of New York, the Episcopal Bishop McIlvaine of Ohio, and the eminent politician Thurlow Weed of Albany. They visited the capitals of Europe, mingled in the society about the courts and the circles of the upper classes, counseled with the diplomatists, corrected erroneous ideas, explained the true nature of the American controversy, and generally exerted no little influence in the prevention of intervention and the preservation of peace. They were received with hospitality, though they doubtless encountered many foreigners, and found the real or imaginary pretensions of interest predominant when they would appeal to higher principles. It was the deliberate testimony of Archbishop Hughes on his return: "Let America be prepared. There is no love for the United States on the other side of the water. Generally speaking on the other side of the Atlantic the United States are ignored if not despised; treated in conversation in the same contemptuous language as we might employ towards the inhabitants of the Sandwich Islands or Washington Territory, or Vancouver's Island, or the settlement of the Red River, or of the Hudson's Bay Territory."*

The affairs of Mexico though not immediately connected with the war for the Union, were yet felt to bear a cer-

* Archbishop Hughes to the Hon. W. H. Seward, New York, November 1st, 1862.

tain relation to it—for the occupation of the United States with domestic difficulties, undoubtedly gave a coveted opportunity for the European powers to set on foot an active interference with the sister republic. A convention was entered into by the sovereigns of Great Britain, Spain and France, in October, 1861, by which these powers mutually engaged to send a naval and military expedition to seize and occupy the fortresses and military positions on the coast of Mexico, to enforce a demand from the authorities of that state "for more efficacious protection for the persons and properties of their subjects as well as a fulfillment of the obligations contracted towards their majesties by the republic." By a special article the invading parties engaged not to seek for themselves in these coercive measures "an acquisition of territory, nor any special advantage, and not to exercise in the internal affairs of Mexico any influence of a nature to prejudice the right of the Mexican nation to choose and to constitute freely the form of its government." After the convention was signed the United States, as a nation, also having "claims" against the country, were to be invited to participate in the convention — a privilege which President Lincoln was not likely, with the traditions of the Monroe doctrine handed down by his predecessors, to avail himself of. So the United States accepting the declarations of the limited objects of the convention, calmly looked on, while Spain, with her fleet and army, followed by the ships of France and England at the close of the year, appeared and took possession of Vera Cruz, which was quietly abandoned to them. The liberal party, headed by President Juarez, meanwhile prepared to resist the further invasion, while the invaders relied upon the friendly aid of the disaffected Church party, who had been driven from power. As a measure of policy, Juarez was ready to negotiate with the invaders, and did make some terms with the Spanish and English officers, which, together with the jealousies which had sprung up among the parties, led to their withdrawal in the following April from the expedition. The French were then left alone to carry out the plans of the Emperor. Their General Lorencez advancing with an inadequate force into the interior, was defeated by the Mexicans, and what with the enemy and the climate, suffered grievously during the summer. This aroused the government at home, and General Forey was sent from France with a large body of reinforcements. On his arrival at Vera Cruz, in September, he issued a proclamation, in which he paraded the beneficent motives of France in making war, not upon the people, but against "a handful of men, without scruple and conscience," and the intention, when "the Mexican people shall be liberated by our arms," to leave them "free to elect the government which they please." The advance of General Forey towards the capital was interrupted by a serious defeat before Puebla, which carried the war, with its international consequences, into another year.

Returning to domestic affairs, the December report to Congress of the Secretary of the Treasury, Mr. Chase, was a long and elaborate document, amply setting forth the previous financial history of the war, and the policy by which he proposed to regulate its burdens in the future. The expenditures of the year were in excess of previous estimates, a result naturally to be expected with the continuance of the war; but owing to a successful system of finance the receipts increased in proportion with the outlay. More than two hundred and fifty millions had yet to be provided for by Congress, to meet the expenditure of the current year—the excess beyond Mr. Chase's calculations of December, 1861. He had then estimated the probable debt of the nation on the 1st of July, 1863, at about nine hundred millions; he now extended the sum to about eleven hundred millions, with an advance by the end of the following year to about seventeen hundred millions. The receipts from customs in this latter year he calculated would be seventy millions, and the product of internal duties one hundred and fifty millions. By a skilful employment of the means placed at his disposal by Congress, he had reduced the average rate of interest paid by the Government to four and three-fifths per cent. As a supplement to the loans already authorized by Congress, the Secretary again urged the organization of banking associations under a general act, according to the plan which he had proposed in his report of the previous year.* Its main feature was the supply by the Government to such associations, of circulating notes on the security of United States bonds deposited in the Treasury. The central idea of the scheme, as stated by Mr. Chase, was "the establishment of one sound, uniform circulation, of equal value throughout the country, upon the foundation of national credit combined with private capital." Its advantages in absorbing the public securities, providing a home market, and giving steadiness to their value, were obvious, while the measure was free from the objections of Government interference formerly urged against a national bank. It would be voluntary, gradually come into use, and meet the necessities of the times. Nor would its least recommendation be that it would supply "a firm anchorage to the union of the States. Every banking association (urged the Secretary) whose bonds are deposited in the Treasury of the Union; every individual who holds a dollar of the circulation secured by such deposit; every merchant, every manufacturer, every farmer, every mechanic, interested in transactions dependent for success on the credit of that circulation, will feel as an injury every attempt to rend the national unity, with the permanence and stability of which all their interests are so closely and vitally connected." For the immediate wants of the Government, the Secretary recommended a resort to loans rather than an indefinite increase of the issue of bank notes, which would involve the mischief of a constantly depreciating popular currency. For the encouragement of bondholders, he presented a flattering picture of the advancing resources of the American Republic, in the vast undeveloped mining and agricultural regions, and the wealth to be added to the country by immigration. "With such resources," said he, "at the disposal of the Republic, no one need be alarmed lest the United States may become unable to pay the interest on its debt, so to reduce the principal to whatever point the public interest may indicate. The Republic is passing through the pangs of a new birth to a nobler and higher life. Twice already she has paid off a national debt contracted for the defence of her rights; the obligations of that which she now incurs for the preservation of her existence will be not less sacredly fulfilled."

The reports of the Secretary of War and of the Navy exhibited an extraordinary development of the national resources. By the former it appeared that the armies operating in ten military departments constituted, according to recent official returns, a force of 775,336 officers and privates fully equipped; that the number had since been increased to over 800,000, and when the quotas were filled up would reach a million. The present naval force afloat or near completion was reported by Secretary Welles at 427 vessels, carrying 3,268 guns—an increase during the year of 123 vessels, carrying 711 guns. Of these, 104, with 1415 guns, were sailing vessels, and 323, with 1853 guns,

* Ante, Vol. II., p. 198.

were steam vessels. In the latter were included 54 iron-clad vessels of various constructions, of which 28 were in the seaboard and 26 in the Western waters.

The close of the year was marked by an extraordinary declaration of opinion on the means and objects of the war, by the Confederate President, Jefferson Davis. We have already noticed the angry terms of his retaliatory proclamation, especially directed against General Butler and the officers of his command, at New Orleans."* The loss of that city and the movement of the Union armies in Tennessee doubtless furnished the motives for his visit to the Southwest, for the purpose of organizing its defence and reassuring the spirit of its inhabitants. Certainly no one was more likely to appreciate the importance of the region. The *Chattanooga Rebel* recorded his arrival at that place by way of Knoxville, on the 11th of December, accompanied by General Joe Davis and Colonel Fitzhugh Lee, of his staff. The journalist was struck with the simplicity of his travelling arrangement, chronicling them with an absurd comparison with the imaginary state of President Lincoln—an amusing specimen of the ridiculous representations of the North, current with the Southern press. "A live President," says this editor, "is still something of a curiosity in Tennessee, notwithstanding she has been visited by many, and her own sacred soil is to-day the resting place of a Jackson and a Polk. . . . His dress was plain and unassuming, and his baggage limited to a single leather valise, with the initials "J. D." marked upon the side. Attended by one body servant alone; his mode of travel was without ostentation or parade, and I could not help contrasting the President of the young Confederacy, travelling securely as a citizen, and incognito, from one extreme of his native Southern land to the other, without even so much as a body-guard, with the miserable despot of Abolitiondom carricoling through the streets of Washington with a file of armed dragoons each side of his coach of state, and in constant apprehension of the assassin's dagger in his own capital." Leaving Chattanooga for Murfreesboro, Davis witnessed a grand review of the Confederate army under Bragg, Polk, Breckinridge, Hardee, and other division generals. Arriving at Jackson, in his old home in Mississippi, the Confederate President was called upon by a committee of the House of Representatives to address the Legislature, when, breaking the silence that he had generally preserved, consented to deliver a lengthened speech on the 26th of December. On this occasion he spoke without reserve, and uttered many memorable sayings, which were often afterwards called to mind in the progress of the war. He was one of those, he said, "who, from the beginning predicted war as the consequence of secession,"—war, which he attributed to the wickedness of the North, of whose "malignant ferocity" he had previously warned his fellow citizens, and now, "after what had happened during the last two years," expressed his "wonder that we consented to live for so long a time in association with such miscreants, and have loved so much a government rotten to the core. Were it even to be proposed again to enter into a Union with such a people I could no more consent to do it than to trust myself in a den of thieves. . . . There is indeed a difference between the two peoples. Let no man hug the delusion that there can be renewed association between them. Our enemies are a traditionless and homeless race; from the time of Cromwell to the present moment they have been disturbers of the peace of the world. Gathered together by Cromwell from the bogs and fens of the North of Ireland and of England, they commenced by disturbing the peace

* Vol. ii. p. 582.

of their own country; they disturbed Holland, to which they fled, and they disturbed England on their return. They persecuted Catholics in England, and they hung Quakers and witches in America." Dwelling at length on the subject of the conscription, which he admitted had excited considerable opposition, he endeavored to parry the charge of favoring the rich at the expense of the poor, in the exemption of persons having charge of twenty or more negroes. This, he said, "was not to draw any distinction of classes, but simply to provide a force in the nature of a police force, sufficient to keep our negroes in control," stating that "most of the wealthiest and most distinguished families of the South have representatives in the ranks." Of the present military situation, he said, reviewing the recent movements, "Vicksburgh and Port Hudson are the real points of attack. Every effort will be made to capture those places with the object of forcing the navigation of the Mississippi, of cutting off our communications with the trans-Mississippi department, and of severing the western from the eastern portion of the Confederacy. Let them all who have at heart the safety of the country, go without delay to Vicksburgh and Port Hudson; let them go for such length of time as they can spare—for thirty or sixty, or for ninety days. Let them assist in preserving the Mississippi River, that great artery of the country, and thus conduce more than in any other way to the perpetuation of the Confederacy and the success of the cause." Recurring to the conscription for filling up the ranks, he made an admission of a probability often urged at the North, for accepting no half-way accommodation. "Cast your eyes forward," said he "to that time at the end of the war, when peace shall *nominally* be proclaimed—for peace between us and our hated enemy will be liable to be broken at short intervals for many years to come—cast your eyes forward to that time, and you will see the necessity for continued preparation and unceasing watchfulness." Of the continuance of the war, he said: "I have been one of those who, from the beginning, looked forward to a long and bloody war; but I must frankly confess that its magnitude has exceeded my expectations. The enemy have displayed more power, and energy, and resources than I had attributed to them. Their finances have held out far better than I imagined would be the case. But I am also one of those who felt that our final success was certain, and that our people had only to be true to themselves to behold the Confederate flag among the recognized nations of the earth. The question is only one of time. It may be remote, but it may be nearer than many people suppose. It is not possible that a war of the dimensions that this one has assumed, of proportions so gigantic, can be very long protracted. The combatants must be soon exhausted. But it is impossible, with a cause like ours, we can be the first to cry: 'Hold, enough.'" Looking at the prospects of the Confederacy in Europe, he remarked:—"In the course of this war our eyes have been often turned abroad. We have expected sometimes recognition and sometimes intervention at the hands of foreign nations, and we had a right to expect it. Never before in the history of the world had a people so long a time maintained their ground, and showed themselves capable of maintaining their national existence, without securing the recognition of commercial nations. I know not why this has been so, but this I say, 'Put not your trust in princes,' and rest not your hope on foreign nations. This war is ours: we must fight it out ourselves; and I feel some pride in knowing that so far we have done it without the good-will of anybody. It is true that there are now symptoms of a change in public opinion abroad. They give us their admiration—they sometimes even say to us God speed—and in the remarkable book written by Mr. Spence, the question of secession has been discussed with more of ability than it ever has been even in this country. Yet England still holds back, but France, the ally of other days, seems disposed to hold out to us the hand of fellowship. And when France holds out to us her hand, right willingly will we grasp it." Recurring to the immediate prospects of the war at home he renewed the expression of his anxiety for the defence of the Mississippi. "There are now," said he, "two prominent objects in the programme of the enemy. One is to get possession of the Mississippi River and to open it to navigation, in order to appease the clamors of the West, and to utilize the capture of New Orleans, which has thus far rendered them no service. The other is to seize upon the capital of the Confederacy, and hold this, but as a proof that the Confederacy has no existence. We have recently repulsed them at Fredericksburgh, and I believe that under God and by the valor of our troops the capital of the Confederacy will stand safe behind its wall of living breasts. Vicksburgh and Port Hudson have been strengthened, and now we can concentrate at either of them a force sufficient for their protection. I have confidence that Vicksburgh will stand as before, and I hope Johnston will find generals to support him if the enemy dare to land. Port Hudson is now strong. Vicksburgh will stand, and Port Hudson will stand; but let every man that can be spared from other vocations, hasten to defend them, and thus hold the Mississippi River, that great artery of the Confederacy, preserve our communications with the trans-Mississippi department, and thwart the enemy's scheme of forcing navigation through to New Orleans. By holding that section of the river between Port Hudson and Vicksburgh, we shall secure these results, and the people of the West, cut off from New Orleans, will be driven to the East to seek a market for their products, and will be compelled to pay so much in the way of freights, that those products will be rendered almost valueless. Thus, I should not be surprised if the first daybreak of peace were to dawn upon us from that quarter." How these hopes were to be maintained and how far the speaker was justified in looking to the Northwest for friendly aid to the rebellion, belongs to the history of the following year.

CHAPTER LXXXV.

JANUARY TO MARCH, 1863.

The New Year opened with several events of importance in the civil and military history of the country. Foremost among these, partaking of the character of both, was the completion of President Lincoln's formal act of emancipation in accordance with the terms of his proclamation of the 22d of September. The first day of January was named in that instrument as the period when all slaves in the States which should be then in rebellion were to be "thenceforward and forever free," and the freedom thus declared was to be maintained by the entire executive force of the Government.* The time allowed had passed, the opportunity given for

* See Proclamation, ante.

return to the legitimate authority of the Union having been neglected or despised by the rebellious States, and it consequently became the duty of the President to define the portions of the country subject to the edict. This was done in his supplementary Emancipation Proclamation of January 1st, 1863. After reciting the terms or conditions, the substantial portions of the previous Proclamation, the new instrument proceeded—"Now, therefore, I, ABRAHAM LINCOLN, President of the United States, by virtue of the power in me vested as Commander-in-Chief of the Army and Navy of the United States, in time of actual armed rebellion against the authority and Government of the United States, and as a fit and necessary war measure for suppressing said Rebellion, do, on this first day of January, in the year of our Lord one thousand eight hundred and sixty-three, and in accordance with my purpose so to do, publicly proclaimed for the full period of one hundred days from the day first above-mentioned, order and designate as the States, and parts of States, wherein the people thereof, respectively, are this day in rebellion against the United States, the following, to wit: Arkansas, Texas, Louisiana, (except Parishes of St. Bernard, Plaquemines, Jefferson, St. John, St. Charles, St. James, Ascension, Assumption, Terre Bonne, Lafourche, St. Marie, St. Martin, and Orleans, including the City of New-Orleans), Mississippi, Alabama, Florida, Georgia, S. Carolina, N. Carolina, and Virginia, (except the forty-eight counties designated as West Virginia, and also the counties of Berkeley, Accomac, Northampton, Elizabeth City, York, Princess Ann and Norfolk, including the cities of Norfolk and Portsmouth,) and which excepted parts are, for the present, left precisely as if this Proclamation were not issued. And by virtue of the power and for the purpose aforesaid, I do order and declare that ALL PERSONS HELD AS SLAVES within said designated States and parts of States, ARE, AND HENCEFORWARD SHALL BE, FREE! and that the Executive Government of the United States, including the Military and Naval authorities thereof, will recognize and maintain the freedom of said persons, and I hereby enjoin upon the people so declared to be free, to abstain from all violence, unless in necessary self-defense; and I recommend to them that in all cases, when allowed, they labor faithfully for reasonable wages. And I further declare and make known, that such persons, of suitable condition, will be received into the armed service of the United States, to garrison forts, positions, stations, and other places, and to man vessels of all sorts in said service. And upon this act, sincerely believed to be an act of justice, warranted by the Constitution, upon military necessity, I invoke the considerate judgment of mankind and the gracious favor of Almighty God." The number of slaves in the rebellious States affected by this Proclamation, according to the census of 1860, was over three millions. About 800,000 in Delaware, Maryland, Kentucky, Tennessee, Missouri, and the excepted parts of Virginia and Louisiana, remained. Of these, more than one-half were about equally divided between Kentucky and Tennessee.

The new Proclamation, like its predecessor, was attended with less immediate and discernible excitement than might have been anticipated from the utterance of a decree involving a social and political revolution of such magnitude. This arose from the uncertainty as to the time and manner in which the emancipation would be practically secured. It, in fact, exclusively depended upon the progress and success of the war, and it is not to be wondered at that the mind of the public was more intent upon each day's fortune in the field than upon this element of the future. Two parties, however, felt its importance, the foes of slavery in the North, who hailed the act as a triumph of modern civilization, and the pro-slavery politicians of the Border States, who recognized in it the death-blow to the peculiar institution. "With the New Year," said Governor Andrew, of Massachusetts, in a special proclamation called forth by the occasion, "America commences a new era of national life, in which we invoke the blessing of Heaven upon our country and its armies, with renewed faith in the favor of Almighty God." On the other hand, Governor Robinson, of Kentucky, addressed the Legislature of the State, denouncing the Proclamation as an usurpation of power by the President, a fatal blow to the interests of Kentucky, and a step calculated to increase to the uttermost the hate of the Confederate States. In the National House of Representatives the measure met with a similar diversity of opinion from the Border State Men and the Republican majority. An attempt to censure the Proclamation as indicating a policy of emancipation "not calculated to hasten the restoration of peace, not well chosen as a war measure, and an assumption of power dangerous to the rights of citizens and to the perpetuity of a free people," was promptly defeated; while the same resolution, introduced by Fessenden, with the negatives stricken out, was passed a few days after.*

Simultaneously with the issue of the Emancipation Proclamation on the 1st of January, the act of Congress, passed by the Senate at the previous session and by the House of Representatives about a fortnight before, admitting West Virginia as a State of the Union, was signed by the President. The act recited the proceedings of the popular Convention at Wheeling, November, 1861, their ratification by the people at a general election in the following May, and the concurrent action of the recognized Legislature of Virginia. The claims of the latter which represented only the loyal portion of the State had been admitted in the reception by Congress of Senators and Members of the House. The Virginia Representatives in Congress, in fact, voted for the bill creating the new State. Until the next general census, West Virginia was declared to be entitled to three members in the House of Representatives. The people within its limits having since the adoption of their State constitution, expressed a wish to change one of its articles by which the children of slaves born after the 4th of July, 1863, were to be free, and all slaves at that time, under the age of ten years, were to be free at the age of twenty-one, and all slaves over ten and under twenty-one, were to be free on arriving at the age of twenty-five, and no slave to be permitted to come into the State for permanent residence, it was provided, that when these provisions were duly incorporated in the Constitution and ratified by a popular vote, it shall be lawful for the President of the United States to issue his Proclamation, stating the fact, and upon the expiration of sixty days thereafter, the admission of the State was to be complete. The conditions of the act of Congress having been complied with, on the twentieth of the following June, Arthur J. Boreman, who had been elected Governor of the new State, was duly inaugurated at Wheeling, succeeding to the authority which had been of late exercised by Governor Pierpont. Addressing the Senate and House of Delegates, Governor Boreman declared the determination of his people to maintain the Government in pursuing the war to the suppression of the rebellion, while he pledged himself to the furtherance of education and the material interests of the State. Its territory included forty-eight counties, irregularly bounded by the Ohio on the west, and by a zig-zag line on the east, following the chain of

* Proceedings of Congress, Dec. 11 and 15, 1863.

the Alleghanies from Kentucky to the Potomac in the vicinity of Williamsport. The white population in 1860 was about 335,000, the number of slaves about 13,000. In agricultural and mineral resources and the facility of river communication West Virginia promised the most inviting rewards to free labor.

The admission by Congress of Western Virginia as an independent State, was noticed by Governor Letcher of old Virginia in the Confederacy, in his message to the Senate and House of Delegates in January. "It clearly," said he, "indicates that the Government had no longer a hope of accomplishing the subjugation of the South; and they are looking to boundary in the adjustment of the controversy which they have provoked. They have overrun much of our State; and this new State thus formed embraces counties both sides of the Blue Ridge. If in any adjustment the portion of our territory embraced by these counties is to be regarded as part of the Northern Government, it requires no prophet to decide what the future of so much as remains is to be. It is bound necessarily to be free territory. I cannot suppose, in any treaty of peace that may be agreed upon, Virginia will ever recognize the division of her territory, or ever assent to a treaty that will strip her of any portion of her domain. Nor can I think that the Confederate Government will ever assent to such an arrangement. Whenever a settlement shall be made, come when it may, Virginia is to be regarded as a whole, her territory is to be preserved intact, and she is to take her place in the Southern Confederacy as she separated from the old Government. Her proportions are not to be diminished. Virginia is to be in the future as Virginia was in the past. She is to be as she has been. 'The Old Dominion,' full and perfect in all respects. We cannot give up a foot of the Northwest nor of the middle West—not a foot on the Potomac borders, not a foot on the Peninsula, nor on the Bay, nor on the James River. It is better that this war should continue for an indefinite period of time, than that Virginia shall be even partially dismembered. Let every Virginian, then, kneeling at the altar, swear that the old Commonwealth shall remain one and indivisible, and that he will never assent to an adjustment which will take from her one square foot of her territory."

The last day of the old year and the first of the new brought two signal disasters to the Navy, in the loss of the Monitor and the Harriet Lane. The former, after various duty in the waters of the Chesapeake, the scene of her original memorable exploit, left Fortress Monroe in tow of the steam gunboat Rhode Island, on her way to the South, on the afternoon of the 29th of December. The sea was tranquil, the weather warm and favorable, and there was promise of a good voyage, as the vessel the next day passed Hatteras shoals in safety. That night, however, a severe storm of wind and rain set in from the southwest, driving the waves furiously over the low deck and against the tower. The water entered every crevice for the admission of air, and presently the vessel sprung a leak. "It was," in the narrative of one of the officers, "about 9 o'clock, and the pumps were set in motion. They rapidly gained on the water, but in about half an hour they kept about even pace with each other. The gale had increased to a hurricane; the Monitor reeling and shuddering from end to end. Faster and faster the water came in. It was gaining on the pumps. By 10½ o'clock the water was reported gaining rapidly. A few minutes later, and the report was that it would soon be up to the fires. This again was followed by the report that the vessel could not live more than two or three hours longer. The water rapidly neared the fires; when they were put out the pumps could not be worked. When it was reported that the Monitor could not stand it more than an hour or two longer, signals of distress were at once made. Red, white, and blue rockets were thrown up, and were answered by the Rhode Island. This was at 11 o'clock, when it had been decided as impossible to save the vessel, and attention was turned to saving their own lives. One of the hawsers connecting the Monitor with the Rhode Island had parted between 8 and 9 o'clock. When the Rhode Island answered, a voice on the Monitor cried out through a trumpet that they were in a sinking condition. Those appealed to on the Rhode Island went to work with the utmost speed to send boats to the rescue.

"It was a most daring undertaking, but they got out a launch and manned her, and riding on the crests and sinking in the hollows of waves, she made toward the Monitor. At this time the sky was filled with clouds, through which a little light from the moon appeared, so that objects could be distinguished. The remaining hawser is now cut so that the boats shall not get entangled; the hawser becomes entangled with the paddle-wheel of the Rhode Island; the rope clogs the wheel, and the Rhode Island, a large war steamer, is drifting toward the Monitor; the launch is between the two vessels thus nearing each other, and seems doomed to destruction; the launch reaches the side of the iron-clad. The proximity is dangerous to all, for two or three lurches and the sharp prow of the Monitor will stave in the wooden walls of the steamer. All feel that they shall go to the bottom. There is a terrible silence, so far as those on the Monitor are concerned. As two or three jump out of the boat, the oars are seen to flash in the air; the launch is heard crashing; in a second the crew have sprang on the deck of the Monitor. Simultaneously the hawser is cleared from the paddle-wheel, and the Rhode Island runs off, without the fatal shock, to a safe distance. While the vessels lay alongside, several of the Monitor's crew sprang for the ropes that dangled from the side of the Rhode Island, and some succeeded in climbing up, while others were washed into the sea. The crew of the launch now sprang back into her, but those of the Monitor were reluctant to trust themselves to make the attempt, as several were washed off the deck by the great seas washing over. They clung, therefore, to the top of the turret, fearing they might share the fate they had witnessed overtaking others, preferring their chance to live a little longer, although there was the moral certainty they could not remain and live long. Finally the launch was filled, having taken on probably some fifteen from the Monitor. All that were on deck at the time got in, and the launch was ordered off. Some stuffed the crushed side with pea-pickets, while others bailed out, and the rowers tried to get to the steamer, which was their only hope. Meanwhile, the Rhode Island had launched a whaleboat. The sea, which was terrific, dashed the whaleboat upon the launch with terrible ferocity. One of the officers in the launch sprang over towards the side and stretched out both his arms to break the blow and turn the course of the boat. This he succeeded in doing, but not without considerable injury to himself. Getting close to the steamer, the men spring for the ropes, and some lose their hold, and are swallowed by the sea, although nearly every one in the boat is saved. The whaleboat saved others from the iron-clad. A third rescuing boat was sent, commanded by Mr. Brown, a brave man, and skilful in management of a boat. This has not been heard from, but it may have picked up some survivors, and have got safely to some other vessel. The Monitor went down about 2 o'clock in the morning."* The boat of the Rhode Island, commanded by Acting Master Brown, had made two trips to the sinking vessel, and had started on the third when the Monitor went down. As Mr. Brown approached her within a quarter of a mile, he saw the light on the flagstaff settle gradually in the water. On arriving at what he supposed to be the position of the vessel, he could perceive no other trace of her except the eddy caused by her sinking; nor could he find any of her crew in the water to rescue. Starting on his return to the Rhode Island he lost sight of her the weather being overcast with a slight rain. The rest of the night was anxiously passed in an effort to keep in the track of the coasting vessels, which was successful, a schooner in the employ of the Government coming in sight in the forenoon and taking the party on board.†

Commander Bankhead, in command of the Monitor at the time of the disaster, with six of his officers and forty men, were brought back in safety on the Rhode Island to Fortress Monroe. Four officers and twelve men of the Monitor were lost, and one officer and seven men of the Rhode Island in their efforts to save the men on the iron-clad.

The capture of the Harriet Lane on the morning of the first of January, was attended with circumstances of a still more painful character, realizing to the full the confusion and disaster which sometimes overtake the most confident military preparations. The harbor of Galveston, Texas, in which this action occurred, had, with the city since its surrender in October to Commander Renshaw, been held by that officer, with the small naval and military force at his command. The defences had been captured after a feeble resistance, "the guns of a formidable looking battery on Pelican Island, from which," wrote Commander Renshaw to Admiral Farragut, "we anticipated a heavy fire, proving to be 'Quakers,' and the bursting of a 11-inch shell from the Owasco over their heavy 10-inch columbiad, mounted on Fort Point, causing a panic in the fort." But though the city was surrendered, the island on which it was situated was imperfectly held, while the enemy were in force at the outer extremity of the railroad bridge connecting it with the main land, with the back country to draw upon for men and supplies. The Union occupation, so small was the number of troops landed, depended almost entirely upon the presence of the gun-boats, and the resources of these were comparatively limited. The conquest had been effected by Commander Renshaw with four steamers, the Harriet Lane and Owasco, and two Northern ferry boats, the Westfield and Clifton, fitted out as gun-boats. These were joined at the end of December by two other vessels, the gun-boat Corypheus and steamer Sachem, the latter in "a broken down condition." The United States troops on shore at this time consisted of 260, rank and file, commanded by Colonel Burrel, of the 42d Massachusetts volunteers, occupying, by advice of Commander Renshaw, a wharf in the town.

A letter written from the harbor by Commander Wainwright of the Harriet Lane, a few weeks earlier, on the 11th of December, will show the peculiar condition of affairs at the place. "We are occupying," he wrote, "a very disagreeable position, lying off the town holding the harbor, but without sufficient force to occupy the city. The Confederates, who hold Virginia Point, on the mainland, about five miles off, and have free access to the town over the railway bridge which connects Galveston Island with the main. They also hold a battery guarding this end of the

* Account of the loss of the Monitor by Assistant-Surgeon G. W Weeks, N. Y. *Tribune*, Jan. 6, 1863.

† Report of Commander Trenchard, of the Rhode Island, to Secretary Welles, Jan. 10, 1863.

bridge, the water being so shallow that we cannot get within gunshot of either. They are in and out all the time, which renders it unsafe for us to go in shore, as we should be liable to be gobbled up at any moment. So we have to stick to our vessels, and feel the want of exercise on *terra firma* sadly. We have constant reports that we are to be attacked, both from water and shore, which keeps us constantly on the alert. We have so many rumors that we are getting tired of hearing them, and would rather prefer some demonstration on the part of the enemy to the never-ending suspense and anxiety on the subject. We should not care a sixpence for the whole party if we had room enough to move about in, but we are anchored in a sort natural canal where there is not sufficient space to turn round. You have to be pointed face before you can go either way. If they come at us with their light draft boats, which are able to go anywhere in the bay, you can see what an advantage they have over us. However, I think we will give a good account of them, if they come. We understand that John Magruder says, if our troops do not arrive pretty soon and beat him off, he will drive us out of the bay. John will have to get up early in the morning. Still, we shall be very glad when the troops make their appearance, so that we can sleep in peace."

In this position of the blockade, for it was little more, an attack, both by land and water, on the Union forces, was arranged by the enemy now led by the Confederate General Magruder, who, after his campaign in Virginia, and his unfortunate assault on McClellan's artillery at Malvern Hills, had been relieved in that department and subsequently been placed in command in Texas. The first day of the new year was chosen for the assault. At half-past one in the morning—we cite the account of the court of inquiry afterwards instituted by Admiral Farragut, in whose department the affair occurred—"it being bright moonlight, some two or three rebel steamers were discovered in the bay above by the Clifton. The Westfield, from the other channel, likewise made the same discovery. Very soon after, our troops on shore learned through their pickets, that the artillery of the enemy was in possession of the market place, about one-quarter of a mile distant. The attack commenced on shore about 3 A. M., by the enemy upon our troops, which were defended by the Sachem and Corypheus with great energy; our troops only replying with musketry, having no artillery. About dawn the Harriet Lane was attacked, or rather attacked two rebel steamers, one of which, the Bayou City, was armed with a 68-pounder rifle gun, had 200 troops, and was barricaded with cotton bales some 20 feet from the water line. The other, the Neptune, was similarly barricaded and was armed with two small brass pieces and 160 men (both were common river steamers). The Harriet Lane was under way in time and went up to the attack firing her bow gun, which was answered by the rebels, but their 68-pounder burst at the third fire. The Harriet Lane ran into the Bayou City carrying away her wheel-guard, which did her little or no damage. The other rebel steamer then ran into the Harriet Lane, but was so disabled by the collision that she was soon afterward obliged to back in the flats, where she sank in about eight feet of water, near to the scene of action. The Bayou City turned and ran into the Harriet Lane, and she remained secured to her by catching under her guard, pouring in incessant volleys of musketry, as did also the other steamers, which was returned by the Harriet Lane, with musketry. This drove the Harriet Lane's men from her guns, and probably wounded Commander Wainwright and

Lieut.-Commander Lee, the latter mortally. She was then carried by boarding, by the Bayou City, her Commander summoned to surrender, which he refused, gallantly defending himself with his revolver until killed.

" But five of the Harriet Lane's men were killed and five wounded—one hundred and ten, exclusive of officers and wounded, were landed on shore, prisoners. Her Commander and First Lieutenant were buried on the following day on shore, in the cemetery, with the honors of war, and her other officers paroled. The Owasco, which had been anchored below the town, coaling, the night before, got under way, moved up at the commencement of the attack, and engaged the enemy's artillery on shore. When it was light enough for her to observe that there were two rebel steamers alongside the Harriet Lane, she moved up to her assistance, grounding several times in so doing, owing to the narrowness of the channel. She could only occasionally bring her 11-inch gun to bear. She was soon driven back by the incessant fire of the enemy's musketry, and when the howitzers of the Harriet Lane opened on her, she concluded she had been captured and backed down below the Sachem and Corypheus, continuing her engagement with the enemy on shore. She had all her rifle-gun crew wounded when above, and lost in all one man killed and fifteen wounded. The Clinton, before the action commenced, went around into Bolivar channel, to render assistance to the Westfield, who had got under way when the rebel steamers were first discovered, soon afterward got hard and fast ashore, at high water, and then made a signal for assistance. While the Clifton was in the act of rendering this assistance, the flashes of the enemy's guns were first seen in the town. Commander Renshaw then directed Lieutenant-Commander Law to leave him and to return to the town. The moon had now gone down, and it became quite dark, yet the Clifton with some difficulty got around into the other channel, opening the batteries upon Fort Point, which the rebels now had possession of, shelling them out and driving them up the beach as she neared the town. Here she anchored and continued the engagement, but did not proceed up to the rescue of the Harriet Lane, owing to the failure of the Owasco, the intricacy of the channel, and the apprehension of killing the crew of the Harriet Lane, who were then exposed by the rebels on her upper deck.

"It was now about 7 30 A. M. A white flag was hoisted on the Harriet Lane. A boat bearing a flag of truce, with a rebel officer and an Acting Master of the Harriet Lane, came down to the Clifton, informing her commander of the capture of the Harriet Lane, the death of her Commander and First Lieutenant, and the killing and wounding of two-thirds of her crew, all of which was corroborated by the Acting-Master. Major Smith, their commander, now proposed that our vessels should all surrender, and that one should be allowed, with the crews of all, to leave the harbor ; otherwise they would proceed down with the Harriet Lane and all their steamers (three more of which had appeared in sight after daylight, but were neither armed nor barricaded), and proceed to capture the gunboats in line. Lieutenant-Commander Law replied that he was not the commanding officer, and he could not imagine that such could be accepted ; but that he would take the Acting-Master of the Harriet Lane, and proceed over to the Westfield, and tender his proposal to Commander Renshaw. This he did, and went in his own boat. Flags of truce were at this time flying on our vessels, and by the parties on shore. During the absence of Lieutenant-Commander Law, and under these flags of truce, the rebels cooly made prisoners of our troops on shore, got more of their artillery into position, and towed the Harriet Lane alongside the wharf, though it had been understood that everything should remain in *statu quo* until an answer should have been received. Commander Renshaw refused to accede to the proposition, directed Lieutenant-Commander Law to return and get all the vessels out of port as soon as possible, and as he found he could not get the Westfield afloat, he should blow her up and go on board the army transports Saxon and M. A. Boardman, which were lying near him, with his officers and crew. Upon Lieutenant-Commander Law's return to his vessel, he proceeded to carry out these directions. The flags of truce were hauled down, the enemy firing upon the vessels as we then left the harbor.

"When the Clifton was half way toward the bar, her Commander was informed, by a boat from the Westfield, that in the explosion of that vessel, which they observed some half hour before, Commander Renshaw, Lieut. Zimmerman, Engineer Green, and some ten or fifteen of the crew had perished—the explosion being premature. Lieutenant-Commander Law now being commanding officer, proceeded to cross his vessel over the bar, and finally concluded to abandon the blockade altogether, considering the Owasco as his only efficient vessel, and regarding her as not equal to resist an attack from the Harriet Lane, should she come out for that purpose. The vessels which were left in possession of the enemy were the Harriet Lane and two coal barks, the Cavallo and Elias Pike. The only injury sustained by the Harriet Lane, appears to have been from an 11-inch shell under her counter, fired by the Owasco, and the damage to her guard from the collision."

The following is the official report of this affair sent by General Magruder from his headquarters at Galveston to the Confederate Government at Richmond: "This morning, the first January, at three o'clock, I attacked the enemy's fleet and garrison at this place, and captured the latter and the steamer Harriet Lane, and two barges, and a schooner of the former. The rest, some four or five, escaped ignominiously under cover of a flag of truce. I have about 600 prisoners, and a large quantity of valuable stores, arms, etc. The Harriet Lane is very little injured. She was carried by boarding from two high-pressure cotton steamers manned by Texas cavalry and artillery. The line troops were gallantly commanded by Colonel Green, of Sibley's Brigade, and the ships and artillery by Major Leon Smith, to whose indomitable energy and heroic daring the country is indebted for the successful execution of a plan which I had considered for the destruction of the enemy's fleet. Colonel Bagby, of Sibley's Brigade, also commanded the volunteers from his regiment for the naval expedition, in which every officer and every man won for himself imperishable renown."

Following this disaster at Galveston came the loss, off the harbor, of the United States steamer Hatteras in an encounter with Captain Semmes' rebel steamer Alabama. "On the afternoon of the 11th of January," as the affair is narrated by the commander of the Hatteras, Lieutenant R. G. Blake, "at half-past three o'clock, while at anchor in company with the fleet under Commander Bell, off Galveston, Texas, I was ordered by a signal from the United States flag-ship Brooklyn to chase a sail to the southward and eastward. I got under way immediately and steamed in the direction indicated. After some time the strange sail could be seen from the Hatteras, and was ascertained to be a steamer, which fact was communicated to the flag-ship by signal. I continued the chase and rapidly gained upon the suspicious vessel. Knowing the slow rate of the Hatteras, I at once suspected that deception was being practised, and at once ordered the ship to be cleared for action, with everything in readiness for a determined and vigorous defence. When within about four miles of the vessel I observed that she had ceased to steam, and was lying broadside on and awaiting us. It was nearly seven o'clock and quite dark, but notwithstanding the obscurity of the night, I felt assured from the general character of the vessel and her manœuvres that I should soon encounter the Alabama. Being able to work only four guns on the side of the Hatteras, two short thirty-two pounders, one thirty-pounder rifled Parrott gun, and one twenty-pounder rifled gun, I concluded to close with her, so that my guns might be effective if necessary. I came within easy speaking distance, about seveny-five yards, and upon asking what steamer is that, received the answer: Her Britannic Majesty's ship Vixen. I replied that I would send a boat aboard, and immediately gave the order. In the mean time, both vessels were changing their positions, the stranger endeavoring to gain a desirable position for a raking fire. Almost simultaneously with the piping away of the boat, the stranger craft again replied, We are the Confederate steamer Alabama, which was accompanied with a broadside. I at the same moment returned the fire. Being well aware of the many vulnerable points of the Hatteras, I hoped by closing with the Alabama to be able to board her, and thus rid the seas of this piratical craft. I steamed directly for the Alabama, but she was enabled by her great speed, and the foulness of the bottom of the Hatteras and consequently her diminished speed, to thwart my attempt when I had gained a distance of but thirty yards from her.

"At this range musket and pistol-shots were exchanged. The firing continued with great vigor on both sides. At length a shell entered amidships in the hold, setting fire to it, and at the same instant—as I can hardly divide the time—a shell passed through the sick-bay and exploded in an adjoining compartment, also producing fire; another entered the cylinder, filling the engine-room and deck with steam, and depriving me of any power to manœuvre the vessel or to work the pumps, upon which the reduction of the fire depended. With the vessel on fire in two places, and far beyond human power, a hopeless wreck upon the waters, with her walking-beam shot away, and her engine rendered useless, I still maintained an active fire, with the double hope of disabling the Alabama and attracting the attention of the fleet off Galveston, which was twenty-eight miles distant. It was soon reported to me that the shells had entered the Hatteras at the water-line, tearing off sheets of iron, and that the water was rushing in, utterly defying every attempt to remedy the evil, and that she was rapidly sinking. Learning this melancholy truth, and seeing that the Alabama was on my port-bow, entirely beyond range of my guns, doubtless preparing for a raking fire across the deck, I felt I had no right to sacrifice uselessly, and without any desirable result, the lives of all under my command, and to prevent the blowing up of the Hatteras from the fire, which was making much progress, I ordered the magazine to be flooded, and afterward a lee-gun to be fired. The Alabama then asked if assistance was desired, to which an affirmative answer was given. The Hatteras was now going down, and in order to save the lives of my officers and men, I caused the armament on the port-side to be thrown overboard. Had I not done so, I am confident the vessel would have gone down with many brave hearts and valuable lives. After considerable delay, caused by the report that a steamer was seen coming from

Galveston, the Alabama sent us assistance, and every living being was conveyed safely from the Hatteras to the Alabama. Ten minutes after leaving Hatteras, she went down, bow first, with her pennant at her mast-head, with all her muskets and stores of every description, the enemy not being able, owing to her sinking so rapidly, to obtain a single weapon. Two firemen were killed on board the Hatteras and five men were wounded, and several were reported missing. The Alabama in this contest had a decided superiority in the weight of metal, and her construction, her machinery being below the water-line. The distance between the two vessels during the action varied from twenty-five to one hundred yards. Lieutenant Blake and his men were landed at Kingston, Jamaica."*

We have seen in the last chapter the appeal of Jefferson Davis to his people in the South-west; his return to the Confederate capital was marked by the exhibition of a temper equally unfavorable to peace, and, if possible, more contemptuous of the North. In a speech which he delivered "to a respectable audience," as described by the *Richmond Enquirer*, after characterizing the Confederacy as "the last hope for the perpetuation of that system of government which our fathers founded—the asylum of the oppressed, and the home of true representative liberty," he said, "you have shown yourselves in no respect to be degenerate sons of your fathers. You have fought mighty battles, and your deeds of valor will live among the richest spoils of Time's ample page. It is true you have a cause which binds you together more firmly than your fathers were. They fought to be free from the usurpations of the British crown, but they fought against a manly foe; you fight against the offscourings of the earth." As if this were not enough, he added, in reference to the course of General Butler at New Orleans, and the emancipation proclamation, "They have come to disturb your social organizations on the plea that it is a military necessity. For what are they waging war? They say to preserve the Union. Can they preserve the Union by destroying the social existence of a portion of the South? Do they hope to reconstruct the Union by striking at everything which is dear to men? By showing themselves so utterly disgraced that if the question was proposed to you whether you would combine with hyenas or Yankees, I trust that every Virginian would say, "Give me the hyenas." Reviewing the recent actions at Fredericksburg, the victory of "our glorious Lee, the valued son emulating the virtues of the heroic Light-horse Harry, his father," at Murfreesboro' and Vicksburg, he again avowed his hope from the divisions of the North-west. "Out of this victory at Vicksburg," alluding to the repulse of Sherman in December, "is to come that dissatisfaction in the North-west, which will rive the power of that section; and thus we see in the future the dawn, first separation of the North-west from the Eastern States, the discord among them which will paralyze the power of both; then for us future peace and prosperity."

In his annual message to the Confederate Congress a few days later, President Davis renewed his declarations of persistence in the struggle in which he had led the South. "The anticipations," said he, "with which we entered into the contest have now ripened into a conviction, which is not only shared with us by the common opinion of neutral nations, but is evidently forcing itself upon our enemies themselves. If we but mark the history of the present year by resolute perseverance in the path we have hitherto pursued, by vigorous effort in the development of all our resources for defence, and by the

* Lieutenant-Commanding Blake to Secretary Welles. Kingston, Ja., January 31, 1863.

continued exhibition of the same unfaltering courage in our soldiers and able conduct in their leaders as have distinguished the past, we have every reason to expect that this will be the closing year of the war. The war, which in its inception was waged for forcing us back into the Union, having failed to accomplish that purpose, passed into a second stage, in which it was attempted to conquer and rule these States as dependent provinces. Defeated in this second design, our enemies have evidently entered upon another, which can have no other purpose than revenge, and thirst for blood, and plunder of private property. But however implacable they may be, they can have neither the spirit nor the resources required for a fourth year of a struggle uncheered by any hope of success, kept alive solely for the indulgence of mercenary and wicked passions, and demanding so exhausting an expenditure of blood and money as has hitherto been imposed on their people. The advent of peace will be hailed with joy; our desire for it has never been concealed; our efforts to avoid the war, forced on us as it was by the lust of conquest and the insane passions of our foes, are known to mankind. But, earnest as has been our wish for peace, and great as have been our sacrifices and sufferings during the war, the determination of this people has, with each succeeding month, become more unalterably fixed to endure any sufferings and continue any sacrifices, however prolonged, until their right to self-government and the sovereignty and independence of these States shall have been triumphantly vindicated and firmly established."

He then passed to an extended review, partly of complaint, partly of appeal, of the relations between the Confederacy and the neutral powers of Europe. Their neutrality, he asserted, had been "rather nominal than real, and that recognized neutral rights had been alternately asserted and waived in such a manner as to bear with great severity on us, and to confer signal advantages on our enemy. * * Proudly self-reliant, the Confederacy, knowing full well the character of the contest into which it was forced, with full trust in the superior qualities of its population, the superior valor of its soldiers, the superior skill of its generals, and, above all, in the justice of its cause, felt no use to appeal for the maintenance of its rights to other earthly aids, and it began and has continued this struggle with the calm confidence ever inspired in those who, with consciousness of right, can invoke the Divine blessing on their cause." Citing the language of the French minister's recent dispatch in the correspondence with England and Russia, he seemed to entertain the expectation of an early recognition by France of the Confederacy. "As this government has never professed the intention of conquering the United States but has simply asserted its ability to defend itself against being conquered by that power, we may safely conclude that the claims of this Confederacy to its just place in the family of nations cannot long be withheld after so frank and formal an admission of its capacity to cope, on equal terms, with its aggressive foes, and to maintain itself against their attempts to obtain decisive results by arms."

From this the message turned to denunciation of what were characterized as "renewed examples of every conceivable atrocity committed by the armed forces of the United States," particularly referring to General McNeil of Missouri as the "murderer of seven prisoners of war in cold blood; to General Butler in New Orleans, and General Milroy in Western Virginia. "The Government of the United States," it was said, "after promising examination and explanation in relation to the charges made against General Benjamin F. Butler, has, by its subsequent silence after repeated efforts on my part to obtain some answer on the subject, not only admitted his guilt, but sanctioned it by acquiescence; and I have accordingly branded this criminal as an outlaw, and directed his execution in expiation of his crimes if he should fall into the hands of any of our forces."

In relation to President Lincoln's emancipation proclamation it was said, "We may well leave it to the instincts of that common humanity which a beneficent Creator has implanted in the breasts of our fellow-men of all countries, to pass judgment on a measure by which several millions of human beings of an inferior race—peaceful and contented laborers in their sphere—are doomed to extermination, while at the same time they are encouraged to a general assassination of their masters by the insidious recommendation "to abstain from violence unless in necessary self-defence." Our own detestation of those who have attempted the most execrable measure recorded in the history of guilty man is tempered by profound contempt for the impotent rage which it discloses. So far as regards the action of this government on such criminals as may attempt its execution, I confine myself to informing you that I shall—unless in your wisdom you deem some other course more expedient—deliver to the several State authorities all commissioned officers of the United States that may hereafter be captured by our forces in any of the States embraced in the proclamation, that they may be dealt with in accordance with the laws of those States providing for the punishment of criminals engaged in exciting servile insurrection. The enlisted soldiers I shall continue to treat as unwilling instruments in the commission of these crimes, and shall direct their discharge and return to their homes on the proper and usual parole."

The message concluded with a general congratulation on the development of the resources of the Confederacy. "Our armies are larger, better disciplined and more thoroughly armed and equipped than at any previous period of the war; the energies of a whole nation, devoted to the single object of success in this war, have accomplished marvels, and many of our trials have by a beneficent Providence been converted into blessings. The magnitude of the perils which we encountered has developed the true qualities and illustrated the heroic character of our people, thus gaining for the Confederacy from its birth a just appreciation from the other nations of the earth. The injuries resulting from the interruption of foreign commerce have received compensation by the developments of our internal resources. Cannon crown our fortresses that were cast from the proceeds of mines opened and furnaces built during the war. Our mountain caves yield much of the nitre for the manufacture of powder, and promise increase of product. From our own foundries and laboratories, from our own armories and work-shops we derive, in a great measure, the warlike material, the ordnance and ordnance stores which are expended so profusely in the numerous and desperate engagements that rapidly succeed each other. Cotton and woollen fabrics, shoes and harness, wagons and gun-carriages, are produced in daily increasing quantities by the factories springing into existence. Our fields, no longer whitened by cotton that cannot be exported, are devoted to the production of cereals and the growth of stock formerly purchased with the proceeds of cotton. In the homes of our noble and devoted women—without whose sublime sacrifices our success would have been impossible—the noise of the loom and the spinning-wheel may be heard throughout the land. With hearts swelling with gratitude, let us, then, join in returning thanks to God, and in beseeching the continuance of His protecting care over our cause, and the restoration of peace, with its manifold blessings, to our beloved country.

"JEFFERSON DAVIS."

The thirty-seventh National Congress closed on the 4th of March, having, in the short session, with singular unanimity and devotion to business, placed the Government in a strong and independent position for the conduct of the war. Its most important measures were those relating to finance, and the levies for the national army. An "Act to provide ways and means for the support of the Government," authorized the issue of six per cent bonds, treasury notes, and United States notes, to the extent of nine hundred millions of dollars. The amount of the last, or currency not bearing interest, was limited, including what had been previously issued, to one hundred and fifty millions. A fractional currency, in lieu of postage and revenue stamps, was authorized to the extent of fifty millions. By the side of this loan bill, an act, in general agreement with the recommendations of the Secretary of the Treasury was passed, to provide a national currency, secured by a pledge of United States stocks. A separate bureau was created in the treasury department, to be presided over by an officer entitled the Comptroller of the Currency, under the general direction of the Secretary of the Treasury. On the formation of banking associations of a capital stock of not less than fifty thousand dollars, and in cities whose population is over ten thousand, of not less than one hundred thousand dollars; when such companies shall have been entitled to commence business by at least one-third of their capital having been paid in, and shall have delivered to the Treasurer of the United States any United States bonds bearing interest to an amount not less than one-third of the capital stock paid in; then they were entitled to receive from the Comptroller of the Currency circulating notes equal in amount to ninety per cent of the current market value of the bonds so deposited, the notes so issued at no time to exceed the amount actually paid in of the capital stock. The entire amount of circulating notes was limited by the act to three hundred millions of dollars, one-half of which was to be apportioned to the States and Territories, according to representative population, the other half according to the existing capital, banking capital, and business. The effect of this new banking system was, of course, as had been often shown by Secretary Chase, to strengthen the public credit, and so provide for the support of the war, by providing a permanent set of creditors to absorb the Government securities, while facilities were given for a safe and uniform enlargement of the popular currency.

By the "Act for enrolling and calling out the national forces," the whole military power of the country was placed at the disposal of the President. All able-bodied male citizens of the United States, and persons of foreign birth who shall have declared on oath their intention to become citizens, between the ages of twenty and forty-five, with a brief list of exceptions, were declared liable to perform military duty when called out by the President for that purpose. The exceptions, beside those physically and mentally unfit, and those disqualified by conviction of a felony, were limited to the Vice-President of the United States, the judges of the various courts of the United States, the heads of the various executive departments of the Government, the governors of the several States, and several cases for the protection of the families of the poor. Thus, the only son of a widow, or of aged or infirm parent or parents, or the only brother of orphan children not twelve years old, or the father of motherless children of the like age, dependent upon his labor for support, were exempted. Where there were two or more sons of aged or infirm parents, the father, or, if he were not living, the mother might elect which son shall be exempt. Where a father and sons were in the same family and household, and two of them were in the military service as non-commissioned officers, musicians, or privates, the residue of such family and household, not exceeding two, were to be exempted. These few cases constituted all the exemptions. Clergymen, it will be observed, teachers, and students, who had been heretofore generally exempted by the militia laws of the several States, under this new Act became subject to military duty. The enrollment and organization of this force was placed directly in the hands of the national executive, who was authorized to appoint a provost-marshal for each congressional district of the States. The forces were to be enrolled in two classes, the first comprising persons between the ages of twenty and thirty-five years, and all unmarried persons between the ages of thirty-five and forty-five. The second class, comprising all others, was not to be called into service until those of the first class shall have been called. The President was authorized to call forth the national forces by draft during the present rebellion, making allowance in assigning the number to the several districts, for the volunteers and militia already furnished, so as to equalize the burden of military service. Any person drafted might furnish an acceptable substitute, or pay to such person as the Secretary of War may authorize to receive it, such sum not exceeding three hundred dollars, as the Secretary may determine, for the procuration of such substitute, such sum to be fixed at a uniform rate at the time of ordering the draft; and thereupon such person so furnishing the substitute or paying the money, shall be discharged from further liability under that draft. The Act was passed in the House of Representatives by a vote of 115 to 48 ; in the Senate by 35 to 6.

An Act passed relating to Habeas Corpus authorized the President during the present rebellion, whenever in his judgment the public safety may require it, to suspend the privilege of the writ in any case throughout the United States, or any part thereof. Various provisions were also included in the Act, regulating judicial proceedings in suits or prosecutions brought against any officer, or other person, for arrests or imprisonments made during the rebellion, by virtue, or under color of any authority from the President or Congress.

An important series of resolutions regarding foreign intervention were introduced in the Senate, by Mr. Sumner, Chairman of the Committee of Foreign Relations, at the close of the session. They were induced by the action of France and the European courts in the previous season, the constant popular agitation of this subject abroad, and particularly by a communication which had been recently made in February from the French Government, through its minister at Washington, to the Secretary of State, suggesting the appointment by the United States Government of commissioners, to meet on neutral ground commissioners of the insurgents, when, without arrest of the armies in the field, differences might be discussed with a view to a pacification. Mr. Seward replied to this communication in an able state paper, addressed to the French Government through the American minister in Paris. He saw in the suggestion which had been made "nothing less than a proposition that, while this Government is engaged in suppressing an armed insurrection, with the purpose of maintaining the constitutional national authority, and preserving the integrity of the country, it shall enter into diplomatic discussion with the insurgents upon the questions whether that authority shall not be renounced, and whether the country shall not be delivered over to disunion, to be quickly followed by ever-increasing anarchy." If the Government could compromise its authority by entering on such debates, the discussion, he thought, with the present pretensions and temper of the insurgent chiefs, would be futile. "It is true, indeed," he added, "that peace must come at some time, and that conferences must attend, if they are not allowed to precede the pacification. There is, however, a better form for such conferences than the one which M. Drouyn de l'Huys suggests. The latter would be palpably in derogation of the Constitution of the United States, and would carry no weight, because destitute of the sanction necessary to bind either the disloyal or the loyal portions of the people. On the other hand, the Congress of the United States furnishes a constitutional forum for debates between the alienated parties. Senators and representatives from the loyal portion of the people are there already, freely empowered to confer; and seats also are vacant, and inviting senators and representatives of this discontented party who may be constitutionally sent there from the States involved in the insurrection. Moreover, the conferences which can thus be held in Congress have this great advantage over any that could be organized upon the plan of M. Drouyn de l'Huys, namely—that the Congress, if it were thought wise, could call a national convention to adopt its recommendations, and give them all the solemnity and binding force of organic law. Such conferences between the alienated parties may be said to have already begun. Maryland, Virginia, Kentucky, Tennessee, and Missouri—States which are claimed by the insurgents—are already represented in Congress, and submitting with perfect freedom and in a proper spirit their advice upon the course best calculated to bring about, in the shortest time, a firm, lasting, and honorable peace. Representatives have been sent also from Louisiana, and others are understood to be coming from Arkansas. There is a preponderating argument in favor of the Congressional form of conference over that which is suggested by M. Drouyn de l'Huys, namely, that while an accession to the latter would bring this Government into a concurrence with the insurgents in disregarding and setting aside an important part of the Constitution of the United States, and so would be of pernicious example, the Congressional conference, on the contrary, preserves and gives new strength to that sacred writing which must continue through future ages the sheet anchor of the Republic."

In this way Mr. Seward quietly disposed of the French suggestion of a domestic conference between the parties to the war. The resolutions of Mr. Sumner, which were adopted by large majorities—a vote of 31 to 5 in the Senate, of 103 to 28 in the House—"in order to remove for the future all chance of misunderstanding on this subject, and to secure for the United States the full enjoyment of that freedom from foreign intervention, which is one of the highest rights of independent States," thus declared the convictions of Congress. "*Resolved*, That while in times past the United States have sought and accepted the friendly mediation or arbitration of foreign powers for the pacific adjustment of international questions where the United States were the party of the one part and some other sovereign power the party of the other part, and while they are not disposed to misconstrue the natural and humane desire of foreign powers to aid in arresting domestic troubles which, widening in their influence, have afflicted other countries, especially in view of the circumstance, deeply regretted by the American people, that the blow aimed by the rebellion at the national life has fallen heavily upon the laboring population of Europe; yet, notwithstanding these things, Congress cannot hesitate to regard every proposition of foreign interference in the present contest as so far unreasonable and inadmissible that its only explanation will be found in a misunderstanding of the true state of the question, and of the real character of the war in which the Republic is engaged. *Resolved*, That the United States are now grappling with an unprovoked and wicked rebellion, which is seeking the destruction of the Republic, that it may build a new power, whose corner-stone, according to the confession of its chiefs, shall be slavery; that for the suppression of this rebellion, and thus to save the Republic, and to prevent the establishment of such a Power, the National Government is now employing armies and fleets, in full faith that through these efforts all the purposes of conspirators and rebels will be crushed; that while engaged in this struggle, on which so much depends, any proposition from a foreign power, whatever form it may take, having for its effect the arrest of these efforts, is, just in proportion to its influence, an encouragement to the rebellion and to its declared principles, and on this account is calculated to prolong and embitter the conflict, to cause increased expenditure of blood and treasure, as to postpone the much desired day of peace; that with these convictions, and not doubting that every such proposition, although made with good intent, is injurious to the national interests, Congress will be obliged to look upon any further attempts in the same direction as an unfriendly act, which it earnestly deprecates, to the end that nothing may occur abroad to strengthen the rebellion, or to weaken those relations of good will with foreign powers which the United States are happy to cultivate. *Resolved*, That the rebellion, from its beginning, and far back even in the conspiracy which preceded the outbreak, was encouraged by the hope of support from foreign powers; that its chiefs frequently boasted that the people of Europe were so far dependent upon the regular supplies of the great Southern staple, that sooner or later their governments would be constrained to take side with the rebellion in some effective form, even to the extent of forcible intervention, if milder form did not prevail; that the rebellion is now sustained by this hope, which every proposition of foreign interference quickens anew, and that without this life-giving support, it must soon yield to the great and paternal authority of the National Government; that considering these things which are aggravated by the motive of the resistance thus encouraged, the United States regret that foreign powers have not frankly told the chiefs of the rebellion that the work in which they are engaged is hateful, and that a new government, such as they seek to found, with slavery as its corner-stone, and with no other declared object of separate existence, is so far shocking to civilization and the moral sense of mankind that it must not expect welcome or recognition in the commonwealth of nations. *Resolved*, That the United States, confident in the justice of their cause, which is the cause also of good government and of human rights everywhere among men, anxious for the speedy restoration of peace, which shall secure tranquillity at home, and remove all occasion for complaint abroad; and awaiting with well-assured trust the final suppression of the rebellion, through which all these things, rescued from present danger, will be secured forever, and the Republic, one and indivisible, triumphant over its enemies, will continue to stand an example to mankind—hereby announce as their unalterable purpose that the war will be vigorously prosecuted, according to the humane principles of Christian States, until the rebellion shall be suppressed, and they reverently invoke upon their cause the blessings of Almighty God. *Resolved*, That the President be requested to transmit a copy of these resolutions, through the Secretary of State, to the ministers of the United States in foreign countries, that the declaration and protest herein set forth may be communicated by them to the governments to which they are accredited."

At the end of the session a resolution was introduced in the Senate by Harlan of Iowa, "That, devoutly recognizing the supreme authority and just government of Almighty God in all the affairs of men and of nations, and sincerely believing that no people, however great in numbers and resources, or however strong in the justice of their cause, can prosper without His favor, and at the same time deploring the national offences which have provoked His righteous judgment, yet, encouraged in this day of trouble by the assurances of His word to seek Him for succor according to His appointed way, through Jesus Christ, the Senate of the United States do hereby request the President of the United States, by his proclamation, to designate and set apart a day for national prayer and humiliation, requesting all the people of the land to suspend their secular pursuits and unite in keeping the day in solemn communion with the Lord of Hosts, supplicating Him to enlighten the councils and direct the policy of the rulers of the nation, and to support all our soldiers, sailors, and marines, and the whole people in the firm discharge of duty until the existing rebellion shall be overthrown, and the blessings of peace restored to our bleeding country."

The resolution was adopted, and President Lincoln accordingly, on the 30th of March issued the following proclamation: "*Whereas*, The Senate of the United States, devoutly recognizing the supreme authority and just government of Almighty God in all the affairs of men and of nations, has, by a resolution, requested the President to designate and set apart a day for national prayer and humiliation; and *Whereas*, It is the duty of nations as well as of men to own their dependence upon the overruling power of God, to confess their sins and transgressions in humble sorrow, yet with assured hope that genuine repentance will lead to mercy and pardon, and to recognize the sublime truths announced in the Holy Scriptures and proven by all history, that those nations only are blessed whose God is the Lord; and, inasmuch as we know that by His divine law nations, like individuals, are subjected to punishments and chastisements in this world, may we not justly fear that the awful calamity of civil war which now desolates the land, may be but a punishment inflicted upon us for our presumptuous sins, to the needful end of our national reformation as a whole people? We have been the recipients of the choicest bounties of Heaven. We have been preserved these many years in peace and prosperity. We have grown in numbers, wealth and power, as no other nation has ever grown. But we have forgotten God. We have forgotten the gracious hand which preserved us in peace, and multiplied and enriched and strengthened us; and we have vainly imagined, in the deceitfulness of our hearts, that all these blessings were produced by some superior wisdom and virtue of our own. Intoxicated with unbroken success, we have become too self-sufficient to feel the necessity of redeeming and preserving grace, too proud to pray to the God that made us! It behooves us, then, to humble ourselves before the offended power, to confess our national sins, and to pray for clemency and forgiveness. Now, therefore, in compliance with the request, and fully concurring in the views of the Senate, I do by this my proclamation designate and set apart Thursday, the 30th day of April, 1863, as a day of national humiliation, fasting, and prayer. And I do hereby request all the people to abstain on that day from their ordinary secular pursuits, and to unite at their several places of public worship and their respective homes, in keeping the day holy to the Lord, and devoted to the humble discharge of the religious duties proper to that solemn occasion. All this being done in sincerity and truth, let us then rest humbly in the hope, authorized by the Divine teachings, that the united cry of the nation will be heard on high and answered with blessings, no less than the pardon of our national sins, and restoration of our now divided and suffering country to its former happy condition of unity and peace."

President Jefferson Davis had also this season issued his proclamation, appointing a day of prayer and humiliation. It was dated at the end of February, and read: "It is meet that, as people who acknowledge the supremacy of the living God, we should be ever mindful of our dependence on Him, and should remember that to Him alone can we trust our deliverance, that to Him is due the devout thankfulness for signal mercies bestowed on us, and that by prayer alone can we hope to receive continued manifestation of that protecting care which has hitherto shielded us in the midst of trials and dangers. In obedience tc this precept, we have from time to time been gathered together with prayers and thanksgiving, and He has been graciously pleased to hear our supplications, and to grant abundant exhibitions of His favor to our arms and our people. Through many conflicts we have now attained a place among nations which commands their respect, and let the enemies who encompass us around and seek our destruction see that the Lord of Hosts has again taught them the lesson of His inspired word, 'that the battle is not to the strong,' but to whomsoever He willeth to exalt. Again an enemy, with loud boasting of power, of their armed men and mailed ships, threaten us with subjugation, and with evil machinations seek, even in our homes and at our own firesides, to pervert our men servants and our maid servants into accomplices of their wicked designs. Under these circumstances it is my privilege to invite you once more to meet together and prostrate yourselves in humble supplication to Him who has been our constant and never-failing support in the past, and to whose protection and guidance we trust for the future. To this end I, Jefferson Davis, President of the Confederate States of America, do issue this, my proclamation, setting apart Friday, the 27th day of March, as a day of fasting, humiliation and prayer. I do also invite the people of the said States to repair on that day to their usual places of public worship, there to join in prayer to Almighty God that he will continue his merciful protection over our cause; that he will scatter our enemies and set at nought their evil designs, and that he will graciously restore to our beloved country the blessings of peace and security."

CHAPTER LXXXVI.

GENERAL HUNTER'S SOUTH CAROLINA DEPARTMENT. JANUARY–JUNE, 1863.

On the 20th of January General Hunter, having returned from his temporary absence at the North, resumed command at Port Royal of the Department of the South. Little had been done in that quarter, beyond the vigilant blockading service, since the death of General Mitchel, at the end of October. It was a season of preparation for future conflict, while the monitors and ironclads from which much was expected in future operations were being completed at the North. The most celebrated of these vessels, the *Monitor*, we have seen, was lost at the close of the year on her way to the South; her companion, the *Passaic*, with the *Montauk*, and the formidable battery the *New Ironsides*, made their appearance at Port Royal simultaneously with the return of General Hunter. Active operations were now promised, a new series of stringent army regulations looking to employment in the field. Brigadier-General Saxton about the same time reported to the Secretary of War the complete organization of the colored 1st Regiment of South Carolina Volunteers, concerning which there had been some difficulties,* which had now passed away. "In organization, drill, discipline, and *morale*, for the length of time it has been in service," he wrote, "this regiment is not surpassed by any white regiment in this department. Should it ever be its good fortune to get into action, I have no fears but it will win its own way to the confidence of those who are willing to recognize courage and manhood, and vindicate the wise policy of the Administration in putting these men into the field, and giving them a chance to strike a blow for the country and their own liberty."* The capacity of the regiment was presently tested in a foraging exhibition along the coast of Georgia, and up the St. Mary's river in Florida, in the course of which they were several times in conflict with the enemy, and fought with distinguished courage. "At Township, Florida, a detachment of the expedition," says the commander, Colonel Higginson, "fought a cavalry company which met us unexpectedly on a midnight march through pine woods, and which completely surrounded us. They were beaten off with a loss on our part of one man killed and seven wounded, while the opposing party admits twelve men killed, including Lieutenant Jones, in command of the company, besides many wounded. Nobody knows anything about these men who has not seen them in battle. There is a fiery energy about them beyond anything of which I have ever read, unless it be the French Zouaves. It requires the strictest discipline to hold them in hand."†

The comparative quiet which had for some time prevailed in the vicinity of Charleston was broken a few days after the arrival of General Hunter, by a vigorous dash of the rebel navy in the harbor on the blockading squadron. On the 29th of January a valuable prize had been made by the gunboat *Unadilla* of the *Princess Royal*, an ironclad steamer, laden with Whitworth guns

* Ante, vol. ii. p. 587.

* Brigadier-General R. Saxton to Secretary Stanton, Beaufort, S. C., January 25, 1863.

† Colonel-Commandant T. W. Higginson to Brigadier-General Saxton, February 1, 1863.

and other munitions of war, from London, by way of Bermuda, a capture which was seriously felt by the Confederates. While this prize was lying off the harbor, preparatory to being sent north, about four o'clock on the morning of the 31st, during the obscurity of a thick haze, the moon having just set, two ironclad gunboats came out of Charleston by the main ship channel, unnoticed by the squadron, and commenced a raid upon the blockading fleet, which at this time was mostly composed of the light class of purchased vessels. The first assault was made upon the steamer *Mercedita*, formerly a merchant vessel, by a ram commanded by the rebel flag-officer, D. N. Ingraham, formerly of the United States service. A graphic account is given of the assault by Captain F. S. Stellwagen, of the *Mercedita*. "Particular vigilance," says he, "was exhibited by the officers and crew in the expectation of a vessel to run the blockade. At three o'clock in the morning we had slipped our cable and overhauled a troop-steamer running for the channel. At four I lay down. Lieutenant-Commander Abbot was on deck giving an order to Acting-Master Dwyer, about recovering the anchor, when they saw a smoke and the faint appearance of a vessel close at hand. I heard them exclaim, 'She has black smoke!' 'Watch, man the guns!' 'Spring the rattle!' 'Call all hands to quarters!' Mr. Dwyer came to the cabin door, telling me 'A steamboat was close aboard.' I was then in the act of getting my pea-jacket, and slipped it on as I followed him out. I jumped to the poop-ladder; saw the smoke and a low boat, apparently a tug, although I thought it might be a little propeller for the squadron. I sang out, 'Train your guns right on him—be ready to fire as soon as I order.' I hailed the steamer, 'Ahoy! Stand clear of us and heave to. What steamer is that?' I then ordered my men to fire on him, and told him: 'You will be into us. What steamer is that?' His answer to the first and second hail was: 'Halloo!' The other replies were indistinct, either by intention, or from having spoken inside of his mail armor, until in the act of striking us with his prow, when he said: 'This is the Confederate States steam-ram.' I repeated the order, 'Fire!' 'Fire!' 'Fire!' but no gun could be trained on him, as he approached us on the quarter, and struck us just abaft our after-mast with a thirty-two pounder, and fired a heavy rifle through us diagonally, penetrating the starboard side through our Normandy condenser, the steam-drum of our port boiler, and exploding against the port side of the ship, blowing a hole in its exit some four or five feet square. The vessel was instantly filled and enveloped with steam. Reports were brought to me: 'That we were shot through both boilers; that the fires were put out by the steam and smoke; that a gunner and one man were killed, that a number of men were badly scalded; that the water was over the fire-room floor, and that the vessel was sinking fast.' The ram had cut us through at and below the water-line on one side, and the shell had burst on the other side almost at the water's edge. After the ram struck she swung around under our starboard counter, her prow touching us, and hailed: 'Surrender or I'll sink you. Do you surrender?' After receiving the reports, I answered: 'I can make no resistance, my boiler is destroyed.' The rebel then cried out: 'Do you surrender?' I said, 'Yes,' having found my moving power destroyed, and that I could bring nothing to bear but muskets against his shot-proof coating. He hailed several times to 'send a boat,' and threatened to fire again. After some delay a boat was lowered, and Lieut.-Commander Abbott asked if he should go in her, and asked for orders what to say. I told him to see what they demanded, and to tell him the condition we were in. He proceeded aboard, and, according to their demand, gave his parole on behalf of himself and all the officers and crew. The ram having been detained a half-hour or more, now ran out for the steamer *Keystone State*, which vessel and three others we tried to alarm by lights."

The part borne in this disastrous affair by the *Keystone State* is thus related by her Commander, William E. Leroy: "At five o'clock in the morning," says he, "while at anchor off the main entrance of the harbor of Charleston, the ship was approached by what was supposed to be a steamer, but regarding her appearance as suspicious, I ordered the cable slipped, and fired a gun, which was responded to by a shell, when I ordered the guns to be fired as they could be brought to bear upon the object. On putting my head to the eastward it was discovered that there was one on either quarter, and we made them out from their peculiar construction to be ironclads after the model of the Merrimac. Owing to a fire in the hold, we stood to the northward about ten minutes, and shoaling water kept south-east about ten minutes, to enable us to subdue the fire; and then I turned around, and, under full steam, proposed attempting to run down the ram; but about six A. M. a shell from one of them entered on the port-side under the forward wheel-house guard, passing through the port steam-chimney, and landed in the starboard, depriving us of our motive power. Ten rifle-shell struck the ship, and two burst on the quarter-deck; most of them striking the hull, being near and below the water-line. Our steam-chimneys being destroyed, our motive power was lost, and our situation became critical. There were two feet of water in the ship, and leaking badly, the water rising rapidly and the fire-hold on fire. Others of the squadron coming along, the ram that had injured us so much altered her course, and before our wheels entirely stopped we were enabled to get a hawser from the Memphis, and were taken in tow. I regret to report our casualties very large. Some twenty were killed and twenty wounded. Among the killed I have to mention the surgeon of the ship, Assistant-Surgeon Jacob H. Gotwold, who was killed while in the act of rendering assistance to some of the wounded." There were no casualties on the other vessels, which suffered little injury; the rebel rams, on the gathering of the Union fleet, retiring, and taking refuge in the Swash channel, behind the shoals The *Mercedita* and *Keystone State* were taken to Port Royal for repairs.

A great effort was made by the Confederate authorities to turn this affair to account, by representing it as an effectual raising of the blockade. A joint proclamation, in grossly exaggerated terms, was issued from Charleston, the day of the attack, signed by General Beauregard, who had been placed in command of the troops at this place, and Flag-officer Ingraham, setting forth that the Confederate States' naval force on the station had sunk, dispersed, or driven off and out of sight for the time the entire hostile fleet, "and that, therefore, we, the undersigned, commanders respectively of the naval and land forces in this quarter, do hereby formally declare the blockade by the United States of the said city of Charleston, South Carolina, to be raised by a superior force of the Confederate States, from and after this 31st day of January, A. D. 1863." Notice to the same effect was given by Benjamin, the Secretary of State, to the foreign consuls and agents of the Confederacy, but without result upon the conduct of foreign governments, by whom Beauregard and his companions, to the contrary notwithstanding, the blockade was still considered, as it was, practically effective in spite of this slight interruption.

The day before the assault on the *Mercedita*, the gunboat *Isaac Smith*, originally a cattle barge on the Hudson river, was captured by the enemy while reconnoitering the Stono river. Batteries were opened from both shores, which rendered the vessel unmanageable.

A few days previously to this affair off Charleston, Admiral Dupont had sent the ironclad "monitor" *Montauk*, Commander Worden to the Ogeechee river, opening into Ossabaw Sound, on the Georgia coast, and running parallel with the Savannah river, and affording an approach from the west at a distance of some ten miles to the city of Savannah. In this stream the Confederate steamer *Nashville*, which we have noticed as having escaped from Beaufort, N. C., in March of the previous year,* to Georgetown, where Lieutenant Pegram relinquished his command, had, after various successful trips as a blockade runner between Charleston, Wilmington, and Nassau, been in July compelled to take refuge from the pursuit of the Union fleet. She was soon followed up, and successfully blockaded in her new quarters. For seven months she had thus been confined to the river, the defences of which had been meanwhile created and strengthened by various obstructions, and the erection of Fort McAllister at an advantageous bend of the stream. To destroy these works and capture the *Nashville*, was the object proposed for the navy. It was known that the *Nashville*, now fitted as a privateer, was ready for sea, and it was rumored that the *Fingal*, a British steamer, converted into a formidable ironclad war-vessel at Savannah, would come from that port to her assistance. With these inducements for action, Commander Worden began the attack on the fort with the *Montauk*, *Seneca*, and three other gunboats of the blockading squadron, on the 27th of January. For five hours through the forenoon an "artillery duel" was kept up, chiefly between the fort and the monitor, the latter being struck thirteen times, with little or no damage. A few indentations on her iron surface were the only injuries she sustained. She was the greater part of the action within about 1,600 yards of the fort, upon which no serious impression seems to have been made. Another attempt was made by Commander Worden with the same force on Sunday, the 1st of February, at as close quarters as the obstructions of stakes and torpedoes, and natural difficulties of the river permitted, within a thousand yards of the battery, but with no better success. In this second action the *Montauk* received sixty-one shots; her smoke-stack was riddled with balls, and her flag-staff carried away, yet she came out without serious injury. The fort was somewhat damaged in this engagement; a 30-pounder was dismounted, and the parapet badly torn in several places. Major Gallie was killed, and seven privates injured by concussion. The only result thus far appeared to be to test the defensive qualities of the "monitor."

The *Nashville* continued concealed and protected behind Fort McAllister through the month of February to the 27th, when, at evening, she was observed in motion above the battery by Commander Worden. "A reconnoissance immediately made," says he, in his report of the next day to Admiral Dupont, "proved that in moving up the river she had grounded in that part of the river known as the seven-miles' reach. Believing that I could, by approaching close to the battery, reach and destroy her with my battery, I moved up at daylight this morning, accompanied by the blockading fleet in

* Ante, vol. ii., pp. 150–152, and 397.

these waters, consisting of the *Seneca*, Lieut.-Commander Gibson; the *Wissahickon*, Lieut.-Commander Davis, and the *Dawn*, Acting Lieut.-Commander Barnes. By moving up close to the obstructions in the river, I was enabled, although under a heavy fire from the battery, to approach the *Nashville*, still aground, within the distance of 1,200 yards. A few well-directed shells determined the range, and soon succeeded in striking her with 11-inch and 15-inch shells. The other gunboats maintained a fire from an enfiladed position upon the battery, and the *Nashville* at long range. I soon had the satisfaction of observing that the *Nashville* had caught fire, from the shells exploding in her, in several places; and in less than twenty minutes she was caught in flames forward, aft, and amidships. At 9.20 A.M. a large pivot-gun, mounted abaft her foremast, exploded from the heat, at 9.40 her smoke-chimney went by the board, and at 9.55 her magazine exploded with terrific violence, shattering her in smoking ruins. Nothing remains of her. The battery kept up a continuous fire upon this vessel, but struck her but five times, doing no damage whatever. The fire upon the other gunboats was wild, and did them no damage whatever. After assuring myself of the complete destruction of the *Nashville*, I, preceded by the wooden vessels, dropped down beyond the range of the enemy's guns. In so doing, a torpedo exploded under this vessel, inflicting, however, but little injury. I beg leave, therefore, to congratulate you, sir, upon this final disposition of a vessel which has so long been in the minds of the public as a troublesome pest."

Still another demonstration was made upon Fort McAllister by Commander Drayton, the ranking officer, on the 3d of March, when the fleet in Ossabaw Sound was reinforced by two new monitors which had recently arrived at Port Royal. Three mortar-boats were also added to the attacking force. The latter, sheltered by a bend of the stream, opened fire, followed by three monitors, the *Passaic*, *Patapsco* and *Nahant*, which, from the narrow channel, could advance only in line. For four hours in the forenoon, and again in the afternoon, fire was kept up from these vessels, the foremost, the *Passaic*, having a range of about 1,900 yards, the *Montauk* and wooden vessels being in the rear, and taking no part in the action. The mortar-boats continued firing during the night. The result was as little decisive as before, the strength of the monitors being fully proved, and the sand fort, protected from a concentrated attack by the channel and obstructions, though often struck, resisting without serious damage the mass of metal thrown upon it. There were no casualties on the Union side. After this third trial, the fleet of monitors returned to Port Royal to prepare for the attack on Charleston.

There were now stirring notes of preparation in this quarter. The army at Port Royal, in view of the projected naval attack, had been strengthened by a considerable reinforcement of troops from the North Carolina department, led by General Foster. On their arrival there was some conflict of authority between that officer and General Hunter, which led to the retirement of the former, leaving his troops in the department. General Hunter, on the 5th of March, issued a general order, announcing the long-expected forward movement, in which every man in his command was promised the consideration due his services. "Soldiers of the department of the South," said he, "after long and wearying delays, due to causes over which no one in this department had control, we have at length the cheering prospect of active and very important service. Soldiers of the Tenth Army Corps, you are stimulated by every consideration of honor to vie with the gallant men from the department of North Carolina, who have been sent by Government to take part with you in the dangers and the glory of operations now pending. Officers and men of the command, you are adjured to the performance of every duty. All who earn distinction, no matter how humble their positions, have my pledge that their services shall be honorably acknowledged, and the acknowledgment pressed to their advantage. Commanding officers of divisions, brigades and regiments, in making their reports to these headquarters, will give the name of every officer, and a full descriptive list of every non-commissioned officer and soldier of their commands who has attracted their observation as behaving with special gallantry or good conduct, in order that the names of all such may be published with honor at their own homes; and all who are thus mentioned may rely that no effort shall be lacking on the part of the Major-General Commanding to secure their promotion. Should any officers neglect their men, or evince the least disposition to shrink at any moment from the proper responsibilities of their commissions, they will be likewise reported and held amenable to the severest penalties denounced by military law for misconduct in presence of the enemy. Should private soldiers distinguish themselves while officers become liable to censure, it would be treason to the country not to compel an exchange of places."

That the troops in the department might be placed in active service, General Hunter, at the same time, ordered that the able-bodied male negroes between the ages of eighteen and fifty, within the military lines of the department, be drafted to serve for a garrison force, as non-commissioned officers and soldiers in the regiments and brigades being organized by Brigadier-General Saxton, who was specially authorized to raise such troops by the War Department. "Suddenly released," said General Hunter, in his order, "from the cruel restraints of chattel slavery, and still pursued into freedom by the curse of that ignorance which slavery fostered as its surest weapon and most effective shield — the Major-General Commanding believes that the discipline of military life will be the very safest and quickest school in which these enfranchised bondsmen can be elevated to the level of our higher intelligence and cultivation; and that their enrollment in regular military organizations, and the giving them in this manner a legitimate vent to their natural desire to prove themselves worthy of freedom, cannot fail to have the further good effect of rendering less likely mere servile insurrection, unrestrained by the comities and usages of civilized warfare."*

Nor was General Beauregard, on the other hand, indifferent to the arrivals and preparations at Port Royal. He had actively employed his engineering ability in pushing on the harbor defences of Charleston, and at the first symptoms of the impending attack, had, on the 18th February, issued the following proclamation: "It has become my solemn duty to inform the authorities and citizens of Charleston and Savannah that the movements of the enemy's fleet indicate an early land and naval attack on one or both cities, and to urge that persons unable to take an active part in the struggle, shall retire. It is hoped, however, that this temporary separation of some of you from your homes will be made without alarm or undue haste, thus showing that the only feeling which animates you in this hour of supreme trial is the right of being able to participate in the defence of your homes, your altars, and the graves of your kindred. Carolinians and Georgians! The hour is at hand to prove your country's cause. Let all

* General Order, Hilton Head, March 6, 1863.

able-bodied men from the seaboard to the mountains rush to arms. Be not too exacting in the choice of weapons. Pikes and scythes will do for exterminating your enemies, spades and shovels for protecting your firesides. To arms, fellow-citizens! Come to share with us our danger, our brilliant success, our glorious death."

An expedition to Florida in March for the purpose of establishing a base of operations on the St. John's, again brought into action the colored troops raised in the department. Colonel Higginson led the way with his colored regiment and two companies of another under Colonel Montgomery, of Kansas fame, who had entered heartily into this work of the military organization of the negroes. Jacksonville was again occupied and courageously held by the new troops. At the end of the month they were reinforced by ten regiments,—Colonel Rust's 8th Maine, and Colonel Chatfield's 6th Connecticut. Colonel Rust, who from his rank assumed command, found, on his arrival, the enemy in the neighborhood, led by General Finnegan, threatening active hostilities from the line of the railway to Tallahassee. "When I reached Jacksonville, on the 23d," says Colonel Rust, "a rebel battery, mounted on a platform car propelled by a locomotive, was shelling the town. The gunboat *Norwich*, which accompanied me, engaged it, replying vigorously, as did also a rifled Parrot 32-pounder on shore. The enemy were soon driven back. He was, as I afterward learned, making a reconnoissance, which it was his plan to follow up by an attack in force after nightfall. He expected to make the attack so close as to render our gunboats unavailable from the danger of their shells falling among our men. Everything remained quiet during that night. The fact that our pickets had previously been drawn in at night to the edge of the town encouraged this plan, which was frustrated by the arrival of the Eighth Maine regiment. and placing a night picket afterwards at a distance.

"On the night of the 24th the locomotive battery again approached and threw several 68-pound rifled shells striking several buildings, but injuring no one. On Wednesday, a reconnoissance in force, commanded by Colonel Higginson and consisting of five companies of the Eighth Maine, under Lieut.-Colonel Twitchell, four companies of the Sixth Connecticut, under Major Meeker, and a portion of Colonel Higginson's colored regiment, advanced along the railroad upward of four miles, driving in General Finnegan's pickets, but were not able to overtake the enemy. After proceeding as far as was deemed advisable, and the enemy showing no disposition to accept battle, our forces commenced to return. Soon after the locomotive battery appeared and threw several shells, but was careful to keep out of reach of our rifles. One of its shells killed Privates Hoole and Goodwin, and severely wounded Willis, all of Captain McArthure's, Co. I, Eighth Maine Volunteers, who were the only persons killed or wounded after my arrival. On this occasion all the troops behaved exceedingly well. Colonel Montgomery, with about one hundred and twenty men of his regiment, accompanied by Captain Stedman, of the gunboat *Paul Jones*, made a successful expedition to Pilatka, seventy-five miles up the river, taking prisoners a Lieutenant and fourteen men, with their arms. The Lieutenant violated his parole of honor, and escaped. A quantity of cotton, rifles, horses, and other property amounting in value to several thousand dollars, has been captured. In accordance with a Special Order received from Headquarters Department of the South, I withdrew all the United States forces from Jacksonville, Fla., on the 31st March, and embarked them on board transports, part of which had just arrived for that purpose.

While the evacuation was taking place, several fires were set—a portion of them undoubtedly by secessionists. The fires were not confined to the lines of any regiment. Perhaps twenty-five buildings were destroyed. On my arrival I found that many buildings had been burned, some by rebels, others by the Union forces from a military necessity. Many Union families came away with us, our soldiers freely making all possible room for them on the transports."*

The preliminary preparations at Port Royal having been completed for the attack on Charleston, the vessels of the fleet and transports through the month of March were quietly forwarded to the place of rendezvous on North Edisto river, where they might readily pass to the immediate scene of operations. It was important for the movements of the iron clads over the bar at Charleston to get the advantage of the high spring tides at the beginning of April, and Admiral Dupont, who led the naval part of the expedition, watched the opportunity with anxiety. On the 5th of April, after several days of high wind, the sea being perfectly smooth and the tides favorable, the fleet left its anchorage, and early in the forenoon arrived at the blockading station off Charleston harbor. Here, as at the first entrance to Port Royal, Commander Boutelle, of the Coast Survey, assisted in sounding and marking out the channel,—a new one, formed by the sinking of the "stone fleet," which was found of a greater depth of water than the old. These and other preliminaries occupied the day. Early on the following morning of the 6th, the iron-clad fleet crossed the bar and was ranged opposite Morris Isand at the southern entrance of the harbor within a mile of the shore, but that day was lost for active operations by a thick haze which prevented any observations of the shore. It consisted of nine vessels, arranged according to the progamme of Admiral Dupont, in the following order: the *Weehawken*, Captain John Rodgers; the *Passaic* Captain Percival Drayton; the *Montauk*, Commander John L. Worden; the *Patapsco*, Commander Daniel Ammen; the *New Ironsides*, the flagship, Commodore Thomas Turner; the *Catskill*, Commander George W. Rodgers; the *Nantucket*, Commander Donald McN. Fairfax; the *Nahant*, Commander John Downes; the *Keokuk*, Lieutenant-Commander Alexander C. Rhind. The flagship *New Ironsides*, a formidable iron-covered battery or steam-frigate, mounted eighteen guns; sixteen 11-inch and two 200 pounder Parrotts; the rest were of the monitor class, and had each two guns, mostly an 11-inch and 15-inch gun in a single turret, with the exception of the *Keokuk*, which had two turrets with an 11-inch gun in each. The *Canandaigua*, and four other gunboats of the squadron, constituted a reserve outside the bar.

A correspondent, who witnessed the scene and had excellent opportunities of information, thus describes the defences of the harbor to be met by an invading fleet: "We are facing Fort Sumter and looking directly up the harbor. We have, accordingly, Sullivan's Island on our right hand and Morris Island on our left. These two islands end each in curved points of land and at their nearest approach are separated by an interval of a mile, formed by the entrance to the harbor, and just on the middle of this passage and right between the two points of land stands Fort Sumter, built on an artificial island made in mid-channel. Both Morris and Sullivan's Islands are scarcely removed above the level of the sea, which, indeed, would probably invade and cover them were it not that the margin of the islands on their sea frontage is marked by a continuous nar-

* Colonel Commanding, John D. Rust to Lieut-Colonel C. J. Halpine, A. A. G. Department of the South, Hilton Head April 4, 1863.

row strip of low sand hills some five or six feet in height. Behind the second ridge of the islands are alternate salt marsh, sand and clumps of wood of live-oak, palmetto and tangled tropical undergrowths. With Sullivan's Island on our right we run the eye up to its upper or north end formed by Breach Inlet. Guarding this point is Breach Inlet battery—a powerful sand work having a circular dome-like bomb-proof magazine in its centre. It is, however, three miles from the entrance of the harbor and will not be able to molest our ships on their passage. Its chief value has been to aid blockake runners, as it covers Maffit's Channel (the passage through which the great majority of these craft run in) from the approach of our blockaders. At present it will serve to oppose our landing troops at Breach Inlet should the attempt be made. Coming down along the shore of Sullivan's Island, from Breach Inlet, we next reach Fort Beauregard, a powerful sand battery, mounting very heavy guns, and situated on the turn of the Island a little right of the "Moultrie House" hotel, from which it is separated only by five intervening seashore houses. Next, to the right of the channel up, and opposite Fort Sumter is Fort Moultrie, which has been prodigiously strengthened by the rebel engineers both in its means of offence and of defence. Looking up the harbor, and still to the right, the eye takes in the extensive line of works, *en cremaillaire*, called the Redan, and which has been formed by throwing up intrenchments on the line of the breakwater erected some years ago by the United States Government for the protection of that portion of the harbor. Beyond the Redan up near the head of the harbor, on an island appears Castle Pinckney in the vista, looking like the "Battery" in New York city as seen from the sea-entrance. So far as the eye can see we have now exhausted the fortifications on the right hand side of the harbor. It now remains briefly to glance at those that line the left hand side. In the meanwhile, Fort Sumter rises up conspicuously before us in mid-channel. We can see every brick in its walls. Two faces out of its five, and two angles only, come within sight from our point of view, namely, the south face, on which the sally-port and wharf are placed, and the eastern face. It was pierced for two tiers of guns, but the lower embrasures had been filled in to strengthen it. From the top of the fort frown the barbette guns, which comprise all the heaviest portion of its armament. You can count distinctly each barbette gun—one, two, three, four, five on this ; one, two, three, four on that, and so on all round, and it is easy to see that the ordnance is of the most formidable character. From a flag-staff on one of the angles of the fort, floats the Confederate flag ; from a flag-staff on the opposite angle, floats the Palmetto flag. Passing now to the left hand side of the harbor, on James Island, we first have the Wappoo battery, near Wappoo Creek, effectually commanding the embouchure of Ashley River and the left side of the city. Next coming down, we have Fort Johnston, and between it and Castle Pinckney, on an artificial island raised by the rebels on the "middle ground," is Fort Ripley. Coming down to Cumming's Point, directly opposite Moultrie, is the Cumming's Point battery, named by the rebels Battery Bee, after the General of that name ; south of Battery Bee, on Morris Island, is Fort Wagoner, a very extensive sand battery of the most powerful construction. Half-way down Morris Island, again, from Fort Wagener, is a new sandwork erected by the rebels since I surveyed the ground from the blockading fleet, a fortnight ago. Finally, down at Lighthouse Inlet, which divides Morris from Folly Island, is another fortification, covering an attempt at a landing at that point.

Such is the formidable panorama the eye takes in, in sweeping around the harbor and its approaches."

The next day, Saturday, the 7th, was favorable for the movement. "Precisely at half-past twelve o'clock," continues the correspondent just cited, "the fleet begins to move on to the attack. The line of battle is formed in the order assigned to each ship in the Admiral's programme, the *Keokuk*, which brings up the rear of the line, lying down nearly opposite Lighthouse Inlet, the others extending on at intervals of a cable's length—the *Weehawken* leading the van. The wooden gunboat fleet lies in reserve outside the bar, close by the position occupied by the blockaders. The head of the line is some four miles from the position the fleet is to make before opening fire, and all the batteries on Morris Island—they must pass within easy range of each—have to be run. The fleet is hardly in motion, however, when the leading vessel, the *Weehawken*, stops, and all the others have to stop, also. The cause of this delay, as we afterwards learned, was the derangement of a raft which had been attached to the *Weehawken* for the purpose of exploding torpedoes and clearing away obstructions. This instrument is one of the inventions of Mr. Ericsson's fertile genius, and consists of a raft about twelve feet square, composed of transverse timbers, eighteen inches in thickness, fitting on to the prow of the vessel. From the forward part of this raft, suspended from a cable, six feet in the water was to be a large projectile, containing several thousand pounds of powder, so constructed that the line of fraction would be forward and laterally, and capable of being exploded from the turrret by means of a lanyard. One of the two of these rafts which had been brought down was attached to the *Weehawken*, which for this reason was assigned the leading position in the line. Owing to the purely experimental character of the device, however, the projectile was not attached to the raft, but in its place a number of grappling-irons had been affixed, which it was hoped would be found of service in exploding and tearing out torpedoes. In the course of getting under way, these grapplings had become fouled in the anchor cable, and this was the cause of the delay of the *Weehawken* and of the whole fleet. It takes an hour to set this matter to rights, and at half-past one o'clock the fleet is once more under way.

"Slowly the leading vessel, followed by the other eight ironclads, moves up the Main Ship Channel—the shore of Morris Island, against which from our point of view they seem to rest, forming a fixed point, by which we measure the progress of the fleet. The first battery to whose fire it will be exposed is Fort Wagener, and one fixes his eye on it, and on the *Weehawken*, approaching nearer and nearer, for the fleet will there undergo its first fiery baptism. Now then she comes within range of the fort; no fire. She passes across it; still no fire! The second ship comes up, and meets the same silent reception; and so on, one by one, till, with the *Keokuk*, the whole nine file by without a single shot from this seemingly formidable work. Meantime, while the fleet is passing Wagener unmolested, the leading vessel has come up with the next rebel work—Battery Bee. The same silent reception for her; the same silent reception for the whole fleet! What is the meaning of this? The enemy is obviously holding back his fire until he can deliver it with the greatest possible effect. The line has now passed across the front of Morris Island and rounds to make the entrance of the harbor, coming up within the circle of the fire of Fort Sumter and the batteries on Sullivan's Island. In an instant a hollow square of smoke rises from the top of Sumter—a hollow square of flame shoots up—a crash counterfeiting 'Jove's dread clamors' bursts on the ear, and a whole broadside streams down from the barbette guns. It is precisely four minutes past three in the afternoon. While the *Weehawken* is receiving this fire, the others are gradually coming up to the same position; but the leading vessel, instead of passing on above Sumter, so as to place herself in the prescribed station opposite the northwest face, sheers off to the right, and hangs estopped between Sumter and Moultrie! From our point of view, no cause for this unlooked-for development can be perceived, but to those on the *Weehawken* it is only too apparent. Stretching from a point close to the northeastern angle of Fort Sumter, completely across the channel to Fort Moultrie, is a stout hauser, floating on lager-beer casks, on which are hung nets, seines and cables, strung with torpedoes. The vessel comes afoul of this, whisks up the nasty entanglements with its propeller, is thus deprived of all motive power, and is at the mercy of the current, to be drifted ashore into the hands of the rebels. If this fatality was not actually realized by the ironclads, it was owing to the admirable skill of the Captains of the foremost ships, who when their vessels were just on the point of fouling sheered off, and saved themselves and the fleet.

"The right hand channel being thus obstructed, it remains to see what can be done with the left, between Sumter and Cumming's Point. But this, too, is still more effectually blockaded by a row of piles rising ten feet above the water, and extending across the whole width of the passage. Looking up the harbor, another row of piles discloses itself, stretching across from Fort Ripley on the middle ground to Fort Johnson. It does not stretch entirely across, however, for midway is an opening, inviting the passage of the fleet. Submerged in the water, underneath that opening, is a torpedo filled with—incredible though the statement may seem, it is an actual fact—*five thousand pounds* of powder! Futhermore, above this first line of piles is a second, and above the second a third—while above all, and just behind the upper line of obstructions, are the three rebel ironclads-drawn up in battle array, and vomiting huge clouds of smoke. You can readily conceive that this unlooked-for estoppel utterly deranged the original intentions. The rebels were quite as well aware as we that the northwest face of Sumter is its weakest point; that it was, in fact, never finished, and, therefore, that it would be first attacked; and they used every means which admirable engineering skill could suggest to prevent our reaching it. Thus brought to a pause, it only remained for the ironclads to take up such positions as they could. And the complication was further increased by the ill-behavior of the flagship, the *Ironsides*. While steaming along up through the passage in front of Sumter she is caught by the tide-way, and veered off from her course, and her huge iron frame refusing to obey her rudder, she becomes in great part unmanageable. This embarrassed not her only, but all that portion of the fleet following her. The two Monitors immediately behind (the *Catskill* and the *Nantucket*) fell foul of her, the one on one side, and the other on the other, and it was full fifteen minutes before they could be got clear, and pass on.

"In this plight it only remained for Admiral Dupont to signal to the fleet to disregard the movements of the flagship. This he did, and the ships then assumed such positions as were available and they could gain, the whole number being at the mouth of the harbor, between Cumming's point and Sullivan's Island, and opposite the northeast and eastern face of Fort Sumter, at distances of from six hundred to a thousand yards. While the maneuvers rapidly indicated in these paragraphs are going on, you must not suppose the enemy is inactive. The powerful work on Cumming's Point, named Battery Bee, opens, the long range rifle ordnance of Fort Beauregard join in, Moultrie hurls its heavy metal, the fifty guns that line the Redan swell the fire, and the tremendous armament of Sumter vomits forth its fiery hail. There now ensues a period of not more than thirty minutes, which forms the climax and white heat of the fight; for though from the time when fire was opened on the head of the approaching line to the time when the retiring fleet passed out of the enemy's range, there was an interval of two hours and a half (from half-past two till five), yet the essence of the fight was shut up in those thirty tremendous minutes. The best resources of the descriptive art, I care not in whose hand, are feeble to paint so terrific and awful a reality. Such a fire, or anything even approaching it, was simply never seen before. The mailed ships are in the focus of a concentric fire of the five powerful works already indicated, from which they are removed only from five to eight hundred yards, and which in all could not have mounted less than three hundred guns. And, understand, these not the lighter ordnance, such as 32 or 42-pounders, which form the ordinary armament of forts, but of the very heaviest calibre—the finest and largest guns from the spoils of the Norfolk Navy-yard, the splendid and heavy 10 and 11-inch guns cast at the Tredegar works and the most approved English rifled guns (Whitworth and others), of the largest calibre made. There was something almost pathetic in the spectacle of those little floating circular towers, exposed to the crushing weight of those tons of metal, hurled against them with the terrific force of modern projectiles, and with such charges of powder as were never before dreamed of in artillery firing. During the climax of the fire a hundred and sixty shots were counted in a single minute! Some of the commanders of the ironclads afterwards told me that the shot struck their vessels as fast as the ticking of a watch, and not less than thirty-five hundred rounds could have been fired by the rebels during the brief engagement!

"While the fleet is receiving the fire from the forts, what, in the meantime, are the ironclads doing in return? On the order being given to disregard the movements of the flagship, the brilliantly audacious Rhind ran his vessel, the *Keokuk*, up through the others and laid it seemingly under the very walls of Sumter, and within a little more than five hundred yards from it. Close behind him, within six hundred yards of the fort, is the *Catskill*, commanded by George Rodgers, a soul of courage all compact; and to both of them one could not help applying the exclamation of Nelson at Trafalgar—"See how Collingwood, that noble fellow, carries his ship into the fight?" Close by is the *Montauk*, commanded by the heroic Worden; while not far removed are the *Passaic*, the *Patapsco*, the *Nahant*, the *Nantucket*, the *Weehawken*, and the *Ironsides*. The whole fleet is devoting itself mainly to the face of Sumter presented to it, with the exception of the *Ironsides*, which, from its position, can do better work on Fort Moultrie, and is pouring forth its terrific broadside from its seven 10-inch guns on that work. Could you look through the smoke, and through the flame-lit ports, into one of those revolving towers, a spectacle would meet your eye such as Vulcan's stithy might present. Here are the two huge guns which form the armament of each Monitor—the one 11 and the other 15 inches in diameter of bore. The gunners begrimed with powder and stripped to the waist are loading the gun. The charge of powder—thirty-five pounds to each charge—is passed up rapidly from below; the shot, weighing 420 pounds, is hoisted up by mechanical appliances to the muzzle of the gun, and rammed home ; the gun is run out to the port, and tightly 'compressed ;' the port is open for an instant, the Captain of the gun stands behind, lanyard in hand—'Ready, fire!" and the enormous projectile rushes through its huge parabola, with the weight of ten thousand tons, home to its mark. That mark is the face of Sumter, which already displays palpable proofs of the horrid impact. Half a dozen ugly pock marks show conspicuous, and a huge crater is formed in the parapet near the eastern angle. We look with interest at these effects, and look forward with good hope to seeing a breach at length effected, if only the ironclads can remain long enough under fire to batter away. If only they could have remained. But what craft, pray, *could* remain under such a hurricane of fire? And what is this coming down out of the fight? It is the *Keokuk*—we know her by her double turret. She has defied Sumter under its very walls, and now comes out to report to the flagship that she has received her death-blow, and is in a sinking condition! The flagship herself has had one of her port shutters shot away, thus exposing her gun-deck, and red-hot shot has penetrated her wooden bows. In addition, three others showed signs of disablement, and there was little more than sufficient daylight left for the fleet to gain its old anchorage. At 5 o'clock the Admiral makes signal to retire.

"The *Nahant* received in all thirty wounds, several of them bad fractures of the deck and sides, below and above the water-line. The most fatal blow, however, was given by a heavy rifled shot, which struck the pilot-house, and dislodged several of the bolts, one of which, driven violently inwards, wounded all of the three inmates of the pilot-house—the Captain (Captain Downs, Massachusetts), the pilot (Isaac Sofield, New Jersey), and the Quartermaster (Edward Cobb, Massachusetts). The Quartermaster had been struck by the bolt on the back of the skull which received a compound comminuted fracture. When I saw the poor fellow, late at night, he was in a state of coma, his life ebbing away. He died this morning. The pilot's wound was a severe contusion of the neck and shoulder, and he is doing well. The Captain received merely a slight contusion of the foot. Other bolts were driven in, in the turret also, and the following were wounded: John McAllister, seaman (Canada), concussion of brain; John Jackson, seaman (Massachusetts), Roland Martin, Seaman (Massachusetts), and James Murry, seaman (Massachusetts), slightly hurt by flying bolts in the turret. The *Passaic* also received twenty five or thirty wounds. The most extraordinary shot was from a large 10-inch rifled projective, which struck the top of the turret, scooping out a huge portion of the iron, breaking all of the eleven plates of an inch thickness each, and spending its force on the pilot-house (which is placed on top of the turret), in which it made a crater three inches deep, and producing such a shock on the pilot-house as to start its top and raise it up three inches! Had not the force of the impact been broken on the turret, there can be little doubt that this shot would have gone clean through the pilot-house. Another shot hit the turret, forcing the place struck inwards, and producing a big swell on the interior. The same shock disabled the carriage of the 11-inch gun, while portions of the interior iron casting fell down, and lodging in the groove of the turret stopped its revolution. The *Nantucket*, besides receiving a number of wounds, had her turret so jarred that the cover of the port could not be opened, and consequently the 15-inch gun could not be used. In addition, the other Monitors each received shots, more or less, though not disabling them. Thus the *Catskill* was hit twenty times. The worst wound was from a rifled shot, which broke the deck-plating forward, going through it, breaking a beam beneath, and spending its force on an iron stanchion, which it settled half an inch. The *Ironsides* was frequently struck. One of the shots broke off and carried away one of her port shutters, and her wooden bows were penetrated by shell, though they were prevented from doing the damage they otherwise must have done, by Commodore Turner's precaution of protecting the exposed part of the vessel with sandbags. But the poor *Keokuk*—she, of all others, was the most fearfully maltreated. This vessel was struck *ninety* times, and she had nineteen holes above and below the water-line, some of a size through which a boy might crawl. Her turrets (five and three-quarters inches of iron in thickness) were fairly riddled and came out of the contest mere sieves. During the action twelve of her men were wounded, among whom was her commander, the gallant Rhind. During the night her pumps were kept at work, to throw out the leaks she was making. The sea had become somewhat rough, however, and was washing in through the holes in her bows. By daylight it became obvious that she must sink. I had remained on board the *Catskill* during the night, and at seven o'clock word was brought down that the *Keokuk*, which was hard by us, had made a signal of distress. Passing up on deck, we saw she was rapidly settling forward. At her signal, boats and tugs had come to her assistance, and were busy removing her wounded men. Barely time enough was afforded to get off them and her crew, for she had settled so much that the water was pouring into her turrets. Two or three of the men, indeed, had to jump into the sea, and were hauled into the small boats. Suddenly she gives a lurch to one side, and a lurch to the other, and plunges under. She went down at eight o'clock at the spot of her original anchorage, near Lighthouse Inlet, and all that is visible of her is the upper portion of her smoke-stack. Thus ended the brief and glorious career of this interesting vessel—the first ironclad ever sunk in battle. Her story must form a most important chapter in the history of these new engines of naval warfare, and her fate presents an astounding example of the frightful power of modern projectiles."*

The military force of General Hunter under these circumstances, numbering it is said but seven thousand men, brought to Stono Inlet, were not called into action, their employment depending upon the success of the naval operations. All that General Hunter in fact could do, was to bear his testimony to the gallantry of the fleet, which he did in the following letter to Admiral Dupont the day after the engagement: "Not knowing what have been the results of your attack of yesterday, so far as Fort Sumter is concerned, I cannot but congratulate you upon the magnificent manner in which the vessels under your command fought. A mere spectator, I could do nothing but pray for you, which, believe me, I did most heartily, for you and all the gallant men under your command, who sailed so calmly and fearlessly into and under and through a concentric fire which has never heretofore had a parallel in the history of warfare. That you are uninjured, and so many of your command fit for service, is a cause of deep gratitude to Almighty God. I confess, when the *Weehawken* first ran under Sumter's guns, receiving the casemate and barbette broadsides from that work simultaneously with the similar broadsides from Fort Moultrie and all the other works within range, I fairly held my breath until the smoke had cleared away, not

* Correspondence of the *New York Times* (W. Swinton) Off Charleston Harbor, April 8th, 1863.

expecting to see a vestige of the little vessel which had provoked such an attack. With each of the others the same scene was re-enacted, my interest in the fate of the *Ironsides* being, perhaps, the keenest from my knowledge of her vulnerability, and of the deep loss the country would sustain if anything was to happen to you. Thank God for the results as far as they go. May He have you in his keeping through whatever chances are yet before you. No country can ever fail that has men capable of suffering what your ironclads had yesterday to endure." In the account of the action published in the *Charleston Mercury* of the 11th of April, it is stated that by an estimate made from Sullivan's Island, "about eighty shots were fired at Fort Sumter where Colonel Alfred Rhett was in command, forty of which struck the work. One 10-inch gun was temporarily disabled by a shot. One columbiad of old pattern burst. One 7-inch rifled gun dismounted by recoil, and one gun was disabled for a few moments by fracture of the elevating screw through recoil. Not a person was killed in Fort Sumter from any cause. Sergeant Faulkner, and privates Chaplin, Minnix, and Penn, Company B, were injured by a shower of bricks thrown from a traverse on the rampart by a large shot of the enemy. A drummer-boy, Ahrens, was struck on the head by the explosion of a shell over the parade. A negro laborer was also wounded. All, we learn, are doing well, and there is no danger of losing a life or a limb. The regimental ensign was pierced near the centre by a ball. The Confederate flag was also perforated. There was but one casualty at Fort Moultrie. A shot from one of the Monitors cut away the flag-staff, a few feet above the parapet, and the staff fell upon private Lusby, Company F, First South Carolina [regular] infantry, inflicting injuries, from the effects of which he soon died."

On the 10th, a few days after the engagement, General Beauregard issued the following congratulatory order on the event: "The Commanding General is gratified to have to announce to the troops the following joint resolutions unanimously adopted by the Legislature of the State of South Carolina: *Resolved*, That the General Assembly reposes unbounded confidence in the ability and skill of the Commanding General of this Department, and the courage and patriotism of his brave soldiers, with the blessing of God, to defend our beloved city, and to beat back our vindictive foes. *Resolved*, That his Excellency the Governor be instructed to communicate this resolution to General Beauregard. Soldiers! the eyes of your countrymen are now turned upon you, on the eve of the second anniversary of the 13th of April, 1861, when the sovereignty of the State of South Carolina was triumphantly vindicated within the harbor which we are now to defend. The happy issue of the action on the 7th instant—the stranded, riddled wreck of the iron-mailed *Keokuk*—her baffled coadjutors forced to retire beyond the range of our guns, have inspired confidence in the country that our ultimate success will be complete. An inestimably precious charge has been committed to your keeping, with every reliance on your manhood and enduring patriotism."

No new operations of moment for some time occurred in the Department, with the exception, perhaps, of the destructive raids in the beginning of June, led by Colonel Montgomery, with several companies of negro soldiers, assisted by gunboats at landing on the Combabee river, where many valuable plantations were destroyed, and on the coast of Georgia, when serious damage was inflicted on Brunswick and Darien in an ascent of the Altamaha river. Early in June General Gillmore arrived as the successor to General Hunter.

This change was announced in the following order, dated Port Royal, June 12: "Major-General David Hunter, Commanding Department of the South, hereby announces that he has been temporarily relieved from command of the Department, and ordered to report to the Adjutant-General, United States Army, for special service, and that Brigadier-General Q. A. Gillmore has been assigned by the President to the command of the Department of the South. In turning over command to his successor, Major-General Hunter congratulates the troops of the Department, that in General Gillmore they will find an officer well known to them, and whose worth they have long since learned to estimate; and it is the earnest hope of General Hunter that the same skill, perseverance, and gallantry, which so largely contributed to the reduction of Fort Pulaski, more than a year ago, may be equally successful in whatever enterprises General Gillmore shall next be engaged in."

CHAPTER LXXXVII.

GENERAL HOOKER'S CAMPAIGN IN VIRGINIA. JANUARY—MAY, 1863.

The Army of the Potomac having been sufficiently recruited, after the battle of December, to warrant in the judgment of its commander, General Burnside, another forward movement against the enemy, arrangements were made in the middle of January for the passage of the river above and below Fredericksburg. The army was set in motion on the 13th, and dispositions made for crossing that night, when a tempestuous rainstorm set in, which suddenly softening the roads, arrested the movement at its commencement, and compelled its abandonment. Immediately after this, General Burnside, at his own request, was relieved of the command of the army, and General Joseph Hooker appointed in his place. On the 26th the former took leave of the army in a general order marked by his characteristic candor and feeling—

"The short time," said he, "that he has directed your movements has not been fruitful of victory, nor any considerable advancement of our line, but it has again demonstrated an amount of courage, patience and endurance that, under more favorable circumstances, would have accomplished great results. Continue to exercise these virtues, be true in your devotion to your country and the principles you have sworn to maintain; give to the brave and skillful general, who has long been identified with your organization, and who is now to command you, your full and cordial support and co-operation, and you will deserve success. Your general, in taking an affectionate leave of the army from which he separates with so much regret, may be pardoned if he bids an especial farewell to his long and tried associates of the Ninth Corps. His prayers are that God may be with you, and grant you continued success until the rebellion is crushed."

General Hooker the same day issued his order on assuming command. "He enters," said he, "upon the discharge of the duties imposed by this trust with a just appreciation of their responsibility. Since the formation of the army he has been identified with its history

He has shared with you its glories and reverses, with no other desire than that these relations might remain unchanged until its destiny should be accomplished. In the record of your achievements there is much to be proud of, and with the blessing of God we will contribute something to the renown of our arms and the success of our cause. To secure these ends your commander will require the cheerful and zealous co-operation of every officer and soldier in this army. In equipment, intelligence and valor, the enemy is our inferior. Let us never hesitate to give him battle wherever we can find him. The undersigned only gives expression to the feelings of this army when he conveys to our late commander, Major-General Burnside, the most cordial good wishes for his future."

In the reorganization of the army which followed, Major-Generals Franklin and Sumner were relieved of their commands. The system of Grand divisions was pronounced to be impracticable, a hindrance to the dispatch of current business, and unsuited to the service which the army was liable to be called upon to perform, and the corps organization was adopted in its place. Major-Generals Reynolds, Couch, Meade Sedgwick, Sigel, Slocum, and Brigadier-General Sickels (temporarily) were appointed corps commanders. The cavalry was consolidated into a single corps under command of Brigadier-General Stoneman.

Genoarl Sumner did not long survive this change. He was presently assigned to the command of the Department of Missouri, and was preparing to enter on this new field of duty, when he was suddenly taken ill on a visit to his son-in-law at Syracuse, N. Y. After a few days' illness of congestion of the lungs, he died at that place, on the 21st of March, having just completed his sixty-seventh year. His long service in the army was remembered with gratitude by the country, while his personal virtues had endeared him to all who knew him. "The name of Sumner," said General Halleck in an order of the day, is "identified with nearly every fierce struggle in which the army of the Potomac has been engaged, and every page of its history will perpetuate the fame of this noble soldier. . . . The regrets of the whole army go with him. He will be lamented and remembered, not for his soldiery traits alone, but for his generous and courteous bearing, the offspring of a true and noble nature." At the funeral services at Syracuse several traits of the noble-hearted old warrior were recalled in an address by the Rev. Mr. Canfield. On his death-bed, it was said, "he expressed a feeling of regret that he had not entered into the thickest of the fight at Fredericksburg so that he could have died on the field of battle. A short time before he died, a few drops of wine were given to revive him, when he seized the glass, and waving it above his pillow, exclaimed, 'God save my country, the United States of America.'" His patriotism was always earnest and unhesitating. "All," wrote General McClellan, "recognized the high honor, loyalty and courage of that distinguished veteran. He presented to younger men the highest example of unswerving devotion to his country, and of a firm determination to sacrifice everything that might be necessary in subduing the rebellion and restoring peace and the unity of the nation, by putting forth all the strength of the country to defeat its armed enemies in the field."

The months of February and March and the greater part of April were passed by General Hooker in preparations for resuming active operations as soon as the season permitted. Under the now organization of the army the rumors of disaffection or mistrust which had followed the previous unsuccessful movements disappeared; improvements were made, especially in cutting down the transportation teams and substituting pack mules for wagons, and everything indicated that when the "fighting" Commander gave the word, the advance would be executed with the highest efficiency. Nor, when the time came, was this expectation disappointed. On the 27th of April the movement, the immediate intention of which had been kept carefully concealed, was commenced. The general plan of the new operations was to divert the attention of the enemy in front, push the main force rapidly across one of the upper fords, turn the strong rebel defences of Fredericksburg on the west, and compel the enemy to fight or abandon the road to Richmond. To assist in this movement, General Stoneman, with a large cavalry force, was to hasten forward and cut the railway communications of the enemy at important points in their road.

The initial steps of this movement are thus described by a correspondent: "By Tuesday morning, the 28th, an acute eye might begin to take in a rough outline of a plan from the dispositions then made of the troops. Three of the seven *corps d'armée* composing the Army of the Potomac, namely: the First Corps (Major-General Reynolds), the Third Corps (Major-General Sickles), and the Sixth Corps (Major-General Sedgwick), had been moved from their camp the night before, and had taken up their positions at the same point of the Rappahannock where General Franklin had his crossing at the time of the battle of Fredericksburg, namely, two miles below that city—and covered from the enemy's view by the curtain of hills that fringe the Rappahannock. While these movements are going on, other columns, consisting of the corps of General Meade (the Fifth), and General Slocum (the Twelfth), are moving on different roads, and have taken up positions up the Rappahannock, in the neighborhood of Banks' and United States fords, which are respectively eight and eleven miles above Fredericksburg, and are, it will be remembered, the places selected by General Burnside for his crossing on the occasion of the mud campaign. Before dawn of Tuesday the pontoon boats had been taken from the wagons, a couple of miles below Fredericksburg, and under cover of a very heavy fog, were carried noiselessly down on men's shoulders to the river's brink and deposited in the water. They were immediately manned by the troops of Russell's brigade (Brookes' division, Sixth Army corps), and rapidly pushed over, in the manner taught us by General Hunt at the time of the crossing in December. The rebels here, as at every ford for forty miles up and down the river, were posted along the river's margin in double lines of rifle pits, containing, perhaps, a couple of hundred men each. At the lower crossings, however, they made but a feeble resistance, and in a few moments our men were in possession of both lines of rifle-pits, with the loss of half a dozen men. Indeed, a rebel Lieutenant captured here, a disingenuous young man, told us that they had been expressly instructed not to offer very serious resistance. This being accomplished, the whole of Brookes' division was passed over the three pontoon bridges which were immediately constructed under charge of Chief-Engineer Benham, to hold the position and the bridge-head. A mile and a half below the position of General Sedgwick's bridges, at an estate called Southfield, Reynolds' command was also instructed to effect a crossing. In doing this, however, they were not quite so lucky as those above them. Daylight had come while the engineers were still endeavoring to get the pontoon boats down to the water, but the fire from the rebel sharpshooters, who were placed in rifle-pits which had been thrown up opposite them, also succeeded in delaying operations so much, that it was 10 o'clock in the forenoon before they could be got into the water. To silence the fire of the sharpshooters, Colonel Warner, commanding artillery on the extreme left, under the able Chief of Artillery, General Hunt, brought forty guns to bear upon them. This completely 'corraled' them, for they were afraid of leaving their pits and exposing themselves to the murderous fire of the artillery. This detained them until a force was able to push over in boats, when, charging up the hill, they captured all the men in the first row of rifle-pits, numbering about one hundred and fifty. Immediately after the crossing of this force, a couple of pontoon bridges were built, and General Wadsworth's division of Reynolds' corps was thrown over. General Wadsworth himself, however, did not wait for the completion of the bridges, but while his men were crossing in the open boats, plunged in on horseback and swam his horse over to the other side.

"Thus far, it is to be noticed that but *one* division of each of the two army corps had been sent across the river—the remaining *four* divisions stayed on the other side. But they were not idle. They were put in motion on the hill-slope on one side of the river, and in plain view of the enemy were marched along the crest of the ridge and down, as though to the crossing. But, instead of crossing, they were quietly drawn up *back* through a gully, round the rear of the ridge, and round again on its top. They made the appearance of an army of at least a hundred thousand men, and must have presented the appearance of a *massing* on our side, preparatory to a passage of the river under cover of the night. The same 'circusing' was performed by the artillery, the same by the wagon trains. Was this a *ruse de guerre?* It could hardly be anything else—and yet to any one but a careful observer, even on *our* side, the deception could not have been detected. The effect on the rebels was prompt. Two hours afterward their columns began moving up the Bowling-green road from down the river. Here a considerable force, including the whole of Jackson's corps—first, Trimble's brigade, down opposite Port Royal, then coming up successively, A. P. Hill's brigade, D. Hill's division, and Ealy's brigade—had been posted as a corps of observation. The Bowling-green road is at this point a sunken road; but we soon began to detect at various points the rebel column moving up—we were removed say a couple of miles—the bayonets glistening in the sun. Were the same plains that witnessed the savage fight last December to see a renewal of it to day? There was certainly every appearance of it. Our main force was massed here: a hundred and fifty guns were in position on the heights on our side, and the two divisions across the river were busily engaged strengthening the rebel rifle-pits now occupied by them. In the afternoon I passed over to the old battleground. It was now covered with a beautiful carpet of green; while the brilliant peach and hawthorn blossoms scented the air and delighted the eye. It is a superb plain for a review—several miles in length and one and a half in width—where *both* armies of the Potomac might march and countermarch; but a horrid place for a battle. At the rear of the plain the ridges rise, forming a perfect amphitheatre of hills around, thickly studded with rebel batteries, affording a hideous converging and enfilading fire on any troops attempting to pass across it. In the mind's eye one might see that battle raging and its fierce antagonisms painted on a cartoon of air. History, it is said, repeats itself; but I knew too well General Hooker's ideas on throwing troops against fortifications, when the resources of strategy enable one to circumvent them, to think for a moment that he would repeat that horrid episode. Maugre all the array, therefore, I firmly held to the impression that this was, after all, but a demonstration, and that the hot work would be elsewhere.

"Passing up the river we have fresh confirmation of this. During Sunday and Monday, the 26th and 27th, Howard's corps (the Eleventh), Slocum's corps (the 12th), and General Meade's (the Fifth), had been moving to the upper fords of the Rappahannock. On the night of Tuesday, between 10 P. M. and 2 A. M., Howard's entire corps crossed the Rappahannock on the pontoon bridge at Kelly's Ford, twenty-seven miles above Falmouth. At daylight General Slocum's corps followed, and during the forenoon General Meade's corps was thrown across. This movable column then struck direct for Germania Ford on the Rapidan River, distant twelve miles, one of the main affluents of the Rappahannock, into which it empties at United States Ford. General Meade, however, instead of taking this direction on passing the river, struck a road diverging eastward, and made Ely's Ford on the Rapidan, eight miles nearer than Germania Ford, to the *embouchure* of that stream into the Rappahannock. At Germania Ford, a force of about a hundred and fifty rebel pioneers was discovered building a bridge. These, by a well-executed maneuver, were all captured. Celerity of movement being the chief desideratum, it was resolved immediately to put the troops over by wading—an affair not very easy of execution, for the waters of the Rapidan, even at the ford, come up to a man's shoulder, and the current is very rapid. The men, however, plunged in, many of them stripping and carrying their clothes and cartridge-boxes on their bayonets—and wading over, up to their armpits, amid Homeric scenes of laughter and gayety—a cavalry picket being placed below to catch those that were carried away by the current. In the meantime a foot-bridge had been constructed on the abutments already placed there by the rebels, and during the night the whole remaining force was passed over, the piers being lighted up with huge bon fires. While this was going on at Germania Ford, Meade's troops were crossing at Ely's Ford. Both columns now moved as ordered, for Chancellorsville, at the junction of the Gordonville turnpike with the Culpepper and Orange Court-house plank road—communication being kept up between the two movable columns by a squadron of Pleasanton's cavalry, while another part of the same horsemen moved on the right flank of the outer column to protect it from the rebel cavalry attacks. This maneuver having uncovered United States Ford (which lies between Kelly's Ford and Falmouth — twelve miles from the latter), Couch's corps, which had, for three days, been lying at that point, was passed over the Rappahannock by a pontoon bridge on Thursday, without any opposition or indeed any demonstration more formidable than a brass band playing Hail Columbia. This force also converged toward Chancellorsville, and on Thursday night four army corps, namely, Howard's, Stevens', Meade's and Couch's, were massed at this point. That same night General Hooker and staff reached Chancellorsville, and established his headquarters in the only house there."*

Chancellorsville a clearing at the apex of the two sides of the angle on which the Union forces were drawn up, was distant west by south from Fredericksburg about ten miles. It was a position of importance by its direct communication with the latter city by a plank road and with Orange Court-house and Gordonsville by a road through the Wilder-

* Correspondence *New York Times*, Chancellorsville Va., May 2, 1863.

ness—a desolate region of tangled woods—in its vicinity.

It was at this time, on the 30th, when the strategy of General Hooker had thus far been successfully carried out, that he issued a memorable, congratulatory order to his troops. It is," said he, "with heartfelt satisfaction, that the General Commanding announces to the army that the operations of the last three days have determined that our enemy must ingloriously fly, or come out from behind their defences, and give us battle on our own ground, where certain destruction awaits him. The operations of the Fifth, Eleventh and Twelfth Corps have been a series of splendid successes." The enemy knew their ground and what might be expected from heroic resolution and promptly advanced to meet the Union army on the ground which the latter had selected. It was a situation of affairs which called for energy and decision, and, fortunately for the enemy, General Lee had at his right hand an officer of all others in the Confederate army peculiarly adapted for such an emergency. General "Stonewall" Jackson, the same night that Hooker established his lines across the Rappahannock, was ordered to advance with his corps, including General A. P. Hill's division, two others commanded by Generals Rodes and Colston, to which General Anderson's was added on the way. Friday, the 1st of May, brought the combatants facing each other. The Union force was drawn up, General Howard's 11th Corps, recently General Sigel's, on the extreme right, beyond Chancellorsville, supported on the left by General Sickles' corps, then General Slocum's and Meade's; Couch and Reynolds' corps being in the rear as a reserve and protection to the fords of the Rappahannock. The positions were well taken, the artillery being placed on advantageous points, the woods furnishing ready materials for abattis, which were skillfully employed by the troops. A reconnoissance of the centre by Jackson's advance at once convinced him of the impracticability of a direct attack in front. Leaving the plank road therefore he turned his efforts in another direction in a concentrated assault on the right flank. There were several reconnoissances by General Hooker's army on Friday, which were conducted with energy and success, particularly in a gallant movement by General Sykes' division of Meade's corps on the left, when an important position was gained with hard fighting. The forenoon of Saturday also brought various skirmishes with the enemy on the front in the general direction of the main road from Fredericksburg, in which the Union forces again fully maintained their ground. The event of the day was the grand attack late in the afternoon on the right by "Stonewall" Jackson, who had employed the previous night in cutting a road through the woods beyond the lines in that direction, had succeeded in turning the Union position, and was now about to precipitate his forces on General Howard's command, composed chiefly of German troops, including the divisions of Schurz, Steinerchr and Deven. "About three o'clock," writes an observer of the field, Mr. Crounse, the able correspondent of the *New York Times*, "the pickets on the right of General Slocum's front reported that from a certain position wagons had been seen moving in a westerly direction nearly all day. It was at once surmised that this might be a retreat, but subsequent events proved that it was a part of an affair of altogether another nature. To ascertain, however, what it really was, General Sickles, who was still in reserve, was ordered to make a reconnoissance in heavy force in that direction. This was done with great promptness, and the divisions of General's Birney and Whipple, with General Barlow's brigade, from

Howard's corps, were pushed out to the front, Berdan's brigade of sharpshooters having the advance, and supporting Randolph's battery. Our troops moved rapidly and soon became more or less engaged, especially with the artillery and the sharpshooters as skirmishers. Berdan soon sent in some sixty prisoners, belonging to the Twenty-third Georgia, including one Major, two Captains and three Lieutenants. Being upon the ground, I examined these prisoners, and soon found that the 'wagon train' which we had seen moving during the day was composed mainly of ordinance wagons and ambulances, and that 'Stonewall' Jackson and staff were at the head of a column of troops which the wagons followed. Nothing more was needed to convince us that this daring opponent was executing another of his sudden movements, and it was at once resolved to checkmate him. General Sickles was ordered to push on, and General Williams' division of Slocum's column was ordered to co-operate. Birney pushed ahead with great vigor, and with Randolph's battery soon sent to the rear as prisoners of war the entire remnant of the Twenty-third Georgia regiment, numbering over four hundred officers and men. The column of the enemy which had been moving up this road was now literally cut in two, and General Williams had commenced a flank movement on the enemy's right, which promised the most auspicious results. But at five o'clock a terrific crash of musketry on our extreme right announced that Jackson had commenced his operations. This had been anticipated, but it was supposed that after his column was cut, the corps of General Howard (formerly General Sigel's), with its supports, would be sufficient to resist his approach, and finding that he was himself assailed in the rear, he would turn about and retreat to escape capture. But to the disgrace of the Eleventh Corps be it said, that the division of General Schurz, which was the first assailed, almost instantly gave way. Threats, entreaties and orders of commanders were of no avail. Thousands threw down their guns and soon streamed down the road toward headquarters. The enemy pressed his advantage. General Deven's division, disaffected by the demoralization of the forces in front of him, soon followed suit, and the brave General was for the the second time severely wounded in the foot, while endeavoring to rally his men. General Howard, with all his daring and resolution and vigor, could not stem the tide of the retreating and cowardly poltroons. The brigades of Colonels Bushbeck and McLean only remained fighting, and maintained themselves nobly as long as possible. But they, too, gave way, though in good order, before vastly superior numbers.

"General Hooker now sent to the aid of General Howard the choicest division of his army, the creation of his own hand—the famous Second Division of the Third Corps, commanded by Major-General Berry. Captain Best soon moved his batteries on a ridge running across the road, and after a short but sanguinary contest the further advance of the enemy was stayed. Of course this disaster compelled the recall of Sickles and Slocum, who had been pursuing their work with remarkable vigor. General Williams' division returned only to find a portion of their works filled with the enemy. Sickles' division could not communicate with the rest of the army at all by the way they advanced, and only at great risk by any other route. This was the position at dark, and it did not look very promising. But our energetic commander was more than equal to the emergency. New dispositions to repair this disaster were at once resolved upon. Communication was at once had with Generals Birney and Whipple, and a night attack ordered, to restore the connection of the lines. General Ward's brigade, of General Birney's division, made the attack at eleven at night, aided by Captain Best's guns, massed on the ridge in front of the enemy. Birney's position was on the extreme left of this new line of battle, but Ward's terrific attack was entirely successful, communication was restored, and in a charge made by the brigade, a portion of the artillery lost by Howard was gallantly retaken by General Hobart Ward. This night attack was the most grand and terrific thing of the war. The moon shone bright, and an enemy could be seen at good musket range. The air was very still, and the roar and reverberation of musketry and artillery past all conception. Malvern Hill was a skirmish compared with this, save in the degree of slaughter. But it was successful,—the enemy were driven back nearly half a mile, and our tired men once more slept on their arms. That night's work was ended.

"Now I come to Sunday. It was perfectly evident, from the position of affairs on Saturday night, that there must be a change of our lines, which would throw the enemy out of our rear and into our front again. It will be seen by what skillful generalship the enemy was fought and checked on front, and flank, and rear, while this was being done. General Reynolds' First Army Corps arrived at United States Ford on Saturday afternoon. It was immediately put into position on our right, which was withdrawn from the plank road to the Ely's Ford turnpike. This line was immediately formed by Generals Reynolds and Meade, the latter's position, on the left, having been relieved by General Howard's Eleventh Corps, which, notwithstanding its disorganized condition, was so far reorganized during the night as to be fit for duty again this morning. They were assigned the position on the left, where it was probable there would be little or no fighting, and were protected by the strong works built the day before by General Meade's corps. Our new line now assumed the shape of a triangle, prolonged at the apex, the right of the line being somewhat longer than the left. As the portion of the line on the right was new, time was necessary to fortify and entrench it, and the work was carried on vigorously by the Fifth and First army corps. It was very evident at daylight this morning that the day would bring forth a terrific battle. We knew that the enemy had been reinforcing his line all night, at the expense, undoubtedly, of the strength of his force on our left. His intention was, evidently, to fight for the possession of the plank road, which it was perfectly apparent he must have, as that portion of it which we then held was subject to the enemy's assaults in front and on both flanks. But the possession of this road was not obtained by the enemy save at our own time, at his severest cost, and after one of the most desperate, tenacious and bloody conflicts, for its short duration, of the whole war. At five o'clock, A. M., the rebels could be plainly seen up the plank road, about a mile and a half from the Chancellor House, which General Hooker still retained as his headquarters, though a shell had gone through it the evening before, and another had cut down a tree directly in front of it. Our line of battle was formed with General Berry's gallant division on the right, General Birney next on the left, General Whipple and General Williams supporting. At half past five, A. M., the advance became engaged in the ravine, just beyond the ridge where Captain Best's guns had made their terrific onslaught the night before, and where they still frowned upon the enemy and threatened his destruction.

"The rattle of musketry soon became a long continued crash, and in a few moments, as battalion after battalion became engaged, the roar surpassed all conception, and indicated that the fight would be one of the most terrible nature. General Berry's division, which had checked the enemy's advance the night before, engaged him again, and if it were possible for them to add more laurels to their fame, then they did it thrice over again. The enemy advanced his infantry in overwhelming numbers, and seemed determined to crush our forces. But the brave men of Sickles and Slocum, who fought their columns with desperate gallantry, held the rebels in check, and inflicted dreadful slaughter among them. General French's division was sent in on the right flank of our line at about seven, A. M., and in a short time a horde of ragged, streaming rebels running down the road, indicated that that portion of the enemy's line had been crushed. At eight o'clock, A. M., General French sent his compliments to General Hooker, with the information that he had charged the enemy and was driving him before him. Sickles maintained the attack upon his line with great endurance. The enemy seemed determined to crush him with the immensity of his forces, and, as subsequently shown from the statements of prisoners, five whole divisions of the rebel army were precipitated upon this portion of the line, for from these five divisions we took during the day an aggregate of over two thousand prisoners. The exploits of our gallant troops in those dark, tangled, gloomy woods may never be brought to light; but they would fill a hundred volumes. It was a deliberate, desperate, hand-to-hand conflict, and the carnage was perfectly frightful. Cool officers say that the dead and wounded of the enemy covered the ground in heaps, and that the rebels seemed utterly regardless of their lives, and literally threw themselves upon the muzzles of our guns. Many desperate charges were made during the fight, particularly by Berry's division. General Berry was himself killed while gallantly fighting his brave men. Mott's brigade made fifteen distinct charges, and captured *seven* stands of colors, the Seventh New Jersey, Colonel Francine, alone capturing four stands of colors and five hundred prisoners. General Couch's Second Army Corps, though only in part present, did excellent work. It was General French who charged and drove the enemy on the flank, and it was the indomitable Hancock who gallantly went to the relief of the hard-pressed Sickles.

"The engagement lasted without the slightest intermission from half past five, A. M., to quarter to nine, A. M., when there was a temporary cessation on our part, occasioned by our getting out of ammunition. We held our position for nearly an hour with the bayonet, and then, being re-supplied, an order was given to fall back to the vicinity of the Chancellor House, which we did in good order. Here the contest was maintained for an hour or more, not so severely as before, but with great havoc to the enemy, and considerable loss to ourselves. The vicinity of the Chancellor House was now the theatre of the fight, and my visits to that spot became less frequent. General Hooker maintained his headquarters there until ten, A. M., when it was set on fire by the enemy's shells, and is now in ruins. Chancellorsville is no longer in existence, having perished with the flame, but Chancellorsville is in history, never to be effaced. Our new line was now so far established as to render it safe to withdraw all our forces on that front, which was accordingly done, and at half past eleven, A. M., the musketry firing ceased. The engagement had lasted six hours, but had been the most terrific of the war. Our artillery had literally slaughtered the enemy, and many of the companies had lost heavily in men themselves, but the guns were

John Sedgwick

From the original painting by Nast, in the possession of the publishers.

Johnson, Fry & Co. Publishers New York.

all saved. The enemy was now no longer in our rear, but had been shoved down directly in our front, and is now directly between us and our forces in Fredericksburg, and we were again in an entrenched and formidably fortified position. The enemy has gained some ground, it is true, but at the sacrifice of the flower of his force, five of his seven divisions having been cut to pieces in the effort, and over two thousand of them have fallen into our hands. Our right wing, under Generals Reynolds and Meade, was not engaged, save the division of General Humphreys, which went into the woods on the enemy's left flank, and fought valiantly under their brilliant leader, until their ammunition was exhausted. During the afternoon the enemy made several attempts to force our lines, particularly at the apex of our position, near the Chancellor House, but Captain Weed had massed a large quantity of artillery in such a position as to repulse with great loss everything placed within its range. The enemy tried several batteries and regiments at that point at different times during the afternoon, and they were literally destroyed by the fire of our guns."

From this detail of operations of General Hooker's army on the right we turn to the movements of the corps of General Sedgwick, which had been left in the vicinity of Fredericksburg. "The going down of the sun on Saturday (May 2d)," writes a correspondent who has given an animated account of these spirited proceedings, "found our troops of the left scattering out on both sides of the river, some two miles below the city. The Flying division had advanced to the old Richmond road. General Burk's lay back, nearer to the river. General Howe's and General Newton's forces were on the plain opposite. Under cover of night Generals Howe and Newton crossed over the river. About two o'clock in the morning orders came to move at once on the enemy. The greater portion of the forces moved quietly up the Richmond road and winding down through the gully just below the city reached the outskirts of Fredericksburg between four and five o'clock. Generals Howe's and Newton's divisions were in the advance, then followed the 'flying division,' or 'light brigade,' and General Brooks' forces were extended on the extreme left. Meantime companies of the Fiftieth New York engineers had constructed pontoon bridges directly across to the city, both above and below the Lacey House, and the Forty-second New York, Nineteenth and Twentieth Massachusetts, Fifty-ninth New York and the One Hundred and Twenty-seventh Pennsylvania, constituting Hall's—Dana's old brigade —Second corps, together with three other regiments, including the Second New York and Fifteenth Massachusetts, crossed on the upper bridge and deployed out along the bank above the city. Batteries were also brought up and planted close to the city. The object of this movement to the city was to storm the first line of rebel earthworks above, which General Sumner attempted in vain to take last December. This line of earthworks is about one-third of a mile from the city, extending close along the monument erected to Mary, the mother of Washington, which is erected on a sort of natural bluff. Beneath runs the famous stone wall and a road leading off in the direction of Richmond. Between this road and the city is an open plain commanded by the rebel works. Across this plain and over the stone wall the charging column had to advance before reaching the fortified bluff. About half past five o'clock in the morning Cochrane's old brigade (Newton's division), now commanded by Colonel Shaler, and led by him in person, charged over the plain, and succeeded in nearly reaching the stone wall, but were obliged to fall back. The Sixty-second New York, it is said, endeavored to storm the works before this hour of the morning. The rebels kept up a constant fire of musketry from behind earthworks, buildings and rifle pits, while the guns from above rained down a storm of grape and canister on the troops. General Brooks' division, which was on the extreme left, suffered least, though fired at the most, owing to the fact of most of the enemy's missiles passing over the heads of the troops. It was now eleven o'clock, continuous fighting had been going on for full six hours, and the rebels still held their works. General Sedgwick now determined on having the 'light brigade' charge the heights. Colonel Benham commanding moved his forces along under the protection of abandoned earthworks and the hill-side formed by the sloping down of the plain near the city, until he had arrived directly in front of the most formidable position, known as the "Slaughter pen." Knapsacks and any article of clothing which might impede their rapid movement were cast aside by the men, and they were deployed out in the following order: one half of the Fifth Wisconsin, Colonel Allen, as skirmish line; Thirty-first New York, Colonel Jones, on the left; Sixth Maine, Lieutenant-Colonel Harris commanding, and the remaining portion of the Fifth in the rear of, and supporting the Thirty-first at the same time. At the same time a force consisting of the Forty-third New York and Sixty-first Pennsylvania, and one or two other regiments, were sent up the road at the right of the stone wall. Going on to the regiments of the Light Brigade, prepared for a charge were the Thirty-sixth New York and Seventh Massachusetts, and still further on other regiments. At twenty minutes past eleven the lion-hearted men rose from their feet. Every one of the thousand spectators on the hills in the rear held their breath in terrible suspense, expecting to see them all the next moment prostrate in the dust. 'Forward!' cried the General, and they dashed forward on the open plain, when instantly there was poured upon them a most terrific discharge of grape and canister. Many lay dead, but not one faltered. Full four hundred yards must be passed over before gaining the stone wall. As they press forward, delivering the battle-cheer, which is heard above the roar of artillery, the rebel guns further to the left are turned upon them. But they falter not. A moment more they have reached the stone wall, scaled its sides, are clambering the green bank of the bluff, and precisely as the city clock struck, they rush over the embrasure of the rebel guns and the Heights are ours. The enemy, with the exception of the cannoneers, fled in confusion, secreting themselves in the houses, woods and wherever a place of concealment was afforded. The guns captured proved to be the Washington Artillery, the battery so highly complimented by General Lee in his report of the last battle of Fredericksburg, and which has figured, more or less, since the outbreak of the rebellion. The Sixth Maine were the first regiment to reach the scene. Lieutenant-Colonel Harris, with unparalleled bravery, rushed right up to the mouth of one as it was belching away, and through the mist and smoke his form could just be discerned as he cheered his men forward. He, together with Captain Furlong, were the first to lay hold of the rebel pieces. The rebels succeeded in getting one gun away to some distance, when the force which had gone round to flank the battery perceived it, and immediately starting in hot pursuit, captured it with seventy-five prisoners. A wagon train was ahead which they might have secured, had they not received orders to proceed no further. On the Washington Artillery being surrendered, the other batteries to the right did not make much resistance, but fled hastily before our charging forces. The rebels on the extreme left, in front of the Barnard House, retreated up the hills when we obtained possession of the city.

"The various divisions of the corps (Sixth, General Sedgwick's) moved rapidly forward up the Gordonsville turnpike, to the distance of four miles, skirmishing all the way, where they found the enemy in force, when another battle ensued, in which Brooks', Newton's, and the Flying division, were engaged—the first suffering severely. The rebels were in a woods, and, as we advanced to it, opened a galling fire. Russell's brigade, composed of the 95th and the 117th Pennsylvania, and 121st New York, made a charge, and suffered severely, the Ninety-fifth being almost annihilated. While the battle was progressing, the enemy suddenly commenced firing on our left to the rear, and Brooks' division was obliged to change front. The battle lasted till dark without any decisive results being obtained on either side. During the night the woods took fire, and it is feared that many of the wounded on both sides perished in the flames. Monday morning the rebels suddenly made their appearance on the hills to the left of Fredericksburg, and coming down rapidly, occupied the city, thus getting in the rear of the corps. Most of the supply trains, ambulances, mules and soldiers in the vicinity were taken. One whole corps of the enemy came down and forming in line of battle immediately marched after the corps. The only way of retreat lay by Brooks' Ford, five miles above the city. General Sedgwick was signaled from the opposite side of the river of the condition of affairs, and immediately turning about, formed a line of battle, holding the rebels in check, and working down toward the ford. The lines of battle remained in this condition until about the middle of the day, when the rebels attacked us, and were gallantly repulsed—Howe's division capturing three hundred prisoners. The rebel reinforcements had fought none, while our troops had been fighting, more or less, since the previous Tuesday night. For a time it was feared that the corps could not make communication at Banks' Ford, and that the whole of it must be captured. But by noon, a connection was made, and General Sedgwick sent for supplies. Meantime, the wounded in Fredericksburg were being taken across the pontoons to this side, all of them being got away on the sudden appearance of the enemy on the outskirts above. Skirmishing occurred along the whole line until half-past five o'clock in the evening, when the rebels attacked us from two ways. The Union forces were at the time arrayed in an arc, both wings resting on the river, the right at Banks' Ford. We were arranged in two lines of battle. The enemy attacking the Second division of the Second corps and Howe's at first approaching them diagonally from Fredericksburg and the country directly beyond. General Mills' brigade, consisting of the Thirty-third New York, Seventy-seventh New York, Twentieth New York, Forty-ninth New York, together with the Vermont brigade and Seventh Maine, bore the brunt of the charge, repulsing the enemy handsomely. The Vermont brigade were on the left of General Mills. General Mills' brigade and other troops made a counter charge; but reinforcements coming up to the enemy, we were not able to drive them. The other lines of battle were now attacked by overwhelming numbers and obliged to fall back to the river. Early the next morning (Tuesday, May 5th) the corps succeeded in crossing the river."* The retreat which had been commenced by General Sedgwick's corps was continued

* Correspondence (D. W. Judd) of the *New York Times*, May 6–8, 1863.

by the main army. A heavy rain storm which had set in early on Tuesday morning, causing a sudden rise of the Rappahannock, with the loss of the advantageous position by the disaster to the corps on the right, compelled General Hooker to withdraw his forces across the river. The movement was accomplished with method and success. New roads were opened, the trains and reserve artillery sent back, and in the night the troops crossed on the pontoon bridges constructed by the efficient engineer corps under General Benham. Couch's first Corps was in the advance, General Meade's corps remained in the entrenchments to the last and covered the retreat. On Wednesday the army of the Potomac was again at its old quarters at Falmouth.

The cavaly raid of General Stoneman which had been sent out to cut the enemy's communication was attended with success. Delayed by a series of rain storms for a fortnight, and thus losing the opportunity of anticipating the concentration of the enemy's forces, the entire expedition, 2700 picked men, with a light battery of six pieces, crossed the river at Kelly's Ford on the 29th. "At the time of General Stoneman's crossing, General Averill"—we follow the summary of the movement by one who accompanied it—"started with a column along the end of the Orange and Alexandria Railroad, with the intention of driving Lee and Hampton, who were in that vicinity, to Culpepper and Gordonsville, thus clearing the way for General Stoneman's body of cavalry, who were to accomplish the real objects of the expedition. General Stoneman crossed the Rappahannock at two places below where General Averill crossed, and advanced on the Shepherdsburg road. Sending out a party to reconnoiter toward Shepherdsburg, they came upon the rear pickets of the enemy, who were in force between Stevensburg and the railroad, with General Averill in front: the nature of General Stoneman's expedition did not allow of his remaining there to fight, as to seek a battle would prevent the accomplishment of his designs; he therefore moved on to Raccoon Ford upon the advance. Reaching this place, they found it defended by infantry and artillery. A detachment was therefore sent to cross the Rappahannock, at a point some distance below Raccoon Ford, and then to attack the enemy in the flank and rear. This was successfully accomplished, and the main body crossed safely at Raccoon Ford. The command then proceeded down the direct road to Louisa Courthouse, sending out parties along every intersecting road to destroy bridges and telegraph wires, and to obtain forage and provisions. The bridges over unfordable streams, on the direct road, were left to be guarded by detachments, in case they were required as a line of retreat. Reaching Louisa Courthouse, on the line of the Virginia Central Railroad, expeditions were sent out along the road in either directions to destroy the road, telegraphs, burn the water-tanks, depots, and railroad tires. The expedition toward Gordonsville encountered a force of the enemy, who, by this time, had been driven from Culpepper and Gordonsville by Averill, who did not, however, effect a junction with Stoneman as directed. The enemy were in such force that reinforcements were sent out, and the rebels were driven back to Gordonsville. The destruction of the road was completed, and a party proceeded to tear up the railroad between Gordonsville and Charlottesville. Parties were also sent out from Louisa Courthouse to destroy the bridges over the North Anna River. The command then proceeded through Sauceyville, and rendezvoused at Thompson's Crossroads.

"From there three expeditions were sent out—one along the South Anna River, to destroy the bridges across this unfordable stream; another to destroy the Fredericksburg and Richmond Railroad from Ashland down; also the railroad from Richmond to Hanover Courthouse, to get as near Richmond as possible, and, if practicable, to cross over to Pamunky River, destroying such bridges as it was practicable to destroy, and then to proceed down the Peninsula to West Point; the third expedition was to strike the James River at Columbia, break the locks of the canal, and destroy the bridges as far down the river as might be. This expedition was to cross a small force over the James, at Carterville, and pass down and destroy the railroad bridge on the Richmond and Lynchburg Road, over the Appomattux River. This expedition was not so successful as the others, too much time being expended in an attempt to destroy a stone bridge over which the acqueducts passed. The other expeditions were perfectly successful, tearing up the track for thirty miles, destroying bridges on the Mattapony and Pamunky rivers, and have since reached West Point. Gathering the balance of his force together at Tomson's Cross Roads, General Stoneman prepared to return. By this time, Stuart, Lee and Hampton were in pursuit of the audacious party. The forces of the latter two were driven in the direction of Charlottesville, and Stuart was drawn off in the direction of Guiney's Station by an apparent diversion of our forces in that direction. Having thus separated Stuart's command, General Stoneman started on his return between the two bodies, along the same route he went out. His scouting party encountered the enemy's infantry pickets on the road to Spottsylvania Courthouse, but the command succeeded in safely recrossing the Rapidan and Rappahannock Rivers, swimming the latter. The feat of getting the artillery across the latter stream, the horses swimming and drawing the guns, is certainly worthy of notice. Only one man was lost by drowning. The success of the whole expedition was mainly due to the deception practiced upon the inhabitants. The force was everywhere magnified, and, by scattering in small parties, the delusion was completed by dividing the command into different expeditions. They were enabled to supply themselves with forage and provisions, and thus live upon the country through which they passed. Their pack-mules were sent back the first day out, and officers and men only carried what they could upon their horses. For two days and three nights they never built a fire. In many places they camped as though intending to remain, giving out that they were merely the advance guard of the main army. With telegraphic communication destroyed, and railroads interrupted, this was only too readily believed; the inhabitants were paroled and sent to Richmond. The officers captured were detained as prisoners; among these was Major Johnston of General Stuart's staff. At one place two large houses were found filled with hams. What of this was not needed was destroyed. Twelve hundred hogsheads of tobacco were also captured, most of which were burned. Such horses as could be found were taken, and those worn out by the march were left in their places. It is estimated that the total number of miles travelled by the different expeditions will exceed one thousand."* The portion of the expedition, led by Colonel Kilpatrick, a young cavalry officer and graduate of West Point, who had on several previous occasions distinguished himself in the Virginia campaigns, penetrated within the lines of the enemy's works at Richmond. His brief report of the affair to General Halleck is a model of a soldier's dispatch: "I have the honor to report," says he, "that, by direction of Major General Stoneman, I left Louisa Courthouse on the morning of the third inst.,

* Correspondence *New York Tribune,* May 11, 1863.

with one regiment (the Harris Light cavalry) of my brigade; reached Hungary, on the Fredericksburg Railroad, at daylight on the morning of the fourth, destroyed the depot, telegraph wires and railroad for several miles; passed over to the Brook turnpike; drove in the rebel pickets down the pike, across the Brook; charged a battery and forced it to retire to within two miles of the city of Richmond; captured Lieutenant Brown, Aid-de-Camp to General Winder, and eleven men within the fortifications; passed down to the left to the Meadow Bridge, on the Chickahominy which I burned; ran a train of cars into the river; retired to Hanovertown, on the Peninsula; crossed and destroyed the ferry just in time to check the advance of a pursuing cavalry force; burned a train of thirty wagons, loaded with bacon; captured thirteen prisoners, and encamped for the night five miles from the river. I resumed my march at one A. M. of the fifth; surprised a force of three hundred cavalry at Aylett's; captured two officers and thirty-three men; burned fifty-six wagons and the depot, containing upwards of twenty thousand barrels of corn and wheat, quanties of clothing and commissary stores, and safely crossed the Mattapony and destroyed the ferry again, just in time to escape the advance of the rebel cavalry pursuit. Late in the evening I destroyed a third wagon train and depot, a few miles above and west of Tappahannock, on the Rappahannock, and from that point made a forced march of twenty miles, being closely followed by a superior force of cavalry, supposed to be a portion of Stuart's, from the fact that we captured prisoners from the First, Fifth and Tenth Virginia cavalry. At sundown I discovered a force of cavalry drawn up in line of battle above King and Queen Courthouse. The strength was unknown, but I at once advanced to the attack, only, however, to discover that they were friends—a portion of the Twelfth Illinois cavalry, who had become separated from the command of Lieutenant-Colonel Davis, of the same regiment. At ten A. M., on the seventh, I found safety and rest under our brave old flag, within our lines at Gloucester Point. The raid and march about the entire rebel army, a march of nearly two hundred miles, has been made in less than five days, with a loss of one officer and thirty-seven men, having captured and paroled upward of 300 men."* On his return to the north bank of the Rappahannock, on the sixth, General Hooker issued the following order to his troops: "The Major-General commanding tenders to this army his congratulations on its achievements of the last seven days. If it has not accomplished all that was expected, the reasons are well known to the army. It is sufficient to say they were of a character not to be foreseen or prevented by human sagacity or resources. In withdrawing from the south bank of the Rappahannock before delivering a general battle to our adversaries, the army has given renewed evidence of its confidence in itself and its fidelity to the principles it represents. In fighting at a disadvantage we would have been recreant to our trust, to ourselves, our cause, and our country. Profoundly loyal, and conscious of its strength, the Army of the Potomac will give or decline battle whenever its interest or honor may demand. It will also be the guardian of its own history and its own arms. By our celerity and secrecy of movements, our advance and passage of the rivers was undisputed, and on our withdrawal not a rebel returned to follow. The events of the last week may swell with pride the hearts of every officer and soldier of this army. We have addel new laurels to its former

* J. Kilpatrick, Colonel-Commanding First Brigade, Third Division Cavalry, to Major-General Halleck, Yorktown, Va., May 8th, 1863.

renown. We have made long marches, crossed rivers, surprised the enemy in his intrenchments, and whenever we have fought we have inflicted heavier blows than we have received. We have taken from the enemy five thousand prisoners and fifteen colors, captured and brought off seven pieces of artillery, and placed *hors du combat* eighteen thousand of his chosen troops. We have destroyed his depots filled with vast amounts of stores, damaged his communications, captured prisoners within the fortifications of his capital, and filled his country with fear and consternation. We have no other regret than that caused by the loss of our brave companions, and in this we are consoled by the conviction that they have fallen in the holiest cause ever submitted to the arbitrament of battle."

In a dispatch to President Davis, dated on the third, at Milford, General Lee thus announced his successes on the field. "Yesterday General Jackson penetrated to the rear of the enemy, and drove him from all his positions from the Wilderness to within one mile of Chancellorsville. He was engaged at the same time in front by two of Longstreet's divisions. Many prisoners were taken, and the enemy's loss in killed and wounded is large. This morning the battle was renewed. He was dislodged from all his positions around Chancellorsville, and driven back toward the Rappahannock, over which he is now retreating. We have again to thank Almighty God for a great victory. I regret to state that General Paxton was killed, General Jackson severely, and Generals Heth and A. P. Hill slightly wounded." This was followed on the seventh by a congratulatory address from General Lee to his army: "With heartfelt gratification, the General commanding expresses to the army his sense of the heroic conduct displayed by officers and men during the arduous operations in which they have just been engaged. Under trying vicissitudes of heat and storm you attacked the enemy, strongly intrenched in the depths of a tangled wilderness, and again on the hills of Fredericksburg, fifteen miles distant, and by the valor that has triumphed on so many fields, forced him once more to seek safety beyond the Rappahannock. While this glorious victory entitles you to the praise and gratitude of the nation, we are especially called upon to return our grateful thanks to the only Giver of victory for the signal deliverance He has wrought. It is, therefore, earnestly recommended that the troops unite on Sunday next in ascribing to the Lord of Hosts the glory due his name. Let us not forget in our rejoicing the brave soldiers who have fallen in defence of their country; and, while we mourn their loss, let us resolve to emulate their noble example. The army and the country alike lament the absence for a time of one to whose bravery, energy and skill they are so much indebted for success. The following letter from the President of the Confederate States is communicated to the army as an expression of his appreciation of its success:

"'I have received your dispatch, and reverently unite with you in giving praise to God for the success with which He has crowned our arms. In the name of the people, I offer my cordial thanks to yourself and the troops under your command, for this addition to the unprecedented series of great victories which your army has achieved. The universal rejoicing produced by this happy result will be mingled with a general regret for the good and the brave who are numbered among the killed and wounded.'"

Of the Union losses in this movement to Chancellorsville no exact official returns have as yet been given to the public. An estimate of the day gives the result, exclusive of the loss in Sedgwick's corps, at over 1,500 killed, 9,000 wounded, and about 2,500 prisoners, showing, if the calculation be correct, an unusally large proportion of wounded. General Berry was the most conspicuous of the officers who fall in the engagement. Essentially a man of the people, a representative of the industry and energy of the inhabitants of his native state of Maine, he had risen by his own exertions in the community to posts of honorable distinction in civil and military life and with ardent patriotism had devoted his life to the service of his country.

The enemy, who suffered heavily in casualties to officers, mourned an irreparable loss in General Jackson, whose enthusiasm as a soldier and practical ability in the field had so often on the bloody ground of Virginia turned the tide of battle in favor of the Confederates. The peculiar circumstances of his fall on the field and the incidents of his death-bed were thus related in the *Richmond Enquirer* of May 13th: "General Jackson having gone some distance in front of the line of skirmishers on Saturday evening (the 2d), was returning about eight o'clock, attended by his staff and part of his couriers. The cavalcade was in the darkness of the night mistaken for a body of the enemy's cavalry, and fired upon by a regiment of his own corps. He was struck by three balls, one through the left arm, two inches below the shoulder joint, shattering the bone and severing the chief artery; another ball passed through the same arm between the elbow and the wrist, making its exit through the palm of the hand; a third ball entered the palm of the right hand about its middle, passing through, and broke two bones. He was wounded on the plank road, about fifty yards in advance of the enemy. He fell from his horse, and was caught by Captain Wormley, to whom he remarked, "All my wounds are by own men." He had given orders to fire at anything coming up the road, before he left the lines. The enemy's skirmishers appeared ahead of him, and he turned to ride back. Just then some one cried out, "Cavalry, charge!" and immediately the regiment fired. The whole party broke forward to ride through our line to escape the fire. Captain Boswell was killed, and carried through the line by his horse, and fell among our own men. Colonel Couchfield, chief of staff, was wounded by his side. Two couriers were killed. Major Pendleton, Lieutenants Morrison and Smith, escaped uninjured. General Jackson was immediately placed on a litter and started for the rear. The firing attracted the attention of the enemy, and was resumed by both lines. One litter-bearer was shot down, and the General fell from the shoulders of the men, receiving a severe contusion, adding to the injury of the arm, and injuring his side severely. The enemy's fire of artillery on this point was terrible. General Jackson was left for five minutes, until the fire slackened; then placed in an ambulance, and carried to the field hospital at Wilderness Run. He lost a large amount of blood, and at one time told Dr. McGuire he thought he was dying, and would have bled to death, but a tourniquet was immediately applied. For two hours he was near pulseless from the shock. As he was being carried from the field, frequent inquiries were made by the soldiers, 'Who have you there?' He told the Doctor, 'Do not tell the troops I am wounded.'

"After the reaction, a consultation was held between Drs. Black, Coleman, Walls and McGuire, and amputation was decided upon. He was asked, 'If we find amputation necessary, shall it be done at once?' He replied, 'Yes, certainly, Dr. McGuire — do for me whatever you think is right.' The operation was performed while he was under the influence of chloroform, and was borne well. He slept on Sunday morning, was cheerful, and in every way was doing well. He sent for Mrs. Jackson, asked minutely about the battle, spoke cheerfully of the result, and said: 'If I had not been wounded, or had an hour more of daylight, I would have cut off the enemy from the road to the United States Ford, and we would have had them entirely surrounded, and they would have been obliged to surrender, or cut their way out. They had no other alternative. My troops sometimes may fail in driving the enemy from a position, but the enemy always fail to drive my men from a position.' This was said smilingly. He complained this day of the fall from the litter, although no contusion or abrasion was apparent as the result of the fall. He did not complain of his wounds; never spoke of them unless asked. On Sunday evening he slept well. On Monday he was carried to Chancellor's house, near Guinney's depot. He was cheerful; talked about the battle, gallant bearing of General Rhodes, and said that his Major-General's commission ought to date from Saturday, the grand charge of his old Stonewall brigade, of which he had heard; asked after all his officers; during the day talked more than usual, and said: 'Men who live through this war will be proud to say, "I was one of the Stonewall brigade," to their children.' He insisted that the term Stonewall belonged to them, and not to him. During the ride to Guinney's he complained greatly of heat, and besides wet applications to his wounds, begged that a wet cloth be applied to his stomach, which was done, greatly to his relief, as he expressed it. He slept well on Monday night, and eat with relish the next morning. On Tuesday his wounds were doing very well. He asked, 'Can you tell me, from the appearance of my wounds, how long I will be kept from the field?' He was greatly satisfied when told they were doing remarkably well. He did not complain of any pain in his side, and wanted to see the members of his staff, but was advised not. On Wednesday his wounds looked remarkably well. He expected to go to Richmond this day, but was prevented by rain. This night, while his surgeon, who had slept none for three nights, was asleep, he complained of nausea, and ordered his boy, Jim, to place a wet towel over his stomach. This was done. About daylight the surgeon was awakened by the boy saying, 'The General is in great pain.' The pain was in the right side, and due to incipient pneumonia and some nervousness, which he himself attributed to the fall from the litter. On Thursday Mrs. Jackson arrived, greatly to his joy and satisfaction, and she faithfully nursed him to the end. By Thursday evening all pain had ceased. He suffered greatly from prostration. On Friday he suffered no pain, but prostration increased. On Sunday morning, when it was apparent that he was rapidly sinking, Mrs. Jackson was informed of his condition. She then had free and full converse with him, and told him he was going to die. He said: 'Very good; very good. It is all right.' He had previously said: 'I consider these wounds a blessing. They were given me for some good and wise purpose. I would not part with them if I could.' He asked of Major Pendleton: 'Who is preaching at headquarters to-day?' He sent messages to all the Generals. He expressed a wish to be buried in Lexington, in the valley of Virginia. During delirium his mind reverted to the battlefield, and he sent orders to General A. P. Hill to prepare for action, and to Major Hawks, his commissary, and to the surgeons. He frequently expressed to his aids his wish that Major-General Ewell should be ordered to command his corps."

General Lee announced the death of General Jackson to the army in a general order on the 11th: "With deep grief the Commanding-General announces the death of Lieutenant-General T. J. Jackson, who expired on the 10th inst., at 3.15, P. M. The daring skill and energy of this great and good soldier, by the decree of an all-wise Providence, are now lost to us; but while we mourn his death, we feel that his spirit still lives, and will inspire the whole army with his indomitable courage and unshaken confidence in God as our hope and strength. Let his name be a watchword to his corps, who have followed him to victory on so many fields. Let the officers and soldiers imitate his invincible determination to do everything in the defence of our beloved country."

CHAPTER LXXXVIII.

GENERAL GRANT'S OPERATIONS IN MISSISSIPPI.—SIEGE OF VICKSBURG, JANUARY—JULY, 1863.

When General McClernand, as previously narrated,* at the beginning of January, took command of the "Army of the Mississippi," after the unsuccessful movement upon Vicksburg, his first proceeding was to direct the forces of which he had been placed in charge by General Grant, against Fort Hindman, an important stronghold of the enemy on the Arkansas river, fifty miles above its mouth. Situated at a bend of the stream, this formidable work,—a regularly constructed square bastioned fort, the sides three hundred feet in length, with casemates and surrounded by a wide and deep ditch, mounting eleven guns, including three Columbiads and four Parrotts, with outer defences,—effectually controlled the passage of the river, protected Little Rock, the capital of the State, about a hundred miles above, and sheltered Post Arkansas, the village at which it was built, and the surrounding fertile country. With such advantages it afforded a convenient base of operations for marauding attacks on the Union transports on the Mississippi, and its reduction became a necessary preliminary to the further necessarily protracted movements before Vicksburg. A joint military and naval expedition was led against the work. The land forces under General McClernand consisted of the two corps of his army under Generals Morgan and Sherman, comprising ten brigades of Western troops with artillery and cavalry; while Rear-Admiral David D. Porter detailed for the purpose and commanded in person the three ironclads Louisville, Baron de Kalb and Cincinnati, with all the light draft gunboats of the fleet.

On the 9th of January the naval vessels and transports had ascended the river, and a landing of the troops was effected on the left bank, about four miles below the fort. A portion of the levee at right angles with the river within a mile and a half of the work constituted an outer line of defence, which was further protected by earthworks and rifle-pits. The enemy, however, abandoning the levee, an attempt was made on the 10th to push a body of troops into the interior to make a detour and surround the fort. This was found to be impracticable in consequence of a swamp which lay in the way and it was determined to advance directly to the attack by the road along the river. The ironclads meanwhile were sent up towards the fort to try the range of their guns, while one of the

* Chapter lxxxii.

gunboats cleared out the rifle-pits in front of the troops. The fleet in the afternoon gallantly opened a destructive fire upon the fort at the distance of four hundred yards. Much damage was done to the work, and numbers of the artillery horses in and about were killed. The light draft ironclad Rattler in an enfilading fire was injured in the hull, a heavy shell raking the vessel from stem to stern. The previous night a brigade was landed on the opposite bank, took position and planted a battery above the fort, thus cutting off the escape of the enemy or their reinforcement by water. Early in the afternoon of the next day, the 11th, the joint forces advanced to the grand attack. The troops of both of the army corps were well handled and brought in face of the enemy within two hundred yards of the fort. In approaching the works General Hovey was wounded by the fragment of a shell and the horse of General Thayer was shot under him. The batteries rendered important service in co-operation with the fleet, which was again brought into close quarters with the fort. "I ordered up," says Admiral Porter, "the ironclads, with directions for the Lexington to join in when the former became engaged, and for the frailer vessels to haul up in the smoke and do the best they could. The Rattler, Lieutenant-Commanding Smith, and the Guide, Lieutenant-Commanding Woodworth, did good execution with their shrapnel, and when an opportunity occurred I made them push through by the fort again, also, the ram Monarch, Colonel Charles Ellet; and they proceeded rapidly up the river to cut off the enemy's retreat by the only way he had to get off. By this time all the guns in the fort were completely silenced by the Louisville, Lieutenant-Commanding E. R. Owen, Baron de Kalb, and Cincinnati, and I ordered the Black Hawk up for the purpose of boarding it in front. Being unmanageable, she had to be kept up the narrow stream, and I took in a regiment from the opposite side to try and take it by assault. As I rounded to, to do so, and the gunboats commenced firing rapidly, knocking everything to pieces, the enemy held out a white flag, and I ordered the firing to cease. The army then entered and took possession. Colonel Dunnington, the commander of the fort, sent for me and surrendered to me in person. General Churchill, of the rebel army, surrendered to the military commander. Our army had almost surrounded the fort, and would no doubt have carried it with ease. They enfiladed it with rifled field-pieces, which did much damage to the houses and light work, leaving their mark in all directions."

General McClernand had ordered an assault, and the troops were on all hands pressing eagerly to its execution, when the fort surrendered after three hours and a half hard fighting. The victory was complete. Seven stands of colors, seventeen pieces of cannon of all sorts, three thousand stands of small arms and a vast quantity of ammunition and military and commissary stores were captured. Five thousand prisoners surrendered. The Union loss, as stated by General McClernand, was 129 killed, 831 wounded and 17 missing; that of the enemy in proportion to his numbers, notwithstanding his defences, was much larger. The loss of the fleet was slight. The *Louisville* reported one killed and ten wounded, ten mortally; the *De Kalb* two killed and fifteen wounded. Having forwarded the prisoners of war to St. Louis, and destroyed the enemy's defences, General McClernand, in pursuance of the orders of General Grant, re-embarked his force on the 17th, and sailed for Milliken's Bend.* An expedition about

* Official Reports. Major General McClernand to Lieutenant-Colonel J. A. Rawlins, A. A. G., Dept. of the Tennessee, steamer Tigress, Mississippi river, January 20th,

the same time under General Gorman ascended the White river to Duvall's Bluff, found the enemy's posts deserted, and was prevented following up its advantages as contemplated in an overland attack upon Little Rock by the state of the intermediate country, the land having been flooded by heavy rains, rendering cavalry and artillery movements impracticable.

Milliken's Bend, some fifteen miles above Vicksburg on the Louisiana shore, and the region below to the entrance to the canal commenced the previous season with the view of cutting a communication for the Mississippi across the peninsula, fronting the city, became now the theatre of operations of the army of the Mississippi. General McClernand's force assembled there, the gunboats dropped down to the station, additional troops from Cairo were landed, and on the 28th of January General Grant arrived and took command of the entire army which he was destined to conduct through many scenes of extraordinary labor and peril, through the vicissitudes of numerous conflicts to a triumphant conclusion. It being at the outset the opinion of General Grant "that Vicksburg could only be turned from the south side," to secure an approach in that direction, the first effort of the troops was given to change the course of the river by a modification and enlargement of the old canal. It was expected that by making an entrance some five hundred feet further up the stream the current of the river would be diverted directly into it and the operation be greatly facilitated; while the channel was to be deepened and widened by the spade. Meanwhile it was an object of the first importance to cut off the rebel communication on the river between Vicksburg and Fort Hudson, which General Banks with the fleet of Admiral Farragut was besieging, and to check the receipt of supplies to the confederates from Texas. For this purpose several vessels of the fleet were sent past Vicksburg, a truly desperate undertaking considering the natural defences of the river, the Confederate gunboats to be met, and the extended line of batteries which bristled at every point for the protection of the city. The first adventure of this kind was successfully accomplished by the wooden steam-ram, Queen of the West, Captain Sutherland. It was this vessel, it will be remembered, which was engaged in the remarkable attempt in the previous July to destroy the Arkansas under the guns of the town. The Commander of the ram fleet, Colonel C. R. Ellet, was on the present occasion on board of the Queen, and in his report to Admiral Porter gives the following account of his adventure: "In compliance with your instructions," says he, writing from below Vicksburg on the after part of the second February, "I started on the Queen of the West at three and a half o'clock this morning to pass the batteries at Vicksburg, and sink the rebel steamer lying before that city. I discovered immediately on starting that the change of the wheel from its former position to the narrow space behind the Queen's bulwarks did not permit the boat to be hauled with sufficient accuracy. An hour or more was spent in re-arranging the apparatus, and when we finally rounded the point, the sun had risen, and any advantage which would have resulted from the darkness was lost to us. The rebels opened a heavy fire upon us as we neared the city, but we were only struck three times before reaching the steamer. She was lying in nearly the same position that the Arkansas occupied when General Ellet ran the Queen into her on a former occasion. The same causes which prevented the destruction of the Arkansas, then saved the City of Vicksburg this morning. Her position was such that

1863; Rear Admiral David D. Porter, to the Hon. Gideon Welles. Arkansas Post, January 11th, 1863.

if we had run obliquely into her as we came down, the bow of the Queen would inevitably have glanced. We were compelled to partially round in order to strike. The consequence was that at the very moment of collision, the current, very rapid and strong at this point, caught the stern of my boat, and, acting on her bow as a pivot, swung her round so rapidly that nearly all her momentum was lost. I had anticipated this, and therefore caused the starboard bow gun to be shotted with three of the incendiary projectiles recommended in your orders. As we swung around, Sergeant J. H. Campbell, detailed for that purpose, fired this gun. A 64-pound shell crushed through the barricade just before he reached the spot, but he did not hesitate. The discharge took place at exactly the right moment, and set the rebel steamer in flames, which they subsequently succeeded in extinguishing. At this moment one of the enemy's shells set the cotton near the starboard wheel on fire, while the discharge of our own gun ignited that portion which was on the bow. The flames spread rapidly and the dense smoke rolled into the engine-room suffocated the engineers. I saw that if I attempted to run into the City of Vicksburg again my boat would certainly be burned. I ordered her to be headed down stream and ordered every man to extinguish the flames. After much exertion we finally put the fire out by cutting the burning bales loose. The enemy of course were not idle. We were struck twelve times, and though the cabin door was knocked to pieces no material injury to the boat or to those on board was inflicted. About two regiments of rebel sharpshooters in rifle pits kept up a continual fire, but did no damage. The Queen was struck twice in the hull, but above the water-line. One of our guns was dismounted and ruined. I can only speak in the highest terms of the conduct of every man on board. All behaved with cool, determined courage." The Queen at once proceeded down the river, captured three rebel steamers laden with provisions, and took a number of prisoners, including several officers. She then returned to her station below Vicksburg where she was presently supplied with coal by a barge, which, with the tender De Soto, ran by the rebel batteries unperceived by the sentinels. On the night of the thirteenth, the ironclad gunboat Indianola, with two coal-barges, under cover of a dark, foggy night, succeeded in passing the batteries in spite of their persistent and heavy fire. In the meantime the Queen of the West had proceeded on an expedition up Red River, of much interest, ending with her loss, the details of which are thus vividly narrated in a report to Admiral Porter by Colonel Ellet, on his return to his station below Vicksburg. "I have the honor," says he, "to report to you that I left the landing below Vicksburg, in obedience to your written instructions, on the night of the tenth instant, taking with me the De Soto and coal-barge, and proceeded down the river. We passed Warrenton without interruption, and reached Red River the following evening. I destroyed, as you directed, the skiffs and flat-boats along either shore. I ascended Red River on the morning of the twelfth as far as the mouth of the Atchafalaya. Leaving the De Soto and coal-barge in a secure position, I proceeded down the stream six miles from its mouth. I met a train of army wagons returning from Simmsport. I landed and destroyed them. On reaching Simmsport, I learned that two rebel steamboats had just left, taking with them the troops and artillery stationed at that point. They had left on the bank seventy barrels of Government beef, which I broke up and rolled into the river. I pursued another train of wagons for some distance, but they retreated into the swamps and escaped. One of their wagons, loaded with ammunition and stores, fell into our hands and was destroyed. On her return at night, a party of overseers and other civilians fired into the Queen from behind a levee, and immediately fled under cover of the darkness. First Master J. D. Thompson, a gallant and efficient officer, was shot through the knee. Anchoring at the mouth of the Atchafalaya, I waited until morning, and then returned to the spot from which we had been attacked. All the buildings on three large adjoining plantations were burned by my order. I started up the Red River the same day, and reached Black River by night. On the morning of the fourteenth, when about fifteen miles above the mouth of Black River, a steamboat came suddenly around a sharp bend in the river, and was captured before she could escape. She proved to be the Era, No. 5, laden with forty-five hundred bushels of corn. She had on board two rebel lieutenants and fourteen privates. The latter I at once paroled and set ashore.

"Hearing of three very large boats lying at Gordon's Landing, thirty miles above, I decided on making an effort to capture them, intending to return if I should find the battery at that point too strong, and ascend the Washita. I left the Era and coal-barge in charge of a guard. We reached the bend just below Gordon's Landing before dusk, the dense smoke of several boats, rapidly firing up, could be seen over the tops of the trees as we approached. I ordered the pilot to proceed very slowly, and merely show the bow of the Queen around the point. From the sharp bend which the river makes at this place there was no apparent difficulty in withdrawing out of the range of the enemy's guns, whenever it might be desired. The rebels opened upon us with four 32-pounders the moment we came in sight. Their guns were in a fine position, and at the third shot I ordered Mr. Garvey, the pilot, to back the Queen out. Instead of doing so he ran her aground on the right-hand shore. The position at once became a very hot one. Sixty yards below we would have been in no danger. As it was, the enemy's shot struck us nearly every time. The Chief Engineer had hardly reported to me that the escape-pipe had been shot away, when an explosion below and a rush of steam around the boat told me that the steam-pipe had been cut in two. Nothing further, of course, could be done. I gave orders to lower the yawl at the stern of the Queen, to carry off Captain Thompson, who lay wounded in my stateroom. Some persons had already taken the yawl, however, and it was gone. The other yawl was on the De Soto, a short distance below. Fortunately, the cotton bales with which the Queen was protected afforded an avenue of escape, and a majority of the men and officers succeeded in reaching the De Soto. I ordered this boat to be brought up as far as practicable without being struck, and sent her yawl to the Queen. Lieutenant Tuthill and Third Master Duncan bravely volunteered for the purpose. I remained on the De Soto over an hour, picking up men and cotton bales. Lieutenant Tuthill barely succeeded in escaping from the Queen, the rebels boarding her in skiffs as he escaped. The Queen could easily have been burned, but this could not be done while Captain Thompson was on board, and it was impossible to remove him. All the passages had been blocked up with cotton; the interior of the boat was intensely dark, full of steam, and strewed with shattered furniture. The display of light enabled the batteries to strike her with unerring certainty. To have brought the De Soto alongside would have insured her destruction, as the light of the latter's furnace would have rendered her a conspicuous mark. A dense fog sprang up as we started down in the De Soto, and she lost her rudder by running into the bank. Drifting down fifteen miles, I took possession of the Era, and scuttled and burned the De Soto and barge, knowing that the rebels would lose no time in pursuing. I pushed on down through the fog, throwing the corn off to lighten her. We reached the Mississippi at dawn, opposite Ellis's Cliffs. Mr. Garvey ran the Era, a boat drawing less than two feet of water, hard aground, actually permitting her wheels to make several revolutions after she struck, and it was with the utmost difficulty she could be gotten off. The disloyal sentiments openly expressed by Mr. Garvey, a few hours previous to this occurrence, rendered it necessary for me to place him under arrest, and fixed upon me the unwilling conviction that the loss of the Queen was due to the deliberate treachery of her pilot. It is to be regretted that the unfortunate illness of Mr. Scott Long, who piloted the Queen past Vicksburg, rendered it necessary for me to intrust the management of the Queen to Mr. Garvey.

"The next morning, a short distance below Natchez, I met the Indianola. Captain Brown thought that he might be able to ascend Red River and destroy the battery at Gordon's Landing, and I accompanied him down in the Era, leading the way. I had not gone three miles when a break in the dense fog disclosed a steamer rapidly moving up stream about a mile ahead. I at once rounded to and caused the whistle to be blown to warn Captain Brown of her presence. As soon as the rebel steamer, which was undoubtedly the Webb, perceived the Indianola, she turned and fled. The latter fired two shots at her, but without effect. I learned afterward that three other armed boats had been sent in pursuit of the Era, and had been turned back by the Webb on her retreat. They all went back up Red River. On reaching this stream Captain Brown decided not to ascend it, and I thought it best to return at once. Thinking we might be attacked on the way up, I seized one hundred and seventy-five bales of cotton, and protected the Era's machinery as far as practicable. At St. Joseph I landed and seized the mails, and learned from them that Colonel Adams was waiting for us at Grand Gulf, with two pieces of artillery. Thirty-six shots were fired at the Era while passing the point, none of which took effect. On reaching Island 107, a body of riflemen opened a heavy fire upon the Era from the Mississippi shore. Suspecting it to be a ruse to draw us to the other side of the river, I decided on keeping the right of the Island. The furnace of the Era became so clogged at this point, I found it necessary to stop and have them cleaned out—a delay of twenty minutes being caused by this. The Era had barely passed the Island when a battery of three guns opened upon us from the Louisiana shore. Forty-six shots were fired, but did no injury. At Warrenton the rebels opened fire upon the Era with two rifled 20-pounder guns; they fired twenty-four shots, but did not succeed in striking her. Extraordinary as it may appear, there is every reason to believe that no one was killed on the Queen. It is probably attributable to the fact that those below got into the hold through the numerous hatches, and thus escaped the effects of the steam. Mr. Taylor, of the engineers, is reported to be badly scalded, by a deserter from the Webb. Twenty-four men were taken prisoners, ten of whom were civilians employed on the boat. Assistant-Surgeon Booth was the only commissioned officer captured."*

Shortly after these events, the Indianola, which had continued the blockade of Red River, was attacked on her return, above Grand Gulf, and com-

* Charles R. Ellet, Commanding Ram Fleet, to Rear-Admiral David D. Porter, Commanding Mississippi Squadron, U. S. Steamer Era, N 5, below Vicksburg, Miss., Feb. 21, 1863.

pelled to surrender. The incidents are thus narrated by her commander, Lieutenant George Brown. "About half past nine, P. M., on the night of the 24th, the night being very dark, four boats were discovered in chase of us. I immediately cleared for action, and as soon as all preparations were completed, I turned and stood down the river to meet them. At this time the leading vessel was about three miles below, the others following in close order. As we neared them, I made them out to be the rams Queen of the West and William H. Webb; and two other steamers, cotton-clad and filled with men. The Queen of the West was the first to strike us, which she did, after passing through the coal-barge lashed to our port side, doing us no serious damage. Next came the Webb. I stood for her at full speed. Both vessels came together, bows on, with a tremendous crash, which knocked nearly every one down on board both vessels, doing no damage to us, while the Webb's bow was cut in at least eight feet, extending about two feet above the water line to the kelson. At this time, the engagement became general, and at very close quarters. I devoted but little attention to the cotton-clad steamers, although they kept up a heavy fire with field-pieces and small-arms, as I knew that everything depended on my disabling the rams. The third blow crushed the starboard barge, leaving parts hanging by the lashings, which were speedily cut. The crew of the Indianola not numbering enough men to man both batteries, I kept the forward guns manned all the time, and fired them whenever I could get a shot at the rams. The night being very dark, our aim was uncertain, and our fire proved less effective than I thought at the time. The peep-holes in the pilot-house were so small that it would have been a difficult matter to have worked the vessel from that place in daylight, so that during the whole engagement the pilots were unable to aid me by their knowledge of the river, as they were unable to see anything—consequently they could do no more than obey such orders as they received from me in regard to working the engines and helm. No misunderstanding occurred in the performance of that duty, and I was enabled to receive the first five blows of the rams forward of the wheels, and at such angles that they did no more damage than to start the plating where they struck.

"The sixth blow we received, was from the Webb, which crushed in the starboard wheel, disabled the starboard rudder and started a number of leaks abaft the shaft. Being unable to work the starboard engine, placed us in an almost powerless condition, but I continued the fight until we received the seventh blow, which was given us by the Webb. She struck us fair in the stern, and started the timbers and starboard rudder-box, so that the water poured in in large volumes. At this time I knew that the Indianola could be of no more service to us, and my desire was to render her useless to the enemy, which I did by keeping her in deep water until there was two and a half feet of water over the floor, and the leaks were increasing rapidly as she settled, so as to bring the opening made by the Webb under water. Knowing that if either of the rams struck us again in the stern, which they then had excellent opportunities of doing, on account of our disabled condition, we would sink so suddenly that few, if any, lives would be saved, I succeeded in running her bows on shore by starting the screw engines. As further resistance could only result in a great loss of life on our part, without a corresponding result on the part of the enemy, I surrendered the Indianola, a partially sunken vessel, fast filling with water, to a force of four vessels, mounting ten guns, and manned by over one thousand men. The engagement lasted one hour and twenty-seven minutes. I lost but one killed, one wounded, and seven missing, while the enemy lost two officers and thirty-three men killed, and many wounded. Before the enemy could make any preparations for endeavoring to save the Indianola, her stern was under water. Both rams were so very much crippled, that I doubt whether they would have tried to ram again had not their last blow proved so fatal to us. Both signal-books were thrown in the river by me a few minutes before the surrender. In conclusion, I would state that the nine-inch guns of the Indianola were thrown overboard, and the eleven-inch guns damaged by being loaded with heavy charges and solid shot, placed muzzle to muzzle, and fired by a slow match, so that they were rendered useless. This was done in consequence of the sham Monitor sent from above, having grounded about two miles above the wreck of the Indianola."*

The reference to the "sham Monitor," in the last paragraph deserves more particular mention. The story is happily told in a letter by Admiral Porter. "During the time," says he, "of the running the blockade by the Queen of the West and the Indianola, five of the guns in the forts at Vicksburg were burst and dismounted; therefore, it was an object to make the enemy fire as much as possible. I got a mortar in easy range and opened on that part of the town where there was nothing but army supplies, and soon provoked a fire of four of their heavy batteries. The shell at first fell over the mortar and around it, bursting close to our men, but the range began to grow shorter, until they let us have it all our own way. Finding that they could not be provoked to fire without an object, I thought of getting up an imitation monitor. Ericsson saved the country with an iron one—why could I not save it with a wooden one? An old coal-barge, picked up in the river, was the foundation to build on. It was built of old boards in twelve hours, with pork barrels on top of each other for smoke-stacks, and two old canoes for quarter-boats; her furnaces were built of mud, and only intended to make black smoke and not steam. Without knowing that Brown was in peril, I let loose our monitor. When it was descried by the dim light of the morn, never did the batteries of Vicksburg open with such a din; the earth fairly trembled, and the shot flew thick around the devoted monitor. But she ran safely past all the batteries, though under fire for an hour, and drifted down to the lower mouth of the canal. She was a much better looking vessel than the Indianola. When it was broad daylight they opened on her again with all the guns they could bring to bear, without a shot hitting her to do any harm, because they did not make her settle in the water, though going in at one side and out at another. She was already full of water. The soldiers of our army shouted and laughed like mad, but the laugh was somewhat against them when they subsequently discovered the Queen of the West lying at the wharf at Warrenton. The question was asked, what had happened to the Indianola? Had the two rams sunk her or captured her in the engagement we heard the night before? The sounds of cannon had receded down the river, which led us to believe that Brown was chasing the Webb, and that the Queen had got up past him. One or two soldiers got the monitor out in the stream again, and let her down on the ram Queen. All the forts commenced firing and signaling, and as the monitor approached the Queen she turned tail and ran down the river as fast as she could go, the monitor after her, making all the speed that was

* Geo. Brown, Lt.-Com., U. S. N., to the Hon. Gideon Welles, Washington, D. C., May 28, 1863.

given her by a five-knot current. The forts at Warrenton fired bravely and rapidly, but the monitor did not return the fire with her wooden guns, but proceeded down after the Queen of the West. An hour after this the same heavy firing that we had heard the night before came booming up on the still air." Admiral Porter had not long afterwards the satisfaction to communicate to the Department at Washington an official confirmation of the further success of his humorous experiment on the fears of the rebels. "I have been pretty well assured for some time past," he writes to Secretary Welles on the 10th of March, "that the Indianola had been blown up, in consequence of the appearance of a wooden imitation mortar, which the enemy sunk with their batteries. The mortar was a valuable aid to us. It forced away the Queen of the West, and caused the blowing up of the Indianola. The following is an account of the affair, taken from the *Vicksburg Whig* of the fifth instant:—

'DESTRUCTION OF THE INDIANOLA.—We stated a day or two since that we would not enlighten our readers in regard to a matter which was puzzling them very much. We alluded to the loss of the gunboat Indianola, recently captured from the enemy. We were loth to acknowledge she had been destroyed, but such is the case. The Yankee barge sent down the river last week was reported to be an iron-clad gunboat. The authorities, thinking that this monster would retake the Indianola, immediately issued an order to blow her up. The order was sent down by courier to the officer in charge of the vessel. A few hours afterward another order was sent down, countermanding the first, it being ascertained that the monstrous craft was only a coal-boat; but before it reached the Indianola she had been blown to atoms—not even a gun was saved.'"

This practical joke of the Quaker monitor succeeded so well that a second sham gunboat was sent down the river a week after. As it proceeded in the dark and stormy night past Vicksburg its presence was detected, and the rebel batteries opened resolutely upon the craft with an expenditure of ammunition which greatly delighted the contrivers of the craft, who quietly compared the cost of the Confederate shots with the few dollars expended on the scow. A deserter reported that two of the rebel guns, a thirty-two and sixty-four pounder, were burst on the occasion. The Yankee Doodle, as the craft was called, is described by a correspondent as having "a flag flying at her bow with a scull and cross-bones, and a caricature of the 'Down-Easter' on the wheel-house, with a long tailed coat, a pair of short pantaloons, and his fingers to his nose, assuming a 'can't come it' expression. By such humors was the grimness of the siege with its tedious labors and disappointments relieved.

The canal project or "cut-off" opposite Vicksburg not proving successful—in consequence of the heavy and continuous rains which interrupted the work and, finally, by sweeping away the dam and flooding the district caused its discontinuance,—two other projects of a similar nature were attempted which seemed to promise better results. They were of considerable magnitude and were undertaken with the design of carrying on a series of operations by the lake and river communications in the interior on both sides of the Mississippi. They were known as the Yazoo Pass and Lake Providence routes from their initial points on the river. The former is a narrow and tortuous channel, traversing a region of swamps and connecting the Mississippi a few miles below Helena with the Coldwater river, which after a crooked passage of about forty miles joins the Tallahatchie, that in turn pursues its way some fifty miles when it unites with the Yallobusha, the two forming the Yazoo river, with a course of over two hundred miles to its outlet at the Mississippi, a short distance above Vicksburg. The advantage of securing the navigation of this long and circuitous stream in a route of nearly five hundred miles was to take Yazoo City, a hundred miles above the mouth of the river from which it was named, in the rear of the works at Haines' Bluff, which had heretofore arrested the progress of the fleet from the Mississippi, and to gain a position whence Vicksburg could be approached from the interior. At Yazoo City a fleet of rebel vessels and transports was congregated, the capture or destruction of which was necessary to the success of the invasion. To commence these operations it was necessary to cut the levee at the entrance to Yazoo Pass which had been constructed to shut off the Mississippi and protect the country from inundations. This was done, and the high state of the river favoring the movement General Grant was encouraged to plan an expedition of some magnitude by this route. General McPherson's army corps and a division from each of McClernand's and Sherman's corps were ordered to be in readiness for a grand movement, which was subsequently, in consequence of a difficulty of obtaining a sufficient number of light transports for this peculiar service, limited to a single division. While the forces of General Grant, as he tells us in his report of these operations, "were opening one end of the Pass, the enemy was diligently closing the other end, and in this way succeeded in gaining time to strongly fortify Greenwood, below the junction of the Tallahatchie and Yallobusha. The advance of the expedition, consisting of one division of McClernand's corps, from Helena, commanded by Brigadier-General L. F. Ross, and the Twelfth and Seventeenth regiments of Missouri infantry, from Sherman's corps, as sharpshooters on the gunboats, succeeded in reaching Coldwater on the 2d day of March, after much difficulty, and the partial disabling of most of the boats. From the entrance into Coldwater to Fort Pemberton, at Greenwood, Mississippi, no great difficulty of navigation was experienced, nor any interruption of magnitude from the enemy. Fort Pemberton extends from the Tallahatchie to the Yazoo, at Greenwood. Here the two rivers come within a few hundred yards of each other. The land around the fort is low, and at the time of the attack was entirely overflowed. Owing to this fact no movement could be made by the army to reduce it, but all depended upon the ability of the gunboats to silence the guns of the enemy, and enable the transports to run down and land troops immediately on the fort itself. After an engagement of several hours the gunboats drew off, being unable to silence the batteries. Brigadier-General J. F. Quimby, commanding a division of McPherson's corps, met the expedition under Ross with his division on its return near Fort Pemberton, on the 21st of March, and being the senior, assumed the command of the entire expedition, and returned to the position Ross had occupied." Finally, at the end of March, the project being abandoned, the expedition returned to Helena, when the troops were sent to join the forces before Vicksburg.

Another expedition in March, in this quarter, consisting of five ironclads including the Lafayette, one of the most powerful of the western gunboats, supported by a detachment of General Sherman's command, was conducted by Admiral Porter through Steel's and Black's Bayou, from a point on the Yazoo, with a view of re-entering that river above Haines' Bluff, by Deer Creek and the Sunflower river. Though pushed with great energy and perseverance it met with no better success than the one from above. For eight days the Admiral was in the heart of the country, having worked his way seventy miles through narrow channels choked with fallen trees, at times with barely room for the passage of his vessels, and as he proceeded was beset by the enemy, who placed fresh obstructions in the river, and whose sharpshooters annoyed the crews from the banks. An assistant engineer of one of the tugs was killed and two others seriously wounded, The expedition was compelled to return, when the passage into the Yazoo river had been almost accomplished. It was a scheme from which much was expected by Admiral Porter and General Grant; but the latter had afterwards occasion to regard its failure in a philosophical spirit. "All this," says he, "may have been providential in driving us ultimately to a line of operations which has proven ultimately successful."

The disadvantages under which these entangled inland water routes labored doubtless had their influence in the abandonment of the third great inland project which promised an internal navigation from Lake Providence, on the right bank of the Mississippi, about a hundred miles above Vicksburg, by a chain of bayous to Tensas River, and thence by the Black into the Red River, and so to the Mississippi again in the vicinity of Port Hudson. A canal was made in pursuance of this scheme at Lake Providence and a considerable region of territory flooded by the Mississippi, but the gunboats and transports of Grant's army found their way below Vicksburg by another route. After all these laborious efforts to circumvent the enemy, the gunboats and transports of General Grant's forces took the old route by the direct channel of the Mississippi in defiance of the batteries of Vicksburg.

Another, and, as it proved, unsuccessful effort was made in this direction simultaneously with the return of Admiral Porter from his Deer Creek expedition. Admiral Faragut having, as we shall have occasion to describe more particularly in the next chapter, on the affairs at Port Hudson, passed the batteries at that place with his flag-ship the Hartford and the gunboat Albatross, had now arrived below Vicksburg, and by a messenger sent overland on the right bank of the river, requested aid from the fleet above. General Ellet accordingly ordered the rams Lancaster and Switzerland to proceed down the river. The attempt was made early on the morning of the 25th of March. Lieutenant-Colonel John A. Ellet commanded the Lancaster; Colonel Charles R. Ellet the Switzerland. They were originally light-built wooden river steamers which had been armed for the "flotilla." Both were disabled in passing the batteries, a shot struck the boiler of the Switzerland, exploded, scalding three negroes and the mate, when the vessel floated down the river and was taken in tow of the Albatross. The Lancaster was utterly destroyed. She was repeatedly struck, "one shot almost splitting her hull in twain, several passing through her boilers and cutting her steam-pipe. She soon commenced to sink, but fearing that she might fall into the hands of the rebels, Lieutenant-Colonel Ellet discharged his revolver into the cotton around the boilers and set her on fire. Her bow went under, however, and in a few seconds the vessel disappeared beneath the engulfing waves. One of the pilots lost a leg, and an engineer was slightly scalded. An orderly sergeant was missing and supposed to be drowned. The escape of the remainder of the crew was due to their good conduct and prompt obedience to orders."* The Switzerland was presently refitted, and, with the Hartford and Albatross, rendered efficient service during the next fortnight in engaging the enemy's batteries at

* Dispatch to the Cincinnati Gazette, above Vicksburg, March 25th, 1863.

Grand Gulf, blockading Red River, scouring the Mississippi of rebel transports and destroying a large quantity of corn stored for the Confederates at Bayou Sara.

The next attempt to pass the batteries at Vicksburg was made in force and with decided success preparatory to the grand movement of General Grant upon the enemy's works from a point below the city. Troops might be and presently were sent overland on the Louisiana shore by a march of over thirty miles to New Carthage and beyond below the bend of the river, but gunboats and transports were necessary to silence the batteries on the opposite shore and provide means for the crossing of the soldiers to the proposed field of operations. Old projects of reaching the rear of Vicksburg from above were abandoned and every effort directed to the new and bolder undertaking. The descent of the gunboats, upon which the success of the movement primarily depended, was watched with great interest. It was an undertaking of great peril, as had been fully proved on various previous occasions, and was well calculated to test the spirit of those engaged in it. Eight gunboats and three transports were selected for the service, Admiral Porter's "veteran" flag-ship, the Benton, Captain Greer ; the Lafayette, Captain Walker ; the Price, Captain Woodworth, a powerful woodenboat, captured from the rebels at Memphis the previous year ; the Louisville, Captain Owens ; the Carondelet, Captain Murphy ; Pittsburg, Captain Hoel ; the Tuscumbia, Captain Shirk, and the Mound City. All of these, except the Price, were ironclads, and all had such additional protection as could be afforded by bales of cotton and of hay, heavy timbers, railroad iron, and other means which experience had taught to be efficient. The transports were the Forest Queen, Captain Dan Conway, the Henry Clay, commanded by her Mate, both sidewheel steamers, and the propeller Silver Wave, Captain McMillen. They were laden with supplies, and protected as far as possible by hay and cotton, the upper works, as described by a correspondent, being "left to the care of Providence and the bad gunnery of the Confederates." That the service was considered sufficiently hazardous was proved by the refusal of the crew of the Silver Wave, with the exception of Captain McMillen, to proceed in her. Soldiers were, in consequence, put on board and the place of a pilot was supplied by Lieutenant George O'Niel, of the Thirtieth Ohio, who volunteered for the undertaking. Nearly the entire crew of the Henry Clay, it is said, was made up of soldiers. Every man belonging to the Forest Queen volunteered to remain with her. "It is a striking feature," says General Grant of this movement and the readiness of those who executed it, "so far as my observation goes, of the present volunteer army of the United States, that there is nothing which men are called upon to do, mechanical or professional, that accomplished adepts cannot be found for the duty required in almost every regiment." On the evening of the sixteenth of April all was in readiness. The scene at the point of starting with the incidents of the gallant adventure are thus graphically described by a correspondent: "The plan decided upon was that the ironclads should pass down in single file, with intervals between the boats of a few hundred yards, and that when in front of the batteries they should engage them with their broadside guns, making as much smoke as possible, under cover of which the transports should endeavor to pass unseen. A warm, cloudless day was succeeded by a clear twilight, beneath which boats from all points up the river began to assemble at the "Lower Landing"—a place about four miles in a direct line from Vicksburg, and which in daylight affords an extended and detailed view of the city and its fortifications. The *Von Phul*, having on board General Grant and wife, General McClernand and wife, together with several other military officials and ladies, also came down from Milliken's Bend, and took a position just at the head of the canal, where her passengers had a most excellent view of the whole operation. The *Rocket*, with General Thomas, made its appearance near the canal, and landed the General, who proceeded further down in a skiff, and took a position where he could speak the gunboats after passing the main batteries. Other parties proceeded down in skiffs, yawls, tugs, etc., and placed themselves wherever they imagined the best view of the coming spectacle could be obtained. In short, by nine o'clock the audience was all seated, waiting and impatient for the opening of the performance. There were in all perhaps thirty boats at the landing, each of which was black with spectators, of whom not a few were ladies; these, and the stars, were the witnesses, and constituted an audience at once large and respectable. I am bound to say that the stars were the more serious and quiet portion of the gathering: the balance passed the hours of waiting in jokes, laughter, choruses and love-making—which, together with a running fusilade of champagne corks, indicated anything but an appreciation of the fact that the drama about to open was a tragedy instead of a roaring farce.

"Lights twinkled busily from the Vicksburg hillsides until about ten o'clock, when they disappeared, and about the same moment song and laughter on our side were hushed, as a shapeless mass of what looked like a great fragment of darkness was discerned floating noiselessly down the river. It was the Benton—it passed and disappeared in the night, and was succeeded by another bank of darkness—the Lafayette, with the Price lashed to her starboard side. And thus they continued across the narrow vista which opened itself to our eyes, as if huge shadows detached themselves from the darkness above, floated across our vision, and disappeared in the darkness below. Ten of these noiseless shapes revealed themselves and disappeared, and then we knew that all the actors in the play had given us the first scene of the first act. Three-quarters of an hour passed; people heard nothing, save their own suppressed breathings; saw nothing, save a long, low bank of darkness, which, like a black fog, veiled the view below, and joined the sky and river in the direction of Vicksburg. So long a time passed without anything occurring, that people began to believe that the rebels had determined, for some malevolent purpose, to allow the fleet to pass below without obstruction; some men offered bets to back such opinions. However, this supposition was hardly broached ere it was contradicted most emphatically. At just a quarter before eleven, two bright, sharp lines of flame flashed through the darkness, at the extreme right of the Vicksburg batteries; and, in an instant, the whole length of the bluffs was a-blaze with fire. The fleet, which had rounded the Point, and now lay squarely before the city, at once responded by opening their ports and pouring their full broadside of twenty-five heavy guns, charged with grape and shrapnel, directly against the city. A great cloud of smoke rolled heavily over the gunboats, and in this the three transports entered and made their 'best time' down the river. The Forest Queen, which was in the advance, received a shot in the hull, and another through the steam-drum, which disabled her instantly. The Henry Clay, that came next, stopped, to prevent her running into the other, and at the same moment was struck by a shell that set her cotton on fire. The crew, demoralized by the stoppage and terrified by the fire, ran aimlessly around for a few moments, then launched the yawl, sprang into it, and pulled for the shore. The pilot, finding that no engineers obeyed the bells, staid a short time till the fire began to seethe round him, when he seized a plank, jumped overboard, and was picked up by a gunboat. The Clay, in the meantime, became a great blazing mass, that floated down the river until it disappeared below Warrenton. Had she been manned by men of nerve, the fire would have been extinguished and the boat carried through safely; the fact of her floating so far shows that her hull was uninjured. The Forest Queen was taken in tow by a gunboat and towed below without further damage. The Silver Wave did not receive a scratch. The Vicksburg batteries were passed in about an hour and a quarter. Upon reaching Warrenton our gunboats took the initiative by pouring in their broadsides the instant they reached position; and so continuous and terrific was their fire that the enemy scarcely ever attempted a response. In fine, the fleet ran the blockade, losing only the transport Henry Clay, and one man killed, and two others wounded on the Benton. This is all our loss, which, considering the tremendous magnitude of the dangers through which the fleet passed, is next to none at all." *

A week later six additional transport steamers, with officers and crew chosen from the regiments in the vicinity, conducting as many coal-barges, were sent in like manner past Vicksburg. They suffered more or less injury; but all, with one exception, got below the batteries. Two tugs, with four hay barges, also, a few nights after, followed in safety. At the end of April the army was fairly on its way from Milliken's Bend overland and past Richmond by a military road constructed over swamps and bayous for sixty miles to a point opposite Grand Gulf, in easy reach of the new theatre of operations at the Big Black river emptying into the Mississippi at that place.

The movements in this quarter began with an attack by the fleet on the enemy's works at Grand Gulf on the morning of the 29th of April. The navy, it was intended, should silence the guns of the enemy, and the troops land under cover of the gunboats and take the place by storm. "After a fight of five hours and thirty minutes," says Admiral Porter in his dispatch reciting the naval operations at the close of the day to Secretary Welles, "we silenced the lower batteries, but failed to silence the upper one, which was high, strongly built, had guns of very heavy calibre, and the vessels were unmanageable in the heavy current. It fired but feebly toward the last, and the vessels all laid by and enfiladed it, while I went up a short distance to communicate with General Grant, who concluded to land the troops and march over to a point, two miles below Grand Gulf. I sent the Lafayette back to engage the upper batteries, which she did, and drove the persons out of it, as it did not respond after a few fires. At six P. M., we attacked the batteries again, and, under cover of the fire, all the transports passed by in good condition. The Benton, Tuscumbia and Pittsburg were much cut up, having twenty-four killed and fifty-six wounded, but they are all ready for service. We land the army in the morning on the other side, and march on Vicksburg."

A second dispatch of Admiral Porter, three days after, on the 3d of May, concludes the history of the rebel defences at Grand Gulf. "I have the honor," he writes, "to report that I got under way this morning with the Lafayette, Carondelet, Mound City and Pittsburg,

* Correspondence *New York Times*, "Galway," near Vicksburg, April 17, 1863.

and proceeded up to the forts at Grand Gulf, for the purpose of attacking them again, if they had not been abandoned. The enemy had left before we got up, blowing up their ammunition, spiking their large guns, and burying or taking away the lighter ones. The armament consisted of thirteen guns in all. The works are of the most extensive kind, and would seem to defy the efforts of a much heavier fleet than the one which silenced them. The forts were literally torn to pieces by the accuracy of our fire. Colonel Wade, the commandant of the batteries, was killed; also his chief of staff. Eleven men were killed that we know of, and our informant says that many were wounded, and that no one was permitted to go inside the forts after the action except those belonging there. We had a hard fight for these forts, and it is with great pleasure that I report that the navy holds the door to Vicksburg. Grand Gulf is the strongest place on the Mississippi. Had the enemy succeeded in finishing the fortifications, no fleet could have taken them. I have been all over the works, and found them as follows: One fort on a point of rocks, seventy-five feet high, calculated for six or seven guns, mounting two 7-inch rifles and one 8-inch and one Parrott gun on wheels, which was carried off. On the left of this work is a triangular work calculated to mount one heavy gun. These works are connected with another fort by a covered way, and double rifle-pits extending one-quarter of a mile, constructed with much labor, and showing great skill on the part of the constructor. The third fort commands the river in all directions. It mounted one splendid Blakely 100-pounder, one 8-inch, and two 30-pounders. The latter were lying burst or broken on the ground. The gunboats had so covered up everything with earth that it was impossible to see at first what was there, with the exception of the guns that were dismounted or broken. Every gun that fell into our hands was in good condition, and we found a large quantity of ammunition. These are by far the most extensively built works, with the exception of those at Vicksburg, I have seen yet, and I am happy to say that we hold them. I am dismounting the guns, and getting on board the ammunition. Since making the above examination, new forts have been passed nearly finished. They had no guns, but were complete of the kind as regards position, and had heavy field-pieces in them."

A brief dispatch from General Grant, dated the same day, announced his entrance on what proved to be a brilliant course of victories. "We landed at Bruinsburgh, April 30th," says he, moved immediately on Port Gibson, met the enemy, eleven thousand strong, four miles south of Port Gibson, at two A. M., on the 1st instant, and engaged him all day, entirely routing him with the loss of many killed, and about five hundred prisoners, besides the wounded. Our loss is about one hundred killed and five hundred wounded. The enemy retreated toward Vicksburg, destroying the bridges over the two forks of the Bayou Pierre. These were rebuilt, and the pursuit has continued until the present time. Besides the heavy artillery at this place, four field-pieces were captured and some stores, and the enemy were driven to destroy many more. The country is the most broken and difficult to operate in I ever saw. Our victory has been most complete, and the enemy are thoroughly demoralized."* McClernand's Thirteenth Army Corps had taken the lead in the overland march to the Mississippi, and being the first to cross the river was in the advance on the road to Port Gibson from Bruinsburgh. In selecting this point for a landing General Grant had been guided by the information of a

* Gen. Grant to Gen. Halleck, Grand Gulf, May 3, 1863.

negro man, who assured him of the practicability of the road. The battle before Port Gibson was fought on the right by the divisions of Hovey, Carr and Smith, and on the left by the division of Osterhaus, of McClernand's corps. The latter was assisted in the after part of the day by Logan's division of McPherson's corps, which was the next in crossing.

General Grant also in the following order congratulated the soldiers of the Army of the Tennessee on their victory: "Once more I thank you for adding another victory to the long list of those previously won by your valor and endurance. The triumph gained over the enemy near Port Gibson, on the first, was one of the most important of the war. The capture of five cannon and more than one thousand prisoners, the possession of Grand Gulf, and a firm foothold on the highlands between the Big Black and Bayou Pierre, from whence we threaten the whole line of the enemy, are among the fruits of this brilliant achievement. The march from Milliken's Bend to the point opposite Grand Gulf was made in stormy weather, over the worst of roads. Bridges and ferries had to be constructed. Moving by night as well as by day, with labor incessant, and extraordinary privations, endured by men and officers, such as have been rarely paralleled in any campaign, not a murmur or complaint has been uttered. A few days' continuance of the same zeal and constancy will secure to this army crowning victories over the rebellion. More difficulties and privations are before us; let us endure them manfully. Other battles are to be fought; let us fight them bravely. A grateful country will rejoice at our success, and history will record it with immortal honor."

Such was the favorable beginning of General Grant's operations in his new campaign below Vicksburg. While he was at Grand Gulf, his new base of supplies, within a few days of these occurrences, he was further encouraged by news of the success of an adventurous expedition which had traversed the interior of the State of Mississippi, through its entire length, from the southern frontiers of Tennessee to the northern borders of Louisiana, passing between the enemy's great lines of communication, the Mobile and Ohio and Mississippi Central railroads, passing in the rear of the works at Vicksburg and Port Hudson, and coming out triumphantly within the Union lines at Baton Rouge. This was the celebrated cavalry raid of Colonel B. H. Grierson, an Illinois officer of volunteers, who had entered the service at the beginning of the war as Major of the Sixth Illinois Cavalry, had succeeded to the colonelcy of the regiment and had since been efficiently engaged in his duties, quietly working his way to a reputation which pointed him out as the man for this extraordinary service. The details of this expedition are too remarkable to be omitted in a comprehensive narrative of the war. As narrated by Colonel Grierson in his official report they present certainly a most noticeable picture of the internal condition of the South at this period, and of the dangers incurred and difficulties overcome by the military energy of this small but determined band of Western horsemen. After three days of brilliant operations in overcoming the enemy's outposts in Northern Missouri, where a number of prisoners were taken and sent within the Union lines, Colonel Grierson on the 21st of April left Pontotoc on his direct southern course with about nine hundred and fifty men of the Sixth and Seventh Illinois cavalry. At Starkville that day they captured a mail and destroyed a quantity of government property. On the way thence to Louisville, "we moved out," says Colonel Grierson, "on the road about four miles through a dismal swamp near belly deep in mud, sometimes swimming our horses to cross streams, when we encamped for the night in the midst of a violent rain." From this point a battalion was sent four miles to destroy a large tannery and shoe manufactory in the service of the rebels. This was effectually accomplished. Boots, shoes, leather and machinery were destroyed in great quantities, and a rebel quartermaster from Port Hudson captured, "who was laying in a supply for his command." Thence twenty-eight miles, "mostly through a dense swamp, the Noxabee river bottom, for miles belly deep in water so that no road was discernible" to Louisville. The people of the country were taken by surprise and "would not believe us to be anything but Confederates." A detachment was sent forward to Louisville to picket the town till the column had passed, when a guard was left for an hour "to prevent persons leaving with information of the course we were taking, to drive out stragglers, preserve order and quiet the fears of the people. They had heard of our coming a short time before we arrived, and many had left, taking only what they could hurriedly move. The column moved quietly through the town without halting, and not a thing was disturbed. Those who remained at home acknowledged that they were surprised. They had expected to be robbed, outraged, and have their houses burned. On the contrary, they were protected in their persons and property."

"After leaving the town," continues Colonel Grierson in his interesting narrative, "we struck another swamp, in which, crossing it as we were obliged to do in the dark, we lost several animals drowned and the men narrowly escaped the same fate. Marching until midnight we halted until daylight at the plantation of Mr. Estus, about ten miles south of Louisville. The next morning, April 23d, at daylight, we took the road for Philadelphia, crossing Pearl river at a bridge about six miles north of the town. This bridge we were fearful would be destroyed by the citizens to prevent our crossing, and upon arriving at Philadelphia we found that they had met and organized for that purpose, but, hearing of our near approach, their hearts failed, and they fled to the woods. We moved through Philadelphia about three P. M., without interruption, and halted to feed about five miles southeast on the Enterprise road. Here we rested until ten o'clock at night, when I sent two battalions of Seventh Illinois cavalry, under Lieutenant-Colonel Blackburn, to proceed immediately to Decatur, thence to the railroad at Newton Station. With the main force I followed about an hour later. The advance passed through Decatur about daylight, and struck the railroad about six o'clock A. M. I arrived about an hour afterward with the column. Lieutenant-Colonel Blackburn dashed into the town, took possession of the railroad and telegraph, and succeeded in capturing two trains in less than half an hour after his arrival. One of these, twenty-five cars, was loaded with ties and machinery, and the other thirteen cars were loaded with commissary stores and ammunition, among the latter several thousand loaded shells. These, together with a large quantity of commissary and quartermaster's stores, and about five hundred stand of arms stored in the town, were destroyed. Seventy-five prisoners captured at this point were paroled. The locomotives were exploded and otherwise rendered completely unserviceable. Here the track was torn up, and a bridge half a mile west of the station destroyed. I detached a battalion of the Sixth Illinois cavalry, under Major Starr, to proceed eastward, and destroy such bridges, etc., as he might find over the Chunkey river. Having damaged as much as possible the railroad and telegraph, and destroyed all government property in the vicinity of Newton, I moved about four miles south of the road and fed men and horses. The forced marches which I was compelled to make in order to reach this point successfully necessarily very much fatigued and exhausted my command, and rest and food were absolutely necessary for its safety.

"From captured mails and information obtained by my scouts, I knew that large forces had been sent out to intercept our return, and having instructions from Major-General Hurlbut and Brigadier-General Smith to move in any direction from this point which, in my judgment, would be best for the safety of my command and the success of the expedition, I at once decided to move south, in order to secure the necessary rest and food for men and horses, and then return to La Grange through Alabama or make for Baton Rouge, as I might hereafter deem best. Major Starr in the meantime rejoined us, having destroyed most effectually three bridges and several hundred feet of trestle-work and the telegraph, from eight to ten miles east of Newton Station. After resting about three hours, we moved south to Garlandsville. At this point we found the citizens, many of them venerable with age, armed with shot guns and organized to resist our approach. As the advance entered the town these citizens fired upon them and wounded one of our men. We charged upon them and captured several. After disarming them we showed them the folly of their actions and released them. Without an exception they acknowledged their mistake, and declared that they had been grossly deceived as to our real character. One volunteered his services as guide, and upon leaving us declared that hereafter his prayers should be for the Union army. I mention this as a sample of the feeling which exists, and of the good effect which our presence produced among the people in the country through which we passed. Hundreds who are skulking and hiding out to avoid conscription, only await the presence of our arms to sustain them, when they will rise up and declare their principles; and thousands who have been deceived, upon the vindication of our cause, would return to loyalty. After slight delay at Garlandsville, we moved southwest about ten miles and camped at night on the plantation of Mr. Bender, two miles west of Montrose. Our men and horses having become gradually exhausted, I determined on making a very easy march the next day, and looking more to the recruiting of my weary little command than to the accomplishment of any important object; consequently, I marched at eight o'clock the next morning, taking a west and varying slightly to a northwest course. We marched about five miles and halted to feed on the plantation of Mr. Nichols.

"After resting until about two o'clock P. M., during which time I sent detachments north to threaten the line of the railroad at Lake Station and other points, we moved southwest toward Raleigh, making about twelve miles during the afternoon, and halting at dark on the plantation of Dr. Mackadora. From this point I sent a single scout, disguised as a citizen, to proceed northward to the line of the Southern Railroad, cut the telegraph, and, if, possible, fire a bridge or trestle-work. He started on his journey about midnight, and when within seven miles of of the railroad he came upon a regiment of Southern cavalry from Brandon, Mississippi, in search of us. He succeeded in misdirecting them as to the place where he had last seen us, and having seen them well on the wrong road, he immediately retraced his steps to the camp with the news. When he first met them they were on the direct road to our camp, and had they not been turned from their course would have come up with us before daylight. From information received through my scouts and other sources, I found that Jackson and the stations east, as far as Lake Station, had been reinforced by infantry and artillery, and hearing that a fight was momentarily expected at Grand Gulf, I decided to make a rapid march, cross Pearl river, and strike the New Orleans, Jackson and Great Northern Railroad at Hazlehurst, and after destroying as much of the road as possible, endeavor to get upon the flank of the enemy and co-operate with our forces, should they be successful in the attack upon Grand Gulf and Port Gibson. Having obtained during this day plenty of forage and provisions, and having had one good night's rest, we now again felt ready for any emergency. Accordingly, at six o'clock on the morning of the 26th, we crossed Leaf river, burning the bridge behind us to prevent any enemy who might be in pursuit from following; thence through Raleigh, capturing the sheriff of that county with about three thousand dollars in government funds; thence to Westville, reaching this place soon after dark. Passing on about two miles we halted to feed, in the midst of a heavy rain, on the plantation of Mr. Williams. After feeding, Colonel Prince, of the Seventh Illinois cavalry, with two battalions, was sent immediately forward to Pearl river to secure the ferry and landing. He arrived in time to capture a courier, who had come to bring intelligence of the approach of the Yankees, and orders for the destruction of the ferry. With the main column I followed in about two hours. We ferried and swam our horses, and succeeded in crossing the whole command by two o'clock P. M. As soon as Colonel Prince had crossed his two battalions he was ordered to proceed immediately to the New Orleans, Jackson and Great Northern Railroad, striking it at Hazlehurst. Here he found a number of cars containing about six hundred loaded shells and a large quantity of commissary and quartermaster's stores, intended for Grand Gulf and Port Gibson. These were destroyed, and as much of the railroad and telegraph as possible. Here, again, we found the citizens armed to resist us, but they fled precipitately upon our approach.

"From this point we took a northwest course to Gallatin four miles, thence southwest three and a half miles to the plantation of Mr. Thompson, where we halted until the next morning. Directly after leaving Gallatin we captured a 64-pound gun and a heavy wagon-load of ammunition, and machinery for mounting the gun, on the road to Port Gibson. The gun was spiked and the carriages and ammunition destroyed. During the afternoon it rained in torrents, and the men were completely drenched. At six o'clock, the next morning, April 28th, we moved westward; after proceeding a short distance I detached a battalion of the Seventh Illinois cavalry, under Captain Trafton, to proceed back to the railroad at Bahaia and destroy the road, telegraph and all government property he might find. With the rest of the command, I moved southwest toward Union Church. We halted to feed at two o'clock, P. M., on the plantation of Mr. Snyder, about two miles northeast of the church. While feeding our pickets were fired upon by a considerable force. I immediately moved out upon them, skirmished with and drove them through the town, wounding and capturing a number. It proved to be a part of Wirt Adams' Alabama cavalry. After driving them off we held the town and bivouacked for the night. After accomplishing the object of his expedition Captain Trafton returned to us about three o'clock in the morning of the 29th, having come upon the rear of the main body of Adams' command. The enemy having a battery of artillery it was his intention to attack us in front and rear about daylight in the morning, but the appearance of Captain Trafton with a force in his rear changed his purpose, and turning to the right he took the direct road to Port Gibson. From this point I made a strong demonstration toward Fayette, with a view of creating the impression that we were going toward Port Gibson or Natchez, while I quietly took the opposite direction. taking the road leading southeast to Brookhaven on the railroad. Before arriving at this place we ascertained that about five hundred citizens and conscripts were organized to resist us. We charged into the town, when they fled, making but little resistance. We captured over two hundred prisoners, a large and beautiful camp of instruction, comprising several hundred tents and a large quantity of quartermaster's and commissary stores, arms, ammunition, etc. After paroling the prisoners and destroying the railroad, telegraph, and all government property, about dark we moved southward, and encamped at Mr. Gill's plantation, about eight miles south of Brookhaven.

"The following morning we moved directly south along the railroad, destroying all bridges and trestle-work to Bogue Chitto Station, where we burned the depot and fifteen freight cars, and captured a very large secession flag. From thence we still moved along the railroad, destroying every bridge, water tank, etc., as we passed, to Summit, which place we reached soon after noon. Here we destroyed twenty-five freight cars and a large quantity of government sugar. We found much Union sentiment in this town, and were kindly welcomed and fed by many of the citizens. Hearing nothing more of our forces at Grand Gulf, I concluded to make for Baton Rouge, to recruit my command, after which I could return to La Grange through Southern Mississippi and West Alabama, or, crossing the Mississippi river, move through Louisiana and Arkansas. Accordingly, after resting about two hours, we started southwest on the Liberty road, marched about fifteen miles, and halted until daylight on the plantation of Dr. Spurlark. The next morning we left the road and threatened Magnolia and Osyka, where large forces were concentrated to meet us, but instead of attacking those points, took a course due South, marching through woods, lanes and by-roads, and striking the road leading from Clinton to Osyka. Scarcely had we touched this road when we came upon the Ninth Tennessee cavalry, posted in a strong defile, guarding the bridges over Tickfaw river. We captured their pickets, and, attacking, drove them before us, killing, wounding and capturing a number. Our loss in this engagement was one man killed, and Lieutenant-Colonel Wm. D. Blackburn and four men wounded. I cannot speak too highly of the bravery of the men upon this occasion, and particularly of Lieutenant-Colonel Blackburn, who, at the head of his men, charged upon the bridge, dashed over, and by undaunted courage dislodged the enemy from his strong position. After disposing of the dead and wounded, we immediately moved south on the Greensburgh road, recrossing the Tickfaw river, at Edward's bridge. At this point we met Garland's rebel cavalry, and with one battalion of the Sixth Illinois and two guns of the battery, engaged and drove them off without halting the column. The enemy were now on our track in earnest. We were in the vicinity of their strongholds, and from couriers and dispatches which we captured it was evident they were sending forces in all directions to intercept us. The Amite river—a wide and rapid stream—was to be crossed, and there was but one bridge by which it could be crossed, and this was in exceeding close proximity to Port Hudson. This I determined upon securing before I halted. We crossed it at midnight, about two hours in advance of a heavy column of infantry and artillery which had been sent there to intercept us. I moved on to Sandy Creek, where Hughes' cavalry, under Lieutenant-Colonel Wilburn, were encamped, and where there was another main road leading to Port Hudson. We reached this point at first dawn of day, completely surprised and captured the camp with a number of prisoners. Having destroyed the camp, consisting of about one hundred and fifty tents, a large quantity of ammunition, guns, public and private stores, books, papers and public documents, I immediately took the road from Baton Rouge. Arriving at the Commite river, we utterly surprised Stuart's cavalry, who were picketing at this point, capturing forty of them, with their horses, arms and entire camp. Fording the river, we halted to feed within four miles of the town. Major-General Augur, in command at Baton Rouge, having now, for the first, heard of our approach, sent two companies of cavalry, under Captain Godfrey, to meet us. We marched into the town about three o'clock P. M., and were most heartily welcomed by the United States forces at that point.

"Before our arrival in Louisville, Company B, of the Seventh Illinois cavalry, under Captain Forbes, was detached to proceed to Macon, on the Mobile and Ohio Railroad, if possible to take the town, destroy the railroad and telegraph, and rejoin us. Upon approaching the place he found it had been reinforced, and the bridge over the Oka Noxubee river destroyed, so that the railroad and telegraph could not be reached. He came back to our trail, crossed the Southern Railroad at Newton, took a southeast course to Enterprise, where, although his force numbered only thirty-five men, he entered with a flag of truce, and demanded a surrender of the place. The commanding officer at that point asked an hour to consider the matter, which Captain Forbes (having ascertained that a large force occupied the place) granted and improved in getting away. He immediately followed us, and succeeded in joining the column while it was crossing the Pearl river, at Georgetown. In order to catch us, he was obliged to march sixty miles per day for several consecutive days. Much honor is due to Captain Forbes for the manner in which he conducted this expedition. At Louisville I sent Captain Lynch, of Company E, Sixth Illinois cavalry, and one man of his company, disguised as citizens, who had gallantly volunteered to proceed to the Mobile and Ohio Railroad, and cut the wings, which it was necessary should be done to prevent the information of our presence from flying along the railroad from Jackson and other points. Captain Lynch and his comrade proceeded toward Macon, but meeting with the same barrier which had stopped Captain Forbes, could not reach the road. He went to the pickets at the edge of the town, ascertained the whole disposition of their forces and much other valuable information, and returning joined us above Decatur, having ridden without interruption for two days and nights without a moment's rest. All honor to the gallant Captain, whose intrepid coolness and daring characterizes him on every occasion.

"During the expedition we killed and wounded about 100 of the enemy, captured and paroled over 500 prisoners, many of them officers, destroyed between fifty and sixty miles of railroad and telegraph, captured and destroyed over 3,000 stand of arms, and other army stores and Government property to an immense amount; we also captured 1,000 horses and mules. Our loss during the entire journey was three killed, seven wounded, five left on the route sick, the Sergeant, Major, and Surgeon of the Seventh Illinois left, with Lieutenant-Colonel Blackburn, and nine men missing, supposed to have straggled. We marched over 600 miles in less than sixteen days. The last twenty-eight hours we marched seventy-six miles, had four engagements with the enemy, and forded the Comite River, which was deep enough to swim many of the horses. During this time the men and horses were without food or rest. Much of the country through which we passed was almost entirely destitute of forage and provisions, and it was but seldom that we obtained over one meal per day. Many of the inhabitants must undoubtedly suffered for want of the necessaries of life, which have reached most fabulous prices. Two thousand cavalry and mounted infantry were sent from the vicinity of Greenwood and Grenada northeast to intercept us ; 1,300 cavalry and several regiments of infantry with artillery were sent from Mobile to Macon, Meridian, and other points on the Mobile and Ohio road. A force was sent from Canton northeast to prevent our crossing Pearl River, and another force of infantry and cavalry was sent from Brookhaven to Monticello, thinking we would cross Pearl River at that point instead of Georgetown. Expeditions were also sent from Vicksburg, Port Gibson and Port Hudson, to intercept us. Many detachments were sent out from my command at various places to mislead the enemy, all of which rejoined us in safety. Colton's pocket map of the Mississippi, which, though small, is very correct, was all I had to guide me, but by the capture of their couriers, dispatches and mails, and the invaluable aid of my scouts, we were always able by rapid marches to evade the enemy when they were too strong, and whip them when not too large. Colonel Prince, commanding the Seventh Illinois, and Lieutenant-Colonel Loomis, commanding the Sixth Illinois, were untiring in their efforts to further the success of the expedition, and I cannot speak too highly of the coolness, bravery, and above all of the untiring perseverance of the officers and men of the command during the entire journey. Without their hearty co-operation, which was freely given under the most trying circumstances, we could not have accomplished so much with such signal success."

We left General Grant at Grand Gulf on the third of May, celebrating the initial victory of his new campaign in the defeat of the rebel General Bowen at Port Gibson. The enemy was vigorously followed in pursuit, but succeeded with the main body of his forces in escaping by the Big Black river. After ten days' bivouac General Grant put his forces in motion on the direct road to Jackson, the capital of the State.

On arriving at Rocky Springs on the seventh, the three corps of Generals McClernand, McPherson and Sherman, which composed the army, were pushed forward with rapidity. On the eleventh General McClernand had advanced to Hall's Ferry on the Big Black river, General Sherman was at Auburn, six or eight miles to the north-east, and General McPherson about eight miles further in the same direction ; the whole thus presenting an immense line of battle fronting to the north. Sherman's corps being in the centre, McPherson's forming the right and McClernand's the left wing. There had been no fighting up to this time on the road. On the twelfth General McClernand's advance drove in the enemy's pickets, near Hall's Ferry, with brisk skirmishing and little loss on either side. The same day General Steele's advance division of Sherman's corps encountered a body of the enemy, chiefly cavalry, at Fourteen

Mile Creek, but, after some slight skirmishing, the enemy retreated before the inferior force, burning the bridge as they retired. A crossing was, however, speedily constructed, and the corps moved on. General McPherson's corps met with more serious opposition. As it was marching on from Utica, on the branch-road to Jackson, on approaching the town of Raymond, it was met, also on the forenoon of the twelfth, by a body of the enemy under Generals Gregg and Walker, numbering about five thousand. Skirmishing commenced between the cavalry advance and the enemy's cavalry picket, about five miles from the town. Early in the morning General Logan's division which was on the road in the advance, was at once ordered forward to engage the enemy. The battle was opened about ten o'clock, and after a conflict of more than two hours resulted in the defeat of the enemy and their abandonment of Raymond to the Union forces. "Our loss," says General Grant, in a dispatch to General Halleck, "was 51 killed and 180 wounded; that of the enemy was 75 killed (buried by us) and 186 prisoners captured. beside the wounded." Ohio and Illinois troops fought this engagement. Colonel Richards of the Twentieth Illinois was killed; Colonel E. McCook, brother of Major-General McCook, was wounded in the foot. On the rebel side, Colonel McGiffick of the Tenth Tennessee, was killed.

McPherson's division was immediately pushed on, and the next day occupied Clinton, a small town about eight miles west of Jackson, on the Vicksburg railroad. A hundred prisoners were found in the hospitals and paroled; the telegraph office and post-office, with their contents, were seized, and the railway destroyed on both sides of the village for four miles. On the fourteenth, McPherson's corps, followed by General Sherman's, which had now come up, advanced upon Jackson, which was defended by General Joseph E. Johnston, the Confederate Commander of the Western Department, in person. He had just arrived on the spot and had little time to organize his troops which were not sufficient in numbers—being reported at about 9,000—long to withstand the force brought against him. General Crocker's division had the Union advance, and charged gallantly upon the enemy's position on the crest of a hill, in front of the town, driving the foe before them. General Sherman with his forces opportunely coming up on the right completed the discomfiture of the rebels. After a fight of about three hours, with few casualties on either side, the capital of Mississippi was abandoned to General Grant. After setting fire to the buildings filled with commissary and quartermaster's stores, General Johnston had retreated northward. An intelligent correspondent at the place estimates the entire loss in the capture of the position at not over 250 in killed and wounded, and that of the enemy in the various skirmishes much greater. Nearly a thousand prisoners were captured, including several officers.* Jackson was occupied by Sherman's corps for ten days, when it was abandoned after the destruction of the State-house, and the public stores and property.

The capture of Jackson was an important achievement, accomplished with far less of difficulty than was expected, when the army started a week before in this apparently desperate enterprise from the vicinity of Port Gibson. Vicksburg had been flanked, its railway communication with the interior cut off and the forces of General Johnston put to flight. There was, however, a larger army in the field which General Grant must overpower to reap any advantage from his recent exertions. This was the force of General Pemberton, who

* Special Correspondent, "Galway." *New York Times*, Jackson, Miss., May 15th, 1863.

had marched out of Vicksburg, as General Grant was informed, with eighty regiments and ten batteries of artillery, in all about 25,000 men, to attack him in the rear while Johnston assailed him in front. We have just seen the flight of the latter; we have now to record the defeat of the other. Early on the morning of the sixteenth, two days after the occupation of Jackson, the left wing of the army under General McClernand advancing to the line of the railway east of the Black River, in concert with McPherson's and Sherman's corps on their way from Jackson, came upon the main force of General Pemberton in the vicinity of Edwards Station. Three miles southeast of this, as described by a Correspondent, a county road, which runs parallel with the railroad, crosses Champion Hills, through which runs a stream called Baker's Creek. General Hovey, who was in the advance with his division on the road "at nine o'clock, discovered the enemy in front, on Champion Hill, to the left of the road, near Baker's Creek, apparently in force. Skirmishers were thrown out, and the division advanced cautiously and slowly to give McPherson's advance division under Logan time to come within supporting distance. General Hovey's division advanced across the open field at the foot of Champion Hill in line of battle. At eleven o'clock the battle commenced. The hill itself was covered with timber, and is, in fact, but an abrupt terminus of a high ridge running north and south, flanked on both sides by deep ravines and gullies, and in many places covered with an impenetrable growth of scrubby white-oak brush. The rebels appeared deficient in artillery throughout the battle, but opened with rather a heavy fire from a four-gun battery of rifled 6-pounders, planted about 400 yards back from the brow of the hill. The woods on both sides of the road leading up the face of the hill, and winding back on the ridge a mile or more, were filled with sharpshooters, supported by infantry. Here the battle began just as our men entered the edge of the timber, and raged terribly from eleven o'clock till between three and four. General Hovey's division carried the heights in a gallant style, and making a dash on the first battery, drove the gunners from their posts and captured the pieces. The rebels lay thick in the vicinity of the guns. Their horses were more than half killed; gun carriages and caissons were broken, and knapsacks, blankets, small arms and other debris, attested to the deadly struggle. The colors of the Thirty-first Alabama Regiment were captured there. At this juncture, Mitchell's Ohio Battery was opened at about eighty yards from the brow of the hill. The rebels made a dash for it, but the fleetness of the horses prevented its capture. At the same time the rebels appeared with fresh troops on that wing and redoubled their efforts to hold their position and dislodge our troops on the hill. Hovey was slowly driven back to the brow, but a brigade from General Quimby was ordered to his support, and the ground was speedily recovered, and the rebels finally repulsed. At the commencement of the engagement General Logan's Division marched past the brow of the hill, and forming in line of battle on the right of Hovey, advanced in grand style, sweeping everything before them. At the edge of the wood in front of Logan the battle was most desperate. Not a man flinched or a line wavered in this division. All behaved like veterans, and moved to new positions with a conscious tread of victory. Two batteries were captured by this division, and enough hard fighting done to immortalize it. They also captured a large portion of the prisoners, small arms, etc. Between three and four o'clock General Osterhaus and General McArthur's divisions came into action on the extreme left, and completed what had been so auspiciously carried forward. They were both miles away when the engagement began, but were brought forward with all dispatch possible. The enemy were in full retreat soon after, and these divisions pursued till nine o'clock, and encamped at Ward's Station, eight miles beyond the battleground."* Early the next morning, the seventeenth, McClernand's Corps, marched to the Black River bridge of the railroad, sixteen miles to the west of the Champion Hill battleground and twelve miles to the east of Vicksburg. Osterhaus was in advance and found the rebels strongly entrenched on the east bank of the river. Batteries were placed in position playing on the enemy's works. At ten o'clock General Lawler's Brigade of Iowa and Wisconsin troops of General Carr's division gallantly charged across the open fields, two hundred yards in width, making the bayou in front and swarming over the entrenchments. Seventeen cannon were taken inside of the earthworks and about two thousand prisoners. The enemy in the retreat beyond the river set fire to the bridge. Sherman's corps the same day crossed the Black River above at Bridgeport on a pontoon bridge, and the next day McClernand's and McPherson's corps having repaired the bridge which had been partially destroyed joined the forces on the other side before Vicksburg. The various roads were occupied and important positions taken investing the city from the direction of Warrenton, on the left to the bluffs, on the Yazoo River, on the right.

Admiral Porter had, in the meantime, not been idle on the Mississippi. "On the morning of the 15th," says he, in his dispatch announcing the capture of the works at Haines' Bluff, "I came over to the Yazoo, to be ready to cooperate with General Grant. Leaving two of the ironclads at Red river, one at Grand Gulf, one at Carthage, three at Warrenton, and two in the Yazoo, left me a small force—still I disposed of them to the best advantage. On the 18th, at meridian, firing was heard in the rear of Vicksburg, which assured me that General Grant was approaching the city. The cannonading was kept up furiously for some time, when, by the aid of glasses, I discovered a company of our artillery advancing, taking position and driving the rebels before them. I immediately saw that General Sherman's division had come on to the left of Snyder's Bluff, and that the rebels at that place had been cut off from joining the forces in the city. I dispatched the DeKalb, Lieutenant-Commander Walker; Choctaw, Lieutenant-Commander Ramsey; Romeo, Petrel and Forest Rose — all under command of Lieutenant-Commander Breese—up the Yazoo to open communication in that way with Generals Grant and Sherman. This I succeeded in doing, and in three hours received letters from Generals Grant, Sherman and Steele, informing me of this vast success, and asking me to send up provisions, which was at once done. In the meantime, Lieutenant-Commander Walker, in the De Kalb, pushed on to Haines' Bluff, which the enemy had commenced evacuating the day before, and a party remained behind in the hopes of destroying or taking away a large amount of ammunition on hand. When they saw the gunboats, they ran out and left everything in good order, guns, fort, tents and equipage of all kinds, which fell into our hands. As soon as the capture of Haines' Bluff and fourteen guns was reported to me, I shoved up the gunboats from below Vicksburg to fire at the hill batteries, which fire was kept up for two or three hours. At midnight they moved up to the town and opened on it for about an hour, and continued, at intervals during

* Special Dispatches to Chicago, Champion Hills, May 16th, 1863.

the night, to annoy the garrison. On the 19th I placed six mortars in position, with orders to fire night and day as rapidly as they could. The works at Haines' Bluff are very formidable. There are fourteen of the heaviest kind of mounted 8 and 10-inch and 7½-inch rifled guns, with ammunition enough to last a long siege. As the gun-carriages might again fall into the hands of the enemy, I had them burnt, blew up the magazine, and destroyed the works generally. I also burnt up the encampments, which were permanently and well constructed, looking as if the rebels intended to stay for some time. These works and encampments covered many acres of ground, and the fortifications and the rifle-pits proper of Haines' Bluff extend about a mile and a quarter. Such a net-work of defences I never saw. The rebels were a year constructing them, and all were rendered useless in an hour. As soon as I got through with the destruction of the magazines and other works, I started Lieutenant-Commander Walker up the Yazoo river, with sufficient force to destroy all the enemy's property in that direction, with orders to return with all dispatch, and only to proceed as far as Yazoo City, where the rebels have a navy-yard and storehouses. In the mean time General Grant has closely invested Vicksburg, and has possession of the best commanding points. In a very short time a general assault will take place, when I hope to announce that Vicksburg has fallen, after a series of the most brilliant successes that ever attended an army. There has never been a case during the war where the rebels have been so successfully beaten at all points, and the patience and endurance shown by our army and navy for so many months is about being rewarded. It is a mere question of a few hours, and then, with the exception of Port Hudson, which will follow Vicksburg, the Mississippi will be open its entire length."*

An expedition under Commander Walker sent up the Yazoo river by Admiral Porter the day after taking possession of Snyder's Bluff met with perfect success. "As the steamers," reports Admiral Porter, "approached Yazoo City, the rebel property was fired by Lieutenant Brown, of the ram Arkansas, and what he began our forces finished. Three powerful rams were burned, viz: the Mobile, a screw vessel ready for plating; the Republic, being fitted for a ram, with railroad iron plating; and a vessel on the stocks, a monster three hundred and ten feet long and seventy-five feet beam. This vessel was to have been covered with four and a half inch iron plating, and was to have had six engines, four side wheels and propellers. She would have given us much trouble. The rebels had under construction a fine navy-yard, containing fine sawing and planing machines, and extensive machine-shop, carpenter, blacksmith shops, and all the necessary appliances for a large building and repairing yard. Lieutenant-Commander Walker burned all these, with a large quantity of valuable building timber. He also burned a large saw-mill that had been used in constructing the monster ram. The material destroyed, at a moderate estimate, would cost more than two millions of dollars. We had one man killed and seven wounded, by field pieces from the enemy's batteries going up the river, but the wounded are doing well."

Immediately on the arrival of the several corps before Vicksburg, General Grant, relying on the demoralization of the enemy in consequence of their repeated defeats, ordered a general assault on their line before the city on the 19th of May. It was vigorously made, but little impression was made on

* Admiral Porter to Secretary Welles, Flag-ship Blackhawk, Haines' Bluff, May 20, 1863.

the rebel positions. A few days later another general attack was ordered. "There were many reasons," says General Grant, "to determine me to adopt this course. I believed an assault from the position by this time could be made successfully. It was known that Johnston was at Canton with the force taken by him from Jackson, reinforced by other troops from the east, and that more were daily reaching him. With the force I had a short time must have enabled him to attack me in the rear, and possibly succeeded in raising the siege. Possession of Vicksburg at that time would have enabled me to have turned upon Johnston and driven him from the State, and possess myself of all the railroads and practical military highways, thus effectually securing to ourselves all territory west of the Tombigbee, and this before the season was too far advanced for campaigning in this latitude. I would have saved Government sending large reinforcements, much needed elsewhere; and, finally, the troops themselves were impatient to possess Vicksburg, and would not have worked in the trenches with the same zeal, believing it unnecessary, that they did after their failure to carry the enemy's works. Accordingly, on the 21st, orders were issued for a general assault on the whole line, to commence at ten A. M., on the 22d. All the corps commanders set their time by mine, that there should be no difference between them in movement of assault. Promptly at the hour designated, the three army corps then in front of the enemy's works commenced the assault. I had taken a commanding position near McPherson's front, and from which I could see all the advancing columns from his corps, and a part of each of Sherman's and McClernand's. A portion of the commands of each succeeded in planting their flags on the outer slopes of the enemy's bastions, and maintained them there until night. Each corps had many more men than could possibly be used in the assault, over such ground as intervened between them and the enemy. More men could only avail in case of breaking through the enemy's line, or in repelling a sortie. The assault was gallant in the extreme on the part of all the troops, but the enemy's position was too strong, both naturally and artificially, to be taken in that way. At every point assaulted, and at all of them at the same time, the enemy was able to show all the force his works could cover. The assault failed, I regret to say, with much loss on our side in killed and wounded; but without weakening the confidence of the troops in their ability to ultimately succeed. No troops succeeded in entering any of the enemy's works, with the exception of Sergeant Griffith, of the Twenty-first regiment Iowa Volunteers, and some eleven privates of the same regiment. Of these none returned except the sergeant and possibly one man. The work entered by him, from its position, could give us no practical advantage, unless others to the right and left of it were carried and held at the same time."

In co-operation with this assault Admiral Porter directed a vigorous attack from the mortar and gunboats upon the hill and water batteries of the city, inflicting considerable damage. The bombardment was at short range, the vessels advancing to within four hundred and forty yards of the batteries. "It was the hottest fire," says Porter, "the gunboats had ever been under." Unable to gain intelligence of the progress of the army, the gunboats fought on after General Grant's assault had proved unsuccessful. "The army," adds Porter, "has terrible work before them, and are fighting as well as ever soldiers fought before. But the works are stronger than any of us dreamed of. General Grant and his soldiers are confident that the brave and energetic generals in the army will soon overcome all obstacles and carry the works."*

Despairing of taking the city by a sudden assault General Grant now commenced a regular series of siege operations. They were conducted with perseverance and energy by the men of his command, who cheerfully adapted themselves to the new exigencies of the service. Day by day through the month of June the works were pushed closer; mines were constructed with occasional sharp conflicts between the opposing combatants; while the city was continually bombarded. The inhabitants, seeking safety from shot and shell, sheltered themselves in caves excavated in the hillsides. To add to the completeness of the investment and secure protection against the threatened attack of General Johnston on his rear General Grant's army was largely reinforced. Its position resting on the Yazoo and supported by the gunboats was speedily made so strong that the enemy, spite of the urgency of the occasion, which no one better appreciated than President Davis, were evidently unable to make any serious attempt to raise the siege. Admiral Porter, with the gunboats and mortars, steadily assisted the assailants, —on one occasion having to report the loss of one of his vessels, the Cincinnati, which was sunk by the enemy's guns while enfilading some rifle-pits which barred the progress of the left wing of the army. The gunboat went down with her flag flying. Twenty-five on board were killed and fifteen were missing, supposed to be drowned.

On the seventh of June, the military operations of the Department were diversified by a rebel attack on the garrison at Milliken's Bend. Brigadier-General Dennis, in command at that place, had the previous day sent out a reconnoitering party in the direction of Richmond, which, after some skirmishing with the enemy in that vicinity, was pursued on its return. Early the next morning the garrison was attacked by a brigade of the enemy under General McCullough, numbering about 2,500 and 200 cavalry. The Twenty-third Iowa Volunteer Infantry and the African Brigade, in all about a thousand men, met the assault. The African regiments having been drilled but a few days and inexperienced in the use of arms, the enemy succeeded in reaching the works. "Here," says General Dennis, "ensued a most terrible hand-to-hand conflict of several minutes' duration, our men using the bayonet freely, and clubbing their guns with fierce obstinacy, contesting every inch of ground until the enemy succeeded in flanking them, and poured a murderous enfilading fire along our lines, directing their fire chiefly to the officers, who fell in numbers. Not till they were overpowered and forced by superior numbers did our men fall back behind the bank of the river, at the same time pouring volley after volley into the ranks of the advancing enemy. The gunboat Choctaw which had been ordered up by Admiral Porter, now moved into position, and fired a broadside into the enemy, who immediately disappeared behind the levee, but all the time keeping up a fire upon our men. The enemy at this time appeared to be extending his line to the extreme right, but was held in check by two companies of the Eleventh Louisiana Infantry, A. D., which had been posted behind cotton bales, and part of the Old Levee. In this position the fight continued until near noon, when the enemy suddenly withdrew. Our men, seeing this movement, advanced upon the retreating column, firing volley after volley at them while they remained within gunshot. The gunboat Lexington then paid her compliments to the flying foe in several well-directed shots, scattering them in all directions. The enemy's loss in this affair is estimated at about

* Admiral Porter to Secretary Welles, Mississippi Squadron, May 23, 1863.

150 killed and 300 wounded; the number of the Union killed, wounded and missing, the blacks being badly scattered, at 652.* General Grant in reporting this engagement, says, "that notwithstanding the inexperience of the Africans, their conduct is said to have been most gallant, and I doubt not, with good officers, they will make good troops." Adjutant-General Thomas had recently visited the Department with instructions from Washington, and had engaged zealously in organizing the colored regiments. The enemy a week after were routed out of Richmond by an expedition from Young's Point, consisting of General Mowry's command and the Marine Brigade under General R. W. Ellet. The town was completely destroyed in the melée.†

The public, which more than once during the year had been disappointed with false reports of the capture of Vicksburg, now settled down into a certain acquiescence with the delay in the promised achievement, the difficulties of which were but imperfectly understood at a distance, as General Grant from week to week telegraphed "the siege is progressing favorably." As the fourth of July drew near—an opportune day for a decisive movement, when much might be expected from the spirit of the troops—the siege operations were evidently approaching the crisis of a general assault. In anticipation of this on the third, his supplies of provisions being well nigh exhausted, and hopeless of relief from Johnston, General Pemberton, commanding the Confederate forces in the city, addressed a letter, borne by Major-General Bowen, under a flag of truce to General Grant, proposing an armistice and the appointment of three commissioners on each side to arrange terms for the capitulation of the place. "I make this proposition," he wrote, "to save the further effusion of blood which must otherwise be shed to a frightful extent, feeling myself fully able to maintain my position for a yet indefinite period." To this General Grant replied, "Lieutenant-General J. C. Pemberton, Commanding 'Confederate' Forces, etc.: General, your note of this date, just received, proposes an armistice of several hours, for the purpose of arranging terms of capitulation through Commissioners to be appointed, etc. The effusion of blood you propose stopping by this course, can be ended at any time you choose by an unconditional surrender of the city and garrison. Men who have shown so much endurance and courage as those now in Vicksburg, will always challenge the respect of an adversary, and, I can assure you, will be treated with all the respect due them as prisoners of war. I do not favor the proposition of appointing Commissioners to arrange terms of capitulation, because I have no other terms than those indicated above." General Bowen, the bearer of General Pemberton's letter, was received by General A. J. Smith. He expressed a strong desire to converse with General Grant, and accordingly while General Grant, declining this, requested General Smith to say that if General Pemberton desired to see him, an interview would be granted between the lines in McPherson's front at any hour in the afternoon which General Pemberton might appoint. A message was soon sent back to General Smith appointing three o'clock as the hour. General Grant was there with his staff, and with Generals Ord, McPherson, Logan and A. J. Smith. General Pemberton came late, attended by General Bowen and Colonel Montgomery. He was, it is said, much excited in his answers to General Grant. The conversation was held apart between General Pemberton and his officers, and Generals Grant, McPherson and A. J. Smith. The rebels insisted

* Brigadier-General Elias S. Dennis to A. A. G. John A. Rawlins, June 16th, 1863.

† Admiral Porter to Secretary Welles, June 18, 1863.

on being paroled and to march beyond the Union lines, officers and men all with eight days' rations drawn from their own stores, the officers to retain their private property and body servants. General Grant heard what they had to say, and left them at the end of an hour and a half, saying that he would send in his ultimatum in writing, to which General Pemberton promised to reply before night, hostilities to cease in the mean time. General Grant then conferred at his headquarters, with his corps and division commanders, and sent the following letter to General Pemberton, by the hands of General Logan and Lieutenant-Colonel Wilson:

"'GENERAL: In conformity with the agreement of this afternoon, I will submit the following propositions for the surrender of the city of Vicksburg, public stores, etc. On your accepting the terms proposed, I will march in one division as a guard, and take possession at eight A. M. to-morrow. As soon as paroles can be made out, and signed by the officers and men, you will be allowed to march out of our lines, the officers taking with them their regimental clothing, and staff, field and cavalry officers one horse each. The rank and file will be allowed all their clothing, but no other property. If these conditions are accepted, any amount of rations you may deem necessary can be taken from the stores you now have, and also the necessary cooking utensils for preparing them, and thirty wagons also, counting two two-horse or mule teams as one. You will be allowed to transport such articles as cannot be carried along. The same conditions will be allowed to all sick and wounded officers and privates, as fast as they become able to travel. The paroles for these latter must be signed, however, whilst officers are present authorized to sign the roll of prisoners.'"

The officers who received this letter stated that it would be impossible to answer it by night, and it was not till a little before peep o' day that the proposed reply by General Pemberton to General Grant was furnished. It read, "General: I have the honor to acknowledge the receipt of your communication of this date, proposing terms for the surrender of this garrison and post. In the main your terms are accepted; but in justice both to the honor and spirit of my troops, manifested in the defense of Vicksburg, I have the honor to submit the following amendments, which, if acceded to by you, will perfect the agreement between us at ten o'clock to-morrow. I propose to evacuate the works in and around Vicksburg, and to surrender the city and garrison under my command, by marching out with my colors and arms and stacking them in front of my present lines, after which you will take possession; officers to retain their side-arms and personal property, and the rights and property of citizens to be respected."

To this General Grant immediately replied as follows, under date of July 4: "General: I have the honor to acknowledge your communication of the 3d of July. The amendments proposed by you cannot be acceded to in full. It will be necessary to furnish every officer and man with a parole signed by himself, which, with the completion of the rolls of prisoners, will necessarily take some time. Again, I can make no stipulation with regard to the treatment of citizens and their private property. While I do not propose to cause any of them any undue annoyance or loss, I cannot consent to leave myself under restraint by stipulations. The property which officers can be allowed to take with them will be as stated in the proposition of last evening—that is, that officers will be allowed their private baggage and side-arms, and mounted officers one horse each. If you mean by your proposition for each brigade to march to the front of the lines now occupied by it, and stack their arms at ten o'clock, A. M., and then return to the inside and remain as prisoners until properly paroled, I will make no objections to it. Should no modification be made of your acceptance of my terms by nine o'clock, A. M., I shall regard them as having been rejected, and act accordingly. Should these terms be accepted, white flags shall be displayed along your lines to prevent such of my troops as may not have been notified from firing upon your men."

To this General Pemberton immediately answered: "General: I have the honor to acknowledge the receipt of your communication of this date, and in reply to say that the terms proposed by you are accepted."

Thus was Vicksburg surrendered on the national anniversary, and the long series of operations on the Mississippi with which General Grant had been connected since the beginning of the war virtually ended. The terms which were agreed upon he regarded as "more favorable to the Government than an unconditional surrender. It saved us the transportation of them North, which at that time would have been very difficult, owing to the limited amount of river transportation on hand and the expense of subsisting them. It left our army free to operate against Johnston, who was threatening us from the direction of Jackson; and our river transportation to be used for the movement of troops to any point the exigency of the service might require."

The surrender was quietly consummated at the appointed hour on the 4th, according to the stipulation. The rebel troops marched out and stacked arms in front of their works, while General Pemberton appeared for a moment with his staff upon the parapet of the central front. General McPherson directed the occupation of the enemy's works. General Grant was received by General Pemberton on entering the city, "with more marked importance," it is said, "than at the former interview; while in reply he treated General Pemberton with even a greater courtesy and dignity than before."

About thirty-one thousand prisoners were paroled, including eight to ten thousand in hospitals and convalescent camps. In the number were fifteen generals and their staffs, including Lieutenant-General Pemberton, and four major-generals, Smith, Stevenson, Forney and Bowen. Among the brigadier-generals was Stephen D. Lee, of South Carolina, who is described by a correspondent as "the idol of the rebel army—young, quiet, modest, handsome and a dangerous traitor." In reviewing the entire campaign General Grant sums up its result in "the defeat of the enemy in five battles outside of Vicksburg, the occupation of Jackson, the capital of the State, the capture of Vicksburg and its garrison and munitions of war; a loss to the enemy of thirty-seven thousand prisoners, among whom were fifteen general officers; at least ten thousand killed and wounded, and among the killed Generals Tracy, Tilghman and Green; and hundreds and perhaps thousands of stragglers, who can never be collected and reorganized. Arms and munitions of war for an army of sixty thousand men have fallen into our hands, besides a large amount of other public property, consisting of railroads, locomotives, cars, steamboats, cotton, etc., and much was destroyed to prevent our capturing it. The Union losses may be summed up as 1,293 killed, 7,095 wounded, and 537 missing: of these 180 were killed and 718 wounded at Port Gibson; 69 killed and 341 wounded at Raymond; 40 killed and 240 wounded at Jackson; 426 killed and 1,842 wounded at Champion's Hill; 29 killed and 242 wounded at Big Black Railroad Bridge; 545 killed and 3,688 wounded before Vicksburg. Of the large number of the wounded not more than one-half were permanently disabled."* To these statistics we may add a statement of the artillery shots fired during the siege, from the report of Colonel Duff, General Grant's Chief of Artillery. From the time of crossing the Mississippi river, May 1st, till the surrender, July 4th, 18,889 solid shot, 72,314 shell, 47,897 case, 2,723 canister, were expended,—making a total of 141,823. They were used in the several engagements as follows: 3,960 at Port Gibson; 82 in the pursuit from Port Gibson; 620 at Raymond; 476 at Jackson; 3,422 at Champion Hill; 1,297 at Big Black river; 9,598 on the 19th of May (really the first day of the siege); 10,754 on the 22d of May; and 111,614 during the remainder of the siege,—an average of 653 shots for each cannon used. Add to these the musketry, and some idea may be formed of the immense amount of ammunition consumed.†

Admiral Porter, who had shown great activity in the employment of his fleet, bombarding the city with their heavy guns, in mortar vessels, on scows, in guarding the river and in a detachment of his force on shore, reports an expenditure of ammunition from the mortars of 7,000 shells and from the gunboats 4,500. For forty-two days the mortar boats were engaged without intermission in throwing shells into all parts of the city, reaching to a distance of three miles; while the gunboats were constantly shelling the works and co-operating with the left wing of the army. Well might Admiral Porter, looking back at the magnitude of the operations on the Mississippi, add in his dispatch to Secretary Welles announcing the surrender of the city, "History has seldom had an opportunity of recording so desperate a defence on one side, with so much courage, ability, perseverance and endurance on the other."*

The Fourth of July was also signalized on the Mississippi by a vigorous assault upon the works of General Prentiss at Helena, Arkansas, by a well-appointed body of rebels, numbering some nine thousand, gathered by Lieutenant-General Holmes, Major-General Sterling Price, General Marmaduke, General Parsons and other Confederate chieftains of the region, at Little Rock. General Prentiss sustained the attack from daylight till three o'clock in the afternoon, when the rebels were repulsed at all points, leaving twelve hundred prisoners. Their loss in killed and wounded was about five hundred; that of the Union forces, who had the advantage of the breastworks and other defences, about sixty. The gunboat Tyler assisted in this result. This rebel defeat was another serious blow to the Confederate efforts in Arkansas.†

The capture of the army of Pemberton at Vicksburg was rapidly followed by the expulsion of the forces of General Johnston from their position in the rear. In the last days of June, when General Grant was preparing for a final assault upon Vicksburg, Major-General W. T. Sherman was assigned to the duty of meeting Johnston, who had crossed the Black river and then threatened an attack. Johnston, however, did not present himself, and when Vicksburg was taken Sherman was promptly sent in pursuit of him with his own corps and other troops joined to his command. The march was conducted with characteristic vigor. Spite of the fatigue the troops had undergone before Vicksburg in their harassing duties and close quarters under fire during

* Gen. Grant's Official Report to A. A. G. Kelton, Washington, Vicksburg, July 6, 1863.

† Correspondence of the *Chicago Times*, Vicksburg, Aug. 5, 1863.

* Admiral Porter to Secretary Welles, Vicksburg, July 4, 1863.

† Maj.-Gen. S. A. Hurlbut to Gen. Halleck, Memphis, July 5, 1863.

the summer heats, they pursued the enemy over an arid and desolate country, in the words of General Sherman, "in heat and dust for fifty miles, with little or no water, save in muddy creeks, in cisterns already exhausted, and in the surface ponds which the enemy in his retreat had tainted with dead cattle and hogs; crossed Black river by bridges of their own construction and then had to deal with an army which had, under a leader of great renown, been formed specially to raise the siege of Vicksburg, far superior in cavalry, and but little inferior in either infantry or artillery, and drove him fifty miles and left him in full retreat; destroyed those great arteries of travel in the State which alone could enable him to assemble troops and molest our possession of the Mississippi river; and so exhausted the land that no army can exist during this season without hauling in wagons all its supplies." Jackson, invested by the Union forces, was a second time abandoned by the enemy on the 16th of July, when Sherman entered and destroyed what was left of its military and railway resources. In this brief campaign his own losses in killed, wounded and prisoners was less than a thousand, while the enemy lost more than that in prisoners alone.

Simultaneously with this movement upon Jackson, a naval and military expedition under Lieutenant-Commanding Walker and Major-General Herron was sent to rout the enemy and capture their transports at Yazoo City. A reconnoissance of the rebel batteries was made by the gunboats, when General Herron landed his force of five thousand men and a joint attack was made upon the works. The rebels soon fled, previously setting fire to "four of their finest steamers that ran on the Mississippi in times past." The army pursued and a number of captures were made. In this movement the Union gunboat Baron De Kalb ran foul of a torpedo and was sunk by the explosion.

The possession of Vicksburg was now fully assured. One position only on the river was left to the enemy; but the fall of that was now certain. The next chapter relating the capture of Port Hudson will complete the narrative, illustrated by so many deeds of heroism, of the re-opening of the Mississippi.

CHAPTER LXXXIX.

GENERAL BANKS' DEPARTMENT OF THE GULF. SURRENDER OF PORT HUDSON, JULY 7, 1863

General Banks after his period of service with the army in Virginia in the summer of 1862, was employed during the autumn in the northern cities in fitting out an expedition, the destination of which was carefully concealed, some thinking it was intended to co-operate with the army in Virginia by a landing on the Atlantic coast, while various indications pointed to Texas. His preparations for forwarding troops and supplies having been completed, he sailed from New York at the beginning of December in the transport steamer North Star, accompanied by his staff and the officers and men of Colonel Chickering's Forty-first Massachusetts regiment. An extra official, Brigadier-General A. J. Hamilton, with the appointment by the President of provisional or military governor of Texas, was of the party. A native of

Alabama, he had been long a resident of Texas, acquired reputation as a lawyer and politician, and been sent as a representative to the second Congress of President Buchanan's administration. There he had advocated the cause of the Union, and subsequently on his return to Texas had maintained his patriotic course to the last, till he was compelled to flee from his State before the armed usurpation of its rebel population. Escaping through Mexico, he had reached the North in safety, and by his influence and public speeches had done much to enlighten the people on the true nature of the rebellion and strengthening the maintenance of the Union. He was sent on his present mission as a representative of the persons at the South true at heart to their country, and to facilitate their return to their old allegiance. Though Texas was long closed to him, as it turned out, he did good service in Louisiana.

After a favorable voyage, General Banks arrived at New Orleans on the 14th of December, and on the 16th, in accordance with his instructions from Washington, relieved General Butler in command of the Department of the Gulf. The announcement was received with surprise by the country which had witnessed with satisfaction the success of General Butler's administration; nor was any censure intended by the Government in his removal. No reason was given for the proceedings; but it was supposed to be in some way connected with the foreign policy of the Government, General Butler having, as we have seen, in the discharge of his duties, incurred the hostility of the European consuls. It was also said that General Butler having cleared the way as a pioneer in repressing the first fury of the rebellion, a new ruler might profitably introduce some relaxation of his vigorous policy. Something, indeed, of this was attempted by General Banks, but it was found that the decided course of his predecessor had substantially to be maintained. His proclamation on assuming command was judicious and forcible, appealing to the interests rather than the fears of the people he came to govern. "The duty," said he, "with which I am charged requires me to assist in the restoration of the Government of the United States. It is my desire to secure to the people of every class all the privileges of possession and enjoyment which are consistent with public safety, or which it is possible for a beneficent and just Government to confer." Looking at the geographical, and hence the moral condition of the situation, he pronounced "the Valley of the Mississippi the chosen seat of population, product and power on this continent. In a few years twenty-five millions of people, unsurpassed in material resources and capacity for war, will swarm upon its fertile rivers. Those who assume to set conditions upon their exodus to the Gulf count upon a power not given to man. The country washed by the waters of the Ohio, the Missouri and the Mississippi can never be permanently severed. If one generation basely barters away its rights, immortal honors will rest upon another that reclaims them. * * * This country cannot be permanently divided. Ceaseless wars may drain its blood and treasure, domestic tyrants or foreign foes may grasp the sceptre of its power, but its destiny will remain unchanged. It will still be united. God has ordained it. What avails, then, the destruction of the best Government ever devised by man—the self-adjusting, self-correcting Constitution of the United States? People of the Southwest! Why not accept the conditions imposed by the imperious necessities of geographical configurations and commercial supremacy and re-establish your ancient prosperity and renown? Why not become the founder of States which, as the entrepots and depots of your own Central and Upper Valleys, may stand in the affluence of their resources without superior, and in the privileges of the people, without a peer among the nations of the earth." The answer to these questions might be deferred; but there could be but one reply, and that was the practical restoration of the Union. On the 24th of December General Banks again addressed the people of Louisiana in a proclamation, setting forth the conditions of the President's Emancipation Proclamation in special reference to the State. After enjoining patience and forbearance during the unsettled relations of the master and slave to be determined in the future he called attention to the Act of Congress forbidding the return of fugitives by officers of the army. "No encouragement," said he, "will be given to laborers to desert their employers, but no authority exists to compel them to return." He suggested to planters the adoption of some plan by which an equitable proportion of the proceeds of the crops of the coming year be set apart and reserved for the support and compensation of labor. Of the future of the peculiar institution he said, in words of weighty import: "The war is not waged by the Government for the overthrow of Slavery. The President has declared, on the contrary, that it is to restore the 'Constitutional relations between the United States and each of the States' in which that relation is or may be suspended. The resolutions passed by Congress, before the war, with almost unanimous consent, recognized the rights of the States in this regard. Vermont has recently repealed the statutes supposed to be inconsistent therewith. Massachusetts had done so before. Slavery existed by consent and Constitutional guaranty; violence and war will inevitably bring it to an end. It is impossible that any military man, in the event of continued war, should counsel the preservation of slave property in the rebel States. If it is to be preserved, war must cease, and the former Constitutional relations be again established. The first gun at Sumter proclaimed emancipation. The continuance of the contest there commenced will consummate that end, and the history of the age will leave no other permanent trace of the rebellion. Its leaders will have accomplished what other men could not have done. The boldest Abolitionist is a cipher when compared with the leaders of the rebellion. What mystery pervades the works of Providence! We submit to its decrees, but stand confounded at the awful manifestations of its wisdom and power! The great problem of the age, apparently environed with labyrinthic complications, is likely to be suddenly lifted out of human hands. We may control the incidents of the contest, but we cannot circumvent or defeat the end. It will be left us only to assuage the horrors of internecine conflict, and to procrastinate the processes of transition. Local and national interests are therefore alike dependent upon the suppression of the rebellion. No pecuniary sacrifice can be too great an equivalent for peace, but it should be permanent peace, and embrace all subjects of discontent. It is written on the blue arch above us; the distant voices of the future—the waves that beat our coast—the skeletons that sit at our tables and fill the vacant places of desolate and mourning firesides, all cry out that this war must not be repeated hereafter. Contest, in public as in social life, strengthens and consolidates brotherly affection. England, France, Austria, Italy—every land fertile enough to make a history, has had its desolating civil wars. It is a baseless nationality that has not tested its strength against domestic enemies. The success of local interests narrows the destiny of a people, and is followed by secession, poverty and degradation. A divided country and perpetual war make possession a delusion and life a calamity.

The triumph of national interests widens the scope of human history, and is attended with peace, prosperity and power. It is out of such contests that great nations are born. What hallowed memories float around us! New Orleans is a shrine as sacred as Bunker Hill! On the Aroostook and the Oregon the names of Washington, Jackson and Taylor are breathed with as deep a reverence as on the James or the Mississippi. Let us fulfil the conditions of this last great trial, and become a nation—a grand nation—with sense enough to govern ourselves and strength enough to stand against the world united!" When the President's Emancipation Proclamation was confirmed by him on the first of January, portions of Louisiana were specially exempted from its provisions. This left the condition of the negroes subject to the laws of Congress which had been passed and the exigencies of military rule in the Department. The latter of course forbade vagrancy and crime as sources of disorder in the community. It was necessary in some way to adjust the relations of capital and negro labor. This was done by authorizing the Sequestration Commission sitting in the State to establish with the planters a proper system of remuneration for which the negroes should be required to render faithful service. "This," said General Banks, "may not be the best, but it is now the only practical system. Wise men will do what they can when they cannot do what they would. It is the law of success. In three years from the restoration of peace under this voluntary system of labor, the State of Louisiana will produce threefold the produce of its most prosperous year in the past."*

The first military operations in General Banks' department were not successful. We allude to the attempted reinforcement of the inadequate garrison at Galveston, which, as has been related in a previous chapter,* was defeated by a prompt and daring movement of the rebel General Magruder, and resulted in the capture of the troops which had been landed, and of the Harriet Lane, with the loss of the Westfield and several transport vessels of the navy. The next military attempt in the Department was in the region of the Bayou Teche, west of the Mississippi, where a band of armed rebels were giving great annoyance by their depredations, being assisted in their spoliations by a gunboat named the Cotton. To repress these disturbances, General Weitzel, in command of several Eastern and Western regiments at Thibodeaux, crossed to Brashier city on the eleventh of January, embarked his infantry for the ascent of the Atchafalaya in quest of the enemy while the cavalry and artillery proceeded by land. The Cotton took refuge in the Bayou Teche, protected by obstructions in the river and by a battery on shore. Lieutenant-Commander Buchanan brought up a fleet of gunboats to the attack, being supported in his advance by the troops of General Weitzel on both sides of the river. One of the gunboats was turned back by the explosion of a torpedo under her when the gallant Buchanan pushing on in the Calhoun the vessel was exposed to the fire from the rifle-pits on the banks. One of his officers was wounded by his side when he was immediately after fatally struck by a ball below the temple. The Union troops meanwhile were flanking the enemy's rifle-pits and getting into position to direct their batteries upon the Cotton. Being disabled by the fire of the land and naval forces, the gunboat was set on fire in the night to prevent her capture. Satisfied with this result, the gunboats were withdrawn and the troops returned to their encampment at Thibodeaux.

* General Banks' order, Promulgating the President's Emancipation Proclamation, New Orleans, Jan. 29th, 1863.

* Chapter LXXXIV.

In another direction at Baton Rouge a considerable force was stationed, which was being drilled and organized with a view of ulterior operations on the river. Twenty miles above, the enemy was in force at Port Hudson, their most important station on the Mississippi below Vicksburg. Situated on an elevated, almost perpendicular, cliff at a contracted bend of the stream, where the narrowed current ran by with great violence, its formidable line of batteries threatened absolute destruction to any hostile fleet, while on the land side the approach, easily capable of defence, was beset by swamps and other topographical difficulties. The first decided movement made in this quarter was mainly the work of the navy, and was undertaken in aid of the operations of General Grant and Admiral Porter at and below Vicksburg. At the beginning of February, it will be remembered Commander Ellet led the way in the Queen of the West in the passage of the batteries at that place. The primary design was to interrupt the supplies of the enemy from the west of the Mississippi. After inflicting much damage in this way, the vessel was lost by the treachery of a pilot, while ascending Red River. On receiving the news of this disaster, Admiral Farragut in command of the Gulf Fleet, determined to run past the rebel batteries at Port Hudson and assist the operations of Admiral Porter on the river from above. The land forces of General Banks were at the same time to threaten Port Hudson on the rear. The attempt was made in the night of the fourteenth of March. At about ten o'clock P. M. Admiral Farragut led the way at the head of his fleet on the flagship Hartford, accompanied by the gunboat Albatross, made fast to her portside ; the Richmond and Genesee in like manner followed ; next the Monongahela and Kineo, and finally the Mississippi, while a mortar fleet under Commander Caldwell of the Essex was brought up to shell the works. As soon as the Hartford came within range of the rebel batteries, a brisk fire was opened upon her which was returned with shot and shell. In the midst of this fire she succeeded in passing the batteries with the Albatross. The Richmond, Commander Alden, next in the line, was not so fortunate. She had run by the principal batteries and had just rounded the point when she was disabled by a shot which passed through her steam-chest and compelled her to drift down stream with a loss of three killed and ten wounded—among the latter her executive officer, Lieutenant-Com. Cummings, whose leg was severed by a shot from his body. A boatswain's-mate, it is said, "who had both legs, his right arm and left hand cut off by the explosion of a shell, as he fell to the deck, with his last breath, exclaimed, 'Don't give up the ship, lads.'"* The Genesee followed her consort in her retreat. The Monongahela and Kineo were next in the line of battle. Captain McKinstry of the former was wounded early in the action, when the command devolved upon Lieutenant Thomas, who kept the vessel on her course till in the midst of the smoke she grounded under fire of the principal batteries. By the aid of the Kineo, after about half an hour's exertion, she was released, and attempted again to advance, but her machinery was so heated that she was compelled to retire. She lost six killed and twenty wounded. The Mississippi, Commander Melanchthon Smith, the last in the line now advanced. She had made good progress without a single casualty, when, as she was pushing by the town, she grounded on the right bank of the river directly opposite the terminus of the Port Hudson and Clinton Railroad. Her engines, according to the account in the *New Orleans Era*, already cited, "were immediately reversed, and orders were given by Cap-

* *New Orleans Era*, March 19th, 1863.

tain Smith for the men to fire with all possibility, as their safety depended upon keeping the enemy from their guns. The men responded with alacrity, and in the short space of thirty-five minutes they fired two hundred and fifty shots. During this time Engineer Rutherford made every exertion to get the ship afloat, but without success. Captain Smith, finding it impossible to save his vessel, gave orders to make instant preparations to destroy the ship and save the crew. Orders were also given to the Chief Engineer to destroy the engines, and cut the outward connecting pipes. This being done, the water flowed rapidly into the ship. The sick and wounded were conveyed on board of the ironclad ram Essex, and the remainder of the crew were conveyed to the right bank of the river, which had been cleared by the gunboats of rebel sharpshooters. Before the crew left the ship every preparation was made to destroy her by collecting combustibles in the forward and after parts of the ship. Unfortunately, she was fired forward before the order was given. This becoming known to the crew, and there being but three small boats which they could use, many jumped overboard, and it is feared some were drowned in attempting to escape. Some others, seven in all, including Marine-Captain Fontene, Assistant-Engineer Brown and Master's Mate Francis, fell into the hands of the enemy. Just before the order was given to abandon the ship a shot from the enemy entered forward of the wheel, killing Acting-Master Kelly, commanding second division, also killing and wounding all but four men at one of his guns. After seeing that the survivors of his crew were fairly clear of the ship, and every preparation made to ensure her destruction, Commander Smith, accompanied by Lieutenant Dewey, his Executive officer, Ensign Bachelder, and First Assistant Engineer Tower, left the ship and abandoned her to the flames, after having with his own hands spiked most of the guns. As an evidence of the coolness which Captain Smith displayed on this occasion, it is related that in the midst of the death and destruction which surrounded him, while coolly lighting his cigar with steel and flint, he remarked to Lieutenant Dewey, 'It is not likely that we shall escape, and we must make every preparation to insure the destruction of the ship.' As soon as Captain Caldwell of the Essex discovered the flames bursting from the Mississippi, notwithstanding she was within 500 yards of the principal rebel batteries, he steamed up the river and succeeded in taking off from the shore many of the men who had escaped, and in saving many who were still struggling with the current for their lives. The fire having full possession of the ship, raged through her for an hour, greatly lightening her while the water, flowing aft, settled her stern, and she gradually slid off into the current. By a seeming act of Providence, the ship was swung round by the force of the current and headed down stream. The guns of her port battery, which had not been fired, becoming heated, the venerable old frigate paid a parting salute to the rebels at the same time that she fired the minute guns over her own graves. Had the ship floated down stream stern foremost, it is impossible to conjecture what would have been the result, inasmuch as her guns would have been discharged on her own crew, on the neighboring bank. She floated down the stream, her guns discharging, and shells on deck exploding in every direction, until half-past five o'clock, when, having reached a point near which the rebel ram Arkansas was destroyed, she blew up with a concussion which shook the country for miles around. Fragments of the ship drifted past Baton Rouge, and one of the wheel-houses was taken ashore at that point. It is estimated that only sixty-five officers and men belonging to the Mississippi were killed, wounded, and taken prisoners. The officers and crew lost everything except what they stood in. They saved nothing, and left nothing in the hands of the rebels."

This disaster closed the naval engagement. General Banks meanwhile had led his troops from Baton Rouge in three divisions under command of Generals Augur, Grover and Emory to Springfield Cross Roads, about five miles from Port Hudson. There was some skirmishing with the rebel pickets but no important advance beyond. On the night of the fourteenth, the cannonading of the fleet was distinctly heard by the soldiers, who also saw the light of the burning Mississippi. In the morning General Banks announced the passage of the fortifications by Admiral Farragut and retired with his troops to Baton Rouge. "Had our land forces," says General Halleck, in his report of the year's operations, "invested Port Hudson at this time, it could have been easily reduced, as its garrison was weak. This would have opened communication by the Mississippi river with General Grant at Vicksburg. But the strength of the place was not then known, and General Banks resumed his operations by the Teche and Atchafalaya." The passage of the batteries by Admiral Farragut enabled him, as we have seen, to render material assistance to Admiral Porter and the army of General Grant in the passage of the Vicksburg batteries, and especially in the blockade of the Red River. When this was accomplished, he left his flag-ship the Hartford above and returned by the Atchafalaya to take part in the final operations for the reduction of Port Hudson. We now turn to General Banks' operations in Louisiana, west of the Mississippi, in the Teche District. Since the expedition of General Weitzel in January, the rebels in that quarter had erected new fortifications and concentrated their forces, aided by a fleet of gunboats, at several stations on the Teche river, with the intention, it was said, of threatening New Orleans. General Banks, who had no disposition to leave a dangerous foe gathering strength in his rear, abandoning for the time active operations against Port Hudson, advanced with his forces to Berwick, where he arrived on the 11th of April, and commenced a series of active movements, which speedily swept the enemy from their strongholds throughout this central region from the Gulf to the Red River. At the outset of the march on the 12th and 13th there was a prolonged engagement of General Emory and Weitzel's Divisions with the enemy at an entrenched position in the vicinity of Pattersonville, at the mouth of the Teche. Artillery was actively employed, and both parties were assisted by gunboats, the rebels employing the Diana, a national vessel, which they had recently captured. After a series of sharp encounters, the enemy having suffered a heavy loss on the night of the thirteenth, evacuated their positions. Another portion of the Union forces meanwhile led by General Grover had with a fleet of transports and gunboats ascended Grand Lake from Brashear City and effected a landing in the rear of the enemy at Irish Bend. Crossing the Teche at that place, they marched towards Franklin and successfully encountered the enemy on the fourteenth after their retreat from the batteries below. The rebels in these engagements were led by General Dick Taylor, a son of President Zachary Taylor. After these defeats the enemy fled in confusion, burning in their retreat the gunboats Hart and Diana and a fleet of steamers on the Teche, while a valuable transport, the Cornie, was surrendered at Franklin. General Banks advanced with his forces to New Iberia and took possession of and destroyed the important salt-works in the vicinity which had been a constant source of supply to the Confederates. The fleet meanwhile, on the fourteenth, had encountered the rebel ram Queen of the West, which, after her capture on the Red River, had been brought by her new commander, Captain Fuller, into the Atchafalaya river, and had now descended to Grand Lake to attack the advancing Union forces. As she was moving onward to the assault, a shell from one of the gunboats exploded a box of ammunition on her deck, when she was immediately enveloped in flames. Strenuous efforts were made by the fleet to save the lives of her crew and ninety-five were taken from the vessel and the water. About forty it was supposed perished. The vessel was burnt to the water's edge, but her guns were saved.

Encouraged by these brilliant successes, General Banks pushed his forces on rapidly. "On the evening of the seventeenth," to continue the narrative in the words of his official dispatch from Opelousas on the twenty-third, "General Grover, who had marched from New Iberia by a shorter road, and thus gained the advance, met the enemy at Bayou Vermilion. The enemy's force consisted of a considerable number of cavalry, 1,000 infantry, and six pieces of artillery, masked in a strong position on the opposite bank, with which we were unacquainted. The enemy was driven from his position, but not until he had succeeded in destroying the bridge over the bayou by fire. Everything had been previously arranged for this purpose. The enemy's flight was precipitous. The night of the seventeenth and the whole of the next day were occupied in pushing with vigor the reconstruction of this bridge. On the nineteenth the march was resumed, and continued to the vicinity of Grand Coteau, and on the following day our main force occupied Opelousas. The cavalry, supported by one regiment of infantry and a section of artillery, being thrown forward to Washington, on the Courtebleaus, a distance of six miles. The command rested on the twenty-first. Yesterday morning, the twenty-second, I sent out Brigadier-General Dwight with his brigade of Grover's division and detachments of artillery and cavalry, to push forward through Washington toward Alexandria. He found the bridges over bayous Cocodue and Bocuff destroyed, and occupied the evening and night in replacing them by a single bridge at the junction of the two bayous. The people say that the enemy threw large quantities of ammunition and some small arms into bayou Cocodue, and that the Texans declared they were going to Texas. Here the steamer Wave was burnt by the enemy, and the principal portion of her cargo, which had been transferred to a flat, captured by us. A dispatch was found by General Dwight, in which Governor Moore tells General Taylor to retreat slowly to Alexandria, and if pressed to retire to Texas. General Dwight will push well forward to-day, and probably halt to-morrow, to continue his march or return, according to circumstances. * * * An expedition, consisting of the One Hundred and Sixty-second New York, Lieutenant-Colonel Blanchard, one section of artillery, and Barrett's Company B, First Louisiana cavalry, accompanied by Captain Dunham, Assistant Adjutant-General, and First Lieutenant Harwood, Engineers, (both of my staff,) was sent out yesterday morning by way of Barre's Landing, to examine the Bayou Courtableau, in the direction of Butte-a-la-Rose. Last night Captain Dunham reported the road impassable, four miles beyond Barre's Landing, and that the expedition had captured the steamer Ellen, in a small Bayou, leading out of the Courtableau. This capture is a timely assistance to us. I informed you that I had ordered the gunboats to take Butte-a-la-Rose. This was handsomely done without serious loss on the morning of the twentieth inst., by Lieutenant-Commander Cooke, U. S. Navy, with his gunboat and four companies of infantry. We captured here the garrison of sixty men and its commander, two heavy guns in position and in good order, a large quantity of ammunition, and the key of the Atchafalaya. I hope not to be obliged to lose a moment in improving the decisive advantage gained in this section. We have destroyed the enemy's army and navy, and made their organization impossible by destroying or removing the material. We hold the key of the position. Among the evidences of our victory are two thousand prisoners, two transports and twenty guns, (including one piece of the Valvado battery,) taken; and three gunboats and eight transports destroyed. The Union loss in these engagements was very slight."

Following up these advantages on the eighth of May, General Banks had advanced to and occupied Alexandria on the Red River immediately after its capture by the naval force of Admiral Porter in one of his excursions from before Vicksburg. The co-operation of the two armies below and above Port Hudson was thus secured by an interior line of communication, while, what was of the utmost consequence, the Confederate supplies from the west of the Mississippi were effectually cut off. Before the vigorous operations of Admirals Farragut and Porter and Generals Grant and Banks, the vaunted strongholds of the Mississippi at Vicksburg and Port Hudson, it was evident, were doomed to an early surrender.

General Banks immediately after his occupation of Alexandria moved down the Red River, making Semmesport on the Atchafalaya his rendezvous, where, crossing the Mississippi, he landed with a portion of his army on the twenty-first of May at Bayou Sara, a few miles above Port Hudson. An expedition under orders of General Nickerson, consisting of Colonel Davis' First Texas Cavalry and Captain Read's Massachusetts Rifle Rangers, previously sent to the Amite river to destroy the Jackson Railroad, had proceeded as far as Camp Moore, captured a number of prisoners, a considerable amount of cotton and destroyed valuable rebel manufactories. On the twenty-third, a junction was effected with the advance of Major-General Augur and Brigadier-General Sherman who had brought up their forces from Baton Rouge. The Union line now occupied the Bayou Sara road at a distance of five miles from Port Hudson. Major-General Augur had an encounter with a portion of the enemy at Port Hudson Plains on the Bayou Sara road, in the direction of Baton Rouge, which resulted with slight loss in the repulse of the enemy with heavy loss. On the twenty-fifth the enemy, continues General Banks, in his official report,* "was compelled to abandon his first line of works. General Weitzel's brigade, which had covered our rear in the march from Alexandria, joined us on the twenty-sixth, and on the morning of the twenty-seventh a general assault was made upon the fortifications. The artillery opened fire between five and six o'clock, which was continued with animation during the day. At ten o'clock Weitzel's brigade, with the division of General Grover, reduced to about two brigades, and the division of General Emory, temporarily reduced by detachments to about a brigade, under command of Colonel Paine, with two regiments of colored troops, made an assault upon the right of the enemy's works, crossing Sandy Creek, and driving them through the woods to their fortifications. The fight lasted on this line until four o'clock, and was very severely contested. On the left, the infantry did not come up until later in the day; but at two o'clock an

* Major-General Banks to Major-General Halleck, before Port Hudson, May 30th, 1863.

assault was opened on the centre and left of centre by the divisions under Major-General Augur and Brigadier-General Sherman. The enemy was driven into his works, and our troops moved up to the fortifications, holding the opposite sides of the parapet with the enemy on the right. Our troops still hold their position on the left. After dark the main body, being exposed to a flank fire, withdrew to a belt of woods, the skirmishers remaining close upon the fortifications. In the assault of the twenty-seventh, the behavior of the officers and men was most gallant, and left nothing to be desired. Our limited acquaintance of the ground and the character of the works, which were almost hidden from our observation until the moment of approach, alone prevented the capture of the post. On the extreme right of our line I posted the First and Third regiments of negro troops. The First regiment of Louisiana Engineers, composed exclusively of colored men, excepting the officers, was also engaged in the operations of the day. The position occupied by these troops was one of importance, and called for the utmost steadiness and bravery in those to whom it was confided. It gives me pleasure to report that they answered every expectation. Their conduct was heroic. No troops could be more determined or more daring. They made, during the day, three charges upon the batteries of the enemy, suffering very heavy losses, and holding their position at nightfall with the other troops on the right of our line. The highest commendation is bestowed upon them by all the officers in command on the right. Whatever doubt may have existed before as to the efficiency of organizations of this character, the history of this day proves conclusively to those who were in a condition to observe the conduct of these regiments, that the Government will find in this class of troops effective supporters and defenders. The severe test to which they were subjected, the determined manner in which they encountered the enemy, leave upon my mind no doubt of their ultimate success. They require only good officers, commands of limited numbers, and careful discipline, to make them excellent soldiers. Our losses from the twenty-third to this date in killed, wounded and missing, are nearly 1,000, including, I deeply regret to say, some of the ablest officers of the corps." Among the officers killed in this gallant assault were Colonel D. S. Cowles of the 128th New York, Captain Arthur De Wint, from the banks of the Hudson, a gallant young officer of the same regiment. Colonel Payne of the Second Louisiana, General T. W. Sherman, formerly at the head of the South Carolina Department, and now second in command under General Banks, was severely wounded in the right leg with a solid shot while leading the attack. He was removed to New Orleans and amputation performed. Brigadier-General Neal Dow was slightly wounded. The attack was a desperate one, and like that made by General Grant on his arrival in the rear of Vicksburg proved the strength of the enemy's positions, the impracticability of taking them by a sudden assault, and was followed by a regular investment of the place. The enemy now effectually cut off from supplies by the Mississippi were closely besieged on the land sides, the Union lines extending on a semi-circle round their works reaching the river at both extremities. Gradually, day by day, General Banks' batteries were pressed closer, the sharpshooters of the army rendering the rebel armaments comparatively useless. On the fourteenth of June, having in vain appealed to the rebel commander to submit to the necessities of his situation and spare further slaughter by a surrender, after a furious cannonade along the whole line, another desperate assault was made by General Weitzel's and Emory's divisions, the latter led by General Paine. Like the former, though marked by many deeds of heroism, in consequence of the advantages of the enemy's position, it was unsuccessful. General Paine was severely wounded, his left leg being shattered as he was leading the assault. Colonel Bryan of the 175th New York was killed. The New York and New England regiments engaged behaved with great gallantry and suffered heavily. This repulse, however, though falling severely on the assailants did not better the fortunes of the beleaguered garrison, whose fall, cut off as they were from supplies, without hope of relief, could not be long deferred. To shorten this period by decisive military action was evidently the desire of General Banks and his army which had lost nothing in spirit by these unsuccessful trials. Accordingly, the day after this second attempt, he issued the followed order: "The Commanding-General congratulates the troops before Port Hudson upon the steady advance made upon the enemy's works, and is confident of an immediate and triumphant issue of the contest. We are at all points upon the threshold of his fortifications. One more advance and they are ours! For the last duty that victory imposes, the Commanding-General summons the bold men of the corps to the organization of a storming column of a thousand men, to vindicate the Flag of the Union, and the memory of its defenders who have fallen! Let them come forward! Officers who lead the column of victory in this last assault, may be assured of the just recognition of their services by promotion, and every officer and soldier who shares its perils and its glory shall receive a medal fit to commemorate the first grand success of the campaign of 1863 for the freedom of the Mississippi. His name will be placed in General Orders upon the roll of honor. Division Commanders will at once report the names of the officers and men who may volunteer for this service, in order that the organization of the column may be completed without delay." The response to this call was immediate, the list of volunteers being filled in a few hours. Happily their services were not required. The fall of Vicksburg on the fourth of July, gave the respectable sanction of a military necessity to the now unavoidable surrender of Port Hudson. On the eighth of July, Major-General Frank Gardner, in command of the Confederate forces at the latter place, under a flag of truce, sent the following note to General Banks: "Having received information from your troops that Vicksburg has been surrendered, I make this communication to ask you to give me the official assurance whether this is true or not, and if true, I ask for a cessation of hostilities, with a view to the consideration of terms for surrendering this position." To this General Banks immediately replied, communicating an official dispatch which he had received the day before from General Grant, by a gunboat on the river, announcing the surrender, adding, "that under present circumstances he could not, consistently with his duty, consent to a cessation of hostilities for the purpose indicated." General Gardner, on receipt of this the same day, answered, "Having defended this position as long as I deem my duty requires, I am willing to surrender to you, and will appoint a commission of three officers to meet a similar commission, appointed by yourself, at nine o'clock this morning, for the purpose of agreeing upon and drawing up the terms of the surrender, and for that purpose I ask for a cessation of hostilities. Will you please designate a point outside of my breastworks, where the meeting shall be held for this purpose." Commissioners were accordingly appointed, General Charles P. Stone, Colonel Henry W. Birge, of the

Thirteenth Connecticut, who had been placed in command of the thousand Volunteers, and Lieutenant-Colonel R. B. Irwin, being named by General Banks and by the articles of capitulation, "the place of Port Hudson and its dependencies, with its garrison, armament, munitions, public funds, material of war, in the condition as nearly as may be, in which they were at the hour of cessation of hostilities, namely, six o'clock A. M., July eighth, 1863," were duly surrendered. A second article declared, that the surrender to be "qualified by no condition save that the officers and enlisted men composing the garrison shall receive the treatment due to prisoners of war, according to the usages of civilized warfare."

The next day formal possession was taken of the works. The surrender included 6,233 prisoners, 51 pieces of artillery, two steamers, 4,400 pounds of cannon powder, 5,000 small arms, and 150,000 rounds of ammunition. "The good old ship Hartford and the Albatross," we are told, "came down below Port Hudson at once, and were greeted with much enthusiasm after their glorious work." The last stronghold of the rebels on the Mississippi had now fallen, the possession of the river severing the Confederacy, depriving it of its most fertile sources of supply from the West, and leaving for the present only predatory bands of insurgents in that region more dangerous to the people of the country whom they chose to call their friends than to their enemies. The story of that great work of the national armies, the reopening of the Mississippi river from the mouth of the Ohio to the Gulf, deserves and will receive hereafter the highest honors of the historian. The toils, the embarrassments, the energy with which they were met, the sacrifices of fortune, health and life who can recount? For these labors what adequate monument can be reared? But the great river, itself, will tell the tale as its mighty waters, a perpetual bond of Union, bears through the length of the land the ever increasing treasures of wealth and civilization.

CHAPTER XC.

THE SUMMER CAMPAIGN ON THE POTOMAC. BATTLE OF GETTYSBURGH, JULY, 1863.

After the indecisive engagement of General Hooker with the enemy at Chancellorsville in the beginning of May, both armies resumed their old positions on either side of the Rappahannock at Fredericksburg. But it was not the policy of the rebel leaders long to remain inactive. Feeling the pressure of the continued and ineffective war in which while they claimed many victories they had achieved no advantages for their cause, with the prospect before them of an early surrender of Vicksburg and Port Hudson, and the consequent loss of the Mississippi, there was an earnest cry at Richmond for a grand movement upon the North which might be attended with some substantial benefits. Various motives might be given for the repetition of the invasion of Maryland in the hopes entertained from the numbers and well-tried endurance of the rebel army, the expectation of an easy entrance to the wealthy agricultural districts of Maryland and Pennsylvania, the much-needed supplies of food and clothing which might be obtained in the towns, with the paramount temptation of some grand success in battle which would place the capital of the nation at the disposal of the Confederate government. How far the advisers of the movement were encouraged by the differences of opinion in reference to the war which had been of late freely manifested at the North it were vain to inquire. Doubtless something was anticipated from this in case of a decided military success; but little could have been hoped for at the outset from any disaffection of this kind after the experience of General Lee in his appeal to the people of Maryland in his previous invasion of that State. It was a moral necessity that something grand should be attempted by the enemy; and the expectation was reasonable enough that much might be accomplished by the direct forces or chances of war if their army was resolutely put in motion. The military motives of the campaign are stated with moderation by General Lee in his report, though he admits the hope of "other valuable results," which, after all his expectations had failed, he does not think it necessary to enter upon. "The position," says he, "occupied by the enemy opposite Fredericksburg being one in which he could not be attacked to advantage, it was determined to draw him from it. The execution of this purpose embraced the relief of the Shenandoah Valley from the troops that had occupied the lower part of it during the Winter and Spring, and, if practicable, the transfer of the scene of hostilities north of the Potomac. It was thought that the corresponding movement on the part of the enemy, to which those contemplated by us could probably give rise, might offer a fair opportunity to strike a blow at the army therein commanded by General Hooker, and that, in any event, that army would be compelled to leave Virginia, and possibly to draw to its support troops designed to operate against other parts of the country. In this way it was supposed that the enemy's plan of campaign for the Summer would be broken up, and part of the season of active operations be consumed in the formation of new combinations and the preparations that they would require."

With these intentions General Lee, on the third of June began the removal of his troops from Fredericksburg in the direction of the Alexandria Railroad. Longstreet's and Ewell's corps were set in motion, leaving Hill's corps to occupy the lines at Fredericksburg. On the eighth, the two army corps, with the cavalry under Stuart, were concentrated at Culpepper Court-house. The stir in the rebel camp did not escape the notice of General Hooker. On the sixth, he crossed a body of troops at Deep Run, below Fredericksburg, which were entrenched and served as a corps of observation. When he ascertained that the enemy's cavalry were gathering at Culpepper, General Pleasanton was sent with a picked cavalry force, consisting of a body of regulars and Pennsylvanians under General Buford, and portions of several New York, Indiana and Illinois regiments under General Gregg, supported by a column of infantry under the command of Generals Russell and Ames, to anticipate the threatened raid. At dawn, on the morning of the ninth, General Pleasanton's forces crossed the Rappahannock at Beverley and Kelly's Fords. General Buford's brigade first encountered the enemy a short distance south of the ford, when a hand-to-hand engagement commenced, both parties repeatedly charging upon one another, the Union troops mostly with sabres, the Confederates with revolvers. On Gregg's force coming up, the enemy were pursued for several miles to the vicinity of Brandy Station, where they were heavily reinforced from Culpepper, upon which General Pleasanton having accomplished the object of the reconnoissance and ascertained the enemy's strength and intentions, retired across the Rappahannock. The fight was severe. Colonel B. F. Davis, Captain Foote and Lieutenant Cutler of the Eighth New York Cavalry were killed on the field, and other officers of the regiment were severely wounded. Captain Canfield of the Second United States Cavalry and Captain Davis of the Sixth Pennsylvania Cavalry were also among the killed. The Rebel loss in officers and men was also heavy. A number of prisoners were also taken on both sides. General Lee claims the capture of 400 prisoners, three pieces of artillery and several colors. General Pleasanton reported the capture of over 200 prisoners and one battle flag. Which ever side, however, might have inflicted the heaviest loss, the moral advantage was with the assailants. The enemy had been anticipated, and, to a certain extent, crippled as they were entering upon a movement, the success of which depended greatly upon their securely gaining ground at the outset; while the positive information which was gained of their intentions doubtless hastened the movements of Hooker, which effectually thwarted their plans.

The first demonstration of the enemy was in the valley of the Shenandoah, upon the outposts at Winchester and Berryville. General Jenkins, with his cavalry brigade, was sent forward in the direction of the former place to coöperate with the infantry in the proposed expedition, while General Imboden was sent towards Romney to cover the movement and prevent reinforcements to the Union troops from the line of the Baltimore and Ohio Railroad. Both these officers, as we are informed from Lee's report, were in position when General Ewell, with his corps, left Culpepper Court-house on the tenth, the day after the cavalry fight. Crossing the Shenandoah, near Front Royal, he detached General Rodes' division to Berryville, with instructions after dislodging the force stationed there, to cut off communication between Winchester and the Potomac,—while with the divisions of Early and Johnson he advanced directly upon Winchester. Winchester was at this time held by General Milroy with about ten thousand men under his command; General McReynolds was at Berryville, eleven miles to the East, with his brigade; and Martinsburgh was held by General Tyler as an outpost of Harper's Ferry. "Neither Winchester nor Martinsburgh," we are told by General Halleck, was "susceptible of a good defence;" and as early as the eleventh directions were given to withdraw their garrisons to Harper's Ferry. Before the orders were acted upon, the enemy had commenced their attack. On the thirteenth the rebel General Rodes' division appeared before Berryville, when General McReynolds, with his command, fell back to Winchester, pursued by the enemy, a portion of the rear guard escaping in the direction of Harper's Ferry. On arriving at Winchester in the evening, he found General Milroy closely pressed by the enemy. On the evening of the next day, General Early carried the outer works of the town by storm. That night General Milroy, after spiking his guns, left with the whole of his command on his retreat to Harper's Ferry, taking with him his artillery horses and wagons. Four miles from the town, on the Martinsburgh road, he was interrupted by an overwhelming rebel force with artillery, when, says he, "after a desperate fight of two hours, I got through." A cavalry force pursued and picked up many of the fugitives on the route. On reaching Harper's Ferry with the greater part of his command, he telegraphed to Washington, estimating his loss at not exceeding two thousand in killed, wounded and missing.* General Rodes, meanwhile, after driving the Union forces from Berryville proceeded to Martinsburgh,

* Official Telegram from General Milroy, Harper's Ferry, June 16th, 1863.

where, says Lee, he took 700 prisoners, five pieces of artillery and a considerable quantity of stores. General Tyler, with the main body of his command, made good his retreat to Harper's Ferry. The lower part of the valley was thus swept of the Union forces, Lee claiming in the several assaults the capture of more than 4,000 prisoners, 29 pieces of artillery, 270 wagons and ambulances, 400 horses, with a large amount of military stores.

The success was immediately followed up by the passage of a body of 1,500 rebel cavalry, under General Jenkins, across the Potomac and their advance to Chambersburgh, which they entered without opposition on the evening of the fifteenth. This invasion of Pennsylvania with the forward movements of Lee's army, indicating a vigorous campaign, aroused the energies of the military department at Washington. At the first symptoms of danger preparations were made for the defence of Pennsylvania. Harrisburg, tempting the enemy by the prospect of large supplies and other advantages, was made the headquarters of the new department of the Susquehanna under Major-General Couch, while Major-General Brooks was assigned to the department of the Monongahela with his headquarters at Pittsburg. A few days after these appointments, on the fifteenth, President Lincoln issued his proclamation, declaring that "the armed insurrectionary combinations now existing in several of the States, threatening to make inroads into, the States of Maryland, Western Virginia, Pennsylvania and Ohio required immediately an additional military force for the service of the United States." He therefore called for 100,000 militia to serve for six months, from Maryland 10,000, Pennsylvania 50,000, Ohio 30,000, West Virginia 10,000; 20,000 were also called for from New York. Governor Curtin of Pennsylvania at once seconded the appeal in a proclamation, calling upon the citizens of the State "to rise in their might and rush to the rescue in this hour of imminent peril." The Governors of the other States promptly lent their aid. New York and Brooklyn sent eighteen city regiments to Harrisburgh and Baltimore,—wherever they were most required. There was some sluggishness at first in Pennsylvania in responding to the call, requiring the most pointed appeals of its Governor to the inhabitants; but the depredations of the enemy speedily enforced his arguments, and men and money were liberally furnished for the emergency.

It was, as we have seen, the anticipation of Lee that at the first incursion into Pennsylvania, Hooker would withdraw his army from Virginia when he might gain some further advantage by attacking him on his retreat. This expectation was defeated by the prompt and skillful dispositions of the Union commander. On the night of the thirteenth, the division on the south side of the Rappahannock, at Deep Run, recrossed the river in safety, and the following day the headquarters at Falmouth were broken up, the base at Acquia Creek was abandoned, and the whole army was on its march along the roads near the Potomac to the vicinity of the camps before Washington. On the evening of the fifteenth, General Hooker had his headquarters at Fairfax Court-house. On his departure from Falmouth, the corps of General Hill at Fredericksburg was sent to the valley to reinforce Ewell, while Longstreet's corps, augmented by three brigades of General Pickett's division, moving from Culpepper Court-house advanced along the east side of the Blue Ridge occupying Ashby's and Snicker's Gaps. General Stuart's cavalry was in front on the flank of Hooker's army. Here they were met by the Union cavalry under General Pleasanton, who, in several engagements, proved the increased efficiency of this branch of the service and its ability to cope with the most experienced forces of the enemy, to whom, on these occasions, success was of the utmost importance. Stuart, failing to accomplish his purpose of arresting the movement of Hooker's army, was himself driven back to the passes of the Blue Ridge. The main struggle between the two bodies of cavalry took place on the twenty-first of June on the road between Aldie and Ashby's Gap, when the enemy, under Stuart, was pursued in a series of encounters from the vicinity of Middleburgh to Upperville, and were defeated at every point. The Union troops, admirably handled by officers of distinguished reputation in this branch of the service, with the infantry supports fought with the greatest courage and resolution. Generals Buford, Gregg, Kilpatrick—names always mentioned with honor—led the attacks. The result at the close of the day was thus announced by General Pleasanton in a dispatch from his camp near Upperville: "I moved with my command this morning to Middleburgh, and attacked the cavalry force of the rebels under Stuart, and steadily drove him all day, inflicting heavy loss at every stop. We took two pieces of artillery—one being a Blakely gun—together with three caissons, beside blowing one up. We also captured upward of sixty prisoners, and more are coming in—including a Lieutenant-Colonel, Major, and five other officers, besides a wounded Colonel, and a large number of wounded rebels left in the town of Upperville. They left their dead and wounded upon the field. Of the former I saw upward of twenty. We also took a large number of carbines, pistols and sabres. In fact it was a most disastrous day to the rebel cavalry. Our loss has been very small, both in men and horses. I never saw the men and troops behave better, or under more difficult circumstances. Very heavy charges were made and the sabre was used freely, but always with great advantage to us."

While the main armies were thus moving parallel with each other—Hooker, by the line of the railway to Alexandria, Lee, by the valley of the Shenandoah—the rebel advance under Jenkins which we have followed to Chambersburgh, in Pennsylvania, was making the best of its opportunities in seizing supplies of horses and provisions from the townspeople and farmers of the vicinity. After two days' occupation of the place fearing that they might be cut off, they retired to Hagerstown on the seventeenth to keep up their communication with the approaching army of Lee. From that point they hurried to the region on either side of the South Mountain, proceeding to Waynesboro' and threatening Gettysburgh on the east. Harrisburgh and Pittsburg were for the time relieved by the withdrawal of the rebel cavalry. The respite, however, was but for a few days.

From Lee's report, it would appear that the advance of Jenkins was intended as a demonstration to hasten Hooker's army out of Virginia, leaving Longstreet at liberty to occupy the fords of the Potomac below Harper's Ferry. As Hooker, however, persisted in watching his enemy before Washington, Longstreet was withdrawn to the west side of the Shenandoah river to coöperate directly with Hill. This shielded the capital from the danger of immediate attack in the rear, compelling the enemy in their threatened invasion of Maryland to cross the Potomac by its upper fords and gave Hooker the opportunity of following the movement, still keeping his army on the flank of the invading column.

That invasion was now fully determined upon. On the twenty-first Lee issued his general orders for the regulation of his army in obtaining supplies "while in the enemy's country." The Chiefs of the Commissary, Quartermaster, Ordnance and Medical Departments were authorized to make requisitions upon the local authorities or inhabitants for the supplies they might need, payment for which should be tendered, and if refused, receipts should be given for the property taken. If property was withheld or concealed it was liable to peremptory seizure. The day following this order, the twenty-second, Ewell's corps crossed the Potomac and was immediately followed by the corps of Longstreet and Hill, the former crossing at Williamsport, the latter at Shephardstown, the columns uniting at Hagerstown. General Rodes' division advanced and occupied Chambersburgh on the twenty-third; on the twenty-fourth a body of rebel cavalry entered Shippensburgh, and the next day the enemy was at Carlisle, from which General Knipe, who was stationed at the place with two of the New York Militia regiments, retired to Harrisburgh, on the appearance of this superior force. General Ewell on entering Chambersburgh issued an order to the inhabitants forbidding the sale of intoxicating liquors to his command, and admonishing all citizens of the country to abstain from all acts of hostility upon the penalty of "being dealt with in a summary manner." On the twenty-seventh, the main body of Ewell's, Longstreet's and Hill's corps were encamped near Chambersburgh. At this time, says General Lee, "no report had been received that the Federal army had crossed the Potomac, and the absence of the cavalry rendered it impossible to obtain accurate information. In order, however, to retain it on the east side of the mountains after it should enter Maryland, and thus leave open our communication with the Potomac, through Hagerstown and Williamsport, General Ewell has been instructed to send a division eastward from Chambersburgh to cross the South Mountains. Early's division was detached for this purpose, and proceeded as far east as York, while the remainder of the corps proceeded to Carlisle. General Imboden, in pursuance of his instructions, had been actively engaged on the left of General Ewell during the progress of the latter into Maryland. He had driven off the forces guarding the Baltimore and Ohio Railroad, destroying all the important bridges on that route from Cumberland to Martinsburgh, and seriously damaged the Chesapeake and Ohio Canal. He subsequently took position at Hancock, and after the arrival of Longstreet and Hill at Chambersburgh was directed to march by way of McConnellsburgh to that place."

In these movements of the enemy, General Gordon's brigade of Early's division of Ewell's corps, entered Gettysburgh on the twenty-sixth, driving before them a regiment of Pennsylvania Militia which was stationed at an outpost of the town. The importance of the place in reference to the position of the army of invasion, had not been unnoticed by General Couch, and efforts had been made to rouse the spirit of the inhabitants and aid them in their defence by sending troops to the town. The number of these, but few more than the single regiment just spoken of, was of course inadequate to resist the superior forces of the enemy whose entire army on the soil of Pennsylvania was estimated to exceed 100,000, including 90,000 infantry, upwards of 10,000 cavalry and 4,000 or 5,000 artillery.* The condition of Early's men as they appeared on their arrival at Gettysburgh is described by Professor Jacobs of Pennsylvania College at that place, a most intelligent observer of the important scenes which occurred there during the campaign, as "exceedingly dirty, some ragged, some without shoes, and some surmounted by the skeleton of what was once an entire hat, affording unmistakable evidence that they stood in great need of having their scanty ward-

* Everett's Oration at Gettysburgh, p. 9.

it, yet not without the deepest emotion. The sorrow of parting with the comrades of so many battles is relieved by the conviction that the courage and devotion of this army will never cease nor fail; that it will yield to my successor, as it has to me, a willing and hearty support. With the earnest prayer that the triumph of its arms may bring successes worthy of it and the nation, I bid it farewell." General Meade's address on taking command was marked by the simple, earnest tone of a true-hearted, veteran soldier entering upon a new field of duty of which he felt the full responsibility. "By direction of the President of the United States," he said, "I hereby assume command of the Army of the Potomac. As a soldier, in obeying this order, an order totally unexpected and unsolicited, I have no promises or pledges to make. The country looks to this army to relieve it from the devastation and disgrace of a hostile invasion. Whatever fatigues and sacrifices we may be called upon to undergo, let us have in view constantly the magnitude of the interests involved, and let each man determine to do his duty, leaving to an all-controlling Providence the decision of the contest. It is with just diffidence that I relieve in the command of this army an eminent and accomplished soldier, whose name must ever appear conspicuous in the history of its achievements; but I rely upon the hearty support of my companions in arms to assist me in the discharge of the duties of the important trust which has been confided to me." When General Meade thus took command, General Lee, as we have seen, was actively pushing his advance in the direction of Harrisburgh. The rapid gathering of the Union army on his flank now compelled him to concentrate his forces to preserve his communications with the Potomac. Accordingly, as he informs us, Longstreet and Hill were directed to proceed from Chambersburg to Gettysburg, to which point General Ewell was also instructed to march from Carlisle. General Stuart, with his cavalry, were at this time entirely separated from the rest of the Confederate army by the route they had taken crossing the Potomac at Seneca Creek on the right of Meade's army. They were encountered on their northern march by Kilpatrick's division at Hanover to the east of Gettysburg, whence they proceeded to Carlisle, arriving after General Ewell had left.

While such were the movements of Lee's army, General Meade was rapidly concentrating his forces to arrest its further progress. General French now in command at Harper's Ferry was ordered on the twenty-eighth to leave that post, which was represented as destitute of supplies, occupying Frederick with 7,000 of his men and with the remaining 4,000 remove and escort the public property to Washington. On the twenty-ninth Meade's army was in motion, and at night was in position, the left at Emmittsburgh and the right at New Windsor. Buford's division of cavalry was on the left flank with its advance at Gettysburg; Kilpatrick's division, as we have mentioned, was in front at Hanover. The next day, in view of the rapidly approaching conflict, General Meade issued the following circular to the army: "The Commanding General requests that previous to the engagement soon to be expected with the enemy, corps and all other commanding officers address their troops, explaining to them the immense issues involved in the struggle. The enemy is now on our soil. The whole country looks anxiously to this army to deliver it from the presence of the foe. Our failure to do so will leave us no such welcome as the swelling of millions of hearts with pride and joy at our success would give to every soldier of the army. Homes, firesides and domestic altars are involved. The army has fought well heretofore. It is believed that it will fight more desperately and bravely than ever if it is addressed in fitting terms. Corps and other commanders are authorized to order the instant death of any soldier who fails to do his duty at this hour."

On the thirtieth, continues General Meade, in his official report of the Campaign, "the right flank of the army was moved up to Manchester, the left still being at Emmettsburg, in the vicinity of which place three corps—the first, eleventh and third—were collected, under orders of Major-General Reynolds. General Buford having reported from Gettysburg the appearance of the enemy on the Cashtown road in some force, General Reynolds was directed to occupy Gettysburg. On reaching that place on the first of July, General Reynolds found Buford's cavalry warmly engaged with the enemy, who had debouched his infantry through the mountains on the Cashtown road, but was being held in check in a most gallant manner by General Buford's cavalry. Major-General Reynolds immediately moved around the town of Gettysburg, and avdanced on the Cashtown road, and without a moment's hesitation deployed his advance division and attacked the enemy, at the same time sending orders for the Eleventh Corps (General Howard) to advance as promptly as possible. Soon after making his dispositions for the attack, Major-General Reynolds fell mortally wounded, the command of the First Corps devolving upon Major-General Doubleday, and the command of the field on Major-General Howard, who arrived about this time (11:30 A. M.) with the Eleventh Corps, then commanded by Major-General Schurz. Major-General Howard pushed forward two divisions of the Eleventh Corps to support the First Corps, now warmly engaged with the enemy on the ridge to the north of the town, and posted his Third Division, with three batteries of artillery, on Cemetery Ridge, on the south side of the town. Up to this time the battle had been with the forces of the enemy debouching from the mountains on the Cashtown road, known to be Hill's corps. In the early part of the action success was on our side—Wadsworth's division of the First Corps having driven the enemy back some distance, and capturing numerous prisoners, among them General Archer of the Confederate Army. The arrival of reinforcements to the enemy on the Cashtown road, and the junction with Ewell's corps, coming on the York and Harrisburgh roads, which occurred between one and two o'clock P. M., enabled the enemy to bring vastly superior forces against both the First and Eleventh Corps, outflanking our line of battle and pressing it so severely that at about four P. M. Major-General Howard deemed it prudent to withdraw these two corps to Cemetery Ridge, on the south side of the town, which operation was successfully accomplished — not, however, without considerable loss in prisoners, arising from the confusion incident to portions of both corps passing through the town and men getting confused in the streets. About the time of the withdrawal, Major-General Hancock arrived, whom I had dispatched to represent me on the field, on hearing of the death of General Reynolds. In conjunction with Major-General Howard, General Hancock proceeded to post troops on Cemetery Ridge, and to repel an attack that the enemy made on our right flank. The attack, however, was not very vigorous. The enemy, seeing the strength of the position occupied, seemed to be satisfied with the successs he had accomplished, desisting from any further attack this day. About seven P. M., Major-Generals Slocum and Sickles, with the Twelfth Corps, and part of the Third, reached the ground, and took post on the right and left of the troops previously posted."

Turning now to the report of General Lee, we find this engagement of the first of July thus briefly mentioned, together with the motives which induced him to offer battle at this point. "The march toward Gettysburg," says he, "was conducted more slowly than it would have been had the movements of the Federal army been known. The leading division of Hill met the enemy in advance of Gettysburg on the morning of the first of July. Driving back these troops to within a short distance of the town, he there encountered a large force, with which two of his divisions became engaged. Ewell, coming up with two of his divisions by the Heidlersburgh road, joined in the engagement. The enemy was driven through Gettysburg with heavy loss, including about five thousand prisoners and several pieces of artillery. He retreated to a high range of hills south and east of the town. The attack was not pressed that afternoon, the enemy's force being unknown, and it being considered advisable to await the arrival of the rest of our troops. Orders were sent back to hasten their march; and, in the meantime, every effort was made to ascertain the numbers and position of the enemy, and find the most favorable point of attack. It had not been intended to fight a general battle at such a distance from our base, unless attacked by the enemy: but, finding ourselves unexpectedly confronted by the Federal army, it became a matter of difficulty to withdraw through the mountains with our large trains. At the same time the country was unfavorable for collecting supplies while in the presence of the enemy's main body, as he was enabled to restrain our foraging parties by occupying the passes of the mountains with regular and local troops. A battle thus became, in a measure, unavoidable. Encouraged by the successful issue of the engagement of the first day, and in view of the valuable results that would ensue from the defeat of the army of General Meade, it was thought advisable to renew the attack. The remainder of Ewell's and Hill's corps having arrived, and two divisions of Longstreet's, our preparations were made accordingly. During the afternoon intelligence was received of the arrival of General Stuart at Carlisle, and he was ordered to march to Gettysburg, and take position on the left."

We now resume the narrative of General Meade, who fully appreciated the enemy's designs. "Being satisfied," says he, "from reports received from the field that it was the intention of the enemy to support, with his whole army, the attack already made, and reports from Major-Generals Hancock and Howard, on the character of the position being favorable, I determined to give battle at this point, and early in the evening of the first issued orders to all corps to concentrate at Gettysburg, directing all trains to be sent to the rear at Westminster. At eleven P. M. of the first, I broke up my headquarters, which, till then, had been at Taneytown, and proceeded to the field, arriving there at one A. M. of the second. So soon as it was light, I proceeded to inspect the position occupied, and to make arrangements for posting several corps as they should reach the ground. By seven A. M. the Second and Fifth Corps, with the rest of the Third, had reached the ground, and were posted as follows: The Eleventh Corps retained its position on the cemetery side, just opposite to the town. The First Corps was posted on the right of the Eleventh, on an elevated knoll, connecting with the ridge extending to the south and east, on which the Second Corps was placed. The right of the Twelfth Corps rested on a small stream at a point where it crossed the Baltimore Pike, and which formed on the right flank of the Twelfth something of an obstacle. Cemetery Ridge extended in a westerly and southerly direction, gradually diminishing in elevation till it came to a very prominent ridge, called Round Top, running east and west. The Second and Third Corps were directed to occupy the continuation of Cemetery Ridge, on the left of the Eleventh Corps. The Fifth Corps, pending the arrival of the Sixth, was held in reserve. While these dispositions were being made, the enemy was massing his troops on the exterior ridge, distant from the line occupied by us from a mile to a mile and a half. At two P. M. the Sixth Corps arrived after a march of thirty-two miles, accomplished from nine A. M. the day previous. On its arrival being reported, I immediately directed the Fifth Corps to remove over to our extreme left, and the Sixth to occupy its place as a reserve for the right. About three P. M. I rode out to the extreme left to await the arrival of the Fifth Corps and post it, when I found that Major-General Sickles, commanding the Third Corps, not fully apprehending the instructions in regard to the position to be occupied, had advanced, or rather was in the act of advancing his corps a half a mile or three-quarters of a mile in front of the line of the Second Corps, on the prolongation of which it was designed his corps should rest. Having found Major-General Sickles, I was explaining to him that he was too far in advance, and discussing with him the propriety of withdrawing, when the enemy opened upon him with several batteries on his front and his flank, and immediately brought forward columns of infantry, and made a vigorous assault. The Third Corps sustained the shock most heroically. Troops from the Second Corps were immediately sent by Major-General Hancock to cover the right flank of the Third Corps, and soon after the assault commenced the Fifth Corps most fortunately arrived, and took position on the left of the Third. Major-General Sykes' command immediately sending a force to occupy Round-Top Ridge, when a most furious contest was maintained, the enemy making desperate but unsuccessful efforts to secure it. Notwithstanding the stubborn resistance of the Third Corps, under Major-General Birney, Major-General Sickles having been wounded early in the action, the superiority in number of corps in the enemy enabling him to outflank its advance position, General Birney was counseled to fall back and re-form behind the line originally designed to be held.

"In the mean time, perceiving great exertions on the part of the enemy, the Sixth Corps (Major-General Sedgwick) and part of the First Corps (to the command of which I had assigned Major-General Newton), particularly Lockwood's Maryland Brigade, together with detachments from the Second Corps, were all brought up at different periods, and succeeded, together with the gallant resistance of the Fifth Corps, in checking, and finally repulsing the assault of the enemy, who retired in confusion and disorder about sunset, and ceased any further efforts. On the extreme left another assault was, however, made about eight P. M., on the Eleventh Corps, from the left of the town, which was repulsed with the assistance of the troops from the Second and First Corps. During the heavy assault upon our extreme left, portions of the Twelfth Corps were sent as reinforcements. During their absence, the line on the extreme right was held by a very much reduced force. This was taken advantage of by the enemy, who, during the absence of Geary's Division of the Twelfth Corps, advanced and occupied part of the line. On the morning of the Third, General Geary, having returned during the night, was attacked at early dawn by the enemy, but succeeded in driving him back, and occupying his former position. A spirited contest was maintained all morning along this part of the line. General Geary, reinforced by Wheaton's Brigade, Sixth Corps, maintained his position and inflicting very severe losses on the enemy. With this exception the quiet of the lines remained undisturbed till one P. M., on the third, when the enemy opened from over 125 guns, playing upon our centre and left. This cannonade continued for over two hours, when our guns failing to make any reply, the enemy ceased firing, and soon his masses of infantry became visible, forming for an assault on our left and left centre. The assault was made with great firmness, being directed principally against the point occupied by the Second Corps, and was repelled with equal firmness by the troops of that corps, supported by Doubleday's Division and Stannard's Brigade of the First Corps. During the assault, both Major-General Hancock, commanding the left centre, and Brigadier-General Gibbon commanding the Second Corps, were severely wounded. This terminated the battle, the enemy retiring to his lines, leaving the field strewed with his dead and wounded, and numbers of prisoners fell into our hands. Buford's Division of Cavalry, after its arduous services at Gettysburg on the first, was, on the second, sent to Westminster to refit and guard our trains. Kilpatrick's Division, that on the twenty-ninth, thirtieth and first had been successfully engaging the enemy's cavalry, was on the third sent to our extreme left, on the Emmettsburg road, where good service was rendered in assaulting the enemy's line and occupying his attention. At the same time General Gregg was engaged with the enemy on our extreme right, having passed across the Baltimore pike and Bonaughtown roads, and boldly attacked the enemy's left and rear."

The second and third days' battles thus described by General Meade are noticed by General Lee as follows: "The preparations for attack," says he, "were not completed until the afternoon of the second. The enemy held a high and commanding ridge, along which he had massed a large amount of artillery. General Ewell occupied the left of our line, General Hill the centre, and General Longstreet the right. In front of General Longstreet the enemy held a position, from which, if he could be driven, it was thought that our army could be used to advantage in assailing the more elevated ground beyond, and thus enable us to reach the crest of the ridge. That officer was directed to endeavor to carry this position, while General Ewell attacked directly the high ground on the enemy's right, which had already been partially fortified. General Hill was instructed to threaten the centre of the Federal line, in order to prevent reinforcements being sent to either wing, and to avail himself of any opportunity that might present itself to attack. After a severe struggle Longstreet succeeded in getting possession of and holding the desired ground. Ewell also carried some of the strong positions which he assailed, and the result was such as to lead to the belief that he would ultimately be able to dislodge the enemy. The battle ceased at dark. These partial successes determined me to continue the assault the next day. Pickett, with three of his brigades, joined Longstreet the following morning, and our batteries were moved forward to the position gained by him the day before. The general plan of attack was unchanged, except that one division and two brigades of Hill's corps were ordered to support Longstreet. The enemy, in the meantime, had strengthened his line with earthworks. The morning was occupied in necessary preparations, and the battle recommenced in the after noon of the third, and raged with great violence until sunset. Our troops succeeded in entering the advanced works of the enemy, and getting possession of some of his batteries; but our artillery having nearly expended its ammunition, the attacking columns became exposed to the heavy fire of the numerous batteries near the summit of the ridge, and, after a most determined and gallant struggle, were compelled to relinquish their advantage, and fall back to their original positions, with severe loss."

Such, in the narrative of the two commanders, was the memorable battle of Gettysburg, in which, as at Antietam, the invading hosts of Lee were defeated with heavy loss on Northern soil and whence they again turned in flight and dismay, peeled and scattered, to seek refuge beyond the Potomac. The particulars of the flight and pursuit to the close of the campaign are briefly and clearly set forth by General Meade. "On the morning of the fourth," he writes, "reconnoissance developed that the enemy had drawn back his left flank, but maintained his position in front of our left, apparently assuming a new line parallel to the mountains. On the morning of the fifth, it was ascertained that the enemy was in full retreat by the Fairfield and Cashtown roads. The Sixth Corps was immediately sent in pursuit on the Fairfield road, and cavalry on the Cashtown road, and by the Emmettsburg and Monterey Passes. The fifth and sixth of July were employed in succoring the wounded and burying the dead. Major-General Sedgwick, commanding the Sixth Corps, having pushed the pursuit of the enemy as far as the Fairfield Pass and the mountains, and reporting that the Pass was very strong—one in which a small force of the enemy could hold in check and delay for a considerable time any pursuing force—I determined to follow the enemy by a flank movement, and accordingly, leaving McIntosh's brigade of cavalry and Neil's brigade of infantry to continue harrassing the enemy, I put the army in motion for Middletown, and orders were immediately sent to Major-General French, at Frederick, to reoccupy Harper's Ferry and send a force to occupy Turner's Pass in South Mountain. I subsequently ascertained that Major-General French had not only anticipated some of these orders, in part, but had pushed a cavalry force to Williamsport and Falling Waters, where they destroyed the enemy's pontoon bridge, and captured its guard. Buford was at the same time sent to Williamsport and Hagerstown. The duty above assigned to the cavalry was most successfully accomplished, the enemy being greatly harrassed, his trains destroyed, and many captures of guns and prisoners made. After halting a day at Middletown to procure necessary supplies and bring up the trains, the army moved through South Mountain, and by the twelfth of July was in front of the enemy, who occupied a strong position on the heights near the marsh which runs in advance of Williamsport. In taking this position, several skirmishes and affairs had been had with the enemy, principally by the cavalry and the Eleventh and Sixth Corps. The Thirteenth was occupied in reconnoissances of the enemy's position and preparations for an attack; but on advancing on the morning of the fourteenth, it was ascertained that he had retired the night previous by the bridge at Falling Waters and ford at Williamsport. The cavalry in pursuit overtook the rear guard at Falling Waters, capturing two guns and numerous prisoners. Previous to the retreat of the enemy, Gregg's division of cavalry was crossed at Harper's Ferry, and coming up with the rear of the enemy at Charlestown and Shepherdstown, had a spirited contest, in which the enemy was driven to Martinsburg and Winchester, and pursued and harrassed in his retreat. The pursuit was resumed by a flank movement of the army crossing the Potomac at Berlin and moving down the Loudon

Valley. The cavalry were immediately pushed into several passes of the Blue Ridge, and having learned from servants of the withdrawal of the Confederate army from the lower valley of the Shenandoah, the army (the Third Corps, Major-General French, being in advance), was moved into Manassas Gap in the hope of being able to intercept a portion of the enemy in possession of the Gap, was disputed so successfully as to enable the rear guard to withdraw by the way of Strasburgh. The Confederate army retiring to the Rapidan, a position was taken with this army on the line of the Rappahannock, and the campaign terminated about the close of July."

The corresponding portion of General Lee's report narrates the circumstances of his retreat as follows, commencing with the close of the engagement at Gettysburg. "Owing," says he, "to the strength of the enemy's position and the reduction of our ammunition, a renewal of the engagement could not be hazarded, and the difficulty of procuring supplies rendered it impossible to continue longer where we were. Such of the wounded as were in condition to be removed, and part of the arms collected on the field, were ordered to Williamsport. The army remained at Gettysburg during the fourth, and at night began to retire by the road to Fairfield, carrying with it about 4,000 prisoners. Nearly 2,000 had previously been paroled, but the enemy's numerous wounded, that had fallen into our hands after the first and second days' engagements, were left behind. Little progress was made that night, owing to a severe storm, which greatly embarrassed our movements. The rear of the column did not leave its position near Gettysburg until after daylight on the fifth. The march was continued during that day without interruption by the enemy, except an unimportant demonstration upon our rear in the afternoon, when near Fairfield, which was easily checked. Part of our train moved by the road through Fairfield, and the rest by the way of Cashtown, guarded by General Imboden. In passing through the mountains, in advance of the column, the great length of the trains exposed them to attack by the enemy's cavalry, which captured a number of wagons and ambulances; but they succeeded in reaching Williamsport without serious loss. They were attacked at that place on the sixth by the enemy's cavalry, which was gallantly repulsed by General Imboden. The attacking force was subsequently encountered and driven off by General Stuart, and pursued for several miles in the direction of Boonesboro' The army, after an arduous march, rendered more difficult by the rains, reached Hagerstown on the afternoon of the sixth and morning of the seventh July. The Potomac was found to be so much swollen by the rains that had fallen almost incessantly since our entrance into Maryland as to be unfordable. Our communications with the south side were thus interrupted, and it was difficult to procure their ammunition or subsistence, the latter difficulty being enhanced by the high waters impeding the working of neighboring mills. The trains with the wounded and prisoners were compelled to await at Williamsport the subsiding of the river and the construction of boats, as the pontoon-bridge left at Falling Waters had been partially destroyed. The enemy had not yet made his appearance; but, as he was in condition to obtain large reinforcements, and our situation, for the reasons above mentioned, was becoming daily more embarrassing, it was deemed advisable to recross the river. Part of the pontoon-bridge was recovered, and new boats built, so that by the thirteenth a good bridge was thrown over the river at Falling Waters.

"The enemy in force reached our front on the twelfth. A position had been previously selected to cover the Potomac from Williamsport to Falling Waters, and an attack was awaited during that and the succeeding day. This did not take place, though the two armies were in close proximity, the enemy being occupied in fortifying his own lines. Our preparations being completed, and the river, though still deep, being pronounced fordable, the army commenced to withdraw to the south side on the night of the thirteenth. Ewell's corps forded the river at Williamsport, those of Longstreet and Hill crossed upon the bridge. Owing to the condition of the roads the troops did not reach the bridge until after daylight of the fourteenth, and the crossing was not completed until one P. M., when the bridge was removed. The enemy offered no serious interruption, and the movement was attended with no loss of material except a few disabled wagons and two pieces of artillery, which the horses were unable to move through the deep mud. Before fresh horses could be sent back for them the rear of the column had passed. During the slow and tedious march to the bridge, in the midst of a violent storm of rain, some of the men lay down by the way to rest. Officers sent back for them failed to find many in the obscurity of the night, and these, with some stragglers, fell into the hands of the enemy. Brigadier-General Pettigrew was mortally wounded in an attack made by a small body of cavalry, which was unfortunately mistaken for our own and permitted to enter our lines. He was brought to Bunker Hill, where he expired a few days afterward. He was a brave and accomplished officer and gentleman, and his loss will be deeply felt by the country and the army. The following day the army marched to Bunker Hill, in the vicinity of which it encamped for several days. The day after its arrival a large force of the enemy's cavalry, which had crossed the Potomac at Harper's Ferry, advanced toward Martinsburgh. It was attacked by General Fitz Lee, near Kearneysville, and defeated with heavy loss, leaving its dead and many of its wounded on the field. Owing to the swollen condition of the Shenandoah River the plan of operations which had been contemplated when we recrossed the Potomac could not be put in execution, and before the water had subsided the movements of the enemy induced me to cross the Blue Ridge and take position south of the Rappahannock, which was accordingly done."

The losses in this campaign were unusually severe on both sides. That of the Union army, as officially reported by General Meade, was 2,834 killed, 14,709 wounded and 6,643 missing. General Lee, in his report, states, that it is "out of his power to give a correct statement of our casualties which were severe." Some estimate may be formed of their extent from the fact that he left 7,540 wounded on his retreat to be cared for by the Union army, while the entire number of prisoners taken by General Meade was 13,821. The rebel wounded who were removed, the killed and missing are estimated by Mr. Everett "from the best data which the nature of the case admits of," at 23,000.* General Meade reported the capture of three guns, forty-one standards and 24,978 small arms collected on the battle-field.

Both armies mourned the loss of distinguished officers. General John F. Reynolds, who fell in command in the first day's engagement at the beginning of the battle, was a native of Pennsylvania, of a family of Lancaster county, with many claims to distinction in the enterprize and public services of its members. He received a military education at West Point, graduating in 1841, with an appointment in the artillery service. He served with the army in the Mexican war, and subsequently in the Indian campaigns, with great

* Oration at Gettysburg, p. 19.

credit, and at the opening of the war for the Union was promoted Lieutenant-Colonel of the Fourteenth Regiment of Regular Infantry, and shortly after to Brigadier-General of Volunteers. His services in Western Virginia and with the army of the Potomac, in command of a division of General McCall's Pennsylvania Reserves, will be remembered by the reader. Taken prisoner in one of the actions before Richmond, he had been exchanged, and was then employed in command of the troops of his native State raised to repel the first invasion of Lee. In General Hooker's army he had command of the First Corps. His military qualities are spoken of in the highest terms. "Modest, reticent, studious and brave, he was exactingly severe in his discipline and passionately devoted to his command."* General Samuel Kosciusko Zook, who fell on the same day with General Reynolds, was also a native of Pennsylvania, and previous to the war was widely known in connection with the telegraph business as discoverer, inventor and constructor, already an officer of the State Militia. He recruited a regiment of Volunteers in New York, where he resided, and served with it through the campaign of General McClellan on the Peninsula. He was then promoted Brigadier-General of Volunteers—the rank which he held on the field at his death on the soil of his native State. General Gabriel Rene Paul, who fell on the second day of the conflict, was a native of Missouri, a graduate of West Point in 1834, and distinguished himself in the Mexican war, when he was brevetted Major in his regiment, the Seventh Infantry. On the outbreak of the rebellion he was transferred with the full rank of Major to the Eighth Regular Infantry and ordered to service in New Mexico. There he rendered most important services in coöperation with Colonel Canby in defence of the Western posts. For his gallantry in these movements he was promoted a Brigadier-General of Volunteers, and was assigned to duty under General Casey at the National Capital. No less than nine General Union officers were wounded. General Sickles, whose right leg was shattered by a shot, suffered amputation on the field. The other wounded Generals, as enumerated by Mr. Everett, were Generals Barlow, Barnes, Butterfield, Doubleday, Gibbon, Graham, Hancock and Warren.

General Lee in his report records among the casualties "an unusual proportion of distinguished and valuable officers, among them (he continues) I regret to mention the following general officers: Major-Generals Hood, Pender, and Trimble severely, and Major-General Heth slightly wounded. General Pender has since died. This lamented officer has borne a distinguished part in every engagement of this army, and was wounded on several occasions while leading his command with conspicuous gallantry and ability. The confidence and admiration inspired by his courage and capacity as an officer were only equaled by the esteem and respect entertained by all with whom he was associated for the noble qualities of his modest and unassuming character. Brigadier-Generals Barksdale and Garnett were killed, and Brigadier-General Semmes mortally wounded, while leading their troops with the courage that always distinguished them. Brigadier-Generals Kemper, Armistead, Scales, G. T. Anderson, Hampton, J. M. Jones and Jenkins were also wounded. Brigadier-General Archer was taken prisoner. General Pettigrew, though wounded at Gettysburgh, continued in command until he was mortally wounded near Falling Waters."

At the crisis of Lee's invasion of Pennsylvania, on the Fourth of July, Alexander H. Stephens, Vice-President of the Confederate States, presented

* Obituary. *Philadelphia Press*, July 3d, 1863.

himself in a Confederate steamer, under a flag of truce, to Admiral S. H. Lee, in command on the station at Hampton Roads, stating that he was the bearer of a communication in writing from Jefferson Davis, Commander-in-Chief of the land and naval forces of the Confederate States of America, to Abraham Lincoln, Commander-in-Chief of the land and naval forces of the United States of America, and that he desired to proceed in the same Confederate steamer to Washington, and deliver the said communication, attended only by Robert Ould, as secretary, for the purpose of conferring upon the subjects of the aforesaid communication, and the officers and crew of the steamer. The fact of Stephen's arrival was promptly communicated to the Secretary of War and the Navy at Washington, who simply replied, "The request of Alexander H. Stephens is inadmissible. The customary agents and channels are adequate for all needful military communications and conference between the United States forces and the insurgents." So Vice-President Stephens returned rejected to Richmond. A general letter of instructions to him by Jefferson Davis, on setting out on this errand, was afterwards published at Richmond, in which it was stated, "your mission is simply one of humanity, and has no political aspect." It was further said to refer to certain negotiations regarding the exchange of prisoners. Whatever may have been the motives and objects of the proceeding, it assumed importance from the time at which it was made, the high official character of the agent, and the ground which was quietly taken in refusing to receive him.

The interest with which this engagement at Gettysburg was regarded by the country can hardly be over estimated. Occurring on the three days immediately preceding the celebration of the national anniversary, at the close of a period of many difficulties to the administration when, not without serious political opposition it was called to a final struggle at several important points, of the favourable issues of which numbers pretended to despair—it was with a hearty sense of relief doubtless that President Lincoln, on the forenoon of the fourth of July, sent from the capital this encouraging telegraphic despatch to the nation:—"The President announces to the country that news from the Army of the Potomac, up to ten P. M. of the third, is such as to cover that army with the highest honor; to promise a great success to the cause of the Union, and to claim the condolence of all for the many gallant fallen; and that for this, he especially desires that on this day He, whose will, not ours, should ever be done, be everywhere remembered and reverenced with profoundest gratitude." On the same day, General Meade had the satisfaction to issue the following address to his army:—"The Commanding General, in behalf of the country, thanks the Army of the Potomac for the glorious result of the recent operations. Our enemy, superior in numbers, and flushed with the pride of a successful invasion, attempted to overcome or destroy this army. Baffled and defeated he has now withdrawn from the contest. The privations and fatigues the army has endured, and the heroic courage and gallantry it displayed, will be matters of history to be ever remembered. Our task is not yet accomplished, and the Commanding General looks to the army for greater efforts to drive from our soil every vestige of the presence of the invader. It is right and proper that we should, on suitable occasions, return our grateful thanks to the Almighty disposer of events, that, in the goodness of His providence He has thought fit to give victory to the cause of the just." When three days later the despatch of Admiral Porter, announcing the great victory of General Grant, the surrender of Vicksburgh, and its occupation on the Fourth, was received at Washington, the enthusiasm of the country was still further stimulated. The coincidence in connection with previous associations with the day was indeed remarkable. It was familiarly, yet forcibly pointed out by President Lincoln himself in a speech which he made on the evening of the day the news from Vicksburgh was received, when he was waited upon at the White House by a body of citizens eager to express their admiration at these decided successes of the war. "Fellow citizens," said the President, in reply to the congratulations of the crowd, "I am very glad indeed to see you to-night, and yet I will not say I thank you for this call, but I do most sincerely thank the Almighty God for the occasion on which you have called. How long ago is it? Eighty odd years since on the Fourth of July for the first time in the history of the world a nation, by its representatives, assembled and declared as a self-evident truth, 'that all men are created equal.' That was the birthday of the United States of America. Since then the Fourth of July has had several very peculiar recognitions. The two most distinguished men in the framing and support of the Declaration were Thomas Jefferson and John Adams—the one having penned it, and the other sustained it the most forcibly in debate—the only two of the fifty-five who sustained it being elected President of the United States. Precisely fifty years after they put their hands to the paper, it pleased Almighty God to take both from this stage of action. This was indeed an extraordinary and remarkable event in our history. Another President, five years after, was called from this stage of existence on the same day and month of the year; and now in this last Fourth of July, just passed, when we have a gigantic rebellion at the bottom of which is an effort to overthrow the principle that all men were created equal, we have the surrender of a most powerful position and army on that very day, and not only so, but in a succession of battles in Pennsylvania, near to us, through three days, so rapidly fought that they might be called one great battle on the first, second, and third of the month of July: and on the Fourth the cohorts of those who opposed the Declaration that all men are created equal, 'turned tail,' and run. Gentlemen, this is a glorious theme, and the occasion for a speech, but I am not prepared to make one worthy of the occasion. I would like to speak in terms of praise due to the many brave officers and soldiers who have fought in the cause of the Union and liberties of their country from the beginning of the war. These are trying occasions, not only in success, but for the want of success. I dislike to mention the name of one single officer, lest I might do wrong to those I might forget. Recent events bring up glorious names, and particularly prominent ones; but these I will not mention. Having said this much, I will now take the music." A week later the President, assured of the importance of the recent military successes, appointed a day of National Thanksgiving by the following proclamation:—"It has pleased Almighty God to hearken to the supplications and prayers of an afflicted people, and to vouchsafe to the army and the navy of the United States, on the land and on the sea, victories so signal and so effective as to furnish reasonable grounds for augmented confidence that the Union of these States will be maintained, their Constitution preserved, and their peace and prosperity permanently preserved; but these victories have been accorded not without sacrifice of life, limb, and liberty, incurred by brave, patriotic and loyal citizens. Domestic affliction in every part of the country follows in the train of these fearful bereavements. It is meet and right to recognise and confess the presence of the Almighty Father, and the power of His hand equally in these triumphs and these sorrows. Now, therefore, be it known that I do set apart Thursday, the sixth day of August next, to be observed as a day for National Thanksgiving, praise and prayer, and I invite the people of the United States to assemble on that occasion in their customary places of worship, and in the form approved by their own conscience, render the homage due to the Divine Majesty for the wonderful things He has done in the Nation's behalf, and invoke the influence of His Holy Spirit, to subdue the anger which has produced, and so long sustained a needless and cruel rebellion ; to change the hearts of the insurgents ; to guide the counsels of the Government with wisdom adequate to so great a National emergency, and to visit with tender care, and consolation throughout the length and breadth of our land, all those who, through the vicissitudes of marches, voyages, battles and sieges, have been brought to suffer in mind, body or estate, and finally to lead the whole nation through paths of repentance and submission to the Divine will, back to the perfect enjoyment of union and fraternal peace."

CHAPTER XCI.

GENERAL BURNSIDE'S DEPARTMENT OF THE OHIO. MORGAN'S RAID AND CAPTURE. OCCUPATION OF EAST TENNESSEE. MARCH — SEPTEMBER, 1863.

After a short interval of repose following his retirement from the Army of the Potomac, General Burnside was, on the twenty-sixth of March, 1863, placed in command of the Department of the Ohio. It was an important position, requiring the exercise of constant vigilance and authority. The southern borders of Kentucky were infested by guerrillas, and the State was again seriously threatened with invasion, while within the Department a spirit of disaffection to the Government was exhibited, which, though confined to a small minority of disappointed political partisans or sympathizers with the rebellion, was bold in its manifestations, and seriously interfered with the efficient conduct of the war. General Burnside, who had always shown himself a man of resolution, prepared at once to grapple with the situation. One of his first acts was to dismiss from the service the captain of a Kentucky regiment of cavalry "for his disgraceful surrender" of Mount Sterling to a party of guerrillas. A few days after he had the satisfaction to report the rout of the enemy in their raid in Central Kentucky by Brigadier-General Gilmore, who set out from Lexington, and with about twelve hundred of his command, Kentucky and Ohio Cavalry, after an energetic march came up in the neighbourhood of Somerset with a Rebel force of more than twice his numbers under General Pegram. "I attacked the enemy," says General Gilmore in his despatch, "on the thirtieth March in a strong position of his own selection, defended by six cannon, near the town; fought him for five hours, driving him from one position to another ; finally stormed his position, whipped him handsomely, and drove him in confusion toward the river. His loss is over 300 in killed, wounded and prisoners ; ours will not exceed thirty." Night stopped the pursuit, when the enemy recrossed the Cumberland.

General Burnside now turned his attention to the treason at work within his Department, issuing from his headquarters at Cincinnati on the thirteenth of April, his memorable General Order No. thirty-eight. It was in these words:—"The Commanding General publishes, for the information of all concerned, that hereafter all persons found within our lines who commit acts for the benefit of the enemies of our country, will be tried as spies or traitors, and, if convicted, will suffer death. This order includes the following class of persons: carriers of secret mails; writers of letters sent by secret mails; secret recruiting officers within the lines; persons who have entered into an agreement to pass our lines for the purpose of joining the enemy; persons found concealed within our lines belonging to the service of the enemy; and, in fact, all persons found improperly within our lines who could give private information to the enemy; all persons within our lines who harbor, protect, conceal, feed, clothe, or in any way aid the enemies of our country. The habit of declaring sympathies for the enemy will not be allowed in this department. Persons committing such offences will be at once arrested, with a view to being tried as above stated, or sent beyond our lines into the lines of their friends. It must be distinctly understood that treason, expressed or implied, will not be tolerated in this department; all officers and soldiers are strictly charged with the execution of this order." The specifications of this order sufficiently indicate the nature of the disaffection with which General Burnside, in maintaining the authority of the Government, had to contend. The subject was presently brought prominently before the country in the proceedings attending the arrest of the Honorable Clement L. Vallandigham, a member from Ohio of the recent National Congress, who was tried by a military commission for a violation of the order. On or about the first day of May, as it was alleged before the Court, Vallandigham publicly addressed a large meeting of citizens at Mount Vernon, Knox county, Ohio, and in the course of his speech declared the war "wicked, cruel, and unnecessary," "not being waged for the preservation of the Union," but "for the purpose of crushing out liberty, and erecting a despotism;" that the Government of the United States was about to appoint military marshals in every district to restrain the people of their liberties, to deprive them of their rights and privileges, characterizing General Burnside's order, No. thirty-eight, as "a base usurpation of arbitrary authority," and inviting resistance to it by saying, "the sooner the people inform the minions of usurped power that they will not submit to such restrictions upon their liberties the better." A few days after the delivery of the speech, Mr. Vallandigham was arrested, under orders of General Burnside, at his residence at Dayton. The arrest was made by a party of soldiers between two and three o'clock on the morning of the fifth of May. The outer and inner doors were broken open, Mr. Vallandigham was seized, carried to Cincinnati, and there confined in a military prison. On the ninth an application was made in the United States Circuit Court for the Southern District of Ohio, in session in the city, for a writ of habeas corpus, that the prisoner "may be relieved from manifest oppression under color of military authority. The Honorable George E. Pugh appeared for Mr. Vallandigham, and the Honorable Aaron F. Perry and District Attorney Bell for General Burnside. At the opening of the proceedings a statement was submitted by General Burnside, in which he presented his motives in ordering the arrest. He pointed out the injurious consequences which would result to the army of "wholesale criticisms of the policy of the Government" by himself and his officers, reminded the Court that one of the States of his department was at the moment invaded, and three others threatened so that it had become the duty of every citizen, as well as of the soldiers, to avoid saying anything that would weaken the army. "If I were to find a man," he added, "from the enemy's country distributing in my camps speeches of their public men, that tended to demoralize the troops, or to destroy their confidence in the constituted authorities of the Government, I would have him tried, and hung if found guilty, and all the rules of modern warfare would sustain me. Why should such speeches from our own public men be allowed?" In reference to the cry of the danger of usurpation, he pronounced it groundless. "There is no fear," said he, "of the people losing their liberties; we all know that to be the cry of demagogues, and none but the ignorant will listen to it; all intelligent men know that our people are too far advanced in the scale of religion, civilization, education and freedom, to allow any power on earth to interfere with their liberties; but this same advancement in these great characteristics of our people teaches them to make all the necessary sacrifices for their country when an emergency requires. They will support the constituted authorities of the Government, whether they agree with them or not. Indeed, the army itself is a part of the people, and is so thoroughly educated in the love of civil liberty, which is the best guarantee for the permanence of our republican institutions, that it would itself be the first to oppose any attempt to continue the exercise of military authority after the establishment of peace by the overthrow of the Rebellion. No man on earth can lead our citizen soldiery to the establishment of a military despotism, and no man living would have the folly to attempt it. To do so would be to seal his own doom. On this point there can be no ground for apprehension on the part of the people." General Burnside defended his course by the plea of sound military necessity, and the Court, after the arguments on both sides were exhausted by the able counsel, supported him in his course. The writ was refused. Judge Leavitt, in his opinion, patriotically asserted the paramount authority of the President of the United States as Commander-in-Chief, specially charged with the suppression of the Rebellion. "In my judgment," said he, "when the top of the Republic is imperiled, he mistakes his duty and obligation as a patriot who is not willing to concede to the Constitution such a capacity of adaptation to circumstances as may be necessary to meet a great emergency, and save the nation from hopeless ruin."

The Military Commission on the sixteenth of May found Mr. Vallandigham guilty of the charge brought against him, and sentenced him "to be placed in close confinement in some fortress of the United States, to be designated by the Commanding Officer of this Department, there to be kept during the continuance of the war." General Burnside designated Fort Warren, Boston Harbor, as the place of confinement. The sentence was revised by President Lincoln and changed to transportation through the Union lines. Mr. Vallandigham was accordingly sent by way of Louisville to General Rosecrans at Murfreesboro', and by him delivered to the rebel authorities of General Bragg's army in his front. He was there received, travelled through the Southern States, ran the blockade from Wilmington to Bermuda in June, reached Canada and made his residence on the British side at Niagara Falls. There, during the summer, he held correspondence with his political friends of the old Democratic party, who, at a meeting of the Ohio State Convention in June had nominated him for Governor of the State. For several months the Vallandigham grievance was freely agitated before the people; but when they were called in the election in October to express their opinion of his course, he was overwhelmingly defeated at the ballot-box, John Brough, the war candidate, being elected Governor by a majority of 61,020 of the Home votes, and by 39,170 of the Soldiers' votes in the field. 187,562 votes in all were cast for Vallandigham; 288,661 for Brough.

By an order issued on the first of June, General Burnside prohibited the circulation of the New York *World* in his department, alleging the tendency of the opinions and articles habitually published in this journal, being "to cast reproach upon the Government and to weaken its efforts to suppress the rebellion by creating distrust in its war policy, and its circulation in war-time being calculated to exert a pernicious and treasonable influence." The publication of the Chicago *Times* was also, at the same time, ordered to be suppressed "on account of the repeated expression of disloyal and incendiary sentiments." When news of the latter was received at Chicago, a popular meeting gathered in front of the *Times* office, and speeches were made denouncing the order as arbitrary and despotic. The Illinois House of Representatives, in session at Springfield, passed resolutions to the same effect. General Jacob Ammen meantime, to whom General Burnside had entrusted the execution of the order, had arrived at Chicago, before dawn on the morning of the third, sent a body of soldiers who broke into the *Times* office and temporarily took possession of the establishment. Judge Drummond, of the Supreme Court, was applied to for an injunction of the proceedings. While the application was pending, the *Times*, on the fourth, issued a paper, when the office was again taken possession of by the military. In the evening the obnoxious order was revoked by General Burnside in pursuance of instructions from President Lincoln. In the popular discussion on this question strong feelings were elicited on both sides. The evil aimed at by General Burnside was generally admitted; but the public readily acquiesced in the policy of the President's course. It was not advisable in so tender a matter as the liberty of the press to resort to unusual means for its regulation. The precedent might prove a dangerous one in the hands of future partisans, and it would feed, in the mean time, the complaints of the opponents of the administration.

From these measures of repression, General Burnside was now called to provide for the exigencies of active military service in his Department. A rebel raid of Kentucky cavalry across the Ohio into Harrison county, Indiana, in the latter part of June, was repelled with a loss to the invaders of fifty-three prisoners. About the same time, an expedition, led by Colonel S. H. Saunders, from Williamsburgh, in South Eastern Kentucky, consisting of the First Tennessee Cavalry, with two pieces of artillery and some detachments from General Carter's command, penetrated East Tennessee, struck the railroad at Lenox, destroyed the road up to Knoxville, and made a demonstration against that city. The bridges at State Creek, Strawberry Plains and Massey Creek were destroyed; three pieces of artillery, some 200 boxes of artillery ammunition, over 500 prisoners and 2,000 stand of arms were captured. A large amount of military stores and a saltpetre work were destroyed. Colonel Saunders, eluding the rebel forces on his halt, returned by Smith's Gap, having accomplished all this with the loss of one killed, two wounded and a few stragglers.*

The Department was now threatened with a serious inroad by a rebel force of cavalry under the redoubtable Gen-

* Colonel Saunders' Dispatch to General Burnside, June 23d, 1863. General Halleck's Annual Report, November 15th, 1863.

eral John H. Morgan. It was the period of Lee's active movements in Virginia preparatory to his invasion of Maryland and Pennsylvania, with which it was supposed to be the design of Morgan to coöperate. General Halleck, in his Annual Report, says, it was probably his intention after passing through Indiana and Ohio to recross the Ohio River into West Virginia or Pennsylvania, and join Lee's army. The actual history of his expedition we now proceed to narrate, certainly one of the most remarkable in the annals of the war, whether we look to its reckless and desperate character, the resolution with which it was followed up, its spirit of wanton cruelty in its assaults upon life and property, and the extent of country traversed in the vain effort to elude the numerous bands of pursuers who were put upon the track.

General Morgan, his command being strengthened by several picked regiments from the Confederate forces in Tennessee, about 3000 cavalry in all, with a battery of artillery, set out on the twenty-seventh of June, from Sparta, in the northern portion of the State, and by a rapid march entered Kentucky, reaching the Cumberland in the vicinity of Jamestown. Here he was watched by a brigade of cavalry, with artillery, under Colonel Wolford, but managed, on the night of the second of July, to cross the river lower down at Burkesville, the water being high, improvising a number of flats for the occasion. There was some skirmishing with the Union cavalry guarding the fords, and in the vicinity of Columbia, whither the enemy proceeded, encountering a reconnoitering party under Captain Carter, of the First Kentucky, who, making the attack, was himself mortally wounded, and his men driven back towards Jamestown. Morgan then moved on Green River, where, on the morning of the fourth, he found his progress arrested at the turnpike bridge, by 200 men of the Twenty-fifth Michigan cavalry, under Colonel Moore, in an intrenched position. Being summoned to surrender, the Union commander replied, "If it was any other day I might consider the summons, but the Fourth of July is a bad day to talk about surrender, and I must therefore decline." The enemy then attacked the rifle-pits and abattis of timber, and were repulsed with heavy loss. One of Morgan's officers, Captain Cunningham, in a narrative of the expedition, states the number of killed and wounded on his side at about sixty. "Of Morgan's command," says he, "the gallant Colonel Chenault fell pierced through the head by a Minnie ball as he led his men in a charge upon the rifle-pits. The lion-hearted Major Brent also poured out his life-blood upon the field. Indeed, this was the darkest day that ever shone upon our command. Eleven commissioned officers were killed, and nine wounded."*

The enemy, after this disaster, crossed above at New Market, and made their way thence to Lebanon, which they reached on the morning of the fifth. They found the town garrisoned by about 400 of the Twentieth Kentucky, under Colonel Hanson, who, placing his men under shelter in the depot and other buildings, kept up a contest of seven hours with the enemy before he was compelled, by their artillery setting fire to the houses, to surrender. His loss was slight. In the attack the rebel Lieutenant Tom Morgan, a brother of the General, was killed. He was "the idol of the command," says Captain Cunningham; and when he fell, "loud and deep were the maledictions that ascended against the cowardly cravens for seeking shelter in dwelling-houses; and the question was raised as to their right to receive quarter." General Morgan, it is said, "with true Southern chivalry,

* S. P. Cunningham, A. A. A. General Morgan's cavalry division, to the Editor of the Enquirer, Richmond, Va. July 31, 1863.

rode up to Colonel Hanson, after the surrender, and pulled him violently by the beard, and threatened to shoot him."* The town was sacked, and Morgan's command freely supplied with arms and ammunition from the captured regiment. From Lebanon the enemy proceeded to Springfield, on their way toward the Ohio. Colonel Alston, Morgan's chief of staff, being detained in paroling the prisoners, was captured by a squad of Union cavalry. At Bardstown, on the sixth, twenty men of the Fourth United States cavalry were surprised, and after defending themselves in a stable while their ammunition lasted, surrendered. At Shepherdsville, on Salt River, Morgan stopped a passenger train from Louisville. Twenty soldiers in the cars were captured, and the express and mail matter, with the valuables of the passengers, freely pillaged. Passing through Laurenceville, the command reached Brandenburg, on the Ohio, on the seventh, a place which it is said had many Southern sympathizers among its inhabitants. There they were speedily enabled to cross the river by gaining possession of two steamboats which came along opportunely for their purposes. The first which made its appearance from below, the J. T. McCombs, they drew to the landing, hailing her from the wharf-boat at the shore. On her reaching the boat, a concealed body of the rebels hurried on board, and took possession without a struggle. Half an hour afterward, the Alice Dean, a large side-wheel steamer, came in sight, when the pilot of the McCombs was made to signal her for assistance. On the vessels approaching each other, a crowd of Morgan's men boarded the Alice Dean, and again quietly took possession. "As soon as their smart ruses had succeeded," says our narrator, "the rebels set about having a good time. The contents of the safes and storerooms, the silverware of the Dean, the bed blankets, all found new owners. The bars were, of course, points of special attraction, and commissioned officers stationed themselves behind them, dispensing the liquors as long as the stock lasted."

On the morning of the eighth the crossing commenced on the two boats. There was some resistance offered to their passage by a company of home guards, with a single gun, from Leavenworth, in the vicinity, on the Indiana shore. The party, however, was speedily overpowered when Morgan's advance landed. The guards were cut up or captured, and their Parrot gun taken. Two Union gunboats, from Louisville, during the crossing, made their appearance on the river, and opened fire on the steamboats; but having only five-second fuses, and not being able to encounter the rifled guns of the rebels, withdrew from the contest. On the morning of the ninth, Morgan's entire force was landed on the Indiana shore, when the Alice Dean, valued at sixty thousand dollars, was burnt by his orders, the McCombs being spared. The Union force which was gathering on the track of Morgan in full pursuit—Colonel Wolford, with his brigade from Jamestown, joining Generals Hobson and Shackleford at Springfield—arrived at Brandenburg just after the crossing of the enemy. General Hobson was in command, his entire force of Kentucky and Ohio cavalry and mounted infantry, with a howitzer battery and section of artillery, numbering about three thousand. General Judah's division, three regiments of Indiana, Kentucky and Illinois infantry, with two regiments of Michigan cavalry, were also summoned from Southern Kentucky, but not arriving in Louisville till after Morgan had crossed the Ohio, were sent up the river in boats to intercept the rebels on their retreat. General Hobson imme-

* An interesting account of Morgan and his career, published in the N. Y. *Tribune*, September 12, 1863, to which we are mainly indebted for the narrative of this expedition.

diately crossed the river at Brandenburg, landing his force on the Indiana side before dawn of the tenth. The rapid and circuitous subsequent movements of Morgan, though he inflicted great damage by the way, were in reality so many efforts to escape from his pursuers. The alarm was speedily sounded through the Department.—Governor Morton of Indiana, called the people of the State to arms, and the response was universal. In Ohio, Governor Tod was equally on the alert. Large war meetings were held at Columbus, Ohio, and Indianapolis, Indiana. At Louisville, Kentucky, on the recommendation and under the direction of General Boyle, measures were taken to organize the citizens to resist the enemy. At Cincinnati, General Burnside was in consultation with the authorities, providing for the defence of the city. Troops were being gathered on all sides to resist or intercept the invaders. Yet, for two weeks, Morgan, by his boldness and skill, managed to keep ahead of his pursuers, traversing the highways of Indiana and Ohio, and ravaging some of the best portions of those States.

His first demonstration after crossing at Brandenburg was upon Corydon, the capital of Harrison County, Indiana, about fifteen miles due north from the river, and about twenty west from Louisville. The invaders burning and destroying along the way reached this place late in the afternoon of the ninth. "About two hundred home guards showed fight, but the rebels closing in upon them from all sides, they were obliged to surrender, after killing and wounding nine of Morgan's men and losing themselves fifteen. The town was then sacked, and some 300 horses confiscated. Mr. Glenn, the minister, and two other brave men, fired upon the rebels from their houses, for which they were killed. Their property was burned. There Morgan inaugurated a new system of levying contributions by forcing parties to save their property from destruction by paying large ransoms. Three mill-owners paid $1,000 each in this way. Camping for the night near Corydon, Morgan marched next morning upon Salem, on the New Albany and Salem Railroad, where he arrived about ten A. M. Here Colonel Steffna, an ex-army officer, had collected several hundred militia, mostly mounted, but surrendered himself and his command as soon as the rebel artillery showed signs of opening fire upon the town. Pillaging was again indulged in without restraint, Morgan looking on from a hotel porch with a cigar in his mouth. Here more citizens were killed upon slight provocation, and $1,000 per head collected from three additional millers. The depot, five cars, and several small bridges and the water-tanks along the railroad were destroyed, but the damage was all repaired in twenty-four hours. There, as at Corydon, the citizens were compelled to cook for the rebels. At four P. M. they left Salem, going northwardly toward Vienna, where they burned another railroad-bridge, and bivouacked until morning. From Vienna they kept on to the North, through Lexington and Paris to Vernon, on the Ohio and Mississippi Railroad, where they arrived on the evening of the twelfth. Colonel Lowe held this point with about 1,200 militia. Morgan summoned him to surrender, when he replied, 'Come and take me.' Morgan then ordered him to remove the women and children previous to the bombardment of the town. A removal was made, but instead of attacking, the rebels left under cover of the night after doing the railroad as much injury as they could. While Morgan was about Vernon, a detachment of 100 rebels, that had become separated from the main body made an effort to rejoin it by crossing the river at Eighteen Miles Island, above Louisville. Forty-seven managed to swim over, but were captured near Charleston. Nineteen men and forty-four horses were on the island, when the gunboat there discovered them and prevented their crossing by shelling until General Manson, on his way up the river with a brigade of Judah's Division, could land a company and take them prisoners. Twenty-five swam back to the Kentucky bank.

"From before Vernon, Morgan proceeded to Dupont Station on the Madison and Indianapolis Railroad, ten miles south-east of Vernon, where he burnt one large and two small bridges. Next he made for Versailles, reaching it about noon on the twelfth. The town was made to suffer as much from depredations as any yet passed. The County Treasurer was relieved of $5,000 by Morgan, who sarcastically regretted that the county was so poor as not to have any more money on hand. A small body, meantime, had burned another bridge on the Ohio and Marietta Railroad at Osgood Station, and soon after also destroyed that at Long Levy Station, 180 feet long. From Versailles the rebels moved eastward, via Pierceville, and bivouacked on the night of the twelfth at a settlement known as Moore's Hill, about thirty-five miles north-west of Cincinnati. At one A. M. in the morning, they left their bivouac, making for the north-east. They crossed the Indianapolis and Cincinnati Railroad at Weisberg Station, where they had a skirmish with home-guards, and then marched via Dover to Harrison, on the State line, making their noon halt at the latter place. The rebels not only uniformly plundered the stores, public offices and private houses of the town, but also the farm houses along the route. The last part of this infamous business was transacted principally by squads sent to the right and left to gather up horses, provisions and forage. Even women were robbed of their garments and jewelry. Many buggies, rockaways and carriages were now also added to the caravan. Finding plenty of liquor in the towns, most of them kept in a constant state of inebriation and conducted themselves like savages, insulting and threatening everybody, discharging their pieces in every direction, riding about wildly with unearthly whoops and yells.

"Fast as Morgan moved, at the rate of from forty to fifty miles per day, General Hobson followed him with greater swiftness, although laboring under serious disadvantages. He made Corydon at ten A. M., on the tenth, and halted in the evening only two miles West of Salem, having traveled during the day no less than fifty miles. Resuming the march at five A. M., he camped the night of the eleventh at Vienna, where he kept trotting almost without rest in the track of the rebels, until Versailles was reached at five A. M. on the thirteenth, and Harrison on the evening of the same day. At this point, General Hobson had reduced the distance between himself and his game to less than half a day's march. Both Hobson and Morgan had their respective commands considerably reduced in this race through Indiana by the loss of men who gave out on the road. Many of our cavalry were likewise obliged to remain behind, from inability to remount themselves after running down their horses. In this respect Morgan had decidedly the advantage over his pursuers. He had the first chance at the stables on his route, and improved it so thoroughly as to leave but few animals within easy range to replace the worn-out ones of our troopers. Again, Morgan by first drafts upon the pantries and barns, deprived the inhabitants to a great extent of the means of readily feeding the chasing men and beasts, thereby impairing their efficiency and causing loss of time in necessitating foraging tours off the roads. Strongly loyal as the people of Southern Indiana proved themselves, by liberally dispensing to our troops all they had left in provisions and forage, and aiding them otherwise in every way they could, they would have really assisted them much more effectually by responding less expeditiously than they did, under the impulse of fear, to the demands made upon them by the rebels. If they had only forced them to take every thing they wanted, instead of carrying it to them, the pursuers would have been upon them much sooner. That the rebel requisitions were filled with such relative alacrity was mainly due to the fact that the heads of families had mostly hurried to the militia rendezvous, and that only old men, women and children were at home. The comet-like swiftness with which Morgan traversed the southern portion of the State—he desecrated its soil less than four days—made it impossible for the military authorities to make proper use against him of the immense militia force assembled at various points.

"As a prairie fire before the wind, the universal excitement and rising in arms of the people of the threatened regions spread to Ohio, as the enemy advanced toward her border. Governor Tod, as their intention to invade his State became manifest, like Governor Morton, called upon the militia to meet at once in their several counties and repair to certain general points of rendezvous, for the purpose of repelling the insolent foe. The call was answered no less enthusiastically than in Indiana. The direction of Morgan's movements, coupled with the exaggerated reports of his strength, having given rise to not unreasonable apprehensions that the enemy might attempt a *coup de main* against Cincinnati, the people of the Queen City prepared for her defense as vigorously as last Fall in the days of Kirby Smith's imaginary advance in force toward the Ohio. On Saturday and Sunday, the eleventh and twelfth, between 10,000 and 12,000 men were organized into regiments. Major Harris—until last Winter an acting Brigadier and one of the most able, energetic and determined officers in the Army of the Ohio—issued a call for 3,000 mounted volunteers to intercept the rebels, and in less than twenty-four hours that number had reported to him. For want of horses, arms and equipments, however, his plan failed of execution. On the morning of the thirteenth, General Burnside proclaimed martial law, requiring business to be suspended and every able-bodied man to join some organization for the defense of the city. Part of General Judah's division and several regiments from Lexington arriving on that and the previous day the safety of the city was fully assured.

"The rebels, after a brief rest at Harrison, entered Ohio on the afternoon of the thirteenth, after burning the bridge across White Water behind them. Fearing interference with their operations from Cincinnati, probably as much as the city people expected an attack from them, they made for the Great Miama over several roads running close to each other, to save time in crossing and reunite on its left bank. They crossed on the Miamitown, New Baltimore and Coleraine bridges, and continuing on after burning them, bivouacked for the night not more than ten miles north-east of Cincinnati. Early next morning they passed through Glendale and Springdale, where the stables, stores and residences were made to furnish them the usual contributions. Near the former place they crossed the Cincinnati, Hamilton and Dayton Railroad without inflicting much injury. A detachment was sent to visit the neighboring Camp Monroe, but found the larger number of Government mules usually kept there gone. After a short halt at Springdale, they moved on through Sharon and Reading, in a south-easterly direction, to Montgomery.

There they contemplated a visit to Camps Dennison) on the Little Miami, some fifteen miles from Cincinnati) and Shady, at which extensive and valuable improvements had been erected, and a vast amount of public property of every description accumulated. Although it must have been known by that time that Morgan was more anxious to avoid Cincinnati than to attack it, and was going toward Camps Dennison and Shady, none of the troops in the city were to be sent out for their protection. Fortunately, Colonel Neff, their commandant, had energy and foresight enough to prevent any great loss of Government stores. By blocking up the direct road from Glendale, through Milford, constructing rifle-pits and manning them with the six hundred convalescents in Camp Dennison, he forestalled an attack upon the former, and gained time enough, by compelling the rebels to make a detour, to remove the hundreds of teams at Camp Shady, with the exception of fifty wagons, which were captured and destroyed. An attempt upon the railroad bridge over the Miami, near Camp Dennison, failed, the approaching rebels being driven back by a squad of convalescents and some home-guards, with a loss of half a dozen killed and wounded. The rebels struck the Little Miami Railroad at Dangerous Crossing, near Miamiville, and after obstructing the tract, lay in wait for trains. Soon the accommodation train from Morrow came along unsuspectingly, and was run off the track. The train was crowded with people, but only the fireman was killed and one of the brakesmen was injured. About two hundred recruits were aboard, whom they paroled. The cars were burned. Continuing to the south-east, the rebels made Batavia at two, and Williamsburg at three P. M. Four miles from Williamsburg the regiment of Dick Morgan separated from the others, and bearing more to the south, proceeded to Georgetown, and thence to West Union, the county seat of Adams County, where it arrived about midnight and bivouacked. On the fifteenth it went further toward the river, evidently for the purpose of reconnoitering it with a view to crossing into Kentucky, but discovering bodies of militia in every direction, it turned back to the north, and subsequently rejoined the main body about Jacksonville. The latter had pushed on from Williamsburg toward Sardinia, near which place they bivouacked on the night of the fourteenth. On their way they burned two more bridges over White Oak River. In all the numerous flourishing small towns the scenes of pillages and excesses of every kind, previously enacted, were repeated. Their march having taken them through some of the richest counties of the State, their visits to stables had been fruitful of hundreds of fine horses.

"The condition of General Hobson's men and animals upon arriving at Harrison was such that he could not resume his march until three A. M. on the fourteenth. Starting at that hour, he followed in the wake of Morgan until late in the evening, when he bivouacked on the little Miami. Setting out again at two A. M. on the following morning, a bewildered Methodist preacher, who presumed to act as guide, led him nine miles out of the way, for the unnecessary fatigue of which extra march, the well-meaning, but unlucky clerical gentleman had to endure some profanity from the hard-worked troopers. In consequence of this mistake and the previous delay, occasioned by the destruction of bridges, General Hobson could not make Sardinia until evening, thus giving Morgan several additional hours' headway. The head of his column was then about ten, the rear about fourteen, hours behind the enemy. The 'will' of our men was still all that could be expected; but as to the 'flesh,' it almost refused service, and required the good example and some exhortation of the officers to keep the 'chase' in running order. The military authorities at Cincinnati must have felt rather cheap upon learning that the rebels had given them the slip. General Burnside, however, at once directed such measures, in cöoperation with Governor Tod, as best accorded with the shift the 'situation' had taken. General Judah's division was sent up the river, with orders to land at such a point as would enable it to head off Morgan from the south. Bodies of militia were ordered to move so as to effect the same from the north. The military committees of the counties through which the rebels were likely to pass were instructed to delay their movements as much as possible by obstructing the roads in every practicable way. The gunboat squadron was ordered to cruise up and down the river, to foil attempts to cross. Cincinnati was relieved from martial law.

"Making through Sardinia, the rebels reached Winchester at two P. M. on the fifteenth. Here they sacked the Post-office, and stole, beside fifty horses, about $40,000 worth of goods. One firm lost $11,000. They amused themselves by tearing all the loyal banners they could find into shreds and tying them to their mules' tails. From Winchester they went to Jacktown, where they destroyed another bridge, and thence via Wheatridge and Jacksonville, toward Jasper, on the right bank of the Sciota. The inhabitants of this place and surrounding country, under the direction of some militia officers, had commenced obstructing the roads from the west. That region being hilly and the roads winding and narrow, the progress of the rebels might have been greatly procrastinated by falling timber across the latter. Morgan, by a sharp ruse, however, saved himself from serious impediment. He had a telegrapher with an instrument along, whom he sent out with a detachment to operate on the telegraph line between Chillicothe and Piketon, and deceive the people around Jasper as to the bearing of his movements. This he did by dint of a telegram, and the axmen on the roads from Jacksonville went to work on more northerly ones. Nevertheless, by what they had already done, the rebels were detained for several hours six miles from Jasper. A Mr. McDougal, one of our axmen, was caught and killed by them. They entered the town, however, at three P. M., on the sixteenth, and after helping themseves to all that was moveable, partaking of exacted dinners, burning a fine steam-mill and the canal bridges, crossed the Sciota, and having destroyed the fine bridge over it also, proceeded to Piketon, which a militia force had evacuated. In Piketon their conduct was as disgraceful and reckless of private property as ever. The stores were robbed and gutted; women and children insulted and frightened, and several citizens killed upon slight provocation. Being informed about dark of the approach of our cavalry, they left for Jackson, the county seat of Jackson County, where they arrived and went into bivouack at eleven P. M.

"General Hobson broke camp at Sardinia at four P. M. on the sixteenth, and reached Winchester at eight, and tracing the rebels closely at Jasper at two o'clock on the following morning. Here he rested his men until eleven A. M. Resuming his march, he experienced another delay from the destruction of the bridges, his men having to swim the canal, but made Jackson toward evening twelve hours behind the rebels. In all the towns, our troops passed them, and afterward the inhabitants received them with the utmost enthusiasm and hospitality. The women, above all, strove to furnish them with tangible evidence of their good will; not shrinking even from holding, feeding, and watering the horses in order to give the men more time to eat and rest. The kindness showed upon the latter, naturally had an inspiring effect; made them forget their fatigue and stimulated them to renewed efforts, to bring to condign chastisement those that had so shamelessly abused those good loyal people. At Jackson, the rebels, according to their uniform practice, had inflicted great havoc upon the stores. Instigated by some of the vilest of sympathizers of Vallandigham persuasion, they gutted the office of *The Jackson Standard*, the Republican county paper. For this outrage, our troops obtained satisfaction afterward by visiting a smilar fate upon *The Jackson Express*, the organ of the Peace Democracy. *The Standard* was the only newspaper interfered with by the rebels during the whole raid. Having ascertained that several thousand militia had congregated at Berlin, six miles north-east, Morgan made an advance upon that point on the morning of the seventeenth. The commander of the Union forces at Berlin, Colonel Runkle, an experienced officer in the volunteer service, had about 2,500 men, tolerably well armed, but utterly raw, and without any artillery. Notwithstanding the superiority of the rebels in every respect, he determined to hold his ground, acting upon the defensive, in the expectation of keeping them engaged until Hobson could come up. Judiciously posting his men in a sheltered position beyond the town, after obstructing the roads leading to his front, he awaited the approach of the rebels. After entering the town and committing their usual depredations, inclusive of the burning of a mill, their whole force came out and deployed in line, as though they meant to give battle. They opened with their artillery upon Colonel Runkle's men, and felt his flanks for some time, but finally withdrew without a *bona fide* attack, after losing a dozen killed and wounded.

"The demonstration against Berlin proved a fatal move to Morgan. Whether he was tempted into it by the fact that there were 1,200 Government animals at the place, and expected to overcome the protecting force with ease, but was frightened off by the imposing display—covering great weakness—of strength by Colonel Runkle, or intended it merely as a feint to create misimpressions as to the movements by which he hoped to extricate himself from his precarious situation, the waste of time incurred in this venture brought him into the net in which the greater portion of his command were caught. His only road to safety was across the Ohio, and for that he should have made without the least delay, instead of losing half a day in an opposite direction. After destroying a bridge and culvert on the Sciota and Hocking Railroad, the rebels first moved in a southerly direction, with a view to crossing between Portsmouth and Gallipolis; but receiving information of the advance of a large body of troops from the former place, and finding the roads barricaded, turned about to the north, and took the road for Pomeroy, on which they camped in the evening. In the mean time, loyal forces were closing in upon them from all directions. From the north, Colonel Runkle's militia were following him. To the west General Hobson was, as previously stated, at Jackson, within a few hours' ride of them. To the east and south-east, one militia and two volunteer regiments, from General Scammon's Kanawha Valley Division, come down the river from Parkersburg, were watching for them. All the fords between Portsmouth and Pomeroy were guarded by gunboats; and from the south-east General Judah was moving up with his whole division. One brigade of the latter, consisting of the Fifteenth Indiana, Fourteenth Illinois, and parts of the Eleventh Kentucky, and Eighth and Ninth Michigan Cavalry and Henshaw's Battery with General

Judah himself, had landed at Portsmouth, upon information of Morgan's passage of Sciota on the evening of the sixteenth, and immediately landed inland toward Oakhill Station, on the Sciota and Hocking Railroad. The General's guide losing his way, and leading the troops several miles out of the way, they did not reach it until next morning. Learning here that Morgan was at Jackson, and about going eastward, General Judah hurried forward to Centreville, after sending orders to General Manson, who had that morning landed at Portsmouth to follow him with his brigade of infantry. Reaching Centreville late in the evening he bivouacked there for the night.

"Early on the eighteenth, the rebels marched toward Pomeroy, taking two roads—one column going via Wilkesville and the other through Vinton. After crossing Raccoon Creek, and burning all the bridges over it, they were detained two hours near the little town of Linesville by barricades which the Home Guards had built on the road. They appeared before Pomeroy about noon, but finding the roads to the town all blocked up and defended by Home Guards, with whom they skirmished slightly, they made no attempt to force an entrance, but continued east to Chester, which point they reached in the evening, after constant detentions on the road by barricades. Stopping only long enough to burn a bridge over Shady Creek, and make some requisitions for food, they pushed on to the south for Buffington Ford, some eight miles above Pomeroy, and opposite a considerable island bearing the same name. Their advance arrived at the ford at three A. M., and immediately began preparations for crossing. The main body went into bivouack in some corn-fields in the river bottom, to the east of the road they had come and a short distance from the bank, expecting to cross at daybreak, and little dreaming what disasters the morning had in store for them. General Hobson had marched from Jackson at three A. M. on the preceding day, and bivouacked at night around Chester. General Judah arrived at Pomeroy via Potter at four P. M., and, after giving his troops a few hours to enjoy the lavish hospitalities of the citizens, moved on by way of Racine toward Buffington. General Manson's and General Scammon's forces, and the gunboats, likewise proceeded up the river for the same point.

"The rebels planted their artillery at the ford, so as to command the passage. At four o'clock they commenced crossing by means of a scow and swimming, and thus managed to get about fifty over, although Home Guards on the Kentucky side fired upon them. The passage of the river, however, was soon cut short by events to the north and in their rear. General Judah, with his staff and escort, and the advance guard of his cavalry, descended the bluffs, skirting the bottom lands in which the rebels were bivouacking, over the pike from Chester to Buffington, about four o'clock. He had been informed by several parties during the night that Morgan had succeeded in crossing, and hardly looked for the enemy. A dense fog had settled upon the bottom, and although day was breaking, sight for any distance was impossible. When within half a mile of the river, a volley from carbines, shot-guns, and pistols, and orders to halt, suddenly burst upon our advance, and gave unmistakable proof of the presence of the rebels, who had discovered the approach of our troops and prepared for their reception. The road being narrow and fenced, the fog obscuring every thing, and our officers being unacquainted with the locality, the advance was thrown into wild confusion, and officers and men made back in indiscriminate flight toward the bluffs. In their helter-skelter race, they stampeded the horses, pulling one of our pieces in their rear, and rode down Captain Henshaw and his cannoneers, and captured the piece and artillerymen. In this repulse, one of the saddest calamities of the war occurred. The venerable Daniel McCook, the head of the branch of the family that furnished no less than seven distinguished officers to the Union service received a wound from which he died two days afterward. Hearing at Cincinnati that the assassin of his son, General Robert L. McCook, was with Morgan, he gave way to the strong impulse for personal revenge he had felt ever since the former's death, and joined General Judah with his trusty rifle that had served the loyal cause so well on many a field in the Eastern and South-eastern campaigns. After being shot off his horse, he fell for a short time into the hands of some rebel dastards, who robbed the bleeding old man of his watch and several hundred dollars in money. A braver and more ardently loyal heart has not ceased to beat. He was filled with the spirit of the devoted, self-sacrificing, lofty patriotism that illumines the annals of the War of Independence.

"The check received by our troops was of short duration. The fog rising, two sections of our artillery were brought forward and opened upon the enemy, and under this fire the Fifth Indiana and Fourteenth Illinois Cavalry formed and attacked the rebels, driving them back and re-capturing the lost piece and artillerists. Judah's cavalry operated upon the rebel flank. At the same time the Fifth Indiana and Fourteenth Illinois made at them, the head of the column of General Hobson, who had left Chester at three A. M., consisting of the Second and Seventh Ohio Cavalry came upon the rear of the rebels and attacked them at once, vigorously supported by the fire of two howitzers. Simultaneously, a body of our infantry, that had been landed below, advanced up the bottom upon the enemy. The gunboat Moose and armed transport Alleghany had also reached the island and directed the fire of their guns upon the north bank. The rebels being completely hemmed in on three sides, so scattered over the ground that they could not make a concerted defense, and demoralized by excessive fatigues, found themselves reduced to a choice between surrender and flight up the road along the river, the only one left open to them. Colonels Dick Morgan, Basil Duke and Smith, with their respective commands, after vainly trying to obtain better terms, surrendered themselves successively without conditions to General Shackleford. The prisoners numbered about 800. Morgan, with the remainder, fled up the river, leaving behind all his artillery and the stolen vehicles laden with plunder. The point for which he made was a ford about fourteen miles above Buffington, opposite Belleville, on the Kentucky side. Having reached it about dark, he ordered Johnson's regiment to cross at once. The rebel troopers, believing the river fordable, plunged in, but speedily found their horses swimming. Many of their tired horses were unequal to the task, and went down, with some fifty of their riders, including several officers. About 300 succeeded in crossing, with Colonel Johnson himself, when the gunboats appeared once more, and by their fire drove those who endeavored to follow back to the north bank. Johnson and his men managed to work their way through Eastern Kentucky to South-western Virginia.

"As soon as the prisoners were properly disposed of, our cavalry resumed the pursuit of Morgan, under the command of General Shackleford. Receiving information on the way that Morgan was making from Belleville to Humphrey's Ford, further above, he took the shortest route for that point, but arrived near it only in time to see the rebels move off at a gallop in a northern direction. His command being absolutely exhausted, and the sun having set, he reluctantly went into bivouac. About one o'clock, scouts having reported to him that Morgan was moving northward in the direction of Athens, he immediately dispatched a column in pursuit. A few hours later, reports reached him that the rebels were moving westward a few miles north of his bivouac, on roads leading to the river, when he started after them with the rest of his command. This was on the morning of Monday, the twentieth. The rebels first went to Harrisonville, and thence southwardly toward the the river. They approached Cheshire, some miles below Pomeroy, in the course of the afternoon; but General Shackleford was close up with them, and forced them to stand about three P. M. After a brief fight, in which the rebels lost ten men, they sent a flag of truce with an offer of unconditional surrender. General Shackleford supposed, when accepting it, that Morgan and all his men were about delivering themselves up; upon examination, he discovered to his sorry disappointment that only Colonel Coleman and some four hundred men were in his hands, while the rebel chief had again slipped away northwestwardly, with some six hundred men. Vexatious at the discovery that another chase was unavoidable, in view of the wearied condition of his command, he set about with unflagging spirit selecting the freshest men and horses for another pursuit. During the twentieth many small squads of Morgan's men became, voluntarily and involuntarily, detached from the main column, and were picked up by the militia. Over two hundred were picked up in Meigs county alone. The scene of the action at Buffington, and all the roads since traveled by them, were literally strewn with the fruits of their thieving operations, and their arms and equipments. There were buggies, rockaways, spring, and lumber wagons, without number; rolls of silk, muslin, calico, and other dry goods; bags full of men's clothing, hats, boots and shoes, linen, laces, kid gloves, cutlery, men's and women's undergarments—even children's petticoats—lying about in every direction, mingled with carbines, shotguns, rifles, sabres, pistols, and cartridge-boxes. Many of the latter were found to contain jewelry instead of ammunition. The woods were full of horses and mules. In places the ground was covered with pieces of greenbacks and other currency, stolen and torn by the rebels on surrendering. At Buffington, 'help yourselves' was the watchword of the volunteers, militia, and hundreds of countrymen attracted to the spot as to the spoils dropped by the rebels. Of the mercantile wares scarcely anything is likely to find its way back to its owners, and even of the vehicles and horses, many were appropriated without just claim to them. The scanty contents of the captured cartridge-boxes and caissons, demonstrated that the rebels would not have been able to make a protracted fight. The former did not average three rounds and the latter not over twenty.

"At daybreak on the twenty-first General Shackleford was again upon Morgan's track with six hundred and fifty picked troopers, comprising detachments of all the mounted regiments engaged under Hobson and Judah in the pursuit. Among the field officers that accompanied him were Cols. Capron, Buford, and Wolford. The last-mentioned had been on the chase longer than any of the others—fully eighteen days—but would not desist as long as his inveterate enemy, whom he had been hunting and fighting for well nigh two years, was still at large. While Shackleford was renewing the chase to the north, a fleet of light-draught boats was sent up the river with volunteers and militia, infantry and cavalry to observe the fords between Pomeroy and Wheeling. Major-General Brooks commanding the Western District of Pennsylvania, provided means of preventing the enemy from crossing between Wheeling and Pittsburg. To head them off from the north, General Burnside ordered two battalions of cavalry, under Major Way and Rue, to proceed by rail to Columbus, and thence wherever the movements of Morgan would render it most advisable. Governor Tod likewise sent some troops from the State capital eastward and southward for the same purpose, and moved the militia of the south-eastern counties so as to cover the routes likely to be taken by the rebels. With Morgan the question was no longer to depredate and fight, when he could be sure of victory, but to avoid all collisions, hurry far away from our troops, and take out of the State and save what remained of his command. Pushing northward from the river with all speed, he reached the vicinity of Ewington, in Gallia County, some twenty miles west of Gallipolis, on the morning of the twenty-first, and halted to feed his horses in some grain-fields. On the morning previous, 250 militia, under Major Sonntag had started out from Portsmouth to interrupt Morgan. Leaving the Sciota and Hocking Railroad at Portland station, they marched overland for some cross-roads which they were to guard, near the farm on which the rebel horses were being fed. Morgan, perceiving their approach, ordered five of his men to proceed toward them under a flag of truce to demand their surrender. The officer in command upon being told that Morgan had surrounded him with several thousand men and that resistance was useless, the officer forthwith complied with the rebel request. Had he shown but the slightest disposition to fight, the fact, of which he had good opportunity after his capture to satisfy himself, that the rebels had but little ammunition, and half of their number had lost their guns, would have compelled them to avoid a rencounter. As it was, they not only obtained arms for all from their captives, but also enough ammunition for seventeen rounds. The disgrace of this affair was strikingly illustrated by the subsequent voluntary surrender to the disarmed and paroled militia of fifty-seven of the rebels, who intentionally skulked to the rear after Morgan had moved away.

"Continuing toward Berlin, Morgan came unawares upon another party of militia, some two miles from that town, about as strong as the Portsmouth braves and commanded by a Major Slain of Pike County. He, too, surrendered upon demand. To the credit of his men, however, be it recorded, that many cried with indignation at the dishonor brought upon them by him. The rebels paroled them and broke their guns. Crossing the Marietta and Cincinnati railroad at Vinton Station without doing any damage beyond cutting down a telegraph pole, and passing through Zaliska within a short mile north-east of the town of McArthur, he encamped in the evening four miles north of it on the Logan road. Starting at six o'clock the next morning, he kept on north a few miles further, then turned east, going within a mile of the town of New Plymouth, and thence toward the Hocking River, which he crossed not far from Nelsonville. From the left bank of the Hocking he rode through Perry and Muskingum County, capturing in the evening at Deaverstown a scouting party of twenty-five citizens of Zanesville. Keeping Zanesville some fifteen miles to his left, he crossed the Muskingum at Eaglesport at ten A. M. on the twenty-third. Shortly after crossing, Colonel Hill, commanding a militia regiment, came upon him. But Morgan had no stomach for a regular fight, and made off after a slight skirmish. From Eaglesport he went to Cumberland, some twelve miles east of Zanesville. There he met another body of militia about dark; but, passing around them, he moved off to the north-east toward Senecaville. Near Cumberland about sixty of his men detached themselves and went back toward the Muskingum, depredating on their way. A mounted portion of the Eighty-sixth Ohio Infantry made after and captured them the next day. At five o'clock on the morning of the twenty-fourth he struck the Ohio Central Railroad at Campbell's Station, eight miles east of Cambridge. There he burned a railroad bridge, the station buildings, containing about twenty thousand dollars worth of produce, and several carts loaded with tobacco. Ten thousand dollars in currency were taken from the office safe.

"Continuing on due north over the National road, burning all the bridges they passed, the rebels appeared at Washington, an important county town, the people of which had been warned of this visit, and had removed their valuables and horses, at seven A. M. Having procured food for man and beast, the band deliberately betook themselves to eating, resting, and sleeping for several hours in fancied security. At ten o'clock, however, the reports of guns started them abruptly from their enjoyments. Soon their pickets dashed up the streets from the southern end of the town, shouting that the Unionists were coming. A general rush and scramble for horses ensued. Morgan jumped out of the bed he was occupying at the hotel, and was on his steed, and in a few minutes the whole gang were seceding out of the place upon the run. Shackleford's cavalry forces, joined by some mounted infantry under Colonel Wallace, near Senecaville, was upon them. Until Morgan reached the National road he had shown anxiety, ever since leaving the Ohio, to follow less-frequented by-roads rather than the well-traveled highways, flattering himself with the vain hope of deceiving thereby and eluding his pursuers. But the latter gained on him all the time by taking more direct and better roads, abounding with full stables and barns. Steadily they had reduced the separating miles, and at last overtaken their game. As the rebels hurried out of one end of the town, our cavalry galloped in by the other firing at the rear of the flying enemy. The former, upon reaching a hill just beyond the town on the Winchester road, halted, formed, and seemed to be ready to fight. General Shackleford at once dismounted his men for an attack; but as soon as they had got off their horses the rebels fled in the direction of Winchester. Having comparatively fresh horses, while Shackleford's had rode that morning a long and rapid ride, they escaped with a loss of three wounded and four prisoners. From Winchester they went over a circuitous route to Antrim in the north-east corner of Guernsey County; thence north-eastwardly to Londonderry, Smyrna, and and Moorfield. Between the last two places, by burning two bridges across the Stillwater, he gained two hours on his pursuers. From Moorfield, he headed for New Athens; but before reaching the place turned toward Cadiz, in Thomson County, where he arrived at eight A. M., on the twenty-fifth. He aimed now at striking and crossing the Ohio river near Warrenton. Shackleford having taken a shorter road from New Athens, came up with him again at the point it intersects that from Cadiz to the river. An opportunity was here lost to cut the rebels in two by opening upon them first with artillery, instead of attacking them forthwith with cavalry. They succeeded in rushing once more out of sight, and pushed for the river as fast as their horses could carry them. Learning, however, on the way, that it had risen nearly five feet the day before and was impassable, they changed their course, with a view of reaching the river higher above; went to Alexandria and thence across the Columbus and Pittsburg and Steubenville Railroad to Centreville, four miles west of Steubenville, where they appeared in the afternoon. The town being defended by a strong military force, principally from Steubenville, they abstained from a visit to it, and went, after exchanging a few shots, northwardly toward Richmond, twelve miles distant. Shackleford reached Wintersville about half an hour later.

The meshes in which they became, in the end, inextricably entangled, were now rapidly contracting around them. Not only Shackleford, but two other columns of cavalry, composed of fresh men and horses, were on Saturday engaged in the chase, and were fast overtaking them. The latter were the battalions of Majors Way and Rae. Major Way's command came by rail from Columbus direct to the vicinity of Steubenville, disembarked, and immediately got on the track of the rebels. Major Rae's went on the Ohio Central Railroad to Bellair, opposite Wheeling; thence north on the Steubenville and Pittsburg Railroad to Shanghai Station, when, hearing of Morgan's whereabouts in the vicinity of Richmond, he had his men and horses off the cars and on the way to Knoxville in less than an hour. The movements of those mounted bodies pressing after Morgan on Saturday afternoon were almost concentric, so that they neared each other by degrees. Shackleford's cavalry, having all but worn-out horses, could not move as expeditiously as the two others. It formed the reserve, as it were, to Way's and Rae's. The rebel's from Richmond kept to the north on the New Lisbon road, their chief's object being to turn to the east, after reaching a certain cross-road, and make for Smith's Ford, not far from Wellsville. Major Way came up with their rear toward dark and pressed and skirmished with it nearly all night. At last, at eight o'clock in the morning (Sunday, the twenty-sixth), he succeeded in forcing the enemy into a fight between Mechanicsville and Salineville, and after a lively combat of an hour's duration routed them completely, with a loss of about 200 men killed, wounded, and prisoners, and an equal number of horses. After securing his captures, Major Way made after the rest of the rebels, who taxed their animals to the utmost to reach Smith's Ferry. Morgan, who until then had made himself comfortable in a buggy, abandoned it in hot haste and fled with the crowd on horseback. While the rebels were keeping Major Way busy, Major Rae was speeding through Adamsville and other small towns in the southern part of Columbiana, toward the road to Smith's Ferry, which he expected the rebels to take. He was describing one side of a triangle, two of which were being followed by the enemy, and hence had good ground to hope to head them off, although they had several hours' ride the start of him. As he neared the point of intersection, toward noon, clouds of dust revealed that the rebels were before him. He started his men instantaneously upon a gallop; but the enemy having likewise noticed his approach, raced with him successfully for the junction of the roads, and reached and passed it some ten minutes earlier. Luckily Major Rae had provided himself with an excellent guide, who knew of a cut-off road, by which he will yet get between the rebels and the rear. Taking it at once and measuring its length of two miles into a steeple-chase rate of speed, he found to his great delight upon reaching the second cross-road, that he had this time the better of the rebels, although they are already in sight. Disposing his command immediately for action, in and on the right and left of the road, he saw a flag of truce coming toward him, and proceeded to meet it. He was indignant and surprised upon being summoned to surrender! His reply was, that he would charge the rebels if they did not instantly throw down their arms and deliver themselves up as prisoners without conditions. Soon the flag returned, and endeavored to secure better terms, but upon being informed by the Major, that for such they would have to apply to his superiors, accepted the Major's. This finale was enacted about four miles south of Lisbon, between one and two o'clock.

"General Shackleford came up in the course of half an hour with the remainder of our cavalry, when a formal surrender was made to him by Morgan in the shade of an apple-tree belonging to a farm, on which—strange coincidence!—the most lamented victim of the raid, old McCook, formerly resided, and all his sons were born. Morgan affected indifference to and talked lightly of his misfortune. His well-known blooded mare he made over to Major Rae, and his pair of silver-mounted, ivory-handled revolvers to Colonel Wolford. The only officer of prominence taken with him was Colonel Cluke. Shortly after the arrival of General Shackleford, Morgan raised a claim to the privileges of paroles for himself and men. Upon inquiry, it appeared that having captured early in the morning and brought along with him a militia captain and a dozen or so of citizens of New Lisbon, he made an offer of surrender upon condition of being paroled to the former, when the barring of his way by Major Rae had cut off all chance of escape. The captain, unsuspicious of any trickery, too ignorant to perceive the absurdity of receiving a surrender of his captor while still in his hands as a prisoner, and to know the terms of the cartel with the rebel authorities, and dazzled with the prospect of immortalizing himself as the captor of so notorious a character, readily accepted it. General Shackleford at once pronounced the claim preposterous, but was willing to submit it to the consideration of General Burnside, and in accordance with instructions from the latter, received during the evening, he started with the rebel officers on the next morning by rail for Cincinnati, arriving there on Monday evening. His prisoners were provided with temporary and anything but agreeable quarters in the City Prison. Governor Tod, upon being advised of Morgan's pretensions to a parole, had telegraphed for the militia captain, and likewise started with him for Cincinnati. General Burnside, after hearing the captain's statements, sent for Morgan and informed him that his claim was no less ridiculous than arrogant, and that he would have to go to the Ohio Penitentiary, to be confined therein until the Richmond authorities were brought to terms in regard to the exchange of officers. And to the Penitentiary the chief rebel marauder was sent."*

There closes the narrative of this remarkable episode in the history of the war, of less importance than many of its greater conflicts, but which will ever remain of especial interest to the people of the States in which were the scene of these depredations and conflicts. Great battles have more or less resemblance all the world over, whatever the cause which may call the combatants together, while an invasion, like this by Morgan, feelingly brings home to the people the sense of their insecurity when the wholesome restraints of government and law are abrogated by the hand of violence. It is but reasonable to suppose that the rebel chieftain in this raid did quite as much to secure the firm loyalty of the inhabitants of the Northwest as the exhortations of their Governors and the exploits of the grand armies from the beginning of the war. While it showed the people the dangers

**New York Tribune*, September 12, 1863.

to which they were exposed, it at the same time taught them their strength and how to employ it. Well might Governor Tod of Ohio, in his proclamation congratulatory of the event, remark: "Do not, fellow citizens, for a moment doubt that this raid of Morgan will ultimately form a benefit to us as a people." General Burnside also, in a letter of thanks to the Ohio militia, through the Governor, wrote: "The consciousness of ability to protect their homes and the perceived advantage of organization and of some degree of principle will produce good fruit, and I cannot suffer the occasion to pass without congratulating you and the people of Ohio upon the result."*

Morgan was confined in the Penitentiary with thirty other Confederate officers captured with him, as a place of safe keeping in the lack of any secure military prison then at the command of General Burnside. They were by orders of Governor Tod to be kept as far as possible separate and apart from the convicts and subject only to such restraints as were necessary to hold them. That these were not of the most rigorous character was shown by the escape from the prison on the twenty-eighth of the following November, of Morgan, with six of his officers. The escape was effected at night by digging through the floor of a cell of the lower tier to a sewer leading outside the wall, one of the party, Captain Hines, by trade a brickmaker, apparently having had the management of the affair. A reward was offered for the recapture of the leader, who, it was supposed, would make his way to Canada. Assisted by his friends, however, he escaped through the Union lines into Georgia, where, in December, he was heard from, advertising in a Southern paper for recruits to form a new band of followers.

Morgan and his men having been thus for the time disposed of, General Burnside continued his preparations for the long-expected advance into East Tennessee. The absence of the Ninth Army Corps which had been detached from his command to reinforce General Grant before Richmond had somewhat delayed his proceedings, and he was at last compelled to proceed without it, urged forward by the necessity of coöperating with General Rosecrans, who was now, at the middle of August, about to move upon Chattanooga. General Burnside left Camp Nelson on the sixteenth of August. The progress of his army is thus related in an account by Surgeon W. H. Church, Medical Director of the Department of the Ohio, who accompanied the expedition. "General Burnside's command was to march in three columns, one via Loudon, under himself; the second, consisting of the Twenty-third Army Corps, under Major-General Hartsuff via Somerset, and the other under General Julius White via Jamestown. General Burnside, marching via Danville and Stanford, reached Crab Orchard on the twentieth. On the twenty-second he marched to Mount Vernon, twenty miles, and on the following day to Loudon, twenty-five miles. On the twenty-fourth he made Williamsburgh, thirty miles further south. On the twenty-sixth he was joined by General Hartsuff, with the Twenty-third Corps, at Chetwood, twenty-eight miles from Williamsburgh. The enemy being reported near, he directed a cavalry regiment to reconnoitre toward Jackboro'. It met a superior rebel force and routed it, capturing forty-five prisoners. From Chetwood the march was continued across New River up the Cumberland Mountains to Montgomery, situated forty-two miles distant on the summit of the range, where the column arrived on the thirtieth. Here it was met by General White's command. Colonel Burt having been sent forward with a cavalry brigade, reported that

* Major-General Burnside to the Honorable David Tod Cincinnati, July 31, 1863.

General Pegram, with 20,000 cavalry held a very strong position at the Gap near Emory Iron Works, leading into Clinch River Valley. Additional troops were sent forward with the expectation of a battle on the morning of the thirty-first, but with daylight it was discovered that the enemy had fled.

"With the possession of this gap the road to Knoxville was clear. Having reached Emory River, seventeen miles from Montgomery, General Burnside ordered Colonel Foster, with a mounted brigade, to make a forced march over a direct road to Kingston, six miles further. Being anxious to save the most extensive and important bridge over the Tennessee, at Loudon, twenty miles from Kingston, General Burnside directed General Shackleford, with his cavalry brigade, to push on to it as rapidly as possible. Upon arriving within three miles of the bridge, a regiment was deployed as skirmishers, and quickly drove the enemy beyond their rifle-pits covering the approaches to the bridge. They retreated hastily across it, closing the gate behind them. The entire structure being prepared with turpentine and shavings, for immediate destruction, it was wrapped in flames in a few seconds. General Shackleford, finding it impossible to save it, moved off towards Knoxville, after driving the enemy from the opposite bank with shells and musketry. Colonel Foster reached Knoxville on the first of September, and General Burnside left Kingston on the second, and entered Knoxville on the third. Both received perfect ovations upon their entrance. The town was decorated with flags hidden for more than two years, and cheering people lined the streets. A large meeting was held on a subsequent day, and addressed by General Burnside and several leading citizens. The latter congratulated themselves in the most enthusiastic terms upon their deliverance from rebel oppression. On the day after Colonel Foster's arrival a procession of women, whose husbands and relatives were mostly in the Union service, came in from the country. It was nearly a mile long. All along the route of our troops the same unmistakable evidence of all but universal loyalty on the part of the population became manifest. Young men seemed to be mostly absent, but old ones and women by the hundreds received our troops with flags and refreshments on the roads. A great number of men that had lived in hiding places for months, came forth and joined their deliverers. Very valuable machine-shops and founderies, belonged to the rebel Government, were found in Knoxville. Also two million pounds of salt, a large quantity of wheat, (the fruits of the tithe-tax,) and many thousand bags. Three locomotives and a number of cars were captured. General Burnside took for his headquarters the residence of a rebel leader.

"Before leaving Kentucky, General Burnside ordered Colonel De Courcy, with a brigade of infantry, to march upon Cumberland Gap by the direct route through Loudon and Barboursville. Learning, on the fourth, that the rebel force defending the Gap was strong, and likely to offer resistance, he dispatched General Shackleford, with his brigade, on the fifth, from Knoxville, with instructions to seize all avenues of escape to the South. He followed himself, with another body of infantry and cavalry, on the seventh, and arrived within four miles of the Gap on the ninth, after a forced march of sixty miles. De Courcy and Shackleford had both made demands for a surrender, which General Frazier declined. Upon his arrival, General Burnside renewed it, when the rebel commander offered to surrender upon condition that his officers and men were paroled. An unconditional surrender being insisted upon, he yielded. His force consisted of the Second North Carolina, First Virginia, First Georgia regiments, and several companies of artillery. The Georgia regiment was eight hundred strong, and was once before captured by General Burnside, at Roanoke Island. The prisoners were sent North. In explanation of the extraordinary isolation General Frazier was left in, rebel officers asserted that General Bragg had peremptorily ordered him to remain. On the night of the seventh two companies of our troops stole their way through the rebel pickets, and burned a mill that had supplied the rebels with meal, in the very sight of the enemy's camp. This neat performance helped much to hasten the surrender.

"For quickness of movement and complete success without bloodshed, General Burnside's operations are the most noteworthy of the war. All of his troops marched over 250 and a large portion of them over 300 miles, and they averaged twenty miles a day, although they moved over the most difficult roads, crossing several high ranges of mountains and numerous deep streams. In the whole compaign but one casualty occurred, a private, killed in a skirmish of Shackleford's cavalry with the rebel pickets near Tazewell."*

Fourteen pieces of artillery and two thousand prisoners were captured at Cumberland Gap. The loss of this important position was a heavy disaster to the enemy. In his message to the Confederate Congress in the following December, President Davis speaks of the intelligence of the event as a "painful surprise, a disaster laying open Eastern Tennessee and South-western Virginia to hostile operations and breaking the line of communication between the seat of Government and Middle Tennessee." At about the same time the abandonment of Chattanooga by General Bragg and its occupation by the Army of General Rosecrans, to be related in the next chapter, placed this important military region at the disposal of the Union forces.

* Cincinnati Correspondence, *New York Daily Times*, September 14th, 1863.

CHAPTER XCII.

THE DEPARTMENT OF THE CUMBERLAND. GENERAL ROSECRANS' ADVANCE TO CHATTANOOGA AND THE BATTLE OF CHICKAMAUGA—SEPTEMBER, 1863.

AFTER the occupation of Murfreesboro by the Army of the Cumberland at the beginning of the year, some months necessarily elapsed before supplies could be brought up, lines of communication opened, and a sufficient base of operations be established for an effective advance upon the next most important position of the enemy at Chattanooga. In this interval, during the remainder of the winter and the ensuing spring, there were various raids and skirmishes; the rebels frequently making the attack and inflicting heavy loss, while, as usual in the history of these affairs, they were repulsed in the end and gained no advantages to compensate them for their extraordinary efforts.

The first of these assaults was made on the third of February, when the rebel Generals Wheeler, Forrest, Wharton, and Woodward attacked Fort Donelson with 4,000 men and eight pieces artillery. Colonel A. C. Harding of the Eighty-third Illinois, was in command of the post with about 500 available men of his regiment, one company of the Fifth Iowa Cavalry, and Captain Floyd's Battery of Artillery. The enemy began in the afternoon by throwing solid shot into the fort and made several feints of storming the works, while the sharpshooters of the garrison would pick them off as they approached. Forrest twice sent a flag of truce, urging his superior force and demanding a surrender, which Colonel Harding resolutely refused. At eight in the evening the enemy had invested the work on three sides to the river above and below, and were about pressing the final attack which, as the defenders were nearly out of ammunition, promised to be successful. At this moment, however, a fleet of gunboats, under Captain Leroy Fitch, which was convoying a number of transports from below, opportunely arrived on the spot and warned of the attack, skillfully opened fire upon the assailants. The gunboats, effectively placed, swept the enemy from their positions and speedily turned the siege into a retreat. The rebels suffered severely in this affair. Their loss being estimated at 900. That of the garrison was 13 killed and 51 wounded.*

Various desultory engagements which followed are thus enumerated by General Halleck in his Report of the year: "On the 4th of March Colonel Coburn with 1,845 men, attempted a reconnoissance from Franklin toward Springfield, encountering in his way Van Dorn's rebel column, estimated at 7,500. The enemy retreated, drawing Colonel Coburn into a gorge, where he was surrounded and nearly all his force captured. Our loss was 1,406; that of the enemy, 150 killed and 450 wounded. On the 20th of March Colonel Hall, while on a reconnoissance, encountered and defeated the rebel General Morgan with a force of three or four thousand. Our loss was 55. The enemy left 66 on the field, but carried off his wounded, estimated at 300. On the 25th of March the rebel General Forrest made a cavalry raid on the Nashville and Columbia Railroad, burning the bridge and capturing Colonel Bloodgood's command at Brentwood. General Green Clay Smith, arriving opportunely with about six hundred cavalry, attacked the enemy in the rear, and recovered a large portion of the property captured at Brentwood, pursuing the rebels to the Little Harpeth, where they were reinforced. His loss in this attack was 4 killed, 19 wounded, and 4 missing. On the 10th of April a guerrilla force attacked a train near Lavergne, guarded by 400 men. The cars were destroyed and nearly half of the guards killed and wounded. At the same time Van Dorn, with a large mounted force, attacked Franklin, but was repulsed by Major-General Granger, with a loss of 19 killed, 35 wounded left on the field, and 48 prisoners. General James J. Reynolds made a raid upon the Manchester and McMinnville Railroad, destroying the depot, rolling stock, supplies, and other property, and capturing 180 prisoners. Colonel Straight, with about 1,600 men, including reinforcements from General Dodge at Tuscumbia, started on a raid into Georgia to cut the enemy's communication. After heavy losses in skirmishes with Forrest's cavalry, and when near its destination he was forced to surrender. On the 22d of May, Major-General Stanley made a raid upon Middleton, capturing 80 prisoners and 200 horses, 600 stand of arms, and other property. On the 4th of June the rebel General Forrest made a raid upon Franklin, and on the 11th attacked Triune. His losses in these unsuccessful skirmishes were estimated at over 100, while ours were only 17 killed and wounded."

The rebel General Van Dorn, one of

* General Rosecrans to General Halleck, Murfreesboro, February 6. Official report of Lieutenant-Commanding Fitch, February 4. Cairo correspondence *New York Tribune*, February 1. General Halleck's Annual Report, December, 1863

the most efficient and unscrupulous of the rebel officers in the Southwest, shortly after his unsuccessful attack upon Franklin, met with his death at the hands of Doctor Peters, a gentleman with whose wife he had formed a criminal intimacy. The event occurred early in May at Van Dorn's quarters at Spring Hill, in Maury County, Tennessee. The incidents of the affair were related by Parson Brownlow in a letter from Nashville to the *Philadelphia Press*. "The Doctor," he writes, "performed a painful duty when he shot Van Dorn, but it was one of bold and manly daring, without a parallel since this wicked rebellion was inaugurated. He walked into the rebel General's quarters in open daylight, passing the sentinels, and demanded satisfaction for the injuries done him, while the rebel was surrounded by members of his staff, and while he was seated at his table writing. He rose up and read to the Doctor what he had written, and offered as satisfaction. The Doctor told him that was not satisfactory, whereupon Van Dorn ordered him to leave his room, a —— cowardly rascal, or he would kick him out. The Doctor instantly drew a revolver and shot his brains out, wheeled upon his heel, passed out through two gates; mounted his horse and rode off, some three miles, when he had a heavy pair of black whiskers, coming down upon his bosom, shaved close to the face, and a coat of hair, flowing down upon his shoulders cut short. He laid aside a high-crowned fashionable hat, and put on a sleek cap, and, upon arriving at Shelbyville, he learned that the Right Reverend Major-General Bishop Leonidas Polk had ordered his arrest, and started out some cavalry in search of him, with printed bills describing his person. He rode several miles with three of the men, passing with them out of town, but he by no means filled the bill! Thus he escaped detection, and reached Nashville in safety." A Chattanooga correspondent of the *Richmond Enquirer* says of Van Dorn: "Without doubt he acted very badly. Wine and women have ruined him, as they have ruined many another brilliant but reckless man. That Van Dorn was a man of daring genius there can be no doubt. Being handsome, with dark, flashing eyes, a magnificent moustache, a superb rider, a showy address, quick-witted, and graceful, he was also a man of sagacious foresight, keen, intelligent, but was wholly and thoroughly unreliable. He always sacrificed his business to his pleasure. He was never at his post when he ought to be. He was either tied to a woman's apron-strings or heated with wine."[*]

During these months of preparation General Rosecrans anxiously sought to strengthen his army by a thorough system of discipline and to excite a proper sense in the minds of his men of the nature of the conflict in which they were engaged. In reply to a resolution of thanks to the Army of the Cumberland passed by the General Assembly of the State of Ohio, he wrote in February in the strongest terms, characterizing the rebellion as kept alive by "an oligarchy of traitors to their friends, to civil liberty, and human freedom. Crafty as the fox, cruel as the tiger, they cried, 'no coercion,' while preparing to strike us. Bully-like they proposed to fight us because they said they could whip five to one; and now, when driven back, they whine out, 'no invasion;' and promise us of the West permission to navigate the Mississippi, if we would be 'good boys,' and do as they bid us. Wherever they have the power, they drive before them into their ranks the Southern people, and they would also drive us. Trust them not; were they able, they would invade and destroy us without mercy. Absolutely assured

* Correspondence of the *Richmond Enquirer*, Chattanooga, May 12, 1863; *New York Times*, May 19 and 31, 1863.

of these things, I am amazed that any one could think of peace on any terms. He who entertains the sentiment is fit only to be a slave; he who utters it at this time is moreover a traitor to his country, who deserves the scorn and contempt of all honorable men. When the power of the unscrupulous rebel leaders is removed, and the people are free to consider and act for their own interests, which are common with ours under this Goverment, there will be no great difficulty in fraternization. Between our tastes and social life there are fewer differences than between those of the people of the northern and southern provinces of England or Ireland."*

Of slavery, the test question of the day, in the conduct of the war, General Rosecrans, a zealous member of the Roman Catholic Church, wrote to the Reverend Edward Purcell, editor of the *Catholic Telegraph*, at Cincinnati: "I am happy to see the splendid stand you took in the *Telegraph* against slavery, with its horrors, barbarities, and base immoralities. Slavery is dead. Nothing can resuscitate it. To learn this fact fully, you should pay us a visit. There is not a negro in the South who does not know he is free. Around here they have squatted on the plantations, and refuse to work for any one but themselves. They have sown little crops of their own, and the masters have ceased to exercise any control over them. As an indication, I will cite a strong case. The lady of the house where I am staying attempted to punish one of her negro women this morning. I had to step in to save the mistress from being badly used up, as the darkey was belaboring her with the stick intended for her own punishment. '*Ex uno disce omnes.*' It is needless for me to say that I applaud every sentiment you have expressed in the *Telegraph*. Your course is that of a prudent navigator, who, watching the black speck on the horizon, sees it expand into a portentous storm, and calls up his crew to take in sail and prepare for a contest with the elements. The storm will pass away, and you will be found sailing under full sail, while those who took not heed will be scattered by the gale. * * I am heart and hand with you in this cause. Slavery is doomed, and those who would now uphold it will be held up in a very short time to public odium and execration. No statesman will vindicate it, no friend of human progress will stretch forth a hand to break its fall, no lover of humanity and religion will grieve for its overthrow. I have lived long enough in the South to see its workings, its disgusting features, debasing the higher principles of our nature, warring with religion, and patronizing vice and immorality. Almighty God has certainly ordained its destruction in this country, where it has been more offensive and immoral than in any other, and until it is utterly extinct this war cannot, from the nature of things, cease. I am in favor of a cessation of hostilities at as early a day as possible; therefore, I am in favor of the President's Proclamation. This State was made for white people and free labor, and when Slavery no longer blights its borders we may expect to see the church and the school-house take the place of the slave-pen and market."*

A military execution in the Department in June attracted the attention of the public from the station of the persons who suffered the penalty. Toward evening of the 8th, two men rode into Colonel Baird's quarters at Franklin, Tennessee, representing themselves to be Colonel Austin and Major Dunlap, Inspector-Generals of the United States Army. They supported the character

* Major General Rosecrans to the Honorable the General Assembly of the State of Ohio, Murfreesboro, Tennessee February, 1863.

* General Rosecrans to the Reverend E. Purcell, Murfreesboro, April 27, 1863.

by counterfeit official papers from General Rosecrans and a circumstantial story of their being plundered by the enemy on their way. They were admitted to the camp, noted its defenses, and borrowed money from the officer in command. As they were departing in the evening for Nashville, as they pretended, Colonel Baird suddenly suspected that they were spies and ordered their arrest. They were pursued, overtaken, and brought back to the camp. General Rosecrans was telegraphed for information, and replied that no such persons were known to him. The men were then searched at midnight, and the clearest proof of their character as spies were established. The pretended Colonel Austin, the leader of the adventure, proved to be Major Lawrence A. Williams, late of the United States Army, who at the beginning of the war had been aid-de-camp and private secretary to General Scott. In consequence of his family relations, his father, a gallant officer, having fallen in the Mexican war, his Southern proclivities had been tenderly dealt with. He took advantage of his freedom and joined the rebel army. He was a young man of fine appearance and of social accomplishments. His comrade in this fatal adventure was Lieutenant Walter G. Peter, a young officer of the Confederate army. After the search General Rosecrans was again applied to by telegraph for further orders, and sent word, "try them by a court martial, and if found guilty hang them immediately." The court was convened and before daylight the case was decided. At nine the next morning they were executed in presence of the garrison.

The month of June saw the Army of the Cumberland again in motion. General Rosecrans had taken time—spite of the anxiety of the public and the calls of the military rulers at Washington for an early advance—to recruit his army, procure horses for his dismounted cavalry and generally perfect his arrangements, while he prudently watched the dispositions of the enemy in his front. General Bragg, after the battle of Murfreesboro', withdrew his force to Shelbyville, Tullahoma, and the line of the Duck River, which crosses the State in a generally westerly direction to the Tennessee, at its nearest point, about thirty miles south of the line, held by General Rosecrans. The rebel force was understood to be strongly intrenched in its main positions, while in front the occupation of the roads running south from Murfreesboro' with the natural features of the country gave it additional security. It was the plan of General Rosecrans, in his advance, to neutralize these advantages by turning the enemy's position and making a flank attack on their right, reach their immediate base of operations at Tullahoma on the Chattanooga Railroad. He designed this to compel the enemy to an engagement on ground of his own choosing, or drive them to a retreat. The camps were broken up at Murfreesboro' on the 24th of June, when the army began its onward march in three corps, McCook's taking the right, Thomas's the centre, and Crittenden's the left. "By an admirably combined movement," says General Halleck, "General Rosecrans deceived the enemy by a threatened advance in force on their left at Shelbyville, while the mass of his army, in reality, seized Hoover's, Liberty and other Gaps by hard fighting, and moved on Manchester, thus turning the right of the enemy's defense of Duck River, and directly threatening Bragg, who was compelled to fall back to Tullahoma, hotly pursued by Granger, who had brilliantly carried Shelbyville. Dispositions were immediately made to turn Tullahoma, and fall upon the enemy's rear; but Bragg abandoned to us his intrenched camp, and rapidly fell back toward Bridgeport, Ala., pursued as far as practicable by our forces. In the words of General Rosecrans' official report, thus ended a nine days' campaign, which drove the enemy from two fortified positions and gave us possession of Middle Tennessee, conducted in one of the most extraordinary rains ever known in Tennessee at that period of the year, over a soil that becomes almost a quicksand. Our operations were retarded thirty-six hours at Hoover's Gap, and sixty hours at and in front of Winchester, which alone prevented us from getting possession of his communications and forcing the enemy to a very disastrous battle. These results were far more successful than was anticipated, and could only have been retained by a surprise as to the direction and force of our movements. Our losses in these operations were 85 killed, 462 wounded, and 13 missing, making in all 560. The killed and wounded of the enemy is unknown, but we took 1,634 prisoners, of which 59 were commissioned officers. We captured, beside six pieces of artillery, many small-arms, considerable camp equipage, and large quantities of Commissary and Quartermasters' stores." In a telegraphic dispatch from Tullahoma on the 7th of July, to Governor Andrew Johnson, of Tennessee, General Rosecrans couples the retreat of the enemy with the successes gained the same week by General Grant at Vicksburg and General Meade at Gettysburg. "On the 2d of July," said he, "Bragg left this, his last stronghold in Middle Tennessee, and on the 4th the rear of his infantry was over the Cumberland Mountains. We may thank God and congratulate ourselves that the ides of July were auspicious for freedom and for our army—that we have accomplished a great work without bloodshed, and were prevented only by the unprecedented rains from giving the *coup de grace* to Bragg's army." The next step in following up the enemy to their important position at Chattanooga, which was now fortified, and the approaches to which offered the best opportunties of defense was undertaken the following month. The difficulties of the region to a pursuing force were formidable. For the Union army now in position from McMinnville to Winchester, with advances at Pelham and Stevenson, to pass to the coveted Chattanooga from above, the Cumberland mountains to the upper waters of the Tennessee had to be crossed; while the latter river, in its sinuous course, with a continuation of the mountain passes interposed below. As this region, not only in the present campaign but in the future, became the theatre of important military operations, it may be well here to present the outline of its topography with which General Rosecrans opens his Report of the Battle of Chickamauga. "The Cumberland Range is a lofty mass of rocks separating the waters which flow into the Cumberland from those which flow into the Tennessee, and extending from beyond the Kentucky line, in a south-westerly direction, nearly to Athens, Alabama. Its north-western slopes are steep and rocky, and scalloped into coves in which are the heads of numerous streams that water Middle Tennessee. Its top is undulating, or rough, covered with timber, soil comparatively barren, and in dry seasons scantily supplied with water. Its south-eastern slope, above Chattanooga, for many miles, is precipitous, rough and difficult all the way up to Kingston. The valley between the foot of this slope and the river seldom exceeds four or five miles in width, and, with the exception of a narrow border along the banks, is undulating or hilly. The Sequatchie Valley is along the river of that name, and is a cañon, or deep cut-splitting the Cumberland range parallel to its range. It is only three or four miles in breadth and fifty in length, The sides of this valley are even more precipitous than the great eastern and western slopes of the Cumberland, which have just been described. To reach Chattanooga from McMinnville, or north of the Tennessee, it is necessary to turn the head of this valley by Pikeville and pass down the valley of the Tennessee, or to cross it by Dunlap or Thurman. That part of the Cumberland range between Sequatchie and the Tennessee, called Walden's Ridge, abuts on the Tennessee, in high rocky bluffs, having no practicable space sufficient for a good wagon-road along the river. The Nashville and Chattanooga Railroad crosses that branch of the Cumberland range, west of the Sequatchie, through a low gap, by a tunnel, two miles east of Cowan, down the gorge of Big Crow Creek to Stevenson, at the foot of the mountain, on the Memphis and Charleston Railroad, three miles from the Tennessee and ten from Bridgeport. Between Stevenson and Chattanooga, on the south of the Tennessee, are two ranges of mountains, the Tennessee River separating them from the Cumberland. Its channel, a great chasm cut through the mountain masses, which in those places abut directly on the river. These two ranges are separated by a narrow valley through which runs Lookout Creek. The Sand Mountain is next the Tennessee, and its northern extremity is called Raccoon Mountain. Its sides are precipitous and its top barren oak ridges, nearly destitute of water. There are but few, and these very difficult, wagon roads by which to ascend and descend the slopes of this mountain. East of Lookout Valley is Lookout Mountain, a vast palisade of rocks rising 2,400 feet above the level of the sea, in abrupt, rocky cliffs, from a steep wooded base. Its eastern sides are no less precipitous. Its top varies from one to six or seven miles in breadth, is heavily timbered, sparsely settled, and poorly watered. It terminates abruptly upon the Tennessee, two miles below Chattanooga, and the only practical wagon roads across it, are over the nose of the mountain, at this point, one at Johnson's Crook, 26 miles distant, and one at Winston's Gap, 42 miles distant from Chattanooga. Between the eastern base of this range, and the line of the Chattanooga, and Atlanta or Georgia State Railroad are a series of narrow valleys, separated by smaller ranges of hills or low mountains, over which there are quite a number of practicable wagon roads running eastward toward the railroad. The first of these ranges in Missionary Ridge, separating the waters of Chickamauga from Chattanooga Creek. A higher range with fewer gaps on the southeast side of the Chickamauga, is Pigeon Mountain, branching from Lookout, near Dougherty's Gap, some 40 miles south from Chattanooga. It extends in a northerly direction, bearing eastward, until it is lost in the general level of the country near the line of the Chattanooga and Lafayette road. East of these two ranges and of the Chickamauga, starting from Ottowah and passing by Ringgold, to the west of Dalton is Taylor's Ridge, a rough, rocky range, traversable by wagon roads only through gaps generally several miles apart. Missionary Ridge passes about three miles east of Chattanooga, ending near the Tennessee at the mouth of the Chickamauga. Taylor's Ridge, separates the East Tennessee and Georgia Railroad from the Chattanooga and Atlanta Railroad. The junction of these roads is at Dalton, in a valley east of Taylor's Ridge and west of the rough mountain region, in which are the sources of the Cossa River. This valley, only about nine or ten miles wide, is the natural southern gateway into East Tennessee, while the other valleys just mentioned terminate northwardly on the Tennessee to the west of it, and extend in a southwesterly direction toward the line of the Cossa, the general direction of which, from the crossing of the Atlanta road to Rome and thence to Gadsden, is south-west."

With this preliminary view of the theatre of operations we resume the condensed narrative of the campaign presented in the annual report of General Halleck, referring the reader for more particular military details to the long and elaborate report of General Rosecrans. "Having put the railroad to Stevenson in condition to procure supplies, Rosecrans, on the 16th of August, commenced his advance across the Cumberland Mountains, Chattanooga and its covering ridges on the south-east being his objective point. To command and avail himself of the most important passes, the front of his movement extended from the head of Sequatchie Valley in Tennessee, to Athens, Alabama, thus threatening the line of the Tennessee River from Whitsburg to Blythe's Ferry, a distance of over one hundred and fifty miles. The Tennessee River was reached on the 20th of August, and Chattanooga shelled from the north bank on the 21st. Pontoon, boat, raft, and trestle bridges, were rapidly prepared at Caperton's Ferry, Bridgeport, the mouth of Battle Creek and Shell Mound, and the army, except cavalry, safely crossed the Tennessee in the face of the enemy. By the 8th of September, Thomas had moved on Trenton, seizing Frick's and Stevens' Gap on the Lookout Mountain; McCook had advanced to Valley Head and taken Winston's Gap, while Crittenden had crossed to Wauhatche, communicating on the right with Thomas, and threatened Chattanooga by the pass over the point of Lookout Mountain. The first mountain barrier south of the Tennessee being successfully passed, General Rosecrans decided to threaten the enemy's communication with his right while his center and left seized the gaps and the commanding points of the mountains in front. General Crittenden's reconnoissance on the 9th, developed the fact that the enemy had evacuated Chattanooga on the day and night previous. While General Crittenden's corps took peaceable possession of Chattanooga, the objective point of the campaign, General Rosecrans, with the remainder of his army, pressed forward through the difficult passes of the Lookout and Missionary Mountains, apparently directing his march upon Lafayette and Rome. On ascertaining these facts, and that General Burnside was in possession of all East Tennessee above Chattanooga, and hearing that Lee was being rapidly reinforced on the Rapidan, it seemed probable that the enemy had determined to concentrate his forces for the defense of Richmond, or a new invasion of the North. The slight resistance made by him in East Tennessee, and his abandonment without a defense of so important a position as Chattanooga, gave plausibility to the reports of spies and deserters from Lee's army of reinforcements arriving there from Bragg."

To assist Rosecrans in maintaining his advance, Burnside was ordered to connect with the former, at least with his cavalry. "On the 12th," continues General Halleck, "General Rosecrans telegraphed that although he was sufficiently strong for the enemy then on his front, there were indications that the Rebels intended to turn his flanks and cut off his communications; he therefore decided that Burnside should move down his infantry toward Chattanooga, on his left, and that Grant should cover the Tennessee River toward Whitsburg, to prevent any raid into Nashville. He was of opinion that no troops had been sent from Bragg's army, but that Bragg was being reinforced by Loring from Mississippi. On the night of the 13th General Foster telegraphed from Fort Monroe that trains of cars had been heard running all the time, day and night, for the last thirty-six hours, on the Petersburg and Richmond road, evidently indicating a movement of troops in some direction, and on the morning of the 14th, that Longstreet's corps was reported to be going south through North Carolina. General Meade had been directed to ascertain, by giving battle if necessary, whether any of Lee's troops had left. It was not till the 14th, he could give me any information on this point, and then he telegraphed. My judgment formed of a variety of meagre and conflicting testimony, is that Lee's army has been reduced by Longstreet's regiments from Ewell's and Hill's."

On receiving the telegrams of Generals Rosecrans and Foster, General Halleck ordered General Burnside to move down his infantry as rapidly as possible toward Chattanooga, General Hurlbut at Memphis, and General Sherman at Vicksburg, to send all the available forces at those points, to Corinth and Tuscumbia, to operate against Bragg and prevent his turning the right flank of Rosecrans' army and recrossing the river into Tennessee. Generals Schofield and Pope "were directed to send forward to the Tennessee line every available man in their departments; and the commanding officers in Indiana, Ohio, and Kentucky, were ordered to make every possible exertion to secure General Rosecrans' lines of communication. General Meade was urged to attack General Lee's army while in its present reduced condition, or at least prevent him from sending off any more detachments. It seemed useless to send any more troops into East Tennessee or Georgia, on account of the impossibility of supplying them in a country which the enemy had nearly exhausted. General Burnside's army was on short rations, and that of the Cumberland inadequately supplied. General Rosecrans had complained of his inadequate cavalry force, but the stables of his depots were overcrowded with animals, and the horses of his artillery, cavalry and trains were dying in numbers for want of forage. As three separate armies were now to operate in the same field, it seemed necessary to have a single commander in order to secure a more perfect co-operation than had been obtained with the separate commands of Burnside and Rosecrans. General Grant, by his distinguished services and superior rank to all other Generals in the West, seemed entitled to this general command. But unfortunately he was at this time in New Orleans, unable to take the field. Moreover there was no telegraphic communication with him, and the dispatches of the 13th, dictated to him and General Sherman did not reach them till some days after their dates, thus delaying the movements of General Grant's forces from Vicksburg. General Hurlbut, however, had moved the troops of his own corps, then in West Tennessee with commendable promptness. These were to be replaced by reinforcements from Steele's corps, in Arkansas, which also formed part of General Grant's army. Hearing nothing from General Grant or General Sherman's corps at Vicksburg, it was determined on the 23d to detach the Eleventh and Twelfth Corps from the Army of the Potomac, and send them by rail, under the command of General Hooker, to protect Rosecrans' line of communication from Bridgeport to Nashville. It was known that these troops could not go immediately to the front. To send more men to Chattanooga, when those already there could not be fully supplied would only increase the embarrassment, and probably cause the evacuation of that place. In other words, Hooker's command was temporarily performing the duties previously assigned to the reinforcements ordered from Grant's army.

"We now return to General Rosecrans' army, the main body of which we left, on the 14th, in the passes of Pigeon Mountain, with the enemy concentrating his forces near Lafayette to dispute his further advance. Bragg's threatened movements to the right and left were merely cavalry raids to cut Rosecrans' line of supplies and threaten his communications with Burnside. His main army was probably only awaiting the arrival of Longstreet's corps, to give battle in the mountains of Georgia. Of the movements of this corps, so well known to the enemy, we could get no trustworthy information. All we knew positively was, that one of Longstreet's divisions had arrived in Charleston to reinforce that place. It was said that others had gone to Mobile to protect it from an attack by Banks' army. But as there was no real danger of such an attack at that moment, it was more probably on its way to reinforce Bragg's army. But the time of its arrival was uncertain, as we had no reliable information of its departure from Richmond. We knew Bragg had been reinforced by troops sent by Johnson from Mississippi, and it was afterward ascertained that the Rebel authorities had falsely declared as exchanged and released from parole the prisoners of war captured by Grant and Banks at Vicksburg and Port Hudson. This shameful violation of the cartel and of the established usages of civilized warfare was resorted to by the enemy in order to swell the numbers of Bragg's army in the approaching conflict. General Rosecrans' troops were at this time scattered along an extended line from Gordon's Mills to Alpines, a distance of some forty miles. By the 17th, they were brought more within a supporting distance, and on the morning of the 18th, a concentration was begun toward Crawfish Springs, but was slowly executed.

"The battle of Chickamauga commenced on the morning of the 19th, McCook's corps forming the right of our line of battle, Crittenden's the centre, and Thomas' the left. The enemy first attacked our left with heavy masses, endeavoring to turn it, so as to occupy the road to Chattanooga. But all their efforts proved abortive. The centre was next assailed, and temporarily driven back, but, being promptly reinforced, maintained its ground. As night approached, the battle ceased, and the combatants rested on their arms. The attack was furiously renewed on the morning of the 20th against our left centre. Division after division was pushed forward to resist the attacking masses of the enemy, when, according to General Rosecrans' order, General Wood, overlooking the order to close up on Reynolds, supposed he was to support him by withdrawing from the line and passing in the rear of General Brannan. By this unfortunate mistake a gap was opened in the line of battle, of which the enemy took instant advantage, and striking Davis in the flank and rear threw his whole division into confusion. General Wood claims that the orders he received were of such a character as to leave him no option but to obey them in the manner he did. Pouring in through this break in our line, the enemy cut off our right and right centre, and attacked Sheridan's Division, which was advancing to support our left. After a gallant but fruitless effort against the Rebel torrent he was compelled to give way, but afterward rallied a considerable portion of his force, and by a circuitous route joined General Thomas, who now had to breast the tide of battle against the whole Rebel army. Our right and part of the centre had been completely broken and fled in confusion from the field, carrying with them to Chattanooga their commanders, Generals McCook and Crittenden, and also General Rosecrans, who was on that part of the line. His Chief of Staff, General Garfield, however, made his way to the left and joined General Thomas, who still remained immovable

looking rifled cannon, each one of whom I had come to regard with a feeling of almost reverential awe, because upon a dozen battle-fields I had seen them flinging destruction into the ranks of traitors, and never knew them once turned against a legion of my country's enemies which they did not scatter like leaves before the blast. Even in the opinion of the rebels themselves, Loomis had made these guns invincible. They were commanded now by a young man who, possessing naturally the noblest qualities, had thoroughly learned the lessons of his teacher, and promised to prove a most worthy successor, even to Loomis himself—Lieutenant Van Pelt. Van Pelt loved his pieces with the same unselfish devotion which he manifested for his wife. In the desperate conflict which broke around Scribner's brigade, he managed the battery with much dexterity and coolness, and for some moments rocked the very trees over the heads of the rebels by the fiery blasts from his guns. But his horses were shot down. Many of his artillerists were killed or wounded. The infantry supporting him had been compelled to turn and cut their way through the enemy, and a horde of traitors rushed up to the muzzles of the now harmless pieces. Van Pelt now almost alone, stationed himself in front of them and drew his sword. 'Scoundrels,' said he, dare not to touch these guns!' The miserable barbarians, unable to appreciate true heroism, brutually murdered him were he stood. The history of the war furnished not an incident more touching or more sublime than the death of Lieutenant Van Pelt."*

The loss of Union officers in the battle of Chickamauga was heavy. Of the whole number of the army killed upon the scene of the actions 131, and of the wounded about 650 were officers, making, together with the missing, nearly one to every fifteen enlisted men. About forty of these were field officers. But one general officer—General Lytle, whose honorable career from the early campaigns in Western Virginia will be remembered—was killed, though nearly a dozen colonels, acting as brigade commanders, were killed and wounded.* Among the rebel officers killed were Brigadier-General Preston Smith of Tennessee, Brigadier-General Deshler, and Brigadier-General B. H. Helm, a Kentuckian, who, on entering the Southern army as a private, had been Colonel of the First Kentucky Rebel cavalry, and been promoted to the command of a Kentucky brigade at Vicksburg. He was a grandson of Ben Hardin, the celebrated Kentuckian, and had married a half-sister of Mrs. Lincoln, the wife of the President. The loss to the enemy in field officers was heavy, including Colonel R. W. Harper, a Marylander, commanding a brigade; Colonels Bland and Ould of South Carolina, Colonel Hewitt of Kentucky, Colonel Wheaton of Alabama, and others; Major-General Hood, Brigadier-Generals Adams, Gregg and Brown were wounded.† Previously to the engagement, General Bragg, on the 17th of September, from his headquarters in the field, at Lafayette, Ga., issued the following order, indicating his expectations from the conflict: "The troops will be held ready for an immediate move against the enemy. His demonstrations on our flanks have been thwarted, and twice has he retired before us when offered battle. We must now force him to the issue. Soldiers, you are largely reinforced—you must now seek the contest. In doing so, I know you will be content to suffer privations and encounter hardships. Heretofore you have never failed to respond to your General when he has asked a sacrifice at your hands. Rely-

* Chattanooga Correspondence of the *Cincinnati Gazette*, September 25th, 1863.

* Tabular statement furnished by the special correspondent of the *New York Tribune*.

† *Atlanta, Ga. Intelligencer*, September 22d. *New York Tribune*, October 2d, 1863.

ing upon your gallantry and patriotism, he asks you to add a crowning glory to the wreaths you wear. Our credit is in your keeping. Your enemy boasts that you are demoralized, and retreating before him. Having accomplished our object in driving back his flank movement, let us now turn on his main force, and crush it in its fancied security. Your General will lead you. You have but to respond to assure us of a glorious triumph over an insolent foe. I know what your response will be. Trusting in God and the justice of our cause, and nerved by the love of dear ones at home, failure is impossible, and victory must be ours." Though fairly claimed by them as a victory, the enemy had little reason to rejoice over a hardly-fought conflict which had left the coveted prize—Chattanooga—still in the hands of the Union General. This dissatisfaction was shown in the arrest by General Bragg of two of his officers, Generals Polk and Hindman, whom it is stated he charged with disobedience of orders in not bringing on the battle on Sunday, the second day, at an earlier hour, thus losing an important advantage. Whatever the state of the case may have been, the fact of General Polk's removal was announced to the public by himself in the following farewell to the officers and soldiers of his corps, dated Mission Ridge, before Chattanooga, September 30th: "In consequence of an unfortunate disagreement between myself and the Commander-in-Chief of this Department, I have been relieved of my command, and am about to retire from the army. Without attempting to explain the circumstances of this disagreement, or prejudicing the public mind by a premature appeal to its judgment, I must be permitted to express my unqualified conviction of the rectitude of my conduct, and that time and investigation will amply vindicate my conduct on the field of the Chickamauga. I cannot, however, part, even temporarily, with the gallant officers and soldiers of my old corps without the deepest feelings of regret and a heartfelt expression of my gratitude for the courage and devotion they have always manifested while under my command. Belmont, Shiloh, Perryville, Murfreesboro' and Chickamauga, all attest on your part the very highest soldierly qualities, and are crowded with precious memories. Contending with a numerous, well-appointed, and merciless enemy, for all that man holds dear, you have borne unexampled privations with fortitude, fought with undaunted bravery, and ever yielded a cheerful obedience to your officers. Soldiers who struggle in such a cause, and with such hearts, can never be conquered. Clouds and darkness may enshroud you for a time, but the sunlight of the future is bright and glowing. The blood of patriots is never shed in vain, and our final victory is certain and assured. Whoever commands you, my earnest exhortations and request to you is, to fight on and fight ever, with true hearts, until your independence is achieved. Thousands of brave hearts may fall, crushed and bleeding, under the weapons of the foe, or the passions and mistakes of friends, but the great cause must never be sacrificed, or our flag abandoned. Our cause is just, and our duty to our country and God is as clear as the sun in the heavens. I leave my command in the care of the bravest of the brave, who has often led them in the darkest hour of their trials. He and you will have my hopes and prayers to the Ruler of the Universe, for your happiness and success. Your kindness, devotion and respect for me, exhibited during the years of our association, both in camp and in the field, are graven on my heart, and will be treasured there until it ceases to beat."

On the other hand, a document of a more cheering character was issued by the Union commander, General Rosecrans, in the following congratulatory order, dated Chattanooga, October 2d: "ARMY OF THE CUMBERLAND: You have made a grand and successful campaign; you have driven the rebels from Middle Tennessee. You crossed a great mountain range, placed yourselves on the banks of a broad river, crossed it in the face of a powerful, opposing army, and crossed two other great mountain ranges at the only practicable passes, some forty miles between extremes. You concentrated in the face of superior numbers; fought the combined armies of Bragg, which you drove from Shelbyville to Tullahoma, of Johnston's army from Mississippi, and the tried veterans of Longstreet's corps, and for two days held them at bay, giving them blow for blow, with heavy interest. When the day closed you held the field, from which you withdrew in the face of overpowering numbers to occupy the point for which you set out, Chattanooga. You have accomplished the great work of the campaign; you hold the key of East Tennessee, of Northern Georgia, and of the enemy's mines of coal and nitre. Let these achievements console you for the regret you experience that arrival of fresh hostile troops forbade you remaining on the field to renew the battle; for the right of burying your gallant dead, and caring for your brave companions who lay wounded on the field. The losses you have sustained, though heavy, are slight, considering the odds against you and the stake you have won. You hold in your hands the substantial fruits of a victory, and deserve, and will receive, the honors and plaudits of a grateful nation, which asks nothing of even those who have been fighting us but obedience to the Constitution and laws established for our own common benefit. The General commanding earnestly begs every officer and soldier of his army to unite with him in thanking Almighty God for His favors to us. He presents his hearty thanks and congratulations to all the officers and soldiers of this command for their energy, patience and perseverance, and the undaunted courage displayed by those who fought with such unflinching resolution. Neither the history of this war, nor probably the annals of any battle, furnish a loftier example of obstinate bravery and enduring resistance to superior numbers—when troops, having exhausted their ammunition, resorted to the bayonet many times, to hold their positions, against such odds—as did our left and centre, comprising troops from all the corps, on the afternoon of the 20th of September, at the battle of 'Chickamauga.'"

On the 18th of October, General Grant, who had arrived from New Orleans, where he had been suffering from an accident from the fall of his horse, issued a general order at Louisville, Ky., assuming command of his new Military Division of the Mississippi, and announcing that his headquarters "will be in the field." The next day General Rosecrans, at Chattanooga, took leave of the Army of the Cumberland in a farewell order, in which he handsomely complimented his successor, General Thomas. "In taking leave of you," said he, "his brothers in arms, officers and soldiers, he congratulates you that your new commander comes to you not as a stranger. General Thomas has been identified with this army from its first organization, and has led you often in battles. To his renown, precedents, dauntless courage and true patriotism, you may look with confidence, that, under God, he will lead you to victory. The General commanding doubts not you will be as true to yourselves and your country, in the future, as you have been in the past. To the division and brigade commanders he tenders his cordial thanks for their valuable and hearty co-operation in all he has undertaken."

CHAPTER XCIII.

GENERAL GRANT'S CAMPAIGN. BATTLE OF CHATTANOOGA AND SIEGE OF KNOXVILLE, NOVEMBER, 1863.

THE battle of Chickamauga was fought by General Bragg with superior numbers, with the intention of defeating the army of General Rosecrans before it could receive the reinforcements and supplies necessary to maintain it in its advanced position. To render this aid was of course the first object of the Union commanders. General W. T. Sherman's Fifteenth Army Corps which had borne the brunt of the campaign in Mississippi before and after the fall of Vicksburg, had been lately engaged in opening the line of the Memphis and Charleston Railroad eastward toward Huntsville, with the design of effecting a communication with Chattanooga. It was employed on this task, working resolutely in face of the enemy eastwardly from Corinth, through Iuka, when on General Grant's taking command of the departments, a more expeditious movement was ordered. Turning to the left, General Sherman struck the Tennessee at Eastport, crossed the river at that point, and reinforced by a portion of the Sixteenth Corps, hastened his march along the north bank of the river to unite with the right wing of the Army of the Cumberland at Stevenson. On the 16th of November this junction was effected, General Sherman arriving on that day at the headquarters of General Thomas at Chattanooga. General Hooker, in the meantime, several weeks earlier, had by a rapid transit—a portion of his force accomplishing the distance of thirteen hundred miles in five days—brought his corps from Virginia to Bridgeport, Ala., where, after the forced retreat of the rebel raiding party under Wheeler, he kept open the communication of the Union army at this part of the route with its base of supplies at Nashville. The position of the enemy in front of Chattanooga, however, interrupted further communication by the river and the railway on its southern bank the remaining distance of twenty-eight miles to the camp of General Thomas, making it necessary to send supplies by a circuitous and difficult road through the mountains to the rear of the town. The town itself was well fortified and protected against a direct assault, but the river below was commanded by General Bragg's forces at Lookout Mountain and its vicinity. After General Rosecrans' retreat to Chattanooga, consequent on the battle of Chickamauga, the enemy following closely upon his steps, had occupied this mountain and the adjacent one connecting Missionary Ridge running in a south-westerly direction directly in front of the Union camps which were thus freely exposed to view from the heights. A battery of rifled 24-pounders was placed at a commanding point of Lookout Mountain, from which, at a distance of about two and a half miles, shells were thrown into Chattanooga, inflicting, however, little damage. The enemy, also, held Lookout Valley on the westerly side of the mountains where a creek of that name runs into the Tennessee. To dislodge them from this position and open a free passage for supplies was the first effort of General Grant in his new military operations. This was undertaken and successfully accomplished by an expedition planned by General William F. Smith, the chief engineer of Grant's army. On the night of the 26th of October, eighteen hundred men, under General Hazen, were embarked at Chattanooga, in sixty pontoon boats, in which they floated down the Tennessee with the current round the bend of the river past Lookout Mountain, escaping the notice of the rebel pickets, till they arrived at the point proposed, known as Brown's Ferry, six miles by the river from the Union headquarters. Here, on the left bank of the river, a lodgment was effected, the enemy's pickets giving way with slight opposition, when the boat party was promptly reinforced by General Smith, who, with the remainder of his force had crossed the peninsula to the opposite shore, and was waiting the success of the landing. An effort made by the rebel troops in the valley to recover the lost ground was defeated by General Hazen, and a strong position on the river was taken and fortified, and a bridge constructed; artillery was planted so as to command the roads leading from the enemy's main camp in Chattanooga Valley to Lookout Valley.

General Hooker now, with his command, crossed the Tennessee and occupied Lookout Valley, General Geary holding the advance at Wauhatchie, where, early on the morning of the 29th of October, he was attacked by two brigades of Hood's division of Longstreet's corps which he repulsed in a sharp engagement, the New York and Pennsylvania regiments of his division fighting bravely. Major Reynolds, Chief of Artillery, Twelfth Corps, directed the batteries which suffered severely. Lieutenant Edward R. Geary, a son of General Geary, "a brave youth and an officer of rare promise," was killed at one of his guns. The enemy's loss was heavy in killed and prisoners. The result of this and the corresponding movement of Howard's corps in the vicinity, which was also attacked and fought bravely, was to gain command of the river. General Thomas congratulated General Hooker and his troops on "the brilliant success gained over his old adversary, Longstreet," that night. "The bayonet charge of Howard's troops," said he, "made up the sides of a steep and difficult hill, over two hundred feet high, completely routed and driving the enemy from his barricades on its top, and the repulse of Geary's division, of greatly superior numbers, who attempted to surprise him, will rank among the most distinguished feats of arms of this war." The Union loss, as reported by General Halleck, in these operations of the 27th, 28th and 29th of October, in re-opening communications on the south side of the Tennessee River from Chattanooga to Bridgeport, was 76 killed, 339 wounded, and 22 missing; while the estimated loss of the enemy was over 1,500. The possession of Lookout Valley removed the enemy from the borders of the river on which supplies were now transported from Bridgeport by means of a steamer sent down from Chattanooga. The rebels, however, continued to hold Lookout Mountain, from which presently after the arrival, already stated, of General Sherman's corps, they were driven in a concerted movement ending in a decisive victory over the whole Confederate line. The detachment of Longstreet from Bragg's army, with a considerable force, early in November, with the intention of driving Burnside from Knoxville and regaining possession of East Tennessee, favored the plans of General Grant before Chattanooga. While General Hooker held Lookout Valley, facing the enemy on the mountain, and General Thomas occupied the central position with his line of works before Chattanooga, with Missionary Ridge before him, General Sherman was sent with his force to a point on the right bank of the river above the town, with the intention of crossing and seizing the northern extremity of the ridge which was unfortified. The enemy would thus be held by Hooker and Sherman on each flank, while the old army of the Cumberland, under Thomas, would be ready to pierce their centre. The preliminary arrangements were admirably made. Sherman's troops, whose march had been directed through many difficulties of the way with extraordinary energy, took up their position near the mouth of the Chickamauga Creek, and pontoon boats in sufficient numbers were carried overland to secure the passage of the river. One division threatened the enemy's left front in the direction of Trenton.

On Monday, the 23d of November, every thing was in readiness for the projected movement. At half-past 11 on the forenoon of that day, we cite the graphic description of the military events which followed, sent by Quartermaster-General M. C. Meigs from the headquarters of the army at Chattanooga to Secretary Stanton: "General Grant ordered a demonstration against Missionary Ridge, to develop the force holding it. The troops marched out, formed in order, and advanced in line of battle as if on parade. The rebels watched the formation and movement from their picket lines and rifle pits, and from the summits of Missionary Ridge, five hundred feet above us, and thought it was a review and drill, so openly and deliberately, so regularly was it all done. The line advanced, preceded by skirmishers, and at 2 o'clock P. M. reached our picket lines and opened a rattling volley upon the rebel pickets, who replied and ran into their advanced line of rifle-pits. After them went our skirmishers, and into them, along the centre of the line of 25,000 troops which General Thomas had so quickly displayed, until we opened fire. Prisoners assert that they thought the whole movement was a review and general drill, and that it was too late to send to their camps for reinforcements, and that they were overwhelmed by force of numbers. It was a surprise in open daylight. At 3 P. M. the important advanced position of Orchard Knob, and the lines right and left, were in our possession, and arrangements were ordered for holding them during the night.

"The next day at daylight General Thomas had 5,000 men across the Tennessee, and established on its south bank, and commenced the construction of a pontoon bridge about six miles above Chattanooga. The rebel steamer Dunbar was repaired at the right moment, and rendered effective aid in this crossing, carrying over 6,000 men. By nightfall General Thomas had seized the extremity of Missionary Ridge nearest the river, and was intrenching himself. General Howard, with a brigade, opened communication with him from Chattanooga on the south side on the river. Skirmishing and cannonading continued all day on the left and centre. General Hooker scaled the slopes of Lookout Mountain, and from the valley of Lookout Creek drove the rebels around the point, captured some 2,000 prisoners, and established himself high up the mountain side, in full view of Chattanooga. This raised the blockade, and now steamers were ordered from Bridgeport to Chattanooga. They had run only to Kelley's Ferry, whence ten miles of hauling over mountain roads, and twice across the Tennessee on to pontoon bridges, brought us our supplies. All night the point of Missionary Ridge on the extreme left, and the side of Lookout Mountain on the extreme right, blazed with the camp fires of loyal troops. The day had been one of dense mists and rains, and much of General Hooker's battle was fought above the clouds, which concealed him from our view, but from which his musketry was heard. At nightfall the sky cleared, and the full moon, 'the traitor's doom,' shone upon the beautiful scene until 1 A. M., when twinkling sparks upon the mountain side showed that picket skirmishing was going on. Then it ceased. A brigade sent from Chattanooga crossed the Chattanooga Creek and opened communication with Hooker. General Grant's headquarters during the afternoon of the 23d, and the day of the 24th, were in Wood's redoubt, except when in the course of the day, he rode along the advanced line, visiting the headquarters of the several commanders in Chattanooga Valley.

"At daylight on the 25th, the 'stars and stripes' were descried on the peak of Lookout. The rebels had evacuated the mountain. Hooker moved to descend the mountain, and striking Missionary Ridge at the Rossville Gap, to sweep on both sides and on its summit. The rebel troops were seen as soon as it was light enough, streaming regiments and brigades along the narrow summit of Missionary Ridge, either concentrating on the right to overwhelm Sherman, or marching for the railroad, and raising the siege. They had evacuated the Valley of Chattanooga—would they abandon that of Chickamauga? The 20-pounders and 4½-inch rifles of Wood's redoubt opened on Missionary Ridge. Orchard Knob sent its compliments to the ridge, which, with rifled Parrots, answered, and the cannonade thus commenced continued all day. Shot and shell screamed from Orchard Knob to Missionary Ridge, and from Missionary Ridge to Orchard Knob, and from Wood's redoubt over the heads of Generals Grant and Thomas and their staffs, who were with us in this favorable position, from whence the whole battery could be seen as in an amphitheatre. The headquarters were under fire all day long. Cannonading and musketry were heard from General Sherman, and General Howard marched the Eleventh Corps to join him. General Thomas sent out skirmishers, who drove in the enemy's pickets, and chased them into their intrenchments, and, at the foot of Missionary Ridge, Sherman made an assault against Bragg's right, intrenched on a high knob next to that on which Sherman himself lay fortified. The assault was gallantly made. Sherman reached the edge of the crest and held his ground, for, it seemed to me, an hour, but was bloodily repulsed by reserves.

"A general advance was ordered, and a strong line of skirmishers followed by a deployed line of battle, some two miles in length. At the signal of leaden shots from the headquarters on Orchard Knob the line moved rapidly and orderly forward. The rebel pickets discharged their muskets and ran into their rifle-pits. Our skirmishers followed on their heels. The line of battle was not far behind, and we saw the gray rebels swarm out of the ledge line of rifle-pits in numbers which surprised us, and over the base of the hill. A few turned and fired their pieces, but the greater number collected into the many roads which cross obliquely up its steep face, and went on to their top. Some regiments passed on and swarmed up the steep sides of the ridge, and here and there a color was advanced beyond the lines. The attempt appeared most dangerous, but the advance was supported, and the whole line was ordered to storm the heights, upon which not less than forty pieces of artillery, and no one knew how many muskets stood ready to slaughter the assailants. With cheers answering to cheers, the men swarmed upward. They gathered to the points least difficult of ascent, and the line was broken. Color after color was planted on the summit, while musket and cannon vomited their thunder upon them. A well-directed shot from Orchard Knob exploded a rebel caisson on the summit, and the gun was seen galloping to the right, its driver lashing his horses. A party of our soldiers intercepted them, and the gun was captured, with cheers.

A fierce musketry fight broke out to the left, where, between Thomas and Sherman, a mile or two of the ridge was still occupied by the rebels. Bragg left the house in which he had held his headquarters, and rode to the rear as our troops crowded the hill on either side of him. General Grant proceeded to the summit, and then did we only know its height. Some of the captured artillery was put into position. Artillerists were sent for to work the guns. Caissons were searched for ammunition. The rebel log breastworks were torn to pieces, and carried to the other side of the ridge, and used in forming barricades across. A strong line of infantry was formed in the rear of Baird's line, hotly engaged in a musketry contest with the rebels to the left, and a secure lodgment was soon effected. The other assault to the right of our centre gained the summit, and the rebels threw down their arms and fled. Hooker coming in favorable position swept the right of the ridge and captured many prisoners. Bragg's remaining troops left early in the night, and the battle of Chattanooga, after days of maneuvering and fighting, was won. The strength of the rebellion, in the centre is broken. Burnside is relieved from danger in East Tennessee. Kentucky and Tennessee are rescued. Georgia and the South-east are threatened in the rear, and another victory is added to the chapter of 'Unconditional Surrender Grant.'"

"To-night," General Meigs writes, on the 26th, "the estimate of captures is several thousand of prisoners and thirty pieces of artillery. Our loss for so great a victory is not severe. Bragg is firing the railroad as he retreats toward Dalton. Sherman is in hot pursuit. To-day I viewed the battle-field, which extends for six miles along Missionary Ridge, and for several miles on Lookout Mountain. Probably not so well directed, so well ordered a battle has been delivered during the war. But one assault was repulsed, but that assault by calling to that point the rebel reserves, prevented them repulsing any of the others. A few days since Bragg sent to General Grant a flag of truce advising him that it would be prudent to remove any non-combatants who might be still in Chattanooga. No reply has been returned, but the combatants having removed from this vicinity, it is probable that non-combatants can remain without im prudence."

The dispatches of General Grant to General Halleck, announcing the progress of the engagement and its final result, were brief and characteristic. Announcing the preliminary demonstration of the 23d, he writes:

"General Thomas' troops attacked the enemy's left at 2 P. M., to-day, carried first line of rifle-pits, running over the knoll 1,200 yards in front of Wood's Fort and low ridge to the right of it, taking about 200 prisoners, besides killed and wounded; our loss small. The troops moved under fire with all the precision of veterans on parade. Thomas' troops will intrench themselves, and hold their position until daylight, when Sherman will join the attack from the mouth of the Chickamauga, and a decisive battle will be fought."

At the close of the next day, he sent the following:

"The fight to-day progressed favorably. Sherman carried the end of Missionary Ridge, and his right is now at the Tunnel and left at Chickamauga Creek. Troops from Lookout Valley carried the point of the mountain, and now hold the eastern slope and point high up. I cannot yet tell the amount of casualties, but our loss is not heavy. Hooker reports 2,000 prisoners taken, besides which a small number have fallen into our hands from Missionary Ridge."

On the evening of the 25th, he wrote:

"Although the battle lasted from early dawn till dark this evening, I believe I am not premature in announcing a complete victory over Bragg. Lookout Mountain top, all the rifle-pits in Chattanooga Valley, and Missionary Ridge entire, have been carried, and now held by us. I have no idea of finding Bragg here to-morrow."

Nor did he find him. The success of this movement was indeed most brilliant, and appears to have been gained at the decisive moment by the uncontrollable ardor and impetuosity of the Union troops.

"The storming of the Ridge," wrote one of the officers to the War Department, "was one of the greatest miracles in military history. No man who climbs the ascent by any of the roads that wind along its front can believe that 18,000 men were moved upon its broken and crumbling face, unless it was his fortune to witness the deed. It seems as awful as a visible interposition of God. Neither General Grant nor General Thomas intended it. Their orders were to carry the rifle-pits along the base of the ridge, and cut off their occupants; but when this was accomplished, the unaccountable spirit of the troops bore them bodily up the impracticable steeps over the bristling rifle-pits on the crest, and the thirty cannon enfilading every gully. The order to storm appears to have been given simultaneously by Generals Sheridan and Wood, because the men were not to be held back, hopeless as the attempt appeared to military prudence; besides, the Generals caught the inspiration of the men, and were ready themselves to undertake impossibilities.'

"Considering the strength of the rebel position," says General Halleck, in his report of this engagement laid before Congress, "and the difficulty of storming his entrenchments, the battle of Chattanooga must be considered the most remarkable in history. Not only did the officers and men exhibit great skill and daring in their operations on the field, but the highest praise is due to the commanding General for his admirable disposition for dislodging the enemy from a position apparently impregnable. Moreover, by turning his right flank, and throwing him back upon Ringgold and Dalton, Sherman's forces were interposed between Bragg and Longstreet, so as to prevent any possibility of their forming a junction.

"Our loss," adds General Halleck, "in killed, wounded, and missing, is reported at about 4,000. We captured over 6,000 prisoners, besides the wounded left in our hands; 40 pieces of artillery, 5,000 or 6,000 small arms, and a large train. The enemy's loss in killed and wounded is not known." *

The brilliant events at Chattanooga were immediately succeeded by the heroic defense of Knoxville, against which Longstreet had advanced by the line of the East Tennessee and Georgia Railroad. On the 9th of November he attacked, and succeeded in capturing General Burnside's most eastern outposts at Rodgersville, whence the rebel cavalry under General Wheeler advanced towards Knoxville, sixty miles distant, capturing on the 15th, portions of several cavalry regiments at Marysville, fifteen miles from Knoxville, in the direction of the Little Holston. The remainder of the Union cavalry fled to Knoxville, when General Saunders in command of a cavalry brigade at that place, advanced to meet the enemy, but finding them too strong for him, was compelled to retire. The main force of the enemy, meanwhile, under Generals Longstreet, Chatham, and Pegram, advanced by way of Loudon and Lenoir, passing the Tennessee by portions at the former place on the 14th, when the advance was met by General Burnside, and driven back toward the river.

* General Halleck to Secretary Stanton, Washington, D. C., December 6, 1863.

Longstreet in the night crossed the remainder of his troops, and General Burnside the next day (Sunday, 15th), fell back to Lenoir, his rear guard skirmishing heavily with the pursuing enemy. On Monday morning, General Burnside evacuated Lenoir, retiring towards Knoxville, but making a stand to secure the passage of the trains, at Campbell's Station, twelve miles from Knoxville, where a sharp contest was kept up during the day. In the night, the Union troops fell back to Knoxville, and early on the 17th, took up their position in front of the city. The rebels advancing, heavy skirmishing immediately ensued, but the line was firmly held by General William C. Saunders. The contest being resumed the next day, the 18th, this gallant officer was mortally wounded.

The Union forces were now confined to their lines round Knoxville, the city being completely invested. For a fortnight the siege was continued, the enemy being effectually resisted in all their efforts to gain possession of the town. On the 29th, a desperate effort was made to take the works by assault. It is thus described in a special dispatch to the *Chicago Tribune*, dated Knoxville the 30th. "The great rebel blow anxiously anticipated so long, was struck yesterday morning. Reinforced by the troops of Sam. Jones, Jackson and Williams, Longstreet sought to annihilate the Army of the Ohio by *coup de guerre*. He selected seven picked regiments. Skirmishing commenced on Sunday night at 10 o'clock, and continued sharply until near daylight of Monday, on our left front before Fort Saunders, commanded by General Ferrero, and defended by the Seventy-ninth New York, Benjamin's Third U. S. Artillery, and Buckley's Rhode Island Battery. Our pickets were driven in and the enemy had possessed themselves of some rifle-pits, but the Massachusetts boys drove them back when suddenly the rebel storming party, led by the Sixteenth and Seventeenth Georgia and Thirteenth Mississippi, under cover of our own retreating men, came to the assault. They approached to within 100 yards of the fort unharmed. Then commenced a series of desperate and daring attacks, stubborn resistance, death, carnage, and horror scarcely equaled during the war. These men were the veterans of the Potomac—the flower of Longstreet's army—and, confident of promised victory, plunged into a boiling hell of lead. Wires had been stretched from stump to stump in front of the works, by Captain Poe. Over these the advancing enemy fell in confused heaps, with the killed and wounded around them. Our artillerymen hurled shell by hand; forward, over the impediments, came the doomed rebels! Hot, and hotter, became the battle, until the ground over which they passed was carpeted with the slain. The ditch was piled with dead, wounded, and dying. Not one on their side faltered—not a score of the gallant stormers escaped. The sun, rising, looked down through the cold mist and chill frost of that November morning upon the remains of an army. One thousand killed, wounded, and prisoners, was the cost of the assault of Fort Saunders. Nobly has it sustained the reputation of its namesake and revenged his fall! Among the killed is Colonel Girarde, of the Thirteenth Massachusetts. General Burnside offered them an armistice from 10 A. M. to 5 P. M., to remove their wounded, and bury their dead. It was accepted. Our loss will not reach 80, all told. Over 50 of these are the men of the Twenty-seventh Kentucky, captured on the south of the river. Besides 250 prisoners, we have three battle flags. One of them was planted on our works at one time."

General Burnside immediately after this victory on the 30th, issued the following congratulatory order to his troops in the field. "The brilliant

ATTACK ON KNOXVILLE.

From the original painting by Nast in the possession of the publishers

events of the 29th inst., so successful to our arms, seem to present a fitting occasion for the commanding General to thank this army for their conduct through the severe experiences of the past seventeen days, to assure them of the important bearing it has had on the campaign in the West, and to give them the news of the great victory gained by General Grant, toward which their fortitude and their bravery have in a high degree contributed. In every fight in which they have been engaged, and recently in those near Knoxville, at Loudon, at Campbell's Station, and finally around the defenses on both sides of the river, while on the march, and in cold and in hunger, they have everywhere shown a spirit which has given to the Army of the Ohio a name second to none. By holding in check a powerful body of the enemy, they have seriously weakened the rebel army under Bragg, which has been completely defeated by General Grant, and at the latest accounts was in full retreat for Dalton, closely pursued by him, with the loss of 6,000 prisoners, 52 pieces of artillery, and 12 stands of colors. For this great and practical result, toward which the Army of the Ohio has done so much, the commanding General congratulates them, and with the fullest reliance on their patience and courage in the dangers they may yet have to meet, looks forward with confidence, under the blessing of Almighty God to a successful close of the campaign." The assault on Fort Saunders was the final effort of Longstreet before Knoxville. His position was now imperilled by the advance of General Sherman, who after the defeat of Bragg at Chattanooga, was sent with his own and General Granger's forces into East Tennessee, to cut off his retreat and relieve General Burnside. Anticipating his arrival, Longstreet broke up his camps and retreated on the line of the railway toward Virginia. On the 4th of December, General Sherman s advanced guard reached Knoxville, and that night the rear guard of Longstreet's forces abandoned their works. The enemy were pursued on their route by General Foster who came with reinforcements as the successor of General Burnside, who had sometime before tendered his resignation, and now had the good fortune to close his campaign with this resolute and successful defense of Knoxville.

In summing up the campaign in his Official Report, General Grant states the Union losses in the various battles at 757 killed, 4,529 wounded and 330 missing. The loss of the enemy, he says, was probably less, owing to the fact that he was protected by his entrenchments while we were without cover. At Knoxville, however, his loss was many times greater than ours, making his entire loss at the two places equal to, if not exceeding ours. We captured 6,142 prisoners, of whom 239 were commissioned officers, 40 pieces of artillery, 69 artillery carriages and caissons, and 7,000 stand of small arms."*

General Sherman having left the corps of General Granger at Knoxville, returned with the rest of his command to Chattanooga. In the valuable report of his campaign from the time of his departure from the vicinity of Vicksburg, to which we refer the reader for an interesting account of the extraordinary services rendered by his Western army, he says: "In reviewing the facts I must do justice to my command for the patience, cheerfulness and courage which officers and men have displayed throughout, in battle, on the march and in camp. For long periods, without regular rations or supplies of any kind, they have marched through mud and over rocks, sometimes barefooted, without a murmur, without a moment's rest. After a march of over 400 miles

* Major-General Grant to Colonel J. C. Kelton, A. A. G., Washington. Chattanooga, Tenn., December 23d, 1863.

without stop for three successive nights, we crossed the Tennessee, fought our part of the battle of Chattanooga, pursued the enemy out of Tennessee and then turned more than a hundred miles north and compelled Longstreet to raise the siege of Knoxville which gave so much anxiety to the whole country."*

On receipt of the intelligence of these results at Washington, President Lincoln on the 7th of December issued the following Proclamation and recommendation to the country: "Reliable information being received that the insurgent force is retreating from East Tennessee under circumstances rendering it probable that the Union forces cannot hereafter be dislodged from that important position; and esteeming this to be of high national consequence, I recommend that all loyal people do, on receipt of this information, assemble at their places of worship and render special homage and gratitude to Almighty God for this great advancement of the national cause." The next day the President also addressed the following cordial letter to Major-General Grant: "Understanding that your lodgment at Chattanooga and Knoxville is now secure, I wish to tender you and all under your command my more than thanks—my profoundest gratitude for the skill, courage and perseverance with which you and they, over so great difficulties, have effected that important object. God bless you all! A. LINCOLN."

General Grant, on the 10th of December, issued the following congratulatory order to his army from his headquarters at Chattanooga: "The General commanding takes this opportunity of returning his sincere thanks and congratulations to the brave armies of the Cumberland, the Ohio, the Tennessee, and their comrades from the Potomac, for the recent splendid and decisive successes achieved over the enemy. In a short time you have recovered from him the control of the Tennessee River from Bridgeport to Knoxville. You dislodged him from his great stronghold upon Lookout Mountain, drove him from Chattanooga Valley, wrested from his determined grasp the possession of Missionary Ridge, repelled with heavy loss to him his repeated assaults upon Knoxville, forcing him to raise the siege there, driving him at all points, utterly routed and discomfitted, beyond the limits of the State. By your noble heroism and determined courage, you have most effectually defeated the plans of the enemy for regaining possession of the States of Kentucky and Tennessee. You have secured positions from which no rebellious power can drive or dislodge you. For all this the General commanding thanks you collectively and individually. The loyal people of the United States thank and bless you. Their hopes and prayers for your success against this unholy rebellion are with you daily. Their faith in you will not be in vain. Their hopes will not be blasted. Their prayers to Almighty God will be answered. You will yet go to other fields of strife; and with the invincible bravery and unflinching loyalty to justice and right, which have characterized you in the past, you will prove that no enemy can withstand you, and that no defense, however formidable, can check your onward march."

On the 11th of December General Burnside took leave of his army in a general order. "In obedience to orders from the War Department, the commanding General this day resigns to Major-General John G. Foster the command of the Army of the Ohio. On severing the tie which has united him to this gallant army, he cannot express his deep personal feeling at parting with men brought near to him by their mutual experiences in the eventful scenes of the past campaign, and who

* Major-General W. T. Sherman to Brigadier-General John A. Rawlins, Chief of Staff to General Grant. Bridgeport, Ala., December 19th, 1863.

have always, regardless of every privation and of every danger, cheerfully and faithfully performed their duty. Associated with many of their number from the earliest days of the war, he takes leave of this army, not only as soldiers to whose heroism many a victorious battle-field bears witness, but as well-tried friends, who in the darkest hours have never failed him. With the sincerest regret he leaves the department without the opportunity of personally bidding them farewell. To the citizen soldiers of East Tennessee who proved their loyalty in the trenches of Knoxville, he tenders his warmest thanks. With the highest confidence in the patriotism and skill of the distinguished officer who succeeds him, with whom he has been long and intimately connected in the field, and who will be welcomed as their leader by those who served with him in the memorable campaign in North Carolina, and by all as one identified with some of the most brilliant events of the war, he transfers to him the command, assured that under his guidance the bright record of the Army of the Ohio will never grow dim."

CHAPTER XCIV.

DEPARTMENT OF THE SOUTH. SIEGE OF CHARLESTON, Etc. JUNE—DECEMBER, 1863.

Simultaneously with the appointment of General Gilmore in place of General Hunter at the head of the land forces in the Department of the South, Rear-Admiral Andrew H. Foote was appointed to succeed Rear-Admiral Dupont in command of the South Atlantic Blockading Squadron. Previously to surrendering his position Admiral Dupont had the satisfaction of reporting to the Government, at the close of his administration, a memorable achievement of one of the monitors in the department. This was the capture of the rebel ram Atlanta in Warsaw Sound. The enemy had been for months busy equipping this vessel, originally a Clyde-built steamer, the Fingal, which had run the blockade early in the war and had since been confined at Savannah. She had been razeed, her timbers were strengthened, and her sloping sides provided with an outer covering of four inches of solid iron. A formidable ram of iron armed with a torpedo at its extremity extended from her bows. Her engines were powerful and well-built. As abundance of time had been taken and the most liberal means expended in her preparation, corresponding expectations were entertained of her success. At length, having completed her armament, consisting of two 7-inch and two 6-inch rifled guns, and taken on board an ample supply of ammunition and stores for a regular cruise, with a complement, officers and men, of one hundred and sixty-five souls, the Atlanta left Savannah on the evening of the 16th of June, by way of Wilmington, for Warsaw Sound, fully prepared to attack the blockading squadron. Anticipating this attempt of the rebel vessel to get to sea, in consequence of the intelligence which he had received, Admiral Dupont had dispatched, some days before, the Weehawken, Captain John Rodgers, from Port Royal, and the Nahant, Commander J. Downes, from North Edisto, to the assistance of Commander Drake, who, in the Cimerone, was maintaining the inside blockade at Warsaw Sound. At 6 o'clock on the morning of the 17th, the Atlanta, commanded by Captain William A. Webb, formerly of the

United States Navy, came in sight, accompanied by two wooden steamers, filled, it is said, with spectators from Savannah, who, confident of the result, had come out to view the engagement. As she was bearing down reserving her fire for close quarters, she was anticipated by Captain Rodgers, who at once engaged her with the Weehawken. Eleven shots where fired in all—five by the Weehawken and six by the Atlanta. The first 15-inch shot fired by Captain Rodgers took off the top of the Atlanta's pilot-house and wounded two of her three pilots. Another 15-inch shot struck half way up her roof, killing one and wounding seventeen men. In consequence of these injuries, the Atlanta grounded, and immediately after surrendered. The whole action occupied only about fifteen minutes, and was over before the consorts of the Weehawken, hastening to the scene could take part in it. The Weehawken in the contest sustained no injury of any sort. The Atlanta proved to have suffered no serious damage, and was presently brought unaided with her officers and crew to Port Royal.* Reviewing the naval events of the year at its close, Secretary Welles pronounced this "the most marked and extraordinary conflict" in the service during that period; of importance not only for testing the vessels of great disparity in size, but the new 15-inch ordnance, "then for the first time brought into naval warfare, and concerning which there had been, as well as with respect to the vessels themselves, some variety of opinion. This remarkable result (he added) was an additional testimony in favor of the monitor class of vessels for harbor defense and coast service against any naval vessels that have been, or are likely to be, constructed to visit our shores. It appears, also, to have extinguished whatever lingering hopes the rebels may have had of withstanding our naval power by naval means."

To Captain Rodgers himself, Secretary Welles paid a special tribute in a letter from the Navy Department, written on receipt of his dispatch, announcing the capture of the Atlanta. "Your early connection," said he, "with the Mississippi flotilla, and your participation in the projection and construction of the first iron-clads in Western waters; your heroic conduct in the attack on Drury's Bluff; the high moral courage that led you to put to sea in the Weehawken upon the approach of a violent storm, in order to test the seagoing qualities of these new craft, at the time when a safe anchorage was close under your lee; the brave and daring manner in which you, with four associates, pressed the iron-clads under the concentrated fire of the batteries in Charleston harbor, and there tested and proved the endurance and resisting power of these vessels, and your crowning successful achievement in the capture of the Fingal, *alias* Atlanta, are all proofs of a skill and courage and devotion to the country and the cause of the Union, regardless of self, that cannot be permitted to pass unrewarded. To your heroic daring and persistent moral courage, beyond that of any other individual, is the country indebted for the development, under trying and varied circumstances on the ocean, under fire from enormous batteries on land, and in successful encounter with a formidable floating antagonist, of the capabilities and qualities of attack and resistance of the monitor class of vessels and their heavy armament. For these heroic and serviceable acts I have presented your name to the President, requesting him to recommend that Congress give you a vote of thanks, in order that you may be advanced to the grade of Commodore in the American Navy."

* Dispatches, Rear-Admiral Dupont, Hilton Head, June 17th, and of Acting Rear-Admiral S. P. Lee, Newport News, June 22d, 1863.

Rear-Admiral Foote—he had received this promotion for his services on the Mississippi, his commission dating from July 16th, 1862—was on his way to take command of the Southern squadron, when he was arrested at New York by a serious illness, which in a few days resulted in his death. He died in that city on the 26th June, 1863. After the reduction of Island No. Ten, early in the previous year, he had passed some months in retirement while recovering from the effects of his wound, when he was appointed Chief of the Bureau of Equipment and Recruiting, an office the duties of which he discharged with his characteristic energy and ability until his recent appointment as successor to Admiral Dupont. Every honor at New York, where a funeral procession was formed, and at New Haven, where his remains were interred, was paid to this patriotic officer justly characterized by the Secretary of the Navy in a general order, as "the gallant and self-sacrificing Christian, sailor and gentleman."

Admiral John A. Dahlgren was now appointed to the command of the South Atlantic fleet. A native of Pennsylvania, he had entered the Navy in 1826, and had risen to the rank of captain in the service. For several years of late he had held the appointment from which he was now transferred of Chief of the Bureau of Ordnance at Washington. The invention of the gun which bears his name and his scientific attainments, had secured to him a distinguished reputation, and as the service on which he was now sent, looking to the reduction of the forts at Charleston, required new resources in gunnery, his appointment by the side of General Gilmore promised the utmost efficiency in this direction. He proceeded immediately to Port Royal, and on the 6th day of July took command of the squadron.

The direct attack by the fleet on the works in Charleston harbor having failed in April, it was now determined as preliminary to further movements to effect a lodgment on Morris Island, on the northern side, where batteries might be erected capable with the new ordnance of battering down Fort Sumter, and thus opening a way for the operations of the squadron. Heavy concealed batteries were erected by the Union troops under Brigadier-General Vogdes on Folly Island, adjoining Morris Island, on the south, which effectually commanded the entrance to the ship channel on that side. Having concentrated a considerable force at this place at 5 o'clock on the morning of the 10th of July, General Gilmore, in the words of his dispatch to General Halleck on the 12th, "made an attack on the enemy's fortified position on the south end of Morris Island, and after an engagement, lasting three hours and a quarter, captured all his strongholds on that part of the island, and pushed forward my infantry to within 600 yards of Fort Wagner. We now hold all the island except about one mile on the north end, which includes Fort Wagner and a battery on Cummings' Point, mounting at the present time fourteen or fifteen heavy guns in the aggregate. The assaulting column was gallantly led by Brigadier-General Strong. It landed in small boats, under cover of our batteries, on Folly Island, and four monitors, led by Rear-Admiral Dahlgren, which entered the main channel abreast of Morris Island, soon after our batteries opened. The monitors continued their fire during the day, mostly against Fort Wagner. On the morning of the 11th inst., at daybreak, an attempt was made to carry Fort Wagner by assault. The parapet was gained, but the supports recoiled under the fire to which they were exposed, and could not be got up. Our losses in both actions will not vary much from 150 in killed, wounded and missing. We have taken eleven pieces of heavy ordnance and a large quantity of camp equipage. The enemy's loss in killed and wounded will not fall short of 200." The routed Confederate artillery on Morris Island were commanded by Captain Mitchell. Their loss in officers was heavy, including Captain Charles Haskell, Lieutenant John Bee killed, Lieutenant Alston, and a number of captains wounded and prisoners. Captain Langdon Cheeves of the Engineer Corps was killed almost instantly by a shell from a monitor exploding in Battery Wagner, and striking him on the head.

The attack caused great alarm in Charleston. Mayor Macbeth, in anticipation of it, after consultation with General Beauregard, "advised and earnestly requested all women and children and other non-combatants to leave the city as soon as possible;" and the Governor of the State issued a proclamation, calling for 3,000 negroes to work on the fortifications, urging the pressing need of additional measures of defense. The press of the city pointed out the consequences of the fall of Charleston. "With her capture," said the *Courier*, "the whole State would soon be at the mercy of the foe, and the great cause of Southern independence would be put in fearful jeopardy. Nothing but a guerrilla warfare for the Southern and South-western portion of the Confederacy, if not for its whole extent, would then be left us, in manifestation of our undying and unconquerable determination never to submit to Yankee rule. Let us, then, resolve to defend our beloved and time-honored city to the last extremity. First, let us make every possible human effort to wrest the adjacent islands from the enemy, and enable Sumter and our other harbor fortresses, with steam rams, to keep these vandals at bay. Failing in this, and even should Sumter become untenable, then let us resolve on a Saragossa defense of our city, manning and defending every wharf—fighting from street to street and house to house—and, if failing to achieve success, yielding nothing but smoking ruins and mangled bodies as the spoil of the ruthless conqueror." "It appears to us," said the *Charleston Mercury*, "to be useless to attempt to disguise from ourselves the situation. The Yankees having gotten possession of the southern half of Morris Island, there is but one way to save the city of Charleston, and that is by the steady and unflinching use of the bayonet. If the fight on Morris Island is to be now a fight by engineering and cannon merely, the advantage is with the enemy. With their iron-clads on the water and their men in occupation of the land, it is likely to be a mere question of time. The fall of Fort Wagner ends in the fall of Charleston. Fort Sumter, like Fort Wagner, will then be assailable by both land and sea, and the fate of Fort Pulaski will be that of Sumter."

Fort Sumter was to be demolished and Fort Wagner was to be taken, but not without much desperate fighting and Union losses. "Well," said General Gilmore, while congratulating his troops on their victory of the 10th, which "places them three miles nearer the rebel stronghold of Sumter, the first among all our country's defenses against foreign foes that felt the polluting tread of traitors," that "our labors are not over. They are just begun; and while the spires of the rebel city still loom up in the dim distance, the hardships and privations must be endured before our hopes and expectations can find full fruition in victory." A formidable attack was made on Fort Wagner on the night of the 18th of July. It was preceded by a heavy bombardment from the batteries which General Gilmore had erected in the face of the enemy on the island and from the guns of the fleet—the Montauk, the Ironsides, the Catskill, Weehawken and other iron-clads. About three-fourths of the island were at this time in possession of the Union troops. Five batteries had been erected by them in all, containing nine 30-pound and four 20-pound Parrotts, and ten 10-inch mortars on the left, with two 30-pound Parrotts, ten 10-inch mortars and three full batteries of light artillery on the right. The extreme right rested on the ocean beach, the extreme left on the edge of a swamp about 500 yards from the small creek separating Morris Island from James Island. The bombardment of the 17th, which was intended to open at daylight, was delayed by a violent thunder storm in the night. The batteries opened about noon, and in concert with the fleet, poured a tremendous fire upon the apparently doomed fort. This continued through the afternoon into the evening, the fort making little reply during the whole time, and whatever damage may have been sustained, showing no sign of surrender. The casualties during these six hours were few on either side. No one was injured on the monitors or Ironsides, and but one man killed and but one slightly wounded within the batteries.* The casualties within Fort Wagner numbered, it is said, four killed and fourteen wounded; the troops being effectually sheltered by the extensive bomb-proofs and other works erected for their protection. As evening set in and the firing ceased, loud peals of thunder echoed through the sky, with frequent flashes of lightning. Preparations for the assault were now made by General Gilmore. The troops were arranged in three brigades; the first commanded by General Strong, consisted of the Fifty-fourth Massachusetts, Colonel Shaw, colored regiment; the Sixth Connecticut, Colonel Chatfield; the Forty-eighth New York, Colonel Barton; the Third New Hampshire, Colonel Jackson; the Seventy-sixth Pennsylvania, Colonel Green; and the Ninth Maine, Colonel Emery. The Second Brigade, commanded by Colonel Putnam, was composed of the Seventh New Hampshire, the Sixty-second Ohio, Colonel Steele, the Sixty-seventh Ohio, Colonel Vorhees, and the One Hundreth New York. The Third Brigade, under General Stevenson, was organized, but was not brought into action. It was now dusk, when the brigades of Strong and Putnam "were formed in line on the beach, the regiments being disposed in columns, excepting the colored regiment which for some reason was given the post of extreme honor and of danger in the advance, and was drawn up in line of battle, exposing its full front to the enemy. This movement of the troops was observed by Sumter, and fire was at once opened upon them, happily without doing injury, as the shells went over the heads of the men. General Strong's brigade under this fire moved along the beach at slow time for about three-quarters of a mile, when the men were ordered to lie down. In this position they remained half an hour Sumter meanwhile being joined in the cannonade by the rebels in Battery Bee, but without effect upon our troops. It was now quite dark, and the order was given for both brigades to advance, General Strong's leading and Colonel Putnam's within supporting distance. The troops went forward at quick time and in deep silence, until the Fifty-fourth Massachusetts, led by its gallant Colonel Shaw, was within two hundred yards of the work, when the men gave a fierce yell and rushed up the glacis, closely followed by the other regiments of the brigade. The enemy, hitherto silent as the grave, while our men were swarming over the glacis, opened upon them furiously with grape, canister, and a continuous fusilade of small arms. The gallant negroes, however, plunged on regardless of this murderous reception, and many of them crossed the

* The Morris Island correspondence, *New York Tribune*, July 19th, 1863.

ditch, although it contained four feet of water, gaining the parapet. They were dislodged, however, in a few minutes with hand-grenades, and retired helter skelter, leaving more than one-half of their number, including their brave colonel, dead upon the field. The Sixth Connecticut Regiment, under Lieutenant-Colonel Rodman, was next in support of the Fifty-fourth, and they also suffered terribly, being compelled to retire after a stubborn contest. The Ninth Maine, which was next in line, was broken up by the passage of the remnant of the repulsed colored regiment through its lines, and retired in confusion, excepting three companies, which nobly stood their ground. It now devolved upon the Third New Hampshire regiment to push forward, and led by General Strong and Colonel Jackson in person the gallant fellows dashed up against the fort. Three companies actually gained the ditch, and wading through the water found shelter against the embankment. Here was the critical point of the assault, and the Second Brigade, which should have been up and ready to support their comrades of the First, were unaccountably delayed. General Strong then gave the order to fall back, and lie down on the glacis, which was obeyed without confusion. It was while waiting here, exposed to the heavy fire, that General Strong was wounded. A fragment of shell entered his thigh, passing entirely through the fleshy part and making a serious wound, although the bone escaped fracture. The breast of Colonel Jackson's coat was torn off at the same time by a piece of shell, slightly wounding him. Neither of these brave men would lie down to escape the rain of metal, but stood unflinchingly throughout, eliciting the unbounded admiration of their men. Finding that the supports did not come, General Strong gave the order for his brigade to retire, and the men left the field in perfect order. A little while afterward the other brigades came up and made up for their apparent tardiness by glorious deeds of valor. Rushing impetuously up the glacis, undeterred by the fury of the enemy, whose fire was not intermitted for a second, several of the regiments succeeded in crossing the ditch, scaling the parapet and descending into the fort. Here a hand-to-hand conflict ensued. Our men fought with desperation, and were able to drive the enemy from one side of the work to seek shelter between the traverses while they held possession for something more than an hour. This unparalleled piece of gallantry was unfortunately of no advantage. The enemy rallied, and, having received large reinforcements, made a charge upon the band of heroes, and expelled them from their nobly-won position by the sheer force of numbers. One of the regiments engaged in this brilliant dash was the Forty-eighth New York, Colonel Barton, and it came out almost decimated. The most distressing part of its disastrous treatment is, that the enemy did not inflict the damage. It was the result of a mistake on the part of one of our own regiments. The Forty-eighth was among the first to enter the fort, and was fired upon by a regiment that gained the parapet some minutes later, under the supposition that it was the enemy. About midnight the order was given to retire, and our men fell back to the rifle-pits outside of our own works, having engaged in as hotly contested a battle as has ever been fought. Our casualties, as may reasonably be expected, was very large. The list of killed, wounded and missing foots up fifteen hundred and thirty. Among the killed are Colonel Putnam, of the Seventh New Hampshire; Colonel Shaw, of the Fifty-fourth Massachusetts; Lieutenant-Colonel Green, of the Forty-eighth New York; Adjutant Libby, of the Third New Hampshire. General Seymour was wounded in the foot, while directing movements in the field. Colonel Barton of the Forty-eighth New York, was wounded in the thigh by a ball, which flattened against the bone. Lieutenant-Colonel Rodman, of the Sixth Connecticut, was seriously wounded. Lieutenant-Colonel Bedell, of the Third New Hampshire, was taken prisoner."*

By the side of this narrative of the assault by Union brigades we place an account of the defense, which appeared immediately after the action in the *Charleston Courier*. "As the shades of night began to fall," says the writer, "the bombardment measurably relaxed. General Taliaferro, one of 'Stonewall Jackson's veterans,' now promptly ordered every man to the parapet, and they were hardly in their places before word was received that the columns of the enemy were advancing to the attack. Five minutes more and the column was plainly in sight, appearing, according to the statement given the writer, to be seven lines deep. Our batteries remained silent, until the enemy reached the vicinity of our rifle-pits, when grape and canister were thrown into their ranks with fearful precision and execution. Checked for an instant only, they closed up the ragged gaps in their lines, and moved steadily on, until within less than eighty yards. Barely waiting the Unionists to get within a destructive range, our infantry opened their fusilade, and, from a fringe of fire that lined the parapet, leaped forth a thousand messengers of death. Staggering under the shock, the first line seemed for a moment checked, but pushed on by those in the rear, the whole now commenced a charge at a 'double quick.' On they came over the sand hills, tripping and stumbling in the pits their own shells had drug, until they reached the ditch of the battery; then it was but a moment's work for those who survived our terrible fire of musketry, to clamber up the sloping sides of the fortification, and attempt to effect a lodgment. But the men who met them on the parapet were as desperate as themselves, and the contest that ensued was brief and bloody. The antagonists were breast to breast, and Southern rifles and Southern bayonets made short work of human life. We could stop to take no prisoners then. The parapet was lined with dead bodies, white and black, and every second was adding to the number. It was one of those renconters which one side or the other must quickly yield or fly. The enemy took their choice. In less than five minutes, probably, the first line had been shot, bayoneted, or were in full retreat, rolling into the ditch, or dragging their bloody bodies through the sand hills on their hands and knees. But another line came, and another, and another, each reinforcing its predecessor, and the battle waxed hot, fierce and bloody. Finally, however, the whole were driven back, either into the broad trench at the base of the battery, out of reach of our guns, or scampering out of view in the darkness of the night.

"There was now a comparative lull in the firing, but in fifteen or twenty minutes, as the writer has been informed, a second column of Unionists repeated the experiment. The first assault failed utterly, but with the reinforcements that joined the defeated party they came again with such strength and impetuosity that between the extreme darkness of the night, which had now enveloped the entire scene, the difficulty of distinguishing friend and foe, and the confusion incident to such an occasion, some two or three hundred, as is estimated, effected a lodgment in the vicinity of the chambers occupied by two of our guns. Others clambered to the top of the magazine and bomb-proof, while still others, as is said, clustered around a Union flag flying on the ramparts. This position the Federals held for certainly upward of an hour. We were at

* *New York Times*, July 27th, 1863.

first comparatively ignorant of their strength or exact location, but General Taliaferro, with the cool courage in which he is distinguished, made a close personal reconnoissance, and soon had measures perfected for driving them from the work. In the present attitude of conflicting statements we shall not detail the manner in which this was done, but we do know that both Major David Ramsey of the Charleston Battalion was severely wounded, and Captain Ryan, of the Irish Volunteers, killed, while leading a portion of their men on a charge against the obstinate enemy. In the melee which followed the final arrangement of the General, most of the prisoners were captured whom we have in hand. Many escaped over the sides of the battery, but others preferred a voluntary surrender to the risk of being shot in the back. Both the Union land batteries and our own — Sumter and Gregg—were firing at intervals during the engagement and during the retreat, the latter greatly facilitating the 'change of base.' Our total loss is estimated at 24 killed and 70 wounded. The returns are not all in.* Out of seven line officers in the detachment from the 1st S. C. Regulars (Artillery) two only escaped unhurt, Lieutenant Gourdin of Company H, and Lieutenant Youngblood of Company I. The loss of the enemy is variously named; some placing the figures as high as 1,500 killed and wounded. They have probably 500 killed; 231 of their wounded were in the city last night, including several negroes. Of white prisoners we have taken six commissioned officers and ninety-four privates. Of blacks, it is said, we have over twenty, of whom several are severely wounded. A wounded negro is to be put into every ward of the white Yankees. One of the negroes is a remarkably sprightly fellow from Bermuda, where he was educated as a soldier. His position is that of an Orderly Sergeant."

* It was stated in a dispatch by General Beauregard at ut 150 killed and wounded.

General George C. Strong died of his wounds at New York on the 30th of July, a few days after he was brought from Morris Island. He was born at Stockbridge, Vermont, was educated at West Point, where he graduated just previous to the war in which he was employed from the commencement in the most important positions. He was on General McDowell's staff at the battle of Bull Run; was subsequently with General McClellan, and afterwards Assistant Adjutant-General with General Butler at New Orleans, in whose department he also distinguished himself by his conduct in the field. He was an officer devoted to his profession, of high mental and moral qualities, and his early death at the age of thirty-one was much lamented. The Chief of Ordnance to which he was attached, General James W. Ripley, coupled his death in a special announcement with that of another distinguished officer of the department, "first Reno," said he, "and now Strong, both so well known to their corps, and so highly appreciated for the intelligence, zeal and devotion which each brought to the discharge of the particular sphere of duty of his own branch of the service—no less of arduous and important, though less brilliant and striking than that of the battlefield—as each crowned his career and finished his course, as a patriot and soldier ought, in the seal of his lifeblood, set to devotion to his country. Both have set a glorious example in their lives and in their deaths, which will ever endear their memories to their corps, while it should serve as an example and incentive to all to do all and give all in so lofty and glorious a cause."

Colonel Robert G. Shaw, another devoted young officer, who fell in this engagement at the age of 27, was the only son of Francis George Shaw of Staten Island, N. Y. At the outbreak of the war he was a private in the Seventh New York City Regiment, which he accompanied on its first call to Washington. Before its three-months' term of service expired he sought and received a commission in the Second Massachusetts, eminently distinguished for its services in the Virginia campaigns. Narrowly escaping at Cedar Mountain, where his life was saved by his watch, and at Antietam where he was struck by a fragment of a shell which grazed his neck, he was selected for his moral qualities and soldierly accomplishments by Governor Andrew as Colonel of the colored regiment from Massachusetts, the first from any free State mustered into the United States service. He fell at the head of this regiment on the parapet of Fort Wagner while leading the assault as he waved his sword, and cried out, "Onward boys."* Had he not fallen, said General Strong, nothing could have prevented his regiment from entering the fort. "Of a most genial and friendly nature" is the language of an obituary of Colonel Shaw, "of manners as gentle as a woman's, of a native refinement that brooked nothing coarse, of a clear, moral insight, that no evil association could tarnish, of a strength of purpose aiming always at noble ends, of a courage, quiet but cheerful and unwavering, he was one of those characters which attracts and at the same time moulds all others brought under their influence."† An exchange of wounded prisoners was a few days after the engagement agreed upon, after a conference of General Vodges, Colonel Hall and Dr. Cravens, under a flag of truce with General Haywood and other rebel officers. On the afternoon of the 23d the rebel wounded were placed on board a hospital boat, and the next day entered Charleston harbor. The iron-clad and mortar fleet then engaging Fort Wagner as the vessel moved up the channel. She was met by the steamer Alice, a blockade runner from Nassau, which had run into Charleston two nights previous with a cargo of machinery and supplies which she had yet on board. This vessel had been chartered by the authorities in a spirit of bravado it was thought, at the time, to bring down the Union wounded. They were 105 in number, leaving 140 behind in two serious a condition to be moved. It was observed that none of the wounded negro prisoners were among those returned. On being enquired for, Colonel Anderson, the officer in charge, answered that their return was a matter of future consideration with his government. Thirty-eight of the rebel wounded were delivered from the Cosmopolitan, the exchange being made on parole without regard to numbers. Though the Union prisoners had been treated with kindness by the Sisters of Charity and others in Charleston, a correspondent "could not but notice the difference between the condition of the prisoners returned from Charleston, and those rebels who were transported on board the Alice clothed in clean linen and lacking nothing essential to their ease and comfort ; while our poor fellows were laid upon the decks of the Alice in the same tattered and bloody clothes in which they were wounded."*

After this, General Gilmore made vigorous preparations to plant new batteries, armed with the heaviest guns known to the service, commanding Wagner and Fort Sumter. In his previous reduction of Fort Pulaski the heaviest gun which he had employed was the rifle 42-pounder. Now, 200 and 300-pounder Parrott rifle guns were to be used. Some three weeks were passed in erecting the new batteries. The nearest of these batteries were located about

* Letter of Edward L. Pierce to Governor Andrew, Beaufort, South Carolina, July 22d, 1863.

† *New York Tribune*, July 22d, 1863.

* Correspondence of the *Philadelphia Enquirer*, Morris Island, July 25th, 1863.

a mile and three quarters from Sumter, 500 yards from Wagner, and one mile from Battery Gregg, the average range of the batteries being about two miles. As these three works of the enemy were in line with the batteries, Fort Sumter was thus besieged over the heads of the two intermediate garrisons. A grand assault by the army and navy was expected to be made on the 13th of August, but was delayed by the illness of General Gilmore. The batteries were, however, completed and at once secured the range of Sumter. Shell and shot were meantime freely exchanged between Fort Wagner and the batteries. On the 17th, without waiting for the reduction of Wagner, General Gilmore opened fire upon Sumter and continued an active bombardment for a week. The result is told in his dispatch to General Halleck from Morris Island, dated August 24th. "I have the honor," says he, "to report the practical demolition of Fort Sumter as the result of our seven days' bombardment of that work, including two days of which a powerful north-easterly storm most seriously diminished the accuracy and effect of our fire. Fort Sumter is to-day a shapeless and harmless mass of ruins. My Chief of Artillery, Colonel J. N. Turner, reports its destruction so far complete that it is no longer of any avail in the defenses of Charleston. He also says that by a longer fire it could be made more completely a ruin and a mass of broken masonry, but could scarcely be more powerless for the defense of the harbor. My breaching batteries were located at distances varying between 3,330 and 4,240 yards from the work, and now remain as efficient as ever. I deem it unnecessary at present to continue their fire upon the ruins of Sumter. I have also, at great labor, and under a heavy fire from James Island, established batteries on my left, with effective range of the heart of Charleston, and have opened with them, after giving General Beauregard due notice of my intention to do so."

The report of Colonel Turner describes particularly the nature of the injuries inflicted. "At the close of the seven days' bombardment," says he, "the gorge wall of the fort is almost a complete mass of ruins for the distance of several casemates. About midway on this face the ramparts are removed nearly and in places quite to the arches; and, but for the sand-bags with which the casemates were filled, and which has served to sustain the broken arches and masses of masonry, it would have long since been entirely cut away, and with it the arches to the floor of the second tier of casemates. The debris on this front now forms a rampart, reaching as high as the floor of these casemates. The parapet walls of the two north-easterly faces is completely carried away, a small portion only being left in the angle made with the gorge wall, and the ramparts of these faces are also a total ruin. Quite one-half of our projectiles seem to have struck the parade and parapet of these two faces, and judging from the effect that they have had upon the gorge wall, within our observation, the destruction of the masonry on these two sides must be very great, and I am of the opinion that nearly every arch in these fronts must be broken in. But one gun remains in position on these two fronts, and this is in the angle of the gorge, and I think unserviceable. The ruin extends around, taking in the north-eastern face as far as can be seen. A portion of this face, adjoining the angle it makes with the south-easterly face is concealed, but from the great number of missiles which have struck in this angle during the last two days, it cannot be otherwise than greatly damaged, and I do not think any guns can be left on this face in a serviceable condition. The ramparts in this angle, as well as in the south-easterly face, must be plowed up and greatly shattered.

The parapet on this latter face is torn off in many places, as we can see, and I hardly think the platforms of the remaining guns on this face could have escaped. With the assistance of a powful glass, I cannot determine that more than one of these guns can be used, and it has been dismounted once. The carriages of the others are evidently more or less shattered, and such is the parapet and parade in the immediate vicinity of this gun, that it probably could not be served for any length of time."

General Gilmore in his dispatch alludes to a correspondence with General Beauregard. It opened with the following letter from the Union commander, dated Morris Island, August 21st: "GENERAL—I have the honor to demand of you the immediate evacuation of Morris Island and Fort Sumter by the Confederate forces. The present condition of Fort Sumter and the rapid and progressive destruction which it is undergoing from my batteries seem to render its complete demolition within a few hours a matter of certainty. All my heaviest guns have not yet opened. Should you refuse compliance with this demand, or should I receive no reply thereto within four hours after it is delivered into the hands of your subordinate at Fort Wagner for transmission, I shall open fire on the city of Charleston from batteries already established within easy and effective range of the heart of the city." This communication reached the Confederate headquarters at a quarter to 11 o'clock that night, when General Beauregard was absent on a reconnoissance, and being unsigned, was returned to General Gilmore for his signature. It finally reached General Beauregard at his headquarters about 9 o'clock on the morning of the 22d. In the meantime, between 1 and 2 o'clock in the morning, a number of shells were fired by General Gilmore from his battery on the left, most of which fell into Charleston, damaging various buildings but inflicting no loss of life or personal injury. In his reply to General Gilmore's communication, General Beauregard complained of this. "Among nations," said he, "not barbarous, the usages of war prescribe that, when a city is about to be attacked, timely notice shall be given by the attacking commander, in order that non-combatants shall have an opportunity of withdrawing beyond its limits. Generally the time allowed is from one to three days; that is, time for the withdrawal in good faith of at least the women and children. You, sir, gave only four hours, knowing that your notice, under existing circumstances, could not reach me in less than two hours, and not less than the same time would be required for an answer to be conveyed from this city to Battery Wagner. With this knowledge you threaten to open fire on this city, not to oblige its surrender, but to force me to evacuate those works which you, assisted by a great naval force, have been attacking in vain for more than 40 days. Batteries Wagner and Gregg and Fort Sumter are nearly due north from your batteries on Morris Island, and in distance therefrom ranging from half a mile to two and a quarter miles. This city, on the other hand, is to the north-west, and quite five miles distant from the battery which opened against it this morning. It would appear, sir, that, despairing of reducing these works, you now resort to the novel measure of turning your guns against the old men, the women and children, and the hospitals of a sleeping city, an act of inexcusable barbarity from your own confessed point of sight, inasmuch as you allege that the complete demolition of Fort Sumter within a few hours by your guns seems to be a matter of certainty. Your omission to attach your signature to such a grave paper must show the recklessness of the course upon which you have adventured. While the facts that you knowingly fixed a limit for receiving an answer to your demand, which made it almost beyond the possibility of receiving any reply within that time, and that you actually did open one, and throw a number of the most destructive missiles ever used in war into the midst of a city taken unawares and filled with sleeping women aud children, will give you a bad eminence in history—even in the history of this war. I am only surprised, sir, at the limits you have set to your demands. If, in order to obtain the abandonment of Morris Island and Fort Sumter, you feel authorized to fire on this city, why did you not include the works on Sullivan's and James Island, nay, even the city of Charleston in the same demand? Since you have felt warranted in inaugurating this method of reducing batteries in your immediate front which were otherwise found to be impregnable, and a mode of warfare which I confidently declare to be atrocious and unworthy of any soldier, I now solemnly warn you that if you fire again on this city from your Morris Island batteries without giving a somewhat more reasonable time to remove the non-combatants, I shall feel impelled to employ such stringent means of retaliation as may be available during the continuance of this attack. Finally, I reply, that neither the works on Morris Island, nor Fort Sumter, will be evacuated on the demand you have been pleased to make. Already, however, I am taking measures to remove all non-combatants, who are now fully aware and alive to what they may expect at your hands."

This letter was delivered during the day, and was answered in the evening by General Gilmore. His first demand, he said, "should have arrived at your headquarters in time to have permitted your answer to reach me within the limit assigned, namely, four hours. The fact that you were absent from your headquarters at the time of its arrival may be regarded as an unfortunate circumstance for the city of Charleston, but it is one for which I clearly am not responsible. This letter bore date at my headquarters, and was officially delivered by an officer of my staff. The inadvertent omission of my signature doubtless affords grounds for special pleading. But it is not the argument of a commander solicitous only for the safety of sleeping women and children and unarmed men. Your threats of retaliation for acts of mine, which you do not allege to be in violation of the usages of civilized warfare, except as regards the length of time allowed as notice of my intention, are passed by without comment. I will, however, call your attention to the well-established principles that the commander of a place attacked, but not invested, having its avenues of escape open and practicable, has no right to a notice of an intention of bombardment other than that which is given by the threatening attitude of his adversary. Even had not this letter been written, the city of Charleston has had, according to your own computation, forty days' notice of her danger. During that time my attack upon her defenses has steadily progressed. The ultimate object of that attack has at no time been doubtful. If under the circumstances the life of a single non-combatant is exposed to peril by the bombardment of the city, the responsibility rests with those who have first failed to remove the non-combatants or to secure the safety of the city after having held control of all its approaches for a period of nearly two years and a half, in the presence of a threatening force, and who afterward refused to accept the terms upon which the bombardment might have been postponed. From various sources, official and otherwise, I am led to believe that most of the women and children of Charleston were long since removed from that city. But upon your assurance that the city is still full of them, I should suspend the bombardment until 11 o'clock P. M., to-morrow, thus giving you two days from the time you acknowledge to have received my communication of the 21st inst." General Gilmore, also, cordially acceded to the request of the Spanish Consul to suspend the bombardment for twenty-four hours, to allow the subjects of his government to depart from the city.

When General Gilmore, on the morning of the 17th opened all his batteries, Admiral Dahlgren moved up the entire available naval force for an attack upon Wagner and Sumter. Wagner was silenced shortly after 9 o'clock in the forenoon, when the rifle-guns of the Passaic and Patapsco were brought to bear at a distance of 2,000 yards upon the south-east front of Sumter. In the afternoon a fire was kept up upon Wagner. "All went well with us," says Admiral Dahlgren, in his report to Secretary Welles, "save one sad exception, Captain Rodgers, my Chief-of-Staff, was killed, as well as Paymaster Woodbury, who was standing near him. Captain Rodgers had more than once asked on this occasion if he should go with me, as usual, or resume the command of his vessel, the Kaatskill, and he repeated the question twice during the morning, the last time on the deck of the Weehawken, just while preparing to move into action. In each instance, I replied, 'Do as you choose.' He finally said, 'Well, I will go in the Kaatskill, and the next time with you.' The Weehawken was lying about 1,000 yards from Wagner, and the Kaatskill, with my gallant friend, just inside of me, the fire of the fort coming in steadily Observing the tide to have risen a little, I directed the Weehawken to be carried in closer, and the anchor was hardly weighed when I noticed the Kaatskill was also under way, which I remarked to Captain Calhoun. It occurred to me that Captain Rodgers detected the movement of the Weehawken, and was determined to be closer to the enemy if possible. My attention was called off immediately to a position for the Weehawken, and soon after it was reported the Kaatskill was going out of action with a signal flying that the Captain was disabled. He had been killed instantly. It is but natural that I should feel deeply the loss thus sustained for the close and confidential relations which the duties of fleet captain necessarily occasioned, impressed me deeply with the worth of Captain Rodgers. Brave, intelligent, and highly capable, devoted to his duty and to the flag under which he passed his life, the country cannot afford to lose such men. Of a kind and generous nature, he was always prompt to give relief when he could. I have directed that all respect be paid to his remains and the country will not, I am sure, omit to honor the memory of one who has not spared his life in her hour of trial."

Fort Sumter having been thus disabled, it remained for General Gilmore to perfect his operations against Fort Wagner. The siege was pressed with vigor. Offensive and defensive works were constructed by the engineers, important points were courageously seized and the saps, spite of the constant fire of the enemy, were pushed forward to the immediate vicinity of the fort, which was now within close range of Gilmore's formidable heavy artillery. In the first week of September a vigorous bombardment was kept up from the Ironsides and other vessels of the fleet and the batteries on the shore. For several days, particularly on the day and night of the 5th, the firing, as described by the *Charleston Mercury*, "raged with the greatest fury—the shots, many of them coming together as from the broadside of a ship, being often more than sixty to the minute. It is almost impossible to describe the terrible beauty of the scene in Charleston harbor as witnessed on Saturday night from the city. From Moultrie almost to Secessionville a whole semi-circle of the horizon was lit up by incessant flashes from cannon and shell. As peal on peal of artillery rolled across the water, no one could scarcely resist the belief that not less than a thousand great guns were in action. It was a grand chorus of hell, in which Moloch might have assisted, and over which Satan might have presided. All this went on beneath a waning September moon, which, with its warm Southern light, mellowed by a somewhat misty atmosphere, brought out softly, yet distinctly, the most distant outlines of the harbor. The loss of Wagner during this awful bombardment was considerable. Up to 8 o'clock on Sunday, the 6th, it amounted to one hundred and fifty in killed and wounded. Probably many more were added to these casualties in the course of the day. At Gregg there were but eight casualties on Saturday night during the skirmish with the barges. Among them was a Captain of the Twenty-seventh Georgia Volunteers. Under cover of their ceaseless fire, the Yankees had approached on Sunday within forty yards of Wagner."

At length, after a fortnight's persevering labor, General Gilmore's operations were crowned with success. On the 7th September he wrote to General Halleck from his headquarters in the field, "I have the honor to report that Fort Wagner and Battery Gregg are ours. Last night our sappers crowned the crest of the counterscarp of Fort Wagner on the sea-front masking all its guns; and an order was issued to carry the place by assault at 9 o'clock this morning, that being the hour of low tide. About 10 o'clock last night the enemy commenced evacuating the island, and all but seventy-five of them made their escape from Cummings' Point in small boats. Captured dispatches show that Fort Wagner was commanded by Colonel Keitt of South Carolina, and garrisoned by 1,400 effective men; and Battery Gregg by between 100 and 200. Fort Wagner is a work of the most formidable kind, its bomb-proof shelter, capable of holding 1,800 men, remaining intact after the most terrible bombardment to which any work was ever subjected. We have captured nineteen pieces of artillery and a large supply of excellent ammunition. The city and harbor of Charleston are now completely covered by my guns." Several additional pieces of artillery were subsequently found, making with the eleven guns taken when the troops first landed an aggregate of thirty-six pieces captured on the island. The *Charleston Mercury* of the 7th, which we have already cited, thus narrates the circumstances attending the evacuation of the island: "To sum up the events through which we have just passed, Battery Wagner has been subjected during the three last days and nights to the most terrific fire that any earthwork has undergone in all the annals of warfare. The immense descending force of the enormous Parrott and mortar shells of the enemy had nearly laid the wood-work of the bomb-proofs entirely bare, and had displaced the sand to so great a degree that the sally-ports are almost entirely blocked up. The parallels of the enemy yesterday afternoon had been pushed up to the very mouth of Battery Wagner, and it was no longer possible to distinguish our fire from that of the enemy. During the entire afternoon the enemy shelled the sand hills in the rear of Battery Wagner, (where our wounded lay), very vigorously. Under these circumstances, and in view of the difficulties of communication with Cummings' Point, the impossibility of longer holding Morris Island became apparent, and it was determined that strenuous efforts should be made at once to release the brave garrison of the island, who seemed to be almost within the enemy's grasp. This desirable result was accomplished with the most commendable promptitude and success. About 6 o'clock, yesterday afternoon, the orders for the evacuation were delivered to Colonel Keitt, commanding our forces on the island. Every thing was at once made ready for the abandonment of Batteries Wagner and Gregg. The dead were buried, and at nightfall the wounded were carefully removed in barges to Fort Johnson. The guns, which for so many weeks had held the foe at bay, were double-shotted, fired and spiked; the heavier pieces were dismounted, and the carriages rendered worthless. The preliminary preparations being thus completed, the work of embarkation was noiselessly begun, and the brave men of the garrison, in 40 barges, were soon gliding from the beach they had held so stoutly and so long. The evacuation was conducted by Colonel Keitt, assisted by Major Bryan, A. A. G.; and the success with which what has always been considered one of the most difficult feats of warfare has been performed, is worthy of the highest praise. Batteries Gregg and Wagner had both been carefully mined, with a view to blowing them up. It was about 1 o'clock this morning when the last three boats, containing Colonel Keitt and a number of his officers, just left the island. The slow match was lighted by Captain Hugenin at Wagner, and by Captain Lesesne at Gregg; but, owing to some defect in the fuses, no explosion took place at either fort. During the evacuation the enemy was not idle. A constant fire of shell was kept up against Wagner, and his howitzer barges were busily plying about this side of Morris Island, to prevent the retreat of our men. But, fortunately, the night was murky, and all our barges, with the exception of one containing about twelve or fifteen men, passed in safety. * * * Thus ends the defense of Morris Island. The issue has been foreseen since the enemy's first success on the 10th of July. The defense of the island had been prolonged far beyond what was deemed possible at first, and the brave garrisons who have held it deserve the admiration of their countrymen. The aggregate of casualties in the struggle for the island have been on our side, about 700—killed, wounded and missing. The enemy's loss is estimated at about six thousand. The successful evacuation, after the glorious defense of forty-eight days is, under all the circumstances, a most gratifying military event."

An attempt, on the night of the 8th, to take possession of Fort Sumter by a boat expedition from the squadron failed of success. Its failure was announced in the following dispatch, on the 9th, from General Beauregard to Adjutant-General Cooper: "Last night thirty of the launches of the enemy attacked Fort Sumter. Preparations had been made for the event. At a concerted signal all the batteries bearing on Sumter, assisted by one gunboat and a ram, were thrown open. The enemy was repulsed, leaving in our hands 113 prisoners, including 13 officers. We also took four boats and three colors."

On the 15th General Gilmore celebrated the conclusion of the long struggle for the possession of Morris Island in the following General Order: "It is with no ordinary feeling of gratification and pride that the Brigadier-General commanding is enabled to congratulate this army upon the signal success which has crowned the enterprise in which it has been engaged. Fort Sumter is destroyed. The scene where our country's flag suffered its first dishonor, you have made the theatre of one of its proudest triumphs. The fort has been in the possession of the enemy for more than two years, has been his pride and boast, has been strengthened by every appliance known to military science, and has defied the assaults of the most powerful and gallant fleet the world ever saw. But it has yielded to your courage and patient labor. Its walls are now crumbled to ruins, its formidable batteries are silenced, and, though a hostile flag still floats over it, the fort is a harmless and helpless wreck. Forts Wagner and Gregg, works rendered memorable by their protracted resistance, and the sacrifices of life they have cost, have also been wrested from the enemy by your persevering courage and skill, and the graves of your fallen comrades rescued from desecration and contumely. You now hold in undisputed possession the whole of Morris Island, and the city and harbor of Charleston lie at the mercy of your artillery from the very spot where the first shot was fired at your country's flag and the rebellion itself was inaugurated. To you, the officers and soldiers of this command, and to the gallant navy which has co-operated with you, are due the thanks of your commander and your country. You were called upon to encounter untold privations and dangers; to undergo unremitting and exhausting labors; to sustain severe and disheartening reverses. How nobly your patriotism and zeal have responded to the call, the results of the campaign will show, and your Commanding General gratefully bears witness."

Though Sumter was not yet occupied, nor the other powerful forts in the harbor reduced, the army and navy, in the possession of Morris Island, held the key of the position. The firing was kept up at intervals upon the city and Sumter, which now barely enjoyed the barren privilege of flying the rebel flag in the face of the Union army. Forts Wagner and Gregg were enlarged and strengthened by General Gilmore, so as more effectually to command Sumter—which was battered anew, from time to time—and the entrance to the harbor. On the night of the 6th of October, the monotony of the blockading service was varied by the descent from the city of a nondescript steamer with a cigar-shaped hull, carrying a formidable torpedo suspended to her bows. She bore down upon the Ironsides, and, bringing the torpedo against the sides of the frigate, an explosion took place, throwing up a great body of water, and jarring the vessel, but inflicting no serious injury. At the close of the year, Secretary Welles, in the annual report of the Navy Department, thus summed up the results of the operations of the season in the Southern Department "Since the fleet, under Admiral Dahlgren, has remained inside the bar, and we have had possession of Morris Island, the commerce of Charleston has ceased. Not a single blockade-runner has succeeded in reaching the city for months, and the traffic which had been to some extent, and with large profits, previously carried on, is extinguished. As a commercial mart, Charleston has no existence; her wealth, with her trade, has departed. In a military or strategic view the place is of little consequence; and whether the rebels are able by great sacrifice and exhaustion to hold out a few weeks, more or less, is of no importance."

CHAPTER XCV.

NATIONAL AFFAIRS TO THE CLOSE OF 1863.

The ample provision made by the Thirty-seventh Congress for the support of the Government and carrying on the war, opportunely strengthened the hand of the Executive. It was at an anxious moment when they adjourned, when the nation was committed to great military enterprises, especially in the two departments of the Mississippi, upon the success of which the probabilities of an early suppression of the rebellion in a great measure depended. The month of July, bringing the victories of General Grant and General Banks, dispelled all uncertainties which may have hung over the Union prospects in this quarter; while the battle of Gettysburg and the defeat of Morgan in Ohio as effectually extinguished the vaunted rebel expectations of a successful invasion of the North. When the smoke of these engagements, closing so brilliantly the summer campaign, was cleared away, Secretary Seward took advantage of the occasion to present to the foreign governments a statement detailing the progress of the national arms. This communication, dated from the Department of State, August 12th, was addressed to the United States Consuls abroad, with the design "to convince those who seek a renewal of commercial prosperity through the restoration of peace in America, that the quickest and shortest way to gain that desirable end is to withdraw support and favor from the insurgents, and to leave the adjustment of our domestic controversies exclusively with the people of the United States." In this document, it was admitted, "that no great progress had been made by our arms in the East," the reason being given that "the opposing forces there have been too equally matched to allow great advantages to accrue to either party, while the necessity of covering the national capital in all contingencies has constantly restrained our Generals, and forbidden such bold and dangerous movements as usually conduct to brilliant military success." The Secretary, looking with more satisfaction to the West, declared, that in the recent campaign, 50,000 square miles had been reclaimed from the insurgents; while, casting his eye over the previous triumphs of the war, he found that "since the breaking out of the insurrection, the Government had extended its former sway over and through a region of 200,000 square miles, an area as large as Austria or France, or the Peninsula of Spain and Portugal." The insurgents, he calculated, had lost in the various military operations of July one-third of their whole forces. To reinstate himself in the field, Jefferson Davis, "the leader of the seditions," had proclaimed a levy of all the able-bodied men within his military lines, from which they expected to gather a force of from 70,000 to 95,000 conscripts. Against this probable reinforcement, the Secretary set off our already superior armies and their expected increase from the draft ordered by President Lincoln for 300,000 more. This was to replace those whose terms of service had expired and to fill up the ranks of the veteran regiments. "The people," added the Secretary, "just so fast as the evidence for the necessity of the measure is received and digested, submit with cheerfulness to the ascertained demands." As an instance of the resources of the country in the supply of war material, he stated that a requisition for 6,200 re-mount horses was filled, and the animals dispatched from Washington in four days. The national six per cent. loan was purchased at par by our own citizens at the average rate of $1,200,000 a day. Gold was selling in our market at 123 to 128, while in the insurrectionary regions it commanded 1200 per cent. premium.

In regard to the interests of slavery, it was added, "Missouri, Kentucky, Delaware, Maryland—all slave States—support the Federal Government: Missouri has already in Convention ordained the gradual abolition of slavery, to take effect at the end of seven years. Four-fifths of Tennessee, two-thirds of Virginia, the coasts and sounds of North Carolina, half of Mississippi and half of Louisiana, with all their large cities, part of Alabama, and the whole sea coast of Georgia and South Carolina, and no inconsiderable part of the coast of Florida, are held by the United States. The insurgents, with the slaves whom they yet hold, in defiance of the President's proclamation, are now crowded into the central and southern portions of Virginia, North Carolina, South Carolina, Georgia and Alabama, while the pioneer slaveholding insurgents beyond the Mississippi are cut off from the main force. On the other hand, it is less than six months since the laws or customs of the United States would allow a man of African descent to bear arms in defence of his country. There are now in the field 22,000 regularly enlisted, armed and equipped soldiers of that class, while fifty regiments of 2,000 each are in progress of organization, and 62,800 persons of the same class are employed as teamsters, laborers and camp-followers. These facts show that as the insurrection continues, the unfortunate servile population, which was at the beginning an element of its strength, is being transferred to the support of the Union."

The ordinance of emancipation in Missouri alluded to by Secretary Seward, passed by the State Convention on the 1st of July, by a vote of fifty-one yeas against thirty nays, declared, "that slavery, or involuntary servitude, except in punishment of crime, shall cease to exist in Missouri on the 4th of July, 1870, and all slaves within the State on that day are hereby declared to be free. Provided, however, that all persons emancipated by this ordinance shall remain under the control of and be subject to their late owners, or their legal representatives, as servants during the following period, to wit: Those over forty years of age, for and during their lives; those under twelve till they arrive at the age of twenty-three, and those of all other ages till the 4th of July, 1876. The persons, or their legal representatives, who up to the moment of emancipation were owners of slaves hereby freed, shall, during the period for which the service of such freedmen are reserved to them, have the same authority and control over the said freedmen for the purpose of receiving the possessions and services of the same that are now held by the master in respect of his slaves; Provided, however, that after the said 4th of July, 1870, no persons so held to service shall be sold to non-residents or removed from the State by authority of his late owner, or his legal representative. All slaves hereafter brought into the State, and not now belonging to citizens of the State, shall thereupon be free."

While such was the progress of emancipation in a border State, destined in it's history to test this question at the most important eras, the condition of the slave was being determined by the course of the war and its practical enforcement of President Lincoln's proclamation. As the latter had apparently produced no immediate results, its operative force became frequently a subject of discussion, and doubts were expressed in some quarters as to its probable enforcement. The employment of colored troops under the act of Congress, however, led to results which required an authoritative re-assertion of the new rights of the negro. The Solicitor of the War Department, William Whiting, at the end of July, addressed a letter to a convention of colored citizens at Poughkeepsie, N. Y., in which he asserted, "The policy of the Government is *fixed* and immovable. Congress has passed the irrevocable acts of emancipation. The Supreme Court of the United States have unanimously decided that since July 13th, 1861, we have been engaged in a territorial civil war, and have full belligerent rights against the inhabitants of the rebellious districts. The President has issued proclamations under his hand and seal. Abraham Lincoln takes no backward step. A man once made free by law cannot be again made a slave. The Government has no power, if it had the will, to do it. Omnipotence alone can re-enslave a freeman. Fear not the Administration will ever take the back track. The President wishes the aid of all Americans, of whatever descent or color, to defend the country. He wishes every citizen to share the perils of the contest, and to reap the fruits of victory."

Much was said at this time of the denial of the rights of war to the colored soldiers taken prisoners in the late unsuccessful assault on Fort Wagner and of other instances of a similar character. It was in reference, doubtless, to these causes of complaint that President Lincoln, on the 30th of July, issued the following war bulletin: "It is the duty of every government to give protection to its citizens, of whatever class, color or condition, and especially to those who are duly organized as soldiers in the public service. The law of nations and the usages and customs of war, as carried on by civilized Powers, permit no distinction as to color in the treatment of prisoners of war as public enemies. To sell or enslave any captured person on account of his color, and for no offence against the laws of war, is a relapse into barbarism, and a crime against the civilization of the age. The Government of the United States will give the same protection to all its soldiers, and if the enemy shall sell or enslave any one because of his color, the offence shall be punished by retaliation upon the enemy's prisoners in our possession. It is therefore ordered that for every soldier of the United States killed in violation of the laws of war, a rebel soldier shall be executed, and for every one enslaved by the enemy or sold into slavery, a rebel soldier shall be placed at hard labor on the public works, and continued at such labor until the other shall be released, and receive the treatment due to a prisoner of war."

The policy of the President was emphatically declared in a letter, dated August 16th, addressed to the Hon. James C. Conklin, in answer to an invitation to attend a mass meeting of unconditional Union men, to be held at Springfield, Illinois. In this he frankly discussed certain grounds of complaint urged by "peace men" or "copperheads," as they were more frequently called, against the war policy of the administration, reducing the question as was his wont in these arguments at once to its lowest terms. "There are those," said he, "who are dissatisfied with me. To such I would say: You desire peace, and you blame me that we do not have it. But how can we attain it? There are but three conceivable ways. First, to suppress the rebellion by force of arms. This I am trying to do. Are you for it? If you are, so we are agreed. If you are not for it, a second way is to give up the Union. I am against this. If you are, you should say so plainly. If you are not for force, nor yet for dissolution, there only remains some imaginary compromise. I do not believe that any compromise embracing the maintenance of the Union is now possible. All that I learn leads to a directly opposite belief. The strength of the rebellion is its military, its army. That army dominates all the country and all the people within its range. Any offer of terms made by any man or men within that range in opposition to that army, is simply nothing for the present; because such man or men have no power whatever to enforce their side of a compromise, if one were made with them. To illustrate: Suppose refugees from the South and peace men of the North get together in convention and frame and proclaim a compromise embracing a restoration of the Union. In what way can that compromise be used to keep General Lee's army out of Pennsylvania? General Meade's army can keep Lee's army out of Pennsylvania; and I think can ultimately drive it out of existence. But no paper compromise to which the controllers of General Lee's army are not agreed, can at all affect that army. In an effort at such compromise we would waste time, which the enemy would improve to our disadvantage; and that would be all. A compromise, to be effective, must be made either with those who control the rebel army, or with the people first liberated from the domination of that army by the success of our army. Now, allow me to assure you that no word or intimation from the rebel army, or from any of the men controlling it, in relation to any peace compromise, has ever come to my knowledge or belief. All charges and intimations to the contrary are deceptive and groundless. And I promise you that if any such proposition shall hereafter come, it shall not be rejected and kept secret from you. I freely acknowledge myself to be the servant of the people, according to the bond of service, the United States Constitution; and that, as such, I am responsible to them."

Having thus disposed of the uncertain suggestions of compromise, supported by vague rumors, resting on no reliable foundation of overtures from the South. the President proceeded to the real motive of complaint—the proclamation. "But to be plain," he said, "you are dissatisfied with me about the negro. Quite likely there is a difference of opinion between you and myself upon that subject. I certainly wish that all men could be free, while you, I suppose, do not. Yet, I have neither adopted nor proposed any measure which is not consistent with even your view, provided that you are for the Union. I suggested compensated emancipation, to which you replied that you wished not to be taxed to buy negroes. But I had not asked you to be taxed to buy negroes, except in such way as to save you from greater taxation to save the Union exclusively by other means. You dislike the Emancipation Proclamation, and perhaps would have it retracted. You say it is unconstitutional. I think differently. I think that the Constitution invests its Commander-in-Chief with the law of war in time of war. The most that can be said, if so much, is that slaves are property. Is there, has there ever been, any question that by the law of war, property, both of enemies and friends, may be taken when needed? And is it not needed whenever taking it helps us or hurts the enemy? Armies, the world over, destroy enemy's property when they cannot use it; and even destroy their own, to keep it from the enemy. Civilized belligerents do all in their power to help themselves or hurt the enemy, except a few things regarded as barbarous or cruel. Among the exceptions are the massacre of vanquished foes and non-combatants, male and female. But the proclamation, as law, is valid or is not valid. If it is not valid, it needs no retraction. If it is valid, it cannot be retracted, any more than the dead can be brought to life. Some of you profess to think that its retraction would operate favorably for the Union. Why better after the retraction than before the issue? There was more than a year and a half of trial to suppress the rebellion before the proclamation was issued, the last one hundred days of which passed under an explicit notice that it was coming unless averted by those in revolt returning to their allegiance. The war has certainly progressed as favorably for us since the issue of the proclamation as before.

"I know, as fully as one can know the opinions of others, that some of the commanders of our armies in the field who have given us our most important victories, believe the emancipation policy and the aid of colored troops constitute the heaviest blows yet dealt to the rebellion? and that at least one of those important successes could not have been achieved when it was, but for the aid of black soldiers. Among the commanders holding these views are some who have never had any affinity with what is called Abolitionists, or with 'Republican party politics,' but who hold them purely as military opinions. I submit their opinions as being entitled to some weight against the objections often urged that emancipation and arming the blacks are unwise as military measures, and were not adopted as such in good faith.

"You say that you will not fight to free negroes. Some of them seem to be willing to fight for you—but no matter. Fight you then, exclusively, to serve the Union. I issued the proclamation on purpose to aid you in saving the Union. Whenever you shall have conquered all resistance to the Union, if I shall urge you to continue fighting, it will be an apt time then for you to declare that you will not fight to free negroes. I thought that in your struggle for the Union, to whatever extent the negroes should cease helping the enemy, to that extent it weakened the enemy in his resistance to you. Do you think differently? I thought that whatever negroes can be got to do as soldiers, leaves just so much less for white soldiers to do in saving the Union. Does it appear otherwise to you? But negroes, like other people, act upon motives. Why should they do any thing for us, if we will do nothing for them? If they stake their lives for us, they must be prompted by the strongest motive, even the promise of their freedom. And the promise being made, must be kept."

These words were explicit enough, and the argument, of a sufficiently practical character, was certainly enforced by the circumstances of the times. The proclamation was a war measure, and the necessities of the war were enforcing it. In conclusion, the President had his word of good cheer on the present prospect of the struggle. "The signs," said he, "look better. The Father of Waters again goes unvexed to the sea. Thanks to the great Northwest for it. Nor yet wholly to them. Three hundred miles up they met New England, Empire, Keystone, and Jersey, hewing their way right and left. The sunny South, too, in more colors than one, also lent a hand. On the spot their part of the history was jotted down in black and white. The job was a great national one, and let none be banned who bore an honorable part in it. And while those who have cleared the great river may well be proud, even that is not all. It is hard to say that any thing has been more bravely and better done than at Antietam, Murfreesboro', Gettysburg, and on many fields of lesser note. Nor must Uncle Sam's web-feet be forgotten. At all the waters' margins they have been present, not only on the deep sea, the broad bay, and the rapid river, but also up the narrow, muddy bayou, and wherever the ground was a little damp, they have been and made their tracks. Thanks to all! For the great Republic —for the principles by which it lives and keeps alive—for man's vast future—thanks to all! Peace does not appear so distant as it did. I hope it will come soon, and come to stay; and so come as to be worth the keeping in all future time. It will then have been proved that, among freemen, there can be no successful appeal from the ballot to the bullet, and that they who take such appeal are sure to lose their case, and pay the cost. And then there will be some black men who can remember that, with silent tongue, and clenched teeth, and steady eye, and well poised bayonet, they have helped mankind on to this great consummation; while I fear there will be some white men unable to forget that, with malignant heart and deceitful speech, they have striven to hinder it. Still, let us not be over sanguine of a speedy final triumph. Let us be quite sober. Let us diligently apply the means, never doubting that a just God, in his own good time, will give us the rightful result."

The national enrollment, provided for by the Conscription Act of the recent Congress, took place generally throughout the loyal States in the month of June. In several instances, perticularly in Indiana and Ohio, the officers were resisted in the discharge of their duty, and it became necessary to suppress the disturbance by mititary force. It was at a season of strong political feeling, when preparations were making for the annual elections; and the novel conditions of the conscription were unscrupulously made the occasion of violent partizan assaults against the Government. The draft, undoubtedly an unpleasant necessity, was turned to account to influence the elections. It was by many considered imperfect in its provisions, and by all, anxiously regarded as a test of the powers of the Government. Strenuous efforts were made in the different States to fill the quotas under the call of the President for 300,000.

They were but partially successful, and early in July, the enrollment having been completed, the machinery of the draft was set in motion. It was commenced simultaneously in several of the Eastern States, a week succeeding the national anniversary, when the loyalty of the country was stimulated by the victory of Gettysburg, and retreat of the invading army of Lee. In the city of New York the draft was commenced on Saturday, July 11th. The number of men required from the city was 20,000, to which fifty per cent. was to be added to cover exemptions. Over 1,200 names were drawn in one of the districts, the proceedings being witnessed by large numbers of the citizens with apparent good humor. When the drawing, however, was resumed, on Monday, 13th, a different spirit was manifested. The interval of Sunday, it was evident, had been taken advantage of to rouse a spirit hostile to the enforcement of the law. The commutation clause, allowing exemption, on the payment of $300, was invidiously represented as a privilege of the rich at the expense of the poor, and much popular feeling was excited on this account by demagogues who misrepresented the motives of the enactment. Political and other prejudices were also excited among the people, particularly an absurd and unjust apprehension of the competition of the emancipated negro race with the Northern laboring classes, while the compulsory operation of the draft upon those who could not readily escape from it was undoubtedly a prominent cause of disaffection. A riot, in fact, had been organized, and a mob was ready to oppose the further progress of the enrollment. A large number of laboring men, abandoning their usual employments, compelled others to leave their work. A crowd was collected, which gathered at one of the conscription offices where the draft was proceeding. Only a few names had been taken from the wheel.

when the building was furiously assailed with various missiles, the mob rushing in, seizing the records, and putting the officers to flight. The papers were destroyed, and fire was set to the building. The firemen, as they arrived, were forbidden to arrest the flames. Kennedy, the Superintendent of the Police, appearing on the ground, was cruelly maltreated, and with difficulty rescued from his assailants. The mob gathering strength, by the addition of laborers forced to abandon their work, proceeded to further acts of violence. A hotel was pillaged and consumed, and an attack was then made on the Colored Orphan Asylum, on the Fifth Avenue, the fury of the mob being equally directed against the negro population and the Republican officers. As the rioters approached in front, the inmates of the Asylum, 230 children, between the ages of four and twelve years, made their escape under charge of the Matron and Superintendent at the rear. The rioters entered, threw the furniture from the windows, to be carried off by their followers outside, and set fire to the building, which was rapidly consumed; the firemen who assembled, as at the draft office in the morning, being forbidden to arrest the flames. The property destroyed on this occasion was valued at over $70,000. The pillage of the furniture showed that the rioters, whatever their original pretensions were, now intended plunder. The spirit of disorder spread, and the city was everywhere threatened with violence aud robbery. In the absence of the militia, who had been generally summoned to repel the invasion of Pennsylvania, the onerous duty of checking the mob was thrown upon the police, assisted by small detachments of the United States troops from the forts in the harbor and the remnant of militia in the city. The Metropolitan Police at this time numbered about 2,000 men, of whom only 800 could be separated from their special duties to make head against the mob. As parties of the rioters appeared at the same time in different quarters of the city, even this force had to be divided, the largest number in one command being 350. They were assisted to some extent by special policemen sworn in from the citizens. Wherever they appeared, the mob, as in their unsuccessful assault on the *Tribune* office on the evening of Monday, felt the effects of their discipline and organization. On Tuesday afternoon—the mob meanwhile continuing their work of destruction, threatening the city with a general conflagration, pursuing the negroes with fiendish animosity, plundering stores and dwellings, assaulting and robbing citizens—the militia and United States forces, the former under General Sandford, the latter under General Harvey Brown, the defender of Fort Pickens, who was put in command by General Wool, then in the city, at the head of the Eastern Department, were effectively organized in concert with the police. The necessity of prompt action was fully felt. Mayor Opdyke on Monday, and Governor Seymour on Tuesday, had issued proclamations declaring that whatever force might be necessary would be employed for the maintenance of law and order. The latter, on his arrival in the city, addressed a mixed assembly from the steps of the City Hall, appealing to them as his "friends," to assist in preserving "peace and order," and refrain from further riotous acts, and promising to ask the Government for a suspension of the draft.*

The military and police now met the mob with decision wherever it attempted to make head, and after several serious encounters, in which fire-arms were freely employed, the riot was effectually suppressed. For four days the city was, to a great extent, at the mercy of the mob. Eighteen persons were killed by the rioters, eleven of whom were ne-

* *N. Y. Times*, July 15th, 1863.

groes. The latter were hunted with the most revolting cruelty, the weak and inoffensive being cowardly selected as objects of attack. Colonel O'Brien, an officer of the city militia, after sparing the rioters by firing over their heads, was caught by them and fiendishly murdered. Several policemen were killed in the discharge of their duty, or died of their wounds. In two days over fifty buildings were burned. The aggregate amount of property destroyed and stolen was estimated at over a million of dollars. The rioters, on their part, suffered severely. Several hundred of them, it is said, were killed or died of wounds received in conflict with the police and military.*

On Friday, the 17th, when the excitement in the city was subsiding, the venerable Catholic Archbishop Hughes, confined to his house by infirmities, which a few months afterwards resulted in his death, addressed from the balcony a large assembly of Catholic citizens, whom he had invited by a circular addressed "To the men of New York who are now called in many of the papers 'rioters.'" In his speech, adroitly enlisting the sympathy of his audience in a vein of good humor, he counseled them to avoid all revolutionary disturbances, and peacefully abide by the protections of the law.

The reaction on the recovery of the city from this scene of violence was, as might be expected, strongly in favor of the authority of the Government. The draft, on the representation of Governor Seymour, for a time suspended on the ground of alleged inequality in its requisition of men, was the following month enforced in the city without further opposition, General Dix having in the mean time succeeded General Wool, who was now placed on the retired list, in the charge of the Eastern Department. The draft, after various delays, was enforced in twelve States, bringing 50,000 soldiers into the service, and by the commutation clause contributing the large sum of over $10,000,000 to be employed as a fund for procuring substitutes.

The negroes of the city who had been so cruelly persecuted, were promptly relieved by the kindness and liberality of the citizens. A general committee was appointed by the merchants, who received and disbursed over $40,000, spontaneously contributed for the relief of the sufferers, to whom every assistance was given in making good their claims against the city for their losses.* A few months after, when negro enlistments under the new policy of the Government became the order of the day, the Union League, a patriotic organization composed of the most eminent citizens, superintended the raising of several colored regiments. On the departure of one of these, on the 5th of March, 1864, Broadway was the scene of a display which, by its contrast, forcibly recalled the events of the riot week of the previous July. In place of the insults and injuries heretofore offered to this oppressed race, they now, ennobled by the spirit of military service, in their prompt willingness, in the face of every hazard, to take part in the defence of their country, were received with kindness and enthusiasm. A flag was presented to them by the ladies of the city, bearing the motto "God and Liberty," and an eloquent address delivered by President Charles King, of Columbia College.

In this, the speaker, after setting before his hearers the kind motives which had influenced the ladies in the presentation of the flag, made this allusion to the circumstance of the July riots and the present position of the colored race before the country: "To these

* "The Draft Riots in New York, 1863. The Metropolitan Police, etc.. By David M. Barnes."

* "Report of the Merchants' Committee for the Relief of Colored People Suffering from the Riots in the City of New York," with the interesting Report of the Secretary, Mr. Vincent Colyer, included in the pamphlet.

considerations, which may be fitly addressed to all soldiers, I desire to add some that belong to you alone. For, my friends (and I use the expression all the more emphatically that the same expression was, in the fatal month of July, employed by a very high functionary, on a very different occasion and to a very different body of men—to each the choice of and responsibility for his own friends), in addressing you by this name, I address soldiers of order, liberty and law—men who come forth at the call of their country, and in vindication of her outraged Constitution—nay, of the very right of national existence. To you, then, in addition to the appeal suitable to every soldier, lies in a higher and holier sense an appeal as emancipators of your own race, while acting as the defenders and champions of another. You are in arms, not for the freedom and law of the white race alone, but for universal law and freedom; for the God-implanted right of life, liberty, and the pursuit of happiness to every being whom He has fashioned in His own image. When you put on this uniform and swear allegiance to the standard of the Union, you stand emancipated, regenerated, and disenthralled; the peer of the proudest soldier in the land; and withered be the hand and palsied be the tongue that shall ever give consent to your being subject to other treatment at the hands of the enemy, than such as is measured out to other soldiers of the Republic. Prejudice, indeed, and the rancorous hate of brutalized minds and the ingrained meanness of factious partizanship may still throw obstacles in your way, but that way is upward and onward, and your march in it cannot be stopped, cannot be much delayed, unless by your own want of faith and want of work. To your own selves be true, to your high mission as the vindicators and asserters of your worth as men, and you cannot then be false to any one, or fail in any high and honorable endeavor. You may fall, as many of your race did fall with the gallant, good, young Shaw at Wagner, and the ignoble foe thought to dishonor that youthful hero's grave by heaping into it the corpses of his colored soldiers. Dishonored! Who would not die such a death to be worthy of such a grave? Who that rightly feels would exchange that lowly resting-place on the barren shore of South Carolina, lulled by the eternal requiem of the solemn sea, for the proudest mausoleum in the loftiest temple built with human hands? No, no, my friends, you cannot be hindered now in your high calling. It is but to look back for a few years—nay, but for a few months in this city—to realize what a forward step has been taken, and to feel quite sure that in such a path there is no step backward. On! on! then, soldiers of the Twentieth United States Colored Troops, with seried ranks, with faith in yourselves and in your cause, with confidence and affection for your officers, and with humble but earnest trust in God, and you will, you must, in contributing to the rescue of your country and its Constitution, work out your own complete redemption. Already the colored troops of the United States count by tens and twenties of thousands, and nowhere have they turned back from the bloodiest conflict, or failed to follow their leader into the very jaws of death."

On the 15th of September, in accordance with the act of the recent Congress, the President suspended the privilege of the writ of *habeas corpus* in certain specified cases immediately growing out of the war. The following are the terms of the proclamation:

"*Whereas*, The Constitution of the United States has ordained that 'The privilege of the writ of *habeas corpus* shall not be suspended, unless, when in cases of rebellion or invasion, the public safety may require it; and, whereas, a rebellion was existing on the 3d day of March, 1863, which rebellion is still existing; and, whereas, by a statute which was approved on that day, it was enacted by the Senate and House of Representatives of the United States, in Congress assembled, that, during the present insurrection, the President of the United States, whenever, in his judgment, the public safety may require, is authorized to suspend the privilege of the writ of *habeas corpus* in any case throughout the United States or any part thereof; and, whereas, in the judgment of the President the public safety does require that the privilege of the said writ shall now be suspended throughout the United States in cases where, by the authority of the President of the United States, military, naval and civil officers of the United States, or any of them, hold persons under their command or in their custody, either as prisoners of war, spies, or aiders or abettors of the enemy, or officers, soldiers or seamen enrolled, drafted or mustered or enlisted in or belonging to the land or naval forces of the United States, or as deserters therefrom, or otherwise amenable to military law, or to the rules and articles of war, or the rules and regulations prescribed for the military or naval services by the authority of the President of the United States, or for resisting a draft, or for any other offence against the military or naval service; now, therefore, I, Abraham Lincoln, President of the United States, do hereby proclaim and make known to all whom it may concern, that the privilege of the writ of *habeas corpus* is suspended throughout the United States, in the several cases before-mentioned, and that this suspension will continue throughout the duration of the said rebellion, or until this proclamation shall, by a subsequent one, to be issued by the President of the United States, be modified and revoked. And I do hereby require all magistrates, attornies, and other civil officers within the United States, and all officers and others in the military and naval services of the United States, to take distinct notice of this suspension and give it full effect, and all citizens of the United States to conduct and govern themselves accordingly, and in conformity with the Constitution of the United States, and the laws of Congress in such cases made and provided."

The proclamation was thus issued for the protection of the army, the enlistments for which were interfered with, in defiance of higher authority by the local courts. The President had, from time to time, interposed his constitutional executive power in particular cases, and he now made the rule general within the prescribed limits. A few months previously, the President had addressed a letter from the Executive Mansion, dated June 12th, in reply to a series of resolutions communicated by the Hon. Erastus Corning and others, presiding officers of a public meeting, held at Albany, New York, at which the administration was called to account for alleged unconstitutional action in making military arrests. In this letter the President defended his course in the arrests, by the provision of the Constitution, admitting the suspension of the writ "when in cases of rebellion or invasion" the public safety might require it. Reviewing the early circumstances of the rebellion, he remarked, "in certain respects it began on very unequal terms between the parties. The insurgents had been preparing for it more than thirty years, while the Government had taken no steps to resist them. The former had carefully considered all the means which could be turned to their account. It undoubtedly was a well-pondered reliance with them, that, in their own unrestricted efforts to destroy Union, Constitution and law altogether, the Government would, in a great degree, be restrained by the same Constitution and law from arresting their progress. Their sympathizers pervaded all departments of the Government, and nearly all communities of the people. From this material, under cover of 'liberty of speech,' 'liberty of the press,' and '*habeas corpus*,' they hoped to keep on foot among us a most efficient corps of spies, informers, suppliers, and aiders and abettors of their course, in a thousand ways. They knew that, in times such as they were inaugurating, by the Constitution itself, the '*habeas corpus*' might be suspended; but they also knew they had friends who would make a question as to who *was* to suspend it; meanwhile their spies and others might remain at large to help on their cause. Or if, as has happened, the Executive should suspend the writ, without ruinous waste of time, instances of arresting innocent persons might occur, as are always likely to occur in such cases; and then a clamor could be raised in regard to this, which might be, at least, of some service to the insurgent cause. It needed no very keen perception to discover this part of the enemy's programme, so soon as by open hostilities their machinery was fairly put in motion. Yet, thoroughly imbued with a reverence for the guarantied rights of individuals, I was slow to adopt the strong measures which by degrees I have been forced to regard as being within the exceptions of the Constitution, and as indispensable to the public safety." Asserting what is indeed sufficiently evident, that the present was "in fact, a clear, flagrant, and gigantic case of rebellion," he urged the circumstances as strictly within the provisions of the Constitution. He remarked the difference between arrest by process of courts and arrests in cases of rebellion; the latter being distinguished by their magnitude, and being "more for the preventive and less for the vindictive than the former. In such cases (he continued) the purposes of men are much more easily understood than in cases of ordinary crime. The man who stands by and says nothing when the peril of his Government is discussed, cannot be misunderstood. If not hindered, he is sure to help the enemy; much more, if he talks ambiguously—talks for his country with 'buts' and 'its' and 'ands.' Of how little value the constitutional provisions I have quoted will be rendered, if arrests shall never be made until defined crimes shall have been committed, may be illustrated by a few notable examples. General John C. Breckinridge, General Robert E. Lee, General Joseph E. Johnston, General John B. Magruder, General William B. Preston, General Simon B. Buckner, and Commodore Franklin Buchanan, now occupying the very highest places in the rebel war service, were all within the power of the Government since the rebellion began, and were nearly as well known to be traitors then as now. Unquestionably if we had seized and held them, the insurgent cause would be much weaker. But no one of them had then committed any crime defined in the law. Every one of them, if arrested, would have been discharged on *habeas corpus* were the writ allowed to operate. In view of these and similar cases, I think the time not unlikely to come when I shall be blamed for having made too few arrests rather than too many."

In reference to the alleged grievance of Mr. Vallandigham's arrest, he set forth his "hostility to the war on the part of the Union," declaring that his arrest was made "because he was laboring, with some effect, to prevent the raising of troops; to encourage desertions from the army; and to leave the rebellion without an adequate military force to suppress it. He was warring upon the military, and this gave the military constitutional jurisdiction to lay hands upon him." There was, in fact, he maintained, a great distinction between the working of the Constitution in this respect, in circumstances like the present, and those of a period of profound peace and public security. "I can no more," he said, "be persuaded that the Government can constitutionally take no strong measures in time of rebellion, because it can be shown that the same could not be lawfully taken in time of peace, than I can be persuaded that a particular drug is not good medicine for a sick man, because it can be shown not to be good food for a well one. Nor am I able to appreciate the danger apprehended by the meeting that the American people will, by means of military arrests during the rebellion, lose the right of public discussion, the liberty of speech and the press, the law of evidence, trial by jury, and *habeas corpus*, throughout the indefinite peaceful future, which I trust lies before them, any more than I am able to believe that a man could contract so strong an appetite for emetics during temporary illness as to persist in feeding upon them during the remainder of his healthy life."

In allusion to the circumstance that the Albany Committee spoke as "Democrats," he remarked, that "in this time of national peril, I would have preferred to meet you upon a level one step higher than any party platform; because, I am sure that, from such more elevated position, we could do better battle for the country we all love than we possibly can from those lower ones, where, from the force of habit, the prejudices of the past, and selfish hopes of the future, we are sure to expend much of our ingenuity and strength in finding fault with, and aiming blows at each other."

The General on whose judgment Mr. Vallandigham was arrested, he reminded them, was a Democrat; while "the Judge who rejected the constitutional view expressed in these resolutions, by refusing to discharge Mr. Vallandigham on *habeas corpus* is a Democrat of better days than these, having received his judicial mantle at the hands of President Jackson."

The name of Jackson, he added, "recalled an instance of pertinent history. After the battle of New Orleans, and while the fact that the treaty of peace had been concluded was well known in the city, but before official knowledge of it had arrived, General Jackson still maintained martial or military law. Now, that it could be said the war was over, the clamor against martial law, which had existed from the first, grew more furious. Among other things, a Mr. Louaillier published a denunciatory newspaper article. General Jackson arrested him. A lawyer by the name of Morel procured the United States Judge Hall to order a writ of *habeas corpus* to relieve Mr. Louaillier. General Jackson arrested both the lawyer and the Judge. A Mr. Hollander ventured to say of some part of the matter that 'it was a dirty trick.' General Jackson arrested him. When the officer undertook to serve the writ of *habeas corpus*, General Jackson took it from him, and sent him away with a copy. Holding the Judge in custody a few days, the General sent him beyond the limits of his encampment, and set him at liberty, with an order to remain till the ratification of peace should be regularly announced, or until the British should have left the Southern coast. A day or two more elapsed, the ratification of the treaty of peace was regularly announced, and the Judge and others were fully liberated. A few days more, and the Judge called General Jackson into Court and fined him a thousand dollars for having arrested him and the others named. The General paid the fine, and there the matter rested for nearly thirty years, when Congress refunded principal and interest. The late Senator Douglas, then in the House of Representatives, took a leading part in the debates, in which the constitutional question was much discussed. I am not prepared to say whom the journals would show to have voted for the measure. It may be remarked: First, that we had the same Constitution then as now; secondly, that we then had a case of invasion, and now we have a case of rebellion; and, thirdly, that the permanent right of the people to public discussion, the liberty of speech and of the Press, the trial by jury, the law of evidence, and the *habeas corpus*, suffered no detriment whatever by the conduct of General Jackson, or its subsequent approval by the American Congress."

"And yet," President Lincoln added, in conclusion, with his characteristic good temper and moderation, "let me say that, in my own discretion, I do not know whether I would have ordered the arrest of Mr. Vallandigham. While I cannot shift the responsibility from myself, I hold that, as a general rule, the commander in the field is the better judge of the necessity in any particular case. Of course, I must practice a general directory and revisory power in the matter. One of the resolutions expresses the opinion of the meeting that arbitrary arrests will have the effect to divide and distract those who should be united in suppressing the rebellion, and I am specifically called on to discharge Mr. Vallandigham. I regard this as, at least, a fair appeal to me on the expediency of exercising a constitutional power which I think exists. In response to such appeal I have to say, it gave me pain when I learned that Mr. Vallandigham had been arrested; that is, I was pained that there should have seemed to be a necessity for arresting him; and that it will afford me great pleasure to discharge him so soon as I can, by any means, believe the public safety will not suffer by it. I further say, that as the war progresses, it appears to me, opinion and action, which were in great confusion at first, take shape and fall into more regular channels, so that the necessity for strong dealing with them gradually decreases. I have every reason to desire that it should cease altogether, and far from the least is my regard for the opinions and wishes of those who, like the meeting at Albany, declare their purpose to sustain the Government in every constitutional and lawful measure to suppress the rebellion. Still, I must continue to do so much as may seem to be required by the public safety."

On the 3d day of October, President Lincoln, in concert with the customary proceeding of the Governors of the several States, issued the following proclamation, appointing a day of National Thanksgiving:

"The year that is drawing towards its close has been filled with the blessings of fruitful fields and healthful skies. To these bounties, which are so constantly enjoyed that we are prone to forget the Source from which they come, others have been added, which are of so extraordinary a nature that they cannot fail to penetrate and soften even the heart which is habitually insensible to the ever-watchful providence of Almighty God. In the midst of a civil war of unequaled magnitude and severity, which has sometimes seemed to invite and provoke the aggressions of foreign States, peace has been preserved with all nations, order has been maintained, the laws have been respected and obeyed, and harmony has prevailed everywhere, except in the theatre of military conflict, while that theatre has been greatly contracted by the advancing armies and navies of the Union. The needful diversion of wealth and strength from the fields of peaceful industry to the national defence have not arrested the plow, the shuttle, or the ship. The axe has enlarged the borders of our settlements, and the mines, as well of iron and coal as of the precious metals, have yielded even more abundantly than heretofore. Population has steadily increased, notwithstanding the waste that has been made in the camp, the siege, and the battle-field; and the country, rejoicing in the consciousness of augmented strength and vigor, is permitted to expect a continuance of years with large increase of freedom. No human counsel hath devised, nor hath any mortal hand worked out these great things. They are the gracious gifts of the Most High God, who, while dealing with us in anger for our sins, hath nevertheless remembered mercy. It has seemed to me fit and proper that they should be solemnly, reverently, and gratefully acknowledged as with one heart and voice by the whole American people. I do, therefore, invite my fellow-citizens in every part of the United States, and also those who are at sea, and those who are sojourning in foreign lands, to set apart and observe the last Thursday of November next as a day of thanksgiving and prayer to our beneficent Father who dwelleth in the heavens. And I recommend to them that, while offering up the ascriptions justly due to Him for such singular deliverances and blessings, they do also with humble penitence for our national perverseness and disobedience commend to their tender care all those who have become widows, orphans, mourners, or sufferers in the lamentable civil strife in which we are unavoidably engaged, and fervently implore the interposition of the Almighty hand to heal the wounds of the nation, and to restore it, as soon as it may be consistent with the Divine purpose, to the full enjoyment of peace, harmony, tranquillity and union."

The language of the proclamation was considered peculiarly appropriate; and there was a general approval of its issue by the President, as well on the ground of the sentiment of nationality which it inspired, proceeding from the head of the Government, as from the religious propriety of its sentiments.

The Rev. Dr. Muhlenberg, an eminent divine of the Episcopal Church in the city of New York, gracefully made this proclamation the basis of an eloquent anthem which was set to music and generally sung in the services on the appointed day of Thanksgiving. With the consent of the President, it was published, with the title,

THE PRESIDENT'S HYMN.

GIVE THANKS, ALL YE PEOPLE.

1. Give thanks, all ye people, give thanks to the Lord,
Alleluiahs of freedom, with joyful accord:
Let the East and the West, North and South roll along,
Sea, mountain and prairie, one thanksgiving song.

Chorus after each verse.

Give thanks, all ye people, give thanks to the Lord,
Alleluiahs of freedom, with joyful accord.

2. For the sunshine and rainfall, enriching again
Our acres in myriads, with treasures of grain;
For the earth still unloading her manifold wealth,
For the skies beaming vigor, the winds breathing health:
Give thanks—

3. For the Nation's wide table, o'erflowingly spread,
Where the many have feasted, and all have been fed,
With no bondage, their God-given rights to enthrall,
But Liberty guarded by Justice for all:
Give thanks—

4. In the realms of the Anvil, the Loom, and the Plow,
Whose the mines and the fields, to Him gratefully bow
His the flocks and the herds, sing ye hill-sides and vales
On His ocean domains chant His name with the gales.
Give thanks—

5. Of commerce and traffic, ye princes, behold
Your riches from Him whose the silver and gold.
Happier children of Labor, true lords of the soil,
Bless the Great Master-Workman, who blesseth your toil.
Give thanks—

6. Brave men of our forces, life-guard of our coasts,
To your Leader be loyal, Jehovah of Hosts:
Glow the Stripes and the Stars aye with victory bright,
Reflecting His glory—He crowneth the Right.
Give thanks—

7. Nor shall ye through our borders, ye stricken of heart,
Only wailing your dead, in the joy have no part:
God's solace be yours, and for you there shall flow
All that honor and sympathy's gifts can bestow.
Give thanks—

8. In the domes of Messiah, ye worshiping throngs,
Solemn litanies mingle with jubilant songs;
The Ruler of Nations beseeching to spare,
And our empire still keep the elect of His care.
Give thanks—

9. Our guilt and transgressions remember no more;
Peace, Lord! righteous Peace, of Thy gift we implore;
And the Banner of Union, restored by Thy hand,
Be the Banner of Freedom o'er All in the Land.
And the Banner of Union, etc.
Give thanks—

A public letter of President Lincoln, dated October the 5th, addressed to the Hon. Charles D. Drake and others, members of a Missouri delegation sent to Washington to urge changes in the military conduct of that department, exhibits the peculiar difficulties which he was called upon to encounter, in questions arising in the border States. The control of the disaffected citizens of Missouri, with the adjustment of the various conflicting interests in the State, had, as we have seen, caused much embarrassment from the beginning of the war. Abolitionists were at war with the supporters of slavery, and "unconditional" Union men advocated a stringent system of carrying on the war, at least distasteful to numbers who, while not prepared to desert the Union, were disposed to regard with forbearace its open assailants. A desperate assault by border ruffians on the defenceless city of Lawrence, in Kansas, on the night of the 20th of August brought this opposition of views in the State to a crisis. The expedition was led by the Guerrilla Chief Quantrell, who, with about 300 of his followers, crossed the Missouri below Leavenworth, and, marching rapidly to Lawrence, took the town by surprise. Nearly all the houses in the place were set fire to and consumed, and a general onslaught made upon the inhabitants, more than a hundred of whom were killed. Among the latter was General Collamer, the Mayor of the city and his son, and a large number of the most prominent citizens. General James H. Lane was in the city at the time, and, escaping the massacre, hastily gathered a small mounted force, with which he pursued Quantrell's men, who immediately left the town after their bloody foray, with the plunder which they had collected. Numbers of them were killed as they were making their way to their homes in scattered parties. Vengeance was denounced upon the whole border region occupied by the guerrillas. In a speech at a public meeting at Leavenworth, on the 27th day of August, General Lane demanded that there should be an extermination of the first tier of counties in Missouri, and if that were not sufficient, of the second and third, that an effectual barrier might be interposed against such incursions in the future. An assembly of armed loyal men was proposed with the evident intention of carrying the suggestion into effect. General Schofield in command of the department, was denounced for his inefficiency in not suppressing Quantrell and his miscreants.

It was with a demand for the removal of General Schofield and the appointment of General Butler in his place; the breaking up of the system of enrolled militia and the substitution for it of national forces in the State, that the Missouri delegation, already alluded to, came to Washington. Their complaints were brought before the public, and examined by the President, who gave them a dispassionate hearing. His reply was characteristic of his moderation and habit of doing justice to all parties. "Among the reasons given," said he, "enough of suffering and wrong to Union men is certainly, and I suppose truly stated. Yet the whole case as presented fails to convince me that General Schofield, or the enrolled militia, is responsible for that suffering and wrong. The whole can be explained on a more charitable, and, as I think, more rational hypothesis. We are in civil war. In such cases there always is a main question; but in this case that question is a perplexing compound—Union and slavery. It thus becomes a question not of two sides merely, but of at least four sides, even among those who are for the Union, saying nothing of those who are against it. Thus: those who are for the Union *with* but not *without* slavery—those for it *without* but not *with*—those for it *with* or *without*, but prefer it *with*, and those for it *with* or *without*, but prefer it *without*. Among these, again, is a subdivision of those who are for *gradual* but not for *immediate*, and those who are for *immediate* but not for *gradual* extinction of slavery. It is easy to conceive that all these shades of opinion, and even more, may be sincerely entertained by honest and truthful men. Yet, all being for the Union, by reason of these differences, each will prefer a different way of sustaining the Union. At once, sincerity is questioned, and motives are assailed. Actual war coming blood grows hot, and blood is spilled. Thought is forced from old channels into confusion. Deception breeds and thrives. Confidence dies, and universal suspicion reigns. Each man feels an impulse to kill his neighbor, lest he be killed by him. Revenge and retaliation follow. And all this, as before said, may be among honest men only. But this is not all. Every foul bird comes abroad, and every dirty reptile rises up. *These add crime to confusion.* Strong measures deemed indispensable, but harsh at best, such men make worse by mal-administration. Murders for old grudges, and murders for pelf, proceed under any cloak that will best cover for the occasion. These causes amply account for what has occurred in Missouri, without ascribing it to the weakness or wickedness of any General. The newspaper files, those chroniclers of current events, will show that the evils now complained of were quite as prevalent under Fremont, Hunter, Halleck and Curtis, as under Schofield. If the former had greater force opposed to them, they also had greater force with which to meet it. When the organized rebel army left the State, the main Union force had to go also, leaving the department commander at home relatively no stronger than before. Without disparaging any, I affirm with confidence that no commander of that department has, in proportion to his means, done better than General Schofield."

A complaint was made against General Schofield that he had protected the Lawrence murderers by not allowing them to be pursued into Missouri. "While," said the President, "no punishment could be too sudden or too severe for these murderers, I am well satisfied that the preventing of the threatened remedial raid into Missouri was the only safe way to avoid an indiscriminate massacre there, including probably more innocent than guilty. Instead of condemning, I therefore approve what I understand General Schofield did in that respect." In the very request to substitute a national force for the enrolled militia, he saw that the latter was rendering an admitted service, and as there were no United States troops to spare, he sagaciously insisted on the continuance of the militia. In the words of the President: "As to the 'enrolled militia,' I shall endeavor to ascertain better than I now *know, what is its exact* value. Let me say now, however, that your proposal to substitute national force for the 'enrolled militia,' implies that in your judgment the latter is doing something which needs to be done; and if so, the proposal to throw that force away, and to supply its place by bringing other forces from the field where they are urgently needed, seems to me very extraordinary; whence shall they come? shall they be withdrawn from Banks, or Grant, or Steele, or Rosecrans? Few things have been so grateful to my anxious feeling, as when in June last, the local force in Missouri aided General Schofield to so promptly send a large general force to the relief of General Grant, then investing Vicksburg, and menaced from without by General Johnston. Was all this wrong? Should the enrolled militia then have been broken up, and General Herron kept from Grant, to police Missouri? So far from finding cause to object, I confess to a sympathy of whatever relieves our general force in Missouri, and allows it to serve elsewhere." To meet certain "existing evils," the President addressed a letter of special instruction to General Schofield, at once protecting the rights of citizens in the State and strengthening the policy of the administration. In conclusion he said to the Committee "I do not feel justified to enter upon the broad field you present in regard to the political differences between radicals and conservatives. From time to time I have done and said what appeared to me proper to do and say. The public knows it well. It obliges nobody to follow me, and I trust it obliges me to follow nobody. The radicals and conservatives each agree with me in some things and disagree in others. I could wish both to agree with me in all things; for then they would agree with each other, and would be too strong for any foe from any quarter. They, however, choose to do otherwise, and I do not question their right. I, too, shall do what seems to be my duty. I hold whoever commands in Missouri or elsewhere responsible to me, and not to either radicals or conservatives. It is my duty to hear all; but at last, I must, within my sphere, judge what to do and what to forbear."

In anticipation of the expiration of the term of service of part of the United States Volunteer forces in the field, to cover the deficiencies of the late draft, and to provide for the spring campaign, President Lincoln, on the 17th of October, issued a proclamation calling out 300,000 volunteers to serve for three years or the war, not, however, exceeding three years. The Governors of the several States were required to raise their respective quotas, and, in case of any deficiency, a draft was ordered to be made in the States or districts, to commence on the 5th day of January, 1864. Active measures were taken to forward recruiting; the volunteers whose term of service was about to expire generally re-enlisted; and when the day appointed for the draft arrived, an amendment of the Conscription Act of the previous session being then under discussion, the drawing was further postponed. The chief point in the debates on the act, was in reference to the propriety or necessity of retaining the Three Hundred Dollar Exemption Clause. It was finally concluded to retain this with the important restriction that the exemption thus purchased should not continue beyond a single year, when the person relieved would again be subject to draft.

An event of importance occurred in November, in the inauguration of the Soldiers' National Cemetery, at Gettysburg, in a portion of the battle-field. The plan of setting apart the ground as a final resting-place for the defenders of their country who fell in the struggle, was formed soon after the battle by Mr. David Wills, of Gettysburg. Governor Curtin, of Pennsylvania, on being appealed to, entered warmly into the project, and in concert with the Governors of the other States represented in the battle, the necessary land was purchased. The ground was laid out in the form of a semi-circle, with divisions proportioned to the number of those who had fallen from the several States, radiating from a centre, where it was proposed to construct a suitable monument. The remains of soldiers of eighteen States who had fallen in the engagement, were already interred. Of these, 158 were numbered from New York, 139 from Massachusetts, 100 from Pennsylvania, 48 from Michigan, and the other States in proportion; more than 500 who were unknown raising the aggregate to a total of 1,188. The preliminary arrangements having been made, the 19th of November was set apart for the consecration. On that day the town was thronged by an immense concourse of citizens from the loyal States, including President Lincoln, Secretary Seward, and other members of the Cabinet, a number of the Foreign Ministers from Washington, and a large representation of the Governors of the loyal States. After an eloquent oration by the Hon. Edward Everett, in which he narrated the incidents of the memorable battle of July, and happily reviewed the great principles of the war, an ode was sung, and President Lincoln, in a few simple words, announced the dedication of the field. "Four score and seven years ago," said he, "our fathers brought forth upon this continent a new nation, conceived in Liberty, and dedicated to the proposition that all men are created equal. Now we are engaged in a great civil war, testing whether that nation or any nation so conceived and so dedicated can long endure. We are met on a great battle-field of that war. We are met to dedicate a portion of it as the final resting-place of those who here gave their lives that that nation might live. It is altogether fitting and proper that we should do this. But in a larger sense we cannot dedicate, we cannot consecrate, we cannot hallow this ground. The brave men living and dead who struggled here have consecrated it far above our power to add or detract. The world will little note nor long remember what we say here, but it can never forget what they did here. It is for us, the living, rather to be dedicated here to the unfinished work that they have thus far so nobly carried on. It is rather for us to be here dedicated to the great task remaining before us, that from these honored dead we take increased devotion to that cause for which they here gave the last full measure of devotion; that we here highly resolve that the dead shall not have died in vain; that the nation shall, under God, have a new birth of freedom; and that governments of the people, by the people and for the people, shall not perish from the earth."

The 38th Congress, which met at Washington, on the 7th of December, exhibited a good working majority in both branches in favor of the Government; the Senate, a body of fifty, numbering 36 Republicans and unconditional Unionists, and the House of Representatives 102 Republicans and unconditional Unionists, against 75 Democrats. The moral effect of the recent autumnal elections in several of the States, where the greatest opposition had been manifested, was calculated to strengthen the Government vote beyond the political census of the members; for while in the previous year the Government had been censured in the election of opposition members in the late elections large majorities had been given to the Governors and other local officers who were unequivocally supporters of the Administration. In Ohio, the opposition, confident in their pretensions, had, as we have seen, put forward the ultra candidate for Governor, Vallandigham, at the time of the election, exiled for his political offences. His defeat was overwhelming, the Union candidate, Mr. Brough, being elected by a majority of 61,920, which was increased by the soldiers' vote to 101,099. In 1862, the Democrats had carried the State by over 5,000. In Pennsylvania the Republican Governor, Curtin, was elected by a majority of over 15,000; the State in 1862, having shown a Democratic majority of over 3,000. New York, which had elected the Democratic Governor, Seymour, in 1862, by a majority of over 10,000; this year gave over 19,000 majority to the Union State officers. In Connecticut, after a resolute struggle, the Union Governor, Buckingham, was elected over Seymour by nearly 3,000. Massachusetts, Minnesota, Missouri and Wisconsin, at the November elections, all exhibited Union majorities; while in New Jersey, the usual Democratic majorities were considerably reduced. The importance of these results to the Government was much enhanced by the fact that the elections had been preceded by a long, severe and unscrupulous partisan scrutiny of the civil and military policy of the Administration. The country had listened to the objections, heard the explanations freely made in the President's Springfield and Albany letters, and watched the practical operation of the Government measures; and accepting the result, recorded their verdict.

Under these circumstances, President Lincoln met the new Congress with cheerfulness and confidence. His Message opened with a simple expression of gratitude for "the year's abundant harvests and especially for the improved condition of our national affairs." Abroad, he found the Government in peace and friendship with foreign powers. The negotiations with Great Britain, which had been carried on during the year with unwearied assiduity on the part of the Secretary of State and Mr. Adams in London, and which had been mainly directed to secure the aid of the foreign government in thwarting the schemes of Confederate ship-building in their harbors, had been successful. In the language of the President: "The efforts of disloyal citizens of the United States to involve us in foreign wars, to aid an inexcusable insurrection have been unavailing. Her Britannic Majesty's Government, as was justly expected, have exercised their authority to prevent the departure of new hostile expeditions from British ports. The Emperor of France has, by a like proceeding, promptly indicated the neutrality which he proclaimed at the beginning of the contest. Questions of great intricacy and importance have arisen out of the blockade, and other belligerent operations between the Government and several of the maritime powers, but they have been discussed, and, as far as was possible, accommodated in a spirit of frankness, justice, and mutual good will. It is especially gratifying that our Prize Courts, by the impartiality of their adjudications, have commanded the respect and confidence of maritime powers."

After the usual summary of the reports of the secretaries of the several departments, and various suggestions for the further effectiveness of the army and navy, the President proceeded with a brief review of his emancipation policy and an enunciation of an amnesty proclamation, with an exposition of its conditions looking to the future restoration of constitutional authority in the rebellious States. We give this portion of the message entire:

"When Congress assembled, a year ago, the war had already lasted nearly twenty months, and there had been many conflicts on both land and sea, with varying results; the rebellion had been pressed back into reduced limits, yet the tone of public feeling and opinion at home and abroad was not satisfactory. With other signs, the popular elections, then just past, indicated uneasiness among ourselves, while, amid much that was cold and menacing, the kindest words coming from Europe were uttered in accents of pity, that we were too blind to surrender a hopeless cause. Our commerce was suffering greatly by a few armed vessels built upon and furnished by foreign shores, and we were threatened with such additions from the same quarters as would sweep our trade from the sea and raise the blockade. We had failed to elicit from European governments any thing hopeful upon this subject. The preliminary Emancipation Proclamation issued in September, was running its assigned period to the beginning of the new year. A month later the final proclamation came, including the announcement that colored men of suitable condition would be received in the war service. The policy of emancipation and of employing black soldiers gave to the future a new aspect, about which hope, and fear, and doubt contended in uncertain conflict. According to our political system, as a matter of civil administration, the Government had no lawful power to effect emancipation in any State, and for a long time it had been hoped that the rebellion could be suppressed without resorting to it as a military measure. It was all the while deemed possible that the necessity for it might come, and that if it should, the crisis of the contest would then be presented. It came, and, as was anticipated was followed by dark and doubtful days. Eleven months having now passed, we are permitted to take another review. The rebel borders are pressed still further back, and by the complete opening of the Mississippi the country dominated by the rebellion is divided into two distinct parts, with no practical communication between them. Tennessee and Arkansas have been substantially cleared of insurgent control, and influential citizens in each, owners of slaves, and advocates of slavery at the beginning of the rebellion, now declare openly for emancipation in their respective States. Of these States not included in the Emancipation Proclamation, Maryland and Missouri, neither of which three years ago would tolerate any restraint upon the extension of slavery into new territories, only disputed now as to the best mode of removing it within their own limits. Of those who were slaves at the beginning of the rebellion, full 100,000 are now in the United States military service, about one-half of which number actually bear arms in the ranks, thus giving the double advantage of taking so much labor from the insurgent cause, and supplying the places which otherwise must be filled with so many white men. So far as tested it is difficult to say they are not as good soldiers as any. No servile insurrection or tendency to violence or cruelty has marked the measures of emancipation or arming the blacks. These measures have been much discussed in foreign countries, and cotemporary with such discussion, the tone of public sentiment there is much improved. At home, the same measures have been fully discussed, supported, criticised, and denounced, and the annual elections following are highly encouraging to those whose official duty it is to bear the country through this great trial. Thus we have the new reckoning. The crisis which threatened to divide the friends of the Union is past.

"Looking now to the present and future, and with a reference to a resumption of the national authority in the States wherein that authority has been suspended, I have thought fit to issue a proclamation, a copy of which is herewith transmitted. On examination of this proclamation it will appear (as is believed), that nothing is attempted beyond what is amply justified by the Constitution. True, the form of an oath is given, but no man is coerced to take it. The man is only promised a pardon in case he voluntarily takes the oath. The Constitution authorizes the Executive to grant or withhold the pardon at his own absolute discretion, and this includes the power to grant on terms, as is fully established by judicial and other authorities. It is also proffered that if in any of the States named, a State government shall be recognized and guarantied by the United States, and that under it the State shall, on the constitutional conditions, be protected against domestic violence.

"The constitutional obligations of the United States to guarantee to every State in the Union a republican form of government, and to protect the State in the cases stated, is explicit and full But why tender the benefits of this provision only to a State government set up in this particular way? This section of the Constitution contemplates a case wherein the element within a State favorable to republican government in the Union may be too feeble for an opposite and hostile element external to, or even within the State, and such are precisely the cases with which we are now dealing. An attempt to guarantee and protect a revised State government, constructed in whole, or in preponderating part, from the very element against whose hostility and violence it is to be protected, is simply absurd. There must be a test by which to separate the opposing elements so as to build only from the sound, and that test is a sufficiently liberal one which excepts as sound whoever will make a sworn recantation of his former movements. But if it be proper to require as a test of admission to the political body an oath of allegiance to the United States, and to the Union under it, why not also to the laws and proclamations in regard to slavery? Those laws and proclamations were put forth for the purpose of aiding in the suppression of the rebellion. To give them the fullest effect there had to be a pledge for their maintainance. In my judgment they have aided and will further aid the cause for which they were intended. To now abandon them would be not only to relinquish a lever of power, but would also be a cruel and astounding breach of faith. I may add, at this point, while I remain in my present position, I shall not attempt to retract or modify the Emancipation Proclamation, nor shall I return to slavery any person who is free by the terms of that proclamation or by any of the acts of Congress.

"For these and other reasons, it is thought best that support of these measures shall be included in the oath, and it is believed that the Executive may lawfully claim it in return for pardon and restoration of forfeited rights, which he has a clear constitutional power to withhold altogether, or grant upon the terms he shall deem wisest for the public interest. It should be observed, also, that this part of the oath is subject to the modifying and abrogating power of legislation and supreme judicial decision. The proposed acquiescence of the National Executive in any reasonable temporary State arrangement for the freed people is made with the view of possibly modifying the confusion and destitution which must at best attend all classes by a total revolution of labor throughout whole States. It is hoped that the already deeply afflicted people in those States may be somewhat more ready to give up the cause of their affliction, if to this extent this vital matter be left to themselves, while no power of the National Executive to prevent an abuse is abridged by the proposition. The suggestion in the proclamation as to maintaining the political framework of the States on what is called reconstruction, is made in the hope that it may do good without danger of harm. It will save labor, and avoid great confusion. But why any proclamation now upon the subject? This subject is beset with the conflicting views that the step might be delayed too long, or to be taken too soon. In some States the elements for resumption seem ready for action, but remain inactive, apparently for want of a rallying point—a plan of action. Why shall A adopt the plan of B, rather than B that of A? And if A and B should agree, how can they know but that the General Government here will reject their plan? By the proclamation a plan is presented which may be accepted by them as a rallying point, and which they are assured in advance will not be rejected here. This may bring them to act sooner than they otherwise would. The objections to a premature presentation of a plan by the National Executive consists in the danger of committees on points which could be more safely left to further developments. Care has been taken to so shape the *denouement* as to avoid embarrassment from this source, saying that on certain terms certain classes will be pardoned, with rights restored. It is not said that other classes and other terms will never be included, saying that reconstruction will be accepted if presented in a specific way. It is not said it will never be accepted in any other way. The movements by State action for emancipation in several of the States not included in the Emancipation Proclamation, are matters of profound gratulation. And while I do not repeat nor detail what I have heretofore so earnestly urged upon this subject, my general views and feelings remain unchanged ; and I trust that Congress will omit no fair opportunity of aiding these important steps to the great consummation. In the midst of other cares, however important, we must not lose sight of the fact that the war power is still our main reliance. To that power alone can we look for a time to give confidence to the people in the contested regions that the insurgent power will not again overrun them. Until that confidence shall be established, little can be done anywhere for what is called reconstruction. Hence our chiefest care must still be directed to the Army and Navy, which have thus far borne their harder part so nobly and well ; and it may be esteemed fortunate that in giving the greatest efficiency to these indispensable arms we do honorably recognize the gallant men, from commander to sentinel, who compose them, and to whom more than to others the world must stand indebted for the home of freedom disenthralled, regenerated, enlarged, and perpetuated."

The following was the proclamation appended to the message :

PROCLAMATION.

Whereas, In and by the Constitution of the United States, it is provided that the President shall have power to grant reprieves and pardons for offences against the United States, except in cases of impeachment ; and

Whereas, A rebellion now exists whereby the loyal State Governments of several States have for a long time been subverted, and many persons have committed and are now guilty of treason against the United States, and

Whereas, With reference to said rebellion and treason, laws have been enacted by Congress declaring forfeiture and confiscation of property and liberation of slaves, all upon terms and conditions therein stated ; and also declaring that the President was thereby authorized at any time thereafter, by proclamation, to extend to persons who may have participated in the existing rebellion in any State, or part thereof, pardon and amnesty, with such exceptions and at such times and on such conditions as he may deem expedient for the public welfare, and

Whereas, The Congressional declaration for limited and conditional pardon accords with the well-established judicial exposition of the pardoning power, and

Whereas, With reference to the said rebellion the President of the United States has issued several proclamations with provisions in regard to the liberation of slaves, and

Whereas, It is now desired by some persons heretofore engaged in the said rebellion to resume their allegiance to the United States, and to re-inaugurate loyal State Governments within and for their respective States ;

Therefore, I, Abraham Lincoln, President of the United States, do proclaim, declare and make known to all persons who have directly, or by implication, participated in the existing rebellion, except as hereinafter excepted, that a full pardon is hereby granted to them and each of them, with restoration of all rights of property, except as to slaves, and in property cases where the rights of third parties shall have intervened, and upon the condition that every such person shall take and subscribe an oath, and thenceforward keep and maintain said oath inviolate, and which oath shall be registered for permanent preservation, and shall be of the tenor and effect following, to wit :

"I,——, do solemnly swear in the presence of Almighty God, that I will henceforth faithfully support, protect, and defend the Constitution of the United States and the Union of the States thereunder, and that I will, in like manner, abide by and faithfully support all acts of Congress passed during the existing rebellion with reference to slaves, so long and so far as not repealed, modified, or held void by Congress or by decision of the Supreme Court, and that I will in like manner abide by and faithfully support all proclamations of the President made during the existing rebellion having reference to slaves, so long and so far as not modified or declared void by decision of the Supreme Court. So help me God."

The persons excepted from the benefits of the foregoing provisions are all who are or shall have been civil or diplomatic officers or agents of the so-called Confederate Government; all who have left judicial stations under the United States to aid the rebellion; all who are or shall have been military or naval officers of said so-called Confederate Government above the rank of Colonel in the army, of Lieutenant in the navy; all who left seats in the United States Congress to aid the rebellion.

All who resigned commissions in the Army or Navy of the United States, and afterward aided the rebellion, and all who have engaged in any way in treating colored persons or white persons in charge of such, otherwise than lawfully as prisoners of war, have been found in the United States service as soldiers, seamen, or in any other capacity.

And I do further proclaim, declare, and make known, that whenever, in any of the States of Arkansas, Texas, Louisiana, Mississippi, Tennessee, Alabama, Georgia, Florida, South Carolina, and North Carolina, a number of persons, not less than one-tenth in number of the votes cast in such States, at the Presidential election of the year of our Lord 1860, each having taken the oath aforesaid, and not having since violated it, and being a qualified voter by the election law of the State existing immediately before the so-called act of secession, and excluding all others, shall re-establish a State Government, which shall be republican, and in no wise contravening said oath, such shall be recognized as the true Government of the State, and the State shall receive thereunder the benefit of the constitutional provision which declares that

"The United States shall guarantee to every State in this Union a republican form of government, and shall protect each of them against invasion, on application of the Legislature, or of the Executive, when the Legislature cannot be convened, against domestic violence."

And I do further proclaim, declare, and make known that any provision which may be adopted by such State Government in relation to the freed people of such State which shall recognize and declare their permanent freedom, provide for their education, and which may yet be consistent, as a temporary arrangement, with their present condition as a laboring, landless, and houseless class, will not be objected to by the National Executive.

And it is engaged as not improper, that, in constructing a loyal State Government in any State, the name of the State, the boundary, the subdivisions, the Constitution and the general code of laws as before the rebellion, be maintained, subject only to the modifications made necessary by the conditions herein before stated, and such others, if any, not contravening said conditions, and which may be deemed expedient by those framing the new State Government.

To avoid misunderstanding, it may be proper to say that this proclamation, so far as it relates to State Governments, has no reference to States wherein loyal State Governments have all the while been maintained. And for the same reason it may be proper to further say, that whether members sent to Congress from any State shall be admitted to seats constitutionally, rests exclusively with the respective Houses, and not to any extent with the Executive.

And still further, that this proclamation is intended to present the people of the States wherein the national authority has been suspended, and loyal State Governments have been subverted, a mode in and by which the national authority and loyal State Governments may be re-establiscd within said States, or in any of them.

And, while the mode presented is the best the Executive can suggest with his present impressions, it must not be understood that no other possible mode would be acceptable.

Given under my hand at the city of Washington, the 8th day of December, A. D. one thousand eight hundred and sixty-three, and of the independence of the United States of America the eighty-eighth. ABRAHAM LINCOLN.

By the President,

WILLIAM H. SEWARD,

Secretary of State.

The reports of the Departments accompanying the President's message, exhibited an extraordinary development of the resources of the country in meeting the exigencies of the war. This was shown in a striking manner in the statistics furnished by Mr. Stanton, the Secretary of War, of the increase of arms and munitions. Over 2,000 siege and sea-coast artillery had been issued since the war begun, being double the number on hand at its commencement. The number of field artillery had increased from 231 to 2,481; infantry firearms from 437,433 to 1,550,576, and other arms and materials in like proportion. For this supply, the country at the beginning of the war, was almost wholly dependent upon foreign nations; now, added the Secretary, "all these things are manufactured at home, and we are independent of foreign countries not only for the manufacture, but also for the materials of which they are composed. The excellency of the arms and munitions of war of American manufacture which have been supplied by the Ordnance Department to the army has been so obvious that our soldiers are no longer willing to use those which have been imported from other countries. The efforts made during the war to extend and improve the manufacture of arms and munitions, have resulted in discoveries of great importance to the country, in peace as well as war. Among the arts thus improved is the manufacture of wrought iron, now rivalling the qualities of iron of Sweden, Norway and England. This country, until the present year, has relied upon those countries for material to make gun-barrels, bridle-bits, car-wheel tires and other articles requiring iron of fine quality. Iron of our own production is now superior to that obtained abroad."

The interruption of the exchange of prisoners had of late excited much interest in the country. The history of the difficulty and the present phase of the question were thus given in the report of Secretary Stanton, based upon the returns of Major-General Hitchcock, Commissioner of Exchanges. "In the operations of the year, prisoners of war to the number of about 13,000 have fallen into the hands of the enemy, and are now held by them. From the commencement of the rebellion until the War Department came into my charge, there was no cartel or formal exchange of prisoners; but at an early period afterward a just and reasonable cartel was made between Major-General Dix and the rebel General Hill, which, until recently, was faithfully acted upon by both parties. Exchanges under that cartel are now stopped, mainly for the following reasons: First, at Vicksburg over 30,000 rebel prisoners fell into our hands, and over 5,000 more at Port Hudson. These prisoners were paroled and suffered to return to their homes until exchanged, pursuant to the terms of the cartel. But the rebel agent, in violation of the cartel, declared the Vicksburg prisoners exchanged, and without being exchanged the Port Hudson prisoners he, without just cause and in violation of the cartel, declared released from their parole. These prisoners were returned to their ranks and a portion of them were found fighting at Chattanooga, and again captured. For this breach of faith, unexampled in civilized warfare, the only apology or excuse was, that an equal number of prisoners had been captured by the enemy; but on calling for specifications in regard to these alleged prisoners, it was found that a considerable number represented as prisoners were not soldiers, but were non-combatants, citizens of towns and villages, farmers, travellers and others in civil life, not captured in battle, but taken at their homes, on their farms, or on the highway by John Morgan and other rebel raiders, who put them under a sham parole. To balance these men against rebel soldiers taken in the field, would be relieving the enemy from the pressure of war and enable him to protract the contest to indefinite duration. Second, when the Government commenced organizing colored troops, the rebel leader, Davis, by solemn and official proclamation, announced that colored troops and their white officers, if captured, would not be recognized as prisoners of war, but would be given up for punishment to the State authorities. These proceedings of the rebel authorites were met by the earnest remonstrance and protest of this Government without effect. The offers by our Commissioner to exchange man for man, and officer for officer, or to receive and provide for our own soldiers under the solemn guarantee that they should not go into the field until duly exchanged, were rejected. In the mean time, well-authenticated statements show that our troops held as prisoners of war were deprived of shelter, clothing and food, and some have perished from exposure and famine. This savage barbarity could only have been practiced in the hope that this Government would be compelled, by sympathy for the suffering endured by our troops, to yield to the proposition of exchanging all the prisoners of war on both sides, paroling the excess not actually exchanged, the effect of which operation would be to enable the rebels to put into the field a new army, 40,000 strong, forcing the paroled prisoners into the ranks without exchange, as was done with those paroled at Vicksburg and Port Hudson, and also to leave in the hands of the rebels the colored soldiers and officers, who are not regarded by them as prisoners of war, and therefore not entitled to the benefit of the proposed exchange. As the matter now stands, we have over 40,000 prisoners of war ready at any moment to be exchanged, man for man, and officer for officer, to the number held by the rebels. This number is about 13,000, and they are now supplied with food and raiment by this Government, and by our benevolent and charitable associations and individuals. Two prisoners, Captains Sawyer and Flynn, held by the rebels, are sentenced to death by way of a pretended retaliation for two prisoners, tried and shot as spies by command of Major-General Burnside. Two rebel officers have been designated, and are held as hostages for them. The rebel prisoners of war in our possession have heretofore been treated with the utmost humanity and tenderness consistent with security. They have had good quarters, full rations, clothing when needed, and the same hospital treatment received by our own soldiers. Indulgence of friendly visits and supplies was formerly permitted, but they have been cut off since the barbarity practiced against our prisoners became known to the Government. If it should become necessary for the protection of our men, strict retaliation will be resorted to; but while the rebel authorities suffer this Government to feed and clothe our troops held as prisoners, we shall be content to continue to their prisoners in our hands the humane treatment they have uniformly enjoyed."

The report of Secretary Welles, of the Navy, exhibited an increase of 161 vessels and 1,175 guns during the year. When the vessels at present under construction shall be completed, the Navy will number 583 vessels, carrying 4,443 guns. Of these vessels 46 were iron-clad steamers for coast service, and 29 for inland service; 203 side-wheel steamers; 193 screw-steamers, and 112 sailing vessels. The number of seamen in service on the 1st of July, including the Mississippi squadron, was about 34,000. The average monthly enlistments during the year was over 1,500. The number of vessels captured by the squadrons and reported by the Department on the 1st of November, was, exclusive of a large number destroyed on the Mississippi and other rivers, 1,045; of which 547 were schooners, 179 steamers, 131 sloops, 30 brigs, 26 barks, 15 ships, 117 yachts and small boats. The value of prizes sent to the courts for adjudication since the blockade was established, was estimated at not less than $15,000,000.

The financial report of Secretary Chase, a remarkably explicit and well-arranged document, exhibited in the statistics of the year a noticeable agreement with his former calculations. The amount of debt had fallen short of the amount anticipated; while the receipts from all sources of income except internal revenue, exceeded the estimates. The debt on the 1st of July, 1863, was $1,098,793,181; its estimated increase it was now calculated would raise it on the 1st of July, 1864, to $1,686,956,641. It was further calculated that the whole debt will have reached on the 30th of June, 1865, the sum of $2,231,935,190. The leading ideas of the Secretary in the management of his Department were clearly stated by him. He had, he said, "kept four objects in view: moderate interest, general distribution, future controllability, and incidental utility." All of these had, in their several ways, been successfully attained. "Toward the accomplishment of the first object," said the Secretary, the nearest approach that seems possible has been made. The earliest negotiations were at the highest rates of interest; for it is a distinguishing characteristic of our financial history in this rebellion that the public credit, which was at the lowest ebb in the months which preceded its breaking out, has steadily improved in the midst of the terrible trials it has brought upon the country. The first loans were negotiated at seven and thirty-hundredths per cent.; the next at seven; the next at six; more recently large sums have been obtained at five and four; and the whole of the debt, which is represented by United States notes and fractional currency, bears, of course, no interest. The interest on the debt which exists in the form of treasury notes and certificates of indebtedness or of deposits, and is called the temporary debt, is paid in United States notes; while the interest on debt which exists in the form of bonds, and is called funded debt, is paid in coin—a discrimination which is intended to bring the payments of coin interest within moderate compass, and at the same time to offer special inducements to investments in bonds, in order to avoid a too rapid increase of circulating notes and consequent depreciation. The average rate of interest on the whole debt, without regard to the varying margin between coin and notes, was, on the 1st day of July, 1862, 4.36 per cent.; on the 1st day of January, 1863, 4.02 per cent.; on the 1st day of July, 1863, 3.77 per cent.; and on the 1st day of October, 1863, 3.95 per cent. It will not escape observation, that the average rate is now increasing, and it is obvious that it must continue to increase with the increase of the proportion of the interest-bearing to the non-interest-bearing debt. And as the amount of the latter, consisting of United States notes and fractional currency, cannot be materially augmented without evil consequences of the most serious character, the rate of interest must increase with the debt, and approach continually the highest average. That must be greater or less, in proportion to the duration and cost of the war." "The general distribution of the debt had been accomplished by the universal diffusion of the United States notes and fractional currency, by the distribution of certificates among great numbers of contract creditors and temporary depositors, and by arrangements to popularize the loans by giving to the people everywhere opportunities to subscribe for bonds." Under this plan, nearly four hundred millions of dollars in five-twenty bonds in denominations of fifty, one hundred, five hundred and one thousand dollars were distributed among all classes of the people. "The history of the world," adds the Secretary, "may be searched in vain for a parallel case of popular financial support to a national government." The "controllability" of the debt had been provided for by limiting the periods and reserving certain times of payment of the bonds issued. "Incidental utility" had been secured by receiving large sums on temporary deposit and maintaining a fund for their reimbursement which had been used for the convenience of the public. The latter had been further provided for in the uniform currency secured by the issue of United States notes, by which the Government was also strengthened in the general distribution of the debt. As a further advantage in this direction, the Secretary urged anew his system of national banking, which we have already set forth, its great feature being "to make use of a portion of the national debt as security for the national currency." In providing for the needs of the Treasury in the future, the Secretary looked to interest-paying loans, thinking it "clearly inexpedient" to increase the present amount of United States notes or currency as tending inevitably to ruinous depreciations.

The evils of a depreciated currency were fully exhibited in the condition of the finances of the Confederate States. They were candidly admitted and set forth in the report of Secretary Memminger, and the annual message of Jefferson Davis to the Confederate Congress, in terms which were generally received as a virtual confession of the essential weakness of the rebellion and the prospect of its early collapse. President Davis reviewed the financial measures adopted for the support of the confederacy from the beginning of the war. Both he and Secretary Memminger admitted that at that time they even were far from anticipating the extent and duration of the conflict. They had relied upon tariff duties as the least onerous and most politic method of raising a revenue. The blockade had rendered this ineffective, and the magnitude of the war had created unprecedented demands. To support the credit of the bonds into which it was expected that the currency would be converted, a war tax had been imposed which had been received with so much disfavor that in only three of the States, South Carolina, Mississippi and Texas, was it actually collected from the people. About two-thirds of the entire taxable property of the Confederate States consisted of lands and slaves, which under a provision of the Constitution could not be reached until a census had been taken. They had thus far been exempt from taxation. An income tax and a tax in kind on the produce of the soil and licenses on business occupations and professions had been devised to supply the requisite resources. They could not however readily be made available. "In this state of affairs, superinduced almost unavoidably by the fortunes of the war in which we are engaged," says Jefferson Davis, in summing up the result, "the issue of treasury notes have been increased until the currency in circulation amounts to more than $600,000,000, or, more than threefold the amount required by the business of the country." As previous attempts to avoid this ruinous increase by offering inducements to voluntary funding had been unsuccessful, President Davis now declared that "the evil had now reached such a magnitude as to permit no other remedy than the compulsory reduction of the currency to the amount required by the business of the country." This, it was proposed, should be effected by substituting for the outstanding notes interest-bearing bonds, which the holders of the currency would be obliged to take in exchange to render their property of any possible value. In the words of Mr. Memminger, "the Government finds itself unable to comply with the letter of its engagement. It endeavors, then, to comply with its spirit. It tenders the creditor payment of its debt before it is due in a security of greater value. It gives him time to accept the payment, and if he should prefer to retain the obligation, it allows the alternative upon the simple condition that he shall forego the privilege of demanding payment till after the war." The consequences of the non-acceptance of this offer were thus described by the Secretary: "The continuance of the notes as a circulating medium to their present extent involves the ruin of public and private credit, and will deprive the Government of the means of defending the lives and property of its citizens. If the currency remains in its present expanded state, no measure of relief can be made effectual. Prices must advance, and the means of the Government to pay these prices must daily lose efficiency. Taxes become fruitless, by reason of the depreciation of the money. The army can neither be paid, clothed, nor fed; arms and munitions of war can no longer be supplied; the officers of the Government cannot be supported, and the country must succumb." The entire debt of the confederacy was stated by the Secretary in round numbers at $1,000,000,000; of which $800,000,000 are treasury notes, with a prospective increase at the end of 1864 to about $2,500,000,000.

In closing the narrative of the year we have to mention various military events in several of the departments in addition to the more important campaigns and battles of which an account has been already given. The army of the Potomac, after General Meade's pursuit of Lee into Virginia, subsequent to the battle of Gettysburg, had settled down in front of the enemy on the line of the Rapidan. This position was held till October when General Lee setting his forces in motion northwardly from Madison Court House commenced a flank movement which seriously threatened to cut the Union army off from its communications with Washington. General Meade carefully watching the enemy, early ascertained their intentions by the cavalry reconnoissances which he sent out; promptly fell back from the Rapidan to the Rappahannock, and thence by a rapid forced march to the line of Bull Run and the old military position at Centreville. The military incidents of the movements of both armies are thus described by a correspondent: "On the night of Monday the 12th, when the retreat was determined on, the position of the army was as follows: the Third Corps at Freeman's Ford; the Second, Fifth and Sixth, near Brandy Station; the First at Kelly's Ford; Burford's cavalry at Brandy Station; Gregg at Fayetteville; Kilpatrick toward Hartwood. From Madison Court House Lee had pushed directly north to Sperryville; and on Monday night, while we were at the position just indicated, the rebels were advancing across the fords of the Hedgeman River. Thus far the rebels had clearly the advantage of us. They had the shorter line, whether to Washington or any point between them and Washington. Accordingly, for the next two days, Tuesday and Wednesday, it became a regular race between the two armies which should first reach the heights of Centreville. The Second Corps marched all Monday night up to Fayetteville to guard the road, and stayed there till the whole army passed. On Tuesday both armies were pushing forward as fast as they could, parallel to each other and separated by but half a dozen miles or less. At Warrenton, General Lee formed the bold design of sending one of his corps (Hill's) by a rapid *detour* to seize the heights of Centreville, while his other (Ewell's) should fall upon our flank and rear. It was on Wednesday morning, when our whole army passed Cedar Run at Auburn, General Warren's corps (Second) bringing up the rear. To this commander was assigned the duty of covering the trains of the army, which were much delayed in the crossing by the pontoons. The occasion was now an extremely critical one. Ewell had begun pressing severely on our rear, and already on Wednesday morning, at Auburn, the rear-guard became engaged with a portion of his force. A double necessity was upon General Meade: first, he must move with extreme celerity to reach Centreville in advance of Hill, who had the start of him, and was on the shortest line; secondly, he must keep back the enemy from his trains in the rear. The army having passing Auburn, pushed rapidly on toward Catlett's. A couple of miles beyond Auburn, Warren received a message from General Meade to hold on to give him time for his trains. The Second Corps, accordingly, for two hours exhausted all the resources of tactics to keep back the enemy, by forming line of battle, skirmishing, shelling the woods, etc., the enemy making vigorous demonstrations all the while. The task was boldly and bravely and effectually performed by General Warren. About noon he reached Catlett's, and began his retreat toward Bristoe. The latter place was made at 2:45 P. M. on Wednesday. Hill's corps had reached Bristoe about simultaneously with Warren—in fact, had just got ahead of him sufficiently to form a line of battle, which he did perpendicular to the railroad.

"The position was the most perilous one in which a column can be placed—marching by the flank and met by the enemy in line of battle. General Warren was equal to the emergency. The troops were brought up at the run—the First Division (Caldwell's) having come up thus for a mile and a half, laden with eight days' rations. The troops, which had been marching on the left of the railroad, were brought quickly over to the right, and General Warren, seeing that the enemy had neglected to occupy the cut and embankment of the railroad, on the instant jumped his men, unseen, into it. More prudence on the part of the rebel commander, or less sagacity on the part of the Union commander, would have proved the destruction of that corps. The rest of the army had all gone ahead. The First Corps (Newton's) had already reached Manassas. The last one but Warren's, namely, the Fifth, (Sykes',) passed beyond Bristoe simultaneously with Warren's coming up, and just as he got engaged with the enemy, he received from Sykes the comforting intelligence that he "was moving off slowly and in good order!" General Warren had formed his troops under cover of the cut and embankment of the railroad, constituting ready-made breastworks. On the left, he placed a defensive crotchet. Down rushed the enemy, charging on this flank, when suddenly the troops under cover rose up, and at close range poured volley after volley of deadly fire into the ad-

Painted by Alonzo Chappel

Geo. G. Meade

Likeness from a recent Photograph from life

Johnson Fry & Co Publishers, New York

vancing and presently retreating rebels. After twenty minutes' fight, the enemy was glad to make off, leaving 1,000 dead and wounded and 500 prisoners in our hands! It was well that night came on as it did, for just as the sun set, Ewell, who had been following in Warren's rear, came up, but had only time to form line of battle when the darkness interrupted further operations, and the rear guard was able to pass on and join the main body of the army. The repulse at Bristoe completely disconcerted Lee's plans, so far as they embraced the view of getting on the communications of General Meade or reaching Centreville before him. Lee had no longer with him that unmatched executive officer, Stonewall Jackson, unequaled at a rapid march. Hill proved slow and feeble, and instead of striking the head of the Union column he struck its rear, and got badly handled in consequence. From this moment, Lee abandoned all purpose of giving battle, and never advanced the main body of his army much beyond Bristoe. Detachments were, however, sent to follow up the Union force and make demonstrations. On Friday at 11 o'clock A. M., the enemy appeared in front of Blackburn's and Mitchell's Fords, and made a vicious attack on our skirmishers, but were promptly driven back. Stuart's cavalry, meanwhile, was sent by a *detour* round northward and westward; but being checked and repulsed in all their efforts, they gave up the attempt. The rebel army was now set to work to destroy the railroad. Thursday, Friday and Saturday seem to have been employed in this manner, and then Lee began this retrograde movement—the rebel army passing through Greenwich on Sunday, and Warrenton on Monday, and thence down across the Rappahannock, their rear covered by the cavalry."*

* W. Swinton, Army Correspondence *New York Times*, Warrenton, Va., October 22d, 1863.

General Halleck reports the Union loss at Bristoe Station 51 killed and 329 wounded. "We captured," says he, "5 cannon, 2 colors and 450 prisoners in the several skirmishes between the 9th and 23d of October, the casualties in our cavalry corps were 74, and 885 missing. The enemy's loss is not known, but must have been heavy, as we captured many prisoners. Troops sent out from Harper's Ferry forced him to immediately retreat. On the 7th of November, Generals Sedgwick and French attacked the enemy at Rappahannock Station and Kelly's Ford, capturing several redoubts, 4 guns, 8 battle-flags, and about 2,000 prisoners. Our loss in killed and wounded was 370. The enemy now retreated to his old position on the Rapidan."

General Lee, in his official report of this October campaign, reported the capture of 2,436 prisoners, including 41 commissioned officers.

On the 26th, General Meade advanced his army across the Rapidan, with the design of effecting, by a rapid movement, a division of the forces of the enemy; but owing to a defect in his combinations the opportunity was lost of engaging them to advantage, and the army was brought back in safety to its former position. There was some heavy skirmishing in the advance, and a number of prisoners were taken from the enemy. The Union losses in this fruitless campaign were stated at 60 killed and 540 wounded and missing.*

During the period of these campaigns of the Army of the Potomac, the forces in Western Virginia had been generally employed on the defensive with occasional encounters with the enemy, which are thus enumerated by General Halleck: "When Lee's army retreated across the Potomac in July last, Brigadier-General Kelly concentrated all his available force on the enemy's flank,

* *Army and Navy Journal*, December 5th, 1863.

near Clear Springs, ready to co-operate in the proposed attack by General Meade. They also rendered valuable services in the pursuit after Lee had effected his passage of the river. On the 24th of July, Colonel Toland attacked the enemy at Wytheville, on the East Tennessee and Virginia Railroad, capturing 2 pieces of artillery, 700 muskets and 125 prisoners. Our loss was 17 killed and 61 wounded. The enemy's killed and wounded were reported to be 75. In August, General Averill attacked a rebel force under General Sam. Jones at Rocky Gap, in Greenbrier County, capturing 1 gun, 150 prisoners and killing and wounding some 200. Our loss in killed, wounded and missing was 130. On the 11th of September, Imboden attacked a small force of our troops at Moorfield, wounding 15 and capturing about 150. On the 5th of November General Averill attacked and defeated the enemy near Lewisburg, capturing 3 pieces of artillery, 100 prisoners and a large number of small arms, wagons and camp equipage. The enemy's loss in killed and wounded is estimated at 300."

An adventurous raid in December, by General Averill, on the communications of Longstreet, on the Tennessee Railroad, is among the most brilliant episodes of the war. Its incidents are thus briefly narrated by its leader in a report to General Halleck, dated from the camp in Pocahontas County, West Virginia, December 21st: "I have the honor to report that I cut the Virginia and Tennessee Railroad at Salem on the 16th inst., and have arrived safely at this point with my command, consisting of the Second, Third and Eighth Virginia Mounted Infantry, Fourteenth Pennsylvania, Dodson's battalion of Cavalry, and Ewing's Battery at Salem. Three depots were destroyed, containing 2,000 barrels of flour, 10,000 bushels of wheat, 100,000 bushels of shelled corn, 50,000 bushels of oats, 2,000 barrels of meat, several cords of leather, 1,000 sacks of salt, 31 boxes clothing, 20 bales of cotton, a large amount of harness, shoes and saddles, equipments, tools, oil, tar, and various other stores, and 100 wagons. The telegraph wire was cut, coiled and burned for half a mile. The water-station, turn-table and three cars were burned, and the track torn up and rails heated and destroyed as much as possible in six hours. Five bridges and several culverts were destroyed, over an extent of fifteen miles. A large quantity of bridge timber and repairing materials were also destroyed. My march was retarded occasionally by the tempest in the mountains and the icy roads. I was obliged to swim my command, and drag my artillery with ropes across Crog's Creek seven times in twenty-four hours. On my return, I found six separate commands under Generals Early, Jones, Fitz Lee, Imboden, Jackson, Echols and McCoustin, arranged in a line extending from Staunton to Newport, upon all the available roads, to prevent my return. I captured a dispatch from General Jones to General Early, giving me the position, and that of Jackson at Clifton Forge, and Cornington was selected to carry. I marched from the front of Jones to that of Jackson at night. His outposts were pressed in at a gallop by the Eighth Virginia Mounted Infantry, and the two bridges across Jackson's River was saved, although faggots had been piled ready to ignite. My column, about four miles long, hastened across, regardless of the enemy, until all but my ambulances, a few wagons and one regiment had passed, when a strong effort was made to retake the first bridge, in which they did not succeed. The ambulance and some sick men were lost, and by the darkness and difficulties, the last regiment was detained upon the opposite side until morning, when it was ascertained that the enemy seemed determined to maintain his position up the cliffs which overlooked the bridges. I caused the bridges, which were long and high, to be destroyed, and the enemy immediately changed his position to the flank and rear of the detachment which was cut off. I sent orders to the remnants to destroy our wagons, and come to me across the river, or over the mountains. They swam the river with the loss of only four men, who were drowned, and joined me. In the meantime forces of the enemy were concentrating upon me at Collaghan's over every available road but one, which was deemed impracticable, but by which I crossed over the top of the Alleghanies with my command, with the exception of four caissons, which were destroyed in order to increase the teams of the pieces. My loss is 6 men drowned 1 officer and 4 men wounded, and 4 officers and 10 men missing. We captured about 200 prisoners, but have retained but 40 officers and 80 men, on account of their inability to walk. We took also about 150 horses. My horses have subsisted entirely upon a very poor country, and the officers and men have suffered cold, hunger and fatigue with remarkable fortitude. My command has marched, climbed, slid and swam 350 miles since the 8th inst."

The Army of the Potomac, in December, lost one of its most efficient officers in the death of General John Buford, commander of the First Cavalry Division. He died at Washington on the 16th of a lingering illness, contracted in the field from exposure and hard service. A native of Kentucky, and graduate of West Point of 1848, he had from that period served with distinction in the regular army. His command of the cavalry in Virginia, under Generals Banks, Pope and McClellan, his services on the Rappahannock, where he was wounded, his gallant conduct in the expeditions of Stoneman and Pleasanton, will be remembered among the most brilliant incidents of the war. For the eminent service rendered by him and his noble division in front of Gettysburg on the 1st of July, by holding the rebel army in check until the First and Eleventh Corps could arrive into position, he was promoted by the President to the rank of Major-General. He received the commission on his death-bed shortly before he expired. "Spared through the perils of a hundred combats," wrote Major-General Pleasanton, in a general order, announcing his death, "a distinguished commander has thus suddenly fallen by the insidious hand of disease while in the prime of life, and with a glorious future before him. His memory remains to be cherished by his comrades-in-arms with all that is honorable, patriotic, devoted."

A few days later, the papers announced the death of General Michael Corcoran, by injuries received by a fall from his horse while in command of his brigade at Fairfax Court House. After his appointment as Brigadier-General, on his release from his Southern imprisonment, he had organized the brigade known as the Irish Legion. "Ordered to the Department of Virginia, he served with credit in the operations on the Blackwater and Peninsula under Major-General Dix. Transferred to the Twenty-second Corps, in June, 1863, he had, since that date, commanded consecutively a brigade and division occupying Fairfax Court House and surrounding country."*

General Banks having been reinforced from General Grant's army, on the termination of the Mississippi campaign and the reduction of Port Hudson, organized an expedition, at the beginning of September, for the occupation of Sabine City, located at the mouth of the river of that name, on the dividing line between Texas and Louisiana. The

* Order issued by Major-General Augur, commanding Department of Virginia.

defences of the place were supposed to consist of two 32-pounders, *en barbette*, and a battery of field-pieces and two bay-boats converted into rams.* Four thousand men, under command of Major-General Franklin, constituted the military force, which left New Orleans in transports on the 4th, accompanied by a squadron of four gunboats—the steamers Clifton, Sachem, Arizona and Granite City—commanded by acting Volunteer Lieutenant Frederick Crocker. The expedition reached the entrance to the harbor on the 7th. A reconnoissance of the fort was made the next morning by Generals Franklin and Weitzel and Lieutenant-Commanding Crocker. The events of the day are thus narrated in the report of Acting-Commander H. Tibbets, of the Arizona, to Commodore Bell, in command of the West Gulf Blockading Squadron: "At 6 A.M. the Clifton stood in the bay, and opened fire on the fort, to which no reply was made. At 9 A.M. the Sachem, Arizona and Granite City, followed by the transports, stood over the bar, and with much difficulty, owing to the shallowness of the water, reached anchorage, two miles from the fort, at 11 A.M., the gunboats covering the transports. At 3½ P.M. the Sachem, followed by the Arizona, advanced up the eastern channel to draw the fire of the forts, while the Clifton advanced up the western channel, followed by the Granite City, to cover the landing of a division of troops under General Weitzel. No reply to the fire of the gunboats was made until we were abreast of the forts, when they opened with eight guns, three of which were rifled, almost at the same moment. The Clifton and Sachem were struck in their boilers, enveloping the vessels in steam. There not being room to pass the Sachem, this vessel was backed down the channel and a boat was sent to the Sachem which returned with Engineer Munroe and Fireman Linn, badly scalded (since dead). The Arizona had now grounded by the storm; the ebb tide caught her bows and swung her across the channel, and she was with much difficulty extricated from this position, owing to the engine becoming heated by the collection of mud in the boilers. The flags of the Clifton and Sachem were run down and white flags were flying at the fore. As all the transports were now moving out of the bay, this vessel remained, covering their movements until she grounded. She remained until midnight, when she was kedged off, as no assistance could be had from any of the tugs of the expedition." The officers and crews of the gunboats, and about ninety sharpshooters, who were on board, were captured. The Union loss, in killed and wounded, was about thirty. The whole expedition now returned to Brashear City, whence, after a long delay, the army moved forward by Franklin and Vermillionville and occupied Opelousas.* At the beginning of November, General Banks conducted an expedition to the Rio Grande, and took possession of Brownsville, which had become an important depôt of rebel trade in connection with Matamoras.

A daring act of piracy was perpetrated at the beginning of December by a party of rebel desperadoes, who had made their way for the purpose to New York from St. Johns, N. B. The scheme had been set on foot by confederate agents. The plan was to enter as passengers and take possession of the steamer Chesapeake while on her way as one of the regular line from New York to Portland, Me. The Chesapeake sailed from New York on the afternoon of Saturday, December 6th, with twenty-four passengers. Eight of the latter, being part of the rebel adventurers, purchased their tickets in the morning, and came on board with the rest with-

* H. H. Bell, commanding West Gulf Blockading Squadron, *pro tem*, to the Hon. Gideon Welles, September 4th, 1863.

* Report of General Halleck, December, 1863.

out suspicion. Their appearance, as subsequently described by Captain Willett, of the Chesapeake, "was that of persons in very moderate circumstances. and they aided the impression by carrying their own trunks, each one of which, it was observed, two could hardly get along with. When the trunks were on board, they were watched with vigilance by a portion of the gang. The result showed that they were filled with firearms and ammunition. After the first batch had secured their tickets and taken on board their luggage, eight more made their appearance and secured tickets. Meantime the Chesapeake had left her dock, and these last had to row into the stream to take her. They had not shown themselves before, and it was arranged that they should delay until all probabilities of suspicion or interference were at an end. When they reached the vessel they neither recognized nor were recognized by their comrades. The steamer soon after started on her trip, and now it was seen where suspicion could justly have been excited. Each of the sixteen devoted themselves singly to a most curious and inquisitive examination of the vessel; they were cautious about it, it is true, but thorough, posting themselves as to her tonnage, speed, machinery, &c. They were especially curious as to the number of the crew and in regard to the chief engineer, and were very conversative with the firemen, of whom they asked innumerable questions relative to the vessel. The first twenty-four hours of the voyage was pretty constantly occupied by them in gleaning all information and in perfecting their plans for the seizure.

"It was on Sunday evening that the deed of piracy and murder was accomplished. For some hours before the sixteen seemed to have subsided in their curiosity, and to have no other feeling than anxiety to reach their destination. After the officers and crew, save those on duty, had retired, and all was quiet, and every body unsuspecting, the night dark, and the time propitious, the pirates avowed their true character. They had so disposed their numbers that there was no hope of overpowering them. They were posted, armed at the doors of each state-room of the officers and rooms of the crew. They all had six-barreled revolvers. The watchman on the upper deck had been previously silenced by a blow on the head, and secured so that he could give no alarm. The pirates now declared the Chesapeake their own, and threatened to shoot any one who dared question their authority. The steamer was at this time off Cape Cod. They had acted simultaneously, and had most of the men on board, not of their own party, at the mercy of their revolvers. They had manacles ready for those whom they overpowered, which they used whenever there was occasion. Opposition to them appeared entirely futile, and but little was attempted. The pirates exhibited their pride in their triumph by profane allusions to the Yankees, and by insulting remarks to persons on board the vessel. They expressed their decided concurrence in the idea of killing all the Northern men on board, and at a word of command from their leader, appeared ready to enter upon the work. Of a sudden the vessel stopped its movement, and immediately inquiry was made by the pirates as to the reason. It was found that the second engineer had refused to run the steamer. He was met coming from his post by one of the rebels, and accosted fiercely as to his refusal to do his work as before. He refused to have any thing to do with the working of the vessel while the pirates had command. Thereupon he was attacked, and was pursued to the deck by several men, who fired at him with pistols repeatedly. He was entirely defenceless, and finally, being wounded in a number of places, he received a fatal shot, and fell dead to the deck, amid the shouts of his pursuers. He was shortly afterward flung overboard. Captain Willett next appeared upon deck, and on being surrounded by the pirates and interrogated as to his willingness to help them work the steamer, or to surrender the vessel to them quietly, he refused to do so. They then fired several shots, all of which, however, providentially failed to hit him. Over half a dozen shots were aimed at him, after which they finally locked him in the wheel-house. He was entirely unarmed, and the assault upon him, as upon the second engineer, in even greater degree, was cowardly, brutal and dastardly, and done apparently from mere wanton love of cruelty. A number of the crew were also attacked, but all escaped without much injury. The chief engineer, the assistant engineer, and three firemen, were kept by the rebels to work the vessel. The chief engineer was shot in the chin, and the second mate was shot twice in the leg."*

On Tuesday morning the vessel was brought to anchor at the mouth of the Bay of Fundy, whence, proceeding toward St. Johns, she received on board a rebel privateer captain, and discharged her prisoners, placing them on board an English pilot-boat, by means of which they found their way to Portland. On receipt of the news of the piracy, a fleet of United States vessels was sent from New York and Eastern ports in pursuit of the Chesapeake, which it was supposed might be furnished with supplies and attempt to reach the confederate port of Wilmington. Some days were spent in the chase, the Chesapeake dodging her pursuers in the waters of Nova Scotia. At one of her stopping-places, a portion of her stolen cargo was sold to the inhabitants at trifling prices. She was finally taken into Sambro Harbor, near Halifax, where, on the 17th, she was captured by the United States gunboat Ella and Annie, which had been recently taken as a prize in attempting to run the blockade. The crew offered no resistance, mostly leaving the vessel and flying to the woods on the shore. The capture having been made in British waters, the vessel was promptly carried into Halifax and transferred to the British authorities for adjudication. An attempt was made by the Government officers to take the pirates on board in custody, but they were rescued by the crowd of Southern agents and partizans, and escaped arrest. When the case came before the courts, the Chesapeake was promptly awarded to her owners, while steps were taken to follow up the pirates. The Government at Washington, on the instant, apologized to Great Britain for the invasion of her rights in the capture of the vessel in her waters, and thus relieved the affair from international difficulties.

* Statement of Captain Willett, *New York Times*, December 14th, 1863.

CHAPTER XCVI.

MILITARY EVENTS JANUARY AND FEBRUARY, 1864.

THE paucity of military events during these months, while great armies where mustering for the field, was indicative of the narrower limits within which the contest for National supremacy was now withdrawn. With the exception of the old area in Eastern Viginia so often fought over, the battle-grounds of the previous campaigns, were now, for the most part, quietly incorporated in the Union lines. In Tennessee, Arkansas, on the line of the Mississippi and in Louisiana, the work of reconstruction was proceeding under more or less favorable circumstances, with the expectation of speedily including all these regions among the loyal States of the Union. Much, undoubtedly, had yet to be achieved to the west of the Mississippi before the whole territory could be fully restored to its allegiance, and constant vigilance had to be maintained at the various posts on the frontier and on the Mississippi, to protect the border States of the West from invasion, and hold the army communications; but these services belonged to the ordinary routine of garrison duty, and though frequently involving fights with guerrillas, which, at the beginning of the struggle, would have been regarded as battles of moment, at this advanced stage of the conflict, excited little interest with the public. Expectation, both at the North and South, was mainly centred on the great opposing armies of Meade and Lee before Richmond, and of Grant and Johnston in the vicinity of Chattanooga. In these quarters, it was evident, the great campaigns of the spring would be undertaken, and for their accomplishment the resources of both parties would be taxed to the uttermost. Fully conscious of this, both sides were engaged during the winter months in accumulating stores, recruiting the wasted ranks of the old armies, and adding to the numbers in the field. In addition to the 300,000 men called for in the previous October, President Lincoln, on the 1st of February, issued an order for 200,000 more, appointing the 10th day of March for a draft of such portion of the half million as should not then be furnished by the States according to their several quotas. Strenuous efforts by bounties and by means of furloughs to the old regiments in the field, whose terms of service were about to expire, were made and resulted in largely supplying the men called for, so that the draft ordered for March was dispensed with. In fact, so successful had the movements for recruiting proved, that on the 14th of March President Lincoln, in addition to the two calls for 500,000, "in order to supply the force required to be drafted for the Navy, and to provide an adequate reserve force for all contingencies," ordered a further enlistment of 200,000 men, appointing the 15th of April as the period when any deficiencies should be made good by a draft. By an act of Congress, passed in February, amendatory of the Enrollment Act of the previous year, the measure was strengthened by various provisions, checking frauds and evasions, and otherwise rendering the enactment more efficient. The $300 exemption was, after much discussion retained, but with some important limitations. The payment relieved the person from the draft only on that call, while his name was to be retained on the roll, subject to draft in filling that and future quotas; while in no case was the exemption purchased to extend beyond one year. Clergymen were still liable to draft; but a provision was made by which members of religious denominations who should, on being drafted, declare themselves conscientiously opposed to the bearing of arms, and be prohibited from doing so by the rules and articles of faith and practice of said religious denominations, were to be considered non-combatants and assigned to duty in the hospitals, the care of freedmen, or be relieved on payment of $300.

A new and more stringent conscription act was passed in February by the confederate congress in session at Richmond. It was provided by this, that all white men, residents of the confederate States, between the ages of 17 and 50, shall be in the military service for the war. All in the service between 18 and 45 were to be retained during the war. Those between 17 and 18, and between 45 and 50, were to form a reserve for State defence and detail duty. The following exemptions were allowed: "Ministers, superintendents of deaf, dumb and blind, or insane asylums; one editor to each newspaper, and such employees as he may swear to be indispensable; the confederate and State public printers, and the journeymen printers necessary to perform the public printing; one apothecary to each drug-store, who was and has been continuously doing business as such since October 10,1862; physicians over thirty years of age of seven years' practice, not including dentists; presidents and teachers of colleges, academies and schools, who have not less than thirty pupils; superintendents of public hospitals established by law, and such physicians and nurses as may be indispensable for their efficient management; one agriculturist on such farm where there is no white male adult not liable to duty employing fifteen able-bodied slaves, between sixteen and fifty years of age, upon the following conditions: The party exempted shall give bonds to deliver to the government in the next twelve months, 100 pounds of bacon, or its equivalent in salt pork, at government selection, and 100 pounds of beef for each such able-bodied slave employed on said farm, at commissioners' rates. In certain cases this may be commuted in grain or other provisions. The person shall further bind himself to sell all surplus provisions now on hand, or which he may raise, to the government, or the families of soldiers, at commissioners' rates.

An act imposing additional taxes was also passed, and another, in accordance with the recommendation of Secretary Memminger and President Davis, providing for the funding of the outstanding treasury notes or popular currency in confederate bonds. This conversion was, in a measure, rendered compulsory by the refusal to receive the currency after an early day in payment of public dues, and by the imposition of a tax on the notes not funded. By another act, the privilege of the writ of *habeas corpus* was suspended in the following cases: Of treason, or treasonable efforts or combinations, to subvert the government of the confederate States; of conspiracies to overthrow the government, or conspiracies to resist the lawful authority of the confederate States; of combining to assist the enemy, or of communicating intelligence to the enemy, or giving him aid and comfort; of conspiracies, preparations and attempts to incite servile insurrection; of desertions or encouraging desertions; of harboring deserters, and of attempts to avoid military service; Provided, that in cases of palpable wrong and oppression by any subordinate officer, upon any party who does not legally owe military service, his superior officer shall grant prompt relief to the oppressed party, and the subordinate shall be dismissed from office; of spies and other emissaries of the enemy; of holding correspondence or intercourse with the enemy, without necessity, and without the permission of the confederate States; of unlawful trading with the enemy and other offences against the laws of the confederate States, enacted to promote their success in the war; of conspiracies, or attempts to liberate prisoners of war held by the confederate States; of conspiracies, or attempts or preparations to aid the enemy; of persons aiding or inciting others to abandon the confederate cause, or to resist the confederate States, or to adhere to the enemy; of unlawfully burning, destroying or injuring, or attempting to burn, destroy or injure any bridge or railroad, or telegraph line of communication, or other property with the intent of aiding the enemy; of treasonable designs to impair the military power of the government by destroying or attempting to destroy the vessels or arms, or munitions of war, or arsenals, founderies, workshops, or other property of the confederate States."

The rebel congress at its close issued an address to the people of the confederate States, reviewing, from a Southern point of view, the conditions and circumstances of the war, with the object of exciting renewed opposition and stimulating effort for the future. The people were urged to sell "the supplies and resources of the country to the government to support and equip its armies," and the hope was held out to them of securing "peace and freedom." In a proclamation to the soldiers in the field, President Davis assumed a more confident tone. "Soldiers," said he, "by your will—for you and the people are but one—I have been placed in a position which debars me from sharing your dangers, your sufferings, and your privations in the field. With pride and affection my heart has accompanied you in every march; with solicitude it has sought to minister to your every want; with exultation it has marked your every heroic achievement; yet never in the toilsome march, nor in the weary watch, nor in the desperate assault, have you rendered a service so decisive in results as in the last display of the highest quality of devotion and self-sacrifice which can adorn the character of the warrior-patriot. Already the pulse of the whole people beats in unison with yours; already they compare your spontaneous and unanimous offer of your lives for the defence of your country with the halting and reluctant service of the mercenaries who are purchased by the enemy at the price of higher bounties than have hitherto been known in war. Animated by this contrast, they exhibit cheerful confidence and more resolute bearing. Even the murmurs of the weak and timid, who shrink from the trials which make stronger and firmer your noble natures, are shamed into silence by the spectacle which you present. Your brave battle-cry will ring loud and clear through the land of the enemy as well as our own; will silence the vainglorious boastings of their corrupt partizans and their pensioned press, and will do justice to the calumny by which they seek to persuade a deluded people that you are ready to purchase dishonorable safety by degrading submission. Soldiers, the coming spring campaign will open under auspices well calculated to sustain your hopes. Your resolution needed nothing to fortify it. With ranks replenished under the influence of your example, and by the aid of representatives who give earnest of their purpose to add by legislation largely to your strength, you may welcome the invader with a confidence justified by the memory of past victories. On the other hand, debt, taxation, repetition of heavy drafts, dissensions occasioned by the strife for power, by the pursuit of the spoils of office, by the thirst for the plunder of the public treasury, and, above all, the consciousness of a bad cause, must tell with fearful force upon the overstrained energies of the enemy. His campaign of 1864 must, from the exhaustion of his resources of men and money, be far less formidable than those of the last two years, when unimpaired means were used with boundless prodigality, and with results which are suggested by the mention of the names of Shiloh, Perryville, Murfreesboro' and the Chickahominy, Manassas, Fredericksburg and Chancellorsville. Soldiers, assured success awaits us in our holy struggle for liberty and independence, and for the preservation of all that renders life desirable to honorable men. When that success shall be reached, to you, your country's hope and pride, under Divine Providence, will it be due. The fruits of that success will not be reaped by you alone, but your children and your children's children, in long generations to come, will enjoy the blessings derived from you that will preserve your memory ever living in their hearts. Citizen defenders of the homes, the liberties and altars of the confederacy—that the God whom we all humbly worship may shield you with His fatherly care, and preserve you for safe return to the peaceful enjoyment of your friends and the associations of those you most love, is the earnest prayer of your commander-in-chief."

Whilst these preparations were being made for the spring campaign, several military movements were set on foot, with the design of clearing the enemy or checking their movements on the southern and south-western border of the Union lines. Prominent among these was an expedition in force or gigantic raid into the interior of Mississippi. This was composed of two divisions—one of cavalry, under command of General William S. Smith, popularly estimated at about 10,000 in number, to set out from the vicinity of Memphis; the other, consisting of Generals Hurlbut and McPherson's army corps, 21,000 infantry, 1,200 cavalry, and about 40 pieces of artillery, led by General W. T. Sherman, to start from Vicksburg. Both commands were to leave simultaneously, and to meet at a point east of Vicksburg, on the Mobile and Ohio Railroad. General Sherman left on the appointed day, the 3d of February, with twenty days' rations. On the 5th, the advance came up with a body of the enemy's cavalry, under Wait Adams, in the vicinity of Canton, putting them to flight with slight loss. The next day the command entered Jackson, and the enemy was driven across Pearl River. After that the expedition encountered little or no opposition. General Sherman rapidly advanced through Brandon to Morton, where two divisions of General Polk's corps had made disposition for battle. They, however, retreated before the Union force, which reached Meridian on the Mobile and Ohio Railway, 150 miles from Vicksburg, on the 14th, the enemy continuing their retreat eastward. Here General Sherman remained for a week, waiting the arrival of General Smith's cavalry force, in his own words, making in the mean time "the most complete destruction of the railroad ever beheld, south below Quitman; east to Cuba Station; twenty miles north to Lauderdale Springs, and west all the way back to Jackson." The State arsenal at Meridian was destroyed, with its valuable machines for repairs of arms and ordnance stores, also several military buildings and grist-mills. An abundance of provisions was found for the Union army. General Smith, who did not leave Tennessee till the 11th, in consequence of delay in the arrival of part of his force, advanced southerly on the Mobile Railroad by Okolona to

West Point, where his further progress was arrested by a combined force of the enemy under Forrest, Roddy and others. There was some heavy fighting in this vicinity, the enemy charging both in the rear and the advance, and three field-pieces were lost. Thus closely pressed by superior numbers, General Smith resolved upon a retreat, falling back steadily and in defiance of the enemy, crossing the Tallahatchie in safety by forced marches, reached Memphis on the 25th, having done much injury to the railway, destroyed a large quantity of rebel stores, and brought away a great number of negroes and some 300 prisoners. The President's Amnesty Proclamation was extensively circulated throughout the country. General Sherman unable to follow up his successes by extending his march farther into the enemy's country, in the absence of the cavalry force which he had relied upon, retired slowly from Meridian, bringing his force "in splendid condition" to Canton, north of Jackson. On the 27th he reached Vicksburg. A dispatch from Major-General Butterfield, dated Cairo, March 11th, addressed to General Halleck, records the result of the expedition: "General Sherman arrived yesterday at Memphis. His command is all safe. Our total loss in killed, wounded and missing is 170 only. The general result of his expedition, including Smith's and the Yazoo River movements, are about, as follows: 150 miles of railroad, 67 bridges, 7,000 feet of trestle, 20 locomotives, 28 cars, 10,000 bales of cotton, several steam mills, and over 2,000,000 bushels of corn were destroyed. The railroad destruction is complete and thorough. The captures of prisoners exceed all loss. Upward of 8,000 contrabands and refugees came in with various columns."

When the first report of this formidable expedition reached the North, it was conjectured that the movement was, in some way, connected with an attempt to capture Mobile, a supposition which was strengthened by news of a simultaneous attack by Admiral Farragut upon the defences of the city at Grant's Pass. Fort Powell, at this entrance, was bombarded on the 23d, and for several days after by the Admiral's mortar fleet and gunboats, but little impression appears to have been made upon the work. The rumors of an attack on Mobile caused the concentration at that place of a considerable rebel force and facilitated the destruction by General Sherman of its main line of communication with the confederate armies in the field, the Mobile and Ohio Railway.

Simultaneously with the movement of General Sherman, at the beginning of February, an expedition was set on foot by General Gillmore in his Department of the South for the permanent occupation of Florida, on the west bank of the St. Johns River. His object was to procure an outlet for cotton, lumber and other productions of the country; to cut off the enemy's sources of commissary supplies from this grazing region; to obtain negro recruits for the army, and to initiate measures for the speedy restoration of the State to its position in the Union by the reconstruction of a legal State Government in which his assistance was invoked by President Lincoln. Accordingly, on the 5th of February, a force of about 6,000 cavalry, infantry and artillery was embarked at Hilton Head, under command of Brigadier-General Seymour; the fleet entered St. Johns River on the 7th, and effected a landing without opposition the same day at Jacksonville. The few soldiers in the town fled immediately. There were rebel troops at Camp Finnegan, a few miles in the interior and along the line of the railway. General Seymour was directed to move forward his mounted force to Baldwin, 20 miles distant on the Central Railroad, at the junction of the railway from Fernandina. The advance under Colonel Guy

V. Henry, comprising the Fortieth Massachusetts Infantry, the Independent Battalion of Massachusetts Cavalry, under Major Stevens, and Elder's Horse Battery, First Artillery, pushed forward into the interior on the night of the 8th, passed by the enemy drawn up in line of battle at Camp Finnegan, seven miles from Jacksonville, surprised and captured a battery three miles in the rear of the camp about midnight, and reached Baldwin about sunrise the next morning. "At our approach," continues General Gillmore, who joined the command that day, "the enemy absconded, sunk the steamer St. Mary's, and burned 270 bales of cotton a few miles above Jacksonville. We have taken, without the loss of a man, about 100 prisoners, 8 pieces of artillery in serviceable condition and well supplied with ammunition, and other valuable property, to a large amount." On the 10th, a portion of the force was sent forward to Sanderson, twenty miles further on the railway, where a quantity of commissary stores were found in flames, the rebels having just withdrawn to a further station at Lake City, where General Finnegan had gathered the fragment of his command. Colonel Henry advanced to the vicinity of this place, reconnoitred the enemy's force and pursuant to orders retired. On the 14th, the main body of General Seymour's command was concentrated at Baldwin. The casualties of the expedition at this time were few, five killed and ten wounded, and the spoils taken from the enemy considerable. Having thus secured an important foothold in the region, General Gillmore, on the 16th, returned to Hilton Head, leaving General Seymour in command. The latter, desirous of pushing the advantage which he had gained, determined upon a further movement to destroy the railroad near the Savannah River, 100 miles from Jacksonville. General Gillmore, on hearing of this, sent a messenger to arrest the movement; but, before the latter arrived, General Seymour had entered on his march, and was in fact engaged with the enemy at their chosen position. The action which took place was, considering the numbers engaged, one of the most disastrous to the Union troops of the war. On the 29th of February, the greater portion of General Seymour's command—a force stated at about 4,500 infantry, 400 cavalry and 20 cannon—set out from its encampment at Barber's Station, to which it had been advanced, twelve miles distant from Baldwin, with the intention of moving the next day to Lake City on the line of the railway, about sixty miles from Jacksonville. The army reached Sanderson at noon, and, without halting, advanced toward Olustee, a station on the railway, ten miles beyond, where it was expected the enemy would be found. "But instead," in the report of a correspondent with the army, whose account of the engagement we condense, "of coming in contact with the enemy at Olustee, the meeting took place three miles this side, so our troops were not so well prepared for battle as they would have been if Olustee had been the battle-field. Our column moved forward in regular order, the cavalry in the advance, and the artillery distributed along the line of infantry. The road from Barber's to Lake City lies parallel with the railroad, crossing it at intervals on an average of five miles. It was at one of these crossing-points that the fight was commenced. The head of the column reached this point at 2 P. M. The men had not rested from the time they left Barber's, at 7 A. M. The usual halt of a few minutes every hour was of course observed, but we cannot say the troops fairly rested. Neither had they tasted of a mouthful of food. Thus, after a tedious march of sixteen miles, over a road of loose sand, or boggy turf, or covered knee-deep with muddy water, the troops, weary, exhausted, faint, hungry, and ill-conditioned, were suddenly attacked by a large force of the enemy, who had concealed himself behind a thick wood, waiting with complacent satisfaction the entry of our men into his ambush. Before reaching the battle-ground, Colonel Henry, with his cavalry of the Independent Massachusetts Battalion and the Fortieth Massachusetts Mounted Infantry, came upon a party of five mounted rebels who were stationed behind an old deserted mill, a little to the left of the wood. A few shots were exchanged and then the rebels fled in the direction of their main force. Captain Langdon's battery of regular artillery was with Henry's cavalry. At the mill, Colonel Henry halted until Hawley's brigade of infantry and Hamilton's regular battery had come up. With the view of meeting the enemy's pickets, three miles in advance of the mill, two companies of the Seventh Connecticut Regiment were deployed on the left of the railroad, while three companies were left at the mill, for the purpose of supporting the artillery. A small force of cavalry was sent to skirmish on the right of the railroad. Our skirmishers had not advanced a hundred yards when they discovered those of the enemy directly in their front. The result was a brisk fire on both sides, which ended by the enemy's falling back on a second line of skirmishers. Our men continued to drive the rebels back, sometimes on the right and sometimes on the left of the railroad, but principally on the left. While this was going on, two companies of the Fortieth Massachusetts were ordered to the left, with a view of outflanking the enemy's skirmishers. In endeavoring to carry out that order, the Fortieth Massachusetts came upon a heavy line of skirmishers and were compelled to withdraw to their original position.

"Captain Elder, of the First Artillery, in order to ascertain the enemy's force and position, brought one of his pieces into battery on the right and fired one shot, but it did not draw a reply. The Seventh New Hampshire Regiment, in connection with the Seventh Connecticut, was then sent forward to the right, and if possible to break through the enemy's line. This movement brought on hot firing, and it was evident that an engagement was near at hand. At this time our force on the field consisted of the Seventh New Hampshire, the Seventh Connecticut, the Independent Battalion of Massachusetts Cavalry, the Fortieth Massachusetts Mounted Infantry, the Eighth United States Colored, Elder's battery of four and Hamilton's of six pieces. The remainder of the column was halted on the road. While our men were at work on the right, Colonel Henry, in person, went over to the left to reconnoitre, and much to his astonishment discovered that the enemy's right lapped on our left. This was reported to General Seymour, who immediately gave orders for the advance troops and batteries to come into position. The enemy watched the movements with an eager eye, and the moment Hamilton commenced unlimbering his pieces his battery was subjected to a galling fire of musketry. A number of men and several horses were shot before he could get ready to fire one round. The fact that the enemy had a force far superior in point of numbers to our own was now beyond all dispute. The firing became heavier and more destructive as each moment advanced. The railroad as it nears Olustee takes a bend, and behind this bend the rebels had taken their position. In the woods at the rear were their supporters and reserves. We had not a moment to lose. Our men were within one hundred yards of the enemy, and the only thing that could be done was to fight. To retreat at that time was impossible, for the road was filled with troops coming up, and the woods on either side would not admit of passage on the flank. By dint of effort, Captain

Langdon succeeded in getting his four guns in battery on the extreme left, but not until he had lost five or six men and about the same number of horses. It must be borne in mind our batteries were within one hundred yards of the enemy's front. This short distance rendered it a very easy task for the rebels to pick off a man or horse at every discharge of their rifles. At the commencement of the fight, the Eighth United States Colored Troops were supporting Hamilton's battery, but when their assistance was really indispensable, by some strange order they filed to the right in rear of the battery, for the purpose of joining their right on the left of the Seventh Connecticut. At that particular time the movement was decidedly an error, for by carrying it out it left Hamilton's battery unsupported. In an attempt to enfilade the enemy on his right, Hamilton moved forward four pieces; but before he got into position, the rebels on that portion of their line had concentrated all their fire upon him and the Eighth U. S., who had again come up to his support. In twenty minutes' time, Hamilton lost forty-four men, killed and wounded, and forty horses. The Eighth also suffered severely. At no one juncture of the engagement had the fire of the enemy been more severe than at the time Hamilton attempted his enfilade movement. Hamilton knew very well his pieces were in great danger of being captured, and he also had sense enough to know that by taking them to the rear it would instantly cause a panic among the infantry, and so inevitably lose the day for us. The behavior of Captain Hamilton at this critical period of the battle is worthy of special note, and I sincerely believe that it was owing mainly to his persistent efforts that the portion of our line at his battery was not broken and scattered in confusion. He had not only his pieces to command, but his infantry supports to keep from leaving the field. It was in the midst of this destructive fire of the enemy, and while Captain Hamilton was urging the infantry to maintain their line, and at the same time giving orders to his battery, he was struck in the arm by a musket-ball, and shortly after was again hit in the thigh. To add to the misfortune, all his officers (four in number) were wounded. Colonel Charles W. Fribley, of the Eighth United States, was also mortally wounded on this portion of the field. He did not cease for a moment to encourage and rally his men, and by his gallant behavior proved himself to be an officer of no ordinary merit. Captain Hamilton kept his pieces at work until it was evident it would be sure loss to fire another round, and then gave orders to withdraw them. Horses were attached to only four pieces; the horses to the other two had been shot, consequently two guns fell into possession of the enemy. On the right of Hamilton the Seventh Connecticut and the Seventh New Hampshire were doing fearful execution. The Seventh Connecticut especially were standing their ground with marked valor. Every volley from their guns told splendidly on the rebel line. But between the two forces a wide difference existed—the rebels outnumbered us five to one. This crushing superiority gave the two regiments little chance for victory. After losing one-fourth of their number they were compelled to retire to the rear. At the same moment Colonel Barton's brigade, the Forty-seventh, Forty-eighth and One Hundred and Fifteenth New York regiments took the field, coming up in line *en echelon*. On the right was Elder's battery, and on the left Langdon's and one section of the Third Rhode Island. The enemy had four pieces of artillery. On a railroad car he had mounted a heavy gun, supposed to be a 32-pounder, and with this he kept up a regular fire, but not destructive, as the shells passed over the heads of our men. There can be no doubt concerning the fighting qualities of Barton's brigade. On this occasion they fought like tigers, but the same difficulty which opposed Hawley's brigade, presented itself to them, viz., the mass of the enemy.

"The last regiments to enter the field were the First North Carolina, and Fifty-fourth Massachusetts (colored), of Montgomery's brigade. They took a bold position at the front, and maintained their ground with commendable pertinacity. For three and a-half successive hours did our brave regiments combat the enemy before them. The instances of personal daring that occurred in the meantime are numerous. Never before did the troops in this department have such an opportunity for displaying their valor, and on no previous occasion have they exhibited such a high degree of bravery. If the enemy had presented an equal force with our own, or even if it had been only double, no doubt could have been felt as to the final result of the contest. As it was, the enemy resisted us with a force in point of numbers three times that of our own, which, taken together with the circumstance of the long and tedious march and the ill condition of the men, it would be hardly reasonable to suppose that success would be on our side. The effect of our fire, both of musketry and artillery, was fearful. At every discharge, down went a body of rebels. The gallant Elder on the right and the dashing Langdon on the left, made an impression on the rebel lines that will go far to off-set the misfortune that ultimately overtook us. The fight was by no means a trivial encounter; it was a battle hotly contested, fought at close range, face to face and foot to foot. The commanding officers of the various regiments are entitled to unlimited credit for the heroic manner in which they led their men. At the acme of the battle, Colonel Sammons, of the One Hundred and Fifteenth New York, was struck in the foot, and was in consequence compelled to leave the field. His horse was shot from under him. Colonel Moore of the Forty-seventh New York, was also wounded, a ball striking his hand and passing out at the elbow. Colonel Barton had his coat pierced in several places and his horse shot. Colonel Henry had three horses shot, but he himself escaped in a most miraculous manner. Provost-Marshal-General Hall had a horse shot from under him, and as for himself, no one would believe it possible for him to again pass through what he did on that day, and come out unscathed. Lieutenant Jackson, of General Seymour's staff, had two horses shot. General Seymour was not away from the ground for an instant. At first on the right and then on the left, he seemed to be everywhere at one and at the same moment. His aim was apparently to be in the thickest of the fight, and at the front of his troops. At 5 P. M. the fire slackened on both sides; on ours, in consequence of the ammunition giving out, and on the enemy's, because we did not press him. A demonstration by the rebels to capture Langdon's battery, at about the middle stage of the fight was prevented by Langdon, who poured into their line a quick and deadly fire. But in coming from the field he was obliged to leave to the enemy three of his pieces, not because the enemy charged upon them, but for the reason that he did not have horses to draw them off. At 5½ o'clock the heavy firing had ceased. The cessation was simultaneous on both sides. We held our ground till 7 o'clock, and then the order came from General Seymour to gradually retire. The retreat was conducted leisurely and orderly. There was no confusion, no panic, nothing that indicated hurry. Colonel Henry, with his cavalry, brought up the rear. At 3 o'clock Sunday morning (the 21st) our troops were at Barber's. The enemy followed closely, but did not press. A few of their cavalry only kept well up to the rear of Henry's column. At Barber's, our men rested till 9 A. M., and then again took up the line of retreat, reaching Baldwin at about 3 P. M. They halted here a short time, and then went on toward Jacksonville, arriving at the camping ground, six miles out, Monday afternoon. On the way down many of the poor fellows could hardly drag one foot after the other.* The Union loss in this disastrous engagement was estimated at the time at about 1,200 killed and wounded, the former in the usual proportion of one-fifth, a calculation which fell short of the actual number, which was subsequently stated, including the prisoners, at about 1,800. The dead and severely wounded were left on the field. Five guns were lost, and a quantity of muskets and equipments abandoned on the retreat. The loss of the enemy was heavy, exposed as they were to the fire of a larger number of guns in position. Their ineffective pursuit showed the injury they had sustained. General Finnegan, their commander, in a dispatch from the field, hastily estimated his loss at 250 killed and wounded. "Among them," said he, "I mourn the loss of many brave officers and men." Another dispatch, published in a Richmond paper, made the confederate loss about 800. Reinforcements were speedily sent to General Seymour at Jacksonville, which, with the aid of the gunboats, was readily held against the enemy. On the 9th of March, an expedition from Jacksonville captured the town of Pilatka, sixty miles distant.

About 9 o'clock, on the evening of the 17th of February, the Housatonic, a steam-sloop, carrying thirteen guns, was destroyed while on her station on the blockade off Charleston, S. C., by a torpedo, sent down by the enemy. It was a moonlight night, and the usual guards were on the lookout, but the assailant was so nearly submerged that the first indication of its approach, in a slight disturbance of the water, was pronounced by the quartermaster to be caused by a school of fish. It was then about a hundred yards distant. The crew was called to quarters and the engines put in motion, when the torpedo came in contact with the stern, throwing timbers into the air and causing a rapid settling of the vessel, which filled instantly. Two of the boats were lowered and picked up some of the men who had jumped overboard; others took refuge in the rigging and tops, the vessel sinking in twenty-eight feet of water. Five lives were lost. Not more than one minute is said to have elapsed from the time the torpedo was first seen before the Housatonic was struck, and not over three or four minutes between the explosion and the sinking of the ship.*

On the 5th of February, also, the day in which General Seymour's expedition left Hilton Head, a spirited movement was made in Eastern Virginia upon Richmond, with the apparent expectation of taking the rebel capital by surprise, and releasing the Union prisoners who were held there in large numbers. General Butler, who, after his recall from New Orleans, had passed some time without a command, had, in October, been appointed the successor of General Foster to the command of the Eighteenth Army Corps and of the Department of Virginia and North Carolina. His administration at Norfolk, Newport News, Newbern and elsewhere in his department, had been signalized by his usual vigor and sagacity. He had taken in hand the negotiation of the exchange of prisoners with the

* Correspondence *New York Times* ("Whit"), Jacksonville, Fla., February 22d, 1864.

* An interesting narrative of the disaster, in a letter by a correspondent, dated "Off Charleston, February 22d," published in the *Army and Navy Journal*, March 5th, 1864.

rebel authorities at Richmond, in which he had been, in a measure, successful, notwithstanding the anathemas which had been directed against him by Jefferson Davis. At the beginning of February, the garrison at Newbern, in North Carolina, under Brigadier-General Innis N. Palmer, in the absence of Major-General Peck, was threatened by an attack by the confederate General Pickett, who, reinforced from Richmond, was advancing with a considerable body of troops from Kinston. The Union outposts at Bachellor's Creek were driven in, retiring to Newbern with a slight loss of stores and prisoners. An advance was also made by the enemy on the south side of the Trent, in which they suffered a repulse. General Palmer held his position firmly, and the assailants retired to Kinston. The defences of Newbern were strengthened and rendered too powerful for the enemy's attack, which was still threatened. It was at this time that General Butler set on foot the raid upon Richmond. While a movement of a portion of the Army of the Potomac across the Rapidan diverted General Lee's attention in that quarter, Brigadier-General Wistar, with a body of cavalry and mounted infantry, left New Kent Court House on the 5th, and marched rapidly to Bottoms' Bridge on the Chickahominy, with the expectation of making a sudden dash into Richmond. The authorities, however, had taken the alarm and interposed such obstacles of fallen timber at the bridge that the opportunity of a surprise was lost, and General Wistar was compelled to relinquish his object and retire, which he did, sucessfully, with some slight skirmishing with the enemy. Nothing was accomplished beyond exciting a panic at Richmond, the city being thrown into great excitement when news of the advance arrived. A few days after this affair, on the 15th of February, General Butler had the satisfaction to announce to the authorities at Washington the escape of Colonel A. D. Streight with 110 other Union officers from the Libby prison at Richmond and the safe arrival of a number of them within the Union lines at Williamsburg. The escape was a handsome set-off to that of Morgan and his men from the Ohio penitentiary. It was accomplished, without aid from without, by descending by a chimney to the cellar of the building, which was used only as a receptacle for straw and other refuse, and thence tunneling through the wall and under the street outside to the enclosure of a storehouse opposite where they emerged. The undertaking required the utmost patience, self-denial and adroitness at concealment during a month's disgusting labor; with no little heroism in the prospect of encountering the enemy; with the danger and hardships, should they get free of the prison, of a flight through the city and country beyond. All these embarrassments were met, and so successfully, that at the end of a week after the escape of the party on the night of the 9th, only forty-eight, less than half of the number who left the prison were, after the most persevering efforts on the part of the authorities, reported recaptured. The escaped officers for the most part belonged to the Western regiments. Colonel Streight of the Fifty-first Indiana Volunteers, it will be remembered, had been taken prisoner in the preceding May, while at the head of a raiding expedition near Rome, Ga. His capture was considered of great importance, and he had been treated during his captivity with great rigor. After his escape, he addressed an account of his imprisonment and that of his fellow-sufferers at Richmond to the Military Committee of the House of Representatives at Washington, exhibiting the cruelties and barbarities inflicted by the rebel authorities.*

* Colonel Streight's account of his captivity, *New York Times*, March 4th, 1864. An interesting narrative of the

The ineffectual raid in General Butler's department upon Richmond at the beginning of February, was followed up at its close by a more formidable expedition from the Army of the Potomac, planned by General Pleasanton, at the head of the cavalry corps, and led by Brigadier-General Kilpatrick, a young cavalry officer, a graduate of West Point since the beginning of the war, whose dash and spirit had gained him this rapid promotion. The details of the movement are thus given by a correspondent who accompanied the expedition: "The command left Stevensburg, Va., on Sunday night, the 28th of February, and crossed Ely's Ford, on the Rapidan; thence by rapid marches to Spottsylvania, Beaver Dam Station, on the Virginia Central Railroad, to the fortifications of Richmond, crossing the Virginia Central Railroad and the Chickahominy River near the Meadows, the White House Railroad, a little east of Tunstall's Station; thence to New Kent Court House and Williamsburg Court House, where the command arrived on the 3d of March—having been in the saddle nearly all the time from Sunday night, a period of four days, and during the most of that time the men were supplied from rebel larders and their horses from rebel granaries. Nearly 300 prisoners were captured, several hundred horses were pressed into the service, and hundreds of negroes availed themselves of this opportunity to come within our lines, thereby depleting the producing class of the rebel confederacy of just so many able-bodied men. As stated, the command left Stevensburg Sunday evening, and moved toward Ely's Ford. Forty men, under the immediate command of Mr. Hogan, a well-known scout, had the advance. The first of the enemy were met within one mile of the ford—a picket, to give notice should any thing like an enemy approach. This picket, composed of four men, by a little strategy was gobbled, with their horses and accoutrements, without firing a shot or doing any thing to alarm the reserve on the other side of the river—a force consisting of 13 men: 1 captain, 1 lieutenant and 11 privates. Hogan and his party gained the opposite bank, and the night being cloudy, succeeded in enveloping the reserve before they discovered his presence, and captured all but three. From these prisoners the important fact was ascertained that nothing whatever was known by the rebel authorities of the movement then on foot for their discomfiture. Colonel Ulric Dahlgren, accompanied by Major Cook, of the Second New York Cavalry, and a small party of picked men, took the advance after crossing the Rapidan, being engaged on a special mission. The main command moved along with rapidity, taking the road to Spottsylvania Court House. The night was cloudy, and betokened rain; but the roads were good, and every one was pleasant and hopeful. "Let the storm hold off twenty-four hours, and then I don't care," said a prominent officer of the command. Spottsylvania was reached late at night; no halt was made, however, and the corps moved rapidly forward to Beaver Dam, on the Virginia Central Railroad. Captain Estes and Lieutenant Wilson, with a party of men, dashed so suddenly upon this place that the telegraph operator was a prisoner before he had time to announce the arrival of the Yankees—much to his chagrin, for all the other telegraph lines had been cut, and Jeff. Davis, in his anxiety to know what was going on had been telegraphing that station every hour in the day for information. This place was reached at about 5 o'clock P. M., Monday, and the work of destruction was at once commenced. Small parties were sent up and down the rail-

escape of the officers from the Libby prison, published in the Washington (D. C.) Star, February 18th, 1864. *Richmond Enquirer*, February 12th, 1864.

road to tear up the track, burn the culverts and bridges, and destroy the rails by heating and bending them. This was comparatively an easy task; for there were thousands of cords of pine wood, all of which was burned, piled along the track—this being a wood station. A large new brick freight-house, 100 by 25 feet, the telegraph office, passenger depot, engine-house, water-tank, several cars, and a number of outbuildings, were all set on fire. While the command was engaged in this work of destruction, a picket reported the approach of a train loaded with troops from the direction of Richmond, and here commenced the first fighting. General Kilpatrick advanced a column to capture the train, if possible, but the enemy had seen the smoke of the burning station, and approached cautiously. They came on, however, to within two miles of the station, and a portion of the troops were disembarked. A small force was advanced to meet them, and in a charge our troops captured two officers and thirty men. The enemy then fled. Several parties were sent out from this point to destroy the railroad at other points, and bridges on important roads. Major Hall, of the Sixth New York Cavalry, with a party, went to destroy the Fredericksburg and Richmond Railroad bridge over the South Anna, at Taylorsville, but found the place guarded by the Maryland battalion of rebel infantry, who had two pieces of artillery. This command was absent some time on important service, and did not rejoin the main column until the following day in front of Richmond. Not returning at the time expected, a detachment under Captain Hull, of the Second New York, was sent out on a mission, and to find out the whereabouts of Major Hall's party. Hall ran across a superior force, and had a brisk skirmish, in which he lost five men, and was forced to retire. Another party under Captain Plum and Lieutenant Lord was also sent off and returned in safety. The main command, just at nightfall, Monday, moved forward, and during the night crossed the South Anna River. Here the advance had a skirmish with an infantry picket near Taylorsville, and dispersed them. The men crossed, a brief halt was made to feed, when the column at daylight moved 'on to Richmond,' before which, and within the second line of defences, a position was taken at 10½ o'clock the same morning. On the way, Kilby Station, on the Fredericksburg road, was destroyed, and Lieutenant Whitaker, of General Kilpatrick's staff, blew up a stone bridge near Kilby Station, and the track and culverts were destroyed all along in that vicinity. Lieutenant Boyce, of the Fifth New York Cavalry, with twelve men, cut the track and destroyed the telegraph at Guinea Station.

"Tuesday, at 10½ o'clock A. M., found the command passing the outer earthworks on the Brook turnpike, within 3½ miles of Richmond. The arrival of Yankee troops was entirely unexpected, and the indignation of some very good-looking women, standing in front of houses at the roadside, excited much amusement. The advance captured several men on picket duty belonging to the citizen soldiery of Richmond, without firing a shot; and while waiting for the main column to come up, citizens were stopped and questioned with the utmost freedom. They, of course, did not know who their questioners were. Here was obtained a copy of the *Examiner* and *Dispatch*, fresh from the press that morning, announcing some rumors about a brigade of Yankee cavalry having crossed the Rapidan. What their astonishment must have been one hour later to hear Kilpatrick's guns, may be imagined but not described. Moving forward to within the second line of defences going toward the city, the skirmishers encountered the first shot from near the third line, or what is known as Battery

No. 9. Guns were opened on both sides, and a strong line of skirmishers was thrown out. Captain Bacon, with others, charged the Johnnys and drove them inside their works, and a desultory firing was kept up until between 4 and 5 o'clock in the evening, when, for some reason then unknown, the command of Colonel Dahlgren not appearing, General Kilpatrick decided to fall back. The enemy had burned the bridge across Brook Creek in rear of the command, and the column turned off upon the Meadows road, crossing the Fredericksburg and Richmond Railroad and destroying every thing within reach. At night, the command went into camp at a place six miles from Richmond, and two miles from the Chickahominy; there was a slight fall of rain and sleet, and the men built fires, cooked their chickens and bacon, and had turned in for a few hours sleep; but as all persons are doomed to disappointment at some time or other, so it was their lot on this occasion. At about 10½ o'clock, just as the command was fairly asleep—except those on duty—the rebels opened a two-gun battery upon the camp of General Davies' brigade, and immediately after charged the camp of the Seventh Michigan. The men, though taken entirely by surprise, seized their carbines, and under Colonel Litchfield, supported by the First Vermont, Colonel Preston, handsomely repulsed the enemy, who, owing to the camp fires, had decidedly the advantage over our troops, owing to their occupying a position between the enemy and the camp fires. After forcing the enemy back, the Commanding-General decided to move his command again, so as to be ready for any emergency at daylight. In this affair a number of horses were killed, and a few were stampeded by the shrieking shell rushing through the midnight air. The scene, all things considered, was not a very fascinating one to a man of tender nerves. Several men were wounded, and Colonel Litchfield, who was missing, it was feared was also wounded. The enemy had the exact range of General Davies' headquarters, but he remained at his post during the whole attack, which lasted three-quarters of an hour, and was loudly cheered by his command for the noble conduct he displayed on this occasion. The enemy did not seem disposed to follow the rear-guard, and the command moved forward, without interruption, toward the Pamunkey River. The enemy had burned all the boats in this river, so that if it had been desirable to cross, such a movement was entirely impracticable; General Kilpatrick, therefore decided to move across the White House Railroad, and down the Peninsula. During the day, Captain Mitchell of the Second New York, with the bulk of Colonel Dahlgren's command, rejoined the main column, and great was the rejoicing thereat, for nothing had been heard from it since the previous Sunday night. The enemy, Tuesday night and all day Wednesday and Wednesday night, hovered all about the command, and picket skirmishing was almost constantly going on in different directions. Wednesday morning, at about 9 o'clock, a large force of cavalry came upon the rear of the column. General Kilpatrick was not unprepared for this, and decided to give them battle. The First Vermont, under Colonel Preston, ably assisted by Captains Grant and Cummings, and the First Maine, bore the brunt of this fight, which lasted something over an hour, while the Sixth Michigan and other regiments of General Davies' brigade were in position to render whatever assistance might be necessary. Only one charge was made, and that was by Company A, First Maine, led on by Captain Estes, A. A. G., and Captain Cole, when five of the enemy were captured. The enemy, satisfied, no doubt, that they could not scare the command away, sullenly retired, but when the command moved forward, harrassed the rear and flanks. Several times an offer was made, but they refused to accept the offer of battle. On this day (Wednesday) several refugees from Richmond came into camp, and reported the presence of Captain Wilson, of the Second Ohio, who had escaped from the Richmond Bastile, near at hand. For some reason, however, best known to himself, he did not join the command. Wednesday, also, Lieutenant Whitaker was sent to destroy Tunstall's Station on the White House Railroad, but upon arriving there, much to his astonishment, he found the place in flames. From negroes in the vicinity he ascertained that a column of Union cavalry from General Butler's department had just left there. This was the first intimation of assistance being so near at hand. Thursday morning, General Kilpatrick moved toward New Kent Court House, and on the way met Colonel Spear, in command of a cavalry force, looking after General Kilpatrick's command. The meeting was a gratifying one on both sides. Near Kent Court House, the command came across the first negro troops they had ever seen. Here was a full brigade which had been marched up ; and, as the cavalry passed by, cheer after cheer was given by both commands. No brigade ever made a better appearance or a better impression upon those who, for the first time, saw colored troops. A mountain of prejudice was removed in an instant. Between New Kent to Williamsburg, the column was more or less annoyed by bushwhackers. Ten of these rascals were captured. Of our men, one was killed, and several were wounded, and one or two horses were killed.

"Colonel Dahlgren, with a picked command, after leaving the main column, went to Frederick Hall on the Virginia Central Railroad, destroyed that road and the telegraph line, and captured twelve officers who were there on court-martial duty. The James River Canal was then struck eight miles east of Goochland Court House, and between there and Wertham Creek an immense amount of property was destroyed. Six grist-mills in full operation, a saw-mill, six canal-boats loaded with grain, several locks of the canal, works at the coal-pits at Manikin's Bend, and the barn of Secretary Seddon, were all destroyed. It was at this point that Colonel Dahlgren discovered that his guide had deceived him, so as to thwart the principal object of the expedition, and he was immediately hanged to the nearest tree. The command then struck the Plank Road and moved on to Richmond from a westerly direction, and when within three miles of that city had a lively skirmish with some rebel infantry. This was late Tuesday afternoon, and about the time General Kilpatrick retired from the Brook turnpike. Could the command have been there three hours earlier the results of the expedition might have been still more satisfactory. Finding the force too large to operate against with any prospect of success, and not knowing the whereabouts or fate of the main column, Colonel Dahlgren decided to fall back, and, if possible, reach that column, destroying property on the way. Colonel Dahlgren and Major Cook, with about 100 men, went a different route from the main portion of the column, commanded by Captain Mitchell. The latter came in on Wednesday, as stated above ; but of the other command nothing was certainly known. A prisoner, however, stated that a colonel with one foot had been captured. The loss of the whole command by straggling, and in every other way, did not probably exceed 150 men, and after three days' rest the horses and men were ready for duty again wherever their services were needed."*

Colonel Dahlgren, with his command,

* E. A. Paul. Correspondence of the *New York Times*, Williamsburg, Va., March 4th, 1864.

while making his way on the night of the 2d March, along the Mattapony, in King William County, toward West Point, was intercepted by a party of Virginia cavalry, joined by the home-guard of the district. The latter, taking their station on the road, opened fire upon the retreating party, when Colonel Dahlgren, resolving to cut his way through, ordered a charge which he led himself and fell in the onset pierced with a ball. His command was then captured. Colonel Ulric Dahlgren, whose fate the country was called upon to lament, was a young officer of great gallantry, being not yet twenty-two years of age. The son of Admiral Dahlgren, he had been employed, at the outset of the war, with his father in the Navy Ordnance Department. Entering the war as Captain of Artillery, he rendered important aid at Maryland Heights, and subsequently in the Virginia campaigns, and especially with General Burnside at Fredericksburg, and with General Hooker at Chancellorsville. Prior to the battle of Gettysburg he was employed in a roving cavalry commission, in which, among other valuable services, he captured the dispatches of Jefferson Davis to General Lee. On the retreat of the enemy, he was wounded in the charge at Hagerstown in the right foot and compelled to undergo an amputation of the leg which nearly proved fatal. After six months confinement, he reported himself for duty, and, when the present expedition was projected, eagerly sought the service which cost him his life. The body of Colonel Dahlgren was treated by the enemy with great ignominy, and much indignation was expressed in the Richmond journals on the publication of certain papers alleged to have been found on his person. These were, for the most part, directions for the destruction of rebel property held in the war, the release of the Union prisoners at Belle Isle and the entrance into Richmond. As published in the rebel newspapers, they further contained injunctions, that "once in the city, it must be destroyed, and Jeff. Davis and his cabinet killed." The latter, however, was considered of more than doubtful authenticity at the North, and discredited as a forgery. No such order was issued to the men of his command. Unauthenticated, however, as it was, it was caught up by the foreign press sympathizing with the South, and became a text for fresh invectives against the North, though nothing could be more at variance with the toleration and forbearance of the National Government.

In retaliation for the attack by the citizens, claiming to be non-combatants, upon Colonel Dahlgren, General Butler, a few days after, sent a cavalry force under Colonel Onderdonk and Colonel Spear to King and Queen Court House, which came upon a camp of the enemy which was destroyed and a number killed. A large quantity of grain, and several mills and store-houses were burnt.

On the 30th of January, Major-General Schofield was succeeded in the command of the Department of the Missouri by Major-General Rosecrans. In a general order, on assuming his new duties, the latter invoked the assistance "of all true National and Union men without regard to politics, creed or party. The past (said he) should be remembered only for the lessons it teaches, while our energies should be directed to the problem of assuring our future, based firmly on the grandeur of our position and on the true principles of humanity and progress, to universal freedom, secured by just laws."

CHAPTER XCVII.

GENERAL BANKS' DEPARTMENT OF THE GULF. EXPEDITION TO WESTERN LOUISIANA. RAID OF GENERAL FORREST AND MASSACRE AT FORT PILLOW, MARCH-APRIL, 1864.

Turning from these scattered military operations to the Department of the Gulf, we find General Banks on the 11th of January issuing an important proclamation, in accordance with the Amnesty Proclamation of President Lincoln. Being "fully assured that more than a tenth of the population desired the earliest possible restoration of Louisiana to the Union," he invited the loyal citizens to assemble on the 22d of February, and to cast their votes for Governor and other State officers who were to "constitute the civil government of the State, under the Constitution and laws of Louisiana, except so much of the said Constitution and laws as recognize, regulate or relate to slavery, which being inconsistent with the present condition of public affairs, and plainly inapplicable to any class of persons now existing within its limits, must be suspended, and they are hereby declared to be inoperative and void." The oath of allegiance required by the President's proclamation, with the condition affixed to the elective franchise by the Constitution of Louisiana, were prescribed as the qualifications of voters. Officers elected were to be installed on the 4th of March. It was also declared in the proclamation, "in order that the organic law of the State may be made to conform to the will of the people, and harmonize with the spirit of the age, as well as to maintain and preserve the ancient landmarks of civil and religious liberty," an election of delegates to a convention for the revision of the Constitution will be held on the first Monday of April, 1864. Early arrangements were to be made for the election of Members of Congress for the State.

The motives and necessity for these proceedings were thus set forth by General Banks: "The fundamental law of the State is martial law. It is competent and just for the Government to surrender to the people, at the earliest possible moment, so much of military power as may be consistent with the success of military operations; to prepare the way, by prompt and wise measures, for the full restoration of the State to the Union and its power to the people; to restore their ancient and unsurpassed prosperity; to enlarge the scope of agriculture and commercial industry, and to extend and confirm the dominion of rational liberty. It is not within human power to accomplish these results without some sacrifice of individual prejudices and interests. Problems of State, too complicate for the human mind, have been solved by the national cannon. In great civil convulsions, the agony of strife enters the souls of the innocent as well as the guilty. The Government is subject to the law of necessity, and must consult the condition of things, rather than the preference of men; and if so be that its purposes are just and its measures wise, it has the right to demand that questions of personal interest and opinion shall be subordinate to the public good When the national existence is at stake, and the liberties of the people in peril, faction is treason. The methods herein proposed submit the whole question of Government directly to the people: first, by the election of executive officers, faithful to the Union, to be followed by a loyal representation in both Houses of Congress—and then by a Convention which will confirm the action of the people, and recognize the principles of freedom in the organic law. This is the wish of the President. The anniversary of Washington's birth is a fit day for the commencement of so great a work. The immortal Father of his Country was never guided by a more just and benignant spirit than that of his successor in office, the President of the United States. In the hour of our trial let us heed his admonitions. Louisiana, in the opening of her history, sealed the integrity of the Union by conferring upon its Government the Valley of the Mississippi. In the war for independence upon the sea, she crowned a glorious struggle against the first maritime power of the world, by a victory unsurpassed in the annals of war. Let her people now announce to the world the coming restoration of the Union, in which the ages that follow us have a deeper interest than our own, by the organization of a free government, and her fame will be immortal."

Previously to the time appointed for the election, an important order was issued by General Banks, dated February 3d, for the regulation of colored labor on the plantations. This was placed under the direction or superintendence of the Provost-Marshal-General and the parish provost-marshals. It was assumed that "labor was a public duty, and idleness and vagrancy a crime;" and these officers were charged with the enforcement of the necessary regulations, the main object of which was to "strengthen all the advantages which capital derives from labor, and enable the laborer to take care of himself and prepare for the time when he can render so much labor for so much money." Hours of labor were prescribed, and a rate of remuneration, with "just treatment, healthy rations, comfortable clothing, quarters, fuel, medical attendance, and instruction for children." Flogging, and other cruel or unnecessary punishments, were interdicted. At the close of this order, General Banks, in the following terms, required from the people of the State co-operation in his plans for the restoration of civil government, on the penalty of exile. "A more majestic and wise clemency human history does not exhibit. The liberal and just conditions that attend it cannot be disregarded. It protects labor by enforcing the performance of its duty, and it will assist capital by compelling just contributions to the demands of the Government. Those who profess allegiance to other governments will be required, as the condition of residence in this State, to acquiesce, without reservation, in the demands presented by Government as a basis of permanent peace. The non-cultivation of the soil, without just reason, will be followed by temporary forfeiture to those who will secure its improvement. Those who have exercised, or are entitled to the rights of citizens of the United States, will be required to participate in the measures necessary for the re-establishment of civil government. War can never cease except as civil governments crush out contest, and secure the supremacy of moral over physical power. The yellow harvest must wave over the crimson field of blood, and the representatives of the people displace the agents of purely military power. It is therefore a solemn duty resting upon all persons to assist in the earliest possible restoration of civil government. Let them participate in the measures suggested for this purpose. Opinion is free, and candidates are numerous. Open hostility cannot be permitted. Indifference will be treated as crime, and faction as treason. Men who refuse to defend their country with the ballot-box or cartridge-box have no just claim to the benefits of liberty regulated by law. All people not exempt by the law of nations, who seek the protection of the Government, are called upon to take the oath of allegiance in such form as may be prescribed, sacrificing to the public good, and the restoration of public peace, whatever scruples may be suggested by incidental considerations. The oath of allegiance, administered and received in good faith, is the test of unconditional fealty to the Government and all its measures, and cannot be materially strengthened or impaired by the language in which it is clothed. The amnesty offered for the past is conditioned upon an unreserved loyalty for the future, and this condition will be enforced with an iron hand. Whoever is indifferent or hostile must choose between the liberty which foreign lands afford, the poverty of the rebel States, and the innumerable and inappreciable blessings which our Government confers upon its people. May God preserve the Union of the States!"

The election for the State officers was held on the 22d of February, and resulted in the success of the Free State ticket, and the choice of Michael Hahn for Governor, by about 3,000 majority out of a vote of over 8,000. The inauguration on the 4th of March was celebrated in a public square of New Orleans with imposing ceremonies. Ten thousand children of the public schools were assembled on the spot, and added their voices in song to the music of the bands, the firing of artillery, and ringing of the city bells. The Governor, in his inaugural accepting the new order of things, looked forward to the time when the "present population of Louisiana, or if they will not do it, then the emigration that will speedily supersede them," would render the State "the most flourishing portion of the most powerful of all nations."

These civil movements in Louisiana were followed by an imposing military effort to bring the western part of the State, intermediate between Texas and Arkansas, an important field for the operations of the rebel leaders, under subjection to the Union forces. For this purpose a joint military and naval expedition was planned to concentrate on the Red River, open the navigation of that stream to our transports, with the ultimate design of advancing and securing possession of the frontier town of Shreveport, the enemy's depot of supplies, the occupation of which, with the intermediate points, would virtually complete the conquest of the State. The forces at New Orleans and its vicinity were got ready for the movement, under the direction of General Banks, who left New Orleans on the 22d of March to take the field in person, a portion of his army having advanced through the Teche country by way of Opelousas. In the mean time Admiral Porter, with a formidable fleet of gunboats, ascended the Mississippi to the mouth of Red River, where, on the 11th of March, he was met by a fleet of transports conveying a force of about 10,000 men, chiefly of western and northwestern troops of the Sixteenth and Seventeenth Army Corps, under General A. J. Smith, from Vicksburg. General Steele, in command in Arkansas, it was understood was to co-operate with the expedition by an overland movement upon Shreveport, from Little Rock. On the 12th, the fleet steamed up Red River into the Atchafalaya, and anchored in the afternoon at Simmesport. The next day General Smith landed a portion of his troops, and sent forward General Mower, with a brigade, to reconnoitre the enemy's position at Bayou Glace, where they occupied a fortified camp. On his approach this was abandoned, the enemy falling back toward Fort De Russy, a formidable fortification which they had erected with great skill and labor to command the Red River. General Smith, seizing his opportunity, pushed rapidly forward by forced marches the intervening distance of thirty-five miles to a land attack upon the fort before it could be reinforced. By a strenuous effort he reached the vicinity on the afternoon of the 14th, and, without pause, hastened at once to the assault. Cautiously advancing, the action was commenced by an Iowa regiment, as skirmishers, who drew the fire of the enemy, when two batteries were brought into play, and after a brisk cannonade, with sharp musketry fire, for ten hours, the enemy replying with four guns, the order was given to charge, when the fort was successfully stormed, the Fifty-eighth Illinois and Eighth Wisconsin regiments leading the way. Three hundred and twenty-five men were found in the fort, including twenty-four commissioned officers, all of whom were made prisoners. Ten guns were taken, two thousand barrels of powder, and a quantity of stores. The casualties were slight on both sides, the garrison losing five killed and four wounded; the assailants, seven killed and forty-one wounded. Such was the activity of General Smith that the fort was surrendered before the gunboats arrived to take part in its capture. The way was now open to Alexandria, on the Red River, which was immediately occupied by the Union forces, the advance of General Smith's forces, under Brigadier-General Mower, accompanied by Admiral Porter, with his fleet of gunboats, taking possession on the evening of the 16th. A large quantity of cotton was captured, and brought in by the gunboats. Fort De Russy was stripped, and its extensive works blown up by order of General Smith. A few days after, General Banks, with the remainder of his forces, under General Franklin, arrived at Alexandria, and preparations were made for the advance upon Shreveport.

On the 28th March General Lee set out at the head of his cavalry division for Natchitoches, which he took possession of without loss, the enemy, said to be under General Dick Taylor, retreating before him with slight skirmishing. The Union army now advanced to Natchitoches, the fleet of Admiral Porter accompanying it to Grand Ecore, the river station in that vicinity. The military movements which ensued are thus related in the summary of the three days engagements by a Southern journalist: "Our army," says he, "broke camp at Natchitoches on the morning of the 6th April, and marched out on the Shreveport road, the cavalry advancing twenty-one miles, and resting for the night at Crump's Hill, the infantry halting three or four miles to the rear, on the banks of a bayou. On the following morning at daybreak the cavalry again started, and came upon a body of mounted rebels before they had marched two miles. Fighting began at once, and the enemy were rapidly driven before our troops. This running style of fight was kept up for fourteen miles, until they had got two miles beyond Pleasant Hill. Here a force of 2,500 rebel cavalry, commanded by General Green, were found strongly posted on Wilson's plantation. The rebels were deployed along the edge of a dense strip of woods, with an open field in front, over which we had to charge in order to reach them. The only Union soldiers that had advanced far enough to take part in the fight, which was inevitable, was the cavalry brigade of Lee's corps, commanded by Colonel Haral Robinson. As he had either to attack or be attacked, he decided to take the initiative, and he led his men in with such a dash and vigor that at last the enemy was completely whipped and driven from the field. This engagement lasted two hours and a-half, and our losses amounted to about forty killed and wounded, the enemy's being at least as many. Colonel Robinson pursued the retreating rebels as far as Bayou du Paul, where he found they had received heavy reinforcements, including four pieces of artillery, and were again in line of battle waiting attack. As it was nearly dark, and the risk was too great in again attacking with his small force, he placed his men in the most advantageous position available, and awaited the progress of events. Nothing further was accomplished on the first day.

"During the night a brigade of infantry, commanded by Colonel Landrum, came up, and early in the morning of the following day (Friday, the 8th) the march was resumed. The rebels were found to be on the alert and ready for the fray, and fighting commenced almost at once. The disposition of our forces at the beginning of this day's battle was: Colonel Landrum's infantry brigade on the right of the Shreveport road, and Colonel Lucas' cavalry brigade on the left. The skirmishing was fierce, and every foot of ground won from the enemy had to be taken by hard knocks, but at 2 o'clock in the afternoon our forces had compelled the rebels to retreat seven miles. Our losses, as well as the enemy's, were very severe during this time; Lieutenant-Colonel Webb, of the Seventy-seventh Illinois, shot through the head and instantly killed, and Captain Breese, commanding Sixth Missouri Cavalry, severely wounded in the arm, being among the casualties on our side. The enemy were now met in strong force, under command of General Kirby Smith. That General Dick Taylor, Mouton, Green, and Price were also there was afterward ascertained from prisoners, who also stated that they had under them from 18,000 to 22,000 men, while our force comparatively were a mere handful. The rebels occupied a strong position in the vicinity of Sabine Cross Roads, concealed in the edge of a dense wood, with an open field in front, the Shreveport road passing through their lines. General Ransom arriving on the field with his command, formed his line as well as circumstances would permit, after reconnoitering and feeling the rebel position. Colonel Emerson's brigade, of the Thirteenth Corps, was stationed on the left of the line, with Nim's Massachusetts Battery; Colonel Landrum's forces, parts of two brigades, on the right and centre, with Rawles' Battery G, Fifth Regulars, and a battery of the First Indiana Artillery in rear of his right and centre. Colonel Dudley's brigade of cavalry (of Lee's corps) supported the left, and held itself in readiness to repel any attempt to flank; while Lucas protected the right flank. Colonel Robinson, with his brigade, was in rear of the centre, protecting the wagon train which was on the Shreveport road. General Banks and staff rode upon the field by the time this disposition of our forces was effected, and word was sent back to General Franklin to make all speed for the scene of the momentarily expected battle. It was the design of General Banks to remain quiet until the balance of his army came up, and then open the battle himself; but Kirby Smith, knowing his own superiority in numbers, began the conflict before they could arrive.

"About 5 o'clock the firing between the skirmishers became very hot, and in a short time our skirmish line was driven back upon the main body by an overwhelming force. The whole strength of the enemy was then advanced, and heavy and repeated volleys were discharged and replied to on our right and centre. Soon this portion of our line became heavily engaged, and all our available strength was required to prevent its being crushed by the masses of the enemy. Our left, which was now, also, hotly fighting, was necessarily much weakened, and it was observed that a strong body of the enemy was massing in a dense piece of woods, preparatory to dashing down and flanking this end of our line. The danger was plain and imminent, but there was no remedy. General Stone ordered General Lee to have Nim's battery withdrawn, although it was doing great execution, in order that it might not become a prize to the enemy, and General Lee sent his aide-de-camp, Colonel J. S. Brisbin, to withdraw the battery. On reaching the point its removal was found impossible, nearly every one of the horses having been killed. In a few moments more a solid mass of the rebels swept down upon the spot, and four of the guns were taken, the other two being dragged from the field by hand. The havoc made in the ranks of the enemy at this point of the action is represented as appalling, the whole six guns belching forth double charges of grape and canister; and some five or six rounds were fired between the time the rebels left the woods until the artillerymen were forced from their pieces. As the rebels were in mass, the execution such a shower of missiles caused can be easily imagined. The two senior officers of the battery were wounded, Lieutenant Snow mortally, having since died. The forces that made this charge were commanded by the rebel General Mouton, who fell shot through the body with four balls.

"The fighting on all parts of our line was now at short range, and, to use the expression of one of the participants, 'we were holding on by the skin of our teeth only.' It was known that Franklin's troops had been sent for, and anxious and wistful were the glances cast to the rear. General Cameron, with his brigade, came up, and going at once into action on the right, where the battle again waxed hottest, created the impression that the veterans of the Nineteenth had arrived, and a glad and exultant shout went up from our wearied and desperately situated little band. This belief was strengthened by the arrival of General Franklin, who dashed boldly into the thickest of the fray, cap in hand, and cheering on the men. General Banks, too, seemed ubiquitous, riding wherever the men wavered, and by personal example inciting them to renewed deeds of daring and reckless valor. Colonels Clark and Wilson, with other members of the staff, sabre in hand, mixed with the soldiers on foot and horseback, and cheered and encouraged them to continue the unequal fight. But human beings could not longer withstand such fierce and overpowering onslaughts as our men were bearing up against, and our line finally gave way at all points, and the men fell back fiercely contesting the ground they yielded. Unfortunately a sad mishap befell them at this time. The large and cumbersome wagon train blocked up the way; the frightened horses dashed through the infantry lines, entangled themselves with the artillery, and created a momentary but unfortunate confusion. This gave the rebels, who were rapidly pressing us, possession of several pieces of artillery. General Franklin was conspicuous during this part of the day, rallying the men, and two horses were killed under him; Captain Chapman, of his staff, had both feet taken off by a round shot, and the horse of General Franklin was killed at the same time. The enemy followed our men step by step for three and a-half miles, but he was advancing to meet a fearful retribution. The Nineteenth Army Corps had been ordered to stop and form its line of battle; the retreating Union troops passed through this line, and formed in the rear. The rebels, thinking they had repulsed our whole army, dashed impetuously on, and thought the line, but half visible in the woods before them, was another feeble but desperate stand of a few men. General Emory commanded this force, consisting of two full brigades, and he ordered the fire to be reserved until the rebels were within short range, when, from both infantry and artillery posted thickly along his line, a storm of iron and lead was hurled upon the foe that literally mowed them down. The rebels halted in amazement, but still they fought, and bravely. Volley after volley was discharged from each side full into the ranks of their opponents, but neither gave signs of yielding, and night charitably threw her mantle over the ghastly scene, and enforced a cessation of hostilities. The two divisions, under command of General A. J. Smith, belonging to the Sixteenth and Seventeenth Army Corps, had reached Pleasant Hill, and were there halted, General Banks determining to withdraw his army to that point, for the sake of the advantageous position which he could there occupy, knowing that the enemy would follow what they supposed to be a demoralized army. In accordance with this plan of operations, all our men were quietly withdrawn from the enemy's front, and the line of march taken up for Pleasant Hill. This conjunction of his forces was satisfactorily effected, and the result confidently awaited. So well was this movement conducted, that, although the first body started at 10 o'clock, and the remainder were not all under way until nearly day, the rebels had not the slightest suspicion of what was going on.

"At 7 o'clock, on Saturday morning, our forces were all at Pleasant Hill, and the rebels were advancing, cavalry in front, endeavoring to discover our position. Colonel O. P. Gooding, with his brigade of Lee's cavalry corps, was sent on the Shreveport road to meet the enemy and draw him on. He had gone about a mile when he came upon the rebel advance. Skirmishing immediately ensued, and according to the plan he slowly fell back. The fight was very sharp between these cavalry bodies, and Gooding lost nearly forty men in killed and wounded, inflicting, however, as much damage as he received. Among his casualties are Captain Becker and Lieutenant Hall of the Second New York Veteran Cavalry. Lieutenant Hall has since died of his wounds. Colonel Gooding had a narrow escape, a ball passing through and tearing the crown out of his hat, and grazing the skin. The brigade behaved very gallantly, covering General Emory's front until his line was formed. The battlefield of Pleasant Hill is a large, open field, which had once been cultivated, but was now overgrown with weeds and bushes. The slightly elevated centre of the field, from which the name Pleasant Hill is taken, is nothing more than a long mound, hardly worthy the name of hill. A semi-circle belt of timber runs around the field on the Shreveport side. General Emory formed his line of battle on the side facing these woods, General McMillan's brigade being posted on the right, General Dwight's on the centre, and Colonel Benedict's on the left. Taylor's Battery L, First Regulars, had four guns in rear of the left wing, on the left of the Shrēveport road, and two on the road in rear of General Dwight's line. Hibberd's Vermont Battery was on the right. In the rear of Emory, and concealed by the rising ground, were General Smith's tried troops, formed in two lines of battle fifty yards apart. All his artillery was in the front line, a piece, section or battery being on the flank of each regiment, the infantry lying between them. The Thirteenth Corps was in reserve in the rear under General Cameron, General Ransom having been wounded the day before. General Smith was Commander-in-Chief of the two lines back of the crest, while General Mower was the immediate commander of the men. The commander of the right brigade in General Smith's first line was Colonel Lynch; the left brigade was Colonel

Shaw's. The second line, also, consisted of two brigades, the right under control of Colonel ——, and the left commanded by Colonel Hill. Crawford's Third Indiana Battery was posted on the right of the Eighty-ninth Indiana Infantry, and the Ninth Indiana Battery on the right of the line of battle. The Missouri Iron Sun Battery, and others, whose names and numbers we could not ascertain, were also in this section of the battle. The skirmishing was kept up with considerable vigor until about 5 o'clock in the afternoon, when the rebels had completed their arrangements for the attack. At about this hour General Emory's skirmish line was driven in on the right by the rebels, who appeared in large force, coming through the timber above mentioned. They soon reached the open ground, and moved on to the attack in three lines of battle. Our batteries and infantry opened with terrible effect, doing great slaughter with grape and canister, while the enemy's artillery, being in the woods and in bad position, did scarcely any damage. Colonel Benedict's brigade on the left was first engaged, soon followed by Dwight's and McMillan's. The fighting was terrific—old soldiers say it never was surpassed for desperation. Notwithstanding the terrible havoc in their ranks, the enemy pressed fiercely on, slowly pushing the men of the Nineteenth Corps back up the hill, but not breaking their line of battle. A sudden and bold dash of the rebels on the right gave them possession of Taylor's battery, and forced our line still further back. Now came the grand *coup de main.* The Nineteenth, arriving at the top of the hill, suddenly filed off over the hill and passed through the lines of General Smith. We must here mention that the rebels were now in but two lines of battle, the first having been almost annihilated by General Emory, what remained being forced back into the second line. But these two lines came on exultant and sure of victory. The first passed over the knoll, and all heedless of the long line of cannons and crouching forms of as brave men as ever trod mother earth, pressed on. The second line appeared on the crest, and the death-signal was sounded. Words cannot describe the awful effect of this discharge. Seven thousand rifles, and several batteries of artillery, each gun loaded to the muzzle with grape and canister, were fired simultaneously, and the whole centre of the rebel line was crushed down as a field of ripe wheat through which a tornado had passed. It is estimated that 1,000 men were hurried into eternity, or frightfully mangled by this one discharge. No time was given them to recover their good order, but General Smith ordered a charge, and his men dashed rapidly forward, the boys of the Nineteenth joining in. The rebels fought boldly and desperately back to the timber, on reaching which a large portion broke and fled, fully two thousand throwing aside their arms. In this charge, Taylor's battery was retaken, as were also two of the guns of Nim's battery, the Parrot gun taken from us at Carrion Crow last fall, and one or two others belonging to the rebels, one of which was considerably shattered, besides 700 prisoners. A pursuit and desultory fight was kept up for three miles, when our men returned to the field of battle. And thus ended this fearful and bloody struggle for the control of Western Louisiana."*

The loss of General Banks in these actions, at the time we write not officially reported, has been estimated at about 4,000 in all. Twenty cannon, it is said, were left in the hands of the enemy.†

Admiral Porter, in an official report, has given an interesting account of the movements of the smaller vessels of his

* *New Orleans Era*, April 15th, 1864.

† *Army and Navy Journal*, April 30th, 1864.

fleet in their attempted co-operation with General Banks on their way to Shreveport. They had made good progress when their way was stopped by obstructions in the river, and before they could be removed, word was brought of the disaster to the army and the order given to return. The difficulties of navigation was great, and the way was beset by guerrillas. "On the evening of the 12th instant," writes Admiral Porter, "we were attacked from the right bank of the river by a detachment of men of quite another character. They were a part of the army which two or three days previous had gained success over our army, and flushed with victory, or under the excitement of liquor, they appeared suddenly upon the right bank, and fearlessly opened fire on the Osage, Lieutenant-Commander T. O. Selfridge (iron-clad), she being hard aground at the time, with a transport (the Black Hawk) alongside of her, towing her off. The rebels opened with 2,000 muskets, and soon drove every one out of the Black Hawk to the safe casemates of the monitor. Lieutenant Bache had just come from his vessel (the Lexington), and fortunately was enabled to pull up to her again, keeping close under the bank, while the Osage opened a destructive fire on these poor deluded wretches, who, maddened by liquor, and led on by their officers, were vainly attempting to capture an iron vessel. I am told that their hootings and actions baffle description. Force after force seemed to be brought up to the edge of the bank, where they confronted the guns of the iron vessel only to be mowed down by grapeshot and canister. In the mean time Lieutenant Bache had reached his vessel, and widening the distance between them and the Osage, he opened a cross-fire on the infuriated rebels, who fought with such desperation and courage against certain destruction that it could only be accounted for in one way. Our opinions were verified on inspection of some of the bodies of the slain, the men actually smelling of Louisiana rum. The affair lasted nearly two hours before the rebels fled. They brought off two pieces of artillery, one of which was quickly knocked over by the Lexington's guns, the other they managed to carry off. The cross-fire of the Lexington finally decided this curious affair of a fight between infantry and gunboats. The rebels were mowed down by her canister, and finally retreated in as quick haste as they had come to the attack, leaving the space of a mile covered with dead and wounded, and knapsacks. A dying rebel informed our men that General Green had his head blown off, which I do not vouch for as true; if true, it is a serious loss to the rebels. Night coming on, we had no means of ascertaining the damage done to the rebels. We are troubled no more from the right bank of the river, and a party of 500 men, who were marching to cut us off, were persuaded to change their mind after hearing of the unfortunate termination of the first expedition. That same night I ordered the transports to proceed, having placed the gunboats at a point where the rebels had a battery. All the transports were passed safely, the rebels not firing a shot in return to the many that were bursting over the hills."

On reaching Grand Ecore, Admiral Porter found several of the vessels of his fleet detained above the bar by the fall of the river. One of these, the gunboat Eastport, he was subsequently compelled to destroy to prevent her falling into the hands of the enemy. Two transport vessels were also burned for the same reason. The army remained at Alexandria, where General Banks established his headquarters, and waited reinforcements. The march of General Steele through Arkansas, toward Shreveport, with a force stated at 20,000 men, was at first attended with success. After dispersing the enemy, under Price, at various positions, by a rapid march he gained the fortified position of Camden, on the Washita, but was presently compelled, by the gathering forces of the enemy, after the Union losses on the Red River, to return to Little Rock, bringing his army to that point, after several severe conflicts on the way. In an address to his troops, dated Little Rock, May 9, General Steele thus speaks of his campaign: "Although you were compelled to fall back without seeing the main object of the expedition accomplished, you will have the satisfaction of knowing that you have beaten the enemy wherever he has met you in force, and extricated yourselves from the perilous position in which you were placed by the reverses of the co-operating column. This let loose upon you a superior force of the enemy, under one of their best generals, causing the loss of your trains, and the total interruption of your communications, rendering it impossible for you to obtain supplies. You have fallen back over rivers and swamps, while pressed by a superior force of the enemy. This you have done successfully, punishing the enemy severely at the same time." The spring campaign, west of the Mississippi, was thus, upon the whole, disastrous to the Union forces, without, however, any important advantage to the rebels, who had suffered severely in the various engagements.

The closing exploit of the campaign was the dexterous withdrawal of the fleet, which was detained by the continuous fall of the river, above the falls of Alexandria. The details, as presented by Admiral Porter in his official report of May 16th, are of too much interest to be abbreviated. "The water," says he, "had fallen so low that I had no hope or expectation of getting the vessels out this season, and, as the army had made arrangements to evacuate the country, I saw nothing before me but the destruction of the best part of the Mississippi squadron. There seems to have been an especial Providence looking out for us in providing a man equal to the emergency. Lieutenant-Colonel Bailey, Acting Engineer of the Nineteenth Army Corps, proposed a plan of building a series of dams across the rocks at the falls, and raising the water high enough to let the vessels pass over. This proposition looked like madness, and the best engineers ridiculed it; but Colonel Bailey was so sanguine of success, that I requested General Banks to have it done, and he entered heartily into the work. Provisions were short, and forage was almost out, and the dam was promised to be finished in ten days, or the army would have to leave us. I was doubtful about the time, but had no doubt about the ultimate success, if time would only permit. General Banks placed at the disposal of Colonel Bailey all the force he required, consisting of some 3,000 men, and 200 or 300 wagons. All the neighboring steam-mills were torn down for material; two or three regiments of Maine men were set at work felling trees, and on the second day after my arrival in Alexandria from Grand Ecore the work had fairly begun. Trees were falling with great rapidity, teams were moving in all directions, bringing in brick and stone; quarries were opened; flatboats were built to bring stone down from above; and every man seemed to be working with a vigor I have seldom seen equaled, while perhaps not one in fifty believed in the success of the undertaking. These falls are about a mile in length, filled with rugged rocks, over which, at the present state of water, it seemed to be impossible to make a channel.

"The work was commenced by running out from the left bank of the river a tree-dam, made of the bodies of very large trees, brush, brick and stone, cross-tied with heavy timber, and strengthened in every way which ingenuity could devise. This was run out about 300 feet into the river; four large coal-barges where then filled with brick and sunk at the end of it. From the right bank of the river, cribs filled with stone were built out to meet the barges, all of which was successfully accomplished, notwithstanding there was a current running of nine miles an hour, which threatened to sweep every thing before it. It will take too much time to enter into the details of this truly wonderful work; suffice it to say that the dam had nearly reached completion in eight days' working time, and the water had risen sufficiently on the upper falls to allow the Fort Hindman, Osage and Neosho to get down and to be ready to pass the dam. In another day it would have been high enough to enable all the other vessels to pass the upper falls. Unfortunately, on the morning of the 9th instant, the pressure of water became so great that it swept away two of the stone-barges which swung in below the dam on one side. Seeing this unfortunate accident, I jumped on a horse and rode up to where the upper vessels where anchored, and ordered the Lexington to pass the upper falls if possible, and immediately attempt to go through the dam. I thought I might be able to save the four vessels below, not knowing whether the persons employed on the work would ever have the heart to renew the enterprise. The Lexington succeeded in getting over the upper falls just in time, the water rapidly falling as she was passing over. She then steered directly for the opening in the dam, through which the water was rushing so furiously that it seemed as if nothing but destruction awaited her. Thousands of beating hearts looked on anxious for the result. The silence was so great as the Lexington approached the dam that a pin might almost have been heard to fall. She entered the gap with a full head of steam on, pitched down the roaring torrent, made two or three spasmodic rolls, hung for a moment on the rocks below, was then swept into deep water by the current, and rounded safely into the bank. Thirty thousand voices rose in one deafening cheer, and universal joy seemed to pervade the face of every man present. The Neosho followed next, all her hatches battened down, and every precaution taken against accident. She did not fare as well as the Lexington, her pilot having become frightened as he approached the abyss, and stopped her engine, when I particularly ordered a full head of steam to be carried. The result was that for a moment her hull disappeared from sight under the water. Every one thought she was lost. She rose, however, swept along over the rocks with the current, and fortunately escaped with only one hole in her bottom, which was stopped in the course of an hour. The Hindman and Osage both came through beautifully without touching a thing, and I thought if I was only fortunate enough to get my large vessels as well over the falls, my fleet once more would do good service on the Mississippi.

"The accident to the dam, instead of disheartening Colonel Bailey, only induced him to renew his exertions after he had seen the success of getting four vessels through. The noble-hearted soldiers, seeing their labor of the last eight days swept away in a moment, cheerfully went to work to repair damages, being confident now that all the gunboats would be finally brought over. The men had been working for eight days and nights, up to their necks in water, in the broiling sun, cutting trees and wheeling bricks, and nothing but good humor prevailed among them. On the whole, it was very fortunate the dam was carried away, as the two barges that were swept away from the centre swung around against some rocks on the left and made a fine cushion for the vessels, and prevented them, as it afterward appeared, from running on certain destruction. The force of the water and the current being too great to construct a continuous dam of six hundred feet across the river in so short a time, Colonel Bailey determined to leave a gap of fifty-five feet in the dam, and build a series of wing-dams on the upper falls. This was accomplished in three days' time, and on the 11th instant the Mound City, the Carondelet and Pittsburg came over the upper falls, a good deal of labor having been expended in hauling them through, the channel being very crooked, scarcely wide enough for them. Next day, the Ozark, Louisville, Chillicothe and two tugs also succeeded in crossing the upper falls. Immediately afterward, the Mound City, Carondelet and Pittsburg started in succession to pass the dam, all their hatches battened down and every precaution taken to prevent accident. The passage of these vessels was a most beautiful sight, only to be realized when seen. They passed over without an accident, except the unshipping of one or two rudders. This was witnessed by all the troops, and the vessels were heartily cheered when they passed over. Next morning, at 10 o'clock, the Louisville, Chillicothe, Ozark and two tugs passed over without any accident, except the loss of a man, who was swept off the deck of one of the tugs. By 3 o'clock that afternoon, the vessels were all coaled, ammunition replaced, and all steamed down the river with the convoy of transports in company. A good deal of difficulty was anticipated in getting over the bars in lower Red River—depth of water reported only five feet; gunboats were drawing six. Providentially, we had a rise from the back-water of the Mississippi, that river being very high at that time, the back-water extending to Alexandria, 150 miles distant, enabling us to pass all the bars and obstructions with safety. Words are inadequate to express the admiration I feel for the ability of Lieutenant-Colonel Bailey. This is without doubt the best engineering feat ever performed. Under the best circumstances, a private company would not have completed this work under one year, and to an ordinary mind the whole thing would have appeared an entire impossibility. Leaving out his ability as an engineer—the credit he has conferred upon the country—he has saved the Union a valuable fleet, worth nearly $2,000,000; more, he has deprived the enemy of a triumph which would have emboldened them to carry on this war a year or two longer, for the intended departure of the army, was a fixed fact, and there was nothing left for me to do in case that event occurred but to destroy every part of the vessels, so that the rebels could make nothing of them. The highest honors the Government can bestow on Colonel Bailey can never repay him for the service he has rendered the country. To General Banks, personally, I am much indebted for the happy manner in which he has forwarded this enterprise, giving it his whole attention night and day; scarcely sleeping while the work was going on; attending personally, to see that all the requirements of Colonel Bailey were complied with on the instant. I do not believe there ever was a case where such difficulties were overcome in such a short space of time, and without any preparation."

In the same report, Admiral Porter chronicles the loss of two small light-draft gunboats, the Signal and Covington, sent down the river to convoy a quartermaster's boat, the Warren, loaded with cotton and with 400 troops on board. The vessels were fired into by a series of masked batteries established by the enemy, thirty miles below Alexandria. "The first notice the vessel received of the battery was a furious fire which opened on the quartermaster's boat, the Warner, piercing her boilers, and completely disabling her. At the same time, 6,000 infantry opened with musketry, killing and wounding half the soldiers on the vessel. She drifted into the opposite bank, where a number managed to make their escape in the bushes, though many were killed in attempting to do so. The Signal and Covington immediately rounded to and opened their guns on the batteries, and pushed up, endeavoring to secure the Warner from her perilous position. They had, however, as much as they could do to take care of themselves, the cross-fire of the three batteries cutting them up in a terrible manner. Their steam-pipes were soon cut and their boilers perforated with shot, notwithstanding which they fought the batteries for five long hours, the vessels being cut all to pieces and many killed and wounded on board. Acting Volunteer Lieutenant George P. Lord, commanding the Covington, having expended all his shot, spiked his guns, set fire to his vessel, and escaped with what was left of his crew to the shore, and his vessel blew up. The Signal, Acting Volunteer Lieutenant Edward Morgan, still fought his guns for half an hour after the destruction of the Covington. He found it impossible to destroy his vessel by burning, her decks being covered with wounded, and humanity forbade him sacrificing the lives of the noble fellows who had defended their vessel so gallantly. He gave permission to all those who wished to escape to do so; some of them attempted to get away by climbing up the bank; many were killed while doing so by the murderous fire of musketry poured in from the opposite side. The captain remained by the vessel, and was captured, if he remained alive, but I have no information regarding him. The rebels took the guns off her, and, placing her across the channel as an obstruction, sunk her. General Banks, on hearing the news, sent out cavalry to hunt for the unfortunate men, many of whom were picked up and brought into Alexandria. A number escaped down the river and went aboard some light-draught gunboats that were coming up at the time to the scene of action, but were driven back by the superior artillery of the enemy. I feel very much for the poor fellows who fell into the hands of the enemy, as the latter have been very merciless to some of the prisoners they have taken, and committed outrages at which humanity shudders. The vessels will all return to their stations in a few days, as there is no prospect, under present circumstances, of renewing operations in this part of Louisiana, the season having passed for operating with any chance of success."

By an order of the War Department, dated May 7th, Major-General E. R. S. Canby was assigned to the command of the Military Division of West Mississippi, including the Departments of Arkansas and the Gulf. His arrival at the Red River was announced simultaneously with the withdrawal by General Banks of his force from Alexandria.

To the east of the Mississippi River, the important military positions in the southwestern corner of Tennessee was occasionally threatened by the rebel General Forrest, who, at the end of March advancing rapidly from Bolivar, Tenn., appeared with several thousand men before Union City, garrisoned by a small force of about 500 men, under Colonel Hawkins, of the Eleventh Tennessee Union Cavalry, who was compelled to surrender. Pursuing his course thence to Mayfield, General Forrest threatened Columbus and Paducah at the mouth of the Tennessee, appearing before the latter place with a force estimated at over 6,000 men, on the 25th of March. The town was held by Colonel S. G. Hicks, of the Fortieth Illinois Regiment, with about 700 men of the Kentucky and Illinois troops, including 250 colored soldiers in the artillery service. With this force he determined to defend the works at the place. Most of the inhabitants were removed or took their flight across the Ohio. Two gunboats at hand drew up to defend the town. Forrest on his arrival at once disposed his forces for attack, pushing forward his lines and occupying with his sharpshooters the houses commanding the fort. The first advance was met by a deadly fire from the works and repulsed. The gunboats shelled the houses which gave cover to the foe. At this crisis the surrender of the fort was demanded under a flag of truce, and gallantly refused by Colonel Hicks, who replied, that he was placed there to defend the works and should discharge his duty. Forrest's demand was thus stated: "If you surrender, you shall be treated as prisoners of war, but if I have to storm your works, you may expect no quarter." A second charge was made and repulsed, the assailants meanwhile plundering the town and occupying every available house with their sharpshooters. A number of buildings were burnt by them and others the next morning were set on fire by order of Colonel Hicks to prevent annoyance to the men in the fort. After repeated attempts to capture the garrison with his greatly superior force, Forrest, content with the pillage and injury he had inflicted, withdrew in the direction of Columbus. The Union loss is stated at fourteen killed and forty-six wounded; that of the enemy was heavy, being estimated in killed and wounded at over a thousand. Among their slain was Brigadier-General A. P. Thompson.

After various rumors of attack at different points, Forrest appeared before Fort Pillow, on the Mississippi, in Tennessee, on the 12th of April, which he made the scene of the most horrible outrages, utterly abhorrent to humanity. The incidents of this heart-sickening affair are thus detailed in an official report by Senator B. F. Wade and D. W. Gooch, two members of the Joint Committee of Congress on the Conduct of the War, specially sent to investigate the matter. "The garrison at Fort Pillow," according to this report, "amounted to 19 officers and 538 enlisted men, of whom 262 men were colored troops, comprising one battalion of the Sixth United States Heavy Artillery, formerly the First Alabama Artillery of colored troops, under the command of Major L. F. Booth, one section of the Second United States Light Artillery (colored), and one battalion of the Thirteenth Tennessee Cavalry (white), commanded by Major A. F. Bradford. Major Booth was the ranking officer, and was in command of the fort.

"On Monday, the 12th of April, the anniversary of the attack on Fort Sumter in April, 1861, the pickets of the garrison were driven in just before sunrise, that being the first intimation our forces there had of any intention on the part of the enemy to attack the place. Fighting soon became general, and about 9 o'clock Major Bradford succeeded to the command and withdrew all the forces within the fort. They had previously occupied some intrenchments at some distance from the fort and further from the river. The fort was situated on a high bluff, which descended precipitately to the river's edge, the ridge of the bluff on the river side being covered with trees, bushes and fallen timber. Extending back from the river on either side of the fort was a ravine or hollow, the one below the fort containing several private stores and some dwellings, and some Government buildings, containing commissary stores. The ravine above the fort forward, was known as Cold Bank Ravine, the ridge being covered with trees and bushes. To the right or below and a little to the front of the fort was a level piece of ground not quite so elevated as the fort itself, on which had been erected some log huts or shanties, which were occupied by the white troops, and also used for hospital and other purposes. Within the fort tents had been erected with board floors for the use of the colored troops. There were six pieces of artillery in the fort, consisting of two 6-pounders, two 12-pounder howitzers, and two 10-pounder Parrotts. The rebels continued their attack, but up to 2 or 3 o'clock in the afternoon they had not gained any decisive success. Our troops, both black and white, fought most bravely, and were in good spirits. The gunboat number 7 (New Era), Captain Marshall, took part in the conflict, shelling the rebels as opportunity offered. Signals had been agreed upon by which the officers in the fort could indicate where the guns of the boat would be most effective. There being but one gunboat there, no permanent impression appears to have been produced upon the enemy, for as they were shelled out of one ravine they would make their appearance in the other. They would thus appear and retire as the gunboat moved from one point to the other. About 1 o'clock the fire on both sides slackened somewhat, and the gunboat moved out in the river to cool and clean the guns, having fired 282 rounds of shell, shrapnel and canister, which nearly exhausted the supply of ammunition. The rebels, having thus far failed in their attack, now resorted to their customary flags of truce. The first flag of truce conveyed a demand from Forrest for the unconditional surrender of the fort. To this, Major Bradford replied, asking to be allowed one hour with his officers and the officers of the gunboat.

"In a short time the second flag of truce appeared, with a communication from Forrest that he would allow Major Bradford twenty minutes in which to move his troops out of the fort, and if it was not done in that time an assault would be ordered. To this Major Bradford replied that he would not surrender. During the time these flags were flying the rebels were moving down the ravine, and taking positions from which the more readily to charge upon the fort. Parties of them were also engaged in plundering the Government building and commissary and quartermaster stores, in full view of the gunboats. Captain Marshall states, that he refrained from firing upon the rebels, although they were thus violating a flag of truce, for fear that, if they should finally succeed in capturing the fort, they might justify any atrocities that might be committed by saying that they were done in retaliation for his firing while a flag of truce was flying. He says, however, that when he saw the rebels coming down the ravine above the fort, taking positions there, he got under way and stood for the fort; he determined to use what little ammunition he had left in shelling out the ravine. But he did not get up within effective range before the final assault was made. Immediately after the second flag of truce retired, the rebels made a rush from the positions they had so treacherously gained, and had obtained possession of the fort, raising the cry of 'no quarter.' But little opportunity was allowed for resistance. Our troops, black and white, threw down their arms and sought to escape by running down the steep bluff near the fort, and secreting themselves behind trees and logs in the bushes and under the brush; some even jumping into the river, leaving only their heads above the water as they crouched down under the bank. Then followed a scene of cruelty and murder without parallel in civilized warfare, which needed but the tomahawk and scalping-knife to exceed the worst atrocities ever committed by savages. The rebels commenced an indiscriminate slaughter, sparing neither age nor sex, white nor black, soldier nor civilian. The officers and men seemed to vie with each other in the devilish work. Men, women and their children, wherever found, were deliberately shot down, beaten and hacked with sabres. Some of the children, not more than ten years old, where forced to stand up and face their murderers while being shot. The sick and wounded were butchered without mercy, the rebels even entering the hospital buildings and dragging them out to be shot, or killing them as they lay there unable to offer the least resistance. All over the hill-side the work of murder was going on. Numbers of our men were collected together in lines or groups and deliberately shot. Some were shot while in the river, while others on the bank were shot and their bodies kicked into the water, many of them still living, but unable to make exertions to save themselves from drowing. Some of the rebels stood upon the top of the hill or a short distance from its side and called to our soldiers to come up to them, and as they approached, shot them down in cold blood, and if their guns or pistols missed fire, forcing them to stand there until they were again prepared to fire.

"All around were heard cries of 'no quarter,' 'no quarter,' 'kill the damned niggers,' 'shoot them down.' All who asked for mercy were answered by the most cruel taunts and sneers. Some were spared for a time, only to be murdered under circumstances of greater cruelty. No cruelty which the most fiendish malignity could devise was omitted by these murderers. One white soldier, who was wounded in the leg so as to be unable to walk, was made to stand up while his tormentors shot him. Others who were wounded and unable to stand up were held up and again shot. One negro, who had been ordered by a rebel officer to hold his horse, was killed by him when he remonstrated. Another, a mere child, whom an officer had taken up behind him on his horse, was seen by Chalmers, who at once ordered him to put him down and shoot him, which was done. The huts and tents in which many of the wounded had sought shelter were set on fire, both that night and the next morning, while the wounded were still in them, those only escaping who were able to get themselves out, or who could prevail on others less injured to help them out; and even some of these thus seeking to escape the flames were met by these ruffians and beastly shot down, or had their brains beaten out. One man was deliberately fastened down to the floor of a tent, face upward, by means of nails driven through his clothing and into the boards under him, so that he could not possibly escape, and then the tent was set on fire. Another was nailed to the side of a building outside of the fort, and then the building was set on fire and burned. The charred remains of five or six bodies were afterward found, all but one so much disfigured and consumed by the flames that they could not be identified, and the identification of that one is not absolutely certain, although there can hardly be a doubt it was the body of Lieutenant Albertson, Quartermaster of the Thirteenth Tennessee Cavalry, and a native of Tennessee. Several witnesses who saw the remains, and who were personally acquainted with him while living here, testified that it is their firm belief that it was his body that was thus treated.

"These deeds of murder and cruelty closed when night came on, only to be renewed the next morning, when the demons carefully sought among the dead lying about in all directions for any other wounded yet alive, and those they found were deliberately shot. Scores of the dead and wounded were found there the day of the massacre by the men from some of our gunboats, who were permitted to go on shore and collect the wounded and bury the dead. The rebels themselves had made a pretense of burying a great number of their victims, but they had merely thrown them, without the least regard to care or decency, into the trenches and ditches about the fort, or the little hollows and ravines on the hill-side, covering them but partially with earth. Portions of heads and faces, hands and feet, were found protruding through the earth in every direction, and even when your Committee visited the spot, two weeks afterward, although parties of men had been sent on there from time to time to bury the bodies unburied and re-bury the others, and were even then engaged in the same work, we found the evidences of this murder and cruelty still most painfully apparent. We saw bodies still unburied at some distance from the fort, of some sick men who had been met fleeing from the hospital and beaten down and brutally murdered, and their bodies left where they had fallen. We could see the faces and hands and feet of men, white and black, protruding out of the ground, whose graves had not been reached by those engaged in re-interring the victims of the massacre, and although a great deal of rain had fallen within the preceding two weeks, the ground, more especially on the side and at the foot of the bluff, where the most of the murders had been committed, was still discolored by the blood of our brave but unfortunate men; and the logs and trees showed but too plainly the evidences of the atrocities perpetrated there. Many other instances of equally atrocious cruelty might be enumerated; but your Committee feel compelled to refrain from giving here more of the heart-sickening details, and refer to the statements contained in the voluminous testimony herewith submitted. Those statements were obtained by them from eye-witnesses and sufferers. Many of them, as they were examined by your Committee, were lying upon beds of pain and suffering, some so feeble that their lips could with difficulty frame the words by which they endeavored to convey some idea of the cruelties which had been inflicted on them, and which they had seen inflicted on others.

"In reference to the fate of Major Bradford, who was in command of the fort when it was captured, and who had up to that time received no injury, there seems to be no doubt. The general understanding everywhere seemed to be that he had been brutally murdered the day after he was taken prisoner. How many of our troops thus fell victims to the malignity and barbarity of Forrest and his followers cannot be definitely ascertained. Two officers belonging to the garrison were absent at the time of the capture and massacre of the remaining officers; but two are known to be living, and they are wounded and now in the hospital at Mound City. One of them, Captain Porter, may even now be dead, as the surgeons, when your Committee were there, expressed no hope of his recovery. Of the men, from 300 to 400 are known to have been killed at Fort Pillow, of whom at least 300 were murdered in cold blood after the fort was in possession of the rebels and our men had thrown down their arms and ceased to offer resistance. Of the surviving, except the wounded in the hospital at Mound City, and the few who succeeded in making their escape unhurt, nothing definite is known, and it is to be feared that many have been murdered after being taken away from the fort. When your Committee arrived at Memphis, Tenn., they found and examined a man, Mr. McLagan, who had been conscripted by some of Forrest's forces, but who, with other conscripts, had succeeded in making his escape. He testifies that while two companies of rebel troops, with Major Bradford and many other prisoners, were on their march from Brownsville to Jackson, Tenn., Major Bradford was taken by five rebels, one an officer, led about fifty yards from the line of march and deliberately murdered in view of all those assembled. He fell, instantly killed by three musket balls, even while asking that his life might be spared, as he had fought them manfully and was deserving of a better fate. The motive for the murder of Major Bradford seems to have been the simple fact that, although a native of the South, he remained loyal to his Government."*

On Sunday, April 17, an attack was commenced by the confederate Brigadier-General R. F. Hoke, with a force estimated at 10,000 and a heavy artillery train, upon the Union post at Plymouth, N. C., commanded by General Wessells, with about 2,000 effective men. The town, situated on the south bank of the Roanoke, near its entrance into Albemarle Sound, was protected by Forts Gray, Wessells, and Williams and other minor works on the river, and by a squadron of gunboats of inferior construction, but sufficient for the ordinary defence of the region. They were five in number, Lieutenant Commander Flusser, a gallant and much esteemed officer of the Navy in the Miami, being the senior in command. On this occasion, however, they were met by a more powerful antagonist in a ram (the Albemarle), which was brought down the river by the rebels. The first attack made by the enemy upon Fort Gray, about a mile up the river, was gallantly resisted, and in several assaults upon the other forts on Monday they were repulsed with slaughter, the Union gunboats assisting in the work. One of the latter, the Bombshell, was disabled and sunk by the enemy's battery. Early in the morning of Tuesday, before daylight, the rebel ram, a powerful iron-clad vessel, armed with two heavy guns, came down the river, passing Fort Gray and making for the gunboat Southfield formerly a Staten Island ferry-boat in the bay of New York, which she struck with her prow and caused to sink immediately. The Southfield was at the time lashed to the Miami, and the guns of both vessels having been employed the previous evening in firing on the enemy on shore, were loaded with shell. At the first discharge, directed by Lieutenant Commander Flusser himself, he was instantly killed by a fragment of shell which rebounded, piercing his chest and skull. He was a gallant officer of the Navy, and his death was much lamented. The Miami and remaining gunboats were now compelled to retire, and as they were relied upon as the main defence of the town in case of a serious attack, General Wessells was forced on Wednesday, after a further obstinate defence, to surrender with the garrison at Plymouth. The Union loss in killed and wounded was stated at about 150 ; that of the enemy was doubtless much larger. On receipt of this intelligence at Newbern, the headquarters of the Department, Major-General J. G. Peck, issued the following general order, announcing the event to the Army : "With feelings of the deepest sorrow, the Commanding General announces the fall of Plymouth, N. C., and the capture of its gallant commander, Brigadier-General H. W. Wessells, and his command. This result, however, did not obtain until after the most gallant and determined resistance had been made. Five times the enemy stormed the lines of the General, and as many times were they repulsed with great slaughter, and but for the powerful assistance of the rebel iron-clad ram and the floating sharpshooter battery, the "Cotton Plant," Plymouth would still have been in our hands. For their noble defence the gallant General Wessells and his brave band have and deserve the warmest thanks of the whole country, while all will sympathize with them in their misfortune. To the officers and men of the Navy the Commanding General tenders his thanks for their hearty

* Report to both Houses of Congress, May 5th, 1864.

co-operation with the army, and the bravery, determination, and courage that marked their part of the unequal contest. With sorrow he records the death of the noble sailor and gallant patriot, Lieutenant Commander C. W. Flusser, U. S. Navy, who in the heat of battle fell dead on the deck of his ship, with the lanyard of his gun in his hand. The Commanding General believes that these misfortunes will tend not to discourage but to nerve the Army of North Carolina to equal deeds of bravery and gallantry hereafter."

The loss of Plymouth was followed by the evacuation of the town of Washington, on the Pamlico River, when the garrison was taken to reinforce Newbern, the defences of which were strengthened by General Palmer, who succeeded to General Peck in command of the Department. On the 5th of May the rebel ram Albemarle, in company with the Cotton Plant and her capture, the Bombshell, was met in Albemarle Sound by a squadron of Union gunboats, including the Miami, when the Bombshell was retaken and a gallant effort made to run down the Albemarle by Lieutenant-Commander Francis Roe, of the Sassacus. The formidable ram fairly staggered in the encounter when an action ensued between the two vessels sustained by the Sassacus with great gallantry. Though the boiler of the latter was pierced by a 100-pound Parrott shot from her adversary, and the vessel was filled with steam, her guns were so well directed at close quarters, within a few feet, as to enter the port-holes of the Albemarle, and compel her to retire disabled to Plymouth. The Union loss in this affair was eight killed, twenty-six wounded, and several badly scalded by steam. Newbern was thus relieved from a threatened naval attack. For their gallantry in this engagement, the officers of the Sassacus, including James M. Hobbey, the engineer, whose presence of mind was eminently displayed in the action, received various degrees of promotion.*

* See an account of "The Fight with the Albemarle." *Army and Navy Journal*, May 28th, 1864.

CHAPTER XCVIII.

GENERAL GRANT'S CAMPAIGN IN VIRGINIA. FROM THE RAPIDAN TO JAMES RIVER, MAY AND JUNE, 1864.

On the 12th of March, 1864, an important order was issued from the War Department, reorganizing the chief military commands for the ensuing campaign. Major-General Halleck was, at his own request, relieved from duty as General-in-Chief of the Army, and General U. S. Grant, who a short time previously had been nominated by the President and confirmed by the Senate to the high rank of Lieutenant-General, was assigned "to the command of the armies of the United States. The headquarters of the Army (it was added) will be at Washington, and also with Lieutenant-General Grant in the field." Major-General Halleck was assigned to duty in Washington, as Chief of Staff of the Army, under the direction of the Secretary of War and the Lieutenant-General Commanding.

A few days previous to the issuing of this order, on the 9th, General Grant, on his arrival at Washington, was formally presented by President Lincoln with his commission as Lieutenant-General. The ceremony took place in the Cabinet chamber, in the presence of the entire Cabinet, General Halleck, Representative Lovejoy, General Rawlings, and Colonel Comstock of General Grant's staff, the son of General Grant, and Mr. Nicolay, the Private Secretary of the President. General Grant having entered the room, the President arose and addressed him thus: "General Grant—The nation's appreciation of what you have done, and its reliance upon you for what remains to be done in the existing great struggle, is now presented with this commission, constituting you Lieutenant-General in the Army of the United States. With this high honor devolves upon you also a corresponding responsibility. As the country herein trusts you, so, under God, it will sustain you. I scarcely need to add, that with what I here speak for the nation goes my own hearty personal concurrence." To which General Grant replied as follows: "Mr. President—I accept the commission with gratitude for the high honor conferred. With the aid of the noble armies that have fought on so many fields for our common country, it will be my earnest endeavor not to disappoint your expectations. I feel the full weight of the responsibilities now devolving upon me, and I know that if they are met, it will be due to those armies, and above all to the favor of that Providence which leads both nations and men."

The re-organization of the Army of the Potomac under General Meade followed immediately upon the call of General Grant to the chief command. In view of the reduced strength of nearly all the regiments serving in the army, the number of corps was reduced from five to three, leaving the Second, Fifth and Sixth respectively commanded by Majors-General Hancock, G. W. Warren (succeeding Major-General George Sykes) and Sedgwick. The First and Third Corps, lately commanded by Major-Generals W. H. French and John Newton, were distributed among the other corps. Major-General Pleasonton, so honorably distinguished at the head of the Cavalry Corps, was relieved, and Major-General Philip Henry Sheridan assigned to his command. The latter, in the prime of manhood, in his thirty-third year, was, as we have seen, among the foremost for valor and success in the campaigns in Kentucky and Tennessee from Perryville, through the battles of Murfreesboro', Chattanooga, Chickamauga to Missionary Ridge. In selecting him for his new command—of the highest importance and responsibility—General Grant recognized his well-tried ability in the field. The Lieutenant-General immediately on receiving his appointment visited the headquarters of the army at Culpepper, and extended his tour of inspection to the command of General Butler at Fortress Monroe. He was accompanied to the latter place by General W. F. Smith, destined in his command of the Eighteenth Corps, to bear an important part in the ensuing operations on the James River, whither also General Gillmore, with his Tenth Army Corps, was ordered from the scene of his recent operations at Charleston. Every thing on both sides portended an immediate and fiercely contested resumption of the war in Virginia. The rebel conscription had reinforced Lee's veteran army in its long established and well-defended lines formidably entrenched in his most advantageous position south of the Rapidan, with his headquarters at Orange Court House, his left guarded by the southwest Mountains of the Blue Ridge, his right extending to the Rappahannock. To the north of the Rapidan, with its line of communication by the Orange and Alexandria Railroad, lay the Union army, threatening its adversary and guarding the approaches to Washington. General Grant's headquarters was established at Culpepper. On the 8th of April, he issued an order sounding the note of preparation for the impending conflict. Public and private property, for which transportation was not provided, was ordered to the rear; sutlers and civilians, other than Government employees, members of the Sanitary and Christian Commissions, and registered newspaper correspondents, were required to leave within a week, and the granting of furloughs was vigorously interdicted.

At the beginning of May, on the 4th, the following address to the army was issued by General Meade: "Soldiers—Again you are called upon to advance on the enemies of your country. The time and the occasion are deemed opportune by your Commanding-General to address you a few words of confidence and caution. You have been recognized, strengthened and fully equipped in every respect. You form a part of the several armies of your country—the whole under the direction of an able and distinguished General, who enjoys the confidence of the Government, the people and the Army. Your movement being in cooperation with others, it is of the utmost importance that no effort should be left unspared to make it successful. Soldiers, the eyes of the whole country are looking with anxious hope to the blow you are about to strike in the most sacred cause that ever called men to arms. Remember your homes, your wives and children, and bear in mind that the sooner your enemies are overcome the sooner you will be returned to enjoy the benefits and blessings of peace. Bear with patience the hardships and sacrifices you will be called upon to endure. Have confidence in your officers and in each other. Keep your ranks on the march and on the battle-field, and let each man earnestly implore God's blessing, and endeavor by his thoughts and actions to render himself worthy of the favor he seeks. With clear consciences and strong arms, actuated by a high sense of duty, fighting to preserve the Government and the institutions handed down to us by our forefathers, if true to ourselves, victory, under God's blessing, must and will attend our efforts."

The actual movement began on Tuesday, the 3d, when the army broke camp and commenced its Southern march towards Richmond on the right of the enemy's position. Two cavalry divisions under Generals Gregg and Wilson were sent forward with pontoon trains in the afternoon, and about midnight had secured the means of crossing at Ely's and Germanna Fords on the Rapidan. The Second Army Corps, under Hancock, was moved rapidly forward by the former route, and the Fifth and Sixth, under Warren and Sedgwick, took the latter. The enemy appeared taken by surprise, the fords being unguarded; and the passage of the army was successfully accomplished on Wednesday, General Burnside's Ninth Corps being held in reserve on the left bank of the river, and Sheridan's Cavalry to the south in the advance. The route which the army had taken led directly through the wild tract of barren country, known as the Wilderness, the scene of General Hooker's operations of the previous year. Hancock moved in the direction of Chancellorsville, Warren having crossed above was a few miles farther to the west at Old Wilderness Tavern, and Sedgwick in his rear toward the river. The army of General Lee occupying the line from Orange to Louisa Court House was in a position to operate on the flank of the Union forces in their advance to the open country beyond, two roads—the Chancellorsville turnpike, and plank road—striking them at right angles. Lee was prompt to seize this advantage, and accordingly sent forward two corps of his army, Ewell's, by the turnpike, and Hill's by the plank road, to attack his enemy on their advance. The arrival of these forces on Thursday brought on a general engagement. The line of General Grant was parallel with the Germanna road to the west, running generally north and south, Sedgwick holding the right, Warren the centre, and Hancock, who had been ordered round from Chancellorsville, the left. It was the object of Lee in advancing on the cross-roads to divide the army and cut off its communications with the river, with the hope, doubtless, in thus striking it on the march before its position was established, of dealing it an effectual blow. The plan was well conceived, but Grant, though he might have chosen another ground for the struggle, was ready for the emergency. He had determined to go forward at all hazards, and was not to be arrested by the prospect of hard fighting under disadvantageous circumstances in the Wilderness. There were two main actions during the day on the right and left of the Union lines, the enemy in both instances being vigorously assailed. In the words of General Lee's dispatch at evening from the field, "A strong attack was made upon Ewell, who repulsed it, capturing many prisoners and four pieces of artillery. The enemy subsequently concentrated upon General Hill, who, with his and Wilcox's divisions, successfully resisted the repeated and desperate assaults. A large force of cavalry and artillery on our right were driven back by Rossan's brigade. By the blessings of God we maintained position against every effort until night, when the combat closed. We have to mourn the loss of many brave officers and men. Gallant Brigadier-General J. M. Jones was killed, and General Stafford, I fear, mortally wounded, while leading his command with conspicuous valor."

In these encounters, which, from the nature of the ground forbidding generally the use of artillery and cavalry, were mostly confined to infantry, both sides suffered heavily, the fighting being of the most determined character. The losses were large in Warren's corps, which, from its position, bore the brunt of the engagements—Griffin's division leading the attack, succeeded by Wadsworth's and Robinson's. In Hancock's corps the divisions of Birney, Barlow and Gibbon were successively engaged. Birney's division lost its second brigade commander, General Alexander Hays, a native of Pennsylvania. He was a graduate of West Point with Hancock and Pleasonton; had served with distinction in the Mexican War, then left the Army, and at the outbreak of the rebellion relinquished his occupation as an iron manufacturer in his native State to re-enter the service. He was with McClellan on the Peninsula, and had been wounded in command of his brigade at Chancellorsville. He had of late served with distinction in Warren's corps. The fighting of this first day was carried late into the evening, neither party gaining any material advantage. It was but the beginning of a contest to be resumed on the morrow. Burnside's division was brought over the river into the field during the day.

A general attack at daylight was ordered by Grant, and at dawn both armies were resolutely engaged. Victory was eagerly sought by each, and had the ground been such as to admit of manœuvering the large forces opposed to one another, a decisive action might have been fought. As it was, the battle extended along the whole line, a distance of seven miles from Sedgwick's right to Hancock's left. With varying success, a vigorous attempt of the enemy to flank on the right was defeated after a sharp contest. Hancock on the left, prompt in the assault at 5 o'clock in the morning, advanced his forces, increased by several divisions from the other corps, and drove the enemy for two miles till they were reinforced by Longstreet's command, which had lately rejoined Lee's army, and now came up by a rapid march. A number of prisoners were taken by Hancock in this movement. A vigorous attack was made in the afternoon by the joint forces of Longstreet and Hill upon the left and centre, which taxed all the resources of Hancock's command. It was effectually resisted after a short and desperate struggle. A second attempt of the enemy at evening on the right was more successful. General Seymour's brigade at the extremity of the line was routed, and that officer taken prisoner, but by the efforts of General Sedgwick no substantial advantage was gained; Sheridan's cavalry, as before, firmly held the advance on our left. Our losses in the right wing, it was estimated, fell very little below 6,000, of which 4,000 probably occurred during the enemy's assault. Our losses in the Second Corps ranged in the neighborhood of 3,000. Our total loss in the two days' fighting must be not far from 15,000 men. Probably that of the enemy was no less severe. In these battles there was an unusual proportion of wounded among the casualties, arising from the fact that so little artillery was used on either side.* Among the casualties of the rebel officers, General Longstreet was reported wounded.

In a dispatch dated Washington, May 8th, from Stanton, the Secretary of War, to General Dix in command at New York, the first of a series of official statements by which the public was advised of the progress of the campaign, it was announced, "We have no official reports from the front, but the Medical Director has notified the Surgeon General that our wounded were being sent to Washington, and will number from 6,000 to 8,000. The Chief Quartermaster of the Army of the Potomac has made requisition for seven days' grain, and for railroad construction trains, and states the enemy is reported to be retiring. This indicates General Grant's advance, and affords an inference of material success on our part. The enemy's strength has always been most felt in his first blows, and their having failed, and our forces not only having maintained their ground, but preparing to advance, lead to the hope of full and complete success, for when either party fails, disorganization by straggling and desertion commences, and the enemy's loss in killed and wounded must weaken him more than we are weakened."

Brigadier-General James S. Wadsworth, commanding the Fourth Division of General Warren's corps, fell mortally wounded about noon on Friday while leading his troops in action. His death was much regretted. He was one of the most gallant officers who had risen to high command in the army from civil life. The son of one of the wealthiest landed proprietors of the State of New York, he had freely employed his resources in the service of the public. Previous to the war, he was appointed by the Legislature of his State a delegate to the Peace Convention held in Washington in 1861. At the outbreak of the rebellion he promptly came to the support of the Government, and sought employment in the field. As volunteer aid to General McDowell at Bull Run, as Military Governor to the District of Columbia, and as a division commander in the Army of the Potomac at Gettysburg, where he was actively engaged, and elsewhere, he had fully proved his resolution and courage. Various tributes were paid to his memory, among the most significant being that of his political opponent and recent successful competitor for the Governor's Chair of his native State. In a general order issued at Albany on the 10th of May, Governor Seymour wrote: "I announce with painful feelings the loss of James S. Wadsworth in the recent battles on the Rapidan. He met death bravely at the

* *Army and Navy Journal*, May 14th, 1864.

head of the forces under his command. A leading and wealthy citizen, he exercised a wide influence by the vigor and energy of his character. As a public man, he was always decided and resolute in demanding purity of legislation and the economical and wise administration of the affairs of our own State, long prominent among us in civil life. When the war broke out he was prompt and among the first to join the Army. From the outset an ardent supporter of the war, to him belongs the merit of freely periling his own person in upholding the opinions which he advocated. Assigned at once to a high military position, he has been up to the day of his death actively and earnestly devoting himself to the performance of his military duties." On Saturday, the 7th, there was some skirmishing in the morning in front, but it soon became evident that Lee was withdrawing his main force toward Spottsylvania Court House, whither General Grant at once pushed with his army. The Union cavalry, already in advance at Todd's Tavern favored the movement. In the afternoon there was a sharp cavalry engagement with the enemy at the front, which was gallantly maintained by the Union forces under Custer, Gregg, and others.

Leaving General Grant's army in its march, we turn to the movements of General Butler's column, which, while the events we have narrated were going on, had gained a brilliant advantage in another quarter of the military area destined to be of the first importance in the prosecution of the campaign in Virginia. The plan of operations, it is said, was suggested or recommended by General Butler to General Grant when the latter, on assuming command, visited Fortress Monroe. As carried out, it began in a preliminary military occupation and settlement at Yorktown as if for the purpose of advancing by the former direct river and railroad route against Richmond. At Yorktown, accordingly, at the end of April was concentrated a force consisting of the Eighteenth Army Corps, drawn from various posts in North Carolina and Virginia, the command of which was given to Major-General W. F. Smith, familiarly known as "Baldy Smith," one of the most efficient of General Grant's officers in securing his recent victories in the South-west. Co-operating with this command, the Tenth Army Corps of General Gillmore was gathered on the opposite bank of the York River, at Gloucester Point. The show of military preparation was actively kept up in this region, while transports were collecting and the naval equipment set in order for the real movement on the James River, which was to be made simultaneously with the advance of General Grant. To deceive the enemy and distract his attention, a brigade of troops at the very last moment was sent up the York River to the White House Landing, where, at the time General Butler's army was in motion, they were employed in constructing a wharf. The deception was complete. When all was ready, on Wednesday, the 4th, the transport steamers were sent from Fortress Monroe to the mouth of York River to take on board the troops, and that night they were quietly brought down to Hampton Roads. The ascent of the James River was to commence at daybreak, the fleet consisting of the transports, preceded by three army gunboats under Brigadier-General Graham, with a naval force of four monitors, the iron-clad Atlanta and ten gunboats under Rear-Admiral Lee. There was some detention in getting both army corps under way, but at 8 o'clock all preliminaries were arranged, and the expedition began the ascent of the river. The object in view was the occupation of the neck of land at City Point, on the right bank, where the Appomattox empties into the James, a position about fifteen miles from Richmond and ten from Petersburg, consequently threatening both places, and within easy striking distance of the important southern line of railway running between. There were two points on the way up the river at which opposition might be expected, at Wilson's Landing, at a bend of the stream on the left bank about thirty-five miles below Richmond, and at Fort Powhatan, at the next turn on the right. At neither place was there any force to offer resistance to the body of negro troops which General Butler landed to take possession, nor did he meet any opposition on arriving in the afternoon at City Point. The surprise was complete. The troops were landed without difficulty, and before the next morning had secured the station at City Point and a most desirable foothold in the triangular district of Bermuda Hundred, a peninsula bounded on three sides by the Appomattox and winding James River. An easy entrenchment on the west, with the gunboats on the flanks, completed the defences of this enviable position.

The movements of this important day were communicated in the following dispatch of General Butler to General Grant at evening: "We have seized Wilson's Wharf Landing. A brigade of Wild's colored troops are there. At Fort Powhatan Landing, two regiments of the same brigade have landed. At City Point, Hink's division, with the remaining troops and battery, have landed. The remainder of both the Eighteenth and Tenth Army Corps are being landed at Bermuda Hundred, above the Appomattox. No opposition experienced thus far. The movement was apparently a complete surprise. Both army corps left Yorktown during last night. The monitors are all over the bar at Harrison's Landing and above City Point. The operations of the fleet have been conducted to day with energy and success. Generals Smith and Gillmore are pushing the landing of the men. General Graham, with the army gunboats, led the advance during the night, capturing the signal station of the rebels. Colonel West, with 1,800 cavalry, made several demonstrations from Williamsburg yesterday morning. General Kautz left Suffolk this morning, with his cavalry, for the service indicated during the conference with the Lieutenant-General. The New York, flag of truce boat, was found lying at the wharf, with 400 prisoners, whom she had not time to deliver. She went up yesterday morning. We are landing troops during the night, a hazardous service, in the face of the enemy."

Colonel West's cavalry was successful in their diversion of the enemy on the peninsula. Of the expedition of General Kautz, a gallant cavalry officer, distinguished by his recent services in Ohio, we shall have more to relate presently. The day following the landing at City Point a reconnoissance was made of the enemy's position on the Petersburg road by General Heckman, in which there was some skirmishing on the Port Walthall branch of the railway. This was followed on the 7th by the advance of five brigades under General Brooks, in a demonstration upon the railway. While the enemy was engaged with the main force below, the left and centre, under Heckman and Brooks, a brigade on the right, commanded by Colonel Barton of New York, succeeded in striking the railway, setting fire to a bridge and destroying a portion of the track. The enemy bringing up reinforcements, the Union force retired in the afternoon with a loss of about 250 killed and wounded. On the afternoon of the 6th, the Commodore Jones, a small navy gunboat, was destroyed by a torpedo while on a reconnoissance ascending James River. The paymaster, Mr. E. T. Chapman, was killed, and about fifty of the crew killed and wounded. Another attempt in force upon the Petersburg road was made on Monday, the

9th, when Generals Smith and Gillmore struck the railway at Port Walthall and Chester, and advanced to Swift Creek within two miles of Petersburg. Here the enemy was driven from their rifle-pits in a charge by General Heckman, but maintained themselves at an earthwork commanding the passage of the stream. The same day, General Butler, in a dispatch to Secretary Stanton, summed up the operations in his department. An old actor in the Virginia campaigns, it will be seen, is introduced on the stage in General Beauregard, who, with his forces relieved by the departure of Gillmore from before Charleston, was following that officer to the North. "With 1,700 cavalry we have advanced up the Peninsula, forced the Chickahominy, and have safely brought them to our present position. These were colored cavalry, and are now holding position as our advance toward Richmond. General Kautz, with 3,000 cavalry from Suffolk, on the same day with our movement up the James River, forced the Blackwater and burnt the railroad bridge at Stony Creek, below Petersburg, cutting in two Beauregard's forces at that point. We have landed here, intrenched ourselves, destroyed many miles of railroad, and got a position which, with proper supplies, we can hold against the whole of Lee's army. I have ordered up the supplies. Beauregard, with a large portion of his command was left south of the cutting of the railroad by General Kautz. That portion which reached Petersburg under Hill I have whipped to-day, killing and wounding many, and taking many prisoners, after a severe and well-contested fight. Lieutenant-General Grant will not be troubled with any further reinforcements to Lee from Beauregard's forces."

Returning to the army of General Grant, we find the several corps pressing on during the afternoon and night of Saturday toward Spottsylvania Court House, the vicinity of which they reached the next day to find the enemy there already in position. Longstreet, by a forced march with his corps, had gained the advantage. There was opposition at every step. A battle was fought on Saturday by Warren's corps on the Brock Road, from Todd's Tavern, at a clearing near Alsop's farm, in which the enemy, in force, were encountered by the brigades of Bartlett and Robinson, with heavy loss to their commands, General Robinson being severely wounded. At this juncture, General Warren rallied his troops in person, the other portions of his corps were brought up under Generals Crawford and Cutler, who had succeeded Wadsworth, and, after further severe fighting, the rebel position was carried. Warren's loss in this engagement was stated at 1,500.* Fredericksburg, a new and temporary base of supplies and hospital station, was occupied by the Union forces on Sunday night. The number of the wounded at this time was estimated at about 12,000. Monday, the 9th, found the two armies confronting one another, Longstreet and Ewell occupying a formidable ridge before Spottsylvania Court House. There was some cannonading and skirmishing in the forenoon between the two lines, in the course of which the Union army met with a serious disaster, in the loss of General Sedgwick, commanding the Sixth Division. This gallant officer—whose honorable record in the Army of the Potomac is second to none, from its early organization through the stirring engagements at Yorktown, Fair Oaks, in the Seven Days' Battles before Richmond; at Antietam, where he was twice wounded, and subsequently, in command of his corps—after meeting the enemy so often in action, fell, struck by a bullet from a sharpshooter, while directing the mounting of a cannon in

* Swinton's Narrative of the Campaign, *New York Times*, May 13th, 1864.

an intrenchment. The ball had entered the face and passed through the head, causing his death immediately. No officer was more popular in the service, his character being distinguished by amiability, a certain plain sincerity and honesty of purpose, and an invincible devotion to the straightforward duties of his profession, which raised his corps to an honorable distinction in the army. Brigadier-General H. G. Wright, of Sedgwick's corps, was placed in command as his successor.

At evening of Monday, General Hancock, who now held the right of the Union line—Warren having the centre, and Wright the left—advanced against the enemy on a branch of the Po River, at the Block House Road, when a severe contest ensued with heavy losses. There was also some sharp fighting by Burnside's corps on the left. News of the recent engagements and of the advance of General Grant having now reached Washington, showing at least that the retreat after the somewhat similar last year's encounter at Chancellorsville was not to be repeated, the President issued the following brief bulletin, dated "Executive Mansion, May 9th. *To the Friends of Union and Liberty*—Enough is known of army operations within the last five days, to claim our especial gratitude to God. While what remains undone demands our most sincere prayers to, and reliance upon, Him (without whom all human effort is vain), I recommend that all patriots, at their homes, at their places of public worship, and wherever they may be, unite in common thanksgiving and prayer to Almighty God.

"ABRAHAM LINCOLN."

The next day, Tuesday the 10th, was marked by fierce and determined fighting before Spottsylvania, the conflict opening in the morning with a heavy discharge of artillery, now for the first brought into effective use from the Union positions, and skirmishing of Burnside's corps on the left, followed by a vigorous attack of Warren's and Hancock's corps on the enemy's centre. Repeated charges were made with great gallantry, in one of which General James C. Rice, commanding a brigade of the division was killed, a loss much regretted, not merely in the army, where he was greatly beloved by his command, but by a large circle of friends throughout the country, who were acquainted with his ardent patriotism and high religious character. A native of Massachusetts and graduate of Yale College, he had been employed as a teacher and editor in the South, and recently as a lawyer in New York. At the breaking out of the war, led by a pure spirit of devotion to his country, he had joined the Garibaldi Guard, a regiment raised in that city, as a private, and had risen by his ability to the lieutenant-colonelcy of another New York regiment, the Forty-fourth, known as the Ellsworth Avengers, with which he had served through the Peninsula and Maryland campaigns, being promoted colonel; and finally, for his gallantry at Gettysburg, brigadier-general. He was a member of the Presbyterian Church. In the words of his friend, the Rev. Dr. Adams, who pronounced his eulogy when his remains were received in New York on their way to interment at his birthplace: "He loved God and his country, and his country because he loved his God." He died a noble example of the Christian warrior.

Another distinguished general officer fell on the field this day, Brigadier-General Thomas G. Stevenson, in command of a division of Burnside's corps. He died at the early age of twenty-eight. The son of a gentlemen of Boston, Mass., he was led by his rank in the local militia, to recruit an infantry regiment for the war, in command of which he joined General Burnside's North Carolina Expedition, had a distinguished part in the capture of Newbern, and was subsequently engaged in various responsible movements into the interior, being appointed a brigadier-general at the close of 1862. He was afterward in the South Carolina Department, engaged in the operations on Morris Island, previous to his joining his old commander, General Burnside. He was much esteemed by him for his personal and military qualities.

The contest begun on the morning of the 10th resulted, after several hours' hard fighting, in the enemy checking the advance of the Union centre, and turning the right across the Po, so as to compel the withdrawal of Barlow's division of Hancock's corps, at that point, to the east bank. At evening, a gallant assault was made by General Upton's and Russell's brigades of Wright's corps, in which the enemy's works were scaled, the first line of rifle-pits captured, and more than 1,000 prisoners taken, with several guns. This advance, however, was not maintained, and the night, "as always before, closed on a hard-fought but indecisive field. Our loss had been not less than 10,000 men; but the rebels had suffered quite as severely as ourselves."* The campaign, evidently not to be decided by a single battle, was now beginning to take a determinate form, with a prospect of continuous fighting, the two armies being equally matched with a skill on the part of their commanders which would not be likely to allow to either any great advantage. Both armies had fought with desperate heroism and with fearful losses. Lee's army stood firmly across the path successfully contesting the road to Richmond; but General Grant, firmly bent on the object of the campaign, was fully determined, at whatever cost, to continue the struggle. A dispatch which he sent to Secretary Stanton from the field, on the morning of Wednesday 11th, expressed this resolution in pointed terms: "We have now ended," said he, "the sixth day of very heavy fighting. The result to this time is much in our favor. Our losses have been heavy, as well as those of the enemy. I think the enemy's must be greater. We have taken over 5,000 prisoners in battle, while he has taken from us but few except stragglers. I propose to fight it out on this line, if it takes all summer." Wednesday, this day, there was a comparative lull in operations, though skirmishing was kept up during the forenoon, and reconnoitering of the enemy's lines, with a view to further results. In the afternoon, the intense heat which had prevailed during the late period of hard fighting, was allayed by a welcome thunder shower. During the night, Hancock's corps was shifted from his position on the right to the left, occupying the ground between Generals Wright and Burnside. At the dawn of Thursday, the movement, concealed by a thick mist, he pushed forward his command—the divisions of Barlow, Birney, Gibbon, and Mott—gallantly advancing over the intervening ground and taking the enemy completely by surprise, forced the first and second lines of their works, capturing the whole of General Edward Johnson's division and part of Early's, together with Major-General Johnson, General George H. Stuart, and from thirty to forty cannon. About 3,000 prisoners were taken. It was a most gallant assault, and its brilliant execution, in connection with the news just received of Sheridan's successful cavalry raid in the enemy's rear, raised the spirits of the army to a high pitch of enthusiasm. The action now became general. Burnside's and Wright's troops joined in the conflict, while Warren occupied the enemy in front. Roused to the danger, the enemy made repeated attempts to re-occupy the lost works, but were repulsed with heavy slaughter by the Union batteries and the musketry of the infantry; an advantage which the foe, in turn, maintained in front, where they

* *Army and Navy Journal*, May 14th, 1864.

were strongly posted. The contest for the works captured in the morning was continued through the day, Burnside, on the extreme left, being engaged in the afternoon in a stubborn and bloody encounter with the enemy, in which he held his ground, though unable to push the flanking movement of the day further in that quarter. The result of the whole engagement was a brilliant success to the Union arms. At evening, General Grant sent a dispatch to Secretary Stanton: "The eighth day of battle closes, leaving between 3,000 and 4,000 prisoners in our hands for the day's work, including two general officers, and over thirty pieces of artillery. The enemy are obstinate, and seem to have found the last ditch. We have lost no organization, not even a company, whilst we have destroyed and captured one division (Johnson's), one brigade (Dobbs'), and one regiment entire of the enemy." On the 13th, Secretary Stanton announced in a bulletin: "A dispatch from the Commissary of Prisoners at Belle Plain, announces the arrival there of over 7,000 prisoners, including 400 officers, with Major-General Johnson and Brigadier-General Stuart."

Several anecdotes were related of the capture of Johnson's division. "A most interesting scene," writes a correspondent on the field at 7 A. M., "is now before us at headquarters. Major-General Edward Johnson, who, with his whole division, was captured this morning, has just been brought up under charge of an officer, to headquarters in the woods, where Generals Grant and Meade and their staffs are seated around a bivouac fire. General Meade, who had been an old friend of General Johnson, shook hands with him and introduced him to General Grant.

"'Formerly of the Sixth Infantry?' inquires the Lieutenant-General. 'Yes,' replies the rebel General; 'you were of the Fourth, and we were both in the same brigade.' Of course, military etiquette precluded any other inquiries than those of a purely personal character. To the question whether General Wadsworth was dead, he replied that such was his belief, though he was not positive. Our Generals Seymour and Shaler, who were captured in the battle of the Wilderness, he had yesterday seen at Lee's headquarters. Longstreet he reports as severely but not mortally wounded. Almost all the staff appear to have been old friends and acquaintances of Johnson, and numerous mutual inquiries in regard to old army comrades are being made. General Hunt, Chief of Artillery, when he met him, had a mind to make a set speech, but the old familiar formula, 'Ed, I'm glad to see you,' came out in a salutation to which Johnson replied: 'Well, Hunt, under the circumstances, I am not glad to see you.' He spoke of the abomination of such a country as the Wilderness to fight in; spoke of the capture of his division, but said, with a quiet, good-natured manner, that we would have a 'hot time of it yet.'"* When Stuart, on his capture, was brought to General Hancock, the latter, it is said, offered his hand, saying frankly, "'How are you, Stuart?' To this the rebel officer replied, 'I am, General Stuart, of the confederate army; and, under present circumstances, I decline to take your hand.' To this, Hancock promptly and wittily replied, 'And, under any other circumstances, General, I should not have offered it.'"†

On the morning of Friday, the 13th, it was found that the enemy had fallen back on our left to a new defensive position. Encouraged by this success, and the valor of the army in the recent engagements, General Meade issued the following congratulatory order from his headquarters in the field: "Soldiers—The moment has arrived when your

* W. Swinton, *New York Times*, May 14th, 1864.

† *United States Service Magazine*, June, 1864.

Commanding-General feels authorized to address you in terms of congratulation. For eight days and nights, almost without intermission, in rain and sunshine, you have been gallantly fighting a desperate foe, in positions naturally strong, and rendered doubly so by intrenchments. You have compelled him to abandon his fortifications on the Rapidan, to retire and attempt to stop your onward progress, and now he has abandoned the last intrenched position, so tenaciously held, suffering in all a loss of 18 guns, 2 colors, and 8,000 prisoners, including 2 general officers. Soldiers! your heroic deeds, and noble endurance of fatigue and privation, will ever be memorable. Let us return thanks to God for the mercy thus shown us, and ask earnestly for its continuance. Soldiers! your work is not yet over. The enemy must be pursued, and, if possible, overcome. The courage and fortitude you have displayed, renders your Commanding-General confident that your future efforts will result in success. While we mourn the loss of many gallant comrades, let us remember that the enemy must have suffered equal if not greater losses. We shall soon receive reinforcements, which he cannot expect. Let us determine, then, to continue vigorously the work so well begun, and, under God's blessing, in a short time the object of our labors will soon be accomplished."

General Sheridan's cavalry raid, meanwhile, had been eminently successful. After securing the passage of the Rapidan to the army at the fords, and guarding its exposed flank in the advance through the Wilderness, till it was established in safety before Spottsylvania, Sheridan organized an expedition of the boldest character to cut off the enemy's supplies in his rear, and traversing the Peninsula, penetrate the defences of Richmond. The necessary preparations having been completed on Sunday, the 8th, at daylight on the following morning the expedition set out, moving toward Fredericksburg, and then by a southerly course on the road to Childsburg, on the border of the county, turning the enemy's right, and at evening, without opposition, crossing the North Anna at Anderson's Bridge. This brought the advance, Custer's brigade of Merritt's division, within striking distance of the Virginia Central Railroad at the neighboring station, Beaver Dam. During that night, Sheridan—we cite his official dispatches, communicated by Secretary Stanton—"destroyed the enemy's depot at that place, 3 large trains of cars, and 100 cars, 2 fine locomotives, 200,000 pounds of bacon, and other stores, amounting in all to 1,500,000 of rebel rations; also the telegraph and railroad track for about 10 miles, embracing several culverts; recaptured 378 of our men, including 2 colonels, 1 major, and several other officers. On the morning of the 10th he resumed operations, crossing the South Anna at Grand Squirrel Bridge, and went into camp at about daylight. On the 11th he captured Ashland Station, destroyed here one locomotive and a train of cars, an engine house, and two or three government buildings, containing a large amount of stores; also destroyed 6 miles of railroad, embracing 6 culverts, 2 trestle-bridges, and the telegraph wire. About 7 A. M. of the 11th, he resumed the march on Richmond. He found the rebel General Stuart with his cavalry concentrated at Yellow Tavern, immediately attacked him, and after an obstinate contest gained possession of the Brockel turnpike, capturing two pieces of artillery, and driving his forces back toward Ashland, and across the north fork of the Chickahominy. At the same time a party charged down the Brock Road and captured the first line of the enemy's works around Richmond. During the night he marched the whole of his command between the first and second line of the enemy's works on the bluffs overlooking the line of the Virginia Central Railroad and the Mechanicsville Turnpike. After demonstrating around the works, and finding them very strong, he gave up the intention of assaulting, and determined to recross the Chickahominy at Meadow Bridge. It had been partially destroyed by the enemy, but was repaired in about three hours under a heavy artillery fire from a rebel battery. General Merritt made the crossing, attacked the enemy, and drove him off handsomely, the pursuit continuing as far as Gaines' Mills. The enemy, observing the recrossing of the Chickahominy, came out from his second line of works. A brigade of infantry and a large number of dismounted cavalry attacked the divisions of Generals Gregg and Wilson, but after a severe contest were repulsed and driven behind their works. Gregg's and Wilson's divisions after collecting the wounded recrossed the Chickahominy. On the afternoon of the 12th the corps encamped at Walnut Grove and Gaines' Mills. On the morning of the 13th the march was renewed, and we encamped at Bottom's Bridge. The command is in fine spirits. The loss of horses will not exceed 100. All the wounded were brought off, except about thirty cases of mortal wounds, and those were well cared for in the farm-houses of the country. The wounded will not exceed 250, and the total losses not over 350. The Virginia Central Railroad bridges over the Chickahominy and other trestle-bridges, one 60 feet in length, one 30 feet, one 20 feet, and the railroad for a long distance south of the Chickahominy were destroyed. Great praise is given to the division commanders, Generals Gregg, Wilson and Merritt, and Generals Custer and Davis, Colonels Gregg, Divine, Chapman, McIntosh and Gibbs, brigade commanders, and all the officers and men behaved splendidly." To this bulletin was added in a postscript by Secretary Stanton the following additional item of importance, which, unlike many reports of a similar character during the war, proved to be true: "In a dispatch this moment received from Admiral Lee, he reports to the Secretary of the Navy that the Richmond papers of yesterday mentioned the death of General J. E. B. Stuart, shot in battle. This, no doubt, happened in the battle with Sheridan."

From Bottom's Bridge where Sheridan's dispatch left his command, the column proceeded to Turkey Bend on the James River, where they where in immediate communication with General Butler. Generals J. E. B. Stuart and Fitz Hugh Lee were in command of the pursuing cavalry of the enemy, with inferior forces following up the expedition with great spirit. The former fell in the engagement at Yellow Tavern, the heaviest loss to the confederate army in Virginia since the death of his redoutable comrade in arms "Stonewall" Jackson. A native of Virginia and a graduate of West Point of 1854, he had distinguished himself as a cavalry officer in Indian warfare in the West. At the outbreak of the war, he resigned his commission as captain, to take up arms in the rebel service, in which, in command of the confederate cavalry in Virginia, he soon gained a distinguished reputation, and rose to the rank of Major-General. Two other "brave and accomplished" officers of the rebel service fell with him in the action at Yellow Tavern, Colonel H. Clay Pate and Lieutenant-Colonel Robert Randolph.

The funeral of General Stuart at St. James' Church, Richmond, on the 13th, was thus described in a newspaper of that city: "At the appointed hour the cortege appeared in front of the church, and the metallic coffin, containing the remains of the noble soldier whose now silent voice had so often startled the enemy with his stirring battle-cry, was carried down the centre aisle and placed before the altar. Wreaths and a cross of evergreen, interwoven with delicate lilies of the valley, laurel, and other flowers of purist white, decked the coffin. The pall-bearers were General Bragg, Major-General McCown, General Chilton, Brigadier-General Lawton, Commodore Forrest, Captain Lee of the Navy, and General George W. Randolph, formerly Secretary of War. The scene was sad and impressive. President Davis sat near the front, with a look of grief upon his care-worn face, and his Cabinet officers were gathered around, while on either side were the Senators and Representatives of the Confederate Congress. Scattered through the church were a number of generals and other officers of less rank; among the former, General Ransom, commanding the Department of Richmond. Hundreds of faces witnessed the scene; but the brave Fitz Lee and other war-wearied and war-worn men, whom the dead Stuart had so often led where the red battle was fiercest, and who would have given their lives for his were away in the fight, doubtless striking with a double courage as they thought of their fallen General. The short service was read by Rev. Dr. Peterkin, a funeral anthem sung, and the remains were carried out and placed in the hearse, which proceeded to Hollywood Cemetery, followed by a large train of carriages. No military escort accompanied the procession, but the hero was laid in his last resting-place on the hill-side, while the earth trembled with the roar of artillery and the noise of the deadly strife of armies—the one bent upon desecrating and devastating his native land, and the other proudly and defiantly standing in the path and invoking the blessing of Heaven upon their cause, to fight in better cheer for the memory of such as Stonewall Jackson and J. E. B. Stuart."

After the success of General Hancock on the 13th, and the hard fighting which preceded and followed that action, both armies remained for a short time in comparative inaction. The heavy rains and state of the roads necessarily suspended operations in General Grant's army; while the severe labors of the troops, exhausted by incessant engagements and numerous marches and counter-marches, demanded repose. Grant, meanwhile, was receiving reinforcements and the supplies of the enemy, cut off or greatly impeded by the raid of Sheridan, rendered their position every day more precarious. For a week the two armies confronted one another with occasional sharp skirmishes in their firmly held lines at and before Spottsylvania Court House. The wounded of the Union army were sent by way of Fredericksburg to the capital, and fresh troops were arriving in camp. More than 20,000 sick and wounded were transported from the field of battle to the Washington hospital, and more than 8,000 prisoners to prison depots. The cavalry force of the army was strengthened by the addition of several thousand fresh horses. The national force, meanwhile, was recruited by the mustering into the service of over 30,000 volunteers for 100 days at the call of the President. The Secretary of War on the 20th announced that over 25,000 veteran reinforcements, with abundant supplies, had been forwarded to General Grant. It was at this date that the active operations of the campaign were resumed. Several days previously, on the 18th, another effort had been made to assault the enemy's works on the right in which the corps of Wright, Hancock and Burnside engaged with great gallantry with considerable loss, but the line of the fort was found on a near approach too well defended by abattis to promise success, and the attack was abandoned. This was followed the next day by an effort of the Confederate General Ewell to turn our right, which was promptly repulsed. "About 300 prisoners fell into our hands," says Secretary Stanton, "besides many killed and wounded. Our loss foots up a little over 600 wounded and 150 killed and missing." The following day, the 20th, General Grant commenced a new flank movement to turn the right of the enemy's position. The cavalry were sent forward at night and occupied the line of the Fredericksburg and Richmond Railway at Guinney's Station and Bowling Green, followed immediately by Hancock's corps and the next day by Warren's and the remainder of the army. Lee, also, at the same time evacuated Spottsylvania, and began his march southward, moving on a direct interior line to the North Anna, where it was expected he would make a stand. There was but little opposition encountered by the Union troops on the route they had taken as the several corps pushed on to the North Anna River, which Hancock, in the advance, reached on Monday, the 23d, encountering the enemy in the vicinity of Taylor's Bridge, and in a spirited assault forced the position and effected a crossing. Warren succeeded in getting his corps over higher up at Jericho Ford, but was violently attacked on the south branch of the stream. His troops being well handled, Griffin's division bearing the brunt of the engagement, the enemy charging against artillery and "suffering especially from canister," were repulsed with heavy loss. The Union casualties were not large. The next day was spent in getting over the remainder of the army in the face of considerable opposition from the enemy. Grant now took up a position south of the river and prepared to open communication with Port Royal on the Rappahannock, whither his wounded were sent. The enemy in front held a strong position between the North and South Anna, and covering the crossing of the Fredericksburg and the Virginia Central Railways at Sexton's Junction. This was the state of affairs on the 24th, when General Grant, in continuance of his strategy in turning the works at Spottsylvania, resolved upon another flank movement which he carried out with equal success. Under cover of a demonstration on his extreme right, withdrawing his army that night to the north side of the North Anna, he moved by a circuitous route to the eastward by Mongohick Church toward Hanovertown, the place designated for crossing the Pamunkey, a river formed by the junction, some distance above, of the North and South Anna, thus avoiding the passage of the latter stream. This new movement would bring the army in ready communication with the old base of operations at White House where supplies could be received, and were already being forwarded by way of York River. Sheridan, with his cavalry, had already taken his route through King William County, rejoining the army from the James River after his recent successful raid just narrated. He now, leading the advance, on the morning of the 27th, with the First and Second Division of Cavalry, took possession of Hanover Ferry and Hanovertown, finding there only a rebel vedette. General Torbert there captured seventy-five cavalry, including six officers. A dispatch from General Grant's headquarters at Mongohick Church, at 7 A. M. of the 28th, reported, "Every thing goes on finely; weather clear and cool; the troops came up rapidly and in fine spirits, and that the army will be beyond the Pamunkey by noon. Breckinridge is at Hanover Court House, with a force variously estimated at from 3,000 to 10,000. Wickham's and Lomax's brigades of cavalry are also there." The same day, there was a severe engagement between two divisions of the cavalry, Torbert's and Gregg's, sent out on a reconnoissance toward Mechanicsville, at Hawe's Store, a point near Tolopatomy Creek, and a body of the enemy's horse, who were driven about a mile. The Union loss in this sharply-contested affair, was 350 killed and wounded ; about the same with that of the foe. In this advance, the railways in the rear and on the enemy's lines of communication, were not neglected by General Grant, who sent Wilson's cavalry division to break up the track west and north of Sexton's Junction, a work which they successfully accomplished. New lines were now formed, and the two armies confronted one another on the old battle-fields of the Peninsula Campaign of General McClellan before Richmond.

While these operations were going on along the main line, General Butler had not been idle. After the reconnoissances already narrated, he had strengthened his fortifications preparatory to a demonstration upon the enemy's works, sufficient, at least, to hold a considerable portion of Lee's army on the southern side of Richmond. On the 12th of May, General Butler advanced several divisions of Gillmore's and Smith's corps between the railroad and the river toward Richmond, in the direction of Fort Darling, and speedily came upon a body of the enemy, reinforced by North and South Carolina troops, guarding the outer defences of that work. A dispatch was captured from General Beauregard to General Hoke, in command of Drury's Bluff, stating that he would join them as soon as the troops came up. A demonstration was made by General Smith upon the rebel lines, which was followed up the next day, the 13th, by a flanking movement of General Gillmore, who, with a portion of his corps and a brigade of the Eighteenth Corps, assaulted and took the enemy's works on their right. General Smith carried the first line on their left with little loss. The enemy retired into three square redoubts upon which the Union artillery was brought to bear. In the bombardment of the 14th, a magazine in the enemy's defences was exploded. At evening, an attack was made on our lines, and repulsed. The next day, Sunday, it was renewed, and in greater force the following morning, under cover of a thick fog, upon General Smith's line, which was forced back in some confusion and with considerable loss ; General Heckman's brigade of New Jersey and Massachusetts troops suffering severely, that officer, with a large portion of his command, being taken prisoners. At the same time, the enemy made an attack from Petersburg on General Butler's forces, guarding the rear, and were repulsed. After this, "the troops, having been on incessant duty for five days, three of which were in a rain storm, General Butler retired leisurely within his own lines."* A cavalry expedition, which, under cover of this movement had been sent in command of General Kautz to cut the Danville Railroad, near Appomattox Station, was successful in blowing up a bridge at that place, and breaking up the road and destroying government stores at several stations. Returning, they inflicted various damage on the Petersburg and Lynchburg Railway, and that to Weldon at Jarrett's Station. A few days after these events, an assault was made by General Beauregard upon General Butler's lines at Bermuda Hundred, held by Terry's and Ames' divisions of the Tenth Corps. The first attack was made at midnight of the 19th, and was gallantly repulsed. It was resumed the next morning by the enemy in force, and a line of rifle-pits captured, which, after a stubborn contest during the day, were retaken. In one of the onsets the rebel Brigadier-General William S. Walker, commanding the South Carolina brigade was captured. Another attack was made upon Gillmore's corps the following day ; but

* Secretary Stanton to Major-General Dix, May 17th, 1864

that officer firmly held his position, inflicting considerable loss on his assailants. After this the enemy fell back, and a portion of General Butler's force, not required for defensive operations, was transferred under General Smith to the Army of the Potomac. It ascended the York River in transports, and was safely landed, on the 30th of May, at White House.

In co-operation with the advance of General Grant and the main army, certain operations (guarding the right flank) had been going on in the Valley of the Shenandoah and in Western Virginia. General Sigel in command in the Valley, with a small corps of observation, advanced beyond Winchester while a portion of his force was sent on an expedition up the Kanawha Valley to assist General Crook, in that quarter, in his operations upon the Virginia and Tennessee Railroad. This column consisted of selected troops, and included a division of cavalry under Brigadier-General Averill, in all about 2,500 men. The principal object of General Averill's movement, as stated by a correspondent who has given a very interesting account of the expedition, to which we refer the reader,* was to distract the attention of the rebel General Jenkins and the noted John Morgan, and by diverting it toward himself prevent a junction of their forces against General Crook, who designed moving on to Dublin, destroying the stores of the Virginia and Tennessee Railroad at that place, and the bridge (the largest and the finest in the South) on New River, seven miles above. The purpose was well accomplished, General Crook effecting the complete destruction he designed, and General Morgan the while, as it proved, holding himself at Wytheville, southwest, about thirty miles distant on the railroad, in expectation of General Averill." The expedition left Charleston, Western Virginia, May 1st, and on the 7th, 140 miles from the southeast, came up at Abb's Valley with a company of Morgan's men, which they routed. After some further skirmishing, General, Averill, finding Morgan in force beyond, passed by a circuitous route over Walker Mountain, a weary march to Cove Mountain Gap, in the immediate vicinity of Wytheville, on the railroad, his proposed destination. Morgan, anticipating the movement, was met at the Gap, strongly posted with a greatly superior body of cavalry and infantry, with four pieces of cannon. Averill firmly held his ground during the day, the 10th, against repeated assaults (he was wounded in the forehead in the engagement), and at night extricated himself from the perilous situation, with a loss in killed and wounded of 135 men, taking route across Walker Mountain and thence to Dublin, in expectation of meeting with General Crook. The latter he found had preceded him, and accomplished his work of destruction on the railway at his quarter, so that he was compelled to continue his arduous march (being without ammunition), avoiding the enemy in his path, till, having taken the northerly route over the mountains from Christiansburg, he came up with the rear of General Crook's command at Union. The two forces frequently rested at Lewisburg. While Averill was making this diversion, General Crook, besides his injury to the railway, had, in his onward route from Princetown, defeated General A. G. Jenkins, on the 9th, at Cloyd Mountain, and again near Dublin Depot. In this action, Jenkins, who will be remembered as one of the most desperate rebel chieftains in Western Virginia, was mortally wounded. The rebel loss in these engagements was stated at over 600, and 300 prisoners."* While this movement was going on

* D. M. Barnes' Correspondence from Lewisburg, Va., in the *New York Times*, June 10th, 1864.

* Secretary Stanton to General Dix, May 18th, 1864.

in Western Virginia, General Sigel had removed up the valley beyond Winchester. On the 14th of May he was reported at Woodstock, a body of the rebels under Imboden being driven or retiring before his advance through Newmarket. General Breckinridge now appeared upon the field, and an action was fought known as the Battle of Newmarket. The details are thus given by a correspondent: "During Saturday and Saturday night, the entire division of Breckinridge was brought up from Staunton, and on Sunday morning, the 15th, about 10 o'clock, his skirmishers were seen advancing on our right, a little to the west of Newmarket. His command consisted of the troops of Brigadier-General W. L. Jackson (Mudwall), Echols and Imboden, estimated at from 10,000 to 15,000 men, and from 15 to 19 pieces of artillery. His infantry were drawn up in three extended lines, each line under command of its respective general, on three rises of ground, to the west of Newmarket, between the pike and the Shenandoah River. One of these lines was deployed to the left to occupy a slight ravine, for the purpose of flanking our right wing or of surprising one of our batteries. His cavalry was drawn up on the east side of the road, and under cover of the town. His artillery was posted chiefly on the three hills occupied by his infantry. General Sigel was compelled to move up his forces from Woodstock in order to protect those which had been sent forward on the 14th under Colonel Moor, and which had driven Imboden through Newmarket. He broke camp at 4 o'clock in the morning, and reached Newmarket, a distance of nineteen miles, by 11 o'clock. When he came up the forces under Colonel Moor had been placed in position, and were already engaged with the enemy, so that the General was obliged to make his dispositions in accordance with those previously made. He also saw a portion of the cavalry retiring in some disorder and could not rally them so as to make them effective. His line was formed on the right of the pike, fronting Newmarket, his right reaching near the Shenandoah River. His artillery of four batteries extended nearly along his entire front, and one battery was posted on the left of the pike, so that the enemy was exposed to a cross fire, and so that the ravine occupied by the flanking brigade of the enemy was swept by our battery on the left. The infantry were exhausted after their long march and could not go into action in perfect order. The artillery was supported in the beginning by cavalry, for want of sufficient infantry, and for the same reason cavalry had to be used as skirmishers against the enemy's infantry skirmishers; but this was only for a short time. The only infantry regiments that were brought into action were the First and Twelfth Virginia, Fifty-fourth Pennsylvania, Eighteenth Connecticut, One Hundred and Twenty-third Ohio and Thirty-fourth Massachusetts. All these behaved well, but the Thirty-fourth Massachusetts, the First Virginia and the One Hundred and Twenty-third Ohio were most exposed and distinguished themselves for great bravery and endurance. But with all the courage and obstinacy displayed our men were compelled to give way before the dense, extended columns of the enemy, which pressed them hard and fiercely. At first they retired in some disorder, but were rallied as soon as they reached the infantry drawn up in their rear. It would have been in the highest degree hazardous to our supplies, and would have needlessly exposed our troops to have continued this unequal contest, and General Sigel withdrew his command gradually toward Mount Jackson, and on the following day fell back to Strasburg and Middletown."*

* Martinsburg, Va., Correspondence, *New York Tribune*, May 25th, 1864.

A dispatch of Secretary Stanton to General Dix, dated May 17th, gives the following account of this engagement: "Dispatches from General Sigel, received this evening, report, that on Sunday he fought the forces of Echols and Imboden, under Breckinridge at Newmarket; that the enemy's forces were superior in number, and that he gradually withdrew from the battle-field and recrossed the Shenandoah, having lost five pieces of artillery, about 600 killed and wounded and fifty prisoners, but bringing all his train and all the wounded that could be transported from the battle-field. He states that in consequence of the long line and the train that had to be guarded, he could not bring more than six regiments into the fight, besides the artillery and cavalry, and that the enemy had about 7,000 infantry, besides other arms; that his retrograde movement to Strasburg was effected in perfect order without any loss of material or men." Shortly after this event General Sigel was superseded in his command of the Department of Western Virginia. He announced the change to his troops in a general order, dated Cedar Creek, May 21st. Major-General Hunter was his successor. "In leaving the troops under my immediate command," said General Sigel, "I feel it my duty to give my most sincere thanks to the officers and men who have assisted me so faithfully during the last campaign. Having no other wishes or aspirations but to serve and promote the great cause which we are all bound to defend, I hope that final success may crown the indefatigable zeal and good-will of this army." General Sigel was now appointed by General Hunter to the command of the Reserve Division, comprising all of the troops on the Baltimore and Ohio Railroad.

Having thus brought down the narrative of military events in other portions of Virginia, we return to the operations of the main army under General Grant. By the repulse of General Sigel at Newmarket, and that of General Butler before Fort Darling, two eminent generals of the confederate service, Breckinridge and Beauregard were left free to co-operate directly with Lee in the movements immediately before Richmond, where General Grant, as we have seen, had planted himself on the old battle-ground on the left bank of the Chickahominy. Here he was destined to find the enemy too strongly intrenched for a successful attack in front and advance in that direction upon Richmond; but he did not accept the conclusion until after several heroic efforts; nor, should that experiment fail, was he without resources for the future in his masterly strategy and consummate handling of his admirably officered and well-disciplined army. After crossing the Pamunkey, General Grant's army was drawn up on a north and south line, five or six miles in length, from Hanover Court House on the right, crossing and beyond Tolopotamy Creek. Wright's corps was on the right, Hancock's at the centre, and Warren's on the left, with Burnside in the rear. Both flanks were covered by Sheridan's cavalry. The enemy were guarding the line of the Virginia Central Railroad and Chickahominy, on the north of the river, his forces being on the Mechanicsville Road, south of the Tolopotamy Creek Road, between that stream and Hawe's Store, and his right resting on Shady Grove. With these general dispositions of the forces there was some hard fighting growing out of mutual reconnoissances on the 30th of May. There was a sharp cavalry skirmish on the left of our lines, followed by an attack on Warren's corps in that quarter, in the afternoon, by Rhode's division of Ewell's corps and a body of cavalry. "The enemy," says General Grant, in a dispatch, "were easily repulsed, and with very considerable slaughter. To relieve General Warren, and speedily, General

Meade ordered an attack by the balance of our lines. General Hancock, the only one who received the order in time to make the attack before dark, drove the enemy from his intrenched line and held it." Warren, at this point, was within seven miles of Richmond. Birney's division of Hancock's corps the next day carried a portion of the enemy's outer intrenchments. General Sheridan, late in the afternoon, perceiving a force of rebel cavalry at Cold Harbor, in our rear, which proved to be Fitz Lee's division, attacked and, after a hard fight, routed it together with Clingman's brigade of infantry which came to Lee's support. Sheridan remained in possession of the place, reporting, at dark, that he had a considerable number of prisoners, and that there were many rebel dead and wounded on the field.* The contest was renewed with greater numbers the next day, June 1st, when General Grant, having brought down Wright's corps by the rear to the left, where it was joined by General W. F. Smith's command, just arrived from General Butler's department, ordered these forces to sieze and occupy the ground at Cold Harbor, which, being a point of vital importance on the road from our base of supplies at White House, was resolutely disputed by the enemy. Warren, Burnside, and Hancock were held in readiness to advance in their respective points. "The attack," said General Grant, in a dispatch the next day,† "was made with spirit about 5 P. M., continuing until after dark, and resulting in our carrying the enemy's works on the right of the Sixth Corps, where we still hold them, and also the first line in front of Smith. The latter, however, were commanded in the rear, which made those carried untenable. The enemy made repeated assaults on each of the corps not engaged in the main assault, but were repulsed with loss in every instance. Several hundred prisoners were taken. During the night the enemy made several assaults to regain what they had lost, but failed." Our loss in this engagement was estimated at 2,000 killed and wounded. There were no operations the next day, but on the following the contest was renewed, General Grant ordering a general attack on the enemy's lines. Hancock's corps was brought in the night from the right to the extreme left, the order of the army corps from the right now being Burnside, Warren, Smith, Wright, Hancock. The line ran nearly parallel with that of the Chickahominy, at a distance of a mile and a-half to two miles and a-half north of it, the enemy directly in front holding the north bank of the river. Breckinridge's command, it is said, occupied the enemy's right, with Beauregard on the right centre, Longstreet on the left centre, Ewell on the left, and Hill in reserve.* The assault was made by our whole line about 4½ in the morning. "We drove the enemy," says General Grant, in a dispatch at 3 o'clock of that day, "within his intrenchments at all points, but without gaining any decisive advantage. Our troops now occupy a position close to the enemy, at some places within fifty yards, and are remaining. Our loss was not severe, nor do I suppose the enemy to have lost heavily. We captured over 300 prisoners, mostly from Breckinridge." A late official report that day accredited by Secretary Stanton, estimated the number of our killed and wounded at about 3,000. Colonel Hassell of the Thirty-sixth Wisconsin; Colonel Porter of the Eighth New York Heavy Artillery; Colonel Morris of the Sixty-sixth New York were among the killed. General R. O. Tyler was seriously wounded, threatening the loss of a foot. The main fighting in this action

* Dispatch from General Grant communicated by Secretary Stanton, June 2d, 1864.

† Stanton's dispatch of June 2d.

* *Army and Navy Journal*, June 11th, 1864.

at close quarters with the enemy was by Hancock's corps on the left, and by Wright and Smith's forces at the centre. Barlow's division on the extreme left, with Gibbon's, made the attack with great gallantry; the onset of the Sixth Corps was also made with great spirit. The battle was renewed at evening. At 6 P. M., Wilson with his cavalry, fell upon the rear of a brigade of Heth's division, which Lee had thrown around to his left, apparently with the intention of enveloping Burnside. After a short but sharp conflict, Wilson drove them from their rifle-pits in confusion, taking a few prisoners. He had previously fought and routed Gordon's brigade of rebel cavalry. An hour later, and the enemy suddenly attacked Gibbon's division of Smith's command. The battle lasted with great fury for half an hour, the attack being unwaveringly repulsed. In the dispatch of June 4th, from which we have drawn these particulars, Secretary Stanton states our entire loss during these three days' operations around Cold Harbor, as reported by the Adjutant-General, at not exceeding 7,500.

Having thus, as at Spottsylvania, tested the strength of the enemy in a direct attack, and, as in that instance, having found their position too strong and well supported to be taken by assault, General Grant turned his attention to other strategic movements, which he had already conceived, to carry on the campaign with success. These involved no less than the abandonment of his present base of operations and the withdrawal of his army, by what was now characterized as his favorite operation by the left flank, across the intervening country to the south of the James River. To render this new movement successful, it was necessary that time should be gained for the requisite preparations, and the enemy be finally held in check while they were going on. The advanced lines of the army in the immediate presence of the enemy were, accordingly, vigorously maintained, new intrenchments were thrown up at night, and frequent skirmishing took place along the front. Sharpshooting from the enemy's picket lines was particularly annoying and destructive. For several nights after the battle of the 3d, assaults were made by the enemy and repulsed. Hancock's lines were reported by General Grant "within forty yards of the rebel works." At evening of the 7th there was a time of two hours spent in clearing the narrow interval between the two armies of the dead and wounded. The enemy, meanwhile, were strengthening their right on the Chickahominy, at Bottom's Bridge, to anticipate any operation of Grant at that point. Grant's dispatches spoke of changes in the disposition of corps and "contemplated operations." He was receiving reinforcements and organizing the army; and, while supplies were being forwarded, and works thrown up in front, was in reality looking away from the Chickahominy to the James. All his arrangements were made in little over a week. The supplies were diverted from White House, and the railway in its vicinity taken up. The movement of the army was commenced on the night of Sunday, the 12th. The Eighteenth Army Corps, under the command of General W. F. Smith, taking the direction by which it had arrived, marched to White House and was embarked on transports for James River. The other corps were moved across the Chickahominy, taking the lower routes below the enemy's well-guarded position. General Hancock's and General Warren's corps passed the stream at Long Bridge, some six miles from Lee's right at Bottom's Bridge, and marched thence to Wilcox's Landing on the James River. The corps of Wright and Burnside crossed at Jone's Bridge, about four miles further below, and marched to Charles City. The movement was entirely successful, the departure being a surprise to the enemy, and the march so skillfully conducted and with such celerity, that they were unable to offer any resistance. On Monday evening the advance reached Wilcox's Landing, and on Tuesday the whole force crossed the James at Powhatan Point on pontoons, prepared by General Butler for the purpose. General Smith's troops were at the same time coming up the river. In briefly reviewing the movement, General Grant, in a dispatch, says: "Our forces drew out from within fifty yards of the enemy's intrenchments at Cold Harbor, made a flank movement of about fifty-five miles' march, crossing the Chickahominy and James Rivers, the latter 2,000 feet wide and eighty-four feet deep at the point of crossing, without the loss of a wagon or piece of artillery, and only about 150 stragglers picked up by the enemy. In covering this move, Warren's corps and Wilson's cavalry had frequent skirmishing with the enemy, each losing from fifty to sixty killed and wounded, but inflicting an equal if not greater loss upon the enemy.

The motives and promise of the strategy of General Grant were thus summed up by an acute army correspondent frequently cited in these pages. "This splendid stroke," wrote Mr. Swinton, "comparable only to Moreau's passage of the Rhine and flank march on Ulm, stands to-day an accomplished fact: the Army of the Potomac, taken up, as in the arms of a giant, is transported from the Chickahominy and planted south of the James River and south of Richmond. Now begins a new act in the grand war drama. We shall operate on new and unattempted lines, looking to new and hitherto unattainable results. I think there are few military men who do not now feel that the present position of the Army of the Potomac gives us reason to indulge brighter hopes of ultimate success than has been possible at any time since the war began. The south side is the true line of operation against Richmond looking to great ulterior results. Of the three cardinal maxims of strategy, the most important of all prescribes 'to operate on the enemy's communications without endangering your own.' Now, the operations of the Virginia campaign have been conducted under circumstances that made it impossible to apply this principle. General Grant has aimed assiduously to bring on a great decisive field fight with the hope of crushing the rebel army. But from the nature of the country, its prodigious facilities for defence, and the skill of the opposing General, this has been impossible. We gained victories; we steadily pushed the enemy back, and in an unparalleled campaign of twenty-nine days, forced Lee from the Rapidan to the front of Richmond. But no decisive results were accomplished. Lee's army is an army of veterans; it is an instrument sharpened to a perfect edge. You turn its flanks; well, its flanks are made to be turned; that effects little or nothing. All that we can reckon as gained, therefore, is the loss of life inflicted on the enemy, and of having reached a point thus near the objective; but no brilliant military results. In loss of life we were undoubtedly suffering more severely than the rebels; I think we may fairly say in the proportion of five to their three. Now it is obvious that we could not have long stood thus. Whatever preponderance of numbers we might have would soon disappear—would soon become an equality, and presently an inferiority. The rebel army might have been worn away by attrition; but we should ourselves have been exhausted in the process. The hammer would have been broken on the anvil.

"By the present move a new order of operation begins. We not only threaten the communications of the enemy, we plant ourselves across his communications. The communications of the rebel army are the great lines of railroad by Petersburg and Danville and their connections. Richmond, as a city, Richmond as a military centre, is strictly dependent on these lines for its supplies. Cut it off from these and you have a tourniquet around its throat. It may have a month's supplies, or three months', or six months', but these exhausted and it must succumb. If Lee allows himself to be shut up within Richmond, therefore, the problem reduces itself to a repetition of Vicksburg over again. Will he do so? That is a question. But this is the pitiless alternative to which Lee is now reduced: to stay in Richmond and suffer the fatal lines of circumvallation to be drawn around him, or to come out of his works and give battle. Now a fair field-fight is precisely what the Army of the Potomac invites and welcomes; it will gladly give the rebels man for man, and engage to defeat them withal. If Lee is unwilling to run this risk, he retires within the defences of Richmond, and we then hold precisely the relations held by the allies to Napoleon defending Paris in 1814. It was in vain then that that consummate master put forth a generalship that recalled the splendors of the first great Italian campaign; in vain he threw his masses on different points of the investing line. If Lee is not a better general than Napoleon, he can hardly hope for a much better fate. With the Army of the Potomac planted at or north of Petersburg, we there tap the great railroad line connecting Richmond with the Atlantic seaboard and Gulf States. When there, Grant may be able to throw his left across the Danville road, and in this case Richmond is isolated. If his plan does not contemplate so great a development of front, he will at least provide for the effectual destruction of the latter road; and this, as well as the destruction of the Western (Lynchburg) road and the James River Canal, will be an easy prey to our cavalry, which, under the hands of Sheridan, has almost put the rebel cavalry out of existence. The reduction of Fort Darling is an incidental piece of work, which will be gladly contended for by some of the able engineering heads of the Army of the Potomac. In the mean time we have a perfectly secure and convenient base, the James River, to which all the transportation lately at White House has been forwarded."*

* Correspondence *New York Times*, June 18th, 1864.

CHAPTER XCIX.

MILITARY MOVEMENTS IN VIRGINIA. JUNE TO AUGUST, 1864.

In the operations of General Grant against Richmond, in addition to the movements of the main army, there were two objects held in view as requisite to final success. These were the possession or control of the great channels of communication of the rebel capital with the south by the railways leading to Weldon and Danville, on the borders of North Carolina. If these were once seized and held, with the capture of Petersburg on the former line, and Lynchburg on the Tennessee line, flanking the other on the west, the supplies of Richmond would be cut off, and its fall or surrender be secured. At least, nothing could save it but the thorough destruction by Lee of Grant's investing army; and of this, judging from the recent trials of strength of the two forces, there was at this time little probability. We shall see what struggles, immediately upon the arrival of General Grant at the James River, were made for the possession of Petersburg. Previously to that point in the history of the campaign, a movement of some importance was undertaken in the direction of Lynchburg. In the notice, in the last chapter, of the military operations in the valley of the Shenandoah and in Western Virginia, we left the united force of Generals Crook and Averill at Lewisburg, after their successful raid on the Tennessee road, in the vicinity of New River, and recorded the transfer in the valley of General Sigel's command to General Hunter. The latter officer, relieved from the immediate presence of the enemy in his camp at Cedar Creek, near Strasburg, lost no time in re-organizing his forces for a further forward movement. Starting with his command on the 26th of May, he passed through Mount Jackson, and, traversing the recent battle-ground at Newmarket, advanced to Harrisburg, where he ascertained the presence of the enemy a few miles in front at Mount Crawford, where they were guarding the approach to Staunton. Making a feint upon their line at the latter place, he turned off his main force to Port Republic, where some prisoners were taken with a number of cattle, and two government cloth factories destroyed. Resting but a night at this place, he moved on early the following morning, Sunday, June 5th, upon the Staunton road, and met the enemy a few miles out in the vicinity of Piedmont. The cavalry under General Stahel became at once engaged, and drove the enemy some distance, when Brigadier-General Sullivan brought up the infantry to the encounter. The enemy now held a position in the wood, where they were defended by breast-works. Captain Dupont brought the artillery to bear upon them, and various brave efforts were made with skillful manœuvering to dislodge them. A turning with a final charge of cavalry decided the day, after a battle of ten hours' duration. The rebel Commanding-General William E. Jones was killed. General Hunter reported also the capture of 1,500 prisoners—1,000 men and over 60 officers on the field of battle, and 3,000 stand of arms, 3 pieces of artillery, and a vast quantity of stores. The next day he marched into Staunton, where, on the 8th, he was joined by the forces of Crook and Averill, who had crossed the mountains to meet him. A vast quantity of government property was destroyed at Staunton, including army clothing and stores, and railway buildings and factories. The railway was also destroyed in the vicinity on both sides of the town. From Staunton the joint forces advanced to Lexington, in Rockbridge County, which they reached on the 11th, burning the Virginia military institution at that place. The house of Governor Letcher was also burnt. Several canal boats in the vicinity, laden with stores, were destroyed, and guns and ammunition captured. General Hunter, taking the route by Buchanan, struck the Tennessee Railway at Liberty, west of Lynchburg, the vicinity of which place he reached on the 18th, having been joined by Averill's cavalry, which had made a circuitous route, destroying portions of the Lynchburg and Charlottesville Railroad by the way. The enemy having now taken the alarm, reinforcements under General Ewell were sent from Richmond to Lynchburg, which arrived in time to strengthen the defences of the place and arrest the further progress of General Hunter in this quarter. After encountering some loss in a reconnoissance before the town, he withdrew his forces by the line of the railway—not without further opposition

Phil. H. Sheridan

From the original painting by Nast in the possession of the publishers.

Johnson Fry & Co. Publishers, New York.

from a guerrilla force, by the way, in the vicinity of Salem, whence by a northerly route over the Catawba Mountain through Monroe and Greenbrier Counties, resting at Sweet Springs and White Sulphur, he reached a place of security at Gauley. In a dispatch given to the public by Secretary Stanton, on the 28th of June, General Hunter reported that his expedition had been "extremely successful, inflicting great injury upon the enemy, and victorious in every engagement. Running short of ammunition, and finding it impossible to collect supplies while in the presence of an enemy believed to be superior to our force in numbers, and constantly receiving reinforcements from Richmond and other points, I deemed it best to withdraw, and have succeeded in doing so without serious loss."

Simultaneously with this movement of General Hunter upon Lynchburg, and with the advance of General Grant to the James River, General Sheridan, with a cavalry force, was sent to operate upon the enemy's line of communication between Richmond and Gordonsville. On his return, the following official report from him was published by Secretary Stanton: "I crossed," says he, "the Pamunkey River on the 7th inst., marching via Aylett's, and encamped on Herring Creek. On the morning of the 8th, I resumed the march via Polecat Station, and encamped three miles west of the station. On the 9th, I marched through Childsburg and Newmarket, encamping on East-Northeast Creek near Young's Bridge. On the 10th, I marched via Andrew's Tavern and Lerman's Store, crossing both branches of the North Anna, and encamped at Buck Child's, about three miles northeast of Trevilan Station. My intention was to break the railroad at this station, march through Mechanicsville, cut the Gordonsville and Charlottesville Railroad near Lyndsay's House, and then to march on Charlottesville, but on our arrival at Buck Child's I found the enemy's cavalry in my immediate front. On the morning of the 11th, General Torbert, with his division, and Colonel Gregg's division, attacked the enemy. After an obstinate contest they drove him from successive lines of breastworks through an almost impassable forest back on Trevilan Station. In the mean time General Custer was ordered with his brigade to proceed by a country road so as to reach the station in the rear of the enemy's cavalry. On his arrival at this point, the enemy broke into a complete rout, leaving his dead and nearly all his wounded in our hands; also 20 officers, 500 men and 300 horses. These operations occupied the whole of the day At night I encamped at Trevilan Station, and on the morning of the 12th inst. commenced destroying the railroad from this point to Lorraine Court House. This was thoroughly done, the ties burned and the rails rendered unserviceable. The destruction of the railroad occupied until 3 o'clock of the day, when I directed General Torbert to advance with his division, and General Davis' brigade of General Gregg's division in the direction of Gordonsville, and attack the enemy who had concentrated and been reinforced by infantry during the night, and had also constructed rifle-pits at a point about five miles from Gordonsville. The advance was made, but as the enemy's position was found too strong to assault, no general assault was made. On the extreme right of our lines, a portion of Reserve Brigade carried the enemy's works twice, and was twice driven therefrom by infantry. Night closed the contest. I found on examination of the command that there was not a sufficiency of ammunition left to continue the engagement. The next day trains of cars also came down to where we were engaged with the enemy. The reports of prisoners and citizens were, that Pickett's old division was coming to prevent the taking of Gordonsville. I, therefore, during the night and next morning, withdrew my command over the North Anna via Carpenter's Ford, near Miner's Bridge. In addition, the animals were for the two entire days in which we were engaged, without forage. The surrounding country affords nothing but grazing of a very inferior quality and generally at such points as were inaccessible to us. The cavalry engagement of the 12th was by far the most brilliant one of the present campaign. The enemy's loss was very heavy. They lost the following named officers in killed and wounded: Colonel M'Allister, commanding a regiment, killed; Brigadier-General Resser, commanding a brigade, wounded; and Colonel Castor, commanding a regiment, wounded. My loss in killed and wounded will be about 575. Of this number 490 are wounded. I brought off in my ambulances 377, all that could be transported. The remainder were, with a number of rebel wounded that fell into my hands, left behind. Surgeons and attendants were detailed and remained in charge of them. I captured and have now with me 370 prisoners of war, including 20 commissioned officers. My loss in captured will not exceed 160. They were principally from the Fifth Michigan Cavalry. This regiment gallantly charged down the Gordonsville road, capturing 1,500 horses and about 800 men, and were finally surrounded and had to be given up. When the enemy broke they hurried between General Custer's command and Colonel Gregg's brigade, capturing five caissons of Pennington's battery, three of which were afterwards recaptured, leaving in their hands two caissons." General Sheridan's command reached White House on the 20th June, in time to assist in the maintenance of that post, where the force under General Abercrombie had just been unsuccessfully assailed by the rebel cavalry of Fitz Hugh Lee and Hampton. A few days after, Sheridan set out with his large army-train over the Peninsula, crossed the Chickahominy and proceeding by Charles City Court House, though vigorously attacked by the enemy on the way, succeeded in bringing his command to the camp of General Grant, on the James River, without the loss of a gun or wagon, though several hundred men were lost in defending them.

From these outlying operations of the war, we return to the movements of the main army in its new position on the south side of the James River. Petersburg was immediately attacked, a large part of General Grant's forces, as they crossed the river, being forwarded on the instant. A few days before their arrival, General Butler, on the 9th June, had made a demonstration against the city, having sent an expedition, commanded by General Gillmore, composed of two brigades of infantry under General Hinks and Colonel Hawley and a body of cavalry under General Kautz. The forces on the night of June 8th, crossed the Appomattox on a pontoon bridge laid near the Point of Rocks, and in the morning, while General Butler was diverting the attention of the enemy by a bombardment of Fort Clifton, on the right bank of the stream, passed round the work and proceeded toward Petersburg. General Gillmore, with the infantry, advanced by the direct road to the vicinity of the city, drove back an outer skirmish line, and reconnoitered the fortifications, which he judged too strong to be successfully assailed with the force at his command, about 3,500 men. General Kautz, meanwhile, with his cavalry charged the works on the southerly side, carried them, and penetrated into the town, but lacking the expected co-operation of the infantry was compelled to withdraw. He brought with him forty prisoners. Both commands now returned to Bermuda Hundred with trifling loss.

In renewing the attack upon Petersburg with a superior force, General Grant relied upon a surprise of the enemy, whom he had deceived in his march from the Chickahominy. General Lee, aware of the new flanking movement, apparently looked for its object in an attack upon Richmond by Malvern Hills and the north bank of the James River, and consequently left for the time the defences of Petersburg comparatively unguarded. General Grant, as we have seen, struck directly for the south side of the river. The advance of his force crossed the James on Tuesday, the 14th, and while the remainder was coming up the next day, the march to Petersburg was already undertaken. The important military events of the next four days are thus successively related by an army correspondent.* "On Tuesday night, the command of General Smith arrived by transports in the Appomattox, and on the morning of Wednesday, the 15th, passed that river by a pontoon bridge, above Point of Rocks, and began its march toward Petersburg. On landing, General Smith's two divisions of Brooks and Martindale were joined by Hink's division of colored troops, and by Kautz's cavalry division. The colored division followed the cavalry, and being formed in line of battle, pushed forward and carried an outer line of rifle-pits, before Brooks' division, which was to form on the left for a flanking movement, could get into position. Disposition was then made to carry the main line of works, and this, with preliminary skirmishing, consumed the whole afternoon. At 7.30 the line was formed, with Brooks' on the centre, Martindale on the right, and the colored division on the left, with sixteen guns in position. The skirmish line was thrown forward, and this, without the aid of the line of battle, assaulted and entered the works, taking 13 redoubts, 16 guns, and several colors, and between 300 and 400 prisoners. To the colored troops belong the honor of having taken three of the redoubts and six of the guns; and there is the utmost disposition to give them full credit for their steady behavior under fire. It is true, the resistance was not strong, and the works were most imperfectly manned; and these facts should be taken into account, that we may not over-estimate the value of this test of the fighting qualities of the blacks. But duly considering all these, they did bravely and well, and their conduct has gone far to modify the current opinion of our officers, adverse to their ability to stand in line of battle.

"On Thursday morning, 16th, Hancock's corps took position, relieving the divisions of Hinks and Brooks. Birney advanced one brigade of his division, and drove the enemy a considerable distance. In the afternoon the Ninth Corps came up, and took position on the left of the Second, and at 6 o'clock in the evening the divisions of Barlow and Birney, of the Second, in conjunction with the Ninth Corps and a portion of Smith's, assaulted the position to which the enemy had withdrawn, after leaving the line of redoubts. The assault was not attended with much success, and was continued during the night without accomplishing any results of moment.

"The rebels were able to offer stout resistance to our advance on Thursday, because they had in the mean time been heavily reinforced; but in the process of doing this, they were compelled to weaken their force at Bermuda Hundred, in the course of which a blunder occurred that was promptly taken advantage of by General Butler. It appears that the orders were that the troops should not be withdrawn until the head of Longstreet's column, which had the advance of Lee's army, and was making a forced march in the direction of Petersburg, should arrive. Instead of waiting, however, Beauregard with-

* Mr. Swinton, *New York Times*, June 23d, 1864.

drew early on Thursday morning. On becoming aware of this General Butler advanced General Terry's corps (commands of Fisher, Ames and Turner), to develop the whereabouts of the enemy. Advancing, they struck the Richmond and Petersburg Railroad, which was entirely uncovered by the rebel evacuation. Turner and Ames tore up portions of the track for two or three miles, in the vicinity of Port Walthal Junction, while Generals Terry and Foster moved up on the turnpike toward Richmond. They had not advanced far, however, when they discovered Longstreet's column, led by the divisions of Pickett, marching by the flank. General Terry made skillful disposition of his small force of about four thousand, and succeeded in delaying the advance of the rebels for an hour or two, when he received orders to retire to his old position.

"At daylight of Friday, 17th, Burnside on the left of Hancock, and supported by Miles, of the First Division, Second Corps, made an assault on the right of the enemy's line, which had not yet been carried. It captured 3 redoubts, 5 guns, 3 colors, and 450 prisoners. After this the different divisions of the Second Corps were thrown forward; but, though their losses were heavy, they achieved no success. On the right, one division of the Sixth Corps (Neill's), and one division of the Eighteenth (Martindale's), pushed out simultaneously and drove the enemy in very handsomely for three-quarters of a mile. At 4 o'clock in the afternoon another advance was made by the Ninth Corps—divisions of Wilcox and Ledlie. Warren's corps connecting on the left, was also pushed forward to cover the flank. The results on Friday's operation were of a mingled nature—successes and reverses. What is most to be regretted is our loss, Hancock on Thursday and Friday having lost not less than 2,500; Warren 2,000, and Burnside 1,500. During the night of Friday, the enemy abandoned all that portion of the second line which had not been carried during the two previous days, and retired to the third line, which they had meanwhile been constructing. Hereupon the commanding General resolved to make an assault along the whole line for the purpose of carrying the town. This action, therefore, separates itself from the assaults of the two previous days, which may be looked upon as of the nature of preliminary operations. This was an action which was designed to be decisive of operations on the present position. Three different assaults were made during the day—at 4 in the morning, at noon, and at 4 in the afternoon. Space would fail me, even if it was possible for you, away from the ground, to appreciate the maze of tactics through which the bloody action of Saturday wrought its way. We gained ground; it brought our front close up to the rebel lines; but it failed to give us the coveted position, and after severe losses on the part of the Second, Fifth and Ninth Corps, night found the enemy still in possession of his works covering Petersburg."

In acknowledgement of the services of his Eighteenth Army Corps, in their recent campaigning, General W. F. Smith issued the following congratulatory address: "The General commanding desires to express to his command his appreciation of the soldierly qualities which have been displayed during the campaign of the last seventeen days. Within that time they have been constantly called upon to undergo all the hardships of the soldier's life, and be exposed to all of his dangers. Marches under a hot sun have ended in severe battles, and after battle, watchful nights in the trenches gallantly taken from the enemy. But the crowning point of the honor they are entitled to has been won since the morning of the 15th inst., when a series of earthworks, on most commanding positions and of formidable strength, have been carried, with all the guns and materials of war of the enemy, including prisoners and colors. The works have all been held, and the trophies remain in our hands. This victory is all the more important to us, as the troops have never been regularly organized in camps, where time has been given them to learn the discipline necessary to a well organized *corps d'armeé*, but they have been hastily concentrated and suddenly summoned to take part in the trying campaign of our country's being. Such honor as they have won will remain imperishable. To the colored troops comprising the division of General Hinks, the General commanding would call the attention of his command. With the veterans of the Eighteenth Corps, they have stormed the works of the enemy and carried them, taking guns and prisoners, and in the whole affair they have displayed all the qualities of good soldiers." General Grant also paid his tribute to the heroism of his army. "Too much praise," said he, in a dispatch on the 17th, "cannot be given to the troops and their commanders, for the energy and fortitude displayed the last five days. Day and night has been all the same, no delays being allowed on any account." The Union loss in the four days' operations before Petersburg was estimated at over 10,000.

These active operations left General Grant's army in possession of the outer line of intrenchments before Petersburg. The capture of the city by direct assault having been found impracticable, efforts were now made to cut off its supplies in the rear by operations upon the Weldon and Danville roads. A demonstration upon the former by the Jerusalem road on the 21st and 22d, by the Second and Sixth Corps, with a portion of the Fifth, proved unsuccessful. The advance on the first day was resisted, and the enemy, fully warned of the movement, came down in force on the following, under General Hill, and, by a flank attack, striking Barlow's, Mott's, and Gibbon's divisions of the Second Corps, which was separated on the march from the Sixth Corps, and, for the time, unsupported, inflicted upon them a heavy loss, capturing a large number of prisoners, estimated at about 2,000, with four guns; 500, it was said, would probably cover the loss in killed and wounded. The disaster of the day was checked by subsequent movements on the field, in which General Meade brought up the Sixth Corps, and the shattered Second recovered a part of its lost ground. Another attempt upon the railway, the next day, by a portion of Wright's corps was met by the enemy with equal success. A number of prisoners were taken, with a further loss in killed and wounded.

Simultaneously with this movement of the army, a cavalry expedition, composed of Wilson's division and Kautz's brigade, was sent out to break up the line of the Danville Railroad. The force, numbering about 6,000 men, with three batteries of four guns each, half-rifled ordnance and half-light 12-pounders, and one battery of four small mountain-howitzers, left the vicinity of Prince George Court House on the morning of the 22d, struck the Weldon Railroad at Ream's Station, and crossed the country to the Lynchburg Railroad at Ford's Station, where, as at the former place, the track was broken up and the buildings and the other property of the road destroyed. The next day, the 23d, Kautz, taking the lead, reached the junction with the Danville road at Burkesville, where he broke up and burnt several miles of the track. Wilson, following on the Lynchburgh road, encountered a brigade of North Carolina and Virginia troops at Nottoway Court House, and a sharp skirmish ensued with a loss on each side of some sixty or seventy men. On the

24th, Wilson joined Lee on the Danville road, which they traversed to the South, destroying the rails for some thirty miles, to the bridge at Staunton River, which they found effectually guarded. After some sharp skirmishing the force began its return, crossing the country to the Nottoway River, and reaching the Weldon Railroad at the vicinity of Jarrett's Station. Here the enemy were found gathering in force, and a push was made for Ream's Station above; but, finding his command in danger of capture, and being unsupported by the main army, which, as we have just seen, had made little progress in this quarter, Wilson divided his force, that they might break through the lines with as little observation from the foe as possible. Kautz was the first to come in, by hard riding reaching the camp on the 25th, followed by Wilson, who took a more southerly route, a few days later. The whole force which escaped was thoroughly exhausted, having suffered extreme hardship and fatigue by the way. In a dispatch from headquarters on the 3d of July, General Grant thus reported the result of Wilson's operations: "Sixty miles of railroad was thoroughly destroyed. The Danville road, General Wilson reports, could not be repaired in less than forty days, even if all the material were on hand. He has destroyed all the blacksmiths' shops where the rails might be straightened, and all the mills where scantling for the sleepers could be sawed. Thirty miles of the South Side road were destroyed. Wilson brought in about 400 negroes, and many of the vast number of horses and mules gathered by his force. He reports that the rebels slaughtered without mercy the negroes which they retook. Wilson's loss of property is a small wagon-train, used to carry ammunition, his ambulance train, and twelve cannon. The horses of the artillery and wagons were generally brought off. Of the cannon, two were removed from their carriages, the wheels of which were broken, and thrown into the water; and one other gun had been disabled by a rebel shot breaking its trunions before it was abandoned. He estimated his total loss at from 750 to 1,000 men, including those lost from Kautz's division."

The necessary interval of repose in the army of the James River, after the ineffectual movements upon Petersburg, with the withdrawal of Hunter's force to Western Virginia, left the enemy free again to push a column down the valley of the Shenandoah and attempt the passage of the Upper Potomac with the design of a raid or more formidable operations in Maryland. All this they successfully accomplished, though the demonstration in its means and results was of far inferior proportions to the invasion of the previous year, which ended in the battle of Gettysburg. When General Hunter superseded General Sigel in the valley, the latter was placed in command of the defences of the Potomac, in the vicinity of Harper's Ferry. At the beginning of July he had his headquarters at Martinsburg, where a large stock of supplies had been collected, to be forwarded, in case of need, to General Hunter. The prospect of gaining possession of these was probably an additional motive with the enemy in making a fresh incursion at this time, though the prime objects of the expedition were, doubtless, to gather in the ripening crops in the valley, and, by threatening Washington, to compel the reduction of General Grant's force before Richmond, and gain the advantage of public opinion, which any show of power north of the Potomac at this time could not fail to bring with it. The rebel movement down the valley was made with secrecy and success. The entire force of the enemy, as subsequently estimated, numbered about 20,000, including two infantry corps, that of Breckinridge, embracing the divisions of Echols and Ramseur, and that of Rhodes, with his own division and that of Gordon. In addition, there was Ransom's division of cavalry, including the brigade of McCausland, Imboden, Jackson and Johnson, and three batteries of artillery. The infantry was about 15,000 strong, the cavalry about 5,000. The whole was under the command of Major-General Jubal Early.*

The first demonstration of this force was made upon Martinsburg, a portion of Sigel's command at Leetown on its flank, being driven in by the enemy in a sudden attack on the morning of Sunday, July 3d. The town was also threatened on the north. General Sigel at once, with the greater part of his stores, fell back to Harper's Ferry, crossed the river and took up a defensive position on Maryland Heights. The lower counties of the valley were now at the mercy of the enemy, and they freely helped themselves to such supplies as they could furnish, while their force was brought up preparatory to making heavier demands upon the farmers and storekeepers of Maryland and Pennsylvania. On the 14th a party of Mosby's guerrillas crossed the Potomac to Point of Rocks, drove off the Home Brigade and plundered the stores at that place. The next day a squad of the rebel cavalry made their appearance before Hagerstown, and on the following, General Ransom, with McCausland's brigade, entered the place, and demanded $20,000 from the Councilmen, which was paid to save the town from being burnt. After this and other spoliations the enemy left. Two days afterwards the town was again pillaged and a money contribution exacted by a party of raiders under Imboden. The Baltimore and Ohio Railroad was destroyed below Harper's Ferry. The Government at Washington, though unable from the conflictive reports to calculate the probable extent of the invasion, took the alarm, and began to provide new means of defence. President Lincoln called for 12,000 militia from Pennsylvania, an equal number from New York, and 5,000 from Massachusetts. General Couch at Chambersburg, and General Lewis Wallace at Baltimore, became busily engaged in organizing troops for the field. The stores and supplies at Frederick were brought away by the railway to Baltimore and the city, abandoned to the exactions of the enemy, was evacuated by our troops, who fell back to a position a few miles distant south of the Monocacy River at the junction of the roads to Washington and Baltimore. There, on Saturday, the 9th, General Lewis Wallace received the attack of the enemy. "The position," we cite the description, by a correspondent, of the action which ensued, known as the Battle of the Monocacy, "was well taken, and the ground was admirable for open warfare. The troops forming Rickett's division were assigned to the left of the railroad crossing the Baltimore pike, with their front resting on the Buckeystown road, while the remaining portion of General Wallace's forces were posted to the right of the railroad, and to General Tyler, with a small force, the duty of defending the drawbridge crossing the Monocacy, was given. On Saturday morning the rebels commenced advancing with cavalry, feeling our lines, but were promptly repelled, and fell back on their infantry supports. The rebels then brought forward a battery, and obtaining a good position, threw shells to the right of our line, with little effect. In front of our left the enemy threw out infantry skirmishers, after their cavalry had been driven in, and both skirmish lines became engaged by 9 A. M. The engagement soon became general, the enemy, during its progress, developing stronger lines in our front, and bringing forward an additional battery, which they suc-

* *Army and Navy Journal,* July 30th, 1864.

ceeded in planting in a position to enfilade our lines on the left. At this time the right was only subject to occasional skirmishing, the rebels having apparently massed their principal force over in front of our left. At 12 M. the heaviest part of the engagement took place. The rebels advanced upon our men with their lines of battle, determined to break our centre, but after withstanding a terrible fire from our side, they fell back in confusion. At this period our men felt greatly encouraged and began cheering, although it was plainly to be seen the rebels were in superior numbers, and fighting with equal determination. We made several successful charges upon the enemy and captured some prisoners, who represented they had 30,000 men, and were commanded by Ewell. They said they were not all there, but coming up as fast as possible. Toward 3 in the afternoon our ranks were becoming thin, so that our battle line was no stronger than the enemy's skirmish line. The day was lost, yet still the fighting was kept up until it was discovered the enemy had flanked our position. The turnpike bridge over the Monocacy was then destroyed, and an attempt made to destroy the iron bridge, but it failed. The retreat became soon a perfect rout, the enemy's cavalry pursuing closely secured a large number of prisoners. All of our wounded and killed in the latter part of the action were abandoned where they fell. A great number of men, principally slight-wounded, managed to reach the train, stationed at Newmarket, and were immediately sent to Baltimore. The rebels followed our retreating column until they reached Newmarket, where they no longer harassed our rear. General Wallace kept up his march until late at night; the morning found him with the remnant of his men at Ellicott's Mills. Our losses in the fight, which they call the Battle of Monocacy, will approximate close on to 1,600 killed, wounded and missing. Of the wounded, not quite 300 have arrived in all; the balance are supposed to be prisoners. The enemy's loss was, without doubt, greater than ours, as we were strictly on the defensive, and they the assaulting party. Officers present, and who have participated in nearly every battle on the Peninsula, assured me that they had never seen so many rebels before in an open space. They had generally fought them in woods or behind breastworks. To the superiority of numbers only our defeat was due. No men fought better than the old veterans of Rickett's division. I regret to say some of the troopers on the right, said to be 'hundred-day men,' had a terrible *penchant* for the rear."

In an official report after the battle, General Wallace announced to the War Department at Washington, that after fighting the enemy from 9 o'clock in the forenoon till 5 in the afternoon, his forces were at length overpowered by the superior numbers of the enemy, which he estimated to be at least 20,000, and "were forced to retreat in disorder. Our troops (he added) behaved well, but suffered severe loss." Brigadier-General Tyler was reported taken prisoner. He succeeded, however, in eluding the enemy, and reached Ellicott's Mills in safety. The withdrawal of this force left the enemy free to continue their depredations through the central portion of Maryland, an advantage which they availed themselves of the utmost, exacting considerable contributions in the small towns and driving off liberal supplies of live stock from the farmers. The country from the Potomac as far north as Westminster and east to the line of the Central Railroad was freely pillaged. The railroad was broken up at Cockeysville and at Texas, fourteen miles from Baltimore; the bridge at

* Baltimore Correspondence, *New York Times*, July 14th, 1864.

Ashland was burnt and the telegraph line cut. A raiding party under Major Harry Gillmore crossed to the Philadelphia, Baltimore and Wilmington road, and captured and destroyed a train of cars at Magnolia Station. In one of the cars Major-General W. B. Franklin, who was going north from Baltimore, was recognized and taken prisoner. The house of Governor Bradford of Maryland, in the immediate vicinity of Baltimore, who had just issued a stirring proclamation, calling upon the citizens of the State to resist the invasion, was burnt by a small raiding party in retaliation, it was said, for General Hunter's destruction of Governor Letcher's residence at Lexington in his movement upon Lynchburg. The drift of the enemy's movements being eastwardly, General Couch, on the 9th, took possession of Hagerstown on their flank.

The main rebel movement after the action at the Monocacy was towards Washington. They marched by the direct route through Rockville, and onward to the vicinity of the capital, a considerable body making its appearance on the 11th, in front of Fort Stevens, one of the series of works protecting Washington on the northern side. They could have had little hope of success in this quarter so strong and well-placed were the fortifications; but the easy approach to Fort Stevens and the cover of several houses in the vicinity gave the sharpshooters some means of annoyance which General Augur in command in the city determined effectually to check. The arrival of a portion of the Sixth Corps sent from the army of General Grant, and of the Nineteenth Corps which had just reached Fortress Monroe from New Orleans, and had been promptly forwarded, now effectually secured the safety of the capital against any force which the enemy could bring against it. In fact, the advance of a single brigade sent out by General Augur was sufficient to dislodge the advance of the enemy, who were met and put to route in the neighborhood of Silver Springs, the residence of Francis P. Blair, which they had occupied, and which they left filled with their officers and soldiers who had been wounded in the skirmishing in the vicinity. After this, the enemy alarmed at the measures being taken for their capture, gathered in their scattered raiding parties, and taking with them the spoils which they had collected, prepared to recross the Potomac in the vicinity of Poolesville. Whatever the real object of the expedition of General Early had been, in one thing he had succeeded, in securing a very handsome quantity of plunder by his adventurous raid.

One of the chief prizes however, taken on the way, was lost to him. This was Harry Gillmore's prisoner, Major General Franklin. As the tale of his escape forms one of the most interesting personal narratives of adventure of the war, we present the story as it was related by a correspondent, after an interview with General Franklin on his safe arrival at Baltimore. "The General," says he, "had taken the way train for Philadelphia, at 8:40 A. M. from Baltimore, and although hearing of the damage done to the Northern Central Railroad, feeling assured that the rebels would make the attempt to tap the Philadelphia, Wilmington, and Baltimore Railroad, still he supposed that the Directors of the railroad possessed more information in regard to the safety of the train, than was possessed by him and he embarked. Near Magnolia the train was captured by the rebel raiders under Major Gillmore. As soon as General Franklin saw how matters stood, he thought he should escape, being dressed in citizen's clothes; but, as he looked toward the rear door of the car, he saw a rebel standing there as a guard, whom he afterwards learned to be Captain

Owens, who was holding the door to prevent any one from leaving the car. Major Gillmore soon came up, and entered, as if in quest of some one in particular. A Lieutenant-Colonel, who was sick, sat in the seat fronting Franklin, and of him Major Gillmore inquired if he was Major-General Franklin. The Colonel replied he was not; but Gillmore, doubting his word, demanded to see his papers, which, on being shown him, he returned, apparently satisfied. Turning to Franklin, Gillmore inquired his name. Franklin replied, I am he; but added, you should not arrest me; I am disabled; besides, I am in citizen's clothes, and not on duty. Gillmore then said, "Well, come along, General, I will take the risk." Franklin then left the cars, and was handed over to Captain Owens for safe-keeping, while the train was being examined. The General states that he thinks it was a young man about twenty-two years old, rather short and stout, who informed the rebels who he was; for, the very moment the train was stopped, the General noticed him leave the cars, and immediately after, mingling with the rebels. The fire of the burning cars attracted the attention of a gentleman who lived near by, and who came down in his buggy to see what was the matter. The buggy was appropriated by the rebels for General Franklin, who in an hour after his capture was on the road to Towsontown with an escort. I might here state that none of his staff officers were captured. none being with him. He had just returned from a visit to General Grant, and was on thirty days leave of absence. At Towsontown, the party halted and took some refreshment; but the rebels, hearing of the closeness of some Union cavalry, moved on down the Reistertown road and encamped for the night, between the former place and Randallstown, on Mr. Olivers' farm. For a lodging place, they squatted in the corner of a wheat-field near the road. The sentries and Captain Owens guarded General Franklin. The latter, complaining of being tired and weak, lay down and pretended to fall asleep. Soon one of the sentries dropped down by his side. Morpheus claimed him, and in a few moments the remaining sentry fell on his post asleep. Captain Owens, who was on the other side of one of the sentries, had been asleep for some time. Franklin raised himself up, and saw that the motion created no alarm. He then got up on his feet, and walked off to where the buggy was standing, and walking slowly out to the road, passed all the guards, who were asleep. Reaching the road, he ran as fast as possible to the woods, some distance back, and wandering through, reached an opening where thick brush covered the ground. Burrowing a place out in the thickest of the thicket, he laid down and remained there all day on Tuesday. During the day, he could plainly hear the rebels relieving their pickets, and conversing with each other. On Tuesday night he rose from his hiding place, and walked cautiously away. He had not walked far before he saw a house, and although very hungry, he was afraid to enter; but on arriving at the next house, he determined to try to get something to eat, and also to find out the location of the country; but before entering he saw two men leave the house and go to the barn, whence they soon emerged, with their arms filled with hay, and made off toward the woods. The General concluded that they were Unionists and had hid their horses in the woods to prevent capture. On making his situation known to them, he was most kindly cared for, and on Wednesday, one of the farmers rode to Baltimore, and informed the military authorities there where he was. They immediately sent a squadron of cavalry to escort him back, and he arrived early this morning in Baltimore. He took the steamer for Havre de Grace, at 10.

this morning, on his way home. It is said that Gillmore was terribly enraged when he found out that his important prisoner had escaped, and swore he would shoot the guard; but the General thinks that he did not carry his threat into execution.*

The rebel force having now retired across the Potomac, the injuries to the Central Northern Railroad, which had interrupted communication between Washington and the East, were speedily repaired, and the threatened towns of Pennsylvania enjoyed their accustomed repose. The relief, however, was but temporary,—the enemy before the month was over, succeeded in again crossing the river, renewing the panic, and inflicting various damage upon the lower counties of Pennsylvania and the narrow region of Maryland, on their route. On their departure from before Washington, on the 13th, they were followed by General Wright, across the Potomac, into Loudon County where, on the 17th, there was a skirmish of Gen. Crook's cavalry with the foe at Snicker's Gap. This passage, having been cleared, our foes advanced and Crook's command crossed the Shenandoah at Island Ford, but were repulsed on the other side, and driven back by the enemy under Breckinridge. Another portion of our cavalry was also reported at Ashby's Gap, with a loss in both encounters of about 500. This ended the pursuit in this quarter. In another direction, meanwhile, General Averill, who had crossed the Potomac, pressed on from Martinsburg, driving a party of the enemy's cavalry before him to the vicinity of Winchester, where he was met, on the 20th, by a larger force, outside of the intrenchments, which he vanquished after a sharp engagement, capturing four cannon, and a large number of prisoners. The enemy's loss in this affair was between 300 and 400. A few days after, on Sunday the 24th, General Crook, who remained in the vicinity of Winchester, was in turn driven by the enemy who surrounded his force on both flanks, routed his force, and compelled a rapid retreat through Martinsburg across the Potomac. In this retreat, Colonel Mulligan, whose defence of Lexington, Mo., in the early annals of the war, will be remembered by the reader, was killed while commanding his brigade.

The withdrawal of Crook and Averill's forces from Virginia, left the upper fords of the Potomac again open to the enemy who immediately began to cross in scattered parties and renewed their depredations. The most disastrous of these incursions was the descent, on the morning of the 30th July, by a raiding force of about 500 men under the rebel General McCausland, upon the town of Chambersburg on the Pennsylvania border. Having demanded $500,000 from the citizens, with the alternative of burning the town, a sum which it was of course impossible to furnish on the instant, he immediately proceeded to inflict the threatened vengeance. No time was given to remove private property, and barely enough for the citizens to save their families. The town was fired in different quarters, and over 250 of its houses consumed, including all the public buildings, stores, and hotels. About two-thirds of the place was thus consumed. The pecuniary loss was estimated at over 1,000,000 of dollars, a heavy disaster to a country town of 6,000 inhabitants. "The number of persons," says a correspondent, "rendered houseless, will not fall far short of 2,500, and so rapid and thorough was the work of destruction performed that nearly all of this immense number of sufferers have lost their all. In many instances citizens were dispossessed of their watches, personal ornaments and pocketbooks by the rebel soldiers." Says an eye-witness of the scene; "Words cannot por-

* Special dispatch to the *N. Y. Times*, July 15th, 1864.

tray the truly awful sight the ruined town presents to the visitors. It is a scene of utter destruction and ruin that I shall not soon forget. From the depot buildings, which, curiously enough, were permitted to escape the fiery element, up the main street, you pass nothing but smoking and smouldering ruins, the blackened and tottering walls being the only vestige left of the dwellings and places of business. The town itself, like all Pennsylvania towns, is principally composed of brick. When we passed up the street, the heated walls and the scorching sun made it difficult for one to make any progress. For a distance of five blocks past the 'Diamond,' or square of the town, you will not find a single edifice standing. The City Hall, the hotels and principal stores, in the immediate vicinity, are now a mass of hissing and smoking bricks; across the town, for at least three blocks, the same utter destruction attests the severity of the fire and the diabolical skill of the incendiaries. The ruins of the buildings fired are absolute; not a stick, not a plank nor a rafter remain; even the window-sills and door-jams are gone. The shade-trees are withered, the garden-railings have disappeared, and the gardens themselves are covered by the *debris* of the falling walls and out-houses. The bricks composing the sidewalks are blistered, and the stone steps to the piazzas are cracked by the intense heat of the conflagration. One can scarcely imagine the completeness of the destruction unless actual eyesight attests the scene."

The same writer relates the following anecdote of the part borne by a citizen of the town: "Among the tragic events of the day was the shooting of two rebels, by Dr. Andrew Miller, while they were in the act of burning his store and dwelling. I had a conversation with the doctor, and he gave me freely the circumstances of the affair. It appears that after the shop had been set on fire twice by igniting paper, he succeeded in extinguishing the flames, when the wretches re-entered his house, and one of them struck the doctor on the cheek with a bit of burning pine wood dipped in turpentine, and he carries the scar yet. They then caught hold of a demijohn of alcohol, breaking which the flames instantly enveloped the entire store. As the ruffians were making the best of their way out, and coming toward Dr. Miller, he seized a double-barreled gun, each barrel loaded with six slugs, and gave them the contents of a barrel each. The first one was hit in the face, and the other received the charge in his breast. Both fell, and the doctor shut the door, and they were consumed in the funereal pyre their own hands had lighted. Mr. Miller is a man of about forty-five years of age.*

The occupation of the town and the conflagration were the work of but a few hours. General Averill, with his cavalry, entered the place at noon, just as the enemy withdrew, and pursued them on the westerly road through McConnellsburgh, skirmishing with their rear. The next day he followed them to the Potomac at Hancock, where his jaded command prevented further pursuit. The destruction of Chambersburg, and the various minor incursions of the enemy above and below Harper's Ferry, across the Potomac, which ensued, now aroused the Government and the authorities of the border states in this quarter to more effectual exertions. Brigadier-General Kelly and General Averill rendered important services in meeting and defeating the enemy at several points. But the most important measure was a new organization by the War Department of the several military forces in Northern and Western Virginia. In a bulletin of Secretary Stanton, dated the 8th of August, it was announced that Major-General Sheridan, of General Grant's army, was assigned

* *New York Daily Times*, August 2d and 4th, 1864.

to the command of the forces in the Middle Military Division, consisting of the Department of Washington, the Middle Department, and the Department of the Susquehanna and Southwest Virginia. The new commander entered upon his work with his accustomed energy, and, as we shall see, in no long time convinced General Early in the valley that he had a powerful antagonist to deal with.

From these movements on the Potomac, we return to General Grant's army on the James River. After the attempts on the Weldon road, which have been described, the army, which still held its grasp upon the outer works before Petersburg, was engaged in strengthening its lines, pushing forward intrenchments, and planting powerful batteries at convenient points, which kept up, at intervals, a destructive bombardment of the city. On the 4th of July, the fire, in celebration of the National Anniversary, was particularly active. The salutes of the day throughout the Army and the Navy on the James were with shotted guns, a custom kept up by General Grant when, as at the taking of Atlanta and other occasions, he was called upon to celebrate a victory. The enemy occasionally responded, and "artillery duels," with picket firing, spite of all efforts to check the latter, were frequently reported. Our forces having been drawn in from the left for purposes of concentration, the enemy were free to repair the injuries to the Weldon road, which was again put in working order. There were occasional reconnoissances, with skirmishing, during the greater part of July, while a portion of both armies was withdrawn to the Potomac. The heat of the month, of unusual continuance without a respite, was intolerable, and was aggravated by the unintermitted drought. Several changes about the middle of the month were made in the division and corps commanders. General Gillmore, relieved of the command of the Tenth Corps, was succeeded by General Birney from the Second Corps, and General W. F. Smith, of the Eighteenth Corps, was relieved and succeeded by General Ord. The work in the trenches, meanwhile, was diligently kept up, while an extraordinary labor was being performed in the construction of a mine leading to a formidable fort of the enemy's, in front of Burnside's line, and about 2,000 yards southeast from Petersburg. The required length of the mine, to reach the point proposed, was about 500 feet. The suggestion of this work, it is said, was first made to General Grant, by Lieutenant-Colonel Pleasants of the Forty-eighth Pennsylvania Regiment, a practical miner, who, with his regiment, became engaged in its construction. The excavation was made from the side of a ravine surmounted by an earthwork, in a gallery about four feet wide at the bottom and about four and a half feet high, the tunnel sloping upward with the rising ground till the enemy's fort was reached, about twenty feet below the surface. Here two diverging galleries, embracing the area of the fort, were constructed to the right and left of the main channel, in which several chambers were constructed, in which were placed about four tons of powder. Wooden pipes ran about a hundred feet from the chambers toward the mouth of the tunnel, connecting with a fuse to the entrance. The work, in which many difficulties in the way of water, marshy grounds and quicksands had been overcome, was completed by the 25th of July, a month after its commencement. It was now to be fired, and advantage was to be taken of the explosion to pass over the ruins and seize in the tumult a cannonading crest beyond, the possession of which would determine the capture of Petersburg.

The more fully to succeed in this

work, General Grant resorted to strategy. A feint was ordered to be made by a movement of troops to the north bank of the James River, to direct the attention of the enemy in that direction, while the army was being prepared for the assault upon Petersburg. General Foster, with a division of the Tenth Corps, held an advance position on the north of the river at Deep Bottom with the enemy guarding the passage to Richmond in his front. A preliminary demonstration was made in this quarter on the 22d of July, when a brigade was crossed on a newly-constructed pontoon bridge in the vicinity of Foster's camp. Skirmishing with the enemy ensued, the gunboats taking part in the movement. On the night of the 26th, Hancock's Second Corps, followed by two divisions of Sheridan's cavalry also crossed the river, and the next day engaged the enemy in their front at Newmarket, capturing four 20-pounder Parrott guns and taking a number of prisoners. Hancock's corps was chiefly engaged in this affair, which was followed up on the 28th by an advance of the cavalry and some sharp skirmishing with a body of rebel infantry. To add to this show of military operations the covered, empty wagon train of the Sixth Corps was transported across the river by daylight in view of the enemy. The effect of these continued movements was to induce General Lee to withdraw on the 28th and 29th from 15 to 20,000 men from Petersburg to the defence of Richmond in the direction of Malvern Hill. Having secured this object, General Grant, while Lee's troops were on their march secretly brought Hancock's corps back by night to the south of the river.

It now remained to fire the mine and carry out the projected assault on Petersburg. How this was done may be told in the account of a correspondent with the army. "On the evening of Friday, the 29th, the troops were notified that the long-talked-of mine would be exploded at 3½ in the morning, and directed to be in readiness to move forward at a moment's warning. On the explosion of the mine, the division of Brigadier-General Ledlie, supported by the divisions of Brigadier-Generals Wilcox and Potter, was to lead the assault upon the rebel line. The colored troops of Ferrero, who were originally intended to lead the charge, were to remain massed in the rear, awaiting orders. In the mean time the troops on the right and left of our line were to open from their works upon the enemy, while the batteries along our entire front were to withdraw by rapid firing, as much as possible, the attention of the rebel artillery from our advancing column in the centre. Half-past 3 in the morning found our men in the trenches, wide awake and expectant. Every thing being in readiness, the fuse connecting with the remain chamber was lighted. Ten minutes elapsed and yet no explosion. Breathless with suspense the men awaited the result. Half an hour passed by and the silence remained unbroken, and it became evident that the fuse had gone out. But who, with even the probability of safety, dare venture along that dark, dripping passage to examine the fuse, when death in its most horrible form might await its coming! A Lieutenant and Sergeant of the Forty-eighth Pennsylvania step forward and volunteer to enter the tunnel. The proffer of their services is accepted, and they enter the passage. Some delay occurs in the adjustment of the fuses, and meantime a red glow in the east heralds the coming of the sun. At 4½ the fuse is again lighted, and again the men in the trenches clench their guns with a tighter grasp, and await the explosion. Five minutes pass, and all remains silent. The rebels in the fort, unconscious of their doom, sleep on; the sun, as if anxious to witness the spectacle, mounts the horizon, and at that moment the earth heaves and trembles as if shaken by an earthquake. An instant, and then a terrific explosion; huge masses of earth, lifted as a child would toss a marble, men, cannon, caissons, limbers, forges, guns and timbers are belched forth high in air, and descend with a heavy 'thud,' a shapeless, chaotic mass. It is doubtful whether any of the occupants of the fort made their escape from death or capture. Numbers were doubtless engulfed in the yawning crater when the huge mass descended, and if alive, were so deeply entombed as to render extrication impossible. Shapeless masses, once men, were found in the debris, and some were found half buried, and were dug out with bayonets, sticks and swords. An officer, while sitting in the ruins, resting his hand on the loose earth thrown up by the explosion, fancied that he discovered a motion beneath. Taking a piece of board, he commenced exploring the dirt, and in a moment uncovered the face of a rebel who had been buried in the ruins. Strange to say, he was uninjured, although nearly suffocated by his premature burial. The crater formed by the explosion was oblong in shape, about 150 feet in length, and 25 in width. The destruction of the fort was complete. Four companies of the Eighteenth North Carolina Regiment, with a portion of another not known, are supposed to have been buried in the debris.

"So tremendous was the explosion, that many of our own men, on hearing the report and seeing a vast column shooting into the air only a short distance in their front, were for a moment struck with terror. It was but momentary, however, for in less time than I can write it the column which had been massed and waiting in the ravine below charged forward with a wild cheer, drove the astonished rebels from a portion of their line on the right and left of the demolished fort, capturing several colors, of which the division of General Ledlie took two. The division of General Ledlie, which was selected to lead the charge, consisted of two brigades, the first commanded by General Bartlett, and the second by Colonel Marshall. General B.'s brigade consisted of the Ninth, Twenty-first, Thirty-fifth, Fifty-sixth, Fifty-seventh and Fifty-ninth Massachusetts Regiments; that of Colonel Marshall of the One Hundredth Pennsylvania, One Hundred and Seventy-ninth New York, Third Maryland, Second Pennsylvania Heavy Artillery and the Fourteenth New York Heavy Artillery. His division was disposed in column of regiments, the Second Brigade, Colonel Marshall, leading the charge, with the Fourteenth New York Heavy Artillery in the advance. The rebels occupied a strong line of breastworks, with an abatis in front, and in front of the latter tripping wires were strung several inches from the ground, and concealed by a small growth of oats. Between these wires and the abatis sharp stakes were driven, for the purpose of impaling any who might be thrown down by the wires. On reaching the work, General Wilcox deployed to the left of Ledlie and General Potter by the right flank to the right. Under a fierce fire from enfilading batteries and musketry on either flank, they penetrated the abatis, gaining the ruins of the rebel fort, and, re-forming their shattered ranks, prepared to hold the position wrested from the enemy at all hazards. On the report of the explosion of the mine, the artillery along our whole line opened upon the enemy with a fierce and incessant cannonade, which lasted for near two hours, in order to divert the enemy from our main point of attack by inducing him to believe that we were about to open a general engagement. It is evident, however, that the enemy soon discovered our intentions, as trains were heard coming from the direction of Richmond bringing fresh supplies of troops which were soon discovered massed in the rear of the crests beyond the demolished fort. It is impossible to be minute in giving the exact positions of regiments, except that the line was formed from left to right as originally intended, viz.: Wilcox on the left, Ledlie in the centre, and Potter on the right. Exposed as they were in storming the works to a merciless fire both of musketry and artillery, it was impossible to maintain perfect organization, and in some instances portions of regiments of one division were fighting gallantly in another. As the possession of the crest of hills in front of our line was indispensable to us, it became evident that without their possession our troops would ultimately be forced to fall back to their original position. Several charges for its possession were made by our line, but each time the galling fire compelled it to fall back to the works first captured from the enemy. Charges were also frequently essayed by the enemy, but were in a like manner repulsed. At 9 o'clock Ferrero's division of colored troops were brought up to dislodge the enemy from the hill, and, from the gallant style in which they came up, it was believed that their attempt would be successful. Subjected to the same severe ordeal, they wavered a moment, and then breaking in disorder, in spite of the entreaties and threats of their officers, who behaved splendidly, they fell back in confusion through our lines, repulsed and demoralized. It was their first baptism in fire, and, when the severity of the ordeal is considered, the fact that they did fall back is a matter of no great surprise. Finally rallying, they again advanced toward the front, but in vain; it is only to again fall back without the accomplishment of their purpose. Finding the position untenable, General Grant, who had come up to the front before daybreak, ordered our lines to retire to their original position. In the ruins around the immense crater formed by the explosion of the mine were a considerable number of men and officers, including Brigadier-General Bartlett, commanding First, and Colonel Marshall, the Second Brigade of Ledlie's, both reported as captured by the enemy. From the position of the ruins, escape by a retreat to the rear with any degree of safety was impossible, as the only exit was swept by grape and canister, and covered by the muskets of the enemy on either flank. In consequence, it was deemed advisable to leave this party in the ruins until nightfall would permit of their escape. It is believed, however, that all were captured by the enemy. Our total wounded in the hospitals of the Ninth Corps today number 1,450, of which 600 belong to Ferrero's, 308 to Potter's, 332 to Wilcox's and 250 to Ledlie's division. As a large number were left on the field the total loss of the Corps will probably reach 2,000."*

This new attempt having failed of success with a loss in the movements of the day estimated at 5,000, the army again settled down to the usual skirmishing and artillery firing of this irregular siege. To the north of the James river a strong working party was presently engaged, under cover of our advanced batteries on that side, in digging a canal across the peninsula at Dutch Gap for the sake of securing a nearer base of operations against Richmond, flanking several of the enemy's important works and affording a passage for the fleet which was now kept below by the formidable obstructions planted in the six miles circuitous course of the river proposed to be avoided by the new channel.

By the middle of August, General Grant was prepared to renew his attempt upon the southern railway communication of the enemy on the Weldon

* Army Correspondence, *New York Tribune*, August 3d, 1864.

road, which, often threatened, and at times seriously injured, had never thus far been permanently occupied. The effort was again made, and though severely contested, was this time effectual. Military possession was taken of a portion of the road near Petersburg, and it continued to be held. As on the previous occasion, a diversion of the enemy's forces was made by a preliminary movement, resulting in heavy fighting on the north bank of the James. On the night of August 13th, Gregg's cavalry division and General Birney's Tenth Corps crossed the river on the pontoon bridge and joined Foster's brigade in its old position at Deep Bottom, while at the same time Hancock's Second Corps which had been ostentatiously sent down the river on transports, was secretly brought back and united with this force. The next day, Sunday, an oppressively hot day, both corps were engaged in a forward movement upon the enemy's entrenchment covering the road to Richmond immediately in their front. A series of rifle pits and some of the outer works were carried by the Tenth Corps on the left with the capture of four guns and a number of prisoners; while on the centre a portion of Hancock's Corps was repulsed in an advance upon an advantageous position of the enemy, the Union loss of the day being estimated at least a thousand. On the following day there was some heavy cavalry skirmishing on the right where Gregg's division, guarding the flank, reached the Charles City road. On Tuesday the 16th, the weather still continuing oppressively hot, fighting was renewed in an advance by the cavalry and a portion of the Second Corps at Deep Run, on the right, and by the Tenth Corps on the centre. The former was in the nature of a reconnoissance with heavy skirmishing; the latter was something more, a line of the enemy's works being carried after a severe struggle, and again retaken by them, the contest continuing till evening. A rough estimate of the losses of the day in Grant's army assigned 1,000 to the Tenth Corps, 500 to the Second, and 100 to the cavalry. Several hundred prisoners were reported taken from the enemy.*

There was also a minor movement by Major Ludlow, in command of the working party at Dutch Gap, in an advance across the peninsula, assisted by the fire of the gunboats to a position from which after various artillery firing the next day he retired. On the night of the 18th General Birney's line was attacked by the enemy in heavy force, and they were repulsed with great loss. "In front of our colored regiment," wrote General Birney in a dispatch the next day, "eighty-two dead bodies of the enemy are counted. The colored troops behaved handsomely and in fine spirits. The assault was in column, a division strong, and would have carried the works if they had not been so well defended. The enemy's loss was at least a thousand."

While such were the events on the north bank of the James, the recent state of affairs remained for several days as usual on the left before Petersburg till the morning of the 18th, when after a heavy cannonade from the enemy before daylight, General Warren moved with the Fifth Corps from their camp towards the Weldon railroad which he struck about noon at Six-Mile Station. While General Griffin's division remained there breaking up the road, General Ayer's, with Crawford's and Cutter's divisions advanced several miles beyond, when about two-and-a-half miles south of Petersburg they took up a position to the right and left of the railway, and where they received the attack of Hill's Corps which came out to meet them. The enemy charged at first with effect but were afterwards repulsed, the fighting continuing with various vicissitudes during the day, but

* *Army and Navy Journal*, August 27th, 1864.

leaving Warren in possession of the road. Determined to hold it, at night he threw up entrenchments in a heavy rain. The next day while the new line was being strengthened and reinforced to connect with the old position before the city on the right it was assailed in the afternoon in the midst of a heavy rain-storm by General Hill, and the two right divisions of Warren's Corps were driven in, with the capture of a number of prisoners. A similar assault with less success, was made by the enemy on our left. The Ninth Corps now coming up,—to the command of which General Wilcox had a few days before been assigned when General Burnside was relieved—and the artillery being effectively employed, the enemy was driven from the field, and the Union lines reestablished. All this was not accomplished without heavy loss, between two and three thousand prisoners were claimed to be taken by the enemy, while our killed and wounded exceeded a thousand. Secretary Stanton in a dispatch on the 20th, estimated the loss of the enemy during the previous week in killed, wounded and captured at not less than 4,000. The exact numbers in these and other battles of the campaign, must be left to be ascertained by a future scrutiny of official returns, the publication of which, for obvious reasons, was now withheld. Another desperate attempt was made by the enemy on Sunday the 21st, to break up the line now firmly established across the railway. An attack was made in two heavy columns, both of which were repulsed with severe loss, the enemy suffering fearfully from their exposure to the fire from our works. Their loss in killed and wounded was estimated at a thousand, and several hundred prisoners, including several field officers. The loss of officers on the field was large, as usual in these arduous assaults of well defended positions. Hancock's Second Corps, with the portion of the Tenth and the cavalry which had been engaged north of the river, were now withdrawn to the operations before Petersburg. While Warren strengthened his position before the city, a considerable body of infantry with cavalry supports was engaged in the destruction of the railway below. They had been reinforced in this work in the vicinity of Reams Station by the Second Corps, when on the 25th the enemy made an attack upon the latter which General Hancock thus reported on the following day to the Department:—"The attack about 5.30 P. M. was probably intended to be simultaneous, by Wilcox on my centre and Heth on my left. The enemy formed in the woods, placed their artillery in position, opened a heavy cannonade, lasting about fifteen minutes, and then assaulted Miles' force. He resisted tenaciously, but the enemy broke his line. Some of Gibbons' troops were hurried over to repair the damage, and the enemy only gained a slight foothold. They soon attempted my extreme left and drove Gibbons' division from his line. His men had been much wearied in rushing over to General Miles and back during the repeated assaults. General Gibbons succeeded in forming a strong line, and the enemy, who were pressing on with great enthusiasm, were severely checked by the dismounted cavalry under General Gregg, which he handled handsomely. Miles regained most of his intrenchments, distinguishing himself. All he had to work with were such small parties as could be rallied and formed by his staff officers. The fighting was continuous until dark, the enemy being held in check by artillery, dismounted cavalry and skirmishers. At dark we withdrew for the reasons stated. The Chief of Artillery reports that he lost about 250 horses. The enemy made no advance up to a late hour last night, holding as far as could be seen, some of our captured guns with their skirmish line. They must have suffered heavily. My own loss, including cavalry, will perhaps not exceed twelve or fifteen hundred, though this is surmise, as the command is not yet organized. Captain Brownson, of my staff, was mortally wounded during the night. Colonel Walker, A. A. G., is missing. This is acknowledged to have been one of the most determined and desperate fights of the war, resembling Spottsylvania in its character, though the number engaged gives less importance to it. A few more good troops would have given a victory of considerable importance. I forward this forenoon prisoners from the field, from Wilcox's and Heth's divisions. Major Angel, of my staff, saw and conversed with two prisoners of Mahone's division, last night. I do not find them this morning. They said Mahone's division, with the exception of one brigade, was there." This engagement was undoubtedly a heavy disaster to the Union forces engaged—the losses numbering, it is said, about 2,000 prisoners and about 1,000 killed and wounded, with nine cannon of necessity abandoned to the superior force of the enemy, who, however, in their turn suffered heavily. But it did not affect the main object of the movement of which it was but an incident—the occupation of the Weldon road below Petersburg, which continued to be firmly held by General Grant.

CHAPTER C.

GENERAL SHERMAN'S GEORGIA CAMPAIGN—CHATTANOOGA TO ATLANTA, MAY–SEPTEMBER, 1864.

WHEN General Grant, in March, 1864, was called to the head of the army with the rank of Lieutenant-General, and removed his headquarters to the army of the Potomac, the important department in the South, the immediate command of which he necessarily relinquished, was assigned to a well-tried officer, of consummate military experience and resources, Major-General W. T. Sherman. The latter by the order of the War Department of the 12th of March, was placed in command of the Military Division of the Mississippi, composed of the Departments of the Ohio, the Cumberland, the Tennessee, and the Arkansas. Major-General J. B. McPherson, also an officer of rare merit, was assigned to the command of the Department and Army of the Tennessee. Major-General Thomas was in command of the Army of the Cumberland at Chattanooga, and Major-General Schofield of the army of the Ohio at Knoxville. By a subsequent order in April, Major-General Hooker was placed in command of the Eleventh and Twelfth consolidated Corps; Major-General O. O. Howard was assigned to the Fourth Corps, relieving Major-General Granger; Major-General J. M. Schofield to the Twenty-third Corps. Major-General Frank P. Blair having withdrawn the resignation as an army officer which he had tendered on taking his seat in Congress in January, was permitted by the President to resume his rank, and was appointed to the command of the Seventeenth Army Corps. Major-General John M. Palmer now held the command of the Fourteenth Corps, and Major-General John A. Logan of the Fifteenth, General George Stoneman was assigned to the command of a special cavalry force. Major-General John Newton was ordered to report to General Thomas at Chattanooga, to be assigned to duty. With such men as these, and with numerous division commanders of tried merit in the field, General Sherman, at the beginning of May, simultaneously with the advance of the army of the Potomac at the east, began a campaign destined after several months of arduous effort, of most heroic exertion, to attain the object in view from the beginning—the capture of Atlanta.

This, next to Richmond, was the most important position, as a centre of military operations now held by the Confederacy ; and not without reason were the two great armies of the Union at this time directed against these points. With the captures already made, the possession of these cities would assure complete military control of the States in rebellion. In an article on Sherman's projected campaign, while it was still being carried out, a Northern journalist presented this striking view of its main object :—"In the first place, it is Atlanta itself—a modern, well-built city, now approaching its twenty-first year, but still sooner to reach its freedom birthday. Laid out in a circular form, with a radius of about a mile, it contains within its strongly intrenched circumference (now that the war has brought an accretion of a fourth to its numbers,) a population of 20,000 souls. From its protected situation, deep in the interior of the Confederacy, it was chosen at the outset as a great military depot of supplies and of material of war, and, furthermore, as a great military workshop. In this respect it has no equal in the central zone of the Confederacy. It is the Richmond of the West. Here are arsenals, foundries, furnaces, rolling-mills, machine-shops, laboratories, factories, which have been busily supplying the Confederacy with munitions of war for the past three years. Here the finest and largest rolling-mill in the South has been turning out iron rails for roads, and armor-plating for iron-clads, the latter in great abundance. Here are factories for shot and shell, for pistols, powder, cartridges and percussion caps, for gun-carriages, for small arms, for equipments, wagons and harnesses, shoes and clothing, and for many other purposes useful to the rebel commissariat. Here also are railroad repair-shops of incalculable value to the enemy. At least 2,000 people keep this valuable machinery in operation. We, with our surplus Springfields and Lowells, do not appreciate how illy the enemy can spare this single city. As a depot of supplies, also as well as a manufactory, Atlanta has played an important part. But doubtless most of its stores and its completed goods, have already been prudentially removed. Next, Atlanta is one of the chief railroad centres in the Confederacy. Northerly runs the Western and Atlantic road to Chattanooga. Southwesterly, the Atlanta, West Point and Montgomery road, connecting the former point with the capital of Alabama, thence with Mobile on the South, and with the whole Mississippi Valley on the West. Southeasterly runs the important road to Macon, and thence to Savannah. Easterly, the road to Augusta, and again to Savannah and to Charleston. Besides these advantages, there is a topographical one of great importance. The chief military point in all the mountain region of this vicinity is Chattanooga. That we must continue to hold in force at all hazards. Its chief value, however, is in its defensive relation to East Tennessee, because from that point a column can easily throw itself on the communications of any hostile force which has passed through the mountain gaps to ravage the interior of the State. Accordingly, it is the key of all that lies behind its back, or, rather, it is the gate which closes up all that region from assault. But for penetrating Central Georgia,

Atlanta is the true starting point. Atlanta is as essentially the door of Georgia as Chattanooga of Tennessee. Till it is seized, only cavalry can be used by us further South, and their raids must be hurried, temporary, often ineffective, and always hazardous. Even a movable infantry column, like that famous one of Sherman which traversed Mississippi from Vicksburg to Meridian at the opening of this year, would be marched in this quarter with great peril, as the army in Atlanta could harass its rear. Now, betwixt these two main points extend the Alleghanies, ridging the whole face of the country into a mountainous formation. Lookout Mountain, Mission Ridge, Taylor's Ridge, John's Mountain, Dug-Down Mountain, and other parallel ranges, break up the region lying between the Tennessee and the Chattahoochee. So long as our base remains at Chattanooga, the enemy can always force us, in a southward march, to expend a campaign of several months in pressing him to Atlanta. We should have to fight him at long odds in such eyries as Buzzard's Roost, or turn him, as Sherman does, by flanking marches of 150 or 200 miles. But once carried, Atlanta is the new advanced position, and that labor is done once for all. To the southwest the country is still broken with the Alleghany chain, and due south of Atlanta is the formidable ridge of Pine Mountain. But, in the main, the region on the south and southeast is less rugged than that which Sherman's legions have already surmounted, and is less defensible."*

With this view of the military value of Atlanta we can better appreciate the heroic persistency with which General Sherman over a track of more than 130 miles by the most direct railway route, interposing many natural obstacles, affording ready means of resistance, and defended by a resolute foe, sought and obtained the prize. He had opposed to him the second army in the Confederacy, inferior only to that of General Lee in Virginia, commanded by Joseph E. Johnston, one of the most experienced of the rebel officers, and especially chosen by President Davis as best capable to resist the progress of the Union forces in the southwest. Associated with Johnston were the corps commanders Major-Generals Polk, Hardee, Hood, and other well-tried leaders of the war. Numerically, the force of General Sherman was superior. He had at his command, at the start, according to his own official report, a grand aggregate of 98,797 troops, with 254 guns. Of these, 60,773, with 130 guns, were in General Thomas' Army of the Cumberland, in the following proportions: infantry, 54,568; artillery, 2,377; cavalry, 3,828. McPherson's Army of the Tennessee numbered 24,465, with 96 guns, including 22,437 infantry; 1,404 artillery, and 624 cavalry. Schofield's Army of the Ohio numbered 13,559, with 28 guns, including 11,183 infantry, 679 artillery, 1,697 cavalry. This effective force, General Sherman tells us, was maintained during the campaign, the number of men joining from furlough and hospitals about compensating for the loss in battle and from sickness. The enemy's force was estimated by General Sherman at about 55,000 or 60,000, including about 10,000 cavalry under Wheeler. But to compensate for any inequality, the enemy had the advantage of position, their thorough knowledge of an intricate field of operations, an interior line of communication for supplies and reinforcements, while Sherman, at every move departing farther from his base as Johnston approached his, risked every thing on the issue of the campaign. "It must," wrote a correspondent from the field, recording the advance to Resaca, "have been apparent to General Sherman, before throwing his columns through this mountain pass, that the campaign into

* *New York Times*, July 26th, 1864.

Georgia must be either a victory or a Moscow for the Union Army Victorious, the rebel cause in Georgia and the whole South is collapsed. Defeated, the enemy would have it in their power to inflict a heavy blow upon us, such as we have never experienced in the history of the war."*

Under these circumstances, General Sherman, having visited the several commands and fully organized his forces, reduced the trains to the absolute necessities of an army in the field, and otherwise provided for an active, fighting campaign, on the 2d of May set his army in motion in the advance from Chattanooga. The army moved in three columns, General Thomas, in front, advancing upon the line of the enemy on the railroad at Ringgold, while General Schofield with his own and Howard's corps moved down on the left from Cleveland; and McPherson, with the Army of the Tennessee, was prepared to execute a flanking movement on the right. Upon Thomas' advance, little resistance was made by the enemy at their outposts at Ringgold and Tunnel Hill, as they fell back to the stronger position a few miles beyond at Buzzard's Roost. This was a narrow gap in the mountains closing on the south the small valley beyond Tunnel Hill, through which the railway ran to Dalton. On the west it was guarded by the northern extremity of Rocky Faced Ridge, a continuous height of several hundred feet, running for some twenty miles parallel with the railway beyond Resaca. The enemy had planted their works across the valley and occupied the declivities on either side, effectually guarding the passage to Dalton. Several days were passed following May 8 in a reconnoissance of this position, with frequent skirmishing and demonstrations on the enemy. The details of this mountain warfare will, when fully narrated, supply some of the most picturesque incidents of the war. A correspondent who was with the portion of the army which sought to gain a position upon Rocky Faced Ridge, thus describes one of these scenes: "General Hooker," he writes, "had hard fighting on the 9th, on the mountain crest. After skirmishing heavily all the fore part of the day, with his men deployed on the steep hill-sides, among rocks and inaccessible cliffs, he finally assaulted the enemy's position under a murderous fire. The rebel line was carried, and held for a few minutes, but, finding themselves exposed to a raking, plunging fire from a new position, they were compelled to fall back. About fifty men were lost in the assault, the larger proportion wounded. Lieutenant-Colonel McIlvain of the Sixty-fourth Ohio was killed, and each of the other commanders of the regiments engaged were wounded. Major Rust of the Twenty-seventh Illinois had been wounded early in the day. The men and officers behaved with the greatest gallantry, and after the repulse maintained their old position, though subjected to a very heavy fire. Throughout there was continued skirmishing on the west front of Rocky Face, General J. D. Morgan's brigade, the first of the Second Division Fourteenth Corps being still engaged, where they were sent in on the 8th. This made two days and a night in the mountains. The Sixtieth Illinois Volunteers pushed upwards at a position toward the southern extremity of the mountain, and some portion of the troops reached within fifty yards of the rebel riflemen, who fell back to the two gaps or depressions in the crest as the Union troops advanced. They finally reached a perpendicular cliff, under which the rebel sharpshooters could not reach them with their rifles, so they began to throw stones and roll rocks down upon them. Here they remained for some time, within speaking distance, the rebels call-

* Army correspondence, *N. Y. Tribune.* Camp Southwest of Resaca, Ga. May 13th, 1864.

ATTACK AT ROCKY FACE RIDGE, G^a

From the original painting by Chappel, in the possession of the publishers.

Johnson, Fry & Co. Publishers. New York.

ing out to them in the choice phraseology of the chivalry. A corporal of the Sixty-fourth halloed to the rebels, and told them if they would stop firing stones he would read to them the President's proclamation. The offer was at first received with derisive yells; but they soon became quiet, and the corporal read to them the amnesty proclamation. When he came to some part they did not approve, they would set up a fiendish yell, as if in defiance, and then send down an instalment of rocks by way of interlude. But the corporal kept on, in spite of these uncivil demonstrations, and finished the document, when there was another outburst of yells, mingled with laughter, and the old business of tumbling down the rocks, and firing was again resumed."*

The same correspondent, writing a few days later, on the 13th, from the summit, says: "I have just climbed to the top of this ridge, 500 feet high, following the track of Harker's brigade, and of General Judah, who came up last evening. The top of this ridge is nothing but a mass of rock and ledges, a sort of hog's back, not wider than a wagon-track, along which only three or four men can march abreast. At intervals are abrupt and rugged ledges, so broken that a horse cannot travel, and men can only pick their way with difficulty. Our troops, led by the Hundred and Twenty-fifth Ohio, of General Harker's brigade, took the heights yesterday, and advanced to a point one-third of the way along the crest. A mile further on is the cleared knoll used by the rebels for a signal station. Of course, it is impossible to put many men in position in such a place. The enemy have a strong rocky promontory of triangular shape, with an inside earthwork, so elevated above the rocky ridge immediately in front as to render artillery useless. Even musketry fire is wasted against these rocks. One advantage to us is, that much of the enemy's fire passes over the heads of our men. Generals McLean and Wagner of the Fourth Corps are also up here, with evidently more men than can, by any possibility, be well used, except to guard against a flank movement, which seems to be anticipated, up a spur of the mountain near the center of our position. To guard against this, a mile of stone-wall has been constructed along the east edge of the crest, and McLean's brigade is drawn along it in two lines to repel any such attack. Firing is brisk in the front, and some wounded are coming to the rear, among others, Major Rust of the Twenty-seventh Illinois Volunteers, not dangerously wounded in the head; some half a dozen privates have also been wounded. The rebel position is a rocky castle, with no room to approach it on the flanks, except by clinging to the rocky sides of the mountain, where they are exposed to the fire of sharpshooters stationed in the trees and in the fort. General Harker is pitching into the place with a desperate pertinacity, but, I should judge, with poor chances of dislodging the enemy. With the enemy on this crest, the southern end of which leads into Buzzard's Roost Gap, no effort to capture or hold the latter position would be practicable. Hence the necessity of driving them out. A line of rebel works is visible in and extending across the valley to the east, which connects with earthworks on the hither slope of the opposite ridge. A battle in the Alps could only equal the contest now going on here, half-way to the clouds, among rocks and stony gorges of the hills. From this eyrie the whole country lies like a map beneath the eye, now, however, obscured by a thick haze which overspreads the lower hills and valleys. Cannonading is going on toward Buzzard's Roost, but there is no general engagement. The troops perfectly line the crest, lying down

* War correspondent E. S. of the *New York Tribune*, Near Rocky Faced Ridge, May 11th, 1864.

among the rocks until called into action. Having advanced to within about 400 yards of the rebel works, vainly endeavouring to get a view of the position through the trees, and finding the place dangerous, by the frequent arrival of leaden missiles, which pass over singing, or drop among the soldiers, I fall back in good order, to witness what is passing in the valley below. General McLean is about withdrawing his brigade to co-operate with the Twenty-third Army Corps ; and General Wagner is moving one of his regiments down upon the left spur of the mountain, to intercept any rebel approach from that direction. One cannot visit this place without feeling how almost hopeless the task must be to dislodge an enemy thus intrenched by nature. The position may be turned, but it seems as difficult to capture as it would to storm the Palisades from the Hudson. The Engineer corps has been busy felling the trees, which have been converted into abattis to protect the steep sides of the hill, and a space of half a mile is thus laid bare, from which the view is magnificent."

While this skirmishing was going on with a loss of some 800 killed and wounded, chiefly in Geary's and Wood's divisions of Hooker's and Palmer's corps,* General McPherson, according to General Sherman's original intention, was making his way by Snake Creek Gap below, through Rocky Faced Ridge to Sugar Valley on the east opening upon Resaca, a position on the railroad about eighteen miles south of Dalton. "The possession of this," wrote Secretary Stanton in a dispatch to General Dix, "will place a strong corps of veteran troops in the rear of the enemy, while Thomas advances upon the front and Schofield closes in on the flank from Cleveland." The result answered the Secretary's prediction. The rebel General Johnston in consequence of this flanking movement, fell back upon his next strong position at Resaca, which, in consequence of his direct route by the railway, he reached in advance of McPherson's arrival, leaving Dalton open to occupation by Thomas' corps. McPherson having secured the passage through Snake Creek Gap without serious opposition, was followed by the remainder of the army which now took up a position along the Sugar Valley several miles in extent, facing the enemy's line of works at Resaca.

"On the 12th of May," says General Sherman, in his admirable official report of the campaign—the only authentic narrative of these important military movements, "we moved against Resaca, General McPherson on the direct road, preceded by General Kilpatrick's cavalry; General Thomas to come up on his left and General Schofield on his. General Kilpatrick met and drove the enemy's cavalry from a cross road within two miles of Resaca, but received a wound which disabled him and gave the command of his brigade to Colonel Murray, who, according to his orders, wheeled out of the road, leaving General McPherson to pass. General McPherson struck the enemy's infantry pickets near Resaca and drove them within their fortified lines and occupied a ridge of 'bald' hills, his right on the Oostanaula, about two miles below the railroad bridge, and his left abreast the town. General Thomas came up on his left, facing Camp Creek, and General Schofield broke his way through the dense forest to General Thomas' left. Johnston had left Dalton, and General Howard entered it and pressed his rear. Nothing saved Johnston's army at Resaca but the impracticable nature of the country, which made the passage of troops across the valley almost impossible. This fact enabled his army to reach Resaca from Dalton along the comparatively good roads constructed beforehand, partly from the topographi-

* *Army and Navy Journal*, May 21st, 1864.

cal nature of the country, and partly from the foresight of the rebel chief. At all events, on 14th of May, we found the rebel army in a strong position behind Camp Creek, occupying the forts at Resaca, and his right on some high chestnut hills to the north of the town. I at once ordered a pontoon bridge to be laid across the Oostanaula at Lay's Ferry in the direction of Calhoun; a division of the Sixteenth Corps, commanded by General Sweeney, to cross and threaten Calhoun; also the cavalry division of General Garrard to move from its position at Villanow down towards Rome, to cross the Oostanaula and break the railroad below Calhoun and above Kingston if possible, and with the main army I pressed against Resaca at all points. General McPherson got across Camp Creek near its mouth, and made a lodgment close up to the enemy's works, on hills that commanded, with short-range artillery, the railroad and trestle bridges; and General Thomas pressing close along Camp Creek Valley, threw General Hooker's corps across the head of the creek to the main Dalton road, and down to it close on Resaca. General Schofield came up close on his left, and a heavy battle ensued during the afternoon and evening of the 15th, during which General Hooker drove the enemy from several strong hills, captured a 4-gun battery and many prisoners. That night, Johnston escaped, retreating south across the Oostanaula, and the next morning we entered the town in time to save the road bridge, but the railroad bridge was burned. The whole army started in pursuit General Thomas directly on his heels, General McPherson by Lay's Ferry, and General Schofield by obscure roads to the left. We found in Resaca another 4-gun battery and a good lot of stores.

"General McPherson during the 16th, got across at Lay's Ferry, General Thomas had to make some additional bridges at Resaca, but General Schofield had more trouble, and made a wide circuit to the left by Fue's and Field's Ferries across the Connasauga and Coosawatta rivers, which form the Oostanaula. On the 17th, all the armies moved south by as many different roads as we could find, and General Thomas had sent by my orders a division, General Jeff. C. Davis, along the west bank of Oostanaula, to Rome. Near Adairsville we again found signs of the rebel army, and of a purpose to fight, and about sunset of that day General Newton's division in the advance had a pretty sharp encounter with his rear guard, but the next morning he was gone, and we pushed on through Kingston to a point four miles beyond, where we found him again in force on ground comparatively open, and well adapted to a grand battle. We made the proper dispositions. General Schofield approaching Cassville from the north, to which point General Thomas had also directed General Hooker's corps, and I had drawn General McPherson's army from Woodland to Kingston, to be in close support. On the 19th the enemy was in force about Cassville, with strong forts, but as our troops converged on him, again he retreated in the night time across the Etowah river, burning the road and railroad bridges near Cartersville, but leaving us in complete possession of the most valuable country above the Etowah river. Holding General Thomas' army about Cassville, General McPherson's about Kingston, and General Schofield's at Cassville depot and toward the Etowah bridge, I gave the army a few days' rest, and also time to bring forward supplies for the next stage of the campaign. In the mean time General Jeff. C. Davis had got possession of Rome with its forts, some eight or ten guns of heavy calibre, and its valuable mills and foundries. We also secured possession of two good bridges across the Etowah river near Kingston, giving us the means of crossing toward the south. Satisfied that the enemy could and would hold us in check at the Allatoona pass, I resolved, without even attempting it in front, to turn it by a circuit to the right, and having supplied our wagons for twenty days' absence from our railroad, I left a garrison at Rome and Kingston, and on the 23d put the army in motion for 'Dallas.'

"General McPherson crossed the Etowah at the mouth of Conasene creek, near Kingston, and moved for his position to the south of Dallas *via* Van Wert. General Davis's division moved directly from Rome for Dallas by Van Wert. General Thomas took the road *via* Euharlee and Burnt Hickory, while General Schofield moved by other roads more to the east, aiming to come up on General Thomas' left. General Thomas' head of column skirmished with the enemy's cavalry about Burnt Hickory, and captured a courier with a letter of General Johnston, showing that he had detected the move and was preparing to meet us about Dallas. The country was very rugged, mountainous, and densely wooded, with few and obscure roads. On the 25th of May, General Thomas was moving from Burnt Hickory for Dallas, his troops on three roads, General Hooker having the advance. When he approached the Pumpkin Vine Creek, on the main Dallas road, he found a respectable force of the enemy's cavalry at a bridge to his left. He rapidly pushed them across the creek, saving the bridge though on fire, and followed out eastward about two miles, where he first encountered infantry, whose pickets he drove some distance, until he encountered the enemy's line of battle, and his leading division, General Geary's, had a severe encounter. General Hooker's other two divisions were on other roads, and he ordered them in, although the road he was then following, by reason of the presence of the enemy, led him north of Dallas about four miles. It was near 4 o'clock P. M. before General Hooker got his whole corps well in hand, when he deployed two divisions, and, by my order, made a bold push to secure possession of a point known as the 'New Hope' Church, where three roads meet from Ackworth, Marietta, and Dallas. Here a hard battle was fought, and the enemy was driven back to New Hope Church; but, having hastily thrown up some parapets, and a stormy, dark night having set in, General Hooker was unable to drive the enemy from those roads. By the next morning we found the enemy well intrenched substantially in front of the road leading from Dallas to Marietta. We were consequently compelled to make dispositions on a larger scale. General McPherson was moved up to Dallas, General Thomas was deployed against New Hope Church, and General Schofield was directed towards our left, so as to strike and turn the enemy's right. General Garrard's cavalry operated with General McPherson, and General Stoneman with General Schofield. General McCook looked to our rear. Owing to the difficult nature of the ground and dense forests, it took us several days to deploy close to the enemy, when I resolved gradually to work towards our left, and, when all things were ready, to push for the railroad east of Allatoona. In making our development before the enemy about New Hope, many severe sharp encounters occurred between parts of the army, details of which will be given at length in the reports of subordinate commanders. On the 28th, General McPherson was on the point of closing to his left on General Thomas, in front of New Hope Church, to enable me with the rest of the army to extend still more to the left and to envelope the enemy's right, when suddenly the enemy made a bold and daring assault on him at Dallas. Fortunately our men had erected good breastworks, and gave the enemy a terrible and bloody repulse. After a few days' delay, for effect, I renewed my orders to General McPherson to move to his left about five miles, and occupy General Thomas' position in front of New Hope Church, and Generals Thomas and Schofield were ordered to move a corresponding distance to their left. This move was effected with ease and safety on the 1st of June, and, by pushing our left well around, we occupied all the roads leading back to Allatoona and Ackworth, after which I pushed General Stoneman's cavalry rapidly into Allatoona, at the east end of the Pass, and General Garrard's cavalry around by the rear to the west end of the Pass. Both of these commands reached the points designated without trouble, and we thereby accomplished our real purpose of turning the Allatoona Pass.

"Ordering the railroad bridge across the Etowah to be at once rebuilt, I continued working by the left, and on the 4th of June had resolved to leave Johnston in his intrenched position at New Hope Church, and move to the railroad about Ackworth, when he abandoned his intrenchments, after which we moved readily to Ackworth and reached the railroad on the 6th of June. I at once examined in person the Allatoona Pass, and found it admirably adapted to our use as a secondary base, and gave the necessary orders for its defence and garrison, and as soon as the railroad bridge was finished across the Etowah our stores came forward to our camps by rail. At Ackworth General Blair overtook us on the 8th of June with two divisions of the Seventeenth Corps that had been on furlough, and one brigade of cavalry, Colonel Long's, of General Garrard's division, which had been awaiting horses at Columbia. This accession of force about compensated for our losses in battle and the detachment left at Resaca, Rome, Kingston and Allatoona. On the 9th of June our communications in the rear being secure and supplies ample, we moved forward to Big Shanty. Kenesaw, the bold and striking Twin Mountain, lay before us, with a high range of chestnut hills trending off to the northeast terminating to our view in another peak called Brushy Mountain. To our right was the smaller hill called Pine Mountain, and beyond it in the distance Lost Mountain. All these, though links in a continuous chain, present a sharp conical appearance, prominent in the vast landscape that presents itself from any of the hills that abound in that region. Kenesaw, Pine Mountain, and Lost Mountain, form a triangle, Pine Mountain the apex, and Kenesaw and Lost Mountain the base, covering perfectly the town of Marietta and the railroad back to the Chattahoochie. On each of these peaks the enemy had his signal stations. The summits were covered with batteries, and the spurs were alive with men, busy in felling trees, digging pits and preparing for the grand struggle impending. The scene was enchanting, too beautiful to be disturbed by the harsh clamors of war, but the Chattahoochie lay beyond, and I had to reach it. On approaching close to the enemy I found him occupying a line full two miles long, more than he could hold with his force. General McPherson was ordered to move toward Marietta, his right on the railroad, General Thomas on Kenesaw and Pine Mountain, and General Schofield off toward Lost Mountain; General Garrard's cavalry on the left, General Stoneman's on the right, and General McCook looking to our rear and communications. Our depot was at Big Shanty.

"By the 11th of June our lines were close up, and we made dispositions to break the line between Kenesaw and Pine Mountains. General Hooker was on its right and front, General Howard on its left and front, and General Palmer between it and the railroad. During a sharp cannonading from General Howard's right or General Hooker's left, General Polk was killed on the 14th, and on the morning of 15th Pine Mountain was found abandoned by the enemy. Generals Thomas and Schofield advanced, and found him again strongly intrenched along the line of rugged hills connecting Kenesaw and Lost Mountain. At the same time General McPherson advanced his line, gaining substantial advantage on the left. Pushing our operations on the centre as vigorously as the nature of the ground would permit, I had again ordered an assault on the centre, when, on the 17th, the enemy abandoned Lost Mountain and the long line of admirable breastworks connecting it with Kenesaw. We continued to press at all points, skirmishing in dense forests of timber and across most difficult ravines, until we found him again strongly posted and intrenched, with Kenesaw as his salient, his right wing thrown back to cover Marietta, and his left behind Nose's Creek, covering his railroad back to the Chattahoochie. This enabled him to contract his lines and strengthen them accordingly. From Kenesaw he could look down upon our camps and observe every movement, and his batteries thundered away, but did us little harm, on account of the extreme height, the shot and shell passing harmlessly over our heads as we lay close up against his mountain town. During our operations about Kenesaw the weather was villainously bad, and the rain fell almost continuously for three weeks, rendering our narrow wooded roads mere mud gulleys, so that a general movement would have been impossible, but our men daily worked closer and closer to the intrenched foe, and kept up an incessant picket firing galling to him. Every opportunity was taken to advance our general lines closer and closer to the enemy.

"General McPherson, watching the enemy on Kenesaw, and working his left forward, General Thomas, swinging as it were on a grand left wheel, his left on Kenesaw connecting with General McPherson, and General Schofield all the time working to the south and east along the old Sandtown Road. On the 22d, General Hooker had advanced his line, with General Schofield on his right, the enemy, Hood's corps, with detachments from the others, suddenly sallied and attacked. The blow fell mostly on General Williams' division of General Hooker's corps, and a brigade of General Haskall's divisions of General Schofield's army. The ground was comparatively open, and although the enemy drove in the skirmish lines, an advanced regiment of General Schofield, sent out purposely to hold him in check until some preparations could be completed for his reception, yet when he reached our line of battle he received a terrible repulse, leaving his dead, wounded, and many prisoners in our hands. This is known as the affair of the 'Kulp House." Although inviting the enemy at all times to commit such mistakes, I could not hope for him to repeat them after the examples of Dallas and the 'Kulp House,' and upon studying the ground, I had no alternative in my turn but to assault his lines or turn his position. Either course had its difficulties and dangers. And I perceived that the enemy and our own officers had settled down into a conviction that I would not assault fortified lines. All looked to me to "outflank." An army, to be efficient, must not settle down to one single mode of offense, but must be prepared to execute any plan which promises success. I waited, therefore, for the moral effect, to make a successful assault against the enemy behind his breastworks, and resolved to attempt it at that point where success would give the largest fruits of victory. The general point selected was the left center; because, if I could thrust a strong head of column through at that point by pushing it boldly and rapidly two and one half miles, it would reach the railroad below Marietta, cut off the enemy's right and center from its line of retreat, and then, by turning on either part, it could be overwhelmed and destroyed. Therefore, on the 24th of June, I ordered that an assault should be made at two points south of Kenesaw, on the 27th, giving three days' notice for preparation and reconnoissance; one to be made near Little Kenesaw by General McPherson's troops, and another about a mile further south by General Thomas' troops. The hour was fixed, and all details given in Field Orders No. 28, of June 24th. On the 27th of June the two assaults were made at the time and in the manner prescribed, and both failed, costing us many valuable lives, among them those of Generals Harker and McCook; Colonel Rice and others badly wounded. Our aggregate loss being near 3,000, while we inflicted comparatively little loss to the enemy, who lay behind his well-formed breastworks. Failure as it was, and for which I assume the entire responsibility, I yet claim it produced good fruits, as it demonstrated to General Johnston that I would assault, and that boldly; and we also gained and held ground so close to the enemy's parapets that he could not show a head above them. It would not do to rest long under the influence of a mistake or failure, and accordingly General Schofield was working strong on the enemy's left; and on the 1st of July, I ordered General McPherson to be relieved by General Garrard's cavalry in front of Kenesaw, and to rapidly throw his whole army by the right down to and threaten Nickajack Creek and Turner's Ferry, across the Chattahoochie, and I also pushed Stoneman's cavalry to the river below Turner's.

"General McPherson commenced his movement the night of July 2d, and the effect was instantaneous. The next morning, Kenesaw was abandoned, and with the first dawn of day I saw our skirmishers appear on the mountain top. General Thomas' whole line was then moved forward to the railroad, and turned south in pursuit toward the Chattahoochie. In person I entered Marietta at 8½ in the morning, just as the enemy's cavalry vacated the place. General Logan's corps of General McPherson's army, which had not moved far, was ordered back into Marietta by the main road, and General McPherson and General Schofield were instructed to cross Nickajack and attack the enemy in flank and rear, and, if possible, to catch him in the confusion of crossing the Chattahoochie; but Johnston had foreseen and provided against all this, and had covered his movement well. He had intrenched strong *tete de pont* at the Chattahoochie, with an advanced intrenched line across the road at Smyrna camp-meeting ground, five miles from Marietta. Here General Thomas found him, his front covered by a good parapet, and his flanks behind the Nickajack and Rottenwood creeks. Ordering a garrison for Marietta, and General Logan to join his own army near the mouth of Nickajack, I overtook General Thomas at Smyrna. On the 4th of July we pushed a strong skirmish line down the main road, capturing the entire line of the enemy's pits, and made strong demonstrations along Nickajack Creek and about Turner's Ferry. This had the desired effect, and the next morning the enemy was gone, and the army moved to the Chattahoochie, General Thomas' left flank resting on it near Paice's Ferry, General McPherson's right at the mouth of Nickajack, and General Schofield in reserve; the enemy lay behind a line of unusual strength, covering the railroad and pontoon bridges, and beyond the Chattahoochie. Heavy skirmishing along our whole front during the 5th demonstrated the strength of the enemy's position, which could alone be turned by crossing the main Chattahoochie River, a rapid and deep stream, only passable at that stage by means of bridges, except at one or two very difficult fords. To accomplish this result, I judged it would be more easy of execution before the enemy had made more thorough preparation or regained full confidence; and, accordingly, I ordered General Schofield across from his position on the Sandtown road to Smyrna camp ground, and next to the Chattahoochie, near the mouth of Soap's Creek, and effect a lodgment on the east bank. This was most successfully and skilfully accomplished on the 7th of July, General Schofield capturing a gun, completely surprising the guard, laying a good pontoon bridge and a trestle bridge, and effecting a strong lodgment on high and commanding ground, with good roads leading to the east. At the same time, General Garrard moved rapidly on Roswell, and destroyed the factories which had supplied the rebel armies with cloth for years. Over one of these, the woolen factory, the nominal owner displayed the French flag, which was not respected, of course. A neutral surely is no better than one of our own citizens, and we do not permit our own citizens to fabricate cloth for hostile uses. General Garrard was then ordered to secure the shallow ford at Roswell, and hold it until he could be relieved by infantry; and as I contemplated transferring the Army of the Tennessee from the extreme right to the left, I ordered General Thomas to send a division of his infantry that was nearest up to Roswell to hold the ford until General McPherson could send up a corps from the neighborhood of Nickajack. General Newton's division was sent, and held the ford until the arrival of General Dodge's corps, which was soon followed by General McPherson's whole army. About the same time, General Howard had also built a bridge at Powers' Ferry, two miles below General Schofield, had crossed over and taken a position on his right. Thus, during the 9th, we had secured three good and safe points of passage over the Chattahoochie, above the enemy, with good roads leading to Atlanta; and Johnston abandoned his *tete de pont*, burned his bridges, and left us undisputed masters, north and west, of the Chattahoochie, at daylight of the 10th of July.

"This was one, if not the chief object of the campaign, viz.: the advancement of our lines from the Tennessee to the Chattahoochie; but Atlanta lay before us only eight miles distant, and was too important a place in the hands of an enemy to be left undisturbed, with its magazines, stores, arsenals, workshops, foundries, etc., and more especially its railroads, which converge there from the four great cardinal points. But the men had worked hard, and needed rest, and we accordingly took a short spell. But in anticipation of this contingency, I had collected a well appointed force of cavalry, about 2,000 strong, at Decatur, Alabama, with orders, on receiving notice by telegraph, to push rapidly south, cross the Coosa at the railroad bridge on the Ten Islands, and thence by the most direct route to Opelika. There is but one stem of finished railroad connecting the channels of trade and travel between Georgia and Alabama and Mississippi, which runs from Montgomery to Opelika, and my purpose was to break it up effectually, and thereby cut off Johnston's army from that source of supply and reinforcement. General Rousseau, commanding the district of Tennessee, asked permission to command the expedition, and received it. As soon as Johnston was well across the Chattahoochie, and as I had begun to manœuver on Atlanta, I gave the requisite notice, and General Rousseau started punctually on the 10th of July. He fulfilled his orders and instructions to the very letter, whipping the rebel General Clinton en route ; he passed through Talladega, and reached the railroad on the 16th, about 25 miles west of Opelika, and broke it well up to that place ; also three miles of the branch toward Columbus, and two toward West Point. He then turned north, and brought his command safely to Marietta, arriving on the 22d, having sustained a trifling loss, not to exceed thirty men.

The main armies remained quiet in their camps on the Chattahoochie until the 16th of July ; but the time was employed in collecting stores at Allatoona, Marietta, and Vining's Station, strengthening the railroad guards and garrisons, and improving the pier bridges and roads leading across the river. General Stoneman's and McCook's cavalry had scouted well down the river to draw attention in that direction, and all things being ready for a general advance, I ordered it to commence on the 17th ; General Thomas to cross at Powers' and Paice's Ferry bridges, and to march by Buckhead ; General Schofield was already across at the mouth of Soap's Creek, and to march by Cross Keys ; and General McPherson to direct his course from Roswell straight against the Augusta Road, at some point east of Decatur, near Stone Mountain. General Garrard's cavalry acted with General McPherson ; and Generals Stoneman and McCook watched the river and roads below the railroad. On the 17th the whole army advanced from their camps, and formed a general line along the Old Peach Tree Road. Continuing on a general right wheel, General McPherson reached the Augusta railroad on the 18th, at a point seven miles east of Decatur, and with General Garrard's cavalry and General Morgan L. Smith's infantry division of the Fifteenth Corps, broke up a section of about four miles, and General Schofield reached the town of Decatur. On the 19th, General McPherson turned along the railroad into Decatur, and General Schofield followed a road toward Atlanta, leading by Colonel Howard's house and the distillery ; and General Thomas crossed Peach Tree Creek, in force, by numerous bridges in face of the enemy's intrenched lines. All found the enemy in more or less force, and skirmished heavily.

"On the 20th, all the armies had closed in, converging toward Atlanta ; but, as a gap existed between Generals Schofield and Thomas, two divisions of General Howard's corps of General Thomas' army were moved to the left to connect with General Schofield, leaving General Newton's division of the same corps on the Buckhead Road. During the afternoon of the 20th, about 4 P. M., the enemy sallied from his works in force, and fell in line of battle against our right centre, composed of General Newton's division of General Howard's corps, on the main Buckhead road ; of General Hooker's corps next south, and General Johnson's division of General Palmer's corps. The blow was sudden, and somewhat unexpected ; but General Newton had hastily covered his front by a line of rail piles, which enabled him to meet and repulse the attack on him. General Hooker's whole corps was uncovered, and had to fight on comparatively open ground ; and it, too, after a very severe battle, drove the enemy back to his intrenchments, and the action in front of General Johnston was comparatively light, that division being well intrenched. The enemy left on the field over 500 dead, about 1,000 wounded severely, 7 stands of colors, and many prisoners. His loss could not have fallen short of 5,000 ; whereas ours was covered by 1,500 killed, wounded, and missing. The greater loss fell on General Hooker's corps, from its exposed condition. On the 21st, we felt the enemy in his intrenched position, which was found to crown the heights overlooking the comparatively open ground of the valley of Peach Tree Creek, his right beyond the Augusta Road to the east, and his left well toward Turner's Ferry on the Chattahoochie, at a general distance from Atlanta of about four miles. On the morning of the 22d, somewhat to my surprise, this whole line was found abandoned, and I confess I thought the enemy had resolved to give us Atlanta without further contest; but General Johnston had been relieved of his command, and General Hood substituted. A new policy seemed resolved on, of which the bold attack on our right was the index. Our advancing ranks swept across the strong and well-finished parapet of the enemy, and closed in upon Atlanta until we occupied a line in the form of a general circle, of about two miles radius, when we again found him occupying in force a line of finished redoubts, which had been prepared for more than a year, covering all the roads leading into Atlanta; and we found him also busy in connecting those redoubts with curtains strengthened by rifle trenches, abattis, and chevaux-de-frise.

"General McPherson, who had advanced from Decatur, continued to follow substantially the railroad, with the Fifteenth Corps; General Logan, the Seventeenth, General Blair on his left, and the Sixteenth, General Dodge on its right; but as the general advance of all the armies contracted the circle, the Sixteenth Corps, General Dodge, was thrown out of line by the Fifteenth connecting on the right with General Schofield, near the Howard House. General McPherson, the night before, had gained a high hill to the south and east of the railroad, where the Seventeenth Corps had, after a severe fight, driven the enemy, and it gave him a most commanding position, within easy view of the very heart of the city. He had thrown out working parties to it, and was making preparations to occupy it in strength with batteries. The Sixteenth Corps, General Dodge, was ordered from right to left to occupy this position, and make it a strong general left flank. General Dodge was moving by a diagonal path or wagon-track leading from the Decatur Road, in the direction of General Blair's left flank. About 10 A. M., I was in person with General Schofield, examining the appearance of the enemy's lines opposite the distillery, where we attracted enough of the enemy's fire of artillery and musketry to satisfy me the enemy was in Atlanta in force, and meant to fight, and had gone to a large dwelling close by, known as the Howard House, where General McPherson joined me. He described the condition of things on his flank and the disposition of his troops. I explained to him, that if we met serious resistance in Atlanta, as present appearances indicated, instead of operating against it by the left, I would extend to the right, and that I did not want him to gain much distance to the left. He then described the hill occupied by General Leggett's division of General Blair's corps, as essential to the occupation of any ground to the east and south of the Augusta railroad, on account of its commanding nature. I therefore ratified his disposition of troops, and modified a previous order I had sent him in writing to use General Dodge's corps, thrown somewhat in reserve by the closing up of our line, to break up railroad; and I sanctioned its going, as already ordered by General McPherson, to his left, to hold and fortify that position. The General remained with me until near noon, when some reports reaching us that indicated a movement of the enemy on that flank, he mounted and rode away with his staff. I must here also state, that the day before I had detached General Garrard's cavalry to go to Covington, on the Augusta Road, forty-two miles east of Atlanta, and from that point to send detachments to break the two important bridges across the Yellow and Ulcofauhatchee rivers, tributaries of Ocmulgee, and General McPherson had also left his wagon train at Decatur, under a guard of three regiments commanded by Colonel, now General Sprague. Soon after General McPherson left me at the Howard House, as before described, I heard the sounds of musketry to our left rear, at first mere pattering shots, but they soon grew in volume, accompanied with artillery, and about the same time, the sound of guns was heard in the direction of Decatur. No doubt could longer be entertained of the enemy's plan of action, which was to throw a superior force on our left flank, while he held us with his forts in front, the only question being as to the amount of force he could employ at that point. I hastily transmitted orders to all points of our centre and right to press forward and give full employment to all the enemy in his lines, and for General Schofield to hold as large a force in reserve as possible, awaiting developments. Not more than half an hour after General McPherson had left me, viz., about 12½ M., of the 22d, his Adjutant-General, Lieutenant-Colonel Clark, rode up and reported that General McPherson was either dead or a prisoner; that he had ridden from me to General Dodge's column, moving as heretofore described, and had sent off nearly all his staff and orderlies on various errands, and himself had passed into a narrow path or road that led to the left and rear of General Giles A. Smith's division, which was General Blair's extreme left; that a few minutes after he had entered the woods a sharp volley was heard in that direction, and his horse had come out riderless, having two wounds. The suddenness of this terrible calamity would have overwhelmed me with grief, but the living demanded my whole thoughts. I instantly dispatched a staff officer to General John A. Logan, commanding the Fifteenth Corps, to tell him what had happened; that he must assume command of the army of the Tennessee, and hold stubbornly the ground already chosen, more especially the hill gained by General Leggett the night before.

"Already the whole line was engaged in battle. Hardee's corps had sallied from Atlanta, and by a wide circle to the east had struck General Blair's left flank, enveloped it, and his right had swung around until it hit General Dodge in motion. General Blair's line was substantially along the old line of the rebel trench, but it was fashioned to fight outwards. A space of wooded ground of near half a mile, intervened between the head of General Dodge's column and General Blair's line, through which the enemy had poured; but the last order ever given by General McPherson was to hurry a brigade (Colonel Wangelin's) of the Fifteenth Corps across from the railroad to occupy this gap. It came across on the double quick and checked the enemy. While Hardee attacked in flank, Stewart's corps was to attack in front directly out from the main works, but fortunately their attacks were not simultaneous. The enemy swept across the hill which our men were then fortifying, and captured the pioneer company, its tools, and almost the entire working party, and bore down on our left until he encountered General Giles A. Smith's division of the Seventeenth Corps, who was somewhat 'in air,' and forced to fight first from one side of the old rifle parapet and then from the other, gradually withdrawing, regiment by regiment, so as to form a flank to General Leggett's division which held the apex of the hill, which was the only part that was deemed essential to our future plans. General Dodge had caught and held well in check the enemy's right, and punished him severely, capturing many prisoners. Smith (General Giles A.) had gradually given up the extremity of his line and formed a new one, whose right connected with General Leggett, and his left refused, facing southeast. On this ground and in this order the men fought well and desperately for nearly four hours, checking and repulsing all the enemy's attacks. The execution on the enemy's ranks at the angle was terrible, and great credit is due both Generals Leggett and Giles A. Smith and their men for their hard and stubborn fighting. The enemy made no further progress on that flank, and by 4 P. M. had almost given up the attempt. In the meantime Wheeler's cavalry unopposed (for General Garrard was absent at Covington by my order) had reached Decatur and attempted to capture the wagon trains, but Colonel (now General) Sprague, covered them with great skill and success, sending them to the rear of Generals Schofield and Thomas, and not drawing back from Decatur till every wagon was safe except three, which the teamsters had left, carrying off the mules. On our extreme left the enemy had taken a complete battery of six guns, with its horses (Morray's), of the regular army, as it was moving along unsupported and unapprehensive of danger in a narrow, wooded road in that unguarded space between the head of General Dodge's column and the line of battle on the ridge above ; but most of the men escaped to the bushes. He also got two other guns on the extreme left flank, that were left on the ground as General Giles A. Smith drew off his men in the manner heretofore described. About 4 P. M. there was quite a lull, during which the enemy fell forward on the railroad and main Decatur road, and suddenly assailed a regiment which, with a section of guns, had been thrown forward as a kind of picket, and captured the two guns ; he then advanced rapidly and broke through our lines at that point which had been materially weakened by the withdrawal of Colonel Martin's brigade, sent by General Logan's order to the extreme left. The other brigade, General Lightburn, which held this part of the line, fell back in some disorder about four hundred yards, to a position held by it the night before, leaving the enemy for a time in possession of two batteries, one of which a 20-pounder Parrott battery of four guns, was most valuable to us, and separating General Woods' and General Harrow's divisions of the Fifteenth Corps, that were on the right and left of the railroad.

"Being in person close by the spot, and appreciating the vast importance of the connection at that point, I ordered certain batteries of General Schofield to be moved to a position somewhat commanding, by a left flank fire, and ordered an incessant fire of shells on the enemy within sight and the woods beyond, to prevent his re-enforcing. I also sent orders to General Logan, which he had already anticipated, to make the Fifteenth Corps regain its lost ground at any cost, and instructed General Woods, supported by General Schofield, to use his division and sweep the parapet down from where he held it until he saved the batteries and recovered the lost ground. The whole was executed in superb stylé, at times our men and the enemy fighting across the narrow parapet ; but at last the enemy gave way, and the Fifteenth Corps regained its position and all the guns except the two advanced ones, which were out of view, and had been removed by the enemy within his main work. With this terminated the battle of the 22d, which cost us 3,722 killed, wounded and prisoners. But among the dead was Major-General McPherson, whose body was recovered and brought to me in the heat of battle, and I had it sent in charge of his personal staff back to Marietta on its way to his northern home. He was a noble youth, of striking personal appearance, of the highest professional capacity, and with a heart

John A. Logan

From the original painting by Nast in the possession of the publishers.

Johnson, Fry & Co. Publishers, New York.

abounding in kindness that drew to him the affections of all men. His sudden death devolved the command of the army of the Tennessee on the no less brave and gallant General Logan, who nobly sustained his reputation and that of his veteran army, and avenged the death of his comrade and commander. The enemy left on the field his dead and wounded, and about 1,000 well prisoners. His dead alone are computed by General Logan at 3,240, of which number 2,200 were from actual count, and of these he delivered to the enemy, under a flag of truce, sent in by him (the enemy) 800 bodies. I entertain no doubt that in the battle of July 22d the enemy sustained an aggregate loss of full 8,000 men. The next day General Garrard returned from Covington, having succeeded perfectly in his mission, and destroyed the bridges at Ulcofauhatchee and Yellow rivers, besides burning a train of cars, a large quantity of cotton (2,000 bales), and the depots of stores at Covington and Conyer's Station, and bringing in 200 prisoners and some good horses, losing but two men, one of whom was killed by accident. Having therefore sufficiently crippled the Augusta Road, and rendered it useless to the enemy, I then addressed myself to the task of reaching the Macon Road, over which of necessity came the stores and ammunition that alone maintained the rebel army in Atlanta.

"Generals Schofield and Thomas had closed well up, holding the enemy behind his inner entrenchments. I first ordered the army of the Tennessee to prepare to vacate its line and to shift by the right below Proctor's Creek, and General Schofield to extend up to the Augusta Road. About the same time General Rousseau had arrived from his expedition to Opelika, bringing me about 2,000 good cavalry, but of course fatigued with its long and rapid march, and ordering it to relieve General Stoneman at the river about Sandtown, I shifted General Stoneman to our left flank, and ordered all my cavalry to prepare for a blow at the Macon Road, simultaneous with the movement of the army of the Tennessee towards East Point. To accomplish this I gave General Stoneman the command of his own and General Garrard's cavalry, making an effective force of full 5,000 men, and to General McCook I gave his own and the new cavalry brought by General Rousseau, which was commanded by Colonel Harrison of the Eighth Indiana Cavalry, in the aggregate about 4,000. These two well-appointed bodies were to move in concert, the former by the left around Atlanta to McDonough, and the latter by the right on Fayetteville, and on a certain night, viz., July 28th, they were to meet on the Macon Road near Lovejoy's and destroy it in the most effectual manner. I estimated this joint cavalry could whip all Wheeler's cavalry, and could otherwise fully accomplish its task, and I think so still. I had the officers in command to meet me, and explained the movement perfectly, and they entertained not a doubt of perfect success. At the very moment almost of starting, General Stoneman addressed me a note asking permission, after fulfilling his orders and breaking the road, to be allowed, with his command proper, to proceed to Macon and Anderson, and release our prisoners of war confined at those points. There was something most captivating in the idea, and the execution was within the bounds of probability of success. I consented that after the defeat of Wheeler's cavalry, which was embraced in his orders, and breaking the road, he might attempt it with his cavalry proper, sending that of General Garrard back to its proper flank of the army. Both cavalry expeditions started at the time appointed. I have as yet no report from General Stoneman, who is a prisoner of war at Macon; but I know that he dispatched General Garrard's cavalry to Flat Rock for the purpose of covering his own movement to McDonough, but for some reason unknown to me he went off towards Covington and did not again communicate with General Garrard at Flat Rock. General Garrard remained there until the 29th, skirmishing heavily with a part of Wheeler's cavalry and occupying their attention, but hearing nothing from General Stoneman, he moved back to Conyer's, where, learning that General Stoneman had gone to Covington and south on the east side of the Ocmulgee, he returned and resumed his position on our left. It is known that General Stoneman kept to the east of the Ocmulgee to Clinton, sending detachments off to the east which did a large amount of damage to the railroad, burning the bridges of Walnut Creek and Oconee, and destroying a large number of cars and locomotives, and with his main force appeared before Macon. He did not succeed in crossing the Ocmulgee at Macon, or in approaching Andersonville, but retired in the direction whence he came, followed by various detachments of mounted men under a General Iverson. He seems to have become hemmed in, and gave consent to two-thirds of his force to escape back whilst he held the enemy in check with the remainder, about 700 men, and a section of light guns. One brigade, Colonel Adams, came in almost intact. Another, commanded by Colonel Capron, was surprised on the way back and scattered; many were captured and killed, and the balance got in mostly unarmed and afoot, and the General himself surrendered his small command, and is now a prisoner at Macon. His mistake was in not making the first concentration with Generals McCook and Garrard near Lovejoy's, according to his orders, which is yet unexplained.

"General McCook, in the execution of his part, went down the west bank of the Chattahoochie to near Rivertown, where he laid a pontoon bridge with which he was provided, crossed his command, and moved rapidly on Palmetto station of the West Point road, where he tore up a section of track, leaving a regiment to create a diversion towards Campbelltown, which regiment fulfilled its duty and returned to camp by way of, and escorting back the pontoon bridge train. General McCook then rapidly moved to Fayetteville, where he found a large number of the wagons belonging to the rebel army in Atlanta. These he burned to the number of 500, killing 800 mules, and carrying along others, and taking 250 prisoners, mostly quartermasters and men belonging to the trains. He then pushed for the railroad, reaching it at Lovejoy's station at the time appointed. He burned the depot, tore up a section of the road, and continued to work until forced to leave off to defend himself against an accumulating force of the enemy. He could hear nothing of General Stoneman, and finding his progress east too strongly opposed, he moved south and west, and reached Newman on the West Point road, where he encountered an infantry force coming from Mississippi to Atlanta, which had been stopped by the break he had made at Palmetto. This force, with the pursuing cavalry, hemmed him in, and forced him to fight. He was compelled to drop his prisoners and captures and cut his way out, losing some 500 officers and men. Among them a most valuable officer, Colonel Harrison, who, when fighting his men as skirmishers on foot, was overcome and made prisoner, and is now at Macon. He cut his way out, reached the Chattahoochie, crossed and got to Marietta without further loss. General McCook is entitled to much credit for thus saving his command, which was endangered by the failure of General Stoneman to reach Lovejoy's. But on the whole the cavalry raid is not deemed a success, for the real purpose was to break the enemy's communications, which, though done, was on so limited a scale that I knew the damages would soon be repaired.

"Pursuant to the general plan the army of the Tennessee drew out of its lines near the Decatur road during the night of July 26, and on the 27th moved behind the rest of the army to Proctor's Creek, and south to prolong our line due south facing east. On that day, by appointment of the President of the United States, Major-General Howard assumed command of the army of the Tennessee, and had the general supervision of the movement, which was made *en echelon*, General Dodge's corps, Sixteenth, on the left, nearest the enemy, General Blair's corps, Seventeenth, next to come up on its right, and General Logan's corps, Fifteenth, to come up on its right and refused as a flank, the whole to gain as much ground due south from the flank already established on Proctor's Creek as was consistent with a proper strength. General Dodge's men got into line in the evening of the 27th, and General Blair's came into line on his right early on the morning of the 28th, his right reaching an old meeting house called Ezra church, near some large open fields by the poor-house, on a road known as the Bell's Ferry, or Lickskillet road. Here the Fifteenth Corps, General Logan's, joined on and refused along a ridge well wooded, which partially commanded a view over the same fields. About 10 A. M. all the army was in position, and the men were busy in throwing up the accustomed piles of rails and logs, which after awhile assumed the form of a parapet. The skill and rapidity with which our men construct them is wonderful, and is something new in the art of war. I rode along his whole line about that time, and as I approached Ezra church there was considerable artillery firing enfilading the road in which I was riding, killing an orderly's horse just behind my staff. I struck across an open field to where General Howard was standing in the rear of the Fifteenth Corps, and walked up to the ridge with General Morgan L. Smith to see if the battery which enfiladed the main road and line of rail piles could not be disposed of, and heard General Smith give the necessary orders for the deployment of one regiment forward and another to make a circuit to the right, when I returned to where General Howard was, and remained there until 12 o'clock. During this time there was nothing to indicate serious battle save the shelling by one or at most two batteries from beyond the large field in front of the Fifteenth Corps.

"Wishing to be well prepared to defeat the enemy if he repeated his game of the 22d, I had, the night before, ordered General Davis's division of General Palmer's corps, which, by the movement of the Army of the Tennessee, had been left, as it were, in reserve, to move down to Turner's Ferry, and thence toward Whitehall or East Point, aiming to reach the flank of General Howard's new line, hoping that in case of an attack this division would in turn catch the attacking force in flank or rear, at an unexpected moment. I explained it to General Howard, and bade him expect the arrival of such a force in case of battle. Indeed, I expected to hear the fire of its skirmishers by noon. General Davis was sick that day, and Brigadier-General Morgan commanded the division which had marched early for Turner's Ferry, but many of the roads laid down on our maps did not exist at all, and General Morgan was delayed thereby. I rode back to make more particular inquiries as to this division, and had just reached General Davis's headquarters at Proctor's Creek when I heard musketry open heavily on the right. The enemy had come out of Atlanta by the Bell's Ferry road, and formed his masses in the open fields behind a swell of ground, and after the artillery firing I have described, advanced in parallel lines directly against the Fifteenth Corps, expecting to catch that flank in air. His advance was magnificent, but founded in an error that cost him sadly, for our men coolly and deliberately cut down his men, and spite of the efforts of the rebel officers, his ranks broke and fled. But they were rallied again and again, as often as six times at some points, and a few of the rebel officers and men reached our lines of rail piles only to be killed or hauled over as prisoners. These assaults occurred from noon until about 4 P. M., when the enemy disappeared, leaving his dead and wounded in our hands; as many as 642 dead were counted and buried, and still others are known to have been buried which were not counted by the regularly detailed burial parties.

"General Logan on this occasion was conspicuous as on the 22d, his corps being chiefly engaged; but General Howard had drawn from the other Corps, Sixteenth and Seventeenth, certain reserves which were near at hand but not used. Our entire loss is reported less than 600, whereas that of the enemy in killed and wounded not less than 5,000. Had General Davis's division come up on the Bell's Ferry road as I calculated, at any time before 4 o'clock, what was simply a complete repulse would have been a disastrous rout to the enemy; but I cannot attribute the failure to want of energy or intelligence, and must charge it, like many other things in this campaign, to the peculiar tangled nature of the forests and absence of roads that would admit the rapid movement of troops. This affair terminated all efforts of the enemy to check our extensions by the flank, which afterwards proceeded with comparative ease, but he met our extensions to the south by rapid and well constructed forts and rifle pits built between us and the railroad to and below East Point, remaining perfectly on the defensive. Finding that the right flank of the Army of the Tennessee did not reach, I was forced to shift General Schofield to that flank also, and afterwards General Palmer's corps of General Thomas' army. General Schofield moved from the left on the 1st of August, and General Palmer's corps followed at once, taking a line below Utoy Creek, and General Schofield prolonged it to a point near East Point. The enemy made no offensive opposition, but watched our movements and extended his lines and parapets accordingly. About this time several changes in important commands occurred, which should be noted. General Hooker, offended that General Howard was preferred to him as the successor of General McPherson, resigned his command of the Twentieth Corps, to which General Slocum was appointed; but he was at Vicksburg, and until he joined, the command of the corps devolved on General H. S. Williams, who handled it admirably. General Palmer also resigned the command of the Fourteenth Corps, and General Jeff. C. Davis was appointed to his place. Major-General D. S. Stanley had succeeded General Howard in the command of the Fourth Corps.

"From the 2d to the 5th we continued to extend to the right, demonstrating strongly on the left and along our whole line. General Reilley's brigade of General Cox's division, General Schofield's army, on the 5th, tried to break through the enemy's line about a mile below Utoy Creek, but failed to carry the position, losing about 400 men, who were caught in the entanglements and abattis; but the next day the position was turned by General Hascall, and General Schofield advanced his whole line close up to and facing the enemy below Utoy Creek. Still he did not gain the desired foothold on either the West Point or Macon railroad. The enemy's line at that time must have been near fifteen miles long, extending from near Decatur to below East Point. This he was enabled to do by the use of a large force of State militia, and his position was so masked by the shape of the ground that we were unable to discover the weak parts. I had become satisfied that, to reach the Macon road, and thereby control the supplies for Atlanta, I would have to move the whole army; but before beginning I ordered down from Chattanooga four 4½-inch rifled guns, to try their effect. These arrived on the 10th, and were put to work night and day, and did execution on the city, causing frequent fires, and creating confusion, yet the enemy seemed determined to hold his forts, even if the city were destroyed. On the 16th of August I made my Orders, No. 57, prescribing the mode and manner of executing the grand movement by the right flank, to begin on the 18th. This movement contemplated the withdrawal of the Twentieth Corps, General Williams, to the entrenched position at the Chattahoochie bridge, and the march of the main army to the West Point railroad, near Fairborn, and afterwards to the Macon road, at or near Jonesboro,' with our wagons loaded with provisions for fifteen days. About the time of the publication of these orders I learned that Wheeler, with a large mounted force of the enemy, variously estimated from 6,000 to 10,000 men, had passed around by the east and north, and had made his appearance on our lines of communication near Adairsville, and had succeeded in capturing 900 of our beef cattle, and had made a break of the railroad near Calhoun. I could not have asked any thing better, for I had provided well against such a contingency, and this detachment left me superior to the enemy in cavalry. I suspended the execution of my orders for the time being, and ordered General Kilpatrick to make up a well-appointed force of about 5,000 cavalry, and to move from his camp about Sandtown during the night of the 18th to the West Point road, and break it good near Fairborn; then to proceed across to the Macon road, and tear it up thoroughly, to avoid as far as possible, the enemy's infantry, but to attack any cavalry he could find. I thought this cavalry would save the necessity of moving the main army across, and that in case of his success it would leave me in better position to take full advantage of the result.

"General Kilpatrick got off at the time appointed, and broke the West Point road, and afterwards reached the Macon road at Jonesboro', where he whipped Ross's cavalry and got possession of the railroad, which he held for five hours, damaging it considerably; but a brigade of the enemy's infantry which had been dispatched below Jonesboro' in cars was run back, and disembarked, and with Jackson's rebel cavalry made it impossible for him to continue his work. He drew off to the east, and made a circuit, and struck the railroad about Lovejoy's Station, but was again threatened by the enemy, who moved on shorter lines, when he charged through their cavalry, taking many prisoners, of which he brought in seventy, and captured a 4-gun battery, which he destroyed, except one gun, which he brought in. He estimated the damage done to the road as enough to interrupt its use for ten days, after which he returned by a circuit north and east, reaching Decatur on the 22d. After an interview with General Kilpatrick, I was satisfied that whatever damage he had done would not produce the result desired, and I renewed my orders for the movement of the whole army. This involved the necessity of raising the siege of Atlanta, taking the field with our main force, and using it against the communications of Atlanta instead of against its intrenchments. All the army commanders were at once notified to send their surplus wagons, incumbrançes of all kinds, and sick back to our intrenched position at the bridge, and that the movement would begin during the night of the 25th. Accordingly, all things being ready, the Fourth Corps, General Stanley, drew out of its lines on our extreme left, and marched to a position below Proctor's Creek. The Twentieth Corps, General Williams, moved back to the Chattahoochie. This movement was made without loss, save a few things left in our camps by thoughtless officers or men. The night of the 26th the movement continued, the army of the Tennessee drawing out and moving rapidly by a circuit well towards Sandtown and across Camp Creek, the army of the Cumberland below Utoy Creek, General Schofield remaining in position. This was effected with the loss of but a single man in the army of the Tennessee wounded by a shell from the enemy. The third movement brought the army of the Tennessee on the West Point railroad, above Fairborn, the army of the Cumberland about Red Oak, and General Schofield closed in near Digs and Mins. I then ordered one day's work to be expended in destroying that road, and it was done with a will. Twelve and one-half miles were destroyed, the ties burned, and the iron rails heated and tortured by the utmost ingenuity of old hands at the work. Several cuts were filled up with the trunks of trees, with logs, rock, and earth intermingled with loaded shells, prepared as torpedoes, to explode in case of an attempt to clear them out. Having personally inspected this work, and satisfied with its execution, I ordered the whole army to move the next day eastward by several roads. General Howard on the right towards Jonesboro,' General Thomas, the centre, by Shoal Creek church to Couch's on the Decatur and Fayetteville road, and General Schofield, on the left, about Morrow's mills. An inspection of the map will show the strategic advantages of this position. The railroad from Atlanta to Macon follows substantially the ridge or 'divide' between the waters of Flint and Ocmulgee rivers, and from East Point to Jonesboro' makes a wide bend to the east. Therefore the position I have described, which had been well studied on paper, was my first 'objective.' It gave me 'interior lines,' something our enemy had enjoyed too long, and I was anxious for once to get the inside track, and therefore my haste and desire to secure it.

"The several columns moved punctually on the morning of the 29th. General Thomas, on the centre, encountered little opposition or difficulty, save what resulted from the narrow roads, and reached his position at Couch's early in the afternoon. General Schofield, being closer to the enemy, who still clung to East Point, moved cautiously on a small circle around that point, and came into position toward Rough-and-Ready; and General Howard, having the outer circle, had a greater distance to move. He encountered cavalry, which he drove rapidly to the crossing of Shoal Creek, where the enemy also had artillery. Here a short delay occurred, and some cannonading and skirmishing; but General Howard started them again, and kept them moving, passed the Renfro Place on the Decatur Road, which was the point indicated for him in the orders of that day; but he wisely and well kept on, and pushed on toward Jonesboro', saved the bridges across Flint River, and did not halt until darkness compelled him within half a mile of Jonesboro'. Here he rested for the night, and on the morning of August 31st, finding himself in the presence of a heavy force of the enemy, he deployed the Fifteenth Corps, and disposed the Sixteenth and Seventeenth on its flanks. The men covered their front with the usual parapet, and were soon prepared to act offensively or defensively, as the case called for. I was that night with General Thomas at Couch's, and as soon as I learned that General Howard had passed Renfro's, I directed General Thomas to send to that place a division of General Jeff. C. Davis' corps, to move General Stanley's corps in connection with General Schofield's towards Rough-and-Ready, and then to send forward, due east, a strong detachment of General Davis' corps to feel for the railroad. General Schofield was also ordered to move boldly forward and strike the railroad near Rough-and-Ready. These movements were progressing during the 31st, when the enemy came out of his works at Jonesboro', and attacked General Howard in the position described. General Howard was admirably situated to receive him, and repusle the attack thoroughly. The enemy attacked with Lee's and Hardee's corps, and, after a contest of over two hours, withdrew, leaving over 400 dead on the ground; and his wounded, of which about 300 were left in Jonesboro', could not have been much less than 2,500. Hearing the sounds of battle at Jonesboro' about noon, orders were renewed to push the other movements on the left and centre, and about 4 P. M. the reports arrived simultaneously that General Howard had thoroughly repulsed the enemy at Jonesboro'; that General Schofield had reached the railroad a mile below Rough-and-Ready, and was working up the road, breaking it as he went; that General Stanley of General Thomas' army had also got the road below General Schofield, and was destroying it, working south; and that General Baird of General Davis' corps had struck it still lower down, within four miles of Jonesboro'.

"Orders were at once given for all the army to turn on Jonesboro', General Howard to keep the enemy busy whilst General Thomas should move down from the north, with General Schofield on his left. I also ordered the troops, as they moved down, to continue the thorough destruction of the railroad, because we had it then, and I did not know but that events might divert our attention. General Garrard's cavalry was directed to watch the roads to our rear, the north. General Kilpatrick was sent south, down the west bank of Flint, with instructions to attack or threaten the railroad below Jonesboro'. I expected the whole army would close down on Jonesboro' by noon of the 1st of September. General Davis' corps, having a shorter distance to travel, was on time and deployed, facing south, his right in connection with General Howard, and his left on the railroad. General Stanley and General Schofield were coming down along the Rough-and-Ready Road, and along the railroad, breaking it as they came. When General Davis joined to General Howard, General Blair's corps on General Howard's left was thrown in reserve, and was immediately sent well to the right below Jonesboro', to act against that flank along with General Kilpatrick's cavalry About 4 P. M. General Davis was all ready, and assaulted the enemy's lines across open fields, carrying them very handsomely and taking as prisoners the greater part of Govan's brigade, including its commander, with two four-gun batteries. Repeated orders were sent to Generals Schofield and Stanley to hurry up, but the difficult nature of the country and the absence of roads are the reasons assigned why these troops did not get well into position for attack before night rendered further operations impossible. Of course the next morning the enemy was gone, and had retreated South. About 2 o'clock that night, the sound of heavy explosions were heard in the direction of Atlanta, distance about twenty miles, with a succession of minor explosions, and what seemed like the rapid firing of cannon and musketry.

These continued for about an hour, and again about 4 A. M. occurred another series of similar discharges, apparently nearer us and these sounds could be accounted for on no other hypothesis than of a night attack on Atlanta by General Slocum, or the blowing up of the enemy's magazines. Nevertheless, at daybreak, on finding the enemy gone from his lines at Jonesboro', I ordered a general pursuit south, General Thomas following to the left of the railroad, General Howard on its right, and General Schofield keeping off about two miles to the east. We overtook the enemy again near Lovejoy's station, in a strong intrenched position, with his flanks well protected behind a branch of Walnut Creek to the right, and a confluent of the Flint River to his left. We pushed close up and reconnoitered the ground, and found he had evidently halted to cover his communication with the McDonough and Fayetteville Road.

"Rumors began to arrive through prisoners captured that Atlanta had been abandoned during the night of September 1st; that Hood had blown up his ammunition trains, which accounted for the sounds so plainly heard by us and which were yet unexplained, that Stewart's corps was then retreating toward McDonough, and that the militia had gone off toward Covington. It was then too late to interpose and prevent their escape, and I was satisfied with the substantial success already gained. Accordingly, I ordered the work of destroying railroad to cease, and the troops to be held in hand ready for any movement that further information from Atlanta might warrant. General Jeff. C. Davis had been left above Jonesboro', and General Garrard's cavalry was still further back, and the latter was ordered to send back to Atlanta and ascertain the exact truth and the real situation of affairs. But the same night, viz., of September 4th, a courier arrived from General Slocum, reporting the fact that the enemy had evacuated Atlanta, blown up seven trains of cars, and had retreated on the McDonough Road. General Slocum had entered and taken possession on 2d of September.

"The object of my movement against the railroad was, therefore, already reached and concluded, and as it was idle to pursue our enemy in that wooded country with a view to his capture, I gave orders on the 4th for the Army to prepare to move back slowly to Atlanta. On the 5th we drew back to the vicinity of Jonesboro', five miles, where we remained a day. On the 7th we moved to Rough-and-Ready, seven miles, and the next to the camps selected, viz: the Army of the Cumberland grouped round about Atlanta, the Army of the Tennessee about East Point, and that of the Ohio at Decatur, where the men now occupy clean and healthy camps. I have not yet received full or satisfactory accounts of Wheeler's operations to our rear, further than that he broke the road about Calhoun, and then made his appearance at Dalton, where Colonel Laibold held him in check until General Steedman arrived from Chattanooga and drove him off. He then passed up into East Tennessee, and made quite a stay at Athens; but, on the first show of pursuit, he kept on north across the Little Tennessee; and crossing the Holston near Strawberry Plains, reached the Clinch near Clinton, and passed over towards Sequatchee and McMinnville. Thence he seems to have gone to Murfreesboro' and Lebanon, and across to Franklin. He may have committed damage to the property of citizens, but has injured us but little, the railroads being repaired about as fast as he broke them. From Franklin he has been pursued towards Florence, and out of the State by Generals Rousseau, Steedman, and Granger; but what amount of execution they have done to him is not yet reported. Our roads and telegraph are all repaired, and the cars run with regularity and speed. It is proper to remark in this place, that during the operation of this campaign, expeditions were sent out from Memphis and Vicksburgh to check any movements of the enemy's forces in Mississippi upon our communications. The manner in which this object was accomplished reflects credit upon Generals A. J. Smith, Washburne, Slocum, and Mower; and although General Sturgis' expedition was less successful than the others, it assisted us in the main object to be accomplished.

"I must bear full and liberal testimony to the energetic and successful management of our railroads during the campaign. No matter when or where a break has been made, the repair train seemed on the spot, and the damage was repaired generally before I knew of the break. Bridges have been built with surprising rapidity, and the locomotive whistle was heard in our advanced camps almost before the echoes of the skirmish fire had ceased. Some of these bridges—those of the Oostanaula, the Etowah, and Chattahoochie—are fine, substantial structures, and were built in inconceivably short time almost out of material improvised on the spot. Colonel W. W. Wright, who has charge of the 'construction and repairs,' is not only a most skillful, but a wonderfully ingenious, industrious, and zealous officer, and I can hardly do him justice. In like manner the officers charged with running the trains have succeeded to my entire satisfaction, and have worked in perfect harmony with the quartermasters and commissaries, bringing forward abundant supplies with such regularity that at no one time have we wanted for provisions, forage, ammunition, or stores of any essential kind. Colonel L. C. Easton, Chief Quartermaster, and Colonel A. Beckwith, Chief Commissary, have also succeeded, in a manner surprising to all of us, in getting forward supplies. I doubt if ever an army was better supplied than this, and I commend them most highly for it, because I know that more solicitude was felt by the Lieutenant-General commanding, and by the military world at large, on this than on any other one problem involved in the success of the campaign. Captain T. G. Baylor, Chief Ordnance Officer, has in like manner kept the army well supplied at all times with every kind of ammunition. To Captain O. M. Poe, Chief Engineer, I am more than ordinarily indebted for keeping me supplied with maps and information of roads and topography, as well as in the more important branch of his duties in selecting lines and military positions. My own personal staff has been small but select. Brigadier-General W. F. Barry, an officer of enlarged capacity and great experience, has filled the office of Chief of Artillery to perfection, and Lieutenant-Colonel E. D. Kittoe, Chief Medical Inspector, has done everything possible to give proper aid and direction to the operations of that important department. I have never seen the wounded removed from the fields of battle, cared for, and afterwards sent to proper hospitals in the rear, with more promptness, system, care, and success, than during this whole campaign, covering over one hundred days of actual battle and skirmish. My Aides-de-Camp, Major J. C. McCoy, Captain L. M. Dayton, and Captain J. C. Audenried, have been ever zealous and most efficient, carrying my orders day and night to distant points of our extended lines, with an intelligence and zeal that insured the perfect working of machinery, covering from ten to twenty-five miles of ground, when the least error in the delivery and explantion of an order, would have produced confusion; whereas in great measure, owing to the intelligence of these officers, orders have been made so clear that these vast armies have moved side by side, sometimes crossing each others tracks through a difficult country of over a hundred and thirty-eight miles in length, without confusion or trouble. Captain Dayton has also fulfilled the duties of my Adjutant-General, making all orders and carrying on the official correspondence. Three Inspectors-General completed my staff. Brigadier-General J. M. Corse, who has since been assigned the command of a division of the Sixteenth Corps at the request of General Dodge. Lieutenant-Colonel W. Warner, of the Seventy-sixth Ohio, and Lieutenant-Colonel Charles Ewing, Inspector-General of the Fifteenth Corps, and Captain Thirteenth United States Regulars. These officers, of singular energy and intelligence, have been of immense assistance to me in handling these large armies. My three 'armies in the field' were commanded by able officers, my equal in rank and experience. Major-General George H. Thomas, Major-General J. M. Schofield, and Major-General O. O. Howard. With such commanders I had only to indicate the object desired, and they accomplished it. I cannot over-estimate their services to the country, and must express my deep and heartfelt thanks that coming together from different fields, with different interests, they have co-operated with a harmony that has been productive of the greatest amount of success and good feeling. A more harmonious army does not exist."

CHAPTER CI.

OCCUPATION OF ATLANTA BY GENERAL SHERMAN, AND FINAL RAID OF GENERAL MORGAN.

The victory at Atlanta came somewhat unexpectedly upon the public, who had now slowly learnt to make due allowance in their calculations for the proverbial delays of war, and was received with corresponding exhilaration. They had yet to wait for the capture of Richmond; but one of the two great objects of the year was attained, and the achievement gave a new impulse to the work yet to be performed. It came simultaneously, too, with the news of Admiral Farragut's success—to be narrated in a coming chapter—before Mobile, which also added at the time greatly to the popular conviction of the final result of the war. President Lincoln gave expression to this feeling in the issue of a proclamation on the 3d of September, recommending a day of Thanksgiving.

"The signal success," said he, "that Divine Providence has recently vouchsafed to the operations of the United States fleet and army in the harbor of Mobile, and the reduction of Fort Powell, Fort Gaines and Fort Morgan, and the glorious achievements of the army under Major-General Sherman in the State of Georgia, resulting in the capture of the city of Atlanta, call for devout acknowledgment to the Supreme Being, in whose hands are the destinies of nations. It is, therefore, requested that on next Sunday, in all places of worship in the United States, thanksgiving be offered to Him for His mercy in preserving our national existence against the insurgent rebels who have been waging a cruel war against the Government of the United States for its overthrow; and also that prayer be made for Divine protection to our brave soldiers and their leaders in the field who have so often and so gallantly periled their lives in battling with the enemy; and for blessings and comfort from the Father of Mercies to the sick, wounded and prisoners, and to the orphans and widows of those who have fallen in the service of their country; and that He will continue to uphold the Government of the United States against all the efforts of public enemies and secret foes."

President Lincoln also issued a special order tendering "the national thanks to General Sherman and the gallant officers and soldiers of his command before Atlanta, for the distinguished ability, courage and perseverance displayed in the campaign in Georgia, which, under Divine power, resulted in the capture of the city of Atlanta. The marches, battles, sieges and other military operations that have signalized this campaign, must render it famous in the annals of war, and have entitled those who have participated therein, to the applause and thanks of the nation."

In a special Congratulatory Order addressed to his army from his headquarters "In the Field, Atlanta, Ga., Sept. 8, 1864," General Sherman presented this striking summary of the leading incidents of his campaign. "The officers and soldiers," said he, "of the armies of the Cumberland, Ohio, and Tennessee, have already received the thanks of the nation, through its President and Commander-in-Chief; and it now remains only for him who has been with you from the beginning, and who intends to stay all the time, to thank the officers and men for their intelligence, fidelity and courage displayed in the campaign of Atlanta. On the 1st of May our armies were lying in garrison, seemingly quiet from Knoxville, and our enemy lay behind his rocky-faced barrier at Dalton, proud, defiant and exulting. He had had time since Christmas to recover from his discomfiture on the Mission Ridge, with his ranks filled and a new Commander-in-Chief, second to none of the Confederacy in reputation for skill, sagacity, and extreme popularity. All at once our armies assumed life and action and appeared before Dalton; threatening Rocky Face, we threw ourselves upon Resaca, and the rebel army only escaped by the rapidity of its retreat, aided by the numerous roads with which he was familiar, and which were strange to us. Again, he took post in Allatoona, but we gave him no rest; and by a circuit toward Dallas and subsequent movement to Ackworth. we gained the Allatoona Pass. Then followed the eventful battles about Kenesaw, and the escape of the enemy across Chattahoochie river. The crossing of the Chattahoochie and breaking of the Augusta road, was most handsomely executed by us, and will be studied as an example in the art of war. At this stage of our game, our enemies dissatisfied with their old and skillful commander, selected one more bold and rash. New tactics were adopted. Hood first boldly and rapidly, on the 20th of July, fell on our right at Peachtree creek, and lost. Again, on the 22d he struck our extreme left, and was severely punished; and finally again, on the 28th he repeated the attempt on our right, and that time must have been satisfied, for since that date he has remained on the defensive. We slowly and gradually drew our lines from Atlanta, feeling for the railroads which supplied the rebel army and made Atlanta a place of importance. We must concede to our enemy that he met these efforts patiently and skillfully, but at last he made the mistake we had waited for so long, and sent his cavalry to our rear, far beyond the reach of recall. Instantly our cavalry was on his only remaining road, and we followed quickly with our principal army, and Atlanta fell into our possession as the fruit of well concerted measures, backed by a brave and confident army. This completed the grand task which had been assigned us by our Government, and your general again repeats his personal and official thanks to all the officers and men composing this army, for the indomitable courage and perseverance which alone could give success. We have beaten our enemy on every ground he has chosen, and have wrested from him *his own Gate City*, where were located his foundries, arsenals, and workshops, deemed secure on account of their distance from our base, and the seemingly impregnable obstacles supervening. Nothing is impossible to an army like this, determined to vindicate a Government which has rights wherever our flag has once floated, and is resolved to maintain them at any and all costs. In our campaign many, yes, very many of our noble and gallant comrades have preceded us to our common destination, the grave; but they have left the memory of deeds, on which a nation can build a proud history. McPherson, Harker, McCook, and others dear to us all, are now the binding links in our minds that should attach more closely together the living, who have to complete the task which still lays before us in the dim future. I ask all to continue as they have so well begun, the cultivation of the soldierly virtues that have ennobled our own and other countries. Courage, patience, obedience to the laws and constituted authorities of our Government; fidelity to our trusts and good feeling among each other; each trying to excel the other in the presence of those high qualities, and it will then require no prophet to foretell that our country will in time emerge from this war, purified by the fires of war, and worthy its great founder, Washington."

The allusion to the loss of general officers in the campaign, was simple and sincere, and made with a true soldier's instinct of the path of duty. We have seen the warmth with which General Sherman in his official report records the animated youth and services of McPherson. A native of Ohio, a graduate at West Point in 1853 at the head of his class, at the age of twenty-five, he had then been appointed to the Corps of Engineers, and was engaged in its active duties, rising to the rank of Captain. In the first year of the war he was appointed Aide to General Halleck in the West, with the rank of Lieutenant-Colonel. He was Chief Engineer in the army of Tennessee, and conducted some of its most important operations. He was promoted to Major-General of Volunteers in reward for his services in the field. His purity and elevation of character secured him the warmest regard of those who knew him. "Frank, manly, generous, earnest, truthful, kind," writes a friend after his death, "these were his chief characteristics."* The following account of the manner of his death gathered from one of his staff officers appeared in the *Nashville Union* of July 26th: "General McPherson had ridden from left to right of his corps, in superintending the advance of his skirmish line, and was returning again to the right, when a party of rebel bushwackers, in ambush, ran from their covert, between the Sixteenth and Seventeenth Corps, and crying out: "There they come, give them hell," fired. A couple of staff officers and two orderlies accompanied the General, all of whom escaped except the General, who fell and expired almost instantly, the ball having cut the aorta. The enemy rushed forward to rifle the body. Officers and orderlies meeting Colonel Strong, Inspector-General, and Captain Buell, both of General McPherson's staff, accompanied by a few orderlies, related the circumstance. Colonel Strong instantly drew the party into line and ordered a charge. This handful of brave and impetuous men, regardless of the foemen in front, dashed gallantly

* Obituary in the N. Y. *Evening Post*, August 1, 1864.

Jas. B. McPherson

From the original painting by Nast in the possession of the publishers.

Johnson, Fry & Co. Publishers, New York.

ahead and drove off the thieving enemy, and, while Captain Buell with his revolver kept them at bay, Colonel Strong, assisted by the orderlies, lifted the nude body, stripped of every article of clothing save a glove and sock, to his own horse, and bore it safely from the field. Beneath the light glove covering the left hand was a diamond ring, which the vandals failed to discover, and which will be forwarded to the General's friends in Ohio."

A generous tribute was paid by Major-General Howard to the memory of his division commander, General Charles G. Harker. "Strict and exact," says he, "in the performance of his own duty, he obtained the most willing and hearty co-operation from all his officers without apparent effort. The only complaint I ever heard was, that if Harker got started against the enemy he could not be kept back. Yet I never found him other than cool and self-possessed. Whenever anything difficult was to be done, anything that required peculiar pluck and energy, we called on General Harker. At Rocky Face, where his division wrested one half of that wonderful wall of strength from the rebels; at Resaca, where he tenaciously held a line of works close under the rebel fire; at Dallas, where he held on for several days with their lines, in conjunction with his brother officers, and hammered the rebel works at a distance of less than 100 yards; at Mud Creek, where he reinforced the skirmishers and directed their movements with so much skill and vigor as to take and hold a strong line of the enemy's earthworks; in fact, in every place where the corps has been engaged, this noble young man earnestly and heartily performed his part. On the 27th of June he led the terrible assault on the enemy's breastworks. We did not carry them, but part of his command reached the works. A sergeant bearing the colors was bayoneted as he was climbing over. Our beloved and trusted young General was close by, pressing forward his column, when the fatal wound was received." A native of New Jersey, General Harker graduated at West Point in 1858, where he was appointed to a lieutenancy in the Second Infantry, and subsequently became captain in the Fifteenth Regiment of Regulars. At the beginning of the war he had command of an Ohio regiment of volunteers, and became distinguished in the campaigns in Tennessee, being promoted to a brigade for his gallantry at Chickamauga.

Colonel Daniel McCook, acting Brigadier-General, one of the patriotic Ohio family, so distinguished in the volunteer service of the war, was mortally wounded while charging the enemy's works at the battle of Kenesaw Mountain. He was removed to Ohio, where he died at Steubenville on the 17th of July. He bore his father's Christian name, whose death at the hands of Morgan's men while defending his State against the incursion of that rebel leader in July, 1863, will be remembered by the reader. Of the seven sons of this devoted patriot who entered the field three had now fallen with their father.

Such, in the brief, condensed military narrative of the commanding general, is the history of this remarkable campaign, which, in the scene on which it was carried on—the heart of the enemy's country—the resistance to be met and physical difficulties to be overcome, the long line of communications to be guarded, the nice adaptation of means to ends, the patient endurance and persistent effort manifested will ever stand prominently forward in the annals of this heroic war. To pursue the details of this campaign in the reports of subordinate officers and in the stirring recitals of the various correspondents on the field would extend this chapter to a volume. Throughout these months of continuous toil, with their exactions of life and health, we should find a great army, drawn from the Western States, the centre of the Union following their military leader firmly relying on his military genius, and steadily supported by a conviction of the justice of their cause and of its inherent strength and vitality. The story, with all its picturesque incidents, deserves to be, and doubtless will be, recorded in an imperishable form. It will constitute in itself the history of a great war ; but in relation to the gigantic conflict of which it was a part, it will be only one of numerous records, among other campaigns, animated by like motives, for equal courage and endurance.

The conduct of the campaign fastened the attention of the public upon General Sherman. His character, prompt, decided and energetic, was studied in his dispatches, and he at last gained credit for the prescience with which he had anticipated the difficulties of this arduous struggle. Born in Ohio in 1820, of a good family, the son of a judge of the Supreme Court of the State, he had been educated at West Point, graduating sixth in his class at the age of twenty. He then entered the service in the Artillery Corps, served in Florida and in California during the Mexican War ; in 1850 married the daughter of the Hon. Thomas Ewing, of Ohio, and in 1853 resigned his commission and took charge of a banking-house at San Francisco. In 1860 he became President of the State Military Academy of Louisiana, in the duties of which he was engaged at the outbreak of the rebellion. He promptly took sides with the Union, in January, 1861, addressing a letter to Governor Moore, of Louisiana, in which he reminded that personage, who became so active an agent in the revolt, that he had "accepted his position when Louisiana was a State in the Union, and when the motto of the seminary was inserted in marble over the main door—'By the liberality of the General Government of the United States: the Union, *Esto perpetua.*' Recent events," he added, "foreshadowed a great change, and it became all men to choose. If Louisiana withdraws from the Federal Union, I prefer," he wrote, "to maintain my allegiance to the old Constitution as long as a fragment of it survives." The determination of the man was not to be mistaken, and his resignation was accepted. He then presented himself at Washington, warned the new Administration of the danger and magnitude of the impending conflict, in his estimate of which he was in advance of the day, and in June, 1861, was appointed colonel in the regular army. His employment in Virginia, and as successor to General Anderson in Kentucky, will be remembered by the reader, with his reply to Adjutant-General Thomas, after a survey of the condition of the Department, that 200,000 men would be needed to hold the State to its allegiance and maintain an aggressive movement in that quarter against the enemy. For this plain calculation he was considered visionary, and so little disposed to flatter the easy views taken of the rebellion that he was pronounced unpatriotic, and suspicions were even thrown out in the newspapers of his sanity. But the new leader of the West, General Grant, took better note of his abilities, and the stirring campaigns which followed in Tennessee and Mississippi soon established his military reputation.*

A letter which he wrote while in the field before Atlanta, on the 30th of July, exhibits something of his disposition. Under the revised conscription law of Congress permitting recruiting of white and black soldiers in the portion of the rebel States occupied by our forces, an agent from Massachusetts reported himself for this purpose on his line at Chattanooga, and applied to Gen-

* Biographical notice of General Sherman, by Colonel J. M. Bowman. *United States Service Magazine* for August, 1864.

eral Sherman for aid. After naming several appropriate stations in Alabama and elsewhere, General Sherman continued : "I do not see that the law restricts you to black recruits, but you are at liberty to collect white recruits also. It is waste of time and money to open rendezvous in Northwest Georgia, for I assure you I have not seen an able-bodied man, black or white, there, fit for a soldier, who was not in this army or the one opposed to it. You speak of the impression going abroad that I am opposed to the organization of colored regiments. My opinions are usually very positive, and there is no reason why you should not know them. Though entertaining profound reverence for our Congress, I do doubt their wisdom in the passage of this law. 1st. Because civilian agents about an army are a nuisance. 2d. The duty of citizens to fight for their country is too sacred a one to be peddled off by buying up the refuse of other States. 3d. It is unjust to the brave soldiers and volunteers who are fighting, as those who compose this army do, to place them on a par with the class of recruits you are after. 4th. The negro is in a transition state, and is not the equal of the white man. 5th. He is liberated from his bondage by act of war ; and the armies in the field are entitled to all his assistance in labor and fighting, in addition to the proper quotas of the States. 6th. This bidding and bartering for recruits, white and black, has delayed the reinforcement of our armies at the times when such reinforcements would have enabled us to make our successes permanent. 7th. The law is an experiment which, pending war, is unwise and unsafe, and has delayed the universal draft which I firmly believe will become necessary to overcome the widespread resistance offered us ; and I also believe the universal draft will be wise and beneficial ; for under the Providence of God it will separate the sheep from the goats, and demonstrate what citizens will fight for their country, and what will only talk. No one will infer from this that I am not a friend of the negro as well as the white race ; I contend that the treason and rebellion of the master freed the slave, and the armies I have commanded have conducted to safe points more negroes than those of any General officer in the army ; but I prefer negroes for pioneers, teamsters, cooks, and servants, others gradually to experiment in the art of the soldier, beginning with the duties of local garrisons, such as we had at Memphis, Vicksburgh, Natchez, Nashville, and Chattanooga ; but I would not draw on the poor race for too large a proportion of its active, athletic young men, for some must remain to seek new homes and provide for the old and young, the feeble and helpless. These are some of my peculiar notions, but I assure you they are shared by a large proportion of our fighting men."

General Sherman had another opportunity to display his ability with the pen, in a correspondence which took place between him and the rebel General Hood, after the occupation of Atlanta. It was the settled resolution of General Sherman, in accordance with his views of the necessities of the situation, to remove the citizens from the town, and garrison it strictly as a military post. Situated in the heart of the enemy's country, and valuable only as a base of further operations, he could not consent that it should be occupied by a doubtful or disaffected population, composed largely of families many of whose members were in the rebel service. Such an evil might be tolerated and controlled within our lines in Virginia or on the Mississippi ; but General Sherman determined to avoid it at Atlanta. He accordingly announced to General Hood his intention of removing the remaining inhabitants, offering to them the choice of going North or South, and to give them the opportunity of doing so, proposed a cessation of hostilities for ten days. Servants or negro slaves were to be allowed, if they wish to do so, to accompany their masters or mistresses ; otherwise to be sent away or employed by the quartermaster. General Hood accepted the proposition as a matter of necessity, but protested "in the name of the God of humanity against the expulsion of the people of Atlanta from their firesides," declaring, while he agreed to the truce, that General Sherman's purpose "transcends the studied and ungenerous cruelty of acts ever before brought to the attention of mankind, even in the darkest history of war."* To this remonstrance General Sherman replied in a letter dated Atlanta, Sept. 10 : "General J. B. Hood, Commanding Army of the Tennessee Confederate Army. General—I have the honor to acknowledge the receipt of your letter of this date at the hands of Messrs. Ball and Crew, consenting to the arrangements I had proposed to facilitate the removal South of the people of Atlanta who prefer to go in that direction. I enclose you a copy of my orders, which will, I am satisfied accomplish my purpose perfectly. You style the measures proposed 'unprecedented,' and appeal to the dark history of war for a parallel as an act of 'studied and ungenerous cruelty." It is not unprecedented, for General Johnston himself very wisely and properly removed the families all the way from Dalton down, and I see no reason why Atlanta should be excepted. Nor is it necessary to appeal to the dark history of war when recent and modern examples are so handy. You, yourself burned dwelling-houses along your parapet, and I have seen to-day fifty houses that you have rendered uninhabitable because they stood in the way of your forts and men. You defended Atlanta on a line so close to the town that every cannon-shot and many musket shots from our line of investments, that overshot their mark, went into the habitations of women and children. General Hardee did the same at Jonesboro', and General Johnston did the same last summer at Jackson, Miss. I have not accused you of heartless cruelty, but merely instance these causes of very recent occurrence, and could go on and enumerate hundreds of others, and challenge any fair man to judge which of us has the heart of pity for the families of a 'brave people.' I say it is a kindness to these families of Atlanta to remove them now at once from scenes that women and children should not be exposed to, and the brave people should scorn to commit their wives and children to the rude barbarians who thus, as you say, violate the laws of war, as illustrated in the pages of its dark history. In the name of common sense, I ask you not to appeal to a just God in such a sacrilegious manner—you, who, in the midst of peace and prosperity, have plunged a nation into civil war, 'dark and cruel war,' who dared and badgered us to battle, insulted our flag, seized our arsenals and forts that were left in the honorable custody of a peaceful ordnance serjeant, seized and made prisoners of war the very garrisons sent to protect your people against negroes and Indians, long before any overt act was committed by the (to you) hateful Lincoln Government, tried to force Kentucky and Missouri into the rebellion in spite of themselves, falsified the vote of Louisiana, turned loose your privateers to plunder unarmed ships, expelled Union families by the thousand, burned their houses, and declared by act of your Congress the confiscation of all debts due Northern men for goods had and received. Talk thus to the marines, but not to me, who have seen these things, and who will this day make as much sacrifice for the peace and honor of the South, as the best born

* Richmond, *Examiner*, Sept. 19, 1864, cited in New York *Times*, Sept. 22.

Southerner among you. If we must be enemies, let us be men, and fight it out as we propose to-day, and not deal in such hypocritical appeals to God and humanity. God will judge us in due time, and he will pronounce whether it be more humane to fight with a town full of women and the families of a 'brave people' at our back, or to remove them in time to places of safety among their own friends and people."

A somewhat similar correspondence was held between General Sherman and James M. Calhoun, the mayor of Atlanta. The latter, with two members of the City Council, represented the inevitable hardships of the removal, the difficulty of finding shelter in the region to the south already crowded with refugees, and appealed for a withdrawal of the order. To this General Sherman replied on the 12th of September:

"GENTLEMEN—I have your letter of the 11th in the nature of a petition to revoke my orders removing all the inhabitants from Atlanta. I have read it carefully, and give full credit to your statements of the distress that will be occasioned by it, and yet shall not revoke my order, simply because my orders are not designed to meet the humanities of the case, but to prepare for the future struggles in which millions, yea hundreds of millions of good people outside of Atlanta have a deep interest. We must have *peace*, not only at Atlanta, but in all America. To secure this we must stop the war that now desolates our once happy and favored country. To stop war we must defeat the rebel armies that are arrayed against the laws and Constitution which all must respect and obey. To defeat these armies we must prepare the way to reach them in their recesses provided with the arms and instruments which enable us to accomplish our purpose. Now, I know the vindictive nature of our enemy, and that we may have many years of military operations from this quarter, and therefore deem it wise and prudent to prepare in time. The use of Atlanta for warlike purposes is inconsistent with its character as a home for families. There will be no manufactures, commerce or agriculture here for the maintenance of families, and sooner or later want will compel the inhabitants to go. Why not go *now*, when all the arrangements are completed for the transfer, instead of waiting till the plunging shot of contending armies will renew the scene of the past month? Of course I do not apprehend any such thing at this moment, but you do not suppose that this army will be here till the war is over. I cannot discuss this subject with you fairly, because I cannot impart to you what I propose to do, but I assert that my military plans make it necessary for the inhabitants to go away, and I can only renew my offer of services to make their exodus in any direction as easy and comfortable as possible. You cannot qualify war in harsher terms than I will. War is cruelty, and you cannot refine it; and those who brought war on our country deserve all the curses and maledictions a people can pour out. I know I had no hand in making this war, and I know I will make more sacrifices to-day than any of you to secure peace. But you cannot have peace and a division of our country. If the United States submits to a division now, it will not stop, but will go on till we reap the fate of Mexico, which is eternal war. The United States does and must assert its authority wherever it has power; if it relaxes one bit to pressure it is gone, and I know that such is not the national feeling. This feeling assumes various shapes, but always comes back to that of *Union*. Once admit the Union, once more acknowledge the authority of the National Government, and instead of devoting your houses and streets and roads to the dread uses of war, I, and this army, become at once your protectors and supporters, shielding you from danger, let it come from what quarter it may. I know that a few individuals cannot resist a torrent of error and passion such as has swept the South into rebellion; but you can point out, so that we may know those who desire a Government and those who insist on war and its desolation. You might as well appeal against the thunder storm as against these terrible hardships of war. They are inevitable, and the only way the people of Atlanta can hope once more to live in peace and quiet at home is to stop this war, which can alone be done by admitting that it began in error and is perpetuated in pride. We don't want your negroes or your horses, or your houses or your land, or any thing you have; but we do want and will have a just obedience to the laws of the United States. That we will have, and if it involves the destruction of your improvements we cannot help it. You have heretofore read public sentiment in your newspapers, that live by falsehood and excitement, and the quicker you seek for truth in other quarters the better for you. I repeat, then, that by the original compact of Government, the United States had certain rights in Georgia which have never been relinquished, and never will be; that the South began war by seizing forts, arsenals, mints, custom-houses, etc., etc., long before Mr. Lincoln was installed, and before the South had one jot or tittle of provocation. I myself have seen in Missouri, Kentucky, Tennessee and Mississippi, hundreds and thousands of women and children fleeing from your armies and desperadoes, hungry and with bleeding feet. In Memphis, Vicksburg and Mississippi we fed thousands upon thousands of the families of rebel soldiers left on our hands, and whom we could not see starve. Now that war comes home to you, you feel very different—you deprecate its horrors, but did not feel them when you sent car-loads of soldiers and ammunition, and molded shell and shot to carry war into Kentucky and Tennessee, and desolate the homes of hundreds and thousands of good people, who only asked to live in peace at their old homes, and under the Government of their inheritance. But these comparisons are idle. I want peace, and believe it can only be reached through Union and war, and I will ever conduct war purely with a view to perfect and early success. But, my dear sirs, when that peace does come, you may call on me for any thing. Then will I share with you the last cracker, and watch with you to shield your homes and families against danger from every quarter. Now, you must go, and take with you the old and feeble: feed and nurse them, and build for them in more quiet places proper habitations to shield them against the weather, until the mad passions of men cool down, and allow the Union and peace to settle on your old homes at Atlanta."

A military order was issued by General Sherman on the 14th, declaring that "the city of Atlanta being exclusively for warlike purposes, will be at once vacated by all except the armies of the United States, and such civilian employès as may be retained by the proper departments of the Government." By the same order traders, manufacturers and sutlers were strictly forbidden to settle in the limits of fortified places on the line from Chattanooga.

In pursuance of this order, as we learn from a letter of General Sherman, dated Atlanta, September 24, addressed "To the Louisville Agent of the New York Associated Press," in which he denounced as utterly false a statement which had been published that the exiles had been "robbed of everything before being sent into the rebel lines." During the time 446 families were moved South, making 705 adults, 860 children and 479 servants, with 1,651 pounds of furniture and household goods on the average for each family.

There were rumors during September of a peace conference in Georgia, of which the following account was transferred from the *Macon* (Ga.) *Telegraph* to the northern journals: "We have a pretty reliable report of the result of the informal deputation to Governor Brown, to invite him to a peace conference with General Sherman. The latter had this project much at heart, and sent as his messenger a gentleman well known, of high social position in Georgia, to whom he tendered written credentials, if desired. He professed great unwillingness to penetrate further into Georgia and inflict the same devastation and misery which were sown broadcast in his rear. He sent an invitation to Governor Brown and other prominent gentlemen to come up and talk the matter over with him, and see if some scheme could not be devised to withdraw Georgia from the war, and save her people from further suffering. He would like, if Governor Brown desired it, that the latter should ride over the State road to Chattanooga, see 'the condition of his people in the rear, and realize the strong claims upon his sympathy it presented.' The reply of Governor Brown, we understand, was very much to this effect: Tell General Sherman that I understand him only to be a general of one of the Federal armies, while I am merely a governor of one of the Confederate States. I don't see how we can negotiate; or, if we should undertake it, how our negotiations can lead to any practical results."

Governor Brown had issued an important proclamation in July, in answer to a call for reinforcements by General Johnston, in which he summoned into active military service, at Atlanta, all that part of the reserve militia of the State between the ages of fifty and fifty-five years, and all between the ages of sixteen and seventeen. He enforced this call by the following appeal, in which the importance of Atlanta, as a military position, is fully set forth: "Georgians, you must reinforce General Johnston's army, and aid in driving back the enemy, or he will drive you back to the Atlantic, burn your cities and public buildings, destroy your property, and devastate the fair fields of your noble State. If the Confederate Government will not send the large cavalry force (now engaged in raiding and repelling raids) to destroy the long line of railroads over which General Sherman brings his supplies from Nashville, and thus compel him to retreat with the loss of most of his army, the people of Georgia, who have already been drawn upon more heavily in proportion to population than those of any other State in the Confederacy, must at all hazards, and at any sacrifice, rush to the front, and aid the great commander at the head of our glorious self-sacrificing army to drive them from the soil of the Empire State. I beg you, fellow-citizens, to reflect upon the magnitude of the issue. If General Johnston's army is destroyed, the Gulf States are thrown open to the enemy, and we are ruined. If General Sherman's army is cut off, the West is thrown open to us to the Ohio river, and all raids into Mississippi, Georgia, and Alabama, will at once cease. If every citizen of Georgia will do his duty, and the President will permit Kentucky to remain free from raids for a time, and will send Morgan and Forrest to operate upon the railroad line of communication nearly 300 miles in Sherman's rear, which passes over many bridges, and through a country destitute of supplies, the grand army of invasion can be destroyed, and not only our own State, but the Confederacy, delivered from disaster by the triumphant success of our arms."

The raid of General Morgan into Kentucky, alluded to by Governor

Brown, was begun at the end of May, when the notorious guerrilla leader entered the State by Pound Gap, with a force of cavalry estimated at between 2,000 and 3,000. Striking across the eastern portion of the State by Paintsville, Hazel Green, Orangeville, and Flemingsburgh to Maysville, on the Ohio, in a rapid march, they helped themselves to the horses of the farmers by the way, and plundered Union men of various stores and supplies. Gaining confidence by this success, they continued their depredations at Mount Sterling, Paris, Georgetown, and elsewhere ; among other incidents, capturing a train of cars on the Louisville and Frankfort railroad. Falling upon a detached body of Ohio troops, under command of General Hooker, at Cynthiana, General Morgan with his superior force, captured the town, and took the garrison prisoners ; but was overtaken the next day by General Burbridge, who was in command in Kentucky, and who since the beginning of the raid, had traversed the State in vigorous pursuit of the marauders. In a dispatch to the War Department, dated June 10th, at Lexington, he reports that, "after concentrating a force at Beaver Creek, on the Big Shandy, I moved against Morgan's force in Virginia, west as far as Gladeville. Morgan, with 2,500 men, moved into Kentucky, via Whitesbury. I pursued, and by marching ninety miles, in twenty-four hours, came upon him at Mount Sterling, yesterday morning, and defeated him. By stealing fresh horses, he reached Lexington at 2 o'clock this morning. Our forces held the fort, and the rebels did but little damage. He left here at 7 o'clock A. M. for Versailles. I start in pursuit with a fresh force this evening." Hearing of the capture of Hobson's troops, which occurred on the 11th, General Burbridge pushed on to the scene of that disaster ; overtook, and routed the enemy, recovering the spoils which they had taken. "I attacked Morgan," says he, in a dispatch of the 13th, "at Cynthiana, at daylight, yesterday morning. After an hour's hard fighting, completely routed him, killing 300, wounding nearly as many, and capturing nearly 400, besides recapturing nearly 100 of Hobson's command, and over 1,000 horses. Our loss, in killed and wounded, was about 150. Morgan's scattered forces are flying in all directions ; have thrown away arms, are out of ammunition, and are wholly demoralized."

Morgan now disappeared from Kentucky, escaping with his followers into Tennessee. He still, however, kept command of an irregular force with which he continued his depredations in the latter State, where, at the beginning of September, he was surprised at Greenville by a party of Union troops a portion of the command of General Gillem, his force routed, his staff taken prisoners, and he himself was killed in the encounter. The circumstances of this event we find thus related in a Southern journal :* "On Saturday, the 3d of September, accompanied by the brigades of Giltner, Hodges and Smith, and a detachment of Vaughan's, with four pieces of artillery, General Morgan and his staff approached the town of Greenville, Tennessee. Scouts had brought the information that the enemy were not nearer than Bull's Gap, sixteen miles distant ; and, in addition, a guard had been sent into the village to reconnoitre. Upon the report of the entire absence of the enemy, Cassel's battalion, commanded by Captain J. M. Clarke, together with the four guns, were posted some three or four hundred yards from the court-house, when General Morgan and his staff entered and established headquarters at the residence of Mrs. Dr. Williams, near the centre of the town. Shortly after the advent of the guard in town, young

* Reprinted in the New York *Times*, Sept. 17, 1864.

Mrs. Williams (daughter-in-law of the lady at whose house General Morgan had his headquarters) disappeared ; a scout was sent for, but could not find her, and as she returned with the enemy next morning, it appears she had ridden all the way to Bull's Gap and had given information of Morgan's whereabouts and the strength of the guard. Precautions had been taken to prevent the egress of persons who might convey information to the enemy, and all the roads and avenues were picketed. After visiting the camps and seeing that pickets had been duly posted, General Morgan and his staff, at a late hour of the night, retired to rest. Being greatly fatigued, they slept very soundly, and were started from their slumbers about 6 o'clock on Sunday morning by the elder Mrs. Williams, who informed them that the Yankees had surrounded the house. The General and his staff at once sprang from their beds, armed themselves, and rushed out at the opposite door to that at which the Yankees were thundering. On the side of the house where they escaped is a very large yard and garden with a great deal of foliage and a vineyard. These, together with the basement of the old hotel at the southwestern extremity of the grounds, enabled them to conceal themselves for a time, but the Yankees by this time began to appear so thick and fast around them that concealment became hopeless, and they rushed out to attempt to fight their way through, in the hope of succor and assistance from the battalion so near at hand. The officers with General Morgan were Major Gassett, and Captains Withers, Rogers and Clay, and a young gentleman by the name of Johnson, a clerk in the office of the Adjutant-General. At this time they were all, except Withers and Clay, in the basement of the old hotel, occupied by Mrs. Fry (wife of the notorious bushwhacker and murderer, now in our possession), who was all the time calling to the Yankees, informing them of the hiding-place of the 'rebels.' Seeing escape almost helpless, General Morgan directed Major Gassett to examine and see if there was any chance of escape from the front of the basement into the street. Major Gassett look and replied that there was a chance, but it was a desperate one, which General Morgan did not hear, as at that instant the Yankees charged up to the fence separating the hotel from Mrs. Williams' grounds, when the General, with Major Gassett, Captain Rogers and Mr. Johnson sprang out in the direction of the vineyard, when the two latter were captured and the General killed. The latter had just fired his pistol, and was in the act of firing again, when he fell. Captains Withers and Clay had not been able to get out of the house, and had concealed themselves in or near it. Major Gassett, in the meantime, sought shelter in the basement and vineyard alternately, but could not elude the vigilance of Mrs. Fry, who was all the time directing attention to his whereabouts. Being the only rebel left—Withers and Clay having been discovered and betrayed by a negro—Major Gassett's ingenuity was set to work to avoid capture. Mrs. Fry knew he was in the basement, and the Yankees were as thick around him as snakes in harvest. After passing to and fro several times between the basement and the garden, all the time under fire, he finally took shelter in the former, and at an auspicious moment sprang into the street, gave Mrs. Fry a parting blessing in his exit, mounted a horse hitched near by and made his escape. A great many shots were fired by the Yankees, but the only one that took effect was that which killed General Morgan, piercing his right breast and ranging through diagonally. Withers, Rogers, Clay and Johnson are now, we presume, in a Yankee prison, and Major Gassett is again on duty with his command. The General was determined never to surrender, and told the members of his staff they must not give up. He was heard to say, 'They have got us sure,' when he drew his pistol and commenced firing. After General Morgan had been killed, the unfeeling brutes who had murdered him threw his lifeless body across a horse and paraded it through the streets. His body was subsequently sent through the lines by a flag of truce. The remains of General Morgan were interred in Abingdon. The *Virginian* gives the following account of the ceremony: 'On Monday night the remains of General Morgan arrived at Abingdon, and were taken to the residence of Judge Campbell, in the vicinity, where Mrs. Morgan, with one or two relatives, are sojourning. On Tuesday evening at 4 o'clock, funeral services were performed by Chaplain Cameron, and the procession formed by General George B. Crittenden. It was the largest and most imposing procession we have ever seen of the sort in this part of the country.' "

CHAPTER CII.

NAVAL ENGAGEMENT OF THE KEARSARGE AND ALABAMA, JUNE 19TH, 1864.

If some disappointment was experienced in the Northern States on the approach of the National Anniversary at the indecisive results of the campaign in Virginia, and the general state of affairs witnessed in the steady rise of gold to 250 per cent. payable in the Government paper currency, there was something more than a momentary feeling of exultation when news arrived from Europe on the 5th of July of the destruction of the rebel steamer Alabama in an engagement with the United States sloop-of-war Kearsarge. The action was fought in the English channel on the forenoon of June 19th. Captain Semmes in command of the Alabama, after his first cruise in that vessel in the West Indies, and destruction of the United States gunboat Hatteras by a ruse, as recorded in a previous chapter, driven from the vicinity of the Gulf of Mexico, had crossed the Atlantic, and passing beyond the Cape of Good Hope, had continued his depredations with great effect upon American commerce in the eastern seas. Taking refuge from time to time in British harbors, when she was supplied and refitted the Alabama sallied forth to plunder and destroy, burning the merchant vessels she met in her course—no port being open to receive them for condemnation. So Captain Semmes set up his own admiralty court on the deck of his ship, and applied the torch to his captures, taking the crews prisoners and landing them from time to time at such places about the world as might be convenient to him. During the year 1863, the destruction of American ships in the West Indies, the Bay of Bengal and adjoining waters was constantly reported. Various United States war vessels were sent in pursuit of her, prominent among which was the fast sailing steamer Vanderbilt, commanded by Captain Wilkes, but by the adroitness of Captain Semmes, aided by the protection of the harbors in which he took refuge, he was enabled to escape pursuit and keep his vessel afloat for nearly two years after her first fraudulent departure from the English port in which she was built. In the spring of 1864, still continuing her depredations, the Alabama left the Cape of Good Hope for the north Atlantic, arriving at Cherbourg early in June. Here it was the expectation of Captain Semmes to refit for a new career of destruction. The American minister at Paris, Mr. Dayton, remonstrated to the French government against this free employment of their harbors, and Captain Semmes was notified to leave after receiving coals and provisions. The latter, knowing that a United States vessel, the Kearsarge, was on his track and would be waiting for him in the channel, confident of his ability to meet her, determined not to avoid the encounter. He accordingly sent a message to Captain Winslow of the Kearsarge, which the latter received on his arrival from Holland, off Cherbourg on the 14th of June, "begging that the Kearsarge would not depart, as he intended to fight her, and would not delay her but a day or two."* The loyal captain, welcoming the opportunity which he had long sought, held his vessel in readiness for the conflict. It came off, as we have stated, on the 19th. The day was Sunday. At about half-past 9 in the forenoon, the Alabama left the harbor and at twenty minutes past 10 was discovered by the Kearsarge steering for her. To avoid any question of marine jurisdiction, the United States vessel steamed a distance of six or seven miles from the Cherbourg breakwater, when she rounded to and commenced steering for the Alabama. For a similar purpose of preventing any hostilities in French waters, the iron-clad frigate Couronne left the port with the Confederate vessel, and accompanied her five miles to sea. Captain Semmes had spoken freely of his purpose on shore, and it was generally known that the engagement was to come off. A positive rumor of the intention was brought to the United States by the Cunard steamer which left Liverpool on the 18th; but it was received as a doubtful report, the proceeding being so much at variance with the usual course of the Alabama in preying on the defenceless. Previously to leaving Cherbourg, Captain Semmes deposited in a place of safe keeping on shore, his papers and other personal property with sixty chronometers, it is stated, the trophies of his various spoliations of as many merchantmen. On his departure he was accompanied by the Deerhound, a yacht belonging to Mr. John Lancaster, an English gentleman, a member of the Royal Yacht Squadron at Cowes, who happened then to be at Cherbourg on an excursion with his family. Hearing that the fight was to take place, Mr. Lancaster determined to witness it. The day being fine, the contest was also observed at a distance from the heights on the shore—about nine miles—by the inhabitants of Cherbourg and a large Sunday party of excursionists from Paris.

The action was commenced by the Alabama as the Kearsarge approached her within about 1,200 yards, the latter receiving two or three broadsides before a shot was returned. "The action," in the brief narrative of Captain Winslow's dispatches, "continued, the respective steamers making a circle round and round at a distance of about 900 yards from each other. At the expiration of an hour the Alabama struck, going down in about twenty minutes afterwards, and carrying many persons with her. . . . Although we received some twenty-five or thirty shots, twelve or thirteen taking effect in the hull, by the mercy of God we have been spared the loss of any of our lives, whereas in the case of the Alabama, the carnage I learn was dreadful." The only casualties on board the Kearsarge were three persons wounded, William Gwin and James Masbeth, ordinary seamen, se-

* Dispatch of Captain John A. Winslow to the Hon. Gideon Welles, June 19, 1864.

verely, and John W. Dempsey, who had an arm amputated owing to a fracture. When the Alabama was found to be in a sinking state in consequence of the explosion on her sides and between decks of the shells from the Kearsarge, Captain Semmes made an effort to return to the French shore, but the ship filling rapidly, the furnace fires were extinguished and he was compelled to surrender. "Some twenty minutes after," says he in his report, communicated by Mr. Mason to the *London Times*, "the ship being on the point of settling, every man, in obedience to a previous order which had been given the crew, jumped overboard and endeavored to save himself." At this juncture Mr. Lancaster came up with his yacht and rendered Captain Semmes and his crew friendly assistance, rescuing them, in fact, from the power to which they had surrendered. The action and the incidents in which he was concerned, are thus stated by Mr. Lancaster in the log which he kept of the Deerhound:—"Sunday, June 10, 9 A. M. Got up steam and proceeded out of Cherbourg harbor. 10.30.—Observed the Alabama steaming out of the harbor toward the Federal steamer Kearsarge. 11.10—The Alabama commenced firing with her starboard battery, the distance between the contending vessels being about one mile. The Kearsarge immediately replied with her starboard guns; a very sharp, spirited firing was then kept up, shot being sometimes varied by shells. In the manœuvring both vessels made seven complete circles at a distance of from a quarter to a half a mile. At 12 a slight intermission was observed in the Alabama's firing, the Alabama making head sail and shaping her course for the land, distant about nine miles. At 12.30 observed the Alabama to be disabled and in a sinking state. We immediately made toward her, and on passing the Kearsarge were requested to assist in saving the Alabama's crew. At 12.50, when within a distance of 200 yards, the Alabama sank. We then lowered our two boats, and, with the assistance of the Alabama's whale boat and dingy, succeeded in saving about thirty men, including Captain Semmes and thirteen officers. At 1 P. M. we steered for Southampton." Sixty-eight of the officers and crew of the Alabama were carried into Cherbourg by the Kearsarge and were liberated on parole. Fifteen of the men were seriously wounded, two dying on the vessel, making the whole number received on board seventy—six officers and sixty-four men. Nine of the Alabama's crew were rescued by a French pilot boat and also taken to Cherbourg. It was said "that Captain Winslow would have secured the whole of the officers and crew of the Alabama had he not placed too much confidence in the honor of the owner of the yacht; that he considered Captain Semmes and others who escaped as bound in honor to give themselves up, and that he did not pursue and fire upon the Deerhound because he did not believe any one carrying the flag of the Royal Yacht Squadron would act so dishonorably."* Mr. Lancaster replied to this charge in a communication to the newspapers in which it was inserted, claiming that he had acted from motives of humanity, at the request of Captain Winslow to save the men, without any stipulation to deliver the men as prisoners, that if any such condition had been proposed, he "should have declined the task as inconsistent with his notions of honor—to lend my yacht and crew for the purpose of rescuing those brave men from drowning only to hand them over to their enemies for imprisonment, ill treatment, and perhaps execution." The sympathies of Mr. Lancaster, in common with very many of his countrymen were evidently with the rebellion. Captain Winslow addressed a letter to

* *London Daily News* cited in *New York Times*, July 7, 1864.

M. Bonfils, the commercial agent of the Alabama at Cherbourg, in which he claimed the officers and sailors of the Alabama carried into Cherbourg by the French pilot boats as his prisoners, and demanded their formal surrender on board the Kearsarge. "If they should endeavor to free themselves from this obligation under cover of the means which have been used for their escape, they must expect to meet with no mercy another time."

In an official dispatch to Secretary Welles, dated June 21, Captain Winslow gives the following account of the circumstances connected with the rescue of the prisoners by the Deerhound: "I have the honor to report that toward the close of the action between the Alabama and the Kearsarge, all available sail was made on the former for the purpose of again reaching Cherbourg. When the object was apparent, the Kearsarge was steered across the bow of the Alabama for a raking fire, but before reaching this point the Alabama struck. Uncertain whether Captain Semmes was not using some ruse, the Kearsarge was stopped. It was seen shortly afterward that the Alabama was lowering her boats; and an officer came alongside in one of them to say that they had surrendered, and were fast sinking, and begging that boats would be dispatched immediately for saving of life. The two boats not disabled were at once lowered, and as it was apparent the Alabama was settling, this officer was permitted to leave in his boat to afford assistance. An English yacht, the Deerhound, had approached near the Kearsarge at this time, when I hailed and begged the commander to run down to the Alabama, as she was fast sinking and we had but two boats, and assist in picking up the men. He answered affirmatively, and steamed toward the Alabama, but the latter sunk almost immediately. The Deerhound, however, sent her boats and was most actively engaged, aided by several others which had come from shore. These boats were busy in bringing the wounded and others to the Kearsarge, whom we were trying to make as comfortable as possible, when it was reported to me that the Deerhound was moving off. I could not believe that the commander of that vessel could be guilty of so disgraceful an act as taking our prisoners off, and therefore took no means to prevent it, but continued to keep our boats at work rescuing the men in the water. I am sorry to say that I was mistaken. The Deerhound made off with Captain Semmes and others, and also the very officer who had come on board to surrender. I learned subsequently that the Deerhound was a consort of the Alabama, and that she received on board all the valuable personal effects of Captain Semmes the night before the engagement."

"The combatants in this action," says Captain Winslow, "were about equal in match, the tonnage being the same, the Alabama carrying a 100-pound rifle with one heavy 68-pounder and six broadside 32-pounders; the Kearsarge carrying four broadside 32-pounders, two 11-inch and one 28-pound rifle, one gun less than the Alabama. In the wake of the engines on the outside, the Kearsarge had stopped up and down her sheet chains. These were stopped by marline to eye bolts, which extended some twenty feet, and was done by the hands of the Kearsarge; the whole was covered by light plank, to prevent dirt collecting. It was for the purpose of protecting the engines, when there was no coal in the upper part of the bunkers, as was the case when the action took place. The Alabama had her bunkers full and was equally protected. The Kearsarge went into action with a crew of 162 officers and men. The Alabama, by report of the Deerhound's officers, had 150."* If this last number

* Captain Winslow's report to Secretary Welles, and letter published in the *London Daily News*.

is correctly stated, the Alabama lost over thirty in the action. F. A. Graham, gunner of the Kearsarge, reports the expenditure of ordnance on board his vessel. The action lasted, he says, sixty-five minutes, and in that time were fired fifty-five 11-inch 5-seconds shell, eighteen 32-pounders 5-seconds shell, forty-two 32-pounds solid shot, forty-eight 30-pound rifle percussion shell, nine shrapnel and one canister from 12-pound howitzer. Captain Winslow reports, "every officer and man doing their duty, exhibiting a degree of coolness and fortitude which gave promise at the outset of certain victory." He especially mentions the services of his executive officer, Lieutenant-Commander Thornton, the superintendent of the battery during the engagement.

Captain Winslow, a native of North Carolina, and citizen of Massachusetts, entered the navy in 1827, saw various service in different parts of the world, was commissioned Commander in 1855; in 1862 was ordered to the Mississippi flotilla, and on its completion to the command of the Kearsarge, one of the new screw sloops built during the war. Lieutenant-commanding James S. Thornton, a native of New Hampshire, who entered the service in 1841, was with Commodore Farragut as executive officer on board the Hartford at the time of the passage of the forts below New Orleans, at the capture of the city, doing distinguished service on that occasion.

On the receipt of Captain Winslow's first dispatch, Secretary Welles, on the 6th of July, addressed to him the following congratulatory letter from the Navy Department:

"Sir: Your very brief dispatches of the 19th and 20th ult., informing the Department that the piratical craft Alabama or 290 had been sunk on the 19th of June, near Meridan, by the Kearsarge, under your command, were this day received. I congratulate you on your good fortune in meeting this vessel, which had so long avoided the fastest ships, and some of the most vigilant and intelligent officers of the service; and for the ability displayed in this combat you have the thanks of the Department. You will please express to the officers and crew of the Kearsarge the satisfaction of the Government at the victory over a vessel superior in tonnage, superior in number of guns, and superior in the number of her crew. The battle was so brief, the victory so decisive, and the comparative results so striking, that the country will be reminded of the brilliant actions of our infant navy, which have been repeated and illustrated in this engagement. The Alabama represented the best maritime effort of the most skilled English workshops. Her battery was composed of the well-tried 32-pounders of 57 cwt., of the famous 68-pounder of the British Navy, and of the only successful rifled 100-pounder yet produced in England. The crew were generally recruited in Great Britain, and many of them received superior training on board her Majesty's gunnery ship, The Excellent. The Kearsarge is one of the first gunboats built at our navy-yards at the commencement of the Rebellion, and lacks the improvements of vessels now under construction. The principal guns composing her battery had never been previously tried in an exclusively naval engagement, yet in one hour you succeeded in sinking your antagonist, thus fully ending her predatory career, and killed many of her crew, without injury to the Kearsarge or the loss of a single life on your vessel. Our countrymen have reason to be satisfied that in this, as in every naval action of this unhappy war, neither the ship, the guns, nor the crew have been deteriorated, but that they maintain the ability and continue the renown which ever adorned our naval annals. The President has signified his intention to recommend that you receive a vote of thanks, in order that you may be advanced to the grade of Commodore. Lieutenant-Commander James S. Thornton, the executive officer of the Kearsarge, will be recommended to the Senate for advancement ten numbers in his grade, and you will report to the Department the names of any others of the officers or crew whose good conduct on the occasion entitles them to especial mention."

Recurring to this subject in his Annual Report in December, Secretary Welles remarked: "This has been the only fair and open sea fight which our naval men have been able to secure, as yet, during the war; and it occurred in the English Channel, in sight of the two great maritime powers of Europe. In size, armament and complement of men, the combatants were as near equal, perhaps, as could have been arranged. Most of the crew of the Alabama were Englishmen, and the gunners admitted to have been picked men of Her Majesty's gunnery ship the Excellent. Some latent remains of pride which belong to the profession, and which animated his earlier and more honorable life while sailing under the American flag, undoubtedly had an influence in inducing the pirate commander to meet a naval antagonist, after his long career of robbery and plunder of unarmed vessels, in the vain hope that it might, if successful, restore to him some portion of the respect he had forfeited, and, at the same time, relieve him of some of the debasement he has never ceased to feel, even when applauded by these foreign partisans who hated the country he had deserted. But the same dishonor marked his conduct on this occasion as during his whole ignoble career. Before leaving Cherbourg he deposited the chronometers and other trophies of his robberies on shore. When beaten and compelled to surrender, he threw overboard the sword that was no longer his own, and, abusing the generous confidence of his brave antagonist, he stole away in the English tender, whose owner proved himself, by his conduct, a fit companion for the dishonored and beaten corsair. Having surrendered, he cannot relieve himself of his obligations, as a prisoner of war, until he shall be regularly exchanged. He, and each of his surviving officers and crew, whether received upon the Kearsarge or the Deerhound, are, and will be, held to be prisoners of war, and amenable to the laws which govern civilized communities. A predatory rover may set the laws of nations, as well as those of his own country, at defiance, but in doing so he must abide the consequences."

The destruction of the Alabama was followed, in the course of a few months, by the capture of two of the most formidable of the rebel piratical vessels then afloat. One of these, the Georgia, after cruising under the rebel flag, had been taken to Liverpool, where a change of ownership was effected and her armament removed. Setting out thence for Lisbon, Commodore Craven, commanding the Niagara, fell in with her on the voyage, took possession, and sent her as a prize to the United States. The other and better known Confederate vessel, the Florida, was arrested in full career of her depredations. Her history, up to the period of her capture, is thus briefly narrated in the Annual Report of Secretary Welles: "The Florida originally sailed from England under the name of Oreto, and under that name she was, on reaching Nassau, brought before the court through the efforts of the American Consul, who was satisfied that she was in the rebel interest and intended as a rebel cruiser. The neutral authorities decided in favor of the vessel, which was permitted to proceed. Leaving Nassau, she went to Green Bay, where she received on board the armament sent out for her from England, ran into Mobile, changed her name to Florida, and has since, fleeing from all naval vessels, carried on predatory war on American commerce, capturing and destroying unarmed merchantmen, without ever sending in a vessel for adjudication. In February last, availing herself of a dark night, she escaped from Brest, eluding the Kearsarge, which was off that port. In June she visited the neutral port of St. George's, Bermuda, and remained there nine days, receiving all the coal and supplies necessary for a long piratical cruise. Leaving St. George's on the 27th of that month, she remained outside, but in sight, for three or four days, boarding all vessels that approached the island. On the 10th of July she captured the Electric Spark, near our coast, while several vessels were cruising for her, but she escaped, and was next heard from at Teneriffe, on the 4th of August. Subsequently, entering the Bay of San Salvador, Brazil, she encountered the steamer Wachusett, commanded by Commander Collins, to whom she surrendered, and by whom she was brought in a leaky and dilapidated condition to Hampton Roads. Here, while at anchor, an army transport came in collision with the shattered vessel, which sunk, a few days after, near the wreck of the Cumberland."

The "encounter" alluded to in the Bay of San Salvador took place on the morning of the 7th of October. The Florida, commanded by C. Manigault Morris, formerly of the United States navy, on arriving in the port two days previously, found there the United States gunboat Wachusett, Commander Napoleon Collins. Some overtures, according to the report of the rebel officer Morris, appear to have been made to him, indirectly through the United States Consul at Bahia, preliminary to a challenge to fight the Wachusett; but this he refused to receive, alleging that the communication did not recognize the Federal authority of his vessel. Captain Collins promptly determined, after consultation with his officers, to sink the rebel cruiser in port. Accordingly, as the facts were reported on the arrival of the Kearsarge at Boston in the early part of November bringing the intelligence, "at about 3 o'clock the cables were slipped, and the Wachusett steered for the Florida, hitting her on the quarter without doing great injury. Captain Collins now called out to those on board the pirate to surrender or he would sink her. This demand was replied to by the first lieutenant, that 'under the circumstances he surrendered.' A hawser was now made fast, the chain slipped, and the Florida towed to sea. In the melee several pistol shots were fired, and accidentally two guns from the Wachusett. Captain Morris and half the Florida's crew were ashore on liberty. No lives were lost. The Florida was taken completely by surprise; seventy of her men it was known being on shore, and the others, just returned from liberty, were asleep and half intoxicated. The blow given the Florida by the Wachusett carried away the mizzen-mast and main-yard, which fell on the awning, preventing any one from getting up from below. So unconscious was the officer of the deck of the intention of the Wachusett's captain, that he sang out, 'You will run into us if you don't take care,' at the same time calling for a light. Twelve officers and fifty-eight of the crew of the Florida were captured." The captured officers and men of the Florida were transferred, after their arrival at Hampton Roads, to Fort Warren at Boston. It was while the subject of the capture of the vessel and the attendant circumstances were under discussion between the governments of the United States and Brazil, that at the end of November the Florida sank, as stated by Secretary Welles, in Hampton Roads, after having been run into by an army steamer.

The Tallahassee, an English-built blockade-running steamer, was fitted out at Wilmington in August as a Confederate cruiser, and in that capacity immediately began a series of depredations on United States commercial vessels on the coast. As soon as the fact was reported numerous cruisers were sent from the Northern Atlantic ports in quest of her, but she succeeded, after touching at Halifax for supplies, though closely pursued, in reaching Wilmington in safety.

CHAPTER CIII.

NAVAL AND MILITARY OPERATIONS AT MOBILE BAY, AUGUST, 1864.

Simultaneously with the closing events of General Sherman's successful campaign against Atlanta, came the news in rapid sequence of the brilliant operations of Farragut's fleet with the co-operation of the army, in the reduction of the important fortresses at the entrance to Mobile Bay. Atlanta was evacuated on the 1st of September; on the 23d of August, Fort Morgan was unconditionally surrendered. The nation, as we have seen, was called by the President, in a Proclamation of Thanksgiving to rejoice in both events. The old defences of Mobile overcome by Admiral Farragut and his coadjutors, consisted of the forts on either side guarding the entrances to the Bay from the Gulf of Mexico, and the serious military obstructions planted in the main channel, through which a passage must be forced. Situated on the right bank of Mobile river at the head of Mobile Bay, thirty miles from the Gulf, the city of Mobile was immediately protected by a series of redoubts, batteries and entrenchments covering the approaches by land from above and on either side, while the shallow waters of the bay rendered defence easy from below. The city was understood to be garrisoned by a force sufficient to man the fortifications; but the main dependence against attack was placed in the iron-clad fleet which had been diligently prepared, and which was under the command of Admiral Buchanan. This, with the powerful aid of the forts at the mouth of the bay, was relied upon for warding off any assault by sea, and keeping open the communication of the fort by the blockade runners for the much needed supplies from abroad. The rebel fleet was composed of Admiral Buchanan's flag ship, the powerful iron-clad ram, the Tennessee, the iron-clad gunboats Selma, Morgan and Gaines, and other vessels of lighter construction suited for harbor defence. There were two avenues of approach to the bay from the Gulf, and both were well guarded by fortifications. The main entrance on the south by the passage about three miles wide between the eastern extremity of Dauphin Island and Mobile Point was protected by Fort Morgan on the latter and Fort Gaines on the island; while the other passage from Mississippi Sound on the southwest, known as Grant's Pass, was protected by Fort Powell and a battery and earthworks on the mainland. With these means of defence, and a liberal use of obstructions in the channels, the operations of the Union fleet in the Department had long been confined to the usual and somewhat uncertain blockade of the coast. After the fall of New

Orleans, the defences had been menaced by a naval attack: and again, at the beginning of the present year, Admiral Farragut had seriously threatened operations in this quarter; but the first was little more than a reconnoissance, and the second appears to have been intended only as a diversion to second the movements of General Sherman in his expedition across Mississippi. The movements of the fleet and army attending the temporary occupation of Brownsville, and the permanent blockade of the Rio Grande, occupied in the early part of the year the western Gulf squadron commanded by Rear Admiral Farragut, postponing for a time the meditated attack on Mobile. The affair was, however, now to be undertaken in earnest. At the beginning of July the details of the movement combining operations by the land and naval forces of the Department were arranged by the respective commanders, General Canby and Admiral Farragut. "On the 8th of July," says the latter in his official report, "I had an interview with Generals Canby and Granger on board the Hartford, on the subject of an attack upon Forts Morgan and Gaines, at which it was agreed that General Canby would send all the troops he could spare to co-operate with the fleet. Circumstances soon obliged General Canby to inform me that he could not dispatch a sufficient number to invest both forts, and in reply, I suggested that Gaines should be the first invested, engaging to have a force in the Sound ready to protect the landing of the army on Dauphin Island in the rear of that fort, and I assigned Lieut.-Commander De Krafft, of the Conemaugh, to that duty. On the 1st of August, General Granger visited me again on the Hartford. In the meantime, the Tecumseh had arrived at Pensacola, and Captain Craven informed me that he would be ready in four days for any service. We therefore fixed upon the 4th of August as the day for the landing of the troops, and my entrance into the bay; but owing to delays, the Tecumseh was not ready. General Granger, however, to my mortification, was up to the time, and the troops actually landed on Dauphin Island.

"As subsequent events proved, the delay turned to our advantage, as the rebels were busily engaged during the 4th in throwing troops and supplies into Fort Gaines, all of which were captured a few days afterward. The Tecumseh arrived on the evening of the 4th, and every thing being propitious, I proceeded to the attack on the following morning. The vessels outside the bar which were designed to participate in the engagement, were all under way at 5:40 in the morning, in the following order two abreast and lashed together: Brooklyn, Captain James Alden, with the Octarora, Lieut.-Commander C. H. Green, on the port side; Hartford, Captain Percival Drayton, with the Metacomet, Lieut.-Commander J. E. Jenett; Richmond, Captain T. A. Jenkins, with the Port Royal, Lieut.-Commander B Gherardi; Lackawanna, Captain B. Marchand, with the Seminole, Commander E. Donaldson; Monongahela, Commander J. H. Strong, with the Kennebec, Lieut.-Commander W. P. McCann; Ossipee, Commander W. E. Leroy, with the Itasca, Lieut.-Commander George Brown; Oneida, Commander J. R. M. Mullany, with the Galena, Lieut.-Commander C. H. Wells. The iron-clads Tecumseh, Commander T. A. M. Craven; the Manhattan, Commander J. W. A. Nicholson; the Winnebago, Commander M. H. Stevens, and the Chickasaw, Lieut.-Commander T. H. Perkins, were already ahead inside the bar, and had been ordered to keep up their positions on the starboard side of the wooden ships, or between them and Fort Morgan, for the double purpose of keeping down the fire from the water battery and the parapet guns of the fort, as well as to attack the ram Tennessee as soon as the fort was passed. It was only at the urgent request of the Captains and commanding officers that I yielded to the Brooklyn being the leading ship of the line, as she had four chase guns and an ingenious arrangement for picking up torpedoes, and because, in their judgment, the flagship ought not to be too much exposed. This I believe to be an error; for apart from the fact that exposure is one of the penalties of rank in the navy, it will always be the aim of the enemy to destroy the flagship, and, as will appear in the sequel, such attempt was very persistently made, but Providence did not permit it to be successful.

"The attacking fleet steamed steadily up the main ship channel, the Tecumseh firing the first shot at 6:47. At 7:06 the fort opened upon us, and was replied to by a gun from the Brooklyn, and immediately after the action became general. It was soon apparent that there was some difficulty ahead. The Brooklyn, for some cause, which I did not then clearly understand, but which has since been explained by Captain Alden in his report, arrested the advance of the whole fleet, while at the same time the guns of the fort were playing with great effect upon that vessel and the Hartford. A moment after I saw the Tecumseh, struck by a torpedo, disappear instantaneously beneath the waves, carrying with her her Commander and nearly all her crew. I determined at once, as I had originally intended to take the lead, and after ordering the Metacomet to send a boat to save, if possible, any of the perishing crew, I dashed ahead with the Hartford, and the ships followed on, their officers believing that they were going to a noble death with their Commander-in-chief. I steamed through between the buoys where the torpedoes were supposed to have been sunk. These buoys had been previously examined by my Flag-Lieutenant, J. Crittenden Watson, in several nightly reconnoissances. Though he had not been able to discover the sunken torpedoes, yet we had been assured by refugees, deserters and others, of their existence, but believing that from their having been some time in the water they were probably innocuous, I determined to take the chance of their explosion. From the moment I turned to the northwestward to clear the middle ground, we were enabled to keep such a broadside fire upon the batteries of Fort Morgan that their guns did us comparatively little injury. Just after we passed the fort, which was about ten minutes before 8 o'clock, the ram Tennessee dashed out at this ship, as had been expected, and in anticipation of which I had ordered the monitors on the starboard side. I took no further notice of her than to return her fire. The rebel gunboats Morgan, Gaines and Selma were ahead, and the latter particularly annoyed us with a raking fire, which our guns could not return. At two minutes after 8 o'clock I ordered the Metacomet to cast off and go in pursuit of the Selma. Captain Jouett was after her in a moment, and in an hour's time he had her as a prize. She was commanded by P. N. Murphy, formerly of the United States Navy. He was wounded in the wrist; his executive officer, Lieutenant Comstock, and eight of the crew killed, and seven or eight wounded. Lieutenant-Commander Jouett's conduct during the whole affair commands my warmest commendations. The Morgan and Gaines succeeded in escaping under the protection of the guns of Fort Morgan, which would have been prevented had the other gunboats been as prompt in their movements as the Metacomet. The want of pilots, however, I believe, was the principal difficulty. The Gaines was so injured by our fire that she had to be run ashore, where she was subsequently destroyed, but the Morgan escaped to Mobile during the night, though she was chased and fired into by our cruisers.

"Having passed the forts and dispersed the enemy's gunboats, I had ordered most of the vessels to anchor, when I perceived the ram Tennessee standing up for this ship; this was at 8:45 o'clock. I was not long in comprehending her intentions to be the destruction of the flagship. The monitors and such of the wooden vessels as I thought best adapted for the purpose, were immediately ordered to attack the ram, not only with their guns, but bows on at full speed. And then began one of the fiercest naval combats on record. The Monongahela, Commander Strong, was the first vessel that struck her, and in doing so, carried away his own iron prow, together with the cutwater, without apparently doing his adversary much injury. The Lackawanna, Captain Marchand, was the next vessel to strike her, which she did at full speed, but though her stern was cut and crushed to the plank ends for the distance of three feet above the water's edge to five feet below, the only perceptible effect on the ram was to give her a heavy lift. The Hartford was the third vessel which struck her, but as the Tennessee quickly shifted her helm, the blow was a glancing one, and as she rasped along our side we poured our whole broadside of nine-inch solid shot within ten feet of her casement. The monitors worked slowly, but delivered their fire as opportunity offered. The Chickasaw succeeded in getting under her stern, and a fifteen-inch shot from the Manhattan broke through her iron plating and heavy wooden backing, though the missile itself did not enter the vessel.

Immediately after the collision with the flag-ship, I directed Captain Drayton to bear down for the ram again. He was doing so at full speed, when, unfortunately, the Lackawanna ran into the Hartford just forward of the mizzen-mast, cutting her down to within two feet of the water's edge. We soon got clear again, however, and were fast approaching our adversary, when she struck her colors and ran up the white flag. She was at this time sore beset; the Chickasaw was pounding away at her stern, the Ossipee was approaching her at full speed, and the Monongahela, Lackawanna, and this ship were bearing down upon her, determined upon her destruction. Her smoke-stack had been shot away, her steering chains were gone; compelling a resort to her relieving tackles, and several of the port-shutters were jammed. Indeed, from the time the Hartford struck her until her surrender, she never fired a gun. As the Ossipee, Commander Le Roy, was about to strike her, she hoisted the white flag, and that vessel immediately stopped her engine, though not in time to avoid a glancing blow. During the contest with the rebel gunboats and the ram Tennessee, and which terminated by her surrender at ten o'clock, we lost many more men than from the fire of the batteries of Fort Morgan. Admiral Buchanan was wounded in the leg, two or three of his men were killed, and five or six wounded. Commander Johnston, formerly of the United States Navy, was in command of the Tennessee, and came on board the flagship to surrender his sword and that of Admiral Buchanan. The Surgeon, Doctor Conrad, came with him, stated the condition of the Admiral, and wished to know what was to be done with him. Fleet Surgeon Palmer, who was on board the Hartford during the action, commiserating the sufferings of the wounded, suggested that those of both sides be sent to Pensacola, where they could be properly cared for. I therefore addressed a note to Brigadier General R. L. Page, commanding Fort Morgan, informing him that Admiral Buchanan and others of the Tennessee had been wounded, and desiring to know whether he would permit one of our vessels, under a flag of truce, to convey them with, or without, our wounded men to Pensacola, on the understanding that the vessel should take out none but the wounded, and bring nothing back that she did not take out. This was acceded to by General Page, and the Metacomet proceeded on this mission of humanity.

"As I had an elevated position in the main rigging, near the top, I was able to overlook, not only the deck of the Hartford, but the other vessels of the fleet. I witnessed the terrible effects of the enemy's shot, and the good conduct of the men at their guns; and although no doubt their hearts sickened, as mine did, when their shipmates were struck down beside them, yet there was not a moment's hesitation to lay their comrades aside, and spring again to their deadly work. Our little consort, the Metacomet, was also under my immediate eye during the whole action up to the moment I ordered her to cast off in pursuit of the Selma. The coolness and promptness of Lieutenant-Commander Jouett throughout, merit high praise; his whole conduct was worthy of his reputation. In this connection, I must not omit to call the attention of the Department to the conduct of Acting Ensign Henry C. Nields, of the Metacomet, who had charge of the boat sent from that vessel when the Tecumseh sunk. He took her in under one of the most galling fires I ever saw, and succeeded in rescuing from death ten of her crew within six hundred yards of the Fort. I would respectfully recommend his advancement. The commanding officers of all the vessels who took part in the action, deserve my warmest commendations, not only for the untiring zeal with which they had prepared their ships for the contest, but for their skill and daring in carrying out my orders during the engagement. With the exception of the momentary arrest of the fleet when the Hartford passed ahead, and to which I have already adverted, the order of battle was preserved, and the ships followed each other in close order past the batteries of Fort Morgan, and in comparative safety, too, with the exception of the Oneida. Her boilers were penetrated by a shot from the fort, which completely disabled her, but her consort, the Galena, firmly fastened to her side, brought her safely through, showing clearly the wisdom of the precaution of carrying the vessels in two abreast. Commander Mullany, who had solicited eagerly to take part in the action, was severely wounded, losing his left arm. In the encounter with the ram, the commanding officers obeyed with alacrity the order to run her down, and without hesitation exposed their ships to destruction, to destroy the enemy. Our iron-clads, from their slow speed and bad sailing, had some difficulty in getting into and maintaining their position in line as we passed the fort, and in the subsequent encounter with the Tennessee, from the same causes, were not so effective as could have been desired; but I cannot give too much praise to Lieutenant-Commander Perkins, who, though he had orders from the department to return North, volunteered to take command of the Chickasaw, and did his duty nobly.

"The Winnebago was commanded by Commander T. H. Stevens, who volunteered for that position. His vessel steers very badly, and neither of his turrets will work, which compelled him to turn his vessel every time to get a shot, so that he could not fire very often, but he did the best under the circumstances. The Manhattan appeared to work well, though she moved slowly. Commander Nicholson delivered his fire deliberately, and, as before stated, with one of his 15-inch shot broke through the armor of the Tennessee, with his wooden backing, though the shot itself did not enter the vessel. No other shot broke through her armor, though many of her plates were started, and several of her port-shutters jammed by the fire from the different ships. The Hartford, my flagship, was commanded by Captain Percival Drayton, who exhibited throughout that coolness and ability for which he has been long known to his brother officers. But I must speak of that officer in a double capacity. He is the fleet captain of my squadron, and one of more determined energy, untiring devotion to duty, and zeal for the service, tempered by great calmness, I do not think adorns any navy. I desire to call your attention to this officer, though well aware that in thus speaking of his high qualities I am only communicating officially to the department that which it knew full well before. To him, and to my staff in their respective positions, I am indebted for the detail of my fleet. Lieutenant J. Crittenden Watson, my flag-lieutenant, has been brought to your notice in former dispatches. During the action he was on the poop attending to the signals, and performed his duties, as might be expected, thoroughly. He is a scion worthy the noble stock he sprang from, and I commend him to your attention. My Secretary, Mr. McKinley, and Acting Ensign L. H. Brownell, were also on the poop, the latter taking notes of the action, a duty which he performed with coolness and accuracy. Two other acting ensigns of my staff (Mr. Bogart and Mr. Heginbotham) were on duty in the powder division, and, as the reports will show, exhibited zeal and ability. The latter, I regret to say, was severely wounded by a raking shot from the Tennessee, when we collided with that vessel, and died a few hours after. Mr. Heginbotham was a young married man, and has left a widow and one child, whom I commend to the kindness of the department. Lieutenant A. R. Yates, of the Augusta, acted as an additional aid to me on board the Hartford, and was very efficient in the transmission of orders. The last of my staff, and to whom I would call the notice of the department, is not the least in importance. I mean Pilot Martin Freeman. He has been my great reliance in all difficulties in his line of duty. During the action he was in the maintop, piloting the ships into the bay. He was cool and brave throughout, never losing his self-possession. This man was captured early in the war in a fine fishing-smack which he owned, and, though he protested that he had no interest in the war, and only asked for the privilege of fishing for the fleet, yet his services were too valuable to the captors as a pilot not to be secured. He was appointed a first-class pilot, and has served us with zeal and fidelity, and has lost his vessel, which went to pieces on Ship Island. I commend him to the department.

"It gives me pleasure to refer to several officers who volunteered to take any situation where they might be useful, some of whom were on their way North, either by orders of the department or condemned by medical survey The reports of the different commanders will show how they conducted themselves. I have already mentioned Lieutenant-Commander Perkins, of the Chickasaw, and Lieutenant Yates, of the Augusta. Acting Volunteer Lieutenant William Hamilton, late commanding officer of the Augusta Dinsmore, had been invalided by the medical survey, but he eagerly offered his services on board the iron-clad Chickasaw, having had much experience in our monitors. Acting Volunteer Lieutenant P. Giraud, another experienced officer in iron-clads, asked to go in one of these vessels, but as they were all well supplied with officers, I permitted him to go on the Ossipee, under Commander Le Roy. After the action he was given temporary charge of the ram Tennessee. Before closing this report there is one other officer of my squadron of whom I feel bound to speak—Captain

T. A. Jenkins of the Richmond, who was formerly my chief of staff, not because of his having held that position, but because he never forgets to do his duty to the Government, and takes now the same interest in the fleet as when he stood in that relation to me. He is also the commanding officer of the Second Division of my squadron, and as such has shown ability and the most untiring zeal. He carries out the spirit of one of Lord Collingwood's best sayings: 'Not to be afraid of doing too much; those who are, seldom do as much as they ought.' When in Pensacola he spent days on the bar, placing the buoys in the best positions; was always looking after the interest of the service, and keeping the vessels from being detained one moment longer in port than was necessary. The gallant Craven told me only the night before the action in which he lost his life: 'I regret, Admiral, that I have detained you, but had it not been for Captain Jenkins, God knows when I should have been here. When your order came, I had not received an ounce of coal!' I feel that I should not be doing my duty did I not call the attention of the Department to an officer who has performed all his various duties with so much zeal and fidelity." The total casualties in this action, exclusive of those lost in the Tecumseh, were 52 killed and 170 wounded; 20 officers, including Admiral Buchanan, and about 170 men were captured in the Tennessee, and 90 officers and men in the Selma.*

Captain Tunis Augustus McDonough Craven, whose loss, thus deplored by Admiral Farragut, was the heaviest price paid for this great victory, had for thirty-five years been in the service of his country. A native of New Hampshire, he entered the Navy as midshipman in 1829. He was early distinguished by his scientific attainments, being engaged at the National Observatory, and particularly in the operations of the Coast Survey in New York harbor and elsewhere. At the outbreak of the rebellion, Captain Craven, whose instinctive loyalty was keenly alive to the necessities of the situation, was of great service to the country in preserving the posts at Key West and the Tortugas, where he was stationed with his vessel on coast duty. He was subsequently in command of the gunboat Tuscarora, in which his active pursuit of the rebel Alabama will be remembered by the reader. Early in 1864 he was put in command of the monitor Tecumseh, with which it was his fate to perish. "No braver, or better, or more loyal officer," says an obituary notice, "is left in our great Navy than Captain Craven; whose steady goodness and bravery and sense were joined with a modesty so sensitive, that when called on for a speech on a public occasion, he could not say a word, and when at the Sanitary Fair he was called out that he might furnish his autograph, was absolutely so discomposed at the attention as to be unable to write."*

The enemy's fleet having thus been effectually disposed of in the action of the 5th of August, the reduction of the forts at the entrance to the harbor was speedily secured. Fort Powell, protecting Grant's Pass, was evacuated and dismantled the night following, the garrison escaping, but leaving all the guns, eighteen in number, in excellent condition for immediate service. Fort Gaines, on Dauphin Island, after a bombardment by one of the iron-clads, was unconditionally surrendered on the 6th. The articles of capitulation were signed on board the flag-ship Hartford by Admiral Farragut and General Granger on the part of the Union forces, and by Colonel Anderson, the rebel officer in command of the post. By this surrender, 818 prisoners of war were captured, includ-

* Annual Report of Secretary Welles, December 5, 1864.

* *N. Y. Tribune*, August 18, 1864.

ing 46 commissioned officers; 26 guns, a large amount of ordnance stores and ammunition, and subsistence stores for a garrison of about 800 men for twelve months.

All that now remained to obtain full possession of the harbor was the reduction of Fort Morgan. A fortnight was passed in the necessary preparations by the fleet and the land forces of General Granger, the latter having landed on Mobile Point and constructed powerful batteries at short range in the rear of the fort. The attack commenced with a terrific bombardment from the combined forces at dawn on the morning of the 22d. The fire was steadily kept up during the day from the shore batteries, the monitors and ships inside, and the vessels outside the bay. Between 9 and 10 in the evening, a shell from one of the land batteries exploded in the citadel and set it on fire. The bombardment was kept up slowly but steadily through the night, and again became general with the daylight. An hour afterward, at 6 A. M., a white flag was hoisted in the fort, and at 2 in the afternoon the fort was unconditionally surrendered by its commander, Brigadier-General R. L. Page. By this surrender, Major-General Canby reported to the Department at Washington, "We have about 600 prisoners, 60 pieces of artillery, and a large quantity of material. In the twelve hours preceding the surrender, about 3,000 shell were thrown into the fort. The citadel and barracks are entirely destroyed, and the works generally much injured. Many of the guns were spiked, the carriages burned, and much of the ammunition destroyed by the rebels. The losses in the army were one man killed and seven wounded."

In his dispatch to Secretary Welles, Admiral Farragut thus commented on certain circumstances attending the surrender: "I regret," says he, "to state that after the assembling of the rebel officers at the appointed hour, 2 P. M., for the surrender outside the fort, it was discovered on an examination of the interior, that most of the guns were spiked, many of the gun-carriages wantonly injured, the arms, ammunition, provisions, etc., destroyed, and there was every reason to believe this had been done after the white flag had been raised. It was also discovered that General Page and several of his officers had no swords to deliver up, and further, that some of those which were surrendered had been broken. The whole conduct of the officers of Fort Gaines and Fort Morgan presents such a striking contrast in moral principle, that I cannot fail to remark upon it. Colonel Anderson, who commanded the former, finding himself in a perfectly untenable position and encumbered with a superfluous number of conscripts, many of whom were mere boys, determined to surrender a fort which he could not defend, and in this determination was supported by all his officers, save one. But from the moment he hoisted the white flag he scrupulously kept every thing intact, and in that condition delivered it over; whilst General Page and his officers, with a childish spite, destroyed guns which they said they would defend to the last, but which they never defended at all, and threw away or broke those weapons which they had not the manliness to use against their enemies; for Fort Morgan never fired a gun after the commencement of the bombardment and the advance pickets of our army were actually on its glacis. As before stated, the ceremony of surrender took place at 2 P. M., and that same afternoon all the garrison were sent to New Orleans in the United States steamers Tennessee and Bienville, where they arrived safely."

The object of the expedition was now fully secured. The city of Mobile, indeed, was not captured, but the possession of the bay effectually suppressed every attempt to use the harbor as heretofore by blockade-runners, or for the fitting out of confederate piratical cruisers. The country rejoiced in the result, and cheerfully awarded to Admiral Farragut the honors of his continued exploits which, in the judgment of a competent foreign critic, placed him at the head of the living naval commanders of the world.* By an order of President Lincoln, dated at the Executive Mansion, September 3, salutes of one hundred guns were ordered to be fired at the national arsenals and navy yards in commemoration of these "brilliant achievements," while in another order he thus congratulated the officers and men engaged in this series of actions: "The national thanks are tendered by the President to Admiral Farragut and Major-General Canby for the skill and harmony with which the recent operations in Mobile harbor and against Fort Powell, Fort Gaines and Fort Morgan were planned and carried into execution; also to Admiral Farragut and Major-General Granger, under whose immediate command they were conducted, and to the gallant commanders on sea and land, and to the sailors and soldiers engaged in the operations, for their energy and courage, which, under the blessing of Providence, have been crowned with brilliant success, and have won for them the applause and thanks of the nation.

"ABRAHAM LINCOLN."

* "The doughty Admiral's feats of arms place him at the head of his profession, and certainly constitute him the first naval officer of the day, as far as actual reputation, won by skill, courage and hard fighting goes."—*British Army and Navy Gazette.*

CHAPTER CIV.

MILITARY AFFAIRS IN VIRGINIA—GENERAL SHERIDAN'S CAMPAIGN IN THE VALLEY OF THE SHENANDOAH—THE ARMY OF THE JAMES—SEPTEMBER TO DECEMBER, 1864.

IN a previous chapter the narration of military movements in Virginia was brought down to General Sheridan's appointment in August to the command of the Middle Division (including the protection of Washington and the northern portions of Virginia), and the subsequent operations of General Warren in General Grant's army to the south of Petersburg. We resume the record with an account of General Sheridan's stirring campaign in the Valley of the Shenandoah. Immediately after his assumption of the chief command in this quarter on the 8th of August he pushed forward a column from Harper's Ferry up the valley to Winchester and beyond to the strong position of the enemy at Fisher's Hill, in the vicinity of Strasburg, skirmishing with the rear-guards of General Early's force by the way. General Averill had already, on the 7th, gained an important victory over the enemy's cavalry to the west of Moorefield, inflicting a heavy loss, and capturing several hundred prisoners, with four cannon. A flank attack by a party of Moseby's troops on the night of the 13th of August, capturing a supply-train at Berryville, with a threatened movement of Longstreet's corps on the east of the Blue Ridge, determined Sheridan to return to the neighborhood of the Potomac. This movement was facilitated by the defeat of a cavalry advance of Longstreet's corps by General Merritt at Thoroughfare Gap on the 16th. The enemy, however, pursued Sheridan in his retreat, and a sharp engagement was fought on Sunday, the 21st, in the vicinity of Charlestown, covering the withdrawal of the Union troops to Harper's Ferry. Early was left in possession of the valley, Sheridan's efforts being, for the present, confined to the protection of the line of the Potomac. Affairs continued in this position for nearly a month, varied at the end of August and the beginning of September with important reconnoissances, conducted with spirit by our cavalry forces, disclosing the enemy in force from Martinsburg and Charlestown to Winchester. At length, on the 13th of September, after a visit from General Grant at Harper's Ferry, General Sheridan began a decided offensive movement with an important reconnoissance to the crossing of the Summit Point and Winchester road over the Opequan Creek, disclosing the presence of the enemy in force on the west bank of that stream, while Generals Wilson and McIntosh's brigades of cavalry, dashing up the Winchester pike, came in contact with Kershaw's rebel division, charged it, and captured the Eighth South Carolina regiment (sixteen officers and 145 men), its battle-flag, and Colonel Hennegan, commanding brigade, with a loss of only two men killed and two wounded.* In the reconnoissances which followed it was ascertained that the main body of General Early's forces were stationed in the neighborhood of Bunker's Hill and Stephenson's Depot. On the 18th, Gordon's division of infantry was sent by Early to occupy Martinsburg, whence they were speedily driven by Averill's cavalry to Darkesville. This position of the enemy's forces gave General Sheridan an opportunity to strike an effective blow. He determined by a rapid movement to mass his forces on the Winchester and Berryville pike, and attack Early in his rear. Every preparation was made on Sunday, the 18th. The movement began at dawn of the following day, when General Wright's Sixth Corps moved out on the Winchester and Berryville pike, followed by General Emory's Nineteenth Corps and the army of Western Virginia, under General Crook, from Summit Point. A concentration of these forces was effected at the crossing of the Opequan. The way was cleared for a passage of the stream by a gallant charge of Wilson's cavalry, which, having crossed, carried the enemy's field-works on the opposite side at the point of the sabre. The Sixth Corps now followed, and took up a position a mile and a half beyond, awaiting the arrival of the Nineteenth Corps to attack the enemy, who were protected by the woods in front. As a diversion, a portion of the Union cavalry, under Torbert and Averill, was employed in a demonstration on the line of the Opequan, twelve miles distant, at Burn's Ford. Previous to the appearance of the Nineteenth Corps on the field, General Early had moved Gordon's division from Bunker Hill in time to unite with Breckinridge's, Ramsour and Rhode's commands, by which Sheridan's force was now confronted. At noon the advance was sounded, and the action became general. The Sixth and Nineteenth Corps advanced together to the attack, General Crook's command being held in reserve. On their close approach to the enemy's position, the first line was driven back by a cannonade of grape and canister upon the second, and the advance checked 'till counter batteries were opened, and the reserve was brought up, with the addition of a body of Averill's and Merritt's cavalry, under General Torbert, on the right, when, about 3 o'clock, General Sheridan, who was actively engaged on the field throughout the day, ordered a final charge. The encounter was a desperate one, the infantry fighting with

* Major-General Sheridan to Lieutenant-General Grant, near Berryville, September 13.

great energy, and the cavalry, in a brilliant, impetuous onset, breaking the enemy's ranks and driving them in disorderly flight.* The route was complete. "I have the honor to report," wrote General Sheridan to General Grant in a dispatch from Winchester, dated at 7½ in the evening, "that I attacked the forces of General Early, over the Berryville pike, at the crossing of Opequan Creek, and after a most stubborn and sanguinary engagement, which lasted from early in the morning until 5 o'clock in the evening, completely defeated him, driving him through Winchester, capturing about 2,500 prisoners, 5 pieces of artillery, 9 army-flags and most of their wounded. The rebel Generals Rhodes and Gordon were killed, and three other general officers were wounded. Most of the enemy's wounded, and all their killed, fell into our hands. Our losses are severe. Among them is General D. A. Russell, commanding a division in the Sixth Corps, who was killed by a cannon ball. Generals Upton, McIntosh and Chapman were wounded. The conduct of the officers and men was most superb. They charged and carried every position taken up by the rebels from Opequan Creek to Winchester. The rebels were strong in numbers, and very obstinate in their fighting. I desire to mention to the Lieutenant-General commanding the Army the gallant conduct of Generals Wright, Crook, Emory, Torbert, and the officers and men under their command. To them the country is indebted for this handsome victory." To Brigadier-General Stephenson, in command at Harper's Ferry, he wrote: "We have just sent the rebels whirling through Winchester, and we are after them to-morrow. This army behaved splendidly." For this service General Sheridan was appointed a brigadier in the regular army, and assigned to the permanent command of the Middle Military Division.

Brigadier-General Davis A. Russell, who fell in this engagement, was a native of New York, and a graduate of West Point of 1845. He had served with distinction in the Mexican war, and had entered on the present struggle as Lieutenant-Colonel of the Seventh Massachusetts volunteers, attached to the Sixth Army Corps. He was actively engaged in Virginia, and was promoted to a full majority in the regular service for his gallant conduct in the Peninsular campaign. Having been appointed brigadier-general of volunteers, he was in action at Fredericksburg, and subsequently at Gettysburg. In November, 1863, he was assigned, for his military capacity and services, the command of the First Division of the Sixth Corps.

At daylight on the 20th the pursuit of the enemy was continued from Winchester by the cavalry, General Sheridan crossing Cedar Creek in the afternoon and the following morning bringing up his army in front of General Early, who had retreated to his strong position of Fisher's Hill, commanding Strasburg. Here he was assailed, late on the afternoon of the 21st, by the combined Union force and compelled to continue his flight. A dispatch from General Sheridan to General Grant, dated the next day, "six miles from Woodstock," gives the following details of the engagement: "I have the honor to announce that I achieved a signal victory over the army of General Early, at Fisher's Hill. I found the rebel army posted with its right resting on the north fork of the Shenandoah, and extending across the Strasburg Valley westward to North Mountain, occupying a position which appeared almost impregnable. After a great deal of maneuvering during the day, General Crook's command was transferred to the extreme right of the line on North Mountain, and he furiously

* Army correspondence *Baltimore American*. Winchester, Va., September 19.

attacked the left of the enemy's line, carrying every thing before him. While Crook was driving the enemy in the greatest confusion, and sweeping down behind their breastworks, the Sixth and Nineteenth Army Corps attacked the rebel works in front, and the whole army appeared to be broken up. They fled in the utmost confusion. Sixteen pieces of artillery were captured ; also, a great many caissons, artillery horses, etc., etc. I am to-night pushing on down the valley. I cannot say how many prisoners I have captured, nor do I know either my own or the enemy's casualties. Only darkness has saved the whole of Early's army from total destruction. My attack could not be made till 4 o'clock in the evening, which left but little daylight to operate in. The First and Third Cavalry Divisions went down the Luray Valley today, and if they push on vigorously to the main valley, the result of this day's engagement will be still more signal. The victory was very complete." In communicating this dispatch Secretary Stanton added : "It will be remembered that Early's command embraced the 'Stonewall Brigade' and the troops constituting 'Stonewall' Jackson's corps, and was the *elite* of the rebel army." In another dispatch the next day, from Woodstock, where General Sheridan stopped to rest his men and issue rations, he said : "I do not think that there ever was an army so badly routed. The valley soldiers are hiding away and going to their homes." The week closed with a further pursuit of the enemy up the valley. "Dispatches from General Sheridan, up to 11 o'clock Saturday night (the 24th) dated six miles south of Newmarket," reported Secretary Stanton, "have been received. He had driven the enemy from Mount Jackson without being able to bring on an engagement. The enemy were moving rapidly, and he had no cavalry present to hold them. Torbert had attacked Wickham's force at Luray and captured a number of prisoners. Sheridan found rebel hospitals in all the towns from Winchester to Newmarket, and was eighty miles from Martinsburg. Twenty pieces of artillery were captured at Fisher's Hill, together with 1,100 prisoners, a large amount of ammunition, caissons, limbers, etc., etc., and a large quantity of intrenching tools, of small arms and debris. The small towns through the valley have a great many of the rebel wounded. General Stevens reports the arrival at Harper's Ferry of a train of our wounded, twenty captured guns, and eighty additional captured officers."

The next published dispatch from General Sheridan was dated Harrisonburg on the 29th, and recorded the further progress of the campaign : "In my last," he writes to General Grant, "I informed you that I pressed Early so closely through Newmarket, at the same time sending cavalry around his flank, that he gave up the valley and took to the mountains, passing through Brown's Gap. I kept up the pursuit to Port Republic, destroying seventy-five wagons and four caissons. I sent General Torbert, who overtook me at Harrisonburg, to Stanton, with Wilson's division of cavalry and one brigade of Merritt's. Torbert entered Staunton on the 26th, and destroyed a large quantity of rebel Government property, harness, saddles, small arms, hard bread, flour, repair shops, etc. He then proceeded to Waynesboro', destroying the iron bridge over the south branch of the Shenandoah, seven miles of the track, the depot buildings, a Government tannery, and a large amount of leather, flour, etc., at that place. He found the tunnel defended by infantry and retired via Staunton. It is my impression that most of the troops which Early had left passed through the mountains to Charlottesville ; that Kershaw's division came to his assistance, and, I think, passed along the west base of the mountain to Waynesboro'. I am getting from twenty-five to forty prisoners daily, who come from the mountains on each side and deliver themselves up. From the most reliable accounts Early's army was completely broken up and is dispirited. Kershaw had not reached Richmond, but was somewhere in the vicinity of Gordonsville, when he received orders to rejoin Early. The destruction of the grain and forage from here to Staunton will be a terrible blow to them. All the grain, forage, etc., in the vicinity of Staunton was retained for the use of Early's army. All in the lower part of the valley was shipped to Richmond for the use of Lee's army. The country from here to Staunton was abundantly supplied with forage, grain, etc."

General Sheridan remained for several days in the vicinity of Staunton, destroying the enemy's communications and supplies in this quarter, when he withdrew his forces down the valley. On his arrival at Woodstock on the 7th of October, he thus reported to General Grant the results of his recent movements. "I commenced," says he, "moving back from Port Republic, Mount Crawford, Bridgewater, and Harrisonburg yesterday morning. The grain and forage in advance of these points had previously been destroyed. In moving back to this point the whole country, from the Blue Ridge to the North Mountain has been made entirely untenable for a rebel army. I have destroyed over 2,000 barns filled with wheat and hay and farming implements, and over 70 mills filled with flour and wheat; have driven in front of the army over 4,000 head of stock, and have killed and issued to the troops not less than 3,000 sheep. This destruction embraces the Luray Valley and the Little Fort Valley as well as the main valley. A large number of horses have been obtained, a proper estimate of which I cannot now make. Lieutenant John R. Meigs, my engineer officer, was murdered beyond Harrisonburg, near Dayton. For this atrocious act all the houses within an area of five miles were burned. Since I came into the valley from Harper's Ferry, every train, every small party, and every straggler has been bushwhacked by the people, many of whom have protection-passes from commanders who have been hitherto in that valley. The people here are getting sick of the war. Heretofore they have had no reason to complain, because they have been living in great abundance. I have not been followed by the enemy to this point, with the exception of a small force of the rebel cavalry, that showed themselves some distance behind my rear-guard, to-day. A party of 100 men of the Eighth Ohio Cavalry, which I had stationed at the bridge over the North Shenandoah, near Mount Jackson, was attacked by McNeil, with seventeen men, while they were asleep, and the whole party dispersed or captured. I think they will all turn up. I learn that fifty-six of them had reached Winchester. McNeil was mortally wounded, and fell into our hands. This was fortunate, as he was the most daring and dangerous of all the bushwhackers in this section of the country."

Continuing his retreat, General Sheridan reported at Strasburg on the 9th: "In coming back to this point, I was not followed up until late yesterday, when a large force of cavalry appeared in my rear. I then halted my command to offer battle by attacking the enemy. I became satisfied that it was only all the rebel cavalry of the valley, commanded by Rosser, and directed Torbert to attack at daylight this morning and finish this 'savior of the valley.' The attack was handsomely made. Custer, commanding the Third Cavalry Division, charged on the back road, and Merritt, commanding the First Cavalry Division, on the Strasburg pike. Merritt captured five pieces of artillery. Custer captured six pieces of artillery, with caissons, battery forge, etc. The two divisions captured forty-seven wagons, ambulances, etc. Among the wagons captured are the headquarter's wagons of Rosser, Lomax, Wickman, and Colonel Pollard. The number of prisoners will be about 330. The enemy, after being charged by our gallant cavalry, were broken and ran. They were followed by our men on the jump twenty-six miles through Mount Jackson and across the north fork of the Shenandoah. I deem it best to make this delay of one day here and settle this new cavalry general. The eleven pieces of artillery captured to-day make thirty-six pieces captured in the Shenandoah Valley since the 19th of September. Some of the artillery were new, and never had been fired. The pieces were marked 'Tredegar Works.'"

The Union army, for the defence of the valley, was now established along the line of Cedar Creek and the north fork of the Shenandoah, covering the approaches to Winchester and the Manasses railroad to Front Royal, when, on the 15th. General Sheridan departed for Washington on important business, leaving General Wright in command. The several corps were posted on the line of Cedar Creek below Strasburg, Crook's on the left, Emory's in the centre, and the Sixth, under Ricketts, on the right. The cavalry of Merritt and Custer guarded the right wing, and that of General Powell, who had succeeded Averill, the left. The enemy first made their appearance on the 17th, a body of cavalry and infantry skirmishing with Custer's cavalry on the right. A reconnoissance on the left showed no indications of the enemy in that quarter. In the early morning of the 19th, however, they renewed the attack, skirmishing at first in a feint on the right, and then, under cover of a fog, advancing in force on the centre and left. Crook's command was taken by surprise by a flank movement directed by the rebel General Kershaw, who had crossed the north fork of the Shenandoah unperceived by a ford to the east, while Early pushed forward a force in front upon Thorburn's division on Crook's right, and effectually routed the whole corps. Improving his success, Early now attacked the Nineteenth Corps in the centre, captured a portion of its artillery, and put its left to flight. The captured guns were turned upon the Union forces, and hastened the retreat, the trains being now rapidly pushed in the direction of Winchester. The Sixth Corps, meanwhile, was wheeled around to face the enemy and cover the retreat of the other corps. Its commander (Ricketts) in this movement was severely wounded. The enemy, meanwhile, though steadily resisted by Wright's new line, were steadily following up the advantage they had acquired, gaining Middletown on the turnpike, and threatening Newtown beyond, where it was expected the Union army would make a stand. Affairs were in this position when General Sheridan, early in the forenoon, arrived at Winchester on his return from Washington. He saw the situation at a glance, and vigorously applied the whole energy of his nature to retrieve the fortunes of the day. He rode along the lines, and was cheered with enthusiasm by the men, who, under the disposition made by General Wright, were awaiting further attack of the enemy. General Sheridan, it is stated, left Winchester, distant thirteen miles, with an escort of 275 men, and so rapid was his march that, on his arrival near the field on his jaded horse, he had less than thirty men with him.* The sequel, in which

* E. A. Paul, army correspondence *New York Times*, Strasburg, October 20.

a great disaster was changed into a great victory, may be related in his own words: "I have the honor to report," says he, in a dispatch to General Grant, dated Cedar Creek at 10 P. M. on the day of battle, "that my army at Cedar Creek was attacked this morning before daylight, and my left was turned and driven in confusion. In fact, most of the line was driven in confusion, with a loss of twenty pieces of artillery. I hastened from Winchester, where I was, on my return from Washington, and found the armies between Middletown and Newtown, having been driven back about four miles. I here took the affair in hand, and quickly united the corps, formed a compact line of battle just in time to repulse an attack of the enemy, which was handsomely done at about 1 P. M. At 3 P. M., after some changes of the cavalry from the left to the right flank, I attacked with great vigor, driving and routing the enemy, capturing, according to the last report, forty-three pieces of artillery and very many prisoners. I do not know yet the number of my casualties or the losses of the enemy. Wagons, trains, ambulances and caissons in large numbers are in our possession. They also burned some of their trains. General Ramseur is a prisoner in our hands, severely, and perhaps mortally, wounded. I have to regret the loss of General Bidwell killed, and Generals Wright, Grover and Ricketts wounded. Wright is slightly wounded. Affairs, at times, looked badly, but by the gallantry of our brave officers and men disaster has been converted into a splendid victory. Darkness again intervened to shut off greater results. I now occupy Strasburg."

The next day he reported further particulars of the triumph of the army. "We have again," he writes to General Grant, "been favored by a great victory, won from disaster, by the gallantry of our officers and men. The attack on the enemy was made about 3 P. M., by a left half wheel of the whole line, with a division of cavalry turning each flank of the enemy, the whole line advancing. The enemy, after a stubborn resistance, broke and fled, and were pushed with vigor. The artillery captured will probably be over fifty pieces. This, of course, includes what was captured from our troops in the early morning. At least 1,600 prisoners have been brought in; also wagons and ambulances in large numbers. This morning the cavalry made a dash at Fisher's Hill, and carried it, the enemy having fled during the night, leaving only a small rear guard. I have to regret the loss of many valuable officers killed and wounded, among them Colonel Joseph Thorburn, commanding a division of Crook's command, killed; Colonel J. Howard Kitchen, commanding a brigade, wounded; Colonel R. G. McKinzie, commanding a brigade, wounded severely, but would not leave the field. Many of our men captured in the morning have made their escape, and are coming in. Ramseur, commanding a division in Early's army died this morning."

A third dispatch from General Sheridan at Cedar Creek on the afternoon of the 21st completes the story of Early's signal defeat: "I pursued the routed force of the enemy nearly to Mount Jackson, which point he reached during the night of the 19th and 20th, without an organized regiment of his army. From the accounts of our prisoners who have escaped and citizens, the rout was complete. About two thousand of the enemy broke and made their way down through the mountains on the left. Fourteen miles on the line of retreat the road and country were covered with small arms thrown away by the flying rebels and other debris. Forty-eight pieces of captured artillery are now at my headquarters. I think that not less than 300 wagons and ambulances were either captured or destroyed. The accident of the morning turned to our advantage as much as though the whole movement had been planned. The only regret I have is the capture in early morning of from 800 to 1,000 men. I am now sending to the War Department ten battle-flags. The loss of artillery in the morning was seven from Crook, eleven from Emory, six from Wright. From all that I can learn, I think Early's reinforcements were not less than 16,000 men."

On receipt of the news of this victory, General Grant, on the 20th, sent this dispatch to Secretary Stanton: "I had a salute of 100 guns from each of the armies here fired in honor of Sheridan's last victory. Turning what bid fair to be a disaster into a glorious victory stamps Sheridan what I always thought him—one of the ablest of generals." President Lincoln also on the 22d addressed this letter of congratulation to General Sheridan: "With great pleasure I tender to you and your brave army the thanks of the nation, and my own personal admiration and gratitude, for the month's operations in the Shenandoah Valley, and especially for the splendid work of October 19."

The losses in killed and wounded in the engagement at Cedar Creek were, from the nature of the conflict, supposed to be greater on the Union side, "partly on account of the prolonged disaster in the morning, and partly because the enemy's precipitate flight when he had lost the day, and the coming of nightfall, saved him from severer carnage. In prisoners the loss was very equal—about 1,300 on each side.* In addition to the Union officers killed in the battles already noted in the dispatches of General Sheridan, the names of Colonel Charles A. Lowell, of Boston, commanding a brigade, Colonel Higgenbotham, and Major Swart are to be mentioned.

The victory of General Sheridan was acknowledged by General Early in an address to his army dated Valley District, October 22, a somewhat remarkable document, of which the following is a portion: "Soldiers of the Army of the Valley: I had hoped to have congratulated you on the splendid victory won by you on the morning of the 19th at Belle Grove, on Cedar Creek, when you surprised and routed two corps of Sheridan's army, and drove back several miles the remaining corps, capturing eighteen pieces of artillery, 1,500 prisoners, a number of colors, a large quantity of small arms, and many wagons and ambulances, with the entire camps of the two routed corps; but I have the mortification of announcing to you that, by your subsequent misconduct, all the benefits of that victory were lost, and a serious disaster incurred. Had you remained steadfast to your duty and your colors, the victory would have been one of the most brilliant and decisive of the war. You would have gloriously retrieved the reverses at Winchester and Fisher's Hill, and entitled yourselves to the admiration of your country. But many of you, including some commissioned officers, yielding to a disgraceful propensity for plunder, deserted your colors to appropriate to yourselves the abandoned property of the enemy, and subsequently those who had previously remained at their posts, seeing their ranks thinned by the absence of the plunderers, when the enemy, late in the afternoon, with his shattered columns made but a feeble effort to retrieve the fortunes of the day, yielded to a needless panic, and fled the field in confusion, thereby converting a splendid victory into a disaster. Had any respectable number of you listened to the appeals made to you and made a stand, even at the last moment, the disaster would have been averted, and the substantial fruits of victory secured; but under the insane dread of being flanked, and a panic-stricken terror of the ene-

* *Army and Navy Journal*, October 29, 1864.

my's cavalry, you would listen to no appeal, threat or order, and allowed a small body of cavalry to penetrate to our train and carry off a number of pieces of artillery and wagons, which your disorder left unprotected. You have thus obscured that glorious fame won in conjunction with the gallant men of the army of Northern Virginia, who still remain proudly defiant in the trenches around Richmond and Petersburg."

From these brilliant achievements of General Sheridan in the Valley, we turn to the army before Richmond. It was obviously the policy of General Grant while holding the most important army of the Confederacy under General Lee firmly invested in Richmond to take advantage of this restraint by pushing his operations more vigorously in other portions of the rebel States. The Lieutenant General, directing a grand movement in which the forces on the James under his immediate direction formed but a part of a connected whole, was under no necessity of seeking military reputation by hastening the time of action in enterprizes of doubtful result. It was, without question, desirable to capture Richmond; it was no less important to strike at the life of the rebellion in more distant quarters and destroy its military and commercial resources. Thus while during the remaining months of the year little was accomplished in pushing the Union successes before Richmond in the conquest of the enemy's works in that quarter, it was undeniable that General Grant from his tent on the banks of the James was directing the heaviest blows which the rebellion had yet received. His occupation of the lines before Richmond destroyed the enemy's prospect of northern invasion, assured success at Atlanta, and, finally, at Savannah. While Grant was fighting it out on his line in Virginia, it was evident that Lee had few men to spare to assist his subordinate armies in other quarters. Thus while Grant's army was for a time comparatively inactive, it was at no moment ineffective.

After the occupation by General Warren of the Weldon Railroad below Petersburg, in August, there was no demonstration of importance till the close of the following month, when a movement was made in co-operation with General Sheridan's operations in the valley. Picket firing and artillery practice had been kept up, as usual, at intervals, and in the middle of September there had been a bold and successful raid of the enemy, Hampton and Lee's cavalry sweeping round the left of the army before Petersburg to a point on the James River opposite Harrison's Landing, where they captured and drove off a reserved herd of 2,500 cattle. The guard, a detachment of Pennsylvania cavalry, was taken by surprise, and many of them made prisoners. On the alarm being given, a body of cavalry was sent in pursuit, but failed to make any impression on the enemy, who handsomely secured their booty for the rebel camp.

On the 29th of September, a movement was made on both sides of the James upon the enemy's works. During the previous night General Birney's Tenth and General Ord's Eighteenth Corps, which were on duty on the south of the river, were silently brought over on muffled pontoon bridges, the former to Deep Bottom, the latter to Aiken's Landing. General Ord's corps advanced in the morning, at dawn, on the Varina road, driving in the rebel pickets until they came to the outer line of the enemy's fortifications and intrenchments below Chapin's Farm, which were gallantly carried by General Stannard's division. Some fifteen pieces of artillery and from 200 to 300 prisoners were taken. In the capture of this post, known as Battery Harrison,

General Burnham, commanding a brigade, was killed, and General Ord wounded, when the command of the corps devolved upon General Weitzel. The loss in Stannard's division in this action was estimated at about 800. Simultaneously with this success, by which the Union lines were advanced in this quarter, the enemy retiring to an inner line, General Birney moved from Deep Bottom, and carried the Newmarket Road and intrenchments, in the words of General Grant, "scattering the enemy in every direction, though he captured but few." He found the whole country filled with field fortifications. In the attack on the works at Newmarket, General Paine's colored division was in advance and gallantly stormed the breastworks at the point of the bayonet, advancing over the intervening obstacles in face of a murderous fire, with great resolution. Their loss in this assault was about 200 killed and many wounded. Two hours after, the line, of works had been carried," says a correspondent, "I rode on the field and counted 105 dead bodies; nameless black men who had won the title of heroes by their unflinching courage in going through this terrible ordeal."* From Newmarket, whence the enemy now rapidly retreated, General Birney pushed on several miles further, to the junction of the Varina and Newmarket roads, where, at Laurel Hill, he found a formidable line of intrenchments which were twice gallantly but unsuccessfully charged by Foster's division and Birney's colored troops, the latter suffering heavily. A number of officers of the New York regiments were wounded in this assault. This disaster closed the day's proceedings in this quarter, General Birney having reached a point about six miles from Richmond. Whilst these movements were going on General Kautz's cavalry division was employed in a reconnoissance on the right, moving along the Central road, supported by General Terry's division of the Tenth Corps, to the main works, within three miles of the city. The two corps now formed a junction on the line of works which they had captured, where they were next day vigorously assailed by the enemy, who had been brought up in force from Petersburg to regain the lost positions. In this assault the Union troops acting on the defensive had the advantage, and gallantly repulsed the impetuous assaults of the foe. The brunt of the engagement fell upon the Eighteenth Corps, now commanded by General Weitzel. A number of prisoners were taken from the enemy. General Stannard was wounded by the fragment of a shell, which caused him the loss of an arm.

General Grant, having by this series of movements, caused Lee to withdraw a considerable force from his left, on the 30th sent General Meade with portions of the Fifth and Ninth Corps in the direction of Poplar Grove Church, fifteen miles westerly, on the Southside railroad. The latter, after a march of about three miles, encountered the enemy at Peeble's Farm, where he had a line of outer intrenchments protecting the Southside railroad. These were gallantly carried by Griffin's division, when the enemy fell back to their inner line. An attempt to take this was unsuccessful, and the enemy, now largely reinforced, in a counter flanking movement broke in between the two corps and carried off a large number of prisoners. This attack was checked by Griffin's division, fighting being kept up throughout the day, the losses of which, including the prisoners captured, was estimated at about 2,000. A heavy rain fell in the night, during which the Union forces threw up intrenchments, from which, the next day,

* H. J. W., Correspondence of the *New York Times*, Sept. 30.

the enemy attacking Ayres' division of the Fifth Corps, was repulsed. There was also an engagement between Hampton and Gregg's cavalry in the afternoon, on the left flank, in which there were severe losses on both sides, the enemy at first gaining the advantage on the outer line, and being afterwards repelled in their attack on a second position. A reconnoissance of the Boynton plank road, over which, the upper portion of the Weldon road being occupied, supplies were now carried by the rebels, disclosed a force posted for its defence. There was no further advance in this direction, the line of the road being firmly held by the enemy.

On the 7th of October an attack was made on the right flank of the army of the James on the north of the river, where, after the recent actions, the Union line extended in a northeasterly direction from Battery Harrison, across the Newmarket to the Central or Darbytown road, the extreme right being held by Kautz's cavalry. "At 6:30 A. M.," says General Butler, in a dispatch to General Grant in the evening, "the enemy, having moved Field's and Hope's divisions from the left at Chapin's Farm road round to our right at Darbytown road, they attacked with spirit Kautz's cavalry in their intrenchments, and drove him back with small loss of men, but with the loss of his artillery. The enemy suffered very considerable loss in his attack. The enemy then swept down the intrenchments towards Birney, who, having thrown back his right, waited their assault, and repulsed it, with very heavy loss on the part of the enemy. The enemy in the meantime advanced towards New Market, but were met by a force at the Signal Tower. At three P. M. I took the offensive, sending Birney with two divisions up the Darbytown road. The enemy retreated as he advanced, and Birney has reached and occupies the intrenchments which the enemy took from Kautz, and were fortifying for themselves. Our loss has been small, not one-eighth that of the enemy. We have about 100 prisoners." In a subsequent dispatch General Grant stated that the Union loss in this attack did not exceed 300 in killed, wounded and missing, while that of the enemy was estimated at 1,000. The *Richmond Whig* of the 8th, recorded of this battle:—"The gallant General Gregg, commanding a Texas brigade, fell in the advance. Among other casualties we have to report General Bratton, of South Carolina, badly wounded. Colonel Haskell, of the Seventh South Carolina Infantry, severely wounded in the face, and Major Haskin, of the South Carolina Artillery, also wounded. A rumor states that General Geary was killed."

Another attempt was made by General Grant, on the 27th of October to penetrate the enemy's lines, the movement as before being simultaneous on both sides of the James River. General Terry's Tenth Corps, with the Eighteenth, under Weitzel, with Kautz's cavalry were advanced by General Butler threatening the enemy's works on the right, "well toward the Yorktown road, without finding a point unguarded." There was skirmishing by Terry's command with the enemy in his front on the Darbytown road, while Weitzel's force was engaged in an unsuccessful attempt on the rebel works defending an advanced point on the Williamsburgh road. General Holman's colored brigade captured a two gun redoubt in this quarter, on the Richmond and York River Railroad. The demonstration on the part of General Butler appears to have been mainly intended to cover the heavier operations beyond Petersburg, directed against the Southside Railroad. Here, also, nothing of importance was accomplished. An outline of the movement is furnished by a correspondent: "The expedition was formed by the concentration of the greater part of the Army of the Potomac on the left of the line. Enough force being retained to hold the old works, and thence cut loose, moving in a southwesterly direction. The Second Corps moved by the Vaughan road, southwestward, crossing Hatcher's Run, and thence westward, attacking the enemy a little after daylight in the vicinity of Armstrong's saw-mill. Warren moved southwestward by an old wood road, and by improvised roads crossing the Duncan road about a mile north of Armstrong's mill. A short distance beyond this point he encountered the enemy and drove them into their works, but was met by a heavy abattis and withdrew. The Ninth Corps moved on a road parallel with that upon which the Fifth Corps moved and encountered the enemy's works to the right of the point struck by Warren. The Fifth and Ninth Corps lay in line of battle in front of the enemy's works during the day, keeping up a continual skirmishing, but accomplishing nothing. Hancock, without halting, pushed his divisions on to the Boynton plank-road, and one division of Warren's corps was crossed over Hatcher's Run, connecting with Hancock's right. Early in the day, Lee, penetrating the nature of the maneuvre, commenced concentrating his forces in the direction of Hatcher's Run. About 4 P. M., Mahone's division made a charge upon the right flank of the Second Corps. The rebels came in at a point where we had not yet formed the connection between the Second and Fifth Corps. This obliged General Grant to withdraw his forces to a safer position. The enemy's line at the point of attack is a prolongation of his front around Petersburg, and is exceedingly formidable and well chosen. * * * There is no disaster to record ; no repulse to chronicle. Our losses are such as are incident to any encounter with a vigilant and vigorous antagonist. Our forces now rest where they did before this move was initiated, within their impregnable lines. There only remains the addition of another chapter to the marvelous history of the siege of Richmond—a siege more wonderful and now almost as long as that of Sebastopol. By months of arduous labor, Grant has, step by step, pushed his lines of circumvallation and contravallation steadily westward ; tapped their communications by the Weldon road, and gained a position from which he could seriously threaten the Southside road. The same intrenched line that envelopes Petersburg has been extended west and southward to cover the Southside road, and a vault of a dozen miles still brought our army face to face with those tantalizing and troublesome works. In this state of facts no results of value could be hoped for, and, after waiting till Friday night (the 30th) to invite an attack from the enemy, he was compelled to retire. The only misfortune was the advantage gained by the enemy over Hancock's corps, which before the Fifth Corps was able to form connection with it found its right flank turned, and suffered a loss of about 1,000 men."*

The subsequent movements in the Army of the Potomac during the year, were directed against the enemy's line for receiving supplies to the south of Petersburg. On the 1st of December, General Gregg, at the head of a strong cavalry force made a successful raid upon Stony Creek Station on the Weldon Railroad, where there was a store of supplies, this being the depot whence they were transferred by wagoning across to the Southside Railroad. A fort at this place mounting two guns was assaulted and taken by the Pennsylvania cavalry dismounted. One hundred and seventy-five prisoners were taken in the day's operations and a large quantity of provisions destroyed.

* Correspondence of the *New York Times*, Oct. 30th and 31st

This expedition was followed on the 6th by another, led by General Warren, which resulted in the destruction of the Weldon Railroad from Jarrett's, below Stony Creek Station, to Bellfield at the Meherrin River. A cold rain-storm, turning to hail and snow rendered the march, which lasted five days, particularly severe.

CHAPTER CV.

GENERAL HOOD'S INVASION OF TENNESSEE.—CAMPAIGN OF GENERAL THOMAS, NOVEMBER, DECEMBER, 1864.

After the fall of Atlanta in September the operations of the rebel cavalry were directed against General Sherman's extended line of railway communication with Nashville. Toward the close of the month Forrest appeared with a considerable force in Northern Alabama, crossed the Tennessee River, and, on the 20th, captured Athens with its garrison, taking, as he claimed, 1,300 prisoners, two pieces of artillery, and various stores. He broke up the railway on the line below to Decatur, and above on the road to Pulaski, where his further advance in this direction was resisted by General Rousseau, when he moved eastward toward the line of the Nashville and Chattanooga railroad, which he again found guarded by General Rousseau at Tullahoma. About the same time the rebel Generals Wheeler and Rhoddy were reported threatening the railway between Decatur and Chattanooga. General Thomas, in command at Nashville, took prompt measures to repel the raiders, and General Rousseau presently reported the escape of Forrest from his pursuit across the Tennessee in the vicinity of Florence. General Hood, in the meantime, had crossed the Chattahoochee from the Macon railroad and moved on Allatoona, which was attacked by a division of his force, under General French, on the 5th of October. General Sherman, who had been engaged in active preparations to resist this threatened assault on his line of communications, had ordered General Corse with reinforcements from Rome to Allatoona. The enemy's attack was accordingly met and repulsed, General Sherman himself having reached Kenesaw Mountain from Atlanta in time to gain a distant view of the military operations. The enemy lost, he reported, some 200 dead, and more than 1,000 wounded and prisoners, while the Union loss was about 700 in the aggregate. The small garrisons at Big Shanty and Ackworth, north of Allatoona, however, were captured, and about seven miles of the railroad destroyed. "Hood, observing our approach," wrote General Sheridan to General Halleck from Allatoona on the 9th, "has moved rapidly back to Dallas and Van Wert, and I am watching him in case he tries to reach Kingston or Rome. Atlanta is perfectly secure to us, and this army is better off than in camp."

In another direction Major-General Burbridge was at this time employed in a raid from East Tennessee into Southwestern Virginia. On the morning of the 2d, having penetrated the latter State, and forced the enemy from Clinch Mountain and Laurel Gap, he drove him to Saltville, where, guarding the important salt works at that place, he was strongly entrenched on the bluff in strong force under Echols, Williams, Vaughan, and, as it was reported,

Breckinridge. "We at once," says General Burbridge, "attacked the enemy, and drove him from his works on our left and centre, and held him in check on the right, and finally, in spite of artillery and superior numbers, whipped him at every point, and forced him back to his own works."* At evening General Burbridge's ammunition gave out, and he withdrew his command in good order. He estimated the enemy's force at between 6,000 and 8,000. His own was 2,500 engaged. The next day he received orders from General Sherman to return. Subsequently during the month General Breckinridge assumed the offensive in East Tennessee, pressed General Gillem, who was pursuing the enemy in that region, and defeated his force at Morristown, compelling his retreat across the Holston. In December another and successful attempt was made to destroy the works at Saltville, where General Breckinridge now had his headquarters, with detachments of his command under Generals Vaughan, Basil Duke and Dick Morgan advanced in Northeastern Tennessee at Greenville, Jonesboro' and Rogersville. The new expedition was led by General Stoneman, General Gillem, with his brigade, taking the advance, coming up with the enemy under Duke and Morgan at Kingsport, defeating him and capturing Morgan, a brother of the notorious rebel leader John Morgan. General Stoneman pushed on a forced march to Bristol, took the town by surprise, and made many important captures. He then moved upon Abingdon, Va., General Gillem advancing to Marion, routing Vaughan's forces there and pursuing him to Wytheville, destroying the valuable lead mines in the vicinity. A portion of General Burbridge's command being left in the neighborhood of Glade Spring, near Saltville, was attacked by General Breckinridge with a superior force and routed, when General Gillem with his brigade came to the rescue and turned the disaster to a victory, capturing guns and prisoners and putting Breckinridge's forces to flight. Saltville was now exposed, and its extensive salt manufactories were effectually destroyed and the town burnt—a loss to the enemy of the utmost importance. The expedition having accomplished this and other works of devastation, returned to Tennessee with vast spoils of supplies.

After the movement on Allatoona, General Hood, reaching Resaca on the 14th, made a partial attack on that place, which was successfully defended by General Watkins, when Hood advanced and took possession of Dalton, Colonel Johnston surrendering the garrison (about 1,200 men) to the vastly superior force brought against him. The enemy now threatened Chattanooga, but General Sherman was in vigorous pursuit, and Hood, retiring from Dalton, moved westwardly to Lafayette, and thence across the Alabama State line southwest to Jacksonville, where he was reinforced by Beauregard, who, on the 17th, assumed command of the Military Division of the West, as it was termed. In an address to his troops on this occasion he said: "The army of General Sherman still defiantly holds Atlanta. He can and must be driven from it. It is only for the good people of Georgia and the surrounding States to speak the word, and the work is done. We have abundant provisions. There are men enough in the country liable to and able for service to accomplish this result. To all such I earnestly appeal to report promptly to their respective commands, and let those who cannot go see to it that none remain who are able to strike a blow in this critical and decisive hour. * * My countrymen—respond to this call as you have done in days that have passed, and, with the blessing of a kind and overruling Providence, the enemy shall be driven from

* Dispatch to Secretary Stanton, October 8.

your soil. The security of your wives and daughters from the insults and outrages of a brutal foe shall be established soon, and be followed by a permanent and honorable peace. The claims of home and country, wife and children, uniting with the demands of honor and patriotism, summon us to the field. We cannot, dare not, will not fail to respond. Full of hope and confidence, I come to join in your struggles, sharing your privations, and with your brave and true men to strike the blow that shall bring success to our arms, triumph to our cause, and peace to our country."

General Sherman, by his movement in pursuit of Hood, had driven the enemy from his line of communication with Chattanooga, the damage to which was now repaired, and over which supplies were again received at Atlanta. This being accomplished, he prepared to set out with a large part of his army from the latter city in a bold movement through Georgia to the seaboard, while he left General Thomas to meet the further advance of Hood in the direction of the Tennessee River. The two armies, which had been recently confronted, were thus turned away from each other, and leaving their respective bases for a bold and determined movement into the enemy's country.

From Jacksonville Hood's army now marched in a northwesterly direction to Guntersville, on the Tennessee River, which they reached on the 22d, and thence, after some delays, made their way to Florence, in the vicinity of which Forrest had been operating with his cavalry, interrupting communication on the river. On the 28th and 30th, Colonel Morgan's colored regiment at Decatur was attacked by a portion of Rhoddy's cavalry, with a heavy loss to the latter. Hood was now preparing for his advance with his main army into Tennessee, in accordance with an intention announced by Jefferson Davis of inflicting a serious blow in this quarter, from which much was to be expected in aid of the rebel cause, while General Thomas was as diligently maneuvering his forces to guard his northern line of railway and meet the threatened invasion. Several weeks were passed before Hood fairly began his advance, when, on the 20th Nov. he moved northwardly from Florence, between which place and Corinth his forces had been gathered, and advanced to Waynesboro' and Lawrenceburgh, where he outflanked the advanced Union position on the line of the Nashville and Decatur Railroad at Pulaski. From the latter place General Thomas now withdrew his forces to Franklin, on the same road, eighteen miles south of Nashville. In this retreat, which was a preconcerted strategic movement of General Thomas to concentrate his forces for the defence of the latter city, the Union troops were closely pursued by the enemy, whose aggregate strength, including the infantry corps of Stephen D. Lee, Cheatham, Stewart, and Taylor, and Forrest's superior cavalry was estimated at about 40,000. Major-General Schofield was in command of the force at Pulaski, which consisted of General Stanley's Fourth and General Cox's Twenty-third Corps, together with a few regiments which had recently entered the service. There was some sharp fighting on the road to Franklin, at Columbia and Spring Hill, Forrest's cavalry pressing hard upon the column. On the 30th, Schofield occupied Franklin. Here, in the words of an Army correspondent, who has furnished many interesting details of the campaign, they "took position in an open field near the Columbia pike, and formed a line of battle, with both flanks resting upon Harpeth River, which makes a curve like a horse-shoe at this point. To guard against disaster, at such a critical point, while waiting to get the immense trains over the river, a hurriedly-constructed line of breastworks and rifle-pits were thrown across the field, a few yards from the pike, from river to river. The spade and axe had barely finished their performance, when our skirmish line was driven in, and almost simultaneously a mass of moving men came down four lines deep and banged away at the whole Federal column. This was precisely at 4 o'clock P. M. The weight of this assault was felt considerably upon the Federal right, but most particularly upon our centre, which was composed in part of raw recruits, and belonged to a brigade of Wagner's division. The rebels came up to the scratch, as they always do, with great impetuosity, and a portion of Wagner's division broke and ran. The rebel column operating upon our centre perceived this, and rushed right over the works at a charge bayonet, carrying every thing before it, and causing one entire brigade of Wagner's division to scamper to the rear in a thousand directions. These fellows threw down their guns, and in many instances their cartridge-boxes, and other portions of their equipage, which might retard or discommode them in their flight, and went into and behind houses, through bars and over fences, pell-mell, helter-skelter, down the banks of the river, as though the minions of darkness were at their heels. At this juncture, fully realizing their advantage, the rebels dashed upon our right and centre, with fearful vociferations and curses, and with that uniform gallantry which has so often characterized their performances upon a field of action, their intention being to pierce and crush the centre and envelop the right wing. This was where the excessive slaughter of the confederates took place. For, somehow or other, three batteries on the left got in a raking fire of grape and canister, the most destructive of all of the missiles of war, and at one clip knocked the daylight out of a hundred men and disabled five times that number. The whole rebel line wavered, and after receiving another treatment of the same course, fell back across the pike in great disorder. While this was transpiring, Wagner had succeeded in rallying a large portion of his men, who came up to their old position and behaved like veterans during the balance of the engagement, notwithstanding the rebels subsequently made three vicious charges within thirty yards of our works.

"The second charge of the enemy was directed against our right wing, which staggered, but never gave way. The battle was waged with unexampled fury and activity, the green troops in the centre evidently emulating the glorious conduct of their comrades upon the right. About 5 P. M., the artillery firing was quite heavy and continuous, and most damaging, indeed, to the rebel side, who acted chary in the use of ammunition. The enemy threw nothing but shot and shell, while our artillerymen hurled into the rebel ranks every conceivable missile of destruction known. At 5½ o'clock the enemy made another terrific charge upon the centre and right, which was particularly heavy against the former. They succeeded not in their attempt to again dislodge a portion of our raw troops. By some rebel mistake, at this juncture, General Gordon got into a snarl, the consequence of which was that he and about two-thirds of his brigade, in a few moments afterward, found themselves in custody in our rear. The rebels made one more charge, this time on our left. A regiment of Floridians attempted to carry off a section of artillery belonging to the Fifth United States, and got badly cut up during the performance. This battle, by all odds, may be pronounced one of the most gallantly fought of the war, while the results are of a substantial character indeed. The fight proper lasted just two hours, although slight firing by artillery and small arms was kept up until midnight. Major-General

Stanley, commanding the Fourth Corps, got a curious wound. He was struck upon the right side of the neck, the ball passing around over his back, and coming out on the left side. Although his wound was extremely painful, he did not leave the field during the action. General Bradley, commanding a brigade in the First Division, Fourth Corps, was severely wounded in the arm by a minie ball. He will not lose his arm, however. The enemy's loss is not placed less than 6,000, including over 1,000 prisoners and a brigadier-general —Gordon. Our total loss will not exceed 1,000. But all of our wounded were shot in the head, arms or body. This great disparity is owing to the terrible distribution our artillerists made of their grape and canister, which they threw into the rebel ranks with awful effect. Besides, our men engaged were behind a good breastwork, while the rebels fought in an open field. With the invaluable assistance of such general officers as Stanley, Cox, Ruger, Wagner, Opdyke, Wood, and Kimball, General Schofield made a splendid fight, and during the night, after caring for our dead, wounded and prisoners, retired our army to Nashville, according to the orders of General Thomas."*

In this account the Union loss was doubtless underrated. It was afterward stated at 2,500. That of the enemy was acknowledged to be severe, particularly in general officers, showing the desperate nature of the conflict. General Hood in his dispatch to Seddon, the rebel secretary of war, on the 8th, claims the capture of several stands of colors and about 1,000 prisoners. "Our troops," he adds, "fought with great gallantry. We have to lament the loss of many gallant officers and men. Major-General Cleburne and Brigadier-Generals John Williams, Adams, Giest, Strahl, and Granbury were killed. Major-General John Brown, and Brigadier-Generals S. Carter, Marignault, Quarles, Cockerell, and Scott, were wounded. Brigadier-General Gordon was captured."

The battle of Franklin was a most important one, in securing safety, and, ultimately, victory to the Union forces in Tennessee. By General Schofield's gallant defence the enemy were not merely successfully resisted in the first shock of arms, but the prestige and strength of an invading army, largely composed of veterans, commanded by experienced officers, fully equipped and animated in the special work before them by the confidence and hopes of the president of the confederacy, were materially impaired. The first blow of such an army as Hood's, rallying after its recent succession of defeats and advancing in a hostile country should have been so directed as to gain a decided success. As it was, the courage and impetuosity of the enemy were expended in vain. The result was simply to hasten Schofield's march to Nashville. By this retreat, indeed, the central and southern portions of Tennessee were left open to the enemy, who drove out the garrisons and temporarily possessed themselves of various towns and stations ; but the more important posts, as Murfreesboro,' where General Rousseau was stationed, and effectually resisted the enemy, the line of the railroad below from, Stevenson to Chattanooga, at which latter place General Meagher was left in command, were firmly held, and the defences of Nashville, where the main army of General Thomas now rested, proved unassailable. On the night after the battle of Franklin, General Schofield safely withdrew his command to these works. The enemy followed and planted himself within sight of the city on the southerly side throwing up a complete line of entrenchments extending to the Cumberland River on both wings. The Union line of entrenchments

* Benjamin C. Truman, army correspondence *New York Times*, Nashville, December 1.

supported by a chain of forts protected the city, also reaching on each flank to the river, which was patrolled and securely held by gunboats and two iron-clads. Nashville, being built mainly on the southerly side of the river was thus readily defended on the north while the gunboats offered an advantage in moving flanking parties upon the enemy's positions. For nearly a fortnight the two armies stood confronting one another with occasional cannonading and skirmishing, both sides being diligently engaged in fortifying and strengthening the opposing works. Hood delayed the threatened attack, but a portion of his forces was engaged in interrupting communications on the Chattanooga railroad. A demonstration was made against Murfreesboro which was successfully defended by General Rousseau and General Milroy, in command of a post on the line, gallantly attacked and defeated the enemy in the vicinity. This took place on the 7th of December. The weather presently became severely cold, and Hood's army, ill provided for the inclement season, suffered much in consequence. At length, on the 15th, simultaneously as we shall see with General Sherman's arrival at Savannah, General Thomas assumed the offensive and began an attack upon Hood's army, which being followed up without cessation, speedily resulted in the disastrous flight and retreat of the enemy beyond the Tennessee river. The first announcement to the country of this movement was made by Secretary Stanton from Washington in the following dispatch at midnight of the first day of the battle: "The department has just received unofficial dispatches from Nashville, announcing that General Thomas, with the forces under his command, attacked Hood's army in front of Nashville at 9 o'clock this morning, and although the battle is not yet decided, the whole action to-day is described as splendidly successful. Our line advanced on the right five miles. The enemy were driven from the river, from their intrenchments, from the range of hills on which their left rested, and forced back upon his right and centre, and the centre was pushed back from one to three miles, with the loss of seventeen guns and about 1,500 prisoners, and his whole line of earthworks, except a mile of his extreme right, where no serious attempt was made to dislodge him. Our casualties are reported to be light. Hood's whole army, except the cavalry and a small force near Murfreesboro', were engaged." Dispatches from General Thomas the following and successive days announced the continued and victorious encounter and pursuit of the enemy. He was forced at all points and immense captures of guns and prisoners made. The details of the engagements of the two days of battle, the 15th and 16th are thus related by the correspondent already cited: "Early in the morning of the first day, the enemy's line of battle was within musket shot of Nashville, with both flanks resting upon the river, with General Frank Cheatham's corps on the rebel right, crossing the Lebanon, Murfreesboro' and Nolensville pikes; Stephen D. Lee's corps in the centre, crossing the Franklin, Granny White and Hillsboro' pikes, and Stewart on their left, crossing the Harding and Charlotte pikes, and resting on the river a few miles south of the city, and commanded by Hood in person. Our forces were commanded by General Thomas, and moved upon the enemy in the following order: A. J. Smith upon the right, Steedman on the left, and Wood in the centre, with Schofield in reserve, and most of our cavalry, under Generals Johnson, Hatch and Wilson, on the right. Besides, we had gunboats assisting in the protection of our flanks, which rested on the river. A. J. Smith moved out the Sixteenth Corps about 8 o'clock, and skirmished with the enemy until a little before 1

Painted by Thos Nast

Geo H Thomas

Likeness from a recent Photograph from life.

Johnson, Fry & Co. Publishers, New York.

o'clock, with little or no loss to either side, making about a mile in that time. Wood moved out the celebrated Fourth Corps about the same time, and charged two lines of works and captured them before he took his dinner. Generals Beatty's and Elliot's divisions charged with great fury and enthusiasm. and were received in gallant manner by the rebels, who fought with their accustomed desperation. But two rebel batteries were brought to bear upon the two divisions, while six batteries of field artillery, and all the guns on Fort Negley and guns upon Casino and Confiscation. for more than an hour, were employed in hurling destruction into the rebel ranks. Immediately in front of Mrs. Acklin's house the charge was made with unbounded spirit. Post's brigade and a battery of artillery piled into the lines head over heels, and captured 100 men and a section of artillery: General Steedman moved out his men, composed of a portion of his own division, detachments of troops belonging to the different corps with Sherman, and two brigades of colored troops, respectively commanded by Colonels Thomson and Morgan. General Steedman's orders were to make a vigorous attack, for two reasons: General Thomas desired to get possession of a nasty fort upon our extreme left, which commanded our line for two miles to the right, and, further, to deceive Hood, as Smith and Schofield were to turn the enemy's left, had any attempt to crush Steedman taken place. But the rebels did not await the second charge of the two colored brigades, which went right up to the summit of the hill without much wavering, driving the enemy a quarter of a mile, and capturing nearly a hundred prisoners. Up to noon Steedman's troops were pretty actively engaged, the white and the black men, shoulder to shoulder, pitching in like fury, regardless of all considerations of color. At noon Steedman had moved nearly a mile and a half, and had commenced to swing his extreme left in a little from the river. On our extreme right our cavalry had about all they could conveniently attend to during the forenoon, experiencing slight repulses, owing to the fine positions of the enemy. Our infantry and cavalry got some very rough handling just about this time, but were helped out of their dilemma by the gunboats, which came along in the nick of time. The Carondelet three about fifty sixty-four pound shells into the rebel left, driving the troops resting on the river in great confusion, and silencing a battery of artillery.

"In the afternoon Steedman was not so busily engaged as he had been during the early part of the day. His troops, however, were under fire all the while, and behaved with great gallantry. During all these charges, the colored troops hardly gave way. They were admirably handled by Colonels Thomson and Morgan, both brave young men, and as they tugged up the hill the white soldiers upon either side rent the air with vociferations. The negroes, too, as they dashed inside the works, shouted, screamed, yelled, and threw up their hats, notwithstanding they had left nearly 200 of their comrades behind, the bleeding victims of rebel shot and shell. As I said above, of the grand charge which I have described, Steedman moved with little opposition, as the rebels, in contracting their lines, necessarily abandoned some strong positions in his front. Wood's corps stood the brunt of the fight in the afternoon, and added new laurels to its well-known and well-earned fame. A little before 3 o'clock, the Second and Third Divisions made two glorious charges upon a long line of rude rifle-pits. An entire battery of brass guns were captured, but most of the troops ran away, and but few prisoners were captured. Before dark another line of works were taken, Wood's corps sustaining a loss of over 100 men killed and wounded during the charge. He was above an hour from the commencement to the conclusion of this charge, during which time the enemy made very little use of his artillery. At dark the Fourth Corps was four miles from Nashville, having taken half a dozen lines of works, several cannon, and toward 400 prisoners. Although Wood's corps did the hardest fighting in the afternoon, A. J. Smith, in conjunction with the cavalry and a portion of Schofield's corps, made a multiplicity of brilliant movements, resulting in the capture of two batteries of artillery, nearly a 1,000 prisoners, a wagon train, and Generals Lee's and Chalmers' headquarters' trains. This was in a great measure owing to the sagacity and skill of General A. J. Smith, who seems as much at home upon a field of action as one might well imagine. Portions of Schofield's corps were also eminently interested in the taking of the batteries, as were also Hatch's and Johnson's divisions of cavalry. The gunboats kept up their thundering all the latter part of the afternoon, and did considerable execution upon the enemy's left. At dark firing ceased, with the exception that our artillerists threw an occasional shell into the rebel lines. The enemy had been pushed over three miles all round since daylight, although at times the fighting was of the most stubborn character.

"The victory was one of the superbest of the war. Our troops drove the enemy at all points, extending our territory three miles south of our position in the morning. Some five distinct lines of rebel works were taken on the left and centre, and the rebel left broken. We captured eighteen guns, with caissons, etc., all in complete order. We also captured 1,600 prisoners, a large amount of small arms, and a number of wagons. It is believed that our own and the enemy's loss in killed and wounded, is about the same, each side losing between 1,200 and 1,500. The rebels used very little artillery, but used what they did to a purpose. The captured guns were all smooth bores but four, and of excellent wormanship. On account of the rolling condition of the country and the thinness of the forests, the movements of the troops upon both sides were witnessed to much advantage. At one time the entire front of Steedman's and Wood's troops and two corps of the enemy, could be seen distinctly from a safe position. Generals Thomas, Smith, Schofield, Wood, Steedman, Wilson and other general officers, were upon the field all day. No general officer was injured, although Wood liked to have lost his head by a cannon ball twice.

"During the night, General Hood contracted his lines in a remarkable degree, resting his right a short distance east of the Franklin pike, and his left on the Harding pike, making his line of battle less than four miles from flank to flank, although it was double that number of miles in extreme length, owing to its zigzag order upon and near the Franklin pike. He also retired his army from a naturally weak position, and disposed his forces at the base of a range of detached spurs of the Cumberland. It was evident that he intended to make another stand, and it was also evident that the preservation of his rear and his line of retreat upon the Franklin pike, were objects of his particular attention. General Thomas evidently knew what Hood's programme was as well as Hood himself, and at daylight moved Steedman out rapidly upon the left, with orders to swing in and cross the Murfreesboro' and Nolensville pikes. This was done with rapidity, but no captures were made owing to the rebel evacuation of their works on our left during the night. Wood and A. J. Smith moved up to within musket shot of the rebel lines, while Schofield was held partly in reserve on the right and partly in a position to make a rapid dash in conjunction with our cavalry, upon the enemy's left, should the situation suggest such a demonstration. All this transpired before 9 A. M. I went out upon the Granny White pike, a little before night, and watched the movements of our right and the enemy's left until noon. The enemy had a very fine position at the base of a range of hills, extending from the Granny White pike to the Harding pike. He was protected by a line of works which had been hastily constructed near the edge of the woods. Garrard's and McArthur's divisions had to advance through an open field over a mile in length. After getting within 400 yards of the rebels our column went down upon their bellies, and crawled up some fifty or sixty yards closer. Three batteries followed up these two divisions, and when they halted commenced shelling the woods back of the rebel line and some houses on the pike, from behind which about fifty sharpshooters were banging away. Up to near 11 o'clock this was the order of things in front of Smith. About that time the rebels showed their heads in great numbers above the works, and acted as though they intended to charge the three batteries. They came out of their works shortly after, and our batteries were retired temporarily to a safer position. Just before 12, Smith's whole corps from right to left made a desperate charge, but could not carry the works. About 12½ o'clock the attempt was again made, and a portion of the works were carried. McArthur ordered up two 6-gun batteries upon his left, and one battery upon the right of his division, his own and Garrard's men made a charge, the three batteries being advanced so that an enfilading fire could be got in. The whole maneuvre was grand in projection and execution. The artillery did frightful work along the rebel line, our infantry carrying the works during a temporary panic, which was caused by the vigorous hurling of grape and canister into the rebel ranks. In this charge over 200 of the enemy were captured. Smith's whole line then advanced, his right swinging around a little from off the Harding pike and a portion of the Twenty-third Corps falling and making up the gap between the Sixteenth and Hatch's division of cavalry. It was now quite one o'clock, and a most terrible cannonading had opened all along our left and centre. Knowing that Wood and Steedman had a certain amount of work to perform to bring up with Smith, I went over upon the left and centre, where I spent the afternoon until dark, and witnessed, in an unsafe position, more thrilling sights than I have ever seen before. The rebel bullets were whizzing quite uncomfortably, but their artillery, which is the thing that generally produces the demoralization, remained comparatively quiet, and I, in company with two other correspondents, took the chances of the former.

"The Sixth Ohio, and a battery of the Fourth Regular Artillery took a position upon an open field, about fifty feet in the rear of our infantry; to the right of Beatty's division a Michigan battery and two Ohio batteries, took up a position in an open field, near and upon Wood's extreme right, while two batteries got in on the left. From 1 till 2 o'clock these thirty-six guns shelled the rebel position, which was very strong in Wood's front, and particularly strong in front of Steedman.

"At precisely 2 o'clock it commenced to rain, and rained hard during the balance of the day. A little after 2 the Third and First Divisions of Wood's corps made a desperate charge upon the rebel line which was located upon a slight elevation. The firing lasted fully twenty minutes, when the rebels retired in considerable disorder, leaving their dead and wounded and forty odd prisoners in our hands. The rebels had parallel works on this hill, and the two divisions, without orders, with the wildest enthusiasm, charged the other line of works in the face of a deadly volley of musketry and a shower of grape from four Napoleon guns. Really, I discovered no signs of wavering. and the whole drama was in full show. In ten minutes after they rushed into the works, captured 300 men and the battery, which was a splendid one of four guns. Every member of the battery—the Second Louisiana—was either killed, wounded or captured. Smith and Wood were now on an even line, and a frowning-looking eminence, topped with strong works, three regiments of Tennessee infantry and Stamford's Mississippi battery lie before Steedman, who, at this juncture, was in conversation with Wood. Captain Tracy informed me that the two colored brigades would be ordered to storm the hill. I crossed the Franklin pike to see Colonel Thompson, commanding one of the colored brigades, who is a particular friend of mine, when I heard the orders given for the assault. Immediately the two brigades of colored men started up the hill. I crossed back to the right of the Franklin pike, where I could see the whole movement, without placing myself in too great danger. When within about a hundred yards of the crest of the hill the four guns and the infantry poured a broadside into the negroes. when a frightful panic took place upon Steedman's right, resting on the pike. The movement ceased for a few moments, when a couple of our batteries commenced an enfilading fire, and the assaulting party, with an additional brigade of white troops, again attempted the ascent. The rebel infantry blazed away at a fearful rate, and the artillery discharged sixteen shots of canister, which made the assaulting column reel, waver and almost fall back. This was the most exciting picture I had ever seen so close, as I stood, in company with Captain Boyd, of General Miller's staff, about 200 feet to the right of the assaulting party. After a manly struggle, with the loss of over 200 men killed and wounded in the colored brigades, including eight officers; the party reached the top, and with a yell went over the works, captured the entire battery and nearly 300 prisoners. The guns were of the James pattern, were manufactured at Columbus, Ga., and were quite warm when I arrived. Every caisson had been smashed by our artillery, and most of the horses killed, although the guns were in good order. The men composing this battery stood like men to their post—thirty-two out of seventy being killed and wounded. Every officer was killed. As soon as the hill was taken, the colored troops pitched after the retreating rebels, chasing them through a valley nearly a mile. Firing wholly ceased upon the left, which had swung around nearly a mile and a half in two hours. Wood's corps carried another line of works, without much opposition, however, although Post's and Straight's brigades pitched in like good fellows.

"This was a little before 4 o'clock, and, when all was quiet upon the left and centre, a tremendous crush took place upon the right. It only lasted about ten minutes, but the firing was awful during that time. I started to go over to the right, but when half way over, met Captain Burroughs, of General Thomas' staff, who told me that Smith had made a glorious charge, and with the assistance of Schofield, had taken twelve guns, two general officers, and 1,500 prisoners. As I told you in the start, Schofield had a certain plan to carry out if the opportunity presented itself. It did. While Smith was making a charge, Schofield threw his whole corps away round to the right, and shut up toward A. J. Smith's corps in front, the two corps grabbing the number of guns and prisoners stated above in the operation. Darkness came abruptly on, and hostilities ceased. As near as I can judge our loss is about 2,000 in killed and wounded. The enemy's loss in killed and wounded is smaller. We captured about 4,000 prisoners and two general officers. Generals Smith and Schofield captured twelve guns, and I saw Wood's and Steedman's corps capture a like number, while Hatch captured a section of artillery on our extreme right. I started for the city a little before 7 o'clock, at which time all was quiet at the front, and all of our dead, and our own and the rebel wounded had been cared for. Our front occupied a position between eight and nine miles from the city. Rebel prisoners admit their defeat, and deplore their great loss in artillery and prisoners. Orders were issued last night for 5,000 rations for prisoners. General Jackson, captured by Smith, is a major-general, and is an old man. Smith is a middle-aged man, and pays a high compliment to our troops, who, he says, are brave in a fight and magnanimous after victory."*

The dispatch of General Thomas, dated at Headquarters, eight miles from Nashville, at 6 in the evening of the 16th, and addressed to the President of the United States, the Hon. Edwin M. Stanton and Lieutenant.-General Grant, was as follows: "This army thanks you for your approbation of its conduct yesterday, and to assure you that it is not misplaced, I have the honor to report that the enemy has been pressed at all points to-day in his line of retreat to the Brentwood Hills. Brigadier-General Hatch, of Wilson's corps of cavalry, on the right, turned the enemy's left, and captured a large number of prisoners, the number not yet reported. Major-General Schofield's corps, next on the left of cavalry, carried several hills, captured many prisoners and six pieces of artillery. Brevet Major-General Smith, next on the left of Major-General Schofield, carried the salient point of the enemy's line with McMillans' brigade of McArthur's division, capturing. sixteen pieces of artillery, two brigadier-generals and about 2,000 prisoners. Brigadier-General Garrard's division, of Smith's command, next on the left of McArthur's division, carried the enemy's intrenchments, capturing all the artillery an troops of the enemy on the line. Brigadier-General Wood's troops on Franklin pike took up the assault, capturing the enemy's intrenchments; in his retreat captured eight pieces of artillery, something over 600 prisoners, and drove the enemy within one mile of the Brentwood Hill Pass. Major-General Steedman, commanding detachments of the different armies of the Military Division of the Mississippi, most nobly supported General Wood's left, and bore a most honorable part in the operations of the day. I have ordered the pursuit to be continued in the morning at daylight, although the troops are very much fatigued. The utmost enthusiasm prevails. I must not forget to report the operations of Brigadier-General Johnson in successfully driving the enemy, with the cooperation of the gunboats under Lieutenant-Commander Fitch, from their established batteries on the Cumberland River, below the city of Nashville, and of the success of Brigadier-General Coxton's brigade in covering and returning our right and rear. In the operations of yesterday and to-day although I have no report of the number of prisoners captured by Johnson's and Croxton's command, I know they have made a large number. I am also glad to be able to state that the number of prisoners captured yesterday greatly exceeds the number reported by tele-

* Army Correspondence, *New York Times*. Nashville, December 16, midnight.

graph last evening. The woods, fields and intrenchments are strewn with the enemy's small arms abandoned in the retreat. In conclusion, I am happy to state that all this has been effected with but a very small loss to us. Our loss probably does not exceed 3,000 and very few killed."

The pursuit of the next day, the 17th, was thus reported by General Thomas from his headquarters at evening near Franklin: "We have pressed the enemy to-day beyond Franklin, capturing his hospitals, containing over 1,500 wounded and about 150 of our wounded, in addition to the above. General Knipe, commanding a division of cavalry, drove the enemy's rear-guard through Franklin to-day, capturing about 250 prisoners and five battle-flags, with very little loss on our side. Citizens of Franklin represent Hood's army as completely demoralized. In addition to the captures of yesterday, reported in my dispatches of last night, I have the honor to report the capture of General Rucker and about 250 prisoners of the enemy's cavalry, in a fight that occurred about 8 o'clock last night between General Rucker and General Hatch of our cavalry. The enemy has been pressed to-day both in front and on both flanks. Brigadier-General Johnson succeeded in striking him on the flank just beyond Franklin, capturing quite a number of prisoners—number not yet reported. My cavalry is pressing him closely through, and I am very much in hopes of getting many more prisoners to-morrow."

The pursuit, which for the last two days had been continued through a violent storm of rain, over roads almost impassable from mud, was kept up beyond Franklin the next day, to Spring Hill, on the line of the Decatur Railroad, the shattered forces of the enemy hastening on in flight to the Tennessee River, where they lingered for a short time in the vicinity of Florence, previously to crossing into Alabama before the gathering forces of Thomas in their rear. In this retreat there were frequent skirmishes between the rebel General Forrest's and Wilson's Union cavalry, but the state of the roads forbade further effectual pursuit by infantry. The close of the year saw Tennessee thoroughly freed from the presence of the rebel army, and the invasion, from which much had been expected by the enemy, turned into a diastrous flight.

The comparative losses of the two opposing armies in this campaign are thus summed up by the correspondent previously quoted, from information gathered at Nashville.* The Union loss of killed and wounded previously to the battle of Franklin, about 100; at the battle of Franklin (official), 2,100; at the battle of Nashville, on the 15th and 16th (official), 2,900; subsequently, about 1,000—making a total of 6,100, to which is to be added 800 missing. The rebel loss of killed and wounded before the battle of Franklin, about 100; at the battle, 7,000; at Murfreesboro', 100; in the battle at Nashville, 2,500; subsequently, 1,000—a total of 10,700; to which is to be added prisoners taken before the battle of Franklin (official), 100; at that battle (official), 842; at Nashville, first day's fight (official), 2,002; second day's fight, (official), 4,440; taken since, 2,000—a total of killed, wounded and prisoners of 20,084. To this number almost 1,000 deserters are to be added. Sixty-eight pieces of artillery were taken from the enemy; 56 being taken in battle, the rest found abandoned. This calculation, if correct, would imply a loss of about one-half of the estimated numbers of the army which Hood mustered in his invasion of Tennessee.

The retreat of Hood into Mississippi was followed by his removal from his

* Nashville correspondence of the *New York Times*, January 5, 1865.

command. In a parting address to his troops, dated Headquarters Army of the Tennessee, at Tupelo, January 23, he thanked his men for the patience with which they had endured the hardships of the recent campaign, for the conception of which, he said, he was alone responsible, and urged them to support the new commander, General Dick Taylor, who had been appointed his successor.

CHAPTER CVI.

GENERAL SHERMAN'S GEORGIA CAMPAIGN.—ATLANTA TO SAVANNAH, NOVEMBER TO DECEMBER, 1864.

General Sherman having pursued the army of General Hood through Alabama, returned to the line of the Chattanooga and Atlanta Railway, falling back upon Rome and Kingston, at which latter place, on the 9th of November, he issued a special order, reorganizing his army for a new military campaign through Georgia, the objective of which was the possession of the city of Savannah, as a new base of operations on the seaboard. Leaving the Fourth Corps, commanded by General Stanley, and the Twenty-third, commanded by General Schofield, to General Thomas, to cope with Hood, in his advance to Tennessee, he divided his army, for the work before it, into two wings, assigning to the right Major-General Howard, commanding the Fifteenth and Seventeenth Corps of Osterhaus and Frank P. Blair, and to the left, Major-General H. W. Slocum commanding the Fourteenth and Twentieth Corps of Jefferson C. Davis and Williams. Brigadier-General Kilpatrick was assigned the command of the cavalry. The habitual order of march it was ordered, should be, whenever practicable, by four roads, as nearly parallel as possible, and converging at points to be hereafter indicated. There were to be no general trains of supplies, and each corps was to have its limited ammunition and provision train so distributed that in case of danger the advance and rear brigades should be unencumbered by wheels. The separate columns were to start habitually at 7 A. M., and make about fifteen miles a day, unless otherwise ordered. The army was directed to "forage liberally on the country during the march." For this purpose brigade commanders were to organize "good and sufficient foraging parties, under the command of one or more discreet officers," to gather corn or forage of any kind, meat, vegetables, or other necessaries, aiming always to keep on hand ten days' provisions for the men and three days' forage. "Soldiers must not enter the dwellings of the inhabitants or commit any trespass; during the halt or a camp they may be permitted to gather turnips, potatoes, and other vegetables, and drive in stock in front of their camps." The power was entrusted to army corps commanders, to destroy mills, houses, cotton-gins, etc., in districts or neighborhoods where the army was molested by guerrillas or bushwhackers, or the inhabitants should burn bridges, obstruct roads, or otherwise manifest local hostility, but no such devastation was to be permitted where the inhabitants remained quiet. "As for horses, mules, wagons, etc., belonging to the inhabitants, the cavalry and artillery may appropriate freely and without limit; discriminating, however, between the rich, who are usually hostile and the poor or industrious, usually neutral or friendly. Foraging parties may also take mules or horses to replace the jaded animals of their trains, or to serve as pack mules for the regiments or brigades. In all foraging, of whatever kind, the parties engaged will refrain from abusive and threatening language, and may, when the officer in command thinks proper, give written certificates of the facts, but no receipts; and they will endeavor to leave with each family a reasonable portion for their maintenance. Negroes who are able-bodied and can be of service to the several columns, may be taken along; but each army commander will bear in mind that the question of supplies is a very important one, and that his first duty is to see to those who bear arms." A pontoon train fully equipped and organized was assigned to each wing of the army.

Having given these instructions, General Sherman assembled his forces at Atlanta, whence, having sent the sick and wounded and surplus stores of provisions to Chattanooga, and burnt the storehouses, depot buildings, and machine-shops, the public property which might be available to the enemy for the purposes of war, he put his army in motion on its march through the central and wealthiest portions of Georgia. The right wing, under General Howard, moved from Atlanta on the 12th, followed on the 14th by the left, under General Slocum. The respective lines of march followed generally the two lines of railroad traversing the State, the Georgia and Central, running from Savannah to Macon, and thence by a soutwesterly line to Atlanta, a distance in all of nearly 300 miles; and the Georgia Railroad, running north of the former between Atlanta and Augusta, which was connected with the southerly line by way of Waynesboro' and Millen with Savannah. In the area bounded by these lines, resembling a parallelogram with Atlanta, Macon, Augusta and Millen at the four corners, and Milledgeville at a central point in the enclosure, the important movements of General Sherman's army were effected. His strategy consisted in directing the attention of the enemy to Augusta, on the north and Macon on the south, while he quietly marched between these cities, through Milledgeville, and by Millen to the seaboard and the conquest of Savannah.

The details of the movement thus outlined, are thus given in a review of the campaign, by a journalist, prepared from the scattered reports which reached the North from rebel and other sources.* "The right wing moved directly south from Atlanta, to Rough and Ready and Jonesboro' stations on the Macon and Western Railroad. November 16 one column of the right wing passed through Jonesboro', twenty-six miles south of Atlanta, Wheeler's cavalry and Cobb's militia retiring upon Griffin. Another column of the right wing occupied McDonough, November 15, the county seat of Henry County, some distance east of Jonesboro', and about thirty-five miles southeast of Atlanta. Henry County is one of the largest and richest of Georgia, and here our forces found large supplies of provisions and forage. On the 16th, Wheeler engaged our cavalry at Bear Creek station, ten miles north of Griffin, and telegraphed General Hardee that he had 'checked the Yankee advance.' The very same evening, at 6 o'clock, his ragged troopers fell back through Griffin, in the direction of Barnesville, where Cobb's militia had already preceded him. Our cavalry occupied Griffin, the county seat of Spalding County, on the 17th, and on the 18th drove Wheeler out of Barnesville, in Pike County, and through Forsyth, the county seat of Monroe County,

* *New York Times*, December 20, 1864.

seventy-six miles south of Atlanta and twenty-five miles northwest of Macon. This demonstration, though only made by cavalry, completely deceived Cobb, who put all his forces in the intrenchments of that place, and by military impressment put every male resident in the ranks. The right wing moved on from McDonough on the 16th, to Jackson, the county seat of Butts County, and thence to Planter's Factory, on the Ocmulgee River, which was successfully crossed on the 20th, thus leaving Macon on our right and rear, distant about twenty-five miles. This crossing of the Ocmulgee was uncontested. It was the first indication that Sherman would pass by Macon, which is in Bibb County, without an effort to take it. The feint was admirably made by our cavalry, which pressed the rebel forces hotly from Forsyth, and then veering around to the east of Macon, attacked a force of rebels at a point known as East Macon, where we captured a battery, which the rebels claim they retook. This was on the 20th, and on the same day our cavalry advanced to Griswoldville, eight miles east of Macon, where they captured a lumber train, burned a foundry and the chemical works, tore up the railroad and cut the telegraph. At the same time a part of General Howard's command moved rapidly through Monticello, the county seat of Jasper County, where the court house was burned, via Hillsboro', in the southern part of the same county, to Clinton, the county seat of Jones County, for the purpose of striking the Georgia Central Railroad at Gordon, the junction of the branch road to Milledgeville. Having left Cobb's forces in Macon, now in his rear, Sherman sent an infantry force to act as rear-guard to Griswoldville, while he moved toward Oconee, occupied Milledgeville and destroyed the railroad.

"Sherman entered Milledgeville, November 21, having made the march from Atlanta in just seven days, with no haste on the part of any of his columns. Average distance by the route marched, ninety-five miles. On the 22d, the rear-guard at Griswoldville was attacked by a force of rebels from Macon, under General Phillips, composed of three brigades of militia, two regiments of State line troops, and the Augusta and Athens battalions. The rebel account of the battle says that it lasted several hours, and that the gallant Georgia militia charged across an open field, and drove our troops from their line of works. During the night, they say, our troops *retired*—that is, continued their *advance*. As this was but a mere skirmish with the rear-guard of the right wing, the truth of the rebel claim to success may be estimated in the fact that they acknowledge a loss of 614 in killed and wounded, and one of their commanders, General Anderson, was censured for his reckless exposure of the tender militia. He was also severely wounded in the fight. This was the most considerable engagement in the whole march.

"The left wing, under General Slocum, left Atlanta November 14, moving out by the Decatur road a short distance and then branching off to the right and passing through De Kalb County, by way of Flat Rock and Snapping Shoals, to Covington, the county seat of Newton County, which point the advance reached on the 17th, the cavalry pushing on as far as Social Circle, in Walton County, a station on the railroad fifty-two miles east of Atlanta, where the railroad buildings were burned. Covington is situated in the midst of a very fertile country, and foraging was carried on to an extensive degree. A party from one of the brigades of the Twentieth Corps, while out foraging some distance north of the railroad, at Oxford, were fired upon by bushwhackers and one of their number killed. Here the order for relentless devastation of the country was carried out, with a degree of severity which resulted in the destruction of Emory College, at Oxford. It was the property of the Methodist Church, had several fine libraries, a mineralogical cabinet, a fine chemical apparatus, and cost nearly half a million dollars before the war. The plantations in this (Newton) county were thoroughly stripped, and our troops lived on the fat of the land. They were much surprised at the richness of the country they passed through. From Covington General Slocum moved directly east to Madison, the county seat of Morgan County, his cavalry covering his left flank, and destroying the railroad thoroughly. At Madison the railroad buildings, the jail, several warehouses and the market-house were burned. From Madison the left wing moved almost due south upon Eatonton, which is the northern terminus of the Milledgeville branch railway. This point was reached November 21, the same day General Howard's right flank reached Gordon, the southern terminus of the same railroad. General Slocum reached Milledgeville on the 22d, which place proved to be a general point of rendezvous for the two wings. Our army occupied Milledgeville for three days, November 21st to the 24th, when the rear-guard left. General Sherman occupied the executive mansion for his headquarters. Very little property, either public or private, was destroyed. The State House was left standing, though the rebels declare that it was much mutilated. The sudden absquatulation of the rebel legislature disgusted our troops. The members, with Governor Brown, left in great haste on the 18th, some for Macon, some for Augusta, and many on foot, there not being confederate currency enough in Milledgeville to hire a conveyance. Two members paid $1,000 to be carried a distance of eight miles. Governor Brown took the public funds, the public archives, his private carriage and his 'garden sass' (so said the Savannah *Republican*), and fled to Macon, where he opened headquarters in the City Hall, and issued a proclamation. He left 3,000 muskets and several thousand pounds of powder belonging to the State of Georgia, which our troops destroyed. Some of our troops perpetrated a very handsome travestie upon the proceedings of the fleeing legislature. They met at the State House, elected a speaker and clerk, and were introducing bills and resolutions at a fabulous rate, when a courier rushed in, breathless with haste, and shouted 'the Yankees are coming!' whereupon the members dispersed in the most panic-stricken manner, causing an immense deal of amusement. Milledgeville was pretty thoroughly stripped of provisions, as the main portion of the army encamped in that vicinity three days. Every horse and mule that could be found were taken, and the rebels said that there was no use in hiding anything, for 'the Yankees would be sure to find it.' The exhortations of the rebel papers, politicians and others who had nothing to lose, to burn and destroy supplies, had no effect. Every body waited to see his neighbor begin, and entertained the hope that he, at least, might possibly escape without loss. On November 25, the Mayor of Milledgeville sent by courier to Macon, a dispatch begging the people there to send the citizens of Milledgeville meat and provisions, as they were utterly destitute. Sherman's army consumed just one week in moving from Atlanta to Milledgeville, the average distance being ninety-five miles. The movement was deliberate, and fully up to the marching orders. The only resistance met with was that on the right flank of Howard's column, where Cobb and Wheeler were steadily pushed back by Kilpatrick. General Slocum's column was unresisted, and even unmolested save by an occasional guerrilla, and the retaliation against the citizens in such cases was very severe.

"The army left Milledgeville November 24, en route to Millen, through which place it passed on the evening of December 2, camping in the vicinity. The distance from Milledgeville to Millen, the way Sherman marched, is about seventy-four miles, and the distance was accomplished in eight days. The main body crossed the Oconee at Milledgeville, destroying the bridge over that river, and the Railroad bridge over Fisher's Creek, south of the city. A large force of cavalry demonstrated at the Central Railroad bridge over the Oconee, twenty-five miles south-east of Milledgeville, which was defended by earth-works, by the rebel General Wayne, who commanded an improvised brigade of stragglers and militia which had been picked up between Milledgeville and Augusta. This road here runs for several miles through a swamp, which borders the west bank of the Oconee. Wheeler, who had been left in the rear at Macon, took a swift circuit southward, through Twiggs, Wilkinson and Laurens Counties, and crossed the Oconee to Wayne's assistance at Buckeye bridge, eighteen miles below the Railroad bridge. But this availed nothing, for Howard's column, in moving upon Sandersville, in Washington County, marched down the east bank of the Oconee, and Wayne, hearing of it, imagined he was flanked, and on the twenty-fifth retired in precipitate haste to Davisboro, and thence in the direction of Louisville, the county seat of Jefferson County. The advance of Howard's column reached Sandersville November 26. The railroad was cut again, and the depot burned, at Tenille station, immediately south of Sandersville. General Slocum's column crossed the Oconee simultaneously with the right wing, but bore to the northward in its march, aiming for Sparta, a flourishing village, and the county seat of Hancock County. On the evening of the 24th, General Slocum's advance encamped at Devereaux, seven miles west of Sparta, and the cavalry scoured the whole county, one of the most fertile and thickly settled in the whole State, and vast quantities of forage and provisions, many horses and mules were obtained, and much cotton burned. The Georgia Railroad, on General Slocum's left flank was not neglected. While the army lay at Milledgeville, a portion of the cavalry force were roaming unresisted through Morgan, Green and Putnam counties, striking the railroad repeatedly, burning the bridge over the Oconee at Blue Spring, and the buildings at Buckhead in Morgan county, Greensboro in Green county, and Crawfordsville in Talliaferro county.

"When it was demonstrated to a certainty that Sherman was east of the Oconee, the rebels in Savannah and Augusta became greatly frightened. Up to that time many of them were consoled with the idea that after all, Sherman was only on a great raid into the heart of the State, or would yet turn and move westward upon Columbus, Montgomery and Mobile. But such hopes were dispelled when his cavalry were discovered in Washington and Hancock counties. At Augusta, then deemed the object of Sherman's march, preparations for defence went on vigorously. Bragg was summoned from Wilmington, and came, the Augusta papers said, with ten thousand men. Troops came from Charleston, Hampton's cavalry came from Virginia, and the entire population of the city was put under arms, and all the slaves in the surrounding country were impressed to work upon the fortifications. Then began, also, a vigorous system of rebel *brag*. Wheeler was put to his trumps, and required to whip Kilpatrick three times a day, and to invariably close the report of his victory with the announcement, 'after this glorious success *we fell back!*' All this Wheeler most valiantly did, but on one occasion, in a fight near Gibson, the county seat of Glascock County, being required to bring in Kilpatrick's head as a trophy, he humbly apologized with his hat observing that in his haste to fall back, he had left Kilpatrick's head on its shoulders. It was through this march from Milledgeville to Millen, occupied a little over a week, that the movements of Kilpatrick were so vigorous, and his cavalry so ubiquitous, that the position of Sherman's infantry was wholly unknown to the enemy. Howard's column passed through Sandersville November 26, and Louisville November 30. Slocum marched through Sparta, in Hancock County, to Gibson, in Glascock County, and then moved upon Louisville, converging with the right wing near the latter place. The whole army appeared in the vicinity of Millen, December 2. Until it was fully ascertained that Sherman had reached Millen, the rebels believed that he was passing down between the Ogechee and Oconee Rivers, aiming to reach the coast of Darien or Brunswick. Very adroit strategy was necessary at this juncture to conceal the real direction of the march, for had the rebels known in time that Augusta was certainly to be avoided, the entire force there could have been sent down to Millen, and thus thrown in Sherman's front, and resisted or delayed his march upon Savannah, and in the end would have proved a formidable addition to the garrison of that place. Kilpatrick, therefore, pressed Wheeler more vigorously than ever, and the latter fell back toward Augusta, which put him out of Sherman's way most effectually, again leaving him in the rear of the very army whose advance he was endeavoring to resist. It was during these cavalry operations that the fight took place at Waynesboro', December 3d, where Wheeler attacked Kilpatrick, and reported that he had 'doubled him up on the main body.' But Kilpatrick wouldn't stay 'doubled up.' On the next day Wheeler was compelled to made his usual report that he had 'signally repulsed Kilpatrick,' but was 'obliged to *fall back*,' the result of which was that he was driven back through Waynesboro' and beyond Brier Creek, the railway bridge over which was destroyed, within twenty miles of Augusta, which was the nearest approach of our forces to that city. Kilpatrick then took up a position to guard Sherman's rear, and while doing so, his force loaded their wagons with the forage and provisions of Burke County, for use in the less fertile counties in the region of the coast.

"It has been shown that General Sherman's army occupied about eight days in moving from Milledgeville to Millen, an average distance of seventy-five miles. This is only a trifle over nine miles per day, but there is no evidence that he was in motion all the time. On the contrary, the rebels discovered, after he had passed Millen, the real object of his leisurely progress. Fully aware that the resistance at Savannah might be formidable, and that communication with the fleet and the procurement of supplies from Port Royal, might be attended with difficulties consuming considerable time, he paid more attention than usual to foraging in the fertile counties of Jefferson, Washington, Burke, Glascock, Warren and Hancock, all immediately west or southwest of Augusta. The rebels said he stopped to 'grind corn.' But the corn didn't need grinding. The animals ate it in the ear, and the men were not reduced to that article of diet. They brought hard tack enough in their wagons from Atlanta to last them through the journey, and the commissaries issued mainly fresh beef, mutton, pork, poultry, sorghum, etc., obtained in the country. Another object of Sherman's moderate progress, which the rebels were not so ready to acknowledge, was the destruction of the railroads. The railroad bridge over the Oconee was burned after the rebels, under Wayne, had been forced back; and that over the Ogeechee, near Sebastopol Station, twenty-five miles west of Millen, shared a like fate. The track was also destroyed in many localities for miles, extending all the way from Griswoldville to Millen, on the Georgia Central, ninety-seven miles, and from Covington to Crawfordsville, on the Georgia State Road, a distance of sixty miles. Kilpatrick, after driving Wheeler beyond Waynesboro, in the direction of Augusta, December 3d, also tore up the track and burned the bridges over Brier Creek, Buckhead Creek, and several smaller streams. This was on the Waynesboro Branch Railroad, connecting Savannah with Augusta *via* Millen. The object of Sherman's cautious march through Washington and Jefferson Counties, and the point at which he had resolved to strike, which was never for a moment undecided in his own mind, only became apparent to the rebels when it was too late to prevent it. Macon had been threatened, and Cobb's forces shut up in its intrenchments. leaving them useless and in the rear, when Sherman moved on. Augusta was threatened, and all the troops that could be gathered were put in the fortifications. Charleston and Wilmington were denuded for Augusta's defence, and the South Carolina militia were assembled at Hamburgh, opposite to Augusta, to cooperate, if necessary. Thus Savannah was almost overlooked, and when Sherman headed his columns directly and rapidly for the city, which he did on the 4th of December, he left all the rebel forces gathered for his defeat well in his rear, and found a feebly garrisoned city in his front. The situation as viewed by the rebels, when they fully realized this fact, was aptly described by one of the Augusta papers thus, on the 3d of December: 'Sherman has not for a moment hesitated, in our humble judgment, as to the point to be attacked or the road to it. When his forage or provision trains are full he will mass his entire force at Millen; throwing his cavalry to the rear, with his wagon train between the two wings of his army, he will move in compact columns, steadily but cautiously upon the city of Savannah, with no fear of an attack on either flank. The Ogeechee and a few crossings and terrible swamps on his right, and the Savannah river, and its equally swampy banks on his left, both flanks will be most securely covered—a grand desideratum in army movements. And thus situated, he has a march of something over eighty miles to the city of Savannah.' When the Augusta people heard that their city was no longer threatened, they drew a long breath, and congratulated themselves. 'The frowns and sadness with which the countenances of our citizens have been bedecked,' said the *Sentinel*, 'have given way to smiles and mirth.' That is, 'smiles and mirth' because their neighbors in Savannah were to be the recipients of Sherman's favors, and not they.

"From Millen to Savannah is seventy-nine miles. After leaving Millen, General Sherman made rapid and regular marches upon Savannah, and on the 9th General Howard struck the canal which connects the Ogeechee with the Savannah at a point about ten miles in the rear (west) of the city. From this point, and on the evening of the same day, he sent three of his most trusted scouts, Captain Duncan and Sergeants Myron J. Emmick and George W. Quimby, in a small boat down the Ogeechee River, passing Fort McAllister in the night, and communicated on the 11th with the gunboat Dandelion, of Admiral Dahlgren's fleet, off Ossabaw Sound, which immediately took them on board, and arrived at Port Royal harbor on the morning of the 12th. Captain Duncan brought this dispatch from General Howard:

"'HEADQUARTERS ARMY OF THE TENNESSEE,
NEAR SAVANNAH CANAL, *December* 9, 1864.

"' *To the Commander of the United States Naval Forces in the vicinity of Savannah:*

"'SIR—We have met with perfect success thus far. The troops are in fine spirits and near by.

"'Respectfully,

"'O. O. HOWARD, Major-General,
Commanding Right Wing of the Army.'

"This was the first intelligence direct from the army, and completely dispelled all doubts and fears, as well as dissipated an immense amount of rebel bombast and boasting of the impediments and difficulties with which Sherman had met, to say nothing of the repeated total annihilation of Kilpatrick's cavalry, which seems not to have been worthy of mention by General Howard or General Sherman. Wheeler, who at last accounts, was 'hacking away at Sherman's rear,' must have had a dull sabre.

"On the 10th instant, General Sherman had advanced to within five miles of Savannah, where, it was generally understood, the rebels had erected the first of the three lines of defences which protect that city. But with the wise sagacity and the sound military judgment which he possesses, General Sherman made preparations at once, not for an assault upon Savannah, but for the capture of Fort McAllister, thereby opening the Ogeechee River, communicating with the fleet, and making a water base on that river at any point he chose, directly in the rear of Savannah; and also cutting off all communication between Savannah and the southern part of the State, *via* the Savannah, Albany and Gulf Railroad, which has heretofore been an important avenue of supplies to the rebels from the vast numbers of beef cattle from Florida transported over it. Accordingly, a division of troops from the Fifteenth Corps, under General Hazen, was sent down on the 13th, and at 5 o'clock P. M., the fort was gallantly carried by assault, with its entire garrison and stores." The loss in this assault was about ninety in killed and wounded, all of Hazen's division; and that of the enemy, was something less.

"This success was announced to the country in the following dispatch from General Sherman, dated at midnight 'on board Dandelion, Ossabaw Sound,' of the day of the victory: 'To-day at 5 o'clock P. M., General Hazen's division of the Fifteenth Corps carried Fort McAllister by assault, capturing its entire garrison and stores. This opened to us the Ossabaw Sound, and I pushed down to this gunboat to communicate with the fleet. Before opening communication we had completely destroyed all the railroads leading into Savannah, and invested the city. The left is on the Savannah River, three miles above the city, and the right on the Ogeechee, at King's Bridge. The army is in splendid order, and equal to any thing. The weather has been fine, and supplies are abundant. Our march was most agreeable, and we were not at all molested by the guerrillas. We reached Savannah three days ago, but owing to Fort McAllister, could not communicate; but now we have McAllister, we can go ahead. We have already captured two boats on the Savannah River, and prevented their gunboats from coming down. I estimate the population of Savannah at 25,000, and the garrison at 15,000. General Hardee commands. We have not lost a wagon on the trip, but have gathered in a large supply of negroes, mules, horses, etc., and our teams are in far better condition than when we started. My first duty will be to clear the army of surplus negroes, mules and horses. We have utterly destroyed over two hundred miles of rails, and consumed stores and provisions that were essential to Lee's and Hood's armies. The quick work made with McAllister, and the opening of communication with our fleet, and the consequent independence of supplies, dissipates all their boasted threats to head me off and starve the army. I regard Savannah as already gained.'"

General Foster now joined General Sherman, having previously sent an expedition from Hilton Head inland towards Grahamsville to engage the enemy's attention on the line of the Charleston and Savannah railroad. He reported, on the 14th, the city as closely besieged; its capture, with the rebel forces there, confidently expected. It was to be summoned in two days, and if not surrendered, Sherman would open his batteries upon it. General Foster further reported Sherman's army in "splendid condition, having lived, on its march, on the turkeys, chickens, sweet potatoes, and other good things of the richest part of Georgia."

General Sherman was in full communication with the fleet under Admiral Dahlgren, who was prepared to bring all his available force into connection with the army. No further military operations, however, beyond the preparations which were going on for an assault were needed. On the evening of the 22d, General Foster had the satisfaction of following up his previous dispatch with this message to General Grant:* "I have the honor to report that I have just returned from General Sherman's headquarters in Savannah. I send Major Gray, of my staff, as bearer of dispatches from General Sherman to you, and also a message to the President. The city of Savannah was occupied on the morning of the 21st. General Hardee anticipating the contemplated assault, escaped with the main body of his infantry and light artillery, on the morning of the 20th, by crossing the river to Union Causeway, opposite the city. The rebel iron-clads were blown up, and the Navy-yard was burned. All the rest of the city is intact, and contains twenty-thousand citizens, quiet and well-disposed. The captures include eight hundred prisoners, one hundred and fifty guns, thirteen locomotives in good order, one hundred and ninety cars, a large supply of ammunition and materials of war, three steamers and thirty-three thousand bales of cotton safely stowed away in warehouses. All these valuable fruits of an almost bloodless victory have been, like Atlanta, fairly won. I opened communication with the city with my steamers to-day, taking up what torpedoes we could see, and passing safely over others. Arrangements are made to clear the channel of all obstructions."

The message to the President was from General Sherman in these words: "Savannah, Ga., December 22. To his Excellency President Lincoln: I beg to present to you as a Christmas gift, the city of Savannah, with one hundred and fifty heavy guns and plenty of ammunition, and also about twenty-five thousand bales of cotton."

On the 26th, the following order was issued by General Sherman in reference to the military government of the city: "The city of Savannah and surrounding country will be held as a military post and adapted to future military uses, but as it contains a population of some 20,000 people who must be provided for, and as other citizens may come, it is proper to lay down certain general principles, that all within its military jurisdiction may understand their relative duties and obligations. 1st. During war, the military is superior to civil authority, and where interests clash, the civil must give way; yet where there is no conflict, every encouragement should be given to well disposed and peaceful inhabitants to resume their usual pursuits. Families should be disturbed as little as possible in their residence, and tradesmen allowed the free use of their shops, tools, etc. Churches, schools, all places of amusement and recreation should be encouraged, and streets and roads made perfectly safe to persons in their usual pursuits. Passes should not

* Report of Secretary Stanton, Washington, Dec. 17.

be exacted within the line of outer pickets, but if any person shall abuse these privileges by communicating with the enemy, or doing an act of hostility to the Government of the United States, he or she will be punished with the utmost rigor of the law. Commerce with the outer world will be resumed to an extent commensurate with the wants of the citizens, governed by the restrictions and rules of the Treasury Department. 2d. The chief quartermaster and commissary of the army may give suitable employment to the people, white and black, or transport them to such points as they choose, where employment may be had, and may extend temporary relief in the way of provisions and vacant houses to the worthy and needy until such time as they can help themselves. They will select, first, the buildings for the necessary use of the army; next, a sufficient number of stores to be turned over to the treasury agent for trade stores. All vacant storehouses or dwellings, and all buildings belonging to absent rebels, will be construed and used as belonging to the United States until such time as their titles can be settled by the Courts of the United States. 3d. The Mayor and City Council of Savannah will continue and exercise their functions as such, and will, in concert with the commanding officer of the post and the chief quartermaster, see that the fire companies are kept in organization, the streets cleaned and lighted, and keep up a good understanding between the citizens and soldiers. They will ascertain and report to the Chief of Commissary Subsistance, as soon as possible, the names and number of worthy families that need assistance and support. The Mayor will forthwith give public notice that the time has come when all must choose their course, viz: to remain within our lines and conduct themselves as good citizens, or depart in peace. He will ascertain the names of all who choose to leave Savannah, and report their names and residence to the chief quartermaster, that measures may be taken to transport them beyond the lines. 4th. Not more than two newspapers will be published in Savannah, and their editors and proprietors will be held to the strictest accountability, and will be punished severely in person and property for any libellous publication, mischievous matter, premature news, exaggerated statements, or any comments whatever upon the acts of the constituted authorities; they will be held accountable even for such articles though copied from other papers."

The inhabitants promptly acquiesced in the new state of things. No resistance was offered to the new military authority and good order and discipline were maintained on the part of the soldiers, Brigadier-General Geary being placed in command of the post. A meeting of the citizens was called by the Mayor on the 27th inst., for the purpose of taking into consideration "matters relating to the present and future welfare of the city." It was largely attended and resolutions were adopted "That we accept the position. and in the language of the President of the United States, seek to have 'peace by laying down our arms, and submitting to the national authority under the Constitution,' 'leaving all questions which remain to be adjusted by the peaceful means of legislation, conference and votes.' That laying aside all differences and burying by-gones in the grave of the past, we will use our best endeavors to bring back the prosperity and commerce we once enjoyed. That we do not put ourselves in the position of a conquered city asking terms of a conqueror, but we claim the immunities and privileges contained in the proclamation and message of the President of the United States, and in all the legislation of Congress in reference to a people situated as we are; and while we owe on our part a strict obedience to the laws of the United States, we ask the protection over our persons, lives and property recognized by those laws. That we respectfully request his Excellency the Governor, to call a Convention of the people of Georgia, by any Constitutional means in his power, to give them an opportunity of voting upon the question whether they wish the war between the two sections of the country to continue."

On the 8th of January, General Sherman from his headquarters at Savannah, issued a congratulatory order to his army in which he briefly alluded to the prominent events of the campaign: "The General commanding announces to the troops composing the Military Division of the Mississippi that he has received from the President of the United States and from Lieutenant-General Grant letters conveying the high sense and appreciation of the campaign just closed, resulting in the capture of Savannah and the defeat of Hood's army in Tennessee. In order that all may understand the importance of events, it is proper to revert to the situation of affairs in September last. We held Atlanta, a city of little value to us, but so important to the enemy that Mr. Davis, the head of the rebellious faction in the South, visited his army near Palmetto, and commanded it to regain it, as well as to ruin and destroy us by a series of measures which he thought would be effectual. That army, by a rapid march, first gained our railroad near Big Shanty, and afterward about Dalton. We pursued, but it marched so rapidly that we could not overtake it, and General Hood led his army successfully far toward Mississippi, in hopes to decoy us out of Georgia. But we were not then to be led away by him, and purposed to control and lead events ourselves. Generals Thomas and Schofield, commanding the department to our rear, returned to their posts, and prepared to decoy General Hood into their meshes, while we came on to complete our original journey. We quietly and deliberately destroyed Atlanta and all the railroad which the enemy had used to carry on war against us; occupied his State capital, and then captured his commercial capital, which had been so strongly fortified from the sea as to defy approach from that quarter. Almost at the moment of our victorious entry into Savannah came the welcome and expected news that our comrades in Tennessee had also fulfilled, nobly and well, their part; had decoyed General Hood to Nashville, and then turned on him, defeating his army thoroughly, capturing all his artillery, great numbers of prisoners, and were still pursuing the fragments down into Alabama. So complete a success in military operations, extending over half a continent, is an achievement that entitles it to a place in the military history of the world. The armies serving in Georgia and Tennessee, as well as the local garrisons of Decatur, Bridgeport, Chattanooga and Murfreesboro', are alike entitled to the common honor, and each regiment may inscribe on its colors at pleasure the words 'Savannah' or 'Nashville.' The General commanding embraces in the same general success the operations of the cavalry column, under Generals Stoneman, Burbridge and Gillem, that penetrated into Southwestern Virginia, and paralyzed the efforts of the enemy to disturb the peace and safety of the people of East Tennessee. Instead of being put on the defensive, we have, at all points, assumed the bold offensive, and completely thwarted the designs of the enemies of our country."

A few days later, on the 16th, General Sherman, in concert with the Secretary of war, Stanton, who visited Savannah immediately after its capture, issued an important order setting apart the sea islands from Charleston south, the abandoned rice-fields for thirty miles back from the sea and the country bordering the St. John River, Florida, for the settlement of the negroes made free by the acts of war and the Proclamation of the President of the United States. At Beaufort, Hilton Head, Savannah, Fernandina, St. Augustine, and Jacksonville the negroes were permitted to remain in their chosen or accustomed avocations, but on the sea islands and proposed settlements, no white person whatever, unless military officers and soldiers detained for duty were to be allowed to reside; the sole and exclusive management of affairs being left to the freed people themselves subject only to the United States military authority and the acts of Congress. Regulations were made for the allotment of land and for special settlements assigning to each family forty acres of land. Military enlistments of the young and able-bodied were to be encouraged, and the rights to property of such persons for themselves and families were to be duly protected. The regulations were to be carried out by a general officer to be detailed as "Inspector of settlements and plantations," an office to which Brigadier-General Saxton, who had already rendered important services in these relations, was assigned by General Sherman in his order. Communications were opened with the northern Atlantic cities for the purpose of procuring provisions, and it being understood, that many of the population were in danger of want, liberal contributions were collected in Boston, New York and elsewhere, and shiploads of supplies were promptly sent for their relief. The appeal for this purpose at Boston was seconded by Edward Everett in a speech at a public meeting, on the 9th of January, at Faneuil Hall. It was the last honorable duty in the brilliant record of his many services to his country. He became apparently slightly ill during the week, and on the morning, of Sunday the 15th, died suddenly at his residence of apoplexy. The news of his death was immediately communicated to President Lincoln and the Cabinet at Washington, when the following official announcement was made of the event by the Secretary of State: "The President directs the undersigned to perform the painful duty of announcing to the people of the United States that Edward Everett, distinguished not more by learning and eloquence than by unsurpassed and disinterested labors of patriotism, at a period of political disorder, departed this life at 4 o'clock this morning. The several Executive Departments of the Government will cause appropriate honors to be rendered to the memory of the deceased, at home and abroad, wherever the national name and authority are recognized."

CHAPTER CVII.

NATIONAL AFFAIRS TO CLOSE OF 1864.

In our retrospect of national affairs, at the close of the previous year, we left the Thirty-eighth Congress just entered on its First Session. That body sat till the 4th of July—seven months, among the most important in the history of the war. The debates on the general policy of the Government were long, and maintained with energy and perseverance on the part of the members in the "minority," who bent their efforts in particular to ward off the penalties of Confiscation, and check the anti-slavery measures which were every day practically gaining ground, as the armies of the country moved on toward the suppression of the rebellion. Several resolutions, offered at different times, in the nature of overtures of "peace negotiations" with the rebel authorities at Richmond, were promptly laid on the table by a decided vote, the minority in the House of Representatives on these extreme measures being about fifty. Though much time was spent in discussion over the preservation to the States in rebellion, of their old rights under the Constitution, and the policy of arming and freeing the negro population, the result in the end was the same. The Government was sustained in its war policy, and adequate means were provided for carrying out its measures in the field. On the other hand, as the power of the State became assured the majority proved itself less intolerant of opposition. In the early part of the session there was, indeed, much discussion concerning the expressions of certain members with a view to their expulsion. But this after a while wore itself out, explanations were accepted, and the obnoxious members remained at their posts. Senator Davis, of Kentucky, early in January, offered a series of resolutions, in which the phrase occurred:—"The people of the North ought to revolt against the war leaders, and take the matter into their own hands," for which he was arraigned by Senator Wilson, who saw in the words an invitation to revolt, and who introduced a resolution for his expulsion. Mr. Davis denied that his resolution fairly bore this interpretation, maintaining that his object was to induce the whole people North and South to terminate the war by a Constitutional settlement. The explanation was deemed unneçessary, or was accepted by a sufficient number of members to induce Senator Wilson to withdraw his resolution. A resolution offered by Mr. Sumner, requiring that every Senator should, before entering upon his duties, take the special oath of allegiance prescribed by the Act of July, 1862, was adopted. It was generally held to be levelled at Senator Bayard, of Maryland, and was opposed in debate by him and his colleague, Senator Saulsbury, as unconstitutional. On the rule being affirmed by a decided vote, Senator Bayard took the additional oath of loyalty as prescribed, and then on a point of honor and principle, resigned his seat in the Senate. Subsequently in April, in the House of Representatives, a resolution was introduced by Speaker Colfax for the expulsion of Alexander Long, a member from Ohio, who had, in debate, expressed himself strongly in opposition to the war, and in favor of ending it by recognizing the Independent Nationality of the Confederacy. This gave rise to an animated debate, which was continued for several days, at the end of which a resolution, not of expulsion but of censure, was passed. By a vote of eighty to seventy, Mr. Long was "declared to be an unworthy member of this House." The preamble to the resolution substantially set forth "that Alexander Long, a Representative from the Second District of Ohio, by his open declaration in the National Capitol, and by publication in New York, has shown himself to be in favor of the recognition of the so-called Confederacy, now trying to establish itself on the ruins of the country; that, by giving aid and comfort to the enemy in their destructive practices, and to the traitors against the Government within our borders, by assurances of their success, and affirmations of the justice of their cause, and that such conduct is incompatible with his duty as a member of this body."

This was the last of the "purging" resolutions in Congress during this Session. It began to be felt that even the semblance of intolerance should be avoided, however annoying or distasteful might be the utterance of sentiments in opposition to the war, the maintainance of which, to a successful end, was considered by the majority indispensable to the salvation of the State. The Government itself acquiesced in the general lenity or forbearance of sentiment on this subject, as the period for the Presidential election approached, and the military necessities of the country were less urgent. "Peace" measures were freely discussed in public in popular harangues, and the exiled Vallandigham, who had made his way out of the rebel States into Canada, was permitted quietly to cross the frontier and take part in the open assemblies of his friends.

The legislation of the previous Congress left the present little to do but to amend or continue its action, in providing additional means to the Government for the prosecution of the war. These consisted of measures securing increased revenues, granting new facilities for enlistments, and sanctioning the policy of the Administration in regard to Slavery. An ample appropriation bill, meeting the demands of the Secretaries of War and the Navy, was passed; new loans were authorized; a new Tariff act largely increased the duties on imports, and an Internal Revenue Law augmented licenses and taxes. Various special taxes were imposed on manufactures and articles of luxury, and the annual assessment on incomes was increased from three to five per cent. on returns between $600 and $5,000; from five to seven and a-half per cent. on returns between $5,000 and $10,000, and to ten per cent. on all excess over the last sum. A special war tax of five per cent. in addition to the three per cent. already levied was ordered on the incomes of the year 1863. This last item, it was subsequently calculated would produce $35,000,000. A new Enrollment Act, approved July 4, supplementary to an amended Enrollment Bill, passed in February, had placed the whole population of the country, between the ages of twenty and forty-five, not physically or otherwise disqualified from bearing arms, at the disposal of the President. He was authorized to call, at his discretion, for any number of volunteers for one, two, or three years, and in case the quotas assigned to the several districts were not forthcoming at the end of fifty days, he was directed then to order a draft for one year, to fill such quota or any deficient portion of it. In case of such draft no payment of money was to be received as commutation for the service; but a substitute might be provided by the person drafted. Volunteers, under this Act, were to receive Government bounties of $100, $200, and $300, according to their term of service of one, two or three years. Clergymen were not exempted, but conscientious and consistent members of religious denominations, whose rules prohibit the bearing of arms were, according to the provisions of the act in February, when drafted to be considered non-combatants, and assigned to hospital or other duty, or released on payment of three hundred dollars. The distinction of classes, with respect to age and married and unmarried persons within the period exposing to service, was abolished by the act of February. By the last mentioned act, all able bodied male persons of African descent, between the ages of twenty and forty-five, resident in the United States, whether citizens or not, were ordered to be enrolled. If a slave of a loyal master was thus drafted, the bounty of $100 was to be paid to the master; on the latter freeing the slave mustered into the service, he was to be awarded a sum not exceeding three hundred dollars. The supplementary act made it lawful for the Executive of any other State to send recruiting agents into any of the States declared to be in rebellion, except the States of Arkansas, Tennessee and Louisiana, and to recruit volunteers to be credited to the State procuring such enlistment.

The enlistment of negro soldiers, thus authoritatively established, was no longer considered a matter of doubtful policy. Their conduct in the field had fully vindicated the expectations formed by their friends, and obvious considerations sanctioned their enrollment.

Various resolutions were brought forward during the session looking to the final abolition of Slavery in the country, by the military power and the action of Congress. The most conclusive of these was received with favor by the House of Representatives, and authoritatively adopted by the Senate. This was the proposition to abolish the institution by an amendment of the Constitution, under the provisions of that instrument, by which, with the concurrence of two-thirds of both Houses of Congress and the signature of the President, the new article to be introduced might be sent to the Legislatures of the several States, and when ratified by three-fourths of their number, become the supreme law of the land. A joint resolution to this effect was offered by Mr. Trumbull in the Senate, in February. The proposed amendment ran thus:—"*Art.* XIII. *Sec.* 1.—Neither slavery nor involuntary servitude, except as a punishment for crime, whereof the party shall have been duly convicted, shall exist within the United States, or any place subject to their jurisdiction. *Sec.* 2.—Congress shall have power to enforce this Article by appropriate legislation." On the 8th of April, this resolution was passed by the requisite majority in the Senate. The strength of Opposition in the House prevented it receiving the requisite majority in that body. We shall find President Lincoln, at the opening of the next session, earnestly urging the adoption of the resolution as a solution of existing difficulties.

The question of State reconstruction, as the States in rebellion might be brought under the National authority, was much discussed in Congress, and the views of the majority in both Houses were finally expressed in the passage of the following bill: *Be it enacted by the Senate and House of Representatives of the United States of America in Congress assembled*, That in the States declared in rebellion against the United States, the President shall, by and with the advice and consent of the Senate, appoint for each a Provisional Governor, whose pay and emoluments shall not exceed that of a Brigadier General of volunteers, who shall be charged with the civil administration of such State until a State Government therein shall be recognized as hereinafter provided. SEC. 2. *And be it further enacted*, That as soon as the military resistance to the United States shall have been suppressed in any such State, and the people thereof shall have sufficiently returned to their obedience to the Constitution and the laws of the United States, the Provisional Governor shall direct the Marshal of the United States, as speedily as may be, to name a sufficient number of deputies, and to enrol all white male citizens of the United States, resident in the State in their respective counties, and to request each one to take the oath to support the Constitution of the United States, and in his enrollment to designate those who take and those who refuse to take that oath, which rolls shall be forthwith returned to the Provisional Governor; and if the persons taking that oath shall amount to a majority of the persons enrolled in the State, he shall, by proclamation, invite the loyal people of the State to elect delegates to a convention charged to declare the will of the people of the State relative to the re-establishment of a State Government, subject to and in conformity with the Constitution of the United States. SEC. 3. *And be it further enacted*, That the Convention shall consist of as many members as both Houses of the last Constitutional State Legislature, apportioned by the Provisional Governor among the counties, parishes, or districts of the State, in proportion to the white population, returned as electors, by the Marshal, in compliance with the provisions of this act. The Provisional Governor shall, by proclamation, declare the number of delegates to be elected by each county, parish, or election district; name a day of election not less than thirty days thereafter; designate the places for voting in each county, parish, or district, conforming as nearly as may be convenient to the places used in the State elections next preceding the rebellion; appoint one or more commissioners to hold the election at each place of voting, and provide an adequate force to keep the peace during the election. SEC. 4. *And be it further enacted*, That the delegates shall be elected by the loyal white male citizens of the United States, of the age of twenty one years, and resident at the time in the county, parish or district in which they shall offer to vote, and enrolled as aforesaid or absent in the military service of the United States, and who shall take and subscribe the oath of allegiance to the United States, in the form contained in the act of Congress of July 2, 1862; and all such citizens of the United States who are in the military service of the United States, shall vote at the head quarters of their respective commands, under such regulations as may be prescribed by the Provisional Governor for the taking and return of their votes; but no person who has held or exercised any office, civil or military, State or Confederate, under the rebel usurpation, or who has voluntarily borne arms against the United States, shall vote or be eligible to be elected as delegate at such election. SEC. 5. *And be it further enacted*, That the said commissioners, or either of them, shall hold the election in conformity with this act, and, so far as may be consistent therewith, shall proceed in the manner used in the State prior to the rebellion. The oath of allegiance shall be taken and subscribed on the poll-book by every voter in the form above prescribed, but every person known by or proved to the commissioners to have held or exercised any office, civil or military, State or Confederate, under the rebel usurpation, or to have voluntarily borne arms against the United States, shall be excluded though he offer to take the oath; and in case any person who shall have borne arms against the United States shall offer to vote he shall be deemed to have borne arms voluntarily unless he shall prove the contrary by the testimony of a qualified voter. The poll-book, showing the name and oath of each voter, shall be returned to the Provisional Governor by the Commissioners of election, or the one acting, and the Provisional Governor shall canvass such returns, and declare the person having the highest number of votes elected. SEC. 6. *And be it further enacted*, That the Provisional Governor shall, by proclamation, convene the delegates elected as aforesaid, at the capital of the State, on a day not more than three months after the election, giving at least thirty days' notice of such day. In case the said capital shall in his judgment be unfit, he shall, in his proclamation, appoint another place. He shall preside over the deliberations of the convention, and administer to each delegate, before taking his seat in the convention, the oath of allegiance to the United States, in the form above prescribed. SEC. 7. *And be it further enacted*, That the convention shall declare, on behalf of the people of the State, their submission to the Constitution and laws of the United States, and shall adopt the following provisions, hereby prescribed by the United States in the execution of the constitutional duty to guarantee a republican form of government to every State. and incorporate

J. E. Johnston

From the original Painting by Nast in the possession of the Publishers.

Johnson, Fry & Co. Publishers, New York.

them in the Constitution of the State, that is to say: *First*—No person who has held or exercised any office, civil or military, except offices ministerial, and military offices below the grade of Colonel, State or Confederate, under the usurping power, shall vote for or be a member of the Legislature or Governor. *Second*—Involuntary servitude is forever prohibited, and the freedom of all persons is guaranteed in said State. *Third*—No debt, State or Confederate, created by or under the sanction of the usurping power, shall be recognized or paid by the State. Sec. 8. *And be it further enacted*, That when the convention shall have adopted those provisions, it shall proceed to re-establish a republican form of government, and ordain a constitution containing those provisions, which, when adopted, the convention shall by ordinance provide for submitting to the people of the State entitled to vote under this law, at an election to be held in the manner prescribed by the act for the election of delegates; but at a time and place named by the convention, at which election the said electors, and none others, shall vote directly for or against such a constitution and form of State government, and the return of said election shall be made to the Provisional Governor, who shall canvass the same in the presence of the electors, and if a majority of the votes cast shall be for the Constitution and form of government, he shall certify the same, with a copy thereof, to the President of the United States, who, after obtaining the assent of Congress, shall, by proclamation, recognise the Government established, and none other, as the constitutional Government of the State; and from the date of such recognition, and not before, Senators and House of Representatives and electors for President and Vice President may be elected in such State, according to the laws of the United States. Sec. 9. *And be it further enacted*, That if the convention shall refuse to re-establish the State Government on the conditions aforesaid, the Provisional Governor shall declare it dissolved; but it shall be the duty of the President, whenever he shall have reason to believe that when a sufficient number of the people of the State, entitled to vote under this act, in number not less than a majority of those enrolled as aforesaid, are willing to re-establish a State Government on the conditions aforesaid, to direct the Provisional Governor to order another election of delegates to a convention for the purpose and in the manner prescribed in this act, and to proceed in all respects as heretofore provided, either to dissolve the convention, or to certify the State Government re-established by it to the President. Sec. 10. *And be it further enacted*, That, until the United States shall have recognized a Republican form of State Government, the Provisional Governor in each of said States shall see that this act, and the laws of the United States, and the laws of the State in force when the State Government was overthrown by the rebellion, are faithfully executed within the State; but no law or usage whereby any person was heretofore held in solitary servitude shall be recognized or enforced by any court or officer in such State, and the laws for the trial and punishment of white persons shall extend to all persons, and jurors shall have the qualification of voters under the law for delegates to this convention. The President shall appoint such officers provided for by the laws of the State when its Government was overthrown, as he may find necessary to the civil administration of the State, all which officers shall be entitled to receive the fees and emoluments provided by the State law for such officers. Sec. 11. *And be it further enacted*, That until the recognition of a State Government as aforesaid, the Provisional Governor shall, under such regulations as he may prescribe, cause to be assessed, levied and collected, for the year 1864, and every year thereafter, the taxes provided by the laws of such State to be levied during the fiscal year preceding the overthrow of the State Government thereof, in the manner prescribed by the laws of the State as nearly as may be; and the officers appointed as aforesaid are vested with all the powers of levying and collecting such taxes, by distress or sale, as were vested in any officers or tribunal of the State Government aforesaid for those purposes. The proceeds of such taxes shall be accounted for to the Provisional Governor, and by him applied to the expenses of the administration of the laws in such State, subject to the direction of the President, and the surplus shall be deposited in the Treasury of the United States to the credit of such State, to be paid to the State upon an appropriation therefor, to be made when a republican form of government shall be recognized therein by the United States. Sec. 12. *And be it further enacted*, That all persons held to involuntary servitude or labor in the States aforesaid are hereby emancipated and discharged therefrom, and they and their posterity shall be forever free. And if any such persons or their posterity shall be restrained of liberty, under pretence of any claim to such service or labor, the courts of the United States shall, on habeas corpus, discharge them. Sec. 13. *And be it further enacted*, That if any person declared free by this act, or any law of the United States, or any proclamation of the President, be restrained from liberty, with intent to be held in or reduced to involuntary servitude or labor, the person convicted before a court of competent jurisdiction of such act shall be punished by a fine of not less than fifteen hundred dollars, and be imprisoned not less than five nor more than twenty years. Sec. 14. *And be it further enacted*, That every person who shall hereafter hold or exercise any office, civil or military, except offices merely ministerial, and military offices below the grade of Colonel, in the rebel service, State or Confederate, is hereby declared not to be a citizen of the United States."

The bill thus passed did not receive the signature of the President, but a few days after the adjournment on the 8th of July, he issued a Proclamation in reference to his conduct in the matter:—" *Whereas*, At the late session, Congress passed a bill to guarantee to certain States whose Governments have been usurped or overthrown, a republican form of government, a copy of which is hereunto annexed, and *Whereas*, The said bill was presented to the President of the United States, for his approval, less than one hour before the *sine die* adjournment of said session, and was not signed by him, and *Whereas*, The said bill contains, among other things, a plan for restoring the States in rebellion to their proper practical relation in the Union, which plan expressed the sense of Congress upon that subject, and which plan it is now thought fit to lay before the people for their consideration, now, therefore, I, Abraham Lincoln, President of the United States, do proclaim, declare and make known that while I am (as I was in December last, when, by proclamation, I propounded a plan for restoration) unprepared by a formal approval of this bill to be inflexibly committed to any single plan of restoration; and, while I am also unprepared to declare that the Free State Constitutions and Governments already adopted and installed in Arkansas and Louisiana, shall be set aside and held for nought, thereby repelling and discouraging the loyal citizens who have set up the same as to further effort, or to declare a constitutional competency in Congress to abolish Slavery in the States, but am, at the same time, sincerely hoping and expecting that a Constitutional amendment abolishing Slavery throughout the nation may be adopted; nevertheless I am fully satisfied with the system for restoration contained in the bill as one very proper plan for the loyal people of any State choosing to adopt it, and that I am, and at all times shall be, prepared to give the Executive aid and assistance to any such people, so soon as the military resistance to the United States shall have been suppressed in any such State, and the people thereof shall have sufficiently returned to their obedience to the Constitution and the laws of the United States, in which cases Military Governors will be appointed, with directions to proceed according to the bill."

By previous Proclamation, dated, March 20th, President Lincoln had defined the cases in which "insurgent enemies" were entitled to the benefits of his Amnesty Proclamation of the 8th of December, 1863. The latter, he said, had been issued solely with the object "to suppress the insurrection, and restore the authority of the United States." He therefore declared, "that the said Proclamation does not apply to cases of persons who, at the time they seek to obtain the benefit thereof by taking the oath thereby prescribed, are in military, naval or civil confinement or custody, or under bonds or on parole of the civil, military or naval authorities, or agents of the United States, as prisoners of war, or persons detained for offences of any kind, either before or after conviction; and that, on the contrary, it does apply to those persons who, being yet at large and free from any arrest. confinement or duress, shall voluntarily come forward and take the said oath with the purpose of restoring Peace and establishing the National authority. Persons excluded from the amnesty offered in the Proclamation, may apply to the President for clemency like all other offenders, and their application will receive due consideration."

A few days previous to its adjournment, Congress adopted the resolution "That the President of the United States be requested to appoint a day for humiliation and prayer by the people of the United States; that he request his constitutional advisers at the head of the Executive Department to unite with him as Chief Magistrate of the nation, at the City of Washington, and the members of Congress, and all magistrates, all civil, military, and naval officers, all soldiers, sailors and marines, with all loyal and law-abiding people, to convene at their usual places of worship, or wherever they may be, to confess and to repent of their manifold sins; to implore the compassion and forgiveness of the Almighty, that, if consistent with His will, the existing rebellion may be speedily supressed, and the Supremacy of the Constitution and laws of the United States may be established throughout the United States; to implore Him, as the Supreme Ruler of the World, not to destroy us as a people, nor suffer us to be destroyed by the hostility or connivance of other nations, or by obstinate adhesion to our own counsels, which may be in conflict with his eternal purposes, and to implore Him to enlighten the mind of the nation to know and do His will, humbly believing that it is in accordance with His will that our place should be maintained as a united people among the family of nations; to implore Him to grant to our armed defenders and the masses of the people that courage, power of resistance and endurance, necessary to secure that result; to implore Him in His infinite goodness to soften the hearts, enlighten the minds, and quicken the consciences of those in rebellion, that they may lay down their arms and speedily return to their allegiance to the United States, that they may not be utterly destroyed, that the effusion of blood may be stayed, and that unity and fraternity may be restored, and peace established throughout all our borders." In accordance with this resolution the President, on the 7th of July, issued a Proclamation appointing the first Thursday of August to be observed as "a day of National humiliation and prayer."

There were several calls by President Lincoln during the year, for recruiting or enlarging the army. On the 1st of February he issued an order, "that a draft for 500,000 men to serve for three years, or during the war, be made on the 10th day of March next, for the military service of the United States, crediting and deducting therefrom so many as may have been enlisted or drafted into the service prior to the first day of March, and not heretofore credited." This order was understood to supplement and supply the deficiencies under the call of the previous order for 300,000 men, only about half of whom had been secured for the service.

In April, with a view to the exigencies of the coming campaign, President Lincoln accepted the offer of the Governors of the North-western States to furnish 80,000 militia, to be regularly mustered into the service, and relieve veteran regiments in post and garrison duty. These troops were presently brought into the field, and when their term had expired, the President returned them thanks in the following order, dated October 1. "The term of one hundred days for which volunteers from the States of Indiana, Illinois, Iowa and Wisconsin, volunteered under the call of their respective Governors in the months of May and June, to aid the recent campaign of General Sherman, having expired, the President directs an official acknowledgment to be made of their patriotic service. It was their good fortune to render effective service in the brilliant operations in the Southwest, and to contribute to the victories of the national arms over the rebel forces in Georgia under command of Johnson and Hood. On all occasions, and in every service to which they were assigned, their duty as patriotic volunteers was performed with alacrity and courage, for which they are entitled to, and are hereby tendered, the National thanks, through the Governors of their respective States. The Secretary of War is directed to transmit a copy of this order to the Governors of Indiana, Illinois, Iowa and Wisconsin, and to cause a certificate of their honorable services to be delivered to officers and soldiers of the States above named, who recently served in the military force of the United States as volunteers for one hundred days."

Another call was made by the President on the 18th of July, in accordance with the recent act of Congress, passed at the close of the session. In this Proclamation he called "for 500,000 volunteers for the military service; provided, nevertheless, that this call shall be reduced by all credits which may be established under section eight of the aforesaid act, on account of persons who have entered the Naval service during the present rebellion, and by credits for men furnished to the military service in excess of calls heretofore made." He further gave notice that volunteers would be accepted under this call for one, two, or three years, as they may elect, and that according to the directions of the Act, immediately after the 5th day of September, being fifty days from the date of the call, a draft for troops to serve for one year would be made in every district where the quota had failed to be supplied. This notice had the usual effect of stimulating individuals and local corporations, to secure enlistments by extraordinary bounties, and so much was accomplished that the Secretary of War, on the 2nd of September, was evoked in an official bulletin, simultaneously with the announcement of the entrance of General Sherman's advance into Atlanta, to state, "It is ascertained with reasonable certainty that the Naval and other credits required by the Act of Congress will amount to about 200,000, including New York, which has not been reported yet to the Department; so that the President's call of July 10th is practically reduced to 300,000 men to meet and take the place of, *First*—The new enlistments in the navy; *Second*—The casualties of battle, sickness, prisoners and desertion; and, *Third*—The hundred days' troops, and all others going out by expiration of service this Fall. One hundred thousand new troops promptly furnished are all that General Grant asks for the capture of Richmond, and to give a finishing blow to the rebel armies yet in the field. The residue of the call would be adequate for garrisons in forts, and to guard all the lines of communication and supply, free the country from guerrillas, give security to trade, protect commerce and travel, and establish peace, order and tranquility in every State."

The draft, to supply the deficiencies of the quota was finally ordered by the Secretary of War to proceed on the 19th of September. This announcement was supported by the following telegraphic communications from Generals Grant and Sherman. The former wrote from City Point on the 13th to Secretary Stanton: "We ought to have the whole number of men called for by the President in the shortest possible time. Prompt action in filling our armies will have more effect upon the enemy than a victory over them. They profess to believe, and make their men believe, there is such a party North in favor of recognizing Southern independence, that the draft cannot be enforced. Let them be undeceived. Deserters come into our lines daily, who tell us that the men are nearly universally tired of the war, and that the desertions would be more frequent, but they believe peace will be negotiated after the Fall election. The enforcement of the draft and prompt filling up of our armies will save the shedding of blood to an immense degree." General Sherman's communication dated Atlanta, Ga., the same day said: "I am very glad to hear that the draft will be enforced. First, we need the men; second, they come as privates to fill up our old and tried regiments, with their experienced officers already on hand; and third, because the enforcement of the law will manifest a power resident in our Government equal to the occasion. Our Government, though a Democracy, should in times of trouble and danger be able to wield the power of a great nation. All well." These appeals stimulated enlistments; but, in consequence of the credits allowed and other causes, including, in the words of President Lincoln, "the operations of the enemy in certain States, rendering it impracticable to procure from them their full quotas," only half the number of men called for in July were actually obtained. The President was therefore obliged in December to call for an additional number of troops. On the 19th of that month he issued a Proclamation, in accordance with the late act of Congress calling for 300,000 volunteers to serve for one, two or three years. If the call should not be complied with by the 15th of February, 1865, a draft was ordered to supply any deficiency at that time.

The most important of the civil events of the year was the Presidential Election in November. The nominations, in consequence of the peculiar state of the country, the leading parties eagerly watching the progress of affairs to determine upon a policy suited to the times, were delayed to an unusually late period; so that when their action was finally determined upon, the political contest was narrowed to a comparatively short time and the appeal to the people was made on sufficiently definite principles. The first convention for the nomination of candidates was held at Cleveland, Ohio, on the 31st of May. Some 350 delegates were in attendance from fifteen States. General John Cochrane of New York presided. Resolutions were adopted asserting that "the Constitution and Laws of the United States must be maintained," that "rights of free speech, free press and the Habeas Corpus be held inviolate, save in districts where martial law has been proclaimed;" that "the rebellion has destroyed Slavery and the Federal Constitution should be amended to prohibit its re-establishment and to secure to all men absolute equality before the law; that "the national policy known as 'The Monroe Doctrine' has become a recognized principle, and that the establishment of an Anti-republican Government on this continent by any foreign Power cannot be tolerated." It was urged that "the one term policy for the Presidency adopted by the people is strengthened by the force of the existing crisis and should be maintained by Constitutional amendments; and "that the Constitution should be so amended that the President and Vice-President shall be elected by a direct vote of the people." The question of "the reconstruction of the rebellious States" was pronounced to "belong to the people through their representatives in Congress and not to the Executive," and it was declared "that the confiscation of the lands of the rebels and their distribution among the soldiers and actual settlers, is a measure of justice." Having passed these, among other resolutions, the Convention nominated Major General John C. Fremont for President of the United States, and General John Cochrane for Vice-President. General Fremont having resigned his rank in the regular army accepted the nomination. In his letter of acceptance dated New York, June 4th, in reply to the letter of the nominating committee of the Convention, in which he was styled "the standard-bearer of the Radical Democracy of the country," General Fremont expressed himself strongly in hostility to the policy of President Lincoln. "Had Mr. Lincoln," said he, "remained faithful to the principles he was elected to defend, no schism could have been created and no contest could have been possible. This is not an ordinary election, it is a contest for the right even to have candidates and not merely as usual for the choice among them. Now, for the first time since '76, the question of constitutional liberty has been brought directly before the people for their serious consideration and vote. The ordinary rights secured under the Constitution and the laws of the country have been violated, and extraordinary powers have been usurped by the Executive. It is directly before the people now to say whether or not the principles established by the Revolution are worth maintaining." "Of the Cleveland Convention," he said, "the principles which form the basis of its platform have my unqualified and cordial approbation, but I cannot so heartily concur in all the measures which you propose. I do not believe that confiscation extended to the property of all rebels, is practicable, and, if it were so, I don't think it a measure of sound policy. It is a question belonging to the people themselves to decide, and is a proper occasion for the exercise of their original and sovereign authority. As a war measure, in the beginning of a revolt, which might be quelled by prompt severity, I understand the policy of confiscation; but not as a final measure of reconstruction after the suppression of an insurrection. In the adjustments which are to follow peace, no considerations of vengeance can consistently be admitted. The object of the war is to make permanently secure the peace and happiness of the whole country, and there was but a single element in the way of its attainment. This element of Slavery may be considered practically destroyed in the country, and it needs only your proposed amendment of the Constitution to make its extinction complete." If the Republican Convention, about to meet at Baltimore, he said, "will nominate any man whose past life justifies a well-grounded confidence in his fidelity to our cardinal principles, there is no reason why there should be any division among the really patriotic men of the country. To any such I shall be most happy to give a cordial and active support. My own decided preference is to aid in this way, and not to be myself a candidate. But if Mr. Lincoln should be renominated, as I believe it would be fatal to the country to indorse a policy and renew a power which has cost us the lives of thousands of men, and needlessly put the country on the road to bankruptcy there will remain no alternative but to organize against him every element of conscientious opposition with the view to prevent the misfortune of his re-election." "As a preliminary step," he added, "I have resigned my commission in the army. This was a sacrifice it gave me pain to make. But I had for a long time fruitlessly endeavored to obtain service. I make this sacrifice only to regain liberty of speech, and to leave nothing in the way of discharging to my utmost ability the task you have set for me."

The Republican party next held its Convention at Baltimore, on the 7th of June. It was called "The National Union Convention." Ex-Governor Denison of Ohio, was elected President of the Convention. The Hon. Henry J. Raymond of New York, chairman of the Committee on Resolutions, reported the following which were adopted as the platform of the party: "*Resolved*, That it is the highest duty of every American citizen to maintain against all their enemies the integrity of the Union and the paramount authority of the Constitution and laws of the United States; and that, laying aside all differences and political opinions, we pledge ourselves as Union men, animated by a common sentiment, and aiming at a common object, to do everything in our power to aid the Government in quelling by force of arms the rebellion now raging against its authority, and in bringing to the punishment due to their crimes the rebels and traitors arrayed against it. *Resolved*, That we approve the determination of the Government of the United States not to compromise with rebels, or to offer any terms of peace except such as may be based upon an 'unconditional surrender' of their hostility and a return of their just allegiance to the Constitution and laws of the United States; and that we call upon the Government to maintain this position and to prosecute the war with the utmost possible rigor to the complete suppression of the rebellion, in full reliance upon the self-sacrifices, the patriotism, the heroic valor and the undying devotion of the American people to their country and its free institutions. *Resolved*, That as Slavery was the cause and now constitutes the strength of this rebellion, and as it must be always and everywhere hostile to the principles of Republican Government, justice and the national safety demand its utter and complete extirpation from the soil of the Republic [applause], and that we uphold and maintain the acts and proclamations by which the Government, in its own defence, has aimed a death-blow at this gigantic evil. We are in favor, furthermore, of such an amendment to the Constitution, to be made by the people in conformity with its provisions, shall terminate and forever prohibit the existence of Slavery within the limits or the jurisdiction of the United States. *Resolved*, That the thanks of the American people are due to the soldiers and sailors of the army and navy [applause] who have periled their lives in defence of their country, and in vindication of the honor of the Flag; that the nation owes to them some permanent recognition of their patriotism and their valor, and ample and permanent provision for those of their survivors who have received disabling and honorable wounds in the service of the country; and that the memories of those who have fallen in its defence shall be held in grateful and everlasting remembrance. *Resolved*, That we approve and applaud the practical wisdom, the unselfish patriotism and unswerving fidelity to the Constitution and the principles of American liberty with which Abraham Lincoln has discharged, under circumstances of unparalleled difficulty, the great duties and responsibilities of the Presidential office; that we approve and indorse, as demanded by the emergency and essential to the preservation of the nation, and as within the Constitution, the measures and acts which he has adopted to defend the nation against its open and secret foes; that we approve especially the Proclamation of Emancipation, and the employment as Union soldiers of men heretofore held in Slavery [applause]; and that we have full confidence in his determination to carry these and all other constitutional measures essential to the salvation of the country into full and complete effect. *Resolved*, That we deem it essential to the general welfare that harmony should prevail in the National councils, and we regard as worthy of public confidence and official trust those only who cordially indorse the principles proclaimed in these resolutions, and which should characterize the administration of the Government. *Resolved*, That the Government owes to all men employed in its armies, without regard to distinction of color, the full protection of the laws of war [applause], and that any violations of these laws or of the usages of civilized nations in the time of war by the rebels now in arms should be made the subject of full and prompt redress. *Resolved*, That the foreign immigration which in the past has added so much to the wealth and development of resources and increase and power to this nation, the asylum of the oppressed of all nations, should be fostered and encouraged by a liberal and just policy. *Resolved*, That we are in favor of the speedy construction of the railroad to the Pacific. *Resolved*, That the national faith pledged for the redemption of the public debt must be kept inviolate, and that for this purpose we recommend economy and rigid responsibility in the public expenditures, and a vigorous and just system of taxation; that it is the duty of any loyal State to sustain the credit and promote the use of the national currency. *Resolved*, That we approve the position taken by the Government that the people of the United States can never regard with indifference the attempt of any European Power to overthrow by force or to supplant by fraud the institutions of any Republican government on the Western Continent [prolonged applause], and that they will view with extreme jealousy, as menacing to the peace and independence of this our country, the efforts of any such Power to obtain new footholds for monarchial governments, sustained by a foreign military force in near proximity to the United States."

On ballotting for a candidate for President, Mr. Lincoln received 497 votes, cast by the delegates of the several States and Territories, represented as follows:—Maine, 14; New Hampshire, 10; Vermont, 10; Massachusetts, 24; Rhode Island, 8; Connecticut, 12; New York, 68; New Jersey, 14; Pennsylvania, 52; Delaware, 6; Maryland, 14; Louisiana, 14; Arkansas, 10: Tennessee, 15; Kentucky, 22; Ohio, 42; Indiana, 26; Illinois, 32; Michigan, 16; Wisconsin, 16; Iowa, 16; Minnesota, 8; California, 10; Oregon, 6; West Virginia, 10; Kansas, 6; Nebraska, 6; Colorado, 6; Nevada, 6;—twenty-two votes by the Missouri delegates were cast for General Grant. The nomination was then made unanimous. Andrew Johnson, the Military Governor of Tennessee was chosen candidate for Vice-President.

President Lincoln, in a letter dated at the Executive Mansion June 27, thus simply and briefly signified to the committee appointed to confer with him, his acceptance of the nomination:—"The nomination is gratefully accepted, as the Resolutions of the Convention—called the platform—are heartily approved. While the resolution in regard to the supplanting of Republican Government upon the Western Continent is fully concurred in, there might be misunderstanding were I not to say that the position of the Government in relation to the action of France in Mexico, as assumed through the State Department and indorsed by the Convention, among the measures and acts of the Executive, will be faithfully maintained so long as the state of facts shall leave that position pertinent and applicable. I am especially gratified that the soldier and the seaman were not forgotten by the Convention, as they forever must and will be remembered by the grateful country for whose salvation they devote their lives."

It now remained for the Democratic Party to nominate their candidate. Anxiously studying the course of events, the meeting of the Convention was deferred by the leaders to the latest moment. It was not till the 29th of August that this "National Democratic Convention" met at Chicago. Delegates were present from twenty-three States. Mr. August Belmont, a banker of New York city, called the Convention to order, and Governor Horatio Seymour of New York was chosen its Chairman. On taking his seat he denounced the cause of the Administration. "The Democratic party," said he, "will restore the Union because it longs for its restoration; it will bring peace because it loves peace; it will bring back liberty to our land because it loves liberty; it will put down despotism because it hates the ignoble tyranny which now degrades the American people. Four years ago a Convention met in this city, when your country was peaceful, prosperous and united. Its delegates did not mean to destroy our Government, to overwhelm us with debt, or to drench our land with blood; but they were animated by intolerance and fanaticism, and blinded by an ignorance of the spirit of our Institutions, the character of our people, and the condition of our land. They thought they might safely indulge their passions and they concluded to do so. They would not heed the warnings of our fathers, and they did not consider that meddling begets strife. Their passions have wrought out their natural results. They were impelled to spurn all measures of compromise. Step by step they have marched on to results which, on the onset, they would have shrunk with horror from; and even now when war has desolated our land, has laid its heavy burdens upon labor, and when bankruptcy and ruin overhang us, they will not have the Union restored except upon conditions unknown to our Constitution. They will not let the shedding of blood cease, even for a little time, to see if Christian charity or the wisdom of statesmanship may not work out a method to save our country. Nay, more than this, they will not listen to a proposal for peace which does not offer that which this Government has no right to ask. This administration cannot now restore this Union if it would. It has, by its proclamations, by vindictive legislation, and by displays of hate and passion, placed obstacles in its own pathway which it cannot overcome. It has hampered its own freedom of action by unconstitutional ties." This discourse represented the temper of the Convention. It was largely composed of the opponents of the war. Vallandigham of Ohio, late an exile, was one of its members. Its views were definitely expressed in the following resolutions, reported by Mr. Guthrie of Kentucky: "*Resolved*, That in the future as in the past, we will adhere with unswerving fidelity to the Union, under the Constitution, as the only solid foundation of our strength, security and happiness as a people, and as a framework of government, equally conducive to the welfare and prosperity of all the States, both Northern and Southern. *Resolved*, That this Convention does explicitly declare, as the sense of the American people, that after four years of failure to restore the Union by the experiment of war during which, under the pretense of a military necessity, or war power higher than the Constitution, the Constitution itself has been disregarded in every part, and public liberty and private right alike trodden down, and the material prosperity of the country essentially impaired, justice, humanity, liberty and the public welfare demand that immediate efforts be made for a cessation of hostilities, with a view to an ultimate Convention of all the States, or other peaceable means, to the end that at the earliest practicable moment peace may be restored on the basis of the Federal Union of the States. *Resolved*, That the direct interference of the military authority of the United States in the recent elections held in Kentucky Maryland, Missouri and Delaware, was a shameful violation of the Constitution, and a repetition of such acts in the approaching election will be held as revolutionary, and resisted with all the means and power under our control. *Resolved*, That the aim and object of the Democratic party is to preserve the Federal Union and the rights of the States unimpaired, and they hereby declare that they consider the Administrative usurpation of extraordinary and dangerous powers not granted by the Constitution, the subversion of the civil by military law in States not in insurrection, the arbitrary military arrest, imprisonment, trial and sentence of American citizens in States where civil law exists in full force, the suppression of freedom of speech and of the press, the denial of the right of asylum, the open and avowed disregard of States rights, the employment of unusual test oaths, and the interference with and denial of the right of the people to bear arms, as calculated to prevent a restoration of the Union, and the perpetuation of a Government deriving its just powers from the consent of the governed. *Resolved*, That the shameful disregard of the Administration to its duty in respect to our fellow-citizens, who now and long have been prisoners of war in a suffering condition, deserves the severest reprobation on the score alike of public and common humanity. *Resolved*, That the sympathy of the Democratic party is heartily and earnestly extended to the soldiery of our army, who are and have been in the field under the flag of our country, and in the event of our attaining power, they will receive all the care, protection, regard and kindness that the brave soldiers of the Republic have so nobly earned."

There were several prominent candidates before the Convention. Major General McClellan, Ex. Governor Thomas W. Seymour of Connecticut, Governor Seymour of New York, Lazarus W. Powell of Kentucky. General McClellan was evidently regarded as the available candidate, but his nomination was opposed by the ultra opponents of the war. When the ballot was taken he received 162 votes, sixty-four being cast for other candidates, among whom Seymour of Connecticut, was prominent. The nomination of McClellan, on motion of Vallandigham was finally made unanimous. George H. Pendleton of Ohio, was nominated for the Vice Presidency. The Convention then adjourned. The peace policy of its Resolutions was, a few days after, blown to the winds by the intelligence of the victory of General Sherman, in the conquest of Atlanta. Without this, it is probable the result would not have been greatly different. The nation was pledged to the war, and the members of the Convention had overrated the dissatisfaction of the people at its continuance and the policy of the Administration.

General McClellan, as a soldier of the war, felt this shock of opinions, and qualified his reply to the nomination of the Convention with discriminating policy. His letter of acceptance addressed to the Committee was dated Orange, N. J., September 8, and read as follows: *Gentlemen:* I have the honor to acknowledge the receipt of your letter, informing me of my nomination by the Democratic National Convention, recently assembled at Chicago, as their candidate at the next election for President of the United States. It is unnecessary for me to say to you that this nomination comes to me unsought. I am happy to know that when the nomination was made, the record of my public life was kept in view. The effect of long and varied service in the army, during war and peace, has been to strengthen and make indelible in my mind and heart, the love and reverence for the Union, Constitution, laws and flag of our country, impressed upon me in early youth. These feelings have thus far guided the course of my life, and must continue to do so to its end. The existence of more than one Government over the region which once owned our flag is incompatible with the peace, the power and the happiness of the people. The preservation of our Union was the sole avowed object for which the war was commenced. It should have been conducted for that object only, and in accordance with those principles which I took occasion to declare when in active service. Thus conducted, the work of reconciliation would have been easy, and we might have reaped the benefits of our many victories on land and sea. The Union was originally formed by the exercise of a spirit of conciliation and compromise. To restore and preserve it, the same spirit must prevail in our councils and in the hearts of the people. The reëstablishment of the Union in all its integrity, is, and must continue to be, the indipensable condition in any settlement. So soon as it is clear or even probable, that our present adversaries are ready for peace, upon the basis of the Union, we should exhaust all the resources of statesmanship practised by civilized nations, and taught by the traditions of the American people, consistent with the honor and interests of the country to secure such peace, reestablish the Union and guarantee for the future the Constitutional rights of every State. The Union is the one condition of peace—we ask no more. Let me add what I doubt not was, although unexpressed, the sentiment of the Convention, as it is of the people they represent, that when any one State is willing to return to the Union, it should be received at once, with a full guarantee of all its Constitutional rights. If a frank, earnest and persistent effort to obtain those objects should fail, the responsibility for ulterior consequences will fall upon those who remain in arms against the Union. But the Union must be preserved at all hazards. I could not look in the face my gallant comrades of the Army and Navy, who have survived so many bloody battles, and tell them that their labors and the sacrifices of so many of our slain and wounded brethren had been in vain; that we had abandoned that Union for which we have so often periled our lives. A vast majority of our people, whether in the Army and Navy or at home, would, as I would, hail with unbounded joy the permanent restoration of peace, on the basis of the Union under the Constitution, without the effusion of another drop of blood. But no peace can be permanent without Union. As to the other subjects presented in the Resolutions of the Convention, I need only say that I should seek, in the Constitution of the United States and the laws framed in accordance therewith, the rule of my duty, and the limitations of Executive power; endeavor to restore economy in public expenditure, reëstablish the supremacy of law, and by the operation of a more vigorous nationality, resume our commanding position among the nations of the earth. The condition of our finances, the depreciation of the paper money, and the burdens thereby imposed on labor and capital, show the necessity of a return to a sound financial system; while the rights of citizens and the rights of States, and the binding authority of law over President, Army and People, are subjects of not less vital importance in war than in peace. Believing that the views here expressed are those of the Convention and the people you represent, I accept the nomination. I realize the weight of the responsibility to be borne should the people ratify your choice. Conscious of my own weakness, I can only seek fervently the guidance of the Ruler of the Universe, and relying on His all-powerful aid, do my best to restore Union and Peace to a suffering people, and to establish and guard their liberties and rights."

The action of the Chicago Convention and the nomination of General McClellan, was presently followed by the withdrawal of General Fremont from the canvass. In a letter dated Boston, September 21st, he thus expresses his reasons for this course. "The Presidential question," said he, "has in effect been entered upon in such a way that the union of the Republican party has become a paramount necessity. The policy of the Democratic party signifies either separation, or reëstablishment with Slavery. The Chicago platform is simply separation. General McClellan's letter of acceptance is reëstablishment with Slavery. The Republican candidate on the contrary is pledged to the reëstablishment of the Union without Slavery: and, however hesitating his policy may be, the pressure of his party will, we may hope, force him to it. Between these issues, I think, no man of the Liberal party can remain in doubt; and I believe I am consistent with my antecedents in withdrawing, not to aid in the triumphs of Mr. Lincoln, but to do my part toward preventing the election of the Democratic candidate. In respect to Mr. Lincoln, I continue to hold exactly the sentiments contained in my letter of acceptance. I consider that his Administration has been politically, militarily, and financially, a failure, and that its necessary continuance is a cause of regret for the country. There never was a greater unanimity in a country than was exhibited here at the fall of Sumter, and the South was powerless in the face of it. But Mr. Lincoln completely paralyzed this generous feeling. He destroyed the strength of the position and divided the North when he declared to the South that Slavery should be protected. He has built up for the South a strength which otherwise they could have never attained; and this has given them an advocate on the Chicago platform. The Cleveland Convention was to have been the open avowal of that condemnation which men had been freely expressing to each other for the past two years, and which had been made fully known to the President. But in the uncertain condition of affairs leading men were not found willing to make public a dissatisfaction and condemnation which could have rendered Mr. Lincoln's nomination impossible; and their continued silence and support established for him a character among the people which leaves now no choice. United, the Republican party is reasonably sure of success; divided, the result of the Presidential election is, at the least, doubtful." General Cochrane, the nominee for the Vice Presidency, also withdrew, and the slender organization of the "Radical Democracy" was virtually disbanded. There were some mutterings from the ultra Peace Democrats at the letter of McClellan, but for all practical purposes the contest now lay between the Republican and Democratic parties. Lincoln and McClellan were the only candidates in the field.

It was felt from the beginning of the active canvass that the movements of the Democratic party were much impeded by the terms of the Platform adopted in their Convention at Chicago. These Resolutions were strongly burthened with the views of the ultra Peace party and their hostility to the war. Their attacks upon the Government were felt to be virtually in the interests of the Rebellion. Several circumstances combined to render the policy to which the party had committed itself at Chicago peculiarly unpopular. It had generally to contend with the interests of a war in progress which the honor of the nation was concerned to bring to a satisfactory conclusion; and that conclusion could be no other in the judgment of the country than the full restoration of the Union with its present power and authority. To interrupt this war by untimely negotiations or concessions of an armistice was, for obvious reasons, to peril the result. This radical defect in the Platform was perceived at once by many of the shrewd leaders of the party and was virtually acknowledged in the letter of their candidate, General McClellan. It led previous to the election to a considerable defection from the party by "War Democrats" as they were termed, who rejected a policy injurious, as they thought, to the interests of the nation. It so happened too, as we have seen, that the successes of General Grant and especially of General Sherman in Georgia, came opportunely to give a practical effect to the theory of the war and thus greatly strengthen the Administration. The discovery of an organized conspiracy in the Western and Northwestern States, the details of which with particulars of its league of affiliated societies, bent in various ways in giving aid to the enemy by private assistance and if opportunity serves, by open rebellion were laid before the public in an official exposure by Judge-Advocate-General Holt, did much to neutralize that opposition to the Government in the West from which the Democratic leaders, at one time, expected the greatest aid at the election. It was one of the items of their indictment of the Republicans in the Chicago Resolutions, that "the people had been interfered with and denied their right to bear arms." When it was found, by the confession of the Conspirators, for what purpose the arms were being collected, the action of the Government in the arrests and seizures complained of in Indiana and elsewhere was fully vindicated, and the revelation nowhere told with greater effect than in these very Western States, as was evidenced in Indiana particularly. The early autumnal State elections foreshadowed the success of the Republican party in November. Vermont, Maine, Pennsylvania, Ohio, and Indiana, closely contested, elected Republican Governors or added to the ranks of the Republican members in Congress. In Indiana where the Democratic expectations were strongest, the Republican Governor Morton was reëlected by an overwhelming majority. The reëlection of Abraham Lincoln was rendered almost a matter of certainty.

He was ably supported in the canvass by the eloquence and arguments of many distinguished officers of the army and statesmen of reputation. The proposition, under existing circumstances, for "a cessation of hostilities," could not, indeed, be expected to find much favor with soldiers in the field. Leaders like Grant and Sherman supported the Administration. General Butler, General Banks, General Burnside and others defended it before the people. The Veteran General Wool denounced the opposition with characteristic vigor. Major-General John A. Dix, a leader of the "War Democrats," gave to the Government a steady support. "In calling," said he, in a letter addressed in October to a political gathering at Philadelphia, "for a cessation of hostilities the members of the Chicago Convention have, in my judgment, totally misrepresented the feelings and opinions of the great body of the Democracy. The policy produced in its name makes it—so far as such a declaration can—what it has never been before, a Peace party, degrading it from the eminence on which it has stood in every other national conflict. In this injustice to the country, and to a great party identified with all that is honorable in our history, I can have no part. I can only mourn over the reproach which has been brought upon it by its leaders, and cherish the hope that it may hereafter, under the auspices of better counsellors, resume its ancient effective and beneficent influence in the administration of the Government."

Two striking speeches were delivered by Mr. Seward, the Secretary of State, during the canvass on his visits to his home at Auburn, New York, in September, and again on the eve of the election in November. In the former, after reviewing the military and political situations, he thus noticed what had been the main difficulty of the war. "The chief complaint against the President," said he, "is that he will not accept peace on the basis of the integrity of the Union, without having also the abandonment of Slavery. When and where have the insurgents offered him peace on the basis of the integrity of the Union? Nobody has offered it. The rebels never will offer it. They are determined and pledged to rule this Republic or ruin it. I told you here a year ago, that practically Slavery was no longer in question—that it was perishing under the operation of the war. That assertion has been confirmed. The Union men in all the Slave States that we have delivered are even more anxious than we are to abolish Slavery. Witness Western Virginia, Maryland, Missouri, Louisiana, Tennessee, and Arkansas. Jefferson Davis tells you in effect, the same thing. He says that it is not Slavery, but Independence and Sovereignty, for which he is contending. There is good reason for this. A hundred dollars in gold is only a year's purchase of the labor of the working man in every part of the United States. At less than half that price you could buy all the slaves in the country. Nevertheless, our opponents want a distinct exposition of the President's views on the ultimate solution of the Slavery question. Why do they want it? For the same reason that the Pharisees and Sadducees wanted an authoritative resolution of the questions of casuistry which arose in their day. One of those sects believed in a Kingdom to come, and the other denied the resurrection of the dead. Nevertheless, they walked together in loving accord in search of instruction concerning the spirit-world. 'Master,' said they, 'there was a man of our nation who married a wife and died, leaving six brothers. These brothers successively married the widowed woman, and afterward died. And last of all the woman died also. In the resurrection which of the seven shall have this woman to wife.' Now what was it to them whether one or all should have the woman to wife in Heaven? It could be nothing to the Sadducees in any case. What was it to any human being on this side of the grave? What was it to any human being in Heaven except the woman and her seven husbands—absolutely nothing. Yet they would have an answer. And they received one. The answer was that while in this mortal state, men and women shall never cease to marry and to die, there will be in the resurrection neither death nor marrying nor giving in marriage. Although altogether unauthorized to speak for the President upon hypothetical questions, I think I can give an answer upon the subject of Slavery at the present day—an answer which will be explicit, and, I hope, not altogether unsatisfactory. While the rebels continue to wage war against the Government of the United States, the military measures affecting Slavery, which have been adopted from necessity, to bring the war to a speedy and successful end, will be continued, except so far as practical experience shall show that they can be modified advantageously, with a view to the same end. When the insurgents shall have disbanded their armies and laid down their arms, the war will instantly cease, and all the war measures then existing, including those which affect Slavery, will cease also, and all the moral, economical and political questions, as well questions affecting Slavery as others which shall then be existing between individuals and States and the Federal Government, whether they arose before the civil war began, or whether they grew out of it, will, by force of the Constitution, pass over to the arbitrament of courts of law, and to the councils of legislation."

Of the probable method in which this war would be closed, the Secretary said, "I am not unsophisticated enough to expect that conspirators while yet unsubdued, and exercising an unresisted despotism in the insurrectionary States, will either sue for, or even accept, an amnesty based on the surrender of the power they have so recklessly usurped. Nevertheless, I know that if any such conspirator should tender his submission upon such terms, that he will at once receive a candid hearing, and an answer prompted purely by a desire for peace, with the maintenance of the Union. On the other hand, I do expect propositions of peace with a restoration of the Union, to come not from the Confederates in authority, nor through them, but from the citizens and States under and behind them. And I expect such propositions from citizens and States to come over the Confederates in power, just so fast as those citizens and States shall be delivered by the Federal arms, from the usurpation by which they are now oppressed. All the world knows, that so far as I am concerned, and, I believe, so far as the President is concerned, all such applications will receive just such an answer as it becomes a great, magnanimous and humane people, to grant to brethren who have come back from their wanderings to seek a shelter in the common ark of our national security and happiness." The Hon. Salmon P. Chase, late Secretary of the Treasury, supported the administration in an able address in Kentucky, and otherwise rendered efficient aid in the canvass. The Hon. Edward Everett, in a speech at Fanuiel Hall, in October, fully and clearly set forth the grounds of the struggle. In the Democratic ranks, Governor Seymour, of New York, was a prominent representative of his party. The contest was conducted with every advantage of able argument on either side.

On one occasion, President Lincoln himself, spoke a few words on the National question, in reference to certain intimations of his policy which had been thrown out for electioneering purposes. It was on the evening of the 19th of October, when he was serenaded at the Executive Mansion, by a party desirous of expressing their gratification at the adoption in Maryland of the new Constitution, by which slavery was finally to be abolished in the State. "I am notified," said he "that this is a compliment paid me by the loyal Marylanders resident in this district. I infer that the adoption of the new Constitution for the State furnishes the occasion, and that in your view the extirpation of slavery constitutes the chief merit of the new Constitution. Most heartily do I congratulate you and Maryland, and the world upon the event. I regret that it did not occur two years sooner, which, I am sure, would have saved to the nation more money than would have met all the private loss incident to the measure; but it has come at last, and I sincerely hope its friends may fully realize all their anticipations of good from it, and that its opponents may, by its effects, be agreeably and profitably disappointed. A word upon another subject. Something said by the Secretary of State in his recent speech at Auburn, has been construed by some into a threat that if I shall be beaten at the election, I will, between then and the end of my constitutional term, do what I may be able to ruin the Government. Others regard the fact that the Chicago Convention adjourned not *sine die*, but to meet again, if called to do so by a particular individual, as the intimation of a purpose, that if the nominee shall be elected, he will at once seize control of the Government. I hope the good people will permit themselves to suffer no uneasiness on either point. I am struggling to maintain the Government, not to overthrow it. I therefore say, that if I live, I shall remain President until the 4th of next March, and that whoever shall be constitutionally elected, therefore, in November, shall be duly installed as President on the 4th of March, and that in the interval I shall do my utmost, that, whoever is to hold the helm for the next voyage, shall start with the best possible chance to save the ship. This is due to the people, both on principle and under the Constitution. Their will, constitutionally expressed, is the ultimate law for all. If they should deliberately resolve to have immediate peace, even at the loss of their country and their liberties, I know not the power or the right to resist them. It is their own business, and they must do as they please with their own. I believe, however, they are still resolved to preserve their country and their liberty; and in this, in office or out of it, I am resolved to stand by them. I may add, that in this purpose to save the country and its liberties, no classes of people seem so nearly unanimous as the soldiers in the field and the seamen afloat. Do they not have the hardest of it? Who should quail when they do not? God bless the soldiers and seamen, and all their brave commanders."

Previous to the election there were various threats of invasion of the Northern frontier by parties of the insurgents, who had taken refuge in Canada, accompanied by practical demonstrations of violence, which led to active measures being taken by the Government to protect the citizens in that quarter. The New York line was peculiarly liable for attack, and information had been received from Canada of threatened raids and attempts at burning cities at the period of the election, which led the Government to strengthen the command of Major-Gen. Dix, at New York, by a body of regulars. Major-Gen. Butler was sent to aid in these precautionary measures, and quietly taking up his residence in the city of New York, organized a preventive force, which effectually precluded all opposition. Here, as elsewhere on the 8th of November, the appointed day, the Presidential election was held without disturbance. Seldom, in time of peace, on such occasions had there been greater quiet or decorum. The result was decided. The election was held in twenty-five States. In twenty-two, 213 electors were chosen, pledged to the support of Lincoln and Johnston. Gen. McClellan received the electoral votes 21 in all, of but three States, Delaware, Kentucky and New Jersey. The Administration gained also a large popular majority. The total of Lincoln's vote was 2,203,831; that of McClellan was 1,797,019.*

At a late hour in the night of the day of election, the result as already indicated, was announced to President Lincoln at the White House, by a club of Pennsylvanians, when the President thus happily responded:—"Friends and Fellow Citizens: Even before I had been informed by you that this compliment was paid me by loyal citizens of Pennsylvania friendly to me, I had inferred that you were of that portion of my countrymen who think that the best interests of the nation are to be subserved by the support of the present administration. I do not pretend to say that you who think so embrace all the patriotism and loyalty of the country. But I do believe, and I trust, without personal interest, that the welfare of the country does require that such support and endorsement be given. I earnestly believe that the consequences of this day's work, if it be as you assure me, and as now seems probable, will be to the lasting advantage, if not to the very salvation, of the country. I cannot at this hour say what has been the result of the election; but, whatever it may be, I have no desire to modify this opinion—that all who have labored to-day in behalf of the Union organization, have wrought for the best interests of their country and the world, not only for the present, but for all future ages. I am thankful to God for this approval of the people. But while deeply grateful for this mark of their confidence in me, if I know my heart, my gratitude is free from any taint of personal triumph. I do not impugn the motives of any one opposed to me. It is no pleasure to me to triumph over any one; but I give thanks to the Almighty for this evidence of the people's resolution to stand by free government and the rights of humanity." Two days afterwards, the resignation of General McClellan, dated the day of the election, was received by the Adjutant General and accepted.

There were two informal attempts in July at negotiation, or the discussion of terms of peace between the contending parties; and though to neither of these was there attached any definite responsibility, yet they were the means of giving publicity to renewed declarations on the part of President Lincoln and Jefferson Davis, as to the essential conditions of ending the struggle. One of these conferences took place on the British frontier at Niagara Falls, between Messrs. Clement C. Clay, of Alabama, and James P. Holcombe, of Virginia, informally speaking for the rebel Confederacy, and Horace Greeley, of New York, who was in communication on the subject with the authorities at Washington. Mr. Greeley was led to the interview through a preliminary correspondence with Mr. George N. Sanders, a noted confederate agent abroad. The object appears to have been to procure for Messrs. Clay and Holcombe a safe conduct to Washington, where they might, on their own responsibility, discuss with the members of the Administration, or such persons as would listen to them, the national questions at issue. Mr. Greeley, on learning that they were not accredited from Richmond, and bore no propositions of peace, applied to Washington for instructions, when he received the following communication from President Lincoln, which he was authorized to make public. It was thus addressed:—"To Whom it may concern: Any proposition which embraces the restoration of peace, the integrity of the whole Union, and the abandonment of Slavery, and which comes by and with authority that can control the armies now at war against the United States, will be received and considered by the Executive Government of the United States, and will be met by liberal terms on substantial and collateral

* The Tribune Almanac for 1865.

points, and the bearer or bearers thereof shall have safe conduct both ways." On the reception of this declaration, the quasi negotiation at Niagara Falls, which appears to have been a purely personal affair, was rapidly extinguished. The other attempt at negotiation, if the latter term may be applied with propriety, was embraced in the voluntary journey of Col. James F. Jacques, of an Illinois regiment, and Mr. J. R. Gillmore, of Massachusetts, to Richmond, with the intent of conferring with President Jefferson Davis and the Confederate authorities on terms of peace. At the request of President Lincoln, they were passed through the lines by Gen. Grant, who asked in a letter to Gen. Lee, that they be allowed to meet Col. Robert Ould, Commissioner for the exchange of prisoners, the object of the meeting, as he stated, being legitimate with the duties of that officer. In case of Gen. Lee's hesitation, Gen. Grant asked that the request be referred to President Davis for his action. The latter authorized Col. Ould to hold the conference, and the visitors were brought to and lodged under surveillance at the Spotswood House, Richmond, whence, on the 17th July, they addressed the following note to the Hon. J. P. Benjamin, Secretary of State, Confederate States of America: "Dear Sir: The undersigned respectfully solicit an interview with President Davis. They visit Richmond only as private citizens, and have no official character or authority; but they are acquainted with the views of the United States Government, and with the sentiments of the Northern people, relative to an adjustment of the differences existing between the North and the South, and earnestly hope that a free interchange of views between President Davis and themselves may open the way to such *official* negotiations as will result in restoring PEACE to the two sections of our distracted country. They therefore ask an interview with the President, and, waiting your reply, are, truly and respectfully yours." The interview was granted and took place in the evening at the office of Secretary Benjamin, who afterward, in an official "circular," published this account of the conference:—"The President came to my office at 9 o'clock in the evening, and Col. Ould came a few moments later with Messrs. Jacques and Gillmore. The President said to them that he had heard from me that they came as messengers of peace from Mr. Lincoln; that as such they were welcome; that the Confederacy had never concealed its desire for peace, and that he was ready to hear whatever they had to offer on that subject. Mr. Gillmore then addressed the President, and in a few minutes had conveyed the information that these two gentlemen had come to Richmond impressed with the idea that this Government would accept a peace on the basis of a reconstruction of the Union, the abolition of Slavery, and a grant of amnesty to the people of the States as repentant criminals. In order to accomplish the abolition of Slavery, it was proposed that there should be a general vote of all the people of both Confederations, and the majority of the vote thus taken was to determine that, as well as all other disputed questions. These were stated to be Mr. Lincoln's views. The President answered that as these remarks had been prefaced by the remark that the people of the North were a majority, and that a majority ought to govern, the offer was, in effect, a proposal that the Confederate States should surrender at discretion, admit that they had been wrong from the beginning of the contest, submit to the mercy of their enemies, and avow themselves to be in need of pardon for crimes; that extermination was preferable to such dishonor. He stated that if they were themselves so unacquainted with the form of their own Government as to make such propositions, Mr. Lincoln ought to have known, when giving them his views, that it was out of the power of the Confederate Government to act on the subject of the domestic institutions of the several States, each State having exclusive jurisdiction on that point, still less to commit the decision of such a question to the vote of a foreign people ; that the separation of the States was an accomplished fact ; that he had no authority to receive proposals for negotiations except by virtue of his office as President of an independent Confederacy, and on this basis alone must proposals be made to him." The result was that the travellers returned the next day to the Union lines with the full impression that the government at Richmond would receive proposals for peace only on the basis of the recognition of their independence. As this had often been avowed before by the rebel authorities, and was, in fact, a necessity of their position, the issue before the country was stripped of all possible ambiguity. The war must be maintained or the Union abandoned.

It needed no indirect communications with Richmond to ascertain this. The resolve of the Confederates to fight on till their Independence should be secured had been persistently declared. It had been set forth in a studied manifesto of the rebel Congress in June, in which, while deprecating the horrors and responsibilities of the war, and professing a desire for peace, that body asserted its right and determination to maintain the liberties which it assumed to be invaded. "For ourselves," said they, "we have no fear for the result. The wildest pictures ever drawn of a disordered imagination, comes short of the extravagance which could dream of the conquest of eight millions of people, resolved with one mind 'to die freemen rather than to live slaves,' and forewarned by the savage and exterminating spirit in which this war has been waged upon them, and by the mad avowals of its patrons and supporters, of the worse than Egyptian bondage that awaits them in the event of their subjugation."

This confidence in the Confederate resources seemed, indeed, to be somewhat impaired, if we may judge from the language and temper of a speech delivered a few months later, in September, after the fall of Atlanta, by President Jefferson Davis at Macon, Georgia, while on a visit to the Southern States ; but new efforts were made, though the old strength was palpably diminished. Governor Brown of Georgia, had just withdrawn the militia of the State from Hood's army. "What, though misfortune," said Davis, "has befallen our arms from Decatur to Jonesboro, our cause is not lost. Sherman cannot keep up his long line of communication and retreat. Sooner or later he must fall back, and when that day comes, the fate that befel the army of the French Empire in its retreat from Moscow will be reacted. Our cavalry and our people will harass and destroy his army as did the Cossacks that of Napoleon ; and the Yankee General, like him, will escape with only a body-guard. How can this be the most speedily effected ? By the absentees of Hood's army returning to their posts ; and will they not ? Can they see the banished exiles ; can they hear the wail of their suffering countrywomen and children, and not come ? By what influence they are made to stay away it is not necessary to speak. If there is one who will stay away at this hour, he is unworthy the name of Georgian. To the women no appeal is necessary. They are like the Spartan mothers of old. I know of one who has lost all her sons, except one of eight years. She wrote that she wanted me to reserve a place for him in the ranks. The venerable General Polk, to whom I read the letter, knew that woman well, and said it was characteristic of her; but I will not weary you by turning aside to relate the various incidents of giving up the last son to the cause of our country, known to me. Wherever we go we find the hearts and hands of our noble women enlisted. They are seen wherever the eye may fall or the step turn. They have one duty to perform; to buoy up the hearts of the people. I know the deep disgrace felt by Georgia at our army falling back from Dalton to the interior of our State. But I was not of those who considered Atlanta lost when our army crossed the Chattahoochee. I resolved that it should not, and then I put a man in command who I knew would strike a manly blow for the city, and many a Yankee's blood was made to nourish the soil before the prize was won. It does not become us to revert to disaster. Let the dead bury the dead. Let us, with one arm and one effort, endeavor to crush Sherman. * * * You have not many men between eighteen and forty-five left. The boys, God bless the boys, are, as rapidly as they become old enough, going to the field. The city of Macon is filled with stores, sick and wounded. It must not be abandoned when threatened, but when the enemy come, instead of calling upon Hood's army for defence, the old men must fight, and when the enemy is driven beyond Chattanooga, they too can join in the general rejoicing. Your prisoners are kept as a sort of Yankee capital. I have heard that one of their Generals said, that their exchange would defeat Sherman. I have tried every means, conceded every thing to effect an exchange, but to no purpose. Butler, the beast, with whom no Commissioner of Exchange would hold intercourse, had published in the newspapers that if we would consent to the exchange of negroes, all difficulties might be removed. This is reported as an effort of his to get himself whitewashed by holding intercourse with gentlemen. If an exchange could be effected, I don't know but that I might be induced to recognize Butler. But in the future, every effort will be given, as far as possible, to effect the end. We want our soldiers in the field, and we want the sick and wounded to return home. It is not proper for me to speak of the number of men in the field, but this I will say, that two-thirds of our men are absent, some sick, some wounded, but most of them absent without leave. * * * * If one half of the men now absent without leave will return to duty, we can defeat the enemy. With that hope I am going to the front. I may not realize this hope, but I know there are men there who have looked death in the face too often to despond now. Let no one despond. Let no one distrust and remember that if genius is the beau ideal, hope is the reality."

In his Annual Message to the Confederate Congress at Richmond, in November, President Davis reviewed the situation more calmly. He claimed various successes in Louisiana and Texas, and the recovery of extensive districts of Territory to the East of the Mississippi. "The army of General Sherman," he said, "although succeeding at the end of the summer in obtaining possession of Atlanta, has been unable to secure any ultimate advantage from this success." The result, he said, would not have been different if Richmond also had been evacuated. "The Confederacy would have remained as erect and defiant as ever. Nothing could have been changed in the purpose of its Government, in the indomitable valor of its troops, or in the unquenchable spirit of its people. The baffled and disappointed foe would in vain have scanned the reports of your proceedings, at some new Legislative seat, for any indication that progress had been made in his gigantic task of conquering a free people. The truth so patent to us must, ere long, be forced upon the reflectant Northern mind. There is no vital point on the preservation of which the continued existence of the Confederacy depends. There is military success of the enemy which can accomplish its destruction. Not the fall of Richmond, nor Wilmington, nor Charleston, nor Savannah, nor Mobile, nor of all combined, can save the enemy from the constant and exhaustive drain of blood and treasure which must continue until he shall discover that no peace is attainable unless based on the recognition of our indefeasible rights."

In this Message it was stated that the total amount of the public debt, as exhibited on the books of the Register of the Treasury, on the 1st of October, 1864, was $1,147,970,208, of which $339,840,090 were funded debt, bearing interest; $283,880,150 were treasury notes of the new issue, and the remainder consisted of the former issue of treasury notes, about to be converted into other forms of debt. In this statement, it was added, "the foreign debt is omitted. It consists only of the unpaid balance of the loan known as the cotton loan. This balance is but £2,200,000, and is adequately provided for by about 250,000 bales of cotton owned by the Government, even if the cotton be rated as worth but sixpence per pound." The great depreciation of the treasury notes, or paper currency, was admitted and attributed to two causes, "redundancy in amount and want of confidence in ultimate redemption." To remedy this pressing difficulty, it was proposed, "First—That the faith of the Government be pledged that the notes shall ever remain exempt from taxation. Second—That no issue shall be made beyond that which is already authorized by law. Third—That a certain fixed portion of the annual receipts from taxation during the war, shall be set apart specially for the gradual extinction of the outstanding amount, until it shall have been reduced to $150,000,000; and, Fourth—The pledge and appropriation of such proportion of the tax in kind, and for such number of years after the return of peace, as shall be sufficient for the final redemption of the entire circulation."

In the portion of the Message relating to the War Department, the employment of the Slaves in the Army was discussed at some length. The President pronounced the requisition hitherto made for short periods, inadequate to the demands of the service. "In this respect," said he, "the relation of persons predominates so far as to render it doubtful whether the private right of property can consistently and beneficially be continued, and it would seem proper to acquire for the public service the entire property in the labor of the slave, and to pay therefore due compensation rather than to impress his labor for short terms; and this the more especially as the effect of the present law would vest this entire property in all cases, where his slave might be recaptured after compensation for his loss had been paid to the private owner. Whenever the entire property in the service of the slave is thus acquired by the Government, the question is presented, by what tenure he should be held. Should he be retained in servitude, or should his emancipation be held out to him as a reward for faithful service, or should it be granted at once on the promise of such service; and if emancipated, what action should be taken to secure for the freed men the permission of the State from which he was drawn to reside within its limits after the close of his public service. The permission would doubtless be more readily accorded as a reward for past faithful service; and a double motive for zealous discharge of duty would thus be offered to those employed by the Government—their freedom, and the gratification of the local attachment which is so marked a characteristic of the negro, and forms so powerful an incentive to his action. The policy of engaging to liberate the negro on his discharge after service faithfully rendered, seems to me preferable to that of granting immediate manumission, or that of retaining him in servitude. If this policy should recommend itself to the judgment of Congress, it is suggested that, in addition to the duties heretofore performed by the slave, he might be advantageously employed as a pioneer and engineer laborer; and, in that event, that the number should be augmented to forty thousand."

Of the general arming of the slaves, which was now being freely discussed in the Confederacy, he said, "The subject is to be viewed by us, therefore, solely in the light of policy and our social economy. When so regarded, I must dissent from those who advise a general levy and arming of the slaves for the duty of soldiers. Until our white population shall prove insufficient for the armies we require, and can afford to keep in the field, to employ as a soldier, the negro who has merely been trained to labor, and as a laborer, the white man, accustomed from his youth to the use of fire-arms, would scarcely be deemed wise or advantageous by any; and this is the question now before us. But should the alternative ever be presented, of a subjugation or of the employment of the slave, as a soldier, there seems no reason to doubt what should then be our decision"

CHAPTER CVIII.

NATIONAL AFFAIRS TO CLOSE OF 1864.—CONTINUED.

SEVERAL important changes in the Cabinet occurred during the year. At the end of June, Salmon P. Chase, Secretary of the Treasury, tendered his resignation of his office to the President, by whom it was promptly accepted. The immediate cause of this proceeding was stated to be a conflict of opinion between the President and Mr. Chase in reference to appointments to office in the Treasury Department; but other unexplained motives doubtless entered into the affair. The President immediately sent in a message to the Senate, then in session, nominating David Tod, the recent Governor of Ohio, to the office. Before this nomination was acted upon Mr. Tod declined to accept the appointment, which was presently conferred upon the Hon. William Pitt Fessenden, a member of the United States Senate, and holding the important position of Chairman of its Finance Committee. Mr. Fessenden, a native of New Hampshire, now at the age of fifty-eight, had early settled as a lawyer in Portland, Maine, where he had acquired a high reputation in his profession. After serving in the State Legislature, he had been sent to Congress, and since 1854 had been a member of the Senate. His nomination was at once ratified by his associates in that body, while it was received with satisfaction by the country. Mr. Fessenden, who had given a cordial support to the financial measures of Secretary Chase, upon entering on his new office pursued the policy of his predecessor with judgment and discretion. Indispensable new loans were regulated according to the exigency of the moment with due regard to the interests of the State, and the public credit was, as far as possible, maintained by avoiding an expansion of the popular currency. In giving notice of the readiness of the

Treasury Department to receive subscriptions to a new issue of $200,000,000 seven-thirties, convertible into bonds, redeemable after five and payable twenty years from 1867, he issued with the proposal an appeal to the People of the United States, in which, while setting forth various financial inducements, he presented this encouraging view of the national resources and prosperity. "The circumstances," said he, "under which this loan is asked for and your aid invoked, though differing widely from the existing state of affairs three years ago, are such as afford equal encouragement and security. Time, while proving that the struggle for national unity was to exceed in duration and severity our worst anticipations, has tested the national strength and national resources to an extent alike unexpected and remarkable, exciting equal astonishment at home and abroad. Three years of war have burdened you with a debt which but three years since would have seemed beyond your ability to meet. Yet the accumulated wealth and productive energies of the nation have proved to be so vast, that it has been borne with comparative ease, and a peaceful future would hardly feel its weight. As a price paid for national existence and the preservation of free institutions, it does not deserve a moment's consideration. Thus far, the war has been supported and carried on as it only could have been by a people resolved, at whatever cost of blood and treasure, to transmit unimpaired to posterity the system of free Government bequeathed to them by the great men who framed it. This deliberate and patriotic resolve has developed a power surprising even to themselves. It has shown that in less than a century a nation has arisen unsurpassed in vigor and exhaustless in resources, able to conduct through a series of years, war on its most gigantic scale, and finding itself when near its close almost unimpaired in all the material elements of power. It has at the present moment great armies in the field, facing an enemy apparently approaching a period of utter exhaustion, but still struggling with a force the greater and more desperate as it sees, and because it sees, the near approach of a final and fatal consummation." Montgomery Blair, of Maryland, who had held the position of Postmaster-General since the commencement of President Lincoln's Administration, and discharged the duties of the office with eminent ability, resigned in September, and was succeeded by William Dennison, Ex-Governor of Ohio. In December, on the eve of the meeting of Congress, another change occurred in the resignation of the Attorney-General, Edward Bates, of Missouri. He was succeeded by Judge-Advocate-General Holt.

An important appointment was thrown into the hands of the President by the decease, on the 12th of October, of Roger Brook Taney, Chief Justice of the Supreme Court. Born in Calvert County, Maryland, in 1777, his life had been coeval with the existence of the nation. He was educated as a lawyer, and in his earlier years served in the Legislature of his State. General Jackson made him a member of his Cabinet as Attorney-General of the United States, in 1831, and two years after transferred him to the post of Secretary of the Treasury as successor to Mr. Duane, who was displaced for his refusal to remove the Government deposits from the United States Bank. The Senate, on meeting, refused to confirm the appointment, and also rejected his appointment as an Associate Justice of the Supreme Court. On the death of Chief Justice Marshall he was appointed his successor by President Jackson and confirmed, and since 1837 had discharged the duties of this high office. The vacancy created by his death was filled by the appointment by President Lincoln of Mr. Chase, the recent Secretary of the Treasury. The nomination was sent into the Senate on the second day of its session, December 6th, and was immediately and unanimously confirmed by that body.

President Lincoln's Message at the meeting of Congress in December, was a straight forward, business paper. The state of our relations abroad was summed up in a brief sentence: "The condition of our foreign affairs is reasonably satisfactory. Confident in the strength of the nation, he said, in allusion to the quasi-recognition by the foreign powers of the Rebellion: "It is possible that if it were a new and open question, the Maritime Powers, with the light they now enjoy, would not concede the privileges of a naval belligerent to the insurgents of the United States, destitute as they are and always have been, equally of ships and of ports and harbors. Disloyal emissaries have been neither less assiduous nor more successful during the last year than they were before that time in their efforts, under favor of that privilege, to embroil our country in foreign wars. The desire and determination of the Maritime States to defeat that design are believed to be as sincere as, and cannot be more earnest than, our own. Nevertheless, unforeseen political differences have arisen, especially in Brazilian and British ports, and on the northern boundary of the United States, which have required and are likely to continue to require the practice of constant vigilance and a just and conciliatory spirit on the part of the United States, as well as of the nations concerned and their Governments."

After briefly reviewing the financial and other Department reports, in which it was noticeable how well the resources of the country had kept pace with the extraordinary demands upon its energies, and had even exceeded them in the settlement of new States and Territories, the President passed to the presentation of his views on the leading question of the times, in relation to the war and the continuance of Slavery in the country. In these, it will be seen, he urged upon Congress the passage of a law submitting to the Legislatures of the several States an amendment of the Constitution abolishing Slavery at once and for ever. "Important movements," said he, "have occurred during the year to the effect of moulding society for durability in the Union, although short of complete success, it is much in the right direction that 12,000 citizens in each of the States of Arkansas and Louisiana have organized loyal State Governments with free constitutions, and are earnestly struggling to maintain and administer them. The movement in the same direction more extensively, though less definite in Missouri, Kentucky, and Tennessee should not be overlooked. But Maryland presents the example of complete success. Maryland is secure to Liberty and Union for all the future. The genius of rebellion will no more claim Maryland. Like another foul spirit, being driven out it may seek to tear her, but it will woo her no more. At the last session of Congress a proposed amendment of the Constitution abolishing Slavery throughout the United States passed the Senate, but failed for the lack of the requisite two-thirds vote in the House of Representatives. Although the present is the same Congress, and nearly the same members, and without questioning the wisdom or patriotism of those who stood in opposition, I venture to recommend the reconsideration and passage of the measure at the present session. Of course, the abstract question is not changed, but an intervening election shows almost certainly that the next Congress will pass the measure if this does not. Hence there is only a question of time as to when the proposed amendment will go to the States for their action, and as it is to go at all events, may we not agree that the sooner the better. It is not claimed that the election has imposed a duty on members to change their views of their votes any further than an additional element to be considered. Their judgment may be affected by it. It is the voice of the people now for the first time heard upon the question. In a great national crisis like ours unanimity of action among those seeking a common end is very desirable, almost indispensable; and yet no approach to such unanimity is attainable unless some deference should be paid to the will of the majority. In this case the common end is the maintenance of the Union, and among the means to secure that end, such will, through the election, is most clearly declared in favor of such constitutional amendment."

From this the President passed to an exhibition of the assertion of the national will and the substantial strength of the country in population, as shown by the returns of voters in the recent general Election. "The most reliable indication," said he, "of public purpose in this country is derived through our popular elections. Judging by the recent canvass and its result, the purpose of the people within the loyal States, to maintain the integrity of the Union, was never more firm nor more nearly unanimous than now. The extraordinary calmness and good order with which the millions of voters met and mingled at the polls, give strong assurance of this. Not only all those who supported the Union ticket (so called,) but a great majority of the opposing party also may be fairly claimed to entertain and to be actuated by the same purpose. It is an unanswerable argument to this effect, that no candidate for any office whatever, high or low, has ventured to seek votes on the avowal that he was for giving up the Union. There has been much impugning of motives and much heated controversy as to the proper means and best mode of advancing the Union cause, but in the distinct issue of Union or no Union, the politicians have shown their instinctive knowledge that there is no diversity among the people. In affording the people the fair opportunity of showing one to another and to the world this firmness and unanimity of purpose, the election has been of vast value to the national cause. The election has exhibited another fact not less valuable to be known—the fact that we do not approach exhaustion in the most important branch of the national resources. That of living men—while it is melancholy to reflect that the war has filled so many graves and caused mourning to so many hearts, it is some relief to know that, compared with the surviving, the fallen have been so few. While Corps and Divisions and Regiments have formed and fought and dwindled and gone out of existence, a great majority of the men who composed them are still living. The same is true of the Naval service. The election returns prove this. So many voters could not else be found. The States regularly holding elections, both now and four years ago, to wit: California, Connecticut, Delaware, Illinois, Indiana, Iowa, Kentucky, Maine, Maryland, Massachusetts, Michigan, Minnesota, Missouri, New Hampshire, New Jersey, New York, Ohio, Oregon, Pennsylvania, Rhode Island, Vermont, West Virginia and Wisconsin, cast 3,982,011 votes now against 4,870,222 cast then, showing an aggregate now of 3,398,211, to which is to be added 33,762 cast now in the new States of Kansas and Nevada, which States did not vote in 1860—thus swelling the aggregate to 4,075,773, and the net increase during the three years and a-half of war, to 145,751. To this, again, should be added the number of all soldiers in the field from Massachusetts, Rhode Island, New Jersey, Delaware, Indiana, Illinois and California, who, by the laws of those States, could not vote away from their homes, and which number cannot be less than 90,000. Nor yet is this all. The number in organized Territories is triple now what it was four years ago; while thousands, white and black, join us as the National arms press back the insurgent lines—so much is shown affirmatively and negatively by the election. It is not material to inquire how the increase has been produced, or to show that it would have been greater but for the war, which is probably true; the important fact remains demonstrated that we have more men now than we had when the war began; that we are not exhausted nor in process of exhaustion; that we are gaining strength, and may, if need be, maintain the contest indefinitely. This as to men."

Of the position of the Government toward the rebellion, he said, with a blending of leniency and authority—"Material resources are now more complete and abundant than ever. The national resources then are unexhausted, and, as we believe, inexhaustible. The public purpose to reëstablish and maintain the National authority is unchanged, and, as we believe, unchangeable. The manner of continuing the effort remains to choose. On careful consideration of all the evidence accessible, it seems to me that no attempt at negotiation with the insurgent leader could result in any good. He would accept of nothing short of the severance of the Union. His declarations to this effect are explicit and oft repeated. He does not attempt to deceive us. He affords us no excuse to deceive ourselves. We cannot voluntarily yield it. Between him and us the issue is distinct, simple and inflexible. It is an issue which can only be tried by war, and decided by victory. If we yield we are beaten. If the Southern people fail him he is beaten; either way it would be the victory and defeat following war. What is true, however, of him who heads the insurgent cause, is not necessary true of those who follow. Although he cannot reaccept the Union, they can. Some of them we know already desire peace and reunion. The number of such may increase. They can at any moment have peace simply by laying down their arms and submitting to the National authority under the Constitution. After so much the Government could not, if it would, maintain war against them. The loyal people would not sustain or allow it. If questions should remain, we would adjust them by the peaceful means of legislation, conference, courts and votes. Operating only in Constitutional and lawful channels, some in certain and other possible questions are and would be beyond the Executive power to adjust, as for instance, the admission of members into Congress, and whatever might require the appropriation of money. The Executive power itself would be greatly diminished by the cessation of actual war. Pardons and remissions of forfeiture, however, would still be within Executive control. In what spirit and temper this control would be exercised, can be fairly judged of by the past. A year ago general pardon and amnesty, upon special terms, were offered to all except certain designated classes, and it was at the same time made known that the excepted classes were still within contemplation of special clemency. During the year many availed themselves of the general provision, and many more would, only that the signs of bad faith in some led to such precautionary measures as rendered the practical process less easy and certain. During the same time, also special pardons have been granted to individuals of excepted classes, and no voluntary application has been denied. Thus, practically, the door has been for a full year open to all, except such as were not in condition to make free choice; that is, such as were in custody or under constraint. It is still open to all, but the time may come, probably will come, when public duty shall demand that it be closed, and that in lieu, more vigorous measures than heretofore shall be adopted. In presenting the abandonment of armed resistance to the National Authority on the part of the insurgents, as the only indispensable condition to ending the war on the part of the Government, I retract nothing heretofore said as to slavery. I repeat the declaration made a year ago, and that while I remain in my present position I shall not attempt to retract or modify the Emancipation Proclamation. Nor shall I return to slavery any person who is free by the terms of that Proclamation, or by any of the Acts of Congress. If the people should, by whatever mode or means, make it an Executive duty to reënslave such persons, another, and not I, must be their instrument to perform it. In stating a single condition of peace, I mean simply to say that the war will cease on the part of the Government, whenever it shall have ceased on the part of those who began it."

The Treasury Report of Secretary Fessenden amply set forth the provisions by Congress, and the measures taken by his predecessor and himself to supply the National wants and maintain the National credit. The exigencies of the times compelled him to admit the necessity of a departure from the solid rules of finance, in the issue of Government paper not immediately redeemable in specie; and he acknowledged that it was an evil which tended to perpetuate itself. "Of course," said he, "the danger increases with enlarged demands upon the Treasury, growing out of increased expenditures, a rise of prices occasioned by an increase of taxation on articles of consumption, the withdrawal of labor from productive pursuits, accompanied by an aggravated demand for products and material incident to a state of war. The problem to be solved is, how to mitigate the evil if it cannot be fully avoided." This mitigation he found in the restraint of the issue of Government paper by a judicious system of loans, the interest of which being payable in gold, unnecessary expansion of the currency was checked, and a specie standard, in a degree, preserved. The financial measures of the year had thus been confined to the placing of loans in various forms, leaving the amount of currency, not bearing interest, to its former limitation, exclusive of fractional currency and notes issued by National Banks, of $400,000,000 subject to slight occasional increase from the fifty millions held in reserve for the payment of temporary deposits. The whole debt of the country, at the beginning of the fiscal year in July, was stated to be $1,740,690,489.49—an increase during the year of over 618 millions. Assuming the continuance of the present state of affairs, with calculations of various resources, the prospective debt on the 1st of July, 1865, was estimated at $2,223,064,677.51, and $2,645,320,682 at the close of the next fiscal year. The expenditure for the first quarter of the present year, from July to September inclusive, were over 350 millions, which, it was estimated would be increased during the remaining three quarters, to $1,245,729,135.75. This included all unexpended appropriations from former years, and a probable unexpended balance, at the close of the year, of $350,000,000 might be deducted. This vast sum included an estimate for the War Department of over 963 millions, and for the Navy of about forty-three millions, and of over ninety millions of interest on the public debt. The actual receipts of the year ending in July, proved to exceed the estimates previously made. Exclusive of the amount of loans they had reached nearly 266 millions, of which about 102 millions had been derived from Customs, and over 109 millions from Internal Revenue. The latter, it was calculated, might be increased during the present year, under the improved working of the tax, to 300 millions. To provide for the accumulating expenditure, Secretary Fessenden recommended generally, a resort to increased direct taxation on sales and otherwise, and, the interest on bonds, payable in gold, having reached the amount likely to be received from Customs, the issue of bonds or securities bearing interest in currency or paper, convertible into bonds, the interest of which is payable in coin. "Notes, bearing an increased rate of interest, payable in currency," was his suggestion, "redeemable in three or five years, and convertible at maturity into five-twenty bonds, would be preferable in the judgment of the Secretary, to any other form of security. Bonds at long dates, the interest of which is payable in currency at the usual rate, would be less attractive, and, in the end, involve much greater sacrifice. The seven-thirty notes, authorized by the Act of June 30, 1864, and now offered to the public, present as many advantages as any form of currency security, uniting a high rate of interest with convertibility. At the period of their maturity, it may be confidently believed that the country will have been restored to a state of security and peace, with all disturbing elements quieted, and resources increased and increasing—its strength confirmed, and with ability to meet its obligations from its ordinary resources."

In placing further loans, the Secretary looked as heretofore to the home rather than the foreign market, justly considering that the demands of the latter would keep pace with those of the former. "The nation," said he, "has been able thus far to conduct domestic war of unparalleled magnitude and cost without appealing for aid to any foreign people. It was chosen to demonstrate its power to put down insurrection by its own strength, and furnish no pretence for doubt of its entire ability to do so, either to domestic or foreign foe. The people of the United States have felt a just pride in their position before the world. In the judgment of the Secretary, it may well be doubted whether the national credit abroad has not been strengthened and sustained by the fact that foreign investments in our securities have not been sought by us, and whether we have not found a pecuniary advantage in self-reliance." In this view the Secretary was seconded by President Lincoln, who, in his annual Message, recommended to Congress to provide additional inducements to place the loan at home, and, for national considerations, discriminate it as widely as possible among the people. "Held as it is," said he, "for the most part by our own people, it has become a substantial branch of national though private property. For obvious reasons, the more nearly this property can be distributed among all the people the better. To favor such general distribution, greater inducements to become owners might, perhaps, with good effect and without injury, be presented to persons of limited means. With this view, I suggest whether it might not be both expedient and competent for Congress to provide that a limited amount of some future issue of public securities might be held by any bona fide purchaser exempt from taxation and from seizure for debt under such restrictions and limitations as might be necessary to guard against abuse of so important a privilege. This would enable prudent persons to set aside a small annuity against a possible day of want. Privileges like these would render the possession of such securities to the amount limited most desirable to any person of small means, who might be able to save enough for the purpose. The great advantage of citizens being creditors, as well as debtors, with relation to the public debt, is obvious. Men readily perceive that they cannot be much oppressed by a debt which they owe themselves."

The report of Gideon Welles, the Secretary of the Navy, a long and elaborate document, exhibited in detail the naval operations of the year and the statistics of the service. Looking back to the beginning of the war, when the duty was suddenly imposed upon the Nation of maintaining a blockade on a coast line exceeding three thousand five hundred miles—a task unprecedented in history,—he traced the successful efforts which had been made for its accomplishment in a gigantic display of the national resources. At the outset a few wooden ships scattered about the world, and but two hundred men available at the depots, constituted the disposable force for this purpose in the hands of the Secretary. We have recorded in previous chapters, the annual increase and development of this branch of the service. The exhibit of the present year showed a proportional progress not only in the number but the character of the vessels. A total was reported of 671 vessels afloat or in process of construction, mounting 4,610 guns and registering 510,396 tons, being an actual addition to the Navy during the year of 109 vessels and 313 guns. From this latter estimate, however, was to be deducted 26 vessels lost by shipwreck, in battle, capture, &c., during that period. Of this huge array of naval vessels, nearly one-fifth in number and more than one-fourth in guns and tonnage, were screw steamers, especially constructed for the service ; 52 were paddle-wheel steamers and 71 iron-clad vessels of various descriptions. Among the last were the sea-going casemated vessels Dunderberg and New Ironsides, the sea-going turret vessels Puritan, Dictator and Roanoke ; 13 double turreted vessels and more than 30 single turreted, all carrying heavy guns, and few in number but of extraordinary calibre. The construction of many of these vessels of naval design, it was admitted by the Secretary, was a matter of experiment and subject to modifications in the progress of the work. The following statement by the Secretary, presents a comprehensive view of the efforts made in this branch of the service:

"At the commencement of the rebellion the Navy consisted of sailing vessels, a few paddle-wheel steamers, and screw vessels with auxiliary steam-power. Among the latter, the principal and most important were the steam frigates, which, on account of their great draught of water, were unsuitable for any other purpose than that of cruisers on foreign stations as flag-ships, for which indeed they were intended. These vessels had been built to meet the conditions of the day ; some of them, the Mississippi, had been in service for more than twenty years. When constructed, the principal object in view was armament, not speed, and they were equal, if not superior, to the vessels of other naval Powers. For attacks on forts, when accessible to naval attacks, or to protect troops from landing, they can still render service. Time was required to repair and place in proper condition such of these vessels as were dismantled, and also those which were recalled from service abroad. The sailing men-of-war had become useless for fighting purposes. In the emergency that devolved upon it in the beginning of hostilities, the department resorted to the commercial marine, and purchased every available merchant steamer that could advantageously be converted into a naval vessel, and be used to enforce the blockade. The want of a class of small heavily-armed propeller vessels was felt, and the department immediately proceeded, on its own responsibility, and without any appropriation or authorization by Congress, to contract for the construction of twenty-three gunboats, of which the Unadilla, Pinola and Wissahickon may be taken as the type. Some of these vessels were afloat, armed and manned within four months from the date of contract, and participated in the attack on Port Royal ; others took part on the lower Mississippi in passing the forts and in the capture of New Orleans. These gunboats continue to maintain a good reputation, and their steam machinery gives satisfaction. Well adapted as they are for guarding our coast, a larger description was needed for ocean service, and four vessels of the class of the Ossipee, mounting each two guns of eleven inches, were built. There were, also, four vessels of slightly less tonnage constructed, carrying the same armament, of which the Kearsarge is a type. The Shenandoah is the type of six vessels, mounting each three eleven-inch guns, all of which sustain a high reputation. The heavy guns mentioned constitute the principal armament of the several classes named, but they each have in addition from two to six guns of less calibre. All of these vessels are screw steamers, suitable for sea cruising : but for shallow sounds and bays, the rivers and bayous, often narrow and tortuous, another and different class, drawing less water, was found to be necessary, and for them competition was invited. To turn in these frequently restricted channels is difficult, sometimes impossible, and the necessities of the case suggested the principal of a fighting vessel with a double bow and rudder at each end. Twelve paddle-wheel steamers constructed on this principle were built, some in the navy yards and others by contract. The Port Royal and the Sonoma are types of this class. An additional number, amounting to twenty-seven, of these double-bowed paddle-wheel vessels have been built, almost all of them by contract. The Sassacus, which was distinguished in the attack on the rebel ram in Albemarle Sound, the Metacomet, conspicuous in Mobile Bay, and the Eutaw, are types of these vessels. Eight of this class are built or building of iron, and will have strength sufficient for sea service as well as for inland waters. One of them, the Wateree, sent round Cape Horn, reached San Francisco in September last, and is on duty in the Pacific. In order to have armed vessels suitable for naval operations on the Mississippi and its tributaries, the Department invited plans and propositions from shipbuilders and others acquainted with those waters, and the vessels built on those rivers have been chiefly from the plans submitted by parties thus invited. Two of these vessels built at St. Louis, participated in the action with the rebel ram Tennessee, and have done good service in Mobile Bay.

"The entire class of monitor or tureted vessels has been brought into existence during this war, and the coast and harbor iron-clads have been serviceable in James River, at Charleston, and at Mobile. Modifications and improvements have been made in this class of armored vessels. The pressure for iron-clads of light draught, which could ascend the rivers and penetrate the sounds and bays along our coast, was felt to be a necessity. The operations of our armies in the vicinity of the inland waters and adjacent to the rivers, required the constant presence of gunboats. But the men thus employed, as well as the magazines and machinery of the vessels are exposed, especially in the narrow streams with high and wooded banks. Some vessels, and not a few valuable lives, have been lost by these exposures, and in order to afford all possible protection to the gallant men who encounter these dangers, the Department considered it a duty to provide armored vessels of light draught for their security. Contracts were entered into for the construction of twenty vessels on the monitor principle, each to carry two 11-inch guns, in order to be efficient, and to draw seven feet of water. It was ascertained, however, when the first two approached completion, that their draught of water was more than was intended. The heavy armor and the two 11-inch guns, with the machinery to give them proper speed, involved the necessity of enlarging the capacity of each of them. When making these necessary alterations, it was deemed advisable, under applications from some of the commanders of squadrons for boats that should present but a small rise above the surface of the water, to dispense with the turrets in five of these light-draught vessels, with a view to special operations. The remaining fifteen were ordered to be enlarged by raising their decks, thereby giving them additional tonnage and greater draught and making them more efficient, but in other respects, carrying out the original design. This work is now being performed, and most of the vessels are near completion.

"The exigencies of the times and the necessities of the war have stimulated the inventive faculties of our countrymen to vast improvements in vessels, in engines, in ordnance and projectiles. That in some instances they are not at first entirely successful is not surprising. Mistakes and even failures will occur. In nearly every class of vessels that have been built, and especially those that are armored, more or less alterations have been found necessary while they were being constructed. Only two of the monitor class of vessels, the Dictator and Puritan, are proposed for sea-service. Their success, of which the inventor and builder is sanguine, is among the experiments that the period and the exigencies of the country have imposed upon the department. Four turreted vessels have been built in the navy yards, of wood, and cased with iron—differing therein from the original monitors, which are exclusively of iron. One of them, the Monadnock, now in commission, has performed her trips from Boston to Hampton Roads with entire satisfaction, giving assurance that this experiment, deviating, in essential respects, from others, is likely to be successful. The draught of water of the Monadnock is twelve feet, and with two independent screws she has a speed of ten knots. Four other similar vessels, of a still more formidable and invulnerable character, are building. The only sea-going iron-clad ships, besides the two turreted vessels already mentioned, are the New Ironsides, built in 1862; the Roanoke, one of the old frigates which has been armored, and the Dunderberg, a casemate vessel. For this vessel, the contractor has promised a speed of fifteen knots at sea. The Department has, on several occasions, invited propositions for iron, sea-going, armored ships, but Congress having declined to make the necessary appropriations, no measures have been taken for their construction.

"The vessels recently built, and at present constructing in the navy yards, are of wood, the smaller class of them being gunboats. eight of which are of the class of the Nepsic, 600 tons, mounting one heavy pivot and four broadside guns. There are four of the class of the Nantucket, of 900 tons, mounting one heavy pivot, with six broadside guns. In addition to these there are four vessels of the class of the Algona, with a tonnage of 1,350 tons, and proportionate armament. All of these vessels have very considerable steam-power, and will, as some of them have already proved, be efficient cruisers at sea. The immediate wants of the blockade having been supplied by the vessels built and altered in the navy yards, and by purchase of the best merchant steamers capable of bearing heavy armament, the attention of the Department has been bestowed on larger and more important ships, such as would be formidable not only for home defence but for foreign service. The position and influence of a nation among the great commercial and maritime powers of the world are to a great extent dependent upon its naval ability. Limited appropriations have already been made by Congress for vessels of this character. Each succeeding year of this war has produced from foreign shipyards, steamers of greater speed to run the blockade, and the reliable preventive of this illicit trade must be found in vessels of increased steam power. By making them of sufficient size they will be formidable, not only to neutral violators of our laws but to any enemy. On the class of vessel of which some sacrifice of armament has been made to obtain speed, there are seven building, three of which are already launched, and the others will soon be ready. Two of these vessels are being built by contract, and five in the navy yards. This class of vessels is represented by the Ammonsoouc and the Chattanooga. There are also in progress of construction twenty vessels with steam machinery of rather less power, but which are to be much more heavily armed. Ten of these, of the class of the Illinois, the Guerriere and the Java, have covered gun-decks, and will carry twenty heavy guus. Two will have a plating of thin iron as a protection from shells. The remaining ten, of the class of the Contoocook and Manitau, building in the navy yards, are of less size, but with equal machinery, and intended for greater speed. As all of them will be provided with masts and sails, they can be cruising vessels and used on foreign stations."

The total number of men at this time in the naval service was stated at 6,000 officers and 45,000 men. The entire expenditure of the Department since the 4th of March, 1861, including the estimates of the year, was reported at $280,647,261 45. The number of vessels captured by the squadrons during the year was 325, classified as follows; Schooners, 105; steamers, 88; sloops, 40; brigs, 3; barks, 3; small boats, 85. The total number of captures since the commencement of the rebellion is 1,397, viz.: Schooners, 652; steamers, 627, sloops, 171; brigs, 33; barks, 29; ships, yachts and small boats, 117. The gross proceeds arising from the sale of condemned prize property amounts to $14,296,250 51; expenses, $1,237,153 96; leaving for distribution, one-half to the captors, and one-half to the United States as a naval pension fund, $13,190, 841 46.

The Secretary had, of course, the satisfaction to compliment Rear-Admiral Farragut for his exploits at Mobile, and the officers of the navy generally, for their successful maintenance of the blockade and the services of the war. One act of gallantry, in addition to those we have already detailed, elicited his admiration. This was the heroic service performed by Lieutenant W. B. Cushing, in the destruction of the rebel iron-clad ram Albemarle, at Plymouth, North Carolina. This formidable vessel, it will be remembered, had been twice encountered by our fleet, first on occasion of the capture of Plymouth from the inadequate Union force in April, and again in the waters of Albemarle Sound in May. After this last engagement the Albemarle returned to Plymouth, where her presence was a constant threat to the United States vessels traversing the Sound. "As there was no known cause," says Secretary Welles, "to prevent her making another demonstration, a competent naval force was always in readiness to meet her. But the inactivity of awaiting her movements was irksome and paralyzing, and her destruction by other means became an object. Lieutenant W. B. Cushing, a young officer who had on previous occasions gained the admiration of the Department by his daring and venturous heroism, was selected to destroy the Albemarle by a torpedo, properly arranged in a light picket-boat, to be placed at his disposal. The torpedo is the invention of Chief-Engineer W. W. Wood, and possesses extraordinary power. It was arranged and applied to the picket-boat at the suggestion and under the direction of Rear-Admiral F. H. Gregory and his able assistants. Lieutenant Cushing was directed to have the means for carrying out the views of the Department prepared, and when these were completed it was quickly and brilliantly executed. With fourteen brave officers and men, who volunteered for the service, he, on the night of October 27, ascended the Roanoke to Plymouth, assailed the ram at her wharf, though guarded by a military force on shore, as well as by her crew, and sunk her. Only himself and one of his party escaped death or capture."

The details of this gallant adventure were thus narrated in the official report of Lieutenant Cushing to Rear-Admiral Porter, in command of the North Atlantic Squadron. "Albemarle Sound, October 30, 1864. Sir: I have the honor to report that the rebel ironclad Albemarle is at the bottom of Roanoake River. On the night of the 27th, having prepared my steam launch, I proceeded up toward Plymouth, with thirteen officers and men, partly volunteers from the squadron. The distance from the mouth of the river to the ram was about eight miles, the stream averaging in width some 200 yards, and lined with the enemy's pickets. A mile below the town was the wreck of the Southfield, surrounded by some schooners, and it was understood that a gun was mounted there to command the bend. I therefore took one of the Shamrock's cutters in tow, with orders to cast off and board at that point, if we were hailed. Our boat succeeded in passing the pickets, and even the Southfield within twenty yards, without discovery, and we were not hailed until by the look-outs on the ram. The cutter was then cast off and ordered below, while we made for our enemy under full head of steam. The rebels sprung their rattle, rang the bell, and commenced firing at the same time, repeating their hail and seeming much confused. The light of a fire ashore showed me the iron-clad made fast to the wharf, with logs around her about thirty feet from her side. Passing her closely, we made a complete circle so as to strike her fairly, and went into her bows on. By this time the enemy's fire was very severe, but a dose of cannister at short range seemed to moderate their zeal and disturb their aim. Paymaster Swan, of the Otsego, was wounded near me, but how many more I know not. Three bullets struck my clothing, and the air seemed full of them. In a moment we had struck the logs just abreast of the quarter port, breaking them in some feet, our bows resting on them. The torpedo boom was then lowered, and, by a vigorous pull, I succeeded in diving the torpedo under the over-hang, and exploding it at the same time that the Albemarle's gun was fired. A shot seemed to go crushing through my boat, and a dense mass of water rushed in from the torpedo, filling the launch, and completely disabling her. The enemy then continued his fire at fifteen feet range, and demanded our surrender, which I twice refused, ordering the men to save themselves, and removing my own coat and shoes. Springing into the river I swam, with others, into the middle of the stream, the rebels failing to hit us. The most of our party were captured, some were drowned, and only one escaped beside myself, and he in another direction. Acting Master's Mate Woodman, of the Commodore Hull, met him in the water half a mile below the town, and assisted him as best he could, but failed to get him ashore. Completely exhausted, I managed to reach the shore, but was too weak to crawl out of the water until just at daylight, when I managed to creep into the swamp close to the fort. While hiding, close to the path, the Albemarle's officers passed, and I judged from their conversation that the ship was destroyed. Some hours' travelling in the swamp served to bring me out well below the town, when I sent a negro in to gain information and found that the ram was truly sunk. Proceeding through another swamp I came to a creek and captured a skiff belonging to a picket of the enemy, and with this by eleven o'clock the next night, I made my way out to the Valley City. Acting Master's Mate William M. Howeth, of the Monticello, showed, as usual, conspicuous bravery. He is the same officer who has been with me twice in Wilmington harbour. I trust he may be promoted when exchanged, as well as Acting Third Assistant Engineer Stoleburgh, who, being the first time under fire, handled his engine promptly and with coolness. All the officers and men behaved in the most gallant manner. The cutter of the Shamrock boarded the Southfield and found no guns there. Four prisoners were taken there. The ram is now completely submerged, and the enemy have sunk three schooners in the river to obstruct the passage of our ships. I desire to call the attention of the Admiral and Department to the spirit manifested by the sailors on the ships in these sounds. But few hands were wanted, but all hands were eager to go into the action, many offering their chosen shipmates a month's pay to resign in their favor."

As a sequel to this exploit Commander W. H. Macomb, the senior officer on the station, was enabled by the destruction of the Albemarle, to ascend to Plymouth and recapture the town. The rebels were driven from their rifle pits and batteries, and twenty-two cannon, and a considerable amount of ammunition, with thirty-seven prisoners, were captured.

Among the secondary events of the war in the autumn of this year may be ranked the invasion of Missouri by the rebel General Price. This rebel leader who in several previous campaigns had inflicted untold injury upon the State, having gathered together in Arkansas an imposing force of some 15,000 men, with eighteen pieces of artillery, crossed the southern frontier line, by way of Pocahontas and Poplar Bluff early in September. Plundering the farmers of horses to mount his men and impressing the citizens into his force, organized under the command of Generals Shelby, Marmaduke and Frazer, gathered strength for a bold stroke of invasion at the centre of the State. The first detachment of the Union forces was encountered at Pilot Knob where General Thomas Ewing was stationed with a garrison of about a thousand men. Here, on the 26th of September, he was attacked by a superior body of the enemy, and after holding his position against repeated assaults for two days, was compelled to evacuate the place, retreating, with skirmishing along his march to Harrison and thence to Rolla. The main force of the enemy now advanced with little opposition toward the Missouri river which they struck at Jefferson city, threatening the capture of that place. General Rosecrans, in command of the department, meanwhile had organized his forces and taken such steps as not only to protect the State capital but to push the invaders to a disastrous retreat. Major-General Pleasonton was placed in command of the troops in the field, and on his arrival at Jefferson city on the 8th of October sent forward Brigadier-General John B. Sanborn with all the available cavalry force in pursuit of the invaders who were now making their way westward by the line of the river. General Sanborn, with inferior numbers harassed the enemy and attacked them at Booneville, whence Price moved to Marshall and Lexington, freely plundering by the way. General Pleasonton, having now efficiently organized his cavalry force in four brigades under Generals Brown, McNeil, Sanborn, and Colonel Winslow, the last having first arrived from General A. J. Smith's command on the Mississippi, promptly took the offensive. Prior was driven from Lexington on the 20th, and two days after out of Independence where there was some severe fighting. The pursuit was vigorously kept up to the Big Blue river at Byron's Ford, where there was a sharp engagement, and also at Westport, where the enemy was confronted by a portion of General Curtis' Kansas force under General Blunt. Price's army was now driven southerly, and was overtaken after a forced march by Pleasonton's cavalry on the 25th, at a halting place on the Osage river. "The rapidity of the march," says General Pleasonton in his report, "was such that the two brigades, Winslow's (then commanded by Lieutenant-Colonel Benteen) and Phillip's brigade had reached the front, but knowing the importance of time to the enemy I did not hesitate to attack at once, and, after a brilliant charge, the enemy was routed by these troops, and eight guns were captured. Major-General Marmaduke and Brigadier-General Cabell surrendered, and near 1,000 men were taken prisoners, and the enemy began to burn a large number of wagons in his train. The road for the next fifteen miles was strewed with muskets and arms of all kinds, which were secured by General Curtis' command in the rear. Also numerous wagons still burning. Late in the evening I again came up with the enemy, and attacked him with artillery and cavalry, and that night he blew up his ammunition train. The exhausted condition of my men and horses, having marched near 100 miles in two days and a night, and fighting the last thirty miles, required that I should proceed to the vicinity of Fort Scott for forage and subsistence." Farther pursuit was kept up by General Blunt's command, supported by McNeil and Sanborn, till Price with his broken and dispirited forces was driven, without any general engagement, into Arkansas.

At the conclusion of the campaign in November, General Rosecrans issued an elaborate order, commenting upon the gallant conduct of the army. "The substantial results," said he, "of this brilliant series of operations are that while our infantry and dismounted men nobly performed their share of the work by fighting at Pilot Knob and Glasgow, holding the depots and important points, and backing your hazards; the enemy, entering the State with a mounted force of veteran troops, variously estimated at from 15,000 to 20,000 and eighteen pieces of artillery, with vast expectations of revolutionizing the State, destroying Kansas, and operating on the 'Presidential election,' after having added to his force 6,000 Missourians, which General Marmaduke told General Pleasonton were armed and organized into a division, has been defeated in all his schemes, his mischief confined to the narrow belt of country over which he passed, and routed by you in four engagements, he has lost ten pieces of artillery, a large number of small arms, nearly all his trains and plunder, and, besides his killed, wounded and deserters, 1,958 prisoners, which we have now in possession; and the latest reports confirm the statement that when the enemy's forces recrossed the Arkansas, demoralization, desertion and losses had reduced their strength to less than 5,000; but partially armed and mounted, with 3 pieces of artillery, and their horses in the most wretched condition; all this has been accomplished by less than 7,000 cavalry, most of whom never before saw a great battle; and your entire loss in killed, wounded and missing, is only 346, officers and men. The records of this war furnish no more brilliant and decisive results."

Serious complaints were from time to time uttered during the year, as the facts were brought to light by the escaped or exchange of prisoners from the South, of their inhuman treatment by the confederate authorities. We would not willingly reproduce on these pages the revolting and disgusting record of these inflictions which stain with the deepest ignominy the great crime of the rebellion. But some allusion to the matter is needful in a narrative of the progress of the war; and the story will ever be useful as a lesson indicating the character and tendencies, and, perhaps, in some measure, the necessities of this iniquitous struggle on the part of the South. The subject was vividly brought before the country in a report of the United States Sanitary Commission in September. Led by the painful facts which had come to its knowledge in its extraordinary and gigantic mission of charity, that body in April appointed a Committee of unquestionable ability and integrity to investigate the matter in detail. The Committee was composed of six members, Dr. Ellerslie Wallace, the Hon. J. I. Clark Hare and the Rev. Treadwell Walden, of Philadelphia, and Dr. Valentine Mott, Dr. Edward Delafield and Gouverneur M. Wilkins, of New York, all persons well known to the community. The Committee employed several months in their enquiry, visiting the hospitals where the returned prisoners had been received in Annapolis, Baltimore, and elsewhere, examining carefully into their condition and taking the depositions of officers and others as to the treatment they had received. A mass of testimony was collected concerning the barbarities practised at Richmond, at the Libby Prison and more particularly in the camp in its vicinity at Belle Isle. The result of the investigation was expressed by the Committee in the following terms: "It is the same story everywhere: prisoners of war treated worse than convicts, shut up either in suffocating buildings, or in outdoor enclosures, without even the shelter that is provided for the beasts of the field; unsupplied with sufficient food; supplied with food and water injurious and even poisonous, compelled to live in such personal uncleanliness as to generate vermin; compelled to sleep on floors often covered with human filth, or on ground saturated with it; compelled to breathe an air oppressed with an intolerable stench; hemmed in by a fatal dead-line and in hourly danger of being shot by unrestrained and brutal guards; despondent even to madness, idiocy and suicide; sick of diseases, (so congruous in character as to appear and spread like the plague) caused by the torrid sun, by decaying food, by filth, by vermin, by malaria, and by cold; removed at the last moment, and by hundreds at a time, to hospitals corrupt as a sepulchre, there, with few remedies, little care and no sympathy, to die in wretchedness and despair, not only among strangers, but among enemies too resentful to have pity or to show mercy." The utterly lamentable emaciated condition of many of the returned prisoners witnessed to by the medical Commissioners offered a terrible commentary on this bill of indictment against the humanity of the South. When partial exchange of prisoners was shortly after effected in the Southern Departures at Savannah, it was found that the horrors of Belle Isle had been tenfold repeated at the military prison or enclosure at Andersonville, Georgia.* Some mitigation of these sufferings was happily effected before the close of the year, the result of a correspondence between General Lee and General Grant, the rebel authorities taking the initiative, by which it was agreed that either party might send to their prisoners of war such articles of necessity and comfort as might be desirable. This was a decided measure of relief pending the negotiation of the entangled question of a general exchange of prisoners. Early in the following year the exchange of prisoners on the

* See the official rebel reports in a statement in the *New York Times* of *November* 26th and 28th, 1864.

part of the North was placed in the hands of General Grant by whom arrangements were made and carried into effect for a general exchange.

In reference to this subject of the treatment of prisoners, a curious correspondence took place between Mr. Seward, Mr. Adams, and certain English gentlemen who had undertaken to distribute the funds raised at a fair in Liverpool for the benefit of Southern prisoners at the North. Lord Wharncliffe, in England, it seems from the papers laid before Congress, informed Mr. Adams that the Liverpool Bazaar produced about £17,000, and asked permission for an accredited agent to visit the military prisons within the Northern States, and distribute aid to their inmates. He denied that any political end was aimed at, or any imputation that Confederate prisoners were deprived of such attentions as the ordinary rules enjoin. He wrote "The issue of the great contest will not be determined by individual suffering, be it greater or less, and you whose family name is interwoven with American history cannot view with indifference the suffering of American citizens, whatever their state or opinions." Mr. Adams replied that it has never been the desire of the Government to treat with unnecessary or vindictive severity any of the misguided individual parties in this deplorable rebellion, who have fallen into its hands in the regular course of the war, and that he should greatly rejoice if the effects of such sympathy could be extended to ministering to their mental ailment, as well as their bodily suffering, thus contributing to put an end to a struggle which otherwise is too likely to be only procrastinated by their English sympathizers. Mr. Seward replied as follows to the application received through Mr. Adams. "Department of State, Washington, Dec. 5, 1864. Sir: I have received your dispatch of the 18th of November, No. 807, together with the papers therein mentioned, viz.: a copy of a letter which was addressed to you on the 12th of November last, by Lord Wharncliffe, and a copy of your answer to that letter. You will now inform Lord Wharncliffe that permission for an agent of the committee described by him to visit the insurgents detained in the military prisons of the United States, and to distribute among them seventeen thousand pounds of British gold is disallowed. Here it is expected that your correspondence with Lord Wharncliffe will end. That correspondence will necessarily become public. On reading it the American public will be well aware that, while the United States have ample means for the support of the prisoners, as well as for every other exigency of the war in which they are engaged; the insurgents, who have blindly rushed into that condition, are suffering no privations that appeal for relief to charity either at home or abroad. The American people will be likely to reflect that the sum thus insidiously headed in the name of humanity, constitutes no large portion of the profits which its contributors may be justly supposed to have derived from the insurgents, by exchanging with them arms and munitions of war, for the coveted productions of immoral and enervating slave labor, nor will any portion of the American people be disposed to regard the sum thus ostentatiously offered for the relief of captured insurgents as a too generous equivalent for the devastation and dissolution which a civil war promoted and protracted by British subjects, has spread throughout the States, which before were eminently prosperous and happy. Finally, in view of this last officious intervention in our domestic affairs, the American people can hardly fail to recall the warning of the Father of our country directed against two great and intimately connected public dangers, namely: sectional faction and foreign intrigue. I do not think the insurgents have become debased, although they have sadly wandered from the ways of loyalty and patriotism. I think that in common with all our countrymen, they will rejoice in being saved by their considerate and loyal Government from the grave insult which Lord Wharncliffe and his associates, in their zeal for the overthrow of the United States, have prepared for the victims of this unnatural and hopeless rebellion."

The autumn witnessed several desperate attempts of the rebels in Canada to make inroads upon the territory of the United States for the sake of injury and plunder, and doubtless with a further expectation of embroiling the two countries in difficulties. Raids were threatened at Detroit, Ogdensburgh, Buffalo; two small steamers on Lake Erie were taken possession of and burnt by a band of depredators from Canada, who made their escape thither in safety. A still more desperate, and in a great measure successful, effort was made in October, in an attack by a party from across the frontier, upon the village of St. Albans in Vermont. They were some thirty in number, who for several days had been gathering in the town when, on the afternoon of the nineteenth being arrived, they made a simultaneous attack upon three of the banks in the place, took the officers in charge by surprise, and freely pillaged the vaults and drawers. They then made their appearance on the streets and fired recklessly upon the citizens, several of whom were killed and wounded. Supplying themselves with stolen horses from the livery stables, they immediately rode off with their plunder toward the Canada line. The town people, as soon as they perceived the nature of this unexpected assault, which was the work of but half an hour, mounted and followed in pursuit, overtaking a portion of the marauders across the frontier, and succeeding with the aid of the Canadian authorities in arresting their leader, Bennett H. Young, with twelve of his followers. Young claimed to be acting under a Confederate commission, calling himself First Lieutenant Provisional Army Confederate States of America. The raiders were lodged in jail, and after various representations on the part of Vermont and the United States, with delays on the part of the local authorities, the case was brought to a hearing before Justice Coursal of Montreal, on the 13th of December. The Judge then decided on technical grounds that the Court had no jurisdiction, released the prisoners, and restored to them a portion of the money of which they had robbed the St. Alban's banks, another portion of it having been regained by the pursuers at the time of the capture of the depredators. The announcement of this result in the United States excited a strong expression of indignation. General Dix, in command of the Department of the East, in consequence, immediately on the 14th, issued from his head-quarters at New York, the following General Order: "Information having been received at these head-quarters that the rebel marauders who were guilty of murder and robbery at St. Alban's, have been discharged from arrest, and that other enterprises are actually in preparation in Canada, the Commanding General deems it due to the people of the frontier borders to adopt the most prompt and efficient measures for the security of their lives and property. All military commanders on the frontiers are, therefore, instructed, in case further acts of depredation and murder are attempted, whether by marauders or persons acting under commissions from the rebel authorities at Richmond, to shoot down the perpetrators if possible while in the commission of their crimes; or if it be necessary, with a view to their capture, to cross the boundary between the United States and Canada, said commanders are hereby directed to pursue them wherever they may take refuge, and if captured they are, under no circumstances to be surrendered, but are to be sent to these headquarters for trial and punishment by martial law. The Major-General commanding the department will not hesitate to exercise to the fullest extent the authority he possesses under the rules of law recognized by all civilized States, in regard to persons organizing hostile expeditions within neutral territory and fleeing to it for an asylum after committing acts of depredation within our own, such an exercise of authority having become indispensable to protect our cities and towns from incendiarism, and our people from robbery and murder. It is earnestly hoped that the inhabitants of our frontier districts will abstain from all acts of retaliation on account of the outrages committed by rebel marauders, and that the proper measures of redress will be left to the action of the public authorities." The effect of this was to arouse the Canadian authorities to a sense of the danger they were incurring, while at the same time to remove an obvious ground of complaint on the part of Great Britain, the order was disapproved of by the Government at Washington. General Dix accordingly, on the 17th, modified his order by issuing the following: "The President of the United States having disapproved of that portion of Department General Order No. 97, current series, which instructs all military Commanders on the frontier, in certain cases, therein specified to cross the boundary line between the United States and Canada, and directs pursuit into neutral territory, the said instruction is hereby revoked. In case, therefore, of any future marauding expedition into our territory from Canada, military Commanders on the frontier will report to these headquarters for orders before crossing the boundary line in pursuit of the guilty parties." The Canadian authorities meanwhile expressed their disapproval of the action of Judge Coursal, and the Governor-General ordered the re-arrest of the raiders, several of whom, including their leader Young, were retaken and again lodged in jail. To secure the frontier from the repetition of raids of this nature, an order was issued by Secretary Seward requiring persons entering the United States on the frontier to be provided with properly certified passports.

During the course of these proceedings a deliberate attempt, supposed to be the work of Southern emissaries, was made to fire the city of New York. Reports of such an intention had been current, and the Secretary of State, Mr. Seward, had on the second of November issued an official notification on the subject, to the effect that the Department had received information from the British Provinces that a conspiracy was on foot to set fire to the principal cities in the Northern States on the day of the Presidential election. The day of the election, however, passed over without disturbance of this kind, but on the night of the 25th of November, an attempt was made to fire the chief hotels and theatres in the city of New York. Though boldly and skillfully undertaken it proved unsuccessful; the fires were put out before any considerable damage was done, and the only effect was to cause various arrests and a constant supervision by the military authorities and police of dangerous or suspected characters. The following order was issued on this occasion by General Dix: "A nefarious attempt was made last night to set fire to the principal hotels and other places of public resort in this city. If this attempt had succeeded, it would have resulted in a frightful sacrifice of property and life. The evidences of extensive combination, and other facts disclosed to-day, show it to have been the work of rebel emissaries and agents. All such persons engaged in secret acts of hostility here can only be regarded as spies, subject to martial law, and to the penalty of death. If they are detected, they will be immediately brought before a court martial or military commission, and, if convicted, they will be executed without the delay of a single day."

The 24th of November was generally observed throughout the loyal States as a day of national Thanksgiving, in accordance with the following proclamation by President Lincoln, (dated October 20th,) seconded by others from the State Governors: "It has pleased Almighty God to prolong our national life another year, defending us with His guardian care, against unfriendly designs from abroad, and vouchsafed to us, in His mercy, many and signal victories over the enemy, who is of our own household. It has also pleased our Heavenly Father to favor as well our citizens in their homes as our soldiers in their camps and our sailors on the rivers and seas, with unusual health. He has largely augmented our free population by emancipation and by immigration, while He has opened to us new sources of wealth, and has crowned the labor of our working men in every department of industry with abundant reward. Moreover, he has been pleased to animate and inspire our minds and hearts with fortitude, courage and resolution sufficient for the great trial of civil war into which we have been brought by our adherence, as a nation to the cause of freedom and humanity, and to afford to us reasonable hopes of an ultimate and happy deliverance from all our dangers and afflictions. Now, therefore, I, Abraham Lincoln, President of the United States, do hereby appoint and set apart the last Thursday in November next, as a day which I desire to be observed by all my fellow-citizens, wherever they may then be, as a day of thanksgiving and prayer to Almighty God, the beneficent Creator and Ruler of the universe; and I do further recommend to my fellow-citizens aforesaid, that on that occasion they do reverently humble themselves in the dust, and from thence offer up penitent and fervent prayers and supplications to the Great Disposer of Events for a return of the inestimable blessings of peace, union and harmony throughout the land which it has pleased Him to assign as a dwelling-place for ourselves and our posterity throughout all generations."

CHAPTER CIX.

ATTACK ON THE DEFENCES OF WILMINGTON, CAPTURE OF FORT FISHER, DECEMBER, 1864—JANUARY, 1865.

After the partial or entire closing of the ports of Savannah, Charleston, and Mobile, the conquests in North Carolina, and the general establishment of the blockade along the coast, the harbor of Wilmington was the only one of importance left to the rebels by which they might receive supplies from abroad. Dur ng the year, this was the chief resort of the English blockade-runners from Nassau, and owing to the peculiar character of the navigation and the rebel fortifications on the coast, in spite of numerous captures at sea, they were enabled to carry on a profitable trade, introducing ammunition and arms, with various foreign articles of necessity, which were paid for by a liberal exportation of cotton. The attention of the Government at Washington had, of course, early been directed to this convenient channel of supplies, and but for the necessity of extraordinary preparations would long since have attempted its capture. Situated on Cape Fear River thirty miles from the sea, the approach to that stream was protected by formidable forts and batteries at the two main entrances at either extremity of the island stretching across the mouth of the river. The Old or Western inlet was commanded by Forts Caswell and Johnson and the coast fortifications, while the New or Eastern Inlet was defended on Federal Point by Fort Fisher, a newly-erected casemated earthwork of great strength, mounting some forty heavy guns. Other formidable defences stretched along the shore, affording a secure protection to blockade-runners entering the harbor. The two main entrances being forty miles apart, intersected by numerous channels, it was impossible effectually to prevent the English vessels, specially constructed for the purpose, gaining the river. "Convinced," says Secretary Welles in his annual report, "as this department always has been, that it is necessary to take possession of the entrances, so as to permit our armed vessels of light draught to go inside, no opportunity has been omitted to impress the necessity of joint military and naval operations for that purpose. The navy has been at all times ready to perform its part in such an expedition; but the army has not yet been able to unite in a conjoint movement. Neither branch of the service can expect to be successful in an attack upon this position independent of the other. Were there deep water at Wilmington, as at New Orleans, Mobile, and Port Royal, either of those operations could have been repeated at that point, but by reason of the shoalness of the water, an exclusively naval operation cannot be relied upon to be successful."

At length the desirable opportunity, aided by the withdrawal of General Bragg from Wilmington with a large part of his force to look after General Sherman in Georgia, seemed to have arrived. It had long been waited for by Rear-Admiral David D. Porter, who in October had succeeded Acting Rear-Admiral S. P. Lee in command of the North Atlantic Squadron lying at Hampton Roads. There was assembled a truly formidable fleet of more than seventy vessels of war, arrayed in five divisions, including such vessels as the Colorado and Minnesota, each 50 guns, Powhatan 19 guns, the Susquehanna, 16 guns; and the monitors and iron clads, the New Ironsides 18 guns, the Monadnock 4, and the Canonicus, Saugus, Dictator and Mahopac each two. On the 12th and 13th of December, this powerful fleet set sail for North Carolina, followed by a land force under General Butler of about 6,500 effective men, consisting of General Ames' division of the Twenty-fourth Corps and General Paine's division of the Twenty-fifth Corps, under command of Major-General Weitzel. Its destination was Wilmington, and its immediate object was the reduction of Fort Fisher at the New Inlet, the command of which with the inner waters would, it was expected, as effectually close the port against blockade-runners as Admiral Farragut in his recent naval triumph had gained the control of the harbor of Mobile.

The fleet on its passage encountered rough weather off Cape Hatteras, and the monitors were exposed to some dangers; but all weathered the cape, and arrived off Beaufort, where fresh supplies of coal were taken in, and preparations made for the attack upon Wilmington. Several days were passed here by the naval vessels before the expedition finally left and joined the transports off New Inlet; and there were other delays owing to the weather and the season of the year before Admiral Porter was able to begin actual operations against Fort Fisher, the transports being compelled by the exhaustion of their limited stores to visit Beaufort for fresh supplies of coal and water.

The details of the movement as finally arranged are fully supplied by Admiral Porter in his official report to the Secretary of the Navy, dated from his Flagship Malvern at sea, off New Inlet, December 26th, after the action. "I was in hopes," says he, "that I should have been able to present to the nation Fort Fisher and the surrounding works as a Christmas offering, but I am sorry to say it has not been taken yet. I attacked it on the 24th inst. with the Ironsides, Canonicus, Mahopac, Monadnock, Minnesota, Colorado, Mohican, Tuscarora, Wabash, Susquehanna, Brooklyn, Powhatan, Juniata, Seneca, Shenandoah, Patuxent, Ticonderoga, Mackinaw, Maumee, Yantic, Kansas, Iasco, Quaker City, Monticello, Rhode Island, Sassacus, Chippewa, Osceola, Tacony, Pontoosuc, Santiago de Cuba, Fort Jackson and Vanderbilt, having a reserve of small vessels, consisting of the Aries, Howqua, Wilderness, Cherokee, A. D. Vance, Anemone, Æolus, Gettysburg, Alabama, Keystone State, Banshee, Emma Lillian, Tristram Shandy, Britannia, Governor Buckingham and Nansemond. Previous to making the attack, a torpedo on a large scale, with an amount of powder on board supposed to be sufficient to explode the powder magazine of the fort, was prepared with great care, and placed under the command of Commander A. C. Rhind, who had associated with him on this perilous service Lieutenant S. W. Preston, Second Assistant Engineer A. T. Mullen, of the United States steamship Agawam, and Acting Master's Mate Paul Bayard, and seven men. So much had been said and written about the terrible effects of gunpowder in an explosion that happened lately in England, that great results were expected from this novel mode of making war. Every thing that ingenuity could devise was adopted to make the experiment a success. The vessel was brought round from Norfolk with great care and without accident, in tow of the United States steamer Sassacus, Lieutenant Commander J. L. Davis, who directed his whole attention to the matter in hand, and though he experienced some bad weather and lost one of his rudders, he took her safely into Beaufort, where we filled her up with powder and perfected all the machinery for blowing her up. General Butler had arrived at the rendezvous before us, and I hastened matters all that I could, so that no unnecessary delay might be laid to my charge.

"On the 18th inst. I sailed from Beaufort with all the monitors, the New Ironsides, and the small vessels, including the Louisiana, disguised as a blockade-runner, for the rendezvous, twenty miles east of New Inlet, N. C., and found all the larger vessels and transports assembled there, the wind blowing light from the northeast. On the 20th a heavy gale set in from the southwest, and not being able to make a port without scattering all the vessels, I determined to ride it out, which I did without accident of any kind, except the loss of a few anchors, the monitors all behaving beautifully. Only two vessels went to sea in order to avoid the gale, and fared no better than those at anchor. The transports being short of water put into Beaufort, N. C., and were not suitable for riding out at anchor such heavy weather. After the southwester, the wind chopped around to the westward and gave us a beautiful spell of weather, which I could not afford to lose, and the transports with the troops not making their appearance, I determined to take advantage of it and attack Fort Fisher and its outworks. On the 23d, I directed Commander Rhind to proceed and explode the vessel right under the walls of Fort Fisher, Mr. Bradford, of the Coast Survey, having gone in at night and ascertained that we could place a vessel of seven feet draught right on the edge of the beach. Lieutenant R. H. Lamson, commanding the Gettysburg, volunteered to go in the Wilderness, Acting Master Henry Arsy in command, and tow the Louisiana into position. At 10:30 P. M. the powder vessel started toward the bar, and was towed by the Wilderness until the embrasures of Fort Fisher were plainly in sight. The Wilderness then cast off, and the Louisiana proceeded under steam until within 200 yards of the beach and 500 from the fort. Commander Rhind anchored her securely there, and coolly went to work to make all his arrangements to blow her up. This he was enabled to do, owing to a blockade-runner going in right ahead of him, the forts making the blockade-runner signals, which they also did to the Louisiana. The gallant party, after coolly making all their arrangements for the explosion, left the vessel. The last thing they did being to set her on fire under the cabin, and then, taking to their boats, they made their escape off the Wilderness, lying close by. The Wilderness then put off shore with good speed, to avoid any ill effects that might happen from the explosion. At 1:45 on the morning of the 24th, the explosion took place. The shock was nothing like so severe as was expected; it shook the vessels some, and broke one or two glasses, but nothing more.

"At daylight of the twenty-fourth, the fleet got under way, and stood in in line of battle. At 11:30 A. M. the signal was made to engage the forts, the Ironsides leading, and the Monadnock, Canonicus and Mahopac following. The Ironsides took her position in the most beautiful and seamanlike manner, and opened a deliberate fire on the fort, which was firing at her with all its guns, which did not seem numerous in the northeast face, though we counted what appeared to be seventeen guns. But four or five of these were fired from that direction, and they were silenced as soon as the Ironsides opened her terrific battery. The Minnesota then took her position in handsome style, and her guns, after getting the range, were fired with rapidity, while the Mohican, the Colorado, and the large vessels marked on the plan, got to their stations, all firing to cover themselves while anchoring. By the time the last of the large vessels anchored, and got their batteries into play, but one or two guns of the enemy were fired, this *feu d'enfer* driving them all to the bomb-proofs. The small gunboats Kansas, Unadilla, Pequot, Seneca, Pontoosuc, Yantic and Huron took a position on the northward and eastward of the monitors, and enfilading the work. The Shenandoah, Ticonderoga, Mackinaw, Tacony and Vanderbilt took effective positions, as marked on the chart, and added their fire to that already begun. The Santiago de Cuba, Fort Jackson Osceola, Chippewa, Sassacus, Rhode Island, Monticello, Quaker City and Iasco dropped into position, and according to order, and the battle became general. In one hour and fifteen minutes after the first shot was fired, not a shot came from the fort. Two magazines had been blown up by our shells, and the fort set on fire in several places; and such a torrent of missiles were falling into and bursting over it, that it was impossible for any thing human to stand it. Finding that the batteries were silenced completely, I directed the ships to keep up a moderate fire, in the hopes of attracting the attention of the transports and bringing them in. At sunset General Butler came in in his flagship with a few transports, the rest not having arrived from Beaufort. Being too late to do any thing more, I signalled to the fleet to retire for the night to a safe anchorage; which they did without being molested by the enemy.

"There were some mistakes made during the day when the vessels went in to take position. My plan of battle being based on accurate calculations, and made from information to be relied on, was placed in the hands of each Commander, and it seemed impossible to go astray if it was strictly followed. I required those vessels that had not followed it closely to get under way and assume their proper positions, which was done promptly and without confusion. The vessels were placed somewhat nearer to the works, and were able to throw in their shell before falling in the water. One or two leading vessels having made the mistake of anchoring too far off, caused those coming after them to commit a like error, but when they all got into place and commenced work in earnest, the shower of shell (one hundred and fifteen per minute) was irresistible. So quickly were the enemy's guns silenced that not an officer or man was injured. I regret, however, to have to report some severe casualties by the bursting of six 100-pounder Parrot cannon. One burst on board the Ticonderoga, killing six of the crew and wounding seven others; another burst on board the Yankee, killing one officer and two men; another on the Juniata, killing two officers, and wounding and killing ten others; another on the Mackinaw, killing one officer and wounding five men; another on the Quaker City, wounding, I believe, two or three; another on the Susquehanna, killing and wounding seven. I think the bursting of the guns (six in all) much disconcerted the crews of the vessels where the accidents happened, and gave one and all a great distrust of the Parrott 100-pounders, and as subsequent events proved, they were unfit for service, and calculated to kill more of our men than of those of the enemy. Some of the vessels were struck once or twice. The Mackinaw had her boiler perforated with a shell and ten or twelve persons were badly scalded. The Osceola was struck with a shell near the magazine, and was at one time in a sinking condition; but her efficient commander stopped up the leak; while the Mackinaw fought out the battle notwithstanding the damage she received. The Yantic was the only vessel which left the line to report damages.

"Commander John Guest, at the last end of the line, showed unusual intelligence in selecting the position and directing his fire. Twice his guns cut down the flagstaff on the Mound Battery, and he silenced the guns there in a very short time, the Keystone State and Quaker City co-operating effectively. Lieutenant-Commander J. R. Davis, with both rudders disabled, got his vessel, the Sassacus, into close action and assisted materially in silencing the works, and the Santiago de Cuba and Fort Jackson took such positions as they could get, towing other vessels not forming proper lines and throwing them out of place, and fought their guns well. The taking of a new position while under fire, by the Brooklyn and Colorado, was a beautiful sight, and when they got into place both ships delivered a fire that nothing could withstand. The Brooklyn well sustained her proud name under her present commander, Captain James Alden, and the Colorado gave evidence that her commander, Commodore H. K. Thatcher, well understood the duties of his position. The Susquehanna was most effective in her fire, and was fortunate enough to obtain the right position, though much bothered by a vessel near her that had not found her right place. The Mohican went into battle gallantly, and fired rapidly and with effect, and when the Powhatan, Ticonderoga and Shenandoah got into their positions, they did good service. The Pawtuxet fell handsomely into line and did good service with the rest, and the Vanderbilt took position near the Minnesota and threw in a splendid fire. The firing of the monitors was excellent, and when their shells struck great damage was done, and the little gunboats that covered them kept up a fire sufficient to disconcert the enemy's aim. The rebels fired no more after the vessels all opened on them, except a few shots from the Mound and upper batteries, which the Iasco and her consorts soon silenced. Our men were at work at the guns five hours, and glad to get a little rest. They came out of the action with rather a contempt for the rebel batteries, and anxious to renew the battle in the morning.

"On the twenty-fifth all the transports had arrived, and General Butler sent General Weitzel to see me and arrange the programme for the day. It was decided that we should attack the forts again, while the army landed and assaulted them, if possible, under our heavy fire. I sent seventeen gunboats under the command of Captain O. S. Glesson, to cover the troops and assist with their boats in landing the soldiers. Finding the smaller vessels kept too far from the beach which was quite bold, I sent in the Brooklyn, to set them an example, which that vessel did, relying as every commander should, on the information I gave him in relation to the soundings. To this number was added all the small vessels that were covering the coast along. And finally I sent some eight or nine vessels that were acting under Commander Griest in endeavoring to find a way across the bar. This gave 100 small boats to land the troops with: beside those, the army were already provided with about twenty more. At seven, A. M., on the twenty-fifth I made signal to get under way and form in line of battle, which was quickly done. The order to attack was given, and the Ironsides took position in her usual handsome style, the monitors following close after her. All the vessels followed according to orders, and took position without a shot being fired at them, excepting a few shots fired at the four last vessels that got into line. The firing this day was slow, only sufficient to answer the enemy while the army landed, which they were doing five miles to the east of the fleet. I suppose about 3,000 men landed, when I was notified they were re-embarking. I could see our soldiers near the fort reconnoitering and sharpshooting, and was in hopes an assault was deemed practicable. General Weitzel, in person, was making observations about 600 yards off. and the troops were in and around the works. One gallant officer, whose name I do not know, went on the parapet and brought away the rebel flag we had knocked down A soldier went into the works and led out a horse, killing the orderly mounted on him, and taking his dispatches from the body. Another soldier fired his musket into the bombproof among the rebels, and eight or ten others who had ventured near the forts were wounded by our shells.

"As the ammunition gave out the vessels retired from action, and the iron-clads and the Minnesota, Colorado and Susquehanna were ordered to open rapidly, which they did with such effect that it seemed to tear the works to pieces. We drew off at sunset, leaving the iron-clads to fire through the night, expecting the troops would attack in the morning, when we would commence again. I received word from General Weitzel informing me that it was impracticable to assault, and herewith inclose a letter from General Butler, assigning his reasons for withdrawing the troops. I also inclose my answer. In the bombardment of the twenty-fifth the men were engaged firing slowly for seven hours. The rebels kept a couple of guns on the upper batteries firing on the vessels, hitting some of them several times without doing much damage. The Wabash and Powhatan, being within their range, the object seemed mainly to disable them ; but a rapid fire soon closed them up. Every thing was coolly and systematically done throughout the day, and witnessed some beautiful practice. The army commenced landing about two o'clock, Captain Glesson, in the Santiago de Cuba, having shelled Flag Pond Battery to insure a safe landing, and they commenced to re-embark about five o'clock. The weather coming on thick and rainy, about a brigade were left on the beach during the night, covered by the gunboats. As our troops landed, sixty-five rebel soldiers hoisted the white flag, and delivered themselves up, and were taken prisoners by the seamen landing the troops, and conveyed to the Santiago de Cuba; and two hundred and eighteen more gave themselves up to the reconnoitering party, all being desirous to quit the war. I don't pretend to put my opinion in opposition to General Weitzel, who is a thorough soldier and an able engineer, and whose business it is to know more of assaulting than I do. But I can't help thinking that it was worth while to make the attempt, after arriving so far.

"About twelve o'clock I sent in a detachment of double-enders under command of Commander John Guest, to see if I could effect an entrance through the channel. The great number of wrecks on and about the bar has changed the whole formation, and where the original channel was, we found a shallow bar. I sent Lieutenant W. B. Cushing in to sound and buoy out the channel if he could find one, with orders to Commander Guest to drag for torpedoes and be ready to run in by the buoys when ordered. One boat belonging to the Tacony was sunk by a shell, and a man had his legs cut off; still they stuck to their work until ordered to withdraw for other duty.

"In conclusion, allow me to draw your attention to the conduct of Commander Rhind and Lieutenant Preston. They engaged in the most perilous adventure that was, perhaps, ever undertaken, and though no material results have taken place from the effects of the explosion that we know of, still it was not their fault. As an incentive to others, I beg leave to recommend them for promotion. Also that of Lieutenant R. H. Lamson, who piloted them in and brought them off. No one in the squadron considered that their lives would be saved, and Captain Rhind and Lieutenant Preston had made an arrangement to sacrifice themselves in case the vessel was boarded, a thing likely to happen. I inclose herewith the report of Commander Rhind, with the names of the gallant fellows who volunteered for the desperate service. Allow me to mention, also, the name of Mr. Bradford, of the Coast Survey, who has always patiently performed every duty he has been called on to carry out. My thanks are due to Lieutenant-Commander R. R. Breese, Fleet Captain, for carrying about my orders to the fleet during the action, and for his general usefulness; to Lieutenant-Commander H. A. Adams, for promptness in supplying the fleet with ammunition; to Lieutenant M. W. Sanders, Signal Officer, whose whole time was occupied in making signals, and who performed his duty well; and to my aids, Lieutenant S. W. Terry and Lieutenant S. W. Preston, who afforded me valuable assistance. I have not yet received a list of the casualties, but believe they are very few from the enemy's guns. We had killed and wounded about forty-five persons by the bursting of the Parrott guns. I must not omit to pay a tribute to the officers and crews of the monitors, who rode out the heavy gales on an open coast without murmuring or complaining of the want of comfort, which must have been very serious. They have shown a degree of fortitude and perseverance seldom witnessed. Equally brave in battle, they take the closest work with pleasure, and the effect of their shells is terrific. The following are the names of the commanders, and I hope I shall ever keep them under my command: Commanders E. G. Parrott, of the Monadnock, and E. R. Calhoun, of the Saugus; Lieutenant Commanders George L. Belknap, of the Canonicus, and E. E. Potter, of the

Mahopac. There are about 1,000 left on shore by the army, who have not got off yet on account of the surf of the beach. These will be got off in the morning, and then the soldiers will be sent home."

The letter of General Butler alluded to by Admiral Porter, supplies the account of the operations of the troops on landing and their officer's reason for his abandonment of the enterprise. "Upon landing the troops," writes General Butler, "and making a thorough reconnoissance of Fort Fisher, both General Weitzel and myself are fully of the opinion that the place could not be carried by assault, as it was left substantially uninjured as a defensive work, by the navy fire. We found seventeen guns, protected by traverses, two only of which were dismounted, bearing on the beach and covering a strip of land, the only practicable route, not wide enough for a thousand men in line of battle. Having captured Flag Pond Battery, the garrison of which, sixty-five men and two commissioned officers, were taken off by the navy, we also captured Half-Moon Battery, and seven officers and two hundred and eight men of the Third North Carolina Junior Reserves, including its commander, from whom I learned that a portion of Hoke's division, consisting of Kirkland's and Hapgood's brigades, had been sent from the lines before Richmond on Tuesday last, arriving at Wilmington Friday night. General Weitzel advanced his skirmish-line within fifty yards of the fort, while the garrison was kept in their bombproofs by the fire of the navy, and so closely, that three or four men of the picket-line ventured upon the parapet, and through the sally-port of the works, capturing a horse, which they brought off, killing the orderly, who was the bearer of a dispatch from the Chief of Artillery of General Whiting, to bring a light battery within the fort, and also brought away from the parapet the flag of the fort. This was done while the shells of the navy were falling about the heads of the daring men who entered the work; and it was evident, as soon as the fire of the navy ceased because of the darkness, that the fort was fully manned again, and opened with grape and canister upon our picket line. Finding that nothing but the operations of a regular siege, which did not come within my instructions, would reduce the fort, and in view of the threatening aspect of the weather, the wind arising from the south-west, rendering it impossible to make further landing through the surf, I caused the troops with their prisoners to reëmbark; and I see nothing further that can be done by the land forces. I shall therefore sail for Hampton Roads as soon as the transport fleet can be got in order. My engineers and officers report Fort Fisher to me as substantially uninjured as a defensive work."

The following was the reply of Adral Porter, dated December 26: "General, I beg leave to acknowledge the receipt of your letter of this date, the substance of which was communicated to me last night by General Weitzel. I have ordered the largest vessels to proceed off Beaufort to fill up with ammunition, to be ready for another attack in case it is decided to proceed with this matter by making other arrangements. We have not commenced firing rapidly yet, and could keep any rebels inside from moving their head until an assaulting column was within twenty yards of the works. I wish some more of your gallant fellows had followed the officer who took the flag from the parapet, and the brave fellow who brought the horse out from the fort. I think they would have found it an easier conquest than is supposed. I do not, however, pretend to place my opinion in opposition to General Weitzel, whom I know to be an accomplished soldier and engineer, and whose opinion has great weight with me."

On the withdrawal of the troops, General Braxton Bragg, who was in command of the defences of Wilmington, thus addressed President Jefferson Davis: "The enemy has re-embarked under the cover of his fleet. His movement is not developed. I have visited Fort Fisher, and find the damage slight, excepting the buildings not necessary for defence. Only two guns were disabled. The marks remaining indicate that the bombardment was very heavy. Major-General Whiting, commanding the defences at the mouth of the river; Colonel Lamb, commanding the fort, and the officers and men comprising the garrison, deserve especial commendation for the gallantry, efficiency, and fortitude displayed under very trying circumstances."

Thus ended the combined attack in December of Porter and Butler upon the outer defences of Wilmington. General Butler returned with his troops to Hampton Roads, while Admiral Porter having sent for fresh supplies of ammunition, remained waiting further orders off Cape Fear River. Shortly after his return to the Army of the Potomac on James River, General Butler by an order of the President was relieved of his command, and Major-General Ord appointed in his place. In the farewell address of General Butler to his troops he evidently represented the course which he had taken on landing at Federal Point as the cause of his removal. This document read as follows:— "Headquarters, Department of Virginia and North Carolina, Army of the James, Sunday, January 8, 1865. *Soldiers of the Army of the James*—Your commander, relieved by order of the President, takes leave of you. Your conduct in the field has extorted praise from the unwilling. You have endured the privations of the camp and the march without a murmur. You have never failed to attack when ordered. You have stormed and carried works deemed impregnable by the enemy. You have shown the positions to be so by holding them against his fiercest assaults in the attempt to retake them. Those skilled in war have marveled at the obstacles overcome by your valor. Your line of works has excited the wonder of the officers of other nations, who have come to learn defensive warfare from the monuments of your skilled labor. Your deeds have rendered your names illustrious. In after times, your General's proudest memory will be to say, with you, 'I, too, was of the Army of the James.' To share such companionship, is pleasure; to participate in such acts, is honor; to have commanded such an army, is glory. No one could yield it without regret. Knowing your willing obedience to orders, witnessing your ready devotion of your blood in your country's cause, I have been chary of the precious charge confided to me. I have refused to order useless sacrifices of the lives of such soldiers, and I am relieved from your command. The wasted blood of my men does not stain my garments. For my action I am responsible to God and my country.

"*To the Colored Troops of the Army of the James*—In this army you have been treated not as laborers, but as soldiers. You have shown yourselves worthy of the uniform you wear. The best officers of the Union seek to command you. Your bravery has won the admiration even of those who would be your masters. Your patriotism, fidelity, and courage have illustrated the best qualities of manhood. With the bayonet you have unlocked the iron-barred gates of prejudice, opening new fields of freedom, liberty, and equality of rights to yourselves and your race for ever.

"Comrades of the Army of the James, I bid you farewell, farewell!"

The full official report of General Butler was presently published with a special communication and the correspondence of General Grant on the subject, in which it was stated by the latter "that it was never contemplated that General Butler would accompany the expedition, but that Major-General Weitzel was especially named as the commander of it. My hopes of success rested entirely on our ability to capture Fort Fisher, and I had even a hope of getting Wilmington before the enemy could get troops there to oppose us. I knew that the enemy had taken nearly the entire garrison of Wilmington and its dependencies to oppose Sherman. I am inclined to ascribe the delay which has cost us so dearly to an experiment. I refer to the explosion of gunpowder in the open air. My dispatches to General Butler will show his report to be in error where he states that he returned, after having effected a landing, in obedience to my instructions. . On the contrary, these instructions contemplated no withdrawal, or a failure, after a landing was made."

General Grant did not long suffer the affair to remain in this unhappy position. A new expedition, or rather a resumption of the former one, was immediately ordered to renew the attack on Fort Fisher. A military force was organized, consisting of the troops brought back by General Butler, with an additional brigade, and placed under the command of General Alfred Howe Terry, a young officer, a native of Connecticut, who having entered the service from civil life, his profession was that of a lawyer, had been engaged, from the beginning of the war in active duties, in all of which he has approved himself a soldier of eminent spirit and ability. He had borne a distinguished part in the operations on the seaboard in Georgia and South Carolina, at the reduction of Fort Pulaski, and the arduous capture of Morris Island, for which he had been promoted, and risen to the command of a division. In the spring of 1864 he was ordered north with the Tenth Corps to the James River, and had been since prominently engaged in the army movements in that quarter. His appointment to his present command was the highest tribute which could be paid to his efficiency. In the first week in January Major-General Terry had sailed from Hampton Roads, and reached Beaufort, N. C., the place of rendezvous, with his forces. We continue the narrative of events with the official report of subsequent operations by Admiral Porter. "As soon as Major-General Terry," says he, "arrived at Beaufort, which he did on the 8th of January, we arranged together a plan of operations, which have proved successful. The weather was threatening, and I advised the General to get his transports inside the harbor to avoid the violence of the coming gale. Most of them, however, laid outside. The gale blew very heavy for two days and nights—the ships-of-war all held on, and rode out at their anchors, except the Colorado, which vessel was obliged to go to sea, having only one anchor left, with which alone she could not positively have ridden out the gale, the sea being very heavy from the southwest, and breaking clean over the vessels. Knowing that the transports had arrived, the commanders all made strenuous exertions to keep their vessels at anchor off Beaufort, to be ready for the move that was about to be made. Having expended almost every shot and shell in the first bombardment, it became necessary to take in about fifteen thousand more, and fill up with coal, which was done under the most adverse circumstances, the large vessels all laying outside in a heavy sea, and filling up as best they could. The fleet, accompanied by the transports, steamed away on the 12th for Fort Fisher, and the wind being fair and moderate, I was in hopes that we would be able to land the troops by 9 or 10 o'clock that night; the wind changing to southwest, we were obliged to anchor off Half-moon battery for the night. The fleet sailed in three columns. Line No. 1, led by the Brooklyn, Captain James Alden, consisted of the Mohican, Commander Daniel Ammen; Tacony, Lieutenant-Commander W. T. Truxton; Kansas, Lieutenant-Commander G. P. Watmough; Yantic, Lieutenant-Commander T. C. Harris; Unadilla, Lieutenant-Commander F. M. Ramsay; Huron, Lieutenant-Commander T. O. Selfridge; Maumee, Lieutenant-Commander Ralph Chandler; Pequot, Lieutenant-Commander D. L. Braine; Pawtuxent, Commander J. H. Spotts; Seneca, Lieutenant-Commander M. Sicard; Pontoosuc, Lieutenant-Commander W. G. Temple; Nereus, Commander J. C. Howell. Line No. 2—Minnesota, Commander Joseph Lanman, leading, consisted of the Colorado, Commodore H. K. Thatcher; Wabash, Captain M. Smith; Susquehanna, Commodore S. W. Godon; Powhatan, Commodore J. F. Schenck; Juniata, Lieutenant-Commander F. S. Phelps; Shenandoah, Captain D. B. Ridgeley; Ticonderoga, Captain Charles Steedman; Vanderbilt, Captain C. W. Pickering; Mackinaw Commander J. C. Beaumont: Tuscarora, Commander J. M. Frailey. Line No. 3—Santiago de Cuba, Captain O. S. Glisson, leading, consisted of Fort Jackson, Captain B. F. Sands; Osceola, Commander J. M. B. Clitz; Sassacus, Lieutenant-Commander J. L. Davis; Chippewa, Lieutenant-Commander E. E. Potter; R. R. Cuyler, Commander C. H. B. Caldwell; Maratanza, Lieutenant-Commander George W. Young; Monticello, Lieutenant-Commander W. B. Cushing; Alabama, A. V. Lieutenant T. C. Dunn; Rhode Island, Commander S. D. Trenchard; Iosco, Commander John Guest. The reserve division under Lieutenant-Commander J. H. Upshur, in the A. D. Vance, consisted of the Britannia, A. V. Lieutenant W. B. Sheldon; Tristram Shandy, A.V. Lieutenant F. M. Green; Lillian, A. V. Lieutenant T. A. Harris; Fort Donnelson, Acting Master G. W. Frost; Wilderness, Acting Master H. Arey; Aries, A. V. Lieutenant F. S. Wells; Governor Buckingham, A. V. Lieutenant J. McDonald. The Nansemond, Acting Master J. H. Porter; Little Ada, Acting Master F. P. Crafts; Eolus, Acting Master E. S. Keyser, and Republic, Acting-Ensign J. W. Bennett, being used as dispatch vessels.

"Great enthusiasm was displayed in the fleet when it was ascertained that troops had come to renew the attack on Fort Fisher, for great was the disappointment on account of the late failure. Some of the vessels that accompanied the expedition were badly damaged in various ways. The Sassacus had both her rudders disabled, but her energetic commander, Lieutenant Commander J. L. Davis, was ready in time. The Mackinaw, Commander J. C. Beaumont, had one of her boilers knocked to pieces. But her Commander would go on one boiler. The Osceola, Commander J. M. B. Clitz, in the same condition, one boiler smashed up with shot, and a hole near the bottom, was ready for any thing, and I heard no complaints from any one. With such a disposition on the part of the officers, I anticipated the most favorable result. At daylight on the 11th instant, line No. 1 took position within 600 yards of the beach to land the troops, lines No. 2 and No. 3 anchoring close to, and outside of them, and the reserves taking charge of the provision vessels. At 8.30 A. M., the signal was made to the fleet to send boats to transports to land troops. At 2 P. M. we had landed 8,000 men, with twelve days' provisions, and all their entrenching tools. In the mean time, the new Ironsides, Commodore William Radford; Sangus, Commander E. R. Colhoun; Canonicus, Lieutenant-Commander George E. Belknap; Mahopac, Lieutenant-Commander A. W. Weaver, and Monadnock, Commander E. G. Parrott, were ordered in to take a nearer position, the outside vessel, the Ironsides, being one thousand yards from Fort Fisher, which was the principal work, and on which the iron vessels were ordered to pour all their fire, and endeavor to dismount all the guns. They got into position about 8 A. M., and opened fire deliberately. The troops having all landed without opposition, at 3 P. M. I signalled line No. 2 to get under way, and go in and attack. Line No. 1 was signalled to take position in front of the batteries, and line No. 3 was to remain and cover the landing party, and get the field artillery on shore.

"The different lines having formed into line of battle, steamed toward Fort Fisher—the Colorado leading, the Minnesota having got a hawser around a propeller. The vessels took their positions handsomely (having had some practice at that place) and delivered their fire as they fell in. The rapid fire of the monitors and Ironsides kept the rebels partly away from their guns, and they inflicted no damage on the fleet, the firing being very unsteady; indeed I do not see how they could fire at all after lines Nos. 1 and 2 got fairly anchored in position. The bombardment was very rapid and severe. This was continued without intermission from 4 P. M., until some time after dark, when the wooden vessels were ordered to haul out and anchor. The monitors and Ironsides were directed to keep up the fire during the night. The enemy had long ceased to respond to our fire, and kept in his bomb-proofs. I could see that our fire had damaged some of their guns, and I determined that before the army went to the assault there should be no guns within our reach to arrest their progress. Having found that the rebels could still bring some heavy guns to bear, I determined to try another plan, and early on the morning of the 14th, ordered in all the small gunboats carrying 11-inch guns to fire slowly and try and dismount the guns on the face of the works were the assault was to be made. The Brooklyn was ordered to throw a pretty quick fire to keep the rebels from working their guns. The attack was commenced at 1 P. M. and lasted until after dark. One or two guns only were fired this day from the upper batteries, inflicting no serious damage on any of the vessels, except cutting away the mainmast of the Huron, and hitting the Unadilla once or twice. These guns were always silenced when a rapid fire was opened. The attack of the gunboats lasted until long after dark, and one vessel was employed firing (an hour each) throughout the night.

"On this evening General Terry came on board to see me, and arrange the plan of battle for the next day. The troops had got rested after their long confinement on shipboard and sea-voyage, and had recovered from the drenching they received when landing through the surf. Having been long enough on their native element, they were eager for the attack. It was arranged between the General and myself that the ships should go in early, and fire rapidly throughout the day, until the time for the assault arrived. The hour named was 3 P. M. I detailed 1,600 sailors and 400 marines to accompany the troops in the assault—the sailors to board the sea face, whilst the troops assaulted the land side. Most all of the sailors were armed with cutlasses and revolvers, while a number had Sharpes' rifles or short carbines. There was perfect understanding between the General and myself, and a system of signals established (by the army code) by which we could converse at our pleasure, though nearly a mile apart, and amid the din of battle. At 9 A. M., on the 15th, the squadron was signalled to attack in three lines, or assume position marked on the plan herewith enclosed. All the vessels reached position at about 11 A. M., and opened fire as they got their anchors down. The same guns in the upper batteries opened again this day with some effect, but no vessel was injured sufficiently to interfere in the least with her efficiency. The fire was kept up furiously all day. The Mound Hill Battery kept up rather a galling fire with its two heavy guns, but the rebels were driven away from their works into their bomb-proofs, so that no vessel was in the least disabled. At 2 o'clock I expected the signal to "change the direction of their fire," so that the troops might assault. The sailors and marines had worked, by digging ditches, or rifle-pits to within two hundred yards of the fort, and were all ready. The troops, however, did not get into position until later, and at three o'clock the signal came. The vessels changed their fire to the upper batteries—all the steam-whistles were blown, and the troops and sailors dashed ahead, nobly vieing with each other to reach the top of the parapet. We had evidently (we thought) injured all the large guns so that they could not be fired to annoy any one. The sailors took the assault by the flank, along the beach, while the troops rushed in at the left, through the pallisades that had been knocked away by the fire of our guns. All the arrangements on the part of the sailors had been well carried out; they had succeeded in getting up to within a short distance of the fort, and laid securely in their ditches. We had but very few killed and wounded to this point. The marines were to have held the rifle-pits and cover the boarding party, which they failed to do. On rushing through the pallisades, which extended from the fort to the sea, the head of the column received a murderous fire of grape and canister, which did not, however, check the officers and sailors who were leading. The parapets now swarmed with rebels who poured in a destructive fire of musketry. At this moment had the marines performed their duty, every one of the rebels on the parapet would have been killed.

"I witnessed the whole affair; saw how recklessly the rebels exposed themselves and what an advantage they gave our sharpshooters, whose guns were scarcely fired, or fired with no precision. Notwithstanding the hot fire, the officers and sailors in the lead rushed on, and some even reached the parapet, a large number having reached the ditch. The advance was swept from the parapet like chaff, and notwithstanding all the efforts made by the commanders of companies to stop them, the men in the rear, seeing the slaughter in front, and that they were not covered by the marines, commenced to retreat; and, as there is no stopping a sailor if he fails on such an occasion on the first rush, I saw the whole thing had to be given up. In the mean time the troops were more successful on their side. The rebels, seeing so large a body of men coming at them on the seaside, were under the impression that it was the main attack, and concentrated the largest part of their forces at that point; and, when they gave three rebel cheers, thinking that they had gained the day, they received a volley of musketry in their backs from our gallant soldiers, who had been successful in gaining the highest parapet. They commenced with a system of fighting, as has never been beaten. Our soldiers had gained two traverses, while I directed the Ironsides to fire on the traverses occupied by the rebels. Four, five or six traverses were carried by our troops in the space of an hour. These traverses are immense bomb-proofs, about sixty feet long, fifty feet wide, and twenty feet high—seventeen of them in all—being on the northeast face. Between each traverse, or bomb-proof are one or two heavy guns. The fighting lasted until ten o'clock at night, the Ironsides and monitors firing through the traverses in advance of our troops, and the level strip of land, called Federal Point, being enfiladed by the ships to prevent reinforcements reaching the rebels. General Terry himself went into the fort, and I kept up constant communication with him, until three hearty cheers, which were taken up by the fleet, announced the capture of Fort Fisher. Finding that the General felt anxious about the enemy receiving reinforcements, I directed the sailors and marines to relieve the troops in the outer line of our defences, and a large number of soldiers were thus enabled to join our forces in the fort. It will not be amiss for me to remark here, that I never saw any thing like the fearless gallantry and endurance displayed by our troops. They fought like lions, and knew no such word as fail. They finally fought and chased the rebels from traverse to traverse, until they reached Battery Lamb at the Mound—a face of work extending about 1,400 yards in length. At this point the rebels broke and fled to the end of Federal Point. Our troops followed them up, and they surrendered at discretion. Thus ended one of the most remarkable battles on record, and one which will do more damage to the rebel cause than any that has taken place in this war; 2,300 rebels manned Fort Fisher; 1,900 were taken prisoners, the rest were killed and wounded.

" I have since visited Fort Fisher and its adjoining works, and find their strength greatly beyond what I had conceived. An engineer might be excusable in saying they could not be captured, except by regular siege. I wonder even now how it was done. The work, as I said before, is really stronger than the Malakoff Tower, which defied so long the combined power of France and England, and yet it is captured by a handful of men, under the fire of the guns of the fleet, and in seven hours after the attack commenced in earnest.*

"The success is so great that we should not complain. Men, it seems, must die that this Union may live; and the Constitution under which we have gained our prosperity must be maintained. We regret our companions in arms, and shed a tear over their remains; but if these rebels should succeed, we would have nothing but regret left us, and our lives would be spent in terror and sorrow. As soon as the forts were taken, I pushed the light-draught gunboats into the river —that is, as soon as I could find and buoy out a channel and take up the torpedoes, which were very thick. We found the wires leading to many and underrun them with boats. We found the torpedoes too heavy to lift with our ordinary boats, and they must have contained at least a ton of powder. The rebels seemed disposed to pay us back for the famous torpedo Louisiana, which exploded in their harbor and did them no harm. We had some difficulty in getting the vessels across the bar and into the river, as the channel is very narrow and the bar very shoal; a few of them got stuck, but were got off again with the tide. We all came to the conclusion that we had followed the right plan to capture Fort Fisher, one in which the nautical man of any sense will concur. After I got three of the gunboats inside of the bar and under the Mound, the rebels prepared to evacuate Fort Caswell. Two steamers near the fort, which, I think, were the Tallahassee and Chickamauga, were set on fire and blown up, after the rebels set fire to the fort. That blew up last night with a heavy explosion, followed by some minor ones. The barracks were apparently in flames all night, and some little works between this and Caswell blown up. I have sent vessels to see what has been done, and shall be governed accordingly. I think

* In a previous brief dispatch to Secretary Welles, in which he says, "I was in Fort Malakoff a few days after its surrender to the French and British. The combined armies of those two nations were many months capturing that stronghold, and it won't compare either in size or strength to Fort Fisher."

they are burning up every thing in Wilmington, and are getting away as fast as they can. In the mean time a large force of gunboats occupy the river between Caswell and Wilmington; that place is hermetically sealed against blockade-runners, and no Alabamas, or Floridas, or Chickamaugas or Tallahasses will ever fit out again from this port, and our merchant vessels will soon, I hope, be enabled to pursue in safety their avocation.

"We expended in the bombardment about 50,000 shells, and have as much on board. I feel much indebted to the Bureau of Ordinance for so promptly supplying us with ammunition and guns. I regret that some one stopped our supply of coal — which should have been doubly increased—for it came very near defeating this expedition. Had we not been supplied by the army this expedition would have been a failure. We shall move along carefully—have no vessels blown up with torpedoes, if I can help it, and I think we will be in Wilmington before long. You may rest satisfied, sir, that the gate through which the rebels obtained their supplies is closed for ever, and we can sit here quietly and watch the traitors starve. The number of guns captured in these works amount to seventy-five, many of them superb rifled pieces of very heavy calibre. All those facing the ships were dismounted, or injured so they could not be used, or the muzzles were filled up with sand or dirt, which rendered them useless. I only saw two that were not useless. I believe we have burst all the rifled guns left in the fleet—one on the Susquehanna, one on the Pequot, and one on the Osceola—and I think the reputation of these guns is now about ruined."

The total naval loss of killed, wounded and missing in the assault, including a number of seamen blown up afterwards in the fort by the accidental explosion of the magazine, was 309. Among these were the names of Lieutenant S. W. Preston, and Lieutenant B. H. Porter. "They were," says Admiral Porter in another dispatch, "both captured together in the attack on Fort Sumter, and died together in endeavoring to pull down the flag that has so long flaunted in our faces. Lieutenant R. H. Lamson was severely wounded. He was lately associated with Lieutenant Preston in his perilous adventure on the powder boat. Lieutenant George M. Bache was wounded, but not dangerously." The loss in the land force was 11 officers and 77 men killed; 39 officers and 472 men wounded and 92 missing.* A general outline of the assault by General Terry's troops was given in a dispatch from Lieutenant-Colonel C. B. Comstock, Chief Engineer of the army: "After a careful reconnoissance on the 14th it was decided to risk an assault on Fort Fisher; Paine's division with Colonel Abbott's brigade to hold our line, already strong, across the peninsula, and facing Wilmington against Hoke, while Ames' division should assault on the west end. After three hours of heavy navy firing, the assault was made at 3 P. M. on the 15th. Curtis' brigade led, and as soon as it had made a lodgment on the west end of the land front it was followed by Pennybacker's and the latter by Bell's. After desperate fighting, gaining foot by foot, and severe loss, by 5 P. M. we had possession of about half the land front. Abbott's brigade was then taken from our line facing Wilmington, and put into Fort Fisher, and on pushing it forward, at 10 P. M., it took the rest of the work with little resistance—the garrison falling back to the extreme of the peninsular, where they were followed and captured, among others General Whiting and Colonel Lamb, both wounded. Among

* Official numerical reports, published in the New York *Times*, February 1, 1865.

our wounded are the commanders of the three leading brigades ; General Curtiss being wounded, not severely ; but Colonels Pennybacker and Bell dangerously. The land front was a formidable one, the parapet in places fourteen or fifteen feet high ; but the men went at it nobly, under a severe musketry fire. The marines and sailors went up gallantly ; but the musketry fire from the east end of the land front was so severe that they did not succeed in entering the work."

General Terry's official report, dated Headquarters United States Forces on Federal Point, North Carolina, January 25, 1865, completes the narrative with full details of the operations of the land forces from the time of their leaving the James River : "On the 2d of January," says General Terry, "I received from the Lieutenant-General in person orders to take command of the troops destined for the movement. They were 3,300 picked men from the Second division of the Twenty-fourth Army Corps, under Brigadier-General (now Brevet Major-General) Adelbert Ames ; the same number from the Third Division of the Twenty-fifth Army Corps, under command of Brigadier-General Charles J. Paine ; 1,400 men from the Second Brigade of the First Division of the Twenty-fourth Army Corps, under Colonel (now Brevet Brigadier-General) J. C. Abbott, Seventh New Hampshire Volunteers, the Sixteenth New York Independent Battery with four 3-inch guns, and Light Battery E, Third United States Artillery, with six light 12-pounder guns. I was instructed to move them from their positions in the lines on the north side of the James River to Bermuda Landing, in time to commence their embarkation on transport vessels at sunrise on the 4th instant. In obedience to these orders, the movement commenced at noon of the 3d instant. The troops arrived at the landing at sunset, and there bivouacked for the night. The transports did not arrive as soon as they were expected. The first of them made its appearance late in the afternoon of the 4th. One of them, the Atlantic, was of too heavy draft to come up the James ; Curtis' brigade of Ames' division, was, therefore, placed on river steamboats, and sent down the river to be transferred to her. The embarkation of the remainder of the force commenced at sunset of the 4th, and was completed at noon of the 5th inst., each vessel, as soon as it was loaded, was sent to Fort Monroe, and at 9 o'clock P. M. of the 5th the whole fleet was collected in Hampton Roads. The troops were all in heavy marching order, with four days' rations from the morning of the 4th in their haversacks, and forty rounds of ammunition in their boxes. No horses, wagons, or ambulances were taken ; the caissons of the artillery were left behind ; but in addition to the ammunition in the limber chests, 150 rounds per gun, in packing-boxes, were embarked. I went down the river personally with the Lieutenant-General, and on the way received from him additional instructions, and the information that orders had been given for the embarkation of a siege-train, to consist of twenty 30-pounder Parrott guns, four 100-pounder Parrotts, and twenty Coehorn mortars, with a detail of artillerists and a company of engineers, so that in case siege operations should become necessary, the men and material for it might be at hand. These troops, under Brevet Brigadier-General H. L. Abbott were to follow me to Beaufort, North Carolina, and await orders. It was not until this time that I was informed that Fort Fisher was the point against which we were to operate. During the evening of the 5th orders were given for the transports to proceed to sea at 4 o'clock the next morning, and accompanying these orders were sealed letters, to be opened when off Cape

Henry, directing them to rendezvous, in case of separation from the flagship, at a point twenty-five miles off Beaufort, North Carolina. The vessels sailed at the appointed hour. During the 6th instant a severe storm arose, which so much impeded our progress that it was not until the morning of the 8th that my own vessel arrived at the rendezvous; all the others, excepting the flagship of General Paine, were still behind. Leaving Brigadier-General Paine to assemble the other vessels as they should arrive, I went into Beaufort Harbor to communicate with Rear-Admiral Porter, commanding the North Atlantic blockading squadron, with whose fleet the forces under my command were destined to co-operate. During the 8th nearly all of the vessels arrived at the rendezvous; some of them required repairs to their hulls, damaged by the gale, some repairs to their machinery, others needed coal or water. These vessels were brought into the harbor or to the outer anchorage, where their wants were supplied; all the others remained, until the final sailing of the expedition, some twenty to twenty-five miles off the land. The weather continued so unfavorable as to afford no prospect that we would be able to make a landing on the open beach of Federal Point until Wednesday the 11th. On that day Admiral Porter proposed to start, but at high water there was still so much surf on the bar that the iron-clads and other vessels of heavy draught could not be gotten over it; our departure was therefore delayed till the next day. On the morning tide of the 12th the vessels in the harbor passed out, and the whole fleet of naval vessels and transports got under way for this place. As we were leaving, the vessels containing General Abbott's command, came in sight; orders were sent to them to follow us. We did not arrive off Federal Point until nearly nightfall, consequently, and in accordance with the direction of the Admiral, the disembarkation of the troops was not commenced until the next morning. Our subsequent experience fully justified the delay; it would have been extremely difficult to land the men at night.

"At 4 o'clock A. M. of the 13th, the inshore division of naval vessels stood in close to the beach to cover the landing. The transports followed them and took positions as nearly as possible in a line parallel to and about two hundred yards outside of them. The iron-clads moved down to within range of the fort and opened fire upon it. Another division was placed on the northward of the landing-place, so as to protect our men from any attack from the direction of Masonboro Inlet. At 8 o'clock nearly 200 boats, beside steam-tugs, were sent from the navy to the transports, and the disembarkation of men, provisions, tools and ammunition simultaneously commenced. At 3 o'clock P. M. nearly 8,000 men, with three days' rations in their haversacks and forty rounds of ammunition in their boxes, six days supply of hard bread in bulk, 300,000 additional rounds of small arm ammunition, and a sufficient number of intrenching tools had been safely landed. The surf on the beach was still quite high, notwithstanding that the weather had become very pleasant, and owing to it some of the men had their rations and ammunition ruined by water. With this exception no accident of any kind occurred. As soon as the troops had commenced landing pickets were thrown out; they immediately encountered outposts of the enemy, and shots were exchanged with them, but no serious engagement occurred. A few prisoners were taken, from whom I learned that Hoke's rebel division, which it was supposed had been sent further South was still here, and that it was its outposts which we were meeting.

"The first object which I had in view after landing, was to throw a defensive line across the peninsula from Cape Fear River to the sea, facing Wilmington, so as to protect our rear from attack while we should be operating against Fisher. Our maps indicated that a good position for such a line would be found a short distance above the head of Myrtle Sound, which is a long shallow piece of water separated from the ocean by a sand spit of about 100 yards in width, communicates with it by Masonboro Inlet. It was supposed that the right flank of a line at that point would be protected by the Sound, and being above its head, that we should by it control the beach as far up as the inlet, and thus in case of need, be able to land supplies in quiet water there. Our landing place was selected with reference to this idea. An examination made after we landed, showed that the Sound, for a long distance above its head, was so shallow as to offer no obstacle to the passage of troops at low tide, and as the further down the peninsula we should go, the shorter would be our line across it, it was determined to take up a position where the maps showed a large pond occupying nearly one-third of the width of the peninsula, at about three miles from the Fort. Shortly before five o'clock, leaving Abbott's brigade to cover our stores, the troops were put in motion for the last-named point. On arriving at it, the "pond" was found to be a sand-flat, covered with water, giving no assistance to the defence of a line established behind it. Nevertheless, it was determined to get a line across at this place, and Paine's division, followed by two of Ames' brigade, made their way through. The night was very dark; much of the ground was a marsh, and illy adapted to the construction of works, and the distance was found to be too great to be properly defended by the troops which could be spared from the direct attack upon the fort. It was not until nine o'clock P. M. that Paine succeeded in reaching the river. The ground still nearer the fort was then reconnoitered, and found to be much better adapted to our purposes; accordingly, the troops were withdrawn from their last position and established on a line about two miles from the work. They reached this final position about two o'clock, A. M. of the 14th instant. Tools were immediately brought up and intrenchments were commenced. At eight o'clock a good breastwork, reaching from the river to the sea, and partially covered by abattis had been constructed and was in a defensible condition. It was much improved afterward, but from this time our foothold on the peninsula was secure.

"Early on the morning of the 14th, the landing of the artillery was commenced, and by sunset all the light guns were gotten on shore. During the following night they were placed on the line, most of them near the river, where the enemy, in case he should attack us, would be least exposed to the fire of the gunboats. Curtis' brigade of Ames' division was moved down toward Fisher during the morning, and at noon his skirmishers, after capturing on their way a small steamer which had come down the river with shells and forage for the garrison of the fort, reached a small unfinished outwork, in front of the west end of the land front of the work. General Curtis, Lieutenant-Colonel (now Brevet Brigadier-General) Comstock, the chief engineer of the expedition, and myself, under the protection of the fire of the fleet, made a careful reconnoissance of the work, getting within six hundred yards of it. As the result of this reconnoissance, and in view of the extreme difficulty which might be expected in landing supplies and the materiel for a siege on the open and often tempestuous beach, it was decided to attempt an assault the next day, provided that in the mean time the fire of the navy should so far destroy the palisades as to make one practicable. This decision was communicated to Admiral Porter, who at once placed a division of his vessels in a position to accomplish this last-named object. It was arranged, in consultation with him, that a heavy bombardment from all the vessels should commence early in the morning, and continue up to the moment of the assault, and then it should not cease, but should be diverted from the points of attack to other parts of the work. It was decided that the assault should be made at three o'clock P. M.; that the army should attack on the western half of the land face, and that a column of sailors and marines should assault at the north-east bastion. The fire of the navy continued during the night. At eight o'clock A. M. of the 15th all of the vessels, except a division left to aid in the defence of our northern line, moved into position, and a fire, magnificent alike for its power and accuracy, was opened.

" Ames' division had been selected for the assault. Paine was placed in command of the defensive line, having with him Abbott's brigade in addition to his own division. Ames' First Brigade—Curtis'—was already at the outwork above-mentioned ; and in trenches close around it ; his other two brigades, Pennypacker's and Bell's, were moved at noon within supporting distance of him. At two o'clock preparations for the assault were commenced. Sixty sharpshooters from the Thirteenth Indiana Volunteers, armed with the Spencer repeating carbine, and forty others, volunteers from Curtis' brigade, the whole under command of Lieutenant-Colonel Lent, of the Thirteenth Indiana, were thrown forward at a run to within 175 yards of the work. They were provided with shovels, and soon dug pits for shelter, and commenced firing at the parapet. As soon as this movement commenced the parapet of the fort was manned, and the enemy's fire, both of musketry and artillery, opened. As soon as the sharpshooters were in position, Curtis' brigade was moved forward by regiment at the double-quick into line about 475 yards from the work. The men there laid down. This was accomplished under a sharp fire of artillery and musketry, from which, however, they soon sheltered themselves by digging shallow trenches. When Curtis moved from the outwork, Pennypacker was brought up to it, and Bell was brought into line 200 yards in his rear. Finding that a good cover from Curtis' men could be found in the reverse slope of a crest fifty yards in the rear of the sharpshooters, they were again moved forward, one regiment at a time, and again covered themselves in trenches. Pennypacker followed Curtis and occupied the ground vacated by him, and Bell was brought up to the outwork. It had been proposed to blow up and cut down the palisades. Bags of powder, with fuses attached, had been prepared, and a party of axmen organized, but the fire of the navy had been so effective during the preceding night and morning, that it was thought unnecessary to use the powder. The axmen, however, were sent in with the leading brigade, and did good service, making openings in portions of the palisading which the fire of the navy had not been able to reach.

" At 2:25 P. M. all the preparations were completed, the order to move forward was given to Ames, and a concerted signal was made to Admiral Porter to change the direction of his fire. Curtis' brigade at once sprung from their trenches and dashed forward in line ; its left was exposed to a severe enfilading fire, and it obliqued to the right so as to envelop the left of the land front ; the ground over which it moved was marshy and difficult, but it soon reached the palisades, passed through them, and effected a lodgment on the parapet. At the same time the column of sailors and marines, under Fleet Captain K. R. Breese, advanced up the breach in the most gallant manner and attacked the northeast bastion; but, exposed to a murderous fire, they were unable to get up the parapet. After a severe struggle and a heavy loss of valuable officers and men, it became apparent that nothing could be effected at that point and they were withdrawn. When Curtis moved forward, Ames directed Pennypacker to move up to the rear of the sharpshooters, and brought Bell up to Pennypacker's last position, and as soon as Curtis got a foothold on the parapet sent Pennypacker in to his support. He advanced, overlapping Curtis' right and drove the enemy from the heavy palisading, which extended from the west end of the land face to the river, capturing a considerable number of their prisoners; then pushing forward to their left, the two brigades together drove the enemy from about one quarter of the land-face. Ames then brought up Bell's brigade, and moved it between the work and the river. On this side there was no regular parapet, but there was abundance of cover afforded to the enemy by cavities from which sand had been taken for the parapet, the ruins of barracks and storehouses, the large magazine, and by traverses, behind which they stubbornly resisted our advance. Hand to hand fighting of the most desperate character ensued, the huge traverses of the land-face being used successively by the enemy as breast works, over the tops of which the contending parties fired in each other's faces. Nine of these were carried one after the other by our men. When Bell's brigade was ordered into action, I foresaw that more troops would probably be needed, and sent an order for Abbott's brigade to move down from the north line, at the same time requesting Captain Breese to replace them with his sailors and marines. I also directed General Paine to send me one of the strongest regiments of his own division. These troops arrived at dusk and reported to General Ames. At 6 o'clock Abbott's brigade went into the fort; the regiment from Paine's division — the Twenty-seventh United States colored troops, Brevet Brigadier-General A. M. Blackman commanding — was brought up to the rear of the work, where it remained under fire for some time, and was then withdrawn. Until 6 o'clock the fire of the navy continued upon that portion of the work not occupied by us; after that time it was directed on the beach, to prevent the coming up of reinforcements, which it was thought might possibly be thrown over from the right bank of the river to Battery Buchanan. The fighting for the traverses continued till nearly 9 o'clock, two more of them being carried; then a portion of Abbott's brigade drove the enemy from their last remaining strongholds, and the occupation of the work was completed. The same brigade, with General Blackman's regiment, were immediately pushed down the Point to Battery Buchanan, whither many of the garrison had fled. On reaching the Battery all of the enemy who had not been previously captured were made prisoners. Among them were Major-General Whiting and Colonel Lamb, the commandant of the fort. At about 4 o'clock in the afternoon Hoke advanced against our line, apparently with the design of attacking it; but if such was his intention he abandoned it after a skirmish with our pickets. During the day Brevet Brigadier-General H. L. Abbott, Chief of Artillery, was busily engaged in landing artillery and ammunition, so that if the assault failed siege operations might at once be commenced.

"I have no words to do justice to the behavior of both officers and men on this occasion; all that men could do, they did. Better soldiers never fought. Of General Ames I have already spoken in a letter recommending his promotion. He commanded all the troops engaged, and was constantly under fire. His great coolness, good judgment and skill were never more conspicuous than on the assault. Brigadier-General Curtis and Colonels Pennypacker, Bell, and Abbott—the brigade commanders—led them with the utmost gallantry. Curtis was wounded after fighting in the front rank, rifle in hand; Pennypacker, while carrying the standard of one of his regiments, the first man in a charge over a traverse. Bell was mortally wounded near the palisades. Brigadier-General Paine deserves high praise for the zeal and energy displayed by him in constructing our defensive line, a work absolutely essential to our success. Brevet Brigadier-General Blackman deserves mention for the prompt manner he brought his regiment up to the work, and afterward followed up the retreating enemy. To Brevet Brigadier-General C. B. Comstock, Aid-de-Camp on the staff of the Lieutenant-General, I am under the deepest obligations. At every step of our progress I received from him the most valuable assistance. For the final success of our part of the operations the country is more indebted to him than to me. Colonel George S. Dodge, Chief Quartermaster of the Army of the James, accompanied me as Chief Quartermaster of the forces under my command. His able and energetic performance of his multifarious duties was all that could be wished for, and reflected the highest honor upon him. Surgeon Norman S. Barnes, United States Volunteers, Medical Director, and Surgeon A. J. D. Buzzell, Third New Hampshire Volunteers, Medical Inspector of the expedition, discharged their laborious duties on the field and in the hospital in a manner most creditable to their ability and humanity. I desire to express my high appreciation of the services of these officers.

"I should signally fail to do my duty were I to omit to speak in terms of the highest admiration of the part borne by the navy in our operations. In all ranks, from Admiral Porter to his seamen, there was the utmost desire not only to do their proper work, but to facilitate in every possible manner the operations of the land forces. To him and to the untiring efforts of his officers and men are we indebted that our men, stores, tools, and ammunition were safely and expeditiously landed, and that our wounded and prisoners were embarked for transportation to the North; to the great accuracy and power of their fire it is owing that we had not to confront a formidable artillery in the assault, and that we were able with but little loss to push forward the men, preparatory to it, to a point nearly as favorable for it as the one they would have occupied had siege operations been undertaken and the work systematically approached. The assault of the sailors and marines, although it failed, undoubtedly contributed somewhat to our success, and certainly nothing could surpass the perfect skill with which the fleet was handled by its commander. Every request which I made to Admiral Porter was most cheerfully complied with, and the utmost harmony has existed between us from the outset to the present time."

The capture of Fort Fisher was followed the next day by the blowing up by the enemy of Forts Caswell and Campbell on the Old Inlet, and the abandonment of these and the works on Smith's Island and those at Smithville and Reeves' Point. These places were occupied by the navy. The whole number of guns captured in the defences, as reported by Admiral Porter on the 20th, was 168. General Terry reported the number of prisoners 112 commissioned officers, and 1,971 enlisted men. In his dispatch enumerating the different forts taken,* Admiral Porter

* This is the list of the forts with their armaments taken

adds: "We have found in each an Armstrong gun, with the 'broad arrow' on it and the name 'Sir William Armstrong' marked in full on the trunnels. As the British Government claims the exclusive right to use these guns, it would be interesting to know how they came into forts held by the Southern rebels. I find that immense quantities of provisions, stores, and clothing have come through this port into rebeldom. I am almost afraid to mention the amount, but it is enough to supply over 60,000 men. It is all English, and they have received the last cargo; no more will ever come this way. We picked up a telegram from General Lee to his subordinate here, saying that if Forts Fisher and Caswell were not held he would have to evacuate Richmond. He says most truly, and I should not be at all surprised if he left it at any moment. We find this a better place to catch blockade-runners than outside. I had the blockade-runners' lights lit last night, and was obliging enough to answer their signals, whether right or wrong we don't know. Two of them, the Stag and Charlotte, from Bermuda, loaded with arms, blankets, shoes, etc., etc., came in and quietly anchored near the Malvern, and were taken possession of. The Stag was commanded by Richard H. Gayle, a lieutenant in the rebel navy, and belongs to the rebel Government. A number more are expected, and we will, I hope, catch a portion of them. I intrusted this duty to Lieutenant Cushing, who performed it with his usual good luck and intelligence. These two are very fast vessels, and valuable prizes. They threw a portion of their papers overboard immediately on finding they were trapped. The Charlotte brings five English passengers, one of them an English army officer. They all came over, as they expressed it, 'on a lark,' and were making themselves quite 'jolly' in the cabin over their champagne, felicitating themselves on their safe arrival. The Stag received three shots in her as she ran by our blockaders outside."

possession of after the fall of Fort Fisher—a sufficient explanation of the protection given for so long a time to the blockade-runners: Reeves' Point, 2 ten inch guns; above Smithville, 2 ten-inch guns; Smithville, 4 ten-inch guns; Fort Caswell, 10 ten-inch guns, 2 nine-inch, 1 Armstrong, and 4 thirty two's (rifled), 2 thirty-two's (smooth), 3 eight-inch, 1 Parrott twenty-pounder, 3 rifled field pieces, 3 guns buried—29 guns. Forts Campbell and Shaw, 6 ten-inch, 6 thirty-two's (smooth), 1 thirty-two (rifled), 1 eight-inch, 6 field pieces, 2 mortars—22 guns. Smith's Island, 3 ten-inch, 6 thirty-two's (smooth), 2 thirty-two's (rifled), 4 field-pieces, 2 mortars, and 17 guns. Reported at the other end of Smith's Island, 6 guns. Total captured, 83 guns.

CHAPTER CX.

GENERAL SHERMAN'S CAMPAIGN—SAVANNAH, GEORGIA, TO GOLDSBORO, N. C.—FALL OF CHARLESTON AND WILMINGTON, FEBRUARY—MARCH, 1865.

General Sherman did not remain long inactive at Savannah after his brilliant conquest of that city. It was the policy of General Grant to pursue the rebellion to its last extremity without affording its desperate leaders any opportunity to recover from their successive defeats. The proper improvement of time was now fully recognized as the great means of breaking up the military strength of the Confederacy. Thus there was no longer delay in waiting for the opening of a spring campaign. The great battle was fought steadily on all sides during the winter months. Active operations in the field, indeed, were of necessity somewhat checked by the state of the roads in Virginia; but there was less occasion for movement in that quarter where General Grant's army was rendering the best service in inexorably holding the forces of Lee—the last strength of the rebellion—in an iron grasp, compelling inaction on the part of the rebel leader, while every day his skillful combinations, as Sherman overran the Carolinas, hastened the inevitable fate of Richmond, and with the fall of its capital secured the ruin of the confederacy. The city of Savannah, after its occupation by General Sherman, was very quiet and orderly. His army, under excellent discipline, was a safeguard to the inhabitants. Secretary Stanton of the War Department, who visited the place in January, on his return to Washington reported, "the peace and order prevailing at Savannah since its occupation by General Sherman could not be surpassed. Few male inhabitants are to be seen on the streets. Ladies and children evince a sense of security. No instance of disorder, or personal injury, or insults has occurred. Laboring men and mechanics, white and black, are seeking employment. The troops are cheerful and respectful toward every one, and seem to feel themselves much at home and on good behavior as if in their native towns." It was, in fact, the constant effort of General Sherman, in pursuance of the wise policy of the Government, to facilitate in every way by the exercise of a sound authority, the return of the State to its loyalty. The general good behavior of his army on its march was admitted, and tales of its cruelties which had been invented and circulated "to fire the Southern heart" were retracted by a portion of the rebel press. The State, pillaged by native marauders, evidently longed for repose, though it was still governed by the evil influences of the rebellion or the remaining power and authority of the rebel leaders. The question, however, of a return to the Union began to be freely discussed in various quarters. In reply to a citizen of Georgia in the interior, whose name is not given, who had opened a correspondence on the subject, General Sherman wrote from Savannah on the 8th of January:—

"Dear Sir—Yours of the 3d inst. is received, and in answer to your inquiries I beg to state I am merely a military commander, and act only in that capacity; nor can I give any assurances or pledges affecting civil matters in the future. They will be adjusted by Congress when Georgia is again represented there as of old. Georgia is not out of the Union, and therefore the talk of 'reconstruction' appears to me inappropriate. Some of the people have been and still are in a state of revolt; and as long as they remain armed and organized, the United States must pursue them with armies, and deal with them according to military law. But as soon as they break up their armed organizations and return to their homes, I take it they will be dealt with by the civil courts. Some of the rebels in Georgia, in my judgment, deserve death, because they have committed murder and other crimes, which are punished with death by all civilized governments on earth. I think this was the course indicated by General Washington in reference to the Whiskey Insurrection, and a like principle seemed to be recognized at the time of the Burr Conspiracy. As to the Union of the States under our Government, we have the high authority of General Washington, who bade us be jealous and careful of it, and the still more emphatic words of General Jackson, 'The Federal Union, it must and shall be preserved.' Certainly Georgians cannot question the authority of such men, and should not suspect our motives, who are simply fulfilling their commands. Wherever necessary, force has been used to carry out that end; and you may rest assured that the Union will be preserved, cost what it may. And if you are sensible men you will conform to this order of things or else migrate to some other country. There is no other alternative open to the people of Georgia. My opinion is that no negotiations are necessary, nor commissioners, nor conventions, nor any thing of the kind. Whenever the people of Georgia quit rebelling against their Government and elect members of Congress and Senators, and these go and take their seats, then the State of Georgia will have resumed her functions in the Union. These are merely my opinions, but in confirmation of them, as I think, the people of Georgia may well consider the following words referring to the people of the rebellious States, which I quote from the recent annual message of President Lincoln to Congress at its present session: 'They can at any moment have peace simply by laying down their arms and submitting to the national authority under the Constitution. After so much, the Government would not, if it could, maintain war against them. The loyal people would not sustain or allow it. If questions should remain, we would adjust them by the peaceful means of legislation, conference, courts and votes. Operating only in constitutional and lawful channels, some certain and other possible questions are and would be beyond the Executive power to adjust, as, for instance, the admission of members into Congress and whatever might require the appropriation of money. The President then alludes to the general pardon and amnesty offered for more than a year past, upon specified and more liberal terms, to all except certain designated classes, even these being "still within contemplation of special clemency,' and adds: 'It is still so open to all, but the time may come when public duty shall demand that it be closed, and that in lieu more vigorous measures than heretofore shall be adopted.' It seems to me that it is time for the people of Georgia to act for themselves, and return, in time, to their duty to the Government of their fathers."

To give protection to the inhabitants disposed to loyalty and aid in this return to the Union, General Sherman on the 14th of January issued the following order relating to the bands of guerillas who devastated the State: "It being represented that the confederate army and armed bands of robbers, acting professedly under the authority of the confederate government, are harassing the people of Georgia and endeavoring to intimidate them in the efforts they are making to secure to themselves provisions, clothing, security to life and property, and the restoration of law and good government in the State, it is hereby ordered and made public: 1. That the farmers of Georgia may bring into Savannah, Fernandina or Jacksonville, Florida, marketing, such as beef, pork, mutton, vegetables of any kind, fish, etc., as well as cotton in small quantities, and sell the same in open market, except the cotton, which must be sold by or through the Treasury agents, and may invest the proceeds in family stores, such as bacon and flour, in any reasonable quantities, groceries, shoes and clothing, and articles not contraband of war, and carry the same back to their families. No trade-store will be attempted in the interior, or stocks of goods sold for them, but families may club together for mutual assistance and protection in coming and going. 2. The people are encouraged to meet together in peaceful assemblages, to discuss measures looking to their safety and good government, and the restoration of State and National authority, and will be protected by the National army while so doing; and all peaceable inhabitants who satisfy the commanding officers that they are earnestly laboring to that end, must not only be left undisturbed in property and person, but must be protected, as far as possible consistent with the military operations. If any farmer or peaceable inhabitant is molested by the enemy, viz.: the confederate army or guerrillas, because of his friendship to the National Government, the perpetrator, if caught, will be summarily punished, or his family made to suffer for the outrage; but if the crime cannot be traced to the actual party, then retaliation will be made on the adherents to the cause of the rebellion—should a Union man be murdered, then a rebel selected by lot will be shot—or if a Union family be persecuted on account of the cause, a rebel family will be banished to a foreign land. In aggravated cases retaliation will extend as high as five for one. All commanding officers will act promptly in such cases, and report their action after the retaliation is done."

Simultaneously with the date of this order, General Sherman renewed the movement of his forces from Savannah. "I have heretofore explained," says he in his subsequent report at the conclusion of the campaign, "how in the progress of our arms, I was enabled to leave in the West an army, under Major-General George H. Thomas, of sufficient strength to meet emergencies in that quarter, while in person I conducted another army, composed of the Fourteenth, Fifteenth, Seventeenth and Twentieth Corps, and Kilpatrick's division of cavalry, to the Atlantic slope, aiming to approach the grand theatre of war in Virginia by the time the season would admit of military operations in that latitude. The first lodgment on the coast was made at Savannah, strongly fortified and armed, and valuable to us as a good seaport with its navigable stream inland. Near a month was consumed there in refitting the army, and in making proper disposition of captured property and other local matters, but by the 15th of January I was all ready to resume the march. Preliminary to this, General Howard, commanding the right wing, was ordered to embark his command at Thunderbolt, transport it to Beaufort, South Carolina, and thence by the 15th of January make a lodgment on the Charleston Railroad, at or near Pocotaligo. This was accomplished punctually, at little cost, by the Seventeenth Corps, Major-General Blair, and a depot for supplies was established near the mouth of Pocotaligo Creek, with easy water communication back to Hilton Head.

"The left wing, Major-General Slocum, and the cavalry, Major-General Kilpatrick, were ordered to rendezvous about the same time near Robertsville and Coosawhatchie, South Carolina, with a depot of supplies at Pureysburg, or Sister's Ferry, on the Savannah River. General Slocum had a good pontoon-bridge constructed opposite the city, and the 'Union causeway' leading through the low rice-fields opposite Savannah was repaired and 'corduroyed,' but before the time appointed to start, the heavy rains of January had swelled the river, broken the pontoon bridge, and overflowed the whole 'bottom,' so that the causeway was four feet under water, and General Slocum was compelled to look higher up for a passage over the Savannah River. He moved up to Sister's Ferry, but even there the river, with its overflowing bottoms, was near three miles wide, and he did not succeed in getting his whole wing across until during the first week in February. In the mean time General Grant had sent me Grover's division of the Nineteenth Corps to garrison Savannah, and had drawn the Twenty-third Corps, Major-General Schofield, from Tennessee, and sent it to reinforce the command of Major-Generals Terry and Palmer, operating on the coast of North Carolina, to prepare the way for my coming. On the 18th of January I transferred the forts and city of Savannah to Major-General Foster, commanding the Department of the South, imparted to him my plans of operation, and instructed him how to follow my movements inland by occupying in succession the city of Charleston and such other points along the sea-coast as would be of any military value to us. The combined naval and land forces under Admiral Porter and General Terry had, on the 15th of January captured Fort Fisher and the rebel forts at the mouth of Cape Fear River, giving me an additional point of security on the sea-coast. But I had already resolved in my own mind, and had so advised General Grant, that I would undertake at one stride to make Goldsboro', and open communication with the sea by the Newbern Railroad, and had ordered Colonel W. W. Wright, Superintendent of Military Railroads, to proceed in advance to Newbern, and to be prepared to extend the railroad out from Newbern to Goldsboro' by the 15th of March. On the 19th of January all preparations were complete, and the orders of march given. My Chief Quartermaster and Commissary, Generals Easton and Beckwith, were ordered to complete the supplies at Sister's Ferry and Pocotaligo, and then to follow our movements coastwise, looking for my arrival at Goldsboro', North Carolina, about March 15, and opening communication with me from Morehead City.

"On the 22d of January I embarked at Savannah for Hilton Head, where I held a conference with Admiral Dahlgren, United States Navy, and Major-General Foster, commanding the Department of the South, and next day proceeded to Beaufort, riding out thence on the 24th to Pocotaligo, where the Seventeenth Corps, Major-General Blair was encamped. The Fifteenth Corps was somewhat scattered—Woods' and Hazen's division at Beaufort, John E. Smith marching from Savannah by the coast road, and Corse still at Savannah, cut off by the storms and freshet in the river. On the 25th a demonstration was made against the Combahee Ferry and railroad bridge across the Salkehatchie, merely to amuse the enemy, who had evidently adopted that river as his defensive line against our supposed objective, the city of Charleston. I reconnoitered the line in person, and saw that the heavy rains had swollen the river so that water stood in the swamps for a breadth of more than a mile, at a depth of from one to twenty feet. Not having the remotest intention of approaching Charleston, a comparatively small force was able, by seeming preparations to cross over, to keep in their front a considerable force of the enemy disposed to contest our advance on Charleston. On the 27th I rode to the camp of General Hatch's division of Foster's command, on the Tullafulney and Coosawhatchie Rivers, and directed to be evacuated, as no longer of any use to us. That division was then moved to Pocotaligo to keep up the feints already begun, until we should with the right wing move higher up and cross the Salkehatchie about Rivers' or Broxton's Bridge. On the 20th I learned that the roads back of Savannah had at last become sufficiently free of the flood to admit of General Slocum putting his wing in motion, and that he was already approaching Sister's Ferry, whither a gunboat, the Pontiac, Captain Luce, kindly furnished by Admiral Dahlgren, had preceded him to cover the crossing. In the mean time three divisions of the Fifteenth Corps had closed up at Pocotaligo, and the right wing had loaded its wagons and was ready to start. I therefore directed General Howard to move one corps, the Seventeenth, along the Salkehatchie, as high up as Rivers' Bridge, and the other, the Fifteenth, by Hickory Hill, Loper's Cross-roads, Anglesey Post-office, and Beaufort's Bridge. Hatch's division was ordered to remain at Pocotaligo, feigning at the Salkehatchie Railroad Bridge and Ferry, until our movement turned the enemy's position and forced him to fall behind the Edisto.

"The Seventeenth and Fifteenth Corps drew out of camp on the 31st of January, but the real march began on the 1st of February. All the roads northward had for weeks been held by Wheeler's cavalry, who had by details of negro laborers felled trees, burned bridges, and made obstructions to impede our march. But so well-organized were our pioneer battalions, and so strong and intelligent our men, that obstructions seemed only to quicken their progress. Felled trees were removed and bridges rebuilt by the heads of columns before the rear could close up. On the 2d of February the Fifteenth Corps reached Loper's Cross-roads and the Seventeenth was at Rivers' Bridge. From Loper's Cross-roads I communicated with General Slocum, still struggling with the floods of the Savannah River at Sister's Ferry. He had two divisions of the Twentieth Corps, General Williams, on the east bank, and was enabled to cross over on his pontoons the cavalry of Kilpatrick. General Williams was ordered to Beaufort's Bridge, by way of Lawtonville and Allendale, Kilpatrick to Blackville via Barnwell, and General Slocum to hurry the crossing at Sister's Ferry as much as possible, and overtake the right wing on the South Carolina Railroad. General Howard, with the right wing, was directed to cross the Salkehatchie and push rapidly for the South Carolina Railroad at or near Midway. The enemy held the line of the Salkehatchie in force, having infantry and artillery intrenched at Rivers' and Beaufort Bridges. The Seventeenth Corps was ordered to carry Rivers' Bridge and the Fifteenth Corps Beaufort's Bridge. The former position was carried promptly and skillfully by Mower's and Giles A. Smith's divisions of the Seventeenth Corps, on the 3d of February, by crossing the swamp, nearly three miles wide, with water varying from knee to shoulder deep. The weather was bitter cold, and Generals Mower and Smith led their divisions in person, on foot, waded the swamp, made a lodgment below the bridge, and turned on the rebel brigade which guarded it, driving it in confusion and disorder toward Branchville. Our casualties were one officer and seventeen men killed, and seventy men wounded, who were sent to Pocotaligo. The line of the Salkehatchie being thus broken, the enemy retreated at once behind the Edisto, at Branchville, and the whole army was pushed rapidly to the South Carolina Railroad at Midway, Bamberg, or Lowry's Station and Graham's Station. The Seventeenth Corps, by threatening Branchville, forced the enemy to burn the railroad bridge, and Walker's Bridge below, across the Edisto. All hands were at once set to work to destroy railroad track. From the 7th to the 10th of February this work was thoroughly prosecuted by the Seventeenth Corps from the Edisto to Bamberg, and by the Fifteenth Corps from Bamberg up to Blackville. In the mean time General Kilpatrick had brought his cavalry rapidly by Barnwell to Blackville, and had turned toward Aiken, with orders to threaten Augusta, but not to be drawn needlessly into a serious battle. This he skillfully accomplished, skirmishing heavily with Wheeler's cavalry, first at Blackville and afterward at Williston and Aiken. General Williams, with two divisions of the Twentieth Corps, marched to the South Carolina Railroad at Graham's Station on the 8th, and General Slocum reached Blackville on the 10th. The destruction of the railroad was continued by the left wing from Blackville up to Windsor. By the 11th of February all the army was on the railroad from Midway to Johnson's Station, thereby dividing the enemy's forces, which still remained at Branchville and Charleston on the one hand, and Aiken and Augusta on the other.

"We then began the movement on Orangeburgh. The Seventeenth Corps crossed the South Fork of Edisto River at Binnaker's Bridge, and moved straight for Orangeburgh, while the Fifteenth Corps crossed at Holman's Bridge, and moved to Poplar Springs in support. The left wing and cavalry were still at work on the railroad, with orders to cross the South Edisto at New and Guignard's Bridges, move to the Orangeburgh and Edgefield road, and there await the result of the attack on Orangeburgh. On the 12th the Seventeenth Corps found the enemy intrenched in front of the Orangeburgh Bridge, but swept him away by a dash, and followed him, forcing him across the bridge, which was partially burned. Behind the bridge was a battery in position, covered by a cotton and earth parapet, with wings as far as could be seen. General Blair held one division (Giles A. Smith's) close up to the Edisto, and moved the other two to a point about two miles below, where he crossed Force's division by a pontoon bridge, holding Mower's in support. As soon as Force emerged from the swamp, the enemy gave ground, and Giles Smith's division gained the bridge, crossed over, and occupied the enemy's parapet. He soon repaired the bridge, and by 4 P. M. the whole corps was in Orangeburgh, and had begun the work of destruction on the railroad. Blair was ordered to destroy this road effectually up to Lewisville, and to push the enemy across the Congaree and force him to burn the bridges, which he did on the 14th; and without wasting time or labor on Branchville or Charleston, which I knew the enemy could no longer hold, I turned all the columns straight on Columbia. The Seventeenth Corps followed the State road, and the Fifteenth crossed the North Edisto from Poplar Springs at Schilling's Bridge, above the mouth of Cawcaw Swamp Creek, and took a country road which came into the State road at Zeigler's. On the 15th, the Fifteenth Corps found the enemy in a strong position at Little Congaree Bridge (across Congaree Creek), with a *tete-de-pont* on the south side and a well constructed fort on the north side, commanding the bridge with artillery. General Charles R. Woods, who commanded the leading division, succeeded, however, in turning the flank of the *tete-de-pont* by sending Stone's brigade through a cypress swamp to the left; and following up the retreating enemy promptly, he got possession of the bridge and the fort beyond. The bridge had been partially damaged by fire, and had to be repaired for the passage of artillery, so that night closed in before the head of the column could reach the bridge across Congaree River in front of Columbia. That night the enemy shelled our camps from a battery on the east side of the Congaree above Granby. Early next morning, February 16, the head of the column reached the bank of the Congaree, opposite Columbia, but too late to save the fine bridge which spanned the river at that point. It was burned by the enemy. While waiting for the pontoons to come to the front, we could see people running about the streets of Columbia, and occasionally small bodies of cavalry, but no masses. A single gun of Captain De Grass' battery was firing at their cavalry squads, but I checked his firing, limiting him to a few shots at the unfinished State House walls, and a few shells at the railroad depot, to scatter the people who were seen carrying away sacks of corn and meal that we needed. There was no white flag or manifestations of surrender. I directed General Howard not to cross directly in front of Columbia, but to cross the Saluda at the Factory, three miles above, and afterward

Broad River, so as to approach Columbia from the north. Within an hour of the arrival of General Howard's head of column at the river opposite Columbia, the head of column of the left wing also appeared, and I directed General Slocum to cross the Saluda at Zion Church, and thence to take roads direct for Winnsboro', breaking up en route the railroads and bridges about Alston.

"General Howard effected a crossing of the Saluda, near the Factory, on the 16th, skirmishing with cavalry, and the same night made a flying bridge across Broad River, about three miles above Columbia, by which he crossed over Stone's brigade of Wood's division, Fifteenth Corps. Under cover of this brigade a pontoon-bridge was laid on the morning of the 17th. I was in person at this bridge, and at 11 A. M. learned that the Mayor of Columbia had come out in a carriage and made a formal surrender of the city to Colonel Stone, Twenty-fifth Iowa Infantry, commanding Third Brigade, First Division, Fifteenth Corps. About the same time a small party of the Seventeenth Corps had crossed the Congaree in a skiff, and entered Columbia from a point immediately west. In anticipation of the occupation of the city, I had made written orders to General Howard touching the conduct of the troops. These were to destroy absolutely all arsenals and public property not needed for our own use, as well as all railroads, depots and machinery useful in war to an enemy, but to spare all dwellings, colleges, schools, asylums, and harmless property. I was the first to cross the pontoon bridge, and in company with General Howard rode into the city. The day was clear, but a perfect tempest of wind was raging. The brigade of Colonel Stone was already in the city, and was properly posted. Citizens and soldiers were on the streets, and general good order prevailed. General Wade Hampton, who commanded the confederate rear-guard of cavalry, had, in anticipation of our capture of Columbia, ordered that all cotton, public and private, should be moved into the streets and fired, to prevent our making use of it. Bales were piled everywhere, the rope and bagging cut, and tufts of cotton were blown about in the wind, lodged in the trees and against houses so as to resemble a snow storm. Some of these piles of cotton were burning, especially in the very heart of the city, near the court-house, but the fire was partially subdued by the labor of our soldiers. During the day the Fifteenth Corps passed through Columbia and out on the Camden road. The Seventeenth did not enter the town at all; and, as I have before stated, the left wing and cavalry did not come within two miles of the town.

"Before one single public building had been fired by order, the smouldering fires, set by Hampton's order, were rekindled by the wind, and communicated to the buildings around. About dark they began to spread. and got beyond the control of the brigade on duty within the city. The whole of Wood's division was brought in, but it was found impossible to check the flames, which, by midnight, had become unmanageable, and raged until about 4 A. M., when the wind subsiding, they were got under control. I was up nearly all night, and saw Generals Howard, Logan, Woods, and others, laboring to save houses and protect families thus suddenly deprived of shelter and of bedding and wearing apparel. I disclaim on the part of my army any agency in the fire, but on the contrary claim that we saved what of Columbia remains unconsumed. And without hesitation I charge General Wade Hampton with having burned his own city of Columbia, not with a malicious intent, or as the manifestation of a silly 'Roman stoicism,' but from folly and want of sense, in filling it with lint, cotton, and tinder. Our officers and men on duty worked well to extinguish the flames ; but others not on duty, including the officers who had long been imprisoned there, rescued by us, may have assisted in spreading the fire after it had once began, and may have indulged in unconcealed joy to see the ruin of the capital of South Carolina. During the 18th and 19th the arsenal, railroad depots, machine-shops, founderies, and other buildings were properly destroyed by detailed working parties, and the railroad track torn up and destroyed down to Kingsville and the Wateree Bridge, and up in the direction of Winnsboro'."*

Columbia, indeed, suffered heavily from her defenders. A correspondent of the *Richmond Whig*, writing from Charlotte, N. C., February 22, describes the pillage of the city by confederate soldiers on the 15th. "A party of Wheeler's cavalry," he writes, "accompanied by their officers, dashed into town, tied their horses, and as systematically as if they had been bred to the business, proceeded to break into the stores along Main Street and rob them of their contents. A detachment of detailed men fired on one party and drove them out. Captain Hamilton, the Provost-Marshal, with another officer, drew swords and pistols on another party, and succeeded in clearing several establishments ; but the valiant raiders still swarmed like locusts, and to-day, a hundred miles away from Columbia, you may see men smoking the cigars and wearing on their saddles the elegant cloths stolen from the merchants of that city. It is said that two of the 'cavalry' drew pistols on General Hampton, who was attempting to protect a store, and threatened his life. Under these circumstances you may well imagine that our people would rather see the Yankees or old Satan himself than a party of the aforesaid Wheeler's cavalry. The barbarities committed by some of them are represented to be frightful, 'life, liberty, and the pursuit of happiness' being perfectly incompatible with their presence. Common rumor says that Sherman's treatment of citizens and private property was uniformly lenient and conciliatory. His headquarters were at Nickerson's Hotel."

Following this scene of pillage came the conflagration of a great part of the city during the night following Sherman's occupation. The enemy, as related by General Sherman, on retreating had fired various buildings and bales of cotton in the streets. The fire spread as the burning masses were carried by the wind, and, notwithstanding the efforts of General Sherman's troops to arrest the flames, nearly the whole city was laid in ashes. The scene as described by eye witnesses, the fierceness of the conflagration, the terror and bewilderment of the inhabitants, aggravated by their mortification and dismay at the presence of the victorious army, was truly appalling. The capital of South Carolina was paying a fearful penalty for her prominent part in the rebellion.

The surprise of the inhabitants and flight from the deserted city are vividly described by the Charlotte, N. C., correspondent of the *Richmond Whig* already cited. "Sherman's advance on Columbia," he writes, "was unexpected. Sudden as surprising, it found all unprepared for the events which followed, and few cool enough in the crisis to yield to any other than the bent of the first impulse. Hence hundreds are to-day exiles from home who would give almost their all to be safely back. They have learned that being a refugee don't pay. Orangeburg and Kingsville were supposed to be the highest points northward on that line at which Sherman would strike. The people who planned his campaign thought from thence he

* General Sherman's Report of the Campaign, Goldsboro, N. C., April 4, 1865.

would branch off toward Charaff and Fayetteville, leaving Columbia untouched. Four days dispelled the illusion. Our troops fell back until the sounds of cannon reverberated through the city. Then public officers for the first time began to think of removing the Government stores. The instructions from Richmond had left many of them no other discretion. Hurry, excitement, and some confusion became the order of the day. Everybody, public and private, wanted a car. The President of the Charlotte and South Carolina Railroad, Colonel William Johnson, his assistants, Captain Sharp, the agent of transportation, and his aids, now bent their energies to the Herculean task before them, and accomplished all that men could do. The trains from the South Carolina and Greenville roads were run upon the Charlotte track, filled and hurried away to return and fill again. Engines shrieked their signal notes, morning, noon and night. The activity was ceaseless. The depots were crowded with goods of every description. Passenger trains were thronged, ladies and families in their fright undergoing the most grievous torments of travel to escape from what they believed was a doomed city. The city resounded with the rumble of a thousand wheels, all bearing their freight to the grand funnel out of which it was to be discharged. Horses, wagons, negroes, every thing that could aid in the removal of property, was brought into requisition, and between force and persuasion, an immense amount of labor was systematically, rapidly and judiciously employed. By Wednesday night the tide was at its height. The enemy were within three miles. The little army in their front had given back step by step until, flanked out of the fortifications on the opposite side of the Congaree, they retired to the limits of the city itself, where a line of battle again re-formed. Three or four shells thrown at the bridge increased the popular agitation until it became a fever. The stores were closed. Militia and detailed men were at the front. Army trains began to move through, and the truth at last flashed upon the minds of all, that Columbia must inevitably be evacuated. Few slept soundly in their beds during the night that followed. Thursday, the 15th, the enemy opened on the city with shells. Some damage was done, but few casualties are reported. One gentleman only is said to have been killed. The State House, Nickerson's Hotel, *South Carolinian* office, together with some private residences, were paid an iron compliment, and the inmates evacuated with the usual polite formalities of leave-taking. Still the work of removal went bravely forward, and a vast amount was accomplished. The time was too brief, however, to do all, and hundreds of thousands of dollars' worth of public and private property remained in and about the depot, as a prey to the Yankee torch and pilferer.

"The scenes up the railroad may be briefly described. Crowds at every depot seeking temporary shelter ; some getting off, some getting on ; twenty trains thundering one after the other in quick succession ; screaming locomotives, crying babies, tearful women, families traveling in box-cars among piles of bacon, salt, bandboxes, trunks and bedclothes ; a break down near Winsboro ; engine off the track ; ten hours' delay ; enemy reported coming ; more consternation ; a long night ; no wood, no water, no breakfast ; ten carloads of ladies of the Treasury Department in most unattractive morning *dishabille*, with hair unkempt, and hollow, sleepy eyes, shivering about in the red mucilaginous mud ; ten or twelve carloads of Yankee prisoners just ahead, likewise at a dead halt ; the guards around their camp-fires, and the individuals of a cerulean aspect singing with tremendous energy Union songs ; still ahead, the section-masters and bricklayers, with a gang of laborers repairing the road and holding *post-mortem* consultations over the remains of a deserted engine—finally, a run back three miles, a filling of tanks, a fresh start, and arrival at Charlotte. There an avalanche upon the good people, an appeal to hospitality which is most warmly heeded, and a gradual simmering down of all the elements in agitation. Such, in brief, is a history of our evacuation of Columbia."

The announcement of the fall of Columbia was first received at the North in the following extract from the *Richmond Dispatch* of February 18, forwarded by General Grant from City Point:

"Columbia has fallen! Sherman marched into and took possession of the city yesterday morning. The intelligence was communicated yesterday by General Beauregard in an official dispatch. Columbia is situated on the north bank of the Congaree River, just below the confluence of the Saluda and Broad Rivers. From General Beauregard's dispatch, it appears that on Thursday night the enemy approached the south bank of the Congaree, and threw a number of shells into the city. During the night they moved up the river, and yesterday morning forded the Saluda and Broad Rivers. Whilst they were crossing these rivers our troops under General Beauregard evacuated Columbia. The enemy soon after took possession. Through private sources we learn that two days ago, when it was decided not to attempt the defence of Columbia, a large quantity of medical stores, which it was thought it was impossible to remove, were destroyed. The female employees of the Treasury Department had been previously sent off to Charlotte, South Carolina, a hundred miles north of Columbia. We presume the Treasury lithographic establishment was also removed, although as to this we have no positive information. The fall of Columbia necessitates, we presume, the evacuation of Charleston, which, we think likely, is already in process of evacuation."

That event, the necessity of which was thus declared, was already in process of completion. The capture of Branchville had rendered it inevitable. Charleston, with its supplies cut off, with the army of Sherman in the rear, closely beset on James Island by the forces of the department from the South, with Admiral Dahlgren's powerful navy in front, was no longer tenable as a military post. It was only left to General Hardee, who was in command, to escape while he could by the single northerly coast line of railway still open to him. Prominent citizens had already left, the army and stores were being removed, and on the 18th, the date of General Grant's communication, the city was surrendered. The fact was announced in a dispatch of that day to General Halleck by General Gillmore, who, at the opening of the campaign, had succeeded General Foster in command of the Department. It was as follows: "General — The city of Charleston and its defences came into our possession this morning, with over 200 pieces of artillery and a goodly supply of fine ammunition. The enemy commenced evacuating all the works last night, and Mayor Macbeth surrendered the city to the troops of General Schimmelfennig at 9 o'clock this morning, at which time it was occupied by our forces. Our advance on the Edisto and from Bull's Bay hastened the retreat. The cotton warehouses, arsenal, quartermaster's stores, railroad bridges, and two iron-clads were burned by the enemy. Some vessels in the ship-yard were also burned. Nearly all the inhabitants remaining belong to the poorer classes."

Intimation of the evacuation of the city was given to the fleet and the troops in the vicinity during the night by the conflagration and explosion of the rebel guns and rams. The Central Railroad buildings in the upper part of the city, containing a large quantity of provisions and two hundred kegs of powder, were consumed. About half-past 3 in the morning the powder blew up, killing and wounding a considerable number — about 100 it was said—of the poorer citizens who were engaged in gathering for themselves the corn and rice devoted to destruction. The rams in the inner harbor were blown up at daylight. Among the guns destroyed were two 600 - pounders, mounted on the wharf-batteries of the city. They were exploded by being filled with powder, sand, and rock ; the concussion at their being fired, completely shattering the houses in the vicinity. The first of the Union forces who entered the city was Lieutenant-Colonel A. G. Bennett, Twenty-first United States Colored Troops, who arrived about half an hour after the last of the rebel forces left. He was followed by Colonel Ames of the Third Rhode Island Artillery. Troops were sent over to hold the city from James and Morris Islands. General Gillmore arrived about noon from Hilton Head, and on seeing the smoke over the city sailed up the channel, reaching the pier at 2 in the afternoon. Admiral Dahlgren preceded him by about an hour. Captain Henry M. Bregg, of General Gillmore's staff, went over to Fort Sumter in a small boat, and planted the United States flag on the parapet, having for a staff an oar and a boat hook lashed together. He found in the fort four columbiads and five howitzers. The Union troops, on landing at the city, were immediately employed in arresting the conflagration and saving the property of the inhabitants from further destruction. The quantity of cotton destroyed was estimated at about four thousand bales. Much more, it was said, was left distributed in small lots about the city. Eight locomotives and twelve cars were captured. Several hundred deserters concealed in the houses surrendered. Hundreds of others came in from the country afterward. In a second dispatch forwarded on the 26th, General Gillmore reported the actual capture of over 450 pieces of ordnance, being more than double his first estimate. Hardee retreated in the direction of North Carolina with about 12,000 men.

A correspondent with General Gillmore's army, writing from Charleston on the 21st, describes the general condition of the city. "The confused state of affairs," says he, "which prevailed for the first day or two after the evacuation of the city is rapidly assuming a more quiet and satisfactory condition. The citizens of the place are gradually becoming accustomed and reconciled to the new regimé, and do not hesitate to appear on the streets or to visit their places of business. But a few complaints have been made to Provost-Marshal Bennett, by citizens who have sustained some annoyance in the way of having their premises unceremoniously entered by the soldiers, and by other citizens who have had horses, vehicles, and other property suddenly confiscated. In a few days, however, a guard will be organized throughout the city, and the people will be assured of the safety of themselves and their effects. The appearance of the city is desolate in the extreme. While on Morris Island I often heard the report that grass was growing in the streets at the lower end of Charleston, and now I am a witness to the truth of the statement. All along the water front, and in fact, for a long distance up the city, the buildings are either partially or wholly demolished. The walls of some present great, jagged holes, through which a horse and cart could easily pass, and that is the case not only in one but several streets. No wonder the rebels were solicitous to get beyond the reach of our shells. Such a punishment was never before inflicted upon any city. All of the hotels are closed, the furniture and appointments having been removed by the proprietors to the interior of the State some months ago. The Mills House was struck seventeen times, and at last the guests announced that they would not risk their lives by remaining longer in the building. The Charleston Hotel was also struck several times, so that it became necessary to close it. While walking through the upper wards this morning, I was astonished to find that shells had even reached as far as the Georgia Railroad depot, thus showing that they had traveled a distance of five and six miles.

"The first day of our entry into the city I noticed but few citizens made their appearance. I am told that the more prominent secessionists, and a great many of the Union sympathizers have gone into the country. But within the past few days a number of the latter have returned here, bringing their furniture with them. Unmistakably there is a strong Union feeling in Charleston. There is also a secesh element remaining which in course of time will die a natural death. As to the matter of subsistence the supply is limited, consisting mostly of meal and rice. The entire quantity was seized by our authorities on Saturday, and at noon to-day will be turned over to a committee of the citizens, of which committee Dr. A. G. Mackey, one of the staunchest Union men in the place, is a member, to be distributed among the poor of the inhabitants. It seems to be inevitable that to prevent suffering, similar measures to those taken by the North in the case of Savannah must be adopted in behalf of the people of Charleston. It is contemplated by the citizens to hold a public meeting for the purpose of choosing delegates to repair to the North and lay before its people an account of the destitute condition to which the rebellion has reduced them. I have taken special pains to inquire of a number of the inhabitants what general view was entertained in the South as to the results thus far of the war, and in every instance I was informed that the South would do well if it held out two months longer. General Hardee and other rebel military officers said before they left the city that their armies must concentrate in Virginia, or all would certainly be lost. Perhaps it will surprise many to learn that there was really a Union League established in Charleston. Such was the case, and it received the support of hundreds of the citizens, and many of the members were of such prominent standing that the military authorities dare not make open arrests. According to the description given, the most inhuman and outrageous acts of cruelty were committed by the rebels when they evacuated. Women and children who had snatched from the flames a few bags of meal or corn, or an apronful of rice, were pursued by the cavalry and cut down with sabres. The rebels were exasperated to the nature of fiends when they approached a man who showed the least desire to share the fate of the city. Had they been allowed to exercise their own will, not a house would have been left standing."

Writing a few days later, on the 26th the same correspondent says: "The citadel, arsenal, and some other public buildings have, until the past two days, been guarded by colored troops. They are now guarded by the Third Rhode Island Artillery and one other regiment. Nearly all of the colored troops have been taken off of patrol duty and sent to the front, where they will doubtless render efficient service. As a natural consequence, the residents felt *hurt* at seeing their houses placed under the surveillance of colored soldiers, who, perhaps, a short time previous had labored as slaves for the inmates, but, at the same time, they had an opportunity of observing that the colored soldiers were slaves no longer. Since my arrival in this city I have been assured by different parties that their colored servants would not leave them on any account, and that they had become so attached to their homes that no one could entice them away. Within the past twenty-four hours I have learned from a number of the same party that their colored servants had taken 'French leave.' The fact is, the slaves in this city—or those who were formerly slaves—have become imbued with a spirit of freedom, and are determined to bear the yoke no longer. They begin to comprehend the old saying 'that the laborer is worthy of his hire.' From the very first day of the rebellion, there have lived in Charleston men firm and true to the Union. Through evil and good report, reverses and successes, they have always stood on one side — the Union side. Those men are in the city to-day, and we take them by the hand and say, you have done your duty nobly and well. How they managed to meet together and talk over the events of the day, each one giving a free expression to his thoughts, and using his influence to counteract the evil designs of the rebels, is a matter which need not be explained here. It is sufficient to know that they did not fail in their object. Of course we cannot expect to find all the inhabitants of Charleston enlisted in the cause of the Union. We meet rebels daily. We meet rebels who do not hesitate to declare themselves as such, notwithstanding they may be on a mission to the office of the Provost-Marshal for the purpose of asking him to send a guard to protect their property. It is strange how little some people will appreciate the efforts of those who try to render them a service. For four long years have the citizens of this place submitted themselves to the tyranny of fiends, and how any one of them can be otherwise than grateful to the men who liberated them is one of the mysteries of the times. As a redeeming circumstance, however, I will state that our soldiers have not been grossly insulted in the streets. The citizens are disposed to treat them respectfully at any rate."

Again, on March 5: "Under the new order of things the people of Charleston are gradually coming to their senses, and evince a disposition to make the city once more the leading trading mart for this section of the country. When we first took possession the citizens were shy, and hesitated about making their appearance on the street, but now they come forth in swarms, and of course the majority of them profess to be on the side of the Union. Were it not for Northern enterprise, however, Charleston might remain in the same dormant state in which we found it for years. But happily the new comers have infused a spirit of activity into the old inhabitants, and we shall see the city in a few months' time full of life and gayety. Some of the citizens still cling to the hope that the rebel government will eventually succeed in establishing itself on a firm basis, but the same citizens are laughed and jeered at by their more wise neighbors. . . . King Street is alive with business. One is astonished to see how some sutlers and other traders have taken stores and exposed goods for sale. The stores are doing an excellent business, too. From morning till night they are thronged with customers. The great trouble is that the majority of the citizens have rebel money only. They appreciate the fact that this money is worthless; yet they are very reluctant to part with it without receiving a portion of an equivalent in return. The other day I saw a man who had $10,000 in rebel notes, and who was willing to exchange the entire amount for $500 in greenbacks, and could not find a purchaser. Men who, before the war, were the wealthiest in the city, are now in the condition of the poorest. Yesterday a man who, three years ago, was worth $2,000,000, confessed to me that he could not raise twenty dollars in current money if it was demanded of him to save his neck from the gallows. I looked at him, and thought he was just the fellow that the gallows had been waiting for during the past four years. A considerable amount of gold and silver is in circulation. It was the practice of the shrewd ones to turn their rebel rag currency into coin as often as an opportunity offered; hence we see many persons attired in soiled and tattered garments with the real stuff in their pockets. In accordance with a general order, issued at the Post Headquarters, a premium of one hundred per cent. is allowed on gold, and seventy-five per cent. on silver. So far as subsistence stores are concerned, the citizens of Charleston appear to have been better off than their neighbors in Savannah. To be sure, they did not have a large quantity of meal, but of rice and corn they had an abundant supply. A large quantity of rice and corn, stored in public buildings, was seized by our authorities, and turned over to a committee of the citizens, to be distributed among the most needy." *

The fall of Charleston was thus a much less dramatic affair than had been anticipated. Though in the successive assaults of the Army and Navy, and the virtual destruction of Fort Sumter, it had been the scene of many acts of great heroism, it was occupied quietly at last without the expected final struggle for which the Navy was prepared and which the Army anticipated. The siege, dating from the establishment of General Gillmore's troops on Morris Island in July, 1863, had lasted 585 days. It would be a curious account—an inventory of the various ammunition, the powder, shot and shell expended during this year and a half of incessant warfare on this ill-fated spot. A Northern "correspondent," writing from the city on the 23d of February, chronicles some of the results of this continuous bombardment. "About 13,000 shells," says he, "have been thrown into the town — nearly a thousand shells a month. Some were filled with the preparation known as 'Greek fire,' others with incendiary fuses, others with powder only. The shells were fired at a great elevation and were therefore plunging shots—striking a house on the roof and passing down from the attic to the chambers, lower stories, ground floor, and basement. Some exploded in the attic, some in the cellars, some in the chambers, others in the walls. The effect has been a complete riddling of the houses. Brick walls have been blown into millions of fragments, roofs have been torn to pieces—rafters, beams, braces, scantlings have been broken and splintered into jack straws. Churches, hotels, stores, dwellings, public buildings, all have been shattered. There are great holes in the ground where cart-loads of earth have been excavated in a twinkling. To present a lively picture of the place I must incorporate personal adventures into my account. The lower half of the city is called Gillmore's town by the inhabitants. I have made a thorough exploration of Gillmore's town, also of that part of the city still inhabited. We visited the old office of the *Mercury* in Broad Street. A messenger sent by the 'Marsh Angel,' had preceded us, entering the roof, passing into the chimney, and exploding within, dumping several cart-loads of brickbats, mortar and soot into the editorial room, smashing all the windows, and splintering the doors. It

* "Whit," Correspondence *New York Times*, February–March, 1865.

was the room where secession had its incubation. The leading rebellious spirits once sat there in their arm chairs and enthroned King Cotton, and demanded homage to his majesty from all nations. The first shell sent the 'Mercury' up town to a safer locality, but when Sherman began his march into the interior, the 'Mercury' fled into the country to Cheraw, it is said, right into the line of Sherman's advance! The 'Courier' office, in Bay street, had not escaped damage. A shell entered through the roof, went tearing down through the floors, ripping up the boards, breaking the timbers, jarring the plaster from the walls, exploding in the second story, rattling all the tiles from the roof, bursting out the windows, smashing the imposing stone, opening the whole building to the sun-light. Another shell had dashed the sidewalk to pieces and blown a passage into the cellar wide enough to admit a six-horse wagon. Near the 'Courier' office was the Union Bank, Farmers' and Exchange Bank, and the Charleston Bank. They were costly buildings, fitted up with marble mantels, floors of terracotta tiles, counters elaborate in carved work, and with gorgeous frescoing on the walls. There, five years ago, the merchants of the city, the planters of the country, the slave-traders assembled on exchange, talked treason, and indulged in extravagant day-dreams of the future glory of Charleston.

"The rooms are silent now. The oaken doors splintered, the frescoing washed from the walls by the rains which drip from the shattered roof, the desks are kindling wood, the highly-wrought cornice work has dropped from the ceiling to the ground, the tiles are plowed up, the marble mantels shivered, the beautiful plate-glass of the windows lies in a million fragments upon the floor. In short the banks have broke! They helped on the rebellion—contributed of their funds to inaugurate it, and invested largely in the State stock to place the State on a war footing. By a document which has fallen into my hands and which lies before me, I notice that the three banks already named held on January 6, 1862, $610,000 worth of the seven per cent. State stock, issued under the act of December, 1861. They would sell it dog cheap now. Passing from the banks to the hotel I found a like scene of destruction. The door of the Mills House was open. The windows had lost their glazing and were boarded up. Sixteen shots have struck the building. The rooms where secession had been rampant in the beginning, where bottles of wine had been drunk over the fall of Sumter, echoed only to our footsteps. The Charleston Hotel has several great holes in the walls. The churches have not escaped. St. Michael's, the oldest of all, has been repeatedly struck. The pavement is thick with broken glass, whick has been rattled from the windows by the explosion of the shells. All the churches in the lower portion of the city are wrecks. The preachers were early imbued with the spirit of revolt. Episcopalian, Presbyterian, and Baptist—all preached secession.

"Warehouses, stores, dwellings alike are shaken to pieces. The family residences overlooking the bay or battery, as it is called, are windowless, some even without doors. The elaborate centre-pieces of stucco-work in the drawing-rooms have crumbled; the marble mantels are defaced; bedrooms are filled with bricks; the white marble steps and mahogany balusters are shattered; owls and bats can build their nests in the coming spring-time undisturbed in the desolate mansions; the esplanade of the battery, the pleasure-ground of the Charlestonians, their delight and pride, is dug into defensive trenches; there is a breastwork in King street. There are masked batteries along the shore, which show that the determination was fierce for holding the city, even if the iron-clads had succeeded in passing Moultrie. In 1861 the heart of the city was burned out by a great fire, which swept from the Cooper to the Ashley Rivers. Since then there has been no sound of saw or hammer, except in the ship-yards where the gunboats were under construction. Those, like everything else, have been lost labor. Last Saturday they, too, were burned. It is an indescribable scene of desolation and ruin, of roofless, doorless, windowless houses, crumbling walls, upheaved pavements, and grass-grown streets—silent to all sounds of business, and voiceless only to the woe-begone, poverty-stricken, haggard people, who wander up and down amid the ruins, looking to a jubilant past, a disappointed present, and a hopeless future. They are in rags, and their boots are out at the toes, their shoes down at the heels. There is no longer a manifestation of arrogance, lordly insolence, and conscious superiority over the Yankees on the part of the whites."*

The picture of the occupation of Charleston would be incomplete without a glance at its effects upon the colored race in the city. The correspondent just cited, in another letter gives a sketch of the scene. "It is impossible," says he, "for me to give a complete representation of the joy of the freedmen of this city over the arrival of the Yankees. On Monday morning last, when the steamer W. W. Coit, with General Gillmore's flag at the fore and the Stars and Stripes at the stern, steamed up the harbor, with the band playing 'Hail Columbia,' there was a sudden gathering of colored people upon the wharves. They were full of ecstasy. Springing upon the pier before the lines were thrown out, I met a gray-bearded old man, who touched his hat, bowed himself to the ground, and said, 'Good morning, massa.' 'We are Yankees, Uncle. Are you not afraid of us?' I said. 'God bless you, no, massa. I've prayed for you to come, and God has heard me,' he said, grasping my hand. He threw his old battered hat upon the ground, looked upward and poured out his gratitude from an overflowing heart. 'Are you a slave?' 'Yes, massa.' 'Well, you are a slave no longer. You are as free as I am.' 'Is it so, massa?' he asked with indescribable earnestness, and again raising his eyes toward heaven, he gave thanks to God with an emotion such as I never before witnessed.

"Charleston has been one of the great slave marts of the South. She has been the boldest advocate for the re-opening of the slave trade. Her statesmen legislated for it; her ministers of the Gospel upheld it as the best means of Christianizing Africa, and the ultimate benefit of the whole human race. Being thus upheld, as might be expected, the slave-traders set up their auction-block in no out-of-the-way place. A score of men opened offices and dealt in the bodies and souls of men. Among them were T. Ryan & Son, M. M. McBride, J. E. Bowers, J. B. Oaks, J. B. Baker, Wilbur & Son, on State and Chalmers Streets. Twenty paces distant from Baker's is a building bearing the sign, 'Theological Library, Protestant Episcopal Church.' Standing by Baker's door and looking up Chalmers Street to King Street, I read another sign, 'Sunday-School Depository;' also, 'Hibernian Hall,' the building in which the ordinance of secession was signed. In another building, on the opposite corner, is the Registry of Deeds. Near by is the guard-house with its grated windows, its iron bars being an appropriate design of double-edged swords and spears. Thousands of poor slaves have been incarcerated there for no crime whatever, except for being out after 9 o'clock, or for meeting in some

* Correspondence of the *Boston Journal*, Charleston, February 23, 1865.

upper chamber to tell God their wrongs, with no white man present. They ought to have obeyed the injunction of the deep-toned bell of old St. Michael's, which, at 8:30 in the evening in its high and venerable tower, opened its trembling lips and shouted, 'Get you home! get you home!' Always that; always that of command; always of arrogance, superiority, and caste; never of love, good-will, and friendship. On Sunday morning it said to the white man, 'Come and sit in your old-fashioned, velvet-cushioned pews, you rich ones! Go up stairs, you niggers!' I heard the old bell last night at half-past eight. A week ago, at 9 o'clock, the horse patrol dashed through the streets, and all negroes abroad without a pass were marched down to the guard-house. Now, freedmen walk the street at all hours of day and night, unchallenged even by the dusky sentinels pacing their appointed beats, whose only duty is to keep watch against surprise from those who would bring chains and slavery once more to this people. The guard-house doors are wide open. The jailor has lost his occupation. The last slave has been incarcerated within its walls, and St. Michael's curfew shall be sweetest music henceforth and forever. It shall ring the glad chimes of freedom—freedom to come, to go, or to tarry by the way—freedom from sad partings of wife and husband, father and son, mother and child. The brokers in flesh and blood took good care to be well buttressed. They set up their mart in a respectable quarter, with St. Michael's and the guard-house, the Registry of Deeds and the Sunday-School Depository, the court house and the Theological Library around them to uphold and sustain them, and make their calling respectable. But the 'Marsh Angel' has rattled all the glass from the windows of St. Michael's, splintered the pews, and smashed the pulpit. Its messengers have howled over the grave of Calhoun, the apostle of secession, whose bones are moldering in the adjoining cemetery. The same 'Angel' has made a record of its doing in the Registry building. At one stroke it opened the entire front of the Sunday-School Depository to the light of heaven. There is a mass of evidence in the court-room—several cart-loads of brick and plaster introduced by General Gillmore, which the advocates of secession here thought admissable. I entered the Theological Library building through a window from which General Gillmore had removed the sash. A pile of old rubbish lay upon the floor—sermons, tracts. magazines, books, papers, damp, musty, and moldy—turning into pulp beneath the rain-drops which came down through the shattered roof.

"Amid these surroundings was the Slave Mart—a building with a large iron gate in front, above which, in large gilt letters, was the word 'Mart.' The iron gate opened to a hall about sixty feet long by twenty broad, flanked on one side by a long table running the entire length of the hall, and on the other by benches. At the further end a door, opening through a brick wall, gave entrance to a yard. The door was locked. I tried my boot heel, but it would not yield. I called a freedman to my aid. Unitedly we took up a great stone. We gave a blow. Another, and the door of the Bastile went into splinters. Across the yard is a four-story brick building, with grated windows and iron doors—a prison. The yard is walled by high buildings. He who entered there left all hope behind. A small room adjoining the hall was the place where women were subjected to the lascivious gaze of brutal men. There were the steps, up which thousands of men, women and children have walked to their places on the table, to be knocked off to the highest bidder. The thought occurred to me that perhaps Governor Andrew or Wendell Phillips, or William Lloyd Garrison, or Drs. Kirk, Stone, or Rev. Mr. Manning would like to make a speech from those steps. I determined to secure them. While doing so a colored woman came into the hall to see the Yankees. 'I was sold there upon that table two years ago,' said she. 'You never will be sold again; you are free now and forever,' I replied. 'Thank God! Oh, the blessed Jesus, he has heard my prayer. I am so glad, only I wish I could see my husband. He was sold at the same time into the country, and has gone I don't know where.' Thus spake Dinah Moore. In front of the mart was a gilt star—I climbed the post and wrenched it from its spike to secure it as a trophy. A freedman took down the gilt letters for me, and knocked off the great lock from the outer iron gate and the smaller lock from the inner door. The steps and lock are on their way to Boston. The key of the French Bastile hangs at Mount Vernon; the staircase of the temple of Jerusalem, up which the Saviour walked, has been transplanted to Rome; and so, as relics of the American prison-house now and forever being broken up, I have secured these relics that all who love freedom, who have worked and prayed through long and weary years for the overthrow of slavery, who have laid down their sons upon the battlefield to save the land, may behold them. These steps have been wet by many tears; men and women have tottered upon them with trembling limbs and broken hearts. Upon them there has been such weeping and sorrow and sighing as slavery alone of all things on earth can give, weeping which has been, but which shall be no more."

Simultaneously with the news of the fall of Columbia and Charleston came the report of further conquests in the Department of North Carolina where General Schofield with reinforcements, had taken command at the beginning of February. After the capture of Fort Fisher and its defendencies the chief obstacle hindering an advance by water to Wilmington was Fort Anderson on Cape Fear River guarding the immediate approach to the city. It was described as a work of immense strength and great extent, "its sea-front like that of Fort Fisher, being a series of large mounds or traverses rising twenty-five to thirty feet above the water of Cape Fear River, in which it fronts to the North East, and extending in alternating mounds, traverses, angles, embrasures and ditches, enclosing an area of about four square miles. Its object was to cover a system of river obstructions, *Chevaux de frise*, torpedoes, etc., which it would have been impossible to pass while held by the enemy, and it also commanded the right of the enemy's strong line of works on the opposite bank of the river.*" The movement up the river commenced on the 11th of February with a reconnoissance in force by Ames' and Paine's divisions of General Terry's command which was pushed to the enemies lines on the left bank of the river opposite Fort Anderson about twelve miles from Wilmington. There was some sharp skirmishing at the enemy's outposts, General Hoke being in command of the confederate forces, in which the Union colored troops were actively engaged while the Monitor Montauk bombarded the Fort. These preliminary movements were followed up on the 16th by the transfer by General Schofield of General Cox's division of the Twenty-third Corps across from Federal Point to Smithfield whence they advanced on the right bank of the river through swampy and difficult ground to the rear of Fort Anderson. The sequel is related in the dispatch of Admiral Porter on the 19th to the Navy Department. "I have the honor," he writes, "to report the surrender or evacuation of Fort Anderson. General Schofield advanced

* "Army and Navy Gazette," February 25, 1865.

from Smithville with 3,000 men on the 17th inst. At the same time I attacked the works by water, placing the Monitor Montauk close to the works, and infilating them with the Pawtucket, Lenafee, Unadilla and Pequot, the tide and wind not allowing more vessels to get under fire. The fort answered pretty briskly, but quieted down by sunset. On the 18th, at 8 o'clock, I moved up closer with the Montauk, leaving the following by the Mackinaw: Huron, Sassacus, Pontoosuc, Maratango, Lenafee, Unadilla, Pawtucket, Osceola, Shawmut, Seneca,. Wyack, Chippewa and Little Ada, and kept up a heavy fire during the day until late in the afternoon. The enemy's batteries were silenced by 3 o'clock, though we kept up the fire until dusk. We also fired through the night. In the meantime General Schofield was working in the rear of the rebels, to cut them off. The latter did not wait for the army to surround them, but left in the night, taking five or six pieces of light artillery with them, and everything else of any value. At daylight this morning some of our troops that were near by, went in and hoisted the flag on the ramparts, when the firing ceased from the monitors. There were ten heavy guns in Fort Anderson, and a quantity of ammunition. We lost but three killed and five wounded."

In addition to the dispatch of Admiral Porter in relation to the surrender or evacuation of Fort Anderson, information was received at the same time at the Navy Department that Lieutenant Wm. B. Cushing constructed a mock monitor so closely resembling one of those vessels that no difference could be detected at the distance of 100 yards. On Saturday night, the 18th, at about 11 o'clock, this vessel was taken up to within four hundred yards of the fort, and set adrift. As there was a strong flood tide, she moved up the river and passed the fort as if under slow steam. At this time the army had worked about two-thirds of the distance around and in the rear of the fort, and the rebels, no doubt thinking their communications would be cut off both by land and water, hastily escaped by the only avenue open to them, leaving their guns unspiked, their magazines uninjured, etc.

The abandonment of Fort Anderson was speedily followed by the evacuation by General Hoke of Wilmington. The naval and military operations leading to the capture of the city on the 22d, are related in a dispatch of Admiral Porter of that day, to Secretary Welles: "I have," he writes, "the honor to inform you that Wilmington has been evacuated, and is in the possession of our troops. After the evacuation of Fort Anderson, I pushed forward the gunboats up as far as the water would permit. The army pushed up at the same time on the right and left banks of the river. After sounding and buoying out the middle ground at Big Island, I succeeded in getting the gunboats over, and opened fire on Fort Strong, the work commanding the principal obstructions, where the rebels had also sank a barge steamer—the North Eastern. Our fire soon drove the rebels away from the fort. Now and then they would fire a shot, one of which struck the Sassacus below water-mark, and set her leaking badly. She was struck once or twice more, but met with no loss in men. That night (the 20th) the rebels sent down 200 floating torpedoes, but I had a strong force of picket-boats out, and the torpedoes were sunk with musketry. One got in the wheel of the Osceola, and blew her wheelhouse to pieces, and knocked down her bulkhead inboard, and there was no damage to the hull. Some of the vessels picked up the torpedoes with their torpedo-nets. The next morning I spread two fishing nets across the river. Yesterday evening,

General Ames, with his division, moved within a short distance of the fort, and had a sharp encounter with the rebels. On hearing the musketry, and seeing where our troops were, I opened a rapid fire on the fort, and ere long the enemy's line and fort responded with three or four shots, but was soon silenced. This morning we heard that General Terry was within their works, and the road was clear to Wilmington. The Montauk could not get across the shoals without lightening, which was a work of some labor, I had the pleasure of placing the flag on Fort Strong, and at 12 o'clock noon, to-day, we all fire a salute of thirty-five guns, this being the anniversary of Washington's birthday."

The night previous to the evacuation, the enemy destroyed about 1,000 bales of cotton, 15,000 barrels of rosin, an extensive cotton shed and presses, an unfinished iron clad, three large turpentine works and various bridges. About 700 prisoners were captured and some thirty or forty pieces of artillery left in the city.

The capture of Wilmington at this time was of the utmost importance as a base of supplies for the Army of General Sherman in its advance into North Carolina, where he was threatened with considerable opposition by the concentrated forces of the enemy, the retreating forces of Beauregard from Columbia, of Hardee from Charleston, the troops of the Department and reinforcements from Richmond, the whole being now under command of General Joseph E. Johnston.

In accordance with an act of the Richmond Congress passed in January, providing for the appointment of a general-in-chief of the armies of the Confederate States, General Lee was early in February called to that command. His headquarters remained with the army of Northern Virginia at Richmond. The Congress also resolved "That if the President will assign General Joseph E. Johnston to the command of the Army of Tennessee, it will, in the opinion of the Congress of the Confederate States, be hailed with joy by the army and receive the approval of the country." This likewise was accomplished, General Johnston succeeding General Beauregard in command at Charlotte, N. C., on the 25th of February, of "The Army of the Tennessee and all the troops in the Departments of South Carolina, Georgia and Florida." General Beauregard, at his own request, received a subordinate command in Johnston's army. We now resume the narrative by General Sherman of his military operations subsequent to the occupation of Columbia on the 17th of February. "At the same time," says he, "the left wing and cavalry had crossed the Saluda and Broad Rivers, breaking up the railroad about Alston, and as high up as the bridge across Broad River on the Spartanburgh road, the main body moving straight for Winnsboro, which General Slocum reached on the 21st of February. He caused the railroad to be destroyed up to Blackstakes depot, and then turned to Rocky Mount, on the Catawba River. The Twentieth Corps reached Rocky Mount on the 22d, laid a pontoon bridge, and crossed over during the 23d. Kilpatrick's cavalry followed, and crossed over in a terrible rain during the night of the 23d, and moved up to Lancaster, with orders to keep up the delusion of a general movement on Charlotte, N. C., to which General Beauregard, and all the cavalry of the enemy, had retreated from Columbia. I was also aware that Cheatham's corps, of Hood's old army, was aiming to make a junction with Beauregard at Charlotte, having been cut off by our rapid movement on Columbia and Winnsboro. From the 23d to the 26th we had heavy rains, swelling the rivers and making the roads almost impassable. The Twentieth Corps reached Hanging Rock on the 26th, and waited there for the

Fourteenth Corps to cross the Catawba. The heavy rains had so swollen the river that the pontoon bridge broke, and General Davis had very hard work to restore it and get his command across. At last he succeeded, and the left wing was all put in motion for Cheraw. In the meantime the right wing had broken up the railroad to Winnsboro, and thence turned for Peay's ferry, where it was crossed over the Catawba before the heavy rains set in, the Seventeenth Corps moving straight on Cheraw *via* Young's Bridge, and the Fifteenth Corps by Tiller's and Kelly's Bridges. From this latter corps detachments were sent in to Camden, to burn the bridge over the Wateree, with the railroad depot, stores, etc. A small force of mounted men, under Captain Duncan, was also dispatched to make a dash and interrupt the railroad from Charleston to Florence, but it met Butler's division of cavalry, and, after a sharp night's skirmish on Mount Elon, was compelled to return unsuccessful. Much bad road was encountered at Lynch's Creek, which delayed the right wing about the same length of time as the left wing had been on the Catawba. On the 2d of March, the leading division of the Twentieth Corps entered Chesterfield, skirmishing with Butler's division of cavalry, and the next day, about noon, the Seventeenth Corps entered Cheraw, the enemy retreating across the Pedee and burning the bridge at that point. At Cheraw we found much ammunition and many guns, which had been brought from Charleston on the evacuation of that city. These were destroyed, as also the railroad trestles and bridges down as far as Darlington. An expedition of mounted infantry was also sent down to Florence, but it encountered both cavalry and infantry, and returned, having only broken up in part the branch road from Florence to Cheraw.

"Without unnecessary delay the columns were again put in motion, directed on Fayetteville, North Carolina, the right wing crossing the Pedee at Cheraw, and the left wing and cavalry at Sneedsboro. General Kilpatrick was ordered to keep well on the left flank, and the Fourteenth Corps, moving by Love's Bridge, was given the right to enter and occupy Fayetteville first. The weather continued unfavorable and roads bad, but the Fourteenth and Seventeenth Corps reached Fayetteville on the 11th of March, skirmishing with Wade Hampton's cavalry, that covered the rear of Hardee's retreating army, which, as usual, had crossed Cape Fear River, burning the bridge. During the march from the Pedee, General Kilpatrick had kept his cavalry well on the left and exposed flank. During the night of the 9th of March his three brigades were divided to picket the roads. General Hampton detecting this, rushed in at daylight and gained possession of the camp of Colonel Spencer's brigade, and the house in which General Kilpatrick and Colonel Spencer had their quarters. The surprise was complete, but General Kilpatrick quickly succeeded in rallying his men, on foot, in a swamp near by, and by a prompt attack, well followed up, regained his artillery, horses, camp, and everything save some prisoners whom the enemy carried off, leaving their dead on the ground. The 12th, 13th, and 14th were passed at Fayetteville, destroying absolutely the United States arsenal and the vast amount of machinery which had formerly belonged to the old Harper's Ferry United States arsenal. Every building was knocked down and burned, and every piece of machinery utterly broken up and ruined by the First Regiment Michigan engineers, under the immediate supervision of Colonel O. M. Poe, Chief Engineer. Much valuable property of great use to the enemy was here destroyed or cast into the river.

"Up to this period I had perfectly succeeded in interposing my superior army between the scattered parts of the enemy. But I was then aware that the fragments that had left Columbia under Beauregard had been reinforced by Cheatham's corps from the West, and the garrison of Augusta, and that ample time had been given to move them to my front and flank about Raleigh. Hardee had also succeeded in getting across Cape Fear River ahead of me, and could therefore complete the junction with the other armies of Johnston and Hoke in North Carolina. And the whole, under the command of the skillful and experienced Joe Johnston, made up an army superior to me in cavalry, and formidable enough in artillery and infantry to justify me in extreme caution in making the last step necessary to complete the march I had undertaken. Previous to reaching Fayetteville I had dispatched to Wilmington, from Laurel Hill Church, two of our best scouts, with intelligence of our position and my general plans. Both of these messengers reached Wilmington, and on the morning of the 12th of March the army-tug *Davidson*, Captain. Ainsworth, reached Fayetteville from Wilmington, bringing me full intelligence of events from the outer world. On the same day this tug carried back to General Terry, at Wilmington, and General Schofield, at Newbern, my dispatches, to the effect that on Wednesday, the 15th, we would move for Goldsboro', *feigning* on Raleigh, and ordering them to march straight for Goldsboro', which I expected to reach about the 20th. The same day the gunboat *Eolus*, Captain Young, United States Navy, also reached Fayetteville, and through her I continued to have communication with Wilmington until the day of our actual departure. While the work of destruction was going on at Fayetteville, two pontoon bridges were laid across Cape Fear River—one opposite the town, the other three miles below.

General Kilpatrick was ordered to move up the plank-road to and beyond Averasboro. He was to be followed by four divisions of the left wing, with as few wagons as possible; the rest of the train, under escort of two remaining divisions of that wing, to take a shorter and more direct road to Goldsboro'. In like manner, General Howard was ordered to send his trains, under good escort, well to the right, toward Faison's depot and Goldsboro', and to hold four divisions light, ready to go to the aid of the left wing if attacked while in motion. The weather continued very bad, and the roads had become more quagmire. Almost every foot of it had to be corduroyed to admit the passage of wheels. Still time was so important that punctually, according to order, the columns moved out from Cape Fear River on Wednesday, the 15th of March. I accompanied General Slocum, who, preceded by Kilpatrick's cavalry, moved up the river or plank-road that day to Kyle's Landing, Kilpatrick skirmishing heavily with the enemy's rear guard about three miles beyond, near Taylor's Hole Creek. At General Kilpatrick's request, General Slocum sent forward a brigade of infantry to hold a line of barricades. Next morning the column advanced in the same order, and developed the enemy, with artillery, infantry and cavalry, in an intrenched position in front of the point where the road branches off toward Goldsboro' through Bentonville. On an inspection of the map it was manifest that Hardee, in retreating from Fayetteville, had halted in the narrow swampy neck between Cape Fear and South Rivers, in hopes to hold me to save time for the concentration of Johnston's armies at some point to his rear, namely, Raleigh, Smithfield, or Goldsboro'. Hardee's force was estimated at twenty thousand men. It was necessary to dislodge him that we might have the use of the Goldsboro' road, and also to keep up the feint on Raleigh as long as possible. General Slocum was therefore ordered to press and carry the position, only difficult by reason of the nature of the ground, which was so soft that horses would sink everywhere, and even men could hardly make their way over the common pine barren.

The Twentieth Corps, General Williams, had the lead, and Ward's division the advance. This was deployed, and the skirmish line developed the position of a brigade of Charleston heavy artillery armed as infantry (Rhett's,) posted across the road behind a light parapet, with a battery of guns enfilading the approach across a cleared field. General Williams sent a brigade (Case's,) by a circuit to his left that turned this line, and, by a quick charge, broke the brigade, which rapidly retreated back to a second line better built, and more strongly held. A battery of artillery (Winninger's) well posted, under the immediate direction of Major Reynolds, chief of artillery of Twentieth Corps, did good execution on the retreating brigade, and, on advancing Ward's division over this ground, General Williams captured three guns and 217 prisoners, of which 68 were wounded, and left in a house near by with a rebel officer, four men, and five days' rations; 108 rebel dead were buried by us. As Ward's division advanced, he developed a second and a stronger line, when Jackson's division was deployed forward on the right of Ward, and the two divisions of Jeff. C. Davis (Fourteenth) corps on the left, well toward the Cape Fear. At the same time Kilpatrick, who was acting in concert with General Williams, was ordered to draw back his cavalry and mass it on the extreme right, and in concert with Jackson's right to feel forward for the Goldsboro' road. He got in a brigade on the road, but it was attacked by McLaws' rebel division furiously, and though it fought well and hard, the brigade drew back to the flank of the infantry. The whole line advanced late in the afternoon, drove the enemy well within his intrenched line, and pressed him so hard that next morning he was gone, having retreated in a miserable stormy night over the worst of roads. Ward's division of infantry followed to and through Averasboro', developing the fact that Hardee had retreated not on Raleigh but on Smithfield. I had the night before directed Kilpatrick to cross South River at a mill-dam to our right rear and move upon the east side toward Elevation. General Slocum reports his aggregate loss in the affair known as that of Averasboro', at 12 officers and 65 men killed, and 477 wounded. We lost no prisoners. The enemy's loss can be inferred from his dead (108) left for us to bury. Leaving Ward's division to keep to a show of pursuit, Slocum's column was turned to the right, built a bridge across the swollen South River, and took the Goldsboro' road, Kilpatrick crossing to the north, in the direction of Elevation, with orders to move eastward, watching that flank. In the meantime the wagon-trains and guards, as also Howard's column, were wallowing along the miry roads towards Bentonville and Goldsboro'. The enemy's infantry, as before stated, had retreated across our front in the same direction, burning the bridges across Mill Creek. I continued with the head of Slocum's column, and camped the night of the 18th with him on the Goldsboro' road, 27 miles from Goldsboro', about five miles from Bentonville, and where the road from Clinton to Smithfield crosses the Goldsboro' road. Howard was at Lee's store, only two miles south, and both columns had pickets three miles forward to where the two roads came together, and became common to Goldsboro'.

"All the signs induced me to believe that the enemy would make no further opposition to our progress, and would not attempt to strike us in flank while in action. I therefore directed Howard to move his right wing by the new Goldsboro' road, which goes by way of Falling Creek Church. I also left Slocum and joined Howard's column, with a view to open communications with General Schofield, coming up from Newbern. and Terry, from Wilmington. I found General Howard's column well strung out, owing to the very bad roads, and did not overtake him in person till he had reached Falling Creek Church, with one regiment forward to the cross roads near Cox's Bridge across the Neuse. I had gone from General Slocum about six miles, when I heard artillery in his direction, but was soon made easy by one of his staff officers overtaking me, exclaiming that his leading division (Carlin's) had encountered a division of rebel cavalry (Dibbrell's), which he was driving easily. But soon other staff officers came up, reporting that he had developed, near Bentonville, the whole of the rebel army under General Johnston himself. I sent him orders to call up the two divisions guarding his wagon trains, and Hazen's division of the Fifteenth Corps, still back near Lee's store, to fight defensively until I could draw up Blair's Corps, then near Mount Olive Station, and with the remaining three divisions of the Fifteenth Corps come up on Johnston's left rear from the direction of Cox's Bridge. In the mean time, while on the road, I received couriers from both Generals Schofield and Terry. The former reported himself in possession of Kinston, delayed somewhat by want of provisions, but able to march so as to make Goldsboro' on the 21st; and Terry was at or near Falson's depot. Orders were at once dispatched to Schofield to push for Goldsboro' and to make dispositions to cross Little River in the direction of Smithfield as far as Millard's; to General Terry to move to Cox's Bridge, lay a pontoon bridge, and establish a crossing; and to Blair to make a night march to Falling Creek Church; and at daylight the right wing, General Howard, less the necessary wagon guards, was put in rapid motion on Bentonville. By subsequent reports I learned that General Slocum's head of column had advanced from its camp of March 18, and first encountered Dibbrell's cavalry, but soon found his progress impeded by infantry and artillery. The enemy attacked his head of column, gaining a temporary advantage, and took three guns and caissons of General Carlin's division, driving the two leading brigades back on the main body. As soon as General Slocum realized that he had in his front the whole Confederate army, he promptly deployed the two divisions of the Fourteenth Corps, General Davis, and rapidly brought up on their left the two divisions of the Twentieth Corps, General Williams. These he arranged on the defensive, and hastily prepared a line of barricades. General Kilpatrick also came up at the sound of artillery, and massed on the left. In this position the left received six distinct assaults by the combined forces of Hoke, Hardee, and Cheatham, under the immediate command of General Johnston himself, without giving an inch of ground, and doing good execution on the enemy's ranks, especially with our artillery, the enemy having little or none.

"Johnston had moved by night from Smithfield with great rapidity, and without unnecessary wheels, intending to overwhelm my left flank before it could be relieved by its co-operating columns. But he 'reckoned without his host.' I had expected just such a movement all the way from Fayetteville, and was prepared for it. During the night of the 19th, General Slocum got up his wagon-train, with its guard of two divisions, and Hazen's division of the Fifteenth Corps, which re-inforcement enabled him to make his position impregnable. The right wing found rebel cavalry watching its approach, but unable to offer any serious opposition until our head of column encountered a considerable body behind a barricade at the forks of the road near Bentonville, about three miles east of the battle-field of the day before. This body of cavalry was, however, quickly dislodged, and the intersection of the roads secured. On moving forward, the Fifteenth Corps, General Logan, found that the enemy had thrown back his left flank, and had constructed a line of parapet, connecting with that toward General Slocum, in the form of a bastion, its salient on the main Goldsboro' road, interposing between General Slocum on the west and General Howard on the east, while the flanks rested on Mill Creek, covering the road back to Smithfield. General Howard was instructed to proceed with due caution until he had made strong connection on his left with General Slocum. This he soon accomplished, and by 4 P. M. of the 20th a complete and strong line of battle confronted the enemy in his intrenched position, and General Johnston, instead of catching us in detail, was on the defensive, with Mill Creek and a single bridge to his rear. Nevertheless we had no object to accomplish by a battle, unless at an advantage, and therefore my general instructions were to press steadily with skirmishers alone, to use artillery pretty freely on the wooded space held by the enemy, and to feel pretty strongly the flanks of his position, which were as usual covered by the endless swamps of this region of country. I also ordered all empty wagons to be sent at once to Kinston for supplies, and other impediments to be grouped near the Neuse, south of Goldsboro', holding the real army in close contact with the enemy, ready to fight him if he ventured outside his parapets and swampy obstructions. Thus matters stood about Bentonville on the 21st of March. On the same day General Schofield entered Goldsboro', with little or no opposition, and General Terry had got possession of the Neuse River at Cox's Bridge, ten miles above, with a pontoon bridge laid and a brigade across, so that the three armies were in actual connection, and the great object of the campaign was accomplished.

"On the 21st a steady rain prevailed, during which General Mower's division of the Seventeenth Corps, on the extreme right, had worked well to the right around the enemy's flank, and had nearly reached the bridge across Mill Creek, the only line of retreat open to the enemy. Of course there was extreme danger that the enemy would turn on him all his reserves, and it might be let go his parapet to overwhelm Mower. Accordingly I ordered at once a general attack by our skirmish line from left to right. Quite a noisy battle ensued, during which General Mower was enabled to regain his connection with his own corps by moving to his left rear. Still he had developed a weakness in the enemy's position of which advantage might have been taken; but that night the enemy retreated on Smithfield, leaving his pickets to fall into our hands, with many dead unburied, and wounded in his field hospitals. At daybreak of the 22d pursuit was made two miles beyond Mill Creek, but checked by my order. General Johnston had utterly failed in his attempt, and we remained in full possession of the field of battle.

"General Slocum reports the losses of the left wing about Bentonville at 9 officers and 145 men killed, 51 officers and 816 men wounded, and 3 officers and 223 men missing, taken prisoners by the enemy; total, 1,247. He buried on the field 67 rebel dead, and took 338 prisoners. General Howard reports the losses of the right wing at 2 officers and 35 men killed, 12 officers and 239 men wounded, and 1 officer and 60 men missing; total, 399. He also buried 100 rebel dead, and took 1,187 prisoners. The cavalry of Kilpatrick was held in reserve, and lost but few, if any of which I have no report as yet. Our aggregate loss at Bentonville was 1,646. I am well satisfied that the enemy lost heavily, especially during his assault on his left wing during the afternoon of the 19th; but as I have no data save his dead and wounded left in our hands, I prefer to make no comparisons. Thus, as I have endeavored to explain, we had completed our march on the 21st, and had full possession of Goldsboro', the real 'objective,' with its two railroads back to the seaports of Wilmington and Beaufort, North Carolina. These were being rapidly repaired by strong working parties, directed by Colonel W. Wright, of the railroad department. A large number of supplies had already been brought forward to Kinston, to which place our wagons had been sent to receive them. I therefore directed General Howard and the cavalry to remain at Bentonsville during the 22d, to bury the dead and remove the wounded, and on the following day all the armies to move to the camps assigned them about Goldsboro', there to rest and receive the clothing and supplies of which they stood in need. In person, I went on the 22d to Cox's Bridge to meet General Terry, whom I met for the first time, and on the following day rode into Goldsboro', where I found General Schofield and his army. The left wing came in during the same day and next morning, and the right wing followed on the 24th, on which day the cavalry moved to Mount Olive Station, and General Terry back to Falson's. On the 25th the Newbern Railroad was finished, and the first train of cars came in, thus giving us the means of bringing from the depot at Morehead City full supplies to the army.

"It was all-important that I should have an interview with the General-in-Chief, and presuming that he could not at this time leave City Point, I left General Schofield in chief command, and proceeded with all expedition by rail to Morehead City, and thence by steamer to City Point, reaching General Grant's headquarters on the evening of the 27th of March. I had the good fortune to meet General Grant, the President, Generals Meade, Ord, and others of the Army of the Potomac, and soon learned the general state of the military world, from which I had been in a great measure cut off since January. Having completed all necessary business, I re-embarked on the navy steamer Bat, Captain Barnes, which Admiral Porter placed at my command, and returned via Hatteras Inlet and Newbern, reaching my own headquarters in Goldsboro' during the night of the 30th. During my absence full supplies of clothing and food had been brought to camp, and all things were working well. I have thus rapidly sketched the progress of our columns from Savannah to Goldsboro', but for more minute details must refer to the reports of subordinate commanders and of staff officers, which are not yet ready, but will in due season be forwarded and filed with this report. I cannot, even with any degree of precision, recapitulate the vast amount of injury done to the enemy, or the quantity of guns and materials of war captured and destroyed. In general terms, we have traversed the country from Savannah to Goldsboro', with an average breadth of forty miles, consuming all the forage cattle, hogs, sheep, poultry, cured meats, corn meal, etc. The public enemy, instead of drawing supplies from that region to feed his armies, will be compelled to send provisions from other quarters to feed the inhabitants. Of course, the abandonment to us by the enemy of the whole sea-coast from Savannah to Newbern, North Carolina, with its forts, dock-yards, gunboats, etc., was a necessary incident to our occupation and destruction of the inland routes of travel and supply. But the real object of this march was to place this army in a position easy of supply, whence it could take an appropriate part in the spring and summer campaign of 1865. This was completely accomplished on March 21, by the junction of the three armies and the occupation of Goldsboro'.

"In conclusion, I beg to express in the most emphatic manner my entire satisfaction with the tone and temper of the whole army. Nothing seems to dampen their energy, zeal, or cheerfulness. It is impossible to conceive a march involving more labor and exposure, yet I cannot recall an instance of bad temper by the way, or hearing an expression of doubt as to our perfect success in the end. I believe that this cheerfulness and harmony of action reflects upon all concerned quite as much real honor and fame as 'battles gained' or 'cities won,' and I therefore commend all, general, staff, officers, and men, for these high qualities, in addition to the more soldierly ones of obedience to orders and the alacrity they have always manifested when danger summoned them 'to the front.'" *

* General Sherman to General Halleck, Goldsboro', April 4, 1865.

CHAPTER CXI.

NATIONAL EVENTS—PEACE NEGOTIATIONS, ETC.—THE INAUGURATION OF PRESIDENT LINCOLN, JANUARY TO MARCH, 1865.

THE month of January witnessed a renewal of the attempts at Peace Negotiations leading to a more direct communication on the subject between the Government at Washington and the rebel authorities at Richmond. The way was paved for the subsequent proceedings by an informal visit of Francis P. Blair, Senior, to Richmond. He received an order from President Lincoln on the 26th of December "to pass our lines, go South and return," but received no authority to speak or act for the Government, nor was the President "informed of anything he would say or do on his own account or otherwise." On his arrival at Richmond Mr. Blair had an interview with Jefferson Davis, and received from him the following letter dated January 12th: "Sir,—I have deemed it proper, and probably desirable to you, to give you in this form the substance of the remarks made by me, to be repeated by you to President Lincoln, etc., etc. I have no disposition to find obstacles in forms, and am willing now, as heretofore, to enter into negotiations for the restoration of peace. I am ready to send a commission whenever I have reason to suppose it will be received, or to receive a commission if the United States Government shall choose to send one. Notwithstanding the rejection of our former offers, I would, if you could promise that a commissioner, minister or other agent would be received, appoint one immediately, and renew the effort to enter into a conference with a view to secure peace to the two countries."

On our return to Washington Mr. Blair communicated this letter to President Lincoln, who, in turn on the 18th addressed this letter to Mr. Blair, "Sir,—You having shown me Mr. Davis' letter to you of the 12th inst., you may say to him that I have constantly been, am now, and shall continue ready to receive any agent whom he or any other influential person now resisting the National authority may informally send me with a view of securing peace to the people of our common country."

Mr. Blair revisited Richmond and communicated this letter to Jefferson Davis, and the result was the appointments by him of three Commissioners, Messrs. Alexander H. Stephens, (the Vice-President of the Confederate States) J. A. Campbell and R. M. T. Hunter to proceed to Washington. These gentlemen presented themselves on the 29th at the lines of the Army of the James with a request to pass through. Major-General Ord telegraphed to Washington for instructions and was informed that a messenger would be sent to them without delay. Major Thomas T. Eckert was thereupon sent by the President to confer with the Commissioners and procure their reception by General Ord and passage to Fortress Monroe on the terms of his letter to Mr. Blair of the 18th. Meantime the Commissioners sent a communication on the 30th from Petersburg to General Grant in which they expressed their desire to "pass his lines under safe conduct, and to proceed to Washington, to hold a conference with President Lincoln upon the subject of the existing war, and with a view of ascertaining upon what terms it may be terminated, in pursuance of the course indicated by him in his letter to Mr. Blair of January 18, 1865, of which we presume you have a copy, and if not, we wish to see you in person, if convenient, and to confer with you on the subject."

General Grant immediately received the Commissioners at his headquarters at City Point, and awaited further intelligence from Washington. He was directed to "detain the gentlemen in comfortable quarters" till the arrival of Major Eckert, who would arrange with them the passage to Fortress Monroe. In expectation of their arrival at the latter place, Mr. Seward, Secretary of State, was sent thither by President Lincoln to meet and informally confer with them on the basis of his letter to Mr. Blair. "You will make known to them," writes the President to Mr. Seward in his letter of instructions, "that three things are indispensable, to wit: "First, the restoration of the national authority throughout all the States. Second, no receding by the Executive of the United States, on the slavery question, from the position assumed thereon in the late annual message to Congress, and in the preceding documents. Third, no cessation of hostilities short of an end of the war, and the disbanding of all the forces hostile to the Government. You will inform them that all propositions of theirs not inconsistent with the above will be considered and passed upon in a spirit of sincere liberality. You will hear all they may choose to say, and report it to me. You will not assume to definitely consummate anything."

General Grant was directed at the same time to "let nothing which is transpiring change, hinder or delay his military movements or plans."

Major Eckert reached City Point and had an unsatisfactory communication with the Commissioners on the 1st of February, which seemed likely to close further communication when President Lincoln received the following telegram sent by General Grant to the Secretary of War: "Now that the interview between Major Eckert, under his written instructions, and Mr. Stephens and party, has ended, I will state confidentially, but not officially, to become a matter of record, that I am convinced upon conversation with Messrs. Stevens and Hunter, that their intentions are good, and their desire sincere to restore peace and Union. I have not felt myself at liberty to express even views of my own, or to account for my reticence. This has placed me in an awkward position, which I could have avoided by not seeing them in the first instance. I fear now their going back without any expression to any one in authority will have a bad influence. At the same time I recognize the difficulties in the way of receiving these informal commissioners at this time, and I do not know what to recommend. I am sorry, however, that Mr. Lincoln cannot have an interview with the two named in this dispatch, if not all three now within our lines. Their letter to me was all that the President's instructions contemplated to secure their safe conduct, if they had used the same language to Major Eckert."

This dispatch induced President Lincoln to proceed himself to join Secretary Seward and take part in the proposed interview at Fortress Monroe. He arrived at Hampton Roads on the night of the 2d of February, found the Secretary of State and Major Eckert on a steamer anchored off the shore, and learned of them that the Richmond gentlemen were on another steamer, also anchored off shore in the Roads, and that the Secretary of State had not yet seen or communicated with them.

On the morning of the 3d, continues President Lincoln in his message to Congress on the subject, "the three gentlemen, Messrs. Stephens, Hunter and Campbell, came aboard of our steamer, and had an interview with the Secretary of State and myself of several hours' duration. No question or preliminaries to the meeting was then and there made or mentioned. No other person was present. No papers were exchanged or produced, and it was in advance agreed that the conversation was to be informal and verbal merely. On our part the whole substance of the instructions to the Secretary of State, hereinbefore recited, was stated and insisted upon, and nothing was said inconsistent therewith. While, by the other party it was not said that, in any event or on any condition, they ever would consent to reunion; and yet they equally omitted to declare that they would so consent. They seemed to desire a postponement of that question, and the adoption of some other course first, which, as some of them seemed to argue, might or might not lead to reunion, but which course we thought would amount to an indefinite postponement. The conference ended without results."

To this authoritative statement we may add the equally authentic narrative of the interview by Secretary Seward communicated in a despatch to Mr. Adams at London. After stating the preliminaries already detailed, he adds, "The Richmond party was brought down the James River in a United States steam transport during the day, and the transport was anchored in Hampton Roads. On the morning of the 3d, the President, attended by the Secretary, received Messrs. Stephens, Hunter and Campbell on board the United States steam transport River Queen, in Hampton Roads. The conference was altogether informal. There was no attendance of secretaries, clerks or other witnesses. Nothing was written or read. The conversation, although earnest and free, was calm and courteous and kind on both sides. The Richmond party approached the discussion rather indirectly, and at no time did they make categorical demands or render formal stipulations or absolute refusals. Nevertheless, during the conference, which lasted four hours, the several points at issue between the Government and the insurgents were distinctly raised and discussed fully, intelligently, and in an amicable spirit. What the insurgent party seemed chiefly to favor was a postponement of the question of separation upon which the war is waged, and a mutual direction of the efforts of the Government, as well as those of the insurgents, to some extrinsic policy or scheme for a season, during which passions might be expected to subside, and the armies be reduced, and trade and intercourse between the people of both sections be resumed. It was suggested by them that through such postponement we might now have immediate peace, with some now very certain prospects of an ultimate satisfactory adjustment of political relations between the Government and the States, section or people now engaged in conflict with it. The suggestion, though deliberately considered, was, nevertheless, regarded by the President as one of armistice or truce, and he announced that we can agree to no cessation or suspension of hostilities except on the basis of the disbandment of the insurgent forces, and the restoration of the national authority throughout all the States in the Union. Collaterally, and in subordination to the proposition which was thus announced, the anti-slavery policy of the United States was reviewed in all its bearings, and the President announced that he must not be expected to depart from the positions he had heretofore assumed in his Proclamation of Emancipation, and other documents, as these positions were reïterated in his annual message. It was further declared by the President that the complete restoration of the National authority everywhere was an indispensable condition of any assent on our part to whatever form of peace might be proposed. The President assured the other party that while he must adhere to these positions, he would be prepared, so far as power is lodged with the Executive, to exercise liberality. Its power, however, is limited by the Constitution, and, when peace should be made, Congress must necessarily act in regard to appropriations of money and to the admission of Representatives from the insurrectionary States. The Richmond party were then informed that Congress had on the 31st ult. adopted by a constitutional majority a joint resolution submitting to the several States the proposition to abolish slavery throughout the Union, and that there is every reason to expect that it will be accepted by three-fourths of the States, so as to become a part of the national organic law. The conference came to an end by mutual acquiescence, without producing an agreement of views upon the several matters discussed, or any of them. Nevertheless, it is perhaps of some importance that we have been able to submit our opinions and views directly to prominent insurgents, and to hear them in answer, in a courteous and not unfriendly manner."

The return of the Commissioners to Richmond was made the occasion of another attempt "to fire the Southern heart." On the 6th of February Jefferson Davis sent a message to the Confederate Congress accompanying the report of the Commissioners. "Having recently," said he, "received a written notification which satisfied me that the President of the United States was disposed to confer informally with unofficial agents that might be sent by me, with a view to the restoration of peace, I requested Hon. Alexander H. Stephens, Hon. R. M. T. Hunter, and Hon. John A. Campbell to proceed through our lines to hold a conference with Mr. Lincoln, or such persons as he might depute to represent him. I herewith submit for the information of Congress the report of the eminent citizens abovenamed, showing that the enemy refuse to enter into negotiations with the Confederate States or any one of them separately, or to give our people any other terms or guarantees than those which a conqueror may grant, or permit us to have peace on any other basis than our unconditional submission to their rule, coupled with the acceptance of their recent legislation, including an amendment to the Constitution for the emancipation of negro slaves, and with the right on the part of the Federal Congress to legislate on the subject of the relations between the white and black population of each State. Such is, as I understand, the effect of the amendment to the Constitution which has been adopted by the Congress of the United States."

The report of Messrs. Stephens, Hunter and Campbell, addressed to the President of the Confederate States, was as follows: "Sir,—Under your letter of appointment of 28th ultimo, we proceeded to seek an informal conference with Abraham Lincoln, President of the United States, upon the subject mentioned in your letter. The conference was granted, and took place on the 3d instant on board a steamer anchored in Hampton Roads, where we met President Lincoln and Hon. Mr. Seward, Secretary of State of the United States. It continued for several hours, and was both full and explicit. We learned from them that the message of President Lincoln to the Congress of the United States in December last, explains clearly and distinctly his sentiments as to terms, conditions, and method of proceeding by which peace can be secured to the people. And we were not informed that they would be modified or altered to obtain that end. We understood from him that no terms or proposals of any treaty or agreement, looking to an ultimate settlement, would be entertained or made by him with the authorities of the confederate States, because that would be a recognition of their existence as a separate Power, which, under no circumstances would be done; and, for like reason, that no such terms would be entertained by him from States separately; that no extended truce or armistice, as at present advised, would be granted or allowed, without satisfactory assurances, in advance, of a complete restoration of the authority of the Constitution and laws of the United States over all places within the States of the Confederacy; that whatever consequences may follow from the re-establishment of that authority, must be accepted; but that the individuals subject to pains and penalties under the laws of the United States, might rely upon a very liberal use of the power confided to him to remit those pains and penalties if peace be restored. During the conference, the proposed amendments to the Constitution of the United States, adopted by Congress on the 31st ultimo, was brought to our notice. These amendments provide that neither slavery nor involuntary servitude, except for crime, should exist within the United States or any place within their jurisdiction, and that Congress should have the power to enforce this amendment by appropriate legislation."

On the evening of the 6th, in response to the call of Governor Smith, of Virginia, a meeting was held at the African Church at Richmond, the object of which, in the words of the *Richmond Dispatch*, "was to hurl back into Lincoln's teeth the insult put upon the Southern people by his answers to the confederate commissioners. After an address by the Governor, President Davis spoke: To be true to himself, said he, he had never entertained much hope of effecting honorable terms so long as our cause was meeting with reverses, but under the circumstances, when semi-official representatives had so frequently visited our government, intimating that negotiations might result in a satisfactory adjustment of our difficulties, and when it was plain that the sufferings of the people dictated that every effort on his part should be made to bring about a cessation of hostilities, he felt it his duty, as he had always done, to appoint those whom he regarded as among the best men we had, who were most calculated to heal the existing breach which severed us, and to obtain that independence for the confederacy from the Federal Government, which no other power on the face of the earth but the Yankees would think of denying. As to the conditions of peace, President Davis emphatically asserted that nothing save the independence of the confederacy could ever receive his sanction. He had embarked in the cause with the full knowledge of the tremendous odds against us. But with the approval of a just Providence, which he conscientiously believed was on our side, and the united resolve of our people, he doubted not that victory would yet crown our labors. In his correspondence with Lincoln, that functionary had always spoken of the United States and the confederacy as our afflicted country; but in his replies, he (the speaker) had never failed to refer to them as separate and distinct governments. And sooner than we should ever be united again, he would be willing to yield up everything he has on earth, and if it were possible, would sacrifice a thousand lives before he would succumb." These declarations of Jefferson Davis were followed by the passage of a series of violent resolutions denouncing the terms of President Lincoln as a "gross insult," and pledging the Commonwealth of Virginia to a hearty continuance of the war.

At a second meeting held a few days after, at the same place, speeches were delivered by Mr. Hunter, one of the Commissioners, Mr. Benjamin, a member of the rebel Cabinet, and others, of a like inflammatory character. Mr. Hunter "noticed the legislation of the United States Government in relation to the people of the confederate States. The confiscation laws, the decree of emancipation, the constitutional amendment, etc., were passed in review. If anything more were wanted, said Mr. Hunter, to show the full animosity which has been exhibited toward us, it is found in their refusal to enter into negotiations with us, whether with our confederate or State government. They negotiate with the meanest Indian tribe but with a population numbering between 7,000,000 and 10,000,000 of people, they have no terms, will enter into no agreement. Suppose we were rebels, as they say we are; no great civil war was ever settled without negotiation. The British Government held the Colonists to be rebels, yet in 1778 they sent commissioners hither authorized to confer and treat with any government or with individuals, and to arrange for truce, armistice, or peace. Strong governments have always esteemed it a part of duty and of wisdom, after vindicating their power, to extend liberal terms to those who had been in armed opposition, in order to reconcile them to their sway and make them contented subjects. The President of the United States had proposed nothing of this sort. He did nothing and offered nothing to soothe the reluctance or mitigate the severities of submission. It is impossible that he could have supposed peace attainable on his terms with such an armed force as the confederates have in the field. He required that we should confess ourselves rebels, and as such responsible for the blood that has been shed; to submit without conditions; to submit to laws by which our property is declared confiscated, and our lives forfeited. He promises, indeed, that he would show leniency in the exercise of the pardoning power; but could a people accustomed to be free consent to hold their lives, their property, their security, at the will of one man, and not under the guarantee of the laws? [Voices, 'Never! never!'] In the Government to which they were thus required to submit unconditionally, it was not promised that they should even have a voice. It was distinctly left uncertain whether they should be allowed any representation. President Lincoln had told our commissioners—had told him (Mr. Hunter)—that should we elect representatives and send them to the Washington Congress, he (President Lincoln) would be in favor of receiving them, but he was only one man, and whether or not they would be received was uncertain. Such was the inducement held out to us, such the proposed basis of pacification." *

"I believe," said Mr. Benjamin on this occasion, "that when Blair came to Richmond there was an opportunity for suspending fighting and bloodshed, in which time measures might be taken for restoration of peace, but none of us for a moment dreamed of reconstruction. Is it wonderful that our President, whose only defect is that he is too tender-hearted, should have yielded to the temptation of trying to stop the bloodshed of his countrymen, of which every drop seemed to come from his own heart? The Vice-President was confident of the feasibility of his own theory, which we were not, and what better could we do than to send him to attempt to make a favorable impression upon the enemy? We knew its failure would be the signal for a grand uprising of the people, which was the only element necessary to success. We hear it now in the improved tone of public sentiment. What is our present duty? We want means. Are they in the country? If so, they belong to the country, and not to the man who chances to hold them now. They belong either to the Yankees or to the confederate States. I would take every bale of cotton in the land. I have a few bales left in my distant Southern home, which is a free gift to my country. But why speak of myself? I speak of my noble State of Louisiana. Let me point you back to 1862, when the city of New Orleans fell under the domination of the enemy. As Farragut's fleet ascended the river and rounded the crescent approaching the city, what greeted his eye? On that bright, balmy spring day the air was murky with smoke. Everything was lined with cotton burning upon the levee. The citizens did not ask to whom it belonged. The Yankees wanted it; and they should not have it. But a few weeks ago Sherman penetrated Savannah, and what was presented there? With full time for the citizens to prepare in advance, with a thousand plausible excuses of interested selfishness, the cotton was left in the belief that the Yankees would give them something for it. This all now goes to the Yankees, who gloatingly said not that, 'We have got Savannah,' but that 'We have got $18,000,000 worth of cotton.' And this, while on the banks of the Mississippi and the waters bordering on my State, 300,000 bales of cotton were sacrificed to the cause. I now ask has any man a right to hold a bale of cotton from his country? No! I will say something in regard to tobacco. Take all the cotton and tobacco, and make it the basis of means without which we cannot go on. I want more. I want all the bacon, every thing which can feed soldiers, and I want it as a free gift to the country. Talk of rights! What rights do the arrogant invaders leave you? I want another thing. War is a game that cannot be played without men. Where are the men? I am going to open my whole heart to you. Look to the trenches below Richmond. Is it not a shame that men who have sacrificed all in our defence should not be reinforced by all the means in our power? Is it any time now for antiquated patriotism to argue refusal to send them aid, be it white or black? I will now call your attention to some figures, which I wish you to seriously ponder. In 1860 the South had 1,664,000 arms-bearing men. How many men have the Yankees sent against us. In

* *Richmond Sentinel*, February 10, 1865.

1851, 654,000; in 1862, 740,000; in 1863, 700,000; in 1864 they called out 1,500,000. Here you have figures that they brought out 3,000,000 men against 1,664,000 confederates, who lived at the beginning of the war to draw a sword in their country's service. Our resources of white population have greatly diminished, but you had 680,000 black men of the same ages, and could Divine prophecy have told us of the fierceness of the enemy's death-grapple at our throats, could we have known what we now know, what Lincoln has confessed, that without 200,000 negroes which he stole from us, he would be compelled to give up the contest, should we have entertained any doubts upon the subject? I feel that the time is rapidly coming on when the people will wonder that they ever doubted. Let us say to every negro who wishes to go into the ranks on condition of being made free, 'Go and fight—you are free.' If we impress them, they will go against us. We know that every one who who could fight for his freedom has no chance. The only side that has had advantage of this element is the Yankee people, that can beat us to the end of the year in making bargains. Let us imitate them in this. I would imitate them in nothing else." *

This attempt, which sufficiently displayed the weakness of the sinking confederacy, was the last public effort in Richmond to rouse the State to a renewed prosecution of the unhallowed cause in which it had already wasted its strength and treasure.

These were brave words spoken by Davis, Benjamin, and the rest; but they were evidently uttered to cover the nakedness of a position every day growing more desperate. Richmond was in danger, and with Richmond would fall the confederacy. The real situation of affairs was candidly stated in an able article in the *Richmond Examiner* of February 27th, which proved prophetic. "In the extraordinary message," says the writer, "which Mr. Davis recently addressed to Congress,* he declared that 'if the campaign against Richmond had resulted in success instead of failure—if we had been compelled to evacuate Richmond as well as Atlanta—the confederacy would have remained as erect and defiant as ever. Nothing could have been changed in the purpose of its government, in the indomitable valor of its troops, or in the unquenchable spirit of its people. The baffled and disappointed foe would in vain have scanned the reports of your proceedings at some new legislative seat for an indication that progress had been made in his gigantic task of conquering a free people. There are no vital points, on the preservation of which the continued existence of the confederacy depends. There is no military success of the enemy which can accomplish its destruction. Not the fall of Richmond, nor Wilmington, nor Charleston, nor Savannah, nor Mobile, nor of all combined, can affect the issue of the present contest.' In the African Church, a fortnight ago, he reiterated these extravagant propositions. Mr. Benjamin afterward took up the theme on the same rostrum, and spoke of evacuating this city with equal flippancy. Inconsiderate persons and newspapers, we observe with pain, repeat the same ideas; as if they positively desired the country to be taught that the abandonment of this vital position would not only be of no injury to the confederacy, but of positive advantage. Let not this fatal error be harbored till it takes root in the imagination. The evacuation of Richmond would be the loss of all respect and authority toward the confederate government, the disintegration of the army, and the abandonment of the scheme of an independent Southern Confederation. The war would after that speedily degenerate into an

* *Richmond Sentinel*, February 10, 1865.

* Ante p. 484.

irregular contest, in which passion will have more to do than purpose; which would have no other object than the mere defense or present safety of those immediately persisting in it. The hope of establishing a confederacy and securing its recognition among nations, would be gone for ever. The common sense of the country, the instinct of every man and woman in the land, contradicts the idea that any possibility of an independent South would remain after its capital was abandoned, its government set adrift, and its army withdrawn into the solitudes of the interior.

"It is idle to pretend that Richmond is of no more importance than Savannah, Atlanta, Mobile or Norfolk, and that its fall would not be fatal to the confederacy. If it had not been a vital point, why has so much effort been expended for its reduction and its defense? It has been the great objective point of the enemy through four successive campaigns. The confederacy has spared no pains or exertions, no cost of blood or treasure, to make good its defense. It is the capital of the last of the border States, commanding the entire portion of Virginia east of the Alleghanies, and the most important division of North Carolina. It is situated 140 miles from the sea, yet large ships can unload from its wharves. The occupation of Richmond in strong force by the enemy would necessarily drive the confederate armies out of Virginia, and render all Eastern North Carolina untenable; and, once gained by a power having command of the water, it could never, under any contingency, be recovered by the confederacy. Each contestant in the war has made Richmond the central object of all its plans and all its exertions. It has become the symbol of the confederacy. Its loss would be material ruin to the cause, and in a moral point of view, absolutely destructive, crushing the heart and extinguishing the last hope of the country. Our armies would lose the incentive inspired by a great and worthy object of defense. Our military policy would be totally at sea; we would be without a hope or an object; without civil or military organization; without a treasury or a commissariat; without the means of keeping alive a wholesome and active public sentiment; without any of the appliances for supporting a cause depending upon the popular faith and enthusiasm; without the emblems of the semblance of authority. The withdrawal of the army from Richmond into the interior would so narrow the area of conscription as greatly to reduce our military strength. As the army would dwindle in numbers, it would move more and more rapidly westward, and before reaching the banks of the Mississippi would have degenerated into a mere body guard for a few officers. From the hour of giving up the seat of government, our cause would sink into a mere rebellion in the estimation of foreign powers, who would cease to accord to us the rights of belligerents; while the enemy would be free to treat our officers and soldiers as traitors and criminals; so that every 'rebel' would fight thenceforth with a halter round his neck.

"Virginia, though slow to come into the Confederacy, has been throughout the contest its main stay and support. It has borne the brunt of every campaign. It has suffered the ravages of war more severely than all the other States together. Every county in the State has felt the hand of the enemy. Its richest and best districts have been utterly desolated. Its sufferings have not only been severe beyond description, but continuous and unceasing. For four years it has been the common campaign and battle-ground for the largest armies and bloodiest conflicts of modern times. No country in the world ever sustained as heavy losses, has endured as hard a fate with more heroism or fortitude. The evacuation of Richmond would be the abandonment of Richmond —for ever—and without any rational hope of a return. Is it possible that such a desertion could be contemplated after the events of this war? Even if the act were not suicidal in policy, could the confederacy now consent to cast away this worn and devastated but still powerful Commonwealth as an old shoe that could be put to no further use? Aside from the disgrace that would attach to such ingratitude, the confederacy could not afford to put General Grant into possession of Richmond, a depot and base a hundred and forty miles from the sea, and in the midst of Southern Virginia, yet with water-carriage to the door, and thus relinquish its last hold on the last of the border States. It could not be expected to continue the struggle with any hope of success, after abandoning States whence its most numerous recruits are obtained, a soil on which its arms have been uniformly victorious, and withdrawing to States where defeat has constantly attended them. The abandonment of Virginia would be equivalent to executing a quit-claim deed to all the border States, together with Tennessee and North Carolina. Two lines of railways radiate from here into the most populous and influential districts of this latter State, subjecting its best portions to the control of any considerable military power having its base at Richmond. Is the confederacy's wealth in population and territory now so great that it can afford to make a voluntary donation of all this territory, restricting its jurisdiction to the Gulf States, and South Carolina, already overrun?

"If Richmond be held but another six months, the fate of the confederacy will have been favorably decided. The people will cling to the cause as long as the seat of government is secure. Recent misfortunes will have awakened foreign powers to the dangers which would result to themselves from the restoration of the Union and pacification of this continent, now possessing a trained soldiery more numerous and formidable than any army in Richmond. So long as Richmond and Virginia are ours, the very reverses which have been sustained will nerve our people to renewed exertion, and beguile the enemy into a false confidence. The war cannot be carried on much longer against us if we prove but true to ourselves; and the single test of success will be our determination and ability to hold Richmond. Other cities may fall, the rest of the confederacy may succumb, but the cause still remains safe so long as Richmond and Virginia are held."

Still another attempt at negotiation to rescue the confederacy from its impending ruin was made by President Davis at the end of February. It grew out of an interview between General Ord and General Longstreet on the subject of the exchange of prisoners, the management of which had been placed in the hands of General Grant, and who, as we have stated, was carrying it on to a successful result. In consequence of some discussion of the general subject of the war between Ord and Longstreet, President Davis, on the 28th of February, gave the following instructions to General Lee:

"Sir—You will learn by the letter of General Longstreet the result of his second interview with General Ord. The point as to whether yourself or General Grant should invite the other to a conference is not worth discussing; only you think the statements of General Ord renders it probably useful that the conference suggested should be had, you will proceed as you may prefer, and are clothed with all the supplemental authority you may need in the consideration of any proposed, or for a military convention, or the appointment of a commissioner to enter into such an arrangement as will cause at least temporary suspension of hostilities."

General Lee, accordingly, on the 2d of March, addressed the following letter to General Grant:

"GENERAL—Lieut.-General Longstreet has informed me that in a recent conversation between himself and Major-General Ord, as to a possibility of arriving at a satisfactory adjustment of the present unhappy difficulties by means of a military convention, General Ord states that if I desired to have an interview with you on the subject, you would not decline, provided that I had authority to act. Sincerely desiring to leave nothing untried which may put an end to the calamities of war, I propose to meet you at such convenient deemed place as you may designate, with hope that upon an interchange of views it may be found practicable to submit the subjects of controversy between the belligerents to a convention of the kind mentioned. In such event, I am authorized to do whatever the result of the proposed interview may render necessary or advisable. Should you accede to this proposition, I would suggest that, if agreeable to you, we meet at the place selected by Generals Ord and Longstreet for the interview, at 11 A. M. on Monday next."

On the receipt of this, General Grant telegraphed to President Lincoln for instructions, and received a reply which afterwards became of peculiar importance. It was written by President Lincoln himself, immediately on the receipt of General Grant's communication, at the Capitol at Washington, on the night of the 3d of March, the last day of his first term of office. The message, signed by the Secretary of War, was as follows:

"The President directs me to say to you, that he wishes you to have no conference with General Lee unless it be for the capitulation of General Lee's army, or on mere minor and purely military matters. He instructs me to say that you are not to decide, discuss, or confer upon any political question. Such questions the President holds in his own hands, and will submit them to no military conferences or conventions. Meantime, you are to press to the utmost your military advantages."

General Grant, accordingly, on the next day replied to Lee: "I have no authority to accede to your proposition for a conference on the subject proposed. Such authority is vested in the President of the United States alone. General Ord could only have meant I would not refuse an interview on any subject in which I had a right to act, which, of course, would be such as are purely of a military character, and on the subject of exchange which has been intrusted to me."

Previous to this time, in February, General Lee had entered on his new position as general-in-chief of the confederate army, under the circumstances related in the last chapter. On taking command he issued the following general order, dated February 9: "In obedience to General Order No. 3, Adjutant and Inspector-General's Office, 6th of February, I assume command of the military forces of the confederate States. Deeply impressed with the difficulties and responsibility of the position, and humbly invoking the guidance of Almighty God, I rely for success upon the courage and fortitude of the army, sustained by the patriotism and firmness of the people, confident that their united efforts, under the blessing of Heaven, will secure peace and independence. The headquarters of the army, to which all special reports and communications will be addressed, will be, for the present, with the Army of Northern Virginia."

This was followed by an order to his army summoning them anew by the old appeals to the contest, and loudly calling upon deserters, of whom it might be supposed by his earnestness there were many, to return to the ranks. "In entering," said he, "upon the campaign about to open, the general-in-chief feels

R E Lee

From the original painting by Nast in the possession of the publishers.

Johnson, Fry & Co. Publishers New York.

assured that the soldiers who have so long and so nobly borne the hardships and dangers of war, require no exhortation to respond to the calls of honor and duty. With the liberty transmitted by their forefathers, they have inherited the spirit to defend it. The choice between war and abject submission is before them. To such a proposal brave men with arms in their hands can have but one answer. They cannot barter manhood for peace, nor right of self-government for life or property. But justice to them requires sterner admonition to those who have abandoned their comrades in the hour of peril. The last opportunity is offered them to wipe out the disgrace and escape the punishment of their crimes. By authority of the president of the confederate States, pardon is announced to such deserters and men improperly absent as shall return to commands to which they belong within the shortest possible time, not exceeding twenty days from the publication of this order, at the headquarters of the department in which they may be. Those who may be prevented by the interruption of communications, may report within the time specified to the nearest enrolling officer, or other officer on duty, to be forwarded as soon as practicable, and upon presenting the certificate from such an officer, showing compliance with the requirement, will receive the pardon hereby offered those who have deserted to the service of the enemy, or who have deserted after having been once pardoned for the same offence; and those who shall desert or absent themselves without authority, after the publication of this order, are excluded from its benefits. Nor does the offer of pardon extend to other offences than desertion and absence without permission. By the same authority it is also declared that no general amnesty will be again granted, and those who refuse to accept pardon now offered, those who shall hereafter desert or absent themselves without leave, shall suffer such punishment as the court may impose, and no application for clemency will be entertained.

"Taking new resolution from the fate which our enemies intend for us, let every man devote all his energies to the common defence. Our resources, wisely and vigorously employed, are ample, and with a brave army sustained by a determined and united people, success, with God's assistance, cannot be doubtful. The advantages of the enemy will have but little value, if we do not permit them to impair our resolution. Let us then oppose constancy to adversity, fortitude to suffering, courage to danger, with the firm assurance that He who gave freedom to our fathers will bless the efforts of their children to preserve it."

Another call of Lee was quite as significant of the growing weakness of the rebel ranks. He demanded of citizens any carbines, revolvers, pistols, saddles and other equipments of the kind which they might have in their possession, for the purpose of equipping an additional force of cavalry, an arm of the service of which the rebels had once greatly boasted, but in which their inferiority was now grossly apparent.

The question of arming the negroes for service in the war, after much discussion by the rebel press, the confederate authorities at Richmond, the governors of the rebel States, and the rebel congress, was finally determined in March by the passage of the following "Act to increase the military forces of the confederate States: The congress of the confederate States of America do enact, that in order to provide additional forces to repel invasion, maintain the rightful possession of the confederate States, secure their independence and preserve their institutions, the president be and he is hereby authorized to ask for and accept from the owners of slaves the services of such number of able-bodied men as he may deem expedient, for and during the war, to perform military service in whatever capacity he may direct. Section 2. That the general-in-chief be authorized to organize the said slaves into companies, battalions, regiments, and brigades, under such rules and regulations as the secretary of war may prescribe, and to be commanded by such officers as the president may appoint. Section 3. That while employed in the service the said troops shall receive the same rations, clothing, and compensation as are allowed to other troops in the same branch of the service. Section 4. That if, under the previous sections of this act, the president shall not be able to raise a sufficient number of troops to prosecute the war successfully, and maintain the sovereignty of the States and the independence of the confederate States, then he is hereby authorized to call on each State, whenever he thinks it expedient, for her quota of three hundred thousand troops, in addition to those subject to military service under existing laws, or so many thereof as the president may deem necessary, to be raised from such classes of the population, irrespective of color, in each State, as the proper authorities thereof may determine: Provided, that not more than twenty-five per cent. of the male slaves between the ages of eighteen and forty-five in any State shall be called for under the provisions of this act. Section 5. That nothing in this act shall be construed to authorize a change in the relation of the said slaves."

The rebel General Lee had previously given this measure his support in a letter dated Headquarters C. S. armies, February 18, 1865, addressed to the Hon. E. Barksdale, House of Representatives, Richmond. "I have," says he, "the honor to acknowledge the receipt of your letter of the 12th instant, with reference to the employment of negroes as soldiers. I think the measure not only expedient but necessary. The enemy will certainly use them against us if he can get possession of them, and as his present numerical superiority will enable him to penetrate many parts of the country, I cannot see the wisdom of the policy of holding them to await his arrival, when we may by timely action and judicious management use them to arrest his progress. I do not think that our white population can supply the necessities of a long war without overtaxing its capacity and imposing great suffering upon our people; and I believe we should provide resources for a protracted struggle, not merely for a battle or a campaign. In answer to your second question, I can only say that, in my opinion, the negroes, under proper circumstances, will make efficient soldiers. I think we could, at least, do as well with them as the enemy, and he attaches great importance to their assistance. Under good officers and good instruction, I do not see why they should not become soldiers. They possess all the physical qualifications, and their habits of obedience constitutes a good foundation for discipline. They furnish a more promising material than many armies of which we read in history, which owed their efficiency to discipline alone. I think those who are employed should be freed. It would be neither just nor wise, in my opinion, to require them to serve as slaves. The best course to pursue, it seems to me, would be to call for such as are willing to come with the consent of their owners. An impressment or draft would not be likely to bring out the best class, and the use of coercion would make the measure distasteful to them and to their owners. I have no doubt that if congress would authorize their reception into service, and empower the president to call upon individuals or States for such as they are willing to contribute, with the condition of emancipation to all enrolled, a sufficient number would be forthcoming to enable us to try the experiment. If it prove successful, most of the objections to the measure would disappear, and if individuals still remained unwilling to send their negroes to the army, the force of public opinion in the States would soon bring about such legislation as would remove all obstacles. I think the matter should be left, as far as possible, to the people and to the States, which alone can legislate as the necessities of this particular service may require. As to the mode of organizing them, it should be left as free from restraint as possible. Experience will suggest the best course, and it would be inexpedient to trammel the subject with provisions that might, in the end, prevent the adoption of reforms suggested by actual trial."

Attempts were at once made in Richmond to bring a body of negroes into the service. They do not appear, however, to have been attended with much success. Besides its inherent difficulties, the undertaking met with a doubtful support from leading politicians. The act, after having been rejected, was barely passed, and, under the failing fortunes of the confederacy, came too late, at least tor ender any appreciable aid to the army in Virginia. Its moral effect was to confirm the faith of the North, and pretty clearly suggest to the South that slavery itself must now rapidly perish. When General Lee wrote "those who are employed should be freed," he admitted the whole question of the superiority of freedom. Governor Brown, of Georgia, in a message to his legislature about this time, expressed the inevitable result. "Whenever," said he, "we establish the fact that the negroes are a military people, we destroy our theory that they are unfit to be free. When we arm the slaves we abandon slavery." The consequences of the policy were still more strongly stated by R. M. T. Hunter, of Virginia, in the debate on the passage of the act in the rebel senate. "When we left the old Government," he said, "he had thought we had gotten rid for ever of the slavery agitation; that we were entering into a new confederacy of homogeneous States; but, to his surprise, he finds that this government assumes the power to arm the slaves, which involves also the power of emancipation. To the agitation of this question, the assumption of this power, he dated the origin of the gloom which now overspreads our people. They knew that if our liberties were to be achieved, it was to be done by the hearts and the hands of free men. It also injured us abroad. It was regarded as a confession of despair and an abandonment of the ground upon which we had seceded from the old Union. We had insisted that Congress had no right to interfere with slavery, and upon the coming into power of the party who it was known would assume and exercise that power, we seceded. We had also then contended that whenever the two races were thrown together, one must be master and the other slave, and we vindicated ourselves against the accusations of the abolitionists by asserting that slavery was the best and happiest condition of the negro. Now what does this proposition admit? The right of the central government to put the slaves into the militia, and to emancipate at least so many as shall be placed in the military service. It is a clear claim of the central government to emancipate the slaves. If we are right in passing this measure, we were wrong in denying to the old Government the right to interfere with the institutions of slavery and to emancipate slaves. Besides, if we offer slaves their freedom as a boon, we confess that we were insincere, were hypocritical, in asserting that slavery was the best state for the negroes themselves. He had been sincere in declaring that the central government had no power over the institution of slavery, and that freedom would be no boon to the negro. He now believed, as he had formerly said in discussion on the same subject, that arming and emancipating the slaves was an abandonment of this contest—an abandonment of the grounds upon which it had been undertaken. If this is so, who is to answer for the hundreds of thousands of men who had been slain in the war? Who was to answer for them before the bar of heaven? Not those who had entered into the contest upon principle and adhered to the principle, but those who had abandoned the principle. Not for all the gold in California would he have put his name to such a measure as this unless obliged to do it by instructions. As long as he was free to vote from his own convictions nothing could have extorted it from him. Mr. Hunter then argued the necessity of freeing the negroes if they were made soldiers. There was something in the human heart and head that tells us it must be so; when they come out scarred from this conflict they must be free. If we could make them soldiers, the condition of the soldier being socially equal to any other in society, we could make them officers, perhaps, to command white men. Some future ambitious president might use the slaves to seize the liberties of his country and put the white men under his feet. The government had no power under the constitution to arm and emancipate the slaves, and the constitution granted no such great powers by implication. Mr. Hunter then showed from statistics that no considerable body of negro troops could be raised in the States over which the government had control, without stripping the country of the labor absolutely necessary to produce food. He thought there was a much better chance of getting the large number of deserters back to the army than of getting the slaves into it. The negro abhorred the profession of a soldier. The commandant of conscripts, with authority to impress 20,000 slaves, had, between last September and the present time, been able to get but 4,000, and of these 3,500 had been obtained in Virginia and North Carolina, and 500 from Alabama. If he, armed with all the powers of impressment, could not get them as laborers, how will we be able then to get them as soldiers? Unless they volunteer they will go to the Yankees; if we depend upon their volunteering we can't get them, and those we do get will desert to the enemy, who can offer them a better price than we can. The enemy can offer them liberty, clothing, and even farms at our expense. Negroes now were deferred from going to the enemy only by the fear of being put into the army. If we put them in they would all go over."

There were two military executions at New York in February and March of importance in the history of the war. It will be remembered that in the previous September two unarmed passenger steamers on Lake Erie were seized by a piratical crew from Canada, one of the vessels destroyed, and the freight and property taken possession of or thrown overboard. The leader of this enterprise was John Y. Beall, a native of Jefferson County, Virginia, about thirty years of age. He had been educated at the University of Virginia, and had been a member of the Virginia House of Delegates. He owned, and cultivated by slave labor a large plantation in Jefferson County, it was said, and had been in prosperous circumstances. In 1861 he entered the rebel service as captain in one of the regiments of the original "Stonewall brigade." He was afterwards transferred to the navy and received a master's commission, under which he claimed to be acting in the raid from Canada. After this piratical act, Beall appears to have lurked in Canada till December, when he was arrested on the Canadian border by John S. Young, Chief of the New York Metropolitan Detective Police. He was brought to the latter city, lodged in Fort Lafayette, and was there tried by a military commission in February, on charges of "violation of the law of war" and "acting as a spy," on various specifications, of both of which charges he was convicted. In pronouncing his sentence, Major-General Dix, the commanding officer of the district, gave this review of the proceedings:

"The testimony shows that the accused, while holding a commission from the authorities at Richmond as acting master in the navy of the insurgent States, embarked at Sandwich, Canada, on board the Philo Parsons, an unarmed steamer, while on one of her regular trips, carrying passengers and freight from Detroit, in the State of Michigan, to Sandusky, in the State of Ohio. The captain had been induced by Burley, one of the confederates of the accused, to land at Sandwich, which was not one of the regular stopping-places of the steamer, for the purpose of receiving them. Here the accused and two others took passage. At Malden, another Canadian port, and one of the regular stopping-places, about twenty-five more came on board. The accused was in citizen's dress, showing no insignia of his rank or profession, embarking as an ordinary passenger, and representing himself to be on a pleasure trip to Kelley's Island, in Lake Erie, within the jurisdiction of the State of Ohio. After eight hours, he and his associates, arming themselves with revolvers and hand-axes brought surreptitiously on board, rose on the crew, took possession of the steamer, threw overboard part of the freight and robbed the clerk of the money in his charge, putting all on board under duress. Later in the evening he and his party took possession of another unarmed steamer (the Island Queen), scuttled her and set her adrift on the lake. These transactions occurred within the jurisdiction of the State of Ohio, on the 19th day of September, 1864. On the 16th day of December, 1864, the accused was arrested near the Suspension Bridge, over the Niagara River, within the State of New York. The testimony shows that he and two officers of the insurgent States, Colonel Martin and Lieutenant Headley, with two other confederates, had made an unsuccessful attempt, under the direction of the first-named officer, to throw the passenger-train coming from the West to Buffalo, off the railroad track, for the purpose of robbing the express company. It is further shown that this was the third attempt in which the accused was concerned to accomplish the same object; that between two of these attempts the party, including the accused, went to Canada and returned, and that they were on their way back to Canada when he was arrested. In these transactions, as in that on Lake Erie, the accused, though holding a commission from the insurgent authorities at Richmond, was in disguise, procuring information, with the intention of using it, as he subsequently did, to inflict injury upon unarmed citizens of the United States and their private property.

"The substance of the charges against the accused is, that he was acting as a spy, and carrying on irregular or guerrilla warfare against the United States; in other words, that he was acting in the two-fold character of a spy and a guerrilla. He was found guilty on both charges, and sentenced to death; and the Major-General commanding fully concurs in the judgment of the court. In all the transactions with which he was implicated—in one as a chief, and in the other as a subordinate agent—he was not only acting the part of a spy, in procuring information to be used for hostile purposes, but he was also committing acts condemned by the common judgment and the common conscience of all civilized States, except when done in open warfare by avowed enemies. Throughout these transactions, he was not only in disguise, but personating a false character. It is not at all essential to the purpose of sustaining the finding of the court, and yet it is not inappropriate to state, as an indication of the *animus* of the accused and his confederates, that the attempts to throw the railroad train off the track were made at night, when the obstruction would be less likely than in the daytime to be noticed by the engineer or conductor, thus putting in peril the lives of hundreds of men, women and children. In these attempts three officers holding commissions in the military service of the insurgent States were concerned. The accused is shown by the testimony to be a man of education and refinement, and it is difficult to account for his agency in transactions so abhorrent to the moral sense, and so inconsistent with all the rules of honorable warfare.

"The accused, in justification of the transaction on Lake Erie, produced the manifesto of Jefferson Davis assuming the responsibility of the act, and declaring that it was done by his authority. It is hardly necessary to say that no such assumption can sanction an act not warranted by the laws of civilized warfare. If Mr. Davis were at the head of an independent government, recognized as such by other nations, he would have no power to sanction what the usage of civilized States has condemned. The Government of the United States from a desire to mitigate the asperities of war, has given to the insurgents of the South the benefit of the rules which govern sovereign States in the conduct of hostilities with each other; and any violation of those rules should, for the sake of good order here and the cause of humanity throughout the world, be visited with the severest penalty. War, under its mildest aspects, is the heaviest calamity that can befall our race; and he who in a spirit of revenge or with lawless violence transcends the limits to which it is restricted by the common behest of all Christian communities, should receive the punishment which the common voice has declared to be due to the crime. The Major-General commanding feels that a want of firmness and inflexibility, on his part, in executing the sentence of death in such a case, would be an offence against the outraged civilization and humanity of the age. It is hereby ordered, that James Y. Beall be hanged by the neck till he is dead, on Governor's Island, on Saturday, the 18th day of February inst., between the hours of 12 and 2 in the afternoon." This sentence was carried out at the appointed time and place, the prisoner meeting his fate with firmness, and at the end, when asked if he had any thing to say, replying: "I protest against this execution. It is absolute murder—brutal murder. I die in the service and defence of my country."

The second execution to which we have alluded was that of Captain Robert Cobb Kennedy, a leader of a band of conspirators, who came to New York from Canada, and engaged on the night of the 25th of November, 1864, in an attempt to burn the city as previously related. Kennedy was a native of Louisiana. His father was a planter in the State, gave his son the benefit of a good education, and procured him admission to the Military Academy at West Point, where he passed two years. He then returned home, living a planter's life, and on the outbreak of the rebellion engaged in active service in the war. He was reckless and daring, and after several captures and releases was retaken prisoner and lodged in the military prison at Johnson's Island, in Lake Erie. Escaping thence to Canada, he planned there the burning of New York city, for which he was afterwards arrested and suffered death. The particulars of his share in the plot was thus narrated by him in a final confession. "After my escape from Johnson's Island," said he, "I went direct to Canada, where I met a number of confederate officers. They asked me if I was willing to go on an expedition, I said 'Yes, if it's in the service of my country.' To which they replied, 'It's all right,' but gave no intimation as to its nature, nor did I ask for any. I was shortly after sent to New York, where I staid some time. There were eight of us in the party, and after we had been in the city three weeks, we were told that the object of the expedition was to retaliate upon the North for the atrocities of Sheridan in the Shenandoah Valley. It was originally intended to set fire to the city on the night of the Presidential election, but as the phosphorus was not prepared, it was postponed until the night of the 25th of November. Of the eight men who formed the original party, two fled to Canada, leaving but six. I was at first stopping at the Belmont House, in Fulton street, but afterward moved into Prince street. I set fire to FOUR HOTELS, or rather to Barnum's Museum, Lovejoy's Hotel, Tammany Hotel, and the New England House. The others only set fire to the house in which each was stopping, and then cut off. Had the entire eight done as I did, we would have set fire to thirty-two houses, and played a big joke on the Fire Department. I know that I am to be hung for setting fire to Barnum's Museum, but the fact is that that affair was simply a reckless joke. I had no idea of doing it, but when we were in there, for the mere fun of the thing, I emptied a bottle of phosphorus on the floor, just to scare the people. I knew it wouldn't set fire to wood, for we had tried that before, and had at one time about concluded to give it up. There was no fiendishness about it. The Museum was set on fire by merest accident, after I had been drinking, and just for the fun of a scare. After setting fire to my four places, I walked the street all night, until near morning, when I went to the Exchange Hotel. There we all met the next morning and again at night. My friend and I had rooms there, but we sat most of the day in the office, reading the papers, while the detectives, who were thick, watched us. I expected then that I should be caught, and if caught I expected to die. Had I done so then it would have been all right, but I think now it's rather rough. I escaped to Canada, as did all the rest, and very glad I was to get safely across the bridge. I was restless, however, and wanted to rejoin my command. I started with my friend via Detroit. Just before we reached the city he received an intimation that the detectives were on the look-out for us, and giving me a signal, he jumped from the cars. I didn't notice the signal, but kept on and was arrested in the depot. I wish to say that the killing of women and children was the last thing we thought of. We wanted to let the people of the North understand and feel that there are two sides to this war, and that they can't be rolling in wealth and comfort while we at the South are bearing all the hardships and privations. In retaliation for Sheridan's atrocities in the Shenandoah we desired to destroy property, not the lives of women and children, although that would of course have followed in the train."*

Kennedy was tried by a military commission at General Dix's headquarters, New York. He was found guilty of both charges, of being a spy and violating the laws of war in setting fire to hotels in New York. He was executed by hanging within the walls of Fort Lafayette, on the 25th of March. He was much excited at the close, acted with great recklessness and levity, shouting at the last moment a scrap of song,

> "Trust to luck, trust to luck,
> Stare your fate in the face;
> Sure your heart will be aisy
> If it's in the right place."

* New York *Times*, March 26, 1865.

The chief act of the United States Congress in its concluding session, ending the 4th of March, was the passage by the House of Representatives on the 31st of January, of the Constitutional Amendment abolishing slavery, by the decided vote of 119 to 56. It will be remembered that this bill had passed the Senate at the previous session, and that its passage by the House had been urged by the President in his annual message at the opening of Congress in December. It was as follows: Be it resolved by the Senate and House of Representatives of the United States of America in Congress assembled, two-thirds of both houses concurring, that the following articles be proposed to the Legislatures of the several States as an amendment to the Constitution of the United States; when ratified by three-fourths of said Legislatures, shall be valid to all intents and purposes as a part of the said Constitution, namely: Art. 13. Section 1. Neither slavery nor involuntary servitude, except as a punishment for crime, whereof the party shall have been duly convicted, shall exist within the United States, or any place subject to their jurisdiction. Sec. 2. Congress shall have power to enforce this article by appropriate legislation."

On the evening of the day after the passage of this act, President Lincoln was serenaded at the White House by a popular assemblage whom he thus addressed. He said "he supposed the passage through Congress of the Constitutional Amendment for the abolishment of slavery throughout the United States, was the occasion to which he was indebted for the honor of this call. The occasion was one of congratulation to the country and to the whole world. But there is a task yet before us—to go forward and consummate by the votes of the States that which Congress so nobly began yesterday. He had the honor to inform those present that Illinois had already done the work. Maryland was about half through; but he felt proud that Illinois was a little ahead. He thought this measure was a very fitting, if not an indispensable adjunct to the winding up of the great difficulty. He wished the reunion of all the States perfected and so effected as to remove all causes of disturbance in the future, and to attain this end it was necessary that the original disturbing cause should, if possible, be rooted out. He thought all would bear him witness that he had never shrunk from doing all that he could to eradicate slavery, by issuing an Emancipation Proclamation. But that proclamation falls far short of what the amendment will be when fully consummated. A question might be raised whether the proclamation was legally valid. It might be added that it only aided those who came into our lines, and that it was inoperative as to those who did not give themselves up, or that it would have no effect upon the children of the slaves born hereafter. In fact it would be urged that it did not meet the evil. But this amendment is a king's cure for all the evils. It winds the whole thing up. He would repeat that it was the fitting, if not the indispensable adjunct to the consummation of the great game we are playing. He could not but congratulate all present, himself, the country, and the whole world, upon this great moral victory."

Thus the question of the further existence of slavery in the country was submitted to the people to complete, with the formalities of the Constitution, the action which had already been taken by the President in the conduct of the war. Slavery, it was admitted on all sides, was doomed. Like the masts of a ship in an overwhelming storm, it had been severed from the State from necessity and for safety; it was now required permanently to disentangle the vessel from the floating and still perilous fragments of the wreck. The votes of twenty-seven States were needed to complete the requisite three-fourths of the whole, to make the proposed amendment the law of the land. Of the twenty-five States which took part in the last Presidential election, before the 4th of March eighteen had ratified the amendment. Illinois took the lead on the 1st of February, by a decisive vote. Maryland was among the foremost in action, her House of Delegates approving the amendment immediately on its announcement on the 1st of February, by a vote of 53 against 23. The Legislatures of other States then in session, Rhode Island, Pennsylvania, New York, Massachusetts, Michigan, West Virginia, Maine, Missouri, Ohio, Wisconsin, rapidly followed with their ratification of the amendment. Delaware, Kentucky and New Jersey positively rejected it.

A statement addressed by Secretary Fessenden of the Treasury Department, to Congress on the 13th of February, made this exhibit of the national debt: Aggregate debt, bearing interest in coin, $1,087,556,438 80; interest, $63,433,-131 45. Debt bearing interest in lawful money, $608,570,952 44; interest, $29,698,770 41. Debt on which interest has ceased, $350,570 09. Legal tender debt, bearing no interest, $433,160,569. Fractional currency, $24,960,913 93. Total, $2,153,735,444 26. Total interest, $93,131,901 86.

Early in March Secretary Fessenden was succeeded in the Department by Hugh McCullough, a native of Maine, and since 1833 a resident of Indiana. He was educated at Bowdoin College, practiced law in the West, and in 1835 commenced his career as a banker. He was President of the Indiana State Bank from 1855 to May, 1863, when he was appointed Comptroller of the Currency at Washington; from the efficient discharge of the duties of which post he was called to be Secretary of the Treasury. The annual report of the Secretary of War, deferred through the exigencies of the public service was presented at the close of the session of Congress. Its statement of the army material furnished within the preceding twelve months, exhibits the gigantic proportions which the war assumed at its height. The ordinance supplies furnished to the military service during the fiscal year, included 1,441 pieces of ordnance, 1,896 artillery carriages and caissons, 455,910 small arms, 502,044 sets of accoutrements and harness, 1,913,753 projectiles for cannon, 7,624,685 pounds of bullets and lead, 464,549 rounds of artillery ammunition, 152,067 sets of horse equipments, 112,087,553 cartridges for small arms, 7,544,044 pounds of gunpowder.

The ceremonies inaugurating President Lincoln's second term of office took place at the Capitol at Washington, at noon of the 4th of March. The procession from Sixteenth Street and through Pennsylvania Avenue was composed of the city authorities, various companies of firemen and benevolent societies, and a military escort, including two regiments of the Invalid Corps, a squadron of cavalry, a battery of artillery and four companies of colored troops. The oath of office was first administered in presence of the Senate, to the Vice-President elect, Andrew Johnson of Tennessee, by Vice-President Hamlin. In reply to the question whether he was ready to take the oath, Mr. Johnson said "I am," and then, addressing the Senators, continued in this inaugural speech: "I am here to-day as the chosen Vice-President of the United States, and as such, by constitutional provision, I am made the presiding officer of this body. I therefore present myself here in obedience to the high behests of the American people to discharge a constitutional duty, and not presumptuously to thrust myself in a position so exalted. May I at this moment—it may not be irrelevant to the occasion—advert to the workings of our institutions under the Constitution which our fathers framed and Washington approved, as exhibited by the position in which I stand before the American Senate, in the sight of the American people? Deem me not vain or arrogant; yet I should be less than man if, under such circumstances, I were not proud of being an American citizen; for to-day one who claims no high descent, one who comes from the ranks of the people, stands, by the voice of a free constituency, in the second place in this Government. There may be those to whom such things are not pleasing; but those who have labored for the consummation of a free government will appreciate and cherish institutions which exclude none, however obscure his origin, from places of trust and distinction. The people, in short, are the source of all power. You, Senators; you, who constitute the Bench of the Supreme Court of the United States, are but the creatures of the American people; your exaltation is from them: the power of this Government consists in its nearness and approximation to the great mass of the people. You, Mr. Secretary Seward, Mr. Secretary Stanton, the Secretary of the Navy, and the others who are your associates—you know that you have my respect and my confidence—derive not your greatness and your power alone from President Lincoln. Humble as I am, plebeian as I may be deemed, permit me, in the presence of this brilliant assembly, to enunciate the truth that courts and cabinets, the President and his advisers, derive their power and their greatness from the people. A President could not exist here forty-eight hours if he were as far removed from the people as the autocrat of Russia is separated from his subjects. Here the popular heart sustains President and Cabinet officers; the popular will gives them all their strength. Such an assertion of the great principles of this Government may be considered out of place, and I will not consume the time of these intelligent and enlightened people much longer: but I could not be insensible to these great truths when I, a plebeian, elected by the people Vice-President of these United States, am here to enter upon the discharge of my duties. For those duties I claim not the aptitude of my respected predecessor. Although I have occupied a seat in both the House of Representatives and the Senate, I am not learned in parliamentary law, and I shall be dependent on the courtesy of those Senators who have become familiar with the rules which are requisite for the good order of the body and the dispatch of its business. I have only studied how I may best advance the interests of my State and of my country, and not the technical rules of order; and if I err, I shall appeal to this dignified body of representatives of the States for kindness and indulgence. Before I conclude this brief inaugural address, in the presence of this audience—and I, though a plebeian boy, am authorized by the principles of the Government under which I live to feel proudly conscious that I am a man, and grave dignitaries are but men—before the Supreme Court, the representatives of foreign Governments, Senators, and the people, I desire to proclaim that Tennessee, whose representative I have been, is free. She has bent the tyrant's rod, she has broken the yoke of slavery, and to-day she stands redeemed. She waited not for the exercise of power by Congress; it was her own act, and she is now as loyal, Mr. Attorney-General, as is the State from which you come. It is the doctrine of the Federal Constitution that no State can go out of this Union: and moreover, Congress cannot eject a State from this Union! Thank God, Tennessee has never been out of the Union! It is true, the operations of her Government were for a time interrupted; but she is still in the Union, and I am her representative. This day she elects her Governor and her Legislature, which will be convened on the first

Monday of April, and again her Senators and Representatives will soon mingle with those of her sister States; and who shall gainsay it, for the Constitution requires that to every State shall be guaranteed a republican form of government? I am now prepared to take the oath of office and renew my allegiance to the Constitution of the United States."

Mr. Johnson having thus taken the oath of office, the Senate adjourned. President Lincoln then appeared in the Senate Chamber where the oath of office was administered by Chief Justice Chase, in presence of a brilliant assembly of the Cabinet Ministers, heads of bureaus, members of Congress, officers of the Army and Navy and the Diplomatic Corps. This ceremony having been completed, and the morning rain having been succeeded by sunshine, the President then repaired to the balcony and delivered his inaugural address in the open air, in presence of the public. It was as follows:

"Fellow-Countrymen–At this second appearing to take the oath of the Presidential office, there is less occasion for an extended address than there was at the first. Then a statement somewhat in detail of a course to be pursued seemed very fitting and proper. Now, at the expiration of four years, during which public declarations have been constantly called forth on every point and phase of the great contest which still absorbs the attention and engrosses the energies of the nation, little that is new could be presented. The progress of our arms, upon which all else chiefly depends, is as well known to the public as to myself, and it is, I trust, reasonably satisfactory and encouraging to all. With high hope for the future, no prediction in regard to it is ventured. On the occasion corresponding to this four years ago, all thoughts were anxiously directed to an impending civil war. All dreaded it; all sought to avoid it. While the inaugural address was being delivered from this place, devoted altogether to saving the Union without war, insurgent agents were in the city seeking to destroy it without war—seeking to dissolve the Union and divide the effects by negotiation. Both parties deprecated war, but one of them would make war rather than let the nation survive, and the other would accept war rather than let it perish, and the war came. One-eighth of the whole population were colored slaves, not distributed generally over the Union, but localized in the southern part of it. These slaves constituted a peculiar and powerful interest. All knew that this interest was somehow the cause of the war. To strengthen, perpetuate and extend this interest, was the object for which the insurgents would rend the Union by war, while the Government claimed no right to do more than to restrict the territorial enlargement of it. Neither party expected for the war the magnitude or the duration which it has already attained. Neither anticipated that the cause of the conflict might cease with or even before the conflict itself should cease. Each looked for an easier triumph, and a result less fundamental and astounding. Both read the same Bible and pray to the same God, and each invokes His aid against the other. It may seem strange that any men should dare to ask a just God's assistance in wringing their bread from the sweat of other men's faces, but let us judge not, that we be not judged. The prayers of both should not be answered. That of neither has been answered fully. The Almighty has His own purposes. Woe unto the world because of offences, for it must needs be that offences come, but woe to that man by whom the offence cometh. If we shall suppose that American slavery is one of these offences, which in the providence of God must needs come, but which having continued through His appointed time, He now wills to remove, and that He gives to both North and South this terrible war as the woe due to those by whom the offence came, shall we discern there is any departure from those Divine attributes which the believers in a living God always ascribe to him? Fondly do we hope, fervently do we pray, that this mighty scourge of war may speedily pass away. Yet, if God wills that it continue until all the wealth piled by the bondman's two hundred and fifty years of unrequited toil shall be sunk, and until every drop of blood drawn with the lash shall be paid by another drawn with the sword, as was said three thousand years ago; so, still it must be said, that the judgments of the Lord are true and righteous altogether. With malice toward none, with charity for all, with firmness in the right, as God gives us to see right, let us finish the work we are in, to bind up the nation's wounds, to care for him who shall have borne the battle and for his widow and his orphans, to do all which may achieve and cherish a just and a lasting peace among ourselves and with all nations."

The language of this truly Christian document was remarkable. It was in every line inspired by the humane and patriotic heart of one who, in the growing convictions of the country, was every day earning the title, coupling his name with that of Washington, as "*the good President*." Subsequent events gave this address a peculiar significance. Its influence was felt at home; and the friends of the country abroad, perhaps more keenly, by its contrast to the usual cool temper and tone of indifference of State papers, noticed its striking characteristics. An English journal, the *British Standard*, thus expressed the sentiment of intelligent thoughtful observers: "It is the most remarkable thing of the sort ever pronounced by any President of the United States from the first day until now. Its Alpha and its Omega is *Almighty God*, the God of justice and the Father of mercies, who is working out the purposes of His love. It is invested with a dignity and pathos which lift it high above every thing of the kind, whether in the Old World or the New. The whole thing puts us in mind of the best men of the English commonwealth; there is, in fact, much of the old prophet about it."

At the conclusion of the delivery of the address at the Capitol, a national salute was fired by a battery in the vicinity, and the President, seated in an open barouche with his son and Senator Foster of the Committee of Arrangements, was conducted at the head of the procession through Pennsylvania Avenue to the White House. Every thing passed off quietly and in order, nothing occurring to disturb the harmony of the day.

CHAPTER CXII.

THE CAMPAIGN IN VIRGINIA—FALL OF RICHMOND AND SURRENDER OF GENERAL LEE'S ARMY.

THE movement of General Sherman towards North Carolina was the signal for the renewal of active military operations in Virginia, where General Grant, confident of the result, was preparing to strike the decisive blow at the rebel capital. As a preliminary to the final stroke, or rather in continuation of the exhaustive measures which were consuming the military resources of Richmond, a final raid and destruction of its means of supply to the north and west in Virginia was set on foot, and successfully accomplished by General Sheridan. Leaving General Hancock in charge of the middle military division, with his headquarters at Winchester, he left that city on the 26th of February, at the head of a body of cavalry, thoroughly armed and equipped for a long and adventurous expedition. The column marched the first day to Woodstock, a distance of about thirty miles, and the next, fording the swollen north fork of the Shenandoah, a task of much peril and difficulty, passed through Newmarket and encamped at Lacy's Springs. On the following day's march to Middle River some resistance was encountered from a body of rebel cavalry under General Rosser, who made a stand near Mount Crawford, on North River. Upon approaching the town the enemy's pickets fired and fell back across the river. On the bluff Rosser had several hundred men in skirmish line, mostly posted behind a curtain breastwork of rails hastily thrown up. The retreating pickets attempted to destroy the bridge by setting it on fire and tearing up the planking. Fortunately, the wood work was wet, and could not be made to burn easily; they did, however, succeed in getting up enough planking to prevent cavalry crossing; but this was speedily repaired. The river is not fordable near the bridge, and the enemy had decidedly the advantage of position; indeed, Rosser boasted half an hour before, to the citizens in Mount Crawford, that he could hold the place all day against the whole of Sheridan's cavalry with his force—about 400 men. Colonel Capeheart, commanding a brigade of General Custer's division, in the advance, charged with the duty of securing the bridges in the route, examined the position, and decided to flank it by swimming a portion of his command. Lieutenant-Colonel Battersby, with the First New York Lincoln; Major S. B. Howe, with the First Virginia, and Second Virginia, Lieutenant-Colonel Allen, swam across the river about one mile above the bridge. The Third Virginia, Major Witcher, at first deployed as skirmishers on the northern bank, finally crossed below. Not half an hour had elapsed from the initiation of the movement before the enemy skedaddled in a great hurry, leaving two dead men on the ground--one an officer—and several wounded. Colonel Capeheart immediately hurried forward his command, and the advance did not halt until within one mile of Staunton, having chased the enemy at a trot and gallop from Mount Crawford, a distance of eighteen miles, thereby securing the large bridge across Middle River and several smaller bridges over other streams that cross the pike. Besides securing the bridges thirty-seven prisoners, including five officers, seventy horses and mules, fourteen wagons and seven ambulances, the wagons filled with commissary and sutler's stores belonging to Rosser's command were the result of this day's operations. The loss in the brigade was six wounded, none killed. The column encamped for the night near Kline's Mill, on Middle River, with a strong picket advance near Staunton.

"The weather all the next day was the worst or as bad as ever experienced by man. The rain fell in torrents and froze on men's whiskers as fast as it fell, and formed icicles on the limbs of trees. The column was compelled to move at a very slow walk through the deep mud and slush, and men as well as horses were chilled through, boots were filled with water and every rag of clothing was saturated with this element. Yet the troops moved along steadily over hills, through mud-holes and streams regardless of consequences. Staunton was entered without opposition; no halt was made here except to close up the column. The road taken at this point was worse, if possible, than the one we had been travelling over; horses, without riders, could scarcely pull their feet out of the mud, and how animals drawing loaded wagons and artillery could get through did not appear, but it was done. Rosser's men fell back only as fast as the Twenty-second New York moved forward, making a little stand in the mud at Fishersville. Five miles beyond, at Waynesboro', Early, it was known, had concentrated his men to give battle. A portion of his command had fallen back the day before from Fishersville to strengthen the post there. Early told the citizens everywhere they need not be alarmed—Sheridan never could get through Rockfish Gap, and told one of his staff officers (since captured) that as soon as Sheridan found he had to fight infantry he would withdraw. Waynesboro' was finally reached. There, on commanding ground, a ridge of hills skirting the front of the town, could be seen, filled with infantry, extended lines of breastworks made of earth and rails. At this time General Custer was alone with his command upon the ground, Generals Sheridan and Merritt, with the other troops, not coming up until some time after the fight was over. It was, I think, between 1 and 2 o'clock in the afternoon when the advance of the command arrived near Waynesboro'. General Custer, riding along in front of the enemy's line with his staff, inspected it carefully, and then in his energetic way remarked, "I think we can flank them on the (enemy's) left." To many present it seemed as though to offer battle under the circumstances was madness. Not so with the ruling spirit there. Promptly his orders were given, and they were obeyed with unaccountable alacrity. The Second Brigade, being nearest at hand, Wells, its commander, was directed to put a heavy skirmish line of mounted men. In obedience to this order, the Twenty-second New York, Colonel Thompson, and First New Hampshire, Captain Wyatt, were deployed and thrown forward, in a depression of the earth, to within about 1,000 yards of the enemy's position: the line was ordered to be made heavy to deceive the enemy, to make them believe the main attack was to be from the front. A suggestion that so formidable a line would draw out a heavy shell fire from the enemy only elicited the response: "It must be done, shell or no shell." The First Vermont, Lieutenant-Colonel Hall, was next directed to take a position to the left and rear, with orders at a given signal to make a dash to gain a piece of woods opposite the enemy's right, to convey the impression that that portion of their line was in danger. The Eighth New York, Major Compson, was placed in reserve to support the skirmish line on the left of the pike. Only one squadron of the remaining regiment in this brigade, Fifteenth New York, Colonel Coppinger, being present, that was placed also in reserve. The balance of the regiment was on duty at the rear of the whole column.

"Pennington's brigade, the First, next came up, Lieutenant-Colonel Whitaker, Acting Inspector-General, was directed to have three regiments of this command dismounted and guide them through the woods and a ravine, so as to be out of sight of the enemy, to a position on the enemy's extreme left; for fear the enemy might discover this body of men in season to make preparations to meet it, the mounted skirmish line was extended to the right so as to cover the front of this column when in position. Colonel Pennington detached in this important flank duty the Second Ohio, Lieutenant-Colonel A. B. Nettleton; Third New Jersey, Lieutenant-Colonel Robeson; First Connecticut, Major Goodwin, the men all armed with Spencer's carbines. The command reached position without the enemy discovering the movement. The Second New York, Colonel A. M. Randall, and Eighteenth Pennsylvania, Captain Nieman, were held in reserve to the right of the pike. The Third Brigade, commanded by Colonel Capehart, now came up, the First New York (Lincoln), Lieutenant-Colonel J. C. Battersby, was placed on the pike; the Second Virginia, Lieutenant-Colonel William Allen, on the right of the pike. The First Virginia, Major Howe, and Third Virginia, Major Witcher, were placed to the left and rear as a reserve. All the troops except the skirmish line and the flanking party on the right, were in column of fours, ready to charge or be thrown to any part where their services might be needed. Woodruff's artillery (two guns) was just placed to the right of the pike at a distance of 1,900 yards from the enemy's works; to deceive the enemy, the guns were wheeled about and taken to the rear and left of the pike out of sight, but were immediately replaced near the first position again, but so under a rise of ground as not to be seen by the enemy. The enemy cheered when they saw the artillery withdrawn. The position of the several commands was verified and the commanders carefully instructed what to do. While all this was going on the skirmish line kept up a slow fire, which was responded to by the enemy with shot and shell. Every thing being in readiness, General Custer's buglers sounded the advance, when each command sounded the "charge." The First Vermont dashed for the left, threatening the enemy's right; the formidable skirmish line moved up in full view of the enemy and pressed forward just as Pennington, Nettleton and Whitaker, with the Second Ohio in advance—regimental part with the First Connecticut and Third New Jersey close behind—emerged from a piece of woods upon the enemy's extreme left. Woodruff commenced throwing shell from his two guns and every thing was in motion at once; every order was carried out to the letter, and the result was success. The enemy were not a little surprised to see so formidable a body of flankers on their left; an attempt to form a line to meet them proved abortive; on they pressed, and the enemy seeing Custer's reckless fellows marching in upon them from every direction, became panic stricken, broke and ran in terrible confusion, abandoning muskets, flags and artillery. By the time they had fairly got into the village of Waynesboro', a few rods to the rear of their works, the mounted cavalry had charged in upon them, and Yankees and rebels were all mixed up together. The First Vermont moved in from the left, the Eighth New York on the pike, and Capehart with the whole of his brigade at his heels dashed into the village, following the Eighth. The sons of the Ancient Dominion showed no fight at close quarters, but surrendered promptly when ordered to do so, thereby preventing a general slaughter. South River winds its way along just in the rear of Waynesboro', and the only route for the enemy to escape was to cross this. It was not at this time fordable, and the only way for infantry to cross was by a small foot-bridge and by the railroad bridge. A few hundred attempted to escape by the latter route. Colonel Whitaker (who, with Captain Burroughs and some thirty men of the Eighth New York, were the first to cross the stream), with a few men on horseback, cut off the men attempting to escape on the railroad track. Whitaker with a dozen men here captured at least 300 rebels and one battle-flag. Major Compson, Captain Burroughs and Captain Benton, the latter of the Twenty-second New York, made no halt, but pressed on and beyond the mountain, capturing several officers and Early's headquarters flag.

"Capehart did not stop for prisoners or artillery, but struck for the extreme rear, and on he dashed up the mountain, through Rockfish Gap, down the other side, until Colonel Allen and a mixed detachment finally held up at Greenwood Station, eleven miles from Waynesboro', and over the worst road ever traveled. From this point our troopers commenced sweeping in every thing. Just as the troops entered Waynesboro', Early, disgusted, took a car in waiting for him, passed down the road a piece, jumped off and took to the mountains. There were three trains on the track, two of them having locomotives attached with a high head of steam on. These two trains moved off rapidly, but the easterly opening of the railway tunnel through the mountain was reached by the first as the second train passed through. A volley was fired at the engineer, killing two men, one a Major, according to the report of a prisoner since captured, who was on the train, and wounding several others. The engineer was so badly scared that he jumped off and climbed into the mountain. The third train, consisting of sixteen cars, and loaded with commissary stores and ordnance was captured. Five pieces of artillery were captured with this train. Some property was destroyed at the next station, but Greenwood Station was a mine. Not less than $1,000,000 worth of property was destroyed there. Several hundred bales of cotton, about 1,000 horse accoutrements, sabres, muskets, bales of cotton cloth, cases of uniforms and other clothing, and a large lot of commissary stores, were all destroyed, together with railroad depots and other buildings. Wagons, ambulances, artillery, in fact, all the material belonging to Early's grand army was captured and destroyed along the road leading through Rockfish Gap. The wagons were all loaded with army supplies—principally provisions. The property captured and destroyed on the road and at Waynesboro' is valued at another million of dollars—making at least a loss of $2,000,000 (green-backs' value) to the so-called Southern Confederacy. It is believed not a man belonging to Early's command escaped, except the remnant of Rosser's cavalry, numbering about 175 men. Early, Long, Wharton and Lilly were the Generals in the battle on the rebel side. Wharton escaped in the cars, Early to the mountains, and the whereabouts of the others is questionable. It is reported Long concealed himself in town, and that Lilly was either a prisoner or killed; but as to the truth or falsity of these reports I am not able to decide at this time. The result of the day's business foots up as follows: Prisoners captured, 1,303; wagons and ambulances, 150; horses and mules, 800; artillery, with carriages and caissons, 11; battle flags, 9; other flags, 16. The casualties to the Union force was—at Waynesboro', two killed, three severely and four slightly wounded; at Mount Crawford, three slightly wounded. At night, General Custer's whole command moved across the mountain at Rockfish Gap, and encamped within four miles of Greenwood Station, and Generals Sheridan, Merritt and Devin halted at Waynesboro'." *

A dispatch of General Sheridan dated Columbia, Va., March 10, continues the narrative of the expedition to that point. "The night of the defeat of Early this division was pushed across the Blue Ridge, and entered Charlottesville at 2 P. M. the next day. The Mayor of the city and the principal inhabitants came out and delivered up the keys of the public buildings. I had to remain at Charlottesville two days. This time was consumed in bringing over from Waynesboro' our ammunition and pontoon trains. The weather was horrible beyond description, and the rain incessant. The two divisions were during this time occupied in destroying the two large iron bridges, one over the Rivanna River, the other over Morse's Creek, near Charlottesville, and a railroad for a distance of eight miles in the direction of Lynchburg. On the 6th of March, I sent the First Division, General Devin commanding, to Scottsville, on the James River, with directions to send out light parties through the country and destroy all merchandise, mills, factories, bridges, etc., on the Rivanna River, the parties to join the division at Scottsville. The division then proceeded along the canal to Duguidsville, fifteen miles from Lynchburg, destroying every lock, and in many places the bank of the canal. At Duguidsville we hoped to secure the bridge to let us cross the river, as our pontoons were useless on account of the high water. In this, however, we were foiled, as both this bridge and the bridge at Hardwicksville were burned by the enemy upon our approach. Merritt accompanied this division. The third division started at the same time from Charlottesville, and proceeded down the Lynchburg Railroad to Amherst Court House, destroying every bridge on the road, and in many places miles of the road. The bridges on this road are numerous, and some of them 500 feet in length. We have found great abundance in this country for our men and animals; in fact, the canal had been the great feeder of Richmond. At the Rockfish River, the bank of the canal was cut, and at New Canton, where the dam is across the James, the guard lock was destroyed, and the James River let into the canal, carrying away the banks, and washing out the bottom of the canal. The dam across the James at this point was also partially destroyed. I have had no opposition. Every body is bewildered by our movements. I have had no news of any kind since I left. The latest Richmond paper was of the 4th, but contained nothing. I omitted to mention that the bridges on the railroad from Swoop's Depot, on the other side of Staunton, to Charlottesville, were utterly destroyed; also, all bridges for a distance of ten miles on the Gordonsville Railroad. The weather has been very bad indeed, raining hard every day, with the exception of four days since we started. My wagons have, from the state of the roads, detained me. Up to the present time we have captured fourteen pieces of artillery, eleven at Waynesboro' and three at Charlottesville. The party that I sent back from Waynesboro' started with six pieces, but they were obliged to destroy two of the six for want of animals. The remaining eight pieces were thoroughly destroyed. We have captured up to the present time twelve canal boats, laden with supplies, ammunition, rations, medical stores, etc. I cannot speak in too high terms of Generals Merritt, Custer and Devin and the officers and men of their commands. They have waded through mud and water during this continuous rain, and

* Diary of Sheridan's Raid, by E. A. Paul, a correspondent of the New York *Times*, March 21, 1865.

are in fine spirits and health. Commodore Hollins, of the rebel navy, was shot near Gordonsville while attempting to make his escape from our advance in that direction."

On the 15th General Sheridan, in a dispatch communicated to the public by the Assistant Secretary of War, reported from the bridge of the Richmond and Fredericksburg Railroad, across the South Anna River, "that, having destroyed the James River Canal as far to the east as Goochland, he marched up the Virginia Central Railroad at Tollsville, and destroyed it down to Beaver Dam Station, totally destroying fifteen miles of the road. General Custer was then sent to Ashland, and General Bevin to the South Anna bridges, all of which have been destroyed. General Sheridan says the amount of property destroyed in his march is enormous. The enemy attempted to prevent his burning the Central Railroad bridge over the South Anna, but the Fifth United States Cavalry charged up to the bridge, and about thirty men dashed across on foot, driving off the enemy and capturing three pieces of artillery, 20-pounder Parrots." Having with slight loss accomplished this thorough destruction of the enemy's supplies and communications, and thus greatly impoverished the rebel force at Richmond, General Sheridan turned, by the way of the Pamunkey River and the White House, to join General Grant's army to the south of Richmond, where he arrived on the 26th, in time to bear a prominent part in the closing actions of the campaign.

The correspondent whom we have cited, thus sums up in his letter from White House, Va., on the 17th March, the prominent results of the expedition. "For nineteen days General Sheridan has roamed almost at will, with his well-disciplined troopers, throughout that portion of Virginia north of the James River, and, by the exercise of a little strategy, thwarting all attempts of the enemy to impede his progress or interrupt his plans, so that the expedition has been fruitful of more substantial results than any that has preceded it. During this period of time the whole command has been continuously and well supplied with rations obtained from the enemy's storehouses, excepting only the two articles of coffee and sugar. It is true, a certain number of rations were issued to the men at the start, but after the first day's march the soldiers found what they preferred to their ordinary rations. Well-cured bacon and hams, sweet, fresh flour, honey, butter, vegetables, meal, mutton, beef and molasses, were some of the supplies to be obtained almost every day. As a part of the substantial results may be classed the thorough disabling of about 200 miles of railway—principally used for supplying the troops defending Richmond with materials of war and provisions—by the destruction of bridges, culverts and the railway track itself. This work never has been done more thoroughly before. Next, and perhaps the first in importance, is the complete destruction of the James River and Kanawha Canal, passing through one of the most extensive grain-growing districts in the world, and also used most exclusively to feed Lee's army. So completely is this destroyed that years must elapse before it can be repaired again, if at all. Some people, residents near the canal, say that no attempt will be made to repair this great highway during the existing war. The same may be said of the railroads, for the enemy have not the men or material under their command. The destruction of these sources of supply has created a greater panic in Richmond than has existed there before during the war. It has done more to dishearten the people and demoralize the rebel soldiers than all the disasters of the last campaign and the evacuation of seaport towns combined. I know this to be the case, having been in daily communication with Richmond through citizens, prisoners and deserters, for the last two week. The expedition has been a success, also, in the destruction and use of other public property. In this is included all kinds, because every thing practically throughout rebeldom belongs to the Government. The quantity of provisions, grain and forage actually consumed by the troops, and the negroes who fell in with them along the route, was alone immense, but the quantity destroyed was much greater. In materials of war destroyed at one place (Greenwood Station) the loss was estimated by a confederate officer at $2,000,000. Hundreds of hogsheads of leaf tobacco, buildings filled with manufactured tobacco, machinery, cars, cannon, shells, bridges, apple-jack and cotton go to make up a portion of the property destroyed to the value of many millions of dollars, and is just so much of the enemy's capital expended. The column returns to our lines after accomplishing all the work laid out for it almost intact. Only four men have been killed in battle ; three or four severely, and half a dozen slightly wounded. One man died from exposure, and one was drowned in the Shenandoah River. The wear and tear of horse-flesh necessarily has been great, owing to the bad roads and the continuous service, employed without rest ; but a large number of horses and mules were captured, and there are only a few dismounted men. The men themselves were never in better spirits, and were never more disposed to risk their lives for the country, when necessary."

This destructive raid by Sheridan, the report of army movements in General Thomas' command in Tennessee approaching from the west, and the advance of Sherman in North Carolina, with the occupation of Goldsboro' on the 21st of March, warned General Lee in Richmond of the increasing peril of his position. The fatal net was evidently closing around him. If inactive, he must remain to be captured. On the other hand he must escape while opportunity yet remained or defeat the army of General Grant by a desperate assault. In this exigency, seeking to gain some temporary advantage or cover his retreat, he chose the latter. Grant, ready for any event, waiting the time to strike, promptly accepted the challenge, and the result to Lee was utter defeat. The attack precipitating the final conflict was made by the enemy on the morning of Saturday, the 25th of March. The events of the day are thus related by two intelligent correspondents with the two wings of General Grant's Army of the Potomac. "The long-anticipated and carefully-prepared rebel movement which was to 'astonish the world,'" writes Mr. Young from the right wing of the army, at midnight of the day of battle, "took place to-day, and, I have no doubt, did astonish that part of the world within the limited precincts of rebeldom. A few more such surprises will, one would think, be sufficient to bring the leaders of secession to their senses, and convince them of the hopelessness of their struggle to divide and ruin our common country. That the affair of to-day has been in contemplation for a long time, and was fully prepared for, is evident from numerous circumstances brought to our knowledge during the progress of the battle and since its occurrence. For several days past the enemy had been busily engaged concentrating all their best troops and a large number of guns near the point of attack ; had provided an abundance of ammunition, and completed such arrangements as were deemed requisite to enable them to take and hold the desirable position they strove to gain. If they had succeeded in accomplishing their object, they would have severed the communication between this army and City Point, and deprived us of all chance of obtaining supplies thence. We should then have been driven to the extremity of assaulting them in their own intrenchments or abandoning this encampment. In either case they would have acquired a vast advantage over us in comparison to what they can have while our present line is held intact, and they might possibly have inflicted serious injury. Fully aware of this, and realizing that maintaining their position in our front will not longer suffice to keep their army together and quiet the spirit of discontent among their citizens, General Lee determined to make the effort, desperate as it undoubtedly was. The place chosen for the demonstration though not, perhaps, the weakest part of our line, possessed advantages found nowhere else along our front. It was on the extreme right of this army on the south side of the Appomattox, and where the shape of the ground afforded excellent facilities for rapidly intrenching and securing it. It would have given them complete command of the line of our military railroad, and perhaps rendered our position here untenable. In short, if success had crowned their efforts Petersburg would have been freed from our grasp, and Richmond released from its present precarious condition, for a time, at least. Having massed General Gordon's entire command, with the larger portion of General Bushrod Johnson's, on that portion of our front commencing at the south bank of the Appomattox and extending about one mile south, and supplied themselves with ammunition and subsistence for a long struggle, the enemy opened about half-past 4 o'clock this morning, by gobbling up about half a mile of our picket line, and charging immediately with two brigades—Cook's and Ransom's—upon our main line. The attack was so skillfully planned and promptly executed, that before our troops could be got ready for action they were within our works. In fact, the garrison in Fort Steadman were not aware of their danger until the enemy poured over the breastworks in such numbers as to make resistance folly, and they therefore immediately abandoned the fort and retired. Once in the fort, the rebels seized upon the guns and turned them upon our men. Batteries Ten and Eleven, two small redoubts close to Fort Steadman on either side, had to be abandoned as soon as the fort was taken, as had also the lines of works connecting them. Our men were hardly out of these positions ere the rebel gunners took possession and opened fire upon the retiring lines. They next made a dash at Fort Haskell, a large work further to the left, but the garrison, through the vigilance of the commanding officer, Major Woermer, of the Third New Jersey Battery, were on the alert and ready to give the intruders such a reception as to make them recoil. The One Hundredth New York, which was in the fort with the Third New Jersey Artillery, instantly mounted the parapets and poured upon the shrinking columns such a murderous shower of bullets that they did not recover from the shock, but continued to retire toward Fort Steadman. On perceiving this repulse, the rebel gunners in Fort Steadman, turned three guns upon Fort Haskell, and for half an hour poured shot and shell into it as rapidly as the pieces could be worked. The gallant Woermer was not to be outdone in compliments of this character, but replied with equal rapidity and remarkable accuracy, and the garrison nobly kept the rebel assaulting column at bay with their volleys of musketry, aided occasionally by a discharge of canister into the enemy's midst. Meanwhile another rebel column had filed through the breach at Fort Steadman, and, turning to the right, was moving toward the Friend House, General

Wilcox's headquarters. Still another formed into line of battle, and were driving our skirmishers slowly back immediately to the rear of the place of entrance. Captain E. J. Jones, commanding the Eleventh Massachusetts Battery, and Captain Stone, commanding Companies C and I of the Fifth United States Artillery, soon succeeded in getting their guns ready, and opened upon the jubilant enemy, who was apparently having every thing his own way, except the seizure of Fort Haskell. The interruption occasioned by this increased cannonading to the onward movement of the rebels, allowed our skirmishers a breathing spell, and enabled the troops who had been driven from their tents to form and assist them.

" Up to this time only a small portion of Major-General Wilcox's division (the First) had been engaged, but now General Hartrauft appeared on the ground with the Third Division, composed almost entirely of new troops. His quick perception enabled him at once to comprehend the situation of affairs, and he immediately disposed his troops to suit the emergency. Captain Wright, of the Fourteenth Massachusetts Battery; Brevet Major Romer, of the Thirty-fourth New York; Captain Eden, of the Twenty-seventh New York; Captain McClellan, of Company G First New York, and Captain Stone, of Companies C and I of the Fifth U. S. Artillery, also succeeded in getting their guns into position. As General Hartrauft's division now moved up against the foe, firing volley after volley of musketry in rapid succession, their batteries opened, and the fire from the rebel batteries and our batteries in their possession was apparently increased in rapidity. The concentrated fire of such a number of cannon, and the desolating volumes of musketry poured into their ranks by General Hartrauft's command, although withstood manfully for a time, finally became too hot for the soldiers of rebeldom Slowly their line retired, wavered, broke, and they sought shelter in Fort Steadman and the two redoubts on its flank. Steadily the Third Division followed them up step by step. Finally it formed into two lines diagonal with the inner walls of the fort, and charging rapidly, wrapped around it, as it were, completely investing it on three sides, and compelling the rebels it contained to yield themselves up as prisoners of war. Quickly the guns of the fort and redoubts were manned by the gunners of the Nineteenth New York Battery, and with the guns of Fort Haskell, Fort Friend and the field batteries, poured a storm of iron hail after the retreating rebels, who succeeded in getting outside the works, and mowed them down with fearful slaughter until they gained the shelter of their own embankments. General Wheaton's division of the Sixth Corps had been ordered down the line to aid the Ninth in repelling this assault, but it did not arrive on the ground until the rebels were safely beyond their own mud walls, and our forces all in their places on the front, as usual. Thus, the entire honor of the victory rests with the Ninth Corps, and chiefly with the Third Division, under the gallant Hartrauft. General Wilcox's division of the corps were all in the works, and none were engaged except those immediately on the front that was attacked. General Porter's division laid in the works to the left and were not disturbed. General Hartrauft led his division in person, assisted by his own staff, and by Colonel Loring, Captain Van Buren and Captain Goddard, of General Parks' staff. General Parks, the commander of the corps, was not present, being at the time in command of the Army of the Potomac, during General Meade's temporary absence at City Point." On the left wing of the army, writes Mr. Williams, " the operations have extended during the entire day, and at this moment heavy picket firing is going on in front of the Second Corps. The day has been one of great hardship and fatigue to the men, and the fighting has been severe and obstinate. As soon as the orders could be issued, the Fifth, Second and Sixth Corps were set in motion, at about 11 o'clock this morning. The Second was pushed forward over their line of works, and shortly after 8 o'clock the entire corps became very hotly engaged with Johnson's division of Anderson's corps. Steadily advancing, General Humphrey succeeded in driving in the enemy's picket line on to his main line, which speedily moved up to the front, and a desperate engagement took place. After repeated charges, the gallant Second Corps seized the rifle pits of the rebel line, and hold them up to the present time. The Sixth Corps likewise formed line of battle along their main line of defences, and shortly after the Second Corps moved forward General Wright sent his Second and Third Divisions, and the engagement thus became general along the entire left. Driving the picket line before them, the Sixth Corps kept quietly on until they had full possession of the main line of rifle pits, taking a large number of prisoners. As soon as the enemy saw that the Sixth Corps purposed holding the pits, their line of battle came over their works, and charging upon our men pushed them slowly back. General Wright then brought up Wheaton's division of his corps, and with their help the command retained possession of the pits. The fighting on the front of the Second and Sixth Corps was of the most desperate character, and the losses in killed and wounded were heavy on both sides. We have defeated the enemy in his projected breaking through our lines, taken large numbers of his men prisoners, and proved the strength of our positions. We have advanced our lines on the left, captured quite a number of prisoners, and tightened our hold on his communitions *via* the Southside Railroad."*

* New York *Times*, March 28, 1865.

The following was the dispatch of Major-General Parke, dated City Point, the afternoon of the engagement: "The enemy attacked my front this morning at about half-past 4 o'clock, with three divisions under command of General Gordon. By a sudden rush they seized the line held by the Third Brigade, First Division, at the foot of the hill to the right of Fort Steadman, wheeled and overpowering the garrison took possession of the fort. They established themselves upon the hill, turning our guns upon us. Our troops on either flank stood firm. Afterward a determined attack was made upon Fort Haskell, which was checked by part of McLaughlin's brigade, Wilcox's division, and was repulsed with great loss to the enemy. The First Brigade of Hartrauft's division, held in reserve, was brought up, and a check given to any further advance. One or two attempts were made to retake the hill, and were only temporarily successful, until the arrival of the Second Brigade, when a charge was made by that brigade, aided by the troops of the First Division on either flank, and the enemy were driven out of the fort with the loss of a number of prisoners, estimated at 1,800. Two battle-flags have also been brought in. The enemy also lost heavily in killed outside of our lines. The whole line was immediately reoccupied, and the guns retaken uninjured. I regret to add that General McLaughlin was captured in Fort Steadman. Our loss otherwise was not heavy. Great praise is due to Hartrauft for the gallantry displayed in handling his division, which behaved with great skill in this its first engagement." General Hartrauft commanded the Third Division of the Ninth Corps, composed of six newly enlisted regiments of Pennsylvania Volunteers. In acknowledgment of their gallantry he issued this congratulatory order: "With feelings of pride and satisfaction the Brigadier-General commanding tenders his congratulations to the officers and men of his command for their gallant and heroic conduct in the brilliant and triumphant achievement of to-day, which resulted in the recapture of Fort Steadman and the entire line, together with battle-flags, a large number of prisoners and small arms. You have won a name and reputation of which veterans might feel proud, and have proved yourselves worthy of being the associates of the brave soldiers of the old Ninth Corps, and the General commanding hopes that this, your first engagement and signal victory, will nerve and stimulate you for the performance of future deeds of gallantry. To the wounded, and to the families of those who have so nobly fallen in defence of their country, the General commanding tenders his most heartfelt sympathies." General Meade, also, in a General Order, acknowledged the distinguished services of Major-General Parke and Brigadier-General Hartrauft in repairing the disaster with which the day had begun. "The result," said he, "was the thorough defeat of the enemy's plans, the capture of his strongly-intrenched picket line under the artillery fire of his main works and the capture of ten battle-flags and 2,860 prisoners." Two days after the engagement General Grant, in a dispatch to the Secretary of War, thus summed up the results of the day's battle: "The battle of the 25th resulted in the following losses to our side: Second Corps —Killed, 51; wounded, 462; missing, 177. Sixth Corps—Killed, 47; wounded, 401; missing, 30. Ninth Corps—Killed, 68; wounded, 338; missing, 506. Our captures by the Second Corps were 365; by the Sixth Corps, 469; and by the Ninth Corps, 1,049. The Second and Sixth Corps pushed forward and captured the enemy's strong intrenchments and turned it against him and still held it. In trying to retake this the battle was continued until 8 o'clock at night, the enemy losing very heavily. Humphreys estimates the loss of the enemy in his front at three times his own, and General Wright, in his front, as double that of ours. The enemy brought in a flag of truce for permission to collect his dead, which were between their picket line and their main line of fortifications. Permission was granted." President Lincoln, who was at that time on a visit to City Point recruiting his health after a recent illness, was a witness, in company with General Grant, of a portion of the action. On the 27th General Sherman came up to City Point from his army in North Carolina, and had an interview with President Lincoln, Generals Grant, Meade, Ord, Sheridan and others. General Lee's report to Major-General John C. Breckinridge, now the confederate secretary of war, dated at 11 P. M. on the day of the battle, was as follows: "At daylight this morning, General Gordon assaulted and carried the enemy's works at Hare's Hill, capturing nine pieces of artillery and eight mortars, and between 500 and 600 prisoners, among them one brigadier-general and a number of officers of lower grades. The lines were swept for a distance of 400 or 500 yards to the right and left, and two efforts made to recover the captured works were handsomely repulsed; but it was found that the inclosed works in the rear, commanding the enemy's main line, could only be taken at a great sacrifice, and the troops were withdrawn to their original position. It being impracticable to bring off the captured guns owing to the nature of the ground, they were disabled and left. Our loss is reported as not heavy. Among the wounded are Brigadier-General Terry, flesh wound; and Brigadier-General Philip Cooke, flesh wound in arm. All the troops engaged, including two brigades under Brigadier-General Ransom, behaved most handsomely. The conduct of the sharpshooters of Gordon's corps, who led the assault, deserve the highest commendation. This afternoon there was skirmishing on the right, between the picket lines, with varied success. At dark the enemy held a considerable portion of the line farthest in advance of our main works." It was now felt by General Grant that the moment for decided action had come. For nearly a year since the advance across the Rappahannock, the bloody encounters with the enemy in the battles of the Wilderness, the subsequent conflicts on the Peninsula, the occupation of the James River, General Grant, through good and evil report, through disaster and victory, by hard fighting constantly renewed and by consummate strategy, had doggedly adhered to his determination at starting on the campaign to pursue the army of Lee, the last great obstacle in the way of peace to the end. "I will fight it out on this line," said he, undeterred by his first severe losses, "if it takes me all summer." The summer was past in the arduous struggle; but, though the army of the enemy was still unconquered, its strength was much diminished and powerless further to inflict decisive injury; it was firmly held at Richmond in the iron grasp of the indomitable General of the West. The winter had been added to the summer and still Grant, ever tightening his hold, waited patiently the inevitable result. Early spring had come, and as the public were looking forward to the approaching campaign it was already commenced. The grand movement in the south of Sherman and the devastating raid of Sheridan were the preliminaries of the final movement. As the event drew near General Grant wrote to his father at Covington, Ky.: "We are now having fine weather, and I think will be able to wind up matters about Richmond soon. I am anxious to have Lee hold on where he is a short time longer, so that I can get him into a position where he must lose a great portion of his army. The rebellion has lost its vitality, and if I am not mistaken, there will be no rebel army of any great dimensions a few weeks hence. Any great catastrophe to any of our armies would, of course, revive the enemy for a short time, but I expect no such thing to happen."

The grand assault by Lee upon Fort Steadman and the adjacent works, in which a momentary success was turned to a decided defeat, was followed by vigorous action on the part of General Grant. He had already prepared the army for a forward movement. The hospitals had been cleared, the camps stripped of superfluous luggage, civilians removed and every step taken to promote the efficiency of the troops. Admiral Farragut, with a powerful fleet of monitors and iron-clads, threatened the approaches to Richmond by the James. The arrival of General Sheridan's cavalry at City Point on the day following Lee's attack on the forts, completed the military arrangements. Abundant information had reached Grant through deserters and otherwise, of the approaching abandonment of Richmond by the rebel army, which its leaders had doubtless for some time regarded as a probable military necessity. He determined to strike while that army was within his reach.

On the 29th of March what proved to be the final movement was begun. General Sheridan's cavalry command had crossed the Appomattox and moved to the rear of the army before Petersburg. A portion of General Ord's Army of the James had also been brought across the river to join the Army of the Potomac. New dispositions were made to hold the lines before Petersburg while General Warren's Fifth Corps and General Humphrey's Second with the cavalry, were assigned to the new military movement, the object of which was the capture of the Southside Railroad, the consequent fall of Petersburg, and isolation of Lee's army of Northern Virginia

Early on the morning of the 29th, General Sheridan started with his cavalry force, moving down the Jerusalem Plank Road towards Ream's Station, on the Weldon Railroad, crossing which he made for Dinwiddie Court House, and occupied the town. The Second and Fifth Corps were meantime sent across Hatcher's Run, to co-operate with his advance on the Boydtown road. On reaching the Quaker road General Griffin's division of the Fifth Corps were met by the enemy and a sharp conflict ensued, resulting in an aggregate loss on each side of about 500. A heavy rain storm now set in, and greatly impeded the prompt movements of the army. During the night there was a heavy bombardment from the enemy's lines in front of Petersburg, but with no material result. On Thursday the 30th, while the storm continued, a junction was effected between Sheridan's and Warren's commands, and the advance was continued with sharp skirmishing towards the enemy's works on the White Oak road, guarding the approaches to the Southside Railroad, their important position being on their extreme right at the junction of several roads known as Five Forks. The successive dispatches forwarded by President Lincoln from City Point to the Secretary of War at Washington, furnish a graphic outline of the continuance of the conflict. On the afternoon of the next day, the 31st, he transmitted the following: " At 12.30 P. M. to-day, General Grant telegraphed me as follows: 'There has been much hard fighting this morning. The enemy drove our left from near Dabney's House back well toward the Boydtown Plank Road. We are now about to take the offensive at that point, and, I hope, will more than recover the lost ground.' Later, he telegraphed again as follows: 'Our troops, after being driven back to the Boydtown Plank Road, turned and drove the enemy in turn, and took the White Oak road, which we now have. This gives us the ground occupied by the enemy this morning. I will send you a rebel flag captured by our troops in driving the enemy back. There have been four flags captured to-day.' Judging by the two points from which General Grant telegraphs, I infer that he moved his headquarters about one mile since he sent the first of the two dispatches." This was followed, on Saturday the 1st of April, by another, which, says Secretary Stanton, in communicating it to the public " shows that the desperate struggle between our forces and the enemy continues undecided, although the advantage appears to be on our side." President Lincoln's telegram was as follows: " Dispatch just received showing that Sheridan, aided by Warren, had, at 2 P. M., pushed the enemy back so as to retake the Five Forks and bring his own headquarters up to F Boisseau's. The Five Forks were barricaded by the enemy, and carried by Diven's division of cavalry. This part of the enemy seem to be now trying to work along the White Oak road, to join the main force in front of Grant, while Sheridan and Warren are pressing them as closely as possible."

This was succeeded the next day, Sunday, April 2, by another from the President, dated City Point, 8.30 A. M. " Last night General Grant telegraphed that General Sheridan, with his cavalry and the Fifth Corps, had captured three brigades of infantry, a train of wagons, and several batteries, the prisoners amounting to several thousand. This morning General Grant having ordered an attack along the whole line, telegraphed as follows: 'Both Wright and Parke got through the enemy's lines. The battle now rages furiously. General Sheridan, with his cavalry, the Fifth Corps, and Miles' division of the Second Corps, which was sent to him this morning, is now sweeping down from the west. All now looks highly favorable. General Ord is engaged, but I have not yet heard the result in his front," Two hours and a-half later the President telegraphs again: "Dispatches are frequently coming in. All is going on finely. Generals Parke, Wright and Ord's lines are extending from the Appomattox to Hatcher's Run. They have all broken through the enemy's intrenched lines, taking some forts, guns and prisoners. Sheridan, with his own cavalry, the Fifth Corps, and part of the Second, is coming in from the west, on the enemy's flank. Wright is already tearing up the Southside Railroad." And again, at 2 o'clock in the afternoon: at 10.45 A. M. General Grant telegraphs as follows: "Every thing has been carried from the left of the Ninth Corps. The Sixth Corps alone captured more than 3,000 prisoners. The Second and Twenty-fourth Corps captured forts, guns and prisoners from the enemy, but I cannot tell the numbers. We are now closing around the works of the line immediately enveloping Petersburg. All looks remarkably well. I have not yet heard from Sheridan. His headquarters have been moved up to Banks' House, near the Boydtown road, about three miles southwest of Petersburg." Still another communication by the President, at 8.30 in the evening, concludes the story of this decisive day. "At 4.30 P. M. to-day, General Grant telegraphs as follows: 'We are now up and have a continuous line of troops, and in a few hours will be intrenched from the Appomattox below Petersburg to the river above. The whole captures since the army started out will not amount to less than twelve thousand (12,000) men, and probably fifty pieces of artillery. I do not know the number of men and guns accurately, however. A portion of Foster's division, Twenty-fourth Corps, made a most gallant charge this afternoon, and captured a very important fort from the enemy with its entire garrison. All seems well with us, and every thing is quiet with us just now.'" The battles of Sunday decided the fate of Richmond. On the forenoon of that day, while President Jefferson Davis was in church in that city, he received a message from General Lee to the effect that his position was no longer tenable, and that Richmond must be evacuated and the army retreat immediately. Preparations were instantly made for abandoning the works and leaving the city. That night the extensive fortifications before Petersburg and Richmond were deserted by the enemy, leaving the long coveted prize a comparatively easy conquest, at the end, to the army of General Grant.

That conquest was announced to the country on the morning of Monday the 3d of April, in the following bulletins; first, from President Lincoln, at 8.30 A. M., to the Secretary of War: "This morning Lieutenant-General Grant reports Petersburg evacuated, and he is confident that Richmond also is. He is pushing forward to cut off, if possible, the retreating rebel army." A second to Major-General Dix at New York, from Secretary Stanton, at 10 A. M.: "It appears from a dispatch of General Weitzel just received by this Department, that our forces under his command are in Richmond, having taken it at 8.15 this morning." An hour later Secretary Stanton sent the following: "General Weitzel telegraphs as follows: 'We took Richmond at 8.15 this morning. I captured many guns. The enemy left in great haste. The city is on fire in one place. Am making every effort to put it out. The people receive us with enthusiastic expressions of joy. General Grant started early this morning with the army toward the Danville road to cut off Lee's retreating army, if possible. President Lincoln has gone to the front.'" The more prominent particulars of the flight of Davis, the evacuation of the city and the entry of Grant's troops are thus related by a correspondent who entered Richmond with the army on Monday: "Richmond has fallen to the arms of the United States, not by a bloody siege, with all its attendant horrors, but by being surrendered. It is a remarkable fact that yesterday General Robert E. Lee sent a dispatch to the war office in Richmond stating that Grant had driven him one mile and a-half, and that he had suffered severely; that he had taken a position which he could not hold, and requested that the city should be evacuated at 12 o'clock, midnight. Soon after midnight Major-General Weitzel was informed of the fact that the enemy in his front intended to evacuate their lines. He was well aware beforehand that they had buried torpedoes in the ground immediately in front of their redoubts, and consequently that any approach toward them in the night would certainly be attended with great risk. At the earliest dawn of day he sent forward a strong skirmish line toward Fort Gillmore, and so thickly were the torpedoes buried, that the main body could only march by single file. The precaution adopted by the rebels to secure the lives of their men in such treacherous ground proved to be most useful to our soldiers, and saved many lives. A thin stick was placed over each torpedo, and a piece of red muslin attached to it. The Second Brigade of the Third Division of the Twenty-fourth Army Corps had the honor of leading the Army of the James into Richmond, under the command of Brigadier-General Ripley. Major-General Weitzel and his staff headed the column. They encountered no opposition whatever. Halting at the confines of the town, the General sent forward Major Stevens and Major Graves with a small squadron of cavalry, to summon the Mayor to surrender the keys. Joseph Mayo, Esq., received them very civilly and handed over the keys at the City Hall at 7 A. M. General Weitzel entered the city at 8 A. M., and it would be utterly useless to attempt to describe the enthusiastic cheers which greeted him. The white and colored population gave him a most hearty welcome. The rebels who had left the city scarcely two hours when he entered, set fire to many of the most important buildings, and at the time I write they are still burning. All the public buildings that contained government stores are burnt. The best portion of Cary and Main Streets is a heap of ashes. Through the exertions of our men, at once detailed to assist, the fire is gradually subsiding. As there were not more than two fire engines available, the only alternative was to pull down adjacent buildings.

"As soon as possible after the arrival of General Weitzel he issued the orders which I send herewith. The office of headquarters is in the Senate House. The General has taken possession of Mr. Jefferson Davis' mansion for a residence. General Devins has taken up his headquarters at Governor Smith's residence. In the state of confusion that naturally attaches to the position, I cannot pretend to give you a correct estimate of what we have captured. The General estimates the guns captured in position on the fortifications—all, I believe, left uninjured—at from four hundred and fifty to five hundred, many of them of heavy calibre. The notorious Libby Prison and Castle Thunder remain untouched. The former is now tenanted by confederate prisoners captured by us this morning, who did not know that their main army had flown. Mr. Jeff. Davis and his family left Richmond on Wednesday for Charlotte, N. C., and it is stated on good authority that they are on their way to Texas. Mr. Davis returned to Richmond, and was in church yesterday, when a dispatch was handed to him from General Lee, stating that the position of affairs was desperate. He left Richmond at once. An immense amount of tobacco, which was stored in Richmond, has been destroyed. It was intended to have moved it away to

Lynchburg, and several hundred boxes were actually in transitu to that place when Sheridan cut the canal and thus interrupted its removal. The offices of the *Enquirer* and the *Dispatch* newspapers are burnt. The State Court House is destroyed. Mayo's Bridge, the Danville Railroad Bridge and the foot-passenger bridge over the James, are all burnt. The powder magazine at Drury Bluff was destroyed last night, and all the gunboats on the James burnt. Three powder magazines in the vicinity of Richmond were exploded early this morning. General Lee and the remains of his army have retreated toward Danville, and I have it upon good authority that they expect to be reinforced by Hardee and make a stand at that place. It is very doubtful whether they will succeed in getting there. A vast amount of suffering has been caused by the fire. The grounds about the Capitol are covered with the household effects of families burnt out. It was an act of useless cruelty on the part of fugitive rebels and is loudly denounced by all who remain here. I omitted to mention that the main column of the army entered Richmond by the Osborne road. The other portion moved more to the right and entered by the Newmarket road. That the falling back of the rebels was precipitated by the tremendous thrashing General Grant gave them on Sunday, is evidenced by the fact that they left all their tents behind them. Mr. Commissioner Ould, in a letter, formally handed over to General Mulford all the papers in his bureau of exchange of prisoners. All the Union prisoners confined in the Libby and Castle Thunder were sent to Boulware Landing yesterday and exchanged. In closing this dispatch I am happy to be able to state that the fires in the different parts of the city have nearly burnt themselves out. The city is perfectly quiet, and great credit is due to Lieutenant-Colonel Manning, the Provost-Marshal, for the energy and firmness he has displayed in the execution of the very onerous duties imposed upon him on this most eventful day."*

The order of General Weitzel alluded to announced the occupation of the city by the armies of the United States under Lieutenant-General Grant, and assured the people of Richmond that "We come to restore to them the blessings of peace, prosperity and freedom, under the flag of the Union." The citizens were requested "to remain for the present quietly within their houses and to avoid all public assemblages or meetings in the public streets." An efficient provost guard was established and martial law proclaimed.

On the 4th, President Lincoln visited Richmond from City Point. Several incidents attending his arrival are thus related by a correspondent at that city. "The most interesting fact to be recorded to-day is the visit of the President to Richmond. Mr. Lincoln, accompanied by his young son and Admiral Porter, arrived at the Rocketts at 2 P. M., in the Malvern, and proceeded at once to the mansion of Ex-President Davis, now the headquarters of Major-General Weitzel. The arrival of the President soon got noised abroad, and the colored population turned out in great force, and for a time blockaded the quarters of the President, cheering vociferously. It was to be expected, that a population that three days since were in slavery, should evince a strong desire to look upon the man whose edict had struck for ever the manacles from their limbs. A considerable number of the white population cheered the President heartily, and but for the order of the Provost-Marshal, issued yesterday, ordering them to remain within their homes quietly for a few days, without doubt there would have been a large addition to the numbers present.

* R. D. Francis' Correspondence, New York *Times*, Senate House, Richmond, April 3, 1865.

After a short interval, the President held a levee—General Devins introduced all the officers present. The President shook hands with each, and received the hearty congratulations of all. The Presidential party attended by Generals Weitzel, Devins, Shepley, and a brilliant staff of officers, then made a tour around the city—drove rapidly around the capitol—stopping for a few moments to admire Crawford's magnificent statue of Washington, in the grounds of the capital, and returned to General Weitzel's headquarters at 5.30. The President and party left Richmond at 6.30 P. M."*

Among the addresses which were made at impromptu popular gatherings in the country on the receipt of the news of the fall of Richmond, two are worthy of preservation for their significance. The first that we shall cite was spoken by Secretary Seward at Washington—a good-humored presentation of familiar points of the protracted struggle: "I thank my fellow-citizens," said he, "for the honor they do me by calling to congratulate me on the fall of Richmond. I am now about writing my foreign dispatches. What shall I tell the Emperor of China? I shall thank him, in your name, for never having permitted a piratical flag to enter the harbors of the empire. What shall I say to the Sultan of Turkey? I shall thank him for always having surrendered rebel insurgents who have taken refuge in his kingdom. What shall I say to the Emperor of the French? I shall say to the Emperor of the French that he can go to-morrow to Richmond and get his tobacco so long held under blockade there, provided the rebels have not used it up. To Lord John Russell I will say, that British merchants will find the cotton exported from our ports under treaty with the United States, cheaper than cotton obtained by running the blockade. As for Earl Russell himself, I need not tell him that this is a war for freedom and national independence, and the rights of human nature, and not a war for empire; and if Great Britain should only be just to the United States, Canada will remain undisturbed by us, so long as she prefers the authority of the noble Queen to voluntary incorporation in the United States. What shall I tell the King of Prussia? I will tell the King of Prussia that the Germans have been faithful to the standard of the Union, as his excellent Minister, Baron Gerolt, has been constant in his friendship to the United States during his long residence in this country. To the Emperor of Austria I shall say that he has proved himself a very wise man, for he told us in the beginning that he had not sympathy with rebellion anywhere. I do not doubt, fellow-citizens, but that at least you accede to the theory by which I have governed myself during the war, namely, that the rebellion will end in ninety days. I have thought this the true theory, because I never knew a physician able to restore his patient to health unless he thought he could work a cure under the most favorable circumstances in ninety days. Finally, if the American people approve, I will say that our motto in peace shall be what our text has been while in war. Every nation is entitled to regulate its own domestic affairs in its own way, and all are bound to conduct themselves so as to promote peace on earth and good will to mankind."

No one had labored more zealously, with more of wearing toil in the service of the country during the last four years than the Secretary of State and few were better entitled to the reward of perseverance in the enjoyment of the result. Unhappily, a day or two after, Secretary Seward was seriously injured by an accident incurred by the horses of his carriage taking fright. In attempting to escape, he struck the ground; his arm

* R. D. Francis, to the New York *Times*, Richmond April 4

was broken near the shoulder joint and his lower jaw was fractured. President Lincoln, hastening from Richmond, found on his arrival at Washington the Secretary laid up from this disaster, which largely called forth the sympathy of the public.

The other speech at Washington to which we alluded was made by Andrew Johnson, the Vice-President of the United States. It soon acquired an importance undreamt of at the time it was uttered. "We are now, my friends," said he, "winding up a rebellion—a great effort that has been made by bad men to overthrow the Government of the United States, a government founded upon free principles and cemented by the best blood of the Revolution. You must indulge me in making one single remark in connection with myself. At the time that the traitors in the Senate of the United States plotted against the Government, and entered into a conspiracy more foul, more execrable, and more odious than that of Cataline against the Romans, I happened to be a member of that body, and, as to loyalty, stood solitary and alone among the Senators from the Southern States. I was then and there called upon to know what I would do with such traitors, and I want to report my reply here. I said, if we had Andrew Jackson he would hang them as high as Haman. But as he is no more, and sleeps in his grave in his own beloved State, where traitors and treason have even insulted his tomb and the very earth that covers his remains, humble as I am, when you ask what I would do, my reply is, I would arrest them; I would try them; I would convict them, and I would hang them. As humble as I am and have been, I have pursued but one undeviating course. All that I have—life, limb and property—have been put at the disposal of the country in this great struggle. I have been in camp, I have been in the field, I have been everywhere where this great rebellion was; I have pursued it until I believe I can now see its termination. Since the world began, there has never been a rebellion of such gigantic proportions, so infamous in character, so diabolical in motive, so entirely disregardful of the laws of civilized war. It has introduced the most savage mode of warfare ever practiced upon the earth. I will repeat here a remark, for which I have been in no small degree censured. What is it, allow me to ask, that has sustained the nation in this great struggle? The cry has been, you know, that our Government was not strong enough for a time of rebellion; that in such a time she would have to contend against internal weakness as well as internal foes. We have now given the world evidence that such is not the fact, and when the rebellion shall have been crushed out, and the nation shall once again have settled down in peace, our Government shall rest upon a more enduring basis than ever before. But, my friends, in what has the great strength of this Government consisted? Has it been in one man power? Has it been in some autocrat, or in some one man who held absolute government? No! I thank God I have it in my power to proclaim the great truth that this Government has derived its strength from the American people. They have issued the edict; they have exercised the power that has resulted in the overthrow of the rebellion, and there is not another Government upon the face of the earth that could have withstood the shock. We can now congratulate ourselves that we possess the strongest, the freest and the best Government the world ever saw. Thank God that we have lived through this trial! and that, looking in your intelligent faces here to-day, I can announce to you the great fact that Petersburg, the outpost of the strong citadel, has been occupied by our brave and gallant officers and our untiring, invincible soldiers! And not content with that, they have captured the citadel itself, the stronghold of traitors. Richmond is ours! and is now occupied by the forces of the United States! Her gates have been entered, and the glorious Stars and Stripes, the emblem of Union, of power and of supremacy, now float over the enemy's capitol! In the language of another, let that old flag rise higher and higher, until it meets the sun in its coming, and let the parting day linger to play upon its ample folds. It is the flag of your country. It is your flag, it is my flag, and it bids defiance to all the nations of the earth, and to the encroachments of all the Powers combined. It is not my intention to make any imprudent remarks or allusions; but the hour will come when those nations that exhibited toward us such insolence and improper interference in the midst of our adversity, and, as they supposed, of our weakness, will learn that this is a government of the people, possessing power enough to make itself felt and respected. In the midst of our rejoicing we must not forget to drop a tear for those gallant fellows who have shed their blood that their Government might triumph. We cannot forget them when we review the many bloody battle-fields of the war. the new-made graves, our maimed friends and relatives who have left their limbs, as it were, on the enemy's soil, and others who have been consigned to their long, narrow houses with no winding-sheet save their blankets saturated with their blood. One word more and I have done. It is this: I am in favor of leniency; but, in my opinion, evil doers should be punished. [Cries of 'That's so!'] Treason is the highest crime known in the catalogue of crimes; and for him that is guilty of it—for him that is willing to lift his impious hand against the authority of the nation—I would say death is too easy a punishment. My notion is that treason must be made odious, that traitors must be punished and impoverished, their social power broken; that they must be made to feel the penalty of their crimes. You, my friends, have traitors in your very midst, and treason needs rebuke and punishment here as well as elsewhere. It is not the men in the field who are the greatest traitors. It is the men who have encouraged them to imperil their lives, while they themselves have remained at home expending their means and exerting all their power to overthrow the Government. Hence I say this: 'The halter for intelligent, influential traitors.' But to the honest boy, to the deluded man who has been deceived into the rebel ranks, I would extend leniency. I would say, Return to your allegiance, renew your support to the Government and become a good citizen; but the leaders I would hang. I hold, too, that wealthy traitors should be made to remunerate those men who have suffered as a consequence of their crime—Union men who have lost their property, who have been driven from their homes, beggars and wanderers among strangers. It is well to talk about these things here, to-day, in addressing the well-informed persons who compose this audience. You can, to a very great extent, aid in moulding public opinion and in giving it a proper direction. Let us commence the work. We have put down these traitors in arms; let us put them down in law, in public judgment and in the morals of the world. Permit me now to propose three cheers for the capture of Richmond."

The pursuit of the flying enemy was promptly undertaken by General Grant who, leaving Richmond behind him, kept the field in person. The city was occupied on Monday; on Tuesday morning at half-past 3, Grant, who was with General Ord's column of the Army of the James, sent a dispatch to Secretary Stanton from Sutherland

Station on the Southside road, ten miles west from Petersburg announcing that "General Sheridan picked up 1,200 prisoners to-day, and from 300 to 500 more had been gathered by our troops. The majority of the arms that were left in the hands of Lee's army are now scattered between Richmond and where his troops now are. The country is also full of stragglers. The line of retreat is marked with artillery, ammunition, burned or charred wagons, caissons, ambulances, etc."

At the close of the day Grant further sent word to the Secretary of War: "The army is pushing forward in the hope of overtaking or dispersing the remainder of Lee's army. Sheridan with his cavalry and the Fifth Corps is between this and the Appomattox, General Meade, with the Second and Sixth, following. General Ord is following the line of the Southside Railroad. All of the enemy that retains any thing like organization have gone north of the Appomattox, and are apparently heading for Lynchburg. Their losses have been very heavy. Houses through the country are nearly all used as hospitals for wounded men. In every direction I hear of rebel soldiers pushing for home—some in large, some in small squads, and generally without arms. The cavalry have pursued so closely that the enemy have been forced to destroy probably the greater part of the transportation, caissons and munitions of war. The number of prisoners captured yesterday will exceed 2,000. From the 20th of March to the present time our loss in killed, wounded and captured will not probably reach 7,000, of whom 1,500 to 2,000 were captured, and many but slightly wounded. I shall continue the pursuit as long as there appears to be any use in it."

The next day, the 5th, General Grant announced the progress of the pursuit from his advance headquarters at Nottoway Court House, "Last night General Sheridan was on the Danville Railroad south of the Amelia Court House, and sent word to General Meade, who was following with the Second and Sixth Corps by what is known as the River Road, that if the troops could be got up in time he had hopes of capturing or dispersing the whole of Lee's army. I am moving with the left wing, commanded by General Ord, by the Cox, or direct Burkesville road. We will be to-night at or near Burkesville. I have had no communication with Sheridan or Meade to-day; but hope to hear very soon that they have come up with and captured, or broken up, the balance of the Army of Northern Virginia. In every direction we hear of the men of that army going home, generally without arms. Sheridan reports Lee at Amelia Court House to-day."

General Lee had taken the Danville road on which Jefferson Davis with his escort had preceded him escaping with a booty of several millions plundered from the Richmond banks into North Carolina. It was his expectation doubtless to effect a junction of Lee's and John ston's armies, and possibly make a stand at Danville; but this was prevented by the activity of the forces under Grant, who, with the advantage of a shorter line reached Burkesville, the junction of the Southside and Danville roads, before Lee, on his way thither, had traversed the adjacent country.

While General Ord was making his way on the direct line of the railway General Sheridan, with his cavalry force and Warren's Fifth Corps, was traversing Amelia County on the road to Lynchburg. They had several sharp skirmishes on the 3d with the enemy whom they pursued with vigor. Pushing rapidly forward next day, on the 5th, Sheridan's forces was in possession of Jettersville, a station above Burkesville on the Danville road, in near proximity to Lee's army at Amelia Court House. On his arrival at Jettersville at 3 P. M. of the 5th, General Sheridan sent the following dispatch to General Grant: General—I send you the inclosed letter, which will give you an idea of the condition of the enemy and their whereabouts. I sent General Davies' brigade this morning around on my left flank. He captured, at Fame's Cross Roads, five pieces of artillery, about 200 wagons, eight or nine battle-flags, and a number of prisoners. The Second Army Corps is now coming up. I wish you were here yourself. I feel confident of capturing the Army of Northern Virginia if we exert ourselves. I see no escape for Lee. I will put all my cavalry out on our left flank, except McKenzie, who is now on the right."

The intercepted letter inclosed read: "Amelia Court House, April 5. Dear Mamma—Our army is ruined, I fear. We are all safe as yet. Shyron left us sick; John Taylor is well; saw him yesterday. We are in line of battle this evening. General Robert Lee is in the field, near us. My trust is still in the justice of our cause and in God. General Hill is killed. I saw Murray a few moments since. Bernard Terry, it is said, was taken prisoner, but managed to get out. I send this by a negro, I see passing up the railroad to Michlenburg. Love to all. Your devoted son, W. B. Taylor, Colonel."

On the receipt of this in the evening General Grant immediately dispatched a force to occupy Burkesville nine miles distant, while he himself rode over and joined Sheridan at Jettersville. Lee being thus intercepted on his route was compelled to turn his course westwardly in the direction of Lynchburg. He was moving toward Farmville on the 6th, when he was overtaken by Sheridan, brought to action and defeated. At night Sheridan reported to Grant a dispatch which was forwarded to Washington from City Point by President Lincoln announcing a decided victory. "I have the honor," he wrote, "to report that the enemy made a stand at the intersection of the Burke's Station Road with the road upon which they were retreating. I attacked them with two divisions of the Sixth Army Corps, and routed them handsomely, making a connection with the cavalry. I am still pressing on with the cavalry and infantry. Up to the present time we have captured Generals Ewell, Kershaw, Button. Corse, DeBare and Custis Lee, several thousand prisoners, fourteen pieces of artillery, with caissons, and a large number of wagons. If the thing is pressed I think Lee will surrender."

This was followed by a dispatch from General Meade, with further details and the events of the day. "At daylight this morning," he wrote, "I moved the Second, Fifth and Sixth Army Corps along the railroad, in the direction of Amelia Court House. Soon after moving reliable intelligence was received that the enemy was moving toward Farmville. The direction of the Second and Fifth Army Corps was immediately changed from a northerly to a north-westerly direction, and the directing corps, the Second, moving on Deatonville, and the Fifth, heretofore in the centre, moved on the right of the Second, and the Sixth facing about and moving by the left flank, taking position on left of the Second. It was understood that the cavalry would operate on the extreme left. The changes were promptly made. The Second Army Corps soon becoming engaged with the enemy, near Deatonville, drove him by the right across Sailor Creek to the Appomattox. The Fifth Army Corps made a long march, but its position prevented its striking the enemy's column before it had passed. The Sixth Army Corps came up with the enemy about 4 P. M., and in conjunction with the Second on its right and cavalry on its left, attacked and routed the enemy, capturing many prisoners, among them Lieutenant-General Ewell and General Custis Lee. I transmit dispatches both from Generals Humphreys and Wright, which, in justice to these distinguished officers and the gallant corps they command, I beg may be sent to the War Department for immediate publication. It is impossible at this moment to give any estimate in the casualties on either side, or of the number of prisoners taken, but it is evident to-day's work is going to be one of the most important of the recent brilliant operations. The pursuit will be continued as soon as the men have a little rest. Griffin, with the Fifth Army Corps, will be moved by the left, and Wright and Humphreys continue the direct pursuit as long as it promises success." The dispatches of Generals Humphreys and Wright, referred to by General Meade, were as follows. From General Humphreys: "Second Army Corps, Thursday, April 6, 7.30 P. M. Major-General A. S. Webb—Our last fight, just before dark, at Sailor's Creek, gave us two guns, three flags and a considerable number of prisoners, two hundred wagons, seventy ambulances, with mules and horses to about one-half of the wagons and ambulances. There are between thirty and fifty wagons in addition abandoned and destroyed along the road, some battery wagons, forges and limbers. I have already reported to you the capture of one gun, two flags and some prisoners, and the fact that the road for over two miles is strewed with tents, baggage, cooking utensils, some ammunition and material of all kinds. The wagons are across the approach to the bridges, and it will take some time to clear it. The enemy is in position on the heights beyond with artillery. The bridge is partially destroyed, and the approaches on the other side are of soft bottom land. We cannot advance to-morrow in the same manner we have to-day. As soon as I get my troops up a little (we are considerably mixed) I might push a column down to the road to deploy it, but it is evident I cannot follow rapidly during the night." General Wright's dispatch was dated: "Headquarters Sixth Army Corps, Thursday, April 6, 10 P. M. Major-General Webb. Chief of Staff, Army of Potomac—In pursuance of instructions of this morning from Major-General Meade, I moved from Jeffersville by the shortest practicable road to the left of the Deatonville, with the object of there taking position on the left of the Second Army Corps, striking the road running from Deatonville to Burke's Station, at a point a little to the southward of the former place. I found that the Second Army Corps was engaged to the front and right, and the cavalry heavily to my left. Moving down the road towards Burke's Station, perhaps a mile, and turning sharp to the right, I proceeded across toward a nearly parallel road, on which the enemy was moving, and along which he had thrown up a line of intrenchments. As soon as the leading division, General Seymour's, could be formed, it was moved upon the road held by the enemy, which was carried. Then, turning the left, it was advanced down the road against a pretty strong resistance. By this time, Wheaton's division was put in position, as rapidly as possible on Seymour's left. The lines were again advanced and we swept down the road for a distance of about two miles. Arriving at a deep and difficult creek we found the enemy had re-formed his line on the opposite side, where we attacked and drove him to a point, a distance of half a mile further. In the first attack a portion of the cavalry operated on our right flank. In its subsequent attack the mass of cavalry operated on our left and right flank of the enemy. The result has been a complete success. The combined forces captured five general officers; among them Generals Ewell and Custis Lee and a large number of other prisoners. I shall go in camp about two miles beyond this point and await instructions. The First and Third Divisions, Wheaton's and

Seymour's, and the artillery engaged to-day, behaved splendidly. The corps has nobly supported the reputation it earned on the 2d instant, as well as upon its many previous hard-fought battle-fields." General Grant promptly availed himself of this brilliant success, in pushing the enemy. On the 8th, the Secretary of War thus announced his progress: "A telegram from General Grant dated this day, at 12 o'clock noon, at Farmville, 16 miles west of Burke's Station, says that the enemy have been pushed from the road toward Danville, and are now pursued toward Lynchburg, and that he is very confident of receiving the surrender of Lee, and what remains of his army." The confidence expressed by Sheridan and thus repeated by Grant, was not rashly entertained. The latter, indeed, had already, without checking his pursuit of the rebel army, addressed on the 7th the following letter to General R. E. Lee: "General, Commanding Confederate States Armies—The result of the last week must convince you of the hopelessness of further resistance on the part of the Army of Northern Virginia in this struggle. I feel that it is so, and regard it as my duty to shift from myself the responsibility of any further effusion of blood, by asking of you the surrender of that portion of the Confederate States Army, known as the Army of Northern Virginia. Very respectfully, your obedient servant, U. S. Grant, Lieutenant-General, Commanding Armies of the United States." To this Lee, the same day, replied: "April 7, 1865. General—I have received your note of this date. Though not entirely of the opinion you express of the hopelessness of further resistance on the part of the Army of Northern Virginia, I reciprocate your desire to avoid useless effusion of blood, and therefore, before considering your proposition, ask the terms you will offer, on condition of its surrender. R. E. Lee, General. To Lieutenant-General U. S. Grant, Commanding Armies of the United States." The next day General Grant wrote to General Lee: "Your note of last evening in reply to mine of same date, asking the conditions on which I will accept the surrender of the Army of Northern Virginia, is just received. In reply I would say that peace being my first desire, there is but one condition that I insist upon, viz.: That the men surrendered shall be disqualified for taking up arms again against the Government of the United States until properly exchanged. I will meet you, or designate officers to meet any officers you may name for the same purpose, at any point agreeable to you, for the purpose of arranging definitely the terms upon which the surrender of the Army of Northern Virginia will be received. Very respectfully, your obedient servant, U. S. Grant, Lieutenant-General, Commanding Armies of the United States." To this General Lee replied: "General—I received, at a late hour, your note of to-day, in answer to mine of yesterday. I did not intend to propose the surrender of the Army of Northern Virginia, but to ask the terms of your proposition. To be frank, I do not think the emergency has arisen to call for the surrender. But as the restoration of peace should be the sole object of all, I desire to know whether your proposals would tend to that end. I cannot, therefore meet you with a view to surrender the Army of Northern Virginia, but as far as your proposition may affect the Confederate State forces under my command, and tend to the restoration of peace. I should be pleased to meet you at 10 A. M. to-morrow, on the old stage road to Richmond, between the picket lines of the two armies. Very respectfully, your obedient servant, R. E. Lee, General C. S. A." General Grant answered on the 9th: "General R. E. Lee, Commanding C. S. A.: General—Your note of yesterday is received. As I have no authority to treat on the subject of peace, the meeting proposed for 10 A. M. to-day could lead to no good. I will state, however, General, that I am equally anxious for peace with yourself; and the whole North entertain the same feeling. The terms upon which peace can be had are understood. By the South laying down their arms, they will hasten that most desirable event, save thousands of human lives, and hundreds of millions of property not yet destroyed. Sincerely hoping that all our difficulties may be settled without the loss of another life, I subscribe myself, very respectfully, your obedient servant, U. S. Grant, Lieutenant-General United States Army." General Lee's reply the same morning was: "General—I received your note of this morning, on the picket line, whither I had come to meet you and ascertain definitely what terms were embraced in your proposition of yesterday with reference to the surrender of this army. I now request an interview in accordance with the offer contained in your letter of yesterday for that purpose. Very respectfully, your obedient servant, R. E. Lee, General. To Lieutenant-General Grant, Commanding United States Armies." General Grant immediately answered: "General R. E. Lee, Commanding Confederate States Armies —Your note of this date is but this moment, 11.50 A. M., received. In consequence of my having passed from the Richmond and Lynchburg road to the Farmville and Lynchburg road, I am at this writing about four miles west of Walter's Church, and will push forward to the front for the purpose of meeting you. Notice sent to me, on this road, where you wish the interview to take place, will meet me. Very respectfully, your obedient servant, U. S. Grant, Lieutenant-General."

A meeting was now accordingly arranged under a flag of truce at Appomattox Court House, where, at about 2 o'clock P. M., the two Generals met at the house of Mr. Wilmer McLean, where the agreement of surrender was engrossed and signed in accordance with the following final correspondence on the subject: "Appomattox Court House, April 9, 1865. General R. E. Lee, Commanding Confederate States Army. —In accordance with the substance of my letters to you of the 8th inst., I propose to receive the surrender of the Army of Northern Virginia on the following terms, to wit: Rolls of all the officers and men to be made in duplicate, one copy to be given to an officer designated by me, the other to be retained by such officers as you may designate. The officers to give their individual paroles not to take arms against the Government of the United States until properly exchanged, and each company or regimental commander sign a like parole for the men of their commands. The arms, artillery and public property to be parked and stacked and turned over to the officers appointed by me to receive them. This will not embrace the side-arms of the officers, nor their private horses or baggage. This done, each officer and man will be allowed to return to their homes, not to be disturbed by United States authority so long as they observe their parole and the laws in force where they reside. Very respectfully, U. S. Grant, Lieutenant-General." To this General Lee finally replied: "Headquarters Army of Northern Virginia, April 9, 1865. Lieutenant-General Grant, Commanding U. S. A.: General—I have received your letter of this date, containing the terms of surrender of the Army of Northern Virginia, as proposed by you. As they are substantially the same as those expressed in your letter of the 8th inst. they are accepted. I will proceed to designate the proper officers to carry the stipulations into effect. Very respectfully, your obedient servant, R. E. Lee, General." The personal circumstances of the surrender are thus narrated by a correspondent* who obtained his information from an officer who was an eye-witness of the whole scene. "It will be recollected," he writes, "that General Grant's first letter to Lee was dated on the 7th, Friday, the day of the battle of Farmville, and the correspondence was kept up during the following day and up to 11 o'clock on Sunday, as already published. In response to General Grant's last letter, General Lee appeared on the picket line of the Second Corps, Mile's division, with a letter addressed to General Meade, requesting a cessation of hostilities while he considered General Grant's terms of surrender. General Meade replied that he had no authority to accede to the request, but that he would wait two hours before making an attack. In the mean time General Grant sent word to General Meade that he would be up in half an hour, and the matter was turned over to him. A flag of truce proceeded to Appomattox Court House shortly after noon, and at about 2 o'clock P. M. the two Generals met at the house of Mr. Wilmer McLean. General Lee was attended by General Marshal, his Adjutant-General; General Grant, by Colonel Parker, one of his chief Aids-de-Camp. The two Generals met and greeted each other with dignified courtesy, and proceeded at once to the business before them. General Lee immediately alluded to the conditions of the surrender, characterized them as exceedingly lenient, and said he would gladly leave all the details to General Grant's own discretion. General Grant stated the terms of the parole; that the arms should be stacked, the artillery parked, and the supplies and munitions turned over to him, the officers retaining their side-arms, horses and personal effects. General Lee promptly assented to the conditions, and the agreement of surrender was engrossed and signed by General Lee at half-past 3 o'clock. General Lee asked General Grant for an interpretation of the phrase "personal effects," and said that many of his cavalrymen owned their own horses. General Grant said he construed it to mean that the horses must be turned over to the United States Government. General Lee admitted the correctness and justice of the interpretation, when General Grant said he would instruct his officers to allow those men who owned their horses to retain them, as they would need them for the purpose of tilling their farms. General Lee expressed a great sense of gratification for such a generous consideration, and said it would have a very good effect. He subsequently expressed a hope that each soldier might be furnished with a certificate of his parole, as evidence to prevent him from being forced into the army until regularly exchanged. General Grant assented to the suggestion, and the printing presses were soon put to work to print the documents required.

In regard to the strength of his army, General Lee said he had no idea of the number of men that he should be able to deliver up. There had been so many engagements, and such heavy losses from desertion and other causes within the past few days, and the retreat so rapid, that no regular morning reports had been made since leaving Petersburg; but it is generally believed by the best informed officers that Lee surrenders eighteen to twenty thousand men. Of the army horses, wagons, etc., there is yet no official account. General Lee informed General Grant that his men were short of provisions, whereupon General Grant ordered twenty-five thousand rations to be distributed to them. Thus substantially ended the interview. Both Generals were the very impersonation of dignity and courtesy in their bearing. Lee is in fine health, and though apparently impressed with the vital effect and importance of

* Mr. L. L Crounse, of the New York *Times*.

the act he was performing, he was cheerful and pleasant in his demeanor. The house where the stipulations were signed was a fair brick structure, with neat grounds, and quite neatly furnished. The room in which the interview took place was a comfortable parlor, about eighteen by twenty feet, and adorned by the usual furnishing common to the average of Virginia houses. Both Generals were attired in full uniform. Lee wore a very fine sword. Grant had no side-arms, having left camp the day previous, with the intention of being gone but a few hours, but on the contrary being gone all night. When the two Generals first met they were attended only by the staff officers already mentioned; but during the interview, several of our officers entered and were introduced to General Lee, who received them cordially and made no objections to their presence. They were Major-Generals Ord and Sheridan, Brevet Major-General Ingalls, Brigadier-Generals Williams, Rawlins and Barnard, Lieutenant-Colonels Barker, Dent, Badeau, Bowers, A. A. G. Porter, Babcock and Captain Lincoln. Tal. P. Shaffner, Esq., was the only civilian present. It should be said that General Grant had anticipated the surrender for several days, and had resolved beforehand not to require the same formalities which are required in a surrender between the forces of two foreign nations or belligerent powers; that they were our own people, and to exact no conditions for the mere purpose of humiliation.

"After the interview, General Lee returned to his own camp, about half a mile distant, where his leading officers were assembled awaiting his return. He announced the result and the terms, whereupon they expressed great satisfaction at the leniency of the conditions. They then approached him in order of rank, shook hands, expressing satisfaction at his course and their regret at parting, all shedding tears on the occasion. The fact of surrender and the liberal terms were then announced to the troops, and when General Lee appeared among them he was loudly cheered. On Monday, between 9 and 10 o'clock A. M., General Grant and staff rode out in the direction of the rebel lines, and on a hill just beyond the court house, where a full view of the rebel army could be obtained, General Lee was met, attended by but one staff officer and orderlies. The Generals halted, and, seated on their horses, conversed for nearly an hour upon the prospects of the future, each seeming to realize the mighty influence which the events of the present were to have upon it. General Lee signified very emphatically his desire for a total cessation of hostilities, and indicated his intention to do all in his power to effect that end. The best of good feeling prevailed, and this was the last interview between the two commanders. General Grant returned to McLean's house, and soon after Generals Longstreet, Gordon, Pickett and Heth, with a number of staff officers, arrived, and after recognitions and introductions, an hour of very friendly intercourse took place, during which many scenes and incidents of bygone college days and days of service together in the regular Army were revived and retold with much good nature. General Grant gave General Lee and his principal officers passes to proceed whither they wished. The parties then separated, and early on Tuesday morning General Grant and staff left the scene of the great event for their headquarters at City Point, arriving at 4.30 A. M. to-day. General Meade was left in command to superintend the details of the surrender, which would occupy several days, the work of providing each man and officer with an individual parole being a slow and tedious one; part of them are written and part printed by the little printing presses which accompany the headquarters.

"Thus, in exactly two weeks, to almost

an hour, from the time General Grant and staff broke up their headquarters at City Point for the spring campaign, they return with the spring campaign not only complete, but the entire opposing army destroyed, and the war substantially closed. The complete character of the destruction of Lee's army thus accomplished, forcibly appears from these facts, viz.: That when the operations began two weeks ago, his army numbered not less than 65,000 men; that we have captured from him 25,000 prisoners; that his killed and wounded are not less than 14,000; and that the balance of the army deserted on the retreat, or fell into our hands at the surrender. The congratulations at headquarters were very hearty, as the various gentlemen of the staff appeared at their old homes, and as commemorative of their triumphant return, Brady, the eminent photographer of New York, preserved the group, generals and all, for the admiration of all their friends in this and future generations."

Sunday, the 9th of April (Palm Sunday), was the memorable day on which this surrender of Lee's army was effected—a surrender which, with the fall of the rebel capital, virtually ended the existence of the confederacy as a military and civil power. The number of men paroled of Lee's army was 26,115; 15,918 small arms were surrendered; 159 cannon; 71 colors, wagons and caissons, estimated at about 1,100, and horses and mules at 4,000.

The announcement of Lee's surrender was made to the country by Secretary Stanton, in a telegram, dated 9 o'clock, on the evening of the 9th, in the following simple terms: "This Department has received the official report of the surrender, this day, of General Lee and his army to Lieutenant-General Grant, on the terms proposed by General Grant."

To General Grant the Secretary sent the following message from the War Department, about half an hour later: "Lieutenant-General Grant—Thanks be to Almighty God for the great victory with which He has this day crowned you and the gallant armies under your command! The thanks of this Department and of the Government, and of the people of the United States—their reverence and honor have been deserved—will be rendered to you and the brave and gallant officers and soldiers of your army for all time." In commemoration of the event the Secretary of War ordered a salute of 200 guns to be fired at the headquarters of every Army and Department, and at every post and arsenal in the United States, and at the Military Academy at West Point, on the day of the receipt of this order.

While General Sherman was entering North Carolina from the south, General Stoneman, under orders from General Thomas in Tennessee, co-operating in the grand movement, was penetrating the State from the west. Leaving Knoxville at the head of an important cavalry column on the 16th of March, he sent forward detachments of his force on the line of the East Tennessee Railroad, which accomplished their work of cutting off the communications of the enemy, destroying bridges and approaching to the immediate vicinity of Lynchburg in Virginia. With the main body of his forces meanwhile, General Stoneman struck for Greensboro' on the North Carolina Railroad. "Arrived near Salem, North Carolina," says he, in his subsequent report to General Thomas, dated Camp at Statersville, N. C., April 13, "I detailed Palmer's brigade to destroy the bridges between Danville and Greensboro' and between Greensboro' and Yadkin River, and the large depots of supplies along the road. This duty was performed with considerable fighting, the capture of 400 prisoners, and to my entire satisfaction. With the other two brigades (Brown's and Miller's) and the artillery, under the command of

Lieutenant Reagan, we pushed for Salisbury, where we found about 3,000 troops, under command of Major-General W. M. Gardiner, and fourteen pieces of artillery, under the command of Colonel (late Lieutenant-General) Pemberton. The whole formed behind Grant's Creek, about ten miles and a half from Salisbury. As soon as a proper disposition could be made, I ordered a general charge upon the entire line, and the result was the capture of the whole 14 pieces of artillery, 1,364 prisoners, including 55 officers. All the artillery, and 1,104 prisoners are now with us. The remainder of the force was chased through and several miles beyond the town, but scattered and escaped into the woods. We remained at Salisbury two days, during which time we destroyed fifteen miles of track and the bridges toward Charlotte, then moved to this point. From here we shall move to the south side of the Catawba River, and be in position to operate toward Charlotte and Columbia, or upon the flank of an army moving south. The following is a partial list of the public property captured north of Salisbury and destroyed by us: 4 large cotton factories and about 7,000 bales of cotton; 4 large magazines, containing 10,000 stand of small arms and accoutrements; 1,000,000 rounds of small arm ammunition, 1,600 rounds of fixed artillery ammunition and 7,000 pounds of powder; 35,000 bushels of corn, 50,000 bushels of wheat, 160,000 pounds of cured bacon; 100,000 suits of gray uniforms and clothing, 250,000 army blankets, 20,000 pounds of harness leather, 10,000 pounds of saltpetre; also a very large amount of sugar, salt, rice and other stores, and medical supplies valued by the rebel medical directors at $100,000 in gold. In addition to the arsenals at Salisbury, a military shop was being fitted up, and was filled with machinery sent from Raleigh and Richmond, all of which was destroyed. The depots along the route traversed by our various parties have furnished us with abundance. The number of horses and mules captured and taken along the road I have no means of estimating. I can say, however, that we are much better mounted than when we left Knoxville. We have a surplus of led animals, and sufficient besides to haul off all our captives, mount a portion of the prisoners and about a thousand contrabands, and this after crossing Stone Mountains once, and the Blue Ridge three times, and a march made by headquarters, since the 29th of last month, of 500 miles and much more by portions of the command. The rapidity of our movements, in almost every instance, caused our advanced guard to herald our approach, and make the surprise complete." The vigor of General Stoneman's operations rendered Grant's success in Virginia the more certain, and in co-operation with the army of General Sherman secured the early surrender of Johnston in North Carolina.

CHAPTER CXIII.

MILITARY OPERATIONS IN ALABAMA. CAPTURE OF MOBILE. WILSON'S CAVALRY EXPEDITION. MARCH, APRIL, 1865.

WHILE General Sherman was pursuing his triumphant course northwardly through the Carolinas and General Grant was patiently awaiting the decisive moment of action before Richmond, the last stronghold of the enemy to the east of the Mississippi, the well fortified city of Mobile was being vigorously besieged by a combination of the national forces. After the capture and occupation of Wilmington and Charleston in February, Mobile remained the last of the coast cities in the possession of the enemy. Its importance as a commercial port had of course been destroyed by the capture in the previous summer of the forts at the entrance of the harbor. But the city, protected by the obstructions in the upper shallow waters of the bay, by the natural difficulties of approach, and by a chain of important fortifications on the land side, garrisoned by a band of resolute defenders under General D. H. Maury, still, after six months had passed, defied assault. Its further resistance, however, was hopeless in the face of the co-operating Union forces, the powerful fleet of Admiral Thatcher and supporting corps of General Granger in front, and the commands of Generals Smith and Steele, the whole under the command of General Canby, approaching it from the east and west, and the column of General Wilson's cavalry sweeping through the State, cutting off its supplies and communication with the North. Mobile was evidently a doomed city, yet its surrender was not secured without a series of determined efforts, of great gallantry on the part of the investing forces. The movement of troops destined for the assault commenced in General Canby's department of the Gulf, in the latter part of March. The corps of General A. J. Smith had, in the previous month, been detached from General Thomas' Army of the Tennessee and joined by a division of cavalry under General Knipe, had descended the Mississippi and encamped in the vicinity of New Orleans. There it awaited the preparation of a force of cavalry which General Thomas was organizing to be placed under command of General Wilson to sweep the State of Alabama from the north. General Granger's Thirteenth Corps meanwhile was on hand waiting for reinforcements at Mobile Point at the entrance to the harbor, whither General A. J. Smith's corps was brought in transports to Dauphin Island by the 20th of March. The cavalry marched overland from New Orleans. A division, under General Steele, with a colored division and two brigades of white troops, about the same time left Pensacola on an overland march to the scene of operations where the decisive conflict was to be fought to the east of Mobile in gaining possession of Spanish Fort and its line of works which guarded the channel and immediate approach to the city by the river. The rendezvous of the several corps was at a station on Fish River, a stream which empties into Bon Secour Bay, a cove on the east side of Mobile Bay. General Granger's corps moved thither by land from Mobile Point, while General Smith's corps crossed the bay from Dauphin Island on transports. A correspondent who was with the latter, describes the passage up the stream. "On striking the mouth of Fish River, we looked," says he, "for torpedoes and guerrillas; but, on the contrary, eager multitudes of blacks and whites, of both sexes, of all ages and conditions, flocked to the shores, and rent the very air with their vociferations of joy. In many cases, in all probability, these manifestations were of a bogus character; but on the whole it is my impression they were sincere. This is one of the most curious streams I have ever been upon. The water is deep enough for the largest boats that float, but it is so very narrow that boats over 280 feet in length could not turn around; it is also so very crooked that many of the transports were obliged to run their bow into shore, and then throw a line to the opposite bank, and then pull around. The people along the shore actually were wonder-struck; and why shouldn't they have been, to see some of the most gorgeous and luxurious floating palaces of the Mississippi wandering such a stream. The condition of the land, upon either side of the river, is of a marshy nature, generally. There were, however, some few pretty farms under a high state of cultivation. Contrabands in great numbers stood along the shores, many of whom jumped upon our boats as they passed along. One of the great peculiarities of the forests upon either side is the great number of eagles and eagles' nests, many of the latter being larger than a cart wheel." The position of the army at its camping ground on Fish River was sixteen miles below the Spanish fort, and about thirty from Mobile. Twelve miles to the northeast of Mobile on the Tensaw River, was the small town of Blakely, which was defended by extensive works. The movement of the troops from Fish River, with the subsequent military operations, are presented in an interesting narrative by Mr. Benjamin C. Truman, the able correspondent of the New York *Times* already cited. "On the 25th March", he writes, "the Thirteenth Corps moved up the Belle Rose road on the left, and the Sixteenth Corps moved up the Blakely road on the right, proceeded about eight miles and went into camp. On the next day, the 26th, both corps again started, and fetched up before noon, after a little skirmishing, the Thirteenth in front of Spanish Fort, and the Sixteenth about four miles from the works of Blakely. The next morning, Monday, March 27, General Canby, discovering that it would be advisable, if not absolutely necessary, to reduce Spanish Fort before turning on Blakely, ordered McArthur's and Carr's divisions of the Sixteenth Corps to retrograde four miles, and take up a position in front of Spanish Fort, on the right, leaving Garrard's division to keep up a bold front upon the Blakely road, until Steele should arrive. Before 10 o'clock Spanish Fort was completely invested on the land side, Carr's division of the Sixteenth Corps on the right, resting its extreme on Bayou Minnette, and Benton's division of the Thirteenth Corps on the left, its extreme touching at Belle Rose. A few hours' skirmishing developed the fact that Spanish Fort, and a neighboring work called Fort Alexis, were hard nuts to crack. Before dark a terrific cannonading was going on on both sides, which was kept up all night, the enemy's gunboats and two forts in the bay participating. From this time until the fall of Spanish Fort, an incessant cannonade and musketry fire was kept up by both sides. During the two weeks' engagement, new guns of a heavy calibre were mounted every day, until at last some 16 mortars, 20 siege guns and 6 batteries of field artillery were bearing upon the enemy's stronghold. Our men were subjected to the hottest fire, for a while, I think, of the war, from the fact that our lines were in no place less than three-fourths of a mile from the rebel works, and night and day, shot and shell of the most ponderous pattern were projected into our camps indiscriminately from four rebel forts and four rebel gunboats. The officers and men of the fleet, worked bravely and assiduously to get within shelling distance of the enemy's works. On Tuesday, the 28th ult., the gunboat Cherokee got within gunshot of Spanish Fort, and at intervals from that time until its fall hurled a 100-pound shell into the fort. Four monitors were also gradually working their way up, removing here and there a torpedo, which seemed to be the most serious obstacles. On this same evening the splendid double turreted monitor Milwaukee struck one of these marine guns, which exploded and sunk the vessel. The Osage, the next morning, shared the same fate. The Milwaukee sunk in about five feet of water, and the Osage in eight feet. The Osage may be saved. The Milwaukee, however, is almost a total wreck, she having split in two a few days ago. Seven men were lost in all. Besides these two monitors, one tin-clad and a transport were sunk, and another tin-clad burst her boiler.

"Tuesday, the 26th ult., was the last day of rations, and the question of how we should obtain supplies was agitated. The road, which was soft clay, from Darley's Mill was entirely destroyed, and the wharves in the upper bay were all in a dilapidated and rickety condition. General Bailey, of Red River raft fame, however, was sent down to the bay, and in a few hours after he arrived he improvised two landings out of pontoons, and the next day completed two wharves and landed one day's rations for the whole army. From that time the army had full rations. The landing of supplies at Howard and Belle Rose was one of the most difficult jobs of the campaign, and reflects great credit on General Bailey.

"On the 2d inst., General Steel's command, after having cut the Mobile and Montgomery Railroad near Pollard, capturing a train of cars bound to Mobile, containing a large amount of confederate money and confederate postage-stamps, and fighting and killing the rebel General Clanton, and killing and wounding about 200 of his men, and capturing nearly 300 of them; moved up to within one mile of the works at Blakely, and went into camp on the right, with General Hawkins' colored division on the extreme point north. This was done with some opposition, and General Hawkins lost 200 men killed and wounded. The next day a portion of General Granger's corps, which had been removed from the front of Spanish Fort, joined General Steele on his left, and General Garrard's division, of the Sixteenth Corps, moved into the gap between General Veatch's division and Bayou Minnette. General Garrard immediately moved up his skirmish line within 200 yards of the rebel works on the left of Blakely, and drove the enemy's skirmishers into the interior of the fort. While urging his line forward, a 120-pounder from the rebel ram Nashville came so near General Garrard's head, that its velocity nearly stunned him. That night, the investment, at least by land, of Spanish Fort and the works of Blakely was complete, with the exception of a gap between Generals Carr and Garrard, about midmay between Spanish Fort and Blakely, and through which runs the Bayou Minnette. The force in front of Blakely, besides being pretty vigorously shelled by guns from the enemy's works, received particular attention from the gunboats Nashville and Huntsville, which had immediately taken positions so as to enfilade one entire line from right to left. Every half hour, day and night, these boats gave us a 'reminder,' in the shape of a 124-pounder. Despite all obstacles, the most dreaded of which were the torpedoes all along the roads and in front of the forts, and the incessant and vigorous shelling of our lines by the enemy's forts and fleet, on the morning of the 8th inst. our whole line, from the extreme right of the works at Blakely to the extreme left of Spanish Fort, was 400 yards (and less) from the enemy's guns. The disposition of the army was as follows: On the extreme right was Hawkins' division of Steel's command; next (to the left of Hawkins), was Andrews' division of the Thirteenth Corps, but temporarily in command of General Steele; next, Veatch's division of the Thirteenth Corps, and on the extreme left of the Blakely works was Garrard's division of the Sixteenth Corps; Carr's division of the Sixteenth Corps, was on the extreme right of Spanish Fort; McArthur's division of the same corps, was in the centre; and Benton's division of the Thirteenth Corps, was on the extreme left, with about 7,000 cavalry in the rear. Throughout the whole day our artillery was being advanced, while our skirmishers, in many places, were within 200 and 300 yards of the forts. Up to this time our loss, during the fourteen days' siege, and the introductory skirmishing, was about 750 killed and wounded.

"It was agreed upon that an assault upon Spanish Fort should be made by our entire artillery at a little before dark, upon the 8th inst.; and, although it was not generally believed that an opportunity for an attack by the infantry would offer itself, Generals Carr, McArthur and Benton, commanding the three divisions in the immediate front of the work, made reconnoissances in person, from the right to left, to get a view of any weak place which might be brought to light. For some days it had been strongly suspected that a weak place upon the left of the fort existed, although to any observer with an unmilitary eye, this position would seem to have been their strongest, as a high bluff runs parallel with the eastern arm of the Alabama River, and between the base of this elevation and the river, is a low strip of ground covered thickly with young pines and water beeches, and of an exceedingly swampy nature. The left of Red Fork, a neighboring work, containing four guns, projected to within a half of a mile of this point, and in front of it, were three lines of palisades, and other obstructions. The only open space at all was an immense ravine, which had been left uncovered intentionally, from the fact that the guns on the left of Spanish Fort commanded the position, which was also easily enfiladed by one of the enemy's gunboats. It was believed by General Carr, that if he could get enough of guns in position to drive away the gunboats, this fort might be easily carried by assault. Accordingly, eight heavy Parrott's were placed in position, not only to bear upon the gunboats, but to participate in the assault upon Spanish and Red Forts. Colonel Geddes, commanding a brigade in Carr's division, went around to the extreme right, with the exception of one regiment, which was kept in supporting distance of the First Indiana heavy artillery, above mentioned. A wooden gunboat, with a powerful armament for several days had been gradually working its way up; and upon the evening of the 8th, was within half a mile of Fort Alexis. This boat, so the navy boasted, could throw a 100-pounder three miles. 'If this be true,' it was argued by General Carr, 'it can drive the enemy's gunboats up Blakely River;' which proved true, as the following will show: General Carr sent word to General A. J. Smith, saying that he could carry the work in his immediate front if the rebel gunboats could be driven up the river. In a few moments after, Generals Smith and Carr, and Colonel Geddes crept up to within a few yards of the advanced saps on our right; and, after an examination and consultation, unanimously concluded that the enemy's left could be turned, and Geddes received instructions to make an assault at a given time after the commencement of the cannonade, if he should deem it judicious and practicable.

"Although we have all along called the whole thing Spanish Fort, there are in reality, three distinct fortifications. On our left is Fort Alexis, a small, but compactly-built affair, mounting four guns; on our right is Red Fort, which differs not materially in its construction from Fort Alexis, and mounting four guns; in the centre, frowns from an imposing eminence, Spanish Fort, nearly two miles in length, of a rectangular shape, with a capacity, including its water-batteries, for thirty-six guns, and capable of garrisoning 2,500 men. These three forts were manned by members of Hood's army, all under the command of the rebel Brigadier-General Gibson. An inclined plane, which leads to this trio of fortifications, had been arranged in the most mechanically-murderous manner imaginable. A deep ditch at the base of the works, six feet in width, was one obstacle. A little fence, made of telegraph-wire, was the next. In front of this fence was an elaborately constructed *chevaux de frize*, while, in order to proceed thus far, a line of abattis and a line of palisades must be removed. Forty-four guns, of all calibres, frowned upon us from these three forts; while batteries Huger and Tracy in the bay, about a mile north of Spanish Fort, and two gunboats at the mouth of Blakely River, sixteen heavy guns in all, had an enfilading fire upon our line. Our brave boys knew exactly what to contend against, but were all anxious to move upon the works. On our side were arranged a *few* engines of war and a good many thousand brave hearts. None of our artillery was more than three-fourths of a mile from the rebel works. We had bearing upon them, at 5 P. M. on the 8th inst., twenty-four 32-pounder Parrott guns, twelve 8-inch mortars, and some wooden mortars, got up by General McArthur, and eight batteries of field artillery—between 75 and 100 pieces of artillery in all. Two of our gunboats were also in readiness to participate in the 'duel.' Our real line of battle was composed of nearly 20,000 men; with General Carr's division of the Sixteenth Corps, on our right; McArthur's division of the same corps, in the centre, and Benton's division of the Thirteenth Corps, on the left. At a few minutes after 5 o'clock, on the evening of the 8th, a sharp crack of a Rodman gun, away over on the left, announced that the ball had opened. Hardly a moment had elapsed, and the pounding is most terrific all along the line. The sharp salutes of the Rodman, the tearing noise of the Napoleons, the dull, heavy report of the mortars, and the awful roar of the Parrotts can be better imagined than described. Add to this the hissing, cracking and crashing of our own and the enemy's shells, and the awful diapason is at its height. This furious cannonade was kept up without abatement for nearly two hours.

"At sundown there was no abatement of the firing upon our side. For the past hour, however, the enemy's fire had slackened. The rebel gunboats had ceased firing, after the first half hour, altogether. Batteries Huger and Tracy fired a 120-pounder regularly every five minutes. Spanish Fort and Fort Alexis had let up considerably, while Red Fort had almost ceased its fire after the first hour. Just at sundown, and while daylight still lingered, Colonel Geddes gave orders for his brigade to advance upon the rebel left. The Eighth Iowa, Colonel Bell, asked for and received permission to lead the assault. Two minutes after the order was given, the ascent was commenced; the Eighth Iowa leading the advance, followed by those Illinois regiments composing the balance of Geddes' brigade. The brigade gave a shout as it went at its work, and was joined by Colonels Ward's and Moore's brigades of Carr's division, stationed next on the left. The shout was taken up and carried along the whole line. I think if our troops all along the front had made a feint, especially on the left and centre, we might have carried the right with but little loss. But really no part of the line assisted General Carr, except in the way of shouting, which was done without stint. It was now growing dark, but Geddes' brigade was climbing over the inextricable mass of matted timber and brush and other obstructions, right in the face of a murderous fire from the enemy's infantry. Just as they had got within forty yards of the fort, a brace of howitzers opened upon them with grape and canister, when our brave troops—and they must be specially mentioned: the Eighth Iowa, the Eighty-first, One Hundred and Eighth and One Hundred and Twenty-fourth Illinois, never retrograded a step, but pushed on amidst the din and destruction of the enemy's artillery and musketry, and succeeded in getting inside of Red Fort just after dark. Here a regular pitched battle took place, and owing to mismanagement on the part of the rebels, Colonel Geddes whipped every thing to pieces inside of Red Fort; captured nearly 300 prisoners, and tumbled them over into the ditch in Ward's front, where they were taken and sent to the rear. Geddes' brigade, at this juncture, were making preparations to turn the artillery upon Spanish Fort, when a whole division came over from that work into Red Fort, causing our men to get back to their original line. This much, however, was accomplished with but trifling loss, owing to the random and careless firing on the part of the rebel infantry.

"As soon as Geddes' brigade was forced outside of Red Fort, General Gibson, who commanded the three forts, went to evacuating rapidly. It was pitch dark when our troops got well into position on our right, and firing on both sides had in a great measure ceased. The rebels, at intervals, was exceedingly quiet, when all of a sudden, occasionally they would break out with a fire from their artillery and musketry from right to left. 'I believe they are evacuating,' says General Carr. But, evidently their chief in command did not know it, or did not care, for nothing was done to ascertain whether they were evacuating until it was too late. Between 9 and 10 P. M., the bustle and lights inside of the forts, and the continual banging away of their skirmishers told too true that the evacuation of the forts was going on. And so it was, for before half-past 11 P. M., the enemy, after spiking part of his guns, had successfully escaped in small boats across the bay to Mobile. If it had been a clear night, our gunboats, and even our Parrots, on our right, would have prevented this thing. It is a singular fact that the enemy's skirmishers did not know that their comrades had gone until informed by our troops. At precisely 11.30 Colonel Geddes sent word to General Carr that there were no troops in Red Fort, and added that he believed that Spanish Fort was also being evacuated. General Carr answered by directing Colonel Geddes to advance a strong skirmish line, and said that he would send the same order to Colonels Ward and Moore. A little before 12 the entire division moved up behind a strong skirmish line, and without resistance, climbed over the parapets of Spanish and Red Forts. McArthur's division was swept around the front and left of Spanish Fort and marched in without opposition. The Thirteenth Corps encountered slight resistance on the part of some portions of the rebel skirmish line, but, after a few volleys, drove this remnant of the enemy inside of Fort Alexis, where they laid down their arms and surrendered, expressing not only astonishment at the clever manner in which our forces drove them into their works, but indignation at the quiet exit of their comrades in arms. There were about 300 prisoners in this batch, all of whom were escorted to the rear before daylight. The Star Spangled banner was thrown to the breeze from the three forts about 1 o'clock A. M. on the 9th. There were some of the most improved patterns of artillery in the three forts, a greater portion of which was spiked with nails. There were Brookes, Blakelys, Napoleons, howitzers, mortars, and other patterns. They left no small arms behind, but did leave any quantity of ammunition and other war material. I met a prisoner who had been inside of the fort during the whole investment. He said that our artillery demonstration on the evening on the 4th instant and on the night before, was the most awful he had ever witnessed. He said that the rebels lost quite a thousand men in killed and wounded during the siege. The interior of Spanish Fort shows unmistakable signs of the terrible damage done by our destructive guns. The whole interior is in a perfect smash. The earth is full of deep holes and furrows, the cabins are all smashed, or partly smashed, and the parapet, from right to left, is marked in many places by the flight of our shot and shell. All the *debris* of a battle-field met our gaze. The enemy had managed to remove his wounded, but his dead he had left, right where the poor fellows fell. In one corner of the fort was a small graveyard, and in another was a lot of disabled gun-carriages and caissons, and three disabled cannon. The whole scene, as presented on our occupation, was most dismal indeed, and shows what an awful ordeal the poor misguided fellows went through during these two weeks of an incessant storm of shot and shell. Really what that garrison passed through during their struggle to hold Spanish Fort may be easier imagined than otherwise.

"Now I come to the most charming episode of the whole affair—the assault upon and capture of Blakely. Blakely is a small town, above the mouth of the river of that name, located on the eastern shore, about four and a-half miles due north of Spanish Fort, and 12 miles northeast from Mobile. When this town was elevated its projector calculated that Mobile would be thrown in the shade in an amazing short time. True it is, that Blakely is better located as regards health, and the eastern channel can float larger craft than the western. But really Blakely is just no place at all; and were it not for our late victory a mile from its centre, no one out of Alabama would know that such a place existed. The rebel works at Blakely were the last built of all the defences of Mobile, and were not so strong as the works below. The work consists of one huge fortification, running from north to south, nearly three miles in length, its right resting near Bayou Minnette and the left on Blakely River. A little after daylight the whole army were made aware of the fact of Spanish Fort and its neighboring strongholds passing from rebel to Federal possession. Some of our gunboats, with the aid of a score or more of rebel prisoners, went to work clearing the channel of torpedoes, and before noon they had succeeded in removing between thirty and forty, and running up between Red Fort and Blakely. This naval exploit was of the utmost advantage to us, as it would prevent the enemy from getting away; and it was a pretty well understood thing that an assault would be made upon the works in front of Blakely without much delay. Two batteries of Parrots were hurried over on to our extreme right to prevent the rebel transports and gunboats from coming down the river. In brief we hurriedly made every preparation, not only to fight ourselves, but to make the enemy stand and fight us which he did, as the following will show. All the forenoon infantry and artillery crowded over the little pontoon bridge across Bayou Minnette, the artillery taking positions where it could be made serviceable during the assault, and the infantry, or the greater part of it, going to the rear and in reserve. Whether the rebels at Blakely, under General Lyddell, thought they could successfully and permanently check us at this point, or whether they fought because no opportunity for flight presented, of course, I do not know. But true it is that a great deal of bustle took place inside of the works during the forenoon, and an unusual amount of skirmishing outside. General Lyddell commanded the rebels of Blakely and the garrison consisted of two divisions respectively commanded by Generals Cockerill and Thomas. The enemy's works were rather formidable. His artillery swept all the main roads, of which there were four, and his gunboats enfiladed our lines from right to left. In front of the works a good deal of labor had been expended in making their obstructions as complete as possible. As in front of Spanish Fort there were lines of abattis, palisades and *chevaux de frize*, and a wide, deep ditch at the base of the fort. Inside there were over 3,000 men. General Thomas' division, consisting of three brigades of Alabama militia and green troops, was on the right; and General Cockerill's division, consisting of two brigades of veterans, formerly of Hood's army, was on the left. The rebels had no heavy artillery at Blakely, but had eight four-gun batteries, making their works fairly glisten with cannon. Besides other obstructions, there were a great many torpedoes buried, here and there, all along the entire front of the rebel works.

"Our line of battle in front of Blakely were disposed as follows: on our right was a division of colored troops commanded by General Hankins, of Steele's command. In the centre were two divisions of the Thirteenth Corps, commanded by Generals Hatch and Andrews. On the left were General Garrard's division of the Sixteenth Corps. McArthur's and Carr's divisions of the Sixteenth Corps, and Benton's division of the Sixteenth Corps. were near at hand in case their services should be needed. General Steele, about 4 P. M., sent word to General Garrard, asking him if he did not think the rebel works could be carried by assault. General Garrard answered that there was not the slightest chance for a failure, and added that his division was ready to move. General Steele thereupon ordered his men to be ready to assault the works at 5 o'clock. At this point in the day, the artillery firing became quite heavy on both sides, as did also the firing along the skirmish line, for our advance had crept up to within less than a hundred yards of the works. At precisely 5.30 o'clock in the evening the fight commenced on the left. General Garrard, who commanded on the left, had the strongest, if not the finest, division in the army, composed of three brigades, respectively commanded by General Gilbert and Colonels Rinneken and Harris. One-third of this force advanced in a strong line up to within fifty yards of the main works, when a discharge of shell and shrapnel was thrown into them, which was immediately answered by the Seventeenth Ohio Battery. General Garrard and his staff, as soon as the rebel artillery had well opened, moved up to the advanced line cautiously, to pick out the safest avenues for moving up the line, preparatory to a grand charge. They had not gone far, though, before they found there was no choice of ground, and after a brief interview between the General commanding the division and his brigade commanders, General Garrard gave that thrilling command—"Forward!" With a terrible yell, which alone drew the enemy's artillery, the whole division moved forward on a double-quick, as though the men composing it were going to tear every thing to pieces before them.

They had not proceeded very far when they were assailed by a terrible storm of grape and canister. At this discharge the men wavered a little; but General Garrard seeing it, and knowing that his presence would encourage them, rode up to the right of his line and urged his men to go on. It was the hottest work of the day; for, fearing an attack on his right, the enemy had massed nearly two-thirds of his available force in Garrard's front. For one half-hour did our poor fellows feel their way through the almost inextricable obstructions, while in addition to the bursting of shells and the shower of bullets and canister, the very ground shook with the explosions of torpedoes. General Garrard was in the thickest of the fire, directing all the movements. Notwithstanding the awful storm of bullets, in just one hour all the obstructions were passed and our men jumped into the ditches and scrambled over the works. Colonel Rinneken's and General Gilbert's brigades turned the right of the fort and gained its entrance at the same time, capturing the rebel Brigadier-General Thomas and over a thousand men. No sooner was this point gained than a half-dozen flags might be seen all along the parapets, while the most deafening shouts rent the air, which went along the whole line.

"During this time the whole line were actively participating. The centre bore its part bravely. The troops in the centre were composed of one brigade of Veatch's division under command of General Dennis, and two brigades of Andrews' division, respectively commanded by Colonels Spicely and Moore. No sooner had Garrard's division got well at work, than Andrews and Veatch, who were both in command, gave orders to their troops to join in the charge. The scene was less bloody in the centre, and the advance upon the fort less dangerous; but the rebels kept up a tremendous artillery fire, causing many a poor fellow to drop dead while manfully performing his duty. Just as Andrews' division got within about forty yards of the fort, the rebels poured into it a withering fire from eight guns. The Eighty-third Ohio, and Ninety-seventh Illinois, which were in advance as skirmishers, pushed forward, and were on the point of reaching the ditch, when upward of a dozen torpedoes exploded under them, causing considerable confusion. During this confusion the enemy rained a perfect torrent of grape and canister into our ranks, but could not succeed in driving back our advance, which was almost immediately joined by the regular line. General Granger was present during the whole affair, and with his staff was upon a slight elevation about three-quarters of a mile from the works. General A. J. Smith was also upon the ground in a little open place between Andrews' and Garrard's divisions during the entire assault. The column on our right was composed of colored troops, and was commanded by General Hawkins. His brigade commanders were General Pile and Cols. Schofield and Drew. The moment the order was given for the negroes to charge they went at it with characteristic impetuosity. Colonel Drew was on the extreme right, and suffered terribly from the enemy's artillery. It was pretty well toward dark when the colored division got well at work. The ascent reminded me not a little of Overton Hill on the Nashville battle-field; and, as at that place, the colored division was pitted against Mississippi troops. But once did they show any sign of wavering; but General Hawkins sent word that they must move up and take the right of the work, as our troops had got possession of the remainder. "On!" cries the brave white officers, and on went the colored troops, literally carrying every thing before them. At 7 o'clock the national flag was flung to the breeze from the ramparts, and Blakely and all it contained came into our possession. We came into possession of

Blakely just about dark, after one of the most brilliantly successful assaults of the war. The whole line moved like clockwork. The movements of the left, under the command of General Garrard, were the finest and most systematic I have seen upon any battle-field. General Garrard has the credit of capturing two brigadier-generals, while Andrews' division got the third. The rebel gunboats, which we dreaded so much, did not participate, and the opinion prevails that they must have been disabled by the First Indiana Heavy Artillery the day before. We captured Generals Lyddell, Thomas and Cockerill, and Acting Brigadiers Barney and Leary, and 3,300 prisoners, 32 pieces of artillery, 4,000 stand of small arms, 16 battle flags, a vast amount of ammunition, etc., etc. The rebel loss in killed and wounded was about 500. Our loss in killed and wounded in front of Blakely will reach 1,000.

"All day Monday the 10th instant, was spent in reconnoitering on land and in the bay. All the forts on the eastern shore were occupied, and about 4,000 prisoners sent to Fort Gaines. The Sixteenth Corps, General A. J. Smith, received four days' rations, and were under marching orders for the next morning, when they commenced moving up the eastern shore. General Granger's forces received orders to move down to the landing, while General Steele's forces took charge of the captured forts. We got over seventy pieces of artillery in all on the eastern shore, all of which were taken by assault. Some of our gunboats attempted to go up into the Blakely River, after removing over a hundred torpedoes, with a view of reconnoitering the vicinity of Mobile, but were stopped by a terrible fire from Batteries Huger and Tracy in the bay. They fired some 200 shots at our fleet during Monday and Tuesday, and on Tuesday night the garrison evacuated after spiking their guns, twelve in all. On Wednesday morning a number of the tin-clads and all the transports at Howard's Landing and Belle Rose, were loaded with troops from General Granger's command and crossed over the bay. About 8,000 or 10,000 men were crossed without opposition and without injury from torpedoes a few of which remain. The Lama, which took over some 500 troops, on its return trip was blown out of water and totally destroyed. The Athens, a tug-boat, was also destroyed by a torpedo. Each boat lost two men. Guns and forts were now falling into our hands upon all sides. Batteries Huger and Tracy, near the mouth of Blakely River, the water batteries of Choctaw Point, the Spanish River batteries and Forts Truson and Pinto were taken possession of by our navy, while Batteries Gadsen and McIntosh, and the batteries above Dog River, known as the Missouri Batteries, were captured by General Veatch. All of these forts contain each a number of the most improved patterns of heavy artillery. Every thing in the bay fell into our hands except the four rebel gunboats, Morgan, Tuscarora, Nashville and Huntsville, and the enemy's transports, which escaped up the Alabama River. The transports Jeff. Davis and Magnolia were several times struck by our shells and rendered unfit for service a week ago. The Nashville was also considerably damaged by our artillery. All three of these craft were turned up the river in a shaky condition. The rebels commenced evacuating Mobile on Monday night and finished on Tuesday night. The Mayor of Mobile on Wednesday evening met General Granger near the Missouri Batteries, and formally handed over the city, but no Federal troops went into Mobile until yesterday morning.

"On the morning of the 13th, a portion of General Veatch's command went into the city by the shell-road, and run up the Stars and Stripes on the Post Office and Custom House. General Granger arrived a short time after, and General Canby and staff arrived in the city a short time after noon. No unpleasant demonstrations were made either by the citizens of Mobile or by our soldiers, upon the occupation of the haughty city. All the public buildings and stores were closed, and the private residences looked like houses of mourning. Four newspapers immediately suspended publication —the *Register*, *Tribune*, *News*, and one other. The interior of the city is not injured in the least, and the large warehouses on the wharves, most of which are filled with "Confederate government" freight and stores, are unharmed. Although many threats to burn the city were made, not a house, nor a bale of cotton, nor a pound of subsistence, nor a particle of war material were burnt or destroyed. Numbers of dwellings and cottages on the Shiny Hill and Whistler roads were destroyed some time ago, and many beautiful villas and farms met the same fate in order to strengthen the rebel forts west of the city, where it was supposed we would make the attack. All conditions of people are in extreme want, the poorer classes of which immediately besieged our soldiers for something to eat. The forts on the west of the city are the strongest works in the South. There are three lines of forts, the interior of which has a ditch twelve feet deep and forty feet wide. The forts in and around Mobile, and upon the water batteries, mount 150 guns. The captures in Mobile are large—said to be $2,000,000 worth of ammunition and commissary stores, 140 pieces of artillery (some of it spiked), a large amount of cotton, and 1,200 prisoners, counting in the sick, stragglers and deserters. The campaign, on the whole, has been a grand success. From the time our army left Dauphin Island up to the present, our entire loss in killed and wounded barely reaches 2,000 men—I think 1,800 is the correct figure. Our navy sustains the loss of two monitors and five other vessels. We have captured one of the most important seaboard cities in the South, killed and wounded about 1,500 of the enemy, killed 1 brigadier-general, captured, 6,000 prisoners, 17 forts, over 200 pieces of artillery, a vast amount of cotton, ordnance and subsistence stores, and put the remainder to flight, with a strong hope of surrounding it on all sides."

An outline of the march of the cavalry expedition of General Wilson, supplied by a member of his staff, completes the narrative of this decisive campaign in Alabama. "General Wilson and his command left Chickasaw, Ala., on the 22d March. At Ebenezer Church, near Plantersville, a short and sharp engagement occurred with Forrest's cavalry, which resulted in the complete discomfiture of the rebels, and the capture of 300 prisoners. A column was then sent to Tuscaloosa, where a large amount of rebel government property was destroyed. On the 2d of April, Selma was taken by assault, with 2,700 prisoners. There our forces found thirty-two guns in the fortifications of the city, and seventy-five others in the arsenal. The arsenal, which was one of the largest and most important in the confederacy, was destroyed, together with several rolling-mills, magazines, powder-works, a naval foundry and other public property. After a delay of eight days, our forces left Selma, crossing the Alabama River on a pontoon bridge, 850 feet in length, and marched against Montgomery, which was captured without opposition on the 12th. Here they discovered that the rebels had destroyed an immense quantity of cotton, the estimates varying from 30,000 to 90,000 bales, five steamers, about seventy cars and one locomotive. All the bridges between Selma and Montgomery, a distance of about fifty miles, were thoroughly destroyed. The rebel property left behind was of little value, and our forces captured but five guns. Several rolling-mills and foundries were destroyed. From Montgomery the expedition marched on Columbus, Ga., distant a little less than ninety miles. This city was captured by an assaulting column under General Upton, on the night of the 16th. Here 1,200 prisoners and fifty-three guns fell into our hands. The quantity of cotton captured and destroyed was immense, the number of bales being estimated at not less than 100,000. Besides this, our forces destroyed great quantities of military stores, an arsenal, a pistol factory, a sword factory, an accoutrement factory, three military and naval foundries, a rolling-mill, thirteen locomotives, about 100 cars, and several depots and machine-shops. A gunboat, mounting six 7-inch rifled guns, was captured here. While this work of destruction was in progress, La Grange's brigade made a detour to West Point, where the rebel works were taken by assault. The entire garrison, numbering over 300, were captured, and their commander, General Tyler, killed. Here fifteen locomotives, 200 cars, and two large factories were destroyed, as well as immense quantities of quartermaster's and commissary's stores. The destruction of every kind of public property was thorough and complete. Macon surrendered to our forces on the 20th without opposition. Generals Howell Cobb, G. W. Smith, Robertson, McCall and Mercer there fell into our hands. The total captures made by our forces in the course of this astonishing sweep through Alabama and Western Georgia are: 32 guns in position, and 200 in arsenals, nearly 200,000 bales of cotton (destroyed), nearly 400 cars, 34 locomotives, besides an immense amount of miscellaneous military stores; while, as before stated, our losses in all the engagements are less than 350 men. In every respect the expedition was a success, and demonstrative—if further proof of the fact were needed—of the utter hollowness of the confederacy."

CHAPTER CXIV.

THE ASSASSINATION OF PRESIDENT LINCOLN AND INAUGURATION OF PRESIDENT JOHNSON. APRIL, 1865.

The fall of Richmond and surrender of Lee's army to General Grant, the long-expected events which were justly calculated to herald the immediate termination of the war, were received with rejoicings, indeed, by the people of the North, but with a calmness and sobriety befitting the serious nature of the protracted conflict. The war had been undertaken by the Government reluctantly at the outset as a necessary and inevitable measure of self-defence for the maintenance of the Union and the preservation of the liberties of the country; it had been maintained steadily and vigorously under the honorable influences of a sense of duty and patriotism and though its pressure upon life and property was most severe and it had cost unprecedented sacrifices, it had been conducted upon the whole with remarkable moderation and with a rare absence of personal animosity and bitterness of feeling. No misconduct of the foe, who scrupled at no excesses of hostility, in foreign intrigue, in desperate acts of piracy, in reckless invasions of the frontier as at St. Albans, in massacres of a captured garrison as at Fort Pillow, in the mining of the Libby Prison at Richmond, and in the habitual ill treatment of prisoners that were there and in Georgia and elsewhere,—none of these and other offences against humanity, beyond the authority of war itself, could shake the settled equanimity and, under the circumstances of the case, the moral grandeur of the North. This was shown in a marked degree in the character and actions of its Chief Executive, its representative man, chosen originally for his virtues and discretion ; and when these qualities had been fully tested through four years of extraordinary trial, putting them every day to the proof, again reëlected with a national consciousness of his worth which recalled the similar confidence placed under equal responsibilities in the merits of Washington. Abraham Lincoln in his calmness and forbearance, the plain sense of duty, the generosity and magnanimity of his nature, fairly represented the nation in the conduct of its great struggle for life and liberty. As the revolution which separated this country from Great Britain is honored in history by the character of Washington ; so will the completion of the work, in its regeneration forced upon it by the Rebellion, be sanctified in the memory of Lincoln.

"The triumph of the cause, the burden of which he had sustained so prudently and faithfully, brought to him no vulgar gratification but, if possible, an increased sense of duty and responsibility. This was shown in his conduct on his return to Washington with the news of the assured fall of the Confederacy. General Lee surrendered his army to Gen. Grant on the 9th of April ; on the 10th, President Lincoln was waited upon at the Executive mansion by a body of citizens, who came to congratulate him and listen to some expressions of his feelings on the great victory. With a sense of the importance of the occasion he deferred his remarks to the next evening, when the company again assembled, and he thus addressed them in words to be for ever memorable as his last speech to the people and the nation.

Thoughts of the past, and of the victories of the day, it will be observed, little affected his mind in comparison with the interests of the future. He was already turning his attention profoundly, and with his accustomed insight and sagacity, to the pressing problem of reconstruction, and in this, as in all his previous acts and deliberations, he was working his way outwardly into light from the heart of the subject. This consummate method of his intellectual faculties was never more strikingly displayed than in this, their last exercise. He proposed nothing experimental or rash, or authoritative beyond the truthful "logic of events" of which he was the patriotic and disinterested expounder, as of some divine oracle. "We meet this evening," said he, "not in sorrow but in gladness of heart. The evacuation of Petersburgh and Richmond, and the surrender of the principal insurgent army, give hopes of a righteous and speedy peace, whose joyous expression cannot be restrained. In the midst of this, however, He from whom all blessings flow, must not be forgotten. A call for a national thanksgiving is being prepared, and will be duly promulgated. Nor must those whose harder part gives us the cause of rejoicing be overlooked. Their honors must not be parcelled out with others. I myself was near the front, and had the high pleasure of transmitting much of the good news to you. But no part of the honor for plan or execution is mine. To General Grant, his skillful officers and brave men, all belongs, the gallant navy stood ready, but was not in reach to take active part. By these recent successes the reinauguration of the national authority—reconstruction, which has had a large share of thought from the first—is pressed much more closely upon our attention. It is fraught with great difficulty. Unlike a war between independent nations, there is no authorized organ for us to treat with. No one man has authority to give up the rebellion for any other man. We must simply begin with and mould from disorganized and discordant elements. Nor is it a small additional embarrassment that we, the loyal people, differ among ourselves as to the mode, manner and measures of reconstruction. As a general rule, I abstain from reading the reports of attacks upon myself, wishing not to be provoked by that to which I cannot properly offer an answer. In spite of this precaution, however, it comes to my knowledge that I am much censured for some supposed agency in setting up and seeking to sustain the new State Government of Louisiana. In this I have done just so much and no more than the public knows. In the annual message of December, 1863, and the accompanying proclamation, I presented a plan of reconstruction, as the phrase goes, which I promised, if adopted by any State, would be acceptable to and sustained by the Executive Government of the nation. I distinctly stated that this was not the only plan which might, possibly, be acceptable ; and I also distinctly protested that the Executive claimed no right to say when or whether members should be admitted to seats in Congress from such States. This plan was in advance submitted to the then Cabinet, and approved by every member of it. One of them suggested that I should then and in that connection apply the Emancipation Proclamation to the theretofore excepted parts of Virginia and Louisiana, that I should drop the suggestion about apprenticeship for freed people, and that I should omit the protest against my own power in regard to the admission of members to Congress. But even he approved every part and parcel of the plan which has since been employed or touched by the action of Louisiana. The new constitution of Louisiana, declaring Emancipation for the whole State, practically applies the proclamation to the part previously excepted. It does not adopt apprenticeship for freed people, and is silent, as it could not well be otherwise, about the admission of members to Congress. So that as it applied to Louisiana every member of the Cabinet fully approved the plan, the message went to Congress and I received many commendations of the plan, written and verbal, and not a single objection to it, from any professed emancipationist, came to my knowledge until after the news reached Washington that the people of Louisiana had begun to move in accordance with it. From about July, 1862, I had corresponded with different persons supposed to be interested in seeking a reconstruction of a State government for Louisiana. When the message of 1863, with the plan before mentioned, reached New Orleans. General Banks wrote me that he was confident that the people, with his military coöperation, would reconstruct substantially on that plan. I wrote to him to come and try it. They tried it, and the result is known. Such has been my only agency in getting up the Louisiana government. As to sustaining it, my promise is out, as before stated. But as bad promises are better broken than kept, I shall treat this as a bad promise and break it whenever I shall be convinced that keeping it is adverse to the public interest, but I have not yet been so convinced.

"I have been shown a letter on this subject, supposed to be an able one, in which the writer expresses regret that my mind has not seemed to be definitely fixed on the question, whether the seceded States, so called, are in the Union or out of it. It would, perhaps, add astonishment to his regret were he to learn that since I have found professed Union men endeavoring to answer that question I have purposely forborne any public expression upon it. As appears to me, that question has not been, nor yet is a practically material one, and that any discussion of it while it thus remains practically immaterial, could have no effect other than the mischievous one of dividing our friends. As yet, whatever it may become, that question is bad as the basis of a controversy, and good for nothing at all—a merely pernicious abstraction. We all agree that the seceded States, so called, are out of their proper practical relation with the Union, and that the sole object of the Government, civil and military, in regard to those States, is to again get them into their proper practical relation. I believe that it is not only possible, but, in fact, easier, to do this without deciding, or even considering, whether those States have ever been out of the Union, than with it. Finding themselves safely at home, it would be utterly immaterial whether they had been abroad. Let us all join in doing the acts necessary to restore the proper practical relations between those States and the nation, and each forever after innocently indulge his own opinion whether in doing the acts he brought the States from without into the Union, or only gave them proper assistance, they never having been out of it. The amount of constituency, so to speak, on which the Louisiana Government rests, would be more satisfactory to all if it contained 50,000, or 30,000, or even 20,000, instead of 12,000, as it does. It is also unsatisfactory to some that the elective franchise is not given to the colored man. I would myself prefer that it were now conferred on the very intelligent, and on those who serve our cause as soldiers. Still the question is not whether the Louisiana government, as it stands, is quite all that is desirable. The question is, will it be wiser to take it as it is, and help to improve it, or to reject and disperse? Can Louisiana be brought into proper practical relation with the Union sooner by sustaining or by discarding her new State government? Some twelve thousand voters in the heretofore slave State of Louisiana have sworn allegiance to the Union, assumed to be the rightful political power of the State elections, organized a State government, adopted a Free State constitution, giving the benefit of public schools equally to black and white, and empowering the Legislature to confer the elective franchise upon the colored man. This Legislature has already voted to ratify the constitutional amendment recently passed by Congress, abolishing slavery throughout the nation. These twelve thousand persons are thus fully committed to the Union and to perpetuate freedom in the State; committed to the very things, and nearly all things, the nation wants, and they ask the nation's recognition and its assistance to make good this committal. Now if we reject and spurn them we do our utmost to disorganize and disperse them. We in fact say to the white man, you are worthless or worse; we will neither help you, nor be helped by you. To the blacks, we say: This cup of Liberty which these, your old masters, held to your lips, we will dash from you, and leave you to the chances of gathering the spilled and scattered contents in some vague and undefined when, where and how. If this course, discouraging and paralyzing both white and black, has any tendency to bring Louisiana into proper practical relations with the Union, I have not, so far, been able to perceive it. If, on the contrary, we recognize and sustain the new government of Louisiana, the converse of all this is made true. We encourage the hearts and nerve the arms of 12,000 to adhere to their work, and argue for it, and proselyte for it, and fight for it, and feed it, and grow it, and ripen it to a complete success. The colored man, too, in seeing all united, is inspired with vigilance, and energy, and daring to the same end. Grant that he desires the elective franchise, will he not attain it sooner by saving the already advanced steps toward it, than by running backward over them? Concede that the new government of Louisiana is to what it should be as the egg is to the fowl, we shall sooner have the fowl by hatching the egg, than by smashing it.—[Laughter.] Again, if we reject Louisiana we also reject one vote in favor of the proposed amendment to the national constitution. To meet this proposition it has been argued that no more than three-fourths of those States which have not attempted secession are necessary to validly ratify the amendment. I do not commit myself against this further than to say that such a ratification would be questionable, and sure to be persistently questioned, while a ratification by three-fourths of all the States would be unquestioned and unquestionable. I repeat the question. Can Louisiana be brought into proper practical relation with the Union sooner by sustaining, or by discarding her new State government? What has been said of Louisiana will apply to other States. And yet so great peculiarities pertain to each State, and such important and sudden changes occur in the same State, and withal so new and unprecedented is the whole case, that no exclusive and inflexible plan can safely be prescribed as to details and collaterals. Such exclusive and inflexible plan would surely become a new entanglement. Important principles may and must be inflexible. In the present situation, as the phrase goes, it may be my duty to make some new announcement to the people of the South. I am considering, and shall not fail to act when satisfied that action will be proper."

It was while considering this new announcement to the people of the South, doubtless some liberal act of amnesty and generous, patriotic appeal; with words of kindness to the end on his lips, with humility and generosity at heart, that, a few days after, he was suddenly killed by a vulgar assassin.

Shortly after the capture of Charleston in March, an order was issued by the Secretary of war, that the approaching anniversary of the initial act of the war, the attack upon Fort Sumter, should be celebrated with appropriate ceremonies at the recaptured Fort. The order dated March 27th, was as follows: Ordered. *First*—That at the hour of noon on the 14th day of April, 1865, Brevet Maj-Gen. Anderson will raise and plant upon the ruins of Fort Sumter, in Charleston Harbor, the same United States flag that floated over the battlements of that fort during the rebel assault, and which was lowered and saluted by him and the small force of his command, when the works were evacuated, on the 14th day of April, 1861. *Second*—That the flag, when raised, be saluted by one hundred guns from Fort Sumter, and by a national salute from every fort and rebel battery that fired upon Fort Sumter. *Third.*—That suitable ceremonies be had upon the occasion, under the direction of Major-Gen. Wm. T. Sherman, whose military operations compelled the rebels to evacuate Charleston, or in his absence, under the charge of Major-Gen. Q. A. Gillmore, commanding the department.—Among the ceremonies will be the delivery of a public address by the Rev. Henry Ward Beecher. *Fourth.*—That the naval forces at Charleston, and their commander on that station, be invited to participate in the ceremonies of the occasion."

The order was carried out to the letter. Previously to the day a large number of distinguished visitors, General Anderson, General Dix, Captain Fox, the Assistant Secretary of the Navy, President Lincoln's Private Secretary,

Mr. Nicolay, William Lloyd Garrison, Senator Wilson and these with the orator of the day, the Rev. Mr. Beecher, were gathered at Charleston, where on the 13th, tidings reached those who had arrived of the surrender of General Lee, and the virtual fall of the rebellion, an event which was hardly anticipated when the order for the commemoration was first promulgated. The news, of course, gave additional significance to the flag raising. The day, the 14th, proved a fine one, and the programme of the celebration was carried out with every advantage. The area and ruins of the fort were covered with an assemblage of guests and spectators, numbering at least three thousand, one sixth of whom were ladies. Large detachments of white and colored troops were present, including the mariners and sailors who had taken part in the assault on the fort. Among the steamers which brought the guests to the fort from Charleston, was the memorable steamer Planter, Capt. David Small, bearing a large number of the negro population of the city. The monitors and other vessels of Admiral Dahlgren's fleet on the station gaily decorated, surrounded the fort. After prayer by the Rev. Matthew Harris, the army chaplain who had knelt in supplication at the previous raising of the flag when Major Anderson had, at the first symptoms of hostilities, removed his command to the spot from Fort Moultrie, the "old flag" which had been carefully preserved by Major Anderson during four years of war, was again raised by him, and saluted as ordered by one hundred guns from the fort, and a national salute from the fleet, Fort Moultrie and Battery Bee on Sullivan's Island, Fort Putnam on Morris Island and Fort Johnson on James Island, the rebel works which had been raised against Fort Sumter, and for the Confederate defence of the harbor. The Rev. Mr. Beecher's address then followed, kind, considerate and patriotic, celebrating with kindling eloquence the new order of things, and the promised blessing of the future. "On this solemn and joyful day," said he, "we lift to the breeze our father's flag, now again the banner of the United States, with the fervent prayer that God would crown it with honor, protect it from treason, and send it down to our children with all the blessings of civilization, liberty and religion. Terrible in battle, may it be beneficent in peace. Happily no bird or beast of prey has been inscribed upon it. The stars that redeem the night from darkness, and the beams of red light that beautify the morning have been united upon its folds. As long as the sun endures, or the stars, may it wave over a nation neither enslaved nor enslaving. Once, but once, has treason dishonored it. In that insane hour when the guiltiest and bloodiest Rebellion of time hurled their fires upon this fort, you, sir, (turning to Gen. Anderson) and a small heroic band, stood within these now crumbled walls, and did gallant and just battle for the honor and defense of the Nation's banner. In that fire this glorious flag still peacefully waved to the breeze above your head, unconscious of harm as the stars and skies above it. Once it was shot down. A gallant hand, in whose care this day it has been, plucked it from the ground and reared it again, cast down, but not destroyed. After a vain resistance, with trembling hand and sad heart you withdrew it from its height, closed its wings, and bore it far away, sternly to sleep amid the tumults of Rebellion and the thunders of battle. The first act of the war had begun. The long night of four years had set in. While the giddy traitors whirled in a maze of exhilaration, dim horrors were already advancing that were ere long to fill the land with blood. To-day you are returned again. We devoutly join with you in thanksgiving to Almighty God that he has spared your honored life, and vouchsafed to you the honors of this day. The heavens over you are the same. The same shores are here, morning comes and evening as they did. All else how changed! What grim batteries around the burdened shores! What scenes have filled this air and disturbed these waters!—These scattered heaps of shapeless stones are all that is left of Fort Sumter. Desolation broods in yonder sad city; solemn retribution had avenged our dishonored banner. You have come back with honor who departed hence four years ago, leaving the air sultry with fanaticism. The surging crowds that rolled up their frenzied shouts as the flag came down are dead, or scattered, or silent, and their habitations are desolate, ruin sits in the cradle of treason the Rebellion has perished, but there flies the same flag that was insulted. With starry eyes it looks all over the bay for that banner that supplanted it, and sees it not. [Applause.] You that then for the day were humbled, are again to triumph once more and forever. [Applause.] In the storm of that assault, this glorious ensign was often struck, but—memorable fact—not one of its stars was torn out by shot or shell. It was a prophecy. It said, not one State shall be struck from this nation by treason. The fulfillment is at hand. Lifted to the air to-day, it proclaims, after four years of war, not a State is blotted out. Hail to the flag of our fathers and our flag. Glory to the banner that has gone through four years black with tempests of war, to pilot the nation back to peace, without dismemberment, and glory be to God who, above all hosts and banners, had ordained victory and shall ordain peace."

After asserting the paramount necessity on the part of the rebel States of submitting to the national authority, he continued. "There is the Constitution, there are the laws, there is the Government. They rise up like mountains of strength that shall not be moved. They are the condition of peace. One nation under one government without slavery has been ordained and shall stand. There can be peace on no other basis. On this basis reconstruction is easy and needs neither architect nor engineer. Without this basis no engineer or architect shall ever reconstruct these rebellious States. We do not want your cities nor your fields; we do not envy you your prolific and heavens full of perpetual summer. Let agriculture revel here. Let manufactures make every stream twice musical; build fleets in every port; inspire the arts of peace with genius, second only to that of Athens, and we shall be glad in your gladness and rich in your wealth. All that we ask is unswerving loyalty and universal liberty, and that in the name of this high sovereignty of the United States of America we demand, and that, with the blessings of Almighty God, we will have. We raise our father's banner that it may bring back better blessings than those of old, that it may cast out the devil of discord, that it may restore lawful governments and a prosperity purer and more enduring than that which it protected before, that it may win parted friends from their alienation; that it may inspire hope, and inaugurate universal liberty; that it may say to the sword, 'Return to thy sheath,' and to the plow and sickle, 'Go forth;' that it may heal all jealousies, unite all politics; inspire a new national life; compact our strength; purify our principles; enable our national ambitions, and make this people great and strong, not for aggression and quarrelsomeness, but for the peace of the world giving to us the glorious prerogative of leading all nations to juster laws and to more humane politics, to sincerer friendship, to rational, instituted civil liberty, and to universal Christian brotherhood."

Having reviewed the essential elements of the conflict, and traced the rebellion to its source and motives, the orator thus concluded:

"What then shall hinder the rebuilding of this Republic? The evil spirit is cast out; why should not this nation cease to wander among tombs cutting itself? Why should it not come clothed and in its right mind to sit at the feet of Jesus? Is it feared that the Government will oppress the conquered States? What possible motive has the Government to narrow the base of that pyramid on which its own permanence stands? Is it feared that the rights of the States will be withheld? The South is not more jealous of State rights than the North State rights, from the earliest colonial days, have been the peculiar pride and jealousy of New England. In every stage of national formation, it was peculiarly Northern, and not Southern, statesmen who guarded State rights, especially as we were forming the Constitution. But once united, the loyal States gave up forever that which had been delegated to the National Government, and now, in the hour of victory, the loyal States do not mean to trench upon Southern States rights. They will not do it, nor suffer it to be done. There is not to be one rule for high latitudes and another for low. We take nothing from the Southern States that has not already been taken from the Northern. The South shall have just those rights that every Eastern, every Middle, every Western State has—no more, no less. We are not seeking our own aggrandizement by impoverishing the South. Its prosperity is an indispensable element of our own. We have shown by all that we have suffered in war how great is our estimate of the importance of the Southern States of this Union, and we will measure that estimate now in peace by still greater exertions for their rebuilding. Will reflecting men not perceive, then, the wisdom of accepting established facts and with alacrity of enterprise begin to retrieve the past? Slavery cannot come back. It is the interest, therefore, of every man to hasten its end. Do you want more war? Are you not yet weary of contest? Will you gather up the unexploded fragments of this prodigious magazine of Mischief and heap them up for continued explosions? Does not the South need peace? And since free labor is inevitable, will you have it in its worst forms or its best? Shall it be ignorant, impertinent, indolent, or shall it be educated, self-respecting, moral and self-supporting? Will you have men as drudges, or will you have them as citizens? Since they have vindicated the Government and cemented its foundation stones with their blood, may they not offer their tribute of support to maintain it laws and its policy? It is better for religion, it is better for political integrity, it is better for industry, it is better for money, if you will have that motive, that you should educate the black man, and by education make him a citizen. [Applause.] They who refuse education to the black man would turn the South into a vast poorhouse, and labor into a pendulum of necessity, vibrating between poverty and indolence. From this pulpit of broken stone, we speak forth our earnest greeting to all our land; we offer to the President of the United States our solemn congratulations that God has sustained his life and health under the unparalleled burdens and sufferings of four bloody years, and permitted him to behold this auspicious consummation of that national unity for which he has waited with so much patience and fortitude, and for which he has labored with such disinterested wisdom. To the members of the Government associated with him in the administering of perilous affairs in critical times; to the Senators and Representatives of the United States, who have eagerly fashioned the instruments by which the popular will might express and enforce itself, we tender our grateful thanks. To the officers and men of the army, who have so faithfully, skillfully and gloriously upheld their country's authority by suffering, labor and sublime courage, we offer here a tribute beyond the compass of words. Upon these true and faithful citizens, men and women who have borne up with unflinching hope in the darkest hour, and covered the land with their labors of love and charity, we invoke the divinest blessing of Him whom they have so faithfully imitated. But chiefly to Thee, God of our fathers! we render thanksgiving and praise for that wondrous providence that has brought forth from such a harvest of war the seed of so much liberty and peace. We invoke peace upon the North; peace be to the West: peace be upon the South. In the name of God, we lift up our banner and dedicate it to Peace, Union, and Liberty, now and forever more. Amen!"

While prayer, and thanksgivings were thus going up for President Lincoln that "God had sustained his life and health under the unparalleled burdens and sufferings of four bloody years, and permitted him to behold this auspicious consummation," his hours were numbered by the assassin stealthily waiting his opportunity at evening to crown this fair day of rejoicing with an act of everlasting infamy. There was no special celebration of the anniversary of Sumter at the national capital, but the President and General Grant were invited by the manager of Ford's Theatre, to be present at a performance that night of the popular play, "The American Cousin," and the expectation of seeing them there, drew together a large audience. The President accepted the invitation, and occupied a private box over the stage, at the theatre, in company with his wife, a daughter of Senator Harris, and Major Henry R. Rathbone, of the United States Army. Gen. Grant, having left the city during the day, did not attend.

When the performance had reached the second scene of the third act, it was interrupted by the discharge of a pistol shot in the box occupied by the President. It was fired from behind, the ball entering the back part and left side of the President's head, penetrating the brain and rendering him totally insensible. His position as he sat in his chair at the front of the box was not changed; his head was slightly bent forward, and his eyes were closed. On hearing the sound of the pistol fired behind him, Major Rathbone, who was sitting at the extreme left of the box, about seven or eight feet from the President, looking round him saw through the smoke a man between the door and the President. He at the same time heard him shout some words one of which was "Freedom." He instantly sprang toward him, and seized him. The man wrested himself from the Major's grasp, and made a violent thrust at his breast with a large knife. Major Rathbone parried the blow by striking it up, and received a wound several inches deep on his left arm. The man rushed to the front of the box, and the Major attempted to seize him again, but only caught his clothes as he was leaping over the front of the box upon the stage.* The escape of the man from the box, was observed by William J. Hawke, an actor in the play then going forward, who heard him exclaim "*Sic semper tyrannis*," the motto of the State arms of Virginia, as he approached the front and leapt upon the stage, where he fell as he struck the floor, but in a moment got upon his feet and brandishing a large knife, saying "The South shall be free," ran across the stage and made his exit from the house by a passage way through a door in the rear. As the man ran across the stage toward Hawke, the latter recognized him as John Wilkes Booth, a well known actor

* Affidavit of Major Rathbone, Washington, D. C., April 17, 1865.

who had formerly performed at the theatre, and was familiar with the arrangements of the house. The fall of Booth upon the stage was occasioned by one of the spurs which he wore, catching in the fringe of the flag, with which the box in honor of the occasion was draped. The spur was left upon the stage. A single barrel pistol was found in the box, with the hat of the assassin. A horse was in waiting for the assassin in the street at the rear of the theatre, on which he mounted, and, in company with a comrade named Herrold, also mounted, escaped from the city into Maryland.

The President meanwhile was instantly looked to by Major Rathbone, who rushed to the door of the box for the purpose of calling medical aid. On reaching the outer door of the passage way, by which the box was entered from the body of the house, he found it barred by a heavy piece of plank, one end of which was secured in the wall, and the other resting against the door. It had been so securely fastened that it required considerable force to remove, such precaution was taken by the assassin to secure a safe approach to the President, free from interruption from without. On the removal of the bar several surgeons were admitted to the box, the President's wound was hastily examined, and it was determined to remove him from the theatre. He was accordingly carried to a private house opposite the theatre, where he was laid upon a bed in a room on the ground floor. Surgeon-General Barnes and other surgeons and physicians were immediately in attendance ; but it was evident from the outset that the wound was mortal. Secretaries Stanton and Welles, and other members of the Cabinet, with General Halleck, Chief Justice Chase, Senator Sumner, the Rev. Dr. Gurley, of New York, and other persons of distinction watched with him through the night at his bedside, his wife and son Robert being near him. At twenty-two minutes past seven o'clock in the morning of the 15th, he breathed his last. He remained unconscious from the first moment he was struck.

Meanwhile the intense excitement of the city was increased by the intelligence that a brutal assault had been made upon the life of Secretary Seward, as he lay in bed at his residence suffering from the serious effects of the wounds he had recently received, when he was thrown from his carriage.

The circumstances, as subsequently related by Mr. Seward's physician, Dr. T. S. Verdi, were these: "At nine o'clock on the evening of the 14th inst.,"* he writes, "I had left Secretary Seward in a comfortable condition, and his family hopeful of his speedy recovery from an accident which he several days previously met with, his horses having run away and dashed him from the carriage, fracturing his right humerus at the surgical neck, his lower maxillary below the angle, and generally bruising him about the face and neck. At a few minutes after 10 P. M., I was hastily summoned by the colored boy, to attend Mr. Seward, his sons and his attendants, who were, as the messenger expressed it, "murdered by an assassin." Two minutes brought me to the spot. I was the first medical man there. As I glanced around the room, I found terror depicted on every countenance, and blood everywhere. Among the bleeding men and terrified ladies I sought for Mr. Seward. He was lying in his bed, covered with blood, a fearful gaping gash marking his chin and extending below the maxillary bone. His, probably, was the only countenance that did not express fear. Hastily I examined his wounds, and I had the joy to bring the first consolation to that anxious family, in announcing to them that his wounds

* Letter to Dr. W. Tod Helmath, dated Washington, April 21, 1865, published in the Western (St. Louis) Homœopathic Observer.

were not mortal. The carotid artery and jugular vein had not been divided or injured. The gash was semi-circular, commencing just below the high bone of the cheek, and extending downward toward the mouth, and then backward over the submaxillary gland, laying open the inflamed and swollen part of the face and neck, that had been injured by his previous accident. On examining further, I found another stab under the left ear, wounding the parotid gland; but this cut, however, was not very deep. Mr. Seward had lost much blood, and I immediately applied ice, to arrest the bleeding temporarily; after which I was informed that Frederick Seward was in an adjacent room, also injured. I hastily went to him and found him lying on a lounge, with blood streaming over his face. He had been wounded in several places, viz., on the left parietal bone, just about the "parietal eminence;" on the left side of the frontal bone, just about the line of intersection with the parietal bone; with two other light wounds in that neighborhood. The injury on the parietal eminence had evidently crushed the bone, as osseous spiculæ were taken out; but it appeared, however, that the internal table, even if fractured, was not depressed. He was not insensible, but could not articulate. In about an hour, however, after his wounds were dressed, he fell into a slumber from which, for sixty hours, he could not be aroused. I had scarcely finished applying ice to arrest the hemorrhage, when I was told to look at Mr. Aug. Seward, (Major A. H. Seward.) I was truly amazed—"What?" said I, "is there another wounded?" His injuries, however, were comparatively light—one was from a blow with the butt-end of a pistol, on the upper and middle part of the forehead; the other a cut over the metacarpal bone of the thumb of his right hand. Here I was again requested to look at another man. My surprise ceased then—I became horrified. This was the man-nurse, a soldier in attendance on Mr. Seward. (Sergeant George F. Robinson.) I found his wounds were four in number, all from the blade of a knife; three over the right scapular region, and one below it. It was evident, after a careful examination, that the scapula prevented the penetration of the frightful weapon into the chest. After giving to this patient the requisite attendance, I was called to see another man who was wounded. He had received but one stab in the back over the seventh rib, very near the spinal column. The knife must have glanced off, as this cut was long but quite superficial; had it been direct, his right lung would have received an irreparable injury.

"Such is the scene that presented. Now I will relate to you the circumstances I gathered in this horrible attempt at assassination. At 10 o'clock the bell at Mr. Seward's house was rung, and answered by the colored boy, (William Wells, waiter.) As the door opened a very tall man appeared, with a small package in his hand, saying that Dr. Verdi had sent him with a prescription for Secretary Seward, which he must deliver personally. The boy remonstrated with the man, saying that Mr. Seward was asleep, and that he (the servant) would take charge of the prescription. The man said, "No; I have particular directions, and I must deliver them myself." So saying, he walked up stairs; but, treading very heavily, he was reminded by the boy, who was following him, to walk more lightly, in order not to disturb Mr. Seward.

"Mr. Frederick Seward was at this time lying, dressed, on a sofa in his room, (one adjacent to his father's) and hearing heavy footsteps, came into the hall and met the stranger, who attempted to enter his father's room. Frederick expostulated with him, declaring that his father was asleep and could not be seen. Evidently the young man saw mischief in the face of the assassin. Miss Fanny Seward, who was in her father's room, hearing the conversation outside, opened the door to ascertain what was the matter; but Frederick cried out to her to "shut the door." It seems that for two or three minutes the assassin hesitated, or endeavored to enter without making a deadly assault upon Frederick, but meeting with determined opposition, he dealt several blows on young Seward's head, apparently with a pistol, with the intention, probably, of disabling him without killing him. The door was then opened, and the murderer entered, pushing Frederick, already staggering, before him; then disengaging himself from his adversary, asked Miss Fanny, "Is the Secretary asleep?"—at the same instant making a spring for the bed, where the unfortunate man sat, aroused with the frightened conviction of what was to be expected. The next moment the villain dealt him a blow with the deadly knife, which was so violent that (fortunately, we may say) it precipitated him from his bed. In falling, however, he must have received the second blow on the other side of the neck. It must have been at this time that the man-nurse (having been absent at the hospital) returned and attacked the murderer, to prevent him from doing further injury to Mr. Seward. In the endeavor to restrain the ferocity of the assassin the nurse was struck several times, as described above. It was at this moment that the nurse and Frederick, who rallied sufficiently to still use his feeble efforts in behalf of his poor father, were struggling with this man, that Major Augustus Seward, awakened from sleep by the noise and screams of Miss Fanny, came into the room, thinking that probably his father was delirious, and had frightened the attendants, or else that the nurse left to watch during the night was in some way misbehaving himself. The Major, seeing the struggle, and not at all comprehending the facts, took hold of the man, (believing him still to be the nurse) and dragged him to the door. Of course the assassin took advantage of this, and dealing one blow on the head of the Major, (making, however, but a slight wound,) and cutting his hand, as aforesaid, ran down stairs, followed by the Major, who did not know the condition of affairs until he came back to his father's room. The assassin then mounted his horse, which he had left before the door, and rode rapidly away."

There was good reason to believe, also, that an attempt was meditated upon the life of Vice-President Johnson, to be executed at the same time, and also upon General Grant on his expected visit to the theatre.

The announcement of these events by telegraph to the country on the morning of the 15th was received by the nation with the profoundest feeling of honor and pity. There was no vulgar excitement, but a deep sense of the unutterable wrong and injury. It was impossible not to couple these acts with the Rebellion, the great iniquity of which they revealed in all its malignity. The nation, it was felt, had been struck where the blow reached every individual of the country. To assail the Chief Magistrate, whose tenure of office had just been a second time secured by a popular election, was to assault the people themselves. But neither new and increased hatred of the Rebellion, nor the sense of private insult and injury compared for the time with the feelings of sorrow and regret at the loss, in so revolting a manner, of the man, Abraham Lincoln, at a moment when the end had proved his work; when his character for integrity, sagacity, modesty, patient self-sacrifice in the national cause had been so fully demonstrated; in fine, when he had grown, in the face of much prejudice and opposition, by the exercise of his true manly qualities, into the very hearts of the people. The nation, suddenly called upon to lament, mourned his loss as that of a personal friend. This was shown in the simple demonstrations of mourning which everywhere appeared. Without waiting for official orders or influence, on the morning of the 15th, before such directions could be given, places of business were closed and the houses in the large cities and elsewhere almost universally were draped in black. There were few so poor as not to exhibit some badge of sorrow of this kind. Trade was suspended while the people gathered in groups wondering at the calamity or listening to the voices of speakers who gave expression in popular harangues to the common sorrow. The voice of party was hushed. If the assault four years before on Sumter had developed the real unity of the nation, the assassination of the President immeasurably strengthened the sentiment and sanctioned the Union.

Nothing was more noticeable during the period which followed than the calmness and sense of security which were exhibited by the great body of the people. There was not a moment's doubt of the strength and stability of the Government. The finances stood firm, the political confidence undoubting. The recent military suppression of the Rebellion doubtless added to this ; but had it been otherwise, and if General Grant had yet his great victory to win, the result would not have been dissimilar. The Constitution, so often of late severely tried, was equal to this emergency, and the violent assassination of Lincoln at the culmination of an unprecedented civil war, caused no more disastrous effect than had occurred on the peaceful natural deaths of Presidents Harrison and Taylor. Vice-President Johnson succeeded to the Chief Magistracy with no more disturbance than had occurred on the accession of his predecessors, Taylor and Filmore.

Immediately upon the death of President Lincoln, Attorney-General Speed waited upon the Hon. Andrew Johnson and officially informed him of the event by the following communication from the members of the Cabinet :

"Sir,—Abraham Lincoln, President of the United States, was shot by an assassin last evening at Ford's Theatre, in this city, and died at the hour of 7:22 o'clock. About the same time at which the President was shot, an assassin entered the sick chamber of the Hon. W. H. Seward, Secretary of State, and stabbed him in several places in the throat, neck and face, severely, if not mortally wounding him. Other members of the Secretary's family were dangerously wounded by the assassin while making his escape. By the death of President Lincoln the office of President has devolved under the Constitution upon you. The emergency of the Government demands that you should immediately qualify according to the requirements of the Constitution and enter upon the duties of President of the United States. If you will please make known your pleasure, such arrangements as you deem proper will be made. Your obedient servants, Hugh McCulloch, Secretary of the Treasury ; Edwin M. Stanton, Secretary of War ; Gideon Welles, Secretary of the Navy ; William Dennison, Postmaster-General ; J. P. Usher, Secretary of the Interior ; James Speed, Attorney-General. To Andrew Johnson, Vice-President of the United States."

Mr. Johnson requested that the ceremonies take place at his rooms at the Kirkwood House, in this city, at 10 o'clock in the morning. The Hon. Salmon P. Chase, Chief Justice of the United States, was notified of the fact, and desired to be in attendance to administer the oath of office. At the above-named hour the following gentlemen assembled in the Vice-President's room to participate in the ceremony : The

Hon. Salmon P. Chase; the Hon. Hugh McCulloch, Secretary of the Treasury; Mr. Attorney-General Speed; F. P. Blair, sr.; the Hon. Montgomery Blair; Senators Foot, of Vermont, Yates, of Illinois, Ramsay, of Minnesota, Stewart, of Nevada, Hale, of New Hampshire, and General Farnsworth, of Illinois. After the presentation of the above letter, the Chief Justice administered the following oath to Mr. Johnson: "I do solemnly swear that I will faithfully execute the office of President of the United States, and will, to the best of my ability, preserve, protect and defend the Constitution of the United States."

After receiving the oath and being declared President of the United States, Mr. Johnson remarked: "Gentlemen,—I must be permitted to say that I have been almost overwhelmed by the announcement of the sad event which has so recently occurred. I feel incompetent to perform duties so important and responsible as those which have been so unexpectedly thrown upon me. As to an indication of any policy which may be pursued by me in the administration of the Government, I have to say that that must be left for development as the Administration progresses. The message or declaration must be made by the acts as they transpire. The only assurance that I can now give of the future is reference to the past. The course which I have taken in the past in connection with this rebellion, must be regarded as a guarantee of the future. My past public life, which has been long and laborious, has been founded, as I in good conscience believe upon a great principle of right, which lies at the basis of all things. The best energies of my life have been spent in endeavoring to establish and perpetuate the principles of free government, and I believe that the Government, in passing through its present perils, will settle down upon principles consonant with popular rights, more permanent and enduring than heretofore. I must be permitted to say, if I understand the feelings of my own heart, I have long labored to ameliorate and elevate the condition of the great mass of the American people. Toil and an honest advocacy of the great principles of free government have been my lot. The duties have been mine—the consequences are God's. This has been the foundation of my political creed. I feel that in the end the Government will triumph, and that these great principles will be permanently established. In conclusion, gentlemen, let me say that I want your encouragement and countenance. I shall ask and rely upon you and others in carrying the Government through its present perils. I feel in making this request that it will be heartily responded to by you and all other patriots and lovers of the rights and interests of a free people."

Official notice of this assumption of the duties of the Presidency was communicated to the country by Secretary Stanton, coupled with a formal announcement that the President would retain the present Secretaries of departments of his Cabinet, and that "they would go on and discharge their respective duties in the same manner as before the deplorable event that had changed the head of the government."

The arrangements for the funeral of President Lincoln were referred to the members of the Cabinet, and in concert with the family of the deceased it was determined that the remains should be accompanied by a national escort from Washington to his former home at Springfield, Illinois, by way of Baltimore, Harrisburg, Philadelphia, New York, Albany, Buffalo, Cleveland, Columbus, Indianapolis and Chicago. The first of the imposing obsequies which ensued was celebrated on the 19th of April, at the White House at Washington, where the body was lying in State. There were present at these initial funeral ceremonies, which were held in the large East Room of the Presidential mansion, a large array of representative persons, including the diplomatic corps in full dress, the heads of bureaus, the city authorities, various members of Congress, the governors of several of the States, delegates from northern cities, officers of the army and navy, including General Grant and Admiral Farragut, while the Supreme Court was represented by Chief Justice Chase. Precisely at noon President Johnson, with the members of the Cabinet, entered and took their places at the right of the coffin. The services were commenced by the Rev. Mr. Hall reading the opening parts of the Episcopal burial service, including the usual portion of the 15th chapter of St. Paul to the Corinthians. The Right Rev. Bishop Simpson, of the Methodist Episcopal Church, then delivered a prayer, and was followed by the Rev. Dr. Gurley, of the Presbyterian Church, who pronounced an eloquent funeral discourse. The remains were then conveyed in a long and imposing procession to the rotunda of the Capitol, where they lay in state till the 21st, when they were conveyed to Philadelphia according to the programme already indicated. The 19th, the day of the funeral at Washington, was solemnly observed in the Northern cities; the churches were opened and appropriate services were held in concert with those at the national capital. The heart of the people throbbed as that of one man through all the circumstances attending these melancholy events. As the great funeral procession proceeded by railway, all along its course, whether by night or day, it was witnessed by multitudes who awaited its arrival with every demonstration of respect. At the great cities where it rested meetings were held, processions formed and orations delivered. It was a fortnight from the time the remains left Washington before they reached their final resting-place at Springfield. "That rain of tears," says an eloquent witness of the scene,* "was there ever anything like it in our American history? Millions crowded to his funeral. Five hundred thousand, it is estimated, gazed upon that dead face, as onward, by day and night, the sad procession moved through the cities, towns and hamlets of our land. The writer witnessed it at an inland station, where no outward show of preparation could be made. Still there, as elsewhere, while the dark draped car moved slowly through, was there the manifestation of the same substantial sorrow—the silent crowd, the spontaneously uncovered head, while drops were stealing down the manly cheeks and muffled sobs betrayed the female grief. All hearts were softened, all malice silenced, all party spirit hushed."

* Professor Taylor Lewis, of Union College, Schenectady, in an article on Abraham Lincoln, in "Hours at Home," June, 1865

CHAPTER CXV.

CONCLUDING EVENTS OF THE WAR. APRIL—JUNE, 1865.

The surrender of Lee's army to General Grant proved as had been anticipated, the virtual extinction of the military power of the rebellion. Other armies, indeed, remained in the field, Johnston's in North Carolina, the remains of Taylor's forces in Alabama, Maury's fugitives from Mobile, and a considerable force under Kirby Smith in Texas ; but these, one after another at short intervals, followed the precedent which had been set by General Lee, laid down their arms and surrendered to the United States authorities. The process was slightly interrupted in the first instance, that of General Johnston, by a negotiation between that officer and General Sherman, the particulars of which were communicated to the country on the 22d of April, in an official dispatch from Secretary Stanton at the War Department. From this it appeared, that on the 18th of April "an agreement for a suspension of hostilities and a memorandum of what is called a basis for peace" had been entered into between Generals Sherman and Johnston, near Durham's Station, North Carolina, the particulars of which were as follows :

"*First*,—The contending armies now in the field to maintain their *statu quo*, until notice is given by the Commanding General of either one to its opponent, and reasonable time—say forty-eight hours—allowed. *Second*,—The Confederate armies now in existence to be disbanded and conducted to their several State capitals, there to deposit their arms and public property in the State arsenals, and each officer and man to execute and file an agreement to cease from acts of war, and abide action of both State and Federal authority. The number of arms and munitions of war, to be reported to the Chief of Ordnance at Washington City, subject to future action of the Congress of the United States, in the meantime to be used solely to maintain peace and order within the borders of the States respectively. *Third*,—The recognition by the executive of the United States of several State Governments, in their officers and legislatures, taking oath prescribed by the Constitution of the United States, and where conflicting State Governments have resulted from the war, the legitimacy of all shall be submitted to the Supreme Court of the United States. *Fourth*.—The re-establishment of all Federal courts in the several States, with powers as defined by the Constitution and laws of Congress. *Fifth*,—The people and inhabitants of all States to be guaranteed, so far as the Executive can, their political rights and franchise, as well as their rights of persons and property, as defined by the Constitution of the United States and of States respectively. *Sixth*,—The executive authority of the Government of the United States, not to disturb any of the people by reason of the late war, so long as they live in peace and quiet, and abstain from acts of armed hostility, and obey laws in existence at any place of their residence. In general terms, war to cease ; a general amnesty, so far as the executive power of the United States can command, or on condition of disbandment of the Confederate armies, and the distribution of arms and resumption of peaceful pursuits by officers and men as hitherto composing the said armies. Not being fully empowered by our respective principals to fulfil these terms, we individually and officially pledge ourselves to promptly obtain necessary authority, and to carry out the above programme." On receipt of this memorandum a cabinet meeting was immediately held, at which the action of General Sherman was disapproved by President Johnson, by the Secretary of War, by General Grant, and by every member of the cabinet. General Sherman was ordered to resume hostilities immediately, and was directed that the instructions given to General Grant by President Lincoln on a previous occasion,* directing him "not to decide, discuss or confer upon any political question" were approved by President Johnson, and "were reiterated to govern the action of military commanders.' The following comment was appended to the memorandum of negotiation in the dispatch from the War Department. "This proceeding of General Sherman was unapproved for the following among other reasons: *First*,—It was an exercise of authority not vested in General Sherman, and on its face shows that both he and Johnston knew that he (General Sherman) had no authority to enter into any such arrangement. *Second*,—It was a practical acknowledgment of the rebel government. *Third*,—It undertook to re-establish the rebel State government, that had been overthrown at the sacrifice of many thousand loyal lives, and an immense treasure, and placed arms and munitions of war in the hands of the rebels at their respective capitols, which might be used as soon as the armies of the United States were disbanded, and used to conquer and subdue the loyal States. *Fourth*,--By the restoration of the rebel authority in their respective States, they would be enabled to re-establish slavery. *Fifth*,—It might furnish a ground of responsibility by the Federal Government to pay the rebel debt, and certainly subjects loyal citizens of the rebel States to the debt consummated by the rebels in the name of the State. *Sixth*,—It put in dispute the existence of loyal State Governments, and the new State of Western Virginia, which had been recognized by every department of the United States Government. *Seventh*,—It practically abolishes the confiscation laws, and relieved rebels of every degree, who had slaughtered our people, from all pains and penalties for their crimes. *Eighth*,—It gives terms that had been deliberately, repeatedly and solemnly rejected by President Lincoln, and better terms than the rebels had ever asked in their most prosperous condition. *Ninth*,—It formed no basis of true and lasting peace, but relieved rebels from the pressure of our victories, and left them in condition to renew their effort to overthrow the United States Government, and subdue the loyal States, whenever their strength was recruited, and any opportunity should offer."

The immediate circumstances which led to this "negotiation" and the motives which influenced him in making it are narrated by General Sherman in the subsequent final report of his campaign. On the 14th of April, the anniversary of Sumter, when General Sherman had established his head quarters at Raleigh, the enemy being between Greensborough and Hillsborough, he received a communication from General Johnston inquiring "whether in order to stop the further effusion of blood and devastation of property you are willing to make a temporary suspension of active operations, and to communicate with Lieutenant-General Grant, commanding the armies of the United States, the request that he will take like action in regard to other armies, the object being to permit the civil authorities to enter into the needful arrangements to terminate the existing war. To this General Sherman

* Ante p. 562.

replied that he was willing to enter into a conference with regard to a suspension of hostilities, and accordingly, says he in his report, "I agreed to meet General Johnston in person, at a point intermediate between our pickets, on the 17th, at noon, provided the position of the troops remained *statu quo*. I was both willing and anxious to secure a few days, as it would enable Colonel Wright to finish our railroad to Raleigh. Two bridges had to be built, and twelve miles of new road made. We had no iron, except by taking up the branch from Goldsborough to Weldon. Instead of losing by time I gained in every way, for every hour of delay possible was required to reconstruct the railroad to our rear and improve the condition of our wagon road to the front, so desirable in case the negotiations failed, and we be forced to make the race of near 200 miles to head off or catch Johnston, then retreating towards Charlotte. At noon of the day appointed I met General Johnston for the first time in my life, although we had been exchanging shots continually since May, 1863. Our interview was frank and soldier-like, and he gave me to understand that further war on the part of the Confederate troops was folly; that the "cause" was lost, and that every life sacrificed after the surrender of Lee's army was the highest possible crime. He admitted the terms conceded to General Lee were magnanimous, and all he could ask; but he did want some general concessions that would enable him to allay the natural fears and anxieties of his followers, and enable him to maintain his control over them until they could be got back to the neighborhood of their homes, thereby saving the State of North Carolina the devastation inevitably to result from turning his men loose and unprovided on the spot, and our pursuit across the State. He also wanted to embrace in the same general proposition the fate of all the Confederate arms that remained in existence. I never made any concession as to his own army, or assumed to deal finally and authoritatively in regard to any other, but it did seem to me that there was presented a chance for peace that might be deemed valuable to the United States, and was at least worthy the few days that would be consumed in reference. To push an enemy whose commander had so frankly and honestly confessed his inability to cope with me, were cowardly and unworthy the brave men I led. Inasmuch as General Johnston did not feel authorized to exercise power over the armies in Texas, we adjourned to the next day at noon. I returned to Raleigh, and conferred freely with all my general officers, *every one* of whom urged me to conclude terms that might accomplish so complete and desirable an end. All dreaded the necessary laborious march after a fugitive and dissolving army back toward Georgia, over the very country where they had toiled so long. There was but one opinion expressed, and, if contrary ones were entertained they were withheld, or indulged in only by that class who shun the fight and the march, but are loudest, bravest and fiercest when danger is past.

"I again met General Johnston on the 18th, and we resumed the conversation. He satisfied me then of his *power* to disband the rebel armies in Alabama, Mississippi, Louisiana and Texas, as well as those in his immediate command, viz.: North Carolina, Georgia and Florida. The points on which he expresses especial solicitude were lest their States were to be dismembered and denied representation in Congress, or any separate political existence whatever; and the absolute disarming of his men would leave the South powerless and exposed to depredations by wicked bands of assassins and robbers. 'The President's (Lincoln) Message of 1864; his Amnesty Proclamation; General Grant's terms to General Lee, substantially extending the benefit of that Proclamation to all officers above the rank of Colonel; the invitation of the Virginia Legislature to re-assemble in Richmond, by General Weitzel, with the supposed approval of Mr. Lincoln and General Grant, then on the spot; a firm belief that I had been fighting to re-establish the Constitution of the United States; and last, but not least, the general and universal desire to close a war any longer without organized resistance, were the leading facts that induced me to pen the 'memorandum' of April 18, signed by myself and General Johnston. It was designed to be, and so expressed on its face, as a mere 'basis' for reference to the President of the United States and constitutional Commander-in-Chief, to enable him, if he chose, at one blow, to dissipate the power of the Confederacy which had threatened the national safety for years. It admitted of modification, alteration and change. It had no appearance of an ultimatum, and by no false reasoning can it be construed into an usurpation of power on my part. I have my opinions on the questions involved, 'but this forms no part of a military report.'

"Immediately on my return to Raleigh I dispatched one of my staff, Major Hitchcock, to Washington, enjoining him to be most prudent and careful to avoid the spies and informers that would be sure to infest him by the way, and to say nothing to anybody until the President could make known to me his feelings and wishes in the matter. The news of President Lincoln's assassination on the 14th of April (wrongly reported to me by telegraph as having occurred on the 11th), reached me on the 17th, and was announced to my command on the same day, in Field Order No. 56. I was duly informed with its horrible atrocity and probable effect on the country. But when the property and interests of millions still living were involved, I saw no good reason why to change my course, but thought rather to manifest real respect for his memory by following after his death, that policy which, if living, I felt certain he would have approved, or at least not reject with disdain. Up to that hour I had never received one word of instruction, advice or counsel as to the plan or policy of the government, looking to a restoration of peace on the part of the rebel States of the South. Whenever asked for an opinion on the points involved I had always avoided the subject. My letter to the Mayor of Atlanta has been published to the world, and I was not rebuked by the War Department for it. My letter to Mr. ——, of Savannah, was shown by me to Mr. Stanton, before its publication, and all my memory retains of his answer is that he said, like my letters generally, it was sufficiently emphatic and would not be misunderstood. Both these letters asserted my belief that, according to Mr. Lincoln's proclamation and messages, when the people of the South had laid down their arms and submitted to the lawful powers of the United States, *ipso facto*, the war was over as to them, and furthermore, that if any State in rebellion would conform to the Constitution of the United States, cease war, elect Senators and Representatives to Congress, if admitted, (of which each House of Congress alone is the judge,) that State became instanter as much in the Union as New York or Ohio. Nor were I rebuked for these expressions though it was universally known and commented on at the time. And again, Mr. Stanton in person at Savannah, speaking of the terrific expense of the war, and the difficulty of realizing the money for the daily wants of government, impressed me most forcibly with the necessity of bringing the war to a close as soon as possible for *financial reasons*.

On the evening of April 23, Major Hitchcock reported to Morehead City with dispatches, of which fact General Johnston, at Hillsborough, was notified so as to be ready in the morning for an answer. At 6 o'clock, A. M. on the 24th, Major Hitchcock arrived accompanied by General Grant and members of his staff, who had not telegraphed the fact of his coming over our exposed roads for prudential reasons. I soon learned that the memorandum was disapproved, without reasons assigned, and I was ordered to give the 48 hours' notice, and resume hostilities at the close of that time; governing myself by the substance of a dispatch then inclosed, dated March 9, 12 M., at Washington, D. C., from Secretary Stanton to General Grant, at City Point; but not accompanied by any part of the voluminous matter so liberally lavished on the public in the New York papers of the 24th April. That was the first and only time I ever saw that telegram, or had one word of instructions on the important matters involved in it, and it does seem strange to me that every bar-room loafer in New York can read in the morning journals 'official' matter that is withheld from a General whose command extends from Kentucky to North Carolina. Within an hour a courier was riding from Durham's Station toward Hillsborough, with notice to Gen. Johnston of the suspension of the truce, and renewing my demand for the surrender of the armies under his immediate command, (see two dispatches of April 24, 6 A. M.,) and at 12 M. I had the receipt of his picket officer. I therefore published my orders No. 62 to the troops, terminating the truce at 12 M. on the 26th, and ordered all to be in readiness to march at that time, on the routes prescribed in Special Field Orders No. 55, of April 14, from the positions held April 18. General Grant had orders from the President to direct military movements, and I explained to him the exact position of the troops, and he approved of it most emphatically; but he did not relieve me, or express a wish to assume command. All things were in readiness, when, on the evening of the 25th, I received another letter from General Johnston asking another interview to renew negotiations. General Grant not only approved, but urged me to accept, and I appointed a meeting at our former place at noon of the 26th, the very hour fixed for the renewal of hostilities. General Johnston was delayed by an accident to his train, but at 2 P. M. arrived. We then consulted, concluded and signed the final terms of capitulation. These were taken by me back to Raleigh, submitted to General Grant, and met his immediate approval and signature. General Johnston was not even aware of the presence of General Grant at Raleigh at the time. There was surrendered to us the second great army of the so-called Confederacy; and though undue importance has been given to the so-called negotiations which preceded it, and a rebuke and public disfavor cast on me wholly unwarranted by the facts, I rejoice in saying that it was accomplished without further ruin and devastation to the country; without the loss of a single life to those gallant men who had followed me from the Mississippi to the Atlantic; and without subjecting brave men to the ungracious task of pursuing a fleeing foe that did not want to fight." The terms of capitulation were the same which had been concluded upon between General Grant and General Lee in Virginia. The army of Johnston, which General Sherman at the beginning of April had estimated, infantry and artillery, at 35,000, cavalry from 6,000 to 10,000, reduced by escape, desertion or other causes, to about 30,000, thus laid down its arms, the soldiers returning to their several homes, while the main portion of the army of General Sherman leisurely made its way to the national capital. There, on the 30th May, on the eve of its disbandment,

General Sherman took farewell of his well-tried companions in a brilliant special order, in which he briefly alluded to the prominent incidents of the honorable campaigns in which he had led them from victory to victory.

On the 4th of May, General Richard Taylor, on terms similar to those granted to Lee and Johnston, surrendered his entire command to General Canby at Citronella, Alabama, some twenty-five miles above Mobile, and a few days after, on the 9th the rebel naval squadron, which had taken refuge in the Tombigbee river, was surrendered by Commodore Farrand to Acting Rear Admiral Thatcher. Other surrenders by Jeff. Thompson in the West, Mosby in Virginia, and others, were meantime made, leaving Texas the only foothold of an insurgent army. The supposed number of forces in the field and their comparatively unimpaired strength, with the avowed purposes of their leader, Kirby Smith, and various desperate resolves promulgated by his associates, now seemed to threaten further though ineffectual hostilities. General Sheridan was consequently assigned to the command of the Southwest for their subjugation, and reinforcements were ordered to the region; but before any new campaign was organized the influence of the failure of the Rebellion in the East was felt beyond the Mississippi; the army of Kirby Smith was rapidly falling to pieces in consequence of the desertion of his troops, and he was compelled to follow the precedents of his brother officers in timely submission. On the 23d of May arrangements were made at Baton Rouge for the surrender of his forces to General Canby. On the 30th General Kirby Smith, at Houston, issued a final address to his soldiers on abandoning the war. "My purpose," says he, "was to concentrate the entire strength of the department, await negotiation, and, if possible, secure terms alike honorable to soldiers and citizens. Failing in this I intended to struggle to the last; and with an army united in purpose, firm in resolve and battling for the right, I believe God would yet give us the victory. I reached here to find the Texas troops disbanded and hastening to their homes. They had forsaken their colors and their commanders; had abandoned the cause for which we were struggling, and appropriated the public property to their personal use. SOLDIERS: I am left a commander without an army—a General without troops. You have made your choice. It was unwise and unpatriotic, but it is final. I pray you may not live to regret it. The enemy will now possess your country and dictate his own laws. You have voluntarily destroyed our organizations, and thrown away all means of resistance. Your present duties are plain. Return to your families. Resume the occupations of peace. Yield obedience to the laws. Labor to restore order. Strive both by counsel and example to give security to life and property. And may God in his mercy direct you aright, and heal the wounds of our distracted country."

One of the first duties of the government after the assassination of President Lincoln was to pursue and bring to punishment the authors and actors of that great crime. Investigations were at once held, testimony was taken, the military and police were everywhere on the alert. The haunts of the actor Booth, the assassin of the President, were explored, and every step taken to ferret out the plot, the existence of which was evident from the simultaneous attack upon the President and the Secretary, and other circumstances of the case. On the night of the 17th of April, while the officers of the War Department were engaged in arresting the inmates of the house, in Washington, of a Mrs. Surratt, who was suspected of being cognizant of the conspiracy, a man, calling himself Louis Payne, disguised as a laborer, came to the premises, who was also detained, and who was presently identified as the person who had attempted the assassination of Secretary Seward. Another of the persons implicated, George A. Atzeroth, to whom had been assigned the assassination of Vice-President Johnson, was arrested on the 19th in Montgomery County, Maryland. For some days Booth and his accomplices evaded detection. On the 20th of April, six days after the assassination, Stanton, the Secretary of War, issued the following proclamation and offer of reward:

"The murderer of our late beloved President, Abraham Lincoln, is still at large. Fifty thousand dollars reward will be paid by this department for his apprehension, in addition to any reward offered by municipal authorities or State Executives. Twenty-five thousand dollars reward will be paid for the apprehension of G. A. Atzeroth, sometimes called "Port Tobacco," one of Booth's accomplices. Twenty-five thousand dollars reward will be paid for the apprehension of David C. Herrold, another of Booth's accomplices. Liberal reward will be paid for any information that shall conduce to the arrest of either of the above-named criminals or their accomplices. All persons harboring or secreting the said persons, or either of them, or aiding or assisting their concealment or escape, will be treated as accomplices in the murder of the President and the attempted assassination of the Secretary of State, and shall be subject to trial before a military commission, and the punishment of death. Let the stain of innocent blood be removed from the land by the arrest and punishment of the murderers. All good citizens are exhorted to aid public justice on this occasion. Every man should consider his own conscience charged with this solemn duty, and rest neither night nor day until it be accomplished."

Secretary Stanton had, meanwhile, employed Colonel L. C. Baker, of New York, as a special detective of the War Department, to ferret out the conspiracy and arrest the persons implicated. It was soon ascertained that Booth, with his accomplice, Herrold, had taken the route of the lower counties of Maryland, whither they were followed up. At Surratt's tavern, about ten miles from the city, on the road to Bryantown, it was found that Booth and Herrold had been present on the 22d. Booth was, at this time, suffering from the injury to his leg, the fracture of one of the small bones, which he experienced in falling upon the stage at the time of the assassination, and was consequently unable to carry one of the carbines which had been provided there for him and his fellow-traveler, under the direction of Mrs. Surratt, an accomplice, in whose house at Washington the conspirators had been in the habit of meeting. Herrold took one of the carbines, and the two proceeded on horseback towards Bryantown, where Booth found it necessary to call into requisition the services of a former acquaintance, Dr. Samuel A. Mudd, to relieve the pain he was suffering from his leg. The fugitives then passed on, escaping with precarious assistance through a swamp to Swan Point, where they crossed the Potomac into King George County, Virginia. Word was brought of their crossing the river to Colonel Baker, at Washington, by a telegraph operator, on detached service to make observations, with a party of soldiers, who came upon a negro who had noticed the passage of the two men. A detachment of the 16th New York cavalry, mustering about twenty-five, was immediately, on the 24th, dispatched from Washington under direction of Colonel Baker, in command of Lieutenant Doherty, accompanied by Lieutenant-Colonel E. J. Conger, to proceed to Port Royal, and intercept the fugitives on their way through Virginia. The cavalry proceeding down the river landed that night at Belle Plain, and making their way the next day to Port R yal Ferry ascertained that Booth and Herrold had crossed at that place and were on their way towards Bowling Green. Arrived at the latter place the pursuers ascertained that the fugitives were on the road from Port Royal, at the house of a Mr. Garrett. This was on the night of the 26th, and the pursuit was instantly continued to the designated place. After some parleying with the occupants of the house it was learnt that Booth and Herrold were secreted in the barn, whither Lieutenant-Colonel Conger at once proceeded with his command. 'As soon as I got there," says he, in his testimony before the Court, at the trial of the conspirators, "I heard somebody walking on the hay; I stationed men around the barn, and Lieutenant Baker said to one of the young Garretts (there had two of them appeared by this time) 'you must go in the barn and get the arms from this man;' I think he made some objection to going; Baker said he knew you and you must go in; Baker then said to the men inside, that one of the men whom he had been stopping with was coming in to get their arms and they must deliver them up; Garrett went in but came out very soon and said, this man says, 'Damn you! you have betrayed me,' and threatened to shoot me; I asked him how he knew the man was going to shoot him; he said he reached down into the hay and got his revolver. I directed Lieutenant Baker to tell the men inside they were to come out and deliver themselves up, and that if they did not in five minutes we would fire the barn. Booth inquired: 'Who are you; what do you want—what do you want?' Lieutenant Baker said: 'We want you; we know who you are; give up your arms and come out.' Booth replied: 'Give us a little time to consider.' Lieutenant Baker said: 'Very well.' Some ten or fifteen minutes elapsed, probably, before anything further was said. Booth again asked: 'Who are you; what do you want?' I said to Baker: 'Do not by any possible intimation or remark let him know who we are. If he chooses to take us for rebels or friends, we will take advantage of it. We will not lie to him about it, but will not answer any question on that subject. Simply insist on his coming out if he will.' Baker replied to Booth: 'It don't make any difference who we are; we know who you are, and want you.' Booth said: 'This is hard; because it may be I am to be taken by my friends.' Some time during the conversation Booth said: 'Captain, I know you to be a brave man, and believe you to be an honorable one. I have got but one leg; I am a cripple. If you will withdraw your men one hundred yards from the door, I will come out and fight you.' Lieutenant Baker replied: 'We did not come here to fight; we simply came to make you prisoner.' Once after that he said: 'If you will take your men fifty yards from the door, I will come out and fight; give me a chance for my life;' there was the same reply; and then, with a singularly theatrical voice, Booth called out: 'Well, my brave boys, you may prepare a stretcher for me.' I requested one of the Garrett boys to pile some pine boughs against the barn. He soon came to me and said: 'This man says if I put any more brush up there he will put a ball through me:' 'Very well,' said I, 'you need not go there any more;' after awhile Booth said: 'There is a man here who wants to come out: 'Lieutenant Baker said: 'Very well, let him take his arms and come out;' some talk passed between them in the barn; one of the expressions I heard Booth use to Herrold was: 'You damned coward, will you leave me now? But go! go! I would not have you stay with me;' further words ensued between them, which I suppose had reference to bringing out arms, which was one of the conditions on which Herrold was directed to come out. What the words were was not heard. He came to the door and said: 'Let me out.' Lieutenant Baker said to him: 'Hand out your arms.' The reply was: 'I have none.' Baker said: 'You carried a carbine; you must hand it out.' Booth replied, 'The arms are mine; I have got them.' Baker said, 'This man carried a carbine, and must bring it out.' Booth said, 'Upon the word and honor of a gentleman the arms are mine, and I have got them.' I told Lieutenant Baker, 'Never mind the arms, but let the man out.' Herrold put out his hands, and Lieutenant Baker took hold of him and brought him out, and passed him to the rear. I then went round the barn, pulled some straw out, and twisted a little rope as big as your finger, fired it and stuck it back. It seemed to be loose broken hay, that had been taken up from the barn floor. It blazed very rapidly and lit up the barn at once. I looked through one of the cracks, and just then heard something drop on the floor, which I supposed to be Booth's crutch. When I first noticed him, his back was toward me; he was looking toward the front door. He then came back within five feet of the corner of the barn. The only thing I noticed he had in his hand when he came, was a carbine. He raised the carbine to his breast, and looked along the cracks rapidly. He then looked at the fire; and from the expression of his face I am satisfied he looked to see if he could put it out. But he could not; it was burning too rapidly. I started to go around to the front of the barn again, and when I was about around I heard the report of a pistol; I went on round to the door, went in, and found Lieutenant Baker looking at him, and rather holding or raising him up, I said: 'He had shot himself.' Baker said: "He had not.' I asked him where he was shot. He raised him up and the blood ran out of his wound. I then said: 'Yes, he had shot himself.' Lieutenant Baker replied very earnestly, 'He had not.' I said: 'We must carry him out, or this will soon be burning us.' We took him up and carried him out on the grass, a little way from the door, beneath a locust tree. I went back into the barn to see if the fire could be put out; but found it could not, and returned to where he was lying. Before this I supposed him to be dead; he had all the appearance of a dead man; but when I came back his eyes and mouth were moving. I called immediately for water, and put some to his face. He seemed to revive, and attempted to speak. I put my ear down to his mouth, and heard him say, 'Tell my mother I died for my country.' I repeated the words to him and said, 'Is that what you would say?' 'He said, 'Yes.' They carried him to the porch of Garrett's house and laid him on a straw bed or tick. At that time he revived considerably, and could talk in a whisper so as to be intelligibly understood. He could not speak above a whisper. He wanted water; I gave it to him. He wanted to turn on his face; I said to him he couldn't lie on his face. He wanted to be turned on his side. We turned him on his side three times, but he could not lie with any comfort, and asked immediately to be turned back. He asked me to put my hand on his throat and press down, which I did. He said 'harder.' I pressed as hard as I thought necessary. He made a very strong exertion to cough, but was unable to do so. I suppose he thought there was blood in his throat. I asked him to put out his tongue, which he did. I said, 'There is no blood in your throat.' He repeated several times—two or three times at least—'Kill me! kill me!' I replied, 'I do not want to kill you.

I want you to get well.' I then took what things he had in his pocket, and tied them up in a paper. I had previously sent for a physician, who came there to see him. He was not quite dead. He would once, perhaps, in a few minutes gasp. His pulse would almost die out, and then there would be a slight motion again. I left him, with the prisoner Herrold, in charge of Lieutenant Baker, saying that if Booth recovered again to wait an hour, and if likely to recover, to send over to Belle Plain for a surgeon from one of the gunships ; if not, to get the best conveyance he could, and bring him over, dead or alive."

The pistol shot which ended the life of Booth was fired by Sergeant Boston Corbett, who at the trial gave the following testimony, narrating his part in the transaction. After Herrold had left the barn, as just stated, "Detective Lieutenant-Colonel Conger," says he, "came over to the side where I was and directed the barn to be fired. I had been previously standing before a crack in the boards large enough to put in your hand; I knew that Booth could see us and could have picked us off, and he in fact once made the remark, 'I could have picked three or four of your men off. Just draw your men off fifty yards and I will come out.' He used such words many times. When the fire was lighted, which was almost immediately after Herrold had been taken out of the barn, I could see him distinctly in about the middle of the barn. He started at first toward the door, and I had a full front dress view of him. I could have shot him much easier than at the time I did, but as long as he made no demonstration I did not shoot him. I kept my eye on him steadily. He turned toward the other side. He brought his piece up to an aim, and I supposed he was going to fight his way out. I thought the time had come, and I took a steady aim upon him and shot him. The ball entered his head a little back of the ear, and came out a little higher on the other side of the head." Thus miserably perished, by a pistol wound similar to that which he had inflicted, the assassin of Abraham Lincoln. His remains were carried in a rough country cart to Washington and placed on board a vessel of war in the river, where, after being fully identified, they were consigned to an unknown and ignominious burial. Other arrests were made, and on the 10th of May, Herrold, Atzeroth, Payne, Michael O'Laughlin, Edward Spangler, Samuel Arnold, Mary E. Surratt and Samuel A. Mudd, were put upon trial as parties to the conspiracy of assassination before a Military Court at Washington, presided over by General David Hunter. O'Laughlin was charged with lying in wait with the intent to kill General Grant; Spangler, one of the persons employed at Ford's Theatre, was charged with assisting Booth in obtaining access to the President's box the night of the assassination ; Arnold was arraigned as a participator in the plot. The charges against the other parties have been indicated in the statement already given. The trial, which was conducted with great deliberation, and in the course of which various testimony was brought forward bearing upon the conduct of Jefferson Davis and other leaders in the Rebellion, occupied the remainder of May and the month of June. On the 6th of July the verdict of the Court was published, with the approval of President Johnson. Herrold, Atzeroth, Payne and Mrs. Mary E. Surratt were sentenced to be hung; O'Laughlin, Arnold and Dr. Mudd to imprisonment at hard labor for life, and Spangler to be confined at hard labor for six years. By order of President Johnson the execution of the four condemned prisoners was fixed for the following day, Friday, the 7th, and at the appointed time was carried into effect.

The capture of Jefferson Davis, early in May, completed the destruction of what remained of the civil organization of the vaunted Southern Confederacy. After the fall of Richmond Davis fled to North Carolina, and at Danville, on the 5th of April, issued a proclamation, in which he declared that "we have now entered upon a new phase of the struggle. Relieved from the necessity of guarding particular points, our army will be free to move from point to point to strike the enemy in detail far from his base. Let us but will it and we are free. I announce to you, fellow-countrymen, that it is my purpose to maintain your cause with my whole heart and soul; that I will never consent to abandon to the enemy one foot of the soil of any one of the States of the Confederacy; that Virginia, with the help of the people and by the blessing of Providence, shall be held and defended, and no peace ever be made with the infamous invaders of her territory. If, by the stress of numbers, we should ever be compelled to a temporary withdrawal from her limits, or those of any other border State, again and again will we return, until the baffled and exhausted enemy shall abandon in despair his endless and impossible task of making slaves of a people resolved to be free." Such were still the dreams of the rebel chieftain which, a few days after, must have been effectually dissipated by the surrender of Lee's army to General Grant. Upon this event Davis retired with a considerable body-guard through North Carolina, lingering for some time in the State, and pursued thence into South Carolina. On the second of May, President Johnson issued a proclamation to the effect that "*Whereas*, It appears in the Bureau of Military Justice, that the atrocious murder of the late President, Abraham Lincoln, and the attempted assassination of Hon. W. H. Seward, Secretary of State, were incited, concerted and procured by and between Jefferson Davis, late of Richmond, Va., and Jacob Thompson, Clement C. Clay, Beverly Tucker, George N. Sanders, W. C. Cleary and other rebels and traitors against the Government of the United States, harbored in Canada; now, therefore, to the end that justice may be done, I, Andrew Johnson, President of the United States, do offer and promise for the arrest of said persons, or either of them, within the limits of the United States, so that they can be brought to trial, the following rewards: One hundred thousand dollars for the arrest of Jefferson Davis—twenty-five thousand dollars each was offered for the arrest of the others, excepting Cleary, for whom ten thousand dollars was offered." The Provost Marshal General of the United States was directed to cause a description of said persons, with notice of the above rewards, to be published. This, of course, stimulated the pursuit. Davis was closely pursued through Georgia by detachments of General Wilson's cavalry corps and finally captured at daylight on the 10th of May, in the vicinity of Irvinsville, in Wilkinson county, Georgia, about seventy-five miles Southeast of Macon. Deserted by the cavalry escort with which he left North Carolina, Davis was now endeavoring to make his escape to the coast with a small party, consisting of his wife and family, Postmaster-General Reagan of the Confederate cabinet; his private secretary, Colonel Harrison, Colonel Johnson, Aid-de-Camp on Davis' Staff, Colonel Morris and others. His train consisted of five wagons and three ambulances. They were encamped for the night in the woods when they were captured. Lieutenant-Colonel Pritchard, commanding a detachment of the Fourth Michigan Cavalry, of Wilson's Cavalry Corps, took the party by surprize at daylight in their tents. Davis attempted to escape into the woods disguised as a female, by wearing a waterproof cloak as a skirt, and a shawl belonging to one of the ladies of the party but the thin concealment was at once detected, and he was compelled to surrender. An accidental encounter marred the proceedings. Another detachment of cavalry, Lieutenant-Colonel Harden's First Wisconsin, also in pursuit that night, coming up in the darkness was mistaken for the enemy, and in the conflict which ensued two men were killed and four men and an officer wounded. Davis was brought a prisoner to Savannah, and thence carried by sea to Fortress Monroe, where he was confined as a prisoner of state. Alexander H. Stephens, the Vice-President of the Confederacy, who had been arrested in Georgia, was also brought to the North at the same time, and similarly confined at Fort Warren in Boston Harbor. With these events the war was fully terminated. The Confederate armies had surrendered, and the heads of the rebel government were prisoners or fugitives. The military and civil organizations of the great revolt had alike perished. As an immediate consequence, the leading armies of the United States were disbanded or greatly reduced to a force simply adequate for the maintenance of order in the late insurgent districts; the naval equipmedts were in like manner curtailed; restrictions were removed from foreign and internal trade; the new state of affairs were recognized by foreign governments, and before the 4th of July, 1865, with the important exception of the regulations affecting the restoration or reconstruction of civil government in the late rebel States, and the position of parties engaged in the rebellion, the administration of the national affairs had mainly returned to its accustomed channels.

President Johnston entered upon his administration of affairs with declarations of his sentiments on the subject of the revolt, the tendency of which was that while the great mass of offenders should be treated with lenity, the leaders of the rebellion should be punished and the nation taught the heinousness of the crime of Treason. His most important action in the matter at this early period was the issue of the following Amnesty Proclamation on the 29th of May, which indicated his policy towards individuals:

"*Whereas*, The President of the United States, on the 8th day of December, A. D. eighteen hundred and sixty-three, and on the 26th day of March, A. D. eighteen hundred and sixty-four, did, with the object to suppress the existing rebellion, to induce all persons to return to their loyalty, and to restore the authority of the United States, issue proclamations offering amnesty and pardon to certain persons, who had directly or by implication participated in the said rebellion; and *Whereas*, many persons, who had so engaged in said rebellion, have, since the issuance of said proclamations, failed or neglected to take the benefits offered thereby: and *Whereas*, many persons, who have been justly deprived of all claim to amnesty or pardon thereunder, by reason of their participation, directly or by implication, in said rebellion, and continued hostility to the Government of the United States since the date of said proclamation, now desire to apply for and obtain amnesty and pardon; To the end, therefore, that the authority of the Government of the United States may be restored, and that peace, order and freedom may be established, I, Andrew Johnson, President of the United States, do proclaim and declare that I hereby grant to all persons who have directly or indirectly participated in the existing rebellion, except as hereinafter excepted, amnesty and pardon, with restoration of all rights of property, except as to slaves, and except in cases where legal proceedings under laws of the United States providing for the confiscation of property of persons engaged in rebellion have been instituted; but on the condition, nevertheless, that every such person shall take and subscribe the following oath or affirmation, and thenceforward keep and maintain said oath inviolate, and which oath shall be registered for permanent preservation, and shall be of the tenor and effect following, to wit:

"I, ———, do solemnly swear or affirm, in presence of Almighty God, that I will henceforth faithfully support and defend the Constitution of the United States and the Union of the States thereunder. And that I will, in like manner, abide by and faithfully support all laws and proclamations which have been made during the existing rebellion with reference to the emancipation of slaves, so help me God."

"The following classes of persons are excepted from the benefits of this proclamation: *First*—All who are or shall have been pretended civil or diplomatic officers, or otherwise domestic or foreign agents of the pretended Confederate Government. *Second*—All who left judicial stations under the United States to aid the rebellion. *Third*—All who shall have been military or naval officers of said pretended Confederate Government above the rank of Colonel in the army or Lieutenant in the navy. *Fourth*—All who left seats in the Congress of the United States to aid the rebellion. *Fifth*—All who resigned or tendered resignations of their commissions in the army or navy of the United States, to evade duty in resisting the rebellion. *Sixth*—All who have engaged in any way in treating otherwise than lawfully as prisoners of war persons found in the United States service, as officers, soldiers, seamen, or in other capacities. *Seventh*—All persons who have been or are absentees from the United States, for the purpose of aiding the rebellion. *Eighth*—All military and naval officers in the rebel service who were educated by the Government in the Military Academy at West Point, or the United States Naval Academy. *Ninth*—All persons who held the pretended offices of Governors of States in insurrection against the United States. *Tenth*—All persons who left their homes within the jurisdiction and protection of the United States and passed beyond the Federal military lines into the so-called Confederate States, for the purpose of aiding the rebellion. *Eleventh*—All paries who have been engaged in the destruction of the commerce of the United States upon the high seas, and all persons who have made raids into the United States from Canada, or been engaged in destroying the commerce of the United States upon the lakes and rivers that separate the British Provinces from the United States. *Twelfth*—All persons who at the time when they seek to obtain the benefits hereof by taking the oath herein prescribed, are in military, naval, or civil confinement. or custody, or under bonds of the civil, military or naval authorities or agents of the United States, as prisoners of war, or persons detained for offences of any kind either before or after conviction. *Thirteenth*—All persons who have voluntarily participated in said rebellion, and the estimated value of whose taxable property is over twenty thousand dollars. *Fourteenth*—All persons who have taken the oath of amnesty as prescribed in the President's Proclamation of December 8th, A. D., 1863, or an oath of allegiance to the Government of the United States since the dates of said proclamation, and who have not thenceforward kept and maintained the same inviolate—provided that special application may be made to the President for pardon by any person belonging to the excepted classes, and such clemency will be liberally extended as may be consistent with the facts of the case and the peace and dignity of the United States. The Secretary of State will establish rules and regulations for administering and recording the said amnesty oath so as to insure its benefit to the people and guard the Government against fraud."

A few days after this Proclamation of Amnesty, Lieut-General Grant on the second of June issued the following congratulatory address to the armies of the United States previous to their disbandment :—

"Soldiers of the Armies of the United States :—By your patriotic devotion to your country in the hour of danger and alarm, your magnificent fighting, bravery and endurance, you have maintainen the supremacy of the Union and the Constitution, overthrown all opposition to the enforcement of the laws and of the proclamations forever abolishing slavery, the cause and pretext of the rebellion, and opened the way to the rightful authorities to restore order and inaugurate peace on a permanent and enduring basis on every foot of American soil. Your marches, sieges and battles, in distance, duration, resolution and brilliancy of results, dim the lustre of the world's past military achievments, and will be the patriot's precedent in defence of liberty and right in all time to come. In obedience to your country's call, you left your homes and families and volunteered in its defence. Victory has crowned your valor, and secured the purpose of your patriotic hearts ; and with the gratitude of your countrymen and the highest honors a great and free nation can accord, you will soon be permitted to return to your homes and families, conscious of having discharged the highest duty of American citizens. To achieve these glorious triumphs, and secure to yourselves, your fellow countrymen and posterity, the blessings of free institutions, tens of thousands of your gallant comrades have fallen, and sealed the priceless legacy with their lives. The graves of these a grateful nation bedews with tears, honors their memories, and will ever cherish and support their stricken families."

In closing this melancholy record, one of the most sad in human history, of four years of civil war, it is hardly needed to point its moral. That is written in letters of fire in the disasters of the period, and in the utter ruin of the gigantic revolt. We have endeavored to trace the course of the rebellion with calmness and truth, the avoidance of unnecessary comment, leaving facts, so far as they were at hand, while the rebellion was in progress, to tell their own significant story. Such a record is necessarily imperfect. Every day is contributing fresh material for its exhibition. Indeed, a full narrative of these most extraordinary events must be left to the labors of the historian in another generation. But enough, surely, is here recorded to warn faction, in future, of its crime and danger, and to strengthen with an invincible resolve for the preservation of the Nation, the hearts of all true patriots and lovers of their country, consecrated anew by the voluntary labors, the sacrifices, sufferings and death of so many Martyrs.

THE END.

www.ingramcontent.com/pod-product-compliance
Lightning Source LLC
LaVergne TN
LVHW021051110826
845150LV00001B/46

* 9 7 8 1 4 2 5 5 6 7 6 3 7 *